ROAD ATLAS

2023 BRITAIN & IRELAND

C000282911

www.philips-maps.co.uk

First published in 2009 as
Complete Road Atlas Britain and Ireland by Philip's,
a division of Octopus Publishing Group Ltd
www.octopusbooks.co.uk
Carmelite House, 50 Victoria Embankment
London EC4Y 0DZ
An Hachette UK Company
www.hachette.co.uk

Fourteenth edition 2022
First impression 2022

ISBN 978-1-84907-609-8 spiral-bound
ISBN 978-1-84907-608-1 perfect-bound

Cartography by Philip's
Copyright © 2022 Philip's

This product includes mapping data licensed from Ordnance Survey®, with the permission of the Controller of Her Majesty's Stationery Office. © Crown copyright 2022.
All rights reserved. Licence number 100011710.

The map of Ireland on pages XVI–XVII is based upon the Crown Copyright and is reproduced with the permission of Land & Property Services under delegated authority from the Controller of Her Majesty's Stationery Office, © Crown Copyright and database right 2022, PMLPA number 100503, and on Ordnance Survey Ireland by permission of the Government © Ordnance Survey Ireland / Government of Ireland Permit number 9257.

Information for National Parks, Areas of Outstanding Natural Beauty, National Trails and Country Parks in Wales supplied by the Countryside Council for Wales.

Information for National Parks, Areas of Outstanding Natural Beauty, National Trails and Country Parks in England supplied by Natural England. Data for Regional Parks, Long Distance Footpaths and Country Parks in Scotland provided by Scottish Natural Heritage.

Gaelic name forms used in the Western Isles provided by Comhairle nan Eilean.

Data for the National Nature Reserves in England provided by Natural England. Data for the National Nature Reserves in Wales provided by Countryside Council for Wales. Darparwyd data'n ymwneud â Gwarchodfeydd Natur Cenedlaethol Cymru gan Gyngor Cefn Gwlad Cymru.

Information on the location of National Nature Reserves in Scotland was provided by Scottish Natural Heritage.

Data for National Scenic Areas in Scotland provided by the Scottish Executive Office. Crown copyright material is reproduced with the permission of the Controller of HMSO and the Queen's Printer for Scotland. Licence number C02W0003960.

Printed in China

*Data from Nielsen Total Consumer Market 2021 weeks 1-52

CONTENTS

II Key to map symbols

III Smart motorways and motorway service areas

IV Restricted motorway junctions

VI Route planning maps

XVI Road map of Ireland

XVIII Tourism and transport

XX Distances and journey times

1 Key to road map pages

2 Road maps of Britain

161 Urban approach maps

161 Bristol *approaches*
162 Birmingham *approaches*
164 Cardiff *approaches*
165 Edinburgh *approaches*
166 Glasgow *approaches*
167 Leeds *approaches*
168 London *approaches*
172 Liverpool *approaches*
173 Manchester *approaches*
174 Newcastle *approaches*

175 Town plans

175 Aberdeen, Ayr, Bath
176 Birmingham, Blackpool, Bournemouth
177 Bradford, Brighton, Bristol
178 Bury St Edmunds, Cambridge, Canterbury, Cardiff
179 Carlisle, Chelmsford, Cheltenham, Chester
180 Chichester, Colchester, Coventry, Derby
181 Dorchester, Dumfries, Dundee, Durham
182 Edinburgh, Exeter, Gloucester
183 Glasgow, Grimsby, Harrogate
184 Hull, Inverness, Ipswich, Kendal
185 King's Lynn, Lancaster, Leeds
186 London
188 Leicester, Lincoln, Liverpool
189 Llandudno, Llanelli, Luton, Macclesfield
190 Manchester, Maidstone, Merthyr Tydfil
191 Middlesbrough, Milton Keynes, Newcastle, Newport
192 Newquay, Northampton, Norwich, Nottingham
193 Oxford, Perth, Peterborough, Plymouth
194 Poole, Portsmouth, Preston, Reading
195 St Andrews, Salisbury, Scarborough, Shrewsbury,
196 Sheffield, Stoke-on-Trent (Hanley), Southampton
197 Southend, Stirling, Stratford-upon-Avon, Sunderland
198 Swansea, Swindon, Taunton, Telford
199 Torquay, Truro, Winchester, Windsor
200 Wolverhampton, Worcester, Wrexham, York

201 Index to town plans

213 Index to road maps of Britain

Inside back cover:
County and unitary authority boundaries

Road map symbols

M3	Motorway, toll motorway
5 8	Motorway junction – full, restricted access
S S	Motorway service area – full, restricted access
	Motorway under construction
A303	Primary route – dual, single carriageway
S S	Service area, roundabout, multi-level junction
4 5	Numbered junction – full, restricted access
	Primary route under construction
	Narrow primary route
Newbury	Primary destination
A303	A road – dual, single carriageway
	A road under construction, narrow A road
B3089	B road – dual, single carriageway
	B road under construction, narrow B road
	Minor road – over 4 metres, under 4 metres wide
	Minor road with restricted access
2	Distance in miles
TOLL	Toll, steep gradient – arrow points downhill
	Tunnel
	National trail – England and Wales
	Long distance footpath – Scotland
	Railway with station
	Level crossing, tunnel
	Preserved railway with station
	National boundary
	County / unitary authority boundary
	Car ferry, catamaran
	Passenger ferry, catamaran
	Hovercraft
CALAIS	Ferry destination
Ferry	Car ferry – river crossing
	Principal airport, other airport
	National park, Area of Outstanding Natural Beauty – England and Wales National Scenic Area – Scotland Forest park / regional park / national forest
	Beach
	Linear antiquity
	Roman road
1643	Hillfort, battlefield – with date
261	Viewpoint, nature reserve, spot height – in metres
	Golf course, youth hostel, sporting venue
	Camp site, caravan site, camping and caravan site
P&R	Shopping village, park and ride
29	Adjoining page number – road maps

Approach map symbols

M6	Motorway	B1288	B road – dual, single carriageway
	Toll motorway		Minor road – dual, single carriageway
6 5	Motorway junction – full, restricted access		Ring road
S	Service area	3	Distance in miles
	Under construction		Congestion charge area
A6	Primary route – dual, single carriageway		
S	Service area	COSELEY	Railway with station
	Multi-level junction	LOXDALE	Tramway with station
	roundabout	M ⊖ ⊕ ⊚	Underground or metro station
	Under construction		
A195	A road – dual, single carriageway		

Town plan symbols

	Motorway		Bus or railway station building
	Primary route – dual, single carriageway		Shopping precinct or retail park
	A road – dual, single carriageway		Park
	B road – dual, single carriageway		Building of public interest
	Minor through road		Theatre, cinema
→	One-way street	P	Parking, shopmobility
	Pedestrian roads	Bank ⊖	Underground station
	Shopping streets	West St ●	Metro station
	Railway with station	H	Hospital, Police station
City Hall	Tramway with station	PO	Post office

Tourist information

Abbey, cathedral or priory	Farm park	Race course
Ancient monument	Garden	Roman antiquity
Aquarium	Historic ship	Safari park
Art gallery	House	Theme park
Bird collection or aviary	House and garden	Tourist information
Castle	Motor racing circuit	Zoo
Church	Museum	Other place of interest
Country park England and Wales Scotland	Picnic area	
	Preserved railway	

Road map scales

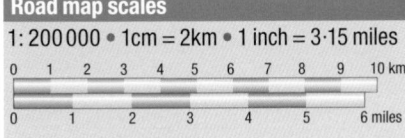

1:200 000 • 1cm = 2km • 1 inch = 3·15 miles

Parts of Scotland

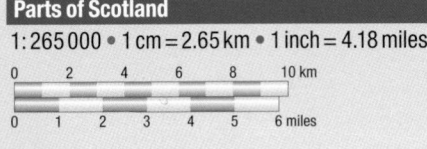

1:265 000 • 1 cm = 2.65 km • 1 inch = 4.18 miles

Scottish Highlands and Islands

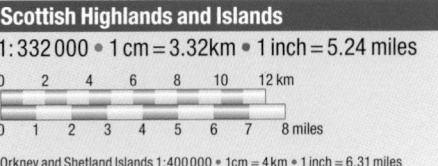

1:332 000 • 1 cm = 3.32km • 1 inch = 5.24 miles

Orkney and Shetland Islands 1:400 000 • 1cm = 4 km • 1 inch = 6.31 miles

Smart motorways and motorway service areas

Smart motorways

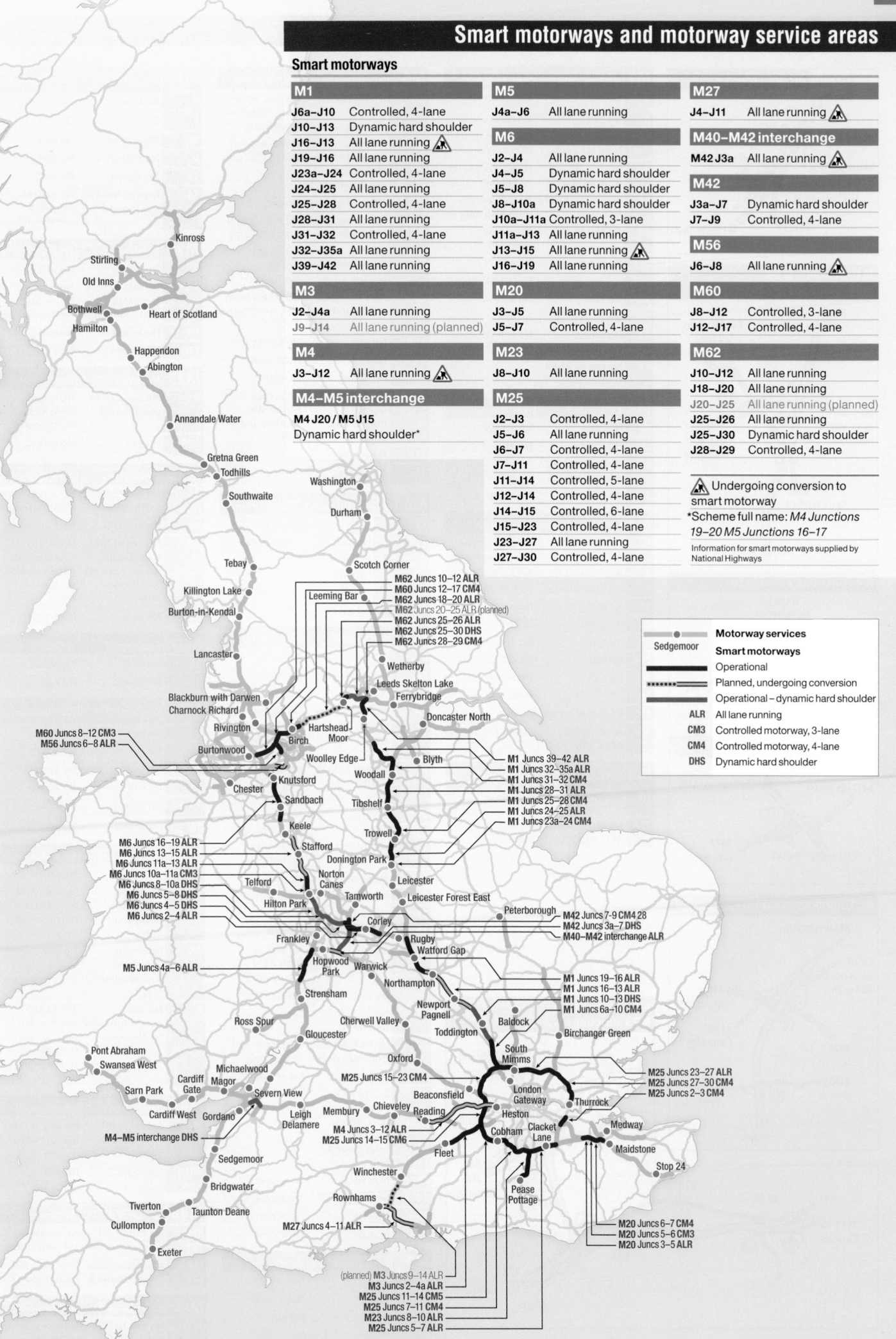

M1	
J6a–J10	Controlled, 4-lane
J10–J13	Dynamic hard shoulder
J16–J13	All lane running
J19–J16	All lane running
J23a–J24	Controlled, 4-lane
J24–J25	All lane running
J25–J28	Controlled, 4-lane
J28–J31	All lane running
J31–J32	Controlled, 4-lane
J32–J35a	All lane running
J39–J42	All lane running

M3	
J2–J4a	All lane running
J9–J14	All lane running (planned)

M4	
J3–J12	All lane running

M4–M5 interchange

M4 J20 / M5 J15
Dynamic hard shoulder*

M5	
J4a–J6	All lane running

M6	
J2–J4	All lane running
J4–J5	Dynamic hard shoulder
J5–J8	Dynamic hard shoulder
J8–J10a	Dynamic hard shoulder
J10a–J11a	Controlled, 3-lane
J11a–J13	All lane running
J13–J15	All lane running
J16–J19	All lane running

M20	
J3–J5	All lane running
J5–J7	Controlled, 4-lane

M23	
J8–J10	All lane running

M25	
J2–J3	Controlled, 4-lane
J5–J6	All lane running
J6–J7	Controlled, 4-lane
J7–J11	Controlled, 4-lane
J11–J14	Controlled, 5-lane
J12–J14	Controlled, 4-lane
J14–J15	Controlled, 6-lane
J15–J23	Controlled, 4-lane
J23–J27	All lane running
J27–J30	Controlled, 4-lane

M27	
J4–J11	All lane running

M40–M42 interchange	
M42 J3a	All lane running

M42	
J3a–J7	Dynamic hard shoulder
J7–J9	Controlled, 4-lane

M56	
J6–J8	All lane running

M60	
J8–J12	Controlled, 3-lane
J12–J17	Controlled, 4-lane

M62	
J10–J12	All lane running
J18–J20	All lane running
J20–J25	All lane running (planned)
J25–J26	All lane running
J25–J30	Dynamic hard shoulder
J28–J29	Controlled, 4-lane

Undergoing conversion to smart motorway

*Scheme full name: *M4 Junctions 19–20 M5 Junctions 16–17*

Information for smart motorways supplied by National Highways

Legend

	Motorway services
Sedgemoor	Smart motorways
	Operational
	Planned, undergoing conversion
	Operational – dynamic hard shoulder
ALR	All lane running
CM3	Controlled motorway, 3-lane
CM4	Controlled motorway, 4-lane
DHS	Dynamic hard shoulder

Restricted motorway junctions

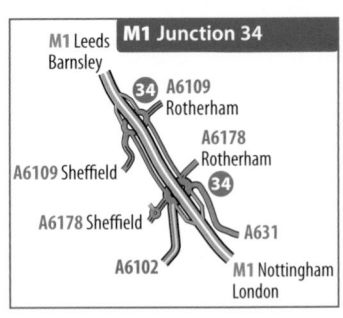

M1 Junction 34

M1 Leeds Barnsley
34
A6109 Rotherham
A6178 Rotherham
A6109 Sheffield
34
A6178 Sheffield
A631
A6102
M1 Nottingham London

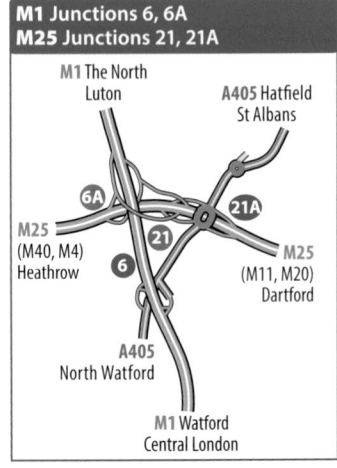

M1 Junctions 6, 6A
M25 Junctions 21, 21A

M1 The North Luton
A405 Hatfield St Albans
6A
21A
M25 (M40, M4) Heathrow
21
6
M25 (M11, M20) Dartford
A405 North Watford
M1 Watford Central London

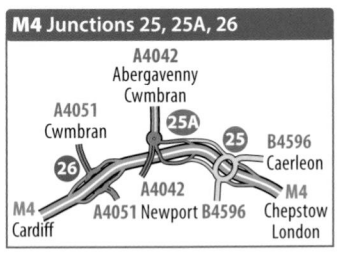

M4 Junctions 25, 25A, 26

A4042 Abergavenny Cwmbran
A4051 Cwmbran
25A
25
B4596 Caerleon
26
A4042
M4 Cardiff
A4051 Newport
B4596
M4 Chepstow London

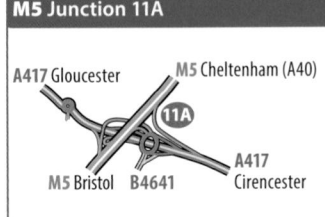

M5 Junction 11A

A417 Gloucester
M5 Cheltenham (A40)
11A
M5 Bristol
B4641
A417 Cirencester

M11 Junctions 13, 14

A14 Huntingdon
A1307 Dry Drayton Oakington
A14 Newmarket
14
A1307 Cambridge
A428 St Neots
A1303 St Neots
13
A1303 Cambridge
M11 London

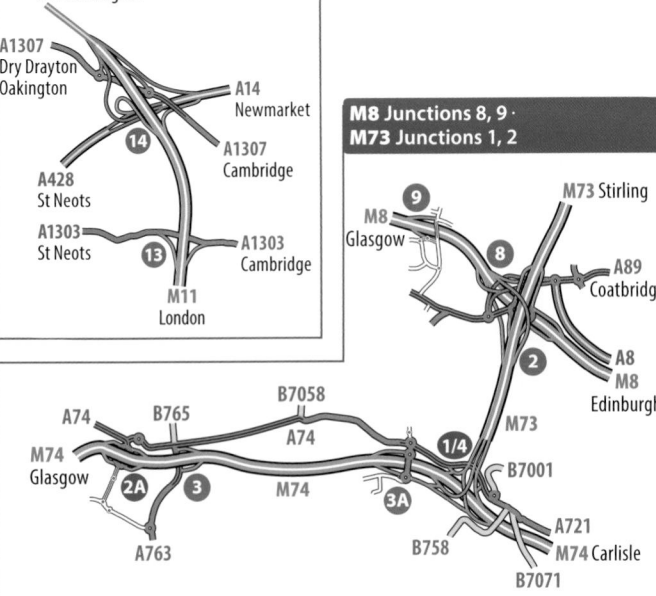

M8 Junctions 8, 9 ·
M73 Junctions 1, 2

M8 Glasgow
9
8
M73 Stirling
A89 Coatbridge
2
A8 M8 Edinburgh
A74
B765
B7058
A74
M74 Glasgow
2A
3
M74
1/4
B7001
M73
3A
A721
B758
M74 Carlisle
A763
B7071

M1	Northbound	Southbound
2	No exit	No access
4	No exit	No access
6A	No exit. Access from M25 only	No access. Exit to M25 only
7	No exit. Access from A414 only	No access. Exit to A414 only
17	No access. Exit to M45 only	No exit. Access from M45 only
19	No exit to A14	No access from A14
21A	No access	No exit
23A		Exit to A42 only
24A	No exit	No access
35A	No access	No exit
43	No access. Exit to M621 only	No exit. Access from M621 only
48	No exit to A1(M) southbound	

M3	Eastbound	Westbound
8	No exit	No access
10	No access	No exit
13	No access to M27 eastbound	
14	No exit	No access

M4	Eastbound	Westbound
1	Exit to A4 eastbound only	Access from A4 westbound only
2	Access from A4 eastbound only	Access to A4 westbound only
21	No exit	No access
23	No access	No exit
25	No exit	No access
25A	No exit	No access
29	No exit	No access
38		No access
39	No exit or access	No exit
42	Access from A483 only	Exit to A483 only

M5	Northbound	Southbound
10	No exit	No access
11A	No access from A417 eastbound	No exit to A417 westbound

M6	Northbound	Southbound
3A	No access.	No exit. Access from M6 eastbound only
4A	No exit. Access from M42 southbound only	No access. Exit to M42 only
5	No access	No exit
10A	No access. Exit to M54 only	No exit. Access from M54 only
11A	No exit. Access from M6 Toll only	No access. Exit to M6 Toll only
20	No exit to M56 eastbound	No access from M56 westbound
20A	No exit	No access
24	No exit	No access
25	No access	No exit
30	No exit. Access from M61 northbound only	No access. Exit to M61 southbound only
31A	No access	No exit
45	No access	No exit

M6 Toll	Northbound	Southbound
T1		No exit
T2	No exit, no access	No access
T5	No exit	No access
T7	No access	No exit
T8	No access	No exit

M8	Eastbound	Westbound
6	No exit	No access
6A	No access	No exit
7	No Access	No exit
7A	No exit. Access from A725 northbound only	No access. Exit to A725 southbound only
8	No exit to M73 northbound	No access from M73 southbound
9	No access	No exit
13	No exit southbound	Access from M73 southbound only
14	No access	No exit
16	No exit	No access
17	No exit	
18		No exit
19	No exit to A814 eastbound	No access from A814 westbound
20	No exit	No access
21	No access from M74	No exit
22	No exit. Access from M77 only	No access. Exit to M77 only
23	No exit	No access
25	Exit to A739 northbound only. Access from A739 southbound only	
25A	No exit	No access
28	No exit	No access
28A	No exit	No access
29A	No exit	No access

M9	Eastbound	Westbound
2	No access	No exit
3	No exit	No access
6	No access	No exit
8	No exit	No access

M11	Northbound	Southbound
4	No exit	No access
5	No access	No exit
8A	No access	No exit
9	No access	No exit
13	No access	No exit
14	No exit to A428 westbound	No exit. Access from A14 westbound only

M20	Eastbound	Westbound
2	No access	No exit
3	No exit. Access from M26 eastbound only	No access Exit to M26 westbound only
10	No access	No exit
11A	No access	No exit

M23	Northbound	Southbound
7	No exit to A23 southbound	No access from A23 northbound
10A	No exit	No access

M25	Clockwise	Anticlockwise
5	No exit to M26 eastbound	No access from M26 westbound
19	No access	No exit
21	No exit to M1 southbound. Access from M1 southbound only	No exit to M1 southbound. Access from M1 southbound only
31	No exit	No access

M27	Eastbound	Westbound
10	No exit	No access
12	No access	No exit

M40	Eastbound	Westbound
3	No exit	No access
7	No exit	No access
8	No exit	No access
13	No exit	No access
14	No access	No exit
16	No access	No exit

M42	Northbound	Southbound
1	No exit	No access
7	No access Exit to M6 northbound only	No exit. Access from M6 northbound only
7A	No access. Exit to M6 southbound only	No exit
8	No exit. Access from M6 southbound only	Exit to M6 northbound only. Access from M6 southbound only

M45	Eastbound	Westbound
M1 J17	Access to M1 southbound only	No access from M1 southbound
With A45	No access	No exit

M48	Eastbound	Westbound
M4 J21	No exit to M4 westbound	No access from M4 eastbound
M4 J23	No access from M4 westbound	No exit to M4 eastbound

M49	Southbound	Northbound
18A	No exit to M5 northbound	No access from M5 southbound

M53	Northbound	Southbound
11	Exit to M56 eastbound only. Access from M56 westbound only	Exit to M56 eastbnd only. Access from M56 westbound only

M56	Eastbound	Westbound
2	No exit	No access
3	No access	No exit
4	No exit	No access
7		No access
8	No exit or access	No exit
9	No access from M6 northbound	No access to M6 southbound
15	No exit to M53	No access from M53 northbound

M57	Northbound	Southbound
3	No exit	No access
5	No exit	No access

M60	Clockwise	Anticlockwise
2	No exit	No access
3	No exit to A34 northbound	No exit to A34 northbound
4	No access from M56	No exit to M56
5	No exit to A5103 southbound	No exit to A5103 northbound
14	No exit	No access
16	No exit	No access
20	No access	No exit
22		No access
25	No access	
26		No exit or access
27	No exit	No access

M61	Northbound	Southbound
2	No access from A580 eastbound	No exit to A580 westbound
3	No access from A580 eastbound. No access from A666 southbound	No exit to A580 westbound
M6 J30	No exit to M6 southbound	No access from M6 northbound

M62	Eastbound	Westbound
23	No access	No exit

M65	Eastbound	Westbound
9	No access	No exit
11	No exit	No access

M66	Northbound	Southbound
1	No access	No exit

M67	Eastbound	Westbound
1A	No access	No exit
2	No exit	No access

M69	Northbound	Southbound
2	No exit	No access

M73	Northbound	Southbound
2	No access from M8 eastbound	No exit to M8 westbound

M74	Northbound	Southbound
3	No access	No access
3A	No exit	No access
7	No exit	No access
9	No exit or access	No access
10		No exit
11	No exit	No access
12	No access	No exit

M77	Northbound	Southbound
4	No exit	No access
6	No exit	No access
7	No exit	
8	No access	No access

M80	Northbound	Southbound
4A	No access	No exit
6A	No exit	No access
8	Exit to M876 northbound only. No access	Access from M876 southbound only. No exit

M90	Northbound	Southbound
1	Access from A90 north-bound only	No access. Exit to A90 south-bound only
2A	No access	No exit
7	No exit	No access
8	No access	No exit
10	No access from A912	No exit to A912

M180	Eastbound	Westbound
1	No access	No exit

M621	Eastbound	Westbound
2A	No exit	No access
4	No exit	
5	No exit	No access
6	No access	No exit

M876	Northbound	Southbound
2	No access	No exit

A1(M)	Northbound	Southbound
2	No access	No exit
3		No access
5	No exit	No exit, no access
14	No exit	No access
40	No access	No exit
43	No exit. Access from M1 only	No access. Exit to M1 only
57	No access	No exit
65	No access	No exit

A3(M)	Northbound	Southbound
1	No exit	No access
4	No access	No exit

A38(M) with Victoria Rd, (Park Circus) Birmingham	
Northbound	No exit
Southbound	No access

A48(M)	Northbound	Southbound
M4 Junc 29	Exit to M4 eastbound only	Access from M4 westbound only
29A	Access from A48 eastbound only	Exit to A48 westbound only

A57(M)	Eastbound	Westbound
With A5103	No access	No exit
With A34	No access	No exit

A58(M)	Southbound
With Park Lane and Westgate, Leeds	No access

A64(M)	Eastbound	Westbound
With A58 Clay Pit Lane, Leeds	No access from A58	No exit to A58

A74(M)	Northbound	Southbound
18	No access	No exit
22		No exit to A75

A194(M)	Northbound	Southbound
A1(M) J65 Gateshead Western Bypass	Access from A1(M) northbound only	Exit to A1(M) southbound only

M3 Junctions 13, 14
M27 Junction 4

M3 Winchester
A335 Chandlers Ford — 13
A27 Romsey
A335 Eastleigh
M3
M27 Southampton Docks New Forest Bournemouth — 4
14
M27 — 4
A33 Southampton
M27 Fareham Portsmouth

M6 Junctions 3A, 4A · **M42** Junctions 7, 7A, 8, 9
M6 Toll Junctions T1, T2

A446 Lichfield
M6 Toll Lichfield
A4091 Tamworth
M42 Derby Burton upon Trent
T2
A4097 Kingsbury
T1
9
A4097 Sutton Coldfield
M42 — A446
M6 Birmingham (N)
4A
8
Coleshill
M42
M6
7A
3A
7
4
A446 Coventry Warwick
M42 Birmingham (S)
M6 Coventry (N & E)

M6 Junction 20 · **M56** Junction 9

M6 Preston Liverpool
A50 Warrington — 20
B5158 Lymm
LYMM SERVICES — S
M56 Manchester
20A
A50 Knutsford Macclesfield
9
M56 Runcorn Chester
20
M6 Birmingham

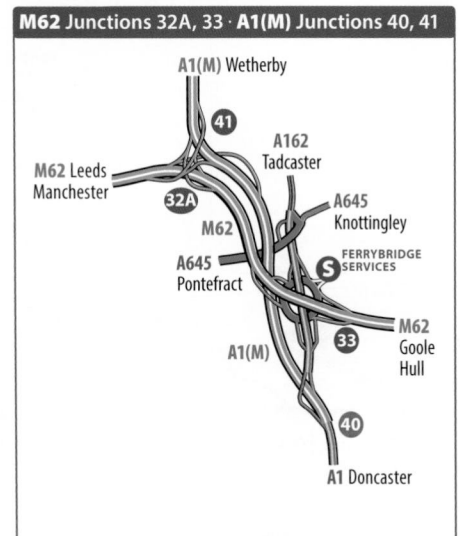

M62 Junctions 32A, 33 · **A1(M)** Junctions 40, 41

A1(M) Wetherby
41
A162 Tadcaster
M62 Leeds Manchester
32A
A645 Knottingley
M62
FERRYBRIDGE SERVICES — S
A645 Pontefract
A1(M)
33
M62 Goole Hull
40
A1 Doncaster

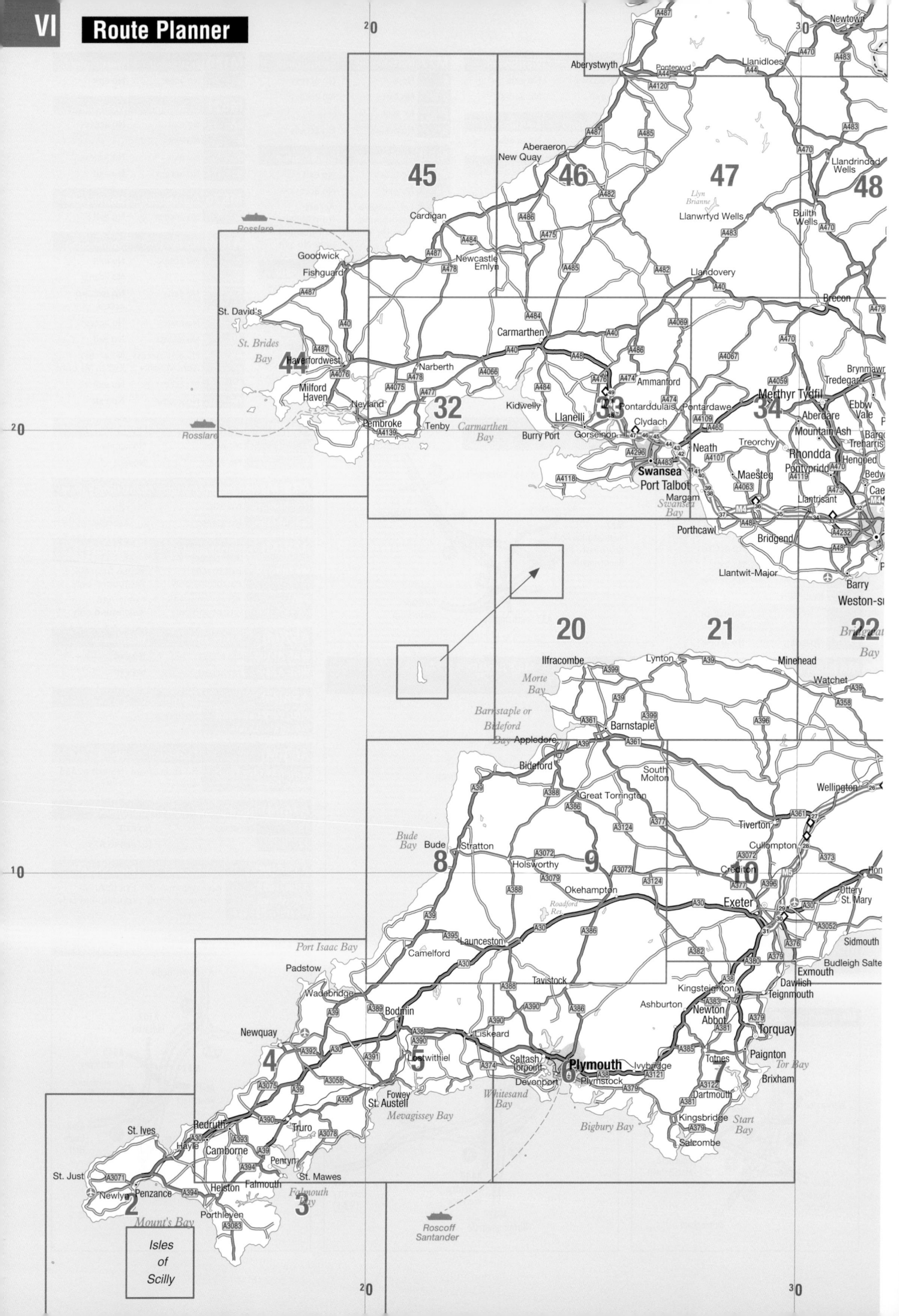

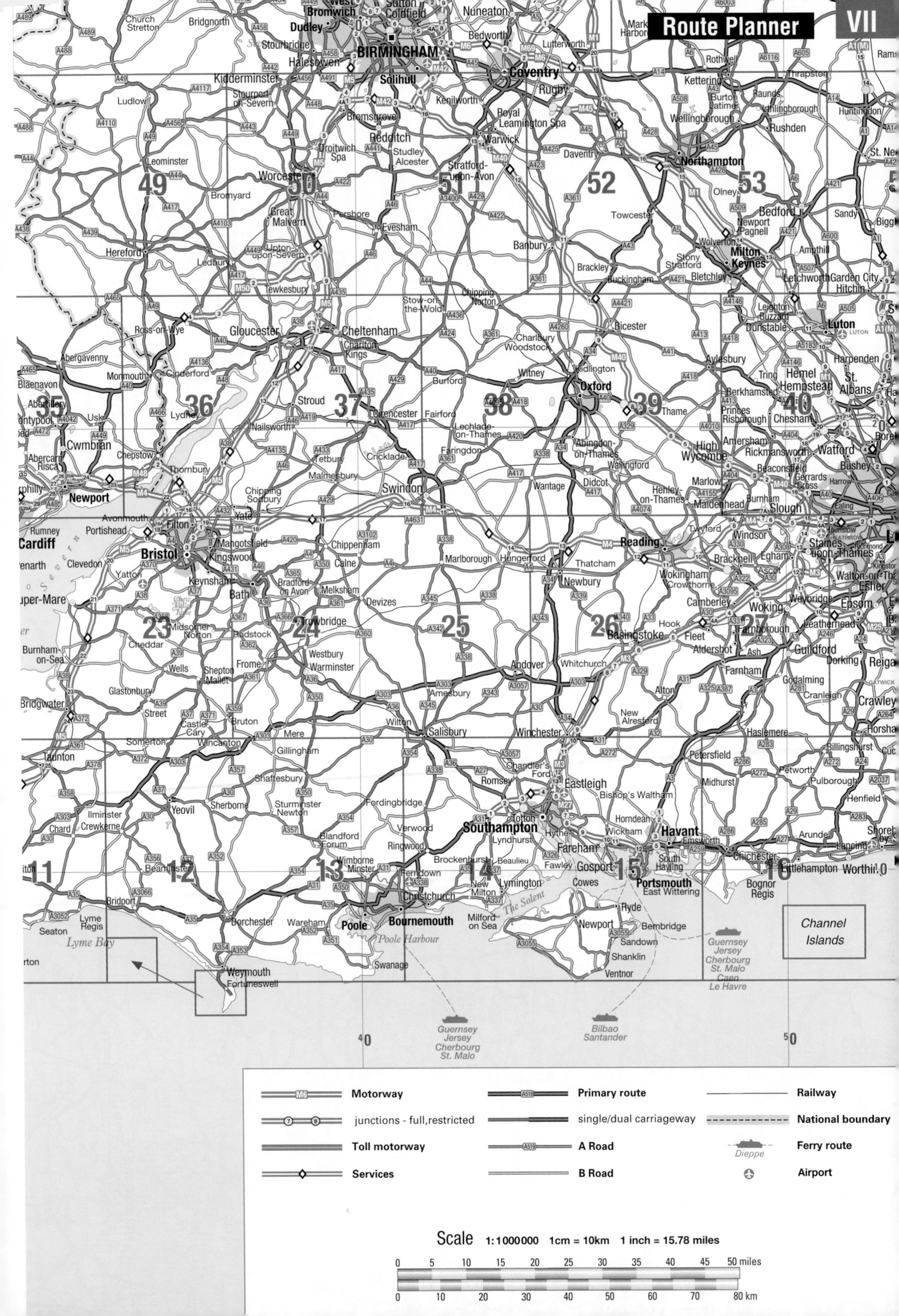

Scale 1:1000000 1cm = 10km 1 inch = 15.78 miles

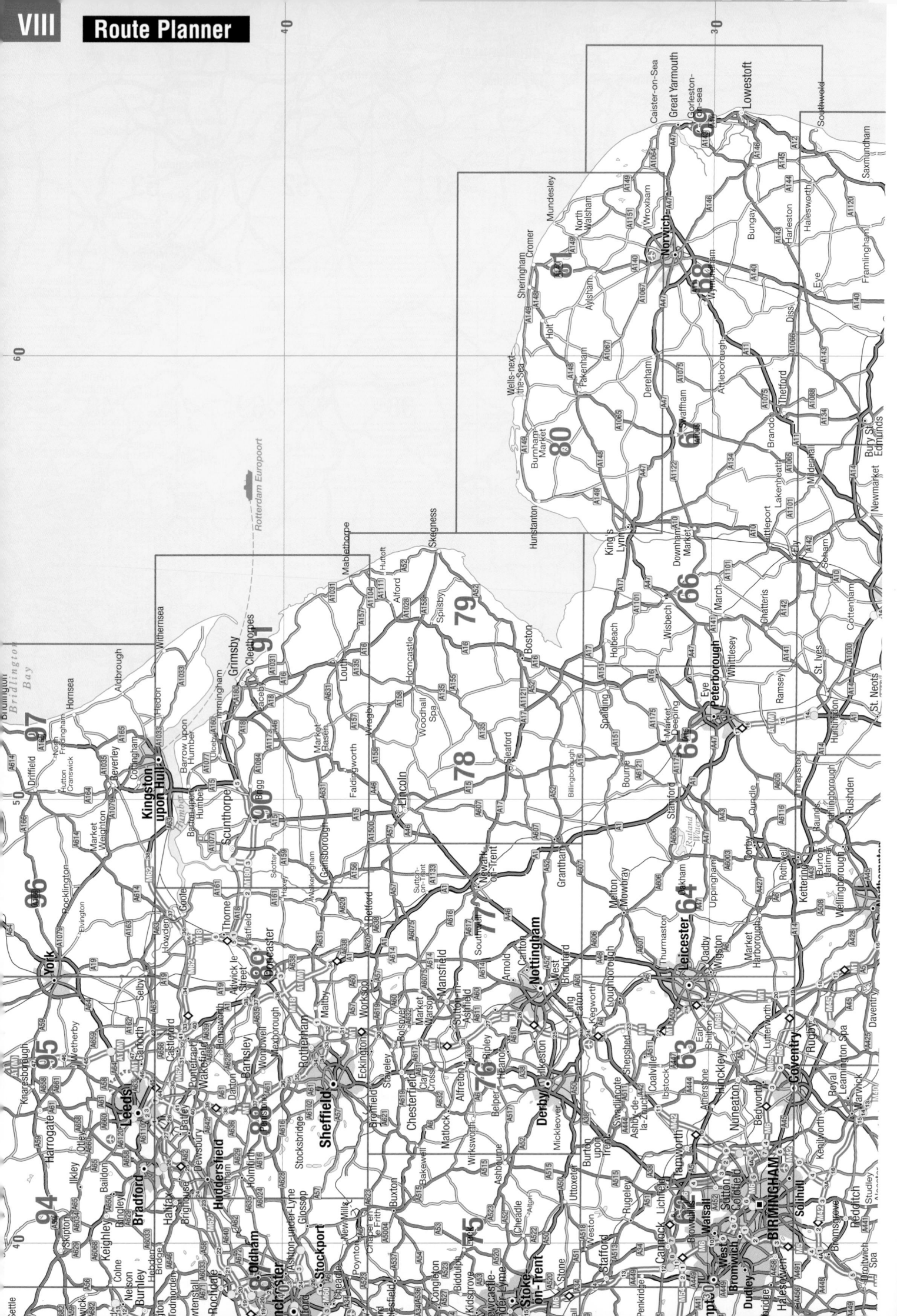

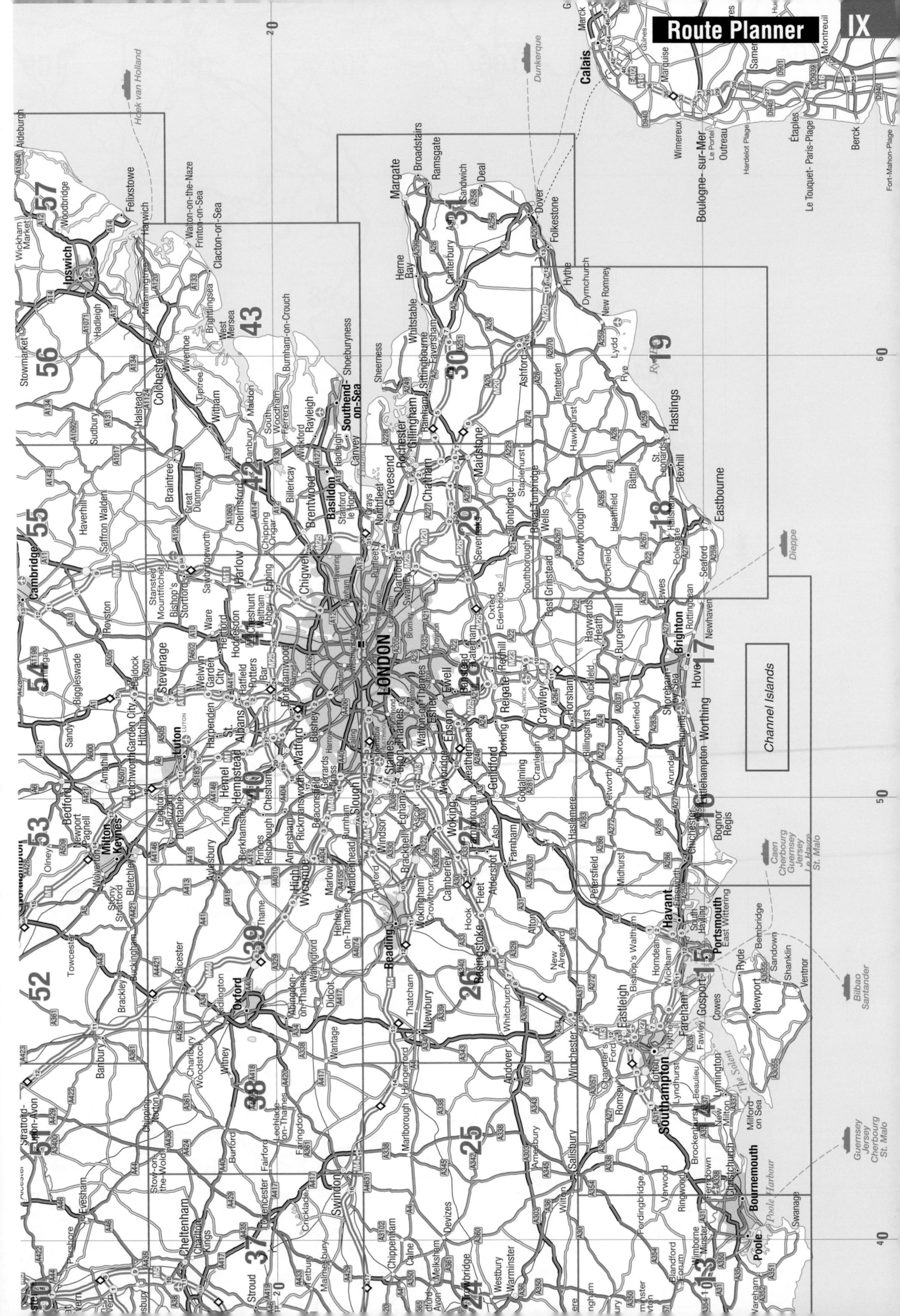

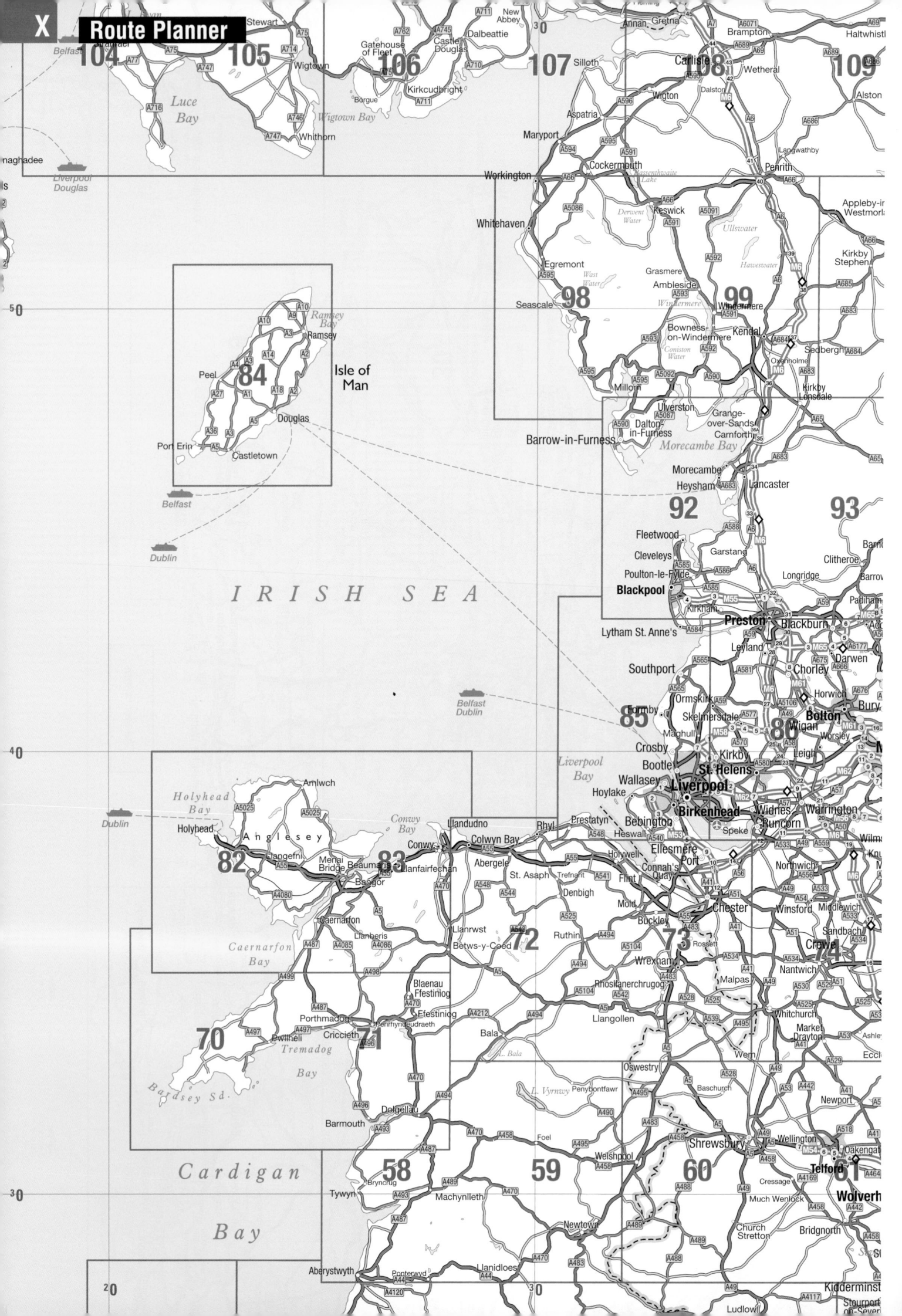

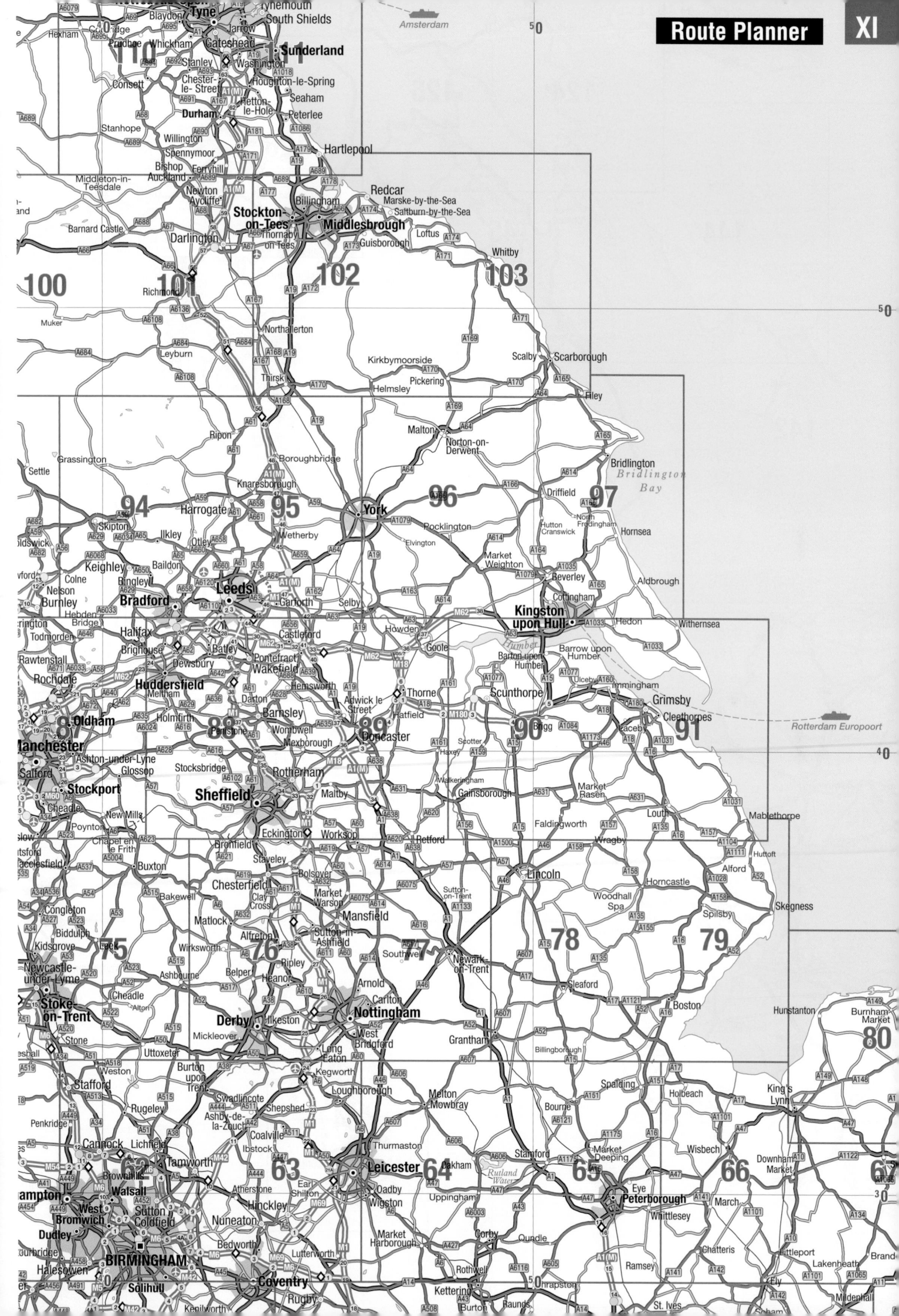

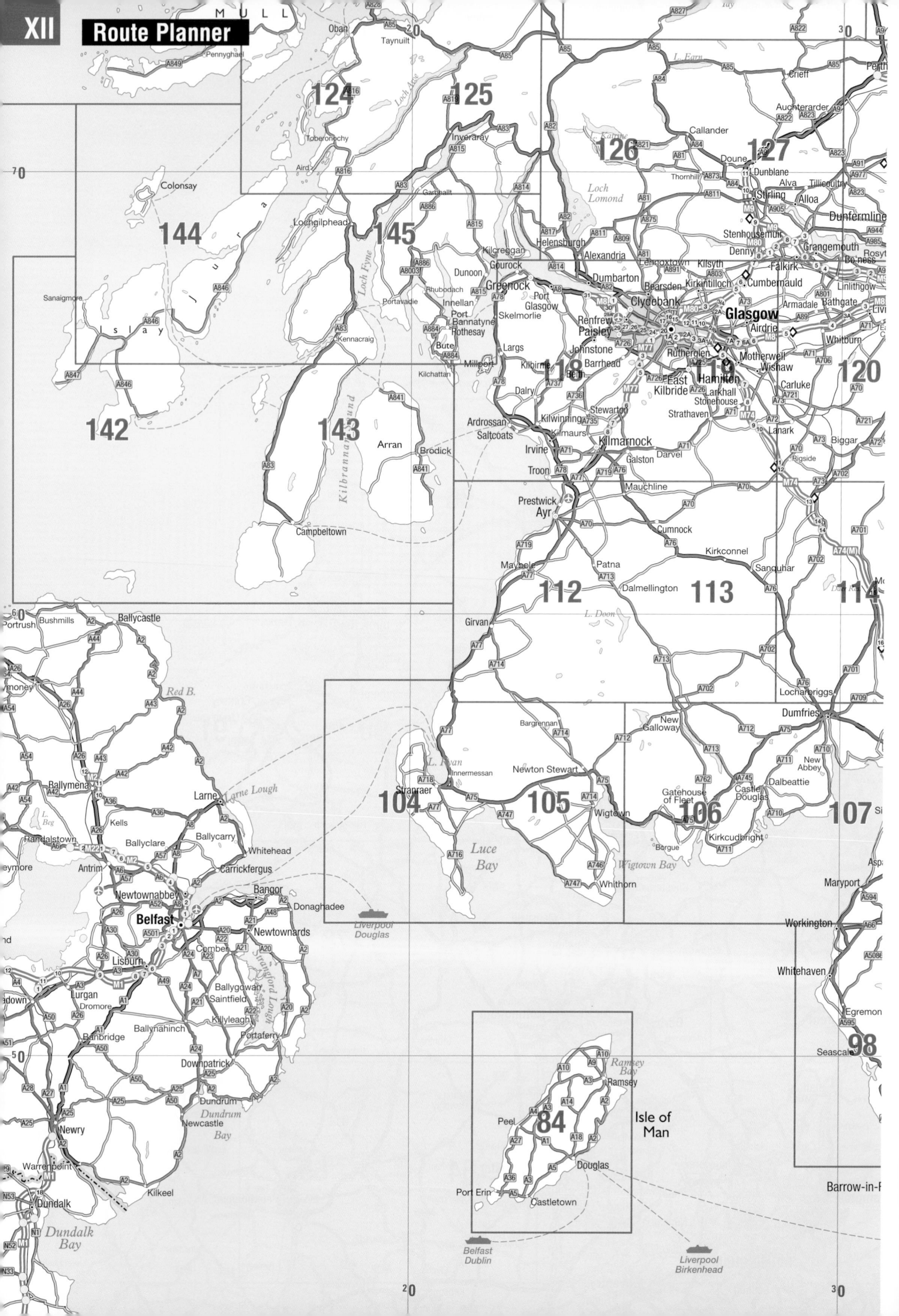

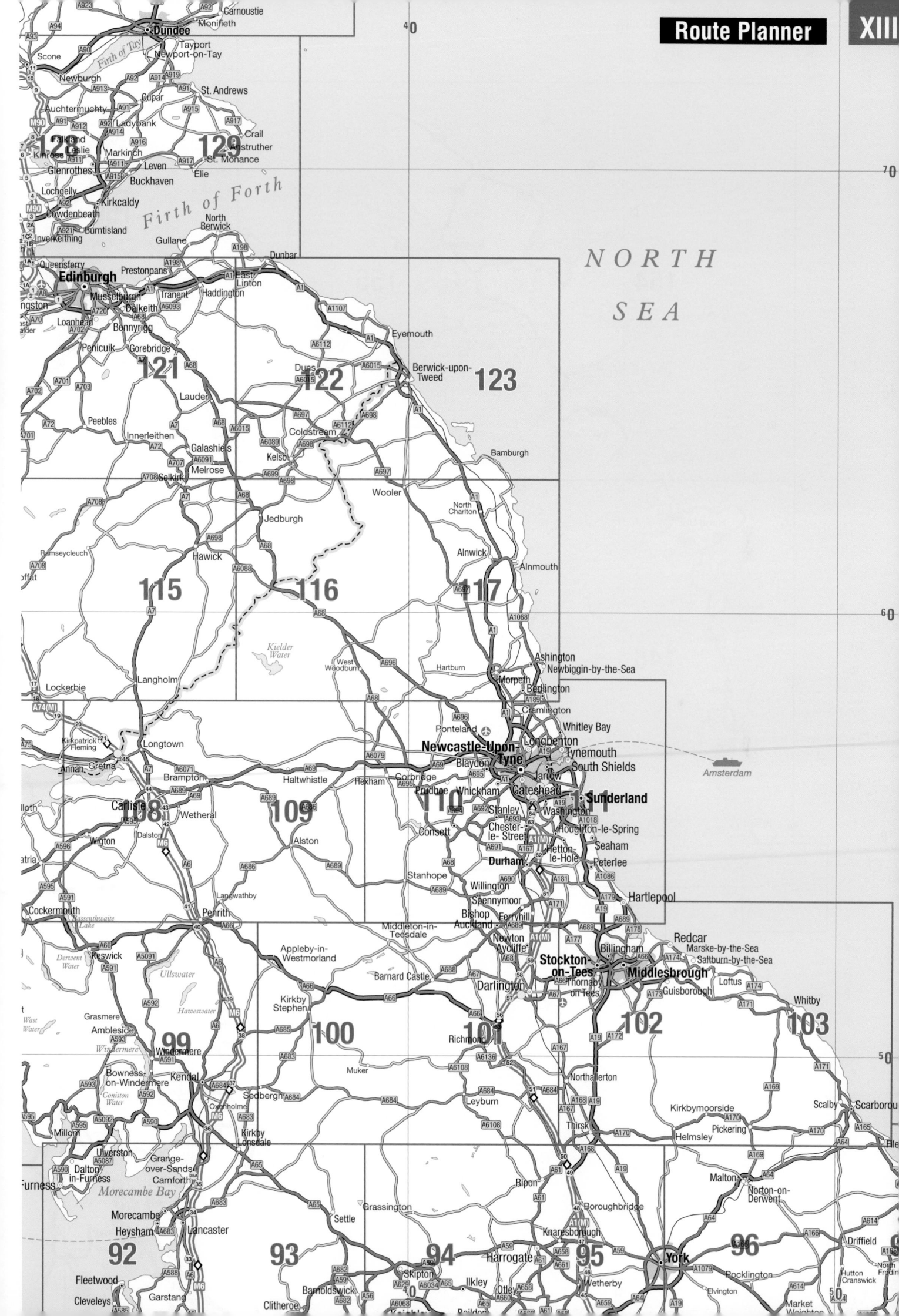

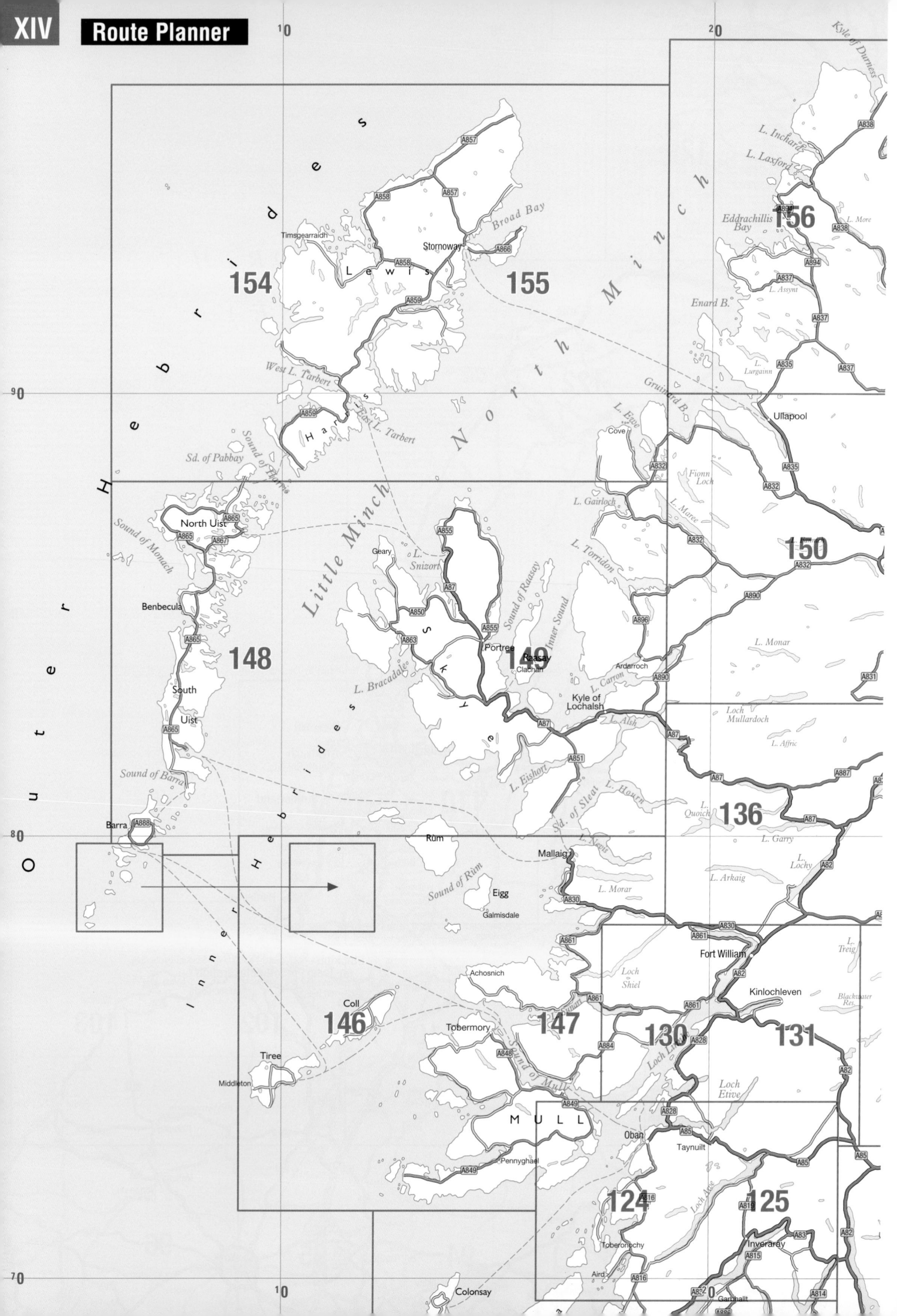

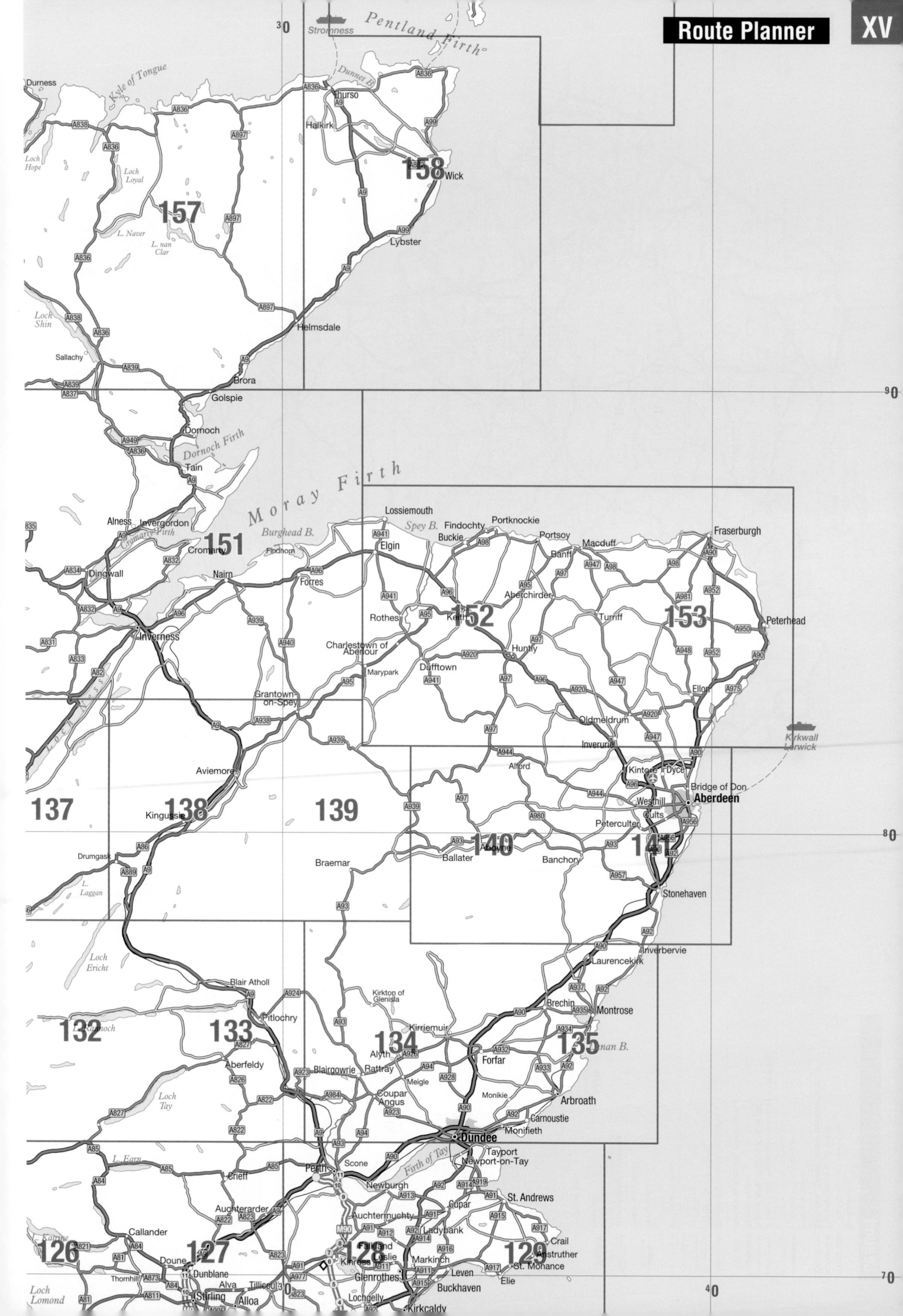

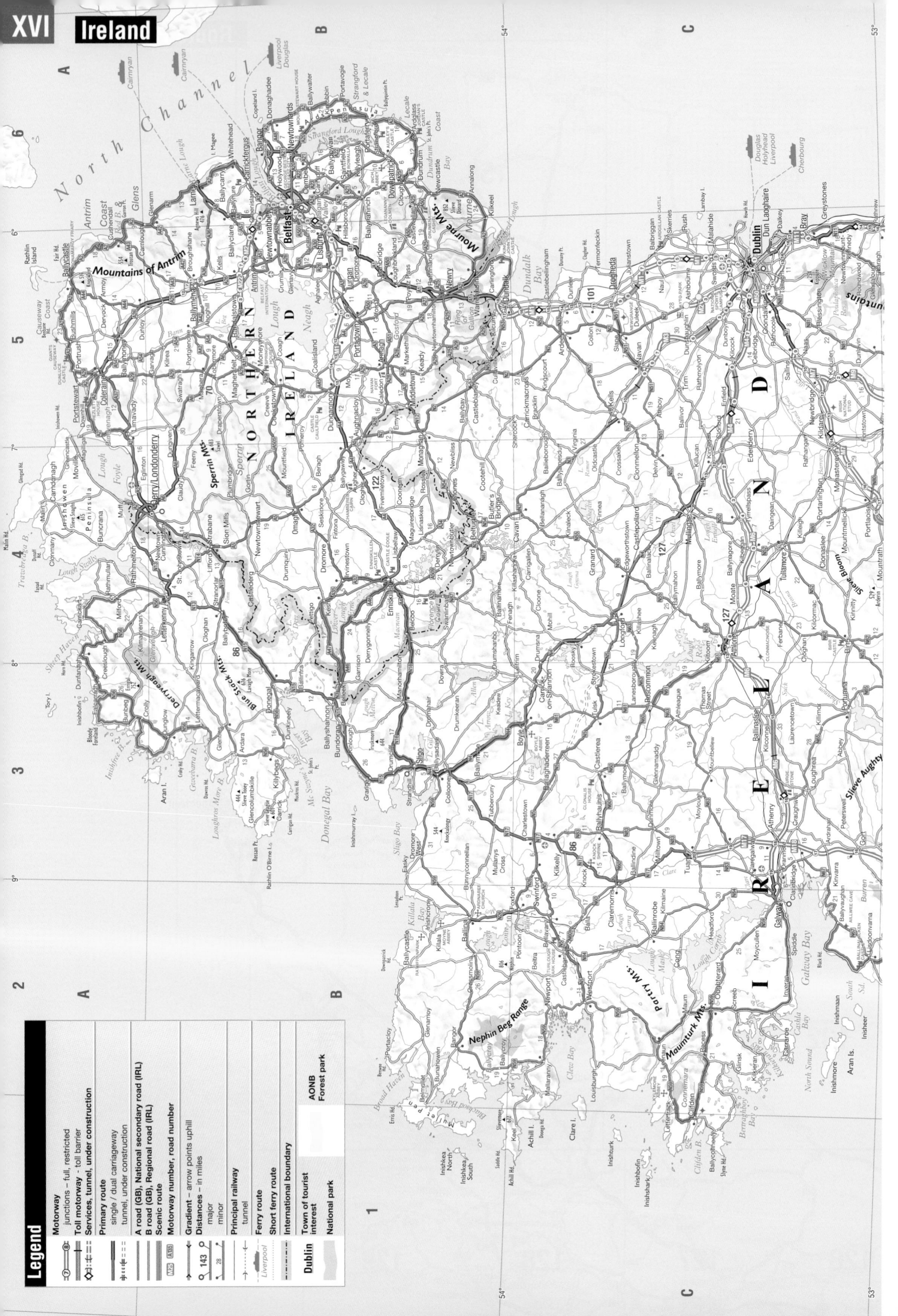

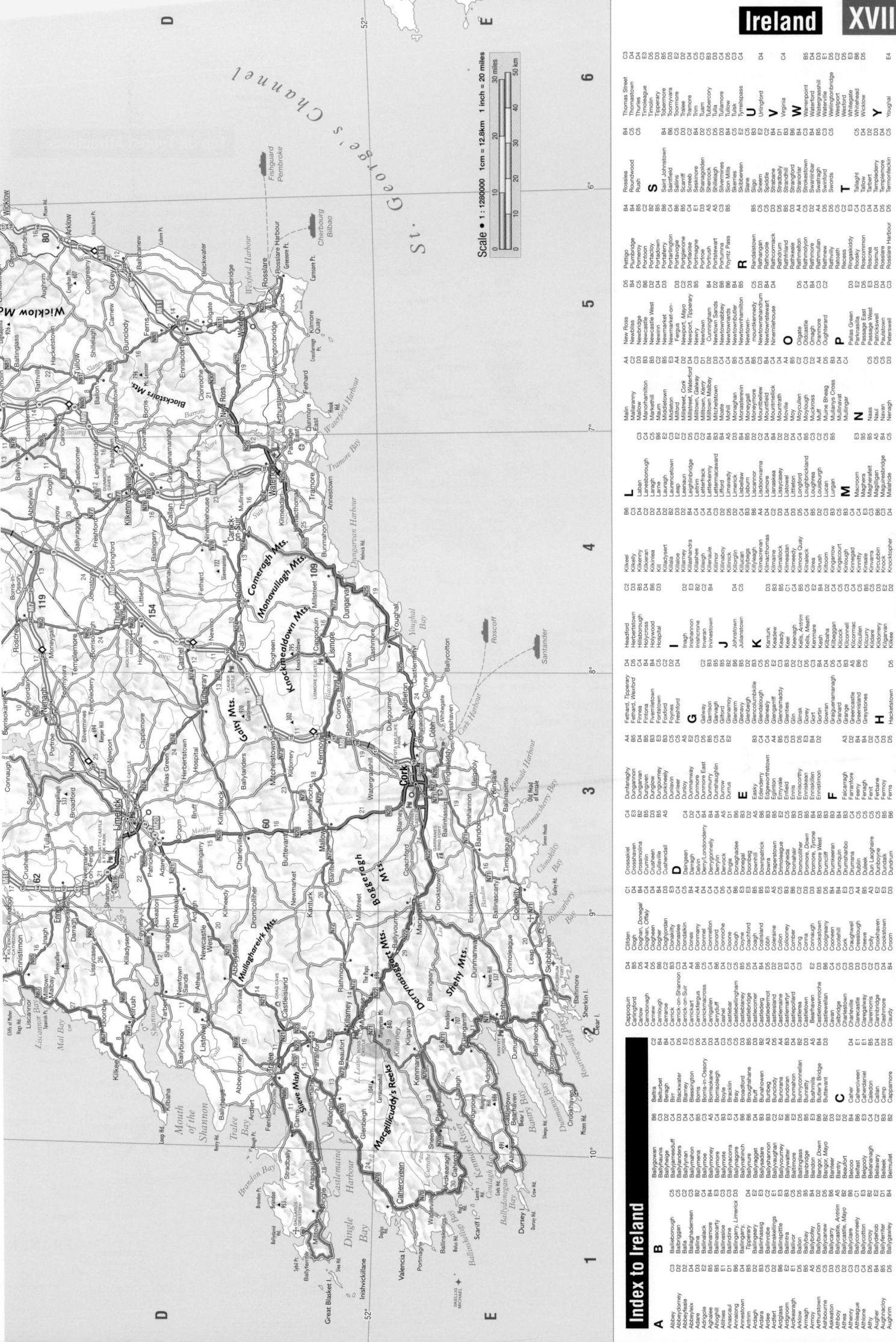

Scale • 1 : 1 280 000   1cm = 12.8km   1 inch = 20 miles

| 0 | 10 | 20 | 30 | 40 | 50 km |
| 0 | 10 | 20 | 30 miles |

St. George's Channel

Index to Ireland

A
Abbey C3
Abbeydorney B4
Abbeyfeale B4
Abbeyleix C4
Adare B4
Aghada C5
Aghdown
Aghavannagh D4
Aglish C5
Ahascragh C3
Allihies A5
Anascaul A5
Annalong E2
Annestown C5
Ardagh B4
Ardara C1
Ardcath D3
Ardee D3
Ardfert B4
Ardfinnan C4
Ardglass E2
Ardgroom A5
Ardmore C5
Ardrahan B3
Arklow D4
Armagh D2
Armoy D1
Arthurstown C5
Ashbourne D3
Ashford D4
Askeaton B4
Athboy D3
Athea B4
Athenry B3
Athleague C3
Athlone C3
Athy D4
Augher D2
Aughnacloy D2
Aughrim D4

B
Bailieborough D3
Balbriggan D3
Ballina B2
Ballinadee C5
Ballinafad C2
Ballinakill C4
Ballinalee C3
Ballinamore C2
Ballinascarty C5
Ballinasloe C3
Ballindine B3
Ballineen C5
Ballingarry, Limerick B4
Ballingarry, Tipperary C4
Ballingeary B5
Ballinhassig C5
Ballinlough C3
Ballinrobe B3
Ballinskelligs A5
Ballinspittle C5
Ballintober C3
Ballintoy D1
Ballivor D3
Ballon D4
Ballybay D2
Ballybofey C2
Ballybunion B4
Ballycanew D4
Ballycastle, Antrim D1
Ballycastle, Mayo B2
Ballyclare E2
Ballyconneely A3
Ballyconnell C2
Ballycotton C5
Ballycumber C3
Ballydehob B5
Ballyferriter A4
Ballygar C3
Ballygawley D2
Ballyhahill B4
Ballyhaise C2
Ballyhaunis C3
Ballyhean B3
Ballyheige B4
Ballyjamesduff D3
Ballylanders C4
Ballyliffin D1
Ballylongford B4
Ballylynan D4
Ballymacarbry C4
Ballymahon C3
Ballymakeery B5
Ballymena E2
Ballymoe C3
Ballymoney D1
Ballymore C3
Ballymote C2
Ballynahinch E2
Ballynure E2
Ballyporeen C4
Ballyragget C4
Ballyronan D2
Ballysadare C2
Ballyshannon C2
Ballyvaughan B3
Ballyvourney B5
Ballywalter E2
Balrothery D3
Baltimore B5
Baltinglass D4
Banagher C3
Banbridge D2
Bandon C5
Bangor, Down E2
Bangor, Mayo B2
Banteer C4
Bantry B5
Beaufort B5
Belcoo C2
Belfast E2
Bellaghy D2
Bellananagh C3
Belleek C2
Belmullet B2
Beltra B6
Belturbet C2
Benagh D4
Birr C3
Blacklion C2
Blarney C5
Blessington D4
Boris C4
Borris-in-Ossory C3
Borrisokane C3
Borrisoleigh C4
Boyle C2
Bracknagh D3
Bray D3
Broadford B4
Broughshane E2
Bruff B4
Bunbeg C1
Bunclody D4
Buncrana D1
Bundoran C2
Bunmahon C5
Burnfort C5
Burnncourt?
Burnchurch?
Burren C3
Bushmills D1
Butler's Bridge C2
Buttevant C4

C
Cappoquin C4
Carlow D4
Carnlough E2
Carndonagh D1
Carracastle C2
Carrick C1
Carrick-on-Shannon C2
Carrick-on-Suir C4
Carrickart C1
Carrickfergus E2
Carrickmacross D3
Carrickmore D2
Carrigaline C5
Carrigallen C2
Carrigtwohill C5
Carryduff E2
Cashel C4
Castlebar B3
Castlebellingham D3
Castleblayney D2
Castlecomer C4
Castleconnell B4
Castledermot D4
Castleisland B4
Castlemaine B4
Castlemartyr C5
Castleplunket C3
Castlepollard C3
Castlerea C3
Castletown D3
Castletownbere A5
Castletownroche C4
Castlewellan E2
Cavan C3
Celbridge D3
Charlestown C2
Charleville C4
Claregalway B3
Claremorris B3
Clarinbridge B3
Clashmore C5
Claudy D2
Clifden A3
Cliffony C2
Clogh C4
Cloghan, Donegal/Offaly C3
Clogheen C4
Clogher D2
Clonakilty C5
Clonard D3
Clonaslee C3
Clonbur B3
Clondalkin D3
Clones C2
Clonmany D1
Clonmel C4
Clonmellon C3
Clonmore C4
Clonony C3
Clonroche D4
Clontibret D2
Cloondara C3
Clough E2
Cloughjordan C3
Cloyne C5
Coachford C5
Coagh D2
Coalisland D2
Cobh C5
Coleraine D1
Collinstown C3
Collon D3
Collooney C2
Comber E2
Cong B3
Conna C5
Cookstown D2
Coolgreany D4
Cooraclare B4
Cootehill D2
Cork C5
Courtmacsherry C5
Craanford D4
Craughwell C3
Creeslough C1
Croagh B4
Crolly C1
Crookhaven B5
Crookstown C5
Croom B4
Crossakiel C3
Crosshaven C5
Crossmolina B2
Crumlin D3
Cullyhanna D2
Cushendall E1

D
Daingean C3
Darragh B4
Delvin C3
Derry D1
Derrygonnelly C2
Derrylin C2
Dervock D1
Dingle A4
Doagh E2
Donabate D3
Donaghadee E2
Donaghmore C4
Donard D4
Donegal C2
Doneraile C4
Doon C4
Doonbeg B4
Douglas C5
Downpatrick E2
Dowra C2
Draperstown D2
Drimoleague B5
Dripsey C5
Drogheda D3
Dromahair C2
Dromcolliher C4
Dromore, Down D2
Dromore, Tyrone D2
Dromore West C2
Drumcliff C2
Drumkeeran C2
Drumshanbo C2
Drumsna C3
Dublin D3
Duleek D3
Dunboyne D3
Dun Laoghaire D3
Dundalk D2
Dundrum E2
Dunfanaghy C1
Dungannon D2
Dungarvan C5
Dungiven D2
Dungloe C1
Dunkineely C2
Dunlavin D4
Dunleer D3
Dunloy D1
Dunmanway B5
Dunmore C3
Dunmore East C5
Dunmurry E2
Dunshaughlin D3
Durrow C4
Durrus B5

E
Easky C2
Edenderry D3
Edgeworthstown C3
Eglinton D1
Emyvale D2
Ennis B3
Enniscorthy D4
Enniscrone B2
Enniskean C5
Enniskerry D3
Enniskillen C2
Ennistimon B3

F
Falcarragh C1
Farranfore B4
Feeny D2
Fenit B4
Ferbane C3
Fermoy C4
Ferns D4
Fethard, Tipperary C4
Fethard, Wexford C5
Finnea C3
Fintona D2
Fivemiletown D2
Fontstown D4
Foxford B2
Foynes B4
Freshford C4

G
Galway B3
Garrison C2
Garvagh D1
Gilford D2
Glandore B5
Glanworth C4
Glaslough D2
Glenamoy B2
Glenarm E2
Glenbeigh A5
Glencolumbkille C2
Glendalough D4
Glenealy D4
Glengarriff B5
Glenties C1
Glin B4
Glinsk B3
Golden C4
Goleen B5
Gorey D4
Gort B3
Gortin D2
Gowran C4
Graiguenamanagh C4
Granard C3
Grange C2
Greencastle E1
Greenisland E2
Greystones D3

H
Hacketstown D4
Headford B3
Herbertstown B4
Hillsborough D2
Hollywood D4
Hospital C4

I
Inagh B4
Inishannon C5
Inishcrone B2
Irvinestown C2

J
Johnstown C4
Julianstown D3

K
Kanturk C4
Keadew C2
Keady D2
Keel A3
Keenagh C3
Kells, Antrim E2
Kells, Meath D3
Kenmare B5
Kesh C2
Kilbaha A4
Kilbeggan C3
Kilcar C2
Kilcock D3
Kilconnell C3
Kilcoole D4
Kilcormac C3
Kilcullen D4
Kilcurry D2
Kildare D4
Kildorrery C4
Kilfenora B3
Kilgarvan B5
Kilkee A4
Kilkeel D2
Kilkenny C4
Kilkieran B3
Kill D3
Killadysert B4
Killala B2
Killaloe B3
Killarney B5
Killashandra C2
Killeagh C5
Killenaule C4
Killimor C3
Killinaboy B3
Killorglin B4
Killucan C3
Killybegs C2
Killyleagh E2
Kilmacrenan C1
Kilmaine B3
Kilmallock C4
Kilmeaden C5
Kilmeage D3
Kilmichael B5
Kilmore Quay C5
Kilrea D1
Kilrush B4
Kiltoom C3
Kingarrow C2
Kingscourt D3
Kinlough C2
Kinnitty C3
Kinsale C5
Kinvarra B3
Kircubbin E2
Knock, Mayo B3
Knock B4
Knocktopher C4

L
Laban C3
Lanesborough C3
Laragh D4
Larne E2
Lauragh A5
Laurencetown C3
Leap B5
Leenaun B3
Leighlinbridge C4
Leitrim C2
Letterkenny C1
Letterfrack A3
Lifford C2
Limavady D1
Limerick B4
Lisbellaw C2
Lisburn D2
Liscannor B3
Liscarroll C4
Lisdoonvarna B3
Lismore C4
Lisnaskea C2
Lispole A4
Lisselton B4
Listowel B4
Littleton C4
Longford C3
Loughbrickland D2
Loughglinn C3
Loughrea C3
Louisburgh B3
Lucan D3

M
Macroom C5
Maghera D2
Magherafelt D2
Maguiresbridge C2
Malahide D3
Malin D1
Mallaranny B2
Mallow C4
Manorhamilton C2
Markethill D2
Maum B3
Middleton C5
Midleton C5
Milford C1
Millstreet, Cork C4
Millstreet, Waterford C4
Milltown, Galway C3
Milltown, Kerry B4
Milltown Malbay B4
Mitchelstown C4
Moate C3
Mohill C2
Monaghan D2
Monasterevin D3
Moneygall C3
Moneymore D2
Mountbellew C3
Mountcharles C2
Mountmellick C3
Mountrath C3
Mountshannon C3
Moville D1
Moy D2
Moycullen B3
Moynalty D3
Muckross B5
Muff D1
Mullagh D3
Mullany's Cross C3
Mullinavat C4
Mullingar C3
Mulranny B2

N
Naas D3
Naul D3
Navan D3
Nenagh C4
New Ross C4
Newbliss C2
Newbridge D3
Newcastle D2
Newcastle West B4
Newinn C4
Newmarket C4
Newmarket-on-Fergus B4
Newport, Mayo B2
Newport, Tipperary C4
Newry D2
Newtown D4
Newtownabbey E2
Newtownards E2
Newtownbutler C2
Newtowncunningham C1
Newtownhamilton D2
Newtownmountkennedy D4
Newtownsandes B4
Newtownshandrum C4
Newtownstewart D2
Ninemilehouse C4

O
Oilgate D4
Oldcastle C3
Omagh D2
Oranmore B3
Oughterard B3

P
Pallas Green C4
Pallasgreen B4
Passage East C5
Passage West C5
Patrickswell B4
Paulstown C4
Petersburg
Pettigo C2
Pomeroy D2
Portadown D2
Portaferry E2
Portarlington C3
Portavogie E2
Portglenone D2
Portlaoise C4
Portmagee A5
Portmarnock D3
Portroe C3
Portrush D1
Portsalon C1
Portumna C3
Poyntz Pass D2

R
Randalstown D2
Rathangan D3
Rathcoole D3
Rathcormack C5
Rathdowney C4
Rathdrum D4
Rathfriland D2
Rathkeale B4
Rathmelton C1
Rathmolyon D3
Rathmore B5
Rathmullan C1
Rathnew D4
Rathvilly D4
Ratoath D3
Recess A3
Ringaskiddy C5
Robertstown D3
Rochfortbridge C3
Roosky C2
Roscommon C3
Roscrea C3
Rosmuk A3
Rosslare D4
Rosslare Harbour D4
Rosslea C2
Roundwood D4
Rush D3

S
Saint Johnstown C1
Saintfield E2
Sallins D3
Scariff C3
Screeb A3
Seaforde E2
Shanagolden B4
Shercock D3
Shillelagh D4
Shinrone C3
Sion Mills D2
Sixmilebridge B4
Skerries D3
Skibbereen B5
Slane D3
Sligo C2
Sneem A5
Spiddal B3
Strabane D2
Stradbally D4
Strandhill C2
Strangford E2
Stranorlar C2
Strokestown C3
Summerhill D3
Swanlinbar C2
Swatragh D2
Swinford C2
Swords D3

T
Tallaght D3
Tallow C5
Tarbert B4
Templederry C4
Templemore C4
Termonfeckin D3
Thomas Street C3
Thomastown C4
Thurles C4
Timoleague C5
Timolin D4
Tipperary C4
Tobercurry C2
Toomyvara C3
Toormore B5
Tralee B4
Tramore C5
Trim D3
Tuam B3
Tubbercurry C2
Tulla B4
Tullamore C3
Tullow D4
Tynemillpass D3

U
Urlingford C4

V
Virginia D3

W
Waterford C4
Watergrasshill C5
Waterville A5
Wellingtonbridge C5
Westport B3
Wexford D4
Whitegate C5
Whitehead E2
Wicklow D4

Y
Youghal E4

Tourism

Tourism symbols

- National Park
- Area of Outstanding Natural Beauty
- National Scenic Area
- Built-up area
- Long distance footpath
- ● Town of tourist interest
- ◆ Other tourist attraction
- ○ Other town

Top Ireland Tourist Attractions

		Visitors in millions (2019)
1.	Guinness Storehouse, Dublin	1.7
2.	Cliffs of Moher Visitor Experience, Clare	1.6
3.	Dublin Zoo, Dublin	1.3
4.	The Book of Kells, Dublin	1.1
5.	Castletown House Parklands, Kildare	1.0
6.	Kilkenny Castle Parklands, Kilkenny	0.9
7.	National Gallery of Ireland, Dublin	0.8
8.	Glendalough Monument & Site, Wicklow	0.7
9.	Tayto Park, Meath	0.7
10.	National Botanic Gardens, Dublin	0.7

Top UK Tourist Attractions

		Visitors in millions (2020)
1.	Tate Modern, London	1.4
2.	Natural History Museum, London	1.3
3.	British Museum, London	1.3
4.	Royal Botanic Gardens, Kew	1.2
5.	National Gallery, London	1.2
6.	Chester Zoo	1.2
7.	RHS Garden Wisley	1.0
8.	Victoria & Albert Museum, London	0.9
9.	Science Museum, London	0.9
10.	Somerset House, London	0.7
11.	Southbank Centre, London	0.7
12.	Horniman Museum and Gardens, London	0.6
13.	ZSL Whipsnade Zoo	0.5
14.	Longleat	0.5
15.	Westonbirt, The National Arboretum	0.5
16.	Attingham Park	0.5
17.	Royal Botanic Garden, Edinburgh	0.5
18.	ZSL London Zoo	0.5
19.	Tower of London	0.4
20.	National Museum of Scotland, Edinburgh	0.4

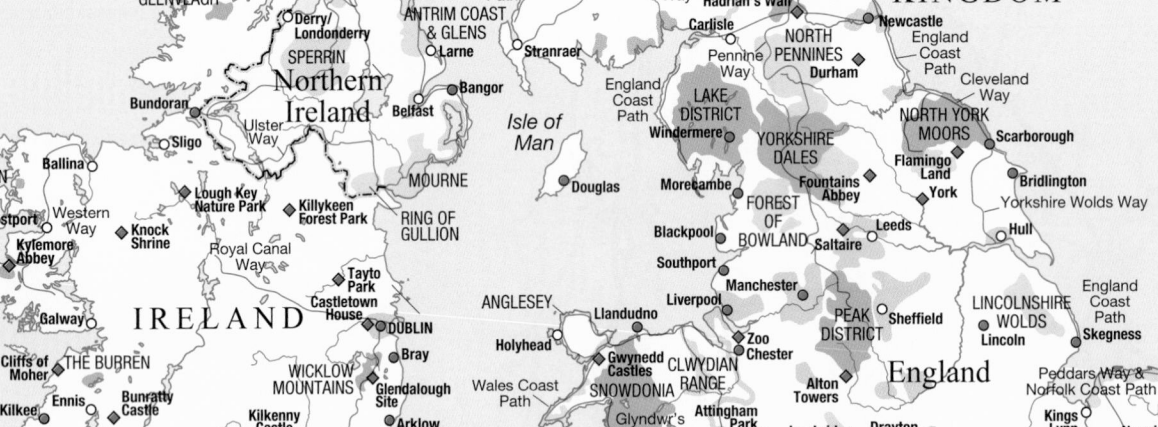

COPYRIGHT PHILIP'S

Transport symbols

- ═══ Motorway
- ── Other important road
- ── Main railway
- ── Main ferry route
- --- Channel Tunnel
- ✈ Main airport
- ⛴ Main ferry port
- o Other town

Top UK Ferry ports

		International passengers in thousands (2020)
1.	Dover	4,376
2.	Holyhead	808
3.	Portsmouth	469
4.	Harwich	347
5.	Hull	227
6.	Newhaven	133
7.	Tyne	115
8.	Pembroke Dock	93
9.	Immingham	83
10.	Plymouth	78

Top UK Airports

		International passengers in millions (2020)
1.	London Heathrow	22.1
2.	London Gatwick	10.2
3.	London Stansted	7.5
4.	Manchester	7.0
5.	London Luton	5.6
6.	Edinburgh	3.5
7.	Birmingham	2.9
8.	Bristol	2.2
9.	Glasgow	1.9
10.	Belfast International	1.7
11.	Liverpool John Lennon	1.3
12.	Newcastle	1.1
13.	Aberdeen	1.0
14.	London City	0.9
15.	East Midlands	0.9
16.	Leeds Bradford	0.8
17.	George Best Belfast City	0.5
18.	Southend	0.4
19.	Doncaster Sheffield	0.3
20.	Southampton	0.3

COPYRIGHT PHILIP'S

Distance table

How to use this table

Distances are shown in miles and kilometres with estimated journey times in hours and minutes.

For example: the distance between Dover and Fishguard is 331 miles or 533 kilometres with an estimated journey time of 6 hours, 20 minutes.

Estimated driving times are based on an average speed of 60mph on Motorways and 40mph on other roads. Drivers should allow extra time when driving at peak periods or through areas likely to be congested.

Supporting

THINK!

Travel safe –
Don't drive tired

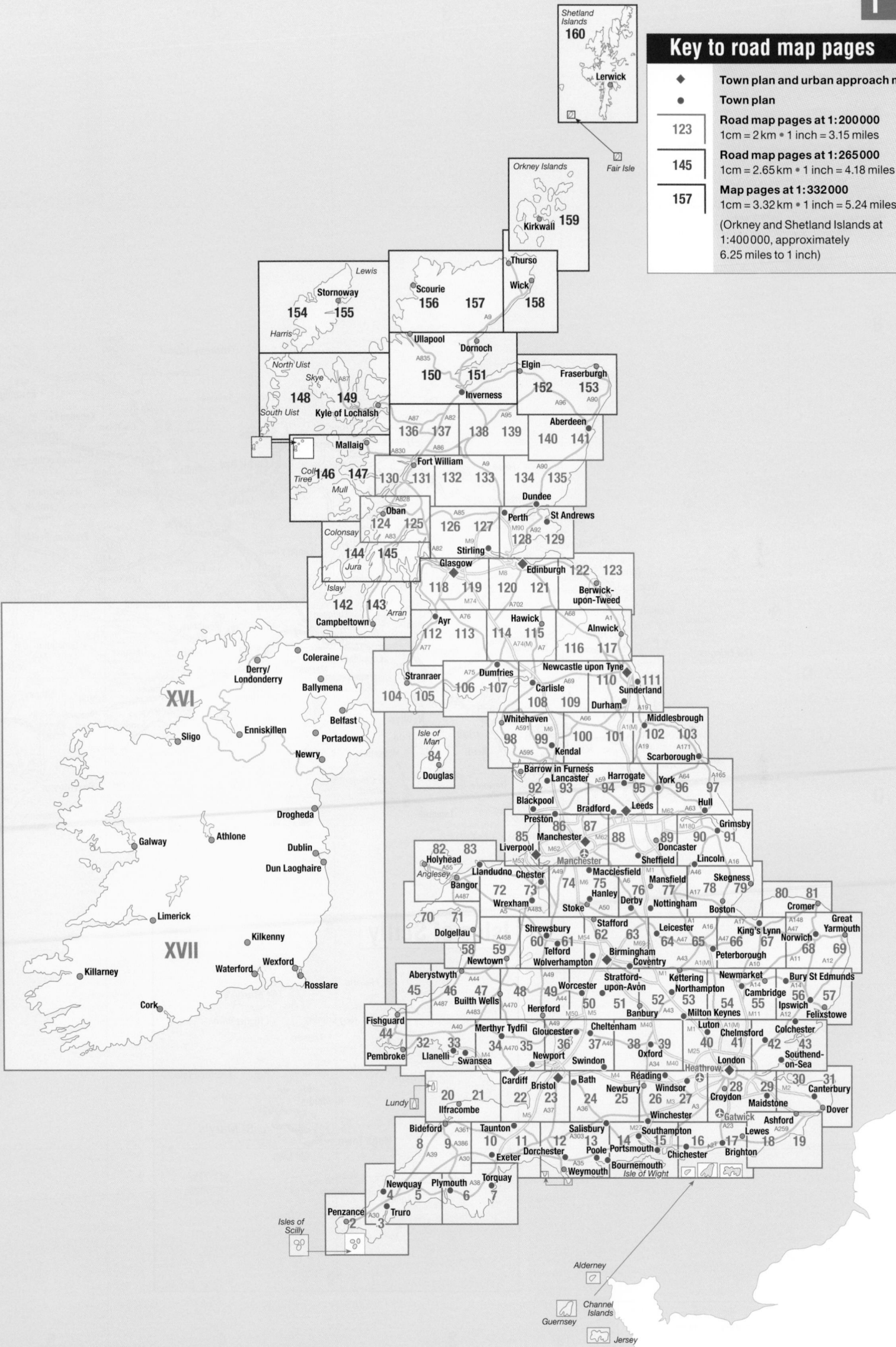

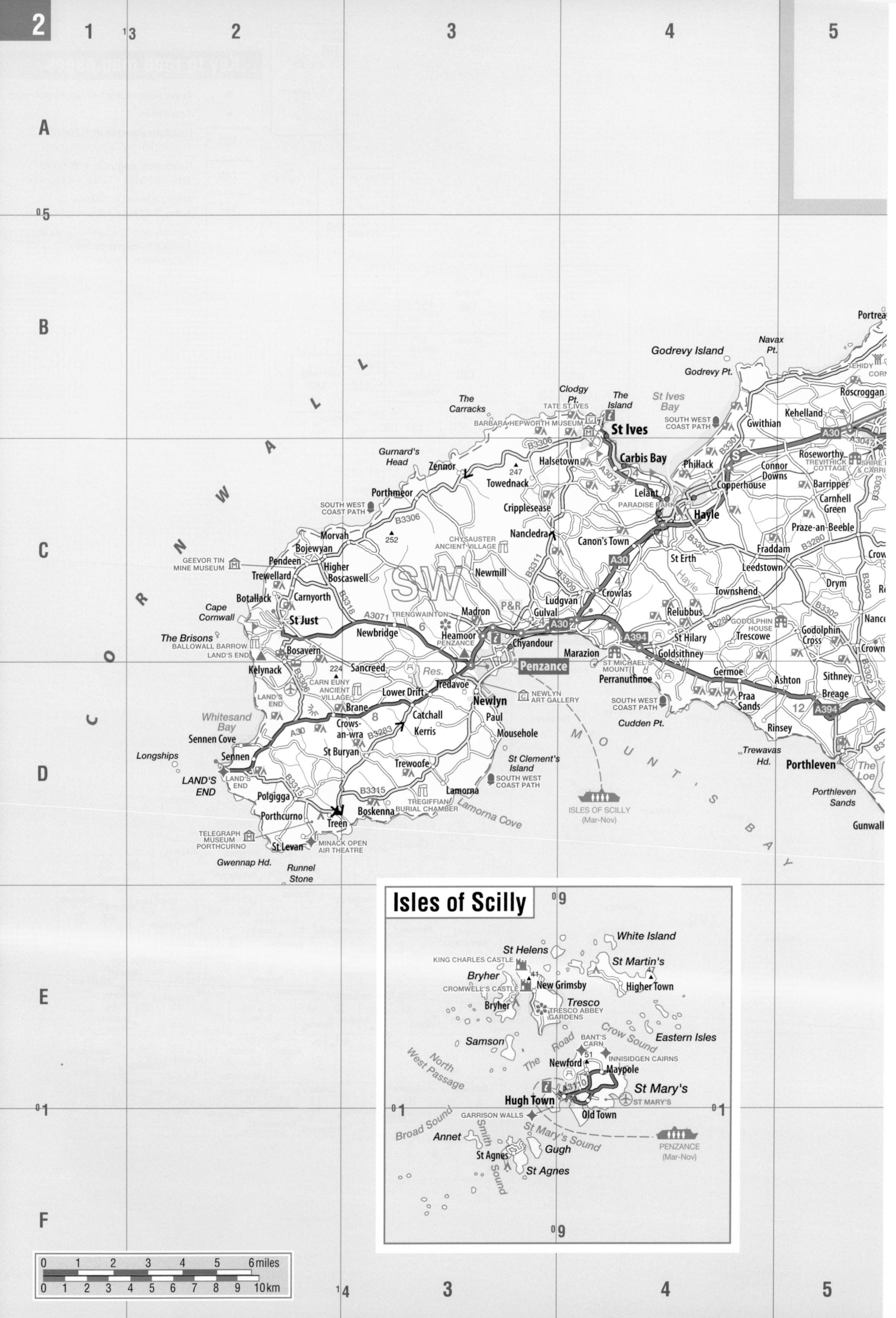

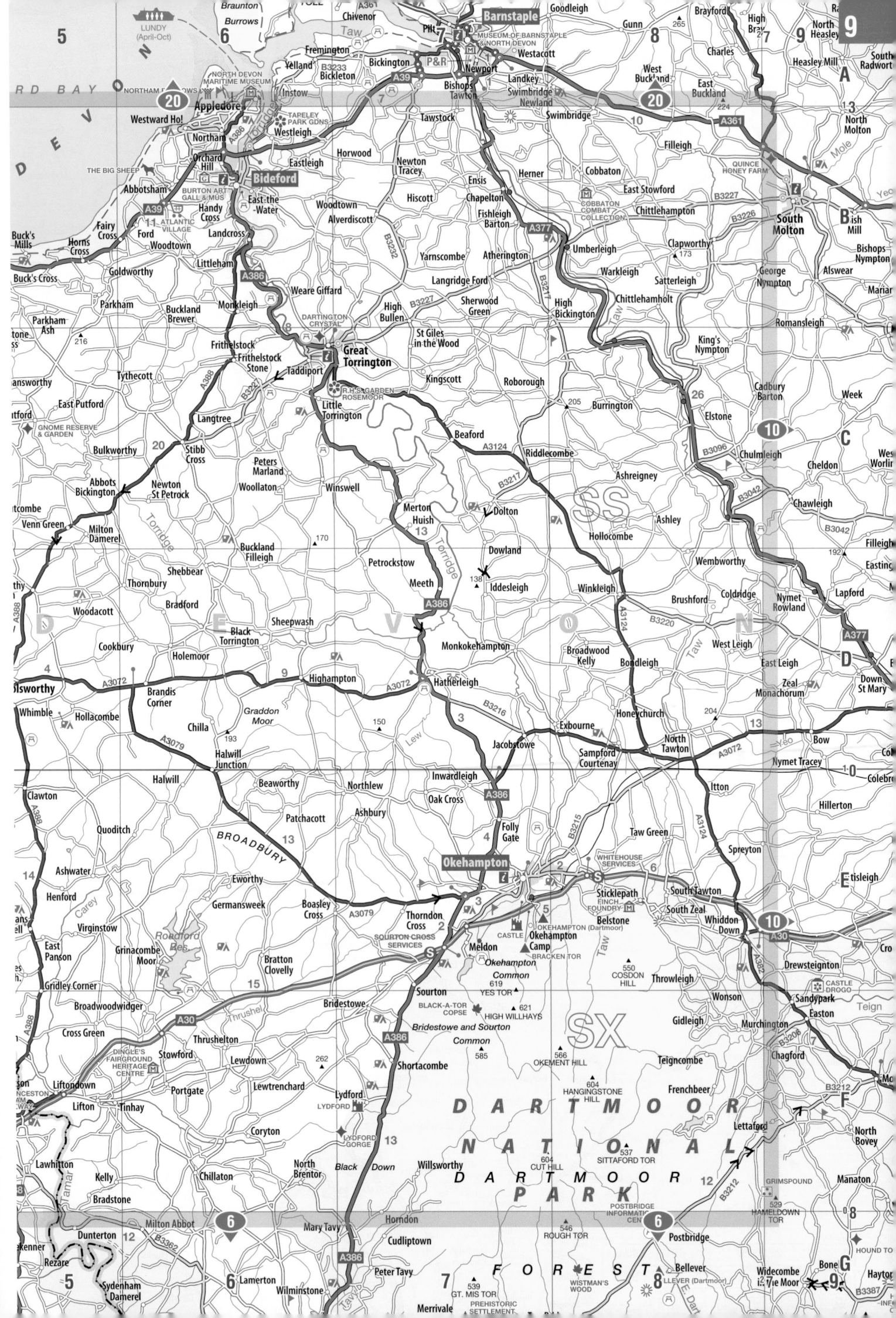

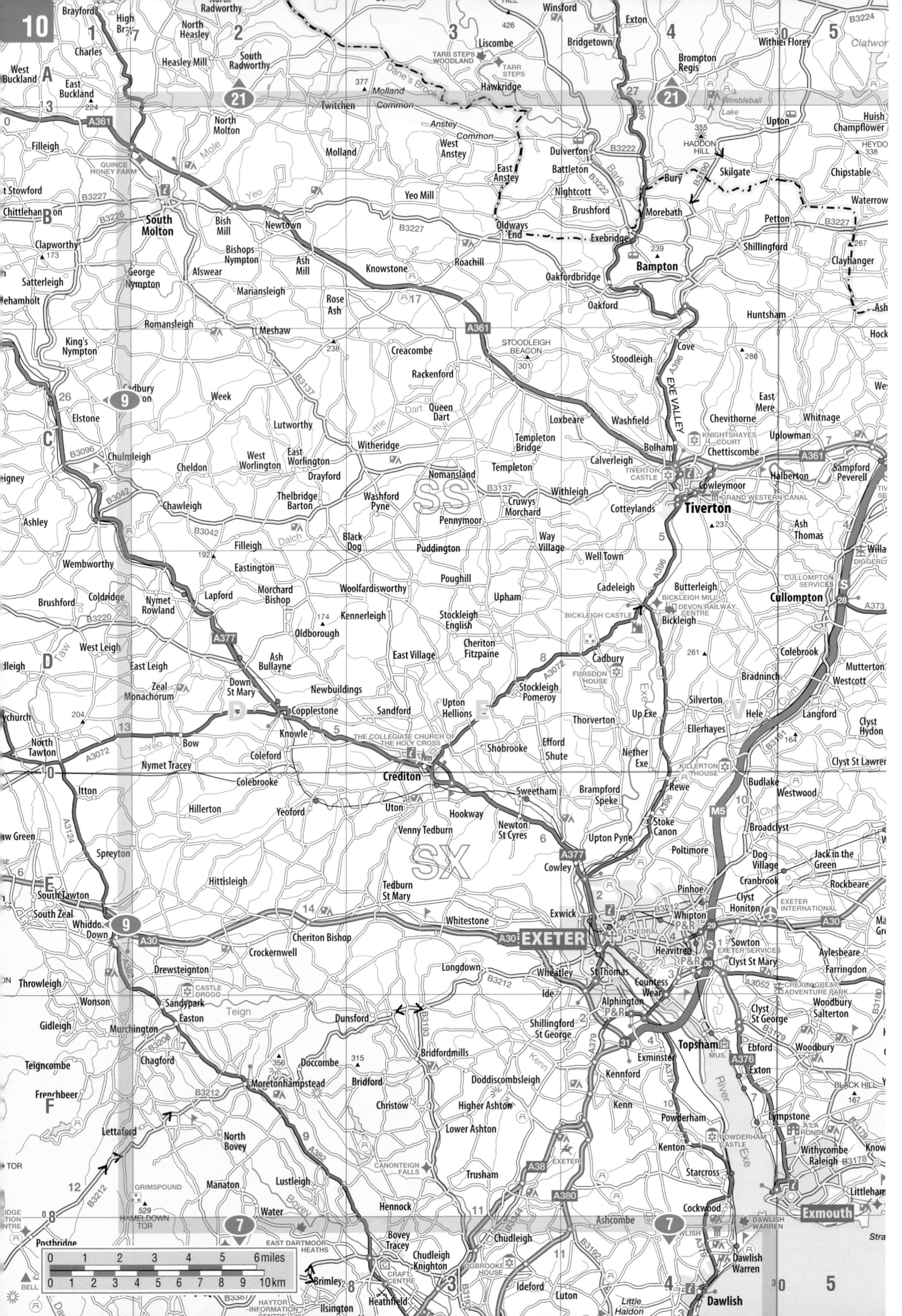

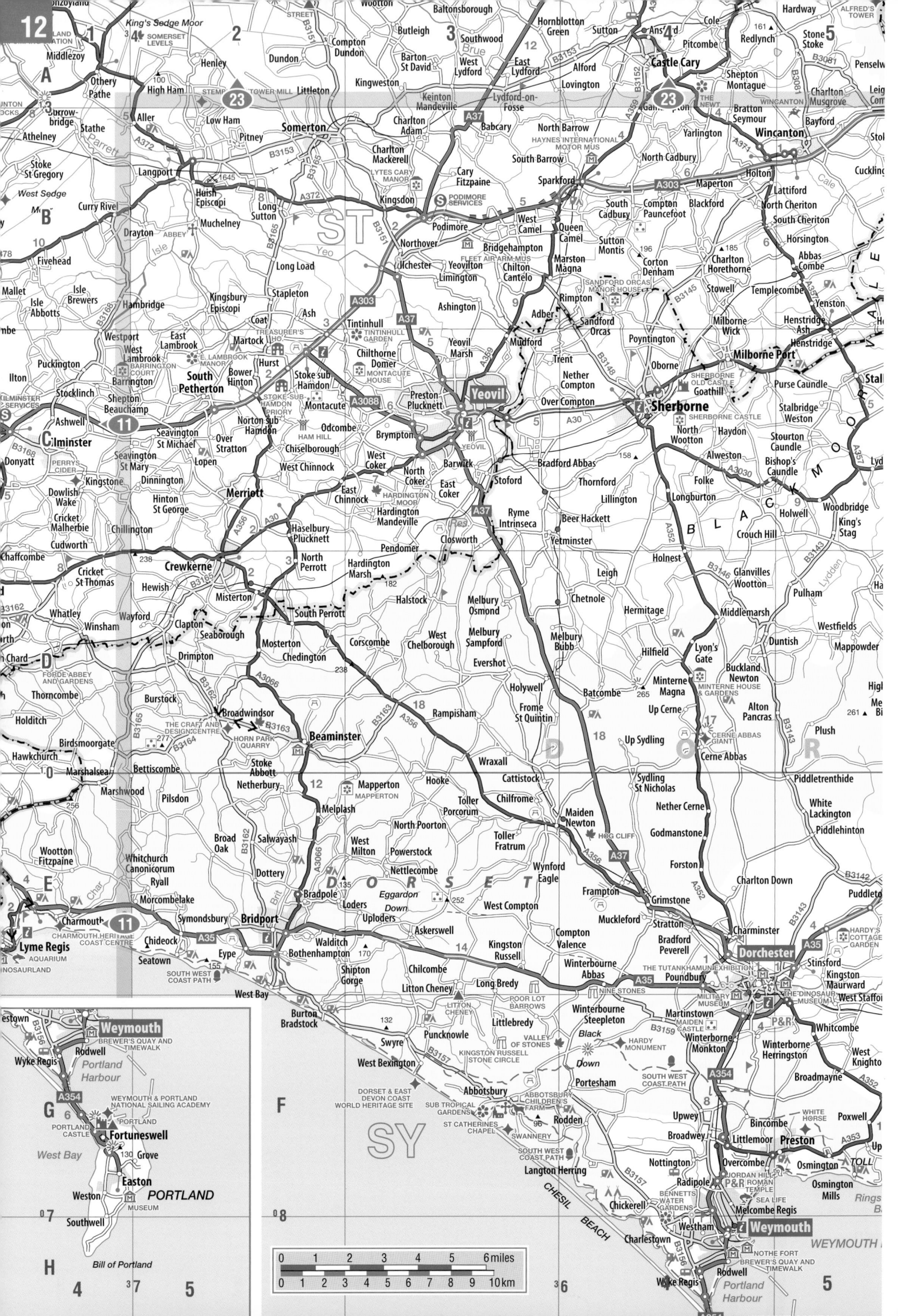

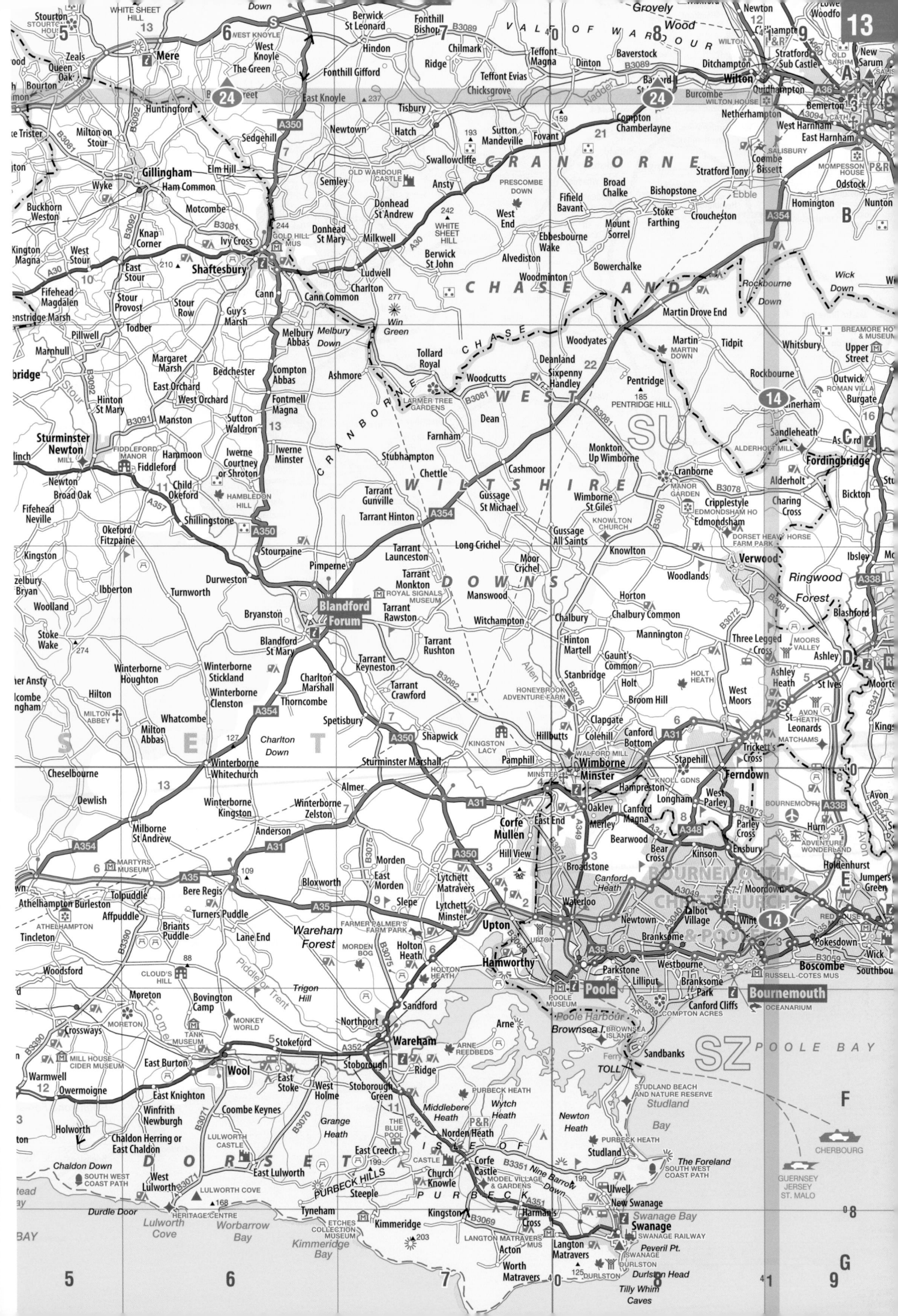

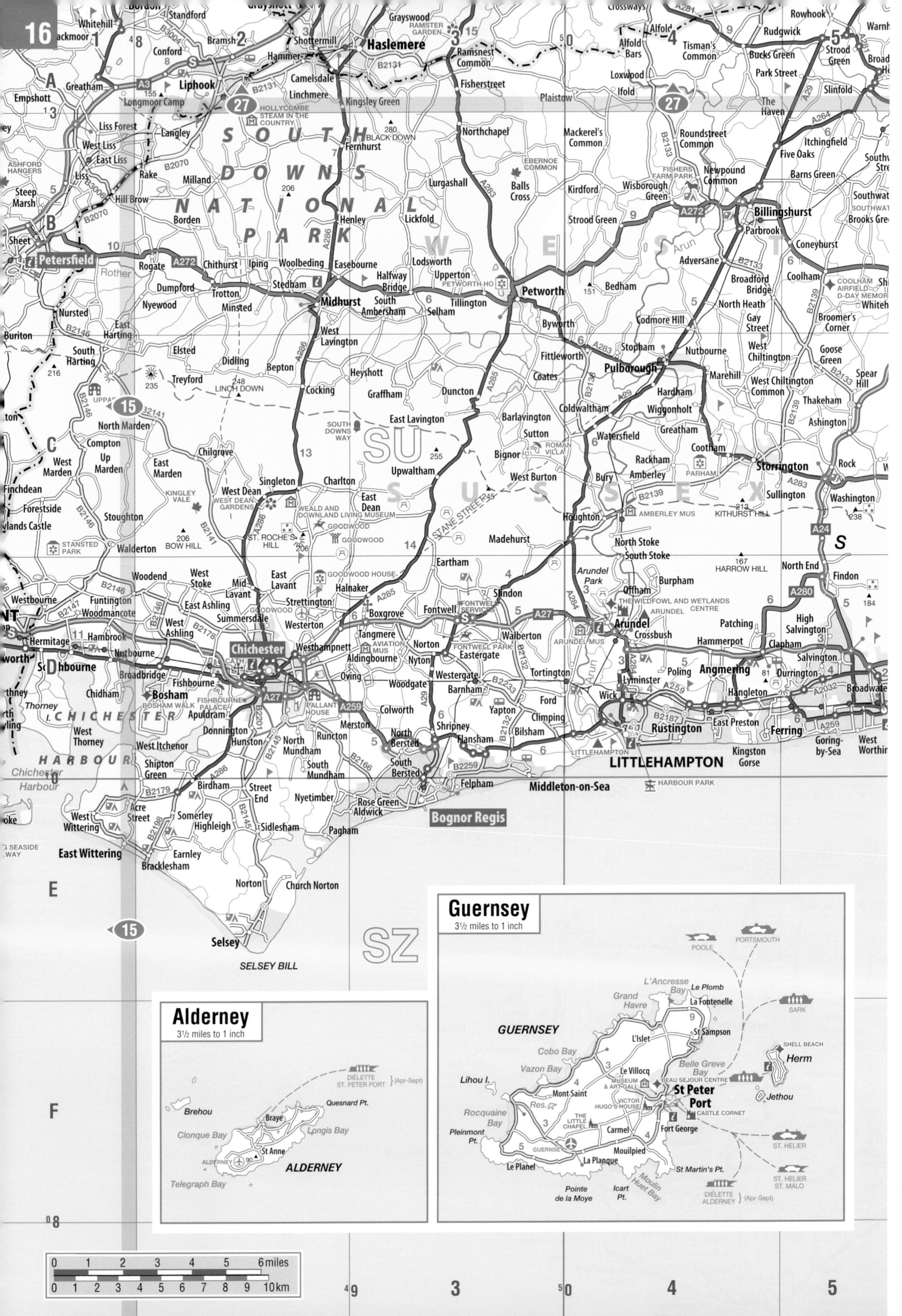

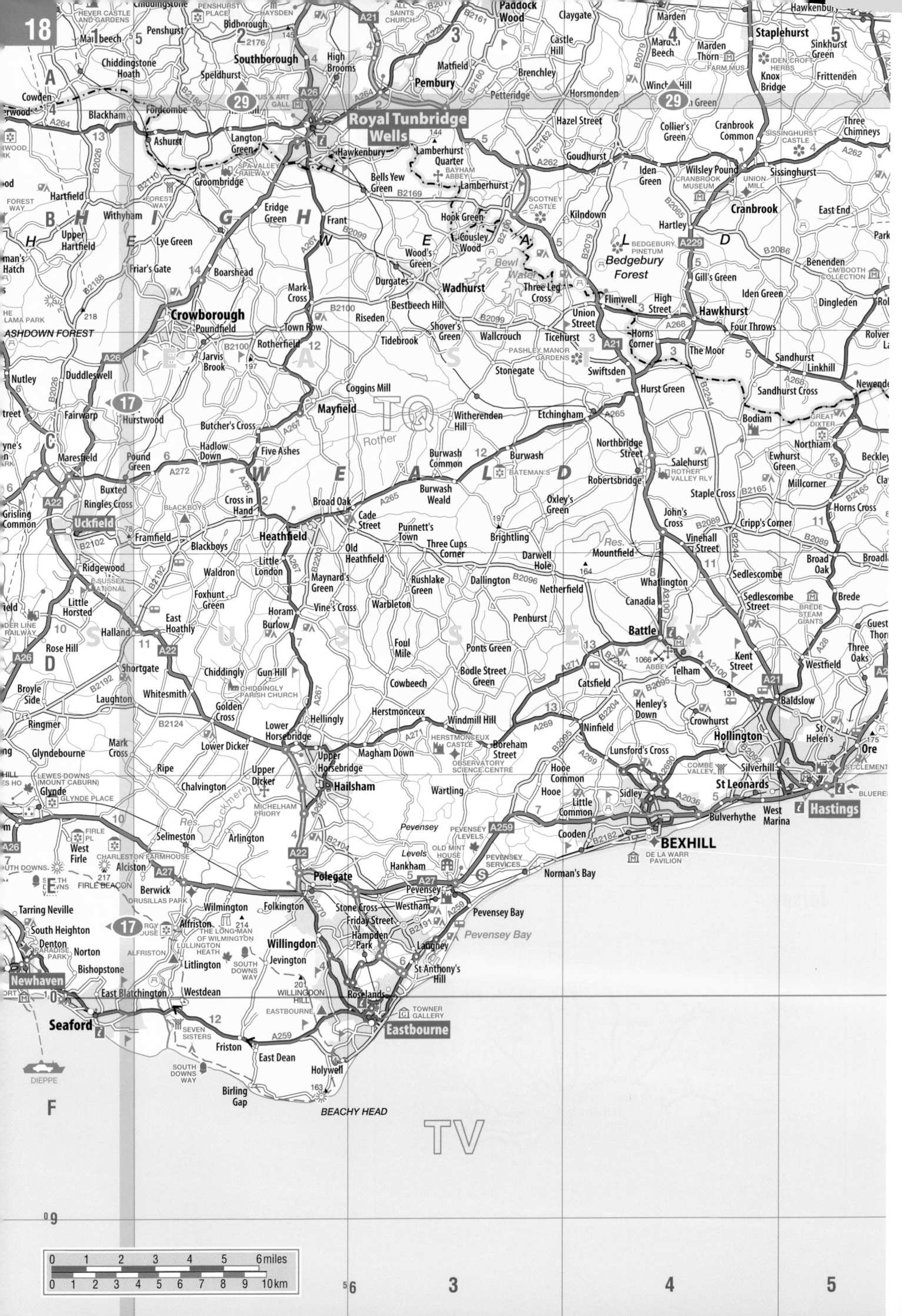

1   3   2   3   2   4   5

A

¹8

B

C

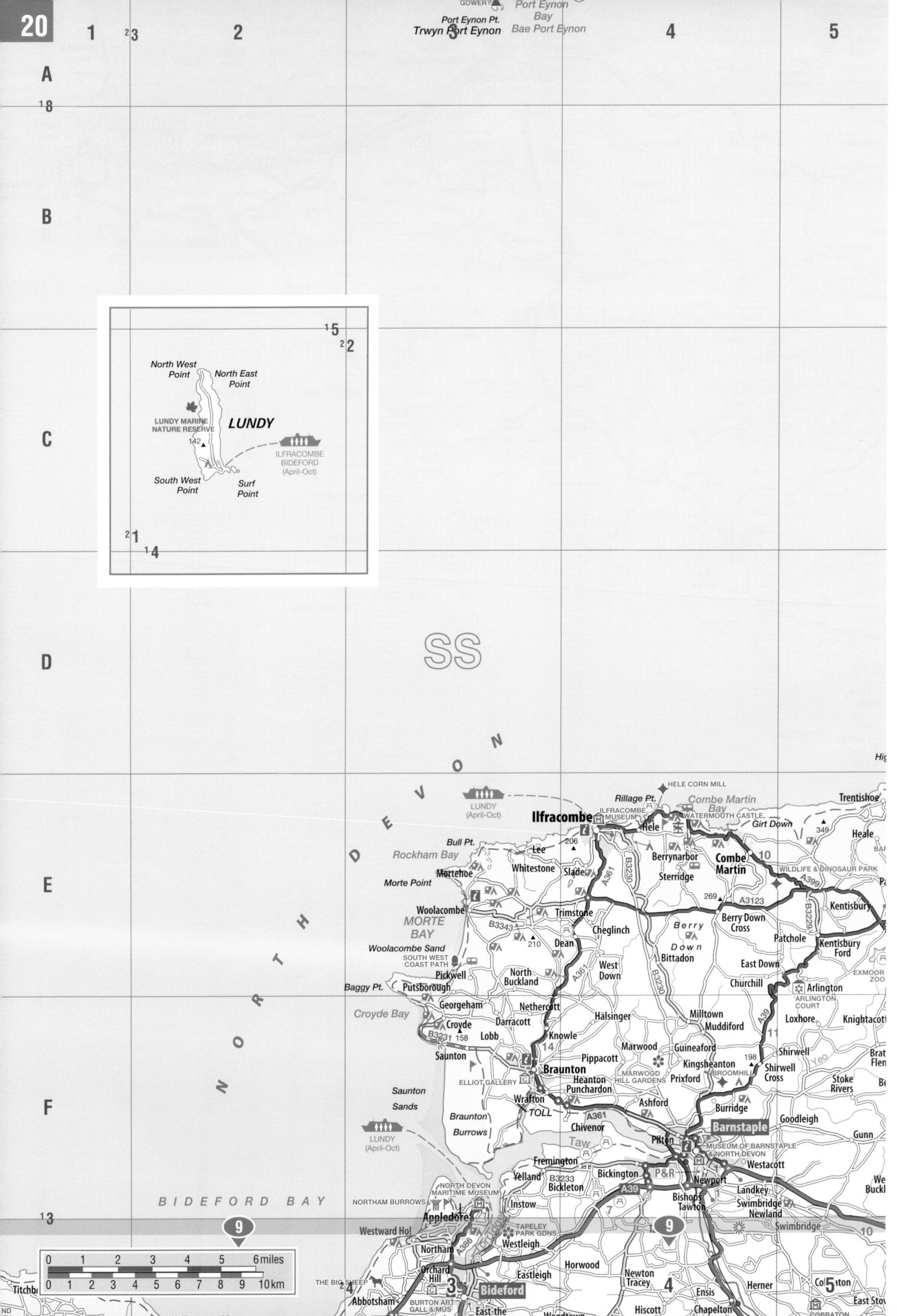

LUNDY

North West Point   North East Point

LUNDY MARINE NATURE RESERVE

142

LUNDY

South West Point   Surf Point

ILFRACOMBE
BIDEFORD
(April-Oct)

¹5
²2

²1
¹4

D

SS

E

NORTH DEVON

LUNDY
(April-Oct)

Rillage Pt.   HELE CORN MILL   Combe Martin Bay   Trentishoe
Ilfracombe   ILFRACOMBE MUSEUM   WATERMOUTH CASTLE   Girt Down   Heale
Bull Pt.   Hele   Berrynarbor   Combe Martin   349
Rockham Bay   Lee   206   Sterridge   10
Mortehoe   Whitestone   Slade   A361   B3230   WILDLIFE & DINOSAUR PARK
Morte Point   Berry Down Cross   269   A3123   Kentisbury   EXMOOR ZOO
Woolacombe   Trimstone   Cheglinch   Berry   Patchole   Kentisbury Ford
MORTE BAY   B3343   Dean   Down   East Down   B3229
Woolacombe Sand   210   West   Bittadon   Churchill   Arlington
SOUTH WEST COAST PATH   Pickwell   North   Down   B3230   ARLINGTON COURT
Baggy Pt.   Putsborough   Buckland   Halsinger   Milltown   Loxhore   Knightacott
Georgeham   Nethercott   Muddiford   A39
Croyde Bay   Darracott   Knowle   Marwood   Guineaford   Shirwell   Yeo   Brat Flen
B3231   158   Croyde   Lobb   Pippacott   MARWOOD HILL GARDENS   Kingsheanton   198   Shirwell Cross   Stoke Rivers
Saunton   14   Braunton   Prixford   BROOMHILL   Ashford   Burridge   Goodleigh
Saunton Sands   ELLIOT GALLERY   Heanton Punchardon   A361   Gunn
Braunton Burrows   Wrafton   Chivenor   Pilton   Barnstaple   Westacott
LUNDY (April-Oct)   TOLL   Taw   P&R   MUSEUM OF BARNSTAPLE & NORTH DEVON   West Buckl
Fremington   Newport   Landkey
NORTH DEVON MARITIME MUSEUM   Yelland   B3233   Bickington   A39   Bishops Tawton   Swimbridge   Newland
BIDEFORD BAY   NORTHAM BURROWS   Instow   Bickleton   Swimbridge
Appledore   ¹3   9   9   10
Westward Ho!   TAPELEY PARK GDNS   Horwood   Newton Tracey   Herner   Col ton
Northam   A386   Westleigh   Eastleigh   East Stou
THE BIG SHEEP   Orchard Hill   3   Bideford   4   Hiscott   Chapelton   5
Titchb ND   Abbotsham   BURTON ART GALL & MUS   East-the   Woodtown   CORRATON

F

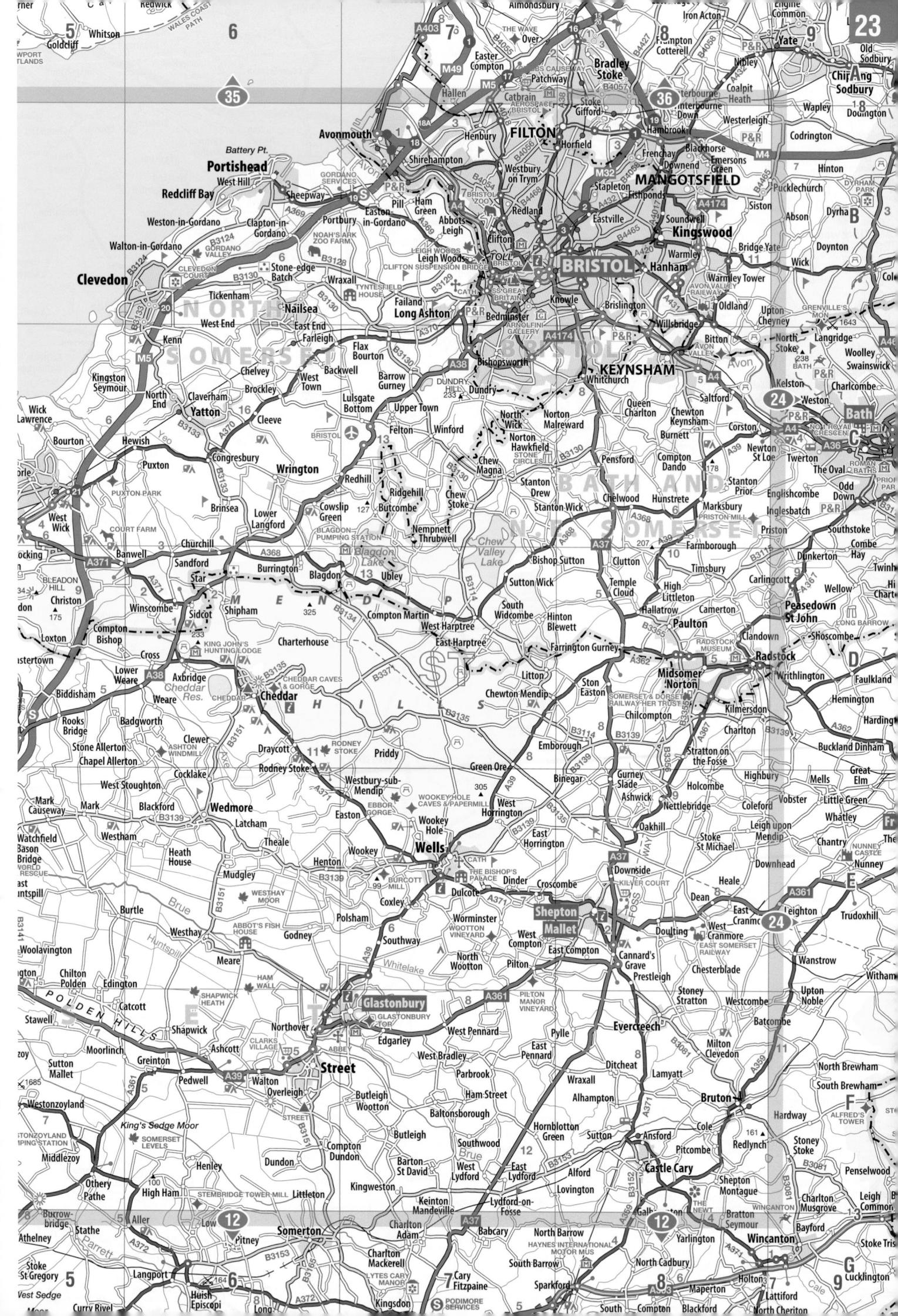

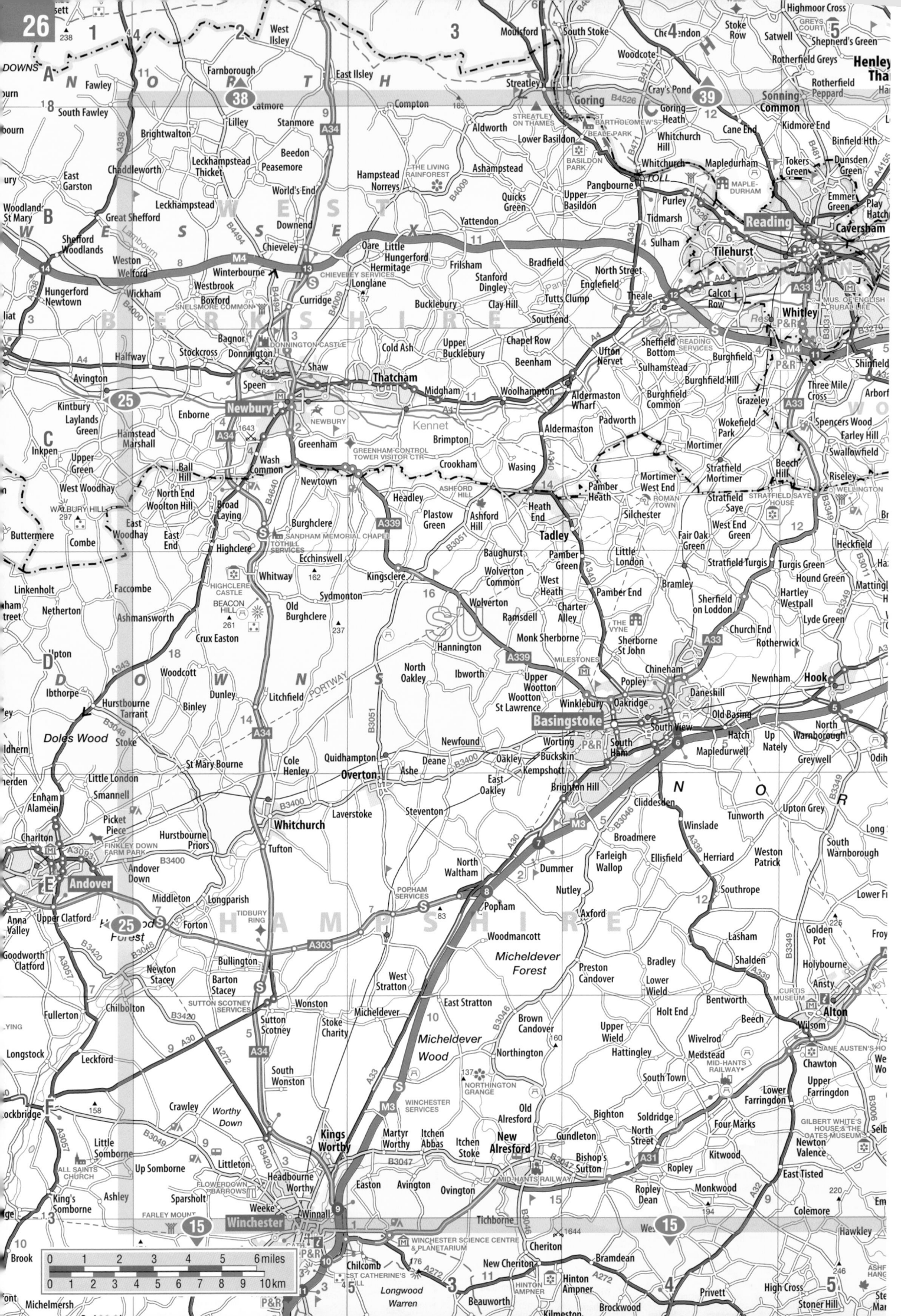

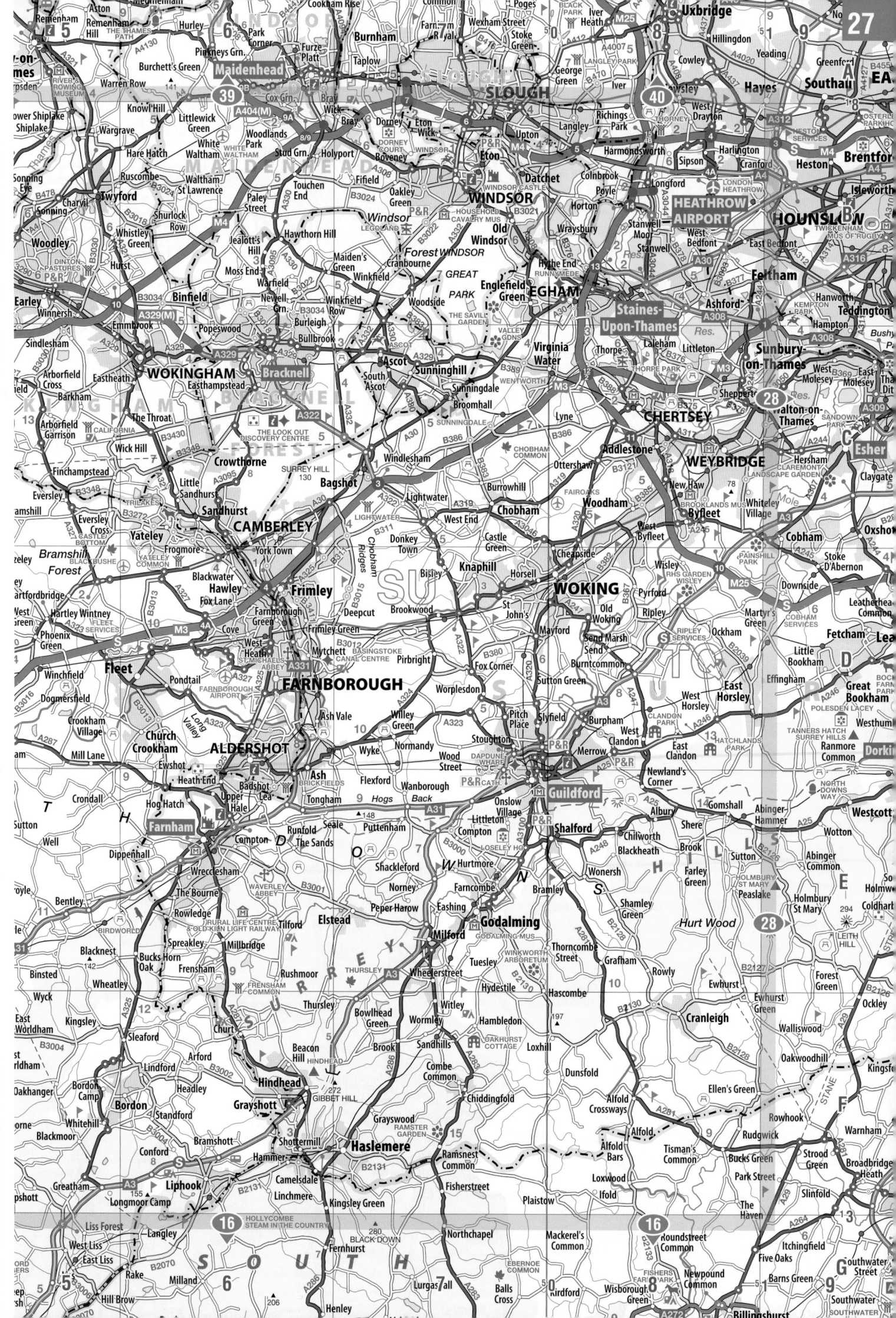

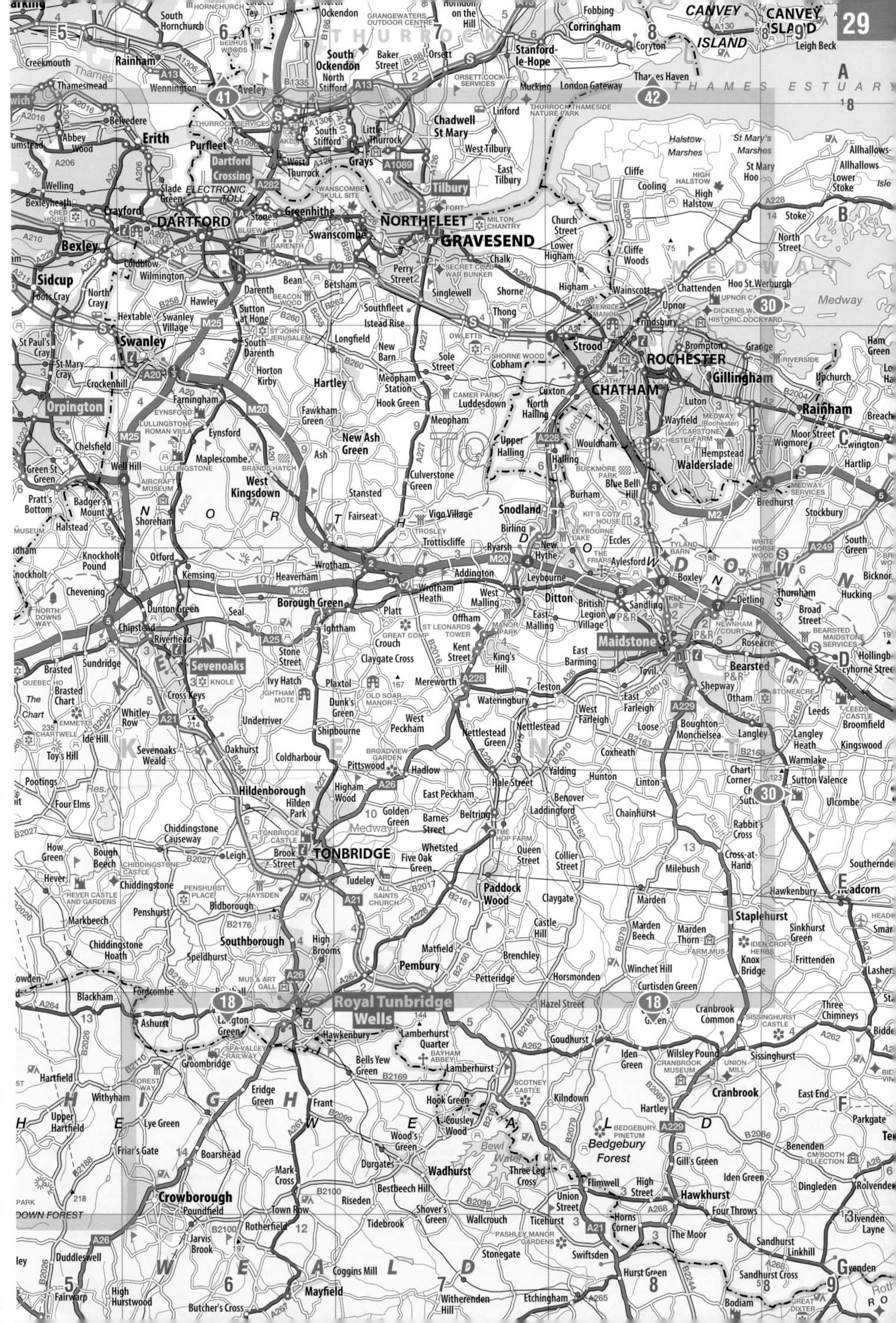

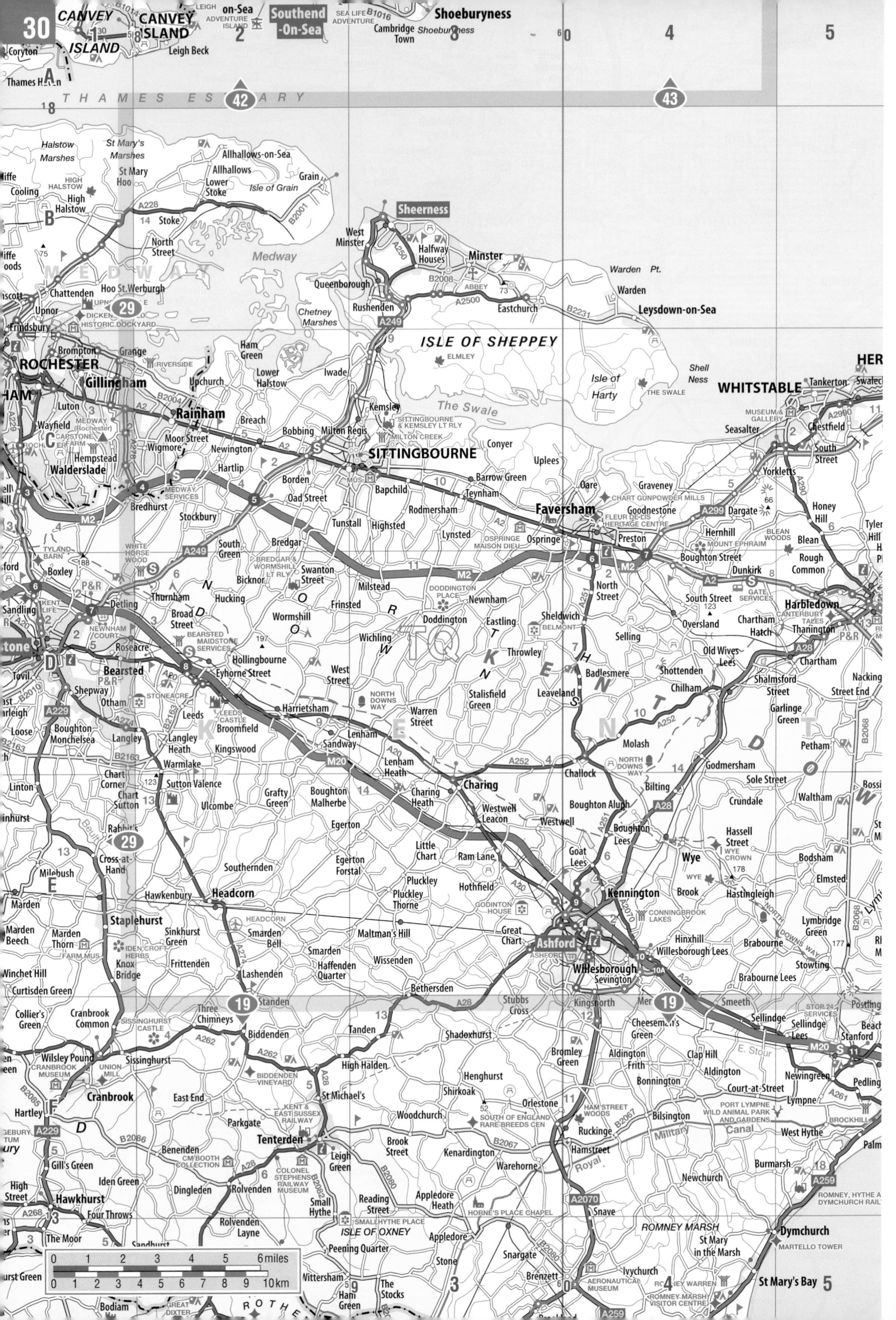

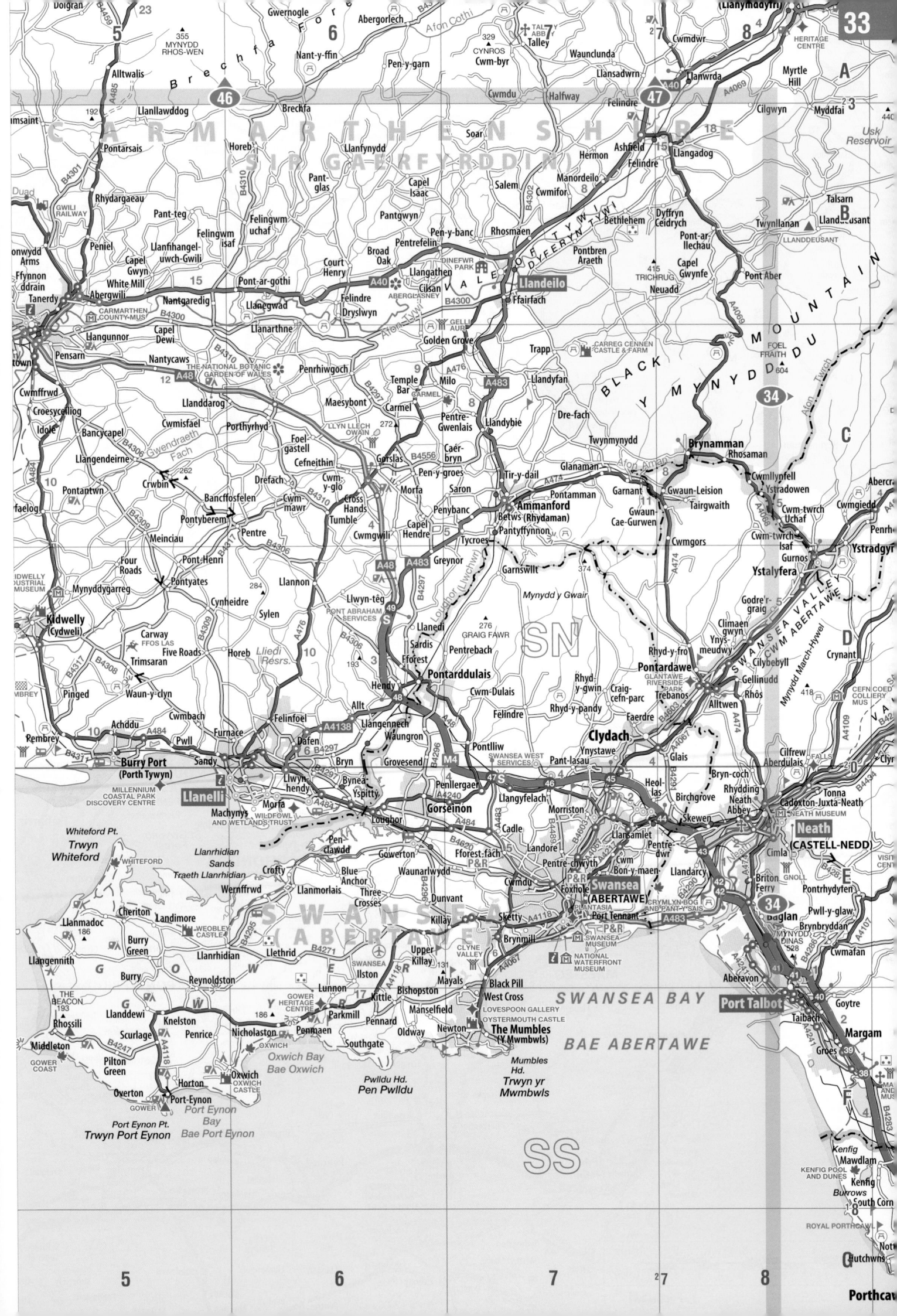

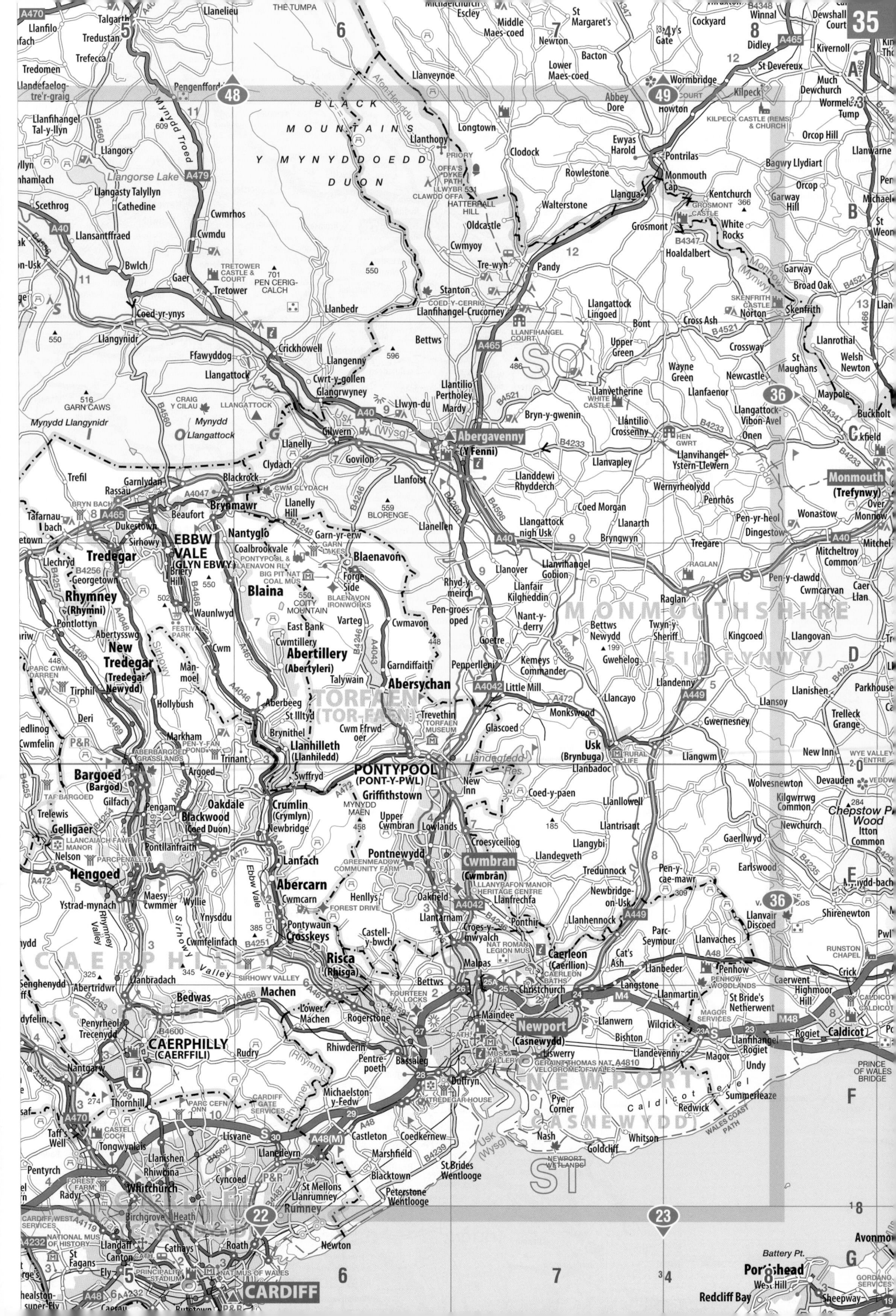

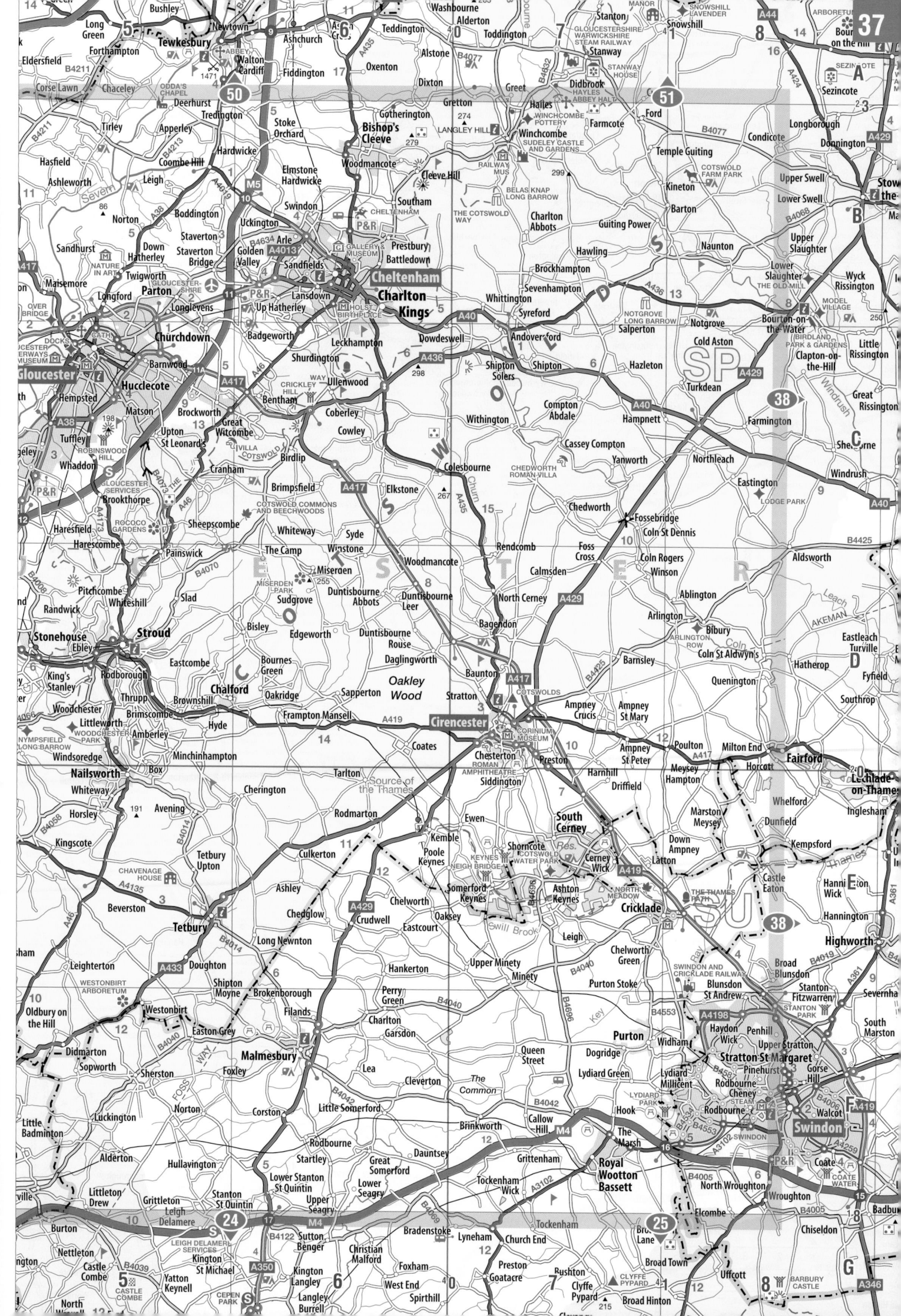

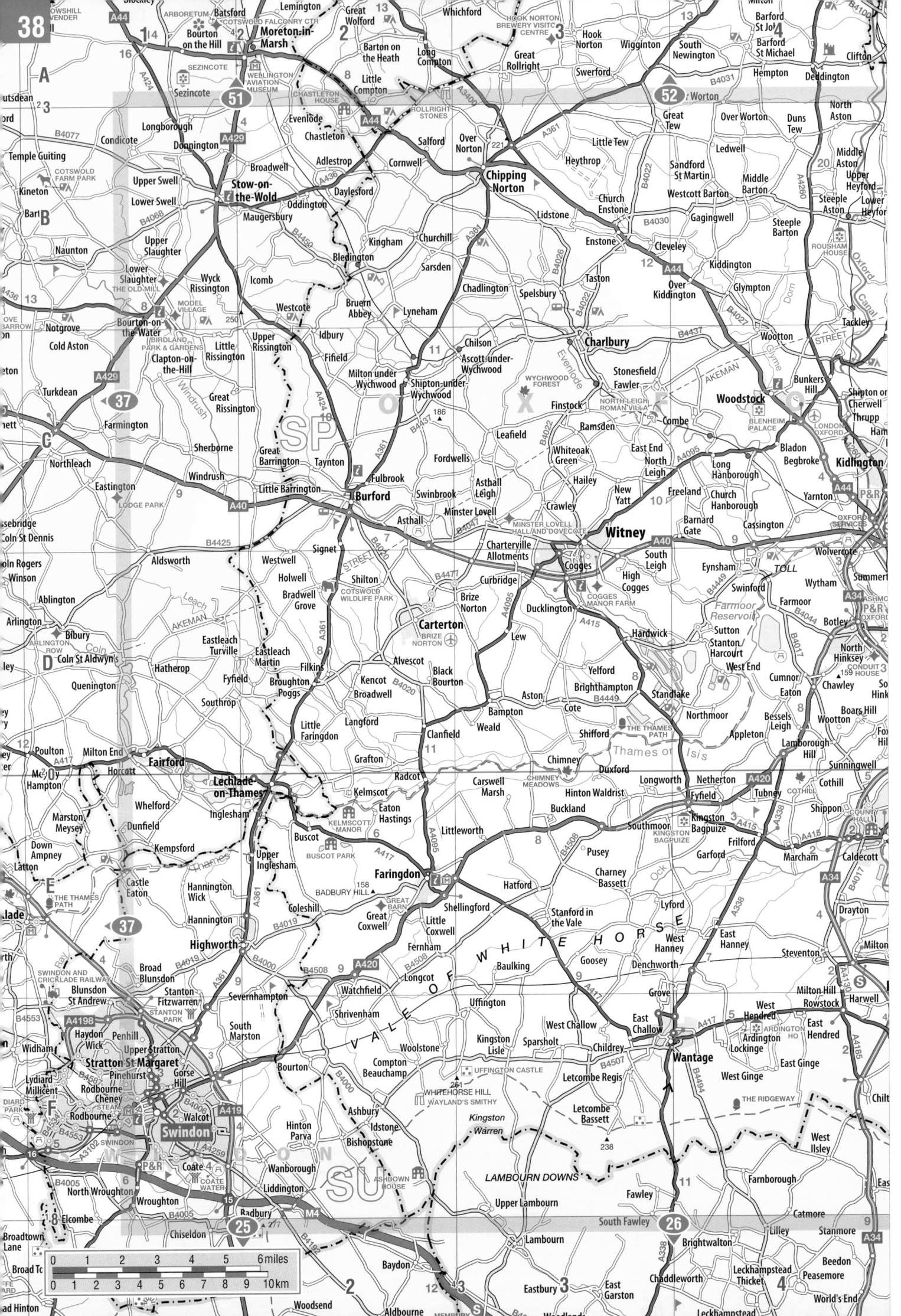

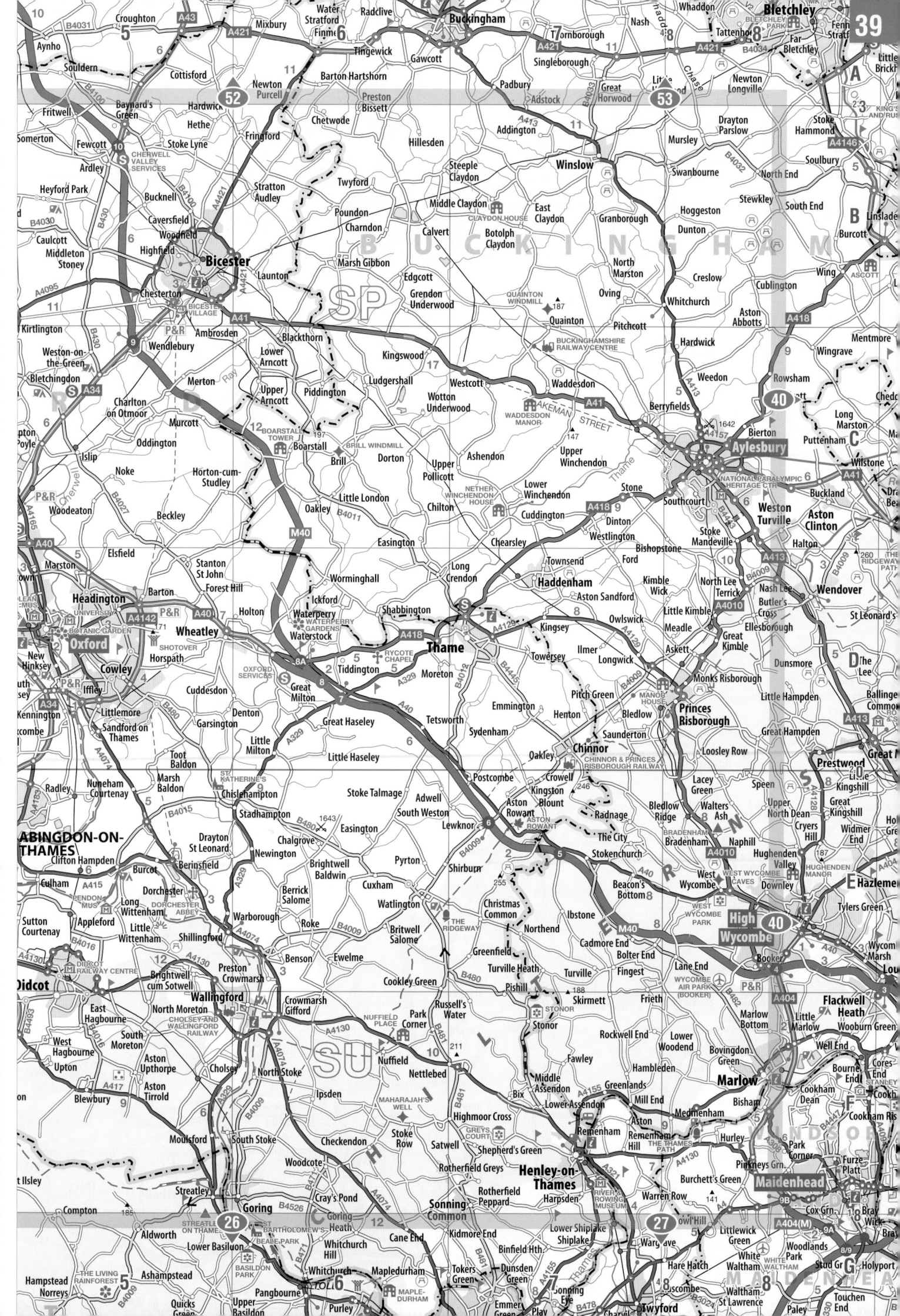

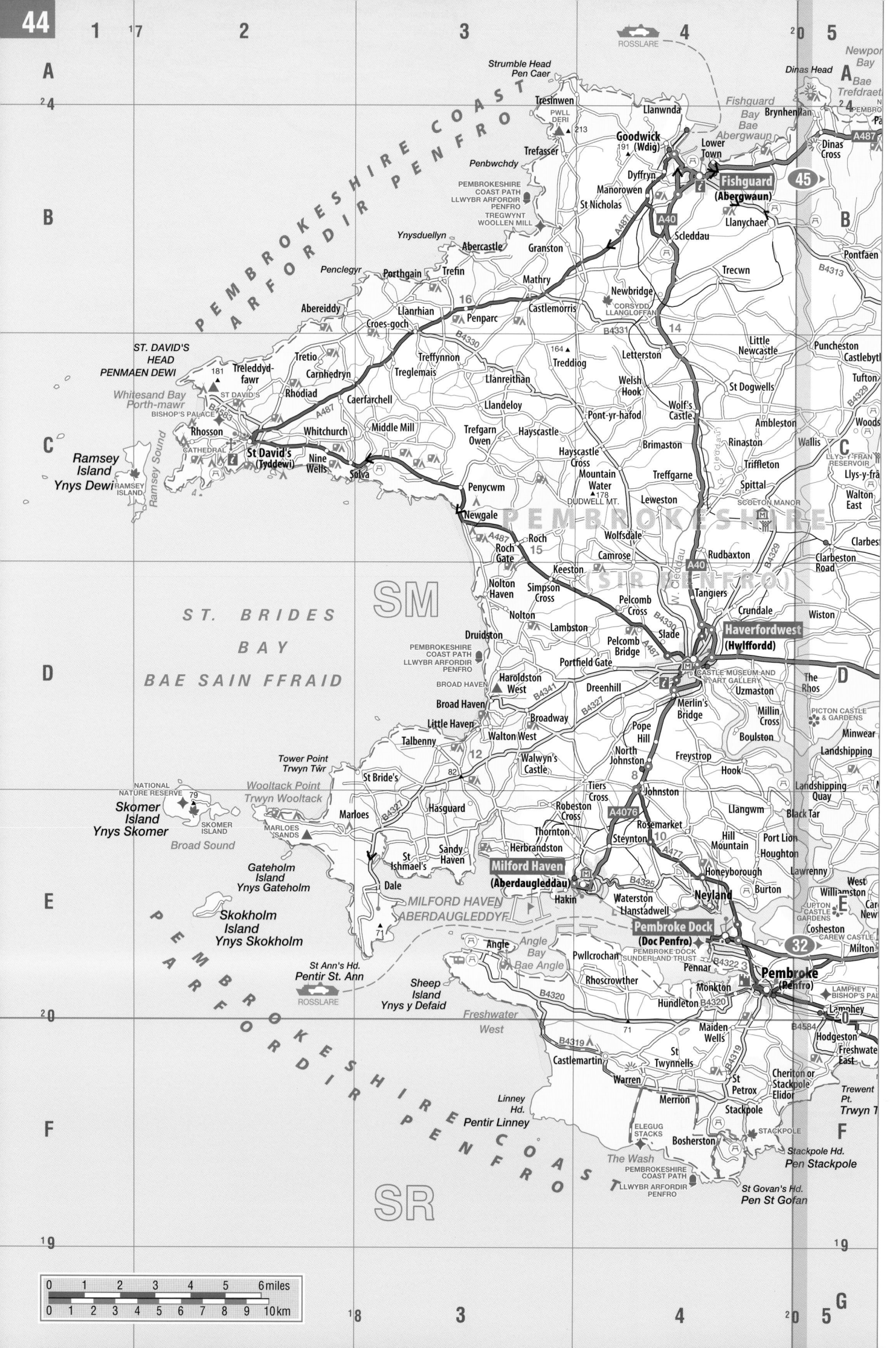

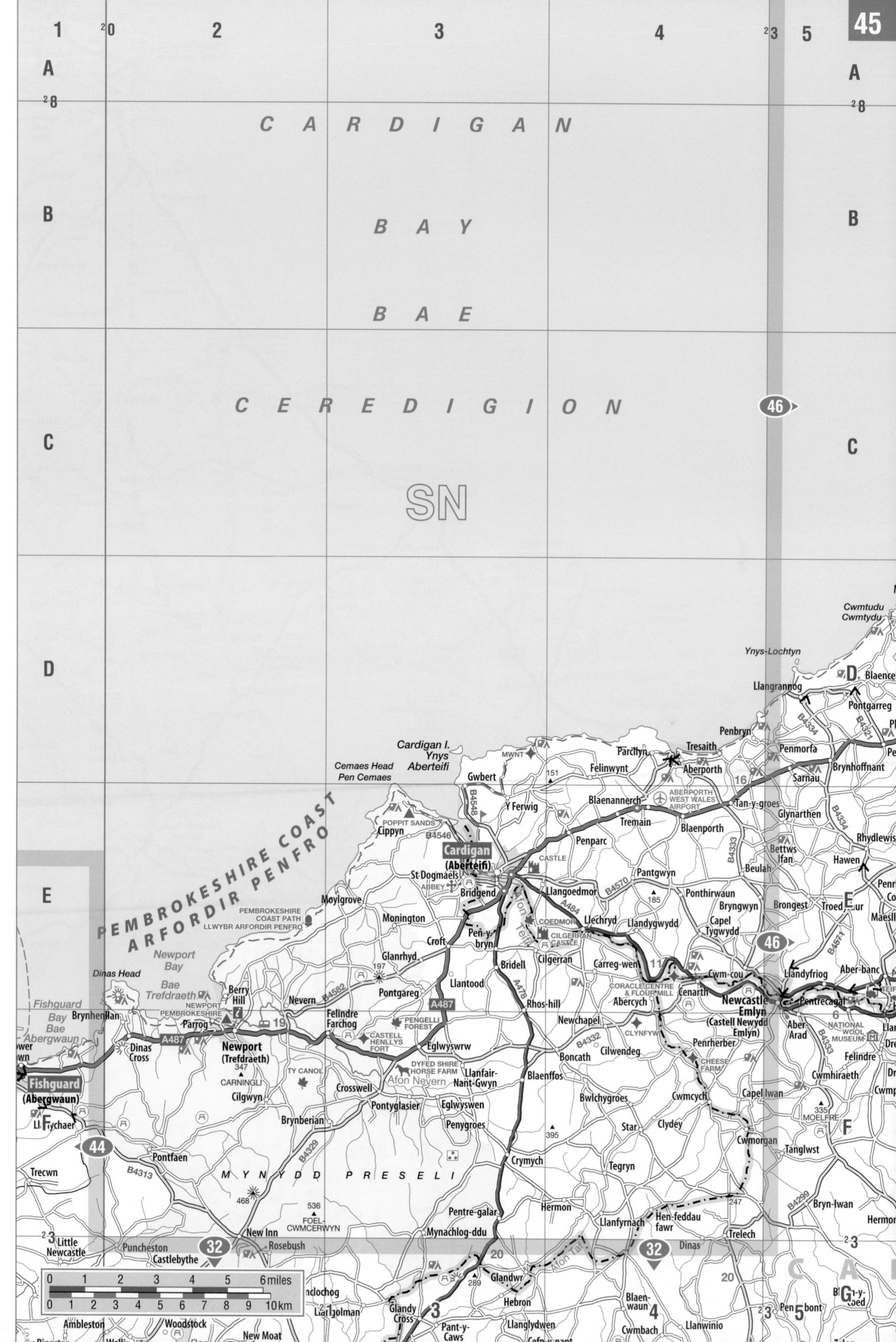

1 20 2 3 4 23 5

A 28 A

CARDIGAN

B BAY B

BAE

CEREDIGION 46

C C

SN

Cwmtudu
Cwmtydu

Ynys-Lochtyn

D Llangrannog D Blaence

Pontgarreg

Penbryn Pl

Cardigan I. Penmorfa Pe
Ynys MWNT Parclyn Tresaith
Cemaes Head Aberteifi Felinwynt Aberporth Brynhoffnant
Pen Cemaes Gwbert ABERPORTH Sarnau
Blaenannerch WEST WALES Tan-y-groes Glynarthen
AIRPORT 16
Y Ferwig Tremain Blaenporth Rhydlewis
POPPIT SANDS Penparc Bettws
Cippyn B4546 Penparc Ifan Beulah Hawen
CASTLE Pantgwyn
Cardigan Pangwyn Ponthirwaun Brongest Penr
(Aberteifi) Llangoedmor 185 Bryngwyn Troed Co
St-Dogmaels Llechryd Llandygwydd Capel Maesll
ABBEY Bridgend COEDMOR Tygwydd
Moylgrove CILGERRAN 46
Monington Pen-y- CASTLE Carreg-wen Cwm-cou Llandyfriog Aber-banc
bryn Cilgerran 11 TEIF
Croft Bridell CORACLE CENTRE Cenarth Pentrecagal
Glanrhyd 197 Rhos-hill & FLOUR MILL Newcastle 6
Llantood Abercych Emlyn NATIONAL
Berry Pontgareg A487 Newchapel (Castell Newydd WOOL
Hill Nevern B4582 A487 Newchapel CLYNFYW Emlyn) Aber MUSEUM Llar
NEWPORT Felindre Newchapel Penrherber Arad Felindre
Parrog PEMBROKESHIRE 19 Farchog PENGELLI B4332 CHEESE Cwmhiraeth Dr
FOREST Boncath Cilwendeg FARM Cwmp
Dinas A487 CASTELL Llanfair- Capel Iwan
Cross HENLLYS Nant-Gwyn Bwlchygroes 335
Newport FORT Blaenffos Cwmcych MOELFRE
Fishguard (Trefdraeth) DYFED SHIRE Star Clydey
(Abergwaun) 347 HORSE FARM Afon Nevern Crymych Cwmorgan Tanglwst
Ll Fychaer CARNINGLI TY CANOL Crosswell Llanfair- Hermor
Cilgwyn Nant-Gwyn Bwlchygroes 247 Bryn-Iwan
44 Pontyglasier Eglwyswen Pentre-galar Hermon Hen-feddau B4299
Pontfaen Brynberian Penygroes Hermon fawr Dinas
Trecwn B4329 Llanfyrnach A
B4313 MYNYDD PRESELI Crymych 247 Trelech
468 Crymych 20 Afon Taf
Little 536 Pentre-galar Hermon
Newcastle FOEL- Llanfyrnach 32 Dinas
Puncheston CWMCERWYN Mynachlog-ddu 20 B
Castlebythe 32 G
Rosebush Glandwr Pen bont Coed

0 1 2 3 4 5 6 miles
0 1 2 3 4 5 6 7 8 9 10 km

nclochog Glandy Glandwr 289 Blaen- 23
Llar olman Cross Hebron waun Pen bont
Ambleston Woodstock Pant-y- Llangivdwen Llanwinio Hermor
New Moat Caws Cwmbach

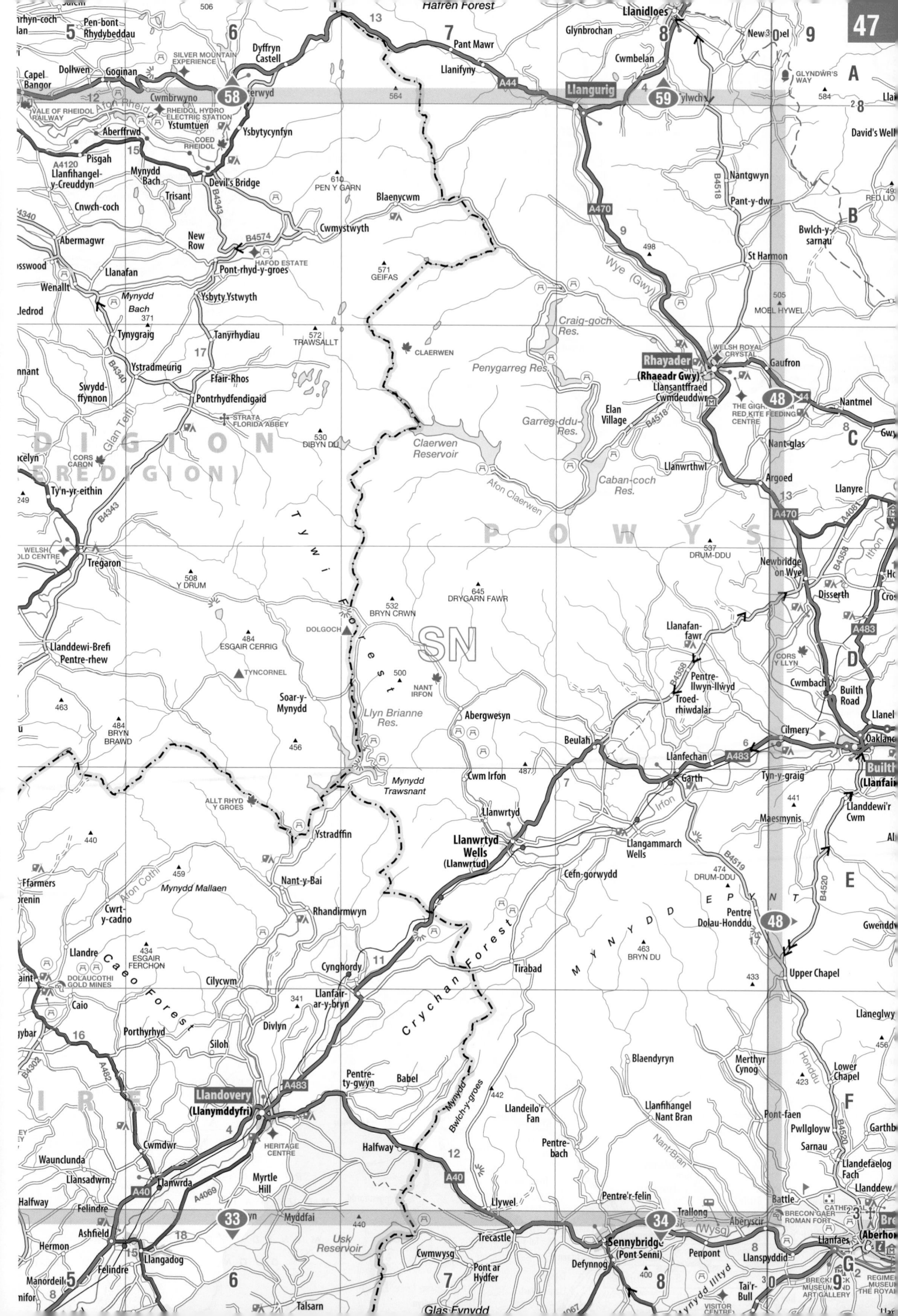

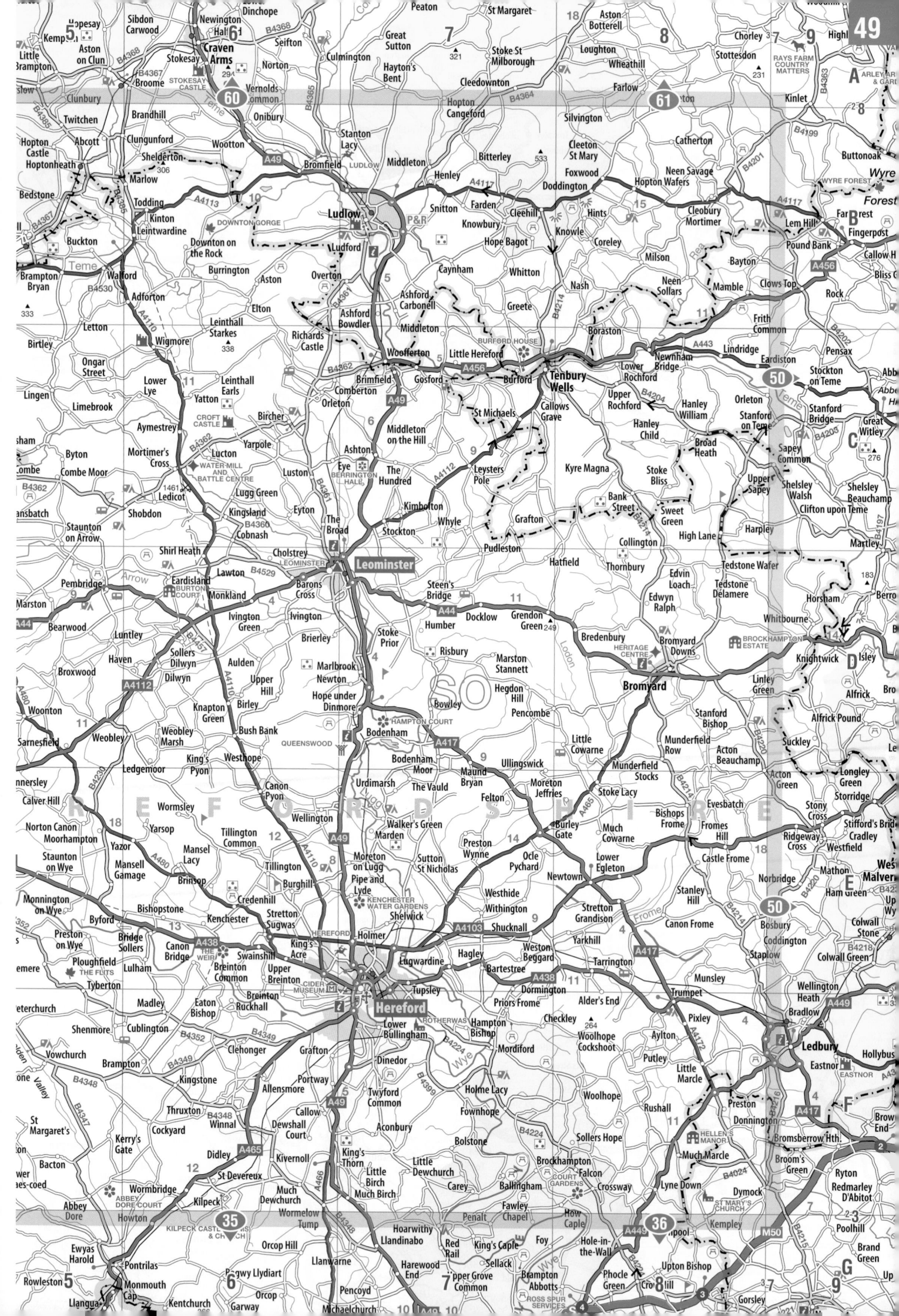

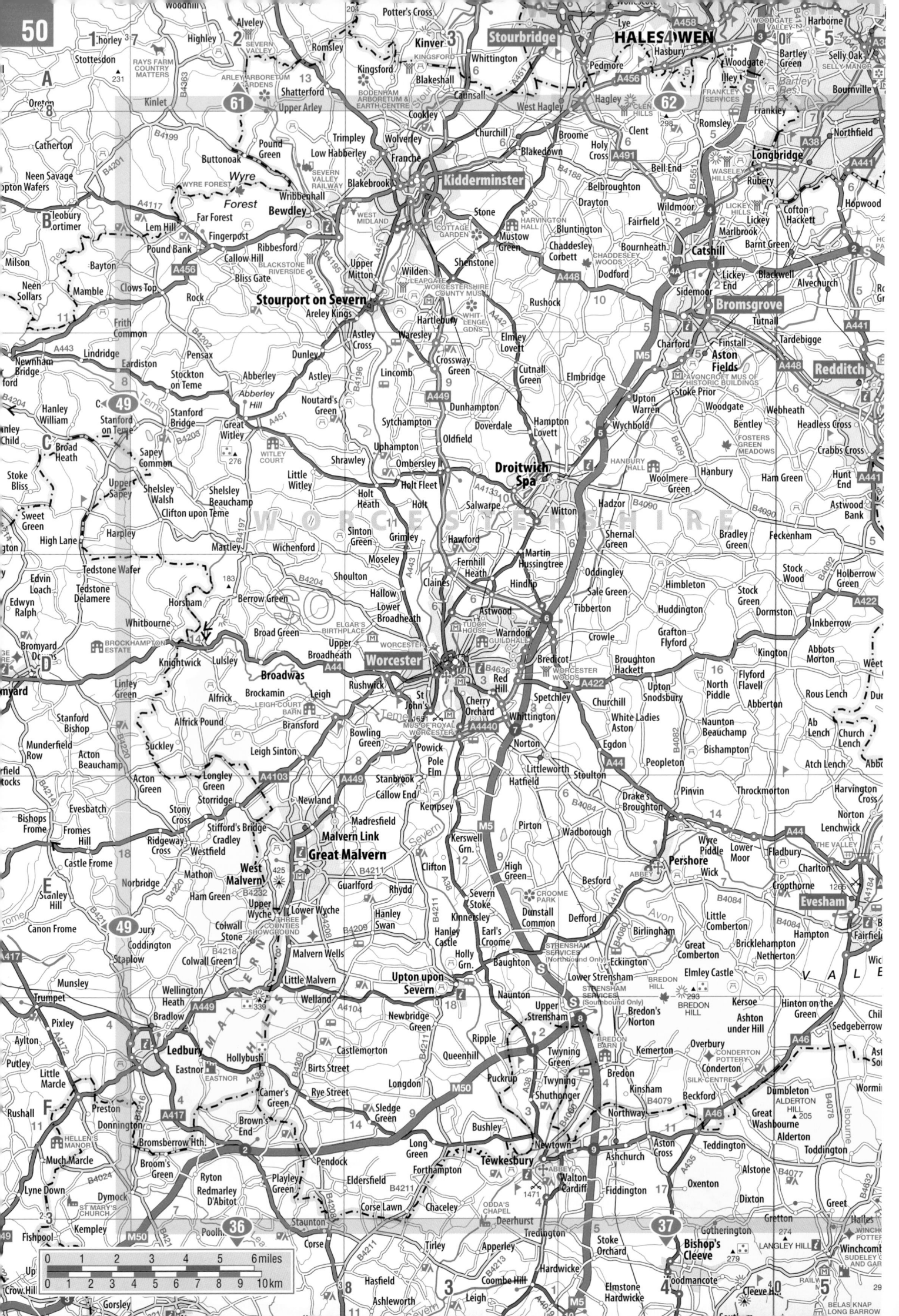

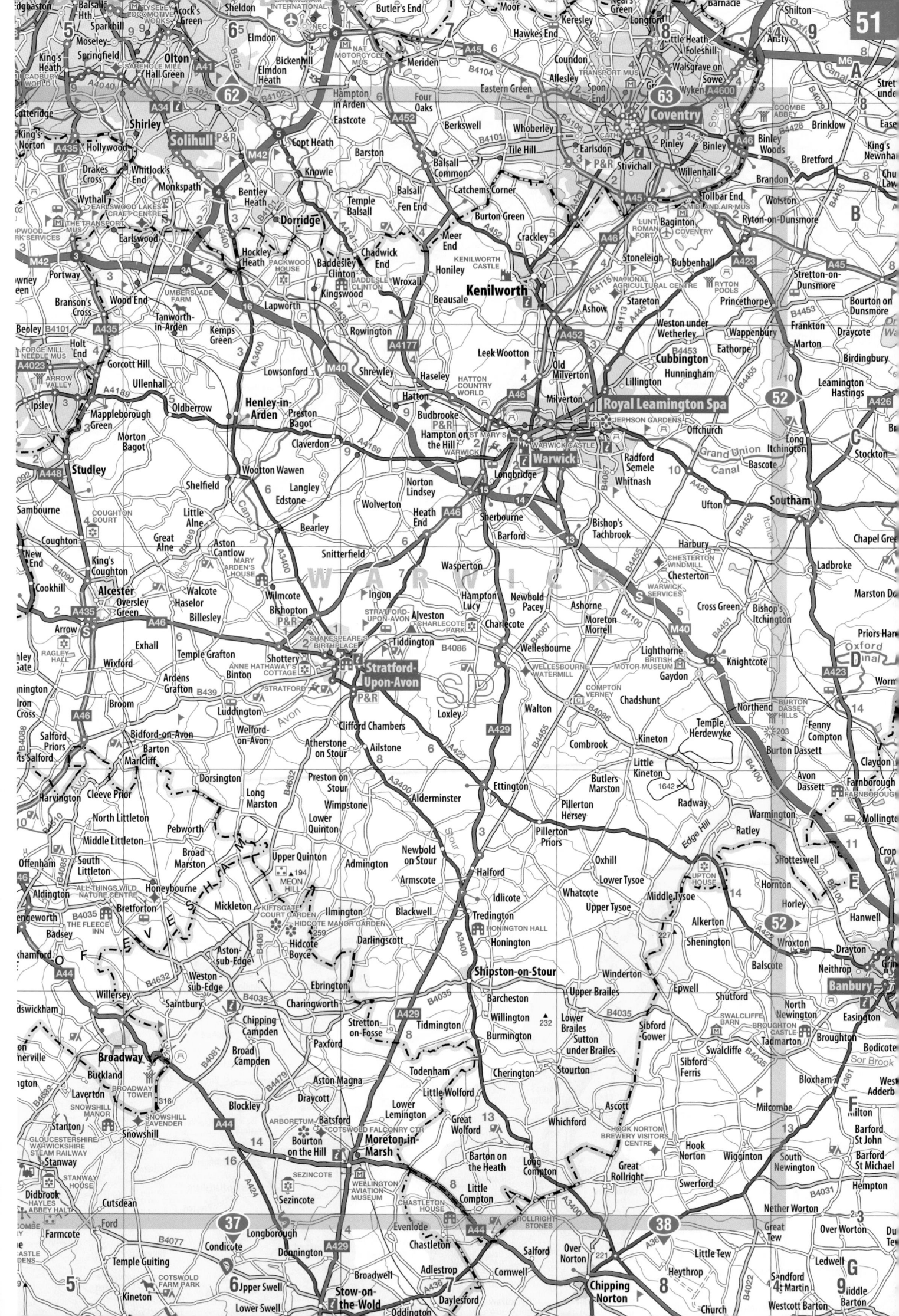

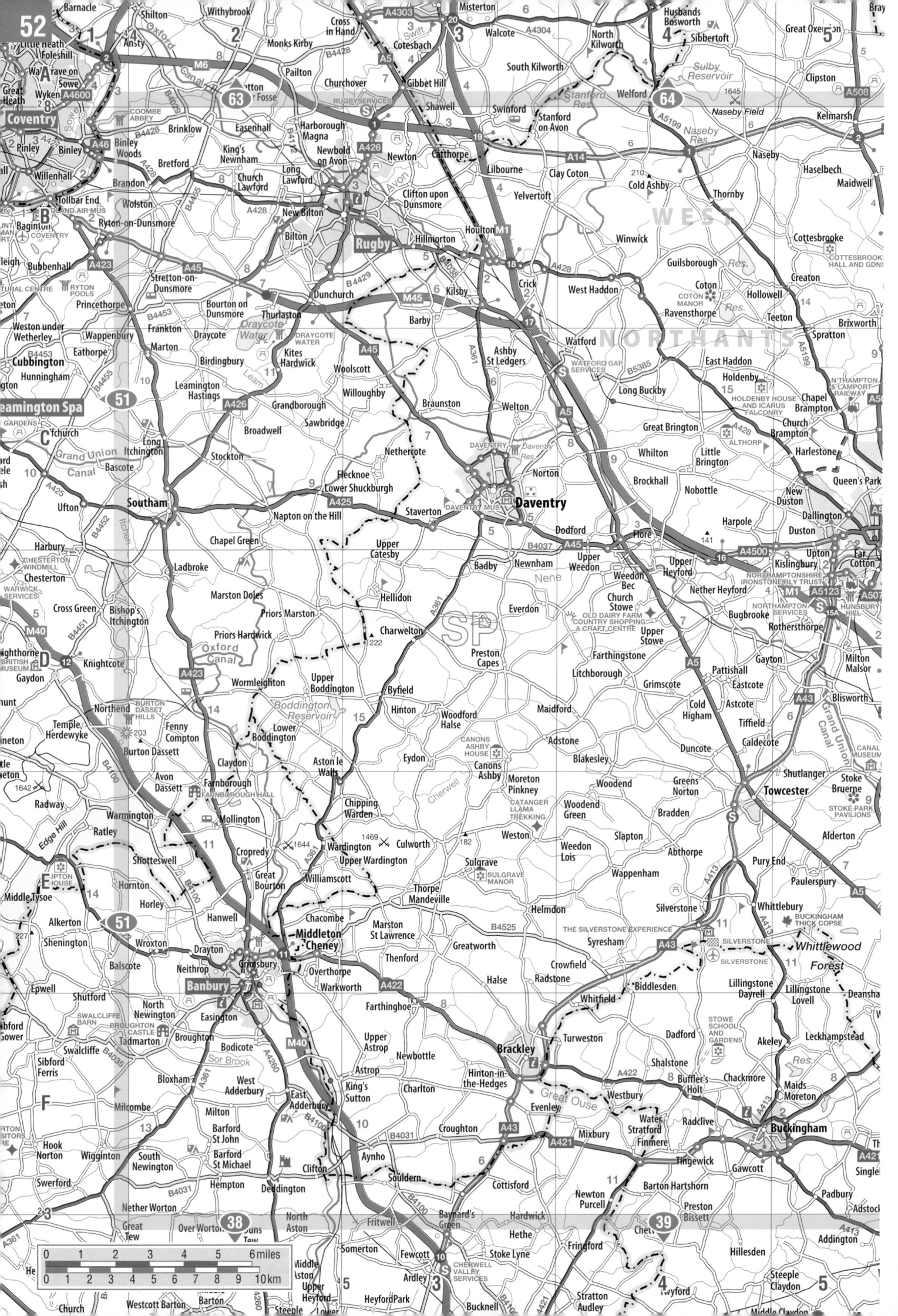

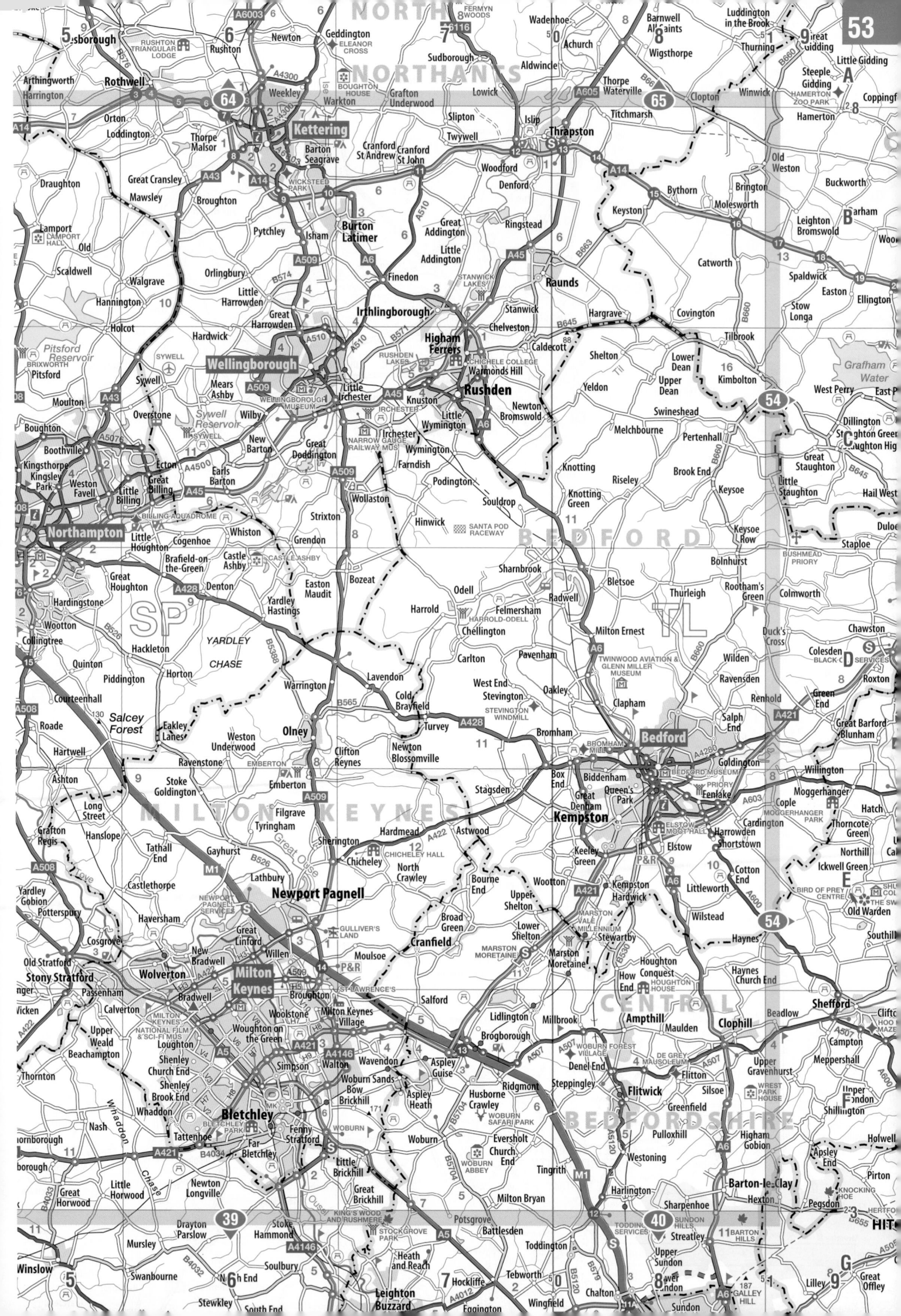

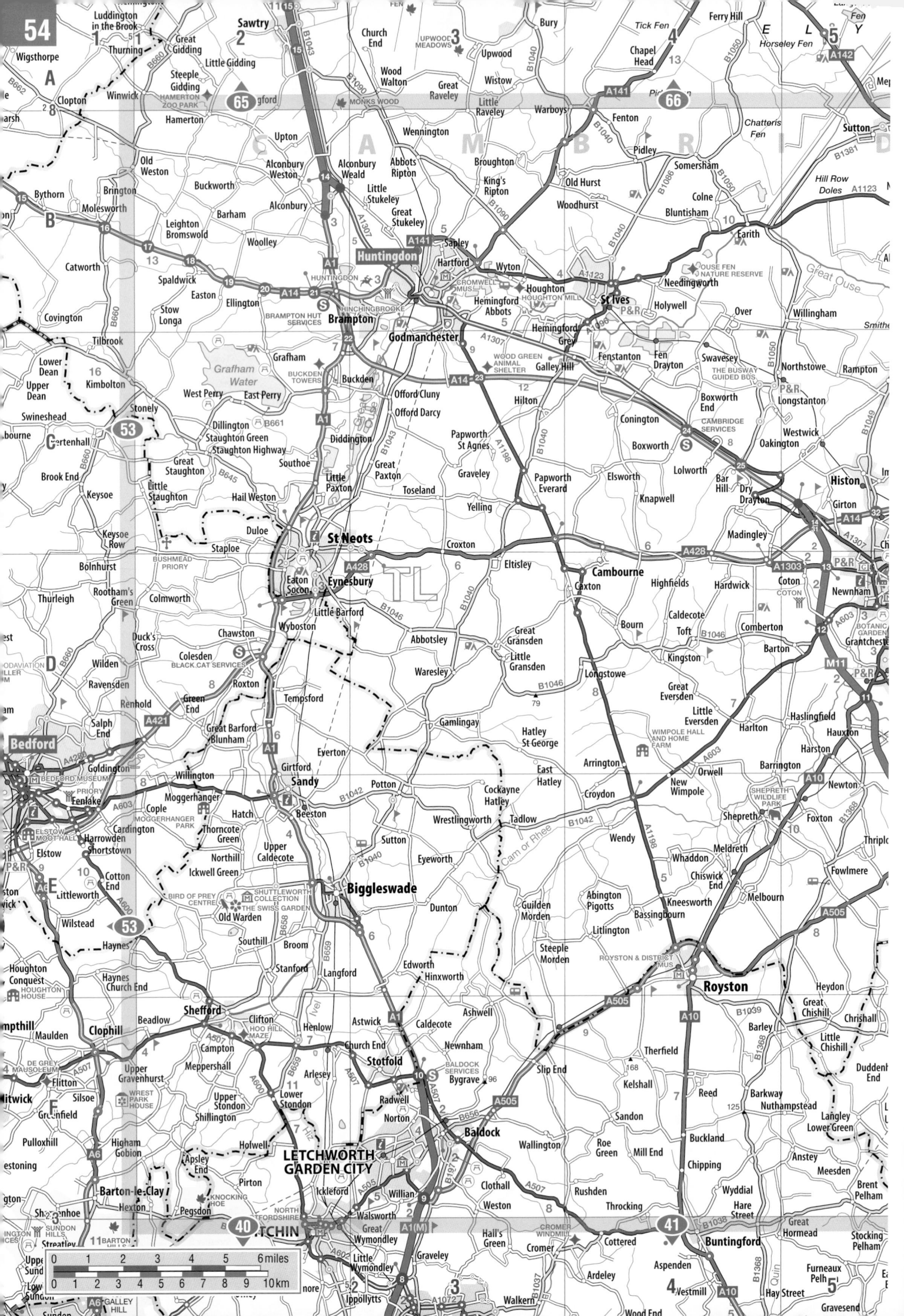

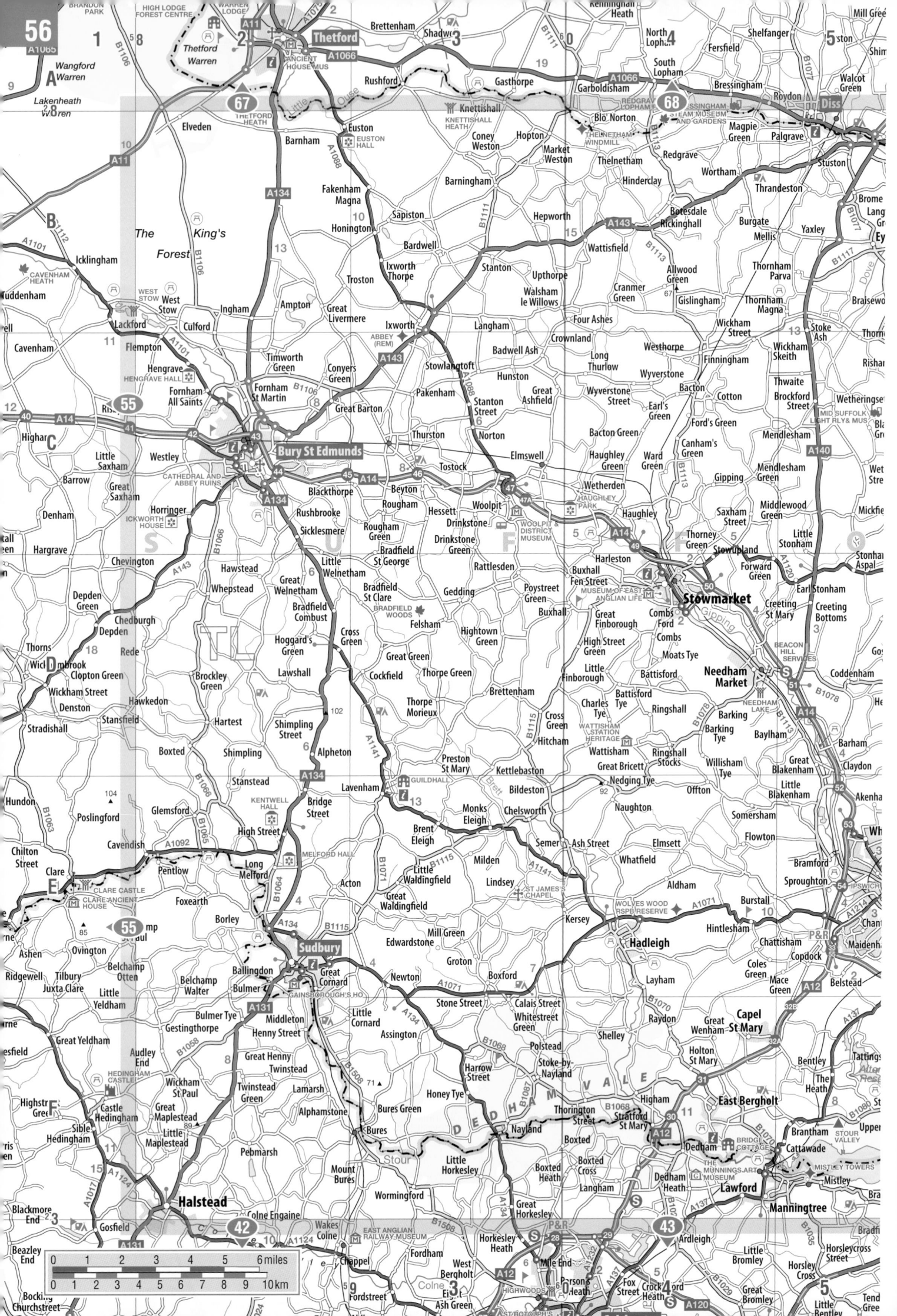

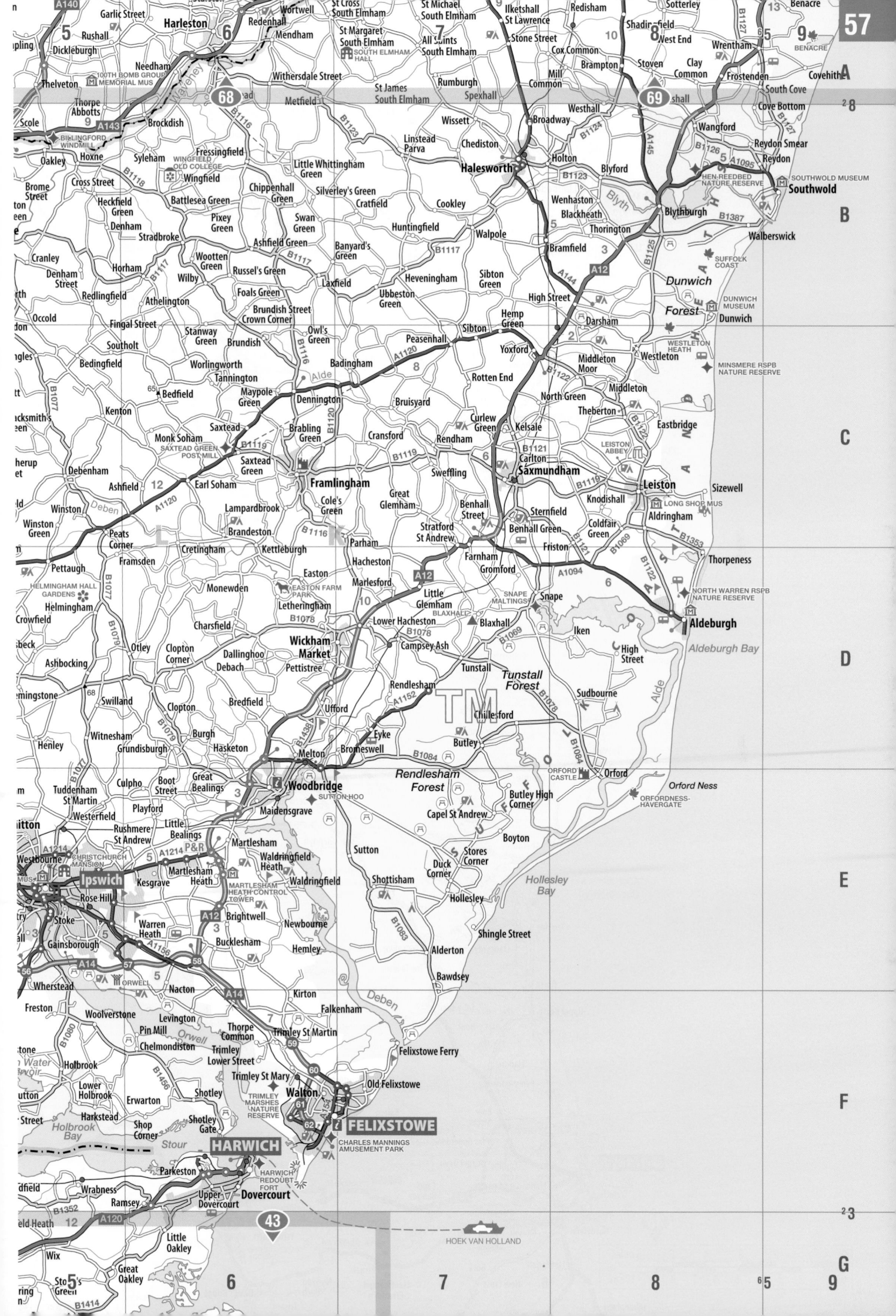

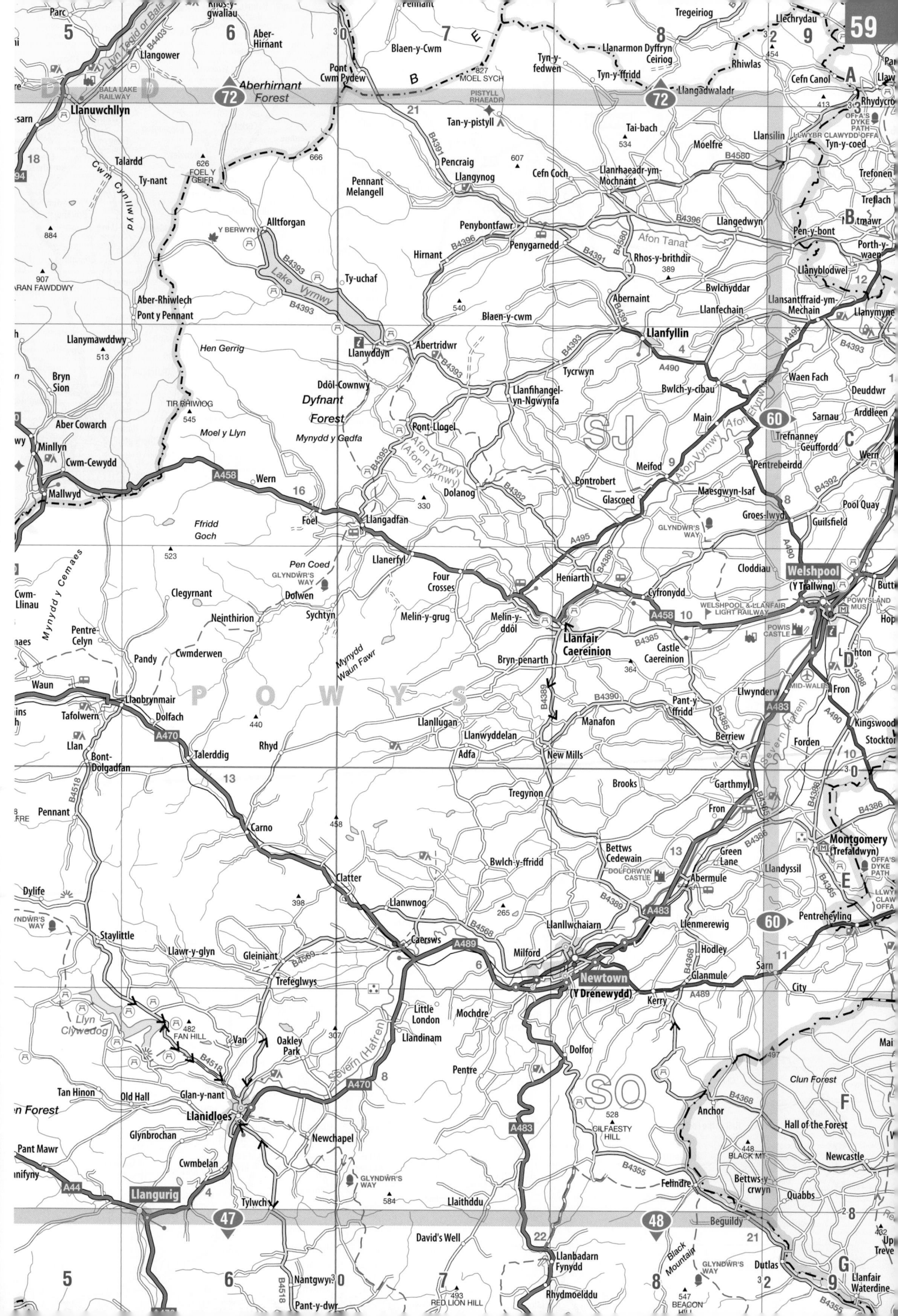

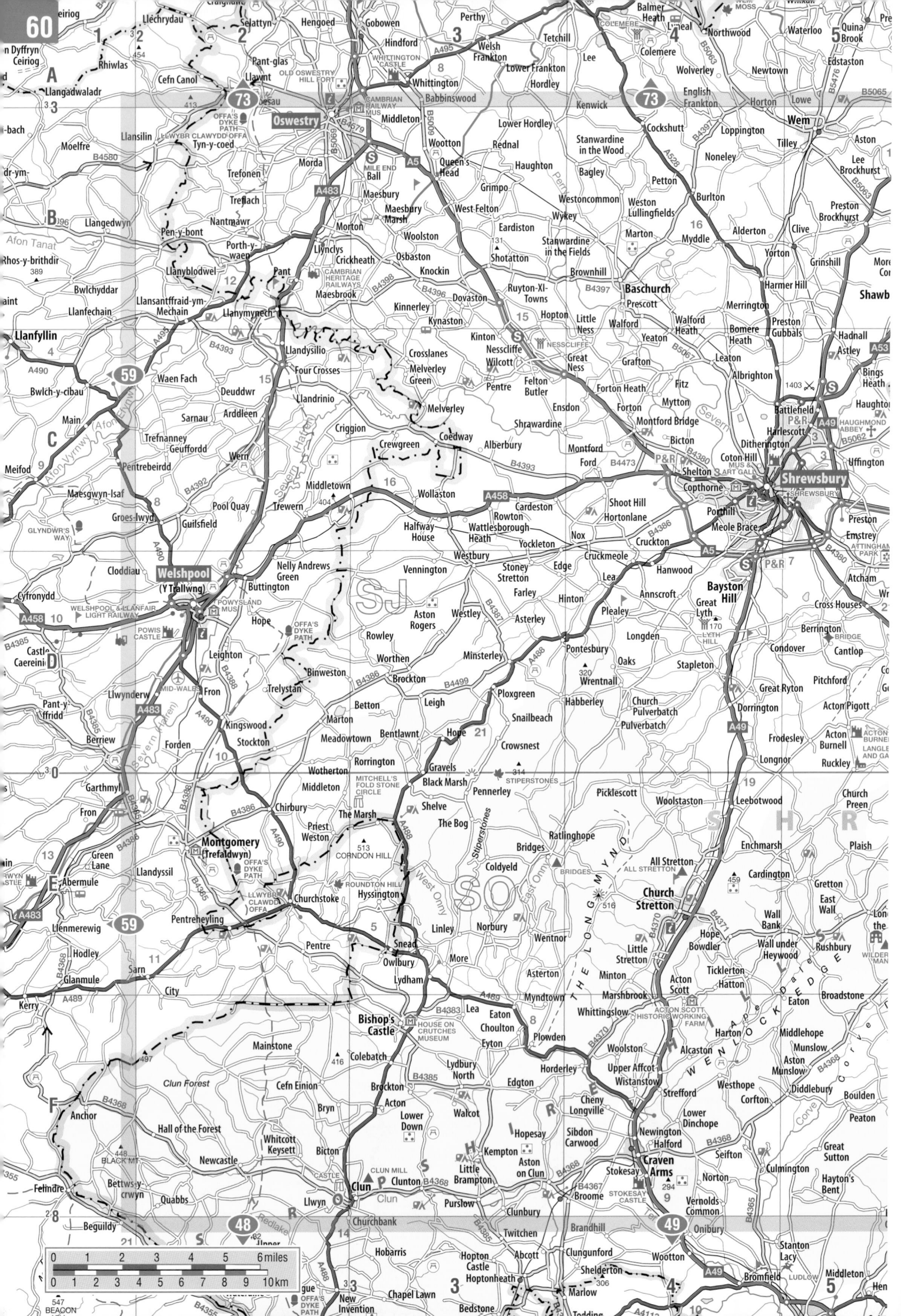

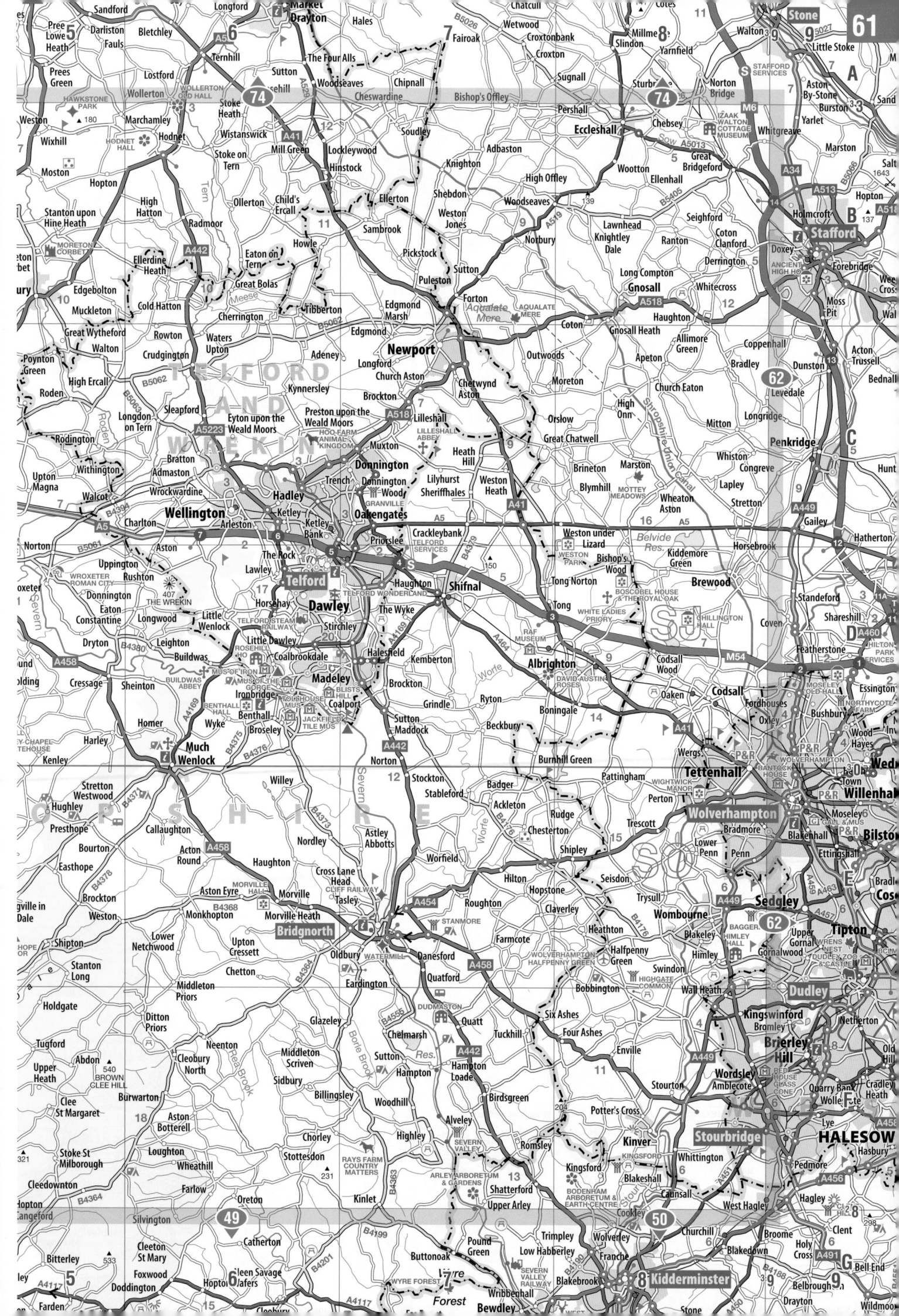

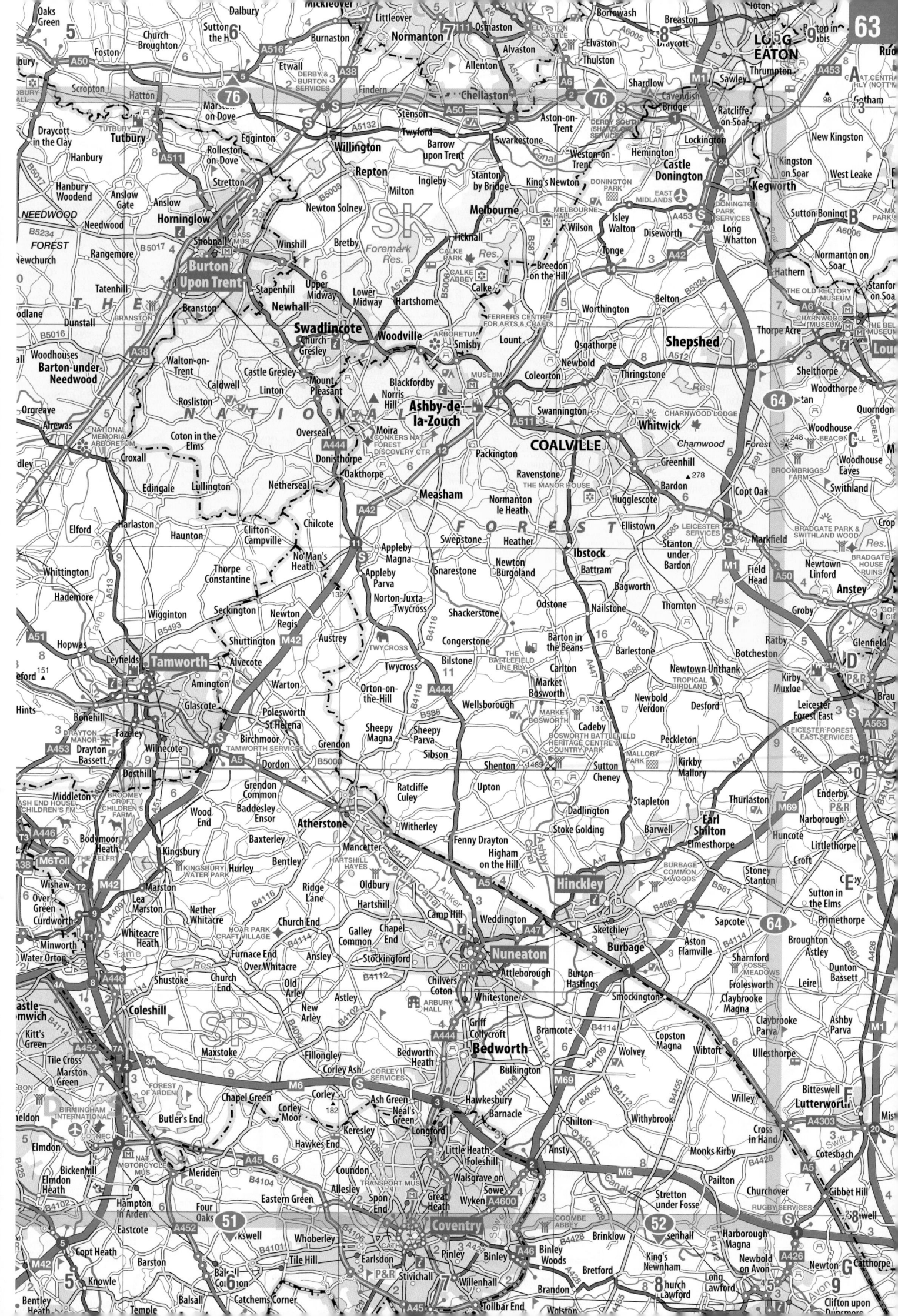

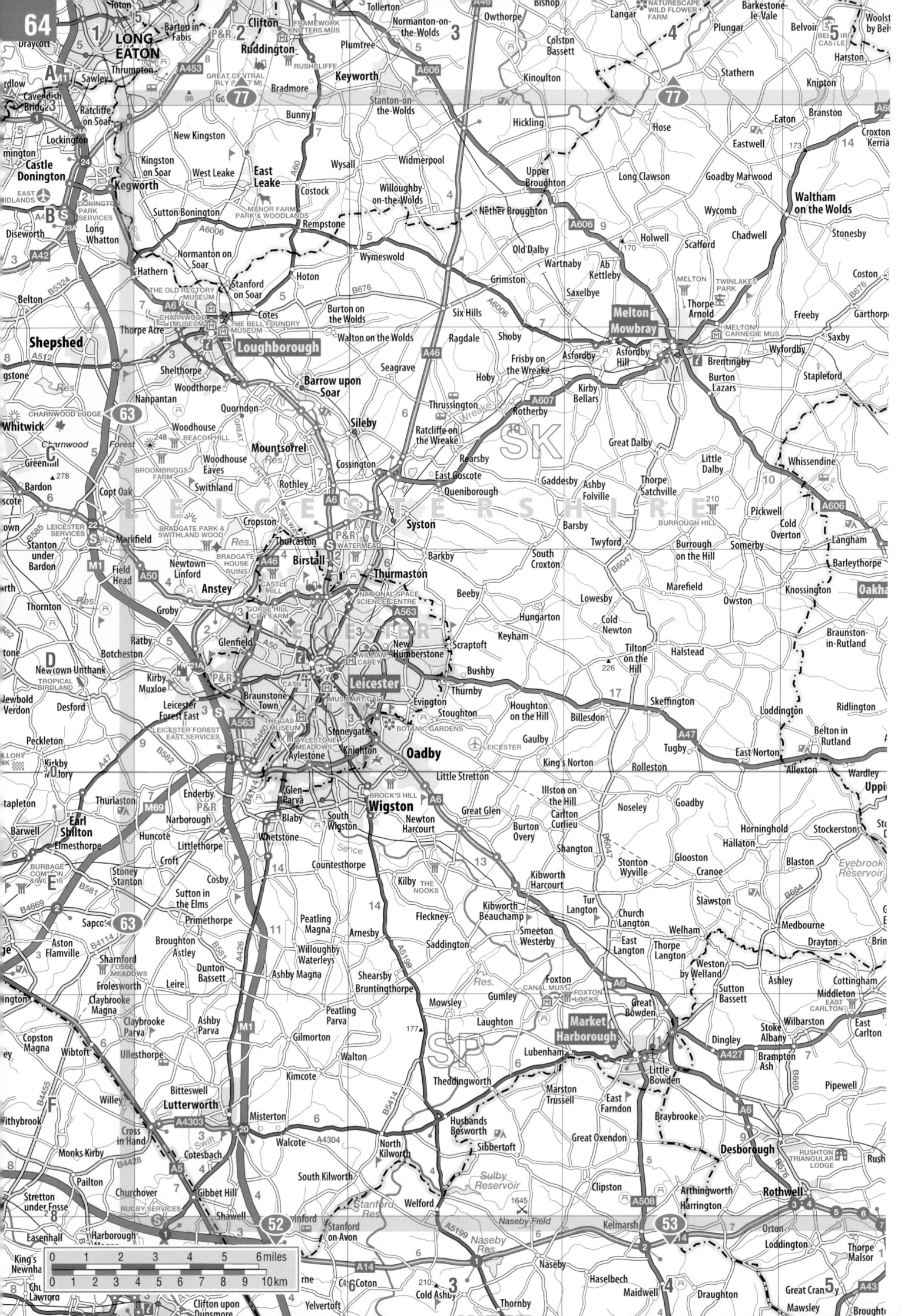

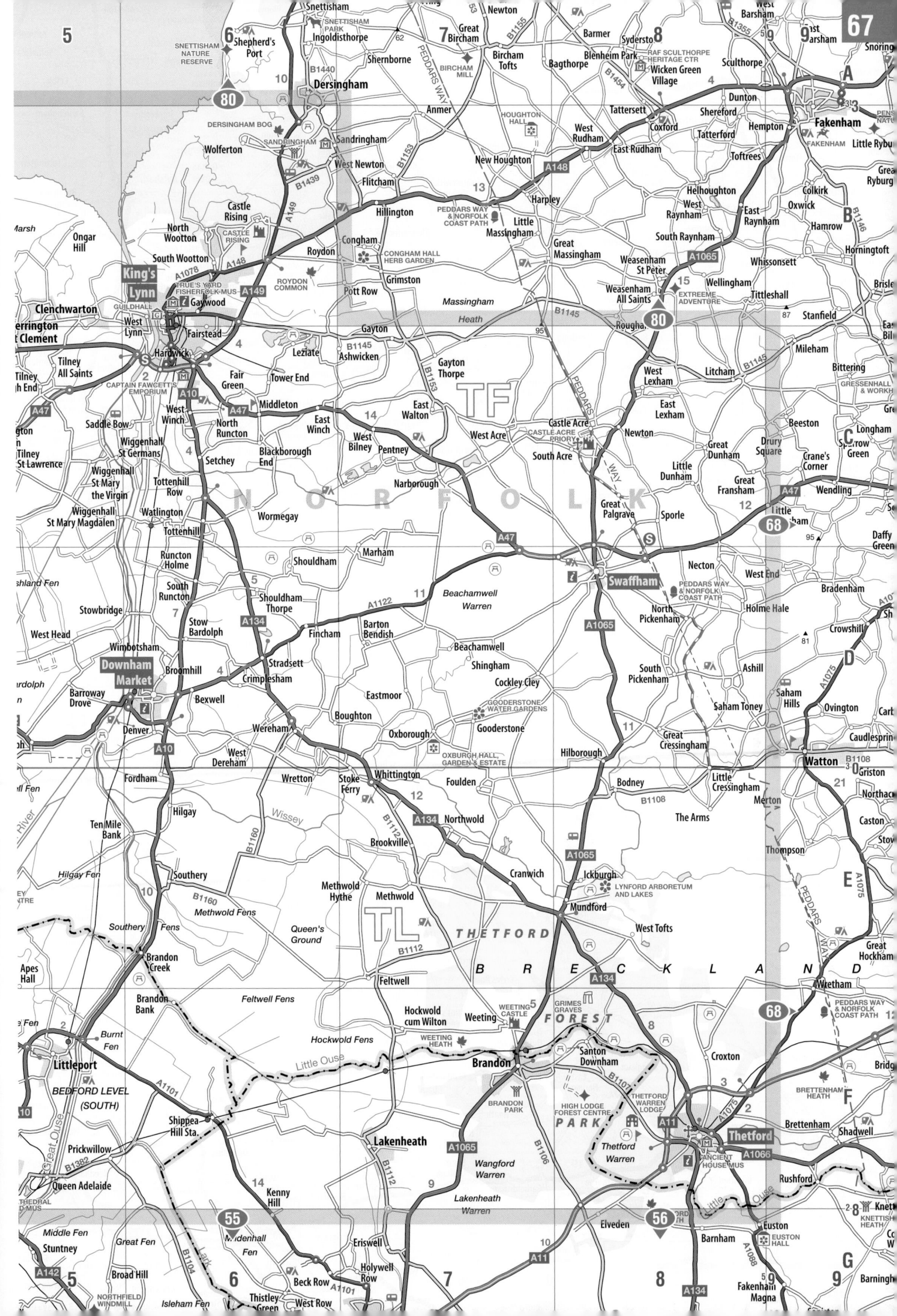

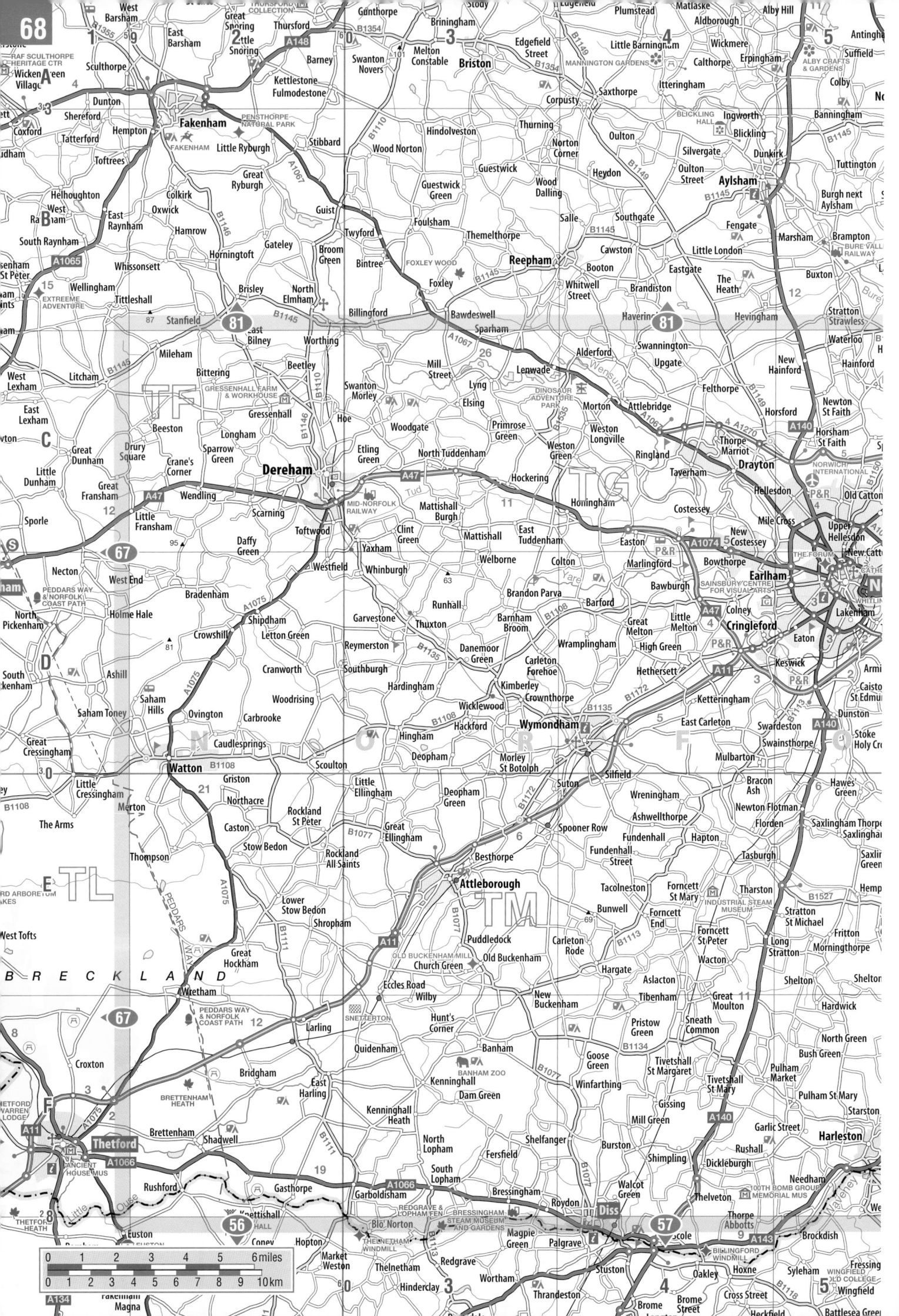

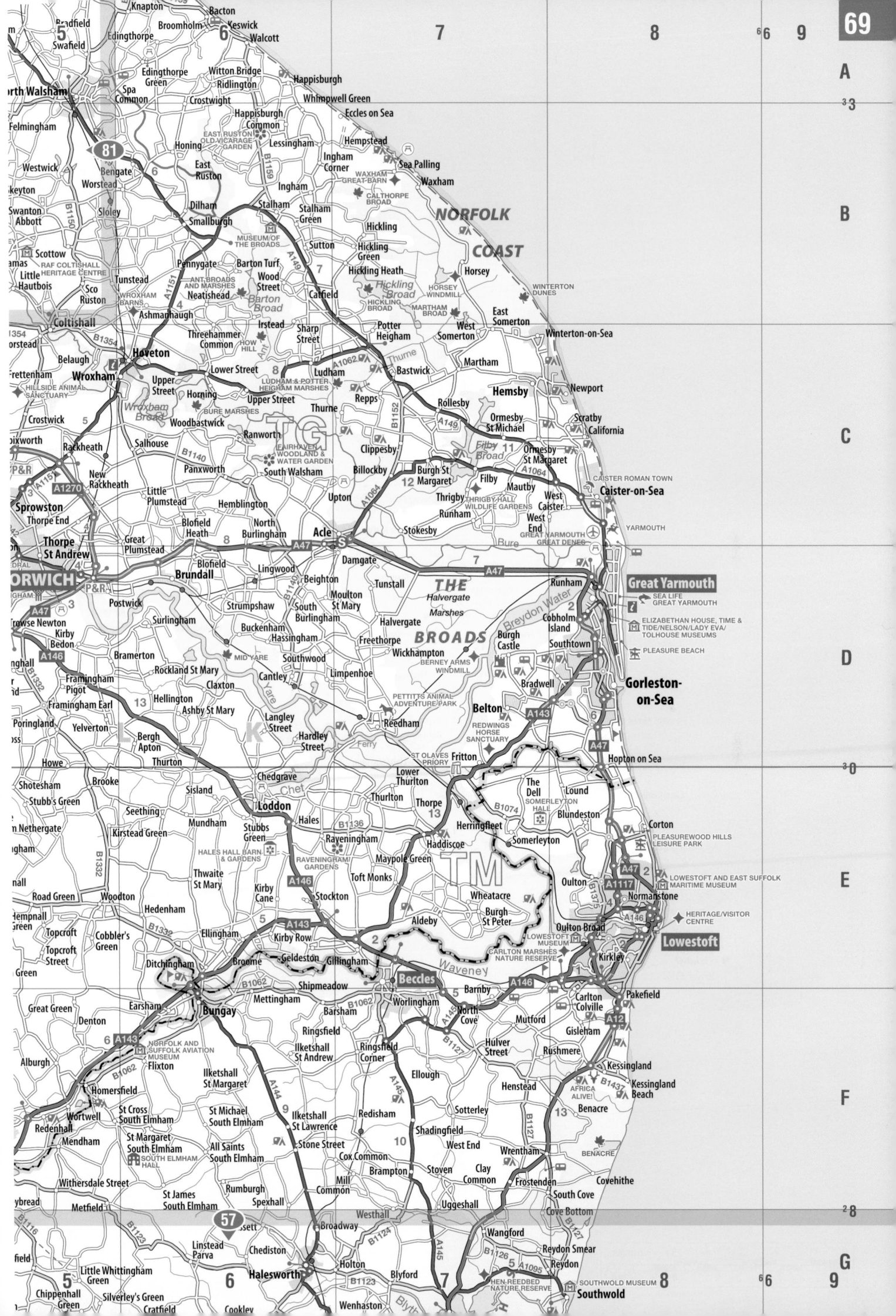

1   1   2   3   4   5

A

CAERNARFON

BAY

B   BAE

CAERNARFON

Malltraeth Bay
Bae Malltraeth

Newborough
Forest

ANGLESEY
MODEL
VILLAGE

Llanddwyn I.
Ynys Llanddwyn

The Bar

Abermenai
Pt.
Trwyn
Abermenai

AIRWORLD
AVIATION MUSEUM

Morfa Dinlle

Dinas Dinlle

Ffrw

Llandwrog

GLYNLLIFO

14

Pontllyfni

Aberdesach

82   Clynnog-fawr   Tain

Gyrn-goch   Capel Uchaf

Bryn-yr-eryr

Trefor

564
YR EIFL

522
GYRN DDU

Llanaelhaearn

509
BWLCH
MAWR

Up
Clyn

Pen-sarn

C   SH

LLYN

Carreg Ddu   Porth
Dinllaen

Pistyll

WALES COAST PATH

B4417   6   Llithfaen

Llwyndyrys

Pencaenewydd

7   Llangybi

Morfa Nefyn   Nefyn

LLYN MARITIME
MUSEUM

Edern

Porth Ysgadan   B4417

Fron

B4354

Llanarmon

Chwilog

Rhos-fawr   Y Ffôr

PENARTH FAWR
MEDIEVAL HOUSE

Tan-y-
graig

Glanrhyd

Rhos-y-llan

CORS
GEIRCH

LLYN

Boduan

A497   7

Llannor

Aberch

HAVEN

D   Tudweiliog

Porth Golmon   14

Dinas

Garnfadryn

Rhyd-y-
clafdy

Efailnewydd

Denio   Pwllheli

Bryn-mawr   Llaniestyn   B4415   Penrhos   7   Carreg yr Imbill

South Beach

Pen-y-graig   Llangwnnadl

Penrhyn Mawr

Ty-hen

Methlem

Pen-y-
groeslon

Bryncroes

Sarn
Meyllteyrn

Botwnnog

Rhedyn   B4413

Nanhoron

Llanbedrog

Mynytho   Trwyn Llanbedrog

Rhydlios   Llandegwning

A499

St Tudwal's
Road
Angorfa St Tudwal

Capel Carmel

Rhoshirwaun

304
MYNYDD
RHIW

PLAS-YN-
RHIW

Llawrdref
Bellaf

Llangian

Abersoch

St Tudwal's Island East
Ynys St Tudwal Dwyrain

Rhiw   Llanengan   St Tudwal's Island West
Ynys St Tudwal Gorllewin

B4413

191

Uwchmynydd   Porth Neigwl or
Hell's Mouth

Llanfaelrhys

Sarn Bach

Bwlchtocyn   Marchroes

Cilan Uchaf

Aberdaron

Bodermid

E   Bardsey Sound
Swnt Enlli

Pen-y-cil

Trwyn Cilan

LLEYN

167

YNYS ENLLI   Bardsey
Island
Ynys Enlli

LLEYN

F

0   1   2   3   4   5   6 miles
0 1 2 3 4 5 6 7 8 9 10km

2   3   4   5

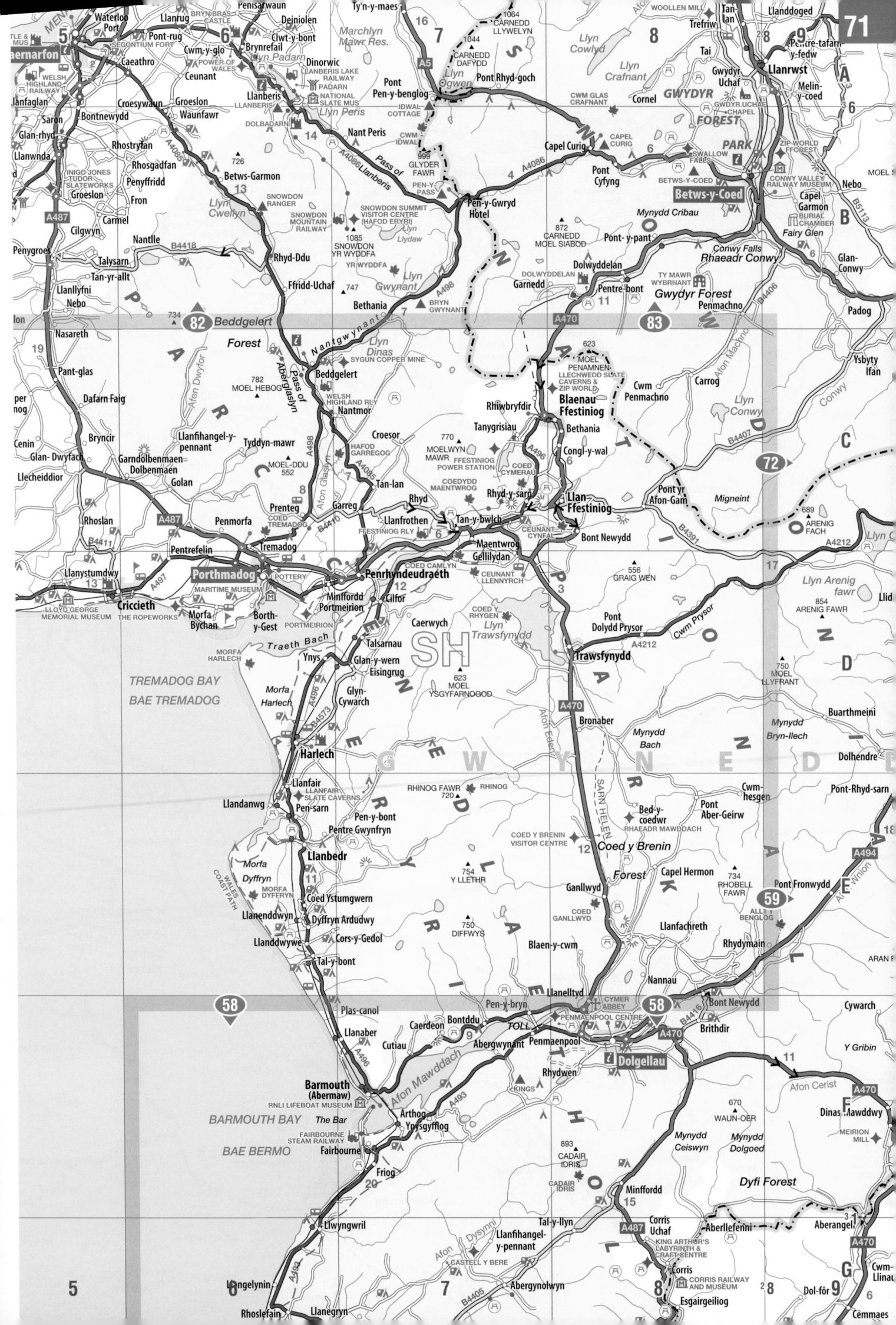

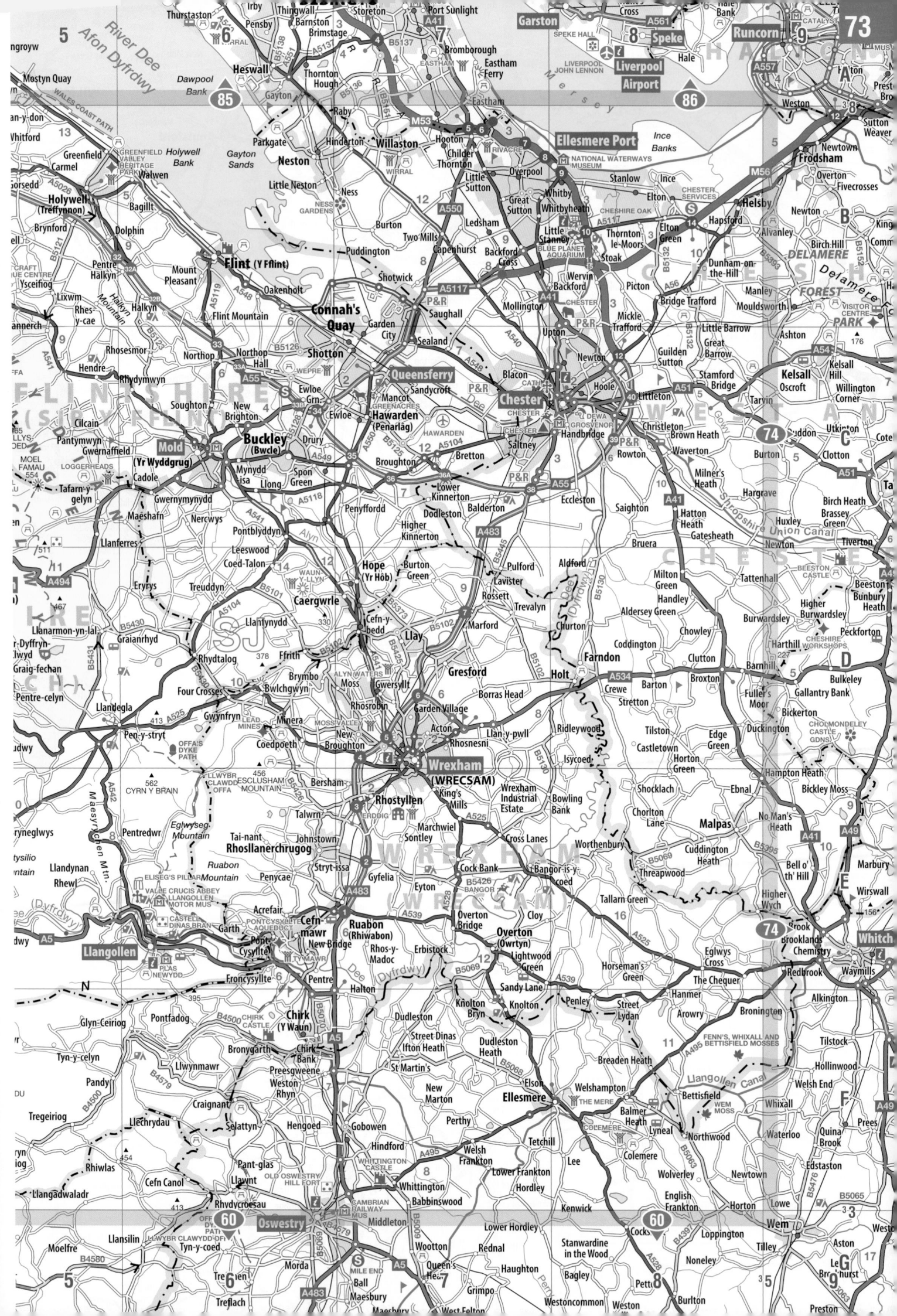

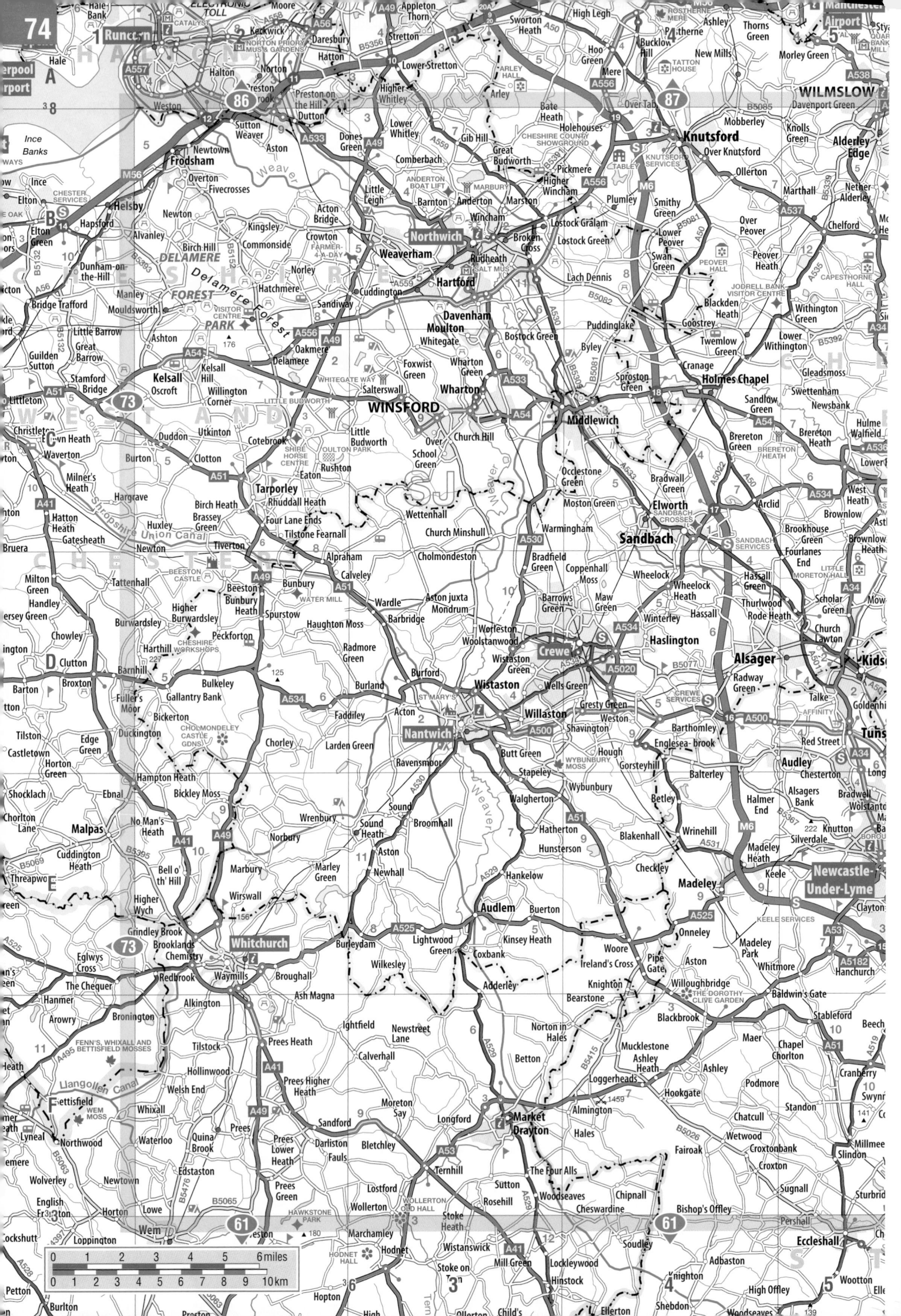

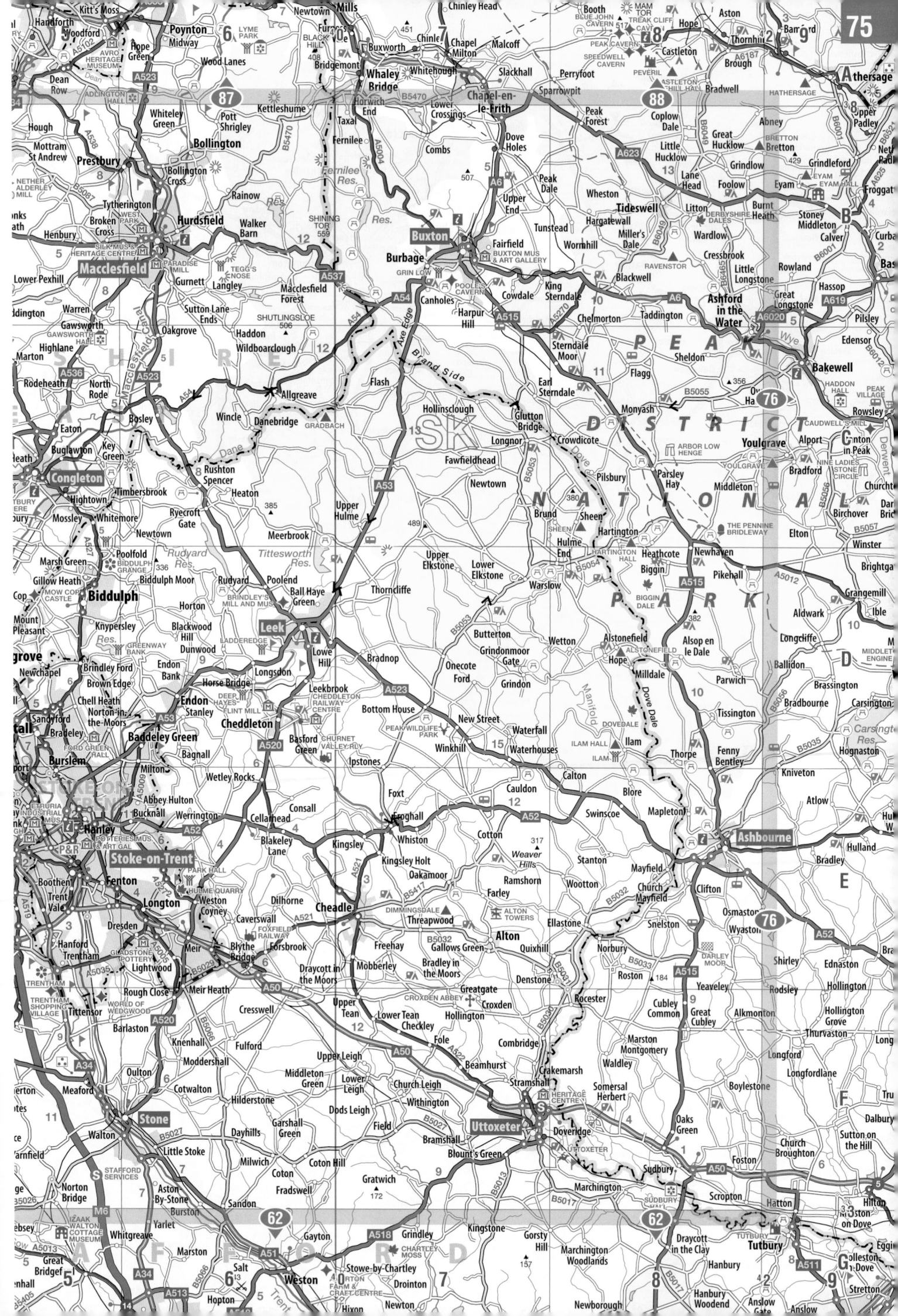

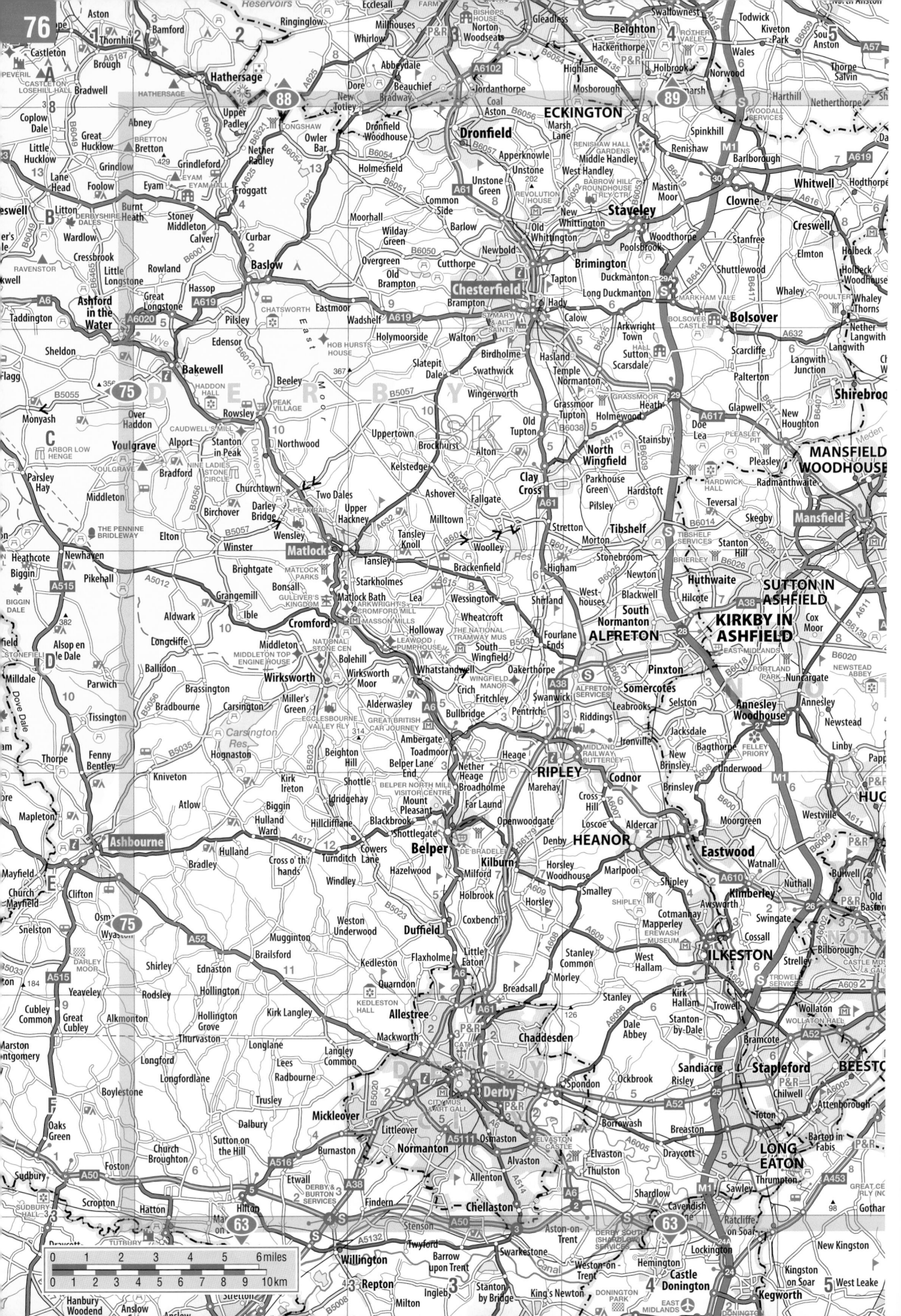

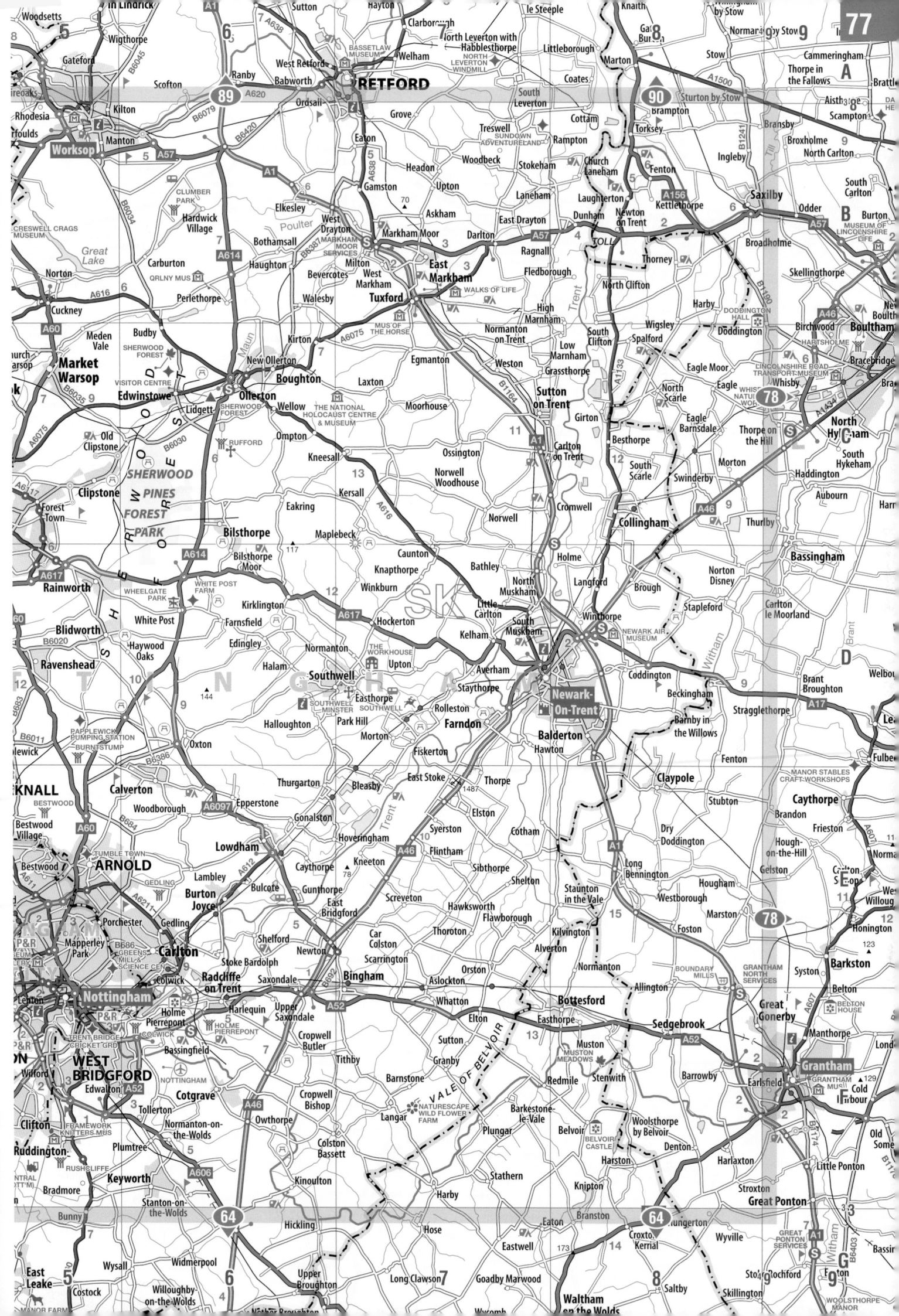

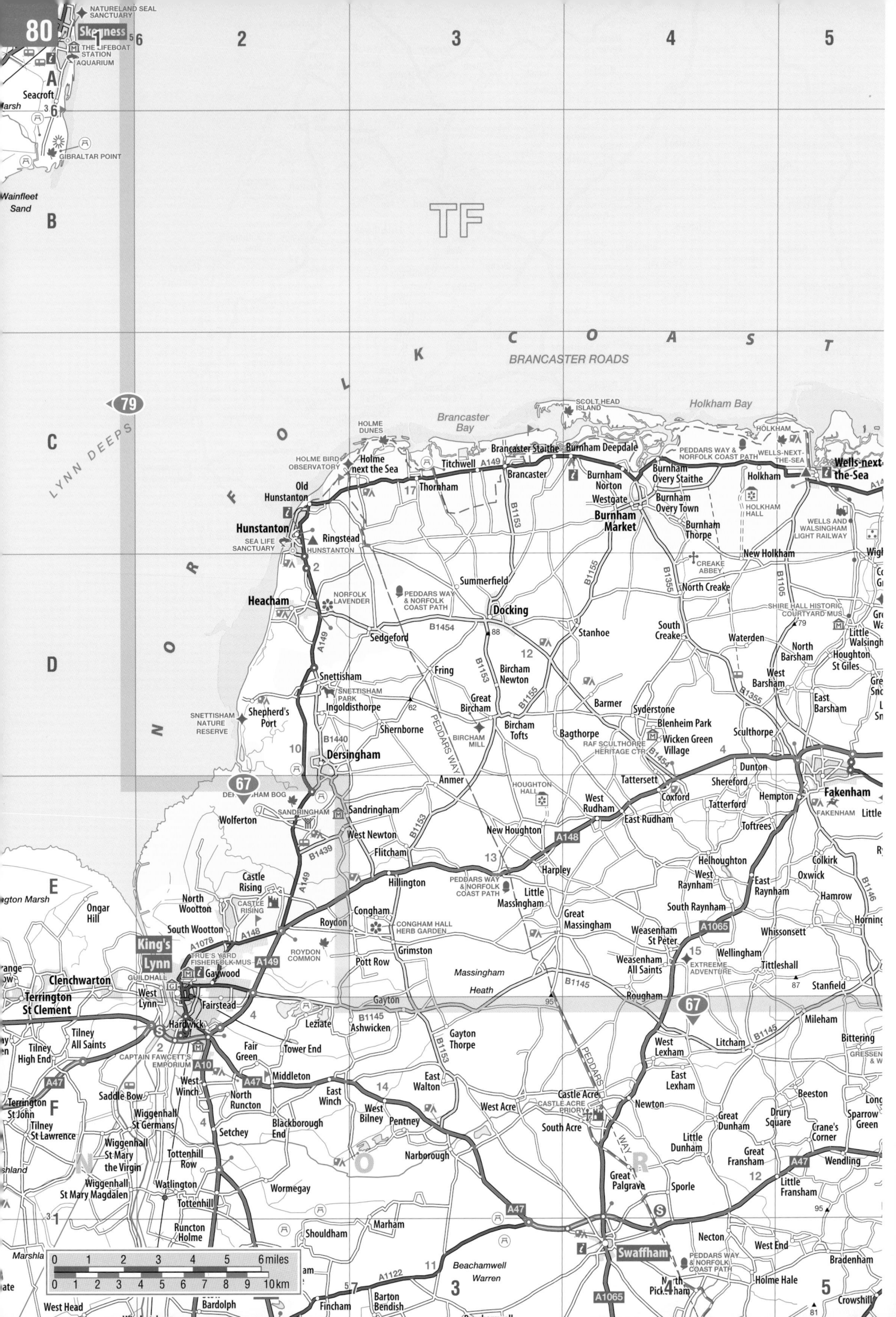

NATURELAND SEAL
SANCTUARY
Skegness
THE LIFEBOAT
STATION
AQUARIUM

A
Seacroft
GIBRALTAR POINT

Wainfleet
Sand

B

TF

NORFOLK COAST

BRANCASTER ROADS

79

SCOLT HEAD
ISLAND   Holkham Bay
HOLKHAM

Brancaster
Bay

LYNN DEEPS

C
HOLME DUNES
HOLME BIRD
OBSERVATORY   Holme
next the Sea   Titchwell   A149
Thornham   Brancaster Staithe Burnham Deepdale   PEDDARS WAY &
NORFOLK COAST PATH   WELLS-NEXT-
THE-SEA   Wells-next-
the-Sea
17   Brancaster
Old
Hunstanton   Burnham
Norton   Burnham
Overy Staithe   Holkham
Hunstanton   Westgate   Burnham
Overy Town   HOLKHAM
HALL   WELLS AND
WALSINGHAM
SEA LIFE   Burnham   Burnham   LIGHT RAILWAY
SANCTUARY   Ringstead   Summerfield   Market   Thorpe
HUNSTANTON   NORFOLK   PEDDARS WAY   CREAKE
LAVENDER   & NORFOLK   ABBEY   SHIRE HALL HISTORIC
2   COAST PATH   Docking   North Creake   COURTYARD MUS   Little
Heacham   79   Walsingham
D   Sedgeford   Stanhoe   South   North
B1454   88   Creake   Waterden   Barsham   Houghton
Snettisham   Fring   12   Bircham   West   St Giles
SNETTISHAM   Newton   Barmer   Syderstone   Barsham   East
PARK   Great   Bircham   Blenheim Park   Barsham
Ingoldisthorpe   62   Bircham   Tofts   Bagthorpe   Wicken Green
SNETTISHAM   Shernborne   BIRCHAM   RAF SCULTHORPE   Village
NATURE   Shepherd's   MILL   HERITAGE CTR   Sculthorpe
RESERVE   Port   4
10   Anmer   Tattersett   Dunton
B1440   HOUGHTON   West   Coxford   Shereford   Hempton
Dersingham   HALL   Rudham   Tatterford   Toftrees   Fakenham
67   East Rudham   FAKENHAM
Wolferton   West Newton   New Houghton   A148   Helhoughton   Colkirk
SANDRINGHAM   Sandringham   Harpley   West   East   Oxwick
B1439   Flitcham   Little   Raynham   Raynham   Hamrow
E   13   Massingham   Great   South Raynham   Horning
Ongar   Hillington   PEDDARS WAY   Massingham
Hill   North   CASTLE   Congham   & NORFOLK   Weasenham
Wootton   RISING   CONGHAM HALL   COAST PATH   St Peter   A1065   Whissonsett
Castle   HERB GARDEN   Weasenham   15   Wellingham
South Wootton   Rising   Roydon   All Saints   EXTREEME
A148   ADVENTURE   Tittleshall
King's   TRUE'S YARD   ROYDON   Grimston   Great   Rough   87   Stanfield
Lynn   FISHERFOLK MUS   A149   COMMON   Pott Row   Massingham   Rougham   67
Clenchwarton   GUILDHALL   Gaywood   Massingham   B1145   Mileham
West   Gayton   Heath   Stanfield
Terrington   Lynn   Fairstead   Bittering
St Clement   Hardwick   Leziate   Gayton   95   West
2   Ashwicken   Thorpe   B1145   Lexham   Litcham   GRESSEN
Tilney   CAPTAIN FAWCETT'S   Fair   B1153   & WI
F   Tilney   All Saints   EMPORIUM   Green   Tower End   East   East
High End   A10   West   Middleton   East   Castle Acre   Lexham   Beeston
Terrington   Saddle Bow   Winch   North   West   Walton CASTLE ACRE   Great   Drury   Long
St John   A47   Runcton   East Winch   West Bilney   West Acre   PRIORY   Newton   Dunham   Square   Sparrow
Tilney   Pentney   Crane's   Green
St Lawrence   Wiggenhall   Setchey   Blackborough   South Acre   Little   Corner
St Germans   End   Dunham   Great   A47
Wiggenhall   Narborough   Fransham   Wendling
St Mary   Great   Little
the Virgin   Tottenhill   Wormegay   Palgrave   Sporle   Fransham   12
Row   95
Wiggenhall   Marham   Great
St Mary Magdalen   Watlington   Palgrave   Necton   West End
1   Tottenhill   Swaffham   Bradenham
Runcton   Shouldham   PEDDARS WAY &
Marshla   Holme   NORFOLK COAST PATH
West Head   Beachamwell   A1122   A1065   North   Holme Hale
Bardolph   Barton   Warren   Pick   ham
Fincham   Bendish   Crowshill
West Head   11   3

0   1   2   3   4   5   6 miles
0 1 2 3 4 5 6 7 8 9 10km

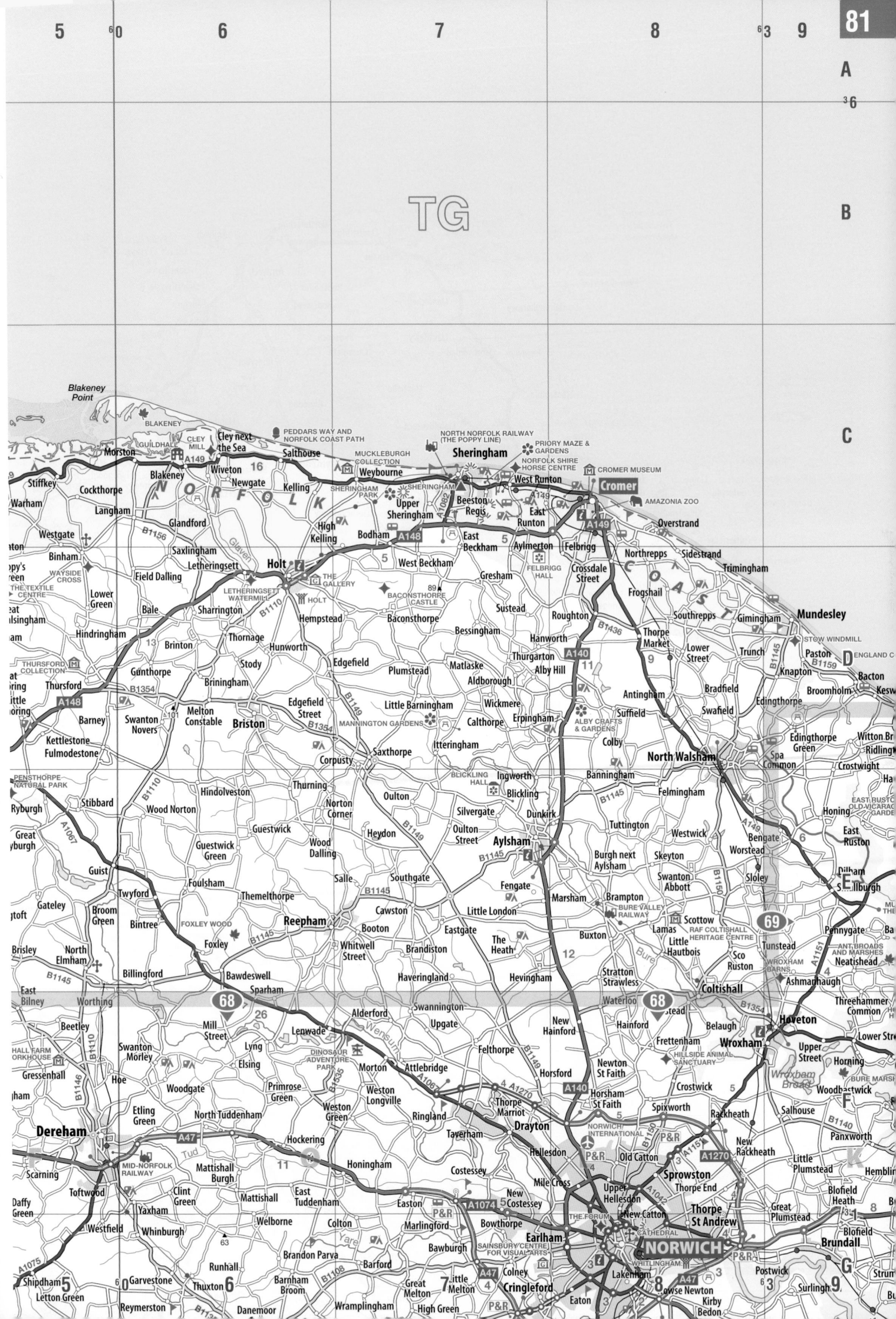

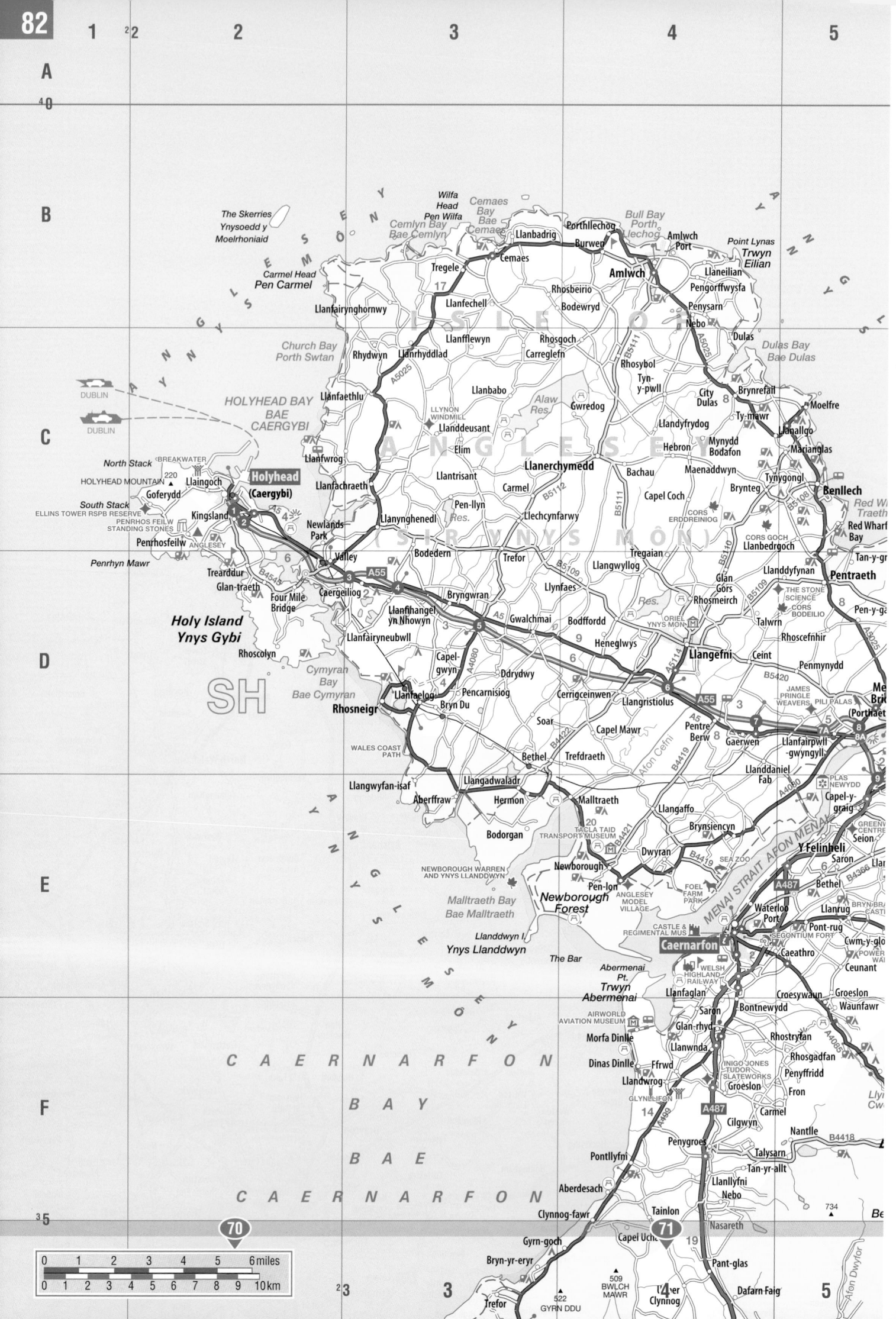

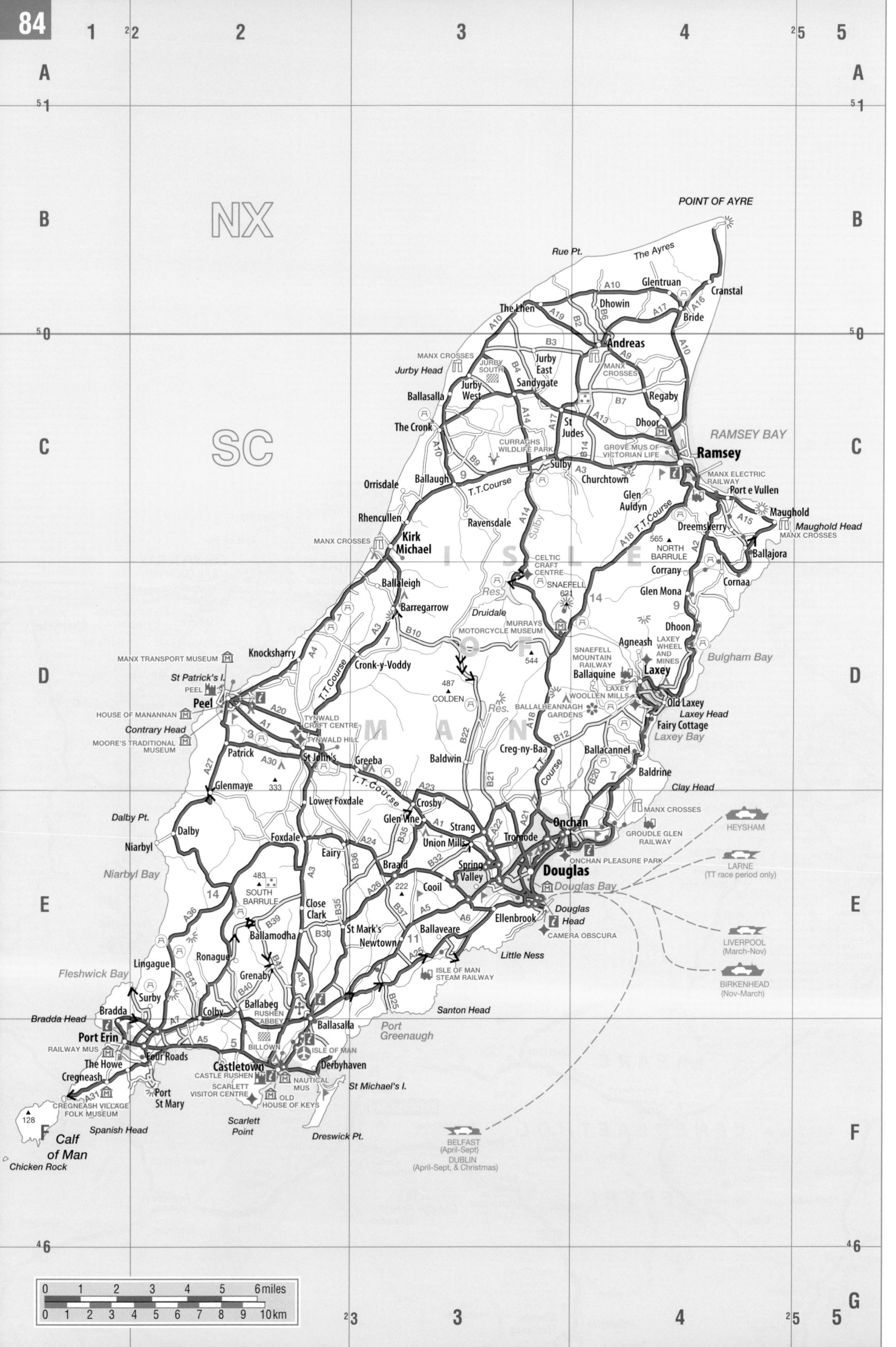

1   2   2   2   3   4   5   5

A

1

B   NX

5   0

C   SC

D

E

F

G

POINT OF AYRE

Rue Pt.
The Ayres
A10   Glentruan
Dhowin   Cranstal
The Lhen   A19   B2   A17   A16   Bride
B6
A10   B3   Andreas   A10
MANX CROSSES   JURBY   SOUTH   Jurby   A9
Jurby Head   East   MANX
Jurby   B4   Sandygate   CROSSES
West
Ballasalla   A14   A17   Regaby   B7   Dhoor
The Cronk   A10   St   B14   RAMSEY BAY
Judes   A13   GROVE MUS OF
A10   CURRAGHS   Dhoor   VICTORIAN LIFE
Orrisdale   Ballaugh   WILDLIFE PARK   B9   Ramsey
9   Sulby   Churchtown   MANX ELECTRIC
Rhencullen   T.T.Course   Glen   A3   RAILWAY
MANX CROSSES   Ravensdale   Auldyn   Port e Vullen
Kirk   Sulby   A18 T.T.Course   A15   Maughold
Michael   CELTIC   Dreemskerry   Maughold Head
Ballaleigh   CRAFT CENTRE   565   NORTH   MANX CROSSES
Barregarrow   SNAEFELL   A2   BARRULE   Ballajora
Res.   621   Corrany   Cornaa
7   B10   Druidale   14   Glen Mona   9
MURRAYS   SNAEFELL   Dhoon
MANX TRANSPORT MUSEUM   A3   7   MOTORCYCLE MUSEUM   MOUNTAIN RAILWAY   Agneash   LAXEY
Knocksharry   Cronk-y-Voddy   544   Ballaquine   WHEEL AND MINES
St Patrick's I.   A4   LAXEY   Bulgham Bay
PEEL   487   Laxey   WOOLLEN MILLS   Laxey
HOUSE OF MANANNAN   Peel   COLDEN   BALLALHEANNAGH   Old Laxey
Contrary Head   A20   Res.   GARDENS   Laxey Head
MOORE'S TRADITIONAL   A1   A18   Fairy Cottage
MUSEUM   TYNWALD   Creg-ny-Baa   Laxey Bay
CRAFT CENTRE   Baldwin   B12   Ballacannel
Patrick   A30   TYNWALD HILL   B22   B20   Baldrine
Glenmaye   333   St John's   Greeba   A23   Clay Head
A27   Lower Foxdale   B21   7
Dalby Pt.   T.T.Course   Crosby   Onchan   MANX CROSSES
Dalby   Glen Vine   A1   Strang   Tromode   GROUDLE GLEN
Niarbyl   Foxdale   A24   Union Mills   B32   Douglas   RAILWAY   HEYSHAM
Eairy   A22   A21   Douglas
Niarbyl Bay   Braaid   B35   Spring   ONCHAN PLEASURE PARK   LARNE
483   B37   Valley   Douglas Bay   (TT race period only)
14   SOUTH   222   Cooil   A5
BARRULE   Close   A26   A6   Ellenbrook   Douglas
Clark   B35   St Mark's   Head
A36   Ballamodha   B30   Newtown   11   CAMERA OBSCURA   LIVERPOOL
Ronague   B39   Ballaveare   (March-Nov)
Lingague   A25   Little Ness
Fleshwick Bay   B40   Grenaby   ISLE OF MAN   BIRKENHEAD
Surby   A3   STEAM RAILWAY   (Nov-March)
Bradda   Colby   Ballabeg   B25   Santon Head
Bradda Head   A7   RUSHEN   Port
Port Erin   Ballasalla   Greenaugh
RAILWAY MUS   A5   5   BILLOWN   ISLE OF MAN
The Howe   Four Roads   NAUTICAL   St Michael's I.
Cregneash   Castletown   MUS
A31   CASTLE RUSHEN   Derbyhaven   BELFAST
128   SCARLETT   Port   OLD   (April-Sept)
Calf   VISITOR CENTRE   St Mary   HOUSE OF KEYS   DUBLIN
of Man   Scarlett   Dreswick Pt.   (April-Sept, & Christmas)
Chicken Rock   Spanish Head   Point

ISLE   OF   MAN

0   1   2   3   4   5   6miles
0   1   2   3   4   5   6   7   8   9   10km

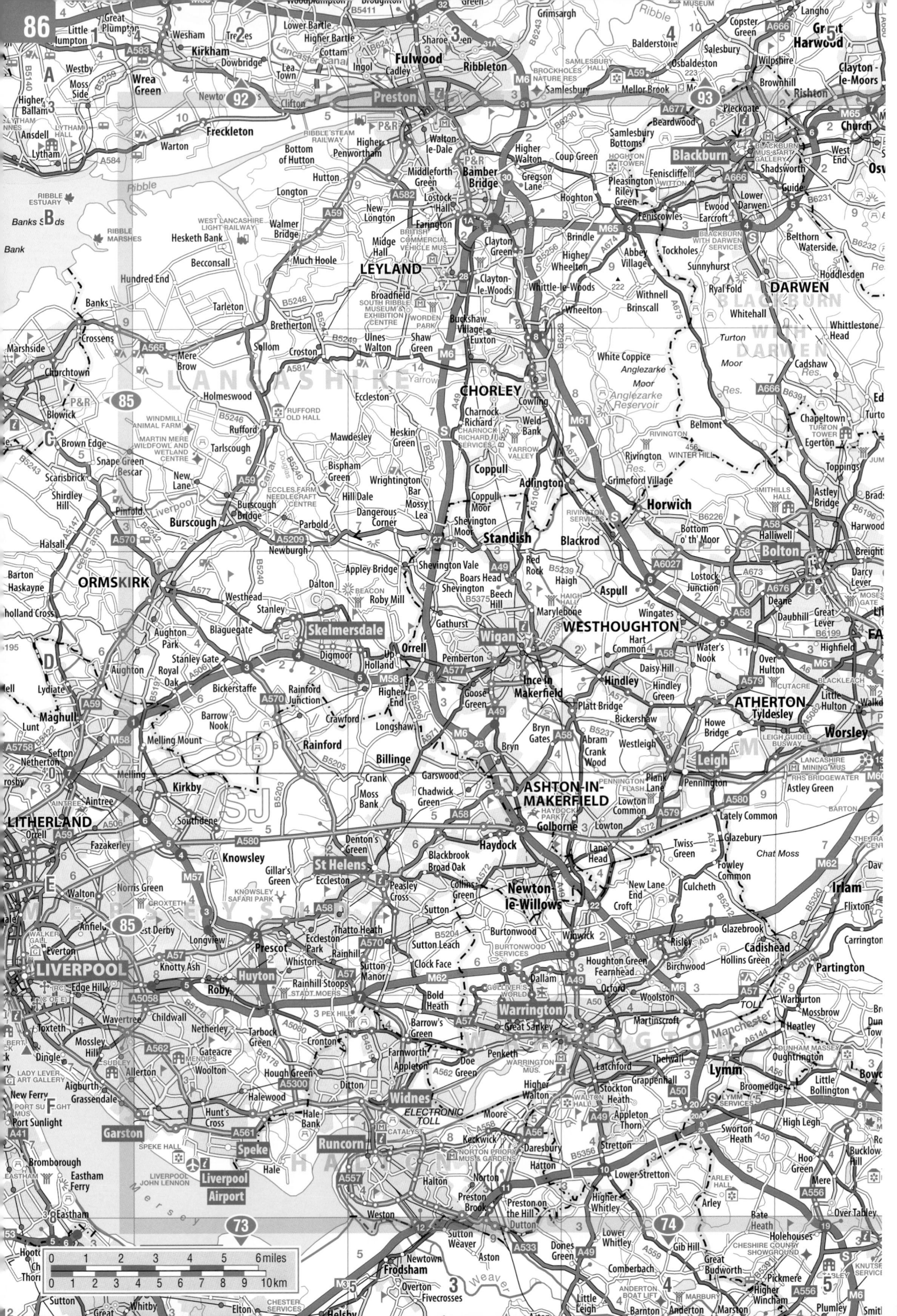

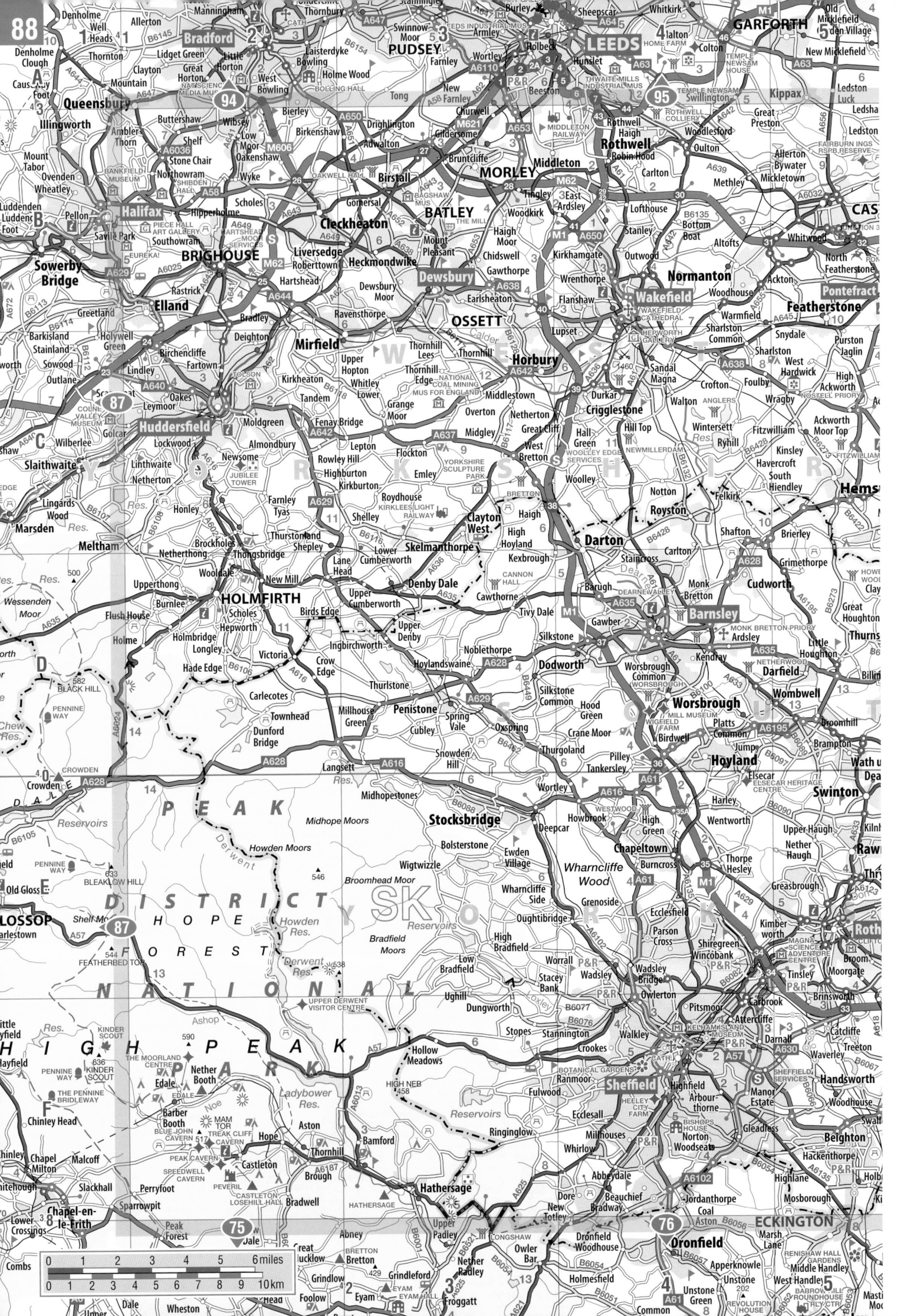

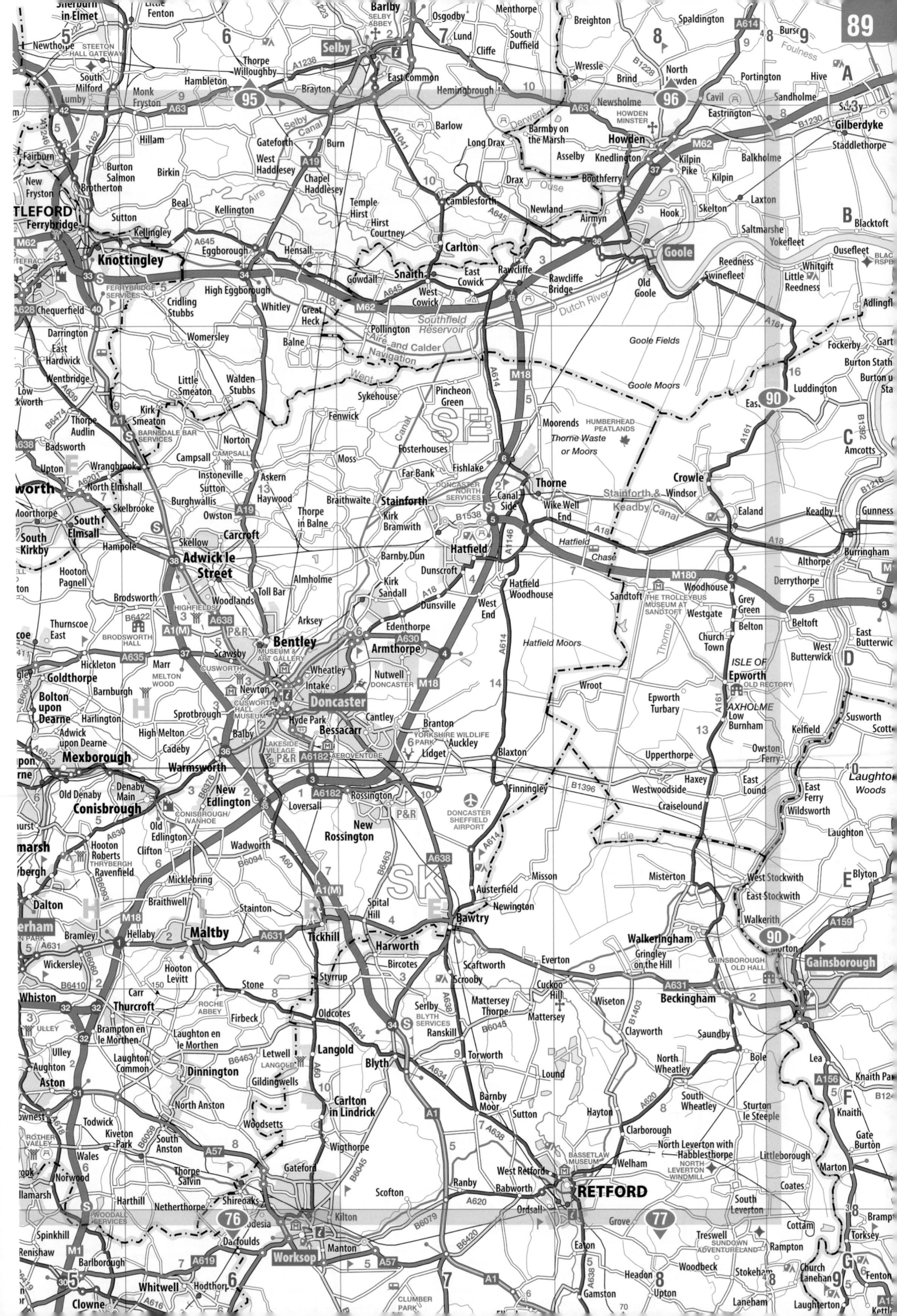

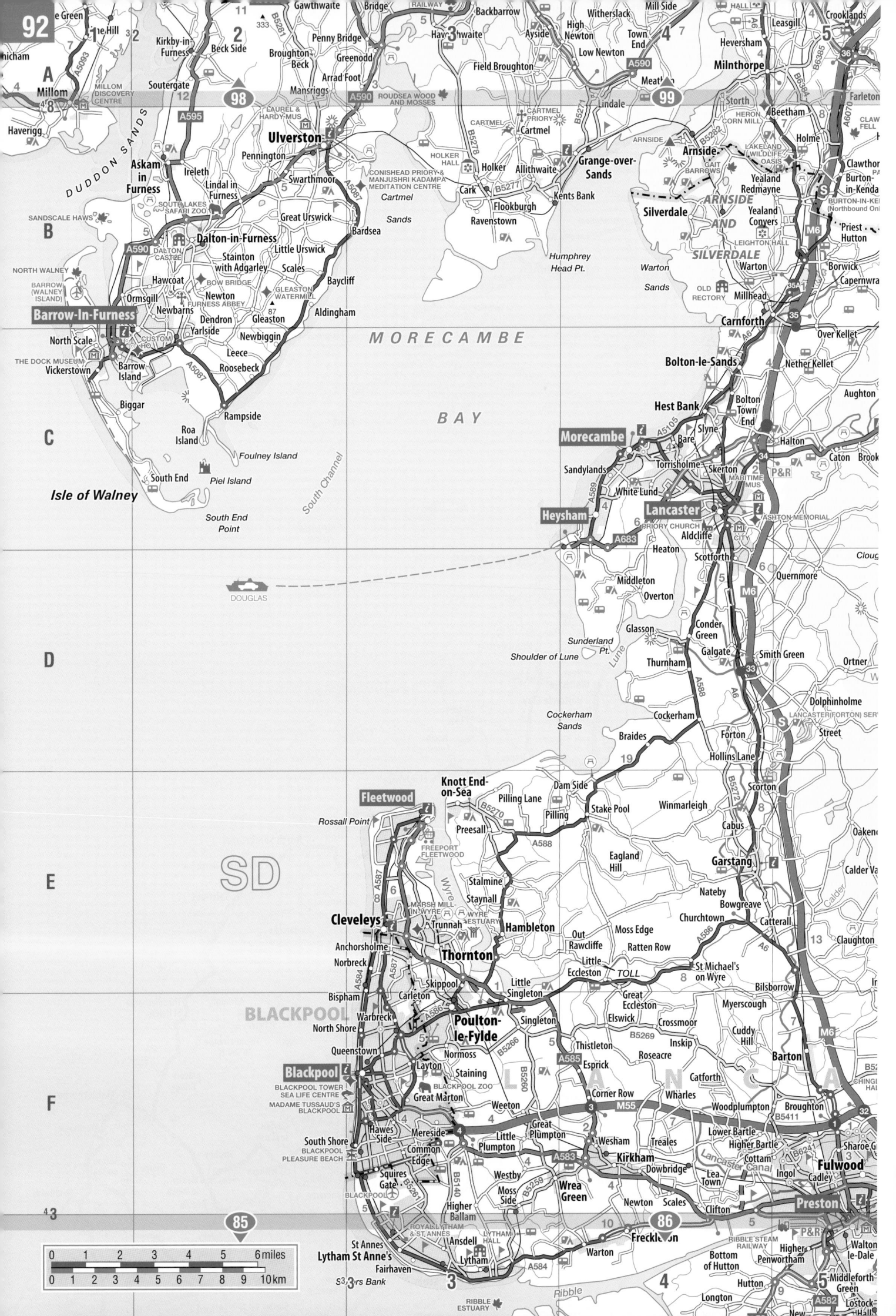

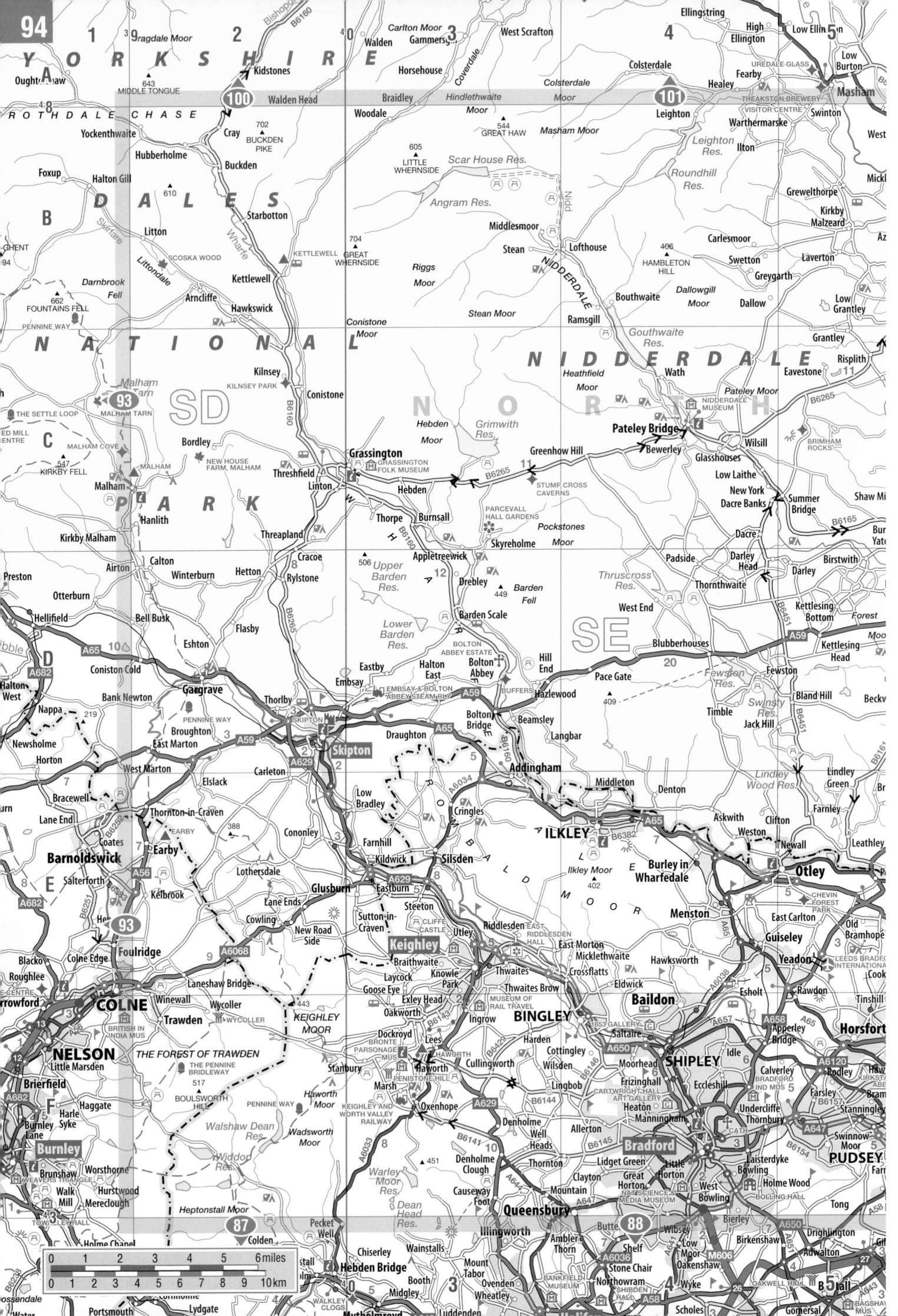

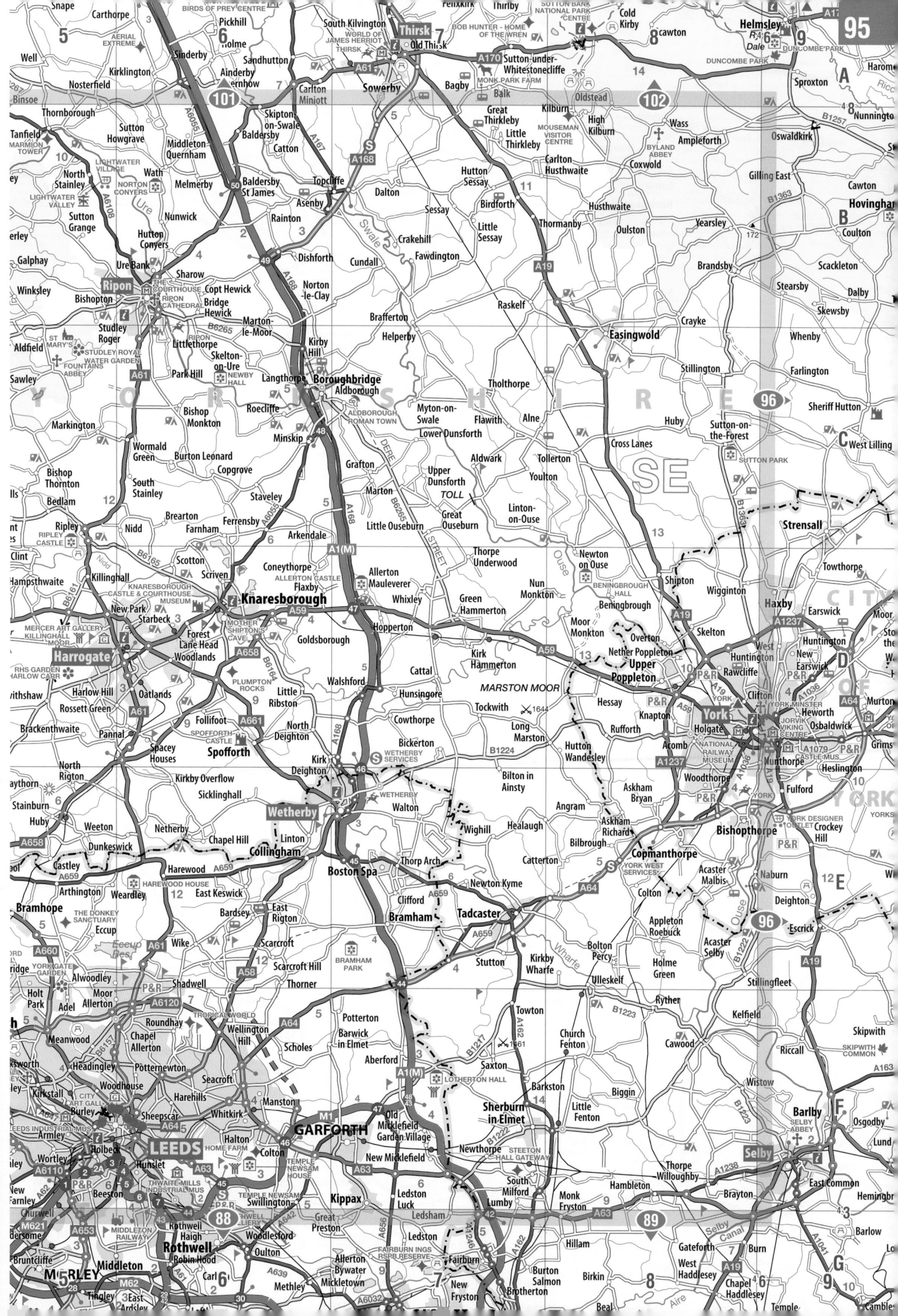

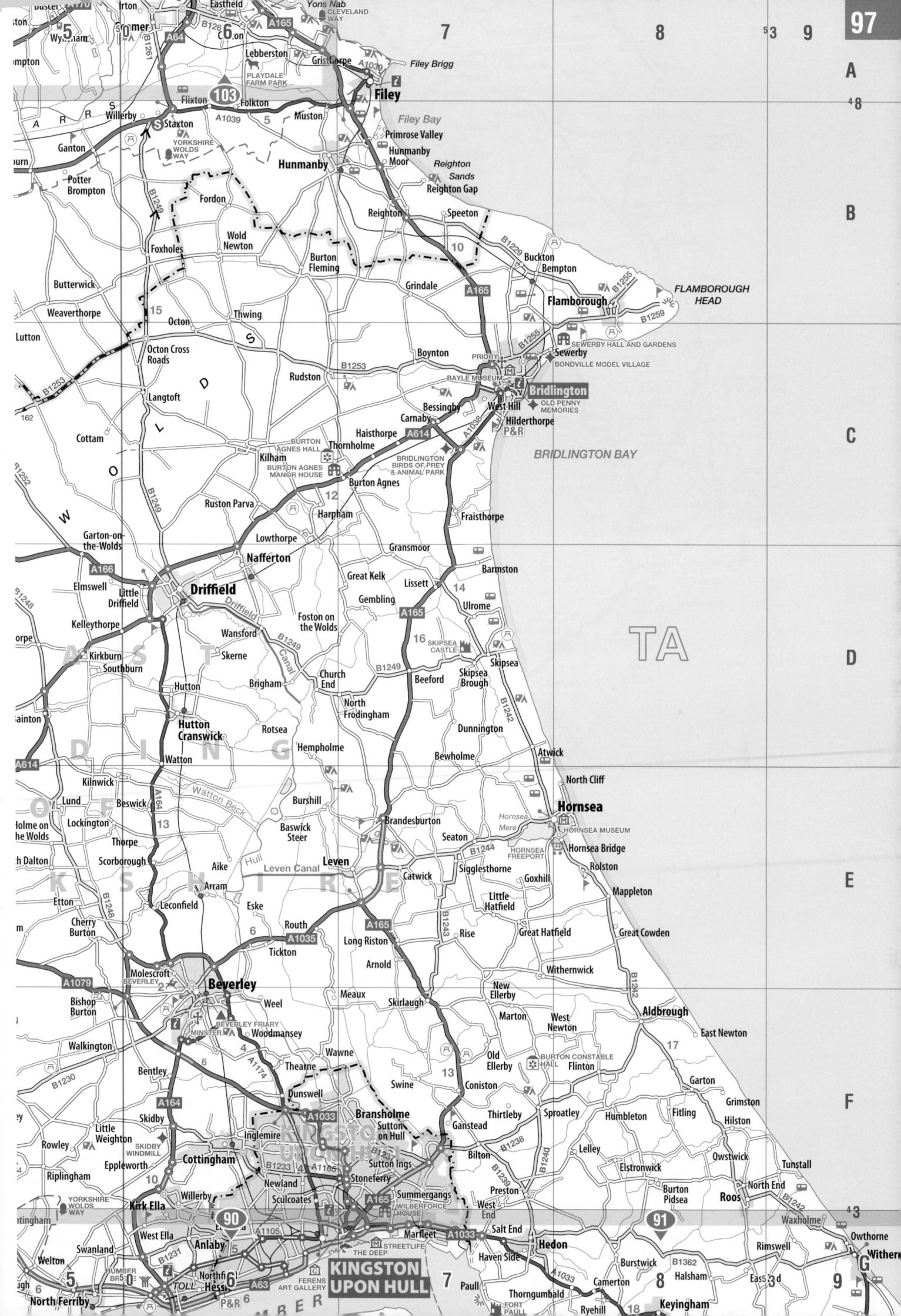

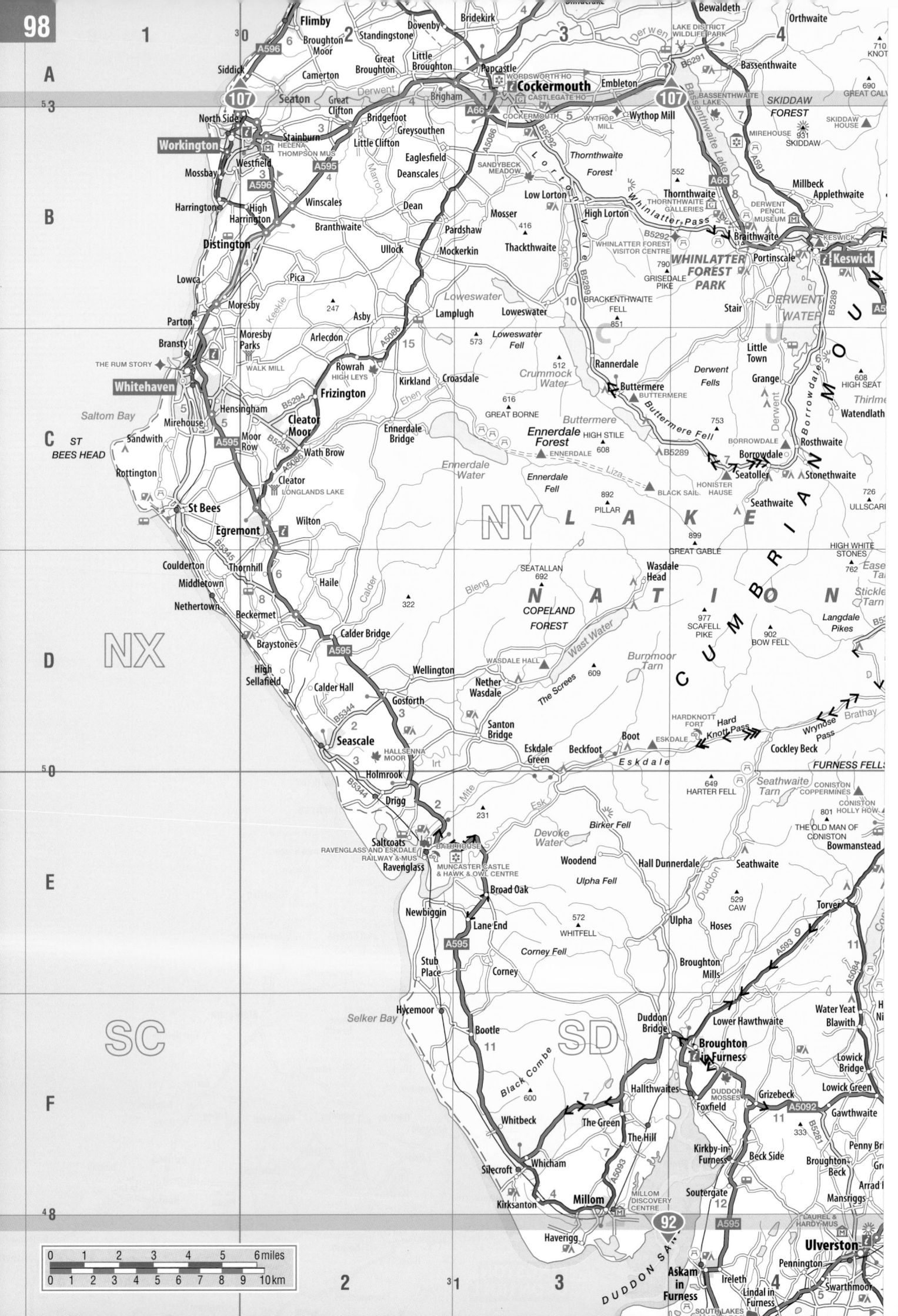

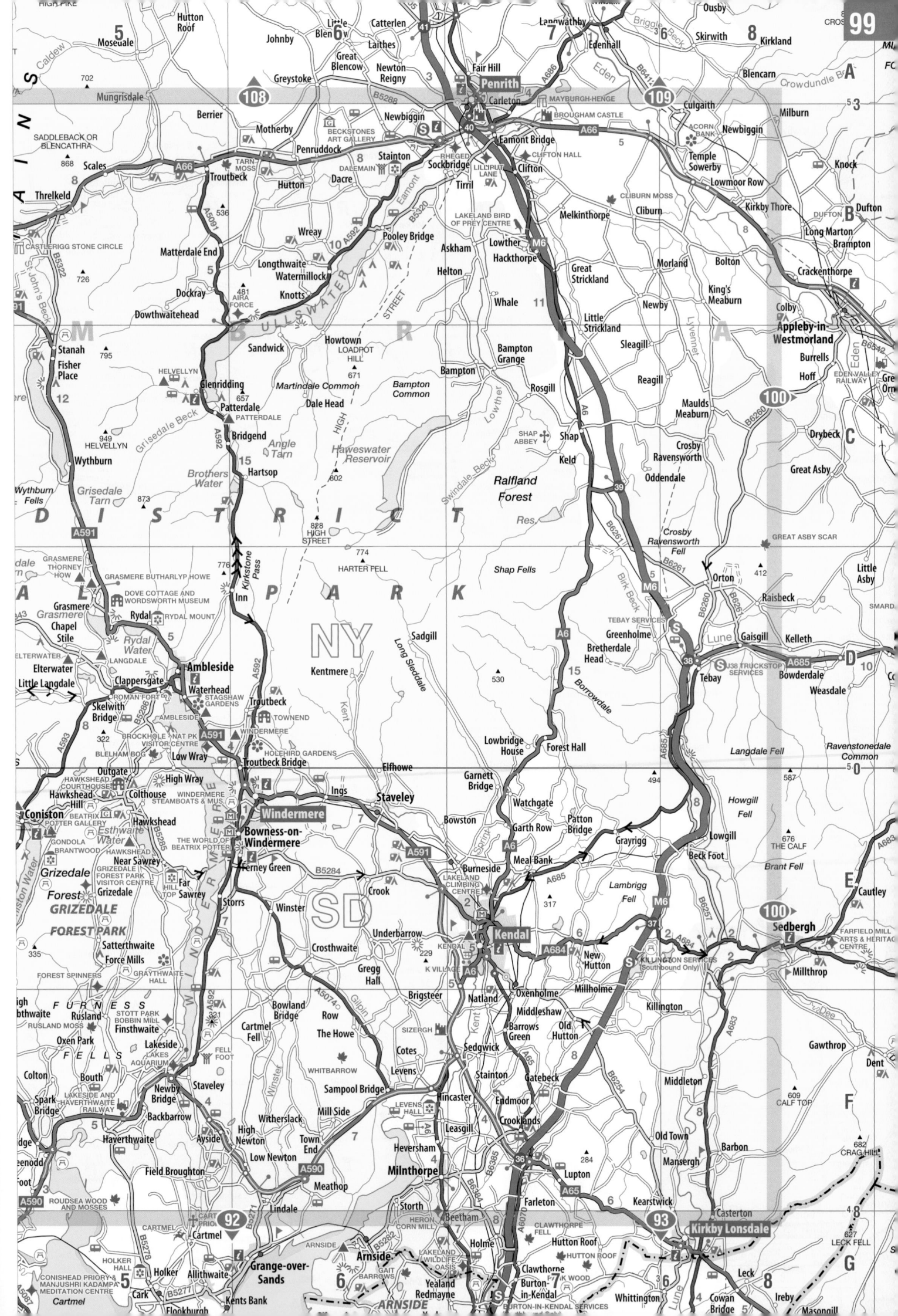

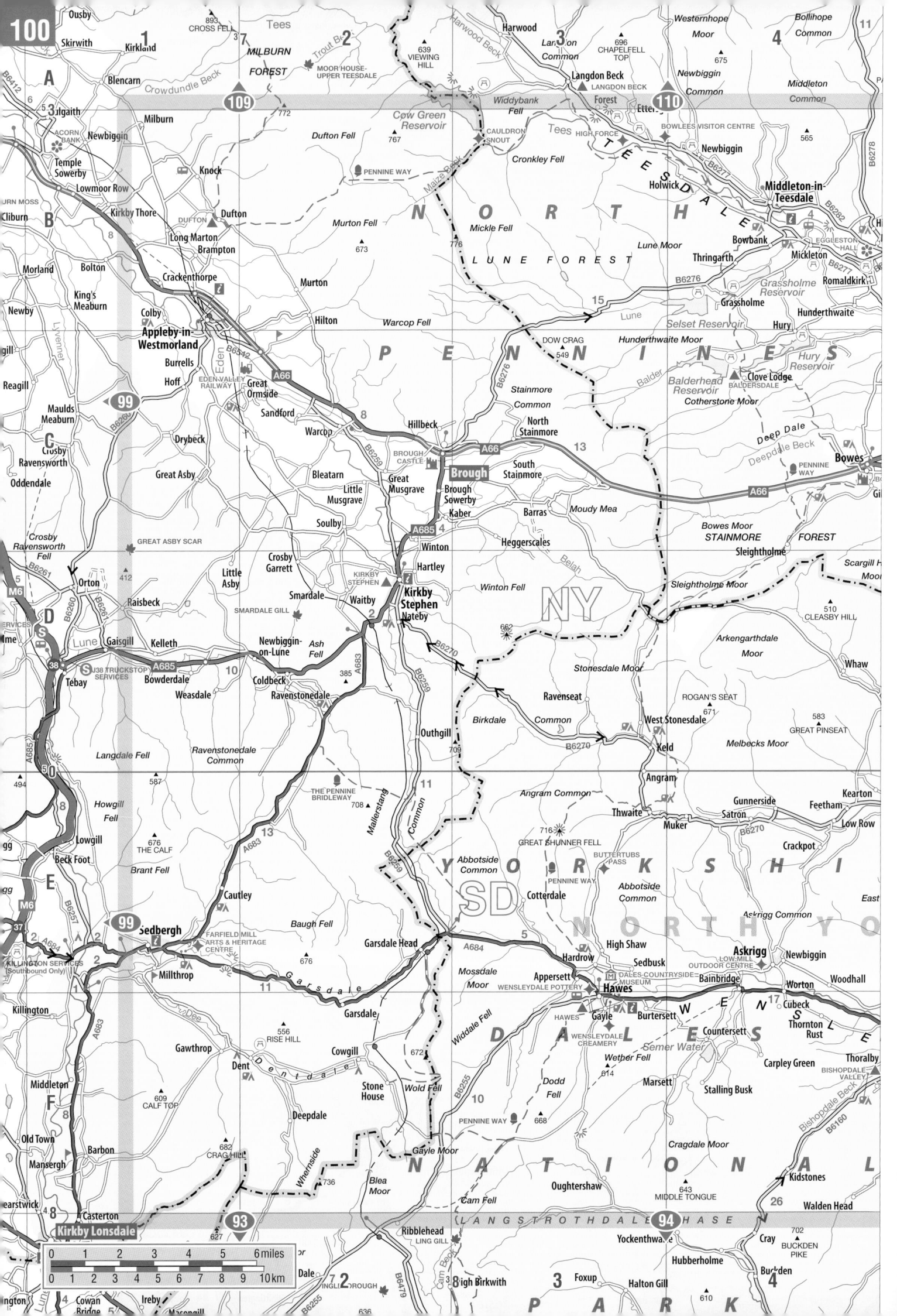

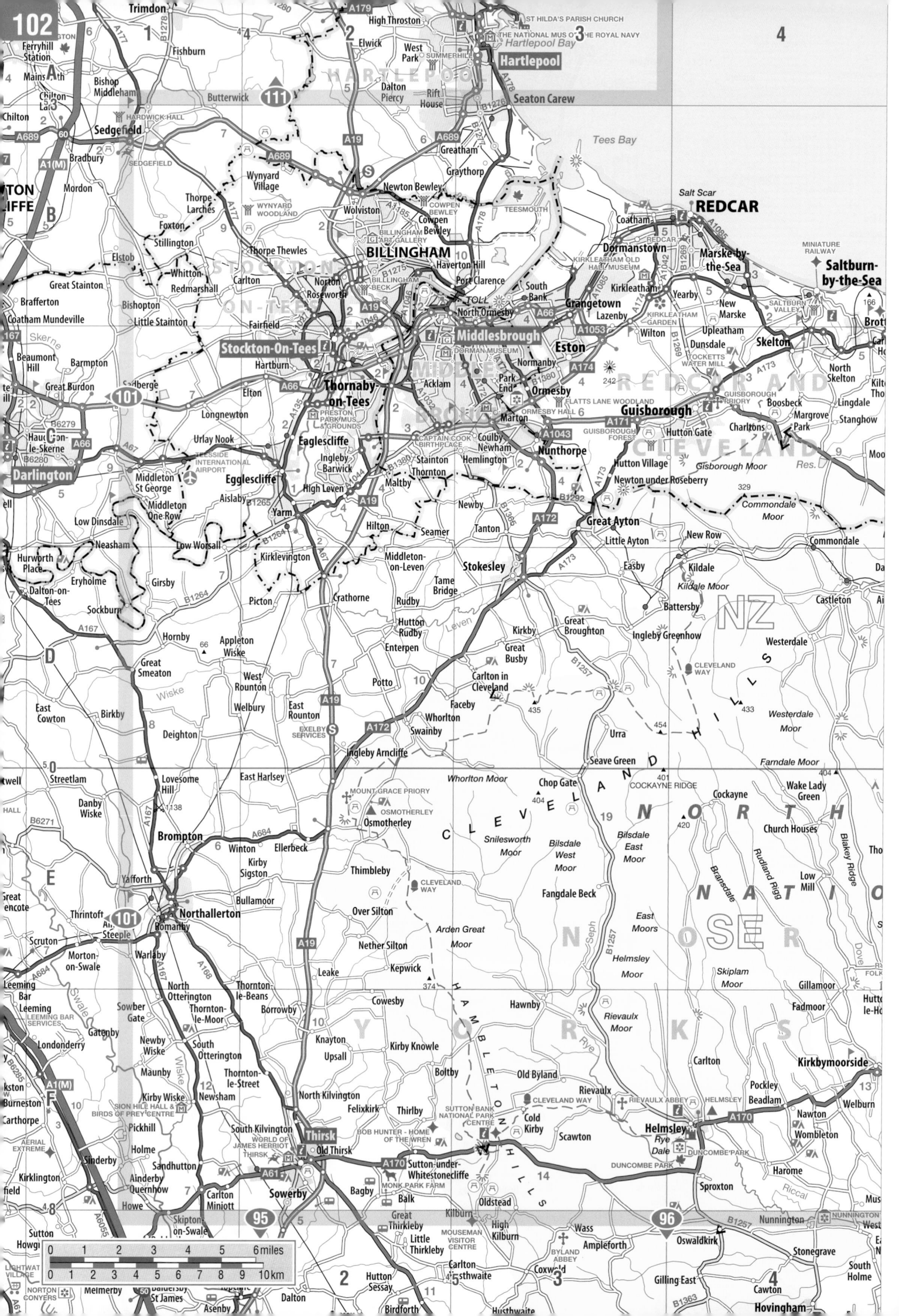

1 8 2 3 0 4 5

CARLETON
CASTLE

Bennane Hd.
112
Colmonell
B734 265 Knockdolian
Heronsford
Glen Tig
A Ballantrae Bay Balkiss
Ballantrae
Downan Pt.
8 Auchencrosh
A77
439
BENERAIRD

B Mark
Milleur Pt. 17 Glen App
257
Corsewall Pt.
Portencalzie Penwhirn
Barnhills Res.
North Cairn Cairnryan
South Cairn Corsewall Braid Fell
B738 Kirkcolm
Dounan Bay Loch Main Water of L
Connell
Mains of Airies Ervie The Wig
Low LOCH RYAN
B798 Salchrie
C Knocknain 6 Auchmant
B738 Leswalt Innermessan
Slouchnawen Craigencross A751
Bay B7043 A718 Black Loch
CASTLE KENNEDY
A77 GARDENS
Glenstockadale White Loch
Stranraer Castle Kennedy
T H Aird Castle Kennedy
Broadsea Bay E CASTLE OF R H I
Knockglass ST JOHN VISITOR Soulsea
STRANRAER CENTRE Loch A75
MUSEUM Mark
Black Hd. 182 Lochans A75
B738 A77 B7077 6
D Dunskey Ho. 5 Awhirk Torrs War
Portpatrick 5 B7084 6
8 Stoneykirk A716
Port of Spittal Bay Luce Se
B7042

Cairngarroch Sandhead
Cairngarroch Bay KIRKMADRINE Sandhead Bay
STONES
Money Hd.
Clachanmore
Hole Stone Bay Ardwell
Ardwell Chapel Rossan
E Mains
Ardwell Pt. Logan 10
Mains
LOGAN
BOTANIC Balgowan Pt.
GARDEN
Mull of Logan
LOGAN FISH POND
MARINE LIFE CENTRE
Port Nessock or Port Logan Bay
4 Port Logan
Cairnywellan Hd. B7065 A716
Clanyard Bay
Low Clanyard
Laggantalluch Hd. Kirkmaiden Drumm
164
F Damnaglaur B7041
Crammag Hd. Ma
Cairngaan

Port Kemin

NW

0 1 2 3 4 5 6 miles
0 1 2 3 4 5 6 7 8 9 10km
9 3 0 4 5

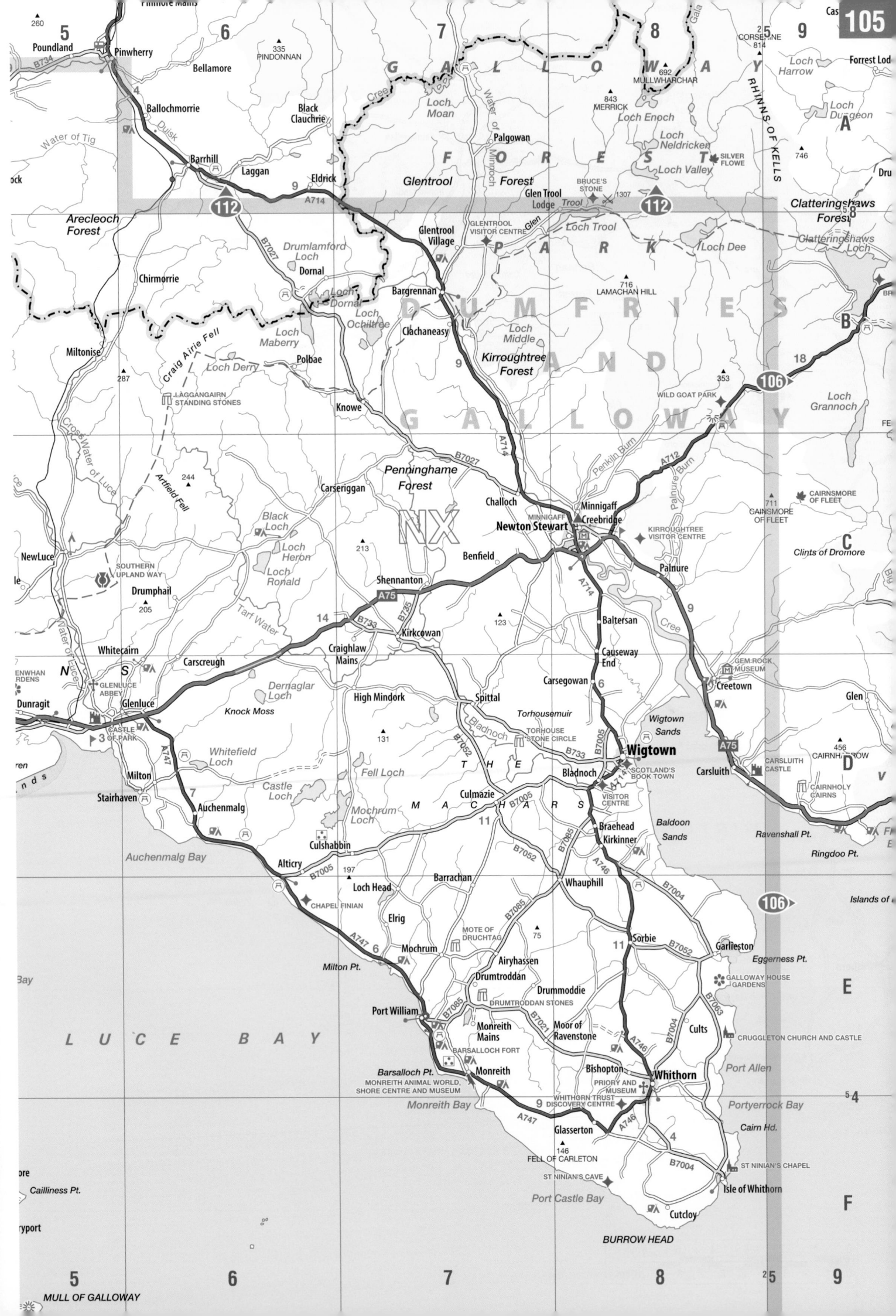

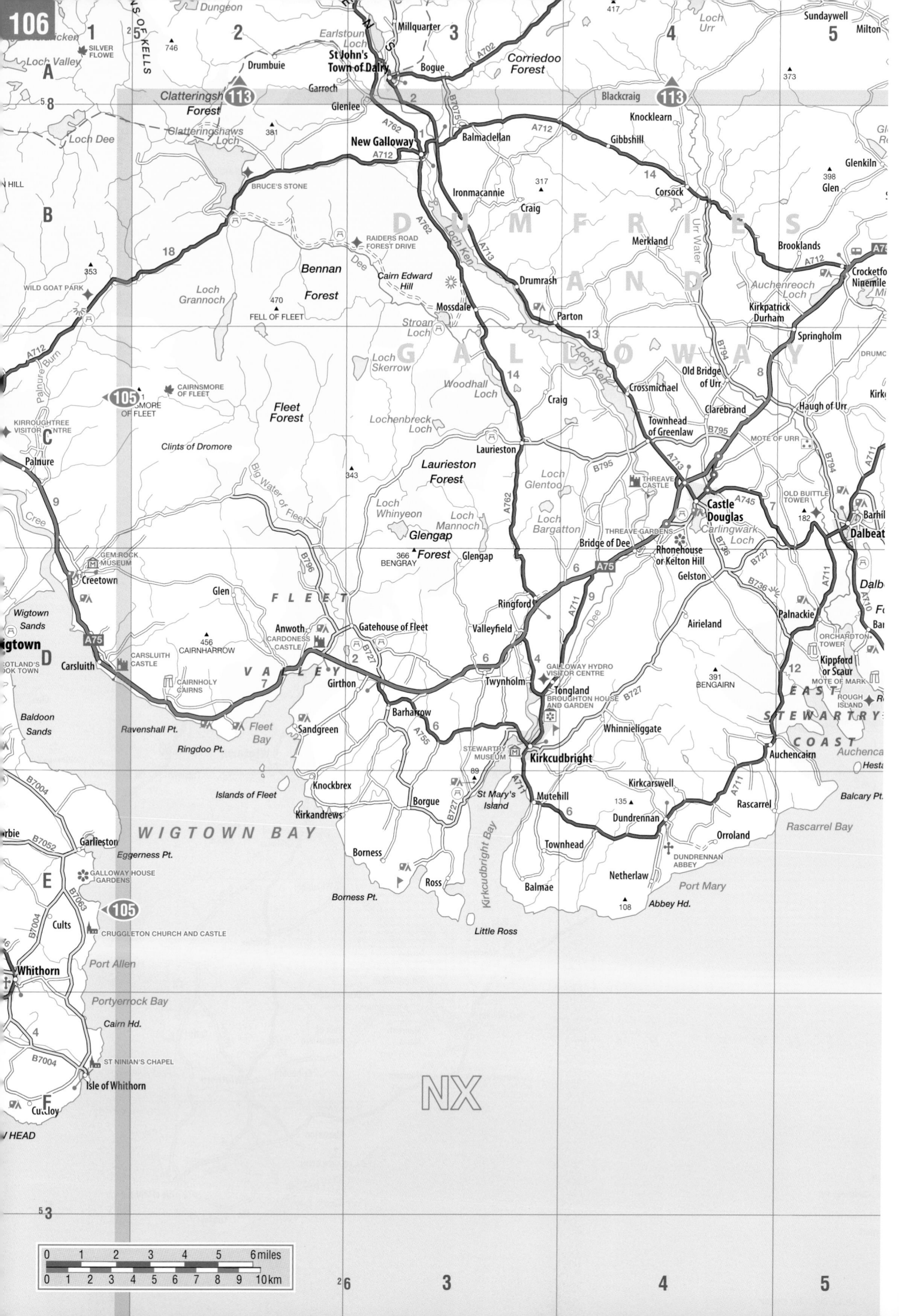

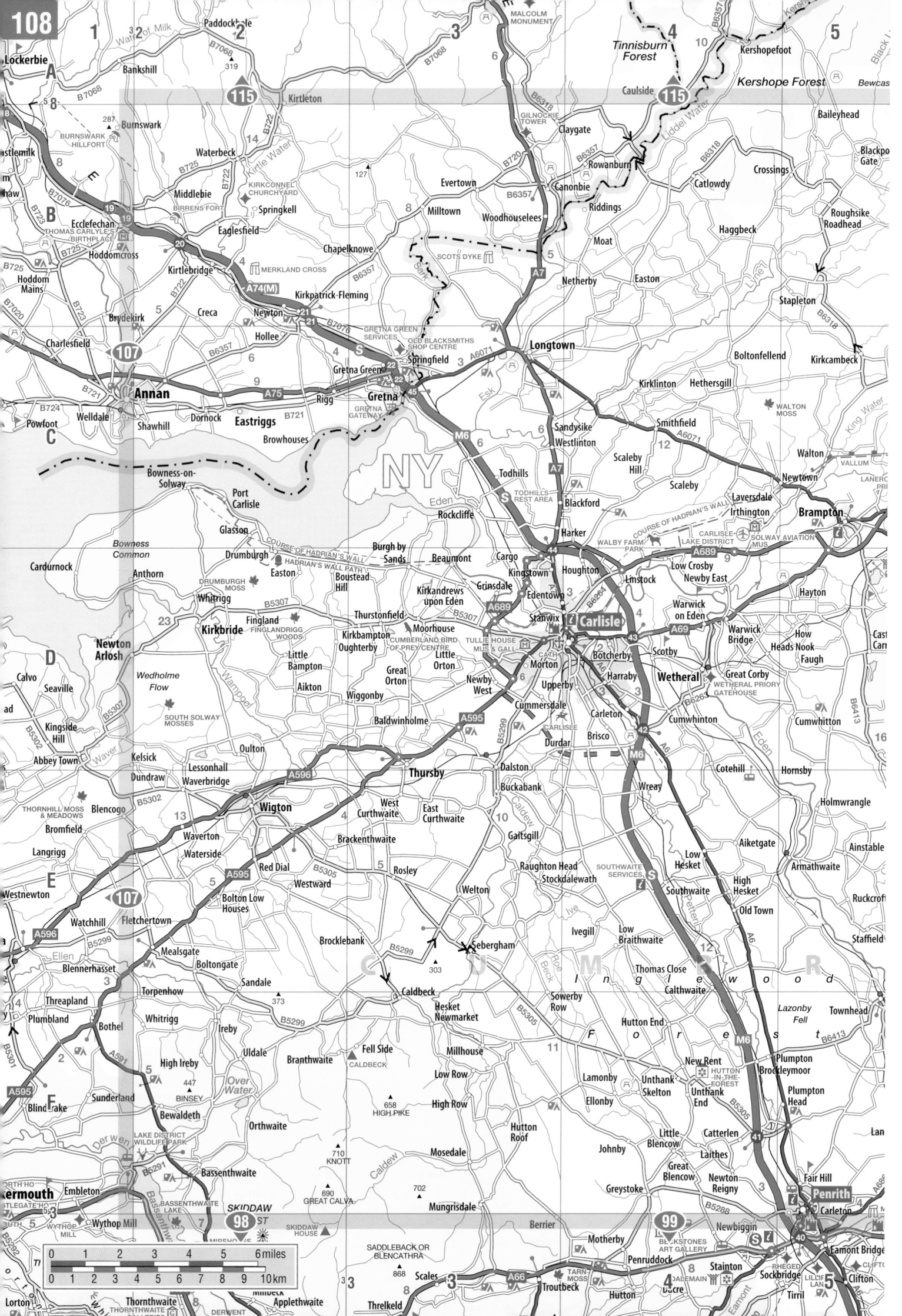

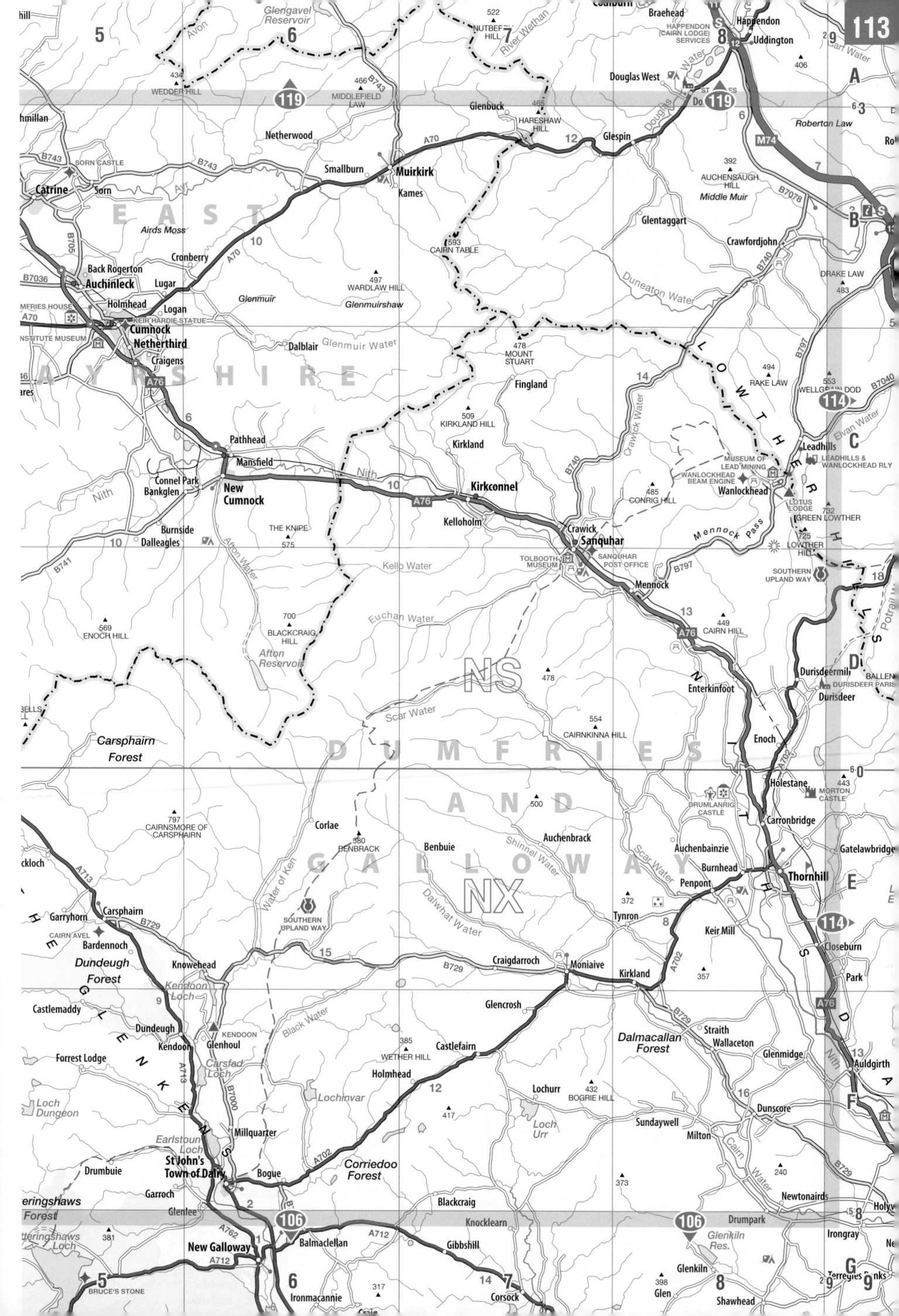

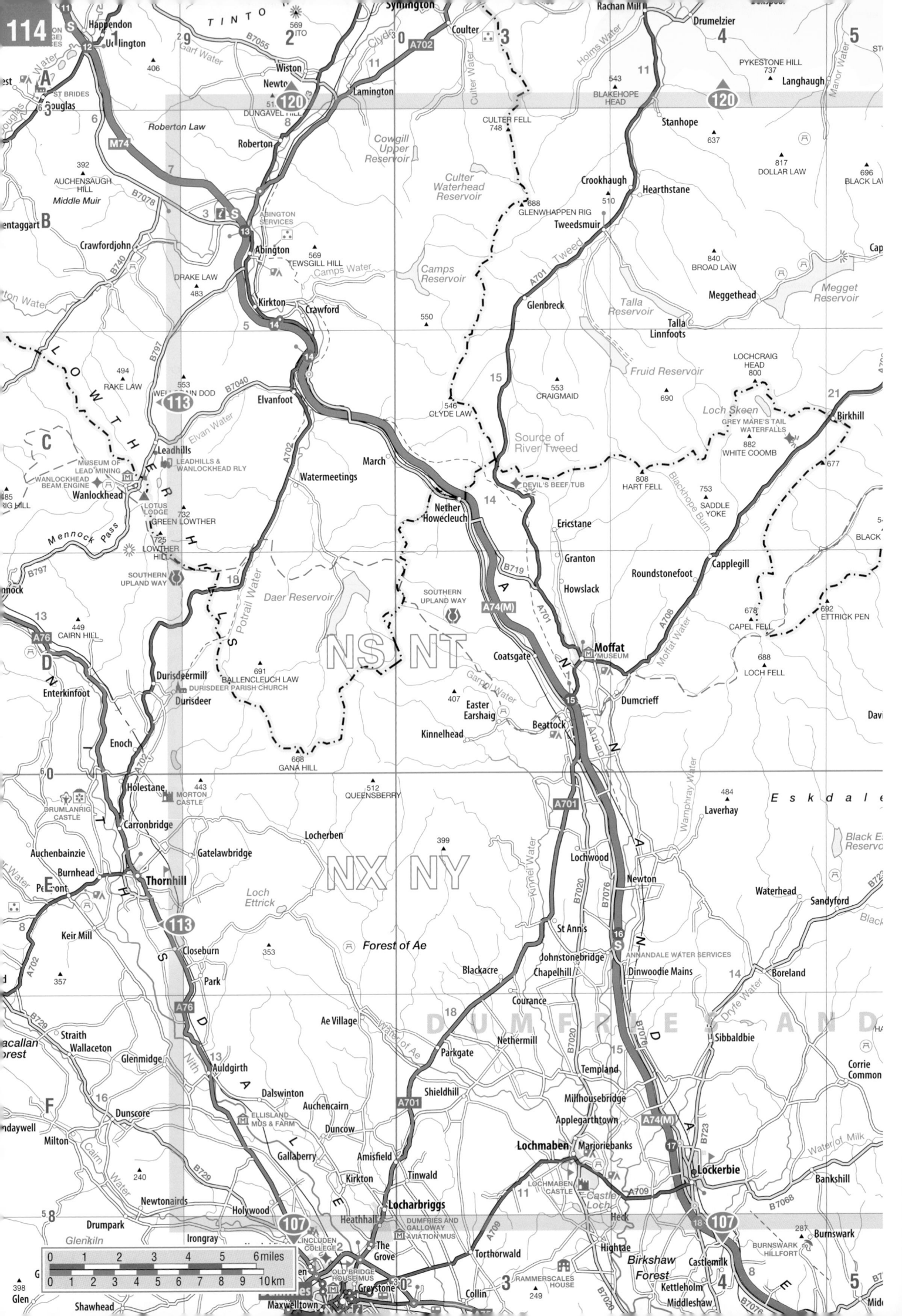

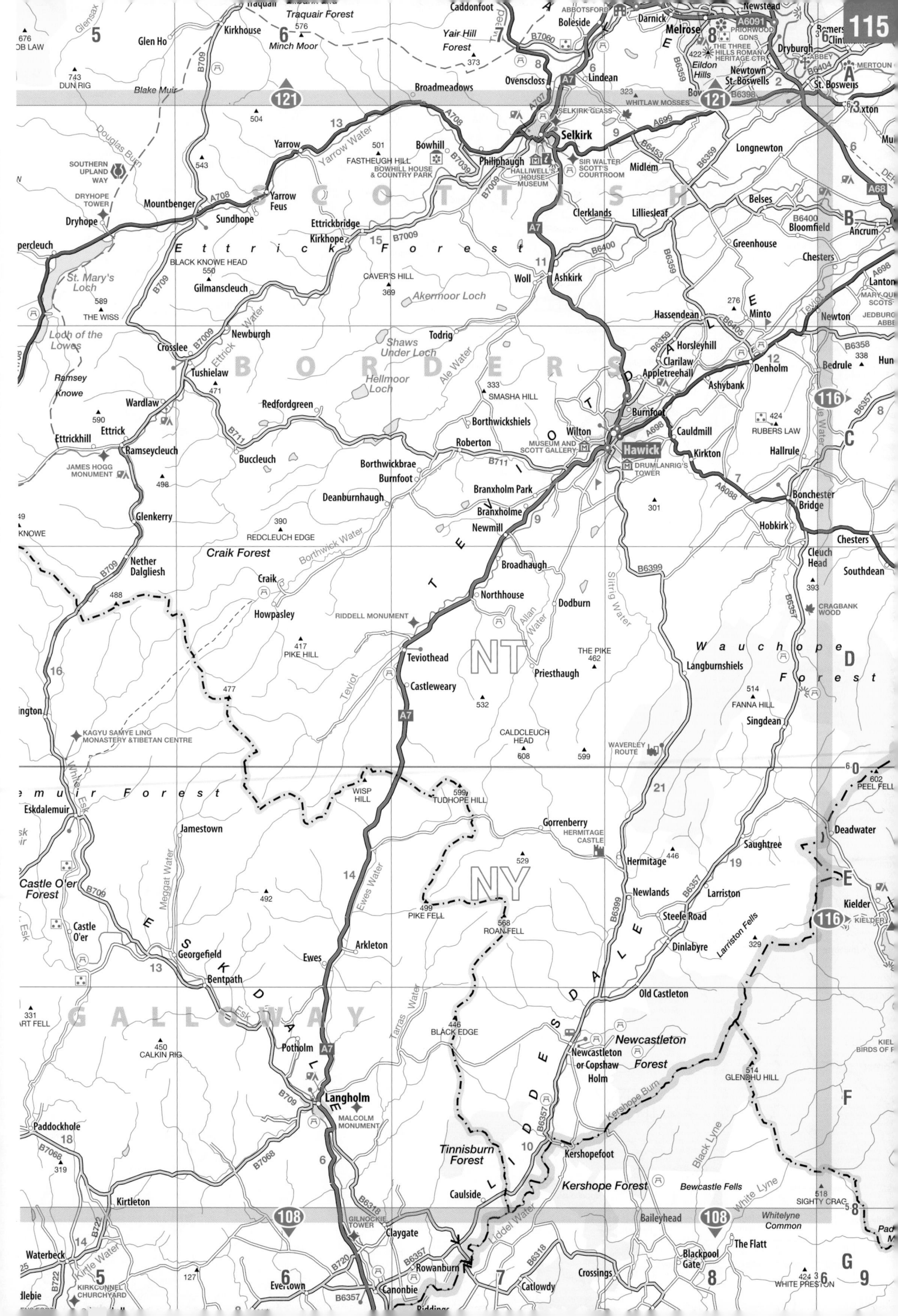

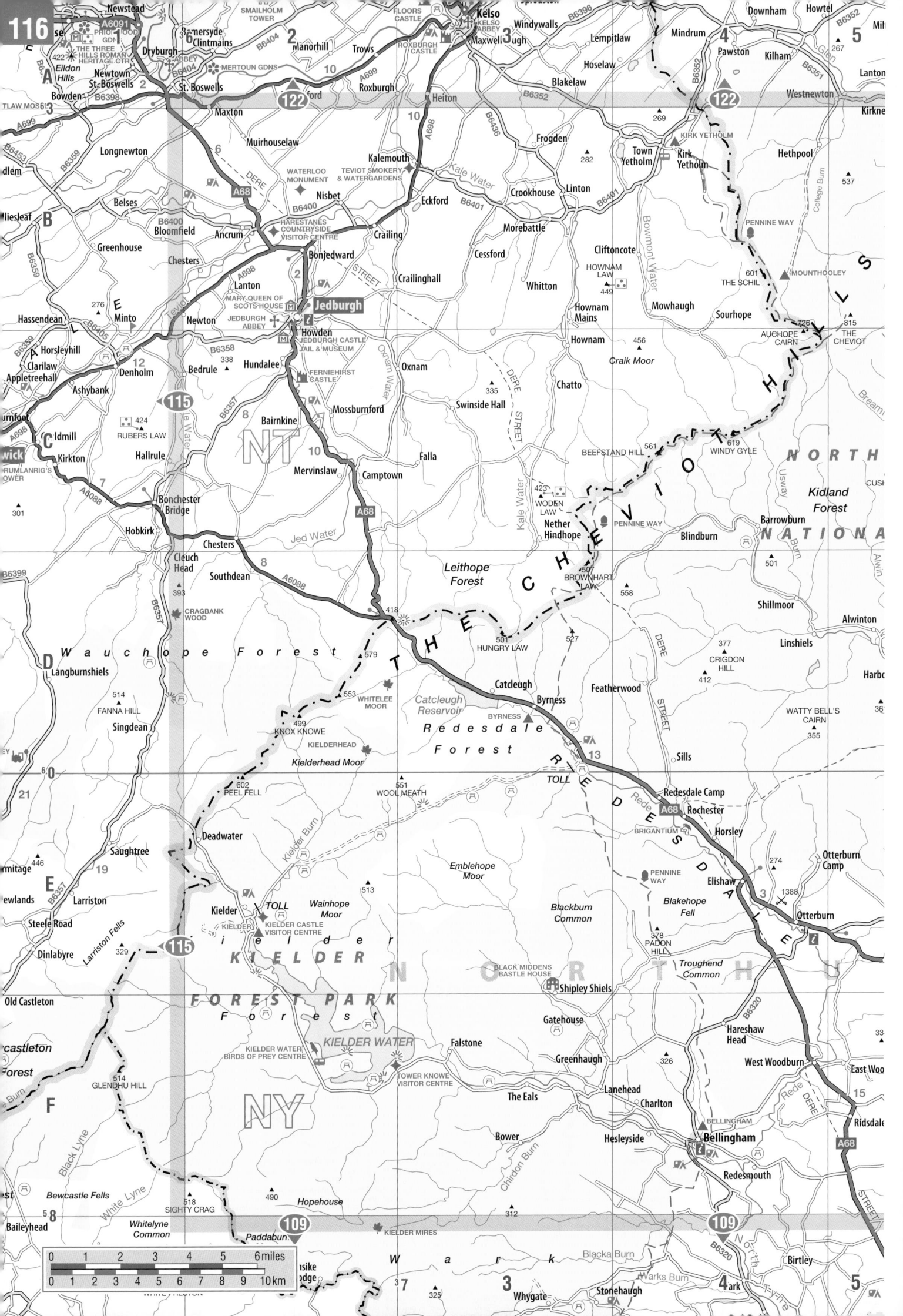

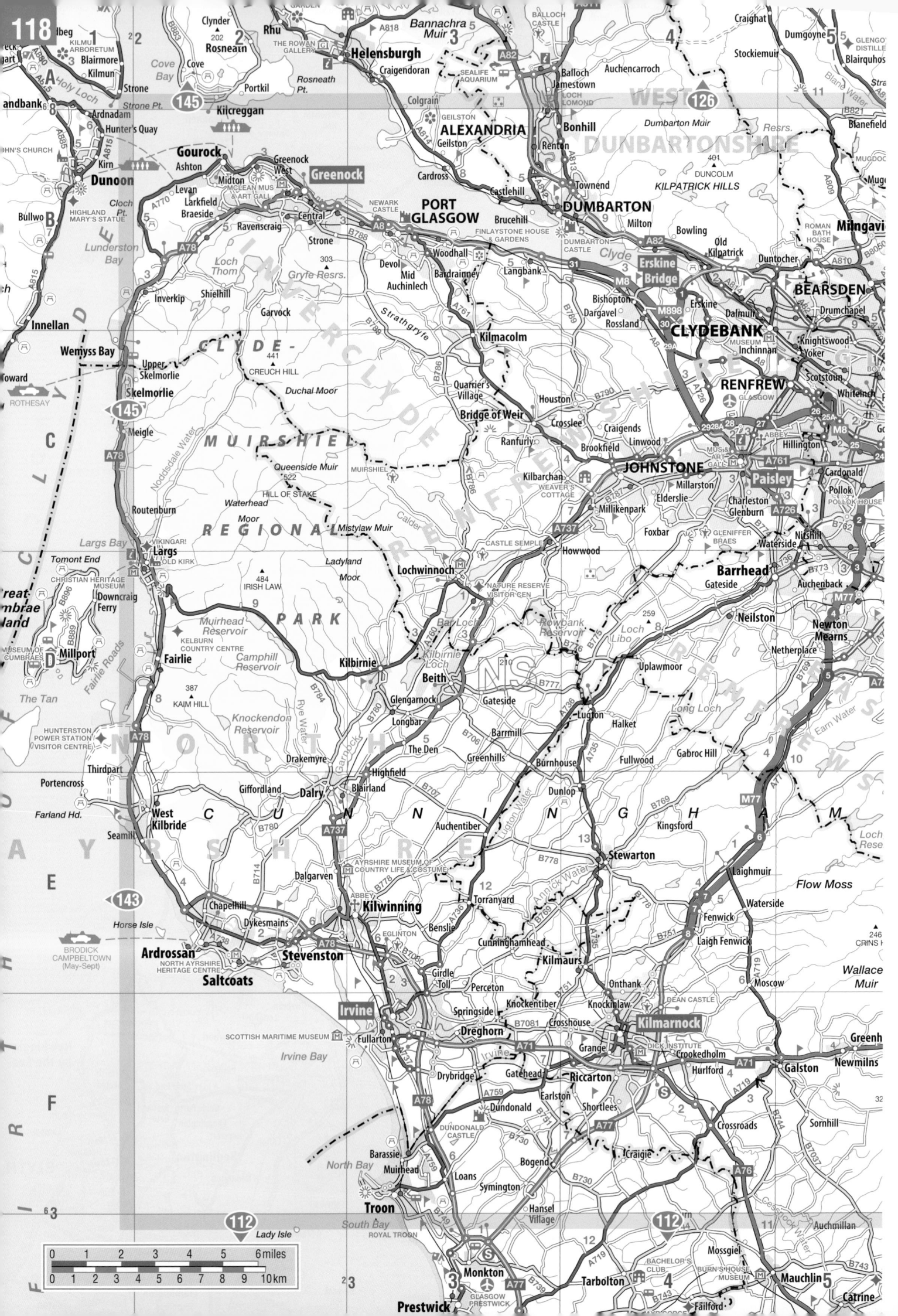

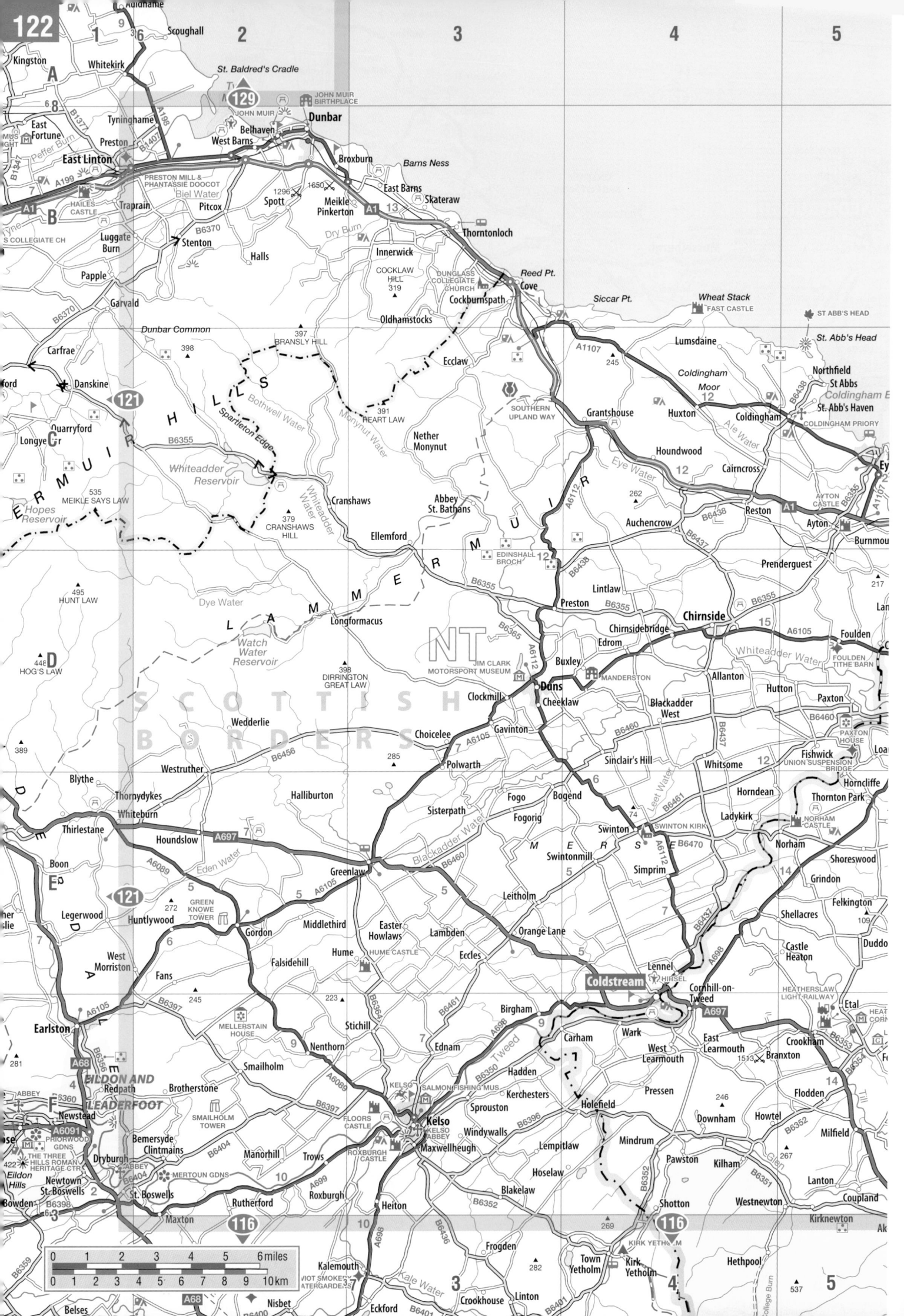

A

B

C

D

E

F

G

5   40   6   7   8   43   9

EYEMOUTH MUSEUM
emouth

Lamberton
Beach

Highfields

Berwick-Upon-Tweed
BERWICK-UPON-TWEED
BARRACKS & MAIN GUARD
BERWICK

East
Ord
Tweedmouth
Spittal

Prior
Park
Redshin Cove

Murton
Thornton
Scremerston

West Allerdean
Shoresdean
Cheswick

Ancroft
Goswick

Haggerston
Berrington
South Low
Beal
Causeway
Holy
Island
Sands
Fenham

Barmoor
Castle
West
Kyloe
Fenwick
Lowick
Kyloe
Hills
East
Kyloe
Buckton

Holburn
Detchant
Middleton

Kimmerston
Hetton
Steads
Budle
North Hazelrigg
Belford
Easington
Waren Mill

Fenton
Town
Nesbit
Spindlestone
Glororum
Burton

Doddington
South
Hazelrigg
Mousen
Bradford
Elford

Newtown
West
Horton
East Horton
Bellshill
Adderstone
Lucker
North
Sunderland

Weetwood Hall
Warenton
ADDERSTONE

117
Chatton
Greendikes
NEWHAM BOG
Warenford
Newham
Hall
Bead
117
Benthall

Wooler
Humbleton
Swinhoe

Earle
Haugh Head
CHILLINGHAM
Chillingham
WILD CATTLE OF
CHILLINGHAM
Newtown
Rosebrough
Newham
Chathill
Fleetham
Newstead

Middleton Hall
Preston
Ellingham
High Newton-
by-the-Sea

NU

NORTH COAST

NORTHUMBERLAND

LINDISFARNE
Emmanuel Hd.
**Holy Island
(Lindisfarne)**
LINDISFARNE CASTLE
Holy
Island
Castle Pt.
HERITAGE
CENTRE
LINDISFARNE
PRIORY

Guile
Pt.

Elwick
Ross
Budle
Bay

Farne
Islands
Staple Sound
BAMBURGH
CASTLE
FARNE ISLANDS
Inner Sound
Bamburgh

Seahouses

Beadnell
Bay

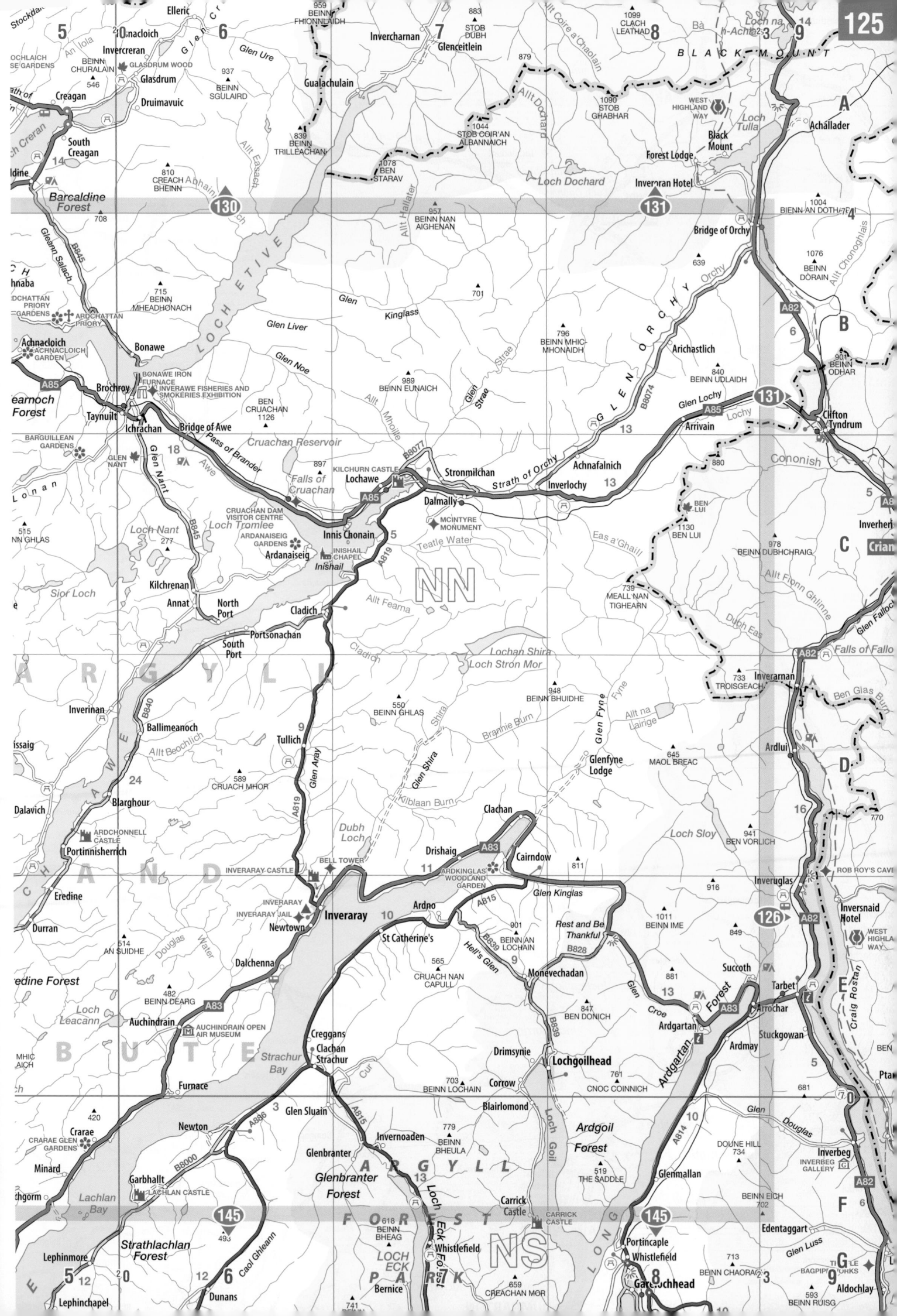

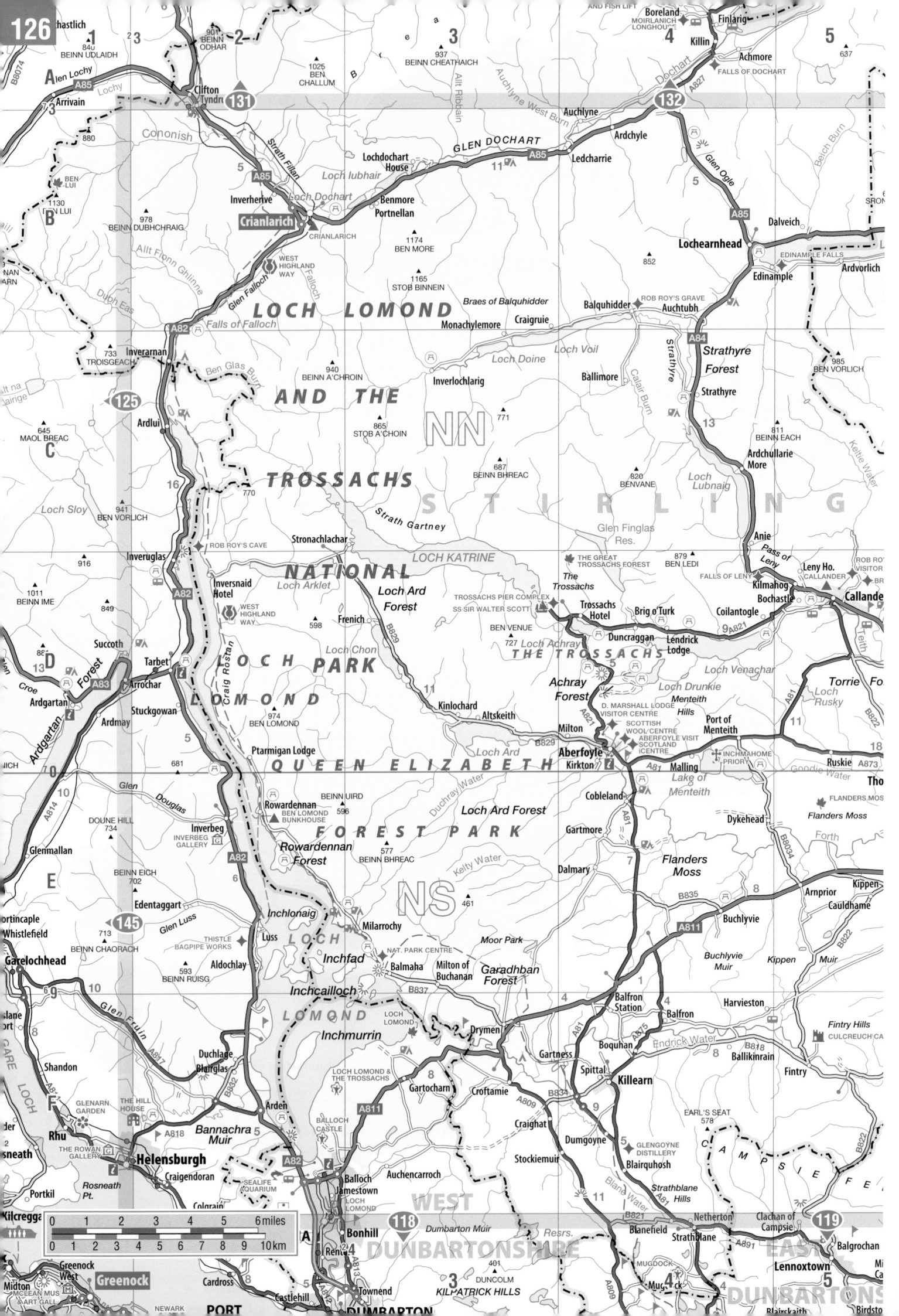

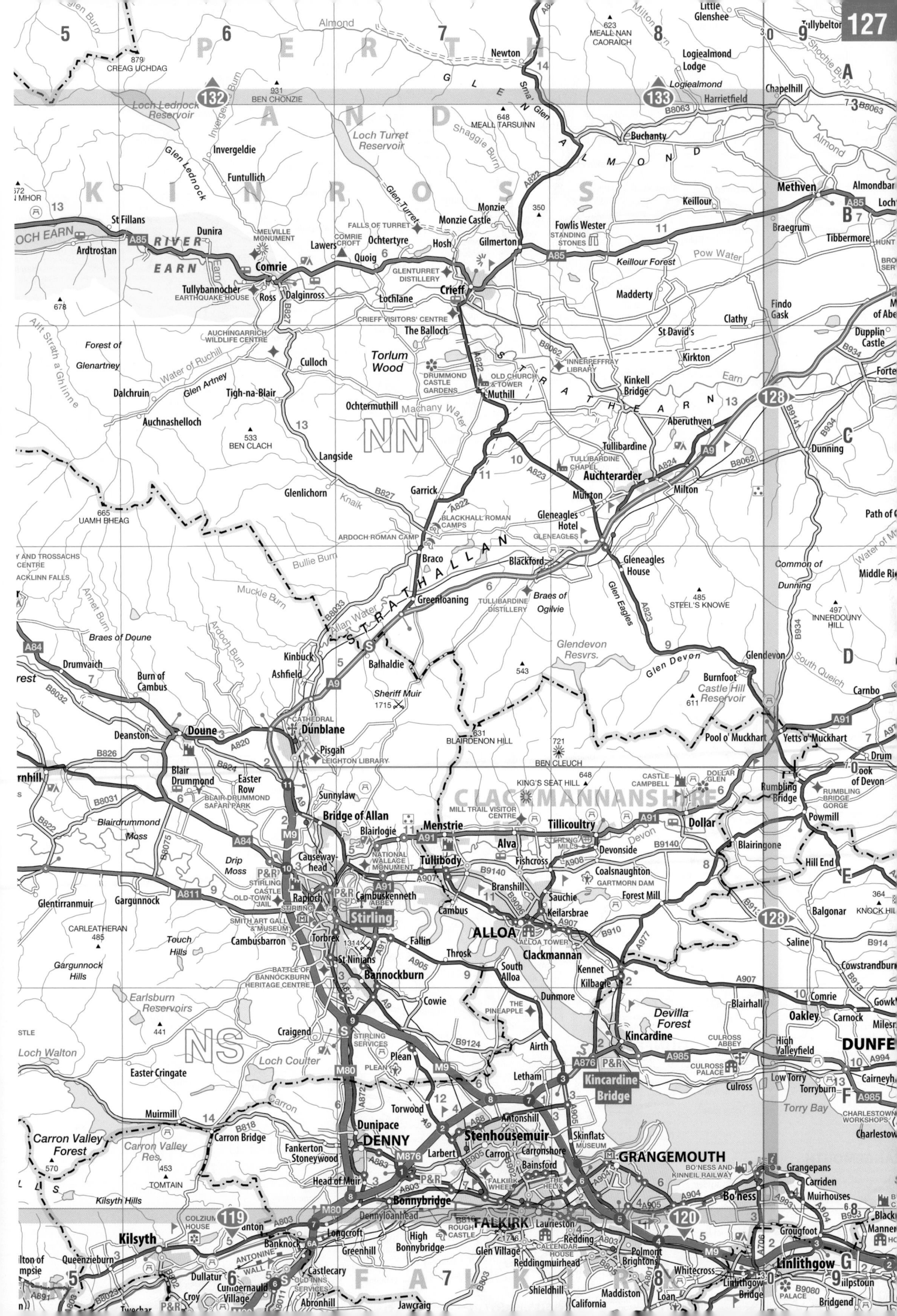

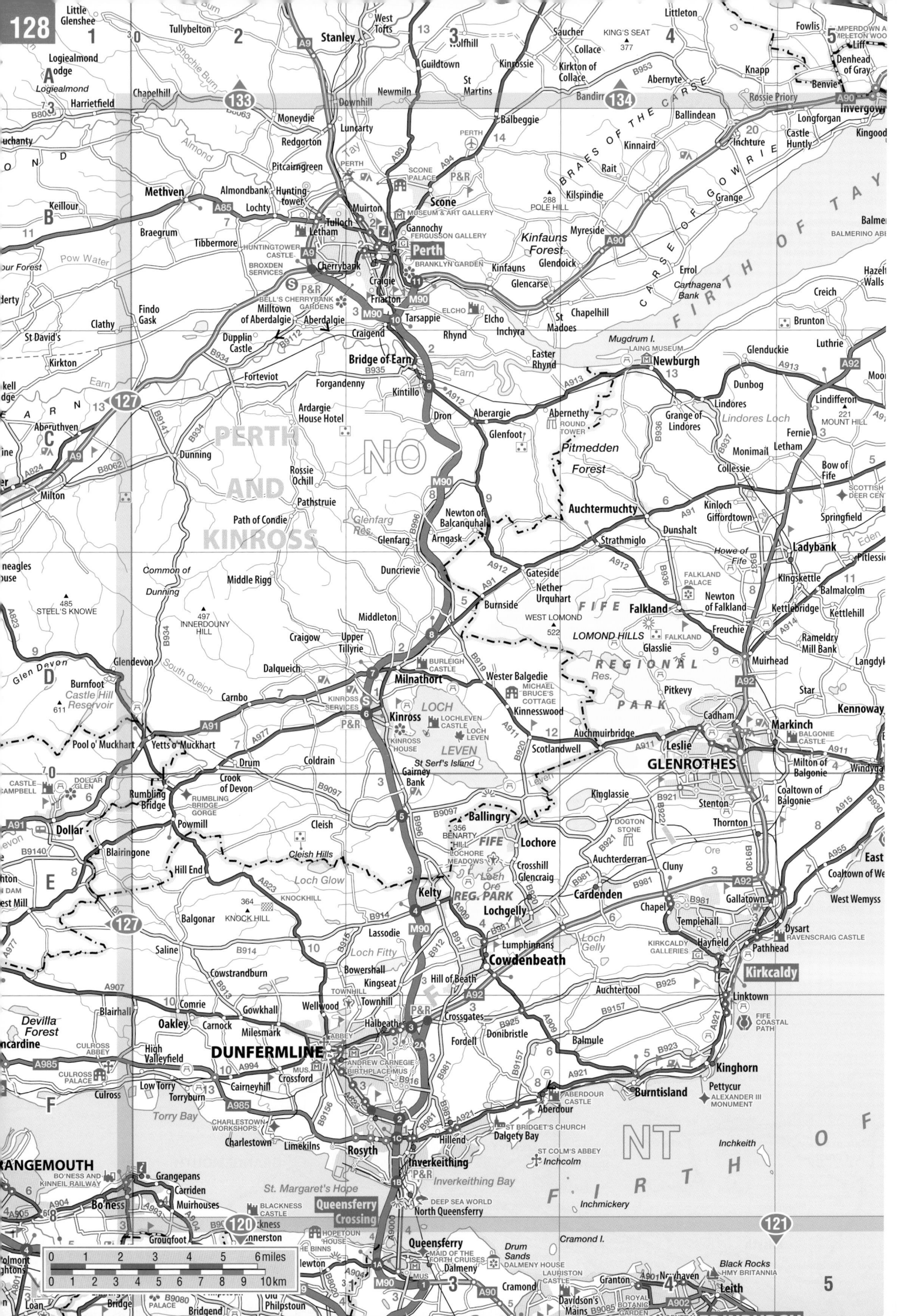

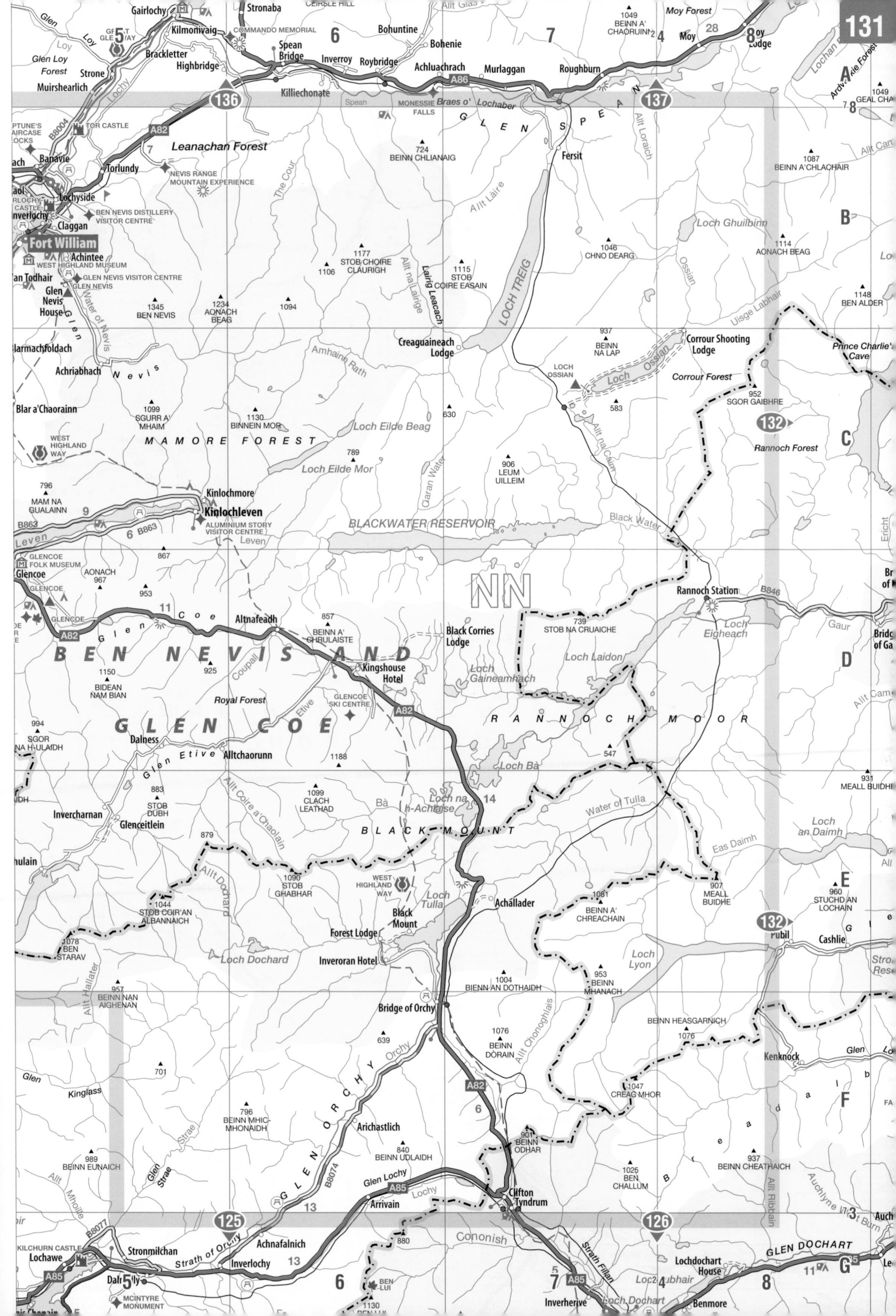

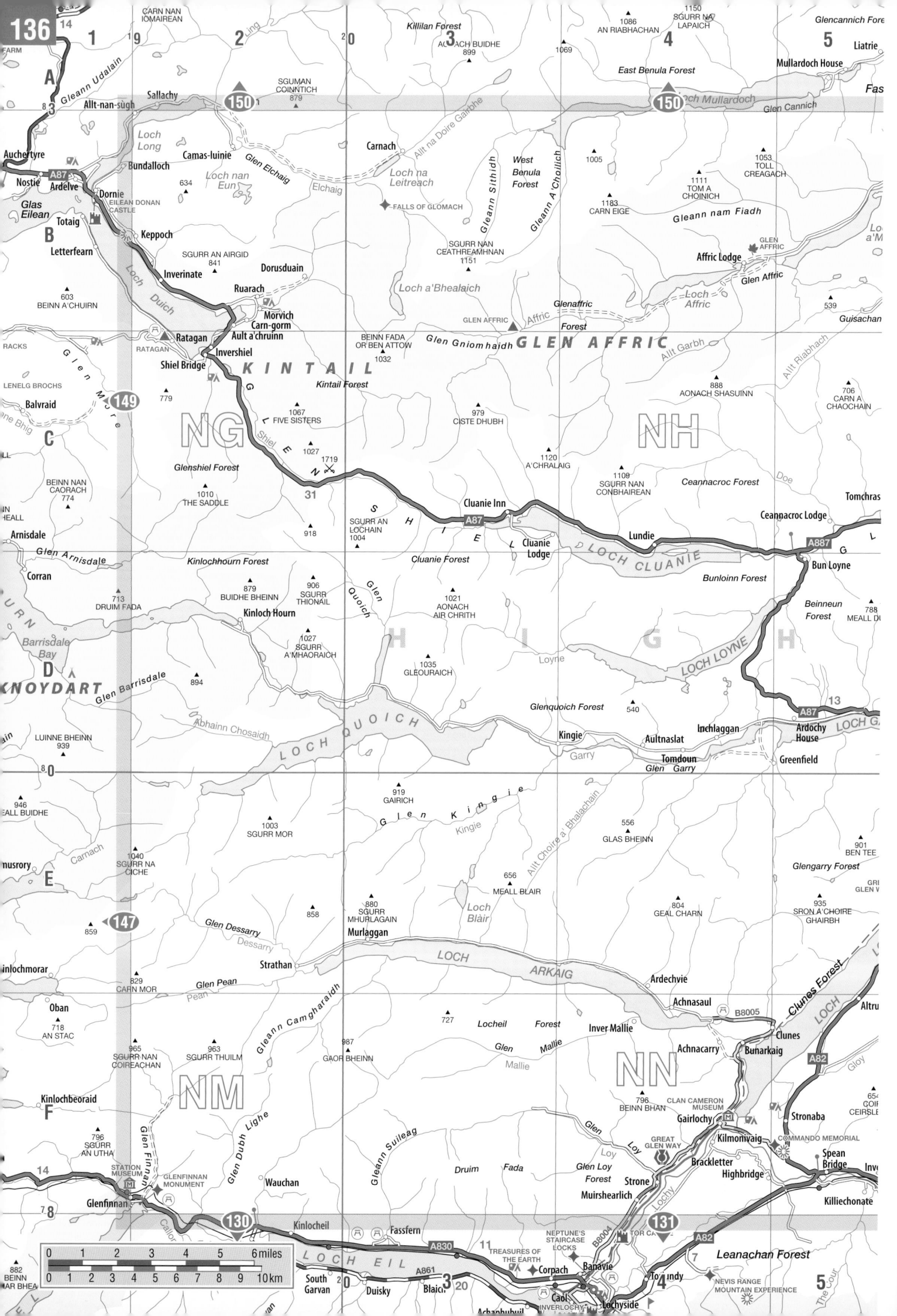

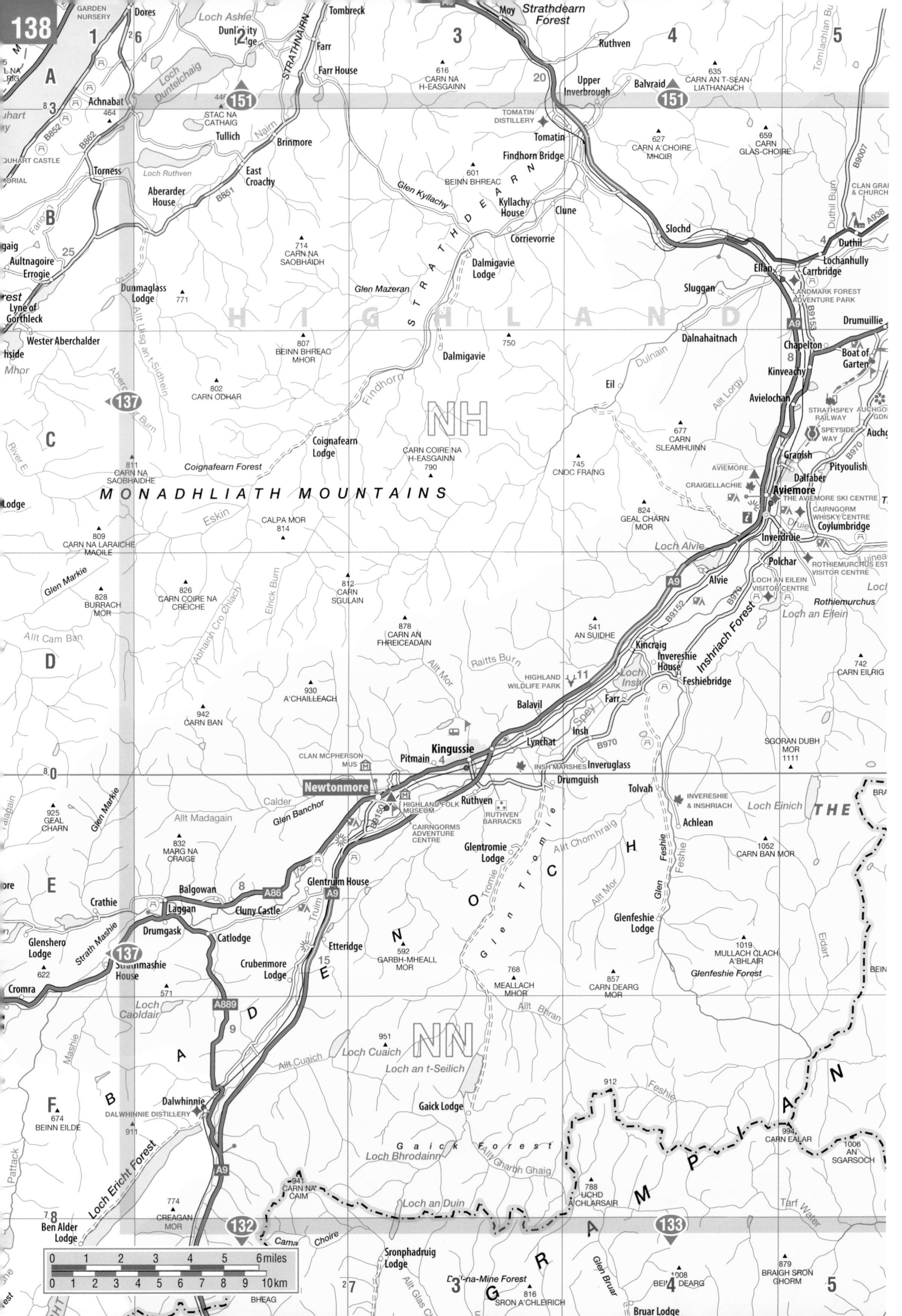

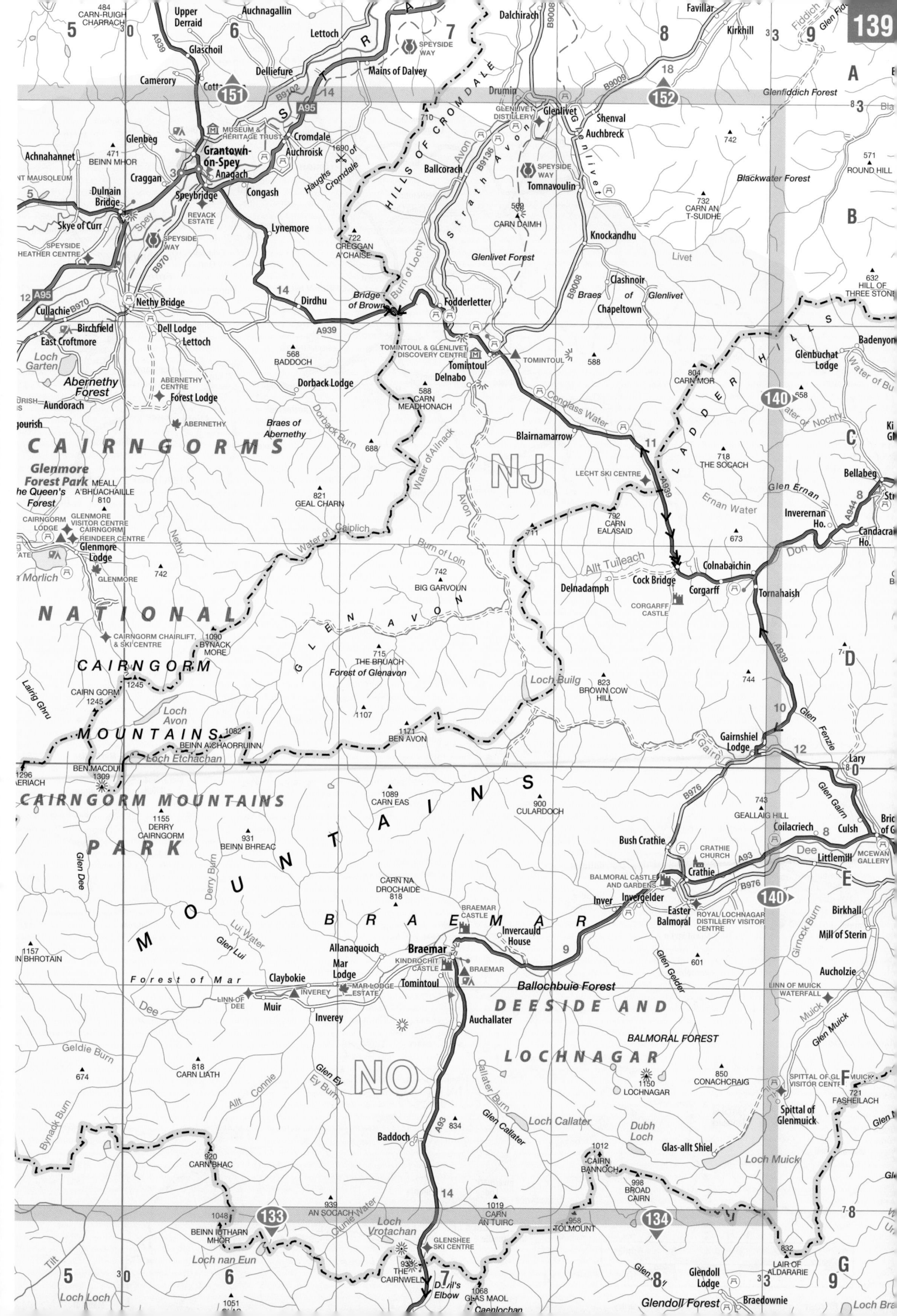

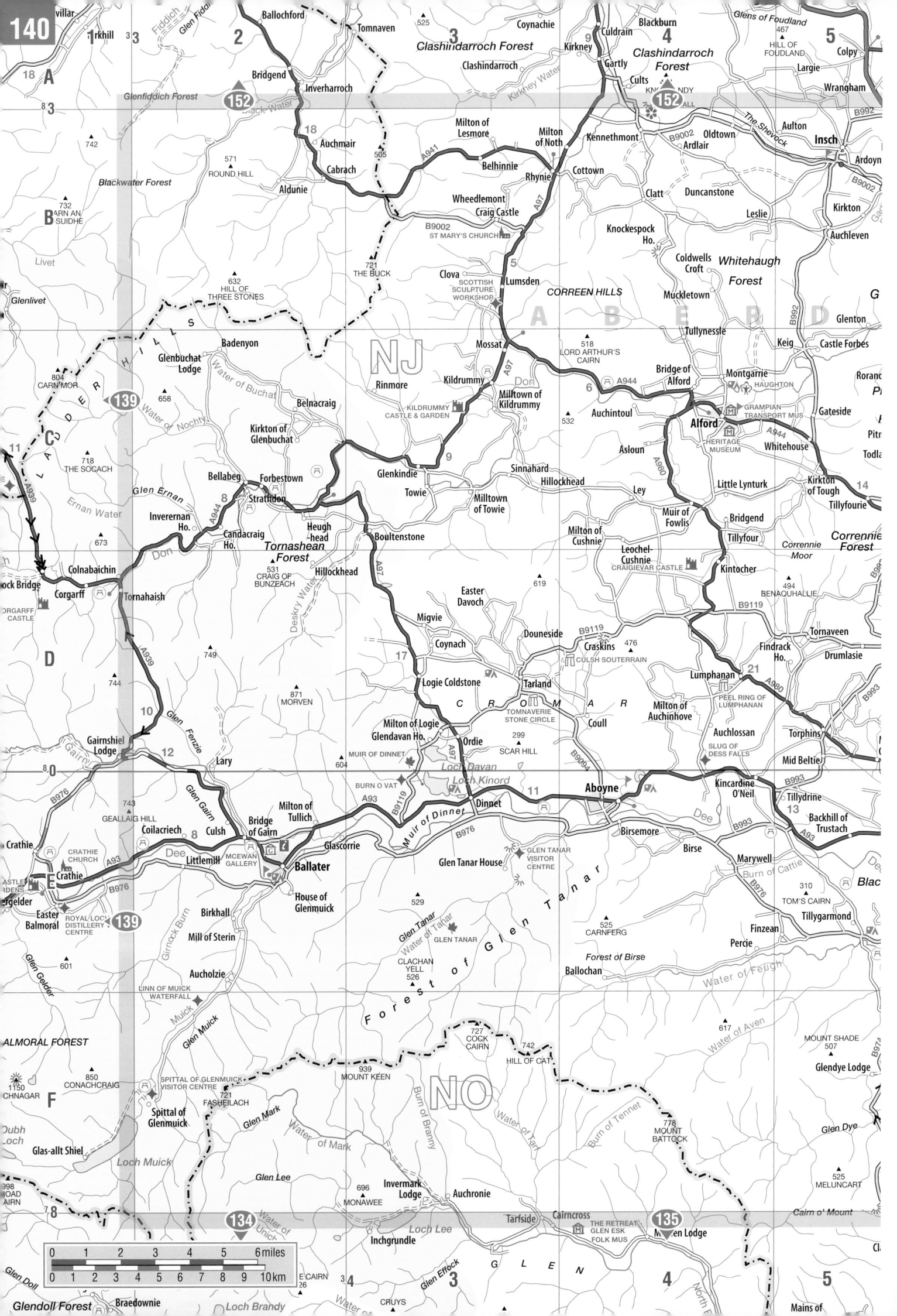

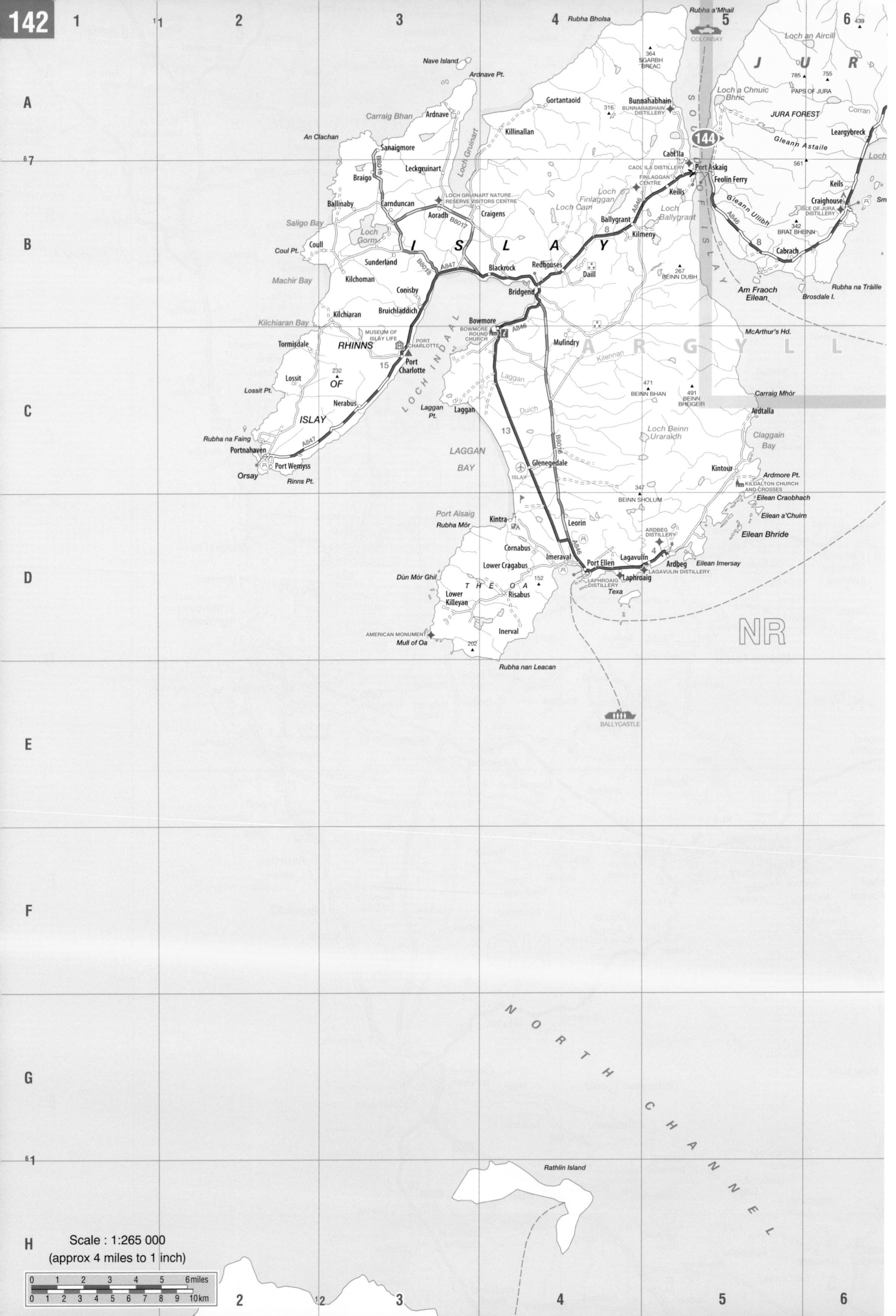

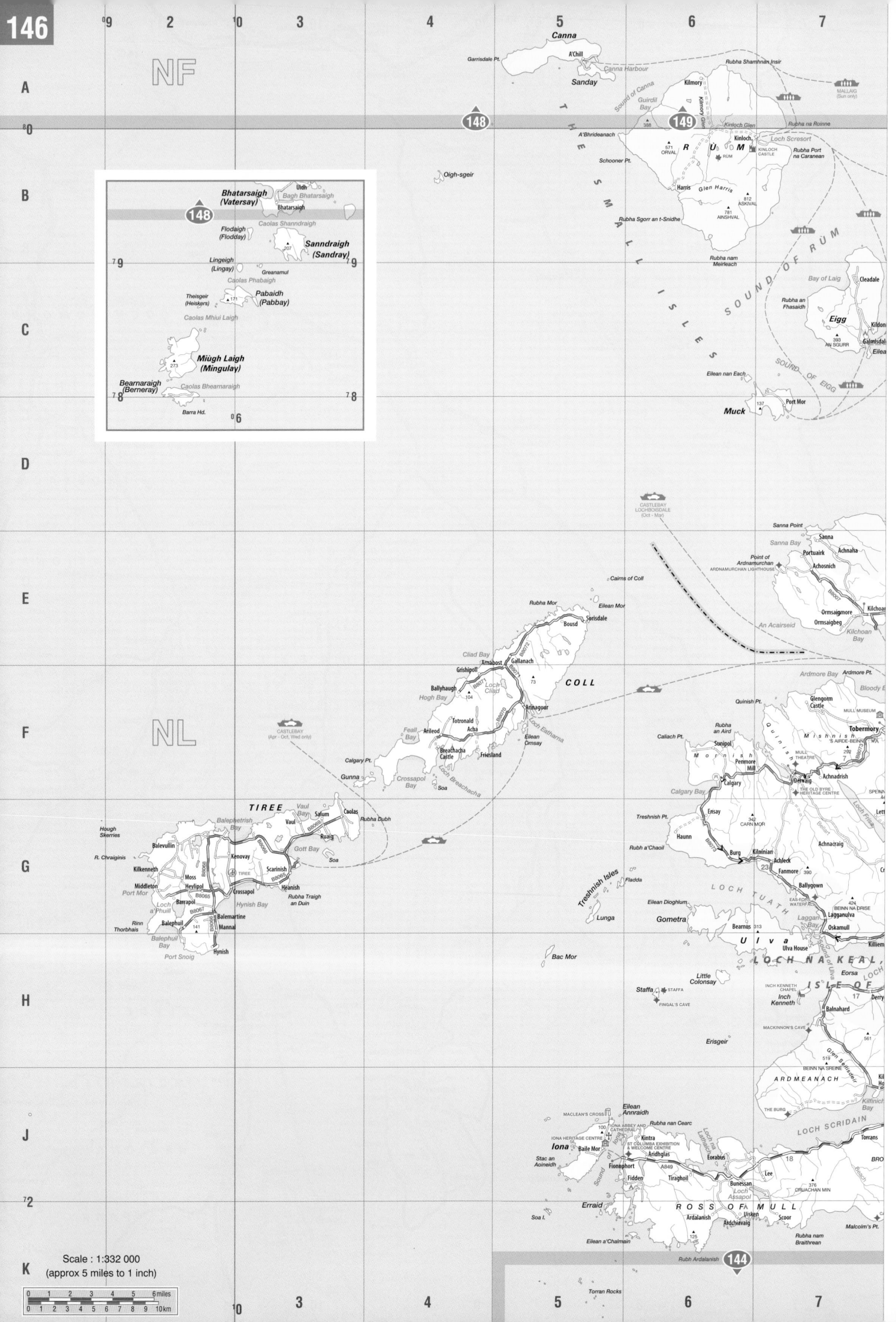

NF

Canna
Garrisdale Pt.
A'Chill
Canna Harbour
Sanday
Sound of Canna
Rubha Shamhnan Insir
Kilmory
Kilmore
Guirdil Bay
Kinloch Glen
MALLAIG
(Sun only)
Rubha na Roinne
THE SMALL ISLES
A'Bhrideanach
588
571 ORVAL
R Ù M
Kinloch
KINLOCH CASTLE
Loch Scresort
Schooner Pt.
Rubha Port na Caranean
Harris
Glen Harris
812 ASKIVAL
781 AINSHVAL
RÙM
Rubha Sgorr an t-Snidhe
Rubha nam Meirleach
SOUND OF RÙM
Bay of Laig
Cleadale
Rubha an Fhasaidh
Eigg
Kildoni
393 AN SGURR
Galmisdale
Eilean
Oigh-sgeir
Eilean nan Each
SOUND OF EIGG
Muck
137
Port Mor

Bhatarsaigh (Vatersay)
Ùidh
Bagh Bhatarsaigh
Bhatarsaigh
148
Flodaigh (Flodday)
Caolas Shanndraigh
Sanndraigh (Sandray)
207
Lingeigh (Lingay)
Greanamul
Caolas Phabaigh
Theisgeir (Heiskers)
171
Pabaidh (Pabbay)
Caolas Mhiui Laigh
Miùgh Laigh (Mingulay)
273
Bearnaraigh (Berneray)
Caolas Bhearnaraigh
Barra Hd.

NL

CASTLEBAY LOCHBOISDALE (Oct - Mar)

Sanna Point
Sanna Bay
Sanna
Point of Ardnamurchan
ARDNAMURCHAN LIGHTHOUSE
Portuairk
Achnaha
Achosnich
An Acairseid
Ormsaigmore
Ormsaigbeg
Kilchoan
Kilchoan Bay

CASTLEBAY (Apr - Oct, Wed only)

Cairns of Coll
Rubha Mor
Eilean Mor
Bousd
Sorisdale
Cliad Bay
Arnabost
Gallanach
Grishipoll
Ballyhaugh
Loch Cliad
104
73
COLL
Hogh Bay
Arileod
Totronald
Acha
Arinagour
Feall Bay
Breachacha Castle
Friesland
Eilean Ornsay
Calgary Pt.
Loch Breachacha
Gunna
Crossapol Bay
Soa
Loch Etharna

Ardmore Bay
Ardmore Pt.
Bloody B
Quinish Pt.
Glengorm Castle
MULL MUSEUM
Caliach Pt.
Rubha an Aird
Mishnish
S'AIRDE-BEINN
292
Tobermory
Mornish
Sunipol
Penmore Mill
Dervaig
Achnadrish
Calgary Bay
Calgary
THE OLD BYRE HERITAGE CENTRE
SPEINN

TIREE
Vaul Bay
Caolas
Salum
Rubha Dubh
Vaul
Ruaig
Balephetrish Bay
Hough Skerries
Balevullin
Gott Bay
Soa
R. Chraiginis
Kenovay
Scarinish
TIREE
Kilkenneth
Moss
Heylipol
Crossapol
Heanish
Middleton
Port Mor
Barrapol
Rubha Traigh an Duin
Loch a'Phuill
Hynish Bay
Balephuil
Balemartine
141
Rinn Thorbhais
Mannal
Balephuil Bay
Hynish
Port Snoig

Treshnish Isles
Fladda
Lunga
Gometra
Bac Mor

Treshnish Pt.
Ensay
342 CARN MOR
Haunn
Burg
Kilninian
23
Achleck
Fanmore
390
Ballygown
Rubh a'Chaoil
Eilean Dioghlum
Bearnus
313
LOCH TUATH
EAS-FORS WATERFALL
BEINN NA DRISE
424
Laggan Bay
Lagganulva
Ulva
Ulva House
Killiem
Eorsa
Little Colonsay
Staffa
STAFFA
FINGAL'S CAVE
INCH KENNETH CHAPEL
Inch Kenneth
Balnahard
Erisgeir
MACKINNON'S CAVE
561
519
BEINN NA SREINE
ARDMEANACH
THE BURG
Kilfinich Ho
LOCH SCRIDAIN

LOCH NA KEAL
ISLE OF

MACLEAN'S CROSS
Eilean Annraidh
Rubha nan Cearc
IONA ABBEY AND CATHEDRAL
100
IONA HERITAGE CENTRE
ST COLUMBA EXHIBITION & WELCOME CENTRE
Kintra
Iona
Baile Mor
Aridhglas
Eorabus
Torrans
Stac an Aoineidh
Sound of Iona
Fionnphort
A849
18
BRO
Fidden
Tiraghoil
Bunessan
Lee
Erraid
Loch Assapol
376 CRUACHAN MIN
Soa I.
ROSS OF MULL
Ardalanish
Uisken
Scoor
Eilean a'Chalmain
125
Rubha nam Braithrean
Malcolm's Pt.
Rubh Ardalanish
Torran Rocks

Scale : 1:332 000
(approx 5 miles to 1 inch)

0 1 2 3 4 5 6miles
0 1 2 3 4 5 6 7 8 9 10km

148

149

144

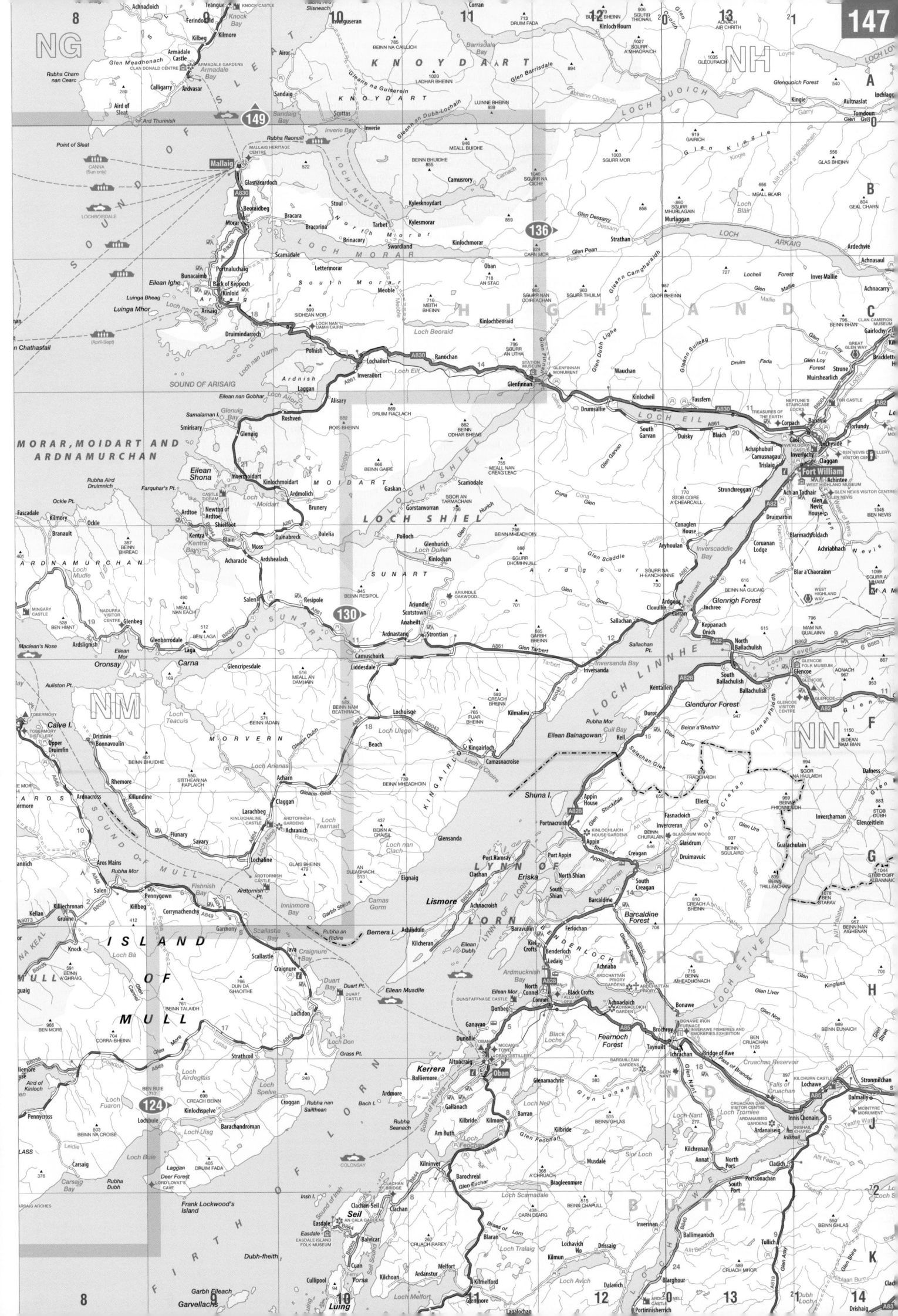

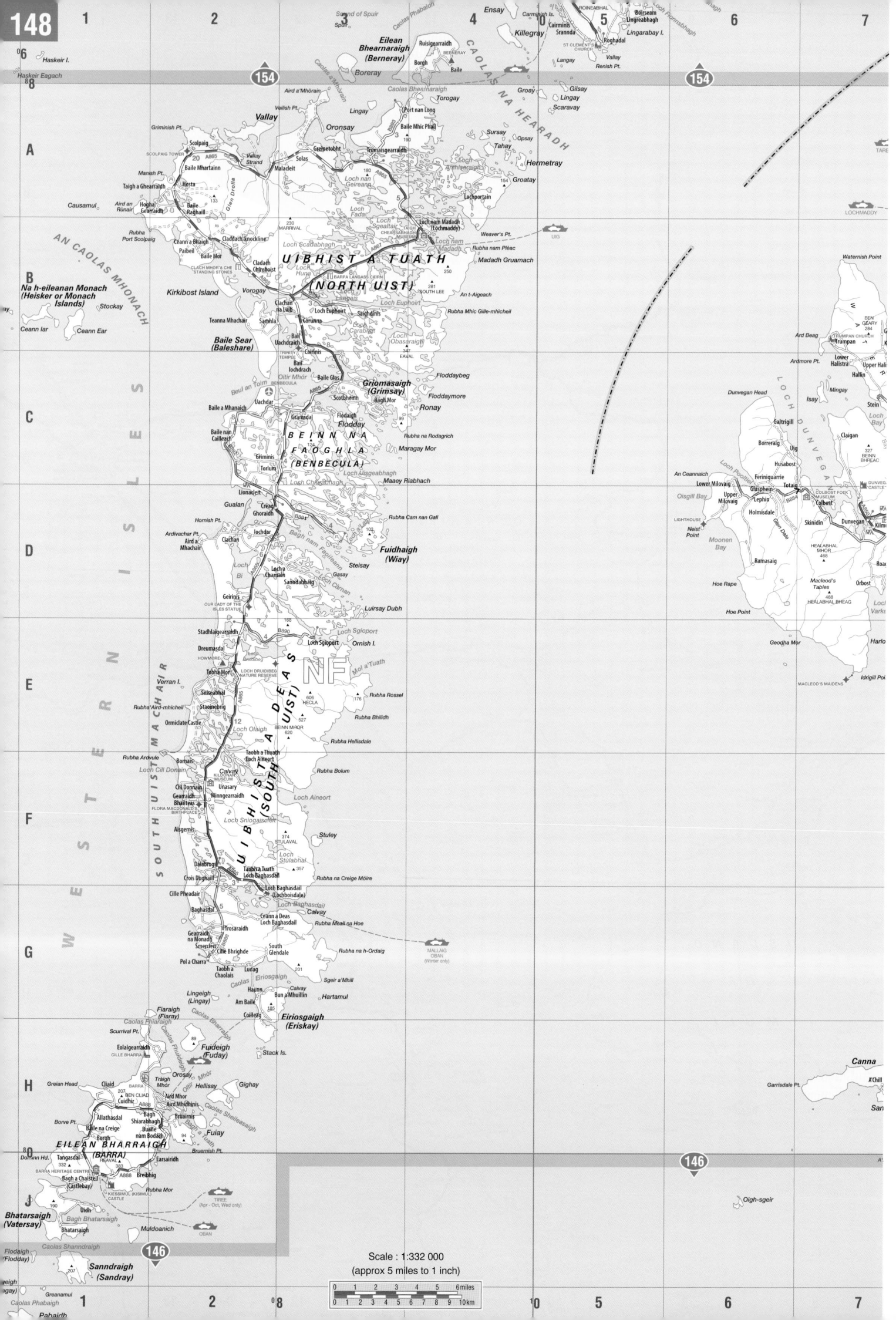

Scale : 1:332 000
(approx 5 miles to 1 inch)

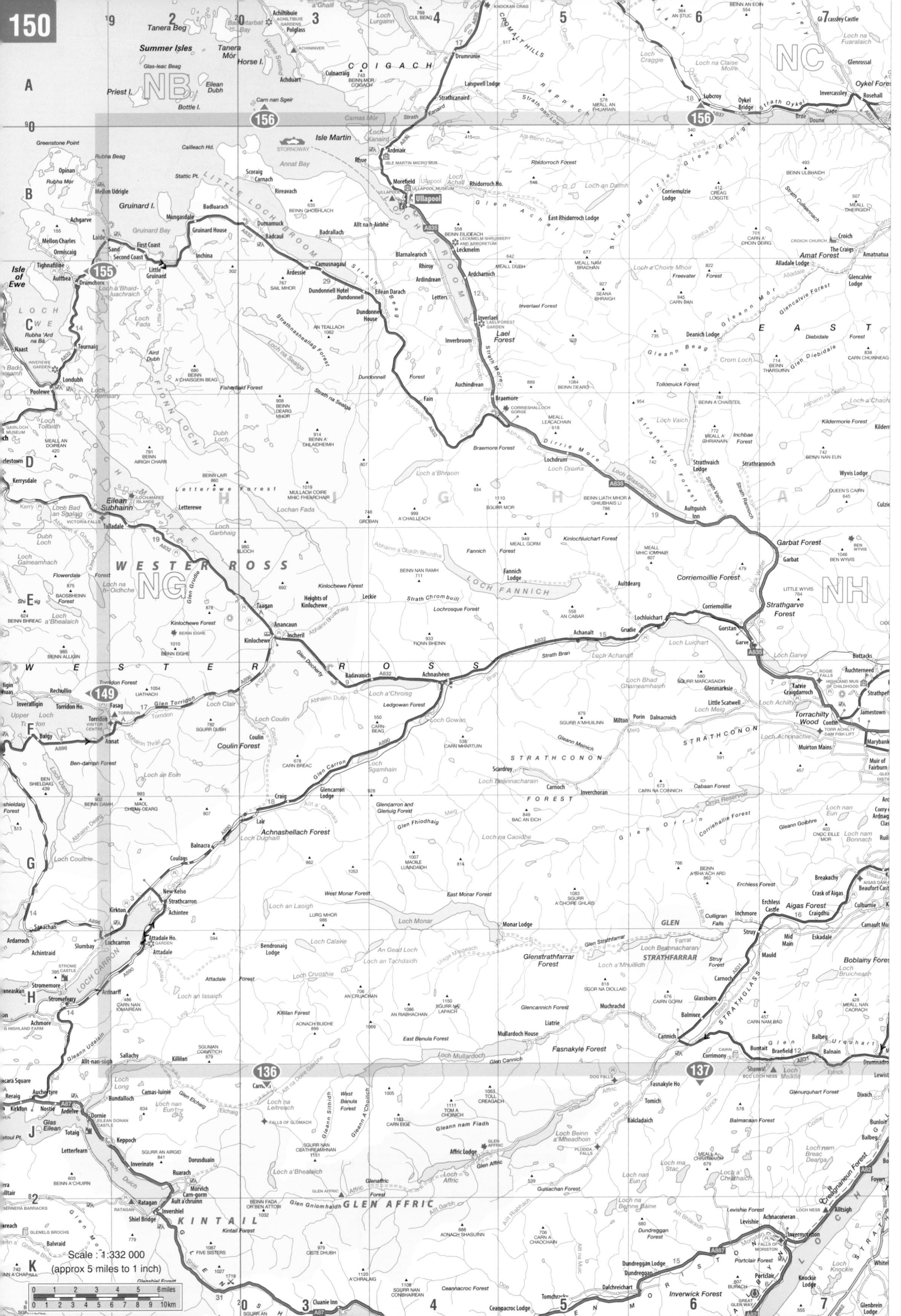

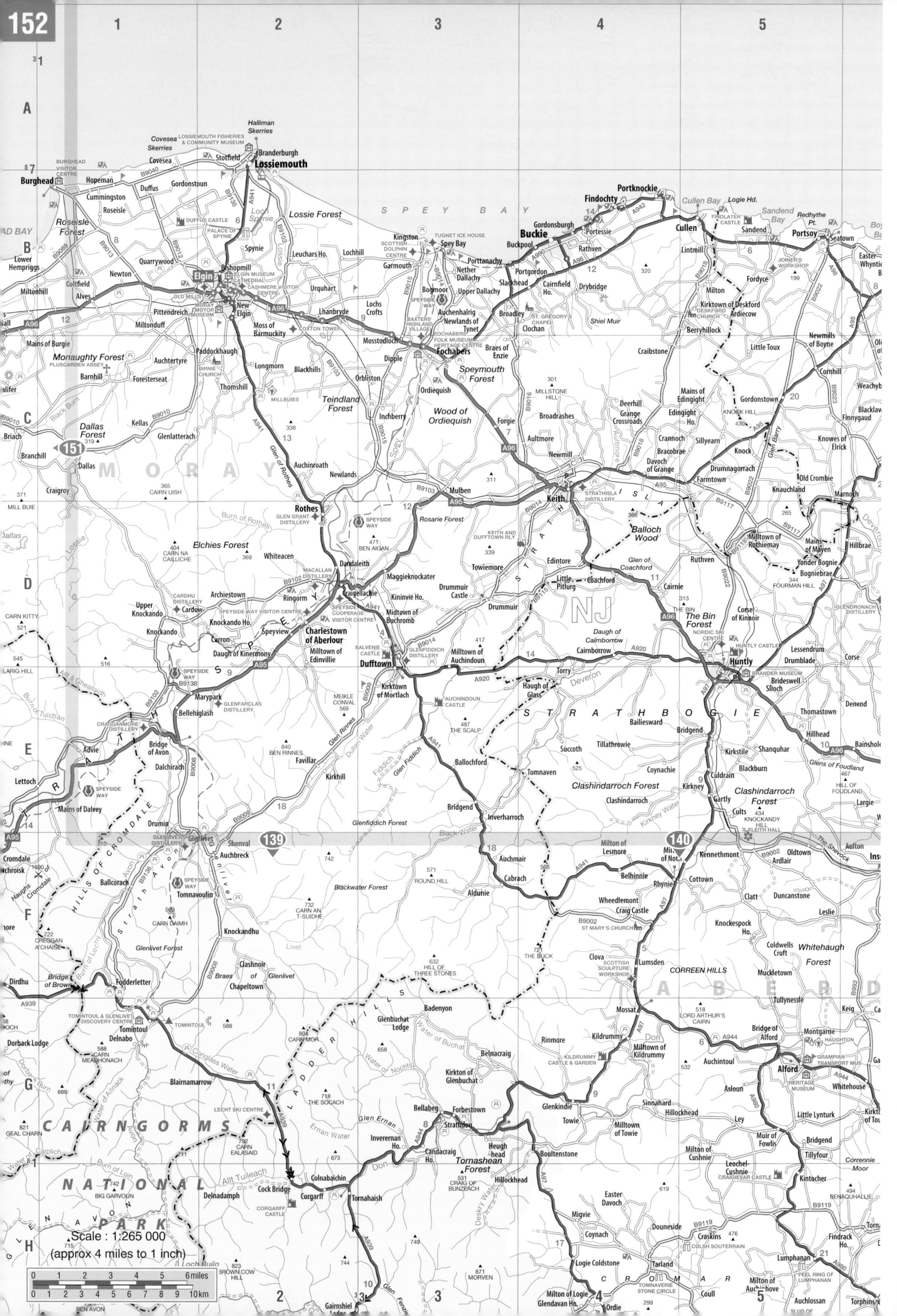

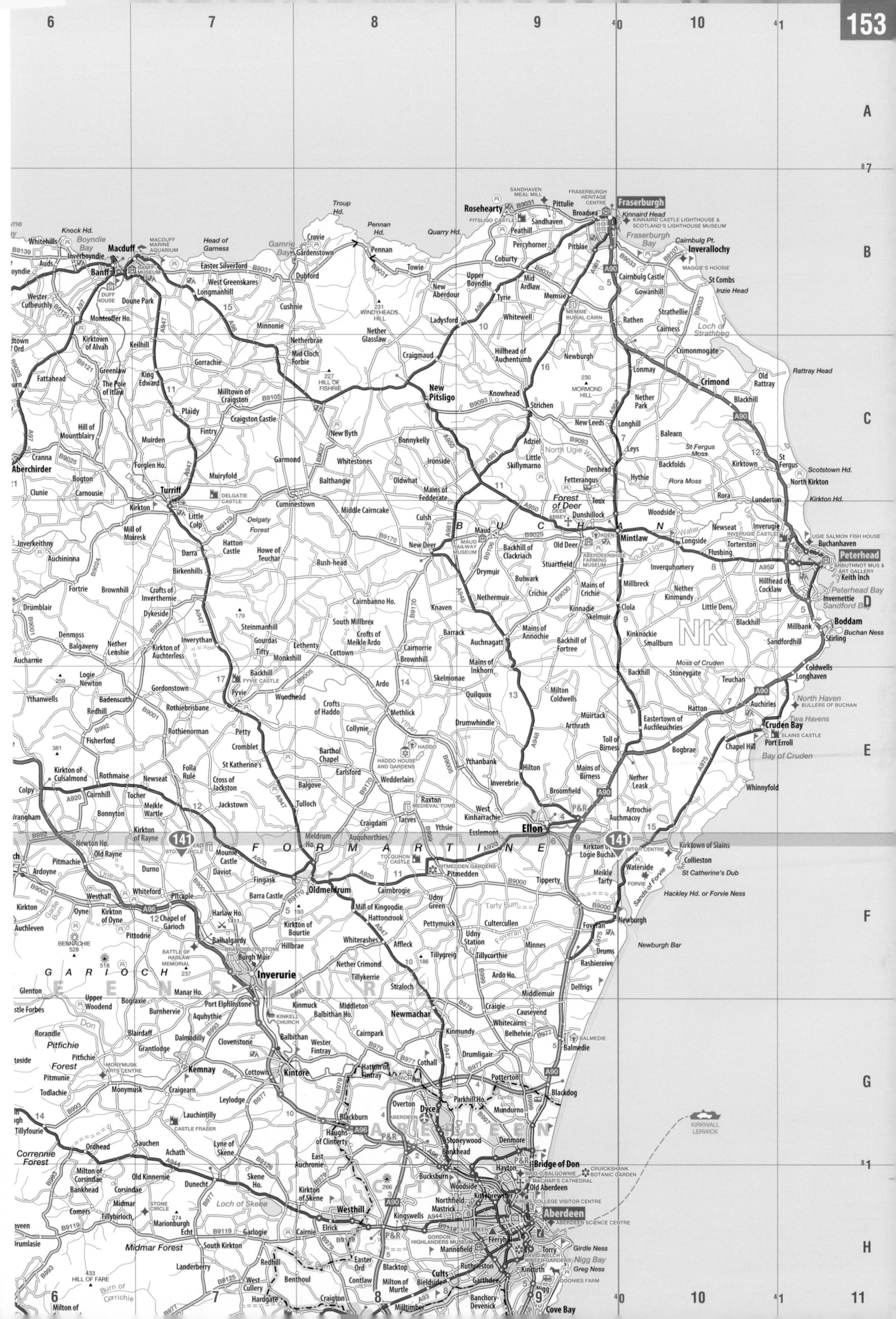

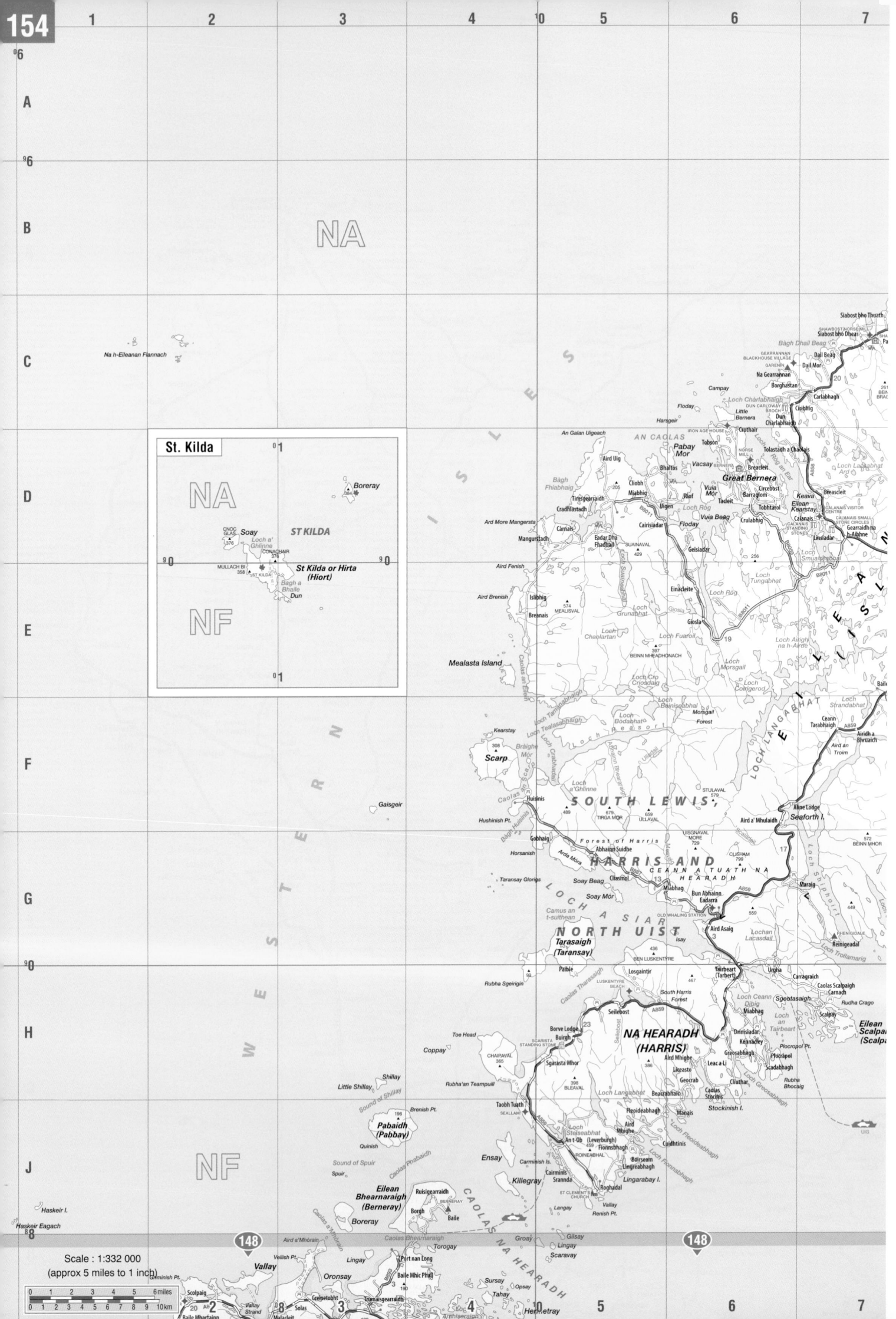

St. Kilda

NA

NF

St Kilda

Soay
CNOC GLAS
376
Loch a' Ghlinne
CONACHAIR
376
MULLACH BI
358
ST KILDA

Boreray
384

ST KILDA

St Kilda or Hirta (Hiort)

Bàgh a' Bhaile
Dun

Na h-Eileanan Flannach

NA

WESTERN ISLES

SIABOST BHO THUATH
SHAWBOST NORSE MILL
Siabost bho Dheas
Bàgh Dhail Beag
GEARRANNAN BLACKHOUSE VILLAGE
GARENIN
Na Gearrannan
Borghastan
Carlabhagh
Dall Beag
Dall Mor
20
BEIN BRAC

Campay
Loch Chàrlabhaigh
DUN CARLOWAY BROCH
Little Bernera
Dun Charlabhaigh
Clèitir
Carlabhagh
Loch Lacasdail Ard

An Galan Uigeach
IRON AGE HOUSE
Floday
Harsgeir
Tobson
Pabay Mor
Vacsay
NORSE MILL
Breascleit
Great Bernera
Loch Ròg an Ear
Tolastadh a Chaolais

Aird Uig
Bhaltos
Cliobh
Miabhig
Riof
Vuia Mor
Bosta
Circebost
Barraglom
Tobhtarol
Keava
Eilean Kearstay
CALANAIS VISITOR CENTRE
CALANAIS STANDING STONES
Dèascleit

Ard More Mangersta
Cradhlastadh
Timsgearraidh
Bàgh Fhabhaig
205
Uigen
Cairisiadar
Floday
Vuia Beag
Crulabhig
CALANAIS SMALL STONE CIRCLES
Gearraidh na h-Aibhne
Linsiadar

Mangurstadh
Càrnais
Eadar Dha Fhadhail
SUAINAVAL
429
Geisiadar
Loch Ròg
256
Loch Smuaisabhal

Aird Fenish
Einacleite
Loch Tungabhat
B8011

Aird Brenish
Islibhig
574 MEALISVAL
Giosla
Loch Grunabhat
Loch Fuaroil
19
Loch Airigh na h-Airde

Breanais
Loch Chaolartan
397
Loch Bhaineabhal
Loch Cro Criosdaig
1079

Mealasta Island
Loch Bodabhato
Forest
Loch Strandabhat
Ceann Tarabhaigh A859
Airidh a' Bhruaich

Loch Tamnabhaigh
Loch Morsgail
Aird an Troim

Kearstay
Loch Teallasabhaigh
Loch Rèasort
Morsgail Forest
572 BEINN MHOR

Bràighe Mor
308
Scarp
Loch a'Ghlinne
WESTERN

Gaisgeir

Caolas an Scarp
Huisinis
SOUTH LEWIS,
STULAVAL 579
Aline Lodge
Seaforth I.

Hushinish Pt.
Bàgh Huisinis
489
679 TIRGA MOR
659 ULLAVAL
17

Gobhaig
Forest of Harris
USGNAVAL MORE 729
Loch Shiphort

Horsanish
Abhainn Suidhe
HARRIS AND
CUSHAM 799
449
RHENIGIDALE

Taransay Glorigs
Arda Mora
Bee
CEANN A TUATH NA HEARADH
Maraig
Reinigeadal

Soay Beag
Clasmol
13
Miabhag
A859
Loch Trollamaig

Soay Mor
Bun Abhainn Eadarra
559

Camus an t-suithean
OLD WHALING STATION
Aird Asaig
Isay
Lochan Lacasdail

Tarasaigh (Taransay)
NORTH UIST
436
BEN LUSKENTYRE

Paibie
Losgaintir
467
Tairbeart (Tarbert)
Urgha
Carragraich
Caolas Scalpaigh
Carnach

Rubha Sgeirigin
LUSKENTYRE BEACH
South Harris Forest
Sgeotasaigh
Rudha Crago

Borve Lodge
23
Seilebost
A859
Loch Ceann Dibig
Miabhag
Loch an Tairbeart
Scalpay
Eilean Scalpaigh (Scalpay)

Toe Head
SCARISTA STANDING STONE
NA HEARADH (HARRIS)
Drinisiadar
Plocropol Pt.

Coppay
Buirgh
Kennacley
Greosabhagh
Plocrapol
Scadabhagh

CHAIPAVAL 365
Sgarasta Mhor
Aird Mhighe
Liceasto
Leac a Li
Geocrab
Cliuthar
Caolas Stocinis
Rubha Bhocaig

Shillay
398 BLEAVAL
Geocrab
Stockinish I.

Little Shillay
Rubha 'an Teampuill
Taobh Tuath
SEALLAM
Loch Langabhat
Beacrabhaic
Manais
UIG

Brenish Pt.
196
An t-Ob (Leverburgh)
Fleoideabhagh
Loch Fleodseabhagh

Pabaidh (Pabbay)
Quinish
Loch Steiseabhat
Aird Mhighe
Fionnsbhagh
Lingreabhagh
Cuidhtinis

Sound of Spuir
Spuir
Ensay
Carminish Is.
Roghadal
Renish Pt.

Eilean Bhearnaraigh (Berneray)
Ruisigearraidh
BERNERAY
Cairminis
Srannda
Killegray
ST CLEMENT'S CHURCH
Vallay

Haskeir I.
Borgh
Baile
Langay
Renish Pt.

Haskeir Eagach
Boreray
Sound of Shillay
Caolas Phabaidh
Caolas na Hearadh
Groay
Gilsay
Lingay

NF
Sound of Spuir
CAOLAS NA HEARADH
Scaravay

Scale : 1:332 000
(approx 5 miles to 1 inch)

0   1   2   3   4   5   6 miles
0 1 2 3 4 5 6 7 8 9 10km

Aird a'Mhorain
Caolas a'Mhorain
Vallay
Gilpinish Pt.
Veilish Pt.
Lingay
Port nan Long
Baile Mhic Phail
Scolpaig
20 A865 2
Valley Strand
Sollas
8
Grenetobht
Trumaisgearraidh
Sursay
Opsay
Tahay
4
Hermetray
5

Baile Mhartainn
Malacleit
Oronsay
3
190

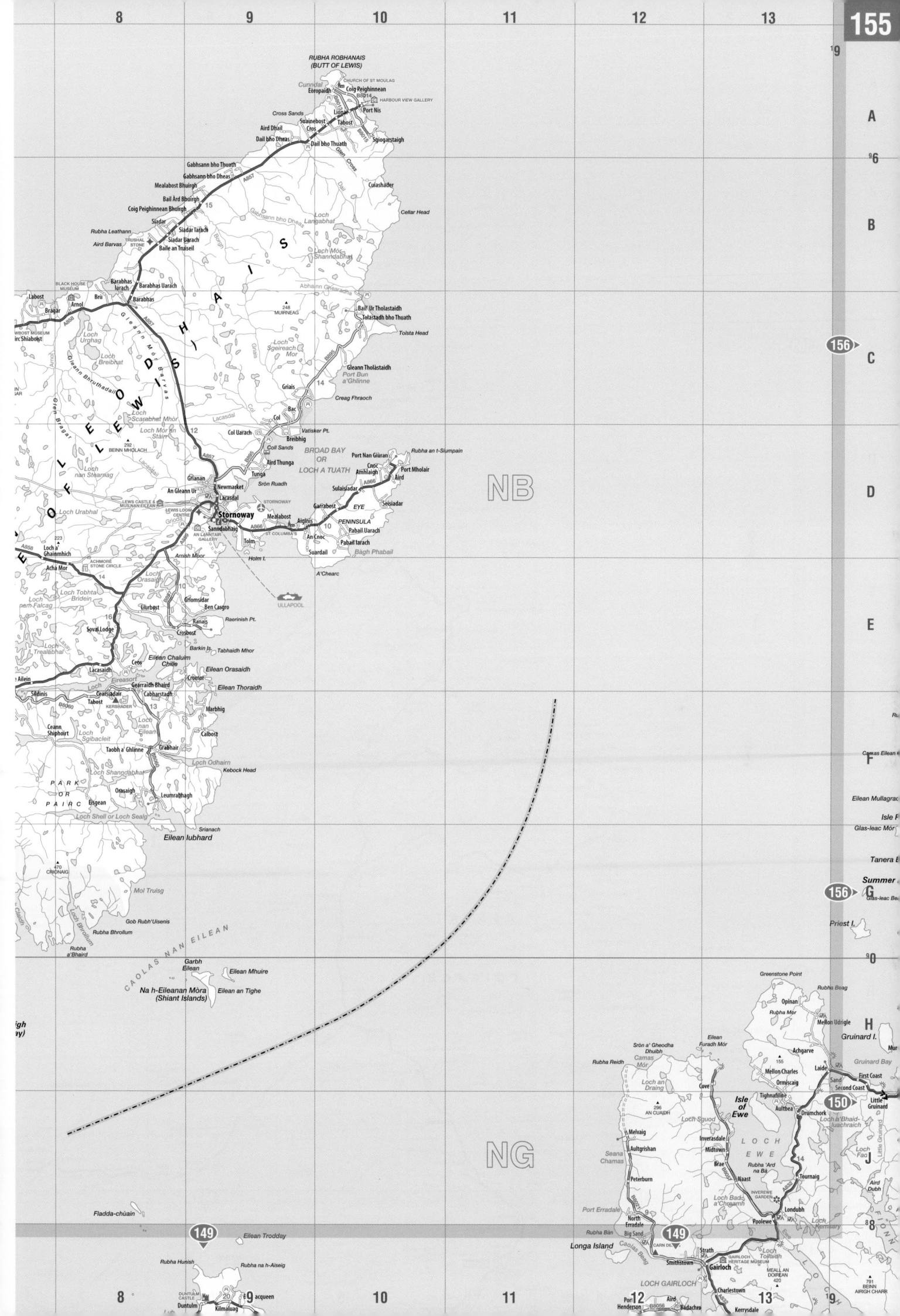

8 9 10 11 12 13

A

B

C

D

E

F

G

H

J

NB

NG

RUBHA ROBHANAIS
(BUTT OF LEWIS)
CHURCH OF ST MOULAG
Cunndal
Eòropaidh
Coig Peighinnean
B8914
HARBOUR VIEW GALLERY
Lional
Port Nis
Cross Sands
Suainebost
Port Nis
Aird Dhail
Cros
Tabost
Dail bho Dheas
Sgiogarstaigh
Dail bho Thuath

Gabhsann bho Thuath
Gabhsann bho Dheas
Mealabost Bhuirgh
Bail Àrd Bhuirgh
Coig Peighinnean Bhuirgh
Siadar
15
Rubha Leathann
Siadar Iarach
Aird Barvas
Siadar Uarach
TRUSHAL STONE
Baile an Truiseil

I S L E   O F   L E W I S

Cuishader
Cellar Head
Loch Langabhat

Loch Mòr Shanndabhat
Abhainn Ghearadha

BLACK HOUSE MUSEUM
Barabhas Iarach
Barabhas Uarach
Labost
Brù
Bragar
Arnol
A858
Barabhas
248 MUIRNEAG
Bail' Ur Tholastaidh
Tolastadh bho Thuath
Tolsta Head

WBOST MUSEUM
irc Shiabost
Loch Urghag
Loch Breibhat
Loch Sgeireach Mòr
Gleann Tholàstaidh
Port Bun a'Ghlinne
156

Gleann Mòr Barvas
Gleann Bhruthadail
Griais
Loch Scarabhat Mhòr
14
Creag Fhraoch
292 BEINN MHOLACH
Loch Mòr an Stàirr
Bac
A857
Col
Col Uarach
Vatisker Pt.
Glen Bragar
Grianan
An Gleann Ur
Newmarket
Coll Sands
Breibhig
Loch nan Stearnag
Aird Thunga
BROAD BAY OR LOCH A TUATH
Port Nan Giùran
Rubha an t-Siumpain
Lacasdal
Tunga
Sròn Ruadh
Cnoc Amhlaigh
Port Mholair
A866
LEWS CASTLE & MUS NAN EILEAN
Stornoway
STORNOWAY
Aird
Loch Urabhal
Loch nan Sgadan
Sulaisiadar
Mealabost
EYE PENINSULA
Seisiadar
Gnoc
Garrabost
223
Loch a' Ghainmhich
Sanndabhaig
Aiginis
Pabail Uarach
LEWIS LOOM CENTRE
AN LANNTAIR GALLERY
An Cnoc
Pabail Iarach
Tolm
ST COLUMBA'S
Suardail
Bàgh Phabail
ACHMORE STONE CIRCLE
Amish Mòr
Holm I.
Acha Mòr
Loch Orasaigh
A'Chearc
14
Loch Tobhta Bridein
Griomsidar
ULLAPOOL
Loch am Falcag
Liurbost
Ben Casgro
16
Ranais
Soval Lodge
Crosbost
Raerinish Pt.
Barkin Is.
Tabhaidh Mhor
Loch Trealabhal
Ceòs
Eilean Chaluim Chille
Lacasaidh
Gearraidh Bhaird
Eilean Orasaidh
Ailein
Crionor
Eilean Thoraidh
Sildinis
Cearsiadar
Cabharstadh
Tabost
KERSHADER
Badgo
13
Marbhig
Ceann Shiphoirt
Loch Sgibacleit
Loch nan Eilean
Calbost
Taobh a' Ghlinne
Grabhair
Loch Odhairn
Loch Shanndabhat
Kebock Head
P A R K   O R   P A I R C
Orasaigh
Leumrabhagh
Eisgean
Loch Shell or Loch Sealg
Srianach
470 CRIONAIG
Eilean Iubhard
Mol Truisg
CAOLAS NAN EILEAN
Gob Rubh'Uisenis
Rubha Bhrollum
Rubha a'Bhaird
Garbh Eilean
Eilean Mhuire
Na h-Eileanan Mòra
(Shiant Islands)
Eilean an Tighe

igh ay)
Fladda-chùain
149
Eilean Troddaÿ

Rubha Hunish
Rubha na h-Aiseig
DUNTULM CASTLE
acqueen
20
Duntulm
Kilmaluag

Rubha Reidh
Eilean Furadh Mòr
Greenstone Point
Rubha Beag
Opinan
Rubha Mòr
Mellon Udrigle
Gruinard I.
Mur
Sròn a' Gheodha Dhuibh
Camas Mòr
155
Achgarve
Gruinard Bay
Mellon Charles
Laide
First Coast
Loch an Draing
Cove
Ormiscaig
Sand
Second Coast
Tighnafiline
150
Little Gruinard
Isle of Ewe
Aultbea
Drumchork
Loch a'Bhaid-luachraich
296 AN CUAIDH
Melvaig
Inverasdale
L O C H   E W E
Loch Faoi
Aultgrishan
Midtown
14
Loch Sguod
Brae
Rubha 'Ard na Bà
Aird Dubh
Peterburn
Naast
Tournaig
Seana Chamas
INVEREWE GARDEN
Port Erradale
Loch Bad a'Chreamh
Londubh
North Erradale
Big Sand
149
Poolewe
Longa Island
Rubha Bàn
CARN DE
Caolas Beag
Strath
Loch Tollaidh
Smithstown
GAIRLOCH HERITAGE MUSEUM
Gairloch
Aird
MEALL AN DOIREAN 420
791 BEINN AIRIGH CHARR
LOCH GAIRLOCH
Port Henderson
B8056
Charlestown
Bàdachro
Kerrysdale

Rudh
Camas Eilean E
Eilean Mullagrac
Isle F
Glas-leac Mòr
Tanera E
Summer
156
Glas-leac Bea
Priest I.

8 9 10 11 12 13

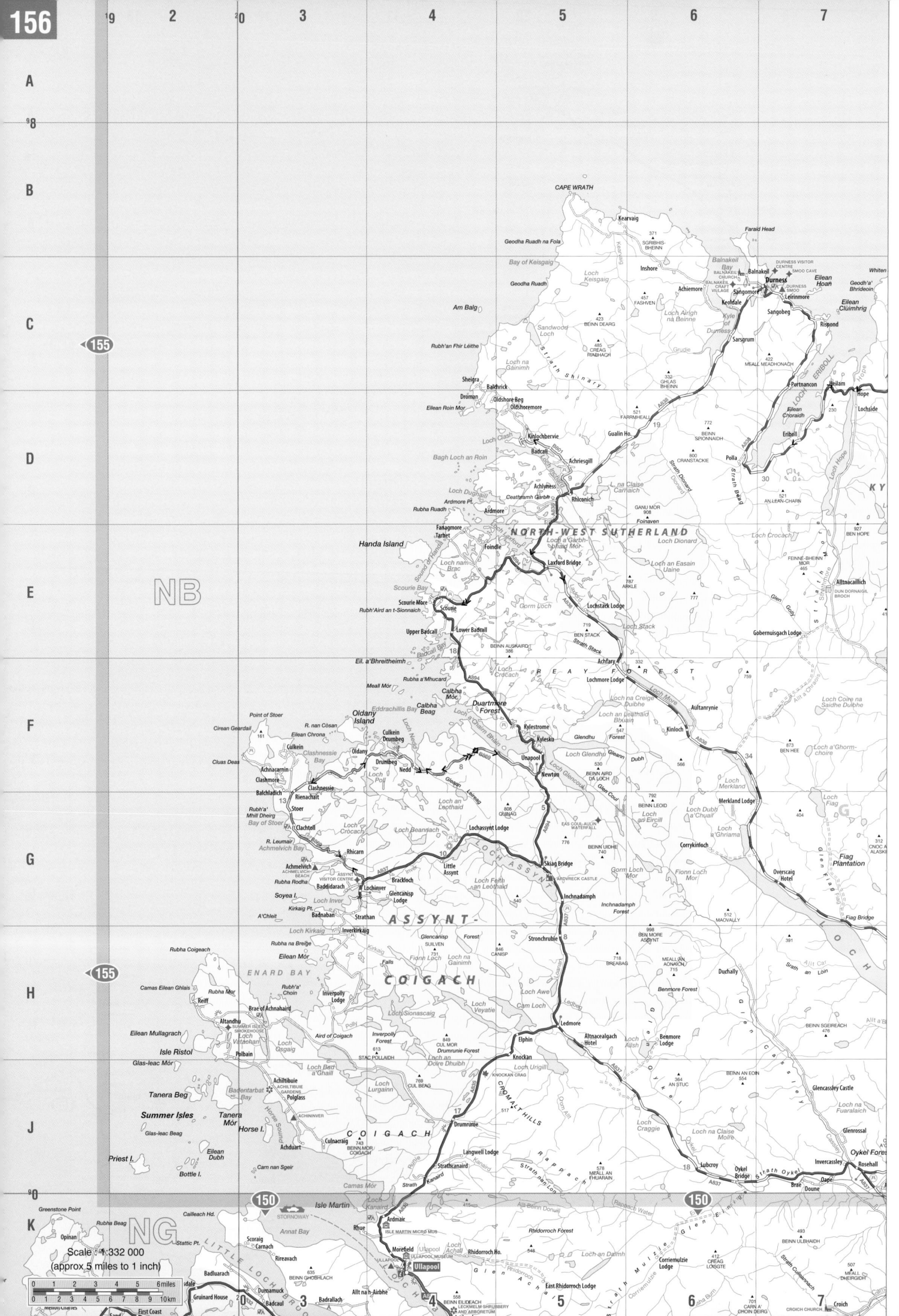

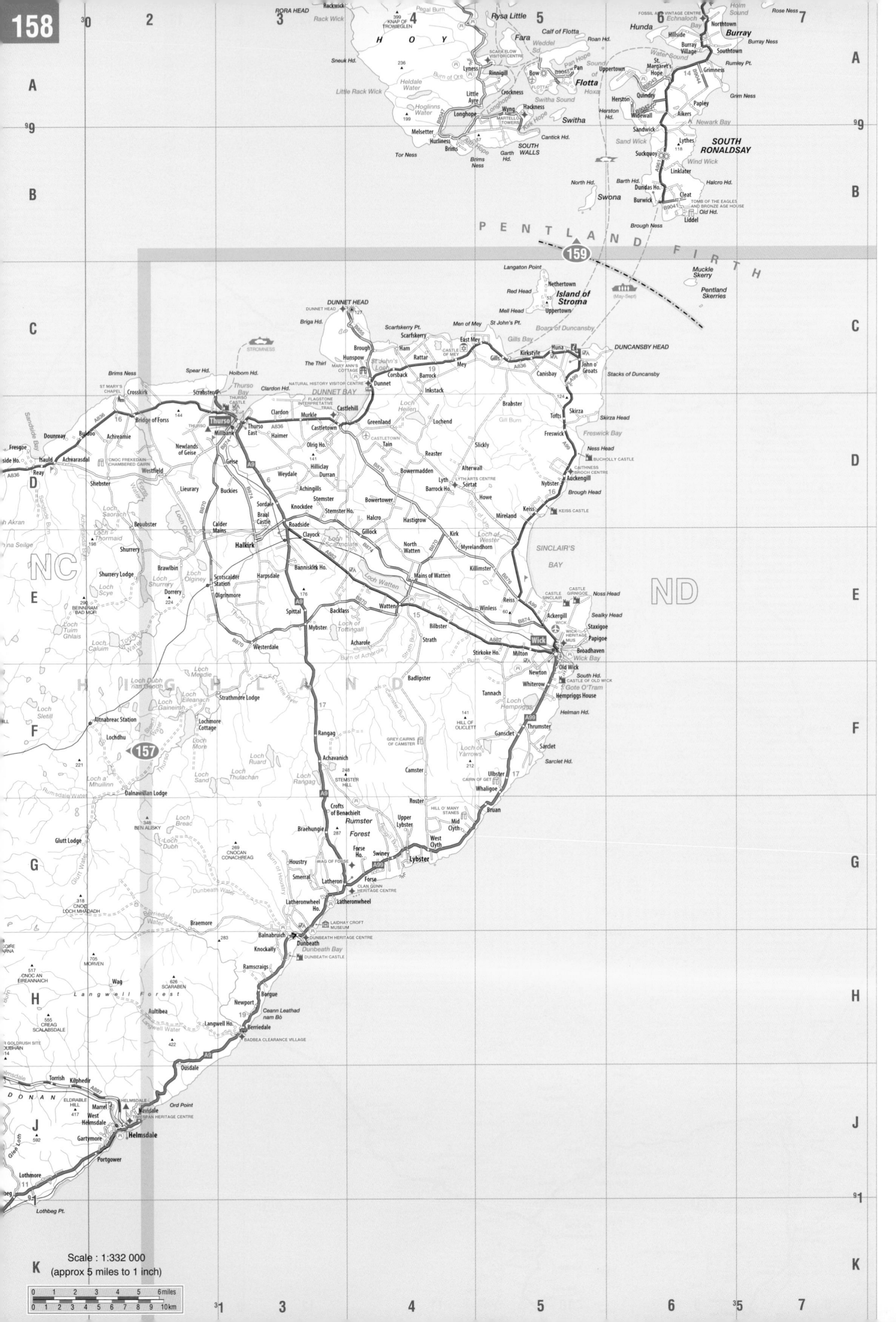

Scale : 1:332 000
(approx 5 miles to 1 inch)

0 1 2 3 4 5 6 miles
0 1 2 3 4 5 6 7 8 9 10km

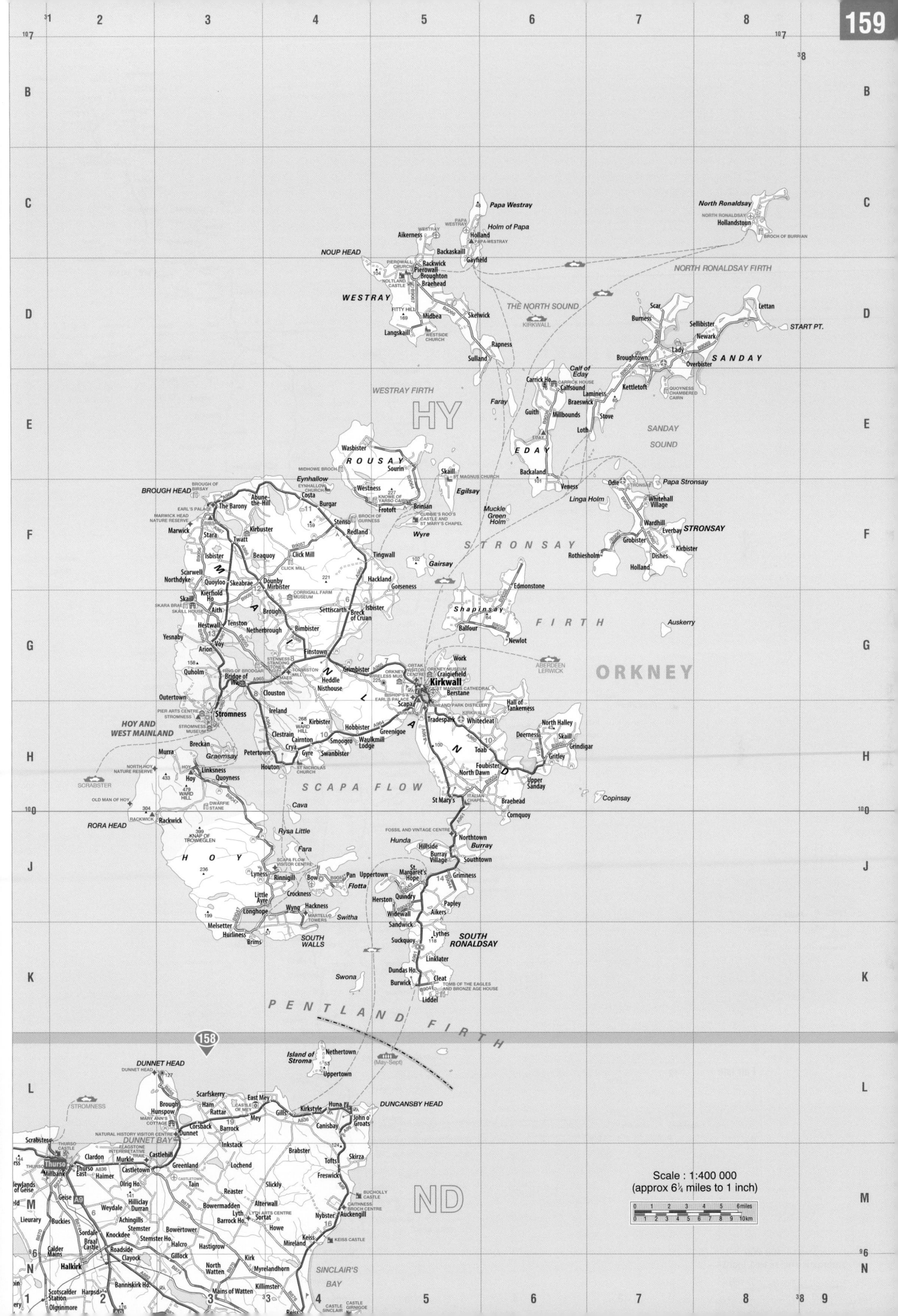

B

C

North Ronaldsay
NORTH RONALDSAY
Hollandstoun
BROCH OF BURRIAN

Papa Westray
PAPA WESTRAY
Holm of Papa
Holland
PAPA-WESTRAY

Aikerness   WESTRAY
Backaskaill
NOUP HEAD   Gayfield

PIEROWALL
CHURCH   Rackwick
104   Pierowall
Broughton
NOLTLAND   Braehead
CASTLE

NORTH RONALDSAY FIRTH

D

FITTY HILL   Skelwick
169   Midbea   THE NORTH SOUND
KIRKWALL
WESTSIDE   Rapness
CHURCH   Langskaill

Sulland

Scar
Burness   Lettan
Sellibister
Newark
Broughtown   Lady   SANDAY
Overbister
Kettletoft   QUOYNESS
CHAMBERED
CAIRN

START PT.

E

WESTRAY FIRTH

HY

Faray

Calf of
Eday
Carrick Ho.   CARRICK HOUSE
Calfsound
Guith   Laminess
Braeswick

ROUSAY
Wasbister
MIDHOWE BROCH   Sourin   Skaill
ST MAGNUS CHURCH
Westness   Egilsay
KNOWE OF   Frotoft
YARSO CAIRN
EYNHALLOW
Eynhallow   Brinian   CUBBIE ROO'S
EYNHALLOW   CASTLE AND
CHURCH   ST MARY'S CHAPEL

Millbounds   Stove
EDAY   Loth
EDAY
Backaland
101   Veness

Odie
STRONSAY   Papa Stronsay
Whitehall
Village

SANDAY
SOUND

F

BROUGH HEAD
BROUGH OF
BIRSAY
Abune-   Costa
the-Hill   Burgar
EARL'S PALACE   The Barony
BIRSAY
MARWICK HEAD   Marwick
NATURE RESERVE   Stara   Twatt
Isbister

Stenso   Redland

Muckle
Green
Holm

Wardhill   Everbay   STRONSAY

Grobister
Rothiesholm   Dishes   Kirbister

Holland

STRONSAY

Tingwall
Hackland

Wyre

G

Scarwell   M
Northdyke   Quoyloo   Skeabrae   Dounby   Mirbister   11
Kierfold   221
Ho.   Brough   CLICK MILL
Skaill   Aith   A
SKARA BRAE   Hestwall   Tenston   Netherbrough   Bimbister
SKAILL HOUSE   Voy   I   Finstown
Yesnaby   Arion   N

Click Mill
102
Gairsay

Gorseness
Isbister
6   CORRIGALL FARM
MUSEUM   Settiscarth   Breck
of Cruan

Work

Shapinsay
64   Balfour
Newlot

FIRTH   Auskerry

ORKNEY

ABERDEEN
LERWICK

H

HOY AND
WEST MAINLAND
SCRABSTER

158
221   Quholm   Bridge
of Waith   A965
RING OF BRODGAR
STENNESS STANDING   L
STONES   TORMISTON
MILL
MAES
HOWE   Heddle   A
Clouston   Ireland   N   Nisthouse
Outertown
Kirbister
268   Hobbister
WARD   Smoogro   D
Clestrain   HILL   Cairston
Crya
Murra   Breckan   Gyre   Swanbister
Graemsay   Petertown   Houton
Linksness   ST NICHOLAS
Hoy   Quoyness   CHURCH
479   Scrabster   Old Man of Hoy   304   DWARFIE
WARD   RACKWICK   STANE
HILL   Rackwick   Cava

Stromness
PIER ARTS CENTRE
STROMNESS
STROMNESS   Stromness
MUSEUM

ORKNEY
WIRELESS MUS   ORKNEY
228   ORKNEY MUSEUM
VISITOR
Grimbister   CENTRE
Kirkwall   Berstane
BISHOP'S &   Scapa
EARL'S PALACE
Craigiefield

Whitecleat
Tradespark
Greenigoe   HIGHLAND PARK DISTILLERY   Hall of
Tankerness
A
100   Toab   Deerness   North Halley
Waulkmill   N   Foubister   Skaill
Lodge   North Dawn   Gritley
D   Upper   Grindigar
Sanday

SCAPA FLOW
St Mary's
Braehead
ITALIAN
CHAPEL   Cornquoy

Copinsay

J

RORA HEAD

390
KNAP OF
TROWIEGLEN
Rysa Little

399   Fara
HOY   Lyness
236   SCAPA FLOW
VISITOR CENTRE
Rinnigill   Bow
Pan
Uppertown   Flotta
Little
Ayre   Crockness
Longhope   Hackness
Wyng   MARTELLO   Herston
199   Melsetter   TOWERS   Swartha
Hurliness   Widewall
Brims   SOUTH
WALLS

FOSSIL AND VINTAGE CENTRE
Northtown
Hunda   Burray
Hillside   Burray
Village   Southtown
St.   14   Grimness
Margaret's
Hope   Quindry   Papley
Sandwick   Aikers
Suckquoy   Lythes   SOUTH
118   RONALDSAY
Linklater

K

Swona   Dundas Ho.
Cleat
Burwick   TOMB OF THE EAGLES
AND BRONZE AGE HOUSE
Liddel

L

P E N T L A N D   F I R T H

158

DUNNET HEAD
DUNNET HEAD   Nethertown
Island of   53
Stroma   Uppertown
(May-Sept)

DUNCANSBY HEAD

STROMNESS

Scarfskerry
Brough   East Mey
Hunspow   Ham   Kirkstyle
MARY ANN'S   Rattar   Huna
COTTAGE   Mey   Gills   John o'Groats
NATURAL HISTORY VISITOR CENTRE   Corsback   Canisbay
DUNNET HEAD   Dunnet   Barrock
FLAGSTONE   A836   Inkstack   19
Scrabster   INTERPRETATIVE
TRAIL   DUNNET BAY   Brabster
144   Thurso   Castlehill   Greenland   324   Skirza
rss   Thurso   Clardon   Castletown   Lochend   Tofts
East   Murkle   Tain   Freswick
Thurso   Haimer   Reaster   BUCHOLLY
Millbank   Olrig Ho.   Slickly   CASTLE
lewlands   Geise   141   Alterwall   CAITHNESS
of Geise   Geise   Hilliclay   Durran   Lyth   BROCH CENTRE
ld   A9   6   Weydale   Bowermadden   Sortat   Nybster
Lieurary   Buckies   Stemster   Howe   Auckengill
Sordale   Bowertower   Barrock Ho.   16
Knockdee   Stemster Ho.   Halcro   Hastigrow
Calder   Braal   Roadside   Gillock   Kirk   KEISS CASTLE
Mains   Castle   Clayock   North   Keiss
Halkirk   Watten   Myrelandhorn   Mireland
Banniskirk Ho.   Mains of Watten   SINCLAIR'S   CASTLE
Scotscalder   Harpsda   Killimster   BAY   GIRNIGOE
Station   3   Reiss   CASTLE
Olgrinmore   CASTLE SINCLAIR

ND

M

Scale : 1:400 000
(approx 6¼ miles to 1 inch)

0   1   2   3   4   5   6 miles
0 1 2 3 4 5 6 7 8 9 10km

N

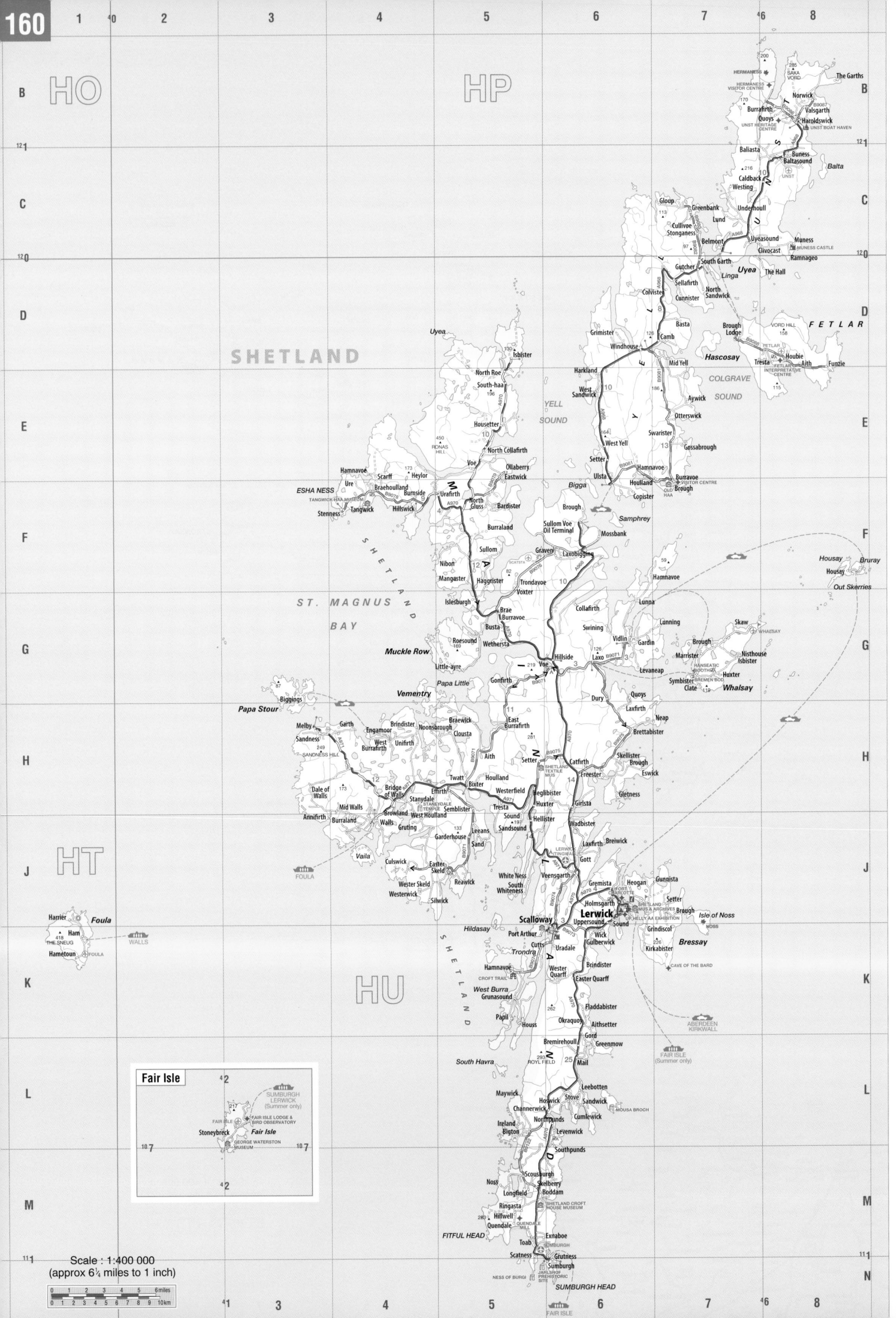

SHETLAND

HO

HP

HERMANESS
HERMANESS VISITOR CENTRE
Norwick
Burrafirth
Quoys
Haroldswick
UNST HERITAGE CENTRE
Baliasta
UNST BOAT HAVEN
Caldback
Westing
Buness
Baltasound
Balta
U N S T
The Garths
SAXA VORD
Valsgarth

Gloup
Greenbank
Cullivoe
Stonganess
Lund
Belmont
Uyeasound
Muness
MUNESS CASTLE
Clivocast
Ramnageo
Gutcher
Sellafirth
Cunnister
North Sandwick
Colvister
South Garth
Uyea
Linga
The Hall

Grimister
Windhouse
Camb
Basta
Mid Yell
Brough Lodge
VORD HILL
FETLAR
FETLAR INTERPRETATIVE CENTRE
Tresta
Houbie
Aith
Funzie
Hascosay
COLGRAVE SOUND
Harkland
West Sandwick
Aywick
Otterswick
Swarister
Gossabrough
Y E L L
Setter
Hamnavoe
West Yell
Ulsta
Houlland
Burravoe
Brough
BURRAVOE VISITOR CENTRE
OLD HAA
Bigga
Copister
Samphrey
Housay
Bruray
Housay
Out Skerries

Uyea
Isbister
North Roe
South-haa

Housetter
RONAS HILL
Voe
North Collafirth
Ollaberry
Eastwick

Hamnavoe
Scarff
Heylor
Ure
Braehoullan
Burnside
ESHA NESS
TANGWICK HAA MUSEUM
Stenness
Tangwick
Hillswick
Urafirth
North Gluss
Bardister

Burraland
Sullom Voe Oil Terminal
Mossbank
Brough
Sullom
Graven
Laxobigging
Hamnavoe
Lunna
Nibon
Mangaster
Haggrister
Trondavoe
Voxter
Collafirth
Lunning
Skaw
WHAESAY
Islesburgh
Brae
Burravoe
Swining
Vidlin
Gardin
Brough
Nisthouse
Isbister
Busta
Roesound
Wethersta
Hillside
Laxo
Levaneap
Marrister
Symbister
Clate
Huxter
Whalsay
HANSEATIC BOOTH
BREMEN BOD
Muckle Row
Little-ayre
Voe
Voe
Dury
Quoys
Laxfirth
ST. MAGNUS BAY
Papa Little
Gonfirth
Neap
Brettabister
Vementry
Biggings
Papa Stour
Melby
Garth
Brindister
Noonsbrough
Braewick
Clousta
East Burrafirth
Sandness
SANDNESS HILL
Engamoor
West Burrafirth
Unifirth
Aith
Setter
Catfirth
Skellister
Brough
Eswick
Gletness
SHETLAND TEXTILE MUS.
Twatt
Houlland
Bixter
Westerfield
Freester
FOULA
Dale of Walls
Bridge of Walls
Efirth
Standale
STANEYDALE TEMPLE
Semblister
Huxter
Girlsta
Mid Walls
Browland
West Houlland
Tresta
Sound
Hellister
Wadbister
Annifirth
Burraland
Walls
Gruting
Garderhouse
Leeans
Sand
Sandsound
Laxfirth
Breiwick
Vaila
Culswick
Easter Skeld
White Ness
South Whiteness
Veensgarth
LERWICK TINGWALL
Gott
Wester Skeld
Reawick
Gremista
Heogan
Gunnista
Westerwick
Silwick
LERWICK
FORT CHARLOTTE
SHETLAND MUS. & ARCHIVES
UP HELLY AA EXHIBITION
Setter
Brough
Isle of Noss
Scalloway
Holmsgarth
Uppersound
Sound
Grindiscol
Kirkabister
Bressay
Hildasay
Port Arthur
Wick
Gulberwick
CAVE OF THE BARD
Trondra
Cutts
Uradale
Hamnavoe
Wester Quarff
Easter Quarff
Brindister
West Burra
Grunasound
Fladdabister
Aberdeen
Kirkwall
Papil
Houss
Okraquoy
Aithsetter
South Havra
ROYL FIELD
Mail
Gord
Greenmow
Bremirehoull
Fair Isle (Summer only)
Leebotten
Maywick
Hoswick
Stove
Sandwick
MOUSA BROCH
Channerwick
Cumlewick
Ireland
Bigton
Northpunds
Levenwick
Southpunds
SHETLAND CROFT HOUSE MUSEUM
Noss
Longfield
Ringasta
Scousburgh
Skelberry
Boddam
Hillwell
Quendale
QUENDALE MILL
Maywick
FITFUL HEAD
Exnaboe
Toab
Scatness
Grutness
Sumburgh
JARLSHOF
NESS OF BURGI
SUMBURGH HEAD
PREHISTORIC SITE

Fair Isle

SUMBURGH LERWICK (Summer only)
FAIR ISLE
FAIR ISLE LODGE & BIRD OBSERVATORY
Stoneybreck
Fair Isle
GEORGE WATERSTON MUSEUM

Harrier
Foula
Ham
THE SNEUG
Hametoun
FOULA
WALLS

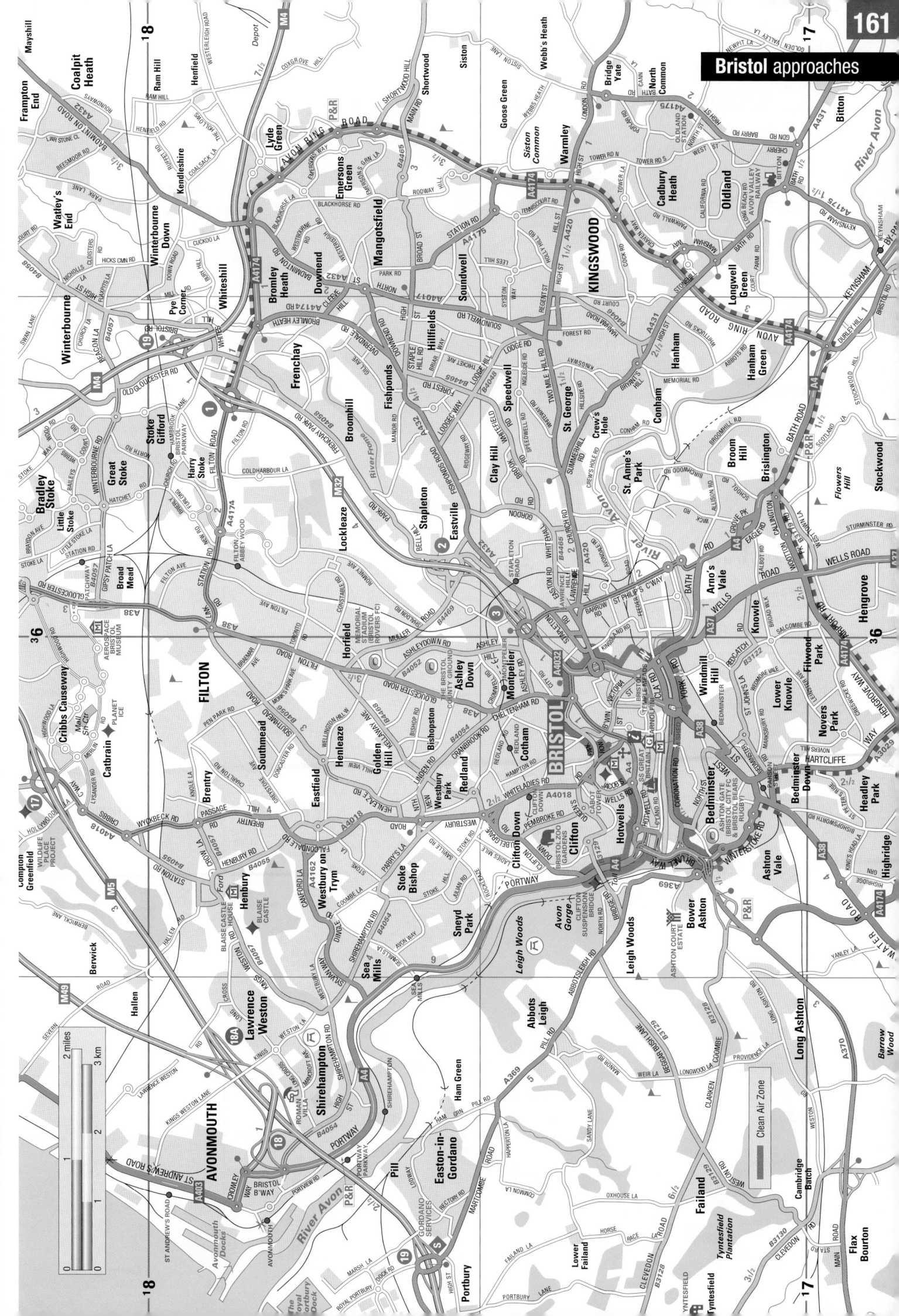

Birmingham approaches

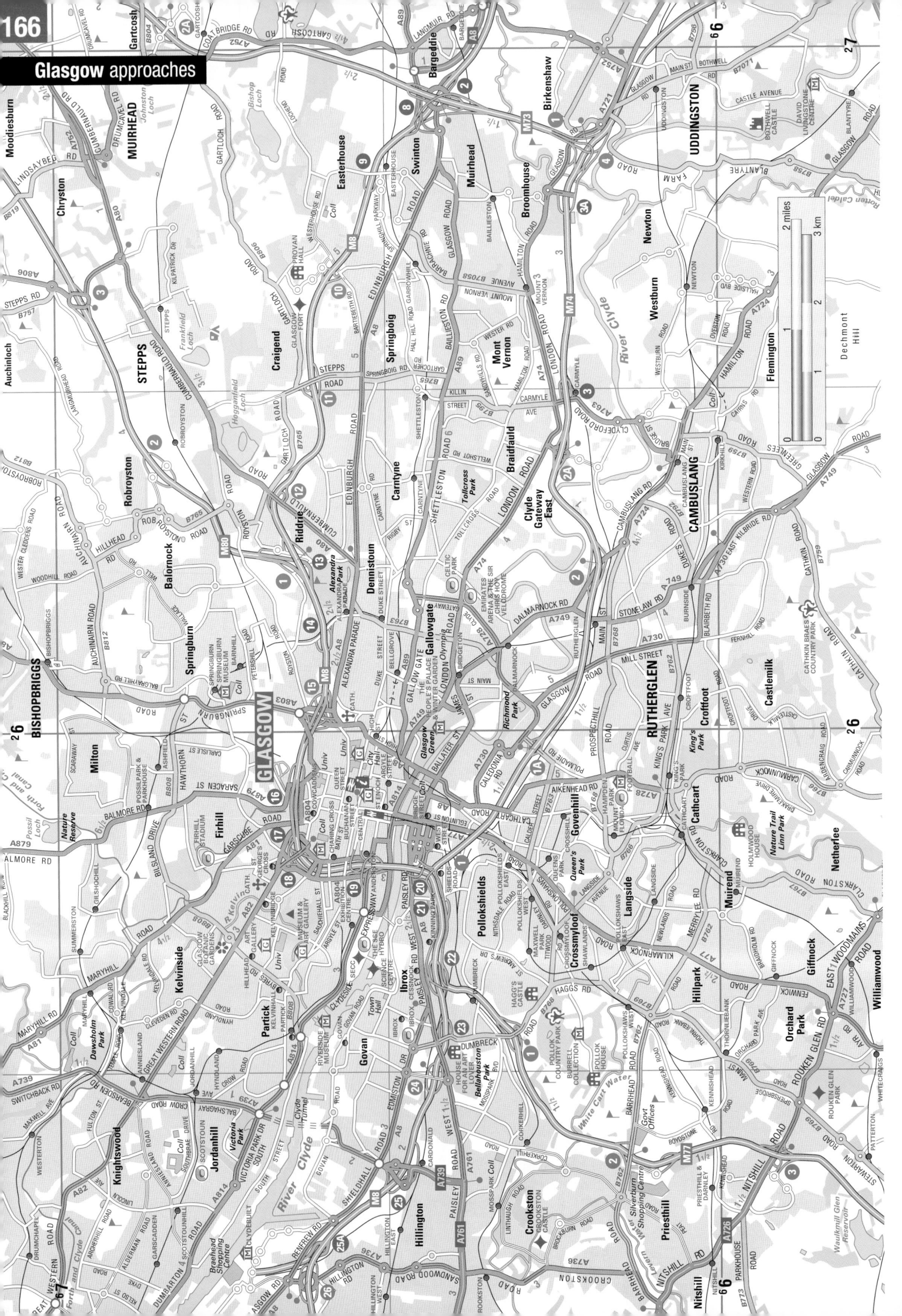

Glasgow approaches

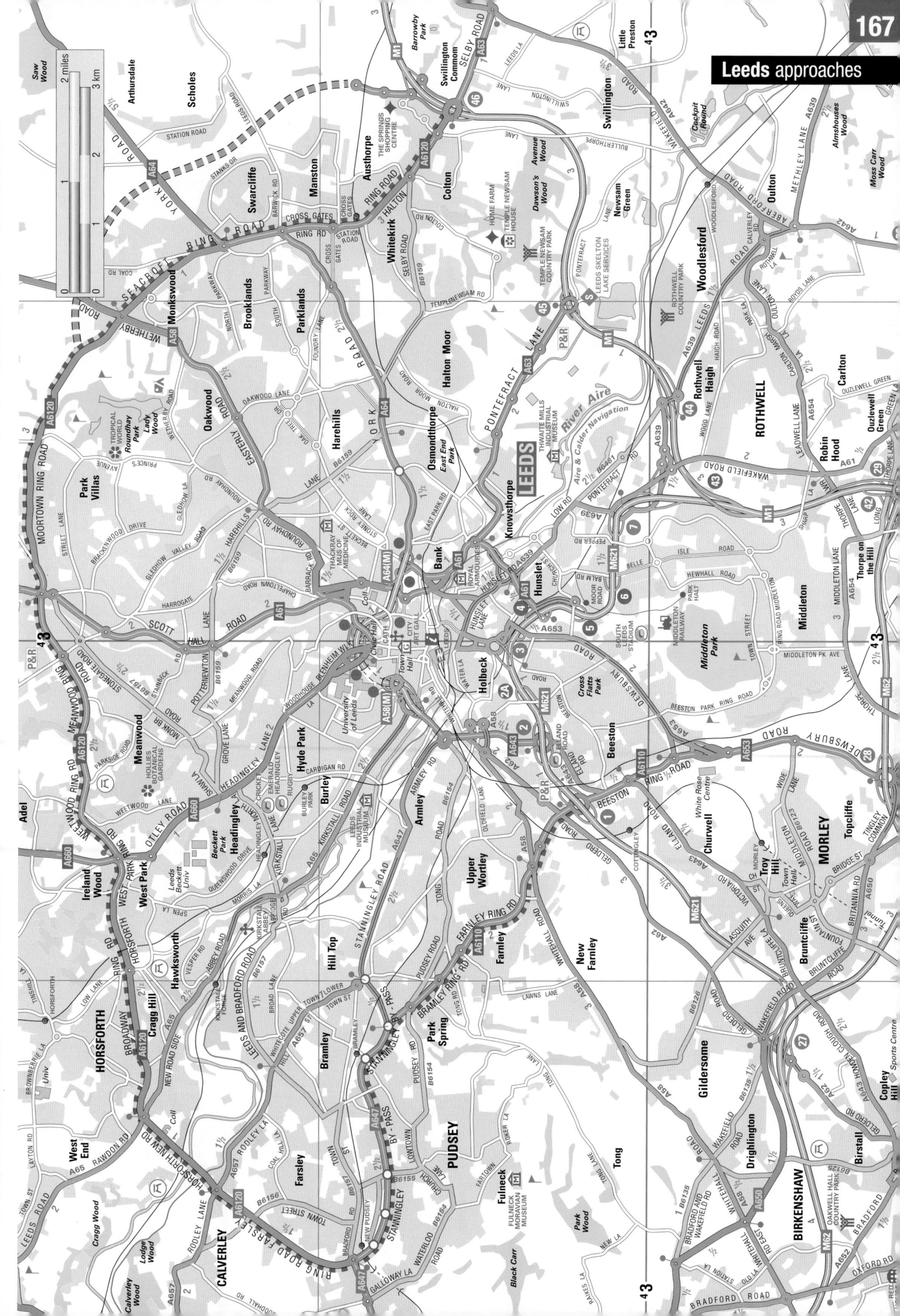

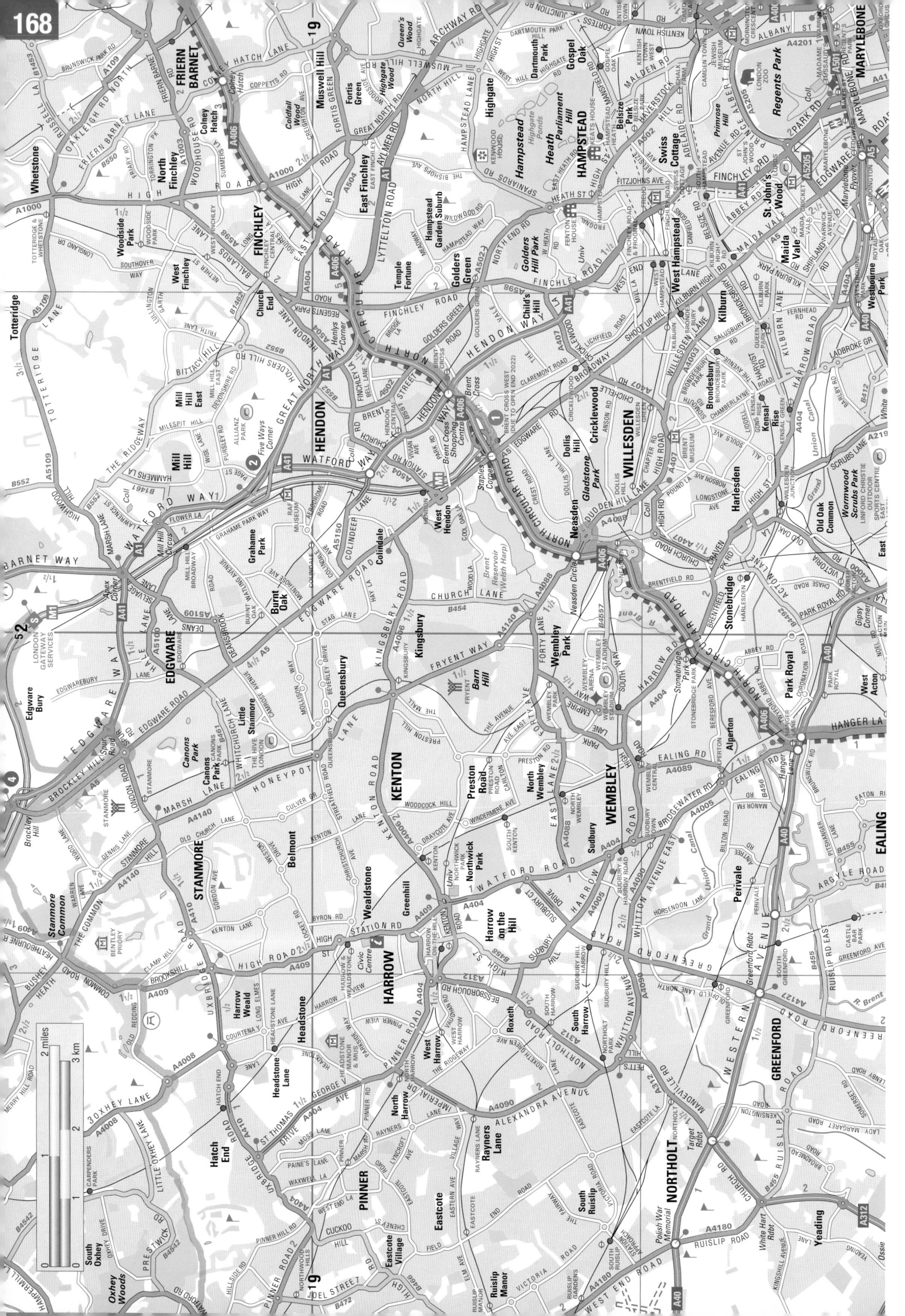

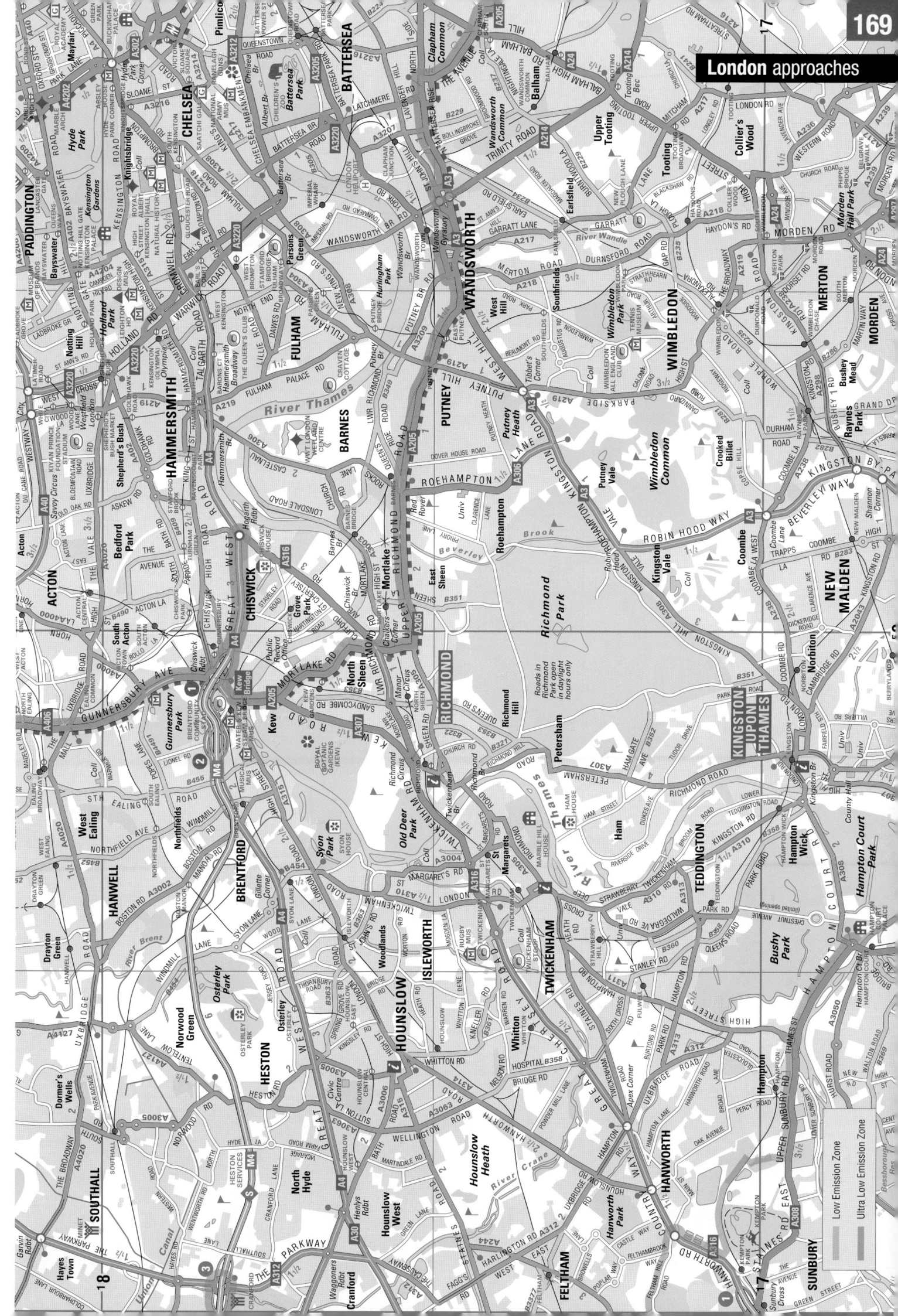

PADDINGTON
CHELSEA
BATTERSEA
Clapham Common
Balham
Tooting
Upper Tooting
Collier's Wood
Hyde Park
Kensington Gardens
Knightsbridge
HAMMERSMITH
FULHAM
WANDSWORTH
West Hill
WIMBLEDON
MERTON
MORDEN
Holland Park
Notting Hill
Shepherd's Bush
River Thames
BARNES
PUTNEY
Putney Heath
Wimbledon Common
Crooked Billet
Raynes Park
ACTON
Bedford Park
CHISWICK
Roehampton
Putney Vale
Kingston Vale
Robin Hood Way
Coombe
NEW MALDEN
West Ealing
Kew
Mortlake
East Sheen
North Sheen
RICHMOND
Richmond Park
Roads in Richmond Park open in daylight hours only
Richmond Hill
KINGSTON UPON THAMES
Norbiton
HANWELL
BRENTFORD
Gunnersbury Park
Syon Park
Old Deer Park
Petersham
Ham
TEDDINGTON
Hampton Wick
Hampton Court Park
SOUTHALL
HESTON
Norwood Green
Osterley Park
ISLEWORTH
TWICKENHAM
Bushy Park
Hampton
Hayes Town
HOUNSLOW
Hounslow West
North Hyde
Hounslow Heath
Whitton
HANWORTH
Hanworth Park
FELTHAM
SUNBURY

Low Emission Zone
Ultra Low Emission Zone

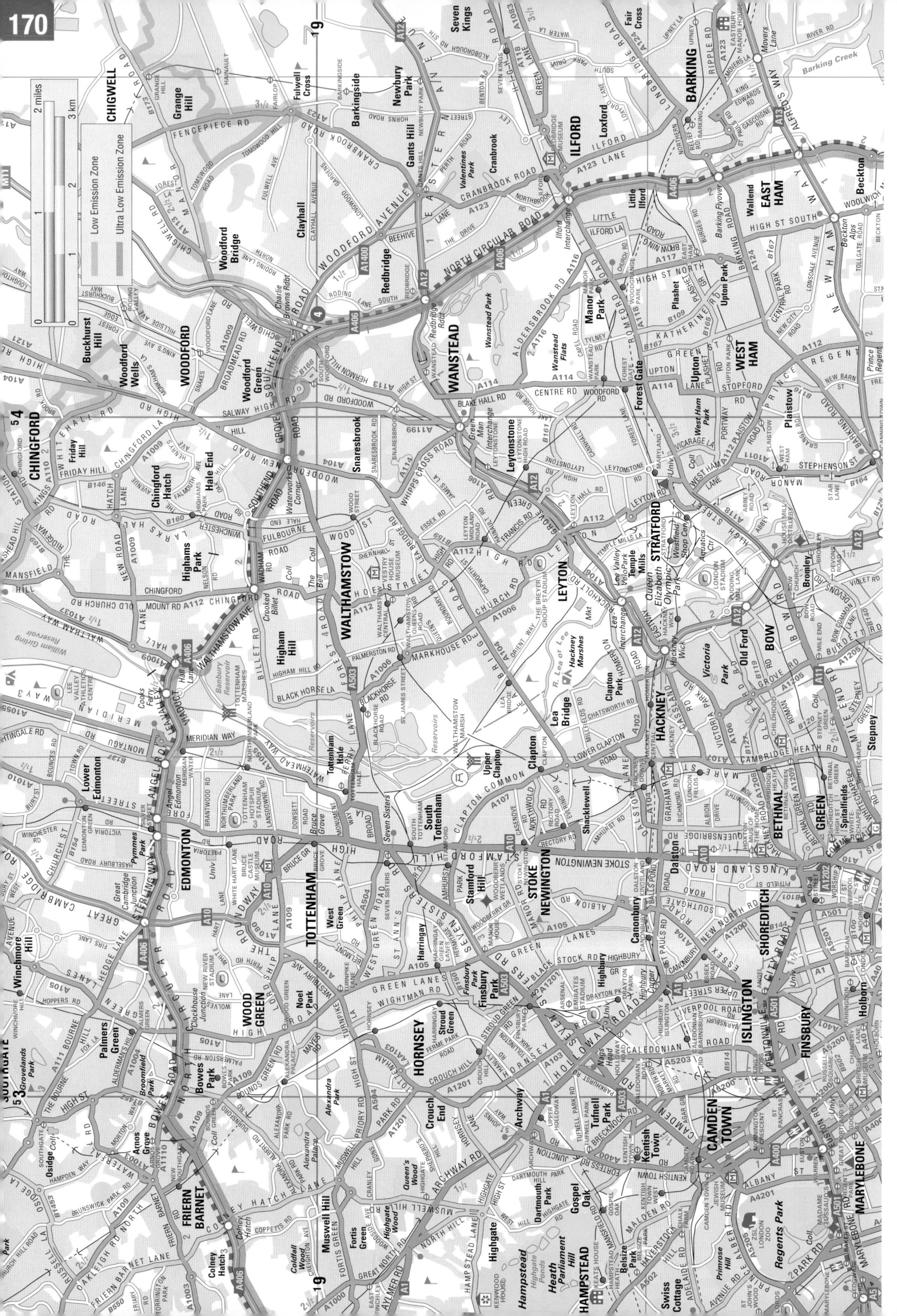

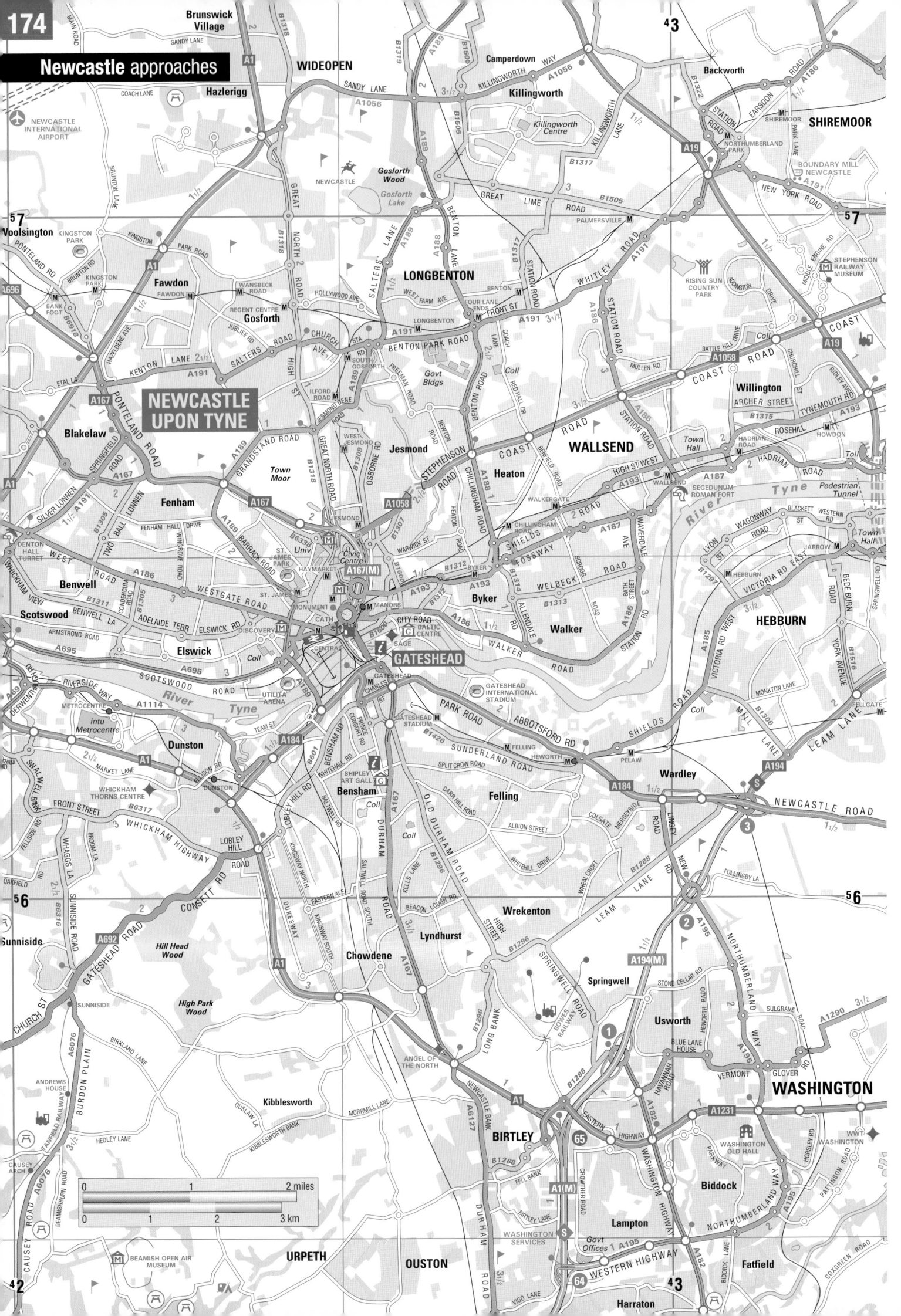

Town plan symbols

Motorway

Primary route – dual, single carriageway

A road – dual, single carriageway

B road – dual, single carriageway

Minor through road

One-way street

Pedestrian roads

Shopping streets

Railway with station

Tramway with station

Underground or Metro station

H Hospital

P Parking

Police

PO Post Office

Shopmobility

Youth hostel

Bus or railway station building

Shopping precinct or retail park

Park

Congestion charge zone

✝ Abbey or cathedral

Ancient monument

Aquarium

Art gallery

Bird collection or aviary

Building of interest

Castle

Church of interest

Cinema

Garden

Historic ship

House

House and garden

Museum

Preserved railway

Roman antiquity

Safari park

Theatre

Tourist information

Zoo

◆ Other place of interest

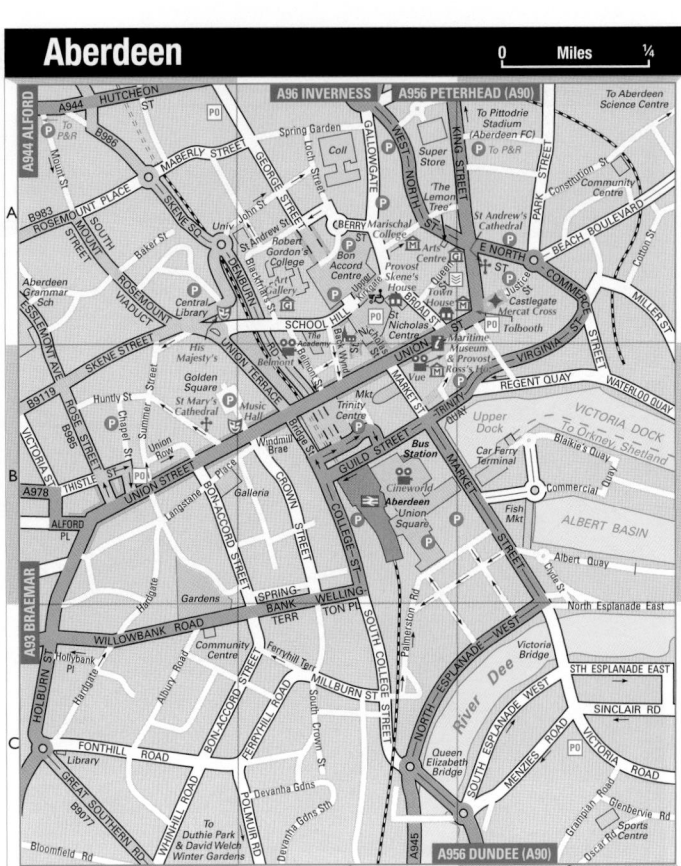

Aberdeen

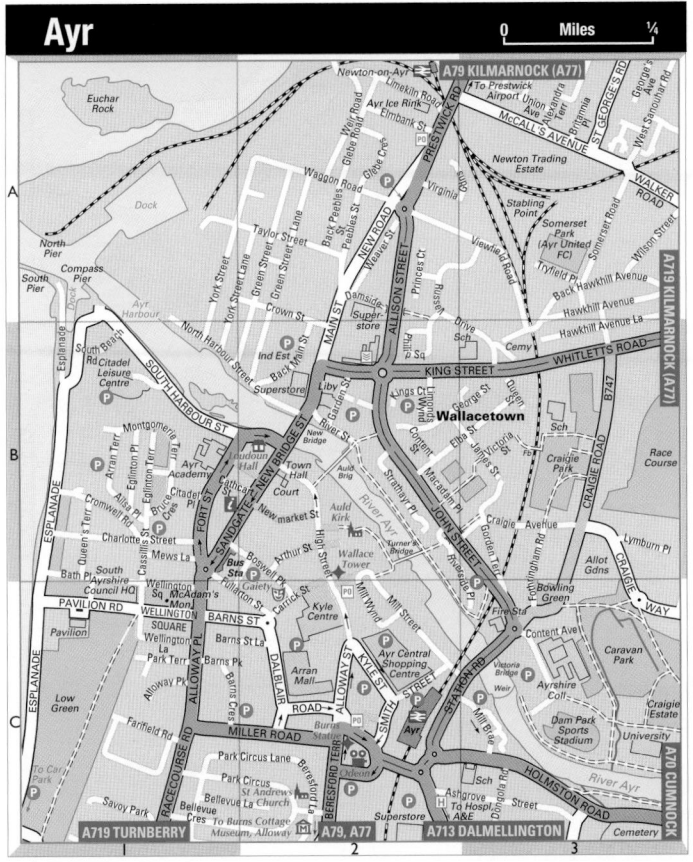

Ayr

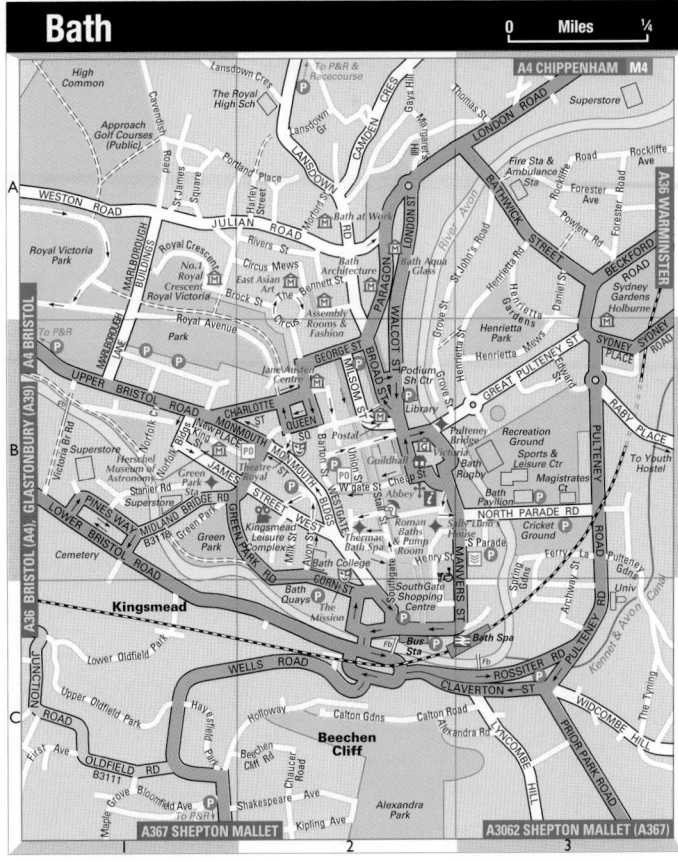

Bath

Birmingham

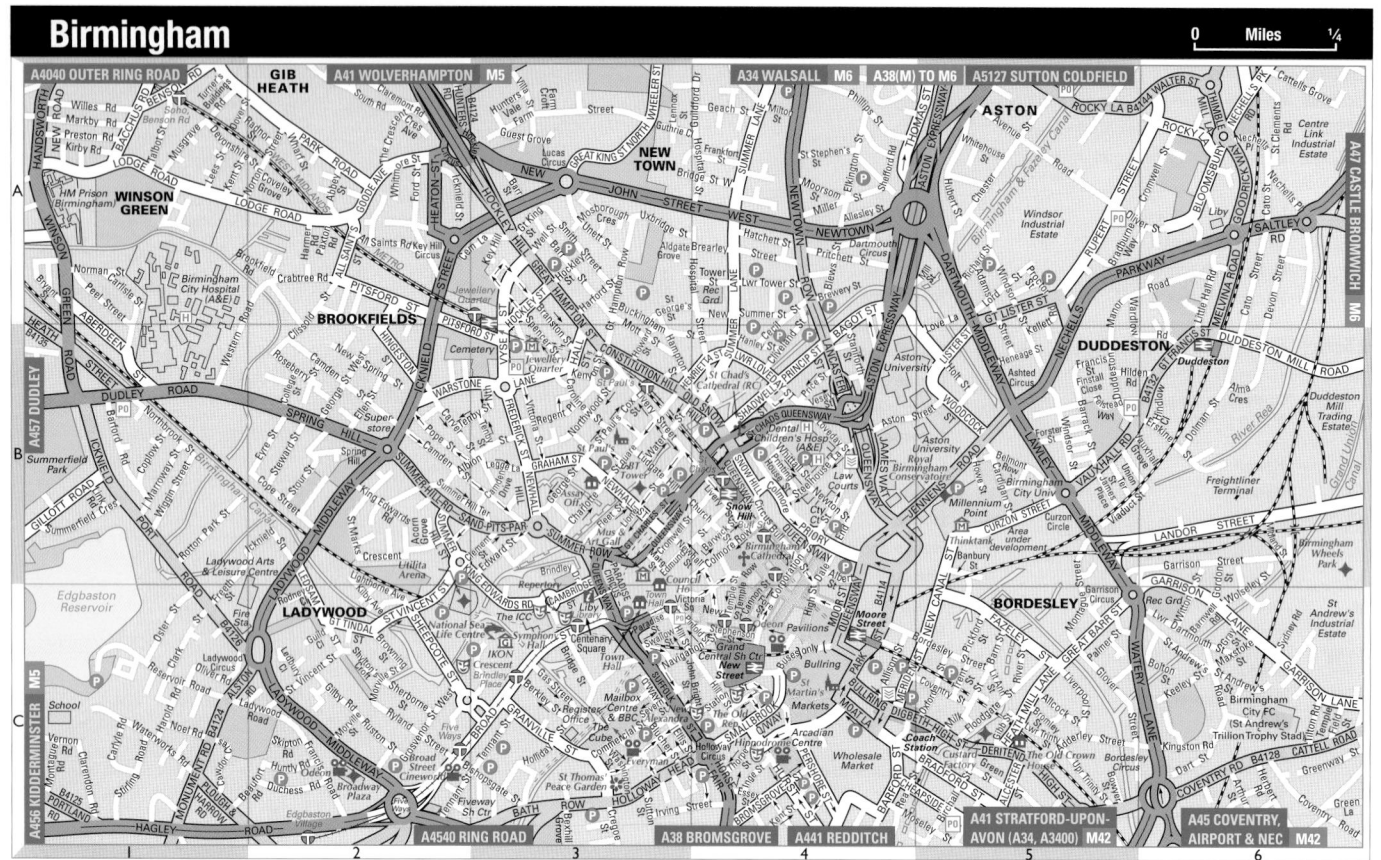

Blackpool

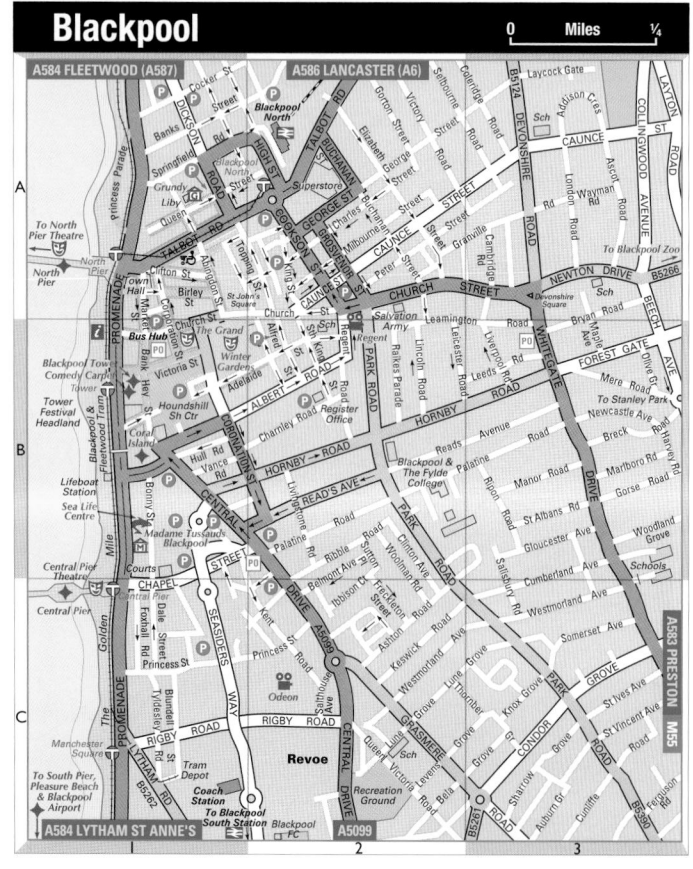

Bournemouth

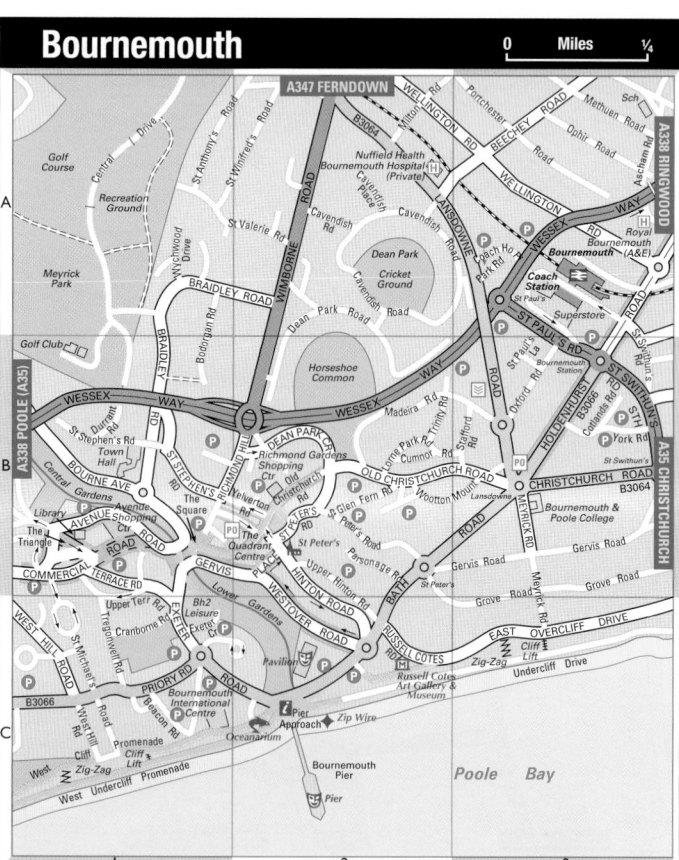

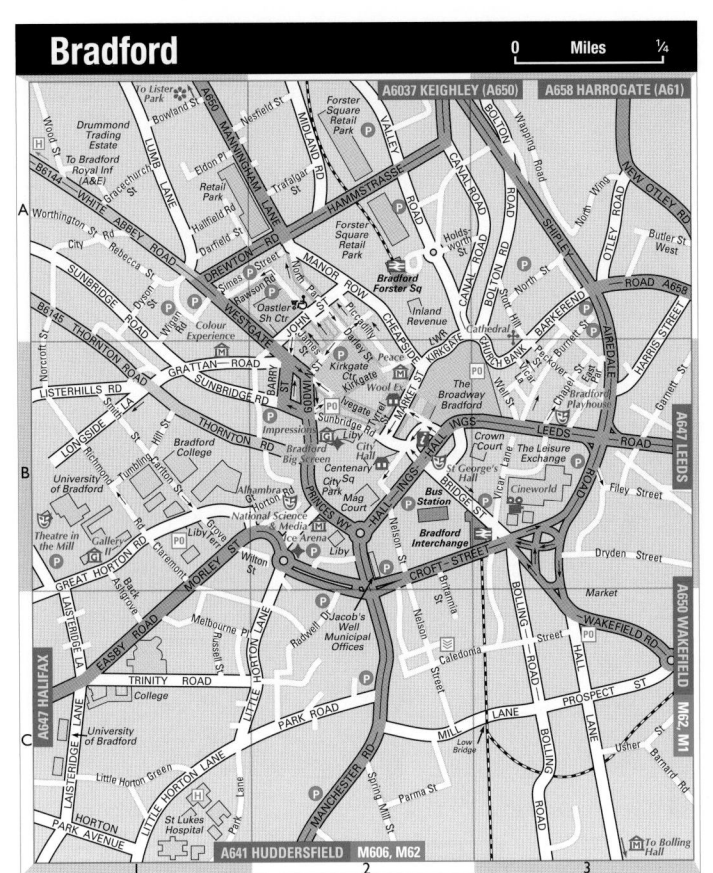

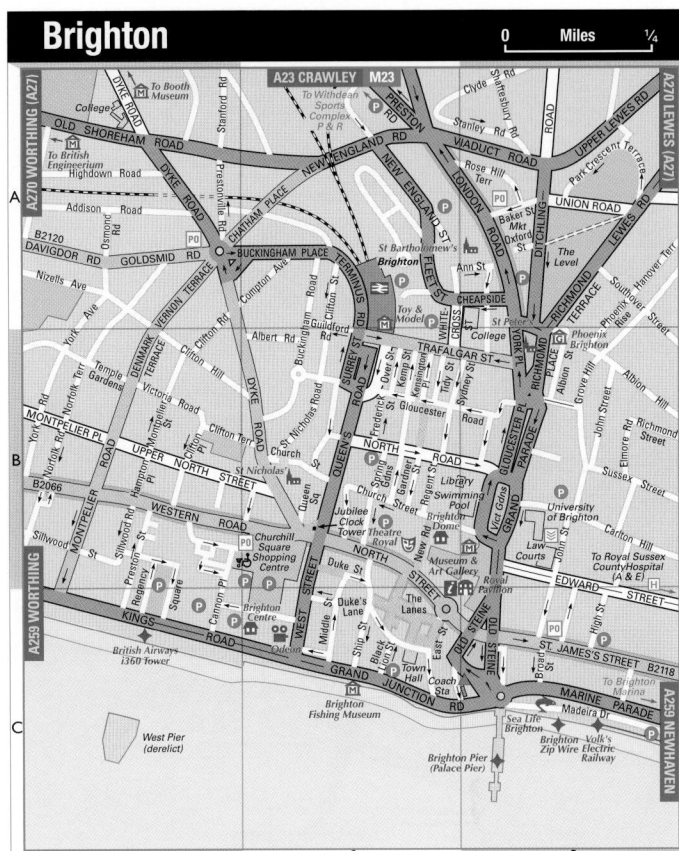

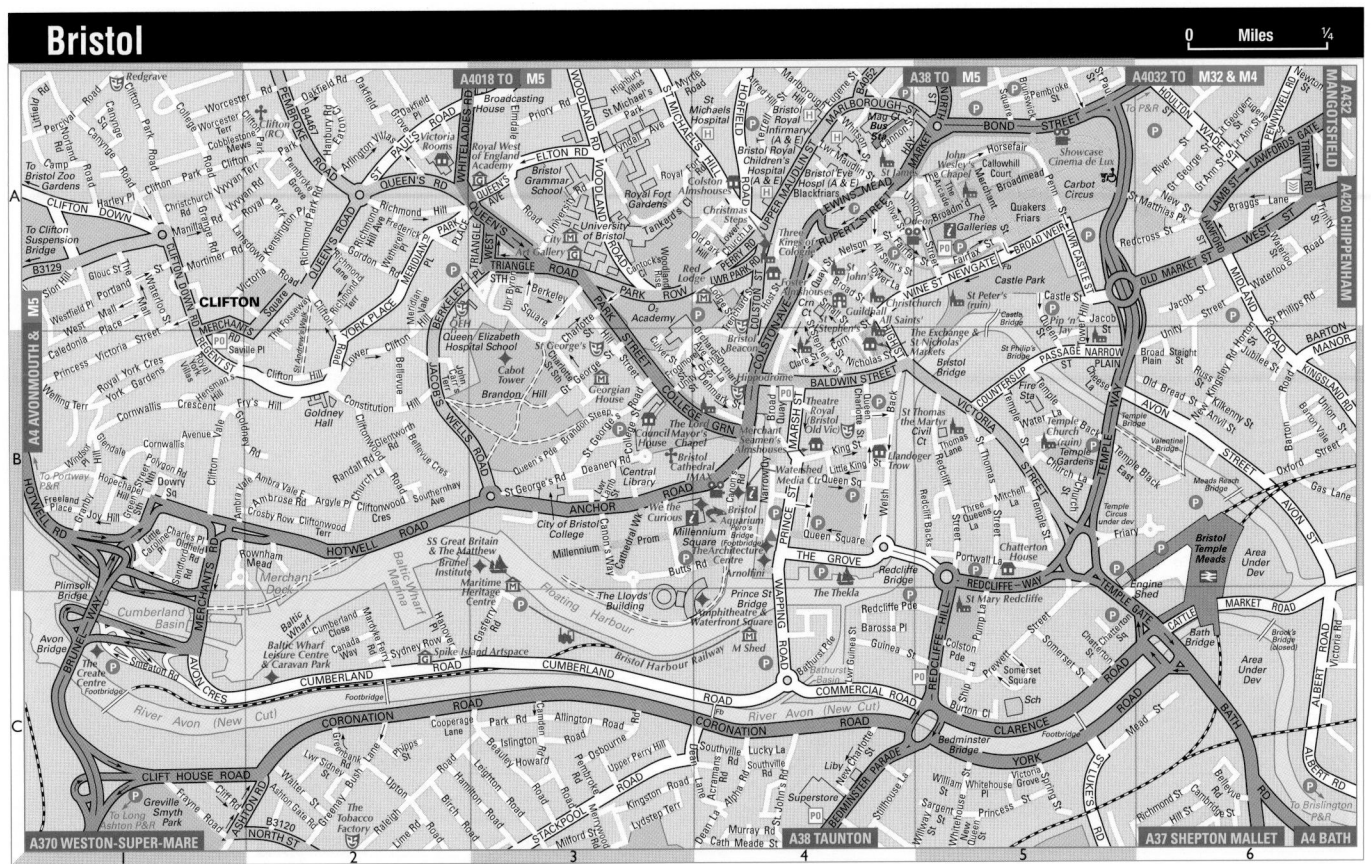

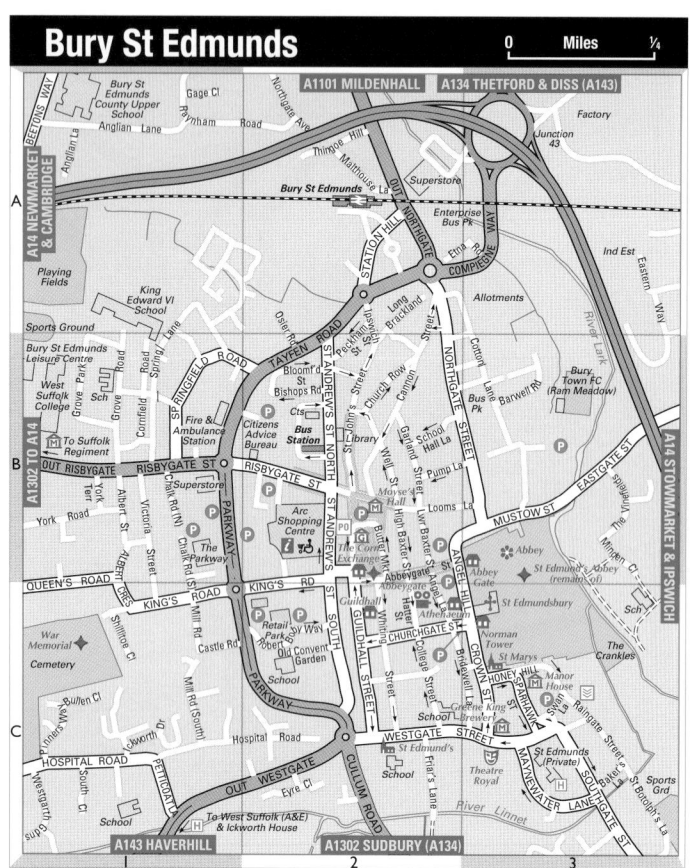

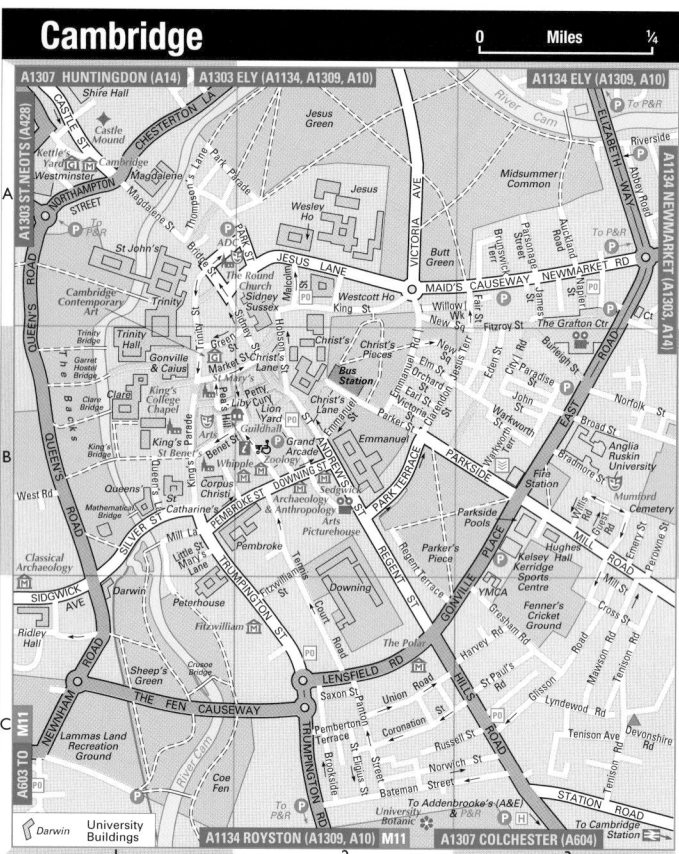

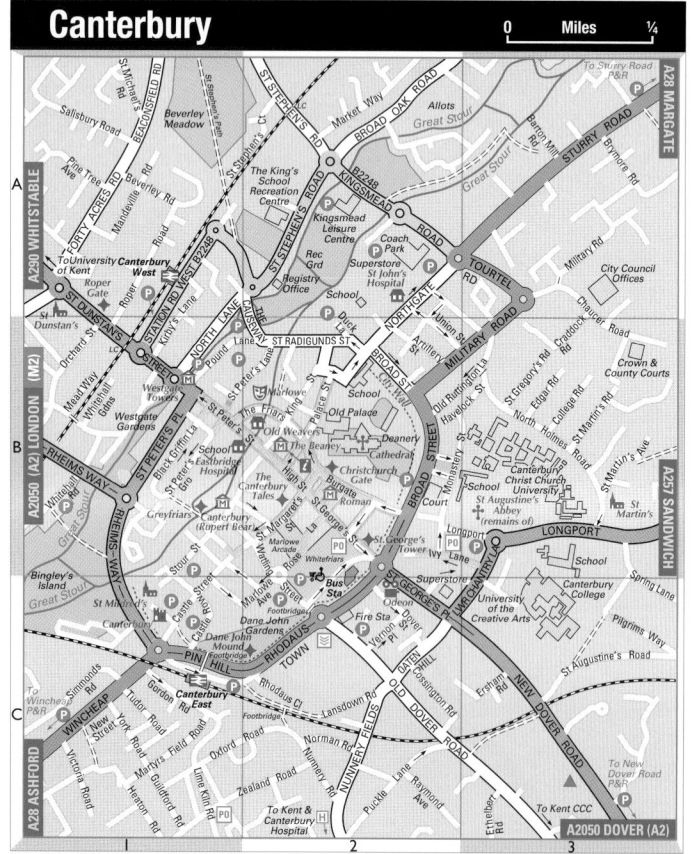

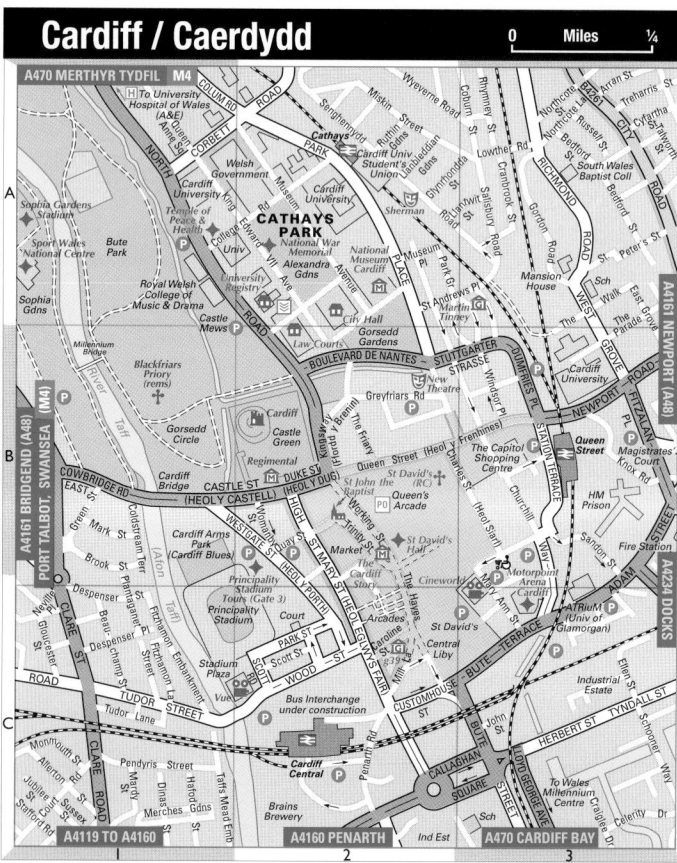

Carlisle

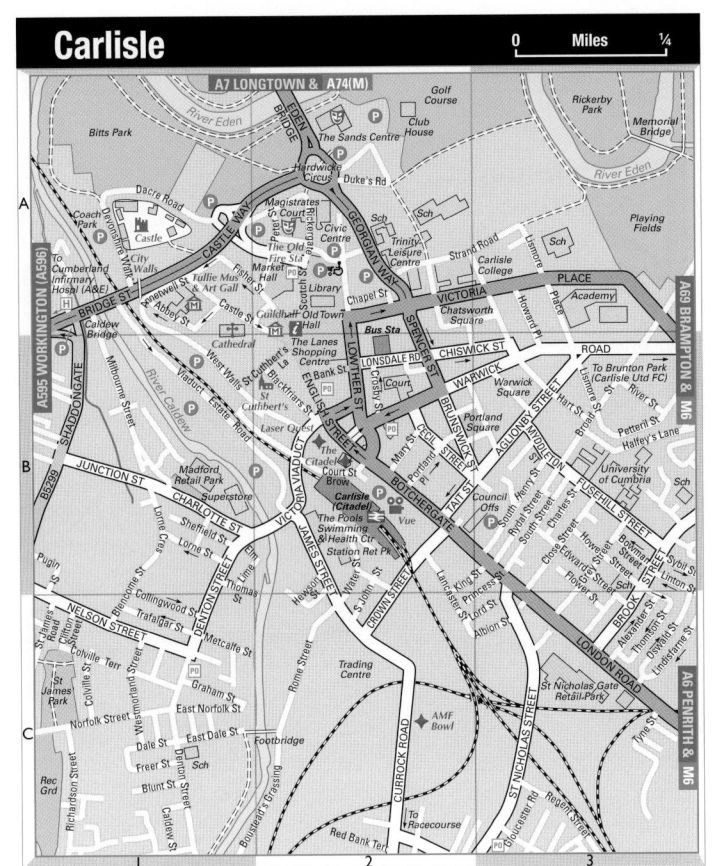

Chelmsford

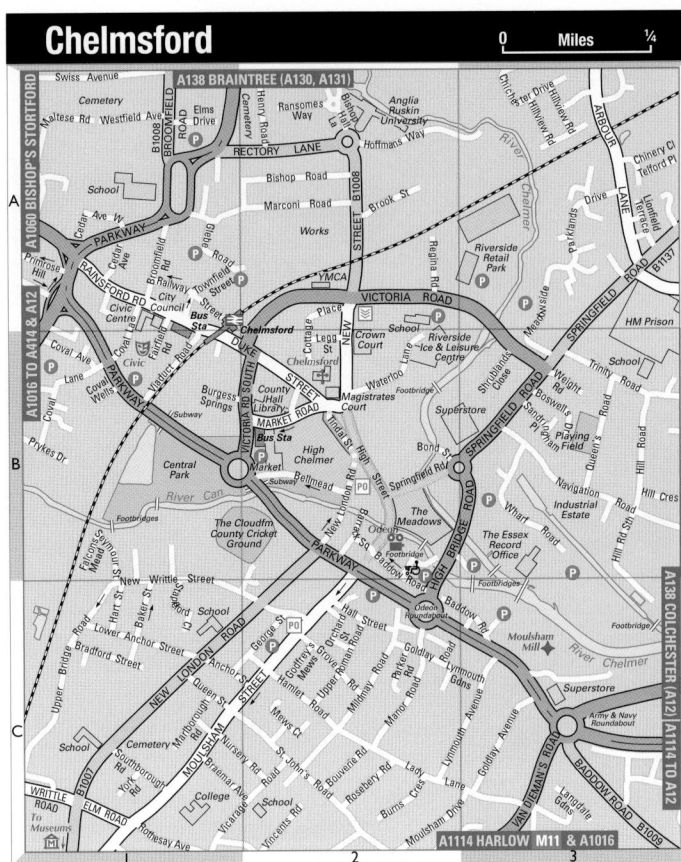

Cheltenham

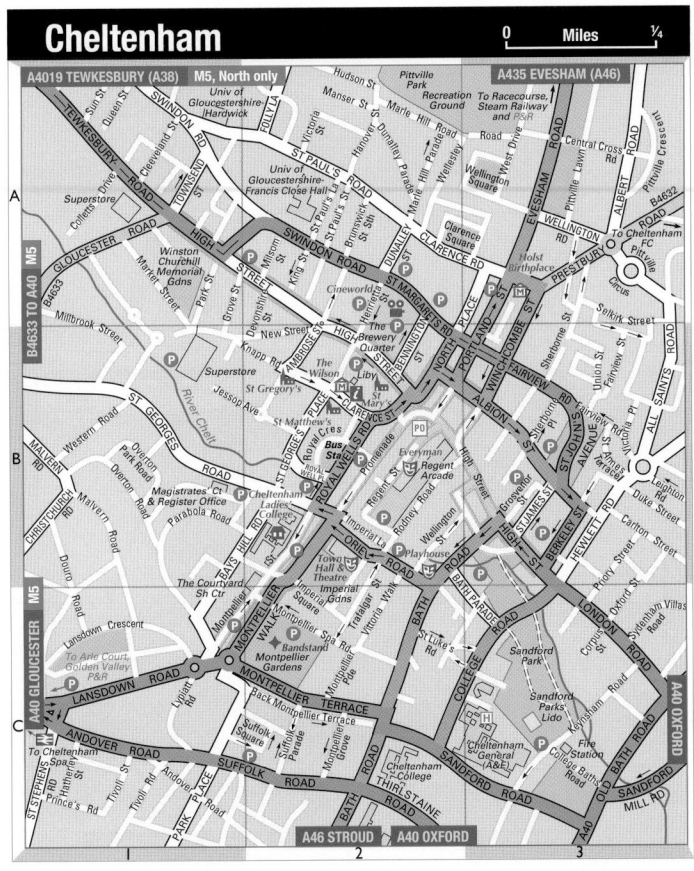

Chester

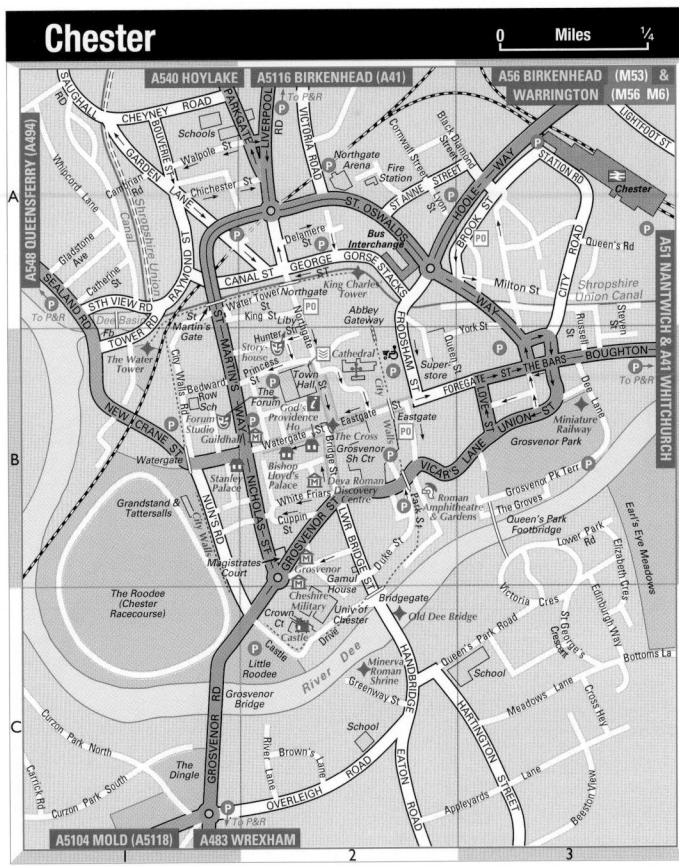

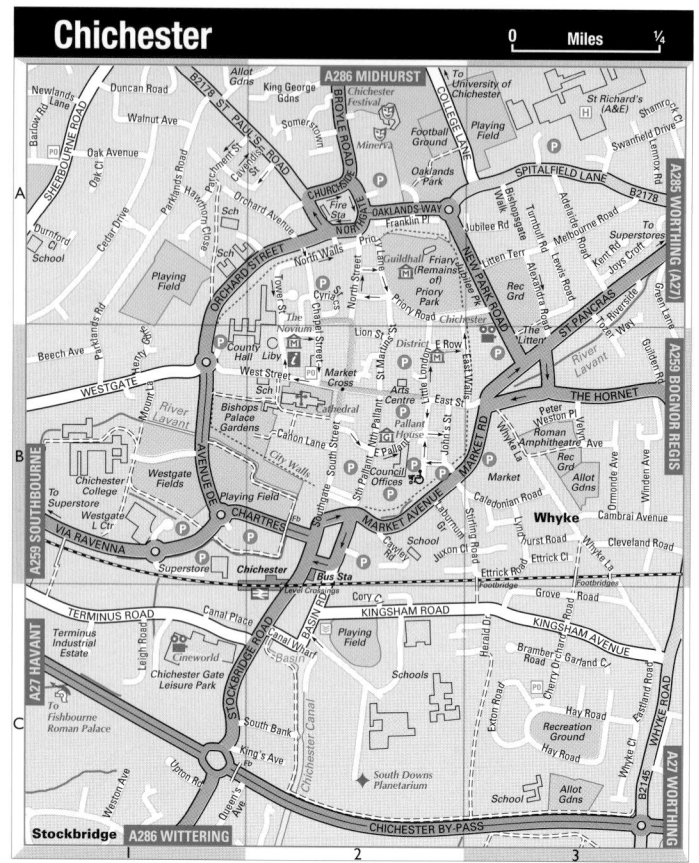

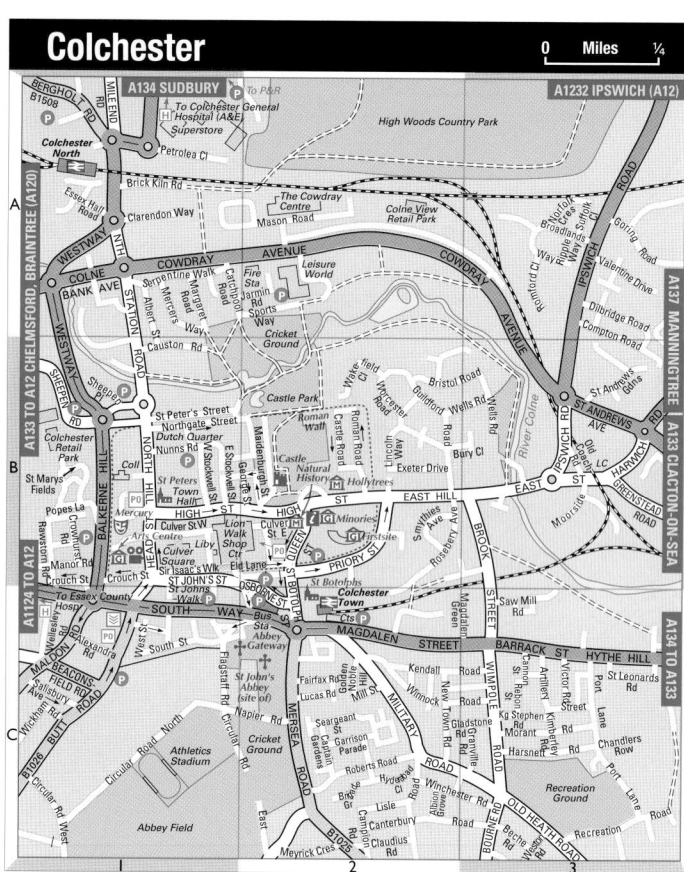

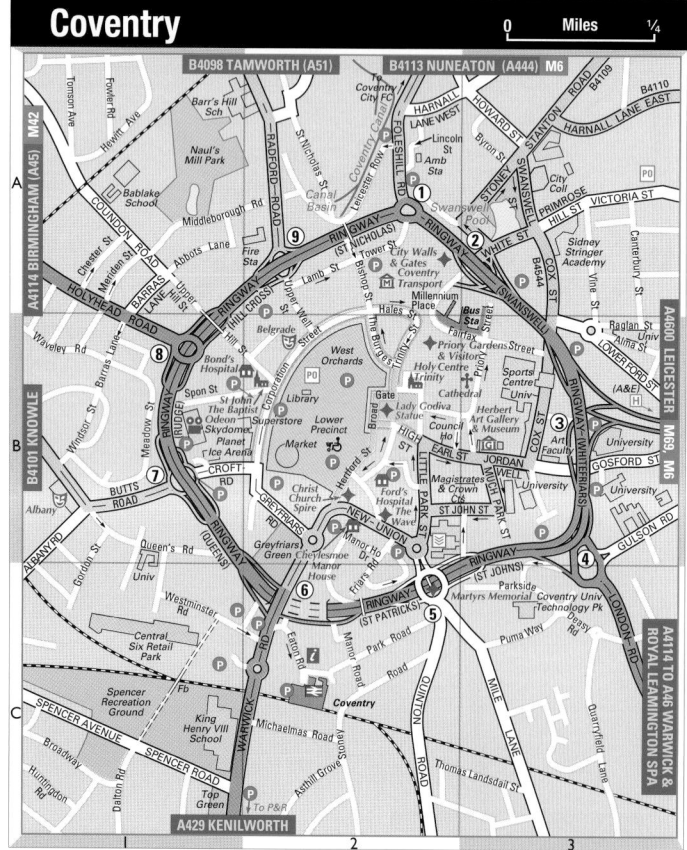

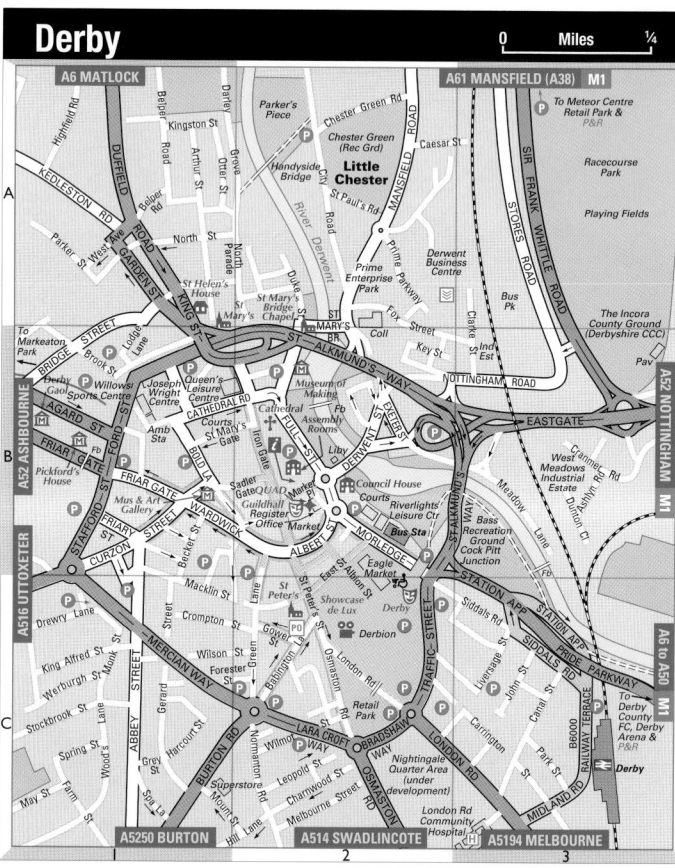

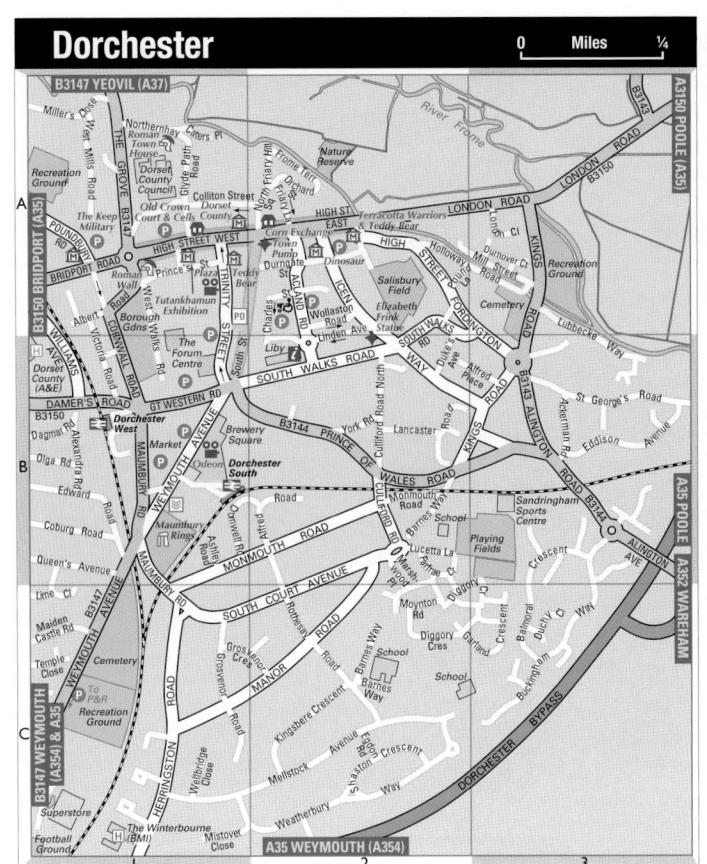

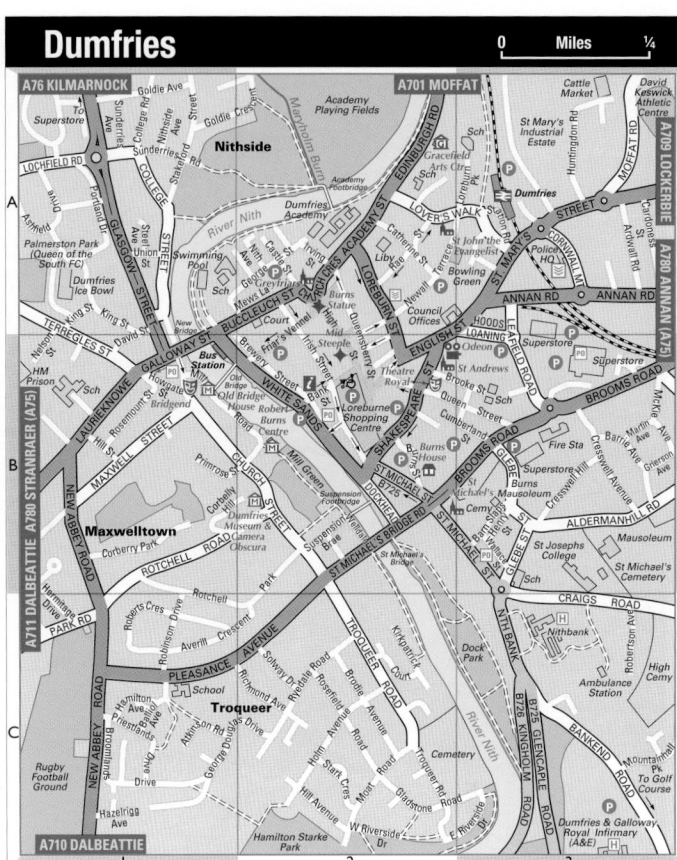

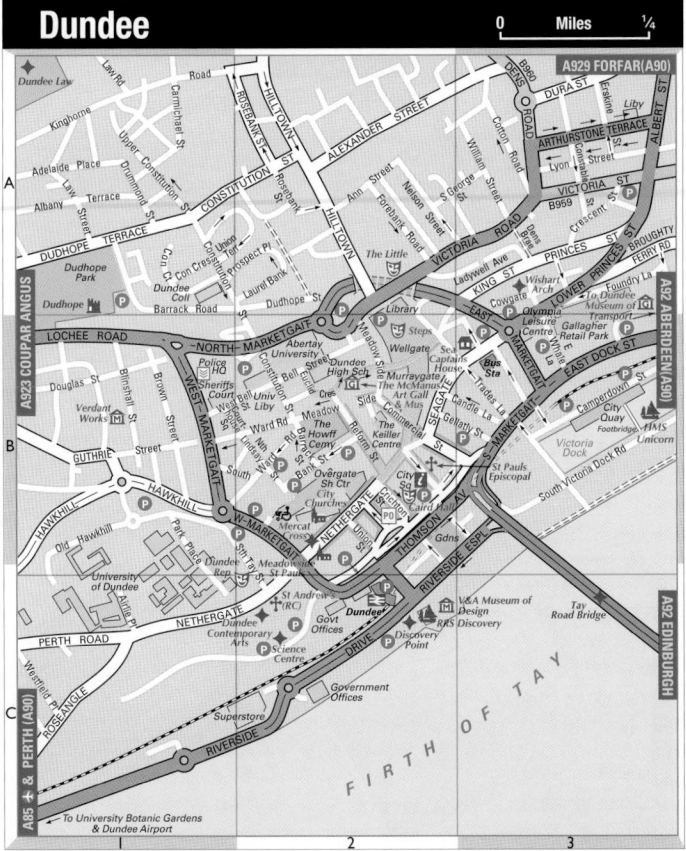

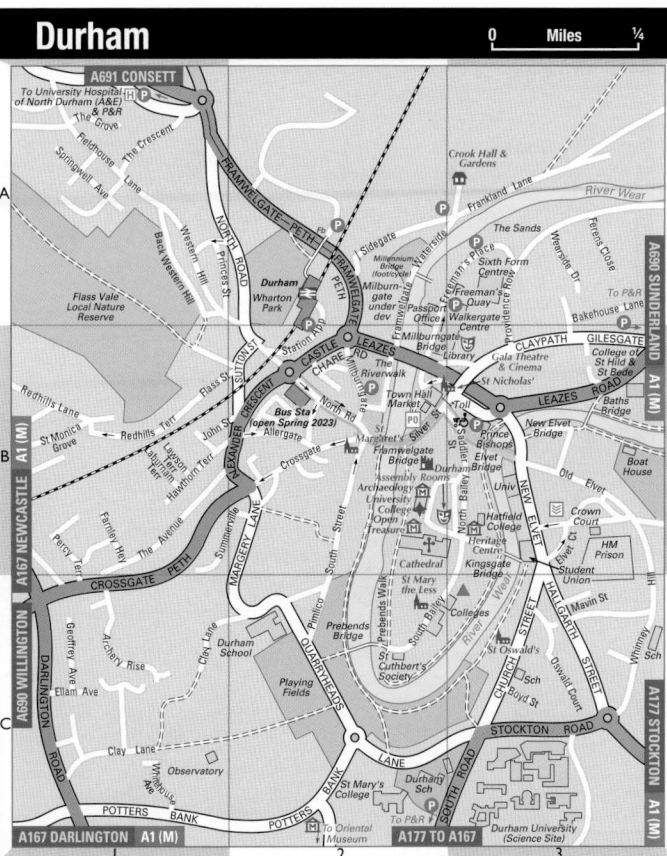

Edinburgh

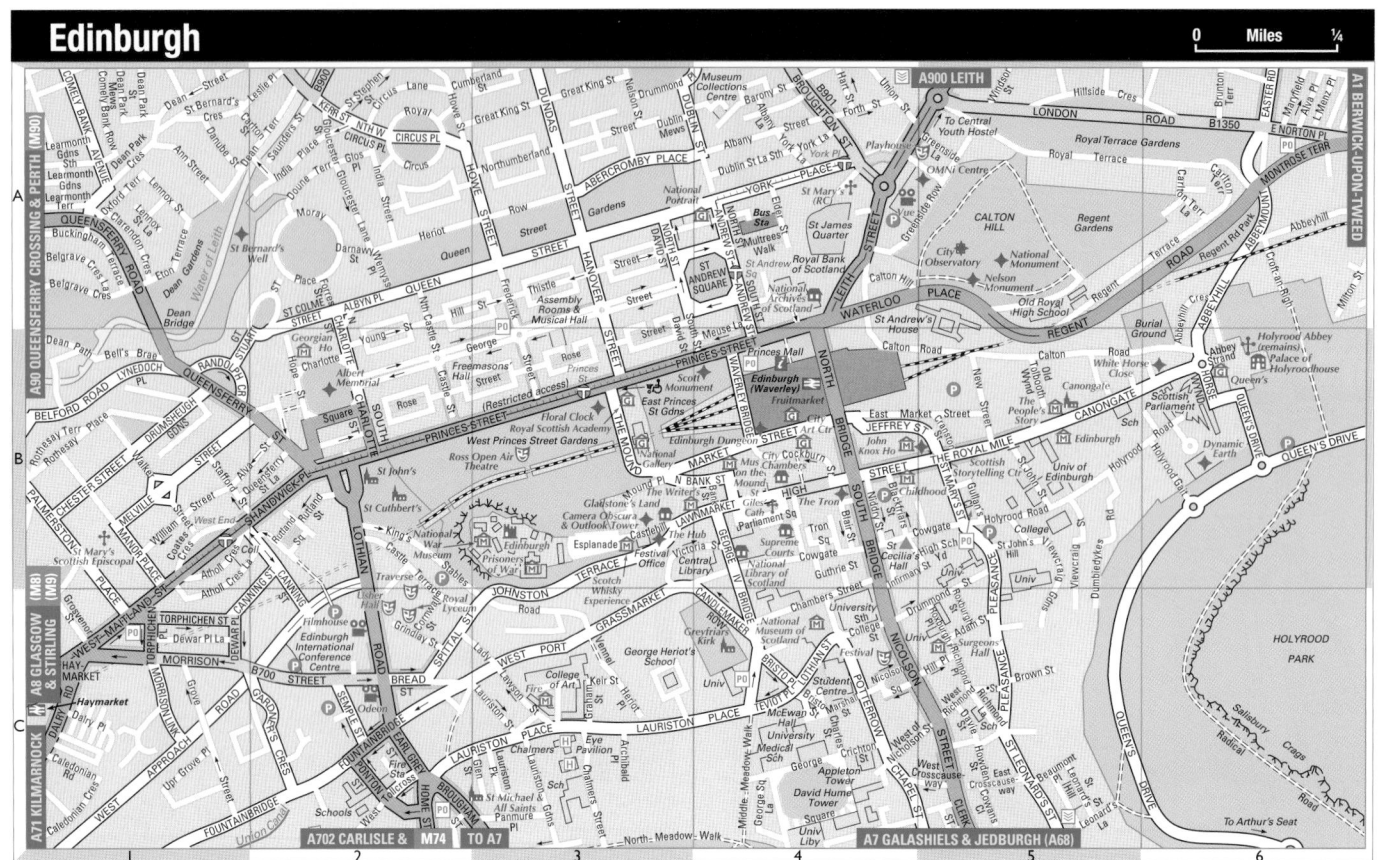

Exeter

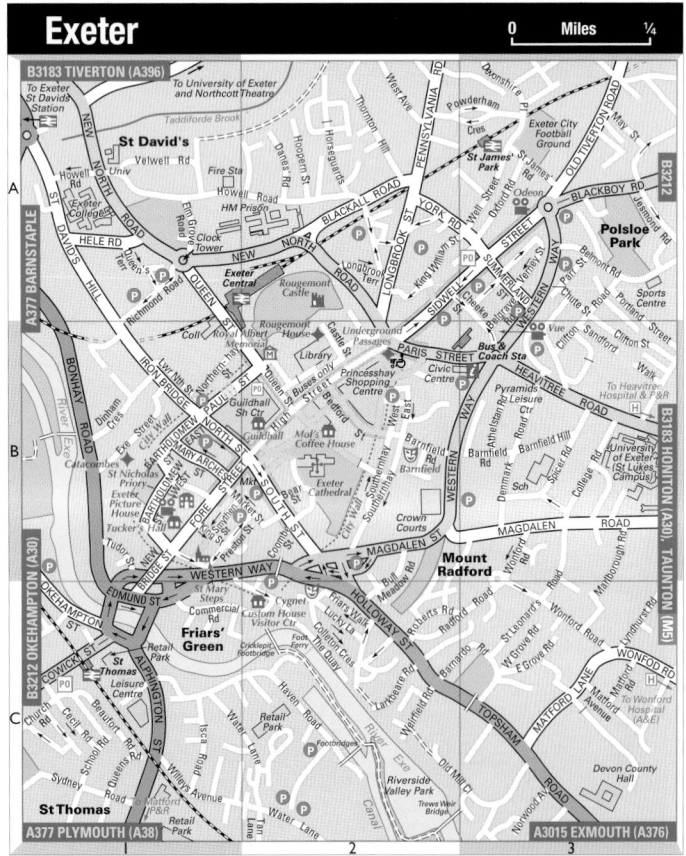

Gloucester

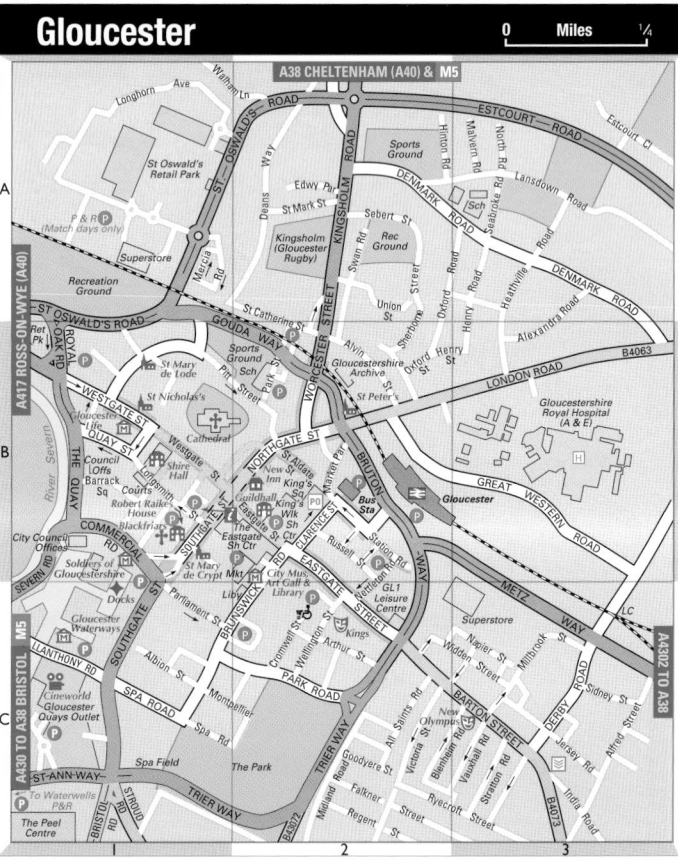

Glasgow

0 Miles ¼

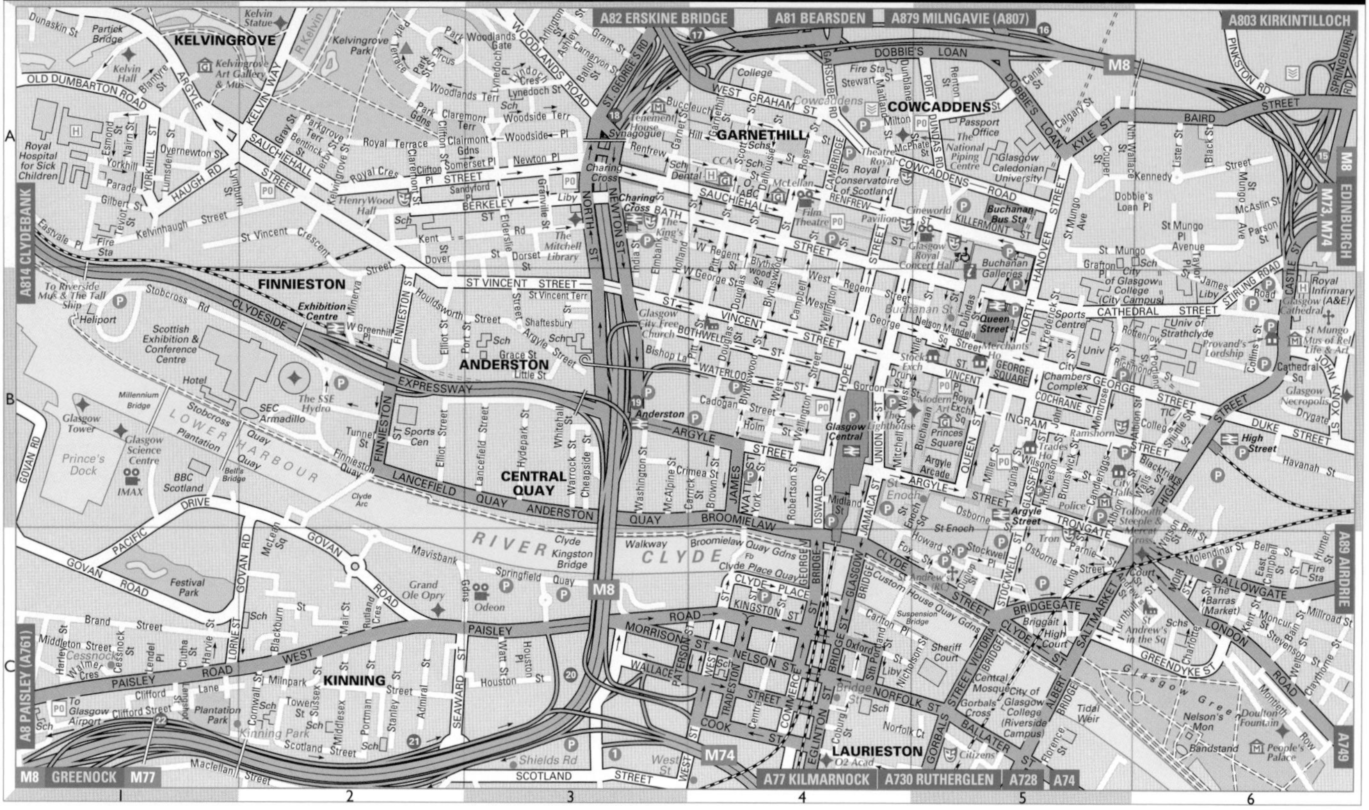

Grimsby

0 Miles ¼

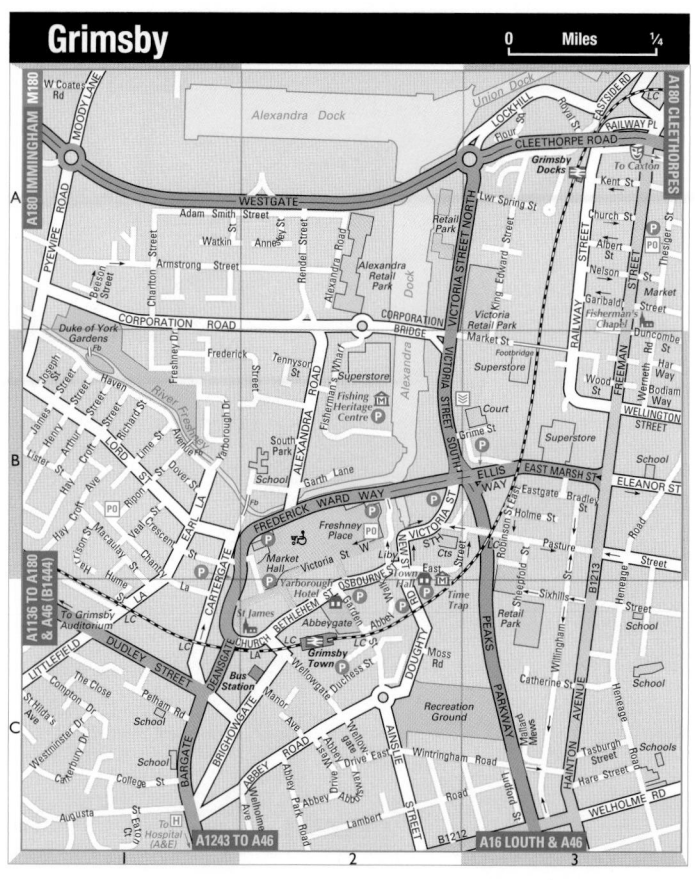

Harrogate

0 Miles ¼

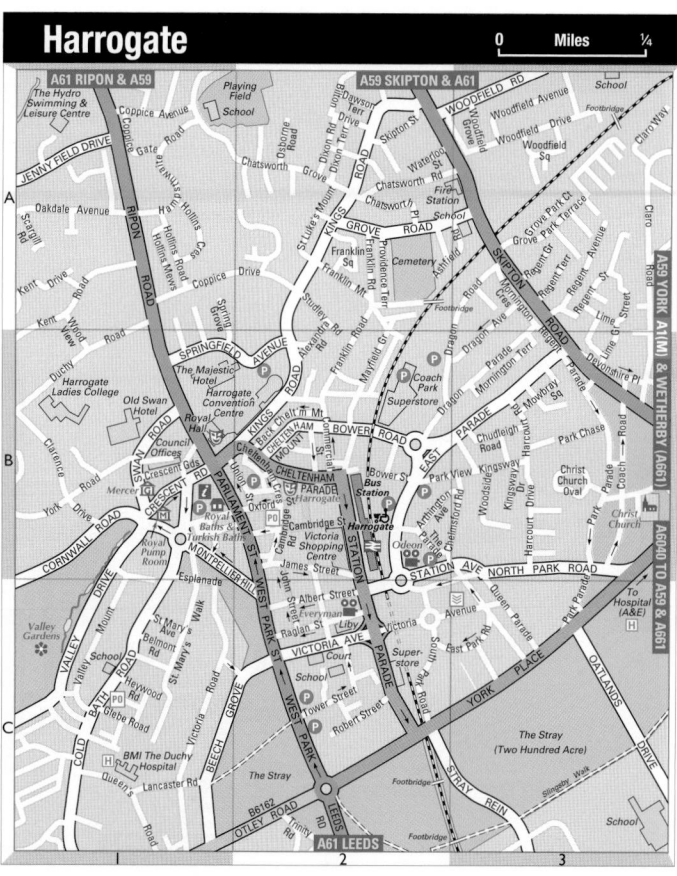

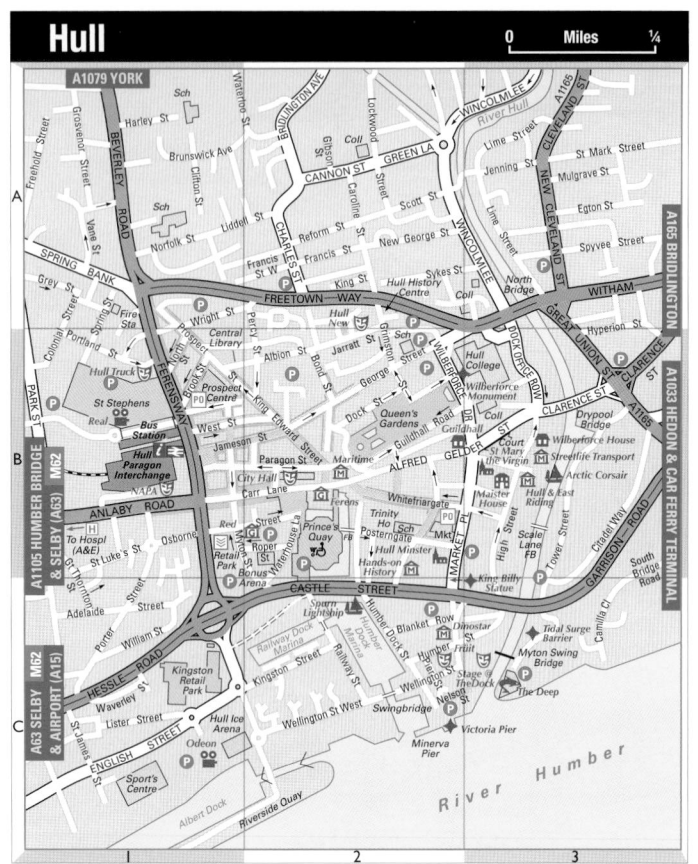

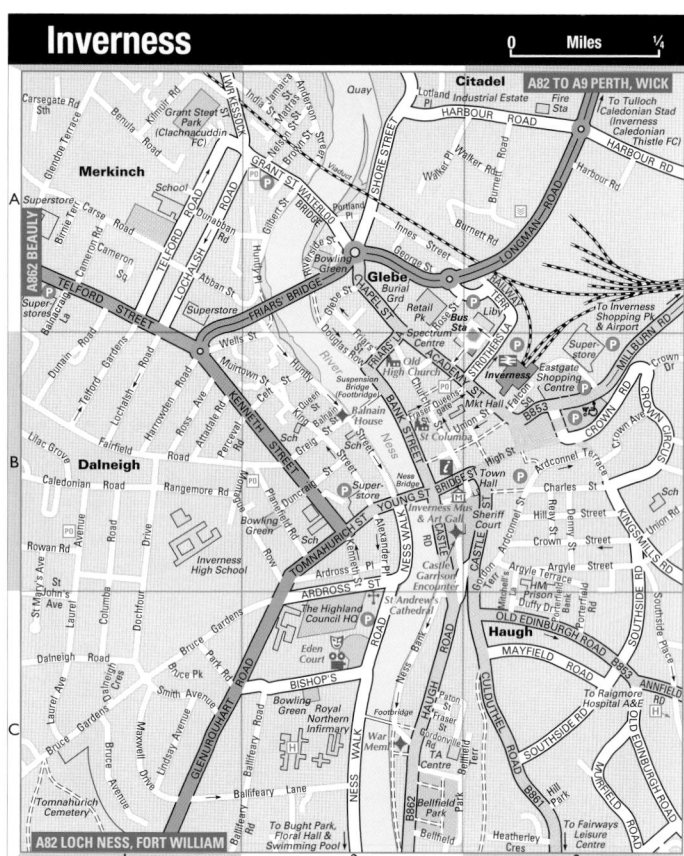

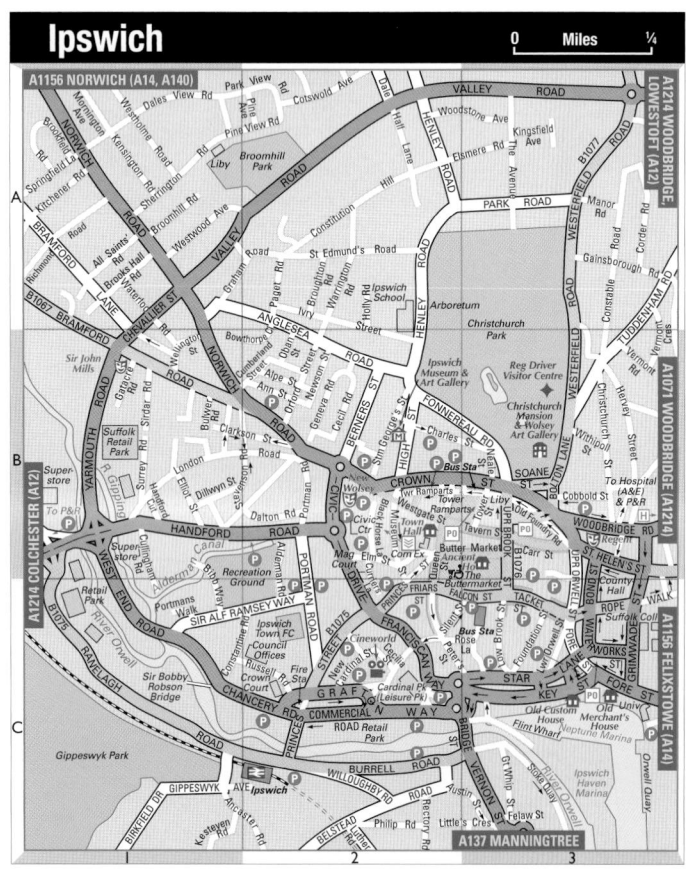

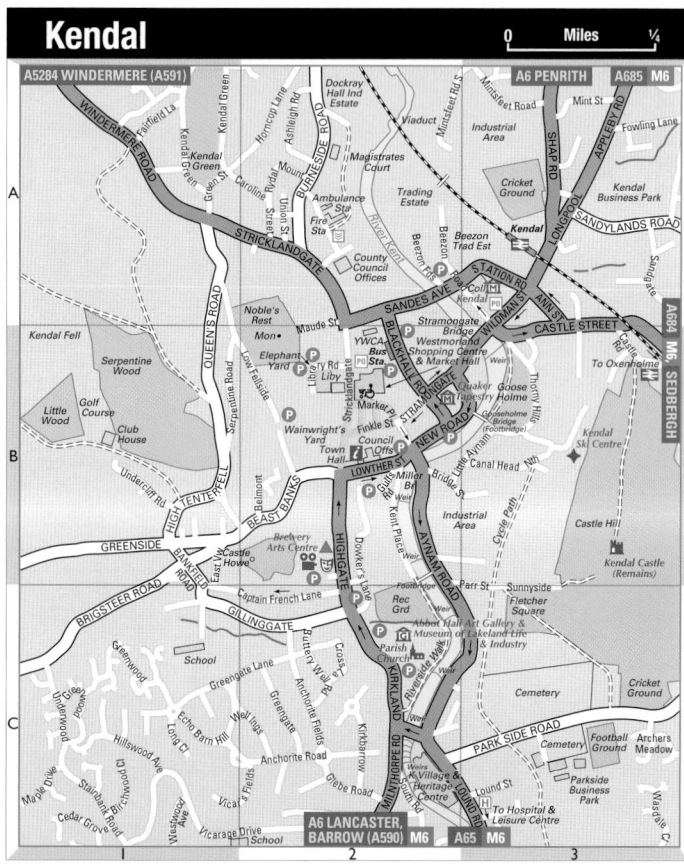

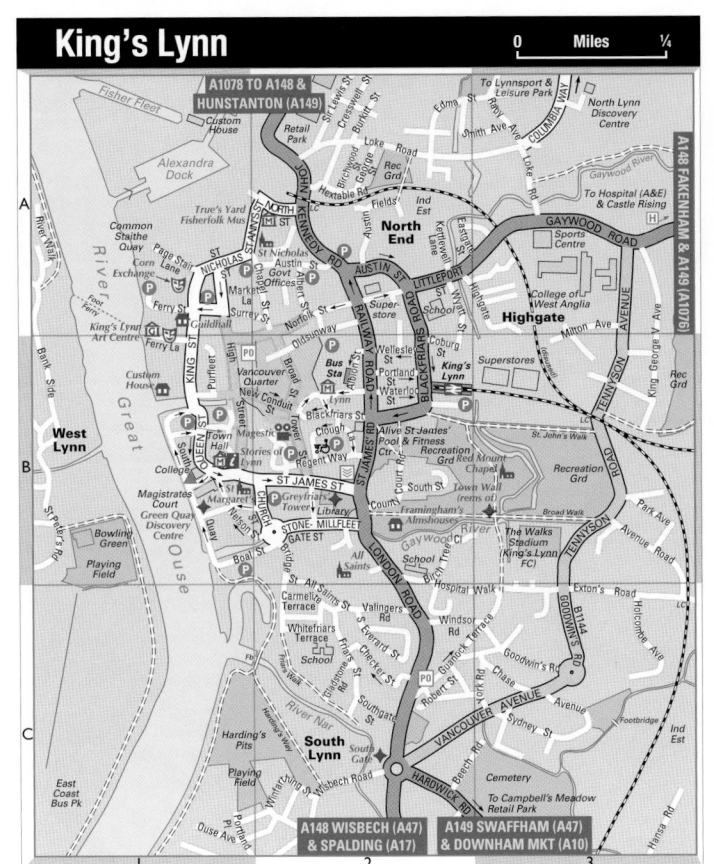

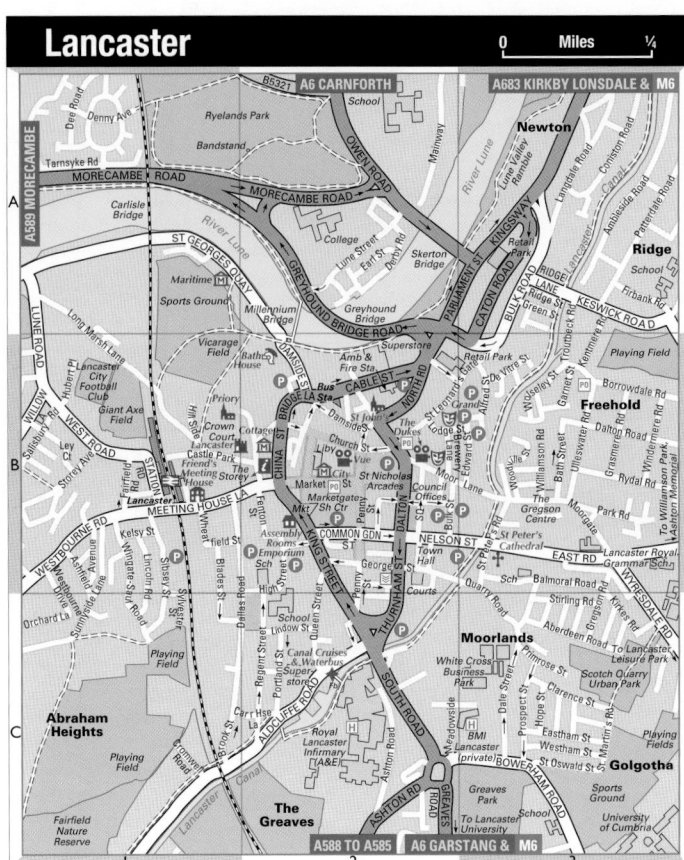

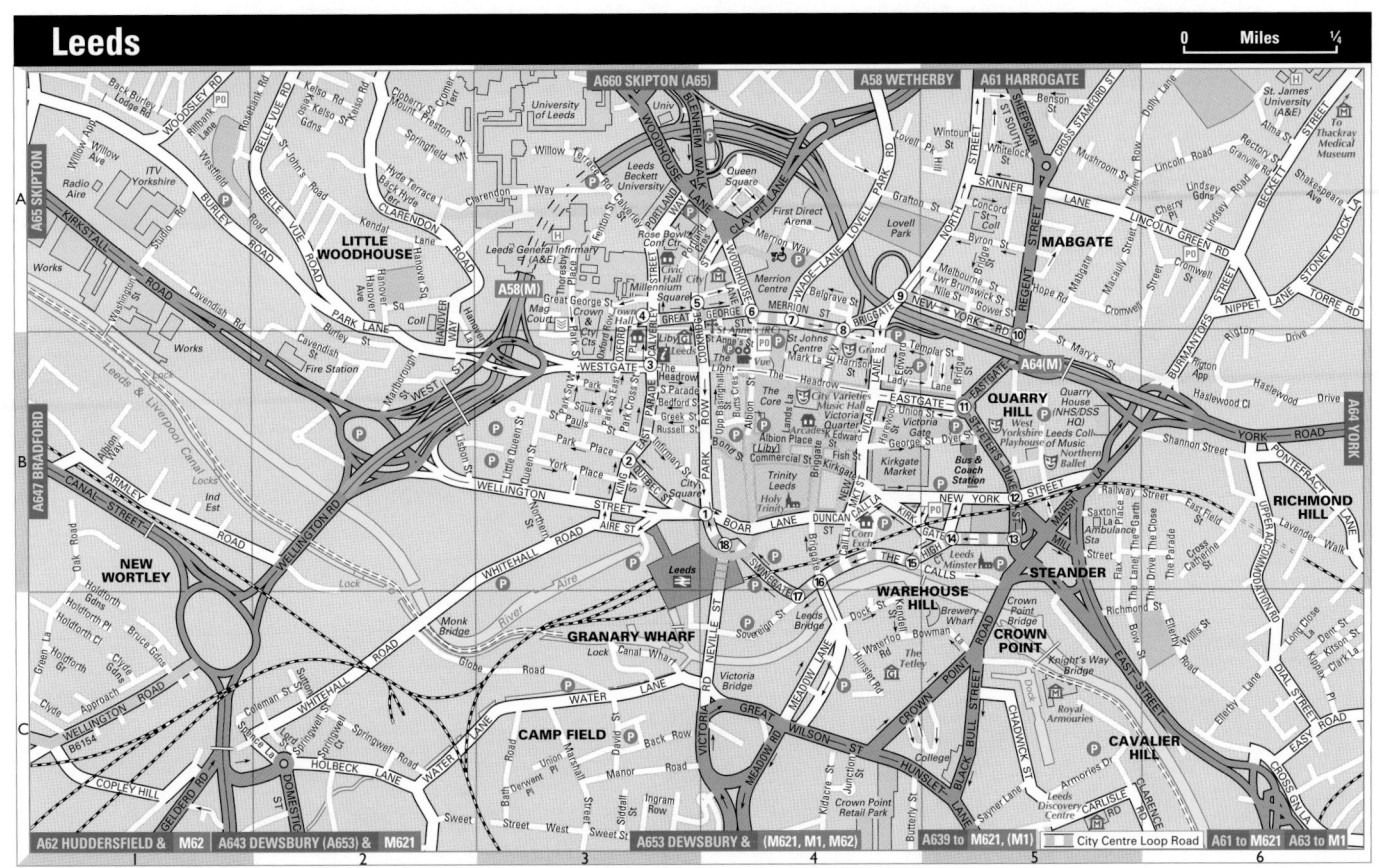

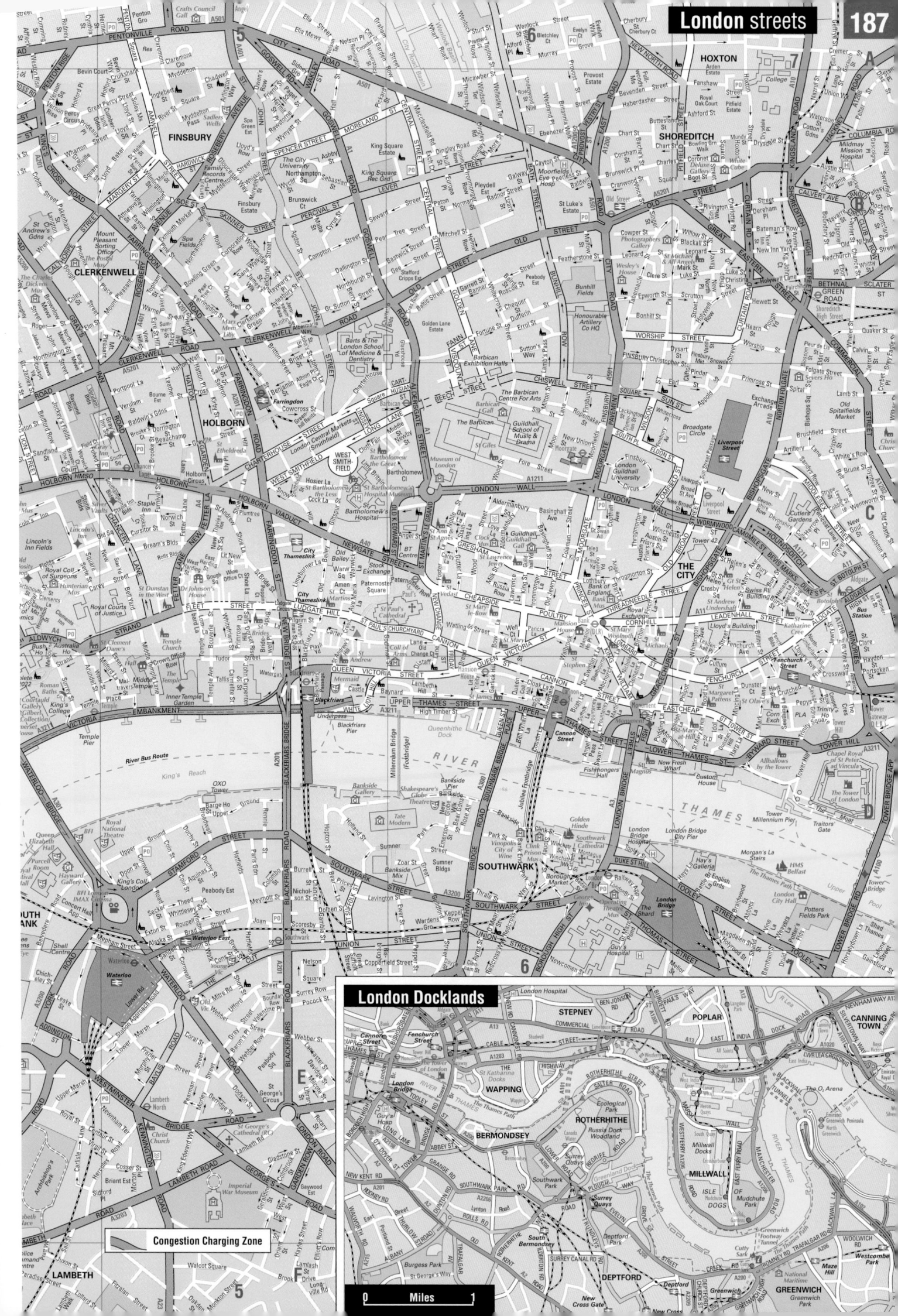

London Docklands

Congestion Charging Zone

0   Miles   1

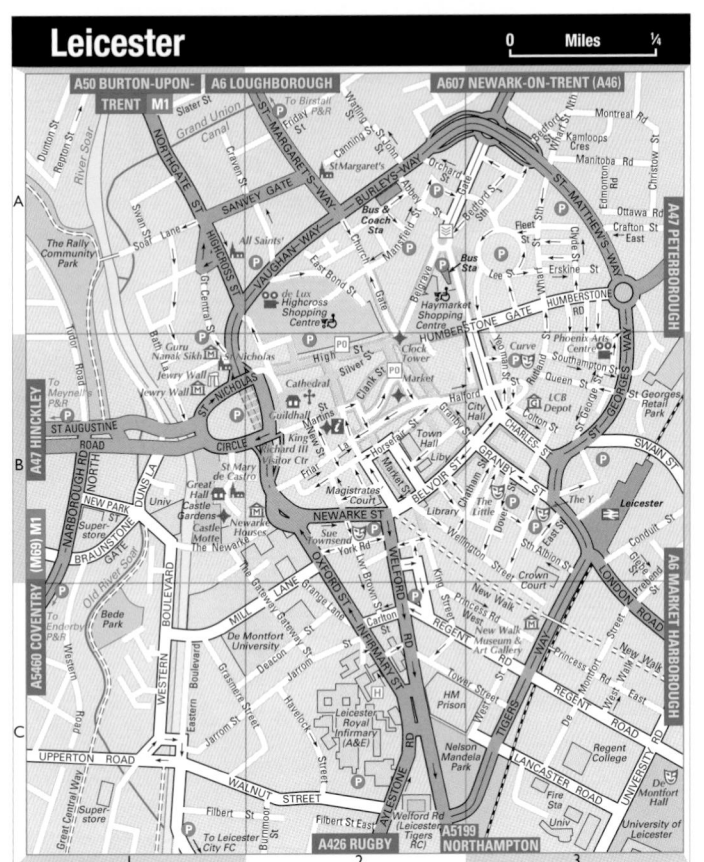

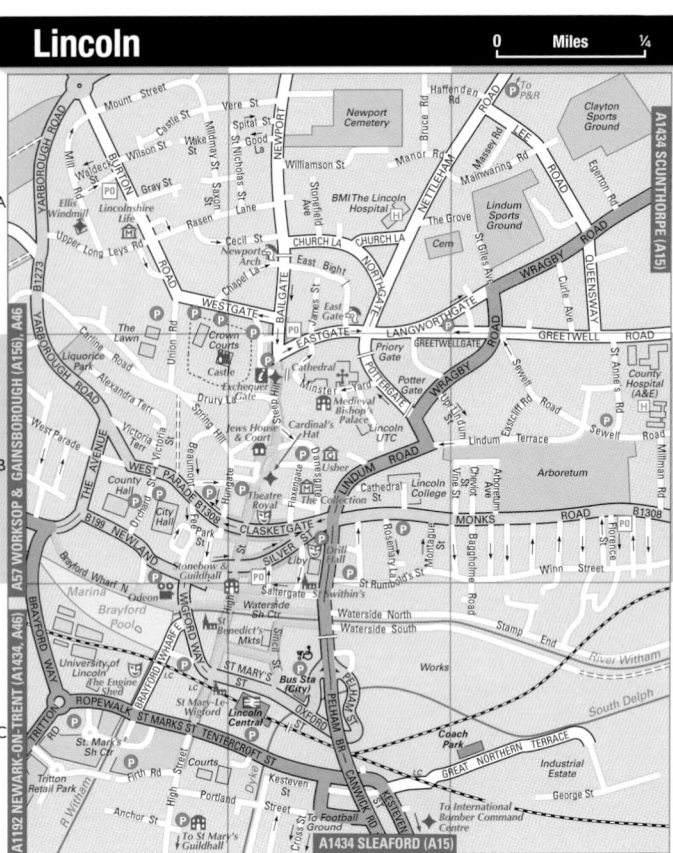

Llandudno
0   Miles   ¼

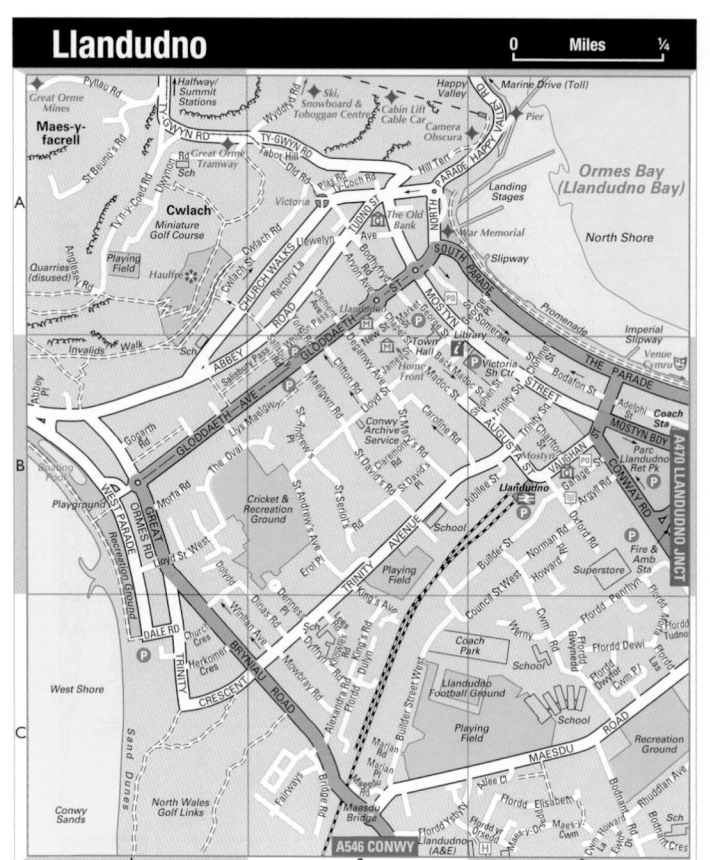

Llanelli
0   Miles   ¼

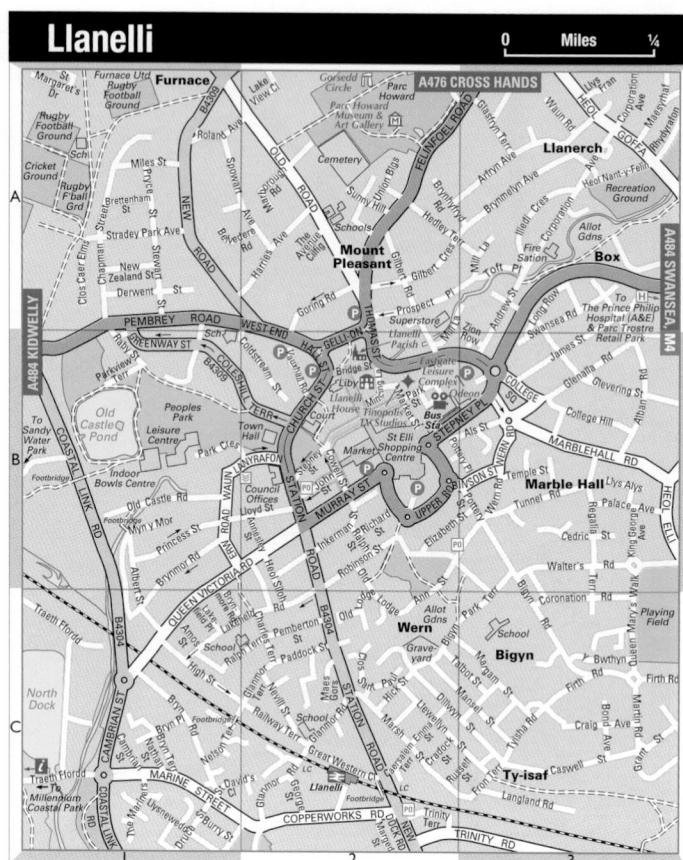

Luton
0   Miles   ¼

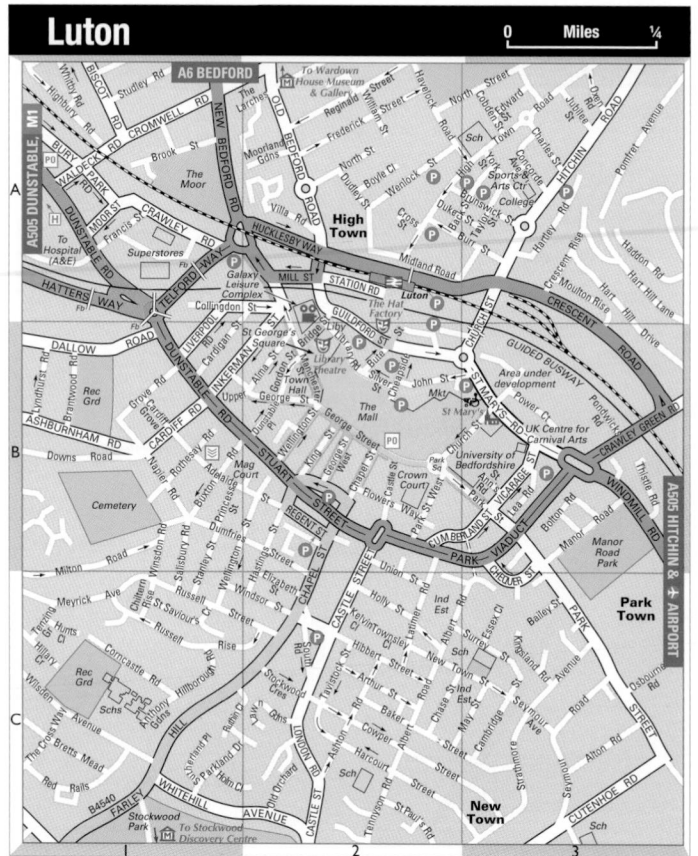

Macclesfield
0   Miles   ¼

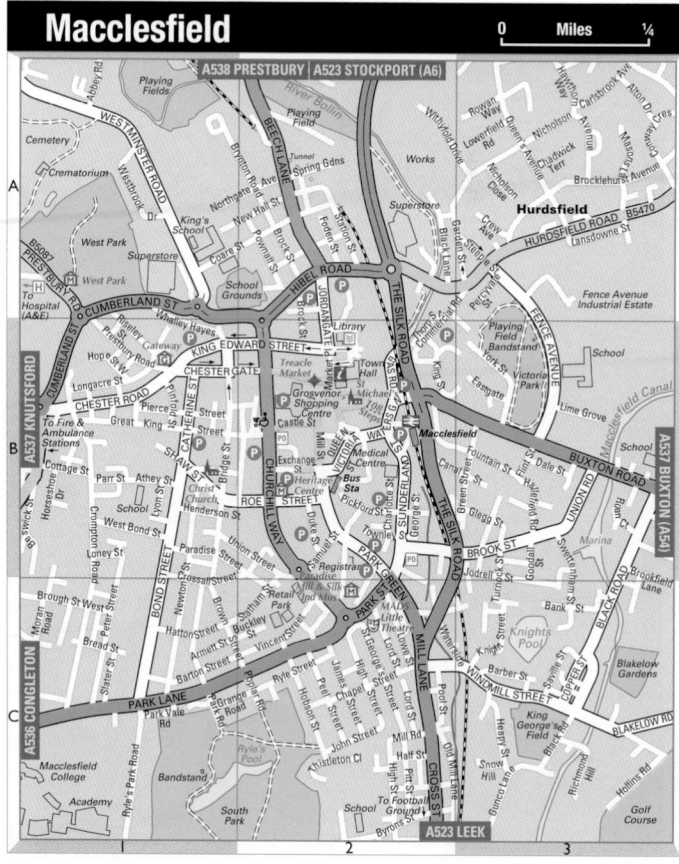

Manchester

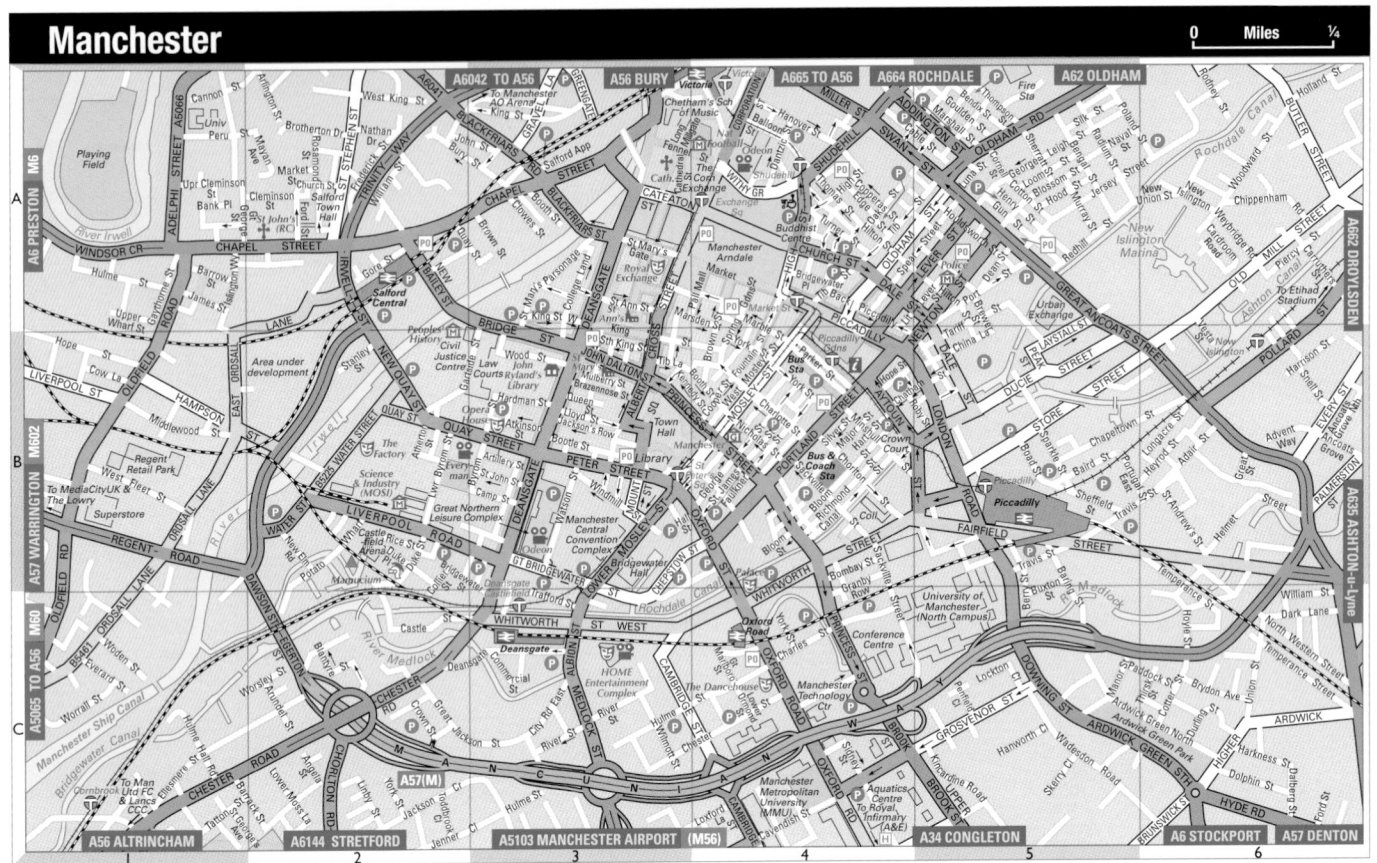

Maidstone

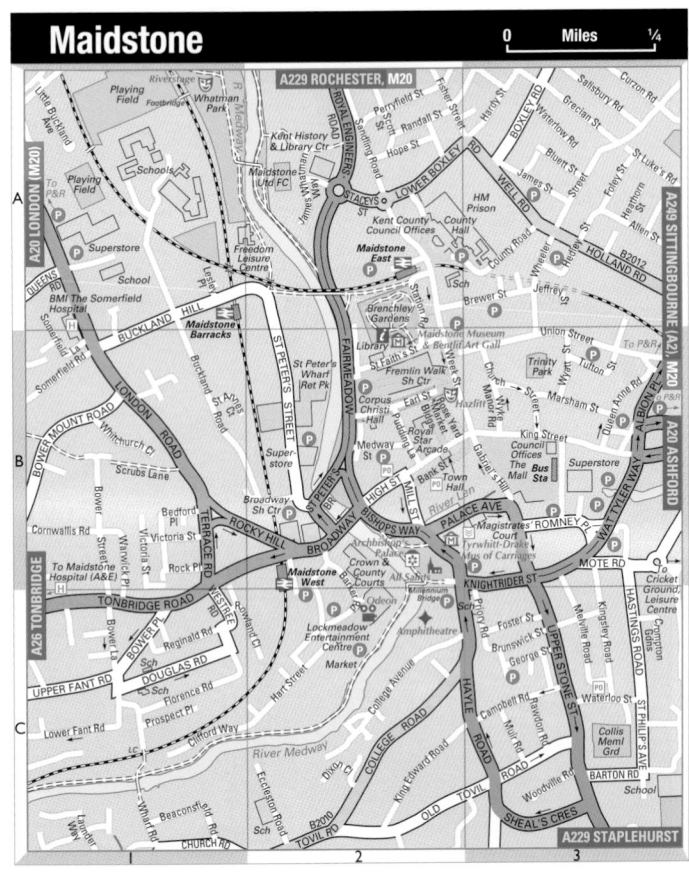

Merthyr Tydfil / Merthyr Tudful

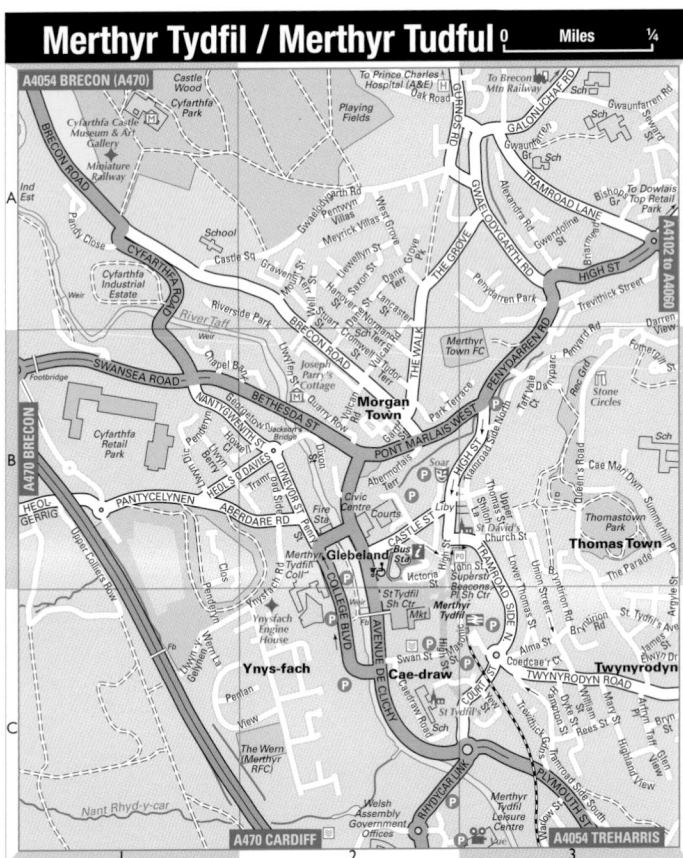

Middlesbrough

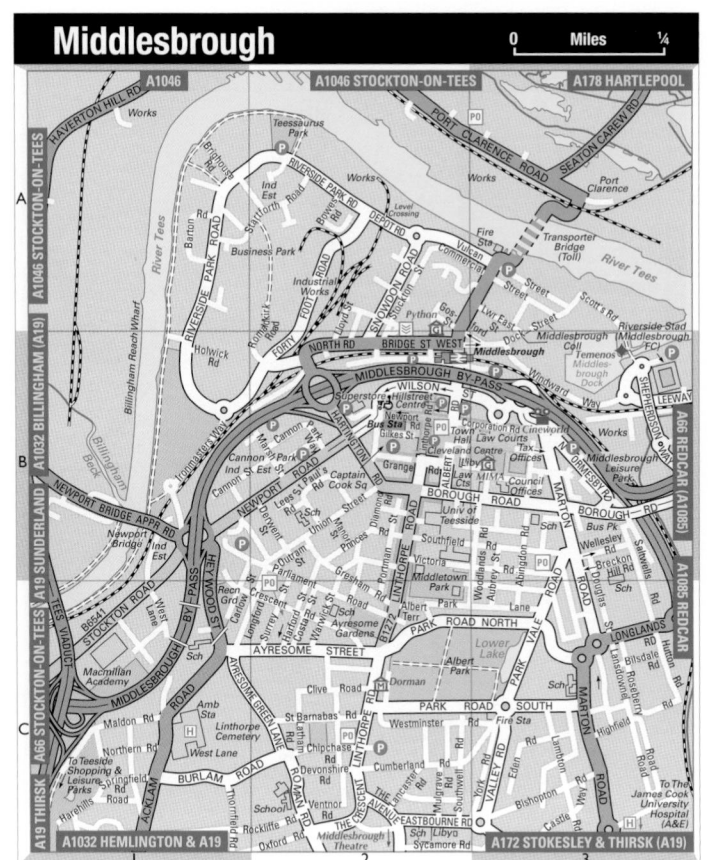

Milton Keynes

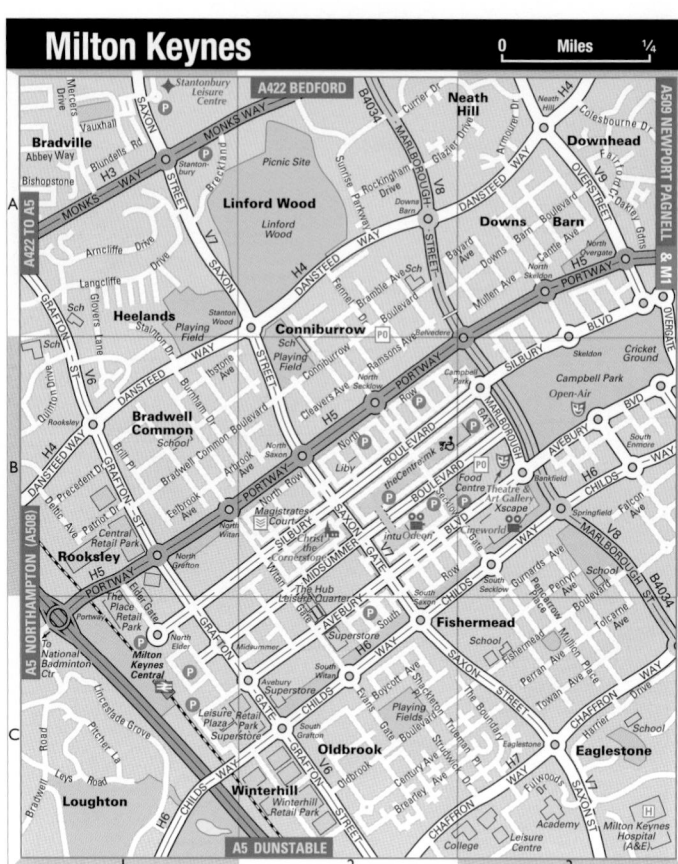

Newcastle upon Tyne

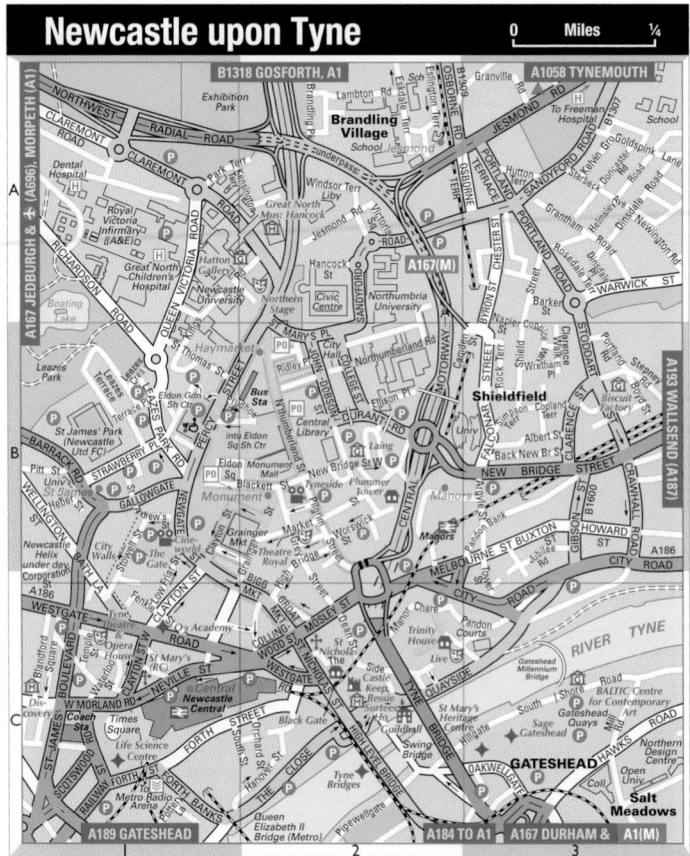

Newport / Casnewydd

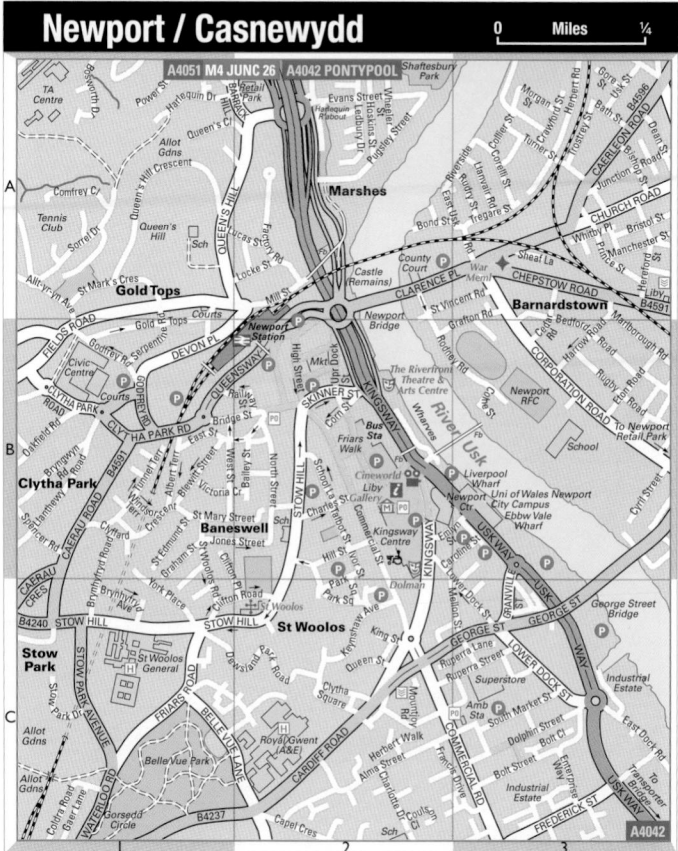

Newquay

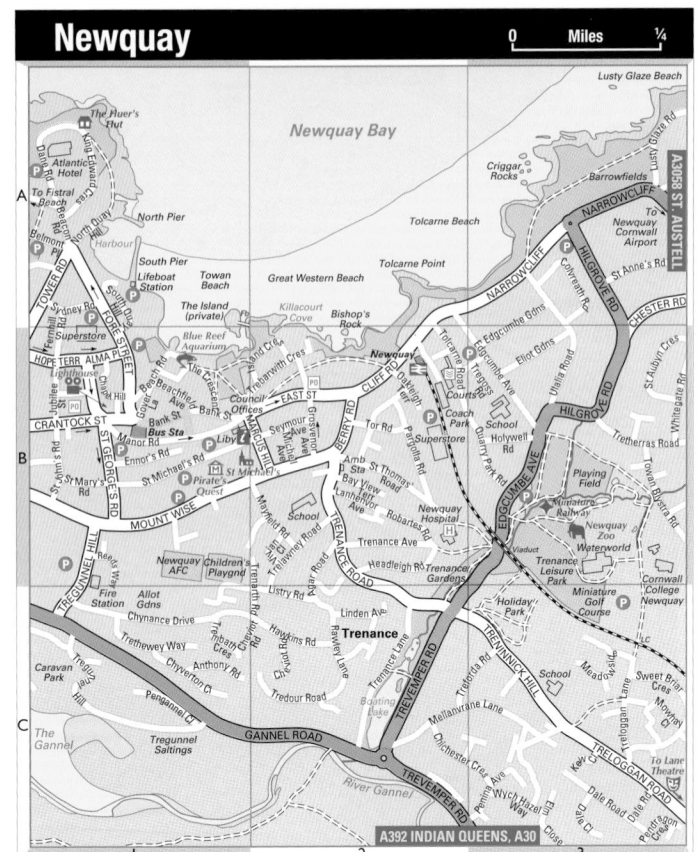

Northampton

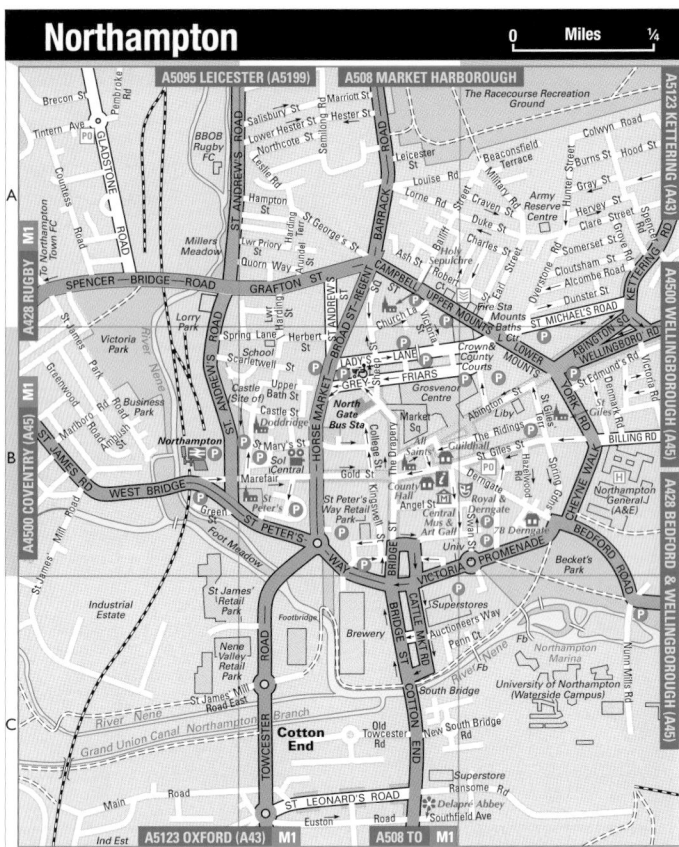

Norwich

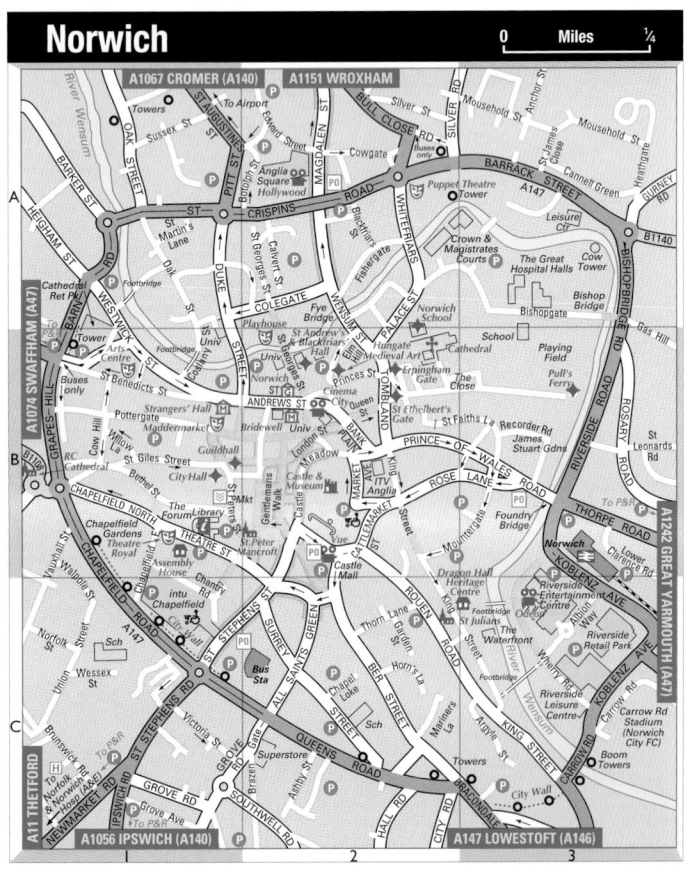

Nottingham

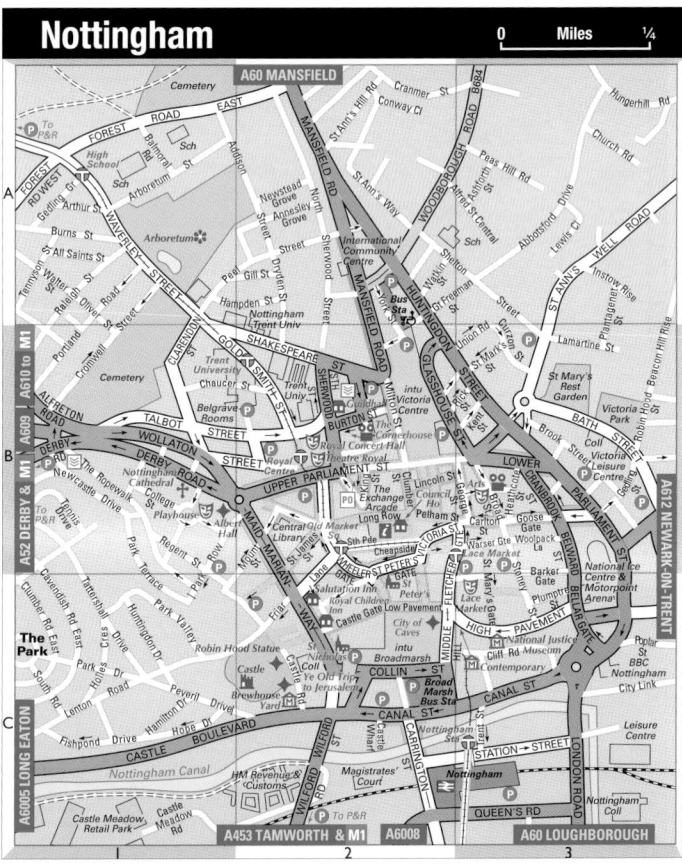

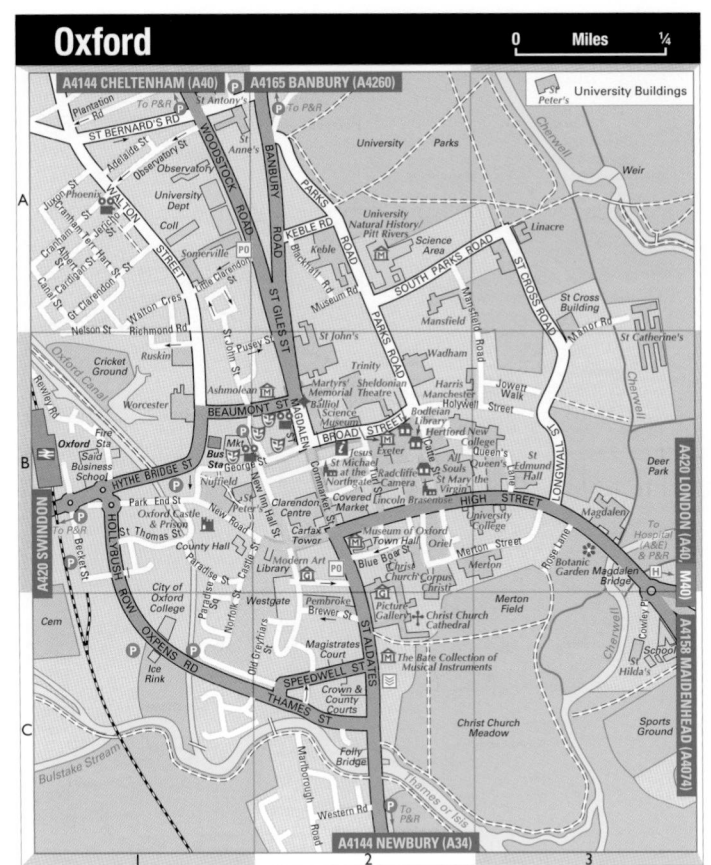

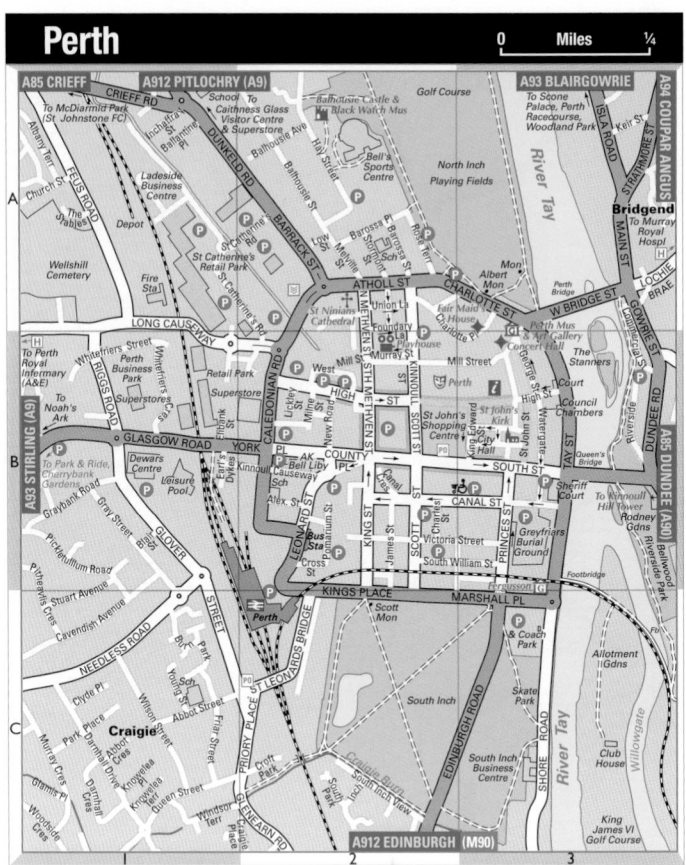

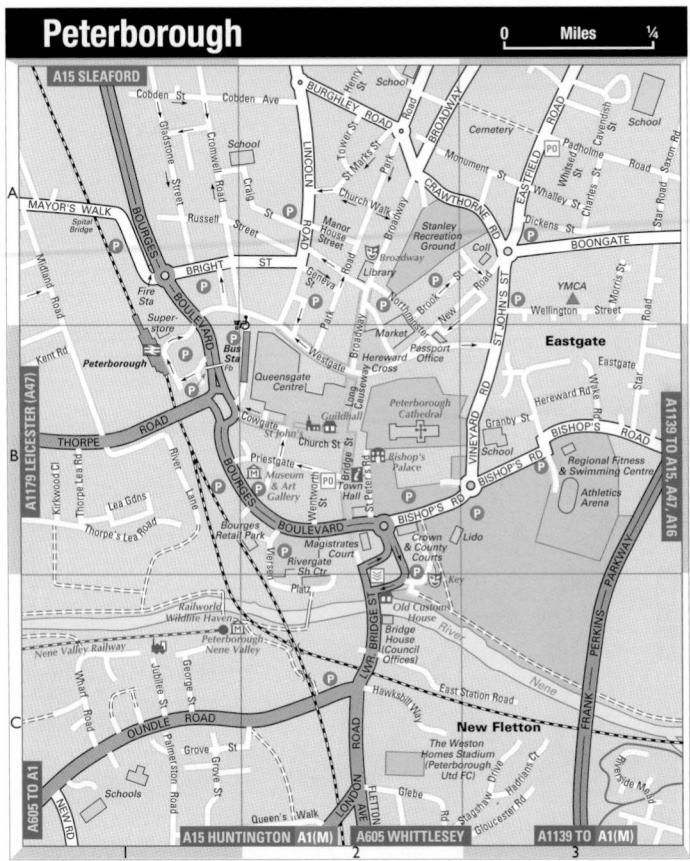

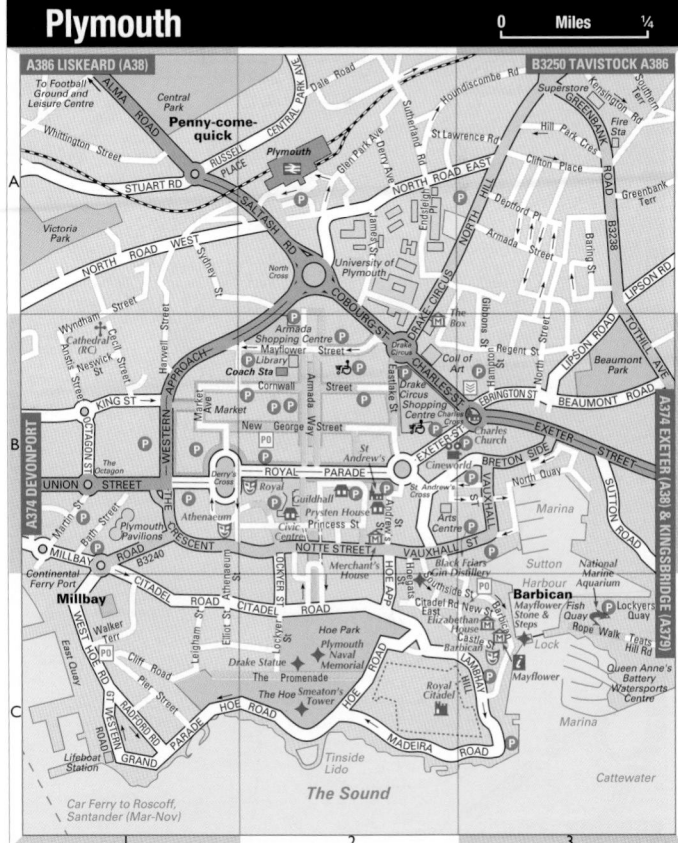

Poole

0 — Miles — ¼

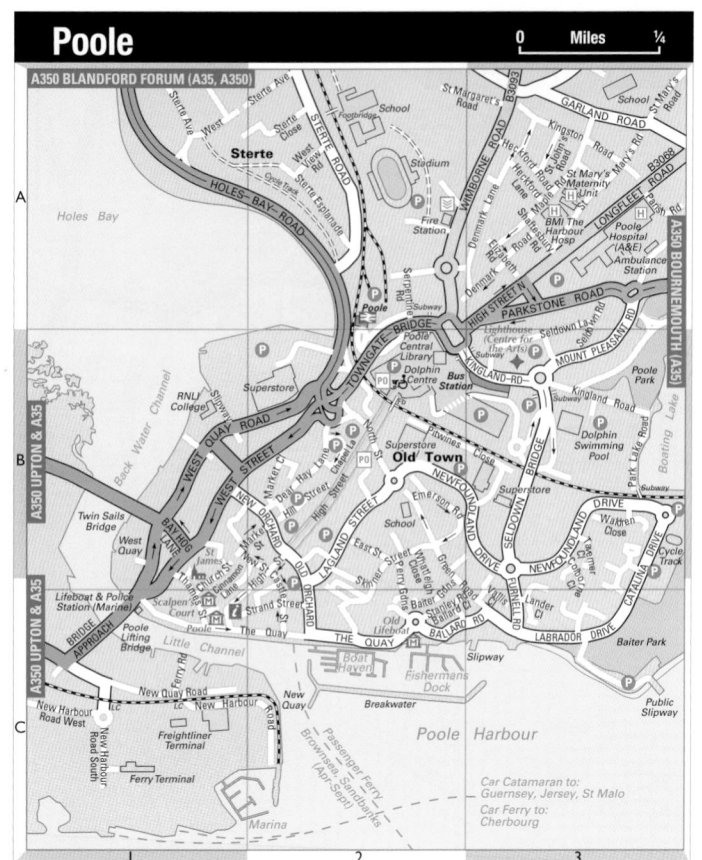

Portsmouth

0 — Miles — ¼

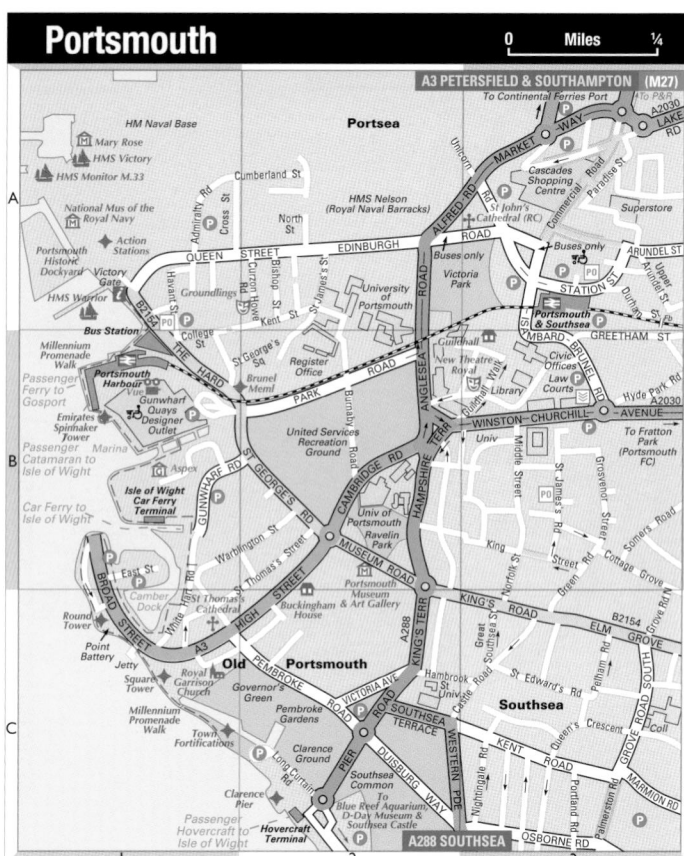

Preston

0 — Miles — ¼

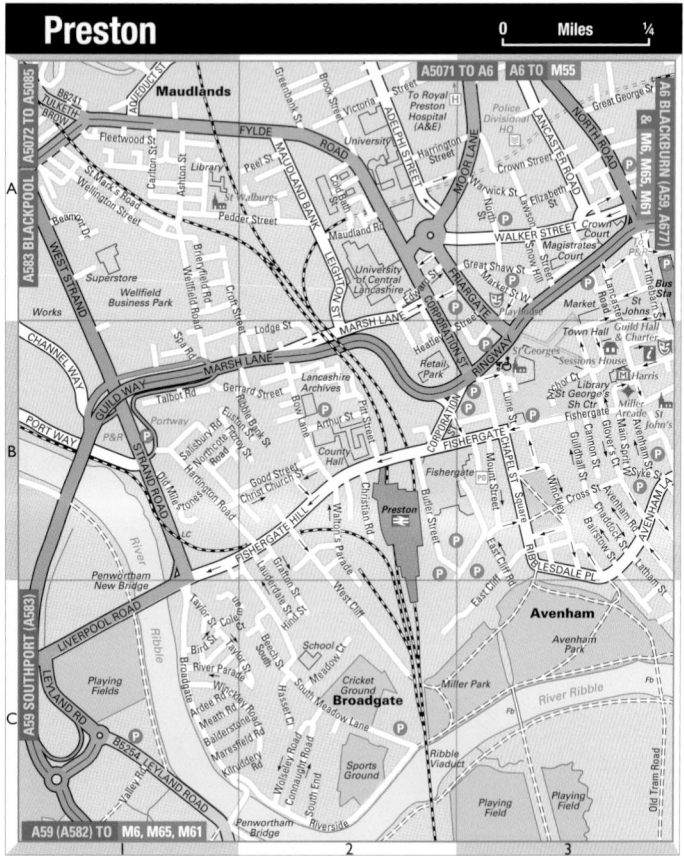

Reading

0 — Miles — ¼

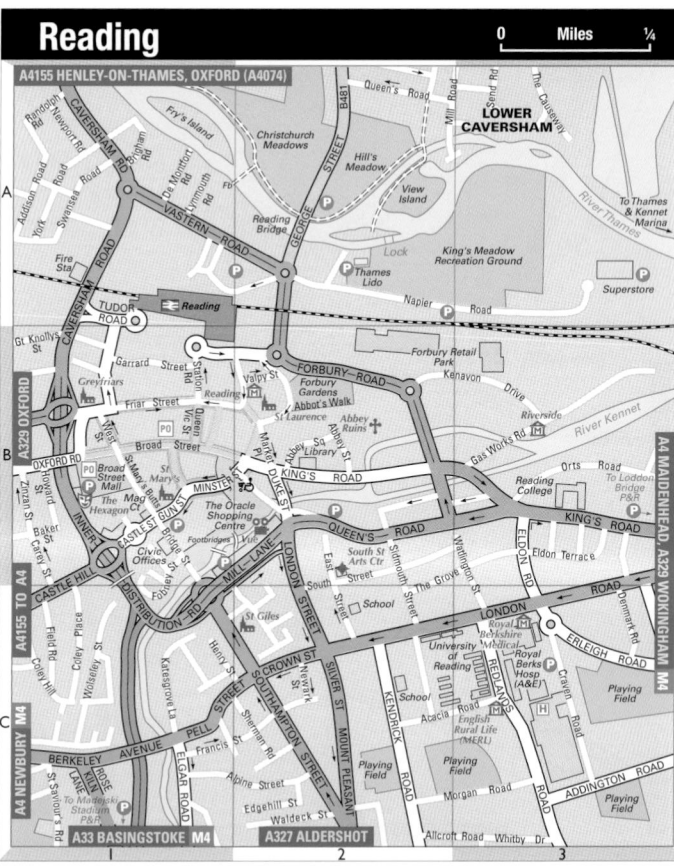

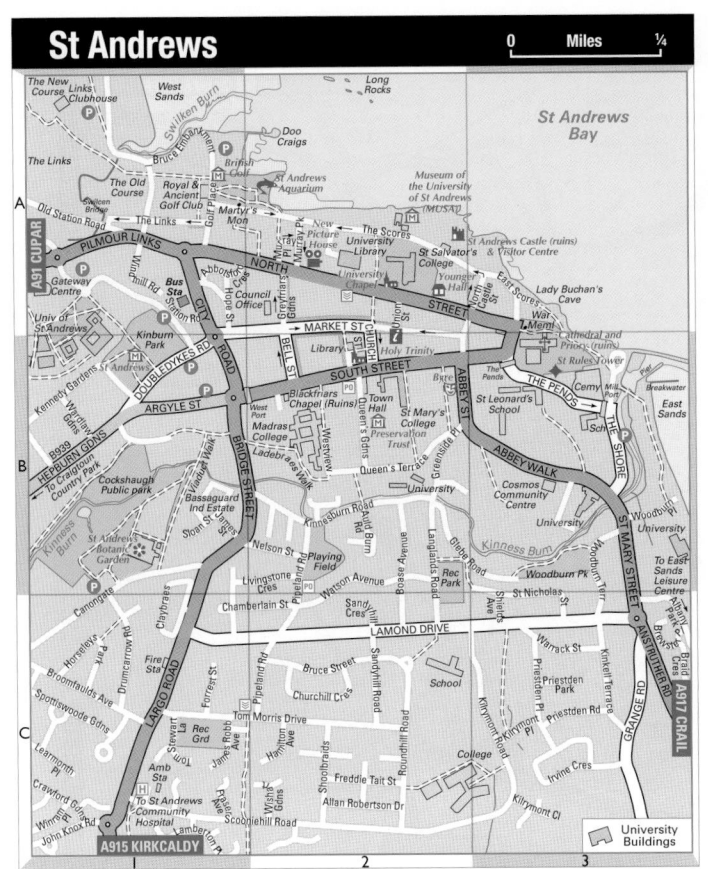

St Andrews

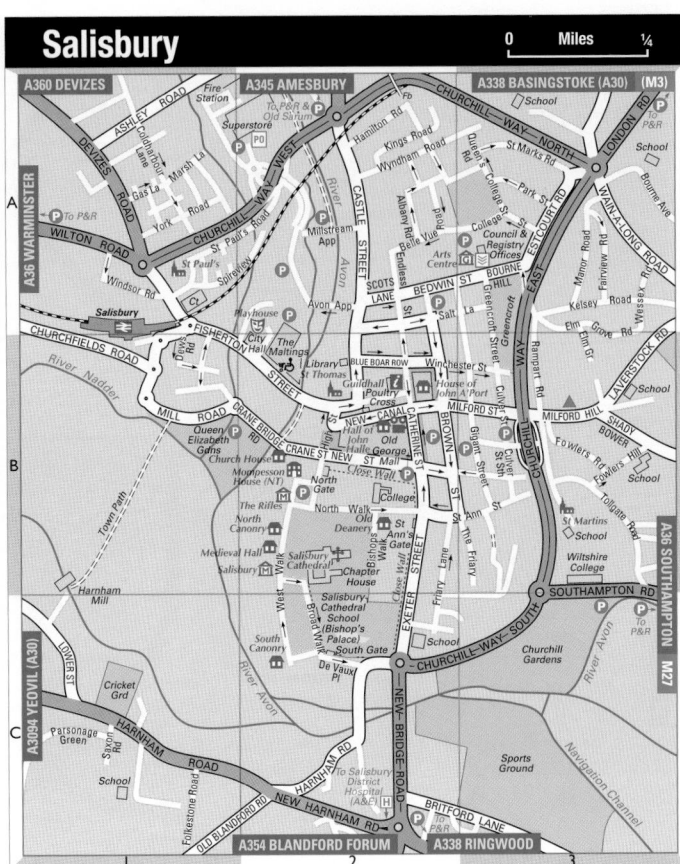

Salisbury

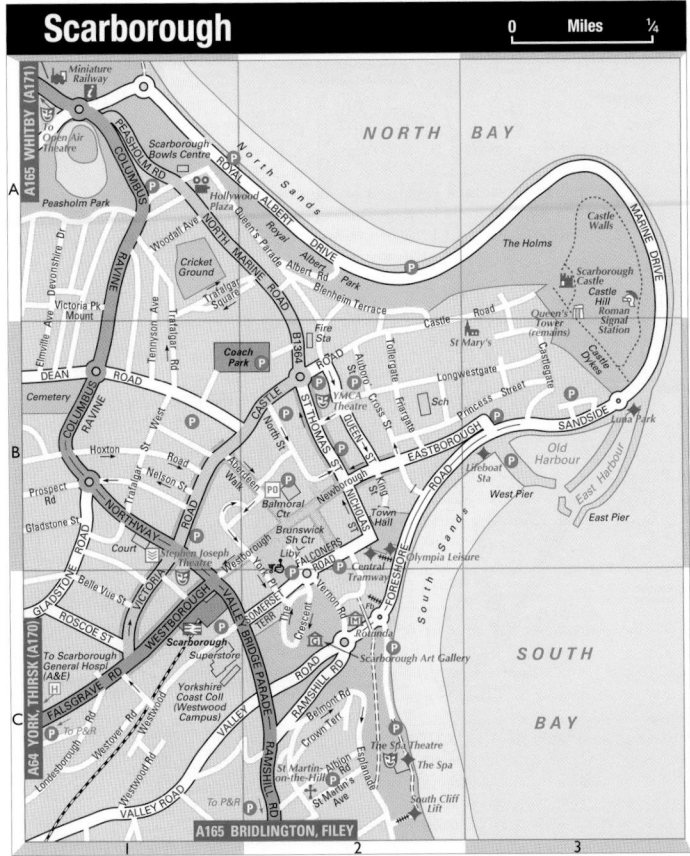

Scarborough

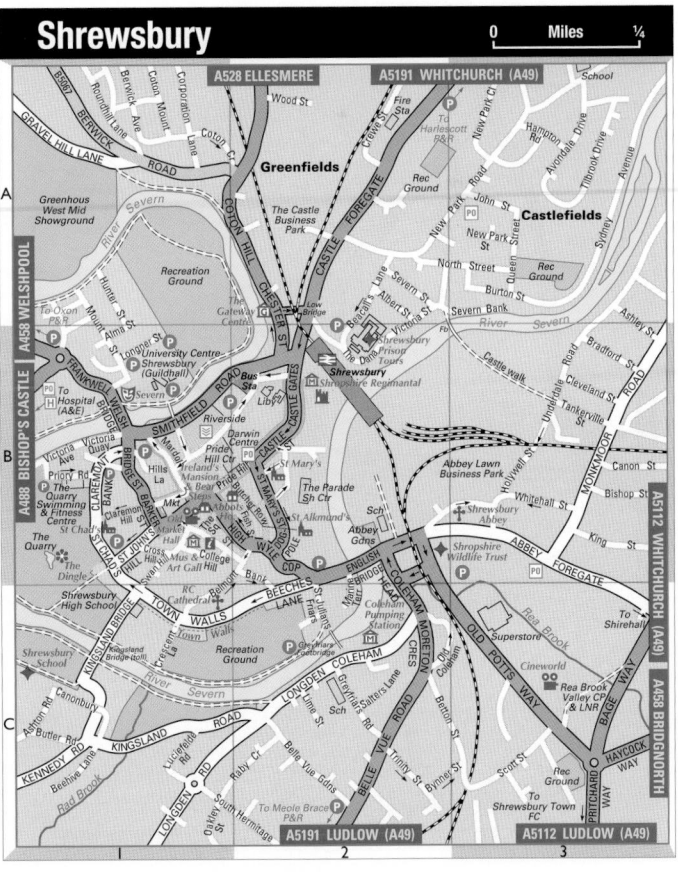

Shrewsbury

Sheffield

0   Miles   ¼

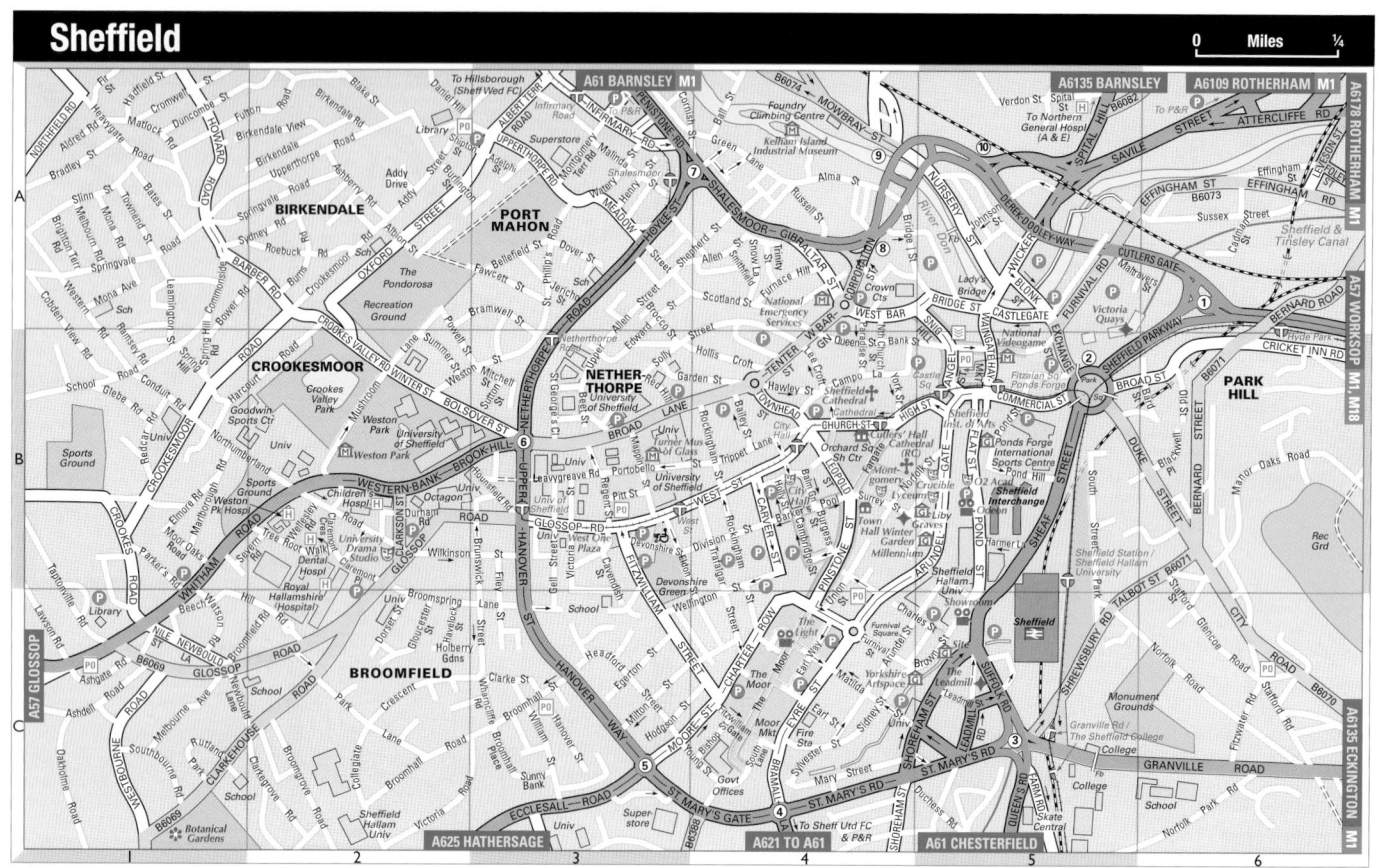

Stoke-on-Trent (Hanley)

0   Miles   ¼

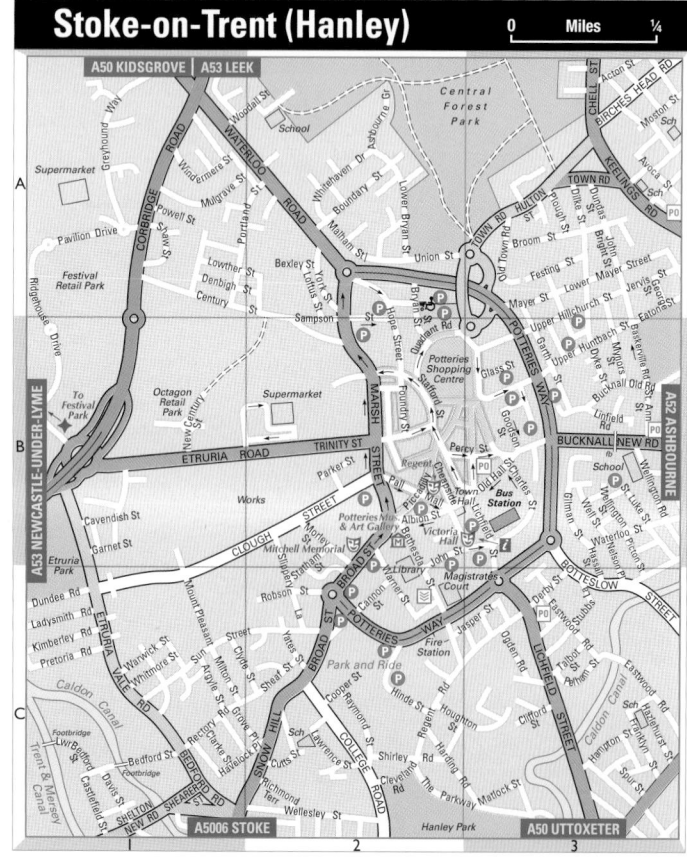

Southampton

0   Miles   ¼

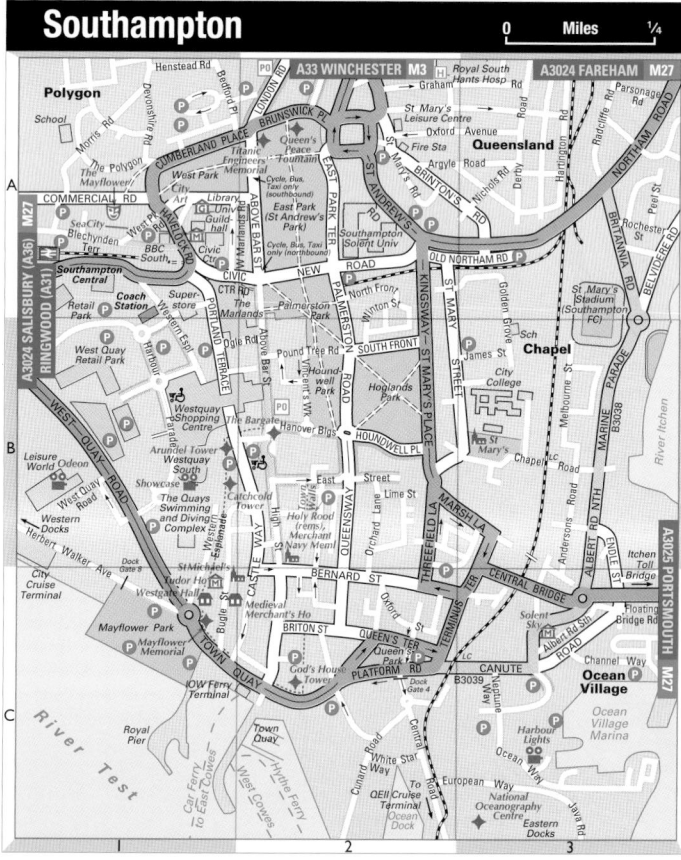

Southend-on-Sea

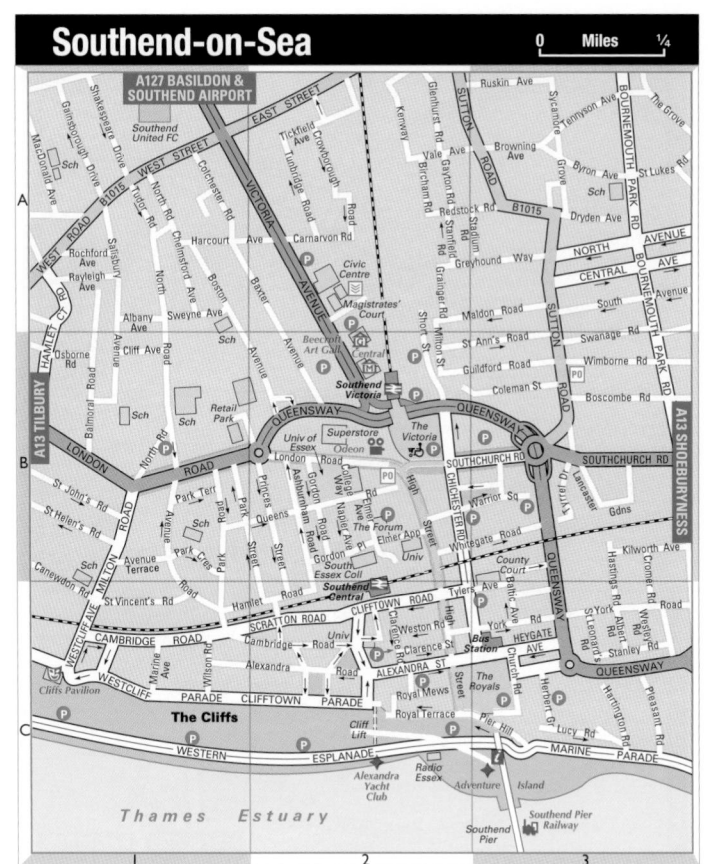

Stirling

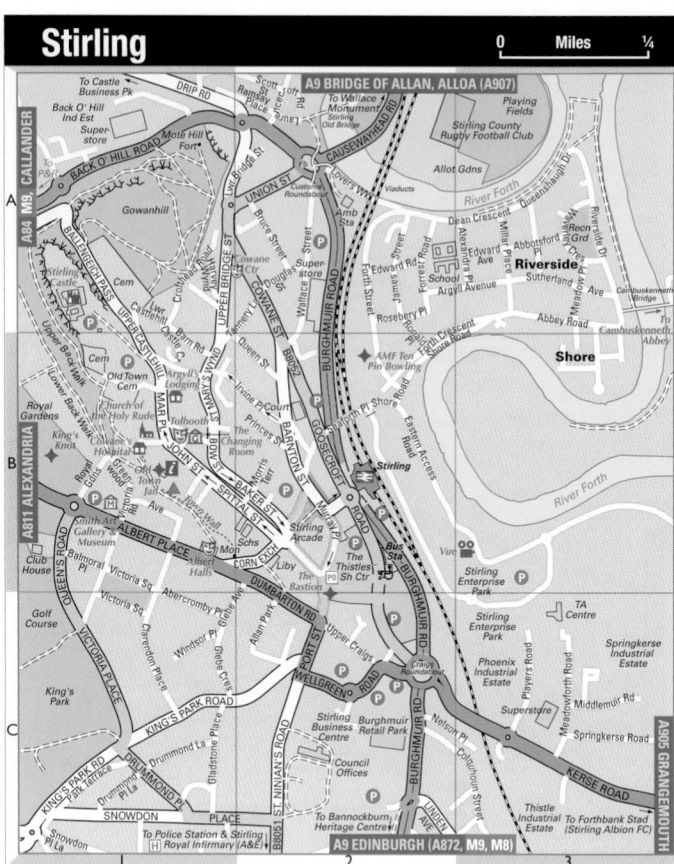

Stratford-upon-Avon

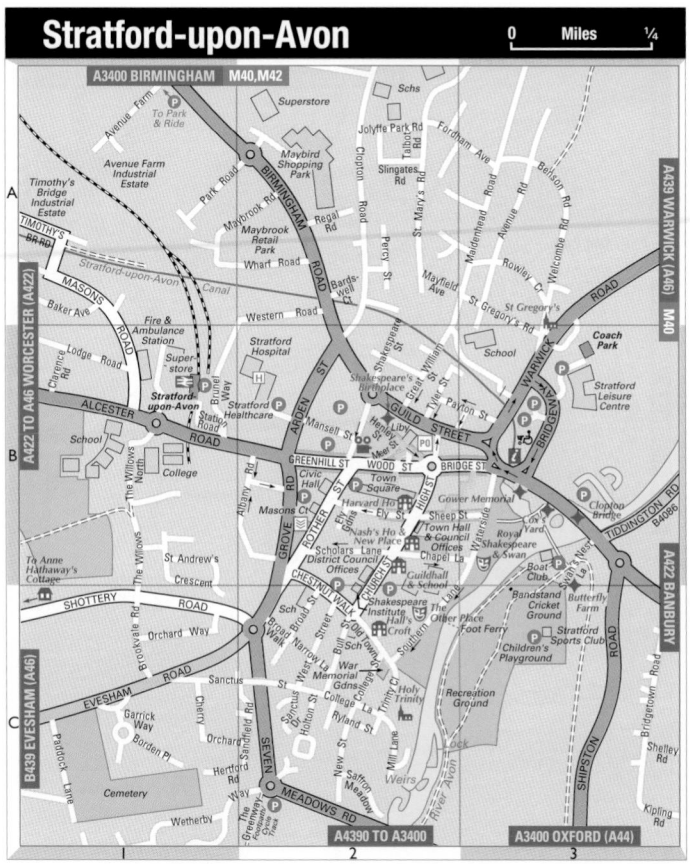

Sunderland

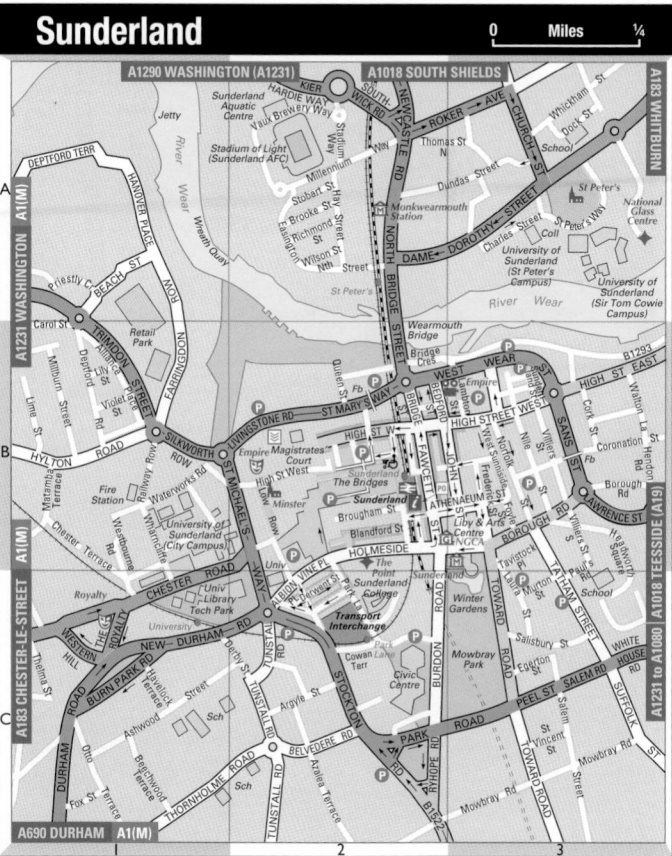

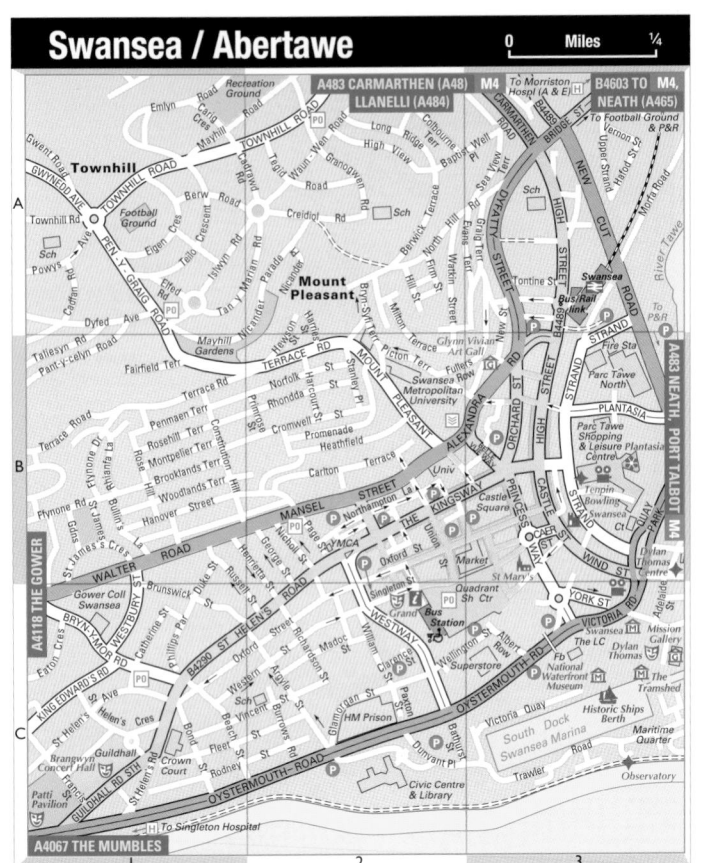

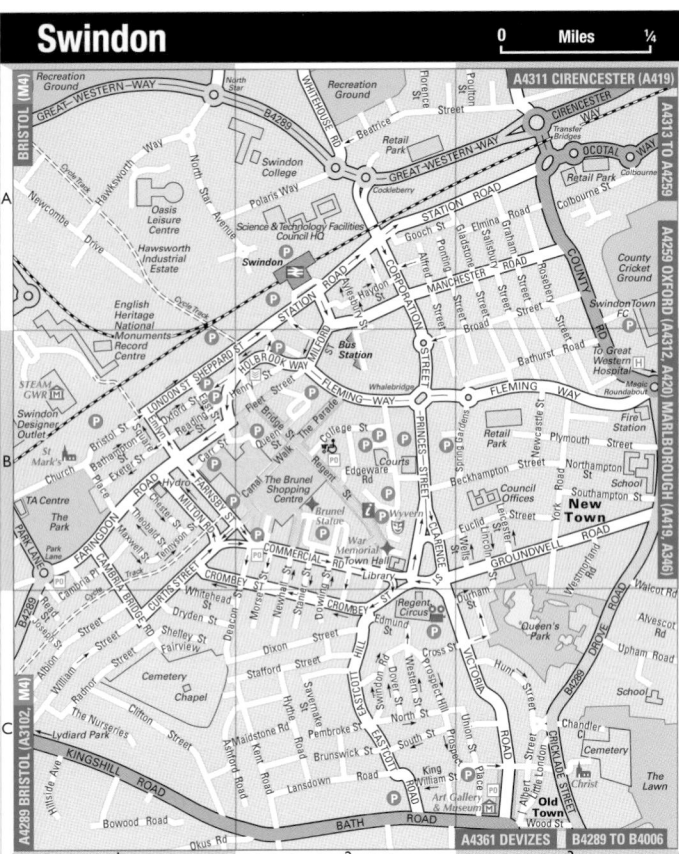

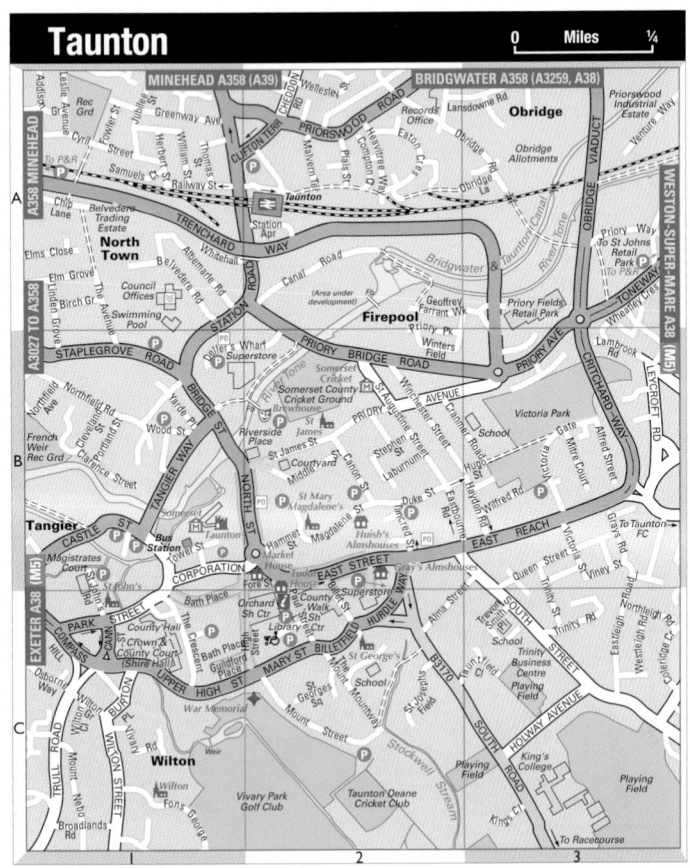

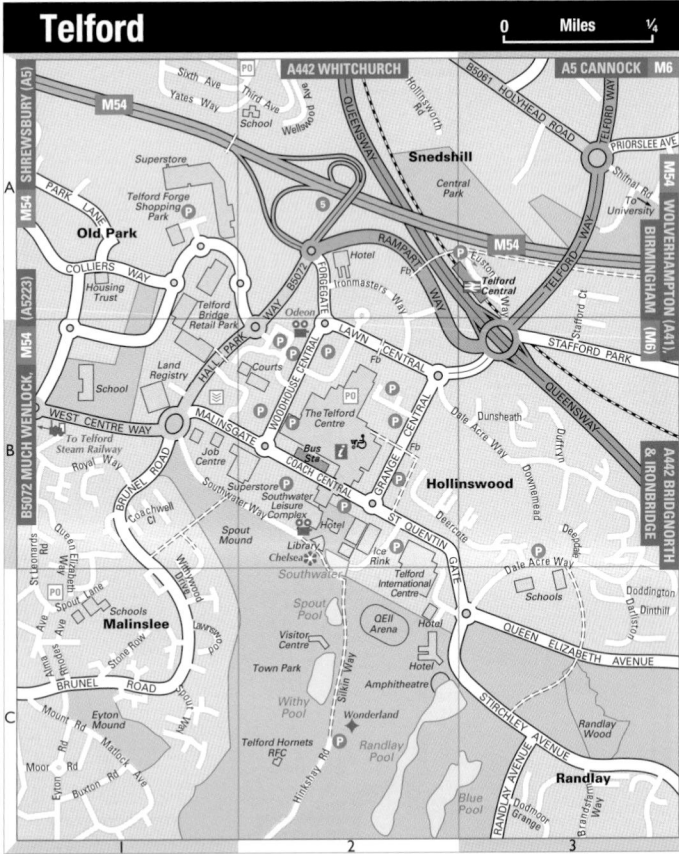

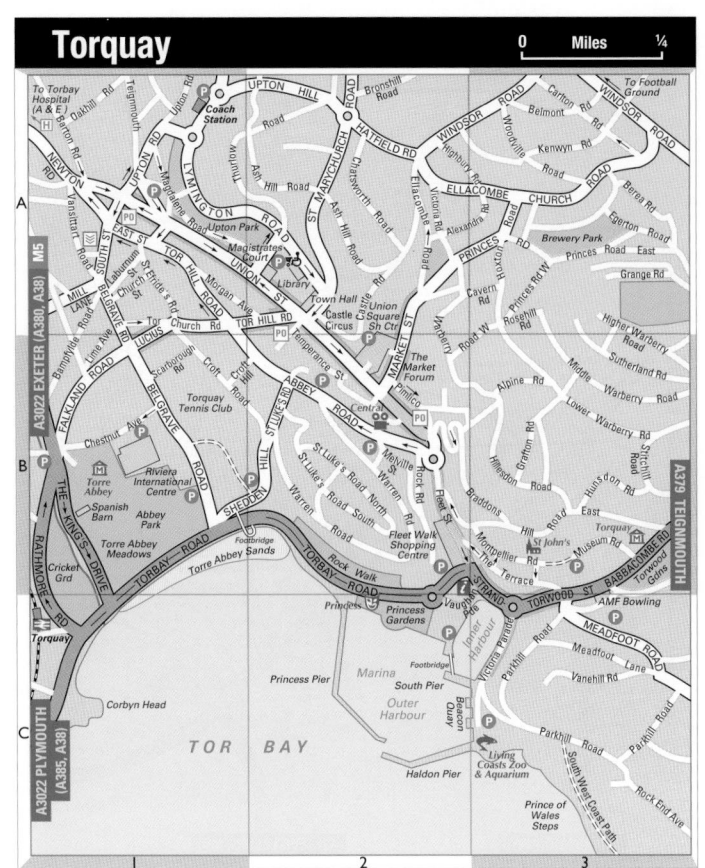

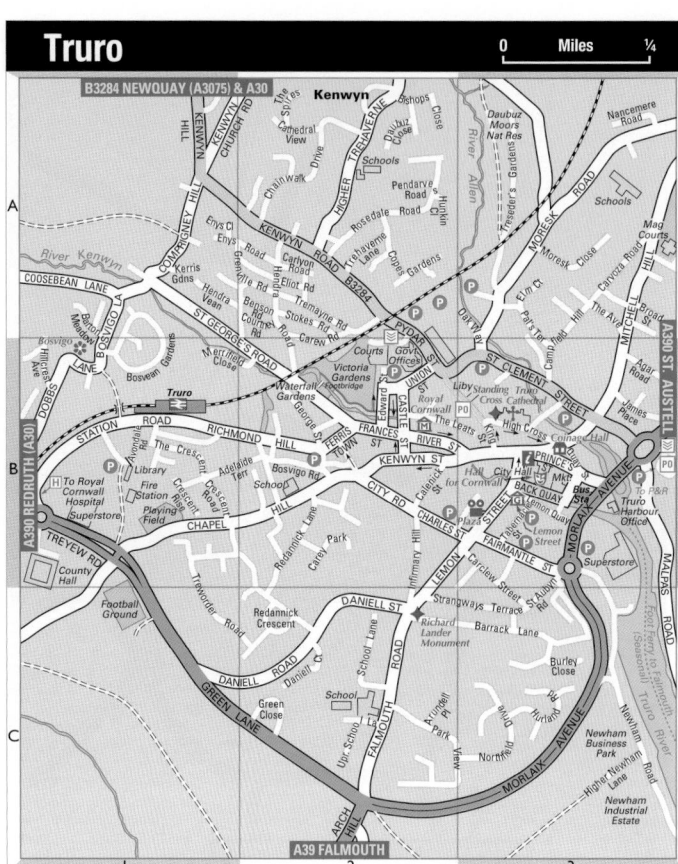

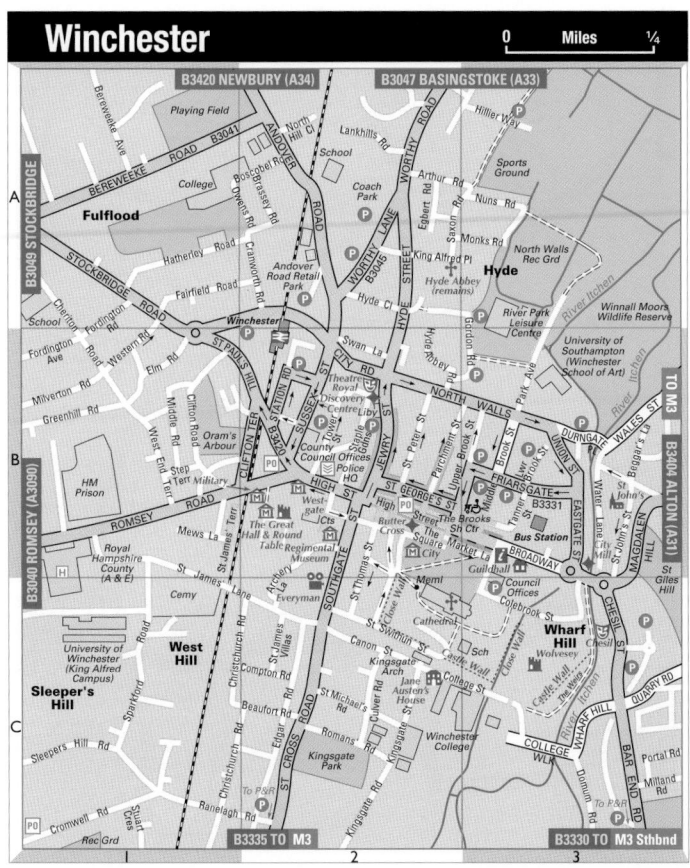

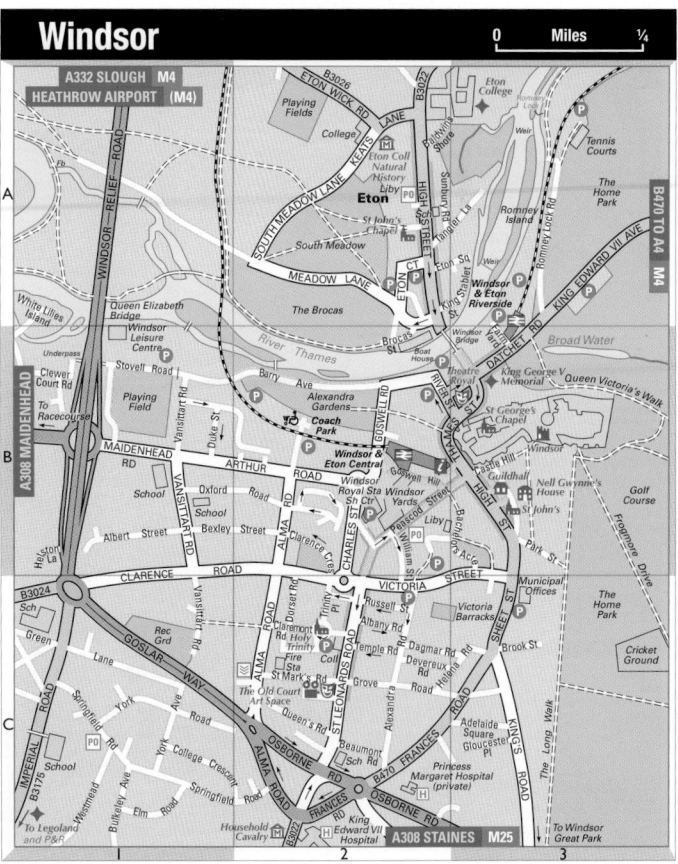

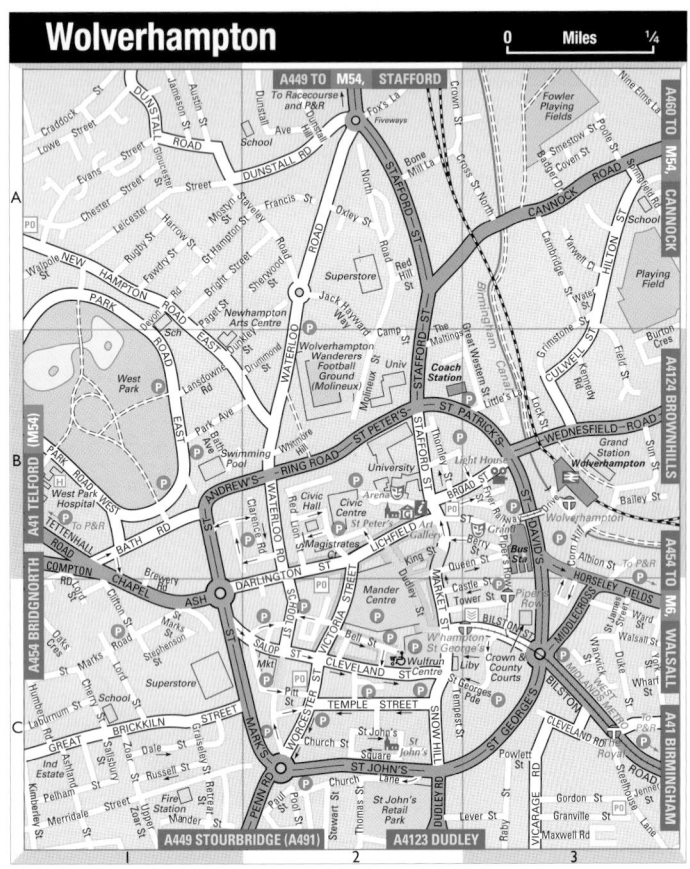

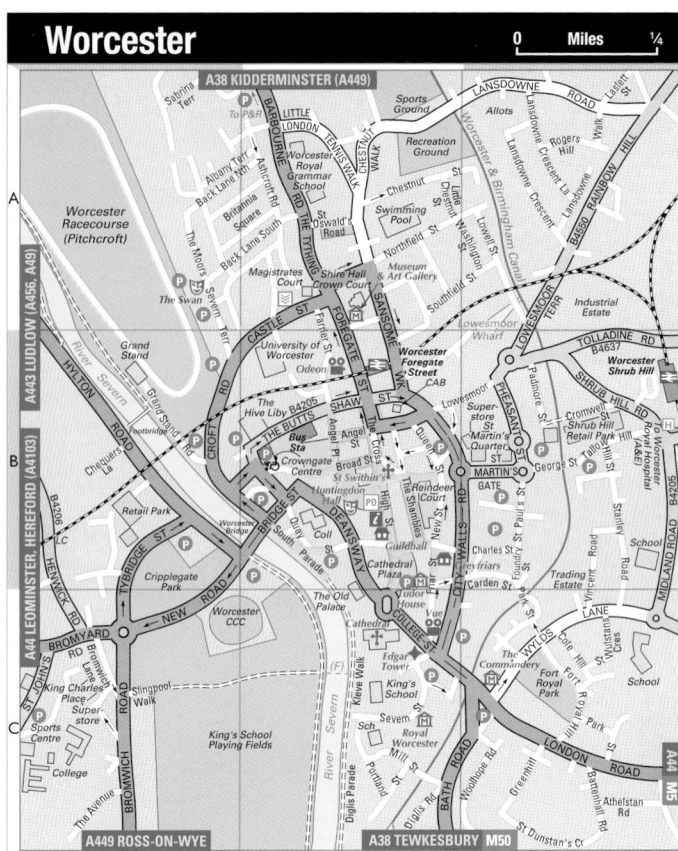

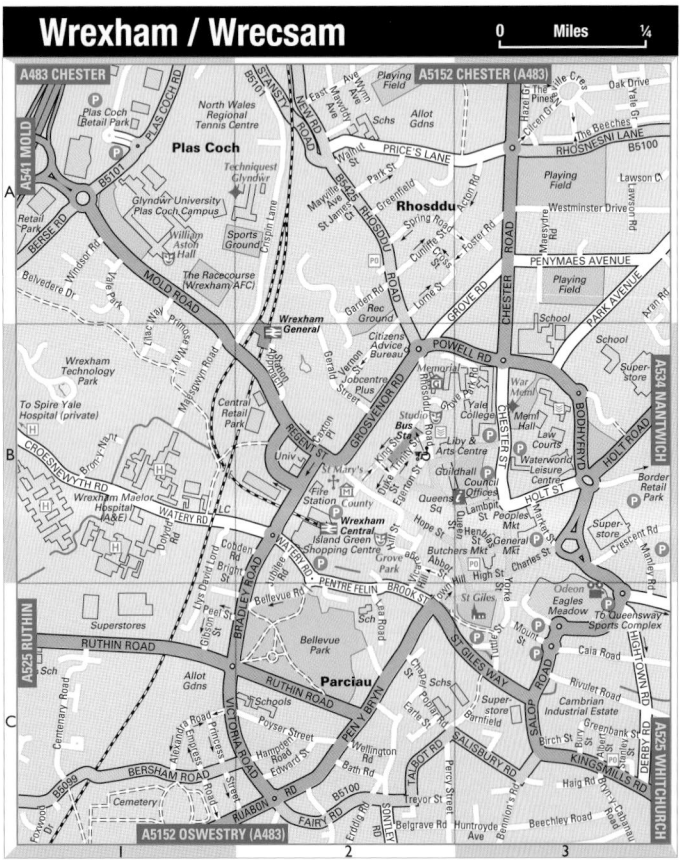

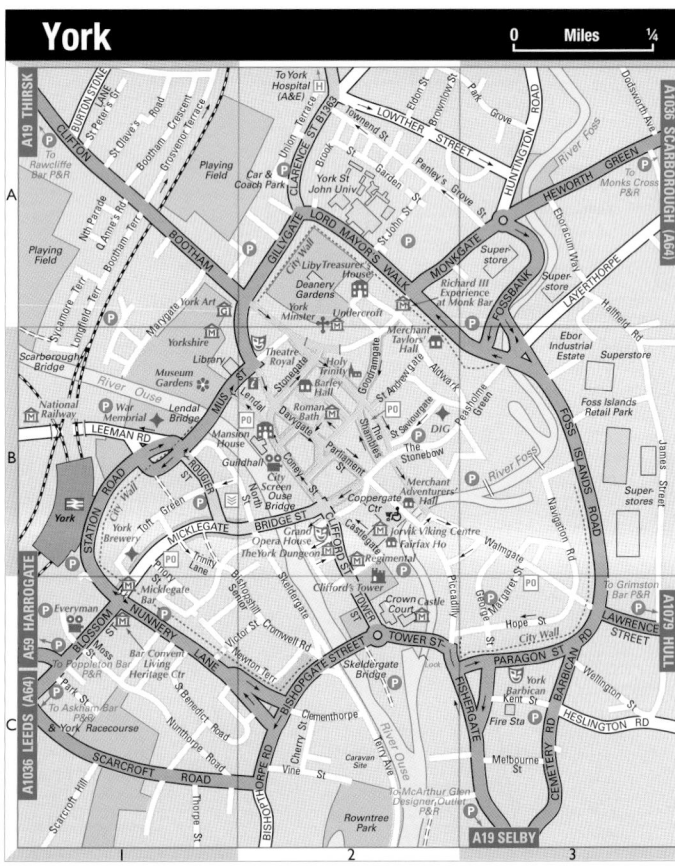

Town plan indexes

Aberdeen 175

Aberdeen ⇌ . . B2
Aberdeen Grammar School . A1
Academy,The . . A1
Albert Basin . . . B3
Albert Quay. . . . B3
Albury Rd C1
Alford Place . . . A2
Art Gallery 🏛 . . A2
Arts Centre A2
Back Wynd A2
Baker St A1
Beach Blvd A3
Belmont 🎭. B2
Belmont St B2
Berry St. A2
Blackfriars St . . . A2
Blaikie's Quay. . . B3
Bloomfield Rd . . . C1
Bon Accord Centre.
Bon-Accord St . . B1/C1
Bridge St B2
Broad St A2
Bus Station B2
Car FerryTerminal . B3
Castlegate A3
Central Library . . A1
Chapel St A2
Cineworld 🎬. . . . B2
Clyde St. B2
College A2
College St B2
Commerce St . . . A3
Commercial Quay . B3
Com Centre . . . A3/C1
Constitution St . . A3
Cotton St. A3
Crown St B2
Denburn Rd A2
Devanha Gardens .
Devanha Gardens South. C2
East North St . . . A3
Esslemont Ave . . A1
Ferryhill Rd C2
FerryhillTerr. . . . C2
Fish Market. B3
Fonthill Rd C1
Galleria A2
Gallowgate. A2
George St A2
Glenbervie Rd. . . C3
Golden Sq. A2
Grampian Rd . . . C3
Great Southern Rd . C1
Guild St B2/C2
Hardgate. B1/C1
His Majesty's Theatre 🎭 A1
Holburn St C1
Hollybank Place . . C1
Huntly St A1
Hutcheon St A1
Information Ctr 🄸 . B2
John St A1
Justice St A3
King St A2
Langstane Place. . B1
LemonTree,The . . A3
Library C1
Loch St A2
Maberly St A1
Marischal Coll 🏛 . A2
Maritime Museum & Provost Ross's House 🏛 B2
Market B2
Market St B2/B3
Menzies Rd C3
Mercat Cross ✦ . . A3
Millburn St C2
Miller St A3
Mount St A1
Music Hall 🎭 . . . A2
North Esp East . . C3
North Esp West. . . C2
Oscar Rd C3
Palmerston Rd . . . C2
Park St A3
Police Station 🛇 . . A1
Polmuir Rd C2
Post Office 🄟 . . A1/A2/A3/B1/C3
Provost Skene's House 🏛 B2
Queen Elizabeth Br C2
Queen St A2
Regent Quay . . . A3
Regent Road. . . . B3
Robert Gordon's College A1
Rose St A1
Rosemount Place. . A1
Rosemount Viaduct A1
St Andrew St . . . A2
St Andrew's Cath ✝ A2
St Mary's Cath ✝ . . B1
St Nicholas Centre . A2
St Nicholas St . . . A2
School Hill A2
Sinclair Rd C3
Skene Sq A1
Skene St B1
South College St . C2
South Crown St . . C2
South Esp East . . C3
South Esp West. . . C3
South Mount St . . A1
Sports Centre . . . C3
Spring Garden . . . A2
SpringbankTerr . . C2
Summer St A1
Superstore A3
Thistle St. A1
Tolbooth 🏛. B2
Town House 🏛. . . B2
Trinity Centre . . . B2
Union Row B2
Union Square . . .
Union St B1/B2
University A2
Upper Dock B3
Upper Kirkgate. . . A2
Victoria Bridge. . . C3
Victoria Dock . . . B3
Victoria Rd C3
Victoria St. B1
Virginia St B3
Vue 🎬. B2
Waterloo Quay . . A3
Wellington Place . . B2
West North St . . . A2
Whinhill Rd C1
Willowbank Rd . . . C1
Windmill Brae . . . B2

Ayr 175

Ailsa Place B1
Alexandra Terr . . . A3
Allison St. B2
Alloway Pk C1
Alloway Place. . . . C1
Alloway St B2
Arran Mall B2
ArranTerr B1
Arthur St. B1
Ashgrove St A2
Auld Brig. B2
Auld Kirk ⛪ B2
Ayr ⇌ B2
Ayr Academy . . . B1
Ayr Central Shopping Centre . B2
Ayr Harbour A1
Ayr Ice Rink. A2
Ayrshire Coll. . . . B1
Back Hawkhill Ave . A3
Back Main St B2
Back Peebles St . . A2
Barns Cres C1
Barns Pk C1
Barns St B1
Barns Street La. . . B1
Bath Place B1
Bellevue Cres . . . C2
Bellevue La C1
Beresford La C2
BeresfordTerr . . . C2
Boswell Park B2
Britannia Place . . . A3
Bruce Cres A1
Burns Statue ✦ . . C2
Bus Sta B2
Carrick St C2
Cassillis St C2
Cathcart St B1
Charlotte St B1
Citadel Leisure Ctr . B1
Citadel Place B1
Compass Pier . . . A1
Content Ave A3
Content St A3
Craigie Ave B3
Craigie Rd B3
Craigie Way B3
Cromwell Rd. . . . A3
Crown St A2
Dalblair Rd C2
Dam Park Sports Stadium. . C3
Damside A2
Dongola Rd C3
Eglinton Place . . . B1
EglintonTerr. B1
Elba St. B2
Elmbank St A2
Esplanade. A1
Euchar Rock A1
Fairfield Rd C1
Fort St B1
Fothringham Rd. . . C1
Fullarton St. C2
Garden St B2
George St B2
George's Ave . . . A3
Glebe Cres A2
Glebe Rd A2
GordenTerr. B1
Green St A2
Green Street La . . A3
Hawkhill Ave. . . . A3
Hawkhill Avenue La B3
High St B2
Holmston Rd. . . . C3
Information Ctr 🄸 . B1
James St B3
John St B2
King St B2
Kings St B2
Kyle Centre. C2
Kyle St B2
Library B2
Limekiln Rd B2
Limonds Wynd . . . B2
Loudoun Hall 🏛 . . B2
Lymburn Place. . . B3
Macadam Place . . B2
Main St C1
Mcadam's Monument C1
Mccall's Ave A3
Mews La C1
Mill Brae C3
Mill St B3
Mill Wynd C2
Miller Rd. C2
MontgomerieTerr . B1
New Bridge. B2
New Bridge St . . . B2
Newmarket St . . . B2
Newton-on-Ayr Station ⇌ A2
North Harbour St . B1
North Pier. A1
Odeon 🎬 B2
Park Circus C1
Park Circus La . . . C1
ParkTerr C1
Pavilion Rd A1
Peebles St A2
Philip Sq B2
Police Station 🛇 . . B2
Prestwick Rd A1
Princes St A1
Queen St. B1
Queen'sTerr B1
Racecourse Rd . . . C1
River St B2
Riverside Place . . . B2
Russell Dr C1
St Andrews Church ⛪ C2
St George's Rd . . . A3
Sandgate B2
Savoy Park C1
Smith St C2
Somerset Park (Ayr United FC) . . A2
Somerset Rd. . . . B1
South Beach Rd . . B1
South Harbour St . B1
South Pier. A1
Station Rd. B2
Strathyar Place . . B2
Taylor St. B2
Town Hall B2
Tryfield Place. . . . B1
Turner's Bridge. . . B2
Union Ave B2
Victoria Bridge. . . C3
Victoria St. B3
Viewfield Rd. . . . A3
Virginia Gdns. . . . A3
Waggon Rd. A3
Walker Rd. A3
WallaceTower ✦. . B2
Weaver St. A3
Weir Rd. A3
Wellington La. . . . C1
Wellington Sq. . . . C1
West Sanouhar Rd . A3
Whitletts Rd. A3
Wilson St. A3
York St. A1
York Street La. . . . B1

Bath 175

Alexandra Park . . C2
Alexandra Rd . . . A2
Ambulance Station A3
Approach Golf Courses (Public) . A1
Archway St. C2
Assembly Rooms & Fashion Mus 🏛 . . A2
Avon St. B2
Barton St. B2
Bath Abbey ✝ . . . B2
Bath Aqua Glass 🏛 B2
Bath at Work Museum 🏛. . . . B2
Bath College B2
Bath Rugby (The Rec) B3
Bath Spa Station ⇌ . C2
Bathwick St A3
Beckford Road . . . A3
Beechen Cliff Rd . . C2
Bennett St. A2
Bloomfield Ave. . . C1
Broad Quay C2
Broad St B2
Brock St A2
Bus Station C2
Calton Gdns C2
Calton Rd. C2
Camden Cres . . . A2
Cavendish Rd . . . A1
Cemetery B1
Charlotte St B1
Chaucer Rd C2
Cheap St. B2
Circus Mews A2
Claverton St C2
Corn St B2
Cricket Ground . . . B3
Daniel St A3
East Asian Art Museum 🏛 A2
Edward St B3
Ferry La. B3
Fire Station B1
First Ave C1
Forester Ave A3
Forester Rd A3
Gays Hill A2
George St B2
Great Pulteney St . B3
Green Park B1
Green Park Rd . . . B1
Green Park Station ✦ B1
Grove St B2
Guildhall 🏛 B2
Harley St A1
Hayesfield Park . . C1
Henrietta Gdns . . A3
Henrietta Mews . . B3
Henrietta Park . . . B3
Henrietta Rd A3
Henrietta St B3
Henry St B2
Herschel Museum of Astronomy 🏛 . B1
High Common . . . A1
Holburne Mus 🏛 . B3
Holloway. C2
James St West . B1/B2
Jane Austen Ctr 🏛 . B2
Julian Rd A1
Junction Rd C1
Kingsmead Leisure Complex. . B2
Kipling Ave C1
Lansdown Cres . . A1
Lansdown Grove . A2
Lansdown Rd . . . A2
Library B2
London Rd A3
London St A2
Lower Bristol Rd. . C1
Lower Oldfield Park . . . C1
Lyncombe Hill . . . C3
Magistrates' Court. B3
Manvers St C2
Maple Grove C1
Margaret's Hill . . . A2
Marlborough Bldgs A1
Marlborough La . . B1
Midland Bridge Rd . B1
Milk St B2
Milsom St B2
Mission,The 🎭. . . A2
Monmouth St . . . B2
Morford St A2
Museum of Bath Architecture 🏛 . . A2
New King St B1
No 1 Royal Cres 🏛 A1
Norfolk Bldgs . . . B1
Norfolk Cres B1
North Parade Rd . . B3
Oldfield Rd C1
Paragon A2
Pines Way B1
Podium Shopping Centre . B2
Police Station 🛇 . . A3
Portland Place . . . A2
Post Office 🄟 . . B2/C2
Postal Museum 🏛 . B2
Powlett St B3
Prior Park Rd C2
Pulteney Bridge ✦ . B2
Pulteney Gdns . . . C2
Pulteney Rd . . . B3/C3
Queen Sq B2
Raby Place C3
Recreation Ground C3
Rivers St B2
Rockliffe Ave A3
Rockliffe Rd A3
Roman Baths & Pump Room 🏛 . . B2
Rossiter Rd C3
Royal Ave A1
Royal Cres A1
Royal High School,The . . A1
Royal Victoria Park. A1
St James Sq A1
St John's Rd A3
Sally Lunn's House ✦ B2
Shakespeare Ave . C2
Shopmobility. . . . B2
South Parade . . . B3
SouthGate Shopping Centre . C2
Sports & Leisure Ctr. B3
Spring Gdns C3
Stall St. B2
Stanier Rd C3
Superstore . . . A3/B1
Sydney Gdns A3
Sydney Place A3
Sydney Rd A3
Theatre Royal 🎭. . B2
Thermae Bath Spa . B2
Thomas St. A3
Tyning,The. A3
Union St B2
University C3
Upper Bristol Rd . . B1
Upper Oldfield Park C1
Victoria Art Gallery 🏛 . . B2
Victoria Bridge Rd . B1
Walcot St B2
Wells Rd C2
Westgate Buildings B2
Westgate St B2
Weston Rd A1
Widcombe Hill . . . C3

Birmingham 176

Abbey St A2
Aberdeen St A1
Acorn Grove. . . . A4
Adams St A5
Adderley St. C6
Albert St B4
Albion St A2
Alcester St C5
Aldgate Grove . . . A3
All Saint's La A2
All Saints Rd A2
Allcock St C6
Allesley St A4
Allison St C4
Alma Cres A6
Alston Rd C6
Arcadian Centre . . C4
Arthur St C6
Assay Office 🏛 . . . B3
Ashted Circus . . . B5
Aston Expressway . A5
Aston St A4
Aston University . B4/B5
Avenue Rd. A1
Bacchus Rd. A1
Bagot St A4
Banbury St B5
Barford Rd B1
Barford St C4
Barn St B5
Barnwell Rd C6
Barr St A3
Barrack St. B5
Barwick St B4
Bath Row. C3
Beaufort Rd C1
Belmont Row . . . B5
Benson Rd A1
Berkley St. C3
Bexhill Grove C3
Birchall St. C5
Birmingham City FC C6
Birmingham City Hospital (A&E) 🏥 . A1
Birmingham City University A3
Birmingham Wheels Park ✦ . . B6
Bishopsgate St . . . C3
Blews St A4
Bloomsbury St . . . A6
Blucher St. C3
Bordesley St C5
Bowyer St C5
Bradburne Way . . A5
Bradford St C5
Branston St A3
Brearley St A4
Brewery St A4
Bridge St C3
Bridge St West . . . A4
Brindley Dr B3
Brindley Place 🎭 . . C3
Broad St C2
Broad Street Cineworld 🎬 . . . C2
Broadway Plaza ✦ . C2
Bromley St C6
Bromsgrove St . . . C4
Brookfield Rd. . . . A2
Browning St. C2
Bryant St A1
Buckingham St . . . A3
Bull Ring B4
Bull St B4
Bullring C4
Cambridge St . . . B3
Camden Dr B3
Camden St B2
Cannon St B4
Cardigan St B5
Carlisle St A1
Carlyle Rd. B1
Caroline St A3
Carver St B2
Cato St A6
Cattell Rd C6
Cattells Grove . . . A6
Cawdor Cres C1
Cecil St B4
Cemetery A2/B2
Cemetery La A2
Centenary Square . B3
Centre Link Ind Est. A5
Charlotte St B3
Cheapside C4
Chester St A5
Children's Hospital (A&E) 🏥 B4
Church St B4
Claremont Rd . . . A2
Clarendon Rd . . . C1
Clark St C1
Clement St B2
Clissold St B2
Cliveland St A4
Coach Station. . . . C5
College St B2
Colmore Circus . . A4
Colmore Row . . . B4
Commercial St . . . C3
Constitution Hill. . . A3
Convention Centre,The C3
Cope St B2
Coplow St B1
Corporation St 📷 . . C4
Council House 🏛 . . B3
County Court B4
Coveley Grove . . . A1
Coventry Rd C6
Coventry St C4
Cox St B3
Crabtree Rd A2
Cregoe St C3
Crescent Ave A2
CrescentTheatre 🎭 C3
Crescent,The. . . . A2
Cromwell St A6
Cromwell St B5
Cube,The. C3
Curzon Circle B5
Curzon St B5
Custard Factory ✦ . C5
Cuthbert Rd B1
Dale End B4
Dart St C6
Dartmouth Circus . A4
Dartmouth Middleway A5
Deritend C5
Devon St A6
Devonshire St . . . A1
Digbeth High St . . C4
Dolman St B6
Dover St B1
Duchess Rd C1
Duddeston ⇌ B6
Duddeston Manor Rd B6
Duddeston Mill Rd . A6
Duddeston Mill Trading Estate . . B6
Dudley Rd B1
Edgbaston Village . C2
Edmund St B3
Edward St B2
Elkington St A4
Ellen St A2
Ellis St C3
Erskine St B6
Essex St C4
Eyre St B2
Farm Croft. A3
Farm St A3
Fazeley St B4/C5
Felstead Way B6
Finstall Close. . . . B5
Five Ways C2
Five Ways 🔘 C2
Fiveway Shopping Centre C2
Fleet St B3
Floodgate St C5
Ford St A2
Fore St B4
Forster St B5
Francis Rd C1
Francis St B5
Frankfort St A4
Frederick St B3
Freeth St C1
Freightliner Terminal B6
Garrison Circus . . . C6
Garrison La C6
Garrison St C6
Gas St C3
Geach St A4
George St B3
George St West . . B2
Gibb St C5
Gilby Rd C2
Gillott Rd B1
Glover St C6
Goode Ave. A1
Goodrick Way . . . A6
Gordon St B6
Graham St B3
Grand Central Shopping Centre . C4
Granville St C3
Gray St C6
Great Barr St C5
Great Charles St . . B3
Great Francis St . . B6
Great Hampton Row A3
Great Hampton St . A3
Great King St A3
Great King St North A3
Great Lister St . . . A5
GreatTindal St . . . B2
Green La C6
Green St C5
Grosvenor St B4
Grosvenor St West C2
Guest Grove A3
Guild Close B2
Guildford Dr A4
Guthrie Close . . . A3
Hagley Rd C1
Hall St A3
Hampton St A3
Handsworth New Rd A1
Hanley St A4
Harford St A3
Harmer Rd A2
Harold Rd C1
Hatchett St A4
Heath Mill La C5
Heath St B1
Heaton St A2
Heneage St B5
Henrietta St A4
Herbert Rd C6
High St C4
High St B6
Hilden Rd C6
Hill St C3/C4
Hindlow Close . . . B6
Hingeston St A2
Hippodrome Theatre 🎭 C4
HM Prison. A1
Hockley Circus . . . A2
Hockley Hill A3
Hockley St A3
Holliday St C3
Holloway Circus . . C4
Holloway Head . . . C3
Holt St B5
Horse Fair. C4
Hospital St A4
Howard St A3
Howe St B5
Hubert St A5
Hunters Rd A3
Hunters Vale A3
Huntly Rd C1
Hurst St. C4
Icknield Port Rd . . B1
Icknield Sq B2
Icknield St A2/B2
IKON 🏛 C3
Information Ctr 🄸 . . C3
Inge St C4
Irving St C3
James Watt Queensway B4
Jennens Rd. B5
Jewellery Quarter ⇌ A3
Jewellery Quarter 🔘 A3
Jewellery Quarter Museum 🏛 . . . A3
John Bright St . . . C4
Keeley St C6
Kellett Rd B5
Kenyon St B3
Key Hill A3
Key Hill Circus . . . A3
Kilby Ave C2
King Edwards Rd . . B2
King Edwards Rd . . C3
Kingston Rd C6
Kirby Rd A1
Ladywood Arts & Leisure Centre . . B1
Ladywood Circus . . C1
Ladywood Middleway . . . C2/C3
Lancaster St A4
Landor St B6
Law Courts B4
Lawley Middleway . B5
Ledbury Close. . . . C2
Ledsam St C2
Lees St A1
Legge La B3
Lennox St A3
Library A6/C3
Library ✦ C1
Lighthorne Ave . . . B3
Link Rd B1
Lionel St B3
Lister St A5
Little Ann St C5
Little Hall Rd A6
Liverpool St C5
Livery St B3/B4
Lodge Rd A1
Lord St A5
Love La A4
Loveday St B4
Lower Dartmouth St C6
Lower Loveday St . A4
Lower Tower St . . A4
LowerTrinty St . . . C5
Lucas Circus A3
Ludgate Hill. B3
Mailbox Ctr & BBC . C3
Margaret St B3
Markby Rd A1
Marroway St B1
Maxstoke St C6
Melvina Rd A6
Meriden St C4
Midland St B6
Milk St C5
Mill St A5
Millennium Point . . B5
Miller St A4
Milton St A4
Moat La C4
Montague Rd . . . C6
Montague St B5
Monument Rd . . . C1
Moor St Queensway C4
Moor Street ⇌ . . . C4
Moorsom St A4
Morville St C2
Mosborough Cres . A3
Moseley St C5
Mott St A3
Mus & Art Gallery 🏛 B3
Musgrave Rd A1
National Sea Life Centre ✦ C3
Navigation St C3
Nechell's Park Rd . A6
Nechells Parkway . B5
Nechells Place . . . A6
New Alexandra 🎭 . C3
New Bartholomew St C5
New Canal St C5
New John St West . A3
New Spring St . . . B2
New St B4
New Street ⇌ C4
New Summer St . . A4
New Town Row . . . A4
Newhall Hill B3
Newhall St B3
Newton St B4
Noel Rd C1
Norman St. A1
Northbrook St . . . B1
Northwood St . . . B3
Norton St A2
Odeon 🎬 C4
Old Crown Ho 🏛 . . C5
Old Rep Theatre,The 🎭 C4
Old Snow Hill A4
Oliver Rd C1
Oliver St A6
Osler St C1
Oxford St C5
Palmer St C5
Paradise Circus. . . B3
Paradise St B3
Park Rd A2
Park St C4
Pavilions C4
Paxton Rd A2
Peel St A1
Pershore St C4
Phillips St A4
Pickford St C5
Pinfold St C3
Pitsford St A2
Plough & Harrow Rd C1
Police Station 🛇 . A4/B4/C2/C4
Post Office 🄟 . A5/B1/B3/B5/C3/C5
Preston Rd A1
Price St B4
Princip St A4
Printing House St . . B4
Priory Queensway . B4
Pritchett St A4
Proctor St A5
Radnor St A2
Rea St C4
Regent Place. . . . B3
Regent Office Rd . . B3
Repertory Theatre 🎭 C3
Reservoir Rd C1
Richard St A5
River St C5
Rocky La A5/A6
Rodney Close . . . C2
Roseberry St B2
Rotton Park St . . . B1
Royal Birmingham Conservatoire ✦ . B5
Rupert St A5
Ruston St C2
Ryland St C2
St Andrew's Ind Est C6
St Andrew's Rd . . . C6
St Andrew's St . . . C6
St Bolton St C6
St Chads 🔘 B4
St Chad's Cathedral (RC) ✝ B4
St Chads Queensway B4
St Clements Rd . . . A6
St George's St . . . A3
St James Place . . . B6
St Marks Cres . . . B2
St Martin's ✝ C4
St Paul's ⇌ B3
St Paul's 🔘 B3
St Paul's Sq B3
St Philip's ✝ B4
St Stephen's St . . . A4
StThomas' Peace Garden ✤ C3
StVincent St C2
Saltley Rd A6
Sand Pits Parade . . B3
Severn St C3
Shadwell St B4
Sheepcote St C2
Shefford Rd. A4
Sherborne St C2
Shylton's Croft . . . C2
Skipton Rd C2
Smallbrook Queensway C4
Snow Hill ⇌ B4
Snow Hill Queensway B4
Soho, Benson Rd 🚃 A1
South Rd A2
Spencer St B3
Spring Hill. B2
Staniforth St A4
Station St C4
Steelhouse La . . . B4
Stephenson St . . . C4
Steward St B2
Stirling Rd C1
Stour St B2
Suffolk St Queensway C3
Summer Hill Rd . . B2
Summer Hill St . . . B2
Summer HillTerr . . B2
Summer La A4
Summer Row B3
Summerfield Cres . B1
Summerfield Park . B1
Sutton St C3
Swallow St C3
Sydney Rd C6
Symphony Hall 🎭 . C3
Talbot St A1
Temple Row. B4
Temple St B4
Templefield St . . . C6
Tenby St B3
Tenby St North . . . B3
Tennant St . . . C2/C3
Thimble Mill La . . . A6
Thinktank (Science & Discovery) 🏛 . . B5
Thomas St A4
Thorpe St C4
Tilton Rd C6
Tower St A4
Town Hall 🏛 B3
Town Hall 🎭 B3
Trent St C5
Turner's Buildings . A1
Unett St A3
Union St B4
UpperTrinity St . . C5
Utilita Arena ✦ . . . C2
Vauxhall Grove . . . B6
Vauxhall Rd B6
Vernon Rd C1
Vesey St B4
Viaduct St B6
Victoria Sq C3
Villa St A3
Vittoria St B3
Vyse St B3
Walter St A6
Wardlow Rd A6
Warstone La B3
Washington St . . . C3
Water La C6
Waterworks Rd . . . C1
Watery La C6
Western Rd B1
Wharf St A3
Wheeler St A3
Whitehouse St . . . A5
Whitmore St A2
Whittall St B4
Wholesale Market . C4
Wiggin St B1
Willes Rd A1
Windsor Ind Est . . A5
Windsor St A5
Windsor St B5
Winson Green Rd . A1
Witton St C6
Wolseley St C6
Woodcock St B5

Blackpool 176

Abingdon St B1
Addison Cres A1
Adelaide St B1
Albert Rd B1
Alfred St B2
Ascot Rd A3
Ashton Rd C2
Auburn Grove . . . C3
Bank Hey St. B1
Banks St A1
Beech Ave C3
Bela Grove C3
Belmont Ave C2
Birley St B1
Blackpool & Fleetwood Tram . . B1
Blackpool & the Fylde College . . . B2
Blackpool FC C2
Blackpool North ⇌ . A2
Blackpool North 🔘 . A2
BlackpoolTower ✦ . B1
Blundell St C1
Bonny St B1
Breck Rd A3
Bryan Rd A3
Buchanan St A2
Bus Hub B1
Cambridge Rd . . . A3
Caunce St A2/A3
Central Dr B1/C2
Central Pier 🔘 . . . C1
Central Pier Theatre 🎭 C1
Chapel St C1
Charles St A2
Charnley Rd B2
Church St A1/A2
Clinton Ave B2
Coach Station . . A2/C1
Cocker St A1
Coleridge Rd A3
Collingwood Ave . . A3
Comedy Carpet ✦ . B1
Condor Grove . . . C3
Cookson St A2
Coronation St . . . B1
Corporation St . . . A1
Courts A1
Cumberland Ave . . C3
Cunliffe Rd A3
Dale St C1
Devonshire Rd . . . A3
Devonshire Sq . . . A3
Dickson Rd A1
Elizabeth St A2
Ferguson Rd C3
Forest Gate B3
Foxhall Rd C1
Freckleton St C2
George St A2
Golden Mile,The . . C1
Gorse Rd B3
Gorton St A2
GrandTheatre,The 🎭 B1
Granville Rd A2
Grasmere Rd C2
Grosvenor St A2
Grundy Art Gallery 🏛 . . A1
Harvey Rd B3
Hornby Rd B2
Houndshill Shopping Centre . B1
Hull Rd B1
Ibbison St C2
Kent Rd C2
Keswick Rd. C3
Knox Grove C3
Laycock Gate A3
Layton Rd A3
Leamington Rd . . . B2
Leeds Rd B2
Leicester Rd B2
Levens Grove C3
Library A1
Lifeboat Station . . . B1
Lincoln Rd B2
Liverpool Rd B2
Livingstone Rd . . . B2
London St B2
Longton Rd C3
Lonsdale Rd B2
Lord St A1
Lune Grove C3
Lytham Rd C1
MadameTussaud's Blackpool 🏛 . . B1
Manchester Sq 🚃 . C1
Manor Rd B3
Maple Ave C3
Market St A1
Marlboro Rd A3
Mere Rd B3
Milbourne St A2
Newcastle Ave . . . B3
Newton Dr A3
North Pier 🔘 B1
North Pier 🎭 A1
North PierTheatre 🎭 A1
Odeon 🎬 C1
Olive Grove B3
Palatine Rd B2
Park Rd B2/C3
Peter St B2
Police Station 🛇 . B1/B2/B3
Portland Rd C2
Princess Pde A1
Princess St C1
Promenade . . . A1/C1
Queen St A1
QueenVictoria Rd . C3
Rawes Pde B2
Reads Ave B2
Regent Rd B2
Ribble Rd B2
Rigby Rd C1/C2
Ripon Rd B3
St Albans Rd A3
St Ives Ave C3
St John's Square . . A1
StVincent Rd A2
Salisbury Rd B3
Salthouse Ave . . . C2
Salvation Army Ctr . A2
Sands Way C1
Sea Life Centre ✦ . . B1
Seasiders Way . . . C1
Selbourne Rd A2
Sharrow Grove . . . A3
Somerset Ave . . . B3
South King St B2
Springfield Rd . . . A1
Sutton Place B2
Talbot Rd A1/A2
Thornber Grove . . C3
Topping St B1
Tower ✦ B1
Town Hall B1
Tram Depot A3
Tyldesley Rd C2
Vance Rd B2
Victoria St B1
Victory Rd A2
Wayman Rd A3
Westmorland Ave . . C2/C3
Whitegate Dr A3
Winter Gardens Theatre 🎭 B1
Woodland Grove . . B3
Woolman Rd B2

Bournemouth 176

Ascham Rd A3
Avenue Rd B2
Ave Shopping Ctr . B1
Bath Rd C2
Beacon Rd C1
Beechey Rd A3
Bodorgan Rd . . . B2
Bourne Ave B1
Bournemouth ⇌ . . A3
Bournemouth & Poole College . . B3
Bournemouth International Ctr. . C1
Bournemouth Pier . C2
Bournemouth Station 🔄 B3
Braidley Rd A1
Cavendish Place. . . A2
Cavendish Rd . . . A2
Central Drive A1
Central Gdns B1
Christchurch Rd . . B3
Cliff Lift C1/C3
Coach House Place . A3
Coach Station A3
Commercial Rd . . . B1
Cotlands Rd B3
Cranborne Rd . . . C1
Cricket Ground . . . A2
Cumnor Rd B2
Dean Park A2
Dean Park Cres . . B2
Dean Park Rd . . . A2
Durrant Rd A1
East Overcliff Dr . . C3
Exeter Cres C1
Exeter Rd C1
Gervis Place B2
Gervis Rd B3
Glen Fern Rd B2
Golf Club A3
Grove Rd B3
Hinton Rd C2
Holdenhurst Rd . . B3
Holmsworth Rd . . A2
Information Ctr 🄸 . . C2
Lansdowne Rd . . . A2
Lansdowne Rd . . . B2
Lorne Park Rd . . . B2
Lower Gdns . . . B1/C2
Madeira Rd A2
Methuen Rd A3
Meyrick Park A1
Meyrick Rd B3
Milton Rd A2
Nuffield Health Bournemouth Hosp (private) 🏥 . . A2
Oceanarium ✦ . . . C2
Old Christchurch Rd B2
Ophir Rd A3
Oxford Rd A3
Park Rd A3
Parsonage Rd . . . B2
Pavilion 🎭 C2
Pier Approach . . . C2
PierTheatre 🎭 . . . C2
Police Station 🛇 . . B1
Portchester Rd . . . B3
Post Office 🄟 . . B1/B3
Priory Rd C1
Quadrant,The . . . B2
Recreation Ground . A3
Richmond Gardens Shopping Centre . B2
Richmond Hill Rd . B1
Russell-Cotes Art Gallery & Mus 🏛 . C2
Russell Cotes Rd . . C2
St Anthony's Rd . . A1
St Michael's Rd . . . C1
St Paul's ⇌ B3
St Paul's La B3
St Paul's Rd B3
St Peter's ✝ B2
St Peter's Rd B2
St Stephen's Rd . B1/B2
St Swithun's Rd . . B3
St Swithun's Rd South B3
StValerie Rd A2
StWinifred's Rd . . A2
Square,The B1
Stafford Rd B3
TerraceRd B1
Tregonwell Rd . . . C1
Triangle,The B1
Trinity Rd B2
Undercliff Drive . . C3
Upper Hinton Rd . . B2
UpperTerr Rd C1
Wellington Rd . . A2/A3
Wessex Way . A3/B1/B2
West Cliff Prom . . . C1
West Hill Rd C1
West Undercliff Promenade C1
Westover Rd B2
Wimborne Rd . . . A1
Wootton Mount . . B2
Wychwood Dr . . . A1
Yelverton Rd B2
York Rd B2
Zig-Zag Walks . . C1/C2
Zip Wire ✦ C2

Bradford 177

Alhambra 🎭 B2
Back Ashgrove . . . B1
Barkerend Rd . . . A3
Barnard Rd C3
Barry St B2
Bolling Rd C3
Bolton Rd A3
Bowland St A1
Bradford Big Screen ✦ . . . B2
Bradford College . . B1
Bradford Forster Square ⇌ A2
Bradford Interchange ⇌ . . . B3
Bradford Playhouse 🎭 . . . B3
Bridge St B2
Britannia St B2
Broadway Bradford,The B2
Burnett St B3
Bus Station B3
Butler St West . . . A3
Caledonia St C2
Canal Rd A2
Carlton St B1
Cathedral ✝ A2
Centenary Sq . . . B2
Chapel St B3
Cheapside A2
Church Bank B2
Cineworld 🎬 C1
City Hall 🏛 B2
City Rd A1
Claremont B1
Colour Experience 🏛 . . . B1
Croft St C2
Crown Court B3
Darfield St A1
Darley St A1
Drewton Rd A1
Drummond Trading Estate . . . A1
Dryden St B3
Dyson St C1
Easby Rd C1
East Parade B3
Eldon Place A1
Filey St B3
Forster Square Retail Park A2
Gallery II 🏛 B1
Garnett St B3
Godwin St B2
Gracechurch St . . A1
Grattan Rd B1
Great Horton Rd . B1/B2
GroveTerr B1
Hall Ings B2
Hall La C3
Hallfield Rd A1
Hammstrasse A2
Harris St B3
Holdsworth St . . . A3
Ice Arena B3
Impressions 🏛 . . . B2
Information Ctr 🄸 . . B2
Inland Revenue . . . B2
Ivegate B2
Jacob's Well B2
Municipal Offices . . B2
James St A2
John St A2
Kirkgate B2
Kirkgate Centre . . B2
Laisteridge La . . . C1
Leeds Rd B3
Leisure Exchange,The . . . B3
Library B1/B2
Listerhills Rd B1
Little Horton Green . C1
Little Horton La . . C1
Longside La B1
Lower Kirkgate . . . B2
Lumb La A1
Magistrates Court . B3
Manchester Rd . . . C2
Manningham La . . A1
Manor Row A2
Market B2
Market St B2
Melbourne Place . . C1
Midland Rd A1
Mill La C3
Morley St B1
National Science and Media Museum 🏛 . B2/C2
Nelson St B2
Nesfield St A2
New Otley Rd . . . A3
Norcroft St B1
North Parade A2
North St A2
North Wing A3
Oastler Shopping Centre A2
Otley Rd A3
Park Ave C1
Park La C1
Park Rd C2
Parma St C2
Peace Museum 🏛 . B2
Peckover St B3
Piccadilly A2
Police Station 🛇 . . A1
Post Office 🄟 . B1/B2/B3/C3
Princes Way B2
Prospect St C2
Radwell Drive . . . C2
Rawson Rd A1

Rebecca St A1
Richmond Rd B1
Russell St C1
St George's Hall B2
St Lukes Hospital C1
Shipley Airedale Rd A3/B3
Shopmobility A2
Simes St A1
Smith St A3
Spring Mill St C2
Stott Hill A3
Sunbridge Rd A1/B1/B2
Theatre in the Mill B1
Thornton Rd A1/B1
Trafalgar St A2
Trinity Rd C1
Tumbling Hill St B1
Tyrrel St B2
Univ of Bradford B1/C1
Usher St C3
Valley Rd A2
Vicar La B3
Wakefield Rd C3
Wapping Rd A3
Well St B3
Westgate A1
White Abbey Rd A1
Wigan Rd A1
Wilton St B1
Wood St A1
Wool Exchange B2
Worthington St A1

Brighton 177
Addison Rd A1
Albert Rd B2
Albion Hill B3
Albion St B3
Ann St A3
Baker St A3
Black Lion St C2
Brighton A2
Brighton Centre C2
Brighton Fishing Museum C2
Brighton Pier (Palace Pier) C3
Brighton Zip Wire C3
British Airways i360 Tower C1
Broad St C3
Buckingham Place A2
Buckingham Rd B2
Cannon Place C1
Carlton Hill B3
Chatham Place A1
Cheapside A3
Church St B2
Churchill Square Shopping Centre B2
Clifton Hill B1
Clifton Place B1
Clifton Rd B1
Clifton St A2
Clifton Terr B1
Clyde Rd A3
Coach Station C3
Compton Ave A2
Davigdor Rd A1
Denmark Terr B1
Ditchling Rd A3
Dome B2
Duke St B2
Duke's La C2
Dyke Rd A1/B2
East St C2
Edward St B3
Elmore Rd B3
Fleet St A2
Frederick St B2
Gardner St B2
Gloucester Place B3
Gloucester Rd B2
Goldsmid Rd A1
Grand Junction Rd C2
Grand Pde B3
Grove Hill B3
Guildford St A2
Hampton Place B1
Hanover Terr A3
High St C3
Highdown Rd A1
Information Ctr C2
John St B3
Jubilee Clock Tower B2
Kemp St B2
Kensington Place B2
Kings Rd C1
Lanes, The C2
Law Courts B3
Lewes Rd A3
Library B2
London Rd A3
Madeira Dr C3
Marine Pde C3
Middle St C2
Montpelier Place B1
Montpelier Rd B1
Montpelier St B1
Mus & Art Gallery B3
New England Rd A2
New England St A2
New Rd B2
Nizells Ave A1
Norfolk Rd B1
Norfolk Terr B1
North Rd B2
North St B2
Odeon C2
Old Shoreham Rd A1
Old Steine C3
Osmond Rd A1
Over St B2
Oxford St A3
Park Crescent Terr A3
Phoenix Brighton B3
Phoenix Rise A3
Police Station B3
Post Office A1/A3/C3
Preston Rd A2
Preston St B1
Prestonville Rd A1
Queen's Rd B2
Queen Sq B2
Regency Sq C1
Regent St B2
Richmond Place B3
Richmond St B3
Richmond Terr A3
Rose Hill Terr A3
Royal Pavilion B2
St Bartholomew's A3
St James's St C3
St Nicholas Rd B2
St Nicholas' B2
St Peter's A3
Sea Life Brighton C3
Shaftesbury Rd A3
Ship St C2
Sillwood Rd B1
Sillwood St B1
Southover St A3
Spring Gdns B2
Stanford Rd A1
Stanley Rd A3
Surrey St B2
Sussex St B3
Swimming Pool B3
Sydney St B3
Temple Gdns B1
Terminus Rd A2
Theatre Royal B2
Tidy St B2
Town Hall C2
Toy & Model Mus A2
Trafalgar St B2
Union Rd A3
Univ of Brighton B3
Upper Lewes Rd A3
Upper North St B1
Viaduct Rd A3
Victoria Gdns B3
Victoria Rd B1
Volk's Electric Railway C3
West Pier (derelict) C1
West St C2
Western Rd B1
Whitecross St B2
YHA C3
London B1
York Place B3
York Rd B1

Bristol 177
Acramans Rd C4
Albert Rd C6
Alfred Hill A4
All Saint's St A4
All Saints' B4
Allington Rd C3
Alpha Rd C4
Ambra Vale B1
Ambra Vale East B2
Ambrose Rd B2
Amphitheatre & Waterfront Sq C4
Anchor Rd B3
Anvil St B6
Arcade, The A5
Architecture Centre, The B4
Argyle Place B2
Arlington Villas A2
Arnolfini B4
Art Gallery A3
Ashton Gate Rd C2
Ashton Rd C1
Avon Bridge C1
Avon Cres C1
Avon St B6
Baldwin St B4
Baltic Wharf C2
Baltic Wharf Leisure Centre & Caravan Park C2
Baltic Wharf Marina C2
Barossa Place C4
Barton Manor B6
Barton Rd B6
Barton Vale B6
Bath Rd C6
Bathurst Basin C4
Bathurst Parade C4
Beauley Rd C3
Bedminster Bridge C5
Bedminster Parade C4
Bellevue B2
Bellevue Cres B2
Bellevue Rd C6
Berkeley Place A2
Berkeley Sq A3
Birch Rd C2
Blackfriars A4
Bond St A5
Braggs La A6
Brandon Hill B3
Brandon Steep B3
Bristol Aquarium B4
Bristol Beacon B4
Bristol Bridge B5
Bristol Cath (CE) B3
Bristol Eye Hospital (A&E) A4
Bristol Grammar School A3
Bristol Harbour Railway C3
Bristol Royal Children's Hosp A4
Bristol Royal Infirmary (A&E) A4
Bristol Temple Meads Station B6
Broad Plain B6
Broad Quay B4
Broad St A4
Broad Weir A5
Broadcasting Ho A3
Broadmead A5
Brunel Institute B3
Brunel Way C1
Brunswick Sq A5
Burton Close C5
Bus Station A4
Butts Rd B3
Cabot Circus A5
Cabot Tower B3
Caledonia Place B1
Callowhill Ct A5
Cambridge St C6
Camden Rd C3
Camp Rd A1
Canada Way C2
Cannon St A4
Canon's Way B3
Cantock's Close A3
Canynge Rd A1
Canynge Sq A1
Castle Park A5
Castle St A5
Cathedral Walk B3
Catherine Meade St C4
Cattle Market Rd C6
Central Library B3
Charles Place B1
Charlotte St B3
Charlotte St South B3
Chatterton Ho B5
Chatterton Sq C5
Chatterton St C5
Cheese La B5
Christchurch A4
Christchurch Rd A1
Christmas Steps A4
Church La B2/B5
Church St B5
City Museum A3
City of Bristol Coll B3
Civil and Family Justice Centre B5
Clare St B4
Clarence Rd C5
Cliff Rd C1
Clift House Rd C1
Clifton Cath (RC) A2
Clifton Down A1
Clifton Down Rd A1
Clifton Hill B2
Clifton Park A1/A2
Clifton Park Rd A1
Clifton Rd A2
Clifton Vale B1
Cliftonwood Cres B2
Cliftonwood Rd B2
Cliftonwood Terr B2
Cobblestone Mews A1
College Green B3
College Rd A1
College St B3
Colston Almshouses A4
Colston Ave B4
Colston Parade C5
Colston St A4
Commercial Rd C4
Constitution Hill B2
Cooperage La C2
Corn St B4
Cornwallis Ave B1
Cornwallis Cres B1
Coronation Rd C2/C4
Council House B3
Counterslip B5
Create Ctr, The C1
Crosby Row B2
Crown Court A4
Culver St B3
Cumberland Basin C1
Cumberland Close C2
Cumberland Rd C2/C3
Dean La C4
Deanery Rd B3
Denmark St B4
Dowry Sq B1
Eaton Cres A2
Elmdale Rd A3
Elton Rd A3
Eugene St A4/A6
Exchange and St Nicholas' Mkts, The B4
Fairfax St A4
Fire Station B5
Floating Harbour C3
Fosseway, The A2
Foster Almshouses A4
Frayne Rd C1
Frederick Place A2
Freeland Place B1
Friary B5
Frogmore St B3
Fry's Hill B2
Galleries shopping centre, The A5
Gas La B6
Gasferry Rd C3
Georgian House B3
Glendale B1
Glentworth Rd B2
Gloucester St A1
Goldney Hall B2
Goldney Rd B1
Gordon Rd A2
Granby Hill B1
Grange Rd A1
Great Ann St A6
Great George Rd B3
Great George St A6/B3
Green St North B1
Green St South B1
Greenay Bush La C2
Greenbank Rd C2
Greville Smyth Park C1
Grove, The B4
Guildhall A4
Guinea St C4
Hamilton Rd C3
Hanbury Rd A2
Hanover Place C2
Harley Place A1
Haymarket A5
Hensman's Hill B1
High St B4
Highbury Villas A3
Hill St B3
Hill St C6
Hippodrome B4
Hopechapel Hill B1
Horfield Rd A4
Horsefair, The A5
Horton St B6
Host St A4
Hotwell Rd B1/B2
Houlton St A6
Howard Rd C3
IMAX Cinema B4
Information Ctr B4
Islington Rd C3
Jacob St A5/A6
Jacob's Wells Rd B2
John Carr's Terr B2
John Wesley's Chapel A5
Joy Hill B1
Jubilee St B6
Kensington Place A2
Kilkenny St B6
King St B4
Kingsland Rd B6
Kingston Rd C3
Lamb St A6
Lansdown Rd A2
Lawford St A6
Lawfords Gate A6
Leighton Rd C3
Lewins Mead A4
Lime Rd C2
Litfield Rd A1
Little Ann St A6
Little Caroline Pl B1
Little George St A6
Little King St B4
Llandoger Trow B4
Lloyds' Building, The C3
Lodge St A4
Lord Mayor's Chapel, The B4
Lower Castle St A5
Lower Church La A4
Lower Clifton Hill B2
Lower Guinea St C4
Lower Lamb St B3
Lower Maudlin St A4
Lower Park Rd A4
Lower Sidney St C2
Lucky La C4
Lydstep Terr C3
M Shed C4
Magistrates' Court A4
Manilla Rd A1
Mardyke Ferry Rd C2
Maritime Heritage Centre B3
Marlborough Hill A4
Marlborough St A4
Marsh St B4
Mead St C5
Merchant Dock B2
Merchant Seamen's Almshouses B4
Merchant St A5
Merchants Rd A1
Merchants Rd C1
Meridian Place A2
Meridian Vale A2
Merrywood Rd C3
Midland Rd A6
Milford St C3
Millennium Prom B3
Millennium Sq B3
Mitchell La B5
Mortimer Rd A1
Murray Rd C4
Myrtle Rd A3
Narrow Plain B5
Narrow Quay B4
Nelson St A4
New Charlotte St C4
New Kingsley Rd B6
New Queen St C5
New St A6
Newgate A5
Newton St A6
Norland Rd A1
North St C2
O2 Academy B3
Oakfield Grove A2
Oakfield Place A2
Oakfield Rd A2
Old Bread St B6
Old Market St A6
Old Park Hill A4
Oldfield Rd B1
Orchard Ave B4
Orchard La B4
Orchard St B4
Osbourne Rd C3
Oxford St B6
Park Place A2
Park Rd C3
Park Row A3
Park St A3
Passage St B5
Pembroke Grove A2
Pembroke Rd A2
Pembroke Rd C3
Pembroke St A5
Penn St A5
Pennywell Rd A6
Percival Rd A1
Pero's Bridge B4
Perry Rd A4
Phipps St C2
Pip 'n' Jay B5
Plimsoll Bridge B1
Police Sta A6
Polygon Rd B1
Portland St A1
Portwall La B5
Post Office A1/A3/A5/B1/B4/C4/C5
Prewett St C5
Prince St B4
Prince St Bridge C4
Princess St C5
Princess Victoria St B1
Priory Rd A3
Pump La C5
QEH Theatre A2
Quakers Friars A5
Quay St A4
Queen Charlotte St B4
Queen Elizabeth Hospital School B2
Queen Sq B4
Queen St A5
Queen's Ave A3
Queen's Parade B3
Queen's Rd A2/A3
Raleigh Rd C2
Randall Rd B2
Red Lodge A4
Redcliffe Backs B5
Redcliffe Bridge B4
Redcliffe Hill C5
Redcliffe Parade C4
Redcliffe St B5
Redcliffe Way B5
Redcross St A6
Redgrave Theatre A1
Regent St B1
Richmond Hill A2
Richmond Hill Ave A2
Richmond La A2
Richmond Park Rd A2
Richmond St C6
Richmond Terr A2
River St A6
Rownham Mead B2
Royal Fort Rd A3
Royal Park A2
Royal West of England Academy A3
Royal York Cres B1
Royal York Villas B1
Rupert St A4
Russ St B6
St Andrew's Walk B2
St George's B3
St George's Rd B3
St James A4
St John's A4
St John's Rd C4
St Luke's Rd C5
St Mary Redcliffe C5
St Matthias Park A6
St Michael's Hill A3
St Michael's Hospital A4
St Michael's Park A3
St Nicholas St B4
St Paul St A5
St Paul's Rd A2
St Peter's (ruin) A5
St Philip's Bridge B5
St Philips Rd A6
St Stephen's B4
St Stephen's St B4
St Thomas St B5
St Thomas the Martyr B5
Sandford Rd B1
Sargent St C5
Saville Place B1
Ship La C5
Shopmobility A5
Showcase Cinema de Lux A5
Silver St A4
Sion Hill A1
Small St A4
Smeaton Rd C1
Somerset Sq C5
Somerset St C5
Southernhay Ave B2
Southville Rd C4
Spike Island Artspace C2
Spring St C5
Superstore C4
SS Great Britain and the Matthew B2
Stackpool Rd C3
Staight St B6
Stillhouse La C4
Sydney Row C2
Tankard's Close A3
Temple Back B5
Temple Back East B5
Temple Bridge B5
Temple Church B5
Temple Circus B5
Temple Gate C5
Temple St B5
Temple Way B5
Terrell St A4
Theatre Royal (Bristol Old Vic) B4
Thekla B4
Thomas La B5
Three Kings of Cologne A4
Three Queens La B5
Tobacco Factory, The C2
Tower Hill B5
Tower La A4
Trenchard St A4
Triangle South A3
Triangle West A3
Trinity Rd A6
Trinity St A6
Tyndall Ave A3
Union St A5
Union St B6
Unity St A6
Unity St B3
University of Bristol A3
University Rd A3
Upper Byron Place A3
Upper Maudlin St A4
Upper Perry Hill C3
Upton Rd C2
Valentine Bridge B6
Victoria Grove C5
Victoria Rd C6
Victoria Rooms A2
Victoria Sq A2
Victoria St B5
Vyvyan Rd A1
Vyvyan Terr A1
Wade St A6
Walter St C2
Wapping Rd C4
Water La B5
Waterloo Rd A6
Waterloo St A1
Waterloo St A6
Watershed Media Centre B4
We the Curious B3
Welling Terr B1
Welsh Back B4
West Mall A1
West St A6
Westfield Place A1
Wetherell Place A2
Whitehouse Place C5
Whitehouse St C5
Whiteladies Rd A2
Whitson St A4
William St C5
Willway St C5
Windsor Place B1
Wine St A4
Woodland Rd A3
Woodland Rise A3
Worcester Rd A1
Worcester Terr A1
YHA B4
York Gdns B1
York Place A2
York Rd C5

Bury St Edmunds 178
Abbey Gardens B3
Abbey Gate B3
Abbeygate B2
Abbeygate St B2
Albert Cres B1
Albert St B1
Angel Hill B2
Angel La B2
Anglian Lane A1
Arc Shopping Ctr B2
Athenaeum C2
Baker's La C3
Barwell Rd B3
Beetons Way A1
Bishops Rd B2
Bloomfield St B2
Bridewell La C2
Bullen Close C1
Bury St Edmunds Station A2
Bury St Edmunds County Upper School A1
Bury St Edmunds Leisure Centre B1
Bury Town FC (Ram Meadow) B3
Bus Station B2
Business Park B3
Butter Mkt B2
Cannon St B2
Castle Rd C1
Cemetery C1
Chalk Rd (N) B1
Chalk Rd (S) B1
Church Row B2
Churchgate St C2
Citizens Advice Bureau B2
College St C2
Compiegne Way A3
Corn Exchange, The B2
Cornfield Rd B1
Cotton Lane B3
Courts B2
Covent Garden C2
Crown St C3
Cullum Rd C2
Eastern Way A3
Eastgate St B3
Enterprise Business Park A2
Etna Rd A2
Eyre Close C2
Fire & Ambulance Station B1
Friar's Lane C2
Gage Close A1
Garland St B2
Greene King Brewery C3
Grove Park B1
Grove Rd B1
Guildhall C2
Guildhall St C2
Hatter St C2
High Baxter St B2
Honey Hill C3
Hospital Rd C1/C2
Ickworth Dr C1
Industrial Estate A3
Information Ctr B2
Ipswich St A2
King Edward VI School A1
King's Rd C1/B2
Library B2
Long Brackland A2
Looms La B2
Lwr Baxter St B2
Malthouse La A2
Manor House C3
Maynewater La C3
Mill Rd C1
Mill Rd (South) C1
Minden Close B3
Moyse's Hall B2
Mustow St B3
Norman Tower C3
Northgate Ave A2
Northgate St B2
Osier Rd A2
Out Northgate A2
Out Risbygate B1
Out Westgate C2
Parkway B1/C2
Parkway, The B1
Peckham St B2
Petticoat La C1
Phoenix Day Hospital C1
Pinners Way C1
Police Station C3
Post Office B2
Pump La B2
Queen's Rd B1
Raingate St C3
Raynham Rd A1
Retail Park C1
Risbygate St B1/B2
Robert Boby Way C2
St Andrew's St North B2
St Andrew's St South B2
St Botolph's La C3
St Edmund's C2
St Edmund's Abbey (Remains) B3
St Edmunds Hospital (Private) C3
St Edmundsbury C3
St John's St B2
St Marys C3
School Hall La B2
Shillitoe Close C1
South Close C1
Southgate St C3
Sparhawk St C3
Spring Lane B1
Springfield Rd B1
Station Hill A2
Swan La C3
Tayfen Rd B2
Theatre Royal C3
Thingoe Hill A2
Victoria St B1
Vinefields, The B3
War Memorial C1
Well St B2
West Suffolk Coll B1
Westgarth Gdns C1
Westgate St C2
Whiting St C2
York Rd B1
York Terr B1

Cambridge 178
Abbey Rd A3
ADC A2
Anglia Ruskin Univ B3
Archaeology & Anthropology B2
Arts Picturehouse B2
Arts Theatre B1
Auckland Rd A3
Backs, The B1
Bateman St C2
Benet St B1
Bradmore St B3
Bridge St A1
Broad St B3
Brookside C2
Brunswick Terr A3
Burleigh St B3
Bus Station B2
Butt Green A2
Cambridge Contemporary Art Gallery B1
Castle Mound A1
Castle St A1
Cemetery B3
Chesterton La A1
Christ's (Coll) B2
Christ's Lane B2
Christ's Pieces B2
City Rd B3
Clare Bridge B1
Clare (Coll) B1
Clarendon St B2
Coe Fen C2
Coronation St C2
Corpus Christi (Coll) B1
Court B3
Cross St C3
Crusoe Bridge C1
Darwin (Coll) C1
Devonshire Rd C3
Downing (Coll) C2
Downing St B2
Earl St B2
East Rd B3
Eden St B3
Elizabeth Way A3
Elm St B2
Emery St B3
Emmanuel (Coll) B2
Emmanuel Rd B2
Emmanuel St B2
Fair St A3
Fen Causeway, The C1
Fenner's Cricket Gd C3
Fire Station B3
Fitzroy St A3
Fitzwilliam Mus C2
Fitzwilliam St C2
Garrett Hostel Bridge B1
Glisson Rd C3
Gonville & Caius (Coll) B1
Gonville Place C2
Grafton Centre, The A3
Grand Arcade B2
Green St B1
Gresham Rd C3
Guest Rd B3
Guildhall B2
Harvey Rd C3
Hills Rd C3
Hobson St B2
Hughes Hall (Coll) B3
Information Ctr B2
James St A3
Jesus (Coll) A2
Jesus Green A2
Jesus La A2
Jesus Terr B3
John St B3
Kelsey Kerridge Sports Centre B3
Kettle's Yard A1
King's Bridge B1
King St A2
King's (Coll) B1
King's College Chapel B1
King's Parade B1
Lammas Land Recreation Gd C1
Lensfield Rd C2
Library B2
Lion Yard B2
Little St Mary's La B1
Lyndewod Rd C3
Magdalene (Coll) A1
Magdalene St A1
Maid's Causeway A3
Malcolm St A2
Market St B1
Mathematical Bridge B1
Mawson Rd C3
Midsummer Comm A3
Mill La B1
Mill Rd B3
Mill St C3
Mumford B3
Museum of Cambridge A1
Museum of Classical Archaeology C1
Napier St A3
New Square A3
Newmarket Rd A3
Newnham Rd C1
Norfolk St B3
Northampton St A1
Norwich St C2
Orchard St B2
Panton St C2
Paradise St B3
Park Parade A1
Park St A2
Park Terr B2
Parker St B2
Parker's Piece B2
Parkside B3
Parkside Pools B3
Parsonage St A3
Pea's Hill B1
Pemberton Terr C2
Pembroke (Coll) B2
Pembroke St B1
Perowne St B3
Peterhouse (Coll) C1
Petty Cury B2
Polar Mus, The C2
Police Station B3
Post Office A3/B2/C1/C2/C3
Queen's La B1
Queen's Rd B1
Queens' (Coll) B1
Regent St B2
Regent Terr B2
Ridley Hall (Coll) C1
Riverside A3
Round Church, The A1
Russell St C2
St Andrew's St B2
St Benet's B1
St Catharine's (Coll) B1
St Eligius St C2
St John's (Coll) A1
St Mary's B1
St Paul's Rd C3
Saxon St C2
Sedgwick Mus B2
Sheep's Green C1
Shire Hall A1
Sidgwick Ave C1
Sidney St A2
Sidney Sussex (Coll) A2
Silver St B1
Station Rd C3
Tenison Ave C3
Tenison Rd C3
Tennis Court Rd B2
Thompson's La A1
Trinity (Coll) A1
Trinity Bridge B1
Trinity Hall (Coll) B1
Trinity St B1
Trumpington Rd C2
Trumpington St B1
Union Rd C2
University Botanic Gardens C2
Victoria Ave A2
Victoria St B2
Warkworth St B3
Warkworth Terr B3
Wesley House (Coll) A2
West Rd B1
Westcott Ho (Coll) A2
Westminster (Coll) A1
Whipple B2
Willis Rd B3
Willow Walk A2
YMCA C3
Zoology B2

Canterbury 178
Artillery St B2
Barton Mill Rd A3
Beaconsfield Rd A1
Beaney, The B2
Beverley Meadow A1
Beverley Rd A1
Bingley's Island B1
Black Griffin La B1
Broad Oak Rd A2
Broad St B2
Brymore Rd A3
Burgate B2
Bus Station C2
Canterbury Castle C1
Canterbury Christ Church University B3
Canterbury College C3
Canterbury East C1
Canterbury Tales, The B2
Canterbury West A1
Castle Row C1
Castle St C1
Cathedral B2
Causeway, The A2
Chaucer Rd A3
Christchurch Gate B2
City Council Offices A3
City Wall B2
Coach park A2
College Rd B3
Cossington Rd C2
Court B2
Craddock Rd A3
Crown & County Courts B3
Dane John Gdns C2
Dane John Mound C1
Deanery B2
Dover St C2
Duck La B2
Eastbridge Hosp B1
Edgar Rd B3
Ersham Rd C3
Ethelbert Rd C3
Fire Station C2
Forty Acres Rd A1
Friars, The B2
Gordon Rd C1
Greyfriars B1
Guildford Rd C1
Havelock St B2
Heaton Rd C1
High St B2
Information Centre A2/B2
Ivy La B2
King St B2
King's School B2/B3
King's School Recreation Ctr, The A2
Kingsmead Leisure Centre A2
Kingsmead Rd A2
Kirby's La B1
Lansdown Rd C2
Lime Kiln Rd C1
Longport B3
Lower Chantry La C3
Mandeville Rd A1
Market Way A2
Marlowe Arcade B2
Marlowe Ave C2
Marlowe Theatre B2
Martyrs Field Rd C1
Mead Way B1
Military Rd B2
Monastery St B2
Museum of Canterbury (Rupert Bear Museum) B1
New Dover Rd C3
New St C1
Norman Rd C2
North Holmes Rd B3
North La B1
Northgate A2
Nunnery Fields C2
Nunnery Rd C2
Oaten Hill C2
Odeon Cinema C2
Old Dover Rd C2
Old Palace B2
Old Ruttington La B2
Old Weavers B2
Orchard St B1
Oxford Rd C1
Palace St B2
Pilgrims Way C3
Pin Hill C1
Pine Tree Ave A1
Police Station C2
Post Office B2, C1
Pound La B1
Puckle La C2
Raymond Ave C2
Recreation Ground A2
Registry Office A2
Rheims Way B1
Rhodaus Close C2
Rhodaus Town C2
Roman Museum B2
Roper Gateway A1
Roper Rd A1
Rose La B2
Shopmobility B2
St Augustine's Abbey (remains) B3
St Augustine's Rd C3
St Dunstan's A1
St Dunstan's St A1
St George's Place C2
St George's St B2
St George's Tower B2
St Gregory's Rd B3
St John's Hosp A2
St Margaret's St B2
St Martin's B3
St Martin's Ave B3
St Martin's Rd B3
St Michael's Rd A1
St Mildred's C1
St Peter's Grove B1
St Peter's La B2
St Peter's Place B1
St Peter's St B1
St Radigunds St B2
St Stephen's Ct A1
St Stephen's Path A1
St Stephen's Rd A2
Salisbury Rd A1
Simmonds Rd C1
Spring La C3
Station Rd West B1
Stour St B1
Sturry Rd A3
Tourtel Rd A3
Tudor Rd C1
Union St B2
University for the Creative Arts C3
Vernon Place C2
Victoria Rd C1
Watling St B2
Westgate Gdns B1
Westgate Towers B1
Whitefriars B2
Whitehall Gdns B1
Whitehall Rd B1
Wincheap C1
York Rd C1
Zealand Rd C2

Cardiff Caerdydd 178
Adam St B3
Alexandra Gdns A2
Allerton St C1
Arran St A3
ATRiuM (University of Glamorgan) C3
Beauchamp St C1
Bedford St A3
Blackfriars Priory (rems) B1
Bvd De Nantes B2
Brains Brewery C2
Brook St B1
Bute Park A1
Bute St C2
Bute Terr C3
Callaghan Sq C2/C3
Capitol Shopping Centre, The B3
Cardiff Arms Park (Cardiff Blues) B1
Cardiff Bridge B1
Cardiff Castle B2
Cardiff Central Station C2
Cardiff Story, The B2
Cardiff Univ A1/A2/B3
Cardiff University Student's Union A2
Caroline St C2
Castle Green B2
Castle Mews A1
Castle St (Heol y Castell) B1
Cathays Station A2
Celerity Drive C3
Central Library C2
Charles St (Heol Siarl) B3
Churchill Way B3
City Hall A2
City Rd A3
Clare Rd C1
Clare St C1
Coburn St A3
Coldstream Terr B1
College Rd A1
Colum Rd A1
Court C2
Court Rd C1
Craiglee Drive C3
Cranbrook St A3
Customhouse St C2
Cyfartha St A3
David's B2/C2
Despenser Place C1
Despenser St C1
Dinas St C1
Duke St (Heol y Dug) B2
Dumfries Place B3
East Grove A3
Ellen St C3
Fire Station B3
Fitzalan Place B3
Fitzhamon Emb C1
Fitzhamon La C1
Friary, The B2
g39 B2
Gloucester St C1
Glynrhondda St A2
Gordon Rd A3
Gorsedd Gdns B2
Green St B1
Greyfriars Rd B2
Hafod St C1
Hayes, The B2
Herbert St C3
High St B2
HM Prison B3
Industrial Estate C3
John St C3
Jubilee St C1
King Edward VII Ave A1
Kingsway (Ffordd y Brenin) B2
Knox Rd B3
Law Courts B2
Llanbleddian Gdns A2
Llantwit St A2
Lloyd George Ave C3
Lower Cathedral Rd B1
Lowther Rd A3
Magistrates Court B3
Mansion House A3
Mardy St C1
Mark St B1
Market B2
Mary Ann St C3
Merches Gdns C1
Mill La C2
Millennium Bridge B1
Miskin St A2
Monmouth St C1
Motorpoint Arena Cardiff C3
Museum Ave A2
Museum Place A2
National Museum Cardiff A2
National War Memorial A2
Neville Place C1
New Theatre B2
Newport Rd B3
Northcote La A3
Northcote St A3
Parade, The A3
Park Grove A4
Park Place A2
Park St C2
Penarth Rd C2
Pendyris St C1
Plantaganet St C1
Post Office B2
Principality Stadium C1
Principality Stadium Tours (Gate 3) B2
Quay St B2
Queen's Arcade B2
Queen Anne Sq A1
Queen St (Heol y Frenhines) B2
Queen St Station B3
Regimental Museums B2
Rhymney St A3
Richmond Rd A3
Royal Welsh College of Music and Drama A1
Russell St A3
Ruthin Gdns A2
St Andrews Place A2
St David's B2
St David's Hall B2
St John the Baptist B2
St Mary St (Heol Eglwys Fair) B2
St Peter's St A3
Salisbury Rd A3
Sandon St B3
Schooner Way C3
Scott Rd C2
Scott St C2
Senghennydd Rd A2
Sherman Theatre A2
Sophia Gardens A1
Sophia Gardens Stadium A1
South Wales Baptist College A3
Sport Wales National Ctr A1
Stafford Rd C1
Stadium Plaza C1
Station Terr B3
Stuttgarter Strasse B2
Sussex St C1
Taffs Mead Emb C1
Talworth St A3
Temple of Peace & Health A1
Treharris St A3
Trinity St B2
Tudor La C1
Tudor St C1
Tyndall St C3
Vue C1
Walk, The A3
Welsh Government A1
West Grove A3
Westgate St (Heol y Porth) B2
Windsor Place B3
Womanby St B2
Wood St C2
Working St B2
Wyeverne Rd A2

Carlisle 179
Abbey St A1
Aglionby St B3
Albion St C3
Alexander St C3
AMF Bowl C2
Annetwell St A1
Bank St B2
Bitts Park A1
Blackfriars St B2
Blencome St C1
Blunt St C1
Botchergate C2
Boustead's Grassing C2
Bowman St B3
Bridge St A1
Broad St B3
Brook St C3
Brunswick St B2
Bus Station B2
Caldew Bridge A1
Caldew St C1
Carlisle (Citadel) Station B2
Carlisle College A2
Castle A1
Castle St A1
Castle Way A1
Cathedral A1
Cecil St B2
Chapel St A2
Charles St B3
Charlotte St B1
Chatsworth Square A2
Chiswick St B2
Citadel, The B2
City Walls A1
Civic Centre A2
Clifton St C1
Close St B3
Collingwood St C1

Colville St C1
Colville Terr C1
Council Offices B3
Court B2
Court St Brow B2
Crosby St B2
Crown St C2
Currock Rd C2
Dacre Rd A1
Dale St C1
Denton St C1
Devonshire Walk A1
Duke's Rd A2
East Dale St C1
East Norfolk St C1
Eden Bridge A2
Edward St B3
Elm St B1
English St B2
Fire Station A2
Fisher St A1
Flower St B3
Freer St C1
Fusehill St B3
Georgian Way A2
Gloucester Rd C3
Golf Course A2
Graham St C1
Grey St B3
Guildhall Mus A2
Halfey's La B3
Hardwicke Circus A2
Hart St B3
Hewson St C2
Howard Place A3
Howe St B3
Information Ctr A2
James St B2
Junction St B1
King St B2
Lancaster St B2
Lanes Shopping Centre, The B2
Laser Quest B2
Library A2
Lime St B1
Lindisfarne St C3
Linton St B3
Lismore Place A3
Lismore St B3
London Rd C3
Lonsdale Rd B2
Lord St C3
Lorne Cres B1
Lorne St B1
Lowther St B2
Madford Retail Pk B1
Magistrates' Ct A2
Market Hall A2
Mary St B2
Memorial Bridge A3
Metcalfe St C1
Milbourne St B1
Myddleton St B3
Nelson St C1
Norfolk St C1
Old Fire Sta, The A2
Old Town Hall A2
Oswald St C3
Peter St A2
Petteril St B3
Pools B2
Portland Place B2
Portland Sq B2
Post Office A2/B2/C1/C3
Princess St C2
Pugin St B1
Red Bank Terr C2
Regent St C3
Richardson St C1
Rickerby Park A3
Rickergate A2
River St B3
Rome St C2
Rydal St B3
St Cuthbert's B2
St Cuthbert's La B2
St James' Park C1
St James' Rd C1
St Nicholas Gate Retail Park C3
St Nicholas St C3
Sands Centre, The A2
Scotch St A2
Shaddongate B1
Sheffield St B1
Shopmobility A2
South Henry St B3
South John St C2
South St B3
Spencer St B2
Station Retail Park B2
Strand Rd A2
Superstore B1
Sybil St B3
Tait St B2
Thomas St B1
Thomson St C3
Trafalgar St C1
Trinity Leisure Ctr A2
Tullie Museum & Art Gallery A1
Tyne St C3
Univ of Cumbria B3
Viaduct Estate Rd B1
Victoria Place A2
Victoria Viaduct B2
Vue B2
Warwick Rd B2
Warwick Sq B3
Water St B2
West Walls B1
Westmorland St C1

Chelmsford 179

Anchor St C1
Anglia Ruskin Univ A2
Arbour La A3
Baddow Rd B2/C3
Baker St C1
Barrack Sq B2
Bellmead B2
Bishop Hall La A2
Bishop Rd A2
Bond St B2
Boswells Dr B3
Bouverie Rd C2
Bradford St C1
Braemar Ave C1
Brook St A2
Broomfield Rd A1
Burgess Springs B3
Burns Cres C2
Bus Station B1/B2
Cedar Ave A1
Cedar Ave West A1
Cemetery A1
Cemetery A2
Cemetery C1
Central Park B1
Chelmsford ✝ B2
Chelmsford ≋ A1
Chichester Dr A3
Chinery Close A3
City Council A1
Civic Centre A1
Civic Theatre B1
Cloudfm County Cricket Gd, The B2
College C1
Cottage Place A2
County Hall B2
Coval Ave B1
Coval La B1
Coval Wells B1
Crown Court B2
Duke St B2
Elm Rd C1
Elms Dr A1
Essex Record Office, The B3
Fairfield Rd B1
Falcons Mead B1
George St C2
Glebe Rd A1
Godfrey's Mews C2
Goldlay Ave C3
Goldlay Rd C2
Grove Rd C2
Hall St C2
Hamlet Rd C2
Hart St C1
Henry Rd A2
High Bridge Rd B2
High Chelmer Shopping Centre B2
High St B2
Hill Cres B3
Hill Rd B3
Hill Rd Sth B3
Hillview Rd A3
HM Prison A3
Hoffmans Way A2
Hospital B2
Lady La C2
Langdale Gdns C3
Legg St B2
Library B2
Lionfield Terr A3
Lower Anchor St C1
Lynmouth Ave C2
Lynmouth Gdns C3
Magistrates Court B2
Maltese Rd A1
Manor Rd C2
Marconi Rd A2
Market B2
Market Rd B2
Marlborough Rd C1
Meadows Shopping Centre, The B2
Meadowside A3
Mews Ct C2
Mildmay Rd C2
Moulsham Dr C2
Moulsham Mill C3
Moulsham St C1/C2
Navigation Rd B3
New London Rd B2/C1
New St A2/B2
New Writtle St C1
Nursery Rd C2
Orchard St C2
Odeon B2
Parker Rd C2
Parklands Dr A3
Parkway A1/B1/B2
Police Station A2
Post Office B2/C2
Primrose Hill A1
Prykes Dr B1
Queen St C1
Queen's Rd B3
Railway St A1
Rainsford Rd A1
Ransomes Way A2
Rectory La A2
Regina Rd A2
Riverside Ice & Leisure Centre B2
Riverside Retail Pk A3
Rosebery Rd C2
Rothesay Ave C1
St John's Rd C2
Sandringham Pl B3
Seymour St B1
Shopmobility B2
Shrublands Close B3
Southborough Rd C1
Springfield Rd A3/B2/B3
Stapleford Close C1
Superstore B2/C3
Swiss Ave A1
Telford Place A3
Tindal St B2
Townfield St A1
Trinity Rd B3
University B1
Upper Bridge Rd C1
Upper Roman Rd C2
Van Dieman's Rd C3
Viaduct Rd B1
Vicarage Rd C1
Victoria Rd A2
Victoria Rd South B2
Vincents Rd C2
Waterloo La B2
Weight Rd B3
Westfield Ave A1
Wharf Rd B3
Writtle Rd C1
YMCA A2
York Rd C1

Cheltenham 179

Albert Rd A3
Albion St B3
All Saints Rd B3
Ambrose St B2
Andover Rd C1
Back Montpellier Terr C2
Bandstand C2
Bath Pde B2
Bath Rd C2
Bays Hill Rd C1
Bennington St B2
Berkeley St B3
Brewery Quarter, The A2
Brunswick St South A2
Bus Station B2
Carlton St B3
Central Cross Road A3
Cheltenham Coll C2
Cheltenham FC A3
Cheltenham General (A&E) C3
Cheltenham Ladies' College B2
Christchurch Rd B1
Cineworld A2
Clarence Rd A2
Clarence Sq A2
Clarence St B2
Cleveland St A1
College Baths Road C3
College Rd C2
Colletts Dr A1
Corpus St C3
Devonshire St A2
Douro Rd B1
Duke St B3
Dunalley Pde A2
Dunalley St A2
Everyman B2
Evesham Rd A3
Fairview Rd B3
Fairview St B3
Fire Station C3
Folly La A2
Gloucester Rd A1
Grosvenor St B3
Grove St A1
Hanover St A2
Hatherley St C1
Henrietta St A2
Hewlett Rd B3
High St B2/B3
Holst Birthplace Museum A3
Hudson St A2
Imperial Gdns C2
Imperial La B2
Imperial Sq C2
Information Ctr B2
Keynsham Rd C3
King St A2
Knapp Rd B2
Lansdown Cres C1
Lansdown Rd C1
Leighton Rd B3
Library B2
London Rd C3
Lypiatt Rd C1
Magistrates' Court & Register Office B1
Malvern Rd B1
Manser St A2
Market St A1
Marle Hill Pde A2
Marle Hill Rd A2
Millbrook St A1
Milsom St A2
Montpellier Gdns C2
Montpellier Grove C2
Montpellier Pde C2
Montpellier Spa Rd C2
Montpellier St C1
Montpellier Terr C2
Montpellier Walk C2
New St B2
North Place B2
Old Bath Rd C3
Oriel Rd B2
Overton Park Rd B1
Overton Rd B1
Oxford St C3
Parabola Rd B1
Park Place C1
Park St A1
Pittville Circus A3
Pittville Crescent A3
Pittville Lawn A3
Pittville Park A2
Playhouse B2
Portland St B3
Prestbury Rd A3
Prince's Rd C1
Priory St B3
Promenade B2
Queen St A1
Recreation Ground A2
Regent Arcade B2
Regent St B2
Rodney Rd B2
Royal Cres B2
Royal Well Place B2
Royal Wells Rd B2
St George's Place B2
St Georges Rd B1
St Gregory's B2
St James St B3
St John's Ave B3
St Luke's Rd C2
St Margarets Rd A2
St Mary's B2
St Matthew's B2
St Paul's La A2
St Paul's Rd A2
St Paul's St A2
St Stephen's Rd C1
Sandford Parks Lido C3
Sandford Mill Road C3
Sandford Park C3
Sandford Rd C2
Selkirk St A3
Sherborne Place B3
Sherborne St B3
Suffolk Pde C2
Suffolk Rd C1
Suffolk Sq C1
Sun St A1
Swindon Rd B2
Sydenham Villas Rd C3
Tewkesbury Rd A1
The Courtyard B1
Thirlstaine Rd C2
Tivoli Rd C1
Tivoli St C1
Town Hall & Theatre B2
Townsend St A1
Trafalgar St C2
Union St B3
University of Gloucestershire (Francis Close Hall) A2
University of Gloucestershire (Hardwick) A1
Victoria Place B3
Victoria St A2
Vittoria Walk C2
Wellesley Rd A2
Wellington Rd A3
Wellington Sq A3
Wellington St B2
West Drive A3
Western Rd B1
Wilson, The B2
Winchcombe St B3
Winston Churchill Meml Gardens A1

Chester 179

Abbey Gateway A2
Appleyards La C3
Bars, The B3
Bedward Row B1
Beeston View C3
Bishop Lloyd's Palace B2
Black Diamond St A2
Bottoms La C3
Boughton B3
Bouverie St A1
Bus Interchange A2
Bridge St B2
Bridgegate C2
Brook St A3
Brown's La C2
Cambrian Rd A1
Canal St A2
Carrick Rd C1
Castle C2
Castle Dr C2
Cathedral B2
Catherine St A1
Cheshire Military Museum C2
Chester ≋ A3
Cheyney Rd A1
Chichester St A1
City Rd A3
City Walls B1/B2
City Walls Rd B1
Cornwall St A2
Cross Hey C3
Cross, The B2
Crown Ct C2
Cuppin St B2
Curzon Park North C1
Curzon Park South C1
Dee Basin A1
Dee La B3
Delamere St A2
Deva Roman Discovery Ctr B2
Dingle, The C1
Duke St B2
Eastgate B2
Eastgate St B2
Eaton Rd C2
Edinburgh Way C3
Elizabeth Cres B3
Fire Station A2
Foregate St B2
Forum Studio B2
Forum, The B2
Frodsham St B2
Gamul House B2
Garden La A1
George St A2
Gladstone Ave A1
God's Providence House B2
Gorse Stacks A2
Greenway St C2
Grosvenor Bridge C1
Grosvenor Mus B2
Grosvenor Park B3
Grosvenor Park Terr C1
Grosvenor Shopping Ctr B2
Grosvenor St B2
Groves Rd B3
Groves, The B3
Guildhall Mus B1
Handbridge C2
Hartington St C3
Hoole Way A2
Hunter St B2
Information Ctr B2
King Charles' Tower A2
King St A2
Library B2
Lightfoot St A3
Little Roodee C2
Liverpool Rd A2
Love St B3
Lower Bridge St B2
Lower Park Rd B3
Lyon St A2
Magistrates Court B2
Meadows La C3
Meadows, The B3
Milton St A3
Minerva Roman Shrine C2
Miniature Railway B3
New Crane St B1
Nicholas St B2
Northgate A2
Northgate Arena A2
Northgate St A2
Nun's Rd B1
Old Dee Bridge C2
Overleigh Rd C2
Park St B2
Police Station B2
Post Office A2/A3
Princess St B2
Queen St B2
Queen's Park Rd C3
Queen's Rd A3
Race Course B1
Raymond St A1
River La C2
Roman Amphitheatre & Gardens B2
Roodee (Chester Racecourse), The B1
Russell St A3
St Anne St A2
St George's Cres C3
St Martin's Gate A1
St Martin's Way A1
St Oswalds Way A2
Saughall Rd A1
Sealand Rd A1
South View Rd A1
Stanley Palace B1
Station Rd A3
Steven St A3
Storyhouse B2
Superstore B2
Tower Rd B1
Town Hall B2
Union St B3
Univ of Chester C2
Vicar's La B2
Victoria Cres C3
Victoria Rd A2
Walpole St A1
Water Tower St A1
Water Tower, The B1
Watergate B1
Watergate St B2
Whipcord La A1
White Friars B2
York St B3

Chichester 180

Adelaide Rd A3
Alexandra Rd A3
Arts Centre B2
Ave de Chartres B1/B2
Barlow Rd A1
Basin Rd C2
Beech Ave B1
Bishops Palace Gardens B2
Bishopsgate Walk A3
Bramber Rd A3
Broyle Rd A2
Bus Station B2
Caledonian Rd B3
Cambrai Ave B3
Canal Place C1
Canal Wharf C2
Canon La B2
Cathedral B2
Cavendish St A1
Cawley Rd B2
Cedar Dr A1
Chapel St A2
Cherry Orchard Rd C3
Chichester ≋ B2
Chichester By-Pass C2/C3
Chichester Coll B1
Chichester Cinema B3
Chichester Festival A2
Chichester Gate Leisure Pk C1
Churchside A2
Cineworld C1
City Walls B2
Cleveland Rd B3
College La A2
Cory Close C2
Council Offices B2
County Hall B2
District B2
Duncan Rd A1
Durnford Close A1
East Pallant B2
East Row B2
East St B2
East Walls B3
Eastland Rd C3
Ettrick Close B3
Ettrick Rd B3
Exton Rd C3
Fire Station A2
Football Ground A2
Franklin Place A2
Friary (Rems of) A2
Garland Close C3
Green La A3
Grove Rd C3
Guilden Rd B3
Guildhall A2
Hawthorn Close A1
Hay Rd C3
Henty Gdns B1
Herald Dr C3
Hornet, The B3
Information Ctr B2
John's St B2
Joys Croft A3
Jubilee Pk A3
Jubilee Rd A3
Juxon Close B1
Kent Rd A3
King George Gdns A2
King's Ave C2
Kingsham Ave C3
Kingsham Rd C2
Laburnum Grove B2
Leigh Rd C1
Lennox Rd A3
Lewis Rd A3
Library B2
Lion St B2
Litten Terr A3
Litten, The A3
Little London B2
Lyndhurst Rd B3
Market B3
Market Ave B2
Market Cross B2
Market Rd B3
Melbourne Rd A3
Minerva A2
Mount La B1
New Park Rd A3
Newlands La A1
North Pallant B2
North St A2
North Walls A2
Northgate A2
Novium, The B2
Oak Ave A1
Oak Close A1
Oaklands Park A2
Oaklands Way A2
Orchard Ave A1
Orchard St A1
Ormonde Ave B3
Pallant House B2
Parchment St A1
Parklands Rd A1/B1
Peter Weston Place B3
Police Station C2
Post Office A1/B2/C3
Priory La A2
Priory Park A2
Priory Rd A2
Queen's Ave C1
Riverside A3
Roman Amphitheatre B3
St Cyriacs A2
St Martins' St B2
St Pancras A3
St Paul's Rd A2
St Richard's Hospital (A&E) A3
Shamrock Close A3
Sherbourne Rd A1
Somerstown A2
South Bank C2
South Downs Planetarium C2
South Pallant B2
South St B2
Southgate B2
Spitalfield La A3
Stirling Rd B3
Stockbridge Rd C1/C2
Swanfield Dr A3
Terminus Ind Est C1
Tower St A2
Tozer Way A3
Turnbull Rd A3
Upton Rd C1
Velyn Ave B3
Via Ravenna B1
Walnut Ave A1
West St B2
Westgate B1
Westgate Fields B1
Westgate Leisure Centre B1
Weston Ave C1
Whyke Close C3
Whyke La B3
Whyke Rd C3
Winden Ave B3

Colchester 180

Abbey Gateway ✝ C2
Albert St A1
Albion Grove C2
Alexandra Rd C1
Artillery St C3
Arts Centre B1
Balkerne Hill B1
Barrack St C3
Beaconsfield Rd C1
Beche Rd C3
Bergholt Rd A1
Bourne Rd C3
Brick Kiln Rd A1
Brigade Grove C2
Bristol Rd B2
Broadlands Way A3
Brook St B3
Bury Close B2
Bus Sta B2
Butt Rd C1
Campion Rd C2
Cannon St C3
Canterbury Rd C2
Captain Gardens C2
Castle B2
Castle Park B2
Castle Rd B2
Catchpool Rd A1
Causton Rd B1
Chandlers Row C3
Circular Rd East C2
Circular Rd North C1
Circular Rd West C1
Clarendon Way A1
Claudius Rd C2
Colchester ≋ A1
Colchester Camp Abbey Field C1
Colchester Retail Pk B1
Colchester Town ≋ C2
Colne Bank Ave A1
Colne View Retail Pk A2
Compton Rd A3
Cowdray Ave A1/A2
Cowdray Ctr, The A2
Crouch St B1
Crowhurst Rd B1
Culver Square Shopping Centre B1
Culver St East B2
Culver St West B1
Dilbridge Rd A3
East Hill B2
East St B3
East Stockwell St B1
Eld La B1
Essex Hall Rd A1
Exeter Dr B2
Fairfax Rd C2
Fire Station A2
Firstsite B2
Flagstaff Rd C1
Garrison Parade C2
George St B2
Gladstone Rd C2
Golden Noble Hill C2
Goring Rd A3
Granville Rd C3
Greenstead Rd B3
Guildford Rd B2
Harsnett Rd C3
Harwich Rd B3
Head St B1
High St B1/B2
High Woods Country Park A2
Hollytrees B2
Hyderabad Close C2
Hythe Hill C3
Information Ctr B2
Jarmin Rd A2
Kendall Rd C2
Kimberley Rd C3
King Stephen Rd C3
Leisure World A2
Library B1
Lincoln Way B2
Lion Walk Shopping Centre B1
Lisle Rd C2
Lucas Rd C2
Magdalen Green C3
Magdalen St C2
Maidenburgh St B2
Maldon Rd C1
Manor Rd B1
Margaret Rd A1
Mason Rd A2
Mercers Way A1
Mercury B1
Mersea Rd C2
Meyrick Cres C2
Mile End Rd A1
Military Rd C2
Mill St C2
Minories B2
Moorside B3
Morant Rd C3
Napier Rd C2
Natural History B2
New Town Rd C2
Norfolk Cres A3
North Hill B1
North Station Rd A1
Northgate St B1
Nunns Rd B1
Odeon B1
Old Coach Rd B3
Old Heath Rd C3
Osborne St B2
Petrolea Close A1
Police Station C1
Popes La B1
Port La C3
Post Office B2/C1
Priory St B2
Queen St B2
Rawstorn Rd B1
Rebon St C3
Recreation Rd C3
Ripple Way A3
Roberts Rd C2
Roman Rd B2
Roman Wall B2
Romford Close A3
Rosebery Ave B2
St Andrews Ave B3
St Andrews Gdns B3
St Botolph St B2
St Botolphs B2
St John's Abbey (site of) ✝ C2
St John's St B1
St Johns Walk Shopping Centre B1
St Leonards Rd C3
St Marys Fields B1
St Peter's St B1
St Peters B1
Salisbury Ave C1
Saw Mill Rd C3
Sergeant St C2
Serpentine Walk A1
Sheepen Place B1
Sheepen Rd B1
Sir Isaac's Walk B1
Smythies Ave B2
South St C1
South Way C1
Sports Way A2
Suffolk Close A3
Superstore A1
Town Hall B1
Valentine Dr A3
Victor Rd C3
Wakefield Close B2
Wellesley Rd C1
Wells Rd B2/B3
West St C1
West Stockwell St B1
Weston Rd C3
Westway A1
Wickham Rd C1
Wimpole Rd C3
Winchester Rd C2
Winnock Rd C2
Worcester Rd B2

Coventry 180

Abbots La A1
Albany B1
Albany Rd B1
Alma St B3
Ambulance Sta A2
Art Faculty B3
Asthill Grove C2
Bablake School A1
Barras La A1/B1
Barr's Hill School A1
Belgrade B2
Bishop St A2
Bond's Hospital B1
Broad Gate B2
Broadway C1
Burges, The B2
Bus Station A3
Butts Radial B1
Byron St A3
Canterbury St A3
Cathedral ✝ B3
Central Six Retail Park C1
Chester St A1
Cheylesmore Manor House B2
Christ Church Spire B2
City Coll A3
City Walls & Gates A2
Corporation St B2
Council House B2
Coundon Rd A1
Coventry Station ≋ C2
Coventry Transport Museum A2
Coventry University Technology Park C3
Cox St A3
Croft Rd B1
Dalton Rd C1
Deasy Rd C3
Earl St B2
Eaton Rd C2
Fairfax St B2
Fire Sta A2
Foleshill Rd A2
Ford's Hospital B2
Fowler Rd A1
Friars Rd C2
Gordon St C1
Gosford St B3
Greyfriars Green B2
Greyfriars Rd B2
Gulson Rd B3
Hales St A2
Harnall Lane East A3
Harnall Lane West A2
Herbert Art Gallery & Museum B3
Hertford St B2
Hewitt Ave A1
High St B2
Hill St B1
Holy Trinity B2
Holyhead Rd A1
Howard St A3
Huntingdon Rd C1
Information Ctr C2
Jordan Well B3
King Henry VIII School C1
Lady Godiva Statue B2
Lamb St A2
Leicester Row A2
Library B2
Lincoln St A2
Little Park St B2
London Rd C3
Lower Ford St B3
Lower Precinct Shopping Centre B2
Magistrates & Crown Courts B2
Manor House Drive B2
Manor Rd C2
Market B2
Martyrs Meml C2
Meadow St B1
Meriden St A1
Michaelmas Rd C2
Middleborough Rd A1
Mile La C3
Millennium Place A2
Much Park St B3
Naul's Mill Park A1
New Union B2
Odeon B1
Park Rd C2
Parkside C3
Planet Ice Arena B1
Post Office A3, B2
Primrose Hill St A3
Priory Gardens & Visitor Centre B2
Priory St B3
Puma Way C3
Quarryfield La C3
Queen's Rd B1
Quinton Rd C2
Radford Rd A2
Raglan St B3
Ringway (Hill Cross) A1
Ringway (Queens) B1
Ringway (Rudge) B1
Ringway (St Johns) B3
Ringway (St Nicholas) A2
Ringway (St Patricks) C2
Ringway (Swanswell) A2
Ringway (Whitefriars) B3
St John St B2
St John the Baptist B2
St Nicholas St A2
Sidney Stringer Academy A3
Skydome B1
Spencer Ave C1
Spencer Rec Gnd C1
Spencer Rd C1
Spon St B1
Sports Centre B3
Stoney Rd C2
Stoney Stanton Rd A3
Superstore B2
Swanswell Pool A3
Thomas Landsdail St C2
Tomson Ave A1
Top Green C1
Tower St A2
Trinity St B2
University B3
Univ Sports Ctr B3
Upper Hill St A1
Upper Well St A2
Victoria St A3
Vine St A3
Wave, The B2
Warwick Rd C2
Waveley Rd B1
West Orchards Shopping Ctr B2
Westminster Rd C1
White St A3
Windsor St B1

Derby 180

Abbey St C1
Agard St B1
Albert St B2
Albion St B2
Ambulance Station B1
Arthur St A1
Ashlyn Rd B3
Assembly Rooms B2
Babington La C2
Bass Recreation Gd B3
Becket St B1
Belper Rd A1
Bold La B1
Bradshaw Way C2
Bradshaw Way Retail Park C2
Bridge St B1
Brook St B1
Burton Rd C1
Bus Station B2
Business Park A3
Caesar St A2
Canal St C3
Carrington St C3
Cathedral ✝ B2
Cathedral Rd B1
Charnwood St C2
Chester Green Rd A2
City Rd A2
Clarke St A3
Cock Pitt Junction B3
Council House B2
Courts B1
Cranmer Rd B3
Crompton St C1
Crown & County Courts B2
Curzon St B1
Darley Grove A1
Derbion C2
Derby ≋ C3
Derby Gaol B1
Derwent Bsns Ctr A2
Derwent St B2
Drewry La C1
Duffield Rd A1
Duke St A2
Dunton Close B3
Eagle Market C2
East St B2
Eastgate B3
Exeter St B2
Farm St C1
Ford St B1
Forester St C1
Fox St A2
Friar Gate B1
Friary St B1
Full St B2
Garden St A1
Gerard St C1
Gower St C2
Green La C2
Grey St C1
Guildhall B2
Handyside Bridge A2
Harcourt St C1
Highfield Rd A1
Hill La C2
Incora County Ground (Derbyshire CCC), The B3
Information Ctr B2
Iron Gate B2
John St C3
Joseph Wright Ctr B1
Kedleston Rd A1
Key St B2
King Alfred St C1
King St A1
Kingston St A1
Lara Croft Way C2
Leopold St C2
Liversage St C3
Lodge La B1
London Rd C2
London Rd Community Hospital C2
Macklin St C1
Mansfield Rd A2
Market B2
Market Place B2
May St C1
Meadow La B3
Melbourne St C2
Mercian Way C1
Midland Rd C3
Monk St C1
Morledge B2
Mount St C1
Mus & Art Gallery B1
Mus of Making B2
North Parade A1
North St A1
Nottingham Rd B3
Osmaston Rd C2
Otter St A1
Park St C3
Parker St A1
Pickford's House B1
Police Station A2, B2
Post Office A1/A2/B1/C2/C3
Pride Parkway C3
Prime Enterprise Pk A2
Prime Parkway A2
QUAD B2
Queens Leisure Ctr B1
Racecourse Park A3
Railway Terr C3
Register Office B2
Riverlights Leisure Centre B2
Sadler Gate B1
St Alkmund's Way B1/B2
St Helens House A1
St Mary's A1
St Mary's Bridge A2
St Mary's Bridge Chapel A2
St Mary's Gate B1
St Paul's Rd A2
St Peter's C2
St Peter's St C2
Showcase De Lux C2
Siddals Rd C3
Sir Frank Whittle Rd A3
Spa La C1
Spring St C1
Stafford St B1
Station Approach C3
Stockbrook St C1
Stores Rd A3
Traffic St C2
Wardwick B1
Werburgh St C1
West Ave A1
West Meadows Industrial Estate B3
Wharf Rd A2
Wilmot St C2
Wilson St C1
Wood's La C1

Dorchester 181

Ackerman Rd B3
Acland Rd A2
Albert Rd A1
Alexandra Rd B1
Alfred Place B3
Alfred Rd B2
Alington Ave B3
Alington Rd B3
Ashley Rd B1
Balmoral Cres C3
Barnes Way B2/C2
Borough Gdns A1
Brewery Sq B1
Bridport Rd A1
Buckingham Way C3
Caters Place A1
Cemetery A3/C1
Charles St A2
Coburg Rd B1
Colliton St A1
Cornwall Rd A1
Cromwell Rd B1
Culliford Rd B2
Culliford Rd North B2
Dagmar Rd B1
Damer's Rd B1
Diggory Cres C2
Dinosaur Mus A2
Dorchester Bypass C2
Dorchester South Station ≋ B1
Dorchester West Station ≋ B1
Dorset County (A&E) B1
Dorset County Council Offices A1
Dorset County Museum A1
Duchy Close C3
Duke's Ave B2
Durngate St A2
Durnover Court A3
Eddison Ave B3
Edward Rd B1
Egdon Rd C2
Elizabeth Frink Statue B2
Farfrae Cres B2
Forum Centre, The B1
Friary Hill A2
Friary Lane A2
Frome Terr A2
Garland Cres C3
Glyde Path Rd A1
Grosvenor Cres C1
Grosvenor Rd C1
Grove, The A1
Gt Western Rd B1
Herringston Rd C1
High St East A2
High St Fordington A2
High Street West A1
Holloway Rd A2
Icen Way A2
Information Ctr B2
Keep Military Museum, The A1
Kings Rd A3/B3
Kingsbere Cres C2
Lancaster Rd B2
Library B1
Lime Close C1
Linden Ave B2
London Close A3
London Rd A2/A3
Lubbecke Way A3
Lucetta La B2
Maiden Castle Rd C1
Manor Rd C2
Market B1
Marshwood Place B2
Maumbury Rd B1
Maumbury Rings B1
Mellstock Ave C2
Mill St A3
Miller's Close A1
Mistover Close C1
Monmouth Rd B1/B2
Moynton Rd C2
Nature Reserve A2
North Sq A2
Northernhay A1
Odeon B1
Old Crown Court & Cells A1
Olga Rd B1
Orchard St A2
Plaza A1
Police Station B1
Post Office A1
Pound Lane A2
Poundbury Rd A1
Prince of Wales Rd B2
Prince's St A1
Queen's Ave B1
Roman Town Ho A1
Roman Wall A1
Rothesay Rd C2
St George's Rd B3
Salisbury Field A2
Sandringham Sports Centre B3
Shaston Cres C2
Smokey Hole La B3
South Court Ave C1
South St B1
South Walks Rd B2
Superstore C3
Teddy Bear Mus A2
Temple Close C1
Terracotta Warriors & Teddy Bear Mus A2
Town Hall A2
Town Pump A2
Trinity St A1
Tutankhamun Ex A1
Victoria Rd B1
Weatherbury Way C2
Wellbridge Close C1
West Mills Rd A1
West Walks Rd A1
Weymouth Ave C1
Williams Ave B1
Winterbourne (BMI) C1
Wollaston Rd A2
York Rd B2

Dumfries 181

Academy St A2
Aldermanhill Rd B3
Ambulance Station C3
Annan Rd A3
Ardwall Rd A3
Ashfield Dr A1
Atkinson Rd C1
Averill Cres C1
Balliol Ave C1
Bank St B2
Bankend Rd C3
Barn Slaps B3
Barrie Ave B3
Beech Ave A1
Bowling Green A3
Brewery St B2
Bridgend Theatre B1
Brodie Ave C2
Brooke St B2
Broomlands Dr C1
Brooms Rd B3
Buccleuch St A2
Burns House B2
Burns Mausoleum B3
Burns St B2
Burns Statue A2
Bus Station B1
Cardoness St A3
Castle St A2
Catherine St A2
Cattle Market A3
Cemetery B3
Cemetery C2
Church Cres A2
Church St B2
College Rd A1
College St A1
Corbelly Hill B1
Corberry Park B1
Cornwall Mt A3
Council Offices A2
Court A2
Craigs Rd C3
Cresswell Ave B3
Cresswell Hill B3
Cumberland St B3
David Keswick Athletic Centre A3
David St B1
Dock Park C3
Dockhead B2
Dumfries ≋ A3
Dumfries Academy A2
Dumfries Ice Bowl A1
Dumfries Museum & Camera Obscura B2

Dumfries & Galloway Royal Infirmary (A&E) Ⓗ C3
East Riverside Dr C3
Edinburgh Rd A2
English St B2
Fire Station B3
Friar's Vennel A2
Galloway St B1
George Douglas Dr C1
George St A2
Gladstone Rd C2
Glasgow St A1
Glebe St B3
Glencaple Rd C3
Goldie Ave A1
Goldie Cres A1
Golf Course C3
Gracefield Arts Centre 🏛 A2
Greyfriars ⛪ A2
Grierson Ave B3
Hamilton Ave C1
Hamilton Starke Pk C2
Hazelrigg Ave C1
Henry St B3
Hermitage Dr C1
High Cemetery C3
High St A2
Hill Ave C2
Hill St B1
HM Prison B1
Holm Ave C2
Hoods Loaning A3
Howgate St B1
Huntingdon Rd A3
Information Ctr ℹ B2
Irish St B2
Irving St A2
King St A1
Kingholm Rd C3
Kirkpatrick Ct C2
Laurieknowe B1
Leafield Rd B3
Library A2
Lochfield Rd A1
Loreburn Pk A3
Loreburn St A2
Loreburne Shopping Centre B2
Lover's Walk A2
Martin Ave B3
Mausoleum B3
Maxwell St B1
McKie Ave B3
Mews La A2
Mid Steeple ✦ B2
Mill Green B2
Mill Rd B1
Moat Rd C2
Moffat Rd A3
Mountainhall Pk C3
Nelson St B1
New Abbey Rd B1/C1
New Bridge B1
Newall Terr A2
Nith Ave A2
Nith Bank C3
Nithbank Hosp Ⓗ C3
Nithside Ave A1
Odeon 🎥 B2
Old Bridge B1
Old Bridge Ho 🏛 B1
Palmerston Pk (Queen of the South FC) A1
Park Rd C1
Pleasance Ave C1
Police HQ A3
Police Sta 🚔 A2/A3
Portland Dr A1
Post Office ✉ B1/B2/B3
Priestlands Dr C1
Primrose St B1
Queen St B3
Queensberry St A2
Rae St A2
Richmond Ave C2
Robert Burns Ctr 🏛 B2
Roberts Cres C1
Robertson Ave C3
Robinson Dr C1
Rosefield Rd C2
Rosemount St B1
Rotchell Park C1
Rotchell Rd B1
Rugby Football Gd C1
Ryedale Rd C2
St Andrews ⛪ B2
St John the Evangelist ⛪ A2
St Josephs College B3
St Mary's Ind Est A3
St Mary's St A3
St Michael St B2
St Michael's ⛪ B2
St Michael's Bridge B2
St Michael's Bridge Rd B2
St Michael's Cemetery B3
Shakespeare St B2
Solway Dr C2
Stakeford St A1
Stark Cres C2
Station Rd A3
Steel Ave A1
Sunderries Ave A1
Sunderries Rd A1
Superstore B3
Suspension Brae B2
Swimming Pool A1
Terregles St B1
Theatre Royal 🎭 B2
Troqueer Rd C2
Union St A1
Wallace St B3
Welldale B2
West Riverside Dr C2
White Sands B2

Dundee 181

Abertay University B2
Adelaide Place A1
Airlie Place C1
Albany Terr A1
Albert St A3
Alexander St A2
Ann St A2
Arthurstone Terr A3
Bank St B2
Barrack Rd A1
Barrack St B2
Bell St B2
Blinshall St B1
Broughty Ferry Rd A3
Brown St B1
Bus Station B3
Caird Hall B2
Camperdown St B3
Candle La B3
Carmichael St A1
City Churches ⛪ B2
City Quay B3
City Square B2
Commercial St B2
Constable St A3
Constitution Cres A1
Constitution Ct A1
Constitution St A1/B2
Cotton Rd A3
Courthouse Sq B1
Cowgate A3
Crescent St A3
Crichton St B2
Dens Brae A3
Dens Rd A3
Discovery Point ✦ C2
Douglas St B1
Drummond St A1
Dudhope Castle 🏰 A1
Dudhope St A2
Dudhope Terr A1
Dundee ⇌ C2
Dundee Contemporary Arts ✦ C2
Dundee High School B2
Dundee Law ✦ A1
Dundee Rep 🎭 C2
Dunhope Park A1
Dura St A3
East Dock St B3
East Marketgait B3
East Whale La B3
Erskine St A3
Euclid Cres B2
Forebank Rd A2
Foundry La A3
Gallagher Retail Pk B3
Gellatly St B3
Government Offices C2
Guthrie St B1
Hawkhill B1
Hilltown A2
HMS Unicorn ✦ B3
Howff Cemetery, The B2
Information Ctr ℹ B2
Keiller Shopping Ctr B2
Keiller Ctr, The B2
King St A3
Kinghorne Rd A1
Ladywell Ave A3
Laurel Bank A2
Law Rd A1
Law St A1
Library A2/A3
Library and Steps Theatre 🎭 A2
Little Theatre, The 🎭 A2
Lochee Rd B1
Lower Princes St A3
Lyon St A3
McManus Art Gallery & Museum, The 🏛 B2
Meadow Side B2
Meadowside St Pauls ⛪ B2
Mercat Cross ✦ B2
Murraygate B2
Nelson St A2
Nethergate B2/C1
North Lindsay St B2
North Marketgait B2
Old Hawkhill B1
Olympia Leisure Ctr B3
Overgate Shopping Centre B2
Park Place B1
Perth Rd C1
Police Station 🚔 B1
Post Office ✉ B2
Princes St A3
Prospect Place A2
Reform St B2
Riverside Dr C2
Riverside Esplanade C2
Roseangle C1
Rosebank St A2
RRS Discovery ⛵ C2
St Andrew's ✝ C2
St Pauls Episcopal ✝ B3
Science Centre ✦ C2
Seagate B2
Sheriffs Court B1
Shopmobility B2
South George St A2
South Marketgait B3
South Tay St B2
South Victoria Dock Road B3
South Ward Rd B2
Tay Road Bridge ✦ C3
Thomson Ave B2
Trades La B3
Union St B2
Union Terr A1
University Library B2
Univ of Dundee B1
Upper Constitution St A1
Verdant Works ✦ B1
V&A Museum of Design 🏛 C2
Victoria Dock B3
Victoria Rd A2
Victoria St A3
Ward Rd B1
Wellgate B2
West Bell St B1
West Marketgait B1/B2
Westfield Place C1
William St A3
Wishart Arch ✦ A3

Durham 181

Alexander Cres B2
Allergate B2
Archery Rise C1
Assembly Rooms 🎭 B2
Avenue, The B1
Back Western Hill A1
Bakehouse La A3
Baths Bridge B3
Boat House B3
Bowling A2
Boyd St C3
Bus Station B2
Castle Chare B2
Cathedral ✝ B2
Church St C3
Clay La C1
Claypath B3
College of St Hild & St Bede B3
County Hospital Ⓗ B1
Crescent, The A1
Crook Hall & Gardens ⌂ A3
Crossgate B2
Crossgate Peth C1
Crown Court B3
Darlington Rd C1
Durham ⇌ A2
Durham Castle 🏰 B2
Durham School C2
Durham University (Science Site) C3
Ellam Ave C1
Elvet Bridge B3
Elvet Court B3
Farnley Hey B1
Ferens Close A3
Fieldhouse La A1
Flass St B1
Flass Vale Local Nature reserve A1
Framwelgate Bridge B2
Framwelgate A2
Framwelgate Peth A2
Framwelgate Waterside A2
Frankland La A3
Freeman's Place A3
Freeman's Quay Leisure Centre A3
Gala Theatre & Cinema 🎭 B3
Geoffrey Ave C1
Gilesgate B3
Grey College C3
Grove, The A1
Hallgarth St C3
Hatfield College B3
Hawthorn Terr B1
Heritage Centre 🏛 B3
HM Prison B3
John St B1
Kingsgate Bridge B3
Laburnum Terr B1
Lawson Terr B1
Leazes Rd B2/B3
Library B2
Margery La B2
Market B2
Mavin St C3
Millburngate B2
Millburngate Bridge B2
Millennium Bridge (foot/cycle) A2
Mountjoy Research Centre C3
Museum of Archaeology 🏛 B2
New Elvet B3
New Elvet Bridge B3
North Bailey B3
North End A1
Observatory C1
Old Elvet B3
Open Treasure 🏛 B2
Oriental Mus 🏛 C2
Oswald Court C3
Passport Office A2
Percy Terr B1
Pimlico C2
Police Station 🚔 B3
Post Office ✉ A1/B2
Potters Bank C1/C2
Prebends Bridge C2
Prebends Walk C2
Prince Bishops Shopping Centre B3
Princes St A1
Providence Row A3
Quarryheads La C2
Redhills La B1
Redhills Terr B1
Riverwalk, The B2
Saddler St B3
St Cuthbert's Society C2
St Margaret's ⛪ B2
St Mary the Less ⛪ C2
St Mary's College C2
St Monica Grove B1
St Nicholas' ⛪ B3
St Oswald's ⛪ C3
Sands, The A3
Shopmobility B3
Sidegate A2
Silver St B2
Sixth Form College A3
South Bailey C2
South Rd C3
South St B2
Springwell Ave A1
Station Approach B2
Stockton Rd C3
Student Union B3
Summerville B1
Sutton St B2
Town Hall B2
Univ Arts Block B3
University Coll ✦ B2
Walkergate Centre A3
Wearside Dr A3
Western Hill A1
Wharton Park A2
Whinney Hill C3
Whitehouse Ave C1
YHA ▲ C3

Edinburgh 182

Abbey Strand B6
Abbeyhill A6
Abbeyhill Cres B6
Abbeymount A6
Abercromby Place A3
Adam St C5
Albany La A4
Albany St A4
Albert Memorial ✦ B2
Albyn Place A2
Alva Place A6
Alva St B1
Ann St A1
Appleton Tower C4
Archibald Place C3
Assembly Rooms & Musical Hall A3
Atholl Crescent B1
Atholl Crescent La C1
Bank St B4
Barony St A4
Beaumont Place C5
Belford Rd B1
Belgrave Cres A1
Belgrave Cres La A1
Bell's Brae B1
Blackfriars St B4
Blair St B4
Bread St C2
Bristo Place C4
Bristo St C4
Brougham St C2
Broughton St A4
Brown St C5
Brunton Terr A6
Buckingham Terr A1
Burial Ground A6
Bus Station A4
Caledonian Cres C1
Caledonian Rd C1
Calton Hill A4
Calton Hill A5
Calton Rd B4
Camera Obscura & Outlook Tower ✦ B3
Candlemaker Row C4
Canning St B2
Canongate B5
Canongate ⛪ B5
Carlton St A1
Carlton Terr A6
Carlton Terrace La A6
Castle St B2
Castle Terr B2
Castlehill B3
Central Library B4
Chalmers Hosp Ⓗ C3
Chalmers St C3
Chambers St C4
Chapel St C4
Charles St C4
Charlotte Sq B2
Chester St B1
Circus La A2
Circus Place A2
City Art Centre 🏛 B4
City Chambers ⌂ B4
City Observatory ✦ A5
Clarendon Cres A1
Clerk St C5
Coates Cres B1
Cockburn St B4
College of Art C3
Comely Bank Ave A1
Comely Bank Row A1
Cornwall St C2
Cowans Close C5
Cowgate B4
Cranston St B5
Crichton St C4
Croft-An-Righ A6
Cumberland St A2
Dalry Place C1
Dalry Rd C1
Danube St A1
Darnawy St A2
David Hume Tower C4
Davie St C5
Dean Bridge A1
Dean Gdns A1
Dean Park Cres A1
Dean Park Mews A1
Dean Park St A1
Dean Path B1
Dean St A1
Dean Terr A1
Dewar Place C1
Dewar Place La C1
Doune Terr A2
Drummond Place A3
Drummond St C5
Drumsheugh Gdns B1
Dublin Mews A3
Dublin St A4
Dublin St La South A4
Dumbiedykes Rd B5
Dundas St A3
Dynamic Earth ✦ B6
Earl Grey St C2
East Crosscauseway C5
East Market St B4
East Norton Place A6
East Princes St Gdns B3
Easter Rd A6
Edinburgh (Waverley) ⇌ B4
Edinburgh Castle 🏰 B3
Edinburgh Dungeon ✦ B4
Edinburgh Int Conference Ctr C2
Elder St A4
Esplanade B3
Eton Terr A1
Eye Pavilion Ⓗ C3
Festival Office B3
Festival Theatre Edinburgh 🎭 C4
Filmhouse 🎥 C2
Fire Station C2
Floral Clock ✦ B3
Forres St A2
Forth St A4
Fountainbridge C2
Frederick St A3
Freemasons' Hall B3
Fruitmarket 🏛 B4
Gardner's Cres C2
George Heriot's School C3
George IV Bridge B4
George Sq C4
George Sq La C4
George St B3
Georgian House 🏛 B2
Gladstone's Land ⌂ B3
Glen St C3
Gloucester La A2
Gloucester Place A2
Gloucester St A2
Graham St C3
Grassmarket C3
Great King St A3
Great Stuart B1
Greenside La A5
Greenside Row A5
Greyfriars Kirk ⛪ C4
Grindlay St C2
Grosvenor St C1
Grove St C1
Gullan's Close B5
Guthrie St B4
Hanover St A3
Hart St A4
Haymarket C1
Haymarket Sta ⇌ C1
Heriot Place C3
Heriot Row A2
High School Yard B5
High St B4
Hill Place C5
Hill St A2
Hillside Cres A5
Holyrood Abbey (Remains) ✝ A6
Holyrood Gait B6
Holyrood Park C6
Holyrood Rd B5
Home St C2
Hope St B2
Horse Wynd B6
Howden St C5
Howe St A2
Hub, The ✦ B3
India Place A2
India St A2
Infirmary St B4
Information Ctr ℹ B4
Jeffrey St B4
John Knox House 🏛 B4
Johnston Terr C3
Keir St C3
Kerr St A2
King's Stables Rd B2
Lady Lawson St C3
Lauriston Gdns C3
Lauriston Park C3
Lauriston Place C3
Lauriston St C3
Lawnmarket B3
Learmonth Gdns A1
Learmonth Terr A1
Leith St A4
Lennox St A1
Lennox St La A1
Leslie Place A2
London Rd A5
Lothian Rd B2
Lothian St C4
Lower Menz Place A6
Lynedoch Place B1
Manor Place B1
Market St B4
Marshall St C4
Maryfield A6
McEwan Hall C4
Medical School C4
Melville St B1
Meuse La B4
Middle Meadow Walk C4
Milton St A6
Montrose Terr A6
Moray Place A2
Morrison Link C1
Morrison St C1
Mound Place B3
Mound, The B3
Multrees Walk A4
Mus Collections Ctr A4
Museum of Childhood 🏛 B5
Museum of Edinburgh 🏛 B5
Museum of Fire 🏛 C3
Museum on the Mound 🏛 B4
National Archives of Scotland ⌂ A4
National Museum of Scotland 🏛 C4
National Gallery 🏛 B3
National Library of Scotland ⌂ B4
National Monument ✦ A5
National Portrait Gallery 🏛 B4
National War Museum 🏛 B3
Nelson Monument ✦ A5
Nelson St A3
New St B5
Nicolson Sq C4
Nicolson St C4
Niddry St B4
North Bank St B3
North Bridge B4
North Castle St A2
North Charlotte St A2
North Meadow Walk C3
North St Andrew St A4
North St David St A3
North West Circus Place A2
Northumberland St A3
Odeon 🎥 C2
Old Royal High School A5
Old Tolbooth Wynd B5
OMNi Centre ✦ A4
Oxford Terr A1
Palace of Holyroodhouse ⛫ B6
Palmerston Place B1
Panmure Place C3
Parliament Sq B4
People's Story, The ⌂ B5
Playhouse Theatre 🎭 A4
Pleasance C5
Police Station 🚔 A4
Ponton St C2
Post Office ✉ A3/B4/B5/C1/C2/C4
Potterrow C4
Princes Mall B4
Princes St B3
Princes St 🚊 B3
Prisoners of War 🏛 B3
Queen's Gallery 🏛 B6
Queen St A2
Queen Street Gdns A3
Queen's Dr B6/C6
Queensferry Rd A1
Queensferry St B1
Queensferry St La B2
Radical Rd C6
Randolph Cres B1
Regent Gdns A5
Regent Rd B5
Regent Rd Park A6
Regent Terr A5
Richmond La C5
Richmond Place C5
Rose St B2
Ross Open Air Theatre 🎭 B3
Rothesay Place B1
Rothesay Terr B1
Roxburgh Place C5
Roxburgh St C5
Royal Bank of Scotland A4
Royal Circus A2
Royal Lyceum 🎭 C2
Royal Mile, The B5
Royal Scottish Academy 🏛 B3
Royal Terr A5
Royal Terrace Gdns A5
Rutland Sq B2
Rutland St B2
St Andrew Sq A4
St Andrew Sq 🚊 A4
St Andrew's House A4
St Bernard's Cres A1
St Bernard's Well ✦ A1
St Cecilia's Hall B4
St Colme St A2
St Cuthbert's ⛪ B2
St Giles' ✝ B4
St James Quarter Shopping Centre A4
St John St B5
St John's ⛪ B2
St John's Hill B5
St Leonard's Hill C5
St Leonard's La C5
St Leonard's St C5
St Mary's A4
St Mary's Scottish Episcopal ✝ B1
St Mary's St B5
St Michael & All Saints ⛪ C3
St Stephen St A2
Salisbury Crags C6
Saunders St A2
Scotch Whisky Experience ✦ B3
Scott Monument ✦ B4
Scottish Parliament B6
Scottish Storytelling Centre ✦ B5
Semple St C2
Shandwick Place B2
South Bridge B4
South Charlotte St B2
South College St C4
South Learmonth Gdns A1
South St Andrew St A4
South St David St A3
Spittal St C2
Stafford St B1
Student Centre C4
Surgeons' Hall 🏛 C5
Supreme Courts ⌂ B4
Teviot Place C4
Thistle St A3
Torphichen Place C1
Torphichen St C1
Traverse Theatre 🎭 B2
Tron Sq B4
Tron, The ✦ B4
Union St A4
University C4
University Library C4
Univ of Edinburgh B5
Upper Grove Place C1
Usher Hall 🎭 C2
Vennel C3
Victoria St B3
Viewcraig Gdns B5
Viewcraig St B5
Vue 🎥 A4
Walker St B1
Waterloo Place A4
Waverley Bridge B4
Wemyss Place A2
West Approach Rd C1
West Crosscauseway C5
West End 🚊 B1
West Maitland St C1
West of Nicholson St C4
West Port C3
West Princes Street Gdns B3
West Richmond St C5
West Tollcross C2
White Horse Close ✦ B6
William St B1
Windsor St A5
Writer's Museum, The 🏛 B4
York La A4
York Place A4
York Place 🚊 A4
Young St B2

Exeter 182

Alphington St C1
Athelstan Rd B3
Barnardo Rd C3
Barnfield Hill B3
Barnfield Rd B2/B3
Barnfield Theatre 🎭 B2
Bartholomew St East B1
Bartholomew St West B1
Bear St B2
Beaufort Rd C1
Bedford St B2
Belgrave Rd A3
Belmont Rd A3
Blackall Rd A2
Blackboy Rd A3
Bonhay Rd B1
Bull Meadow Rd C2
Bus & Coach Sta B3
Castle St B2
Catacombes ✦ B1
Cecil Rd C1
Cheeke St A3
Church Rd C1
Chute St A3
City Wall B1/B2
Civic Centre B2
Clifton Rd B3
Clifton St B3
Clock Tower A1
College Rd B3
Colleton Cres C2
Commercial Rd C1
Coombe St B2
Cowick St C1
Crown Courts B2
Custom House Visitor Centre ⌂ C2
Cygnet Theatre 🎭 C2
Danes' Rd A2
Denmark Rd B3
Devon County Hall C3
Devonshire Place A3
Dinham Cres B1
East Grove Rd C3
Edmund St C1
Elm Grove Rd A1
Exe St B1
Exeter Cathedral ✝ B2
Exeter Central Station ⇌ A1
Exeter City Football Ground A3
Exeter College A1
Exeter Picture Ho 🎥 B1
Fire Station A1
Fore St B1
Friars Walk C2
Guildhall ⌂ B2
Guildhall Shopping Centre B2
Haven Rd C2
Heavitree Rd B3
Hele Rd A1
High St B2
HM Prison A2
Holloway St C2
Hoopern St A2
Horseguards A2
Howell Rd A1
Information Ctr ℹ B3
Iron Bridge B1
Isca Rd C1
Jesmond Rd A3
King St B1
King William St A2
Larkbeare Rd C2
Leisure Centre C1
Library B2
Longbrook St A2
Longbrook Terr A2
Lower North St B1
Lucky La C2
Lyndhurst Rd C3
Magdalen Rd B3
Magdalen St B2
Market B2
Market St B2
Marlborough Rd C3
Mary Arches St B1
Matford Ave C3
Matford La C3
Matford Rd C3
May St A3
Mol's Coffee Ho ⌂ B2
New Bridge St B1
New North Rd A1/A2
North St B1
Northernhay St B1
Norwood Ave C3
Odeon 🎥 A3
Okehampton St C1
Old Mill Close C2
Old Tiverton Rd A3
Oxford Rd A3
Paris St B2
Parr St A3
Paul St B1
Pennsylvania Rd A2
Portland Street A3
Post Office ✉ A3/B2/C1
Powderham Cres A3
Preston St B1
Princesshay Shopping Centre B2
Pyramids Leisure Centre B3
Quay, The C2
Queen St A1
Queen's Terr A1
Queens Rd C1
Radford Rd C2
Richmond Rd A1
Roberts Rd C2
Rougemont Castle 🏰 A2
Rougemont Ho ✦ B2
Royal Albert Memorial Museum 🏛 B2
St David's Hill A1
St James' Pk Sta ⇌ A3
St James' Rd A3
St Leonard's Rd C3
St Mary Steps ⛪ C1
St Nicholas Priory ⛫ B1
St Thomas Sta ⇌ C1
Sandford Walk B3
School Rd C1
Sidwell St A2
Smythen St B1
South St B2
Southernhay East B2
Southernhay West B2
Spicer Rd B3
Sports Centre A3
Summerland St A3
Sydney Rd C1
Tan La C2
Thornton Hill A2
Topsham Rd C3
Tucker's Hall ⌂ B1
Tudor St B1
Underground Passages ✦ B2
University of Exeter (St Luke's Campus) B3
Velwell Rd A1
Verney St A3
Vue 🎥 B3
Water La C1/C2
Weirfield Rd C2
Well St A3
West Ave A2
West Grove Rd C3
Western Way A3/B1/B2
Willeys Ave C1
Wonford Rd B3/C3
York Rd A2

Glasgow 183

Admiral St C2
Albert Bridge C5
Albion St B5
Anderston ⇌ B3
Anderston Quay B3
Argyle Arcade B5
Argyle St A1/A2/B3/B4/B5
Argyle Street ⇌ B5
Arlington St A3
Arts Centre 🏛 B3
Ashley St A3
Bain St C6
Baird St A6
Baliol St A3
Ballater St C5
Barras (Mkt), The C6
Bath St A3
BBC Scotland B1
Bell St C6
Bell's Bridge B1
Bentinck St A2
Berkeley St A3
Bishop La B3
Black St A6
Blackburn St C2
Blackfriars St B6
Blantyre St A1
Blythswood Sq A4
Blythswood St B4
Bothwell St B4
Brand St C1
Breadalbane St A2
Bridge St C4
Bridge St Ⓜ C4
Bridgegate C5
Briggait C5
Broomielaw B4
Broomielaw Quay Gdns B3
Brown St B4
Brunswick St B5
Buccleuch St A3
Buchanan Bus Sta A5
Buchanan Galleries A5
Buchanan St B5
Buchanan St Ⓜ B5
Cadogan St B4
Caledonian Univ A5
Calgary St A5
Cambridge St A4
Canal St A5
Candleriggs B5
Carlton Place C4
Carnarvon St A3
Carrick St B4
Castle St B6
Cathedral Sq B6
Cathedral St B5
Central Mosque C5
Centre for Contemporary Arts 🏛 A4
Centre St C4
Cessnock Ⓜ C1
Cessnock St C1
Charing Cross ⇌ A3
Charlotte St C6
Cheapside St B3
Cineworld 🎥 A5
Citizens' Theatre 🎭 C5
City Chambers Complex B5
City Halls ⌂ B5
City of Glasgow Coll (City Campus) B5
City of Glasgow Coll (Riverside Campus) C5
Clairmont Gdns A2
Claremont St A2
Claremont Terr A2
Claythorne St C6
Cleveland St A3
Clifford La C1
Clifford St C1
Clifton Place A2
Clifton St A2
Clutha St C1
Clyde Arc B2
Clyde Place C4
Clyde Place Quay C4
Clyde St C5
Clyde Walkway C3
Clydeside Expressway B2
Coburg St C4
Cochrane St B5
College St B6
Collins St B6
Commerce St C4
Cook St C4
Cornwall St C2
Couper St A5
Cowcaddens Ⓜ A4
Cowcaddens Rd A4
Crimea St B3
Custom House Quay Gdns C4
Dalhousie St A4
Dental Hospital Ⓗ A4
Derby St A2
Dobbie's Loan A4/A5
Dobbie's Loan Pl A5
Dorset St A3
Douglas St B4
Doulton Fountain ✦ C6
Dover St A2
Drury St B4
Drygate B6
Duke St B6
Dunaskin St A1
Dunblane St A4
Dundas St B5
Dunlop St C5
East Campbell St C6
Eastvale Place A1
Eglinton St C4
Elderslie St A3
Elliot St B2
Elmbank St A3
Esmond St A1
Exhibition Ctr ⇌ B2
Festival Park C1
Film Theatre 🎥 A4
Finnieston Quay B2
Finnieston St B2
Fire Station C6
Florence St C5
Fox St C5
Gallowgate C6
Garnet St A3
Garnethill St A4
Garscube Rd A4
George Sq B5
George St B5
George V Bridge C4
Gilbert St A1
Glasgow Bridge C4
Glasgow Cath ✝ B6
Glasgow Central ⇌ B4
Glasgow City Free Church ⛪ B4
Glasgow Green C6
Glasgow Necropolis ✦ B6
Glasgow Royal Concert Hall 🎭 A5
Glasgow Science Centre ✦ B1
Glasgow Tower ✦ B1
Glassford St B5
Glebe St A6
Gorbals Cross C5
Gorbals St C5
Gordon St B4
Govan Rd B1/C1/C2
Grace St B3
Grafton Place A5
Grand Ole Opry ✦ C2
Grant St A3
Granville St A3
Gray St A2
Greendyke St C6
Grey Eagle St B7
Harley St C1
Harvie St C1
Haugh Rd A1
Havanah St B6
Heliport B1
Henry Wood Hall 🎭 A2
High Court C5
High St B6
High Street ⇌ B6
Hill St A3
Holland St A3
Holm St B4
Hope St A5
Houldsworth St B2
Houston Place C3
Houston St C3
Howard St C5
Hunter St C6
Hutcheson St B5
Hydepark St B3
Imax Cinema 🎥 B1
India St A3
Information Ctr ℹ B5
Ingram St B5
Jamaica St B4
James Watt St B4
John Knox St B6
John St B5
Kelvin Hall ✦ A1
Kelvin Statue ✦ A2
Kelvin Way A2
Kelvingrove Art Gallery & Mus 🏛 A1
Kelvingrove Park A2
Kelvingrove St A2
Kelvinhaugh St A1
Kennedy St A6
Kent Rd A2
Killermont St A5
King St B5
King's, The 🎭 A3
Kingston Bridge C3
Kingston St C4
Kinning Park Ⓜ C2
Kyle St A5
Lancefield Quay B2
Lancefield St B3
Langshot St C1
Lendel Place C1
Lighthouse, The ✦ B4
Lister St A6
Little St B3
London Rd C6
Lorne St C1
Lower Harbour B1
Lumsden St A1
Lymburn St A1
Lyndoch Cres A3
Lynedoch Place A3
Lynedoch St A3
Maclellan St C1
Mair St C2
Maitland St A4
Mansell St C7
Mavisbank Gdns C2
Mcalpine St B3
Mcaslin St A6
McLean Sq C2
McLellan Gallery 🏛 A4
McPhater St A4
Merchants' Ho ⌂ B5
Middlesex St C2
Middleton St C1
Midland St B4
Miller St B5
Millennium Bridge B1
Millroad St C6
Milnpark St C2
Milton St A4
Minerva St B2
Mitchell St West B4
Mitchell Liby, The ✦ A3
Modern Art Gallery 🏛 B5
Moir St C6
Molendinar St C6
Moncur St C6
Montieth Row C6
Montrose St B5
Morrison St C3
Nairn St A1
National Piping Centre, The ✦ A5
Nelson Mandela Sq B5
Nelson St C4
Nelson's Monument C6
Newton Place A3
Newton St A3
Nicholson St C4
Nile St B5
Norfolk Court C4
Norfolk St C4
North Frederick St B5
North Hanover St B5
North Portland St B6
North St A3
North Wallace St A5
O2 ABC A4
O2 Academy ✦ C4
Odeon 🎥 C3
Old Dumbarton Rd A1
Osborne St B5/C5
Oswald St B4
Overnewton St A1
Oxford St C4
Pacific Dr B1
Paisley Rd C3
Paisley Rd West C1
Park Circus A2
Park Gdns A2
Park St South A2
Park Terr A2
Parkgrove Terr A2
Parnie St C5
Parson St A6
Partick Bridge A1
Passport Office A5
Pavilion Theatre 🎭 A4
Pembroke St A3
People's Palace ⌂ C6
Pitt St A4/B4
Plantation Park C1
Plantation Quay B1
Police Mus 🏛 B5
Police Station A4/A6
Port Dundas Rd A5
Port St B2
Portman St C2
Prince's Dock B1
Princes Sq B5
Provand's Lordship ⌂ B6
Queen St B5
Queen Street ⇌ B5
Ramshorn 🎭 B5
Renfrew St A3/A4
Renton St A5
Richmond St B5
Robertson St B4
Rose St A4
Rottenrow B5
Royal Concert Hall 🎭 A5
Royal Conservatoire of Scotland A4
Royal Cres A2
Royal Exchange Sq B5
Royal Highland Fusiliers Mus 🏛 A3
West Glasgow Ambulatory Care Ⓗ A1
Royal Infirmary Ⓗ B6
Royal Terr A2
Rutland Cres C2
St Andrew's in the Square ⛪ C6
St Andrew's (RC) ✝ C5
St Andrew's St C5
St Enoch Ⓜ B5
St Enoch Shopping Centre B5
St Enoch Sq B4
St George's Rd A3
St James Rd B6
St Kent St C6
St Mungo Ave A5/A6
St Mungo Museum of Religious Life & Art 🏛 B6
St Mungo Place A6
St Vincent Cres A2
St Vincent Place B5
St Vincent St B3/B4
St Vincent Terr B3
Saltmarket C5
Sandyford Place A3
Sauchiehall St A2/A4
SEC Armadillo B2
School of Art A4
Sclater St B7
Scotland St C2
Scott St A4
Scottish Exhibition & Conference Ctr B1
Seaward St C2
Shaftesbury St B3
Sheriff Court C5
Shields Rd Ⓜ C3
Shopmobility A5
Shuttle St B6
Somerset Place A2
South Portland St C4
Springburn Rd A6
Springfield Quay C3
SSE Hydro The ⌂ B2
Stanley St C2
Stevenson St C6
Stewart St A4
Stirling Rd B6
Stobcross Quay B1
Stobcross Rd B1
Stock Exchange ⌂ B5
Stockwell Place C5
Stockwell St B5
Stow College A4
Sussex St C2
Synagogue A3
Taylor Place A6
Tenement House 🏛 A3
Teviot St A1
Theatre Royal 🎭 A4
Tolbooth Steeple & Mercat Cross ✦ C6
Tower St C2
Trades House ⌂ B5
Tradeston St C4
Transport Mus 🏛 A1
Tron 🎭 C5
Trongate B5
Tunnel St B2
Turnbull St C5
Union St B4
Univ of Strathclyde B6
Victoria Bridge C5
Virginia St B5
Wallace St C3
Walls St B6
Walmer Cres C1
Warrock St B3
Washington St B3
Waterloo St B4
Watson St B6
Watt St C3
Wellington St B4
West Campbell St B4
West George St B4
West Graham St A4
West Greenhill Pl B2
West Regent St A4
West Regent St B4
West St C4
West St Ⓜ C4
Whitehall St B3
Wilkes St C7
Wilson St B5
Woodlands Gate A3
Woodlands Rd A3
Woodlands Terr A2
Woodside Place A3
Woodside Terr A3
York St B4
Yorkhill Pde A1
Yorkhill St A1

Gloucester 182

Albion St C1
Alexandra Rd B3
Alfred St C3
All Saints Rd C2
Alvin St B2
Arthur St C2
Barrack Square B1

Barton St C2
Blackfriars † B1
Blenheim Rd C2
Bristol Rd C1
Brunswick Rd C2
Bruton Way B2
Bus Station B2
Cineworld C1
City Council Offices B1
City Mus, Art Gallery & Library B2
Clarence St B2
Commercial Rd B1
Council Offices B1
Courts B1
Cromwell St C2
Deans Way A2
Denmark Rd A3
Derby Rd C3
Docks ✦ C1
Eastgate St B2
Eastgate, The B1
Edwy Pde A2
Estcourt Close A3
Estcourt Rd A3
Falkner St C2
GL1 Leisure Centre C2
Gloucester Cath † B1
Gloucester Life B1
Gloucester Quays Outlet C1
Gloucester Sta ≹ B2
Gloucester Waterways C1
Gloucestershire Archive B2
Gloucestershire Royal Hospital (A&E) H B3
Goodyere St C2
Gouda Way A1
Great Western Rd B3
Guildhall B2
Heathville Rd A3
Henry Rd B3
Henry St B2
Hinton Rd A2
India Rd C3
Information Ctr B1
Jersey Rd C3
King's C2
King's Walk Shopping Centre B2
Kingsholm (Gloucester Rugby) A2
Kingsholm Rd A2
Lansdown Rd A3
Library C2
Llanthony Rd C1
London Rd B3
Longhorn Ave A1
Longsmith St B1
Malvern Rd A3
Market B2
Market Parade B2
Mercia Rd A1
Metz Way C3
Midland Rd C2
Millbrook St C3
Montpellier C1
Napier St C3
Nettleton Rd C2
New Inn B2
New Olympus C3
North Rd A3
Northgate St B2
Oxford Rd A2
Oxford St B2
Park & Ride Gloucester A1
Park Rd C2
Park St B2
Park, The C2
Parliament St C1
Peel Centre, The C1
Pitt St B1
Police Station C3
Post Office B2
Quay St B1
Quay, The B1
Recreation Gd A1/A2
Regent St C2
Robert Raikes Ho B1
Royal Oak Rd B1
Russell St B2
Ryecroft St C2
St Aldate St B2
St Ann Way C1
St Catherine St A2
St Mark St A2
St Mary de Crypt B1
St Mary de Lode B1
St Nicholas's B1
St Oswald's Rd A1
St Oswald's Retail Park A1
St Peter's B2
Seabroke Rd A3
Sebert St A2
Severn Rd C1
Sherborne St B2
Shire Hall B1
Sidney St C3
Soldiers of Gloucestershire B1
Southgate St B1/C1
Spa Field C1
Spa Rd C1
Sports Ground A2/B2
Station Rd B2
Stratton Rd C3
Stroud Rd C1
Superstore A1
Swan Rd A2
Trier Way C1/C2
Union St A2
Vauxhall Rd C3
Victoria St C2
Walham Lane A1
Wellington St C2
Westgate Retail Pk B1
Westgate St B1
Widden St C2
Worcester St B2

Grimsby 183

Abbey Drive East C2
Abbey Drive West C2
Abbey Park Rd C2
Abbey Rd C2
Abbey Walk C2
Abbeygate Shopping Centre C2
Abbotsway C2
Adam Smith St A1/A2
Ainslie St C2
Albert St A3
Alexandra Dock A2/B2
Alexandra Rd A2/B2
Alexandra Retail Pk A2
Annesley St A2
Armstrong St A1
Arthur St B1
Augusta St C1
Bargate C1
Beeson St A1
Bethlehem St C2
Bodiam Way B3
Bradley St B3
Brighowgate C1/C2
Bus Station C2
Canterbury Dr C1
Cartergate B1/C1
Catherine St C3
Chantry La B1
Charlton St A1
Church La C2
Church St A3
Cleethorpe Rd A3
Close, The C1
College St C1
Compton Dr C1
Corporation Bridge A2
Corporation Rd A1
Court B2/B3
Crescent St B1
Deansgate C1
Doughty Rd C2
Dover St B1
Duchess St C2
Dudley St C1
Duke of York Gdns B1
Duncombe St B3
Earl La B1
East Marsh St B3
East St B2
Eastgate B3
Eastside Rd A3
Eaton Ct C1
Eleanor St B3
Ellis Way B3
Fisherman's Chapel A3
Fisherman's Wharf B2
Fishing Heritage Centre B2
Flour Sq A3
Frederick St B1
Frederick Ward Way B2
Freeman St A3/B3
Freshney Dr B1
Freshney Place B2
Garden St C2
Garibaldi St A3
Garth La B2
Grime St B3
Grimsby Docks Station A3
Grimsby Town Station C2
Hainton Ave C3
Har Way B3
Hare St C3
Harrison St B1
Haven Ave B1
Hay Croft Ave B1
Hay Croft St B1
Heneage Rd B3/C3
Henry St B1
Holme St B3
Hume St C1
James St B1
Joseph St B1
Kent St A3
King Edward St A3
Lambert Rd C2
Library B2
Lime St B1
Lister St B1
Littlefield La C1
Lockhill A3
Lord St B1
Lower Spring St A3
Ludford St C2
Macaulay St B1
Mallard Mews C3
Manor Ave C2
Market A3
Market Hall B2
Market St B3
Moody Lane A3
Moss Rd C2
Nelson St A3
New St B2
Osbourne St B2
Pasture St B3
Peaks Parkway C3
Pelham Rd C1
Police Station A3
Post Office B1/B2
Pyewipe Rd A1
Railway Place A3
Railway St A3
Recreation Ground C2
Rendel St A2
Retail Park A2/B3
Richard St B1
Ripon St B1
Robinson St East B3
Royal St A3
St Hilda's Ave C1
St James C2
Sheepfold St B3/C3
Sixhills St C3
South Park B2
Superstore B3/B2
Tasburgh St C3
Tennyson St B2
Thesiger St A3
Time Trap C2
Town Hall B2
Veal St B1
Victoria Retail Park A3
Victoria St North A2
Victoria St South B2
Victoria St West B2
Watkin St A1
Welholme Ave C2
Welholme Rd C3
Wellington St B3
Wellowgate C2
Werneth Rd B3
West Coates Rd A1
Westgate A2
Westminster Dr C1
Willingham St C3
Wintringham Rd C2
Wood St B3
Yarborough Dr B1
Yarborough Hotel C2

Harrogate 183

Albert St C2
Alexandra Rd B2
Arthington Ave B2
Ashfield Rd A2
Back Cheltenham Mount B2
Beech Grove C1
Belmont Rd C1
Bilton Dr A2
BMI The Duchy Hospital H C1
Bower Rd B2
Bower St B2
Bus Station B2
Cambridge Rd B2
Cambridge St B2
Cemetery A2
Chatsworth Grove A2
Chatsworth Place A2
Chatsworth Rd A2
Chelmsford Rd B3
Cheltenham Cres B2
Cheltenham Mt B2
Cheltenham Pde B2
Christ Church B3
Christ Church Oval B3
Chudleigh Rd B3
Clarence Dr B1
Claro Rd A3
Claro Way A3
Coach Park B2
Coach Rd B3
Cold Bath Rd C1
Commercial St B2
Coppice Ave A1
Coppice Dr A1
Coppice Gate A1
Cornwall Rd B1
Council Offices B1
Crescent Gdns B1
Crescent Rd B1
Dawson Terr A2
Devonshire Place B3
Dixon Rd A2
Dixon Terr A2
Dragon Ave B3
Dragon Parade B2
Dragon Rd B2
Duchy Rd B1
East Parade B2
East Park Rd C3
Esplanade B1
Everyman B2
Fire Station A2
Franklin Mount A2
Franklin Rd B2
Franklin Square A2
Glebe Rd C1
Grove Park Ct A3
Grove Park Terr A3
Grove Rd A2
Hampsthwaite Rd A1
Harcourt Dr B3
Harcourt Rd B3
Harrogate ≹ B2
Harrogate Convention Centre B1
Harrogate Justice Ctr (Magistrates' and County Courts) C2
Harrogate Ladies College B1
Harrogate Theatre B2
Heywood Rd C1
Hollins Cres A1
Hollins Mews A1
Hollins Rd A1
Hydro Leisure Centre, The A1
Information Ctr B1
James St B2
Jenny Field Dr A1
John St B2
Kent Dr A1
Kent Rd A1
Kings Rd A2
Kingsway B3
Kingsway Dr B3
Lancaster Rd C1
Leeds Rd C2
Lime Grove B3
Lime St A3
Mayfield Grove B2
Mercer B1
Montpellier Hill B1
Mornington Cres A3
Mornington Terr B3
Mowbray Sq B3
North Park Rd B3
Oakdale Ave A1
Oatlands Dr C3
Odeon B2
Osborne Rd A2
Otley Rd C2
Oxford St B2
Parade, The B2
Park Chase B3
Park Parade B3
Park View B2
Parliament St B1
Police Station C3
Post Office B2/C1
Providence Terr A2
Queen Parade C3
Queen's Rd C1
Raglan St C2
Regent Ave A3
Regent Grove A3
Regent Parade A3
Regent St A3
Regent Terr A3
Ripon Rd A1
Robert St C2
Royal Baths & Turkish Baths B1
Royal Pump Room B1
St Luke's Mount A2
St Mary's Ave C1
St Mary's Walk C1
Scargill Rd A1
Skipton Rd A3
Skipton St A2
Slingsby Walk C3
South Park Rd C2
Spring Grove A1
Springfield Ave B1
Station Ave B2
Station Parade B2
Stray Rein C3
Stray, The C2/C3
Studley Rd A2
Superstore B2/C1
Swan Rd B1
Tower St C2
Trinity Rd C2
Union St B2
Valley Dr C1
Valley Gardens C1
Valley Mount C1
Victoria Ave C2
Victoria Rd C1
Victoria Shopping Centre B2
Waterloo St A2
West Park C2
West Park St C2
Wood View A1
Woodfield Ave A3
Woodfield Dr A3
Woodfield Grove A3
Woodfield Rd A3
Woodfield Square A3
Woodside B3
York Place C3
York Rd B1

Hull 184

Adelaide St C1
Albert Dock C1
Albion St B2
Alfred Gelder St B2
Anlaby Rd B1
Arctic Corsair ✦ B3
Beverley Rd A1
Blanket Row C2
Bond St B2
Bonus Arena B2
Bridlington Ave A2
Brook St B1
Brunswick Ave A1
Bus Station B1
Camilla Close C3
Cannon St A2
Caroline St A2
Carr La B2
Castle St C2
Central Library B1
Charles St A2
Citadel Way B3
Clarence St B3
Cleveland St A3
Clifton St A1
Colonial St B1
Court B2
Deep, The C3
Dinostar C2
Dock Office Row B3
Dock St B2
Drypool Bridge B3
Egton St A3
English St C1
Ferens Gallery B2
Ferensway B1
Fire Sta A1
Francis St A2
Francis St West A2
Freehold St A1
Freetown Way A2
FrüitTheatre C2
Garrison Rd B3
George St B2
Gibson St A2
Great Thornton St B1
Great Union St A3
Green La A2
Grey St A1
Grimston St B2
Grosvenor St A1
Guildhall B2
Guildhall Rd B2
Hands-on History B2
Harley St A1
Hessle Rd C1
High St B3
Hull Minster B2
Hull Paragon Interchange Sta ≹ B1
Hull & East Riding Museum B3
Hull Ice Arena C1
Hull City Hall B2
Hull College B3
Hull History Centre A2
Hull New Theatre A2
Hull Truck Theatre B1
Humber Dock Marina C2
Humber Dock St C2
Humber St C2
Hyperion St A3
Information Ctr B2
Jameson St B1
Jarratt St B2
Jenning St A3
King Billy Statue ✦ C2
King Edward St B2
King St A2
Kingston Retail Pk C1
Kingston St C2
Liddell St A1
Lime St A3
Lister St C1
Lockwood St A2
Maister House B3
Maritime Mus B2
Market B2
Market Place B2
Minerva Pier C2
Mulgrave St A3
Myton Swing Bridge C3
Myton St B1
NAPA (Northern Acad of Performing Arts) B1
Nelson St C2
New Cleveland St A3
New George St A2
Norfolk St A1
North Bridge A3
North St B1
Odeon C1
Old Harbour C3
Osborne St B1
Paragon St B2
Park St B1
Percy St A2
Pier St C2
Police Station B1
Porter St C1
Portland St B1
Post Office B1/B2
Posterngate B2
Prince's Quay B2
Prospect Centre B1
Prospect St B1
Queen's Gdns B2
Railway Dock Marina C2
Railway St C2
Real B1
Red Gallery B1
Reform St A2
Retail Park B1
Riverside Quay C2
Roper St B2
St James St C1
St Luke's St B1
St Mark St A3
St Mary the Virgin B3
St Stephens Shopping Centre B1
Scale La Footbridge B3
Scott St A2
South Bridge Rd B3
Sport's Centre C1
Spring Bank A1
Spring St B1
Spurn Lightship C2
Spyvee St A3
Stage @TheDock C3
southwater B3
Sykes St A2
Tidal Surge Barrier ✦ C3
Tower St B3
Trinity House B2
Vane St A1
Victoria Pier ✦ C2
Waterhouse La B2
Waterloo St A1
Waverley St C1
Wellington St C2
Wellington St West C2
West St B1
Whitefriargate B2
Wilberforce Dr B2
Wilberforce Ho B3
Wilberforce Monument ✦ B3
William St C1
Wincolmlee A3
Witham A3
Wright St A1

Inverness 184

Abban St A1
Academy St B2
Alexander Place B2
Anderson St A2
Annfield Rd C3
Ardconnel St B3
Ardconnel Terr B3
Ardross Place B2
Ardross St B2
Argyle St B3
Argyle Terr B3
Attadale Rd B1
Ballifeary La C2
Ballifeary Rd C1/C2
Balnacraig La A1
Balnain House ✦ B2
Balnain St B2
Bank St B2
Bellfield Park C2
Bellfield Terr C3
Benula Rd A1
Birnie Terr A1
Bishop's Rd C2
Bowling Green C2
Bridge St B2
Brown St A2
Bruce Ave C1
Bruce Gdns C1
Bruce Pk C1
Burial Ground A2
Burnett Rd A3
Bus Station B3
Caledonian Rd B1
Cameron Rd A1
Cameron Sq A1
Carse Rd A1
Carsegate Rd Sth A1
Castle Garrison Encounter ✦ B2
Castle Rd B2
Castle St B3
Celt St B2
Chapel St A2
Charles St B3
Church St B2
Columba Rd B1/C1
Crown Ave B3
Crown Circus B3
Crown Dr B3
Crown Rd B3
Crown St B3
Culduthel Rd C3
Dalneigh Cres C1
Dalneigh Rd C1
Denny St B3
Dochfour Dr B1/C1
Douglas Row B2
Duffy Dr C3
Dunabban Rd A1
Dunain Rd B1
Duncraig St B2
Eastgate Shopping Centre B3
Eden Court C2
Fairfield Rd B1
Falcon Sq B3
Fire Station A3
Fraser St B2
Fraser St C2
Friars' Bridge A2
Friars' La B2
Friars' St A2
George St A2
Gilbert St A2
Glebe St A2
Glendoe Terr A1
Glenurquhart Rd C1
Gordon Terr B3
Gordonville Rd C2
Grant St A2
Grant Street Park (Clachnacuddin FC) A1
Greig St B2
Harbour Rd A3
Harrowden Rd B1
Haugh Rd C2
Heatherley Cres C3
High St B3
Highland Council HQ, The C2
Hill Park C3
Hill St B3
HM Prison B3
Huntly Place A2
Huntly St B2
India St A2
Industrial Estate A3
Information Ctr B2
Innes St A2
Inverness ≹ B3
Inverness High Sch B1
Inverness Museum & Art Gallery B2
Jamaica St A2
Kenneth St B2
Kilmuir Rd A1
King St B2
Kingsmills Rd B3
Laurel Ave B1/C1
Library A3
Lilac Grove B1
Lindsay Ave C1
Lochalsh Rd A1/B1
Longman Rd A3
Lotland Place A2
Lower Kessock St A1
Madras St A2
Maxwell Dr C1
Mayfield Rd C3
Millburn Rd B3
Mitchell's La C3
Montague Row B2
Muirfield Rd C3
Muirtown St B1
Nelson St A2
Ness Bank C2
Ness Bridge B2
Ness Walk B2/C2
Old Edinburgh Rd C3
Old High Church B2
Park Rd C1
Paton St C2
Perceval Rd B1
Planefield Rd B2
Police Station A3
Porterfield Bank C3
Porterfield Rd C3
Portland Place A2
Post Office A2/B1/B2
Queen St B2
Queensgate B2
Railway Terr A3
Rangemore Rd B1
Reay St B3
Riverside St A2
Rose St A2
Ross Ave B1
Rowan Rd B1
Royal Northern Infirmary H C2
St Andrew's Cath † C2
St Columba B2
St John's Ave C1
St Mary's Ave C1
Sheriff Court B3
Shore St A2
Smith Ave C1
Southside Place C3
Southside Rd C3
Spectrum Centre B2
Strothers La B3
Superstore A1/B2
TA Centre C2
Telford Gdns B1
Telford Rd A1
Telford St A1
Tomnahurich Cemetery C1
Tomnahurich St B2
Town Hall B3
Union Rd B3
Union St B3
Victorian Market B3
Walker Place A2
Walker Rd A3
War Memorial ✦ C2
Waterloo Bridge A2
Wells St B1
Young St B2

Ipswich 184

Alderman Rd B2
All Saints' Rd A1
Alpe St B2
Ancaster Rd C1
Ancient House B3
Anglesea Rd B2
Ann St B2
Arboretum A2
Austin St C2
Avenue, The A3
Belstead Rd C2
Berners St B2
Bibb Way B1
Birkfield Dr C1
Black Horse La B2
Bolton La B3
Bond St C3
Bowthorpe Close B2
Bramford La A1
Bramford Rd A1
Bridge St C2
Brookfield Rd A1
Brooks Hall Rd A1
Broomhill Park A2
Broomhill Rd A1
Broughton Rd A2
Bulwer Rd B1
Burrell Rd C2
Bus Station B3
Butter Market B2
Buttermarket Shopping Ctr, The B3
Cardinal Park Leisure Park C2
Carr St B3
Cecil Rd B2
Cecilia St C2
Chancery Rd C2
Charles St B2
Chevallier St A1
Christchurch Mansion & Wolsey Art Gallery B3
Christchurch Park A3
Christchurch St B3
Cineworld C2
Civic Centre B2
Civic Dr B2
Clarkson St B1
Cobbold St B3
Commercial Rd C2
Constable Rd A3
Constantine Rd C1
Constitution Hill A2
Corder Rd A3
Corn Exchange B2
Cotswold Ave A2
Council Offices C2
County Hall B3
Crown Court C2
Crown St B2
Cullingham Rd B1
Cumberland St B2
Curriers La B2
Dale Hall La A2
Dales View Rd A1
Dalton Rd B2
Dillwyn St B1
Elliot St B1
Elm St B2
Elsmere Rd A3
Falcon St C2
Felaw St C3
Fire Station C2
Flint Wharf C3
Fonnereau Rd B2
Fore St C3
Foundation St C3
Franciscan Way C2
Friars St C2
Gainsborough Rd A3
Gatacre Rd B1
Geneva Rd B2
Gippeswyk Ave C1
Gippeswyk Park C1
Grafton Way C2
Graham Rd A1
Great Whip St C3
Grimwade St C3
Handford Cut B1
Handford Rd B1
Henley Rd A2
Hervey St B3
High St B2
Holly Rd A2
Ipswich Haven Marina ✦ C3
Ipswich Museum & Art Gallery B2
Ipswich School A2
Ipswich Station ≹ C2
Ipswich Town FC (Portman Road) C2
Ivry St A2
Kensington Rd A1
Kesteven Rd C1
Key St C3
Kingsfield Ave A3
Kitchener Rd A1
Library B2
Little's Cres C2
London Rd B1
Low Brook St C3
Lower Orwell St C3
Luther Rd C2
Magistrates Court B2
Manor Rd A3
Mornington Ave A1
Museum St B2
Neale St B3
New Cardinal St C2
New Cut East C3
New Wolsey B2
Newson St B2
Norwich Rd A1/B1
Oban St B2
Old Custom Ho C3
Old Foundry Rd B3
Old Merchant's House C3
Orford St B2
Paget Rd A2
Park Rd A3
Park View Rd A2
Peter's St C2
Philip Rd C2
Pine Ave A2
Pine View Rd A2
Police Station B2
Portman Rd B2
Portmans Walk C1
Post Office B2
Princes St C2
Prospect St B1
Queen St B2
Ranelagh Rd C1
Recreation Ground B1
Rectory Rd C2
Regent Theatre B3
Reg Driver Visitor Centre ✦ B3
Retail Park C1
Retail Park C2
Richmond Rd A1
Rope Walk C3
Rose La C2
Russell Rd C2
St Edmund's Rd A2
St George's St B2
St Helen's St B3
Sherrington Rd A1
Shopmobility B2
Silent St C2
Sir Alf Ramsey Way C1
Sir Bobby Robson Bridge C1
Sirdar Rd B1
Sir John Mills Theatre B1
Soane St B3
Springfield La A1
Star La C3
Stevenson Rd B1
Stoke Quay C3
Suffolk College C3
Suffolk Retail Park B1
Superstore B1
Surrey Rd B1
Tacket St C3
Tavern St B3
Tower Ramparts B2
Tower Ramparts Shopping Centre B2
Tower St B3
Town Hall B2
Tuddenham Rd A3
University C3
Upper Brook St B3
Upper Orwell St B3
Valley Rd A2
Vermont Cres B3
Vermont Rd B3
Vernon St C3
Warrington Rd A2
Waterloo Rd A1
Waterworks St C3
Wellington St B1
West End Rd B1
Westerfield Rd A3
Westgate St B2
Westholme Rd A1
Westwood Ave A1
Willoughby Rd C2
Withipoll St B3
Woodbridge Rd B3
Woodstone Ave A3
Yarmouth Rd B1

Kendal 184

Abbot Hall Art Gallery & Mus of Lakeland Life & Industry C2
Ambulance Station A2
Anchorite Fields C2
Anchorite Rd C2
Ann St A3
Appleby Rd A3
Archers Meadow C3
Ashleigh Rd A2
Aynam Rd B2
Bankfield Rd B1
Beast Banks B2
Beezon Fields A2
Beezon Rd A2
Beezon Trad Est A3
Belmont B2
Birchwood Close C1
Blackhall Rd B2
Brewery Arts Centre B2
Bridge St B2
Brigsteer Rd C1
Burneside Rd A2
Bus Station B2
Buttery Well Rd C2
Canal Head North B3
Captain French La C2
Caroline St A2
Castle Hill B3
Castle Howe B2
Castle Rd B3
Castle St A3/B3
Cedar Grove C1
Council Offices B2
County Council Offices A2
Cricket Ground A3
Cricket Ground C3
Cross La C2
Dockray Hall Industrial Estate A2
Dowker's La B2
East View B1
Echo Barn Hill C1
Elephant Yard B2
Fairfield La A1
Finkle St B2
Fire Station A2
Fletcher Square C3
Football Ground C3
Fowling La A3
Gillinggate C2
Glebe Rd C2
Golf Course B1
Goose Holme B3
Gooseholme Bridge B3
Green St A1
Greengate C2
Greengate La C1/C2
Greenside B1
Greenwood C1
Gulfs Rd B2
High Tenterfell B1
Highgate B2
Hillswood Ave C1
Horncop La A2
Information Ctr B2
Kendal A3
Kendal Business Park A3
Kendal Castle (Remains) B3
Kendal Fell B1
Kendal Green A1
Kendal Ski Ctr ✦ B3
Kendal Station ≹ A3
Kent Place B2
Kirkbarrow C2
Kirkland C2
Library B2
Library Rd B2
Little Aynam B3
Little Wood B1
Long Close C1
Longpool A3
Lound Rd C3
Lound St C3
Low Fellside B2
Lowther St B2
Magistrates Court A2
Maple Dr C1
Market Place B2
Maude St B2
Miller Bridge B2
Milnthorpe Rd C2
Mint St A3
Mintsfeet Rd A3
Mintsfeet Rd South A2
New Rd B2
Noble's Rest B2
Parish Church C2
Park Side Rd C3
Parkside Business Park C3
Parr St B3
Police Station A2
Post Office A3/B2
Quaker Tapestry ✦ B2
Queen's Rd B1
Riverside Walk C2
Rydal Mount A2
Sandes Ave A2
Sandgate A3
Sandylands Rd A3
Serpentine Rd B1
Serpentine Wood B1
Shap Rd A3
South Rd C2
Stainbank Rd C1
Station Rd A3
Stramongate B2
Stramongate Bridge B2
Stricklandgate A2/B2
Sunnyside C3
Thorny Hills B3
Town Hall B2
Undercliff Rd B1
Underwood C1
Union St A2
Vicar's Fields C2
Vicarage Dr C1/C2
Wainwright's Yard B2
Wasdale Close C3
Well Ings C2
Westmorland Shopping Centre & Market Hall B2
Westwood Ave C1
Wildman St A3
Windermere Rd A1
YHA B2
YWCA B2

King's Lynn 185

Albert St A2
Albion St B2
Alive St James' Swimming Pool B2
All Saints B2
All Saints St B2
Austin Fields A2
Austin St A2
Avenue Rd B3
Bank Side B1
Beech Rd C2
Birch Tree Close B2
Birchwood St A2
Blackfriars Rd B2
Blackfriars St B2
Boal St B1
Bridge St B2
Broad St B2
Broad Walk B3
Burkitt St A2
Bus Station A2
Carmelite Terr C2
Chapel St A2
Chase Ave C3
Checker St C2
Church St B2
Clough La B2
Coburg St B2
Coll of West Anglia A3
Columbia Way A3
Comm Staithe Quay A1
Corn Exchange A1
County Court Rd B2
Cresswell St A2
Custom House A1
East Coast Business Park C1
Eastgate St A2
Edma St A2
Exton's Rd C3
Ferry La B1
Ferry St A1
Framingham's Almshouses B2
Friars St C2
Friars Walk C2
Gaywood Rd A3
George St A2
Gladstone Rd C2
Goodwin's Rd C3
Green Quay Discovery Centre ✦ B1
Greyfriars' Tower ✦ B2
Guanock Terr C2
Guildhall A1
Hansa Rd C3
Harding's Way C2
Hardwick Rd C2
Hextable Rd A2
High St B1
Holcombe Ave C3
Hospital Walk C2
Information Ctr B1
John Kennedy Rd A2
Kettlewell Lane A2
King George V Ave B3
King St B1
King's Lynn Art Centre A1
King's Lynn Sta ≹ B2
Library B2
Littleport St A2
Loke Rd A2
London Rd B2
Lynn Museum B2
Magistrates Court B1
Majestic B2
Market La A1
Millfleet B2
Milton Ave A3
Nar Valley Walk C2
Nelson St B1
New Conduit St B2
Norfolk St A2
North Lynn Discovery Centre ✦ A3
North St A2
Oldsunway B2
Ouse Ave C1
Page Stair Lane A1
Park Ave B3
Police Station B2
Portland Place C1
Portland St B2
Purfleet B1
Queen St B1
Raby Ave A3
Railway Rd A2
Red Mount Chapel B3
Regent Way B2
River Walk A1
Robert St C2
Saddlebow Rd C2
St Ann's St A1
St James St B2
St James' Rd B2
St John's Walk B3
St Margaret's B1
St Nicholas A1
St Nicholas St A1
St Peter's Rd B1
Sir Lewis St A2
Smith Ave A3
South Everard St C2
South Gate ✦ C2
South Quay B1
South St B2
Southgate St C2
Stonegate St B2
Stories of Lynn B1
Surrey St A1
Sydney St C3
Tennyson Ave B3
Tennyson Rd B3
The Walks Stadium (King's Lynn FC) B3
Tower St B2
Town Hall B1
Town Wall (Remains) ✦ B3
True's Yard Fisherfolk Museum A2
Valingers Rd C2
Vancouver Ave C2
Vancouver Quarter B2
Waterloo St B2
Wellesley St B2
Whitefriars Terrace C2
Windsor Rd C2
Winfarthing St C2
Wisbech Road C2
Wyatt St A2
York Rd C3

Lancaster 185

Aberdeen Rd C3
Aldcliffe Rd C2
Alfred St B3
Ambleside Rd A3
Ambulance & Fire Station B2
Ashfield Ave B1
Ashton Rd C2
Assembly Rooms Emporium B2
Balmoral Rd B3
Bath House B2
Bath St B3
Blades St B1
BMI Lancaster (private) H C3
Borrowdale Rd B3
Bowerham Rd C3
Brewery La B2
Bridge La B2
Brook St C1
Bulk Rd A3
Bulk St B2
Bus Station B2
Cable St B2
Canal Cruises & Waterbus ✦ C2
Carlisle Bridge A1
Carr House La C2
Castle B1
Castle Park B1
Caton Rd A3
China St B2
Church St B2
City Museum B2
Clarence St C3
Common Gdn St B2
Coniston Rd A3
Cottage Museum B2
Council Offices B2
Courts B2
Cromwell Rd C1
Crown Court B1
Dale St C3
Dallas Rd B1/C1
Dalton Rd B3
Dalton Sq B2
Damside St B2
De Vitre St B3
Dee Rd A1
Denny Ave A1
Derby Rd A2
Dukes, The B2
Earl St A2
East Rd B3
Eastham St C3
Edward St B3
Fairfield Nature Reserve C1
Fairfield Rd B1
Fenton St B2
Firbank Rd A3
Friend's Meeting House B1
Garnet St B3
George St B2
Giant Axe Field B1
Grand B2
Grasmere Rd B3
Greaves Park C3
Greaves Rd C2
Green St A3
Gregson Ctr, The B3
Gregson Rd C3
Greyhound Bridge A2
Greyhound Bridge Rd A2
High St B2
Hill Side B1
Hope St C3
Hubert Place B1
Information Ctr B2
Kelsy St B1
Kentmere Rd B3
Keswick Road A3
King St B2
Kingsway A3
Kirkes Rd C3
Lancaster City Football Club B1
Lancaster Royal Grammar School B3
Lancaster Sta ≹ B1
Langdale Rd A3
Ley Ct B1
Library B2
Lincoln Rd B1
Lindow St C2
Lodge St B2
Long Marsh La B1
Lune Rd A1
Lune St A2
Lune Valley Ramble A3
Mainway A2
Maritime Mus A1
Marketgate Shopping Centre B2
Market St B2
Meadowside C2
Meeting House La B1
Millennium Bridge A2
Moor La B2
Moorgate B3
Morecambe Rd A1/A2
Nelson St B2
North Rd B2
Orchard La C1
Owen Rd A2
Park Rd B3
Parliament St A3
Patterdale Rd A3
Penny St B2
Police Station B2
Portland St C2
Post Office B2/B3
Primrose St C3
Priory B1
Prospect St C3
Quarry Rd B3
Queen St C2
Regent St C2
Ridge La A3
Ridge St A3
Royal Lancaster Infirmary (A&E) H C2
Rydal Rd B3
Ryelands Park A1
St Georges Quay A1
St John's B2
St Leonard's Gate B2
St Martin's Rd C3
St Nicholas Arcades Shopping Centre B2
St Oswald St C3
St Peter's † B3

St Peter's Rd B3
Salisbury Rd B1
Scotch Quarry Urban Park C3
Sibsey St B1
Skerton Bridge A2
South Rd C2
Station Rd B1
Stirling Rd C3
Storey Ave B1
Sunnyside La C1
Sylvester St C1
Tarnsyke Rd A1
Thurnham St C2
Town Hall B2
Troutbeck Rd B3
Ulleswater Rd B3
Univ of Cumbria C3
Vicarage Field B1
Vue B2
West Rd B1
Westbourne Dr C1
Westbourne Rd B1
Westham St C3
Wheatfield St B1
White Cross Business Park C2
Williamson Rd B3
Willow La B1
Windermere Rd B3
Wingate-Saul Rd B1
Wolseley St B3
Woodville St B3
Wyresdale Rd C3

Leeds 185
Aire St B3
Albion Place B4
Albion St B4
Albion Way B1
Alma St A6
Ambulance Sta B5
Arcades B4
Armley Rd B1
Armories Dr C5
Back Burley Lodge Rd A1
Back Hyde Terr A2
Back Row C3
Bath Rd C3
Beckett St A6
Bedford St B3
Belgrave St A4
Belle Vue Rd A2
Benson St A5
Black Bull St C5
Blenheim Walk A3
Boar La B4
Bond St B4
Bow St C5
Bowman La C4
Brewery C4
Brewery Wharf C5
Bridge St A5/B5
Briggate B4
Bruce Gdns C1
Burley Rd A1
Burley St B1
Burmantofs St B6
Bus & Coach Sta B5
Butterly St C4
Butts Cres B4
Byron St A5
Call La B4
Calls,The B5
Calverley St A3/B3
Canal St B1
Canal Wharf C3
Carlisle Rd C5
Cavendish Rd A1
Cavendish St A2
Chadwick St C5
Cherry Place A6
Cherry Row A5
City Museum A4
City Varieties Music Hall B4
City Sq B3
Civic Hall A3
Clarence Road C5
Clarendon Rd A2
Clarendon Way A3
Clark La C6
Clay Pit La A4
Cloberry St A2
Close,The B6
Clyde Approach C1
Clyde Gdns C1
Coleman St C2
Commercial St B4
Concord St A5
Cookridge St A4
Copley Hill C1
Core,The B4
Corn Exchange B4
Cromer Terr A2
Cromwell St A5
Cross Catherine St B6
Cross Green La C6
Cross Stamford St A5
Crown & County Courts A3
Crown Point Bridge C5
Crown Point Rd C4
Crown Point Retail Park C4
David St C3
Dent St C6
Derwent Place C3
Dial St C6
Dock St C4
Dolly La A6
Domestic St C2
Drive,The B6
Duke St B5
Duncan St B4
Dyer St B5
East Field St B6
East Pde B3
East St C5
Eastgate B5
Easy Rd C6
Edward St B4
Ellerby La C6
Ellerby Rd C6
Fenton St A3
Fire Station B2
First Direct Arena A4
Fish St B4
Flax Place B6
Garth,The B5
Gelderd Rd C1
George St B4
Globe Rd C2
Gower St A5
Grafton St A4
Grand Theatre B4
Granville Rd A6
Great George St A3
Great Wilson St C4
Greek St B3
Green La C1
Hanover Ave A2
Hanover La A2
Hanover Sq A2
Hanover Way A2
Harewood St B4
Harrison St B4
Haslewood Close B6
Haslewood Drive B6
Headrow,The B3/B4
High Court B5
Holbeck La C2
Holdforth Close C1
Holdforth Gardens B1
Holdforth Grove C1
Holdforth Place C1
Holy Trinity B4
Hope Rd A5
Hunslet La C4
Hunslet Rd C4
Hyde Terr A2
Infirmary St B3
Information Ctr B3
Ingram Row C3
ITV Yorkshire A1
Junction St C4
Kelso Gdns A2
Kelso Rd A2
Kelso St A2
Kendal La A2
Kendell St C4
Kidacre St C4
King Edward St B4
King St B3
Kippax Place C6
Kirkgate B4
Kirkgate Market B4
Kirkstall Rd A1
Kitson St C6
Knight's Way Bridge C5
Lady La B4
Lands La B4
Lane,The B5
Lavender Walk B6
Leeds Art Gallery B3
Leeds Beckett Univ A3
Leeds Bridge C4
Leeds Coll of Music B5
Leeds Discovery Centre C5
Leeds General Infirmary (A&E) A3
Leeds Minster B5
Leeds Station B3
Library B3/B4
Light,The B4
Lincoln Green Rd A6
Lincoln Rd A6
Lindsey Gdns A6
Lindsey Rd A6
Lisbon St B3
Little Queen St B3
Long Close La C6
Lord St C2
Lovell Park A4
Lovell Park Hill A4
Lovell Park Rd A4
Lower Brunswick St A5
Mabgate A5
Macauly St A5
Magistrates Court A3
Manor Rd C3
Mark La B4
Marlborough St B2
Marsh La B5
Marshall St C3
Meadow La C4
Meadow Rd C4
Melbourne St A5
Merrion Centre A4
Merrion St A4
Merrion Way A4
Mill St B5
Millennium Sq A3
Monk Bridge C2
Mount Preston St A2
Mushroom St A5
Neville St C4
New Briggate A4/B4
New Market St B4
New York Rd A5
New York St B5
Nile St A5
Nippet La A6
North St A4
Northern Ballet B5
Northern St B3
Oak Rd B1
Oxford Place B3
Oxford Row A3
Parade,The B6
Park Cross St B3
Park La A2
Park Place B3
Park Row B4
Park Sq B3
Park Sq East B3
Park Sq West B3
Park St B3
Police Station B5
Pontefract La B6
Portland Cres A3
Portland Way A3
Post Office B4/B5
Quarry House (NHS/DSS HQ) B5
Quebec St B3
Queen St B3
Radio Aire A1
Railway St B5
Rectory St A6
Regent St A5
Richmond St C5
Rigton Approach B6
Rigton Dr B6
Rillbank La A1
Rosebank Rd A1
Rose Bowl Conference Centre A3
Royal Armouries C5
Russell St B3
St Anne's Cathedral (RC) A4
St Anne's St B4
St James' Hosp A6
St John's Rd A2
St Johns Centre B4
St Mary's St B5
St Pauls St B3
Saxton La B5
Sayner La C5
Shakespeare Ave A6
Shannon St B6
Sheepscar St South A5
Siddall St C3
Skinner La A5
South Pde B3
Sovereign St C4
Spence La C2
Springfield Mount A2
Springwell Ct C2
Springwell Rd C2
Springwell St C2
Stoney Rock La A6
Studio Rd A1
Sutton St C2
Sweet St C3
Sweet St West C3
Swinegate B4
Templar St B5
Tetley,The C4
Thoresby Place A3
Torre Rd A6
Town Hall A3
Trinity Leeds B4
Union Place C3
Union St B5
University of Leeds A3
Upper Accommodation Rd B6
Upper Basinghall St B4
Vicar La B4
Victoria Bridge C4
Victoria Gate B4
Victoria Quarter B4
Victoria Rd C4
Vue B4
Wade La A4
Washington St A1
Water La C3
Waterloo Rd C4
Wellington Rd B2/C1
Wellington St B3
West St B2
West Yorkshire Playhouse B5
Westfield Rd A1
Westgate B3
Whitehall Rd B3/C2
Whitelock St A5
Willis St C6
Willow Approach A1
Willow Ave A1
Willow Terrace Rd A3
Wintoun St A5
Woodhouse La A3/A4
Woodsley Rd A1
York Place B3
York Rd B6

Leicester 188
Abbey St A2
All Saints' A1
Aylestone Rd C2
Bath La A1
Bede Park C1
Bedford St A3
Bedford St South A3
Belgrave Gate A2
Belvoir St B2
Braunstone Gate B1
Burleys Way A2
Burnmoor St C2
Bus & Coach Sta A2
Canning St A2
Carlton St C2
Castle Motte B1
Castle Gardens B1
Cathedral B2
Charles St B3
Chatham St B2
Christow St A3
Church Gate A2
City Hall B3
Clank St B2
Clock Tower B2
Clyde St A3
Colton St B3
Conduit St B3
Crafton St East A3
Craven St A1
Crown Courts B3
Curve B3
De Lux A2
De Montfort Hall C3
De Montfort St C3
De Montfort Univ C1
Deacon St C2
Dover St B3
Duns La B1
Dunton St A1
East St B3
Eastern Boulevard C1
Edmonton Rd A3
Erskine St A3
Filbert St C1
Filbert St East C2
Fire Station C3
Fleet St A3
Friar La B2
Friday St A2
Gateway St C2
Gateway,The C2
Glebe St B3
Granby St B3
Grange La C2
Grasmere St C1
Great Central St A1
Great Hall B2
Guildhall B2
Guru Nanak Sikh Museum B1
Halford St B2
Havelock St C2
Haymarket Shopping Centre A2
High St A2
Highcross Shopping Centre A2
Highcross St A1
HM Prison C2
Horsefair St B2
Humberstone Gate B2
Humberstone Rd A3
Infirmary St C2
Information Ctr B2
Jarrom St C2
Jewry Wall B1
Kamloops Cres A3
King Richard III Visitor Centre B2
King St B2
Lancaster Rd C3
LCB Depot B3
Lee St A3
Leicester Royal Infirmary (A&E) C2
Leicester Station B3
Library B2
London Rd C3
Lower Brown St B2
Magistrates' Court B2
Manitoba Rd A3
Mansfield St A2
Market B2
Market St B2
Mill La C2
Montreal Rd A3
Narborough Rd North B1
Nelson Mandela Pk C2
New Park St B1
New St B2
New Walk C3
New Walk Museum & Art Gallery C3
Newarke Houses B2
Newarke St B2
Newarke,The B1
Northgate St A1
Orchard St A2
Ottawa Rd A3
Oxford St C2
Phoenix Arts Ctr B3
Police Station A3
Post Office A1/B2/C2/C3
Prebend St C3
Princess Rd East C3
Princess Rd West C3
Queen St B3
Rally Com Park,The A2
Regent College C3
Regent Rd C2/C3
Repton St A1
Rutland St B3
St Augustine Rd B1
St Georges Retail Pk B3
St George St B3
St Georges Way B3
St John St A2
St Margaret's A2
St Margaret's Way A2
St Martins B2
St Mary de Castro B1
St Matthew's Way A3
St Nicholas B1
St Nicholas Circle B1
Sanvey Gate A2
Silver St B2
Slater St A1
Soar La A1
South Albion St B3
Southampton St B3
Sue Townsend Theatre B2
Swain St B3
Swan St A1
Tigers Way C3
Tower St C3
Town Hall B2
Tudor Rd B1
Univ of Leicester C3
University Rd C3
Upperton Rd C1
Vaughan Way A2
Walnut St C2
Watling St A2
Welford Rd B2
Welford Rd (Leicester Tigers RC) C2
Wellington St B2
West St C3
West Walk C3
Western Boulevard C1
Western Rd C1
Wharf St North A3
Wharf St South A3
Y Theatre,The B3
Yeoman St B3
York Rd B2

Lincoln 188
Alexandra Terr B1
Anchor St C1
Arboretum B3
Arboretum Ave B3
Avenue,The B1
Baggholme Rd B3
Bailgate A2
Beaumont Fee B1
BMI The Lincoln Hospital A2
Brayford Way C1
Brayford Wharf East C1
Brayford Wharf North B1
Bruce Rd A2
Burton Rd A1
Bus Station (City) C2
Canwick Rd C2
Cardinal's Hat B2
Carline Rd B1
Castle B1
Castle St A1
Cathedral B2
Cathedral St B2
Cecil St A2
Chapel La A2
Cheviot St B3
Church La A2
City Hall B1
Clasketgate B2
Clayton Sports Gd A3
Coach Park C2
Collection,The B2
County Hospital (A&E) B3
County Hall B1
Courts C1
Cross St C2
Crown Courts B1
Curle Ave A3
Danesgate B2
Drill Hall B2
Drury La B1
East Bight A2
East Gate A2
Eastcliff Rd B3
Eastgate B2
Egerton Rd A3
Ellis Windmill A1
Engine Shed,The C1
Exchequer Gate B2
Firth Rd C1
Flaxengate B2
Florence St B3
George St C3
Good La A2
Gray St A1
Great Northern Terr C3
Greetwell Rd B3
Greetwellgate B3
Grove,The A3
Haffenden Rd A2
High St B2/C1
Hungate B2
James St A2
Jews House & Ct B2
Kesteven St C2
Langworthgate A2
Lawn,The B1
Lee Rd A3
Library B2
Lincoln Central Station C2
Lincoln College B2
Lincolnshire Life A1
Lincoln Univ Technical College (UTC) B2
Lindum Rd B2
Lindum Sports Gd A3
Lindum Terr B3
Liquorice Park B1
Mainwaring Rd A3
Manor Rd A2
Market C2
Massey Rd A3
Medieval Bishop's Palace B2
Mildmay St A1
Mill Rd A1
Millman Rd B3
Minster Yard B2
Monks Rd B3
Montague St B2
Mount St A1
Nettleham Rd A2
Newland B1
Newport A2
Newport Arch A2
Newport Cemetery A2
Northgate A2
Odeon C1
Orchard St B1
Oxford St C2
Park St B1
Pelham Bridge C2
Pelham St C2
Portland St C2
Post Office A1/B2/B3
Potter Gate B2
Priory Gate B2
Queensway A3
Rasen La A1
Ropewalk C1
Rosemary La B2
St Anne's Rd B3
St Benedict's C1
St Giles Ave A3
St Mark's Shopping Centre C1
St Marks St C1
St Mary-le-Wigford C1
St Mary's St C2
St Nicholas St A2
St Rumbold's St B2
St Swithin's B2
Saltergate C1
Saxon St A1
Sewell Rd B3
Silver St B2
Sincil St C2
Spital St A2
Spring Hill B1
Stamp End C3
Steep Hill B2
Stonebow & Guildhall C2
Stonefield Ave A2
Tentercroft St C1
Theatre Royal B2
Tritton Rd C1
Tritton Retail Park C1
Union Rd B1
Univ of Lincoln C1
Upper Lindum St B3
Upper Long Leys Rd A1
Usher B2
Vere St A2
Victoria St B1
Victoria Terr B1
Vine St B3
Wake St A1
Waldeck St A1
Waterside North C2
Waterside Shopping Centre C2
Waterside South C2
West Pde B1
Westgate A2
Wigford Way C1
Williamson St A2
Wilson St A1
Winn St B3
Wragby Rd A3
Yarborough Rd A1

Liverpool 188
Abercromby Sq C5
Addison St A3
Adelaide Rd B6
Ainsworth St B4
Albany Rd B6
Albert Edward Rd B6
Angela St C6
Anson St B4
Argyle St C3
Arrad St C4
Ashton St B5
Audley St A4
Back Leeds St A2
Basnett St B3
Bath St A1
Beacon,The B3
Beatles Story,The C2
Beckwith St C3
Bedford Close C5
Bedford St North C5
Bedford St South C5
Benson St C4
Berry St C4
Birkett St A4
Bixteth St B2
Blackburne Place C4
Bluecoat B3
Bold Place C4
Bold St C4
Bolton St B3
Bridport St B4
Bronte St B4
Brook St A1
Brownlow Hill B4/B5
Brownlow St B5
Brunswick Rd A5
Brunswick St B1
Bus Station C2
Butler Cres A6
Byrom St A3
Caledonia St C4
Cambridge St C5
Camden St A4
Canada Blvd B1
Canning Dock C2
Canterbury St A4
Cardwell St C6
Carver St A4
Cases St B3
Castle St B2
Catherine St C5
Cavern Club B3
Central Library A3
Chapel St B2
Charlotte St B3
Chatham Place C6
Chatham St C5
Cheapside B2
Chavasse Park C2
Chestnut St C5
Christian St A3
Church St B3
Clarence St B4
Clayton Square Shopping Centre B3
Coach Station A4
Cobden St A5
Cockspur St A2
College St C3
College St North A5
College St South A5
Colquitt St C4
Comus St A3
Concert St C3
Connaught Rd B6
Cook St B2
Copperas Hill B4
Cornwallis St C3
Covent Garden B2
Craven St A4
Cropper St B3
Crown St B5/C6
Cumberland St B2
Cunard Building B1
Dale St B2
Dansie St B4
Daulby St B5
Dawson St B3
Dental Hospital B5
Derby Sq B2
Drury La B2
Duckinfield St B4
Duke St C3
Earle St A2
East St A2
Eaton St A2
Edgar St A3
Edge La B6
Edinburgh Rd A6
Edmund St B2
Elizabeth St B5
Elliot St B3
Empire Theatre B4
Empress Rd B6
Epstein Theatre B3
Epworth St A5
Erskine St A5
Everyman Theatre C5
Exchange St East B2
FACT C4
Falkland St A5
Falkner St C5/C6
Farnworth St A6
Fenwick St B2
Fielding St A6
Fire Sta A4
Fleet St C3
Fraser St A4
Freemasons Row A2
Gardner Row A3
Gascoyne St A2
George St B2
Gibraltar Road A1
Gilbert St C3
Gildart St A4
Gill St B4
Goree B2
Gower St C2
Gradwell St C3
Great Crosshall St A3
Great George St C4
Great Howard St A1
Great Newton St B4
Greek St B4
Green La B4
Greenside A5
Greetham St C3
Gregson St A5
Grenville St C3
Grinfield St C6
Grove St C5
Guelph St A6
Hackins Hey B2
Haigh St A4
Hall La B6
Hanover St B3
Harbord St C6
Hardman St C4
Harker St A4
Hart St B4
Hatton Garden A2
Hawke St B4
Helsby St B6
Henry St C3
Highfield St A2
Highgate St B6
Hilbre St B4
Hope Place C4
Hope St C4
Hope University A5
Houghton St B3
Hunter St A3
Hutchinson St A6
Information Ctr B4/C2
Institute for the Performing Arts C4
Int Slavery Mus C2
Irvine St B6
Irwell St B2
Islington A4
James St B2
James St Station B2
Jenkinson St A4
John Moores Univ A2/A3/A4/B4/C4
Johnson St A3
Jubilee Drive B6
Kempston St A4
Kensington A6
Kensington Gdns B6
Kensington St A6
Kent St C3
King Edward St A1
Kinglake St B6
Knight St C4
Lace St A3
Langsdale St A4
Law Courts C2
Leece St C4
Leeds St A2
Leopold Rd B6
Lime St B3
Lime St Station B4
Liver St C2
Liverpool Central Station B3
Liverpool Landing Stage B1
Liverpool Institute for Performing Arts (LIPA) C4
Liverpool ONE C2
Liverpool Wheel, The C2
London Rd A4/B4
Lord Nelson St B4
Lord St B2
Lovat St C6
Low Hill A5
Low Wood St A6
Lydia Ann St C3
M&S Bank Arena C2
Mansfield St A4
Marmaduke St B6
Marsden St A6
Martensen St B6
Marybone A3
Maryland St C4
Mason St B6
Mathew St B2
May St B4
Melville Place C6
Merseyside Maritime Museum C2
Metquarter B3
Metropolitan Cathedral (RC) B5
Midghall St A2
Molyneux Rd A6
Moor Place B4
Moorfields B2
Moorfields Sta B2
Moss St A5
Mount Pleasant B4/B5
Mount St C4
Mount Vernon B6
Mulberry St C5
Municipal Buildings B2
Mus of Liverpool C2
Myrtle St C5
Naylor St A2
Nelson St C4
New Islington A4
New Quay B1
Newington St C3
North John St B2
North St A3
North View B6
Norton St A4
O2 Academy B4
Oakes St B5
Odeon B2
Old Hall St A1
Old Leeds St A2
Oldham Place C4
Oldham St C4
Olive St C6
Open Eye Gallery C3
Oriel St A2
Ormond St B2
Orphan St C6
Overbury St C6
Overton St B6
Oxford St C5
Paisley St A1
Pall Mall A2
Paradise St C3
Park La C3
Parker St B3
Parr St C3
Peach St B5
Pembroke Place B4
Pembroke St B5
Philharmonic Hall C5
Phythian Park A6
Pickop St A2
Pilgrim St C4
Pitt St C3
Playhouse Theatre B3
Pleasant St B4
Police HQ C2
Police Sta A4/A6/B4
Pomona St B4
Port of Liverpool Building B2
Post Office A2/A4/A5/B2/B3/B4/C4
Pownall St C2
Prescot St A5
Preston St B3
Princes Dock A1
Princes Gdns A2
Princes Jetty A1
Princes Pde B1
Princes St B2
Pythian St A6
Queen Sq Bus Sta B3
Queensland St C6
Queensway Tunnel (Docks exit) B1
Queensway Tunnel (Entrance) B3
Radio City B2
Ranelagh St B3
Redcross St B2
Renfrew St B6
Renshaw St B4
Richmond Row A4
Richmond St B3
Rigby St A2
Roberts St A1
Rock St B4
Rodney St C4
Rokeby St A4
Romily St A6
Roscoe La C4
Roscoe St C4
Rose Hill A3
Royal Albert Dock C2
Royal Court Theatre B3
Royal Liver Building B1
Royal Liverpool Hospital (A&E) B5
Royal Mail St B4
Rumford Place B2
Rumford St B2
Russell St B4
St Andrew St B4
St Anne St A4
St Georges Hall B3
St John's Centre B3
St John's Gdns B3
St John's La B3
St Joseph's Cres A4
St Minishull St B5
St Nicholas Place B1
St Paul's Sq A2
Salisbury St A4
Salthouse Dock C2
Salthouse Quay C2
Sandon St C5
Saxony Rd B6
Schomberg St A6
School La B2
Seel St C3
Seymour St B4
Shaw St A5
Shopmobility C2
Sidney Place C6
Sir Thomas St B3
Skelhorne St B4
Slater St C3
Smithdown La B6
Soho Sq A4
Soho St A4
South John St B2
Springfield A4
Stafford St A4
Standish St A3
Stanley St B2
Strand St C2
Strand,The B2
Suffolk St C3
Sydney Jones Liby C5
Tabley St C3
Tarleton St B3
Tate Liverpool Gallery C2
Teck St B6
Temple St B2
Titanic Memorial B1
Tithebarn St B2
Town Hall B2
Trowbridge St B4
Trueman St A3
Union St B2
Unity Theatre C4
University C5
Univ of Liverpool B5
Upper Baker St A6
Upper Duke St C4
Upper Frederick St C3
Vauxhall Rd A2
Vernon St B2
Victoria Gallery & Museum B5
Victoria St B2
Vine St C5
Wakefield St A4
Walker Art Gallery A3
Walker St A6
Wapping C2
Water St B1/B2
Waterloo Rd A1
Wavertree Rd B6
West Derby Rd A6
West Derby St B5
Western Approaches War Museum B2
Whitechapel B3
Whitley Gdns A5
William Brown St B3
William Henry St A4
Williamson Sq B3
Williamson St B3
Williamson's Tunnels Heritage Centre C6
Women's Hosp C6
Wood St B3
World Museum, Liverpool A3
York St C3

Llandudno 189
Abbey Place B1
Abbey Rd B1
Adelphi St B3
Alexandra Rd C2
Anglesey Rd A1
Argyll Rd B3
Arvon Ave A2
Atlee Close C3
Augusta St B3
Back Madoc St B2
Bodafon St B3
Bodhyfryd Rd A2
Bodnant Cres C3
Bodnant Rd C3
Bridge Rd C2
Bryniau Rd C1
Builder St B3
Builder St West C2
Cabin Lift A2
Cable Car A2
Camera Obscura A3
Caroline Rd B2
Chapel St A2
Charlton St B3
Church Cres C1
Church Walks A2
Claremont Rd B2
Clement Ave A2
Clifton Rd B2
Clonmel St B3
Coach Station B3
Conway Rd B3
Conwy Archive Service B2
Council St West C3
Cricket and Rec Gd B2
Cwlach Rd A2
Cwlach St A1
Cwm Howard La C3
Cwm Place C3
Cwm Rd C3
Dale Rd C1
Deganwy Ave B2
Denness Place C2
Dinas Rd C2
Dolydd B1
Erol Place B2
Ewloe Dr C3
Fairways C2
Ffordd Dewi C3
Ffordd Dulyn C2
Ffordd Dwyfor C3
Ffordd Elisabeth C3
Ffordd Gwynedd C3
Ffordd Las C3
Ffordd Morfa C3
Ffordd Penrhyn C3
Ffordd Tudno C3
Ffordd yr Orsedd C3
Ffordd Ysbyty C2
Fire & Ambulance Station B3
Garage St B3
George St A2
Gloddaeth Ave B1
Gloddaeth St B2
Gogarth Rd B1
Great Orme Mines A1
Great Ormes Rd B1
Great Orme Tramway A2
Happy Valley A2
Happy Valley Rd A3
Haulfre Gardens A1
Herkomer Cres C1
Hill Terr A2
Home Front Mus B2
Hospice B1
Howard Rd B3
Information Ctr B2
Invalids' Walk B1
James St B2
Jubilee St B3
King's Ave C2
King's Rd C2
Knowles Rd C2
Lees Rd C2
Library B2
Llandudno A2
Llandudno (A&E) C2
Llandudno Sta B3
Llandudno Football Ground C2
Llewelyn Ave A2
Lloyd St B2
Lloyd St West B1
Llwynon Rd A1
Llys Maelgwn B1
Madoc St B2
Maelgwn Rd B2
Maes-y-Cwm C3
Maes-y-Orsedd C3
Maesdu Bridge C2
Maesdu Rd C2/C3
Marian Place C2
Marian Rd C2
Marine Drive (Toll) A3
Market St A2
Miniature Golf Course A1
Morfa Rd B1
Mostyn B3
Mostyn Broadway B3
Mostyn St B3
Mowbray Rd C2
New St A2
Norman Rd B3
North Parade A2
North Wales Golf Links C1
Old Bank,The A2
Old Rd A2
Oval,The B1
Oxford Rd B3
Parade,The B3
Parc Llandudno Retail Park B3
Pier A3
Plas Rd A2
Police Station B3
Post Office A2/B3
Promenade A3
Pyllau Rd A1
Rectory La A2
Rhuddlan Ave C3
St Andrew's Ave B2
St Andrew's Place B2
St Beuno's Rd A1
St David's Place B2
St David's Rd B2
St George's Place A3
St Mary's Rd B2
St Seriol's Rd B2
Salisbury Pass B1
Salisbury Rd B2
Somerset St B3
South Parade A2
Stephen St B3
Tabor Hill A2
Town Hall B2
Trinity Ave B1
Trinity Cres C1
Trinity Sq B3
Tudno St A2
Ty-Coch Rd A2
Ty-Gwyn Rd A1/A2
Ty'n-y-Coed Rd A1
Vaughan St B3
Victoria Shopping Centre B3
Victoria A2
War Memorial A2
Werny Wylan C3
West Parade B1
Whiston Pass A2
Winllan Ave C2
Wyddfyd Rd A2
York Rd A2

Llanelli 189
Alban Rd B3
Albert St B1
Als St B3
Amos St C1
Andrew St A3
Ann St C2
Annesley St B2
Arfryn Ave A3
Avenue Cilfig,The A2
Belvedere Rd A1
Bigyn Park Terr C3
Bigyn Rd C3
Bond Ave C3
Brettenham St A1
Bridge St B2
Bryn Place C1
Bryn Rd C1
Bryn Terr C1
Bryn-More Rd C1
Brynhyfryd Rd A2
Brynmelyn Ave A3
Brynmor Rd B1
Burry St C1
Bus Station B2
Caersalem Terr C2
Cambrian St C1
Caswell St C3
Cedric St B3
Cemetery A2
Chapman St A1
Charles Terr C2
Church St B2
Clos Caer Elms A1
Clos Sant Paul C2
Coastal Link Rd B1/C1
Coldstream St B2
Coleshill Terr B1
College Hill B3
College Sq B3
Copperworks Rd C2
Coronation Rd C3
Corporation Ave A3
Council Offices B2
Court B2
Cowell St B2
Cradock St C2
Craig Ave C3
Cricket Ground A1
Derwent St A1
Dillwyn St C2
Druce St C1
Eastgate Leisure Complex B2
Elizabeth St B2
Emma St C2
Erw Rd B1
Felinfoel Rd A2
Fire Station A3
Firth Rd C3
Fron Terr C3
Furnace United Rugby Football Ground A1
Gelli-On B2
George St C2
Gilbert Cres A2
Gilbert Rd A2
Glanmor Rd C2
Glanmor Terr C2
Glasfryn Terr A3
Glenalla Rd B3
Glevering St B3
Goring Rd A2
Gorsedd Circle A2
Grant St C3
Graveyard C2
Great Western Close C2
Greenway St B1
Hall St B2
Harries Ave A2
Hedley Terr A2
Heol Elli B3
Heol Goffa A3
Heol Nant-y-Felin A3
Heol Siloh B2
Hick St C2
High St C1
Indoor Bowls Ctr B1
Inkerman St A2
Island Place B2
James St B3
John St B2
King George Ave B3
Lake View Close A2
Lakefield Place C1
Lakefield Rd C1
Langland Rd C3
Leisure Centre B1
Library B2
Llanelli House B2
Llanelli Parish Church B2
Llanelli Station C2
Llewellyn St C2
Lliedi Cres A3
Lloyd St B2
Llys Alys B3
Llys Fran A3
Llysnewedd C1
Long Row A3
Maes Gors C2
Maesyrhaf A3
Mansel St C3
Marblehall Rd B3
Marborough Rd A2
Margam St C3
Marged St C2
Marine St C1
Mariners,The C1
Market B2
Market St B2
Marsh St C2
Martin Rd C3
Miles St A1
Mill La A3/B2
Mincing La B2
Murray St B2
Myn y Mor B1
Nathan St C1
Nelson Terr C1
Nevill St C2
New Dock Rd C2
New Rd A1
New Zealand St A1
Odeon B2
Old Lodge C2
Old Rd A2
Paddock St C2
Palace Ave B3
Parc Howard A2
Parc Howard Museum & Art Gallery A2
Park Cres B1
Park St B2
Parkview Terr B1
Pemberton St C2
Pembrey Rd A1
Peoples Park B1
Police Station B2
Post Office B2/C2
Pottery Place B3
Pottery St B3
Princess St B1
Prospect Place A2
Pryce St A1
Queen Mary's Walk C3
Queen Victoria Rd C1
Raby St B1
Railway Terr C2
Ralph St B2
Ralph Terr C1
Regalia Terr B3
Rhydyrafon A3
Richard St B2
Robinson St B2
Roland Ave A1
Russell St C3
St David's Close C1
St Elli Shopping Ctr B2
St Margaret's Dr A1
Spowart Ave A1
Station Rd B2/C2
Stepney Place B2
Stepney St B2
Stewart St A1
Stradey Park Ave A1

Sunny Hill . . A2
Superstore . . A2
Swansea Rd . . A3
Talbot St . . C3
Temple St . . B3
Thomas St . . A2
Tinopolos TV Studios ✦ . . B2
Toft Place . . A3
Town Hall . . B2
Traeth Ffordd . . C1
Trinity Rd . . C3
Trinity Terr . . C2
Tunnel Rd . . B3
Tyisha Rd . . C3
Union Blgs . . A2
Upper Robinson St . B2
Vauxhall Rd . . B2
Walter's Rd . . B3
Waun Lanyrafon . . B2
Waun Rd . . A3
Wern Rd . . B3
West End . . A2
Y Bwthyn . . C3
Zion Row . . B3

London 186

Abbey Orchard St . E3
Abchurch La . . D6
Abingdon St . . E4
Achilles Way . . D2
Acton St . . B4
Addington St . . E4
Air St . . D3
Albany St . . B2
Albemarle St . . D3
Albert Embankment F4
Aldenham St . . A3
Aldersgate St . . C6
Aldford St . . D2
Aldgate ⊖ . . C7
Aldgate High St . . C7
Aldwych . . C4
Allsop Place . . B1
Amwell St . . B5
Angel ⊖ . . A5
Appold St . . C7
Argyle Sq . . B4
Argyle St . . B4
Argyll St . . C3
Arnold Circus . . B7
Artillery La . . C7
Artillery Row . . E3
Association of Photographers Gallery . . B6
Baker St ⊖ . . B1
Baker St . . B1
Baldwin's Gdns . . C5
Baltic St . . B6
Bank ⊖ . . C6
Bank Museum . . C6
Bank of England . . C6
Bankside . . D6
Bankside Gallery . D5
Banner St . . B6
Barbican ⇌⊖ . . C6
Barbican Centre for Arts,The . . C6
Barbican Gallery . C6
Basil St . . E1
Bastwick St . . B6
Bateman's Row . . B7
Bath St . . B6
Bayley St . . C3
Baylis Rd . . E5
Beak St . . D3
Bedford Row . . C4
Bedford Sq . . C3
Bedford St . . D4
Bedford Way . . B3
Beech St . . C6
Belgrave Place . . E2
Belgrave Sq . . E2
Bell La . . C7
Belvedere Rd . . E4
Berkeley Sq . . D2
Berkeley St . . D2
Bernard St . . B4
Berners Place . . C3
Berners St . . C3
Berwick St . . C3
Bethnal Green Rd . B7
Bevenden St . . B6
Bevis Marks . . C7
BFI (British Film Institute) . . D4
BFI London IMAX Cinema . . D5
Bidborough St . . B4
Binney St . . C2
Birdcage Walk . . E3
Bishopsgate . . C7
Blackfriars ⇌⊖ . . D5
Blackfriars Bridge . D5
Blackfriars Passage D5
Blackfriars Rd . . E5
Blandford St . . C1
Blomfield St . . C6
Bloomsbury St . . C3
Bloomsbury Way . . C4
Bolton St . . D2
Bond St ⊖ . . C2
Borough High St . . E6
Boswell St . . C4
Bow St . . C4
Bowling Green La . B5
Brad St . . D5
Bressenden Place . E3
Brewer St . . D3
Brick St . . D2
Bridge St . . E4
Britannia Walk . . B6
British Film Institute (BFI) . . D4
British Library . . B3
British Museum . . C4
Britton St . . B5
Broad Sanctuary . . E3
Broadway . . E3
Brook Dr . . F5
Brook St . . D2
Brunswick Place . . B6
Brunswick Shopping Centre,The . . B4
Brunswick Sq . . B4
Brushfield St . . C7
Bruton St . . D2
Bryanston St . . C1
BT Centre . . C6
Buckingham Gate . . E3
Buckingham Palace . . E3
Buckingham Palace Rd . . F2
Bunhill Row . . B6
Byward St . . D7
Cabinet War Rooms & Churchill Mus . . E3
Cadogan La . . E2
Cadogan Place . . E1
Cadogan Sq . . F1
Caledonian Rd . . A4
Calshot St . . A4
Calthorpe St . . B4
Calvert Ave . . B7
Cambridge Circus . . C3
Camomile St . . C7
Cannon St . . D6
Cannon St ⇌⊖ . . D6
Capel Manor Coll . . B2
Carey St . . C4
Carlisle La . . E4
Carlisle Place . . E3
Carlton House Terr . D3
Carmelite St . . D5
Carnaby St . . C3
Carter La . . C5
Carthusian St . . C6
Cartwright Gdns . . B4
Castle Baynard St . D5
Cavendish Place . . C2
Cavendish Sq . . C2
Caxton Hall . . E3
Caxton St . . E3
Central St . . B6
Chalton St . . B3
Chancery Lane ⊖ . . C5
Chapel St . . E2
Charing Cross ⇌⊖ D4
Charing Cross Rd . . C3
Charles Dickens Museum,The . . B4
Charles II St . . D3
Charles Sq . . B6
Charles St . . D2
Charlotte Rd . . B7
Charlotte St . . C3
Chart St . . B6
Charterhouse Sq . . C5
Charterhouse St . . C5
Cheapside . . C6
Chenies St . . C3
Chesham St . . E2
Chester Sq . . F2
Chesterfield Hill . . D2
Chiltern St . . C2
Chiswell St . . C6
City Garden Row . . A5
City Rd . . B6
City Thameslink ⇌ . C5
City University,The . B5
Claremont Sq . . A5
Clarges St . . D2
Clerkenwell Close . . B5
Clerkenwell Green . B5
Clerkenwell Rd . . B5
Cleveland St . . C3
Clifford St . . D3
Clink Prison Mus . D6
Clock Museum . . C6
Club Row . . B7
Cockspur St . . D3
Coleman St . . C6
Columbia Rd . . B7
Commercial St . . C7
Compton St . . B5
Conduit St . . D2
Constitution Hill . . E2
Copperfield St . . E5
Coptic St . . C4
Cornhill . . C6
Cornwall Rd . . D5
Coronet St . . B7
Courtauld Gallery . . D4
Covent Garden ⊖ . . D4
Covent Garden ✦ . . D4
Cowcross St . . C5
Cowper St . . B6
Cranbourn St . . D3
Craven St . . D4
Crawford St . . C1
Creechurch La . . C7
Cremer St . . A7
Cromer St . . B4
Cumberland Gate . . D1
Cumberland Terr . . A2
Curtain Rd . . B7
Curzon St . . D2
Cut,The . . E5
D'arblay St . . C3
Davies St . . C2
Dean St . . C3
Deluxe Gallery . . B7
Denmark St . . C3
Dering St . . C2
Devonshire St . . C2
Diana, Princess of Wales Meml Walk . E3
Dingley Rd . . B6
Dorset St . . C1
Doughty St . . B4
Dover St . . D2
Downing St . . E4
Druid St . . E7
Drummond St . . B3
Drury La . . C4
Drysdale St . . B7
Duchess St . . C2
Dufferin St . . B6
Duke of Wellington Place . . E2
Duke St . . C2
Duke St . . D3
Duke St Hill . . D6
Duke's Place . . C7
Duncannon St . . D4
East Rd . . B6
Eastcastle St . . C3
Eastcheap . . D7
Eastman Dental Hospital . . B4
Eaton Place . . E2
Eaton Sq . . E2
Eccleston St . . E2
Edgware Rd . . C1
Eldon St . . C6
Embankment ⊖ . . D4
Endell St . . C4
Endsleigh Place . . B3
Euston ⇌⊖ . . B3
Euston Rd . . B3
Euston Square ⊖ . . B3
Evelina Children's Hospital . . E4
Eversholt St . . A3
Exmouth Market . . B5
Fann St . . B6
Farringdon ⇌⊖ . . C5
Farringdon Rd . . C5
Farringdon St . . C5
Featherstone St . . B6
Fenchurch St . . D7
Fenchurch St ⇌ . . D7
Fetter La . . C5
Finsbury Circus . . C6
Finsbury Pavement C6
Finsbury Sq . . B6
Fitzalan St . . F5
Fitzmaurice Place . . D2
Fleet St . . C5
Floral St . . D4
Florence Nightingale Museum . . E4
Folgate St . . C7
Foot Hospital . . B3
Fore St . . C6
Foster La . . C6
Foundling Museum, The . . B4
Francis St . . F3
Frazier St . . E5
Freemason's Hall . . C4
Friday St . . C6
Gainsford St . . E7
Garden Row . . E5
Gee St . . B6
George St . . C1
Gerrard St . . D3
Giltspur St . . C5
Glasshouse St . . D3
Gloucester Place . . C1
Golden Hinde . . D6
Golden La . . B6
Golden Sq . . D3
Goodge St ⊖ . . C3
Goodge St . . C3
Gordon Sq . . B3
Goswell Rd . . B5
Gough St . . B4
Goulston St . . C7
Gower St . . B3
Gracechurch St . . D6
Grafton Way . . B3
Gray's Inn Rd . . B4
Great College St . . E4
Great Cumberland Place . . C1
Great Eastern St . . B7
Great Guildford St . D6
Great Marlborough St . . C3
Great Ormond St . . B4
Great Ormond St Children's Hosp . B4
Great Percy St . . B4
Great Peter St . . E3
Great Portland St ⊖ B2
Great Portland St . . C2
Great Queen St . . C4
Great Russell St . . C3
Great Scotland Yd . D4
Great Smith St . . E3
Great Suffolk St . . D5
Great Titchfield St . C3
Great Tower St . . D7
Great Windmill St . D3
Greek St . . C3
Green Park ⊖ . . D3
Green St . . D2
Greencoat Place . . F3
Gresham St . . C6
Greville St . . B4/C5
Greycoat Hosp Sch . E3
Greycoat Place . . E3
Grosvenor Cres . . E2
Grosvenor Gdns . . E2
Grosvenor Place . . E2
Grosvenor Sq . . D2
Grosvenor St . . D2
Guards Museum and Chapel . . E3
Guildhall Art Gallery . . C6
Guilford St . . B4
Guy's Hospital . . D6
Haberdasher St . . B6
Hackney Rd . . B7
Half Moon St . . D2
Halkin St . . E2
Hall St . . B5
Hallam St . . C2
Hampstead Rd . . B3
Hanover Sq . . C2
Hans Cres . . E1
Hanway St . . C3
Hardwick St . . B5
Harley St . . C2
Harrison St . . B4
Hastings St . . B4
Hatfields . . D5
Hay's Galleria . . D7
Hay's Mews . . D2
Hayles St . . F5
Haymarket . . D3
Hayward Gallery . . D4
Helmet Row . . B6
Herbrand St . . B4
Hercules Rd . . E4
Hertford St . . D2
High Holborn . . C4
Hill St . . D2
HMS Belfast . . D7
Hobart Place . . E2
Holborn ⊖ . . C4
Holborn . . C5
Holborn Viaduct . . C5
Holland St . . D5
Holmes Mus . . B1
Holywell La . . B7
Horse Guards' Rd . . D3
Houndsditch . . C7
Houses of Parliament . . E4
Howland St . . C3
Hoxton Sq . . B7
Hoxton St . . B7
Hunter St . . B4
Hunterian Mus . . C4
Hyde Park . . D1
Hyde Park Cnr ⊖ . . E2
Imperial War Museum . . E5
Inner Circle . . B2
Ironmonger Row . . B6
James St . . C2
James St . . D4
Jermyn St . . D3
Jockey's Fields . . C4
John Carpenter St . D5
John St . . B4
Judd St . . B4
Kennington Rd . . E5
King Charles St . . E4
King St . . D3
King St . . C6
King William St . . C6
King's Coll London . D5
King's Cross ⇌ . . A4
King's Cross Rd . . B4
King's Cross St Pancras ⊖ . . A4
King's Rd . . E2
Kingley St . . C3
Kingsland Rd . . B7
Kingsway . . C4
Kinnerton St . . E2
Knightsbridge ⊖ . . E1
Lamb St . . C7
Lamb's Conduit St . . C4
Lambeth Bridge . . F4
Lambeth High St . . F4
Lambeth North ⊖ . . E5
Lambeth Palace . . E4
Lambeth Palace Rd . E4
Lambeth Rd . . E5
Lambeth Walk . . F4
Lancaster Place . . D4
Langham Place . . C2
Leadenhall St . . C7
Leake St . . E4
Leather La . . C5
Leicester Sq ⊖ . . D3
Leicester St . . D3
Leonard St . . B6
Lever St . . B6
Lexington St . . D3
Lidlington Place . . A3
Lime St . . D7
Lincoln's Inn Fields C4
Lindsey St . . C5
Lisle St . . D3
Liverpool St . . C7
Liverpool St ⇌⊖ . . C7
Lloyd Baker St . . B5
Lloyd Sq . . B5
Lombard St . . C6
London Aquarium . . E4
London Bridge ⇌⊖ . . D6
London Bridge Hospital . . D6
London City Hall . . D7
London Dungeon, The . . E4
London Guildhall University . . C6
London Rd . . E5
London Transport Museum . . D4
London Wall . . C6
London Eye ✦ . . E4
Long Acre . . D4
Long La . . C5
Longford St . . B2
Lower Belgrave St . . E2
Lower Grosvenor Pl . E2
Lower Marsh . . E5
Lower Thames St . . D6
Lowndes St . . E2
Ludgate Circus . . C5
Ludgate Hill . . C5
Luxborough St . . C2
Lyall St . . E2
Macclesfield Rd . . B6
Madame Tussaud's ✦ . . B2
Maddox St . . D2
Malet St . . C3
Mall,The . . E3
Manchester Sq . . C2
Manchester St . . C2
Mandeville Place . . C2
Mansell St . . D7
Mansion House . . C6
Mansion House ⊖ . . D6
Maple St . . C3
Marble Arch ⊖ . . C1
Marble Arch . . D1
Marchmont St . . B4
Margaret St . . C3
Margery St . . B5
Mark La . . D7
Marlborough Rd . . D3
Marshall St . . C3
Marsham St . . E3
Marylebone High St C2
Marylebone La . . C2
Marylebone Rd . . B2
Marylebone St . . C2
Mecklenburgh Sq . . B4
Middle Temple La . . C5
Middlesex St (Petticoat La) . . C7
Midland Rd . . A3
Minories . . C7
Monck St . . E3
Monmouth St . . C4
Montagu Place . . C1
Montagu Sq . . C1
Montagu St . . C4
Montague Place . . C3
Monument ⊖ . . D6
Monument St . . D6
Monument,The ✦ . . D6
Moor La . . C6
Moorfields . . C6
Moorfields Eye Hospital . . B6
Moorgate . . C6
Moorgate ⇌⊖ . . C6
Moreland St . . B5
Morley St . . E5
Mortimer St . . C3
Mount Pleasant . . B5
Mount St . . D2
Murray Grove . . A6
Museum of Garden History . . E4
Mus of London . . C6
Museum St . . C4
Myddelton Sq . . B5
Myddelton St . . B5
National Gallery . . D3
National Hospital . . B4
National Portrait Gallery . . D3
Neal St . . C4
Nelson's Column ✦ . D4
New Bond St . . C2/D2
New Bridge St . . C5
New Cavendish St . . C2
New Change . . C6
New Fetter La . . C5
New Inn Yard . . B7
New North Rd . . A6
New Oxford St . . C3
New Scotland Yard . . E3
New Sq . . C4
Newgate St . . C5
Newton St . . C4
Nile St . . B6
Noble St . . C6
Noel St . . C3
North Audley St . . D2
North Cres . . C3
North Row . . D2
Northampton Sq . . B5
Northington St . . B4
Northumberland Ave . . D4
Norton Folgate . . C7
Nottingham Place . . C2
Obstetric Hosp . . B3
Old Bailey . . C5
Old Broad St . . C6
Old Compton St . . C3
Old County Hall . . E4
Old Gloucester St . . C4
Old King Edward St C6
Old Nichol St . . B7
Old Paradise St . . F4
Old Spitalfields Mkt C7
Old St . . B6
Old St ⇌⊖ . . B6
Old Vic . . E5
Open Air Theatre . . B2
Operating Theatre Museum . . D6
Orange St . . D3
Orchard St . . C2
Ossulston St . . A3
Outer Circle . . B1
Oxford Circus ⊖ . . C3
Oxford St . . C2/C3
Paddington St . . C2
Palace St . . E3
Pall Mall . . D3
Pall Mall East . . D3
Pancras Rd . . A4
Panton St . . D3
Paris Gdn . . D5
Park Cres . . B2
Park La . . D2
Park Rd . . B1
Park St . . D2
Park St . . D6
Parker St . . C4
Parliament Sq . . E4
Parliament St . . E4
Paternoster Sq . . C5
Paul St . . B6
Pear Tree St . . B5
Penton Rise . . B4
Penton St . . A5
Pentonville Rd . . A4/A5
Percival St . . B5
Petticoat La (Middlesex St) . . C7
Petty France . . E3
Phoenix Place . . B4
Phoenix Rd . . A3
Photo Gallery . . D3
Piccadilly . . D2
Piccadilly Circus ⊖ D3
Pitfield St . . B7
Pollock's Toy Museum . . C3
Polygon Rd . . A3
Pont St . . E1
Portland Place . . C2
Portman Mews . . C2
Portman Sq . . C2
Portman St . . C1
Portugal St . . C4
Postal Museum, The . . B4
Poultry . . C6
Primrose St . . C7
Princes St . . C6
Procter St . . C4
Provost St . . B6
Quaker St . . B7
Queen Anne St . . C2
Queen Elizabeth Hall . . D4
Queen Sq . . B4
Queen St . . C6
Queen Street Place . D6
Queen Victoria St . . D5
Queens Gallery . . E3
Radnor St . . B6
Rathbone Place . . C3
Rawstorne St . . B5
Red Lion Sq . . C4
Red Lion St . . C4
Redchurch St . . B7
Redcross Way . . D6
Regency St . . F3
Regent Sq . . B4
Regent St . . C3
Regent's Park . . B2
Richmond Terr . . E4
Ridgmount St . . C3
Rivington St . . B7
Robert St . . B2
Rochester Row . . F3
Ropemaker St . . C6
Rosebery Ave . . B5
Roupell St . . D5
Royal Academy of Arts . . D3
Royal Academy of Dramatic Art (RADA) . . B3
Royal Acad of Music B2
Royal Artillery Memorial ✦ . . E2
Royal College of Nursing . . C2
Royal College of Surgeons . . C4
Royal Festival Hall . . D4
Royal London Hospital for Integrated Medicine . . C4
Royal National Theatre . . D5
Royal National Throat, Nose and Ear Hospital . . B4
Royal Opera Ho . . D4
Russell Sq . . B3
Russell Square ⊖ . . B4
Sackville St . . D3
Sadlers Wells . . B5
Saffron Hill . . C5
St Alban's St . . D3
St Andrew St . . C5
St Bartholomew's Hospital . . C5
St Botolph St . . C7
St Bride St . . C5
St George's Circus . . E5
St George's Rd . . E5
St Giles High St . . C3
St James's Pal . . D3
St James's Park ⊖ . E3
St James's St . . D3
St John St . . B5
St Margaret St . . E4
St Mark's Hosp . . B5
St Martin's La . . D4
St Martin's Le Grand . . C6
St Mary Axe . . C7
St Pancras International ⇌ . . A4
St Paul's ⊖ . . C6
St Paul's Cath ✝ . . C6
St Paul's Churchyard . . C5
St Peter's Hosp . . D4
St Thomas St . . D6
St Thomas' Hosp . . E4
Savile Row . . D3
Savoy Place . . D4
Savoy St . . D4
School of Hygiene & Tropical Medicine C3
Scrutton St . . B7
Sekforde St . . B5
Serpentine Rd . . D1
Seven Dials . . C4
Seward St . . B5
Seymour St . . C1
Shad Thames . . D7
Shaftesbury Ave . . D3
Shakespeare's Globe Theatre . . D6
Shepherd Market . . D2
Sherwood St . . D3
Shoe La . . C5
Shoreditch High St . B7
Shoreditch High St ⊖ . . B7
Shorts Gdns . . C4
Shrek's Adventure ✦ . . E4
Sidmouth St . . B4
Silk St . . C6
Sir John Soane's Museum . . C4
Skinner St . . B5
Sloane St . . E1
Snow Hill . . C5
Soho Sq . . C3
Somerset House . . D4
South Audley St . . D2
South Carriage Dr . . E1
South Molton St . . C2
South Place . . C6
South St . . D2
Southampton Row . C4
Southampton St . . D4
Southwark ⊖ . . D5
Southwark Bridge . . D6
Southwark Bridge Rd . . D6
Southwark Cath ✝ . . D6
Southwark St . . D6
Speakers' Corner . . D1
Spencer St . . B5
Spital Sq . . C7
Stamford St . . D5
Stanhope St . . B3
Stephenson Way . . B3
Stock Exchange . . C5
Stoney St . . D6
Strand . . C5
Stratton St . . D2
Sumner St . . D5
Sutton's Way . . B6
Swanfield St . . B7
Swinton St . . B4
Tabernacle St . . B6
Tate Modern . . D6
Tavistock Place . . B4
Tavistock Sq . . B3
Tea & Coffee Museum . . D6
Temple ⊖ . . D5
Temple Ave . . D5
Temple Place . . D4
Terminus Place . . E2
Thayer St . . C2
Theobald's Rd . . C4
Thorney St . . F4
Threadneedle St . . C6
Throgmorton St . . C6
Tonbridge St . . B4
Tooley St . . D7
Torrington Place . . B3
Tothill St . . E3
Tottenham Court Rd B3
Tottenham Ct Rd ⊖ C3
Tottenham St . . C3
Tower Bridge ✦ . . D7
Tower Bridge App . . D7
Tower Bridge Rd . . E7
Tower Hill . . D7
Tower Hill ⊖ . . D7
Tower of London, The . . D7
Toynbee St . . C7
Trafalgar Square . . D3
Trinity Sq . . D7
Trocadero Centre . . D3
Tudor St . . D5
Turnmill St . . C5
Ufford St . . E5
Union St . . D5
Univ Coll Hosp . . B3
University College London (UCL) . . B3
Univ of London . . C3
Univ of Westminster C2
University St . . B3
Upper Belgrave St . . E2
Upper Berkeley St . . C1
Upper Brook St . . D2
Upper Grosvenor St D2
Upper Ground . . D5
Upper Montague St C1
Upper St Martin's La . . D4
Upper Thames St . . D6
Upper Wimpole St . . C2
Upper Woburn Pl . . B3
Vere St . . C2
Vernon Place . . C4
Vestry St . . B6
Victoria ⇌⊖ . . E2
Victoria Emb . . D4
Victoria Place Shopping Centre . . F2
Victoria St . . E3
Villiers St . . D4
Vincent Sq . . F3
Vinopolis City of Wine . . D6
Virginia Rd . . B7
Wakley St . . B5
Walbrook . . C6
Wallace Collection . . C2
Wardour St . . C3/D3
Warner St . . B5
Warren St ⊖ . . B3
Warren St . . B3
Waterloo ⇌⊖ . . E5
Waterloo Bridge . . D4
Waterloo East ⇌ . . D5
Waterloo Rd . . E5
Watling St . . C6
Webber St . . E5
Welbeck St . . C2
Wellington Arch ✦ . E2
Wellington Mus . . E2
Wells St . . C3
Wenlock St . . A6
Wentworth St . . C7
West Smithfield . . C5
West Sq . . E5
Westminster ⊖ . . E4
Westminster Abbey ✝ . . E4
Westminster Bridge E4
Westminster Bridge Rd . . E5
Westminster Cathedral (RC) ✝ . . E3
Westminster City Hall . . E3
Westminster Hall . . E4
Weymouth St . . C2
Wharf Rd . . A6
Wharton St . . B4
Whitcomb St . . D3
White Cube . . B7
White Lion Hill . . D5
White Lion St . . A5
Whitecross St . . B6
Whitefriars St . . C5
Whitehall . . D4
Whitehall Place . . D4
Wigmore Hall . . C2
Wigmore St . . C2
William IV St . . D4
Wilmington Sq . . B5
Wilson St . . C6
Wilton Cres . . E2
Wimpole St . . C2
Windmill Walk . . D5
Woburn Place . . B4
Woburn Sq . . B3
Women's Hosp . . C3
Wood St . . C6
Woodbridge St . . B5
Wootton St . . D5
Wormwood St . . C7
Worship St . . B6
Wren St . . B4
Wynyatt St . . B5
Young Vic . . E5
York Rd . . E4
York St . . C1
York Terrace East . . B2
York Terrace West . . B2
York Way . . A4

Luton 189

Adelaide St . . B1
Albert Rd . . C2
Alma St . . B2
Alton Rd . . C3
Anthony Gdns . . C1
Arthur St . . C2
Ashburnham Rd . . B1
Ashton Rd . . C2
Back St . . A2
Bailey St . . C3
Baker St . . C2
Biscot Rd . . A1
Bolton Rd . . B3
Boyle Close . . A2
Brantwood Rd . . B1
Bretts Mead . . C1
Bridge St . . B2
Brook St . . A1
Brunswick St . . A3
Burr St . . A3
Bury Park Rd . . A1
Bute St . . B2
Buxton Rd . . B2
Cambridge St . . C3
Cardiff Grove . . B1
Cardiff Rd . . B1
Cardigan St . . A2
Castle St . . B2/C2
Chapel St . . C2
Charles St . . A3
Chase St . . C2
Cheapside . . B2
Chequer St . . C3
Chiltern Rise . . C1
Church St . . B2/B3
Cinema . . A2
Cobden St . . A3
College . . A3
Collingdon St . . A1
Concorde Ave . . A3
Corncastle Rd . . C1
Cowper St . . C2
Crawley Green Rd . . B3
Crawley Rd . . A1
Crescent Rd . . A3
Crescent Rise . . A3
Cromwell Rd . . A1
Cross St . . A2
Cross Way,The . . C1
Crown Court . . B2
Cumberland St . . B2
Cutenhoe Rd . . C3
Dallow Rd . . B1
Downs Rd . . B1
Dudley St . . A2
Duke St . . A2
Dumfries St . . B1
Dunstable Place . . B2
Dunstable Rd . . A1/B1
Edward St . . A3
Elizabeth St . . C2
Essex Close . . C3
Farley Hill . . C1
Flowers Way . . B2
Francis St . . A1
Frederick St . . A2
Galaxy Leisure Complex . . A2
George St . . B2
George St West . . B2
Gordon St . . B2
Grove Rd . . B1
Guildford St . . A2
Haddon Rd . . A3
Harcourt St . . C2
Hart Hill Drive . . A3
Hart Hill Lane . . A3
Hartley Rd . . A3
Hastings St . . B2
Hat Factory,The . . B2
Hatters Way . . A1
Havelock Rd . . A2
Hibbert St . . C2
High Town Rd . . A3
Highbury Rd . . A1
Hightown Community Sports & Arts Ctr . A3
Hillary Cres . . C1
Hillborough Rd . . C1
Hitchin Rd . . A3
Holly St . . C2
Holm . . C1
Hucklesby Way . . A2
Hunts Close . . C1
Inkerman St . . A2
John St . . B2
Jubilee St . . A3
Kelvin Close . . C2
King St . . B2
Kingsland Rd . . C3
Larches,The . . A2
Latimer Rd . . C2
Lawn Gdns . . C2
Lea Rd . . B3
Library . . B2
Library Rd . . B2
Library Theatre . . B2
Liverpool Rd . . B1
London Rd . . C2
Luton Station ⇌ . . A2
Lyndhurst Rd . . B1
Magistrates Court . . B2
Mall,The . . B2
Manchester St . . B2
Manor Rd . . B3
Manor Road Park . . B3
May St . . C3
Meyrick Ave . . C1
Midland Rd . . A2
Mill St . . A2
Milton Rd . . B1
Moor St . . A1
Moor,The . . A1
Moorland Gdns . . A2
Moulton Rise . . A3
Napier Rd . . B1
New Bedford Rd . . A1
New Town St . . C2
North St . . A3
Old Bedford Rd . . A2
Old Orchard . . C2
Osbourne Rd . . C3
Oxen Rd . . A3
Park Sq . . B2
Park St . . B3/C3
Park St West . . B2
Park Viaduct . . B3
Parkland Drive . . C1
Police Station . . B1
Pomfret Ave . . A3
Pondwicks Rd . . B3
Post Office . . A1/B2
Power Court . . B3
Princess St . . B1
Red Rails . . C1
Regent St . . B2
Reginald St . . A2
Rothesay Rd . . B1
Russell Rise . . C1
Russell St . . C1
Ruthin Close . . C2
St Ann's Rd . . B3
St George's Square . B2
St Mary's . . B3
St Marys Rd . . B3
St Paul's Rd . . C2
St Saviour's Cres . . C1
Salisbury Rd . . B1
Seymour Ave . . C3
Seymour Rd . . C3
Silver St . . B2
South Rd . . C2
Station Rd . . A2
Stockwood Cres . . C2
Stockwood Park . . C1
Strathmore Ave . . C2
Stuart St . . B2
Studley Rd . . A1
Surrey St . . C3
Sutherland Place . . C1
Tavistock St . . C2
Taylor St . . A3
Telford Way . . A1
Tennyson Rd . . C2
Tenzing Grove . . C1
Thistle Rd . . B3
Town Hall . . B2
Townsley Close . . C2
UK Centre for Carnival Arts ✦ . . B3
Union St . . B2
University of Bedfordshire . . B3
Upper George St . . B2
Vicarage St . . B3
Villa Rd . . A2
Waldeck Rd . . A1
Wardown House Museum & Gallery . . A2
Wellington St . . B1/B2
Wenlock St . . A2
Whitby Rd . . A1
Whitehill Ave . . C1
William St . . A2
Wilsden Ave . . C1
Windmill Rd . . B3
Windsor St . . C2
Winsdon Rd . . B1
York St . . A3

Macclesfield 189

108 Steps . . B2
Abbey Rd . . A1
Alton Dr . . A3
Armett St . . C1
Athey St . . B1
Bank St . . C3
Barber St . . C3
Barton St . . C1
Beech La . . A2
Beswick St . . B1
Black La . . A2
Black Rd . . C3
Blakelow Gardens . . C3
Blakelow Rd . . C3
Bond St . . B1/C1
Bread St . . C1
Bridge St . . B1
Brock St . . A2
Brocklehurst Ave . . A3
Brook St . . B3
Brookfield La . . B3
Brough St West . . C1
Brown St . . C1
Brynton Rd . . A2
Buckley St . . C2
Bus Station . . B2
Buxton Rd . . B3
Byrons St . . C2
Canal St . . B3
Carlsbrook Ave . . A3
Castle St . . B2
Catherine St . . B1
Cemetery . . A1
Chadwick Terr . . A3
Chapel St . . C2
Charlotte St . . B2
Chester Rd . . B1
Chestergate . . B1
Christ Church . . B1
Churchill Way . . B2
Coare St . . A1
Commercial Rd . . B2
Conway Cres . . A3
Copper St . . C3
Cottage St . . B1
Crematorium . . A1
Crew Ave . . A3
Crompton Rd . . B1/C1
Cross St . . C2
Crossall St . . C1
Cumberland St . . A1/B1
Dale St . . B3
Duke St . . B2
Eastgate . . B3
Exchange St . . B2
Fence Ave . . B3
Fence Ave Ind Est . . A3
Flint St . . B3
Foden St . . A2
Fountain St . . B3
Garden St . . A3
Gas Rd . . B2
Gateway Gallery ✦ . B1
George St . . B2
Glegg St . . B3
Golf Course . . C3
Goodall St . . B3
Grange Rd . . C1
Great King St . . B1
Green St . . B3
Grosvenor Shopping Centre . . B2
Gunco La . . C3
Half St . . C2
Hallefield Rd . . B3
Hatton St . . C1
Hawthorn Way . . A3
Heapy St . . C3
Henderson St . . B1
Heritage Centre . . B2
Hibel Rd . . A2
High St . . C2
Hobson St . . C2
Hollins Rd . . C3
Hope St West . . C1
Horseshoe Dr . . B1
Hurdsfield Rd . . A3
Information Ctr . . B2
James St . . C2
Jodrell St . . B3
John St . . C2
Jordangate . . B2
King Edward St . . B2
King George's Field C3
King St . . B2
King's School . . A1
Knight Pool . . C3
Knight St . . C3
Lansdowne St . . A3
Library . . B2
Lime Grove . . B3
Loney St . . B1
Longacre St . . B1
Lord St . . C2
Lowe St . . C2
Lowerfield Rd . . A3
Lyon St . . B1
Macclesfield Coll . . C1
Macclesfield Sta ⇌ . B2
MADS Little Theatre . . C2
Marina . . B3
Market . . B2
Market Place . . B2
Masons La . . A3
Mill La . . C2
Mill Rd . . C2
Mill St . . B2
Moran Rd . . C1
New Hall St . . A2
Newton St . . C1
Nicholson Ave . . A3
Nicholson Close . . A3
Northgate Ave . . A2
Old Mill La . . C2
Paradise Mill . . C2
Paradise St . . B1
Park Green . . B2
Park La . . C1
Park Rd . . C1
Park St . . C2
Park Vale Rd . . C1
Parr St . . B1
Peel St . . C3
Percyvale St . . A3
Peter St . . C1
Pickford St . . B2
Pierce St . . B1
Pinfold St . . B1
Pitt St . . C2
Police Station . . B2
Pool St . . C2
Poplar Rd . . C2
Post Office . . B2
Pownall St . . A2
Prestbury Rd . . A1/B1
Queen Victoria St . . B2
Queen's Ave . . A3
Registrar . . B2
Retail Park . . C2
Richmond Hill . . C3
Riseley St . . B1
Roan Ct . . B3
Roe St . . B2
Rowan Way . . A3
Ryle St . . C2
Ryle's Park Rd . . C1
St George's St . . C2
St Michael's . . B2
Samuel St . . B2
Saville St . . C3
Shaw St . . B1
Silk Rd,The . . A2/B2
Slater St . . C1
Snow Hill . . C3
South Park . . C1
Spring Gdns . . A2
Statham St . . C2
Station St . . A2
Steeple St . . A3
Sunderland St . . B2
Superstore . . A1/A2/C2
Swettenham St . . B3
Thistleton Close . . C2
Thorp St . . B2
Town Hall . . B2
Townley St . . B2
Treacle Market ✦ . . B2
Turnock St . . C3
Union Rd . . B3
Union St . . B2
Victoria Park . . B3
Vincent St . . C2
Waters Green . . B2
Waterside . . C2
West Bond St . . B1
West Park . . A1
West Park Mus . . A1
Westbrook Dr . . A1
Westminster Rd . . A1
Whalley Hayes . . B1
Windmill St . . C3
Withyfold Dr . . A2
York St . . B3

Maidstone 190

Albion Place . . B3
All Saints . . B2
Allen St . . A3
Amphitheatre ✦ . . C2
Archbishop's Palace . . B2
Bank St . . B2
Barker Rd . . C2
Barton Rd . . C3
Beaconsfield Rd . . C1
Bedford Place . . B1
Bishops Way . . B2
Bluett St . . A3
BMI The Somerfield Hospital . . A1
Bower La . . C1
Bower Mount Rd . . B1
Bower Place . . C1
Bower St . . B1
Boxley Rd . . A3
Brenchley Gardens . A2
Brewer St . . A3
Broadway . . B2
Broadway Shopping Centre . . B2
Brunswick St . . C3
Buckland Hill . . A1
Buckland Rd . . B1
Bus Station . . B3
Campbell Rd . . C3
Church Rd . . C1
Church St . . B3
Cinema . . C2
Clifford Way . . C1/C2
College Ave . . C2
College Rd . . C2
Collis Meml Gdn . . C3
Cornwallis Rd . . B1
Corpus Christi Hall . B2
Council Offices . . B3
County Hall . . A2
County Rd . . A3
Crompton Gdns . . C3
Crown & County Courts . . B2
Curzon Rd . . A3
Dixon Close . . C2
Douglas Rd . . C1
Earl St . . B2
Eccleston Rd . . C2
Fairmeadow . . B2
Fisher St . . A2
Florence Rd . . C1
Foley St . . A3
Foster St . . C3
Freedom Leisure Centre . . A1/A2
Fremlin Walk Shopping Centre . . B2
Gabriel's Hill . . B3
George St . . C3
Grecian St . . A3
Hardy St . . A3
Hart St . . C2
Hastings Rd . . C3
Hayle Rd . . C3
Hazlitt . . B2
Heathorn St . . A3
Hedley St . . A3
High St . . B2
HM Prison . . A3
Holland Rd . . A3
Hope St . . A2
Information Ctr . . B2
James St . . A3
James Whatman Way . . A2
Jeffrey St . . A3
Kent County Council Offices . . A2
Kent History & Library Centre . . A2
King Edward Rd . . C2
King St . . B3
Kingsley Rd . . C3
Knightrider St . . B3
Launder Way . . C1
Lesley Place . . A1
Library . . B2
Little Buckland Ave A1
Lockmeadow Leisure Complex . . C2
London Rd . . B1
Lower Boxley Rd . . A2
Lower Fant Rd . . C1
Magistrates Court . . B3
Maidstone Barracks Station ⇌ . . A1
Maidstone East Station ⇌ . . A2
Maidstone Museum & Bentlif Art Gall . . B2
Maidstone Utd FC . . A2
Maidstone West Station ⇌ . . B2
Mall,The . . B3
Market . . C2
Market Buildings . . B2
Marsham St . . B3
Medway St . . B2
Melville Rd . . C3
Mill St . . B2
Millennium Bridge . . C2
Mote Rd . . B3
Muir Rd . . C3
Old Tovil Rd . . C2
Palace Ave . . B3
Perryfield St . . A2
Police Station . . B3
Post Office . . B2/C3
Priory Rd . . C3

Prospect Place C1
Pudding La B2
Queen Anne Rd B3
Queens Rd A1
Randall St A2
Rawdon Rd C3
Reginald Rd C1
Riverstage A1
Rock Place B1
Rocky Hill B1
Romney Place B3
Rose Yard B2
Rowland Close C1
Royal Engineers' Rd A2
Royal Star Arcade B2
St Annes Ct B1
St Faith's St B2
St Luke's Rd A3
St Peter St B2
St Peter's Bridge B2
St Peter's Wharf Retail Park B2
St Philip's Ave C3
Salisbury Rd A3
Sandling Rd A2
Scott St A2
Scrubs La A1
Sheal's Cres C3
Somerfield La B1
Somerfield Rd B1
Staceys St A2
Station Rd A2
Superstore A1/B2/B3
Terrace Rd B1
Tonbridge Rd C1
Tovil Rd C2
Town Hall B2
Trinity Park B3
Tufton St B3
Tyrwhitt-Drake Mus of Carriages B2
Union St B3
Upper Fant Rd C1
Upper Stone St C3
Victoria St B1
Warwick Place B1
Wat Tyler Way B3
Waterloo St C3
Waterlow Rd A3
Week St B2
Well Rd A3
Westree Rd C1
Wharf Rd C1
Whatman Park A1
Wheeler St A3
Whitchurch Close B1
Woodville Rd C3
Wyatt St B3
Wyke Manor Rd B3

Manchester 190

Adair St B6
Addington St A5
Adelphi St A1
Advent Way B6
Albert Sq B3
Albion St C3
Ancoats Grove B6
Ancoats Grove North B6
Angela St C2
Aquatics Centre C4
Ardwick Green North C5
Ardwick Green Pk C5
Ardwick Green South C5
Arlington St A2
Artillery St B3
Arundel St C2
Atherton St B2
Atkinson St B3
Aytoun St B4
Back Piccadilly A4
Baird St B5
Balloon St A4
Bank Place A1
Baring St B5
Barrack St C1
Barrow St A1
Bendix St A5
Bengal St A5
Berry St C5
Blackfriars Rd A3
Blackfriars St A3
Blantyre St C2
Bloom St B4
Blossom St A5
Boad St B5
Bombay St B4
Booth St A3
Booth St B4
Bootle St B3
Brazennose St B3
Brewer St A5
Bridge St A3
Bridgewater Hall B3
Bridgewater Place A4
Bridgewater St B2
Brook St C4
Brotherton Dr A2
Brown St A3
Brown St B4
Brunswick St C6
Brydon Ave C6
Buddhist Centre A4
Bury St A2
Bus & Coach Sta B4
Bus Station B4
Butler St A6
Buxton St C5
Byrom St B3
Cable St A5
Cambridge St C3/C4
Camp St B3
Canal St B4
Cannon St A1
Cardroom Rd A6
Carruthers St A6
Castle St C2
Castlefield Arena B2
Cateaton St A3
Cathedral A3
Cathedral St A3
Cavendish St C4
Chapel St A1/A3
Chapeltown St B5
Charles St C4
Charlotte St B4
Chatham St B4
Chepstow St B3
Chester Rd C1/C2
Chester St C4
Chetham's School of Music A3
China La B5
Chippenham Rd A6
Chorlton Rd C2
Chorlton St B4
Church St A2
Church St A4
City Park A4
City Rd East C3
Civil Justice Centre B2
Cleminson St A2
Clowes St A3
College Land A3
Collier St B2
Commercial St C3
Conference Centre C4
Cooper St B4
Copperas St A4
Corn Exchange, The A4
Cornbrook C1
Cornell St A5
Corporation St A4
Cotter St C6
Cotton St A5
Cow La B1
Cross St B3
Crown Court B4
Crown St C2
Dalberg St C6
Dale St A4/B5
Dancehouse, The C4
Dantzic St A4
Dark La C6
Dawson St C2
Dean St A5
Deansgate A3/B3/C2
Deansgate Castlefield C3
Deansgate Sta C3
Dolphin St C6
Downing St C5
Ducie St B5
Duke Place B2
Duke St B2
Durling St C6
East Ordsall La A2/B1
Edge St A4
Egerton St C2
Ellesmere St C1
Everard St C1
Everyman B2
Every St B6
Exchange Sq A4
Factory, The B2
Fairfield St B5
Faulkner St B4
Fennel St A3
Fire Sta A5
Ford St A2
Ford St C6
Fountain St B4
Frederick St A2
Gartside St B2
Gaythorne St A1
George Leigh St A5
George St B4
Gore St A2
Goulden St A5
Granby Row B4
Gravel La A3
Great St B6
Great Ancoats St A5
Great Bridgewater St B3
Great George St A1
Great Jackson St C2
Great Marlborough St C4
Great Northern Leisure Complex B3
Greengate A3
Grosvenor St C5
Gun St A5
Hall St B3
Hampson St B1
Hanover St A4
Hanworth Close C5
Hardman St B3
Harkness St C6
Harrison St B6
Hart St B4
Helmet St B6
Henry St A5
Heyrod St B6
High St A4
Higher Ardwick C6
Hilton St A4/A5
Holland St A6
HOME Entertainment Complex C3
Hood St A5
Hope St B1
Hope St B4
Houldsworth St A5
Hoyle St C6
Hulme Hall Rd C1
Hulme St A1
Hulme St C3
Hyde Rd C6
Islington Way A1
Information Ctr B4
Irwell St A2
Jackson Cres C2
Jackson's Row B3
James St A1
Jenner Close C2
Jersey St A5
John Dalton St A3
John Ryland's Library B3
John St A2
Kennedy St B3
Kincardine Rd C5
King St A3
King St West A3
Law Courts B3
Laystall St B5
Lever St A5
Library B3
Linby St C2
Little Lever St A4
Liverpool Rd B2
Liverpool St B1
Lloyd St B3
Lockton Close C5
London Rd B5
Long Millgate A3
Longacre St B6
Loom St A5
Lower Byrom St B2
Lower Mosley St B3
Lower Moss La C2
Lower Ormond St C4
Loxford La C4
Luna St A5
Major St B4
Mamucium B2
Manchester Arndale A4
Manchester Art Gallery B4
Manchester Central Convention Complex B3
Manchester Metropolitan Univ (MMU) B4/C4
Manchester Piccadilly Station B5
Manchester Technology Ctr C4
Mancunian Way C3
Manor St C5
Marble St A4
Market St A2
Market St A4
Market St A4
Marsden St A3
Marshall St A5
Mayan Ave A2
Medlock St C3
Middlewood St B1
Miller St A4
Minshull St B4
Mosley St A4
Mount St B3
Mulberry St B3
Murray St A5
Museum of Science & Industry (MOSI) B2
Nathan Dr A2
National Football Museum A4
Naval St A5
New Bailey St A2
New Elm Rd B2
New Islington A6
New Islington Station B6
New Quay St B2
New Union St A6
Newton St A5
Nicholas St B4
North Western St C6
Oak St A4
Odeon A4/B3
Old Mill St A6
Oldfield Rd A1/C1
Oldham Rd A5
Oldham St A4
Opera House B3
Ordsall La C1
Oxford Rd C4
Oxford Rd C4
Oxford St B4
Paddock St C6
Palace Theatre B4
Pall Mall A3
Palmerston St B6
Parker St B4
Peak St B5
Penfield Close C5
Peoples' History Museum B2
Peru St A1
Peter St B3
Piccadilly A4
Piccadilly B5
Piccadilly Gdns B4
Piercy St A6
Poland St A5
Police Museum A5
Police Station B3/B5
Pollard St B6
Port St A5
Portland St B4
Portugal St East B5
Post Office A2/A4/A5/B3/B4/C4
Potato Wharf B2
Princess St B3/C4
Quay St A2
Quay St B2
Queen St B3
Radium St A5
Redhill St A5
Regent Retail Park B1
Regent Rd B1
Rice St B2
Richmond St B4
River St C3
Roby St B5
Rodney St A6
Rosamond St A2
Royal Exchange A3
Sackville St B4
St Andrew's St B6
St Ann St A3
St Ann's A3
St George's Ave C1
St James St B4
St John St B3
St John's Cathedral (RC) A2
St Mary's B3
St Mary's Gate A3
St Mary's Parsonage A3
St Peter's Sq B3
St Stephen St A2
Salford Approach A3
Salford Central A2
Sheffield St B5
Sherratt St A5
Shopmobility A4
Shudehill A4
Shudehill A4
Sidney St C4
Silk St A5
Silver St B4
Skerry Close C5
Snell St B6
South King St B3
Sparkle St B5
Spear St A4
Spring Gdns A4
Stanley St A2
Store St B5
Superstore B1
Swan St A4
Tariff St B5
Tatton St C1
Temperance St B6/C6
Thirsk St C6
Thomas St A4
Thompson St A5
Tib La B3
Tib St A4
Town Hall (Manchester) B3
Town Hall (Salford) A2
Trafford St C3
Travis St B5
Trinity Way A2
Turner St A4
Union St C6
Univ of Manchester (North Campus) C5
Univ of Salford A1
Upper Brook St C5
Upper Cleminson St A1
Upper Wharf St A1
Urban Exchange A5
Vesta St B6
Victoria A4
Victoria Station A4
Wadesdon Rd C5
Water St B2
Watson St B3
West Fleet St B1
West King St A2
West Mosley St B4
Weybridge Rd A6
Whitworth St B4
Whitworth St West C3
William St A2
William St C6
Wilmott St C3
Windmill St B3
Windsor Cres A1
Withy Grove A4
Woden St C1
Wood St B3
Woodward St A6
Worrall St C1
Worsley St C2
York St B4
York St C2
York St C4

Merthyr Tydfil
Merthyr Tudful 190

Aberdare Rd B2
Abermorlais Terr B2
Alexandra Rd A3
Alma St C3
Arfryn Place C3
Argyle St C3
Avenue De Clichy C2
Beacons Place Shopping Centre C2
Bethesda St B2
Bishops Grove A3
Brecon Rd A1/B2
Briarmead A3
Bryn St C3
Bryntirion Rd B3/C3
Bus Station B2
Cae Mari Dwn B3
Caedraw Rd C2
Castle Sq A1
Castle St B2
Chapel B2
Chapel Bank B1
Church St B3
Civic Centre B2
Clos Penderyn B1
Coedcae'r Ct C3
College Boulevard C2
County and Crown Courts B2
Court St C3
Cromwell St B2
Cyfarthfa Castle, Mus and Art Gallery A1
Cyfarthfa Ind Est A1
Cyfarthfa Park A1
Cyfarthfa Retail Pk B1
Cyfarthfa Rd A1
Dane St A2
Dane Terr A2
Danyparc B3
Darren View A3
Dixon St B2
Dyke St C3
Dynevor St B2
Elwyn Dr C3
Fire Station B2
Fothergill St B3
Galonuchaf Rd A3
Garth St B2
Georgetown B2
Grawen Terr A2
Grove Pk A2
Grove, The A2
Gurnos Rd A2
Gwaelodygarth Rd A2/A3
Gwaunfarren Grove A3
Gwaunfarren Rd A3
Gwendoline St A3
Hampton St C3
Hanover St A2
Heol S O Davies B1
Heol-Gerrig B1
High St A3/B2/B3/C2
Highland View C3
Howell Close B1
Information Ctr B2
Jackson's Bridge B2
James St C3
John St B3
Joseph Parry's Cottage B2
Lancaster St A2
Library B2
Llewellyn St A2
Llwyfen St B2
Llwyn Berry B1
Llwyn Dic Penderyn B1
Llwyn-y-Gelynen C1
Lower Thomas St B3
Market C2
Mary St C3
Masonic St C2
Merthyr Tydfil Coll B2
Merthyr Town FC B3
Merthyr Tydfil Leisure Centre C3
Merthyr Tydfil Sta C3
Meyrick Villas A2
Miniature Railway A1
Mount St A2
Nantygwenith St B1
Norman Terr B2
Oak Rd A2
Old Cemetery B3
Pandy Close A1
Pantycelynen B1
Parade, The B3
Park Terr B2
Penlan View C2
Penry St B2
Pentwyn Villas A2
Penyard Rd B3
Penydarren Park A3
Penydarren Rd B3
Plymouth St C3
Police Station C2
Pont Marlais West B2
Post Office B2
Quarry Row B2
Queen's Rd B3
Rees St C3
Rhydycar Link C2
Riverside Park A1
St David's B3
St Tydfil's C2
St Tydfil's Ave C3
St Tydfil's Square Shopping Centre C2
Saxon St A2
School of Nursing A2
Seward St A3
Shiloh La B3
Stone Circles B3
Stuart St A2
Summerhill Place B3
Superstore B3
Swan St C2
Swansea Rd B1
Taff Glen View C3
Taff Vale Ct B3
Theatre Soar B2
Thomastown Park B3
Tramroad La A3
Tramroad Side B2
Tramroad Side North B3
Tramroad Side South C3
Trevithick Gdns C3
Trevithick St A3
Tudor Terr B2
Twynyrodyn Rd C3
Union St B3
Upper Colliers Row B1
Upper Thomas St B3
Victoria St B2
Vue C3
Vulcan Rd B2
Walk, The B2
Warlow St C3
Well St A2
Welsh Assembly Government Offices C2
Wern La C1
Wern, The (Merthyr RFC) C2
West Grove A2
William St C3
Yew St C3
Ynysfach Engine House C2
Ynysfach Rd C2

Middlesbrough 191

Abingdon Rd C3
Acklam Rd C1
Albert Park C2
Albert Rd B2
Albert Terr C2
Ambulance Station C1
Aubrey St C3
Avenue, The C2
Ayresome Gdns C2
Ayresome Green La C1
Ayresome St C2
Barton Rd A1
Bilsdale Rd C3
Bishopton Rd C3
Borough Rd B2/B3
Bowes Rd A2
Breckon Hill Rd B3
Bridge St West B2
Brighouse Rd A1
Burlam Rd C1
Bus Station B2
Cannon Park B1
Cannon Park Way B2
Cannon St B1
Captain Cook Sq B2
Carlow St C1
Castle Way C3
Chipchase Rd C2
Cineworld B3
Cleveland Centre B2
Clive Rd C2
Commercial St A2
Corporation Rd B2
Costa St C2
Council Offices B3
Crescent Rd C2
Crescent, The C2
Cumberland Rd C2
Depot Rd A2
Derwent St B2
Devonshire Rd C2
Diamond Rd B2
Dock St B3
Dorman Mus C2
Douglas St B3
Eastbourne Rd C2
Eden Rd C3
Fire Sta A3
Forty Foot Rd A2
Gilkes St B2
Gosford St A2
Grange Rd B2
Gresham Rd B2
Harehills Rd C1
Harford St C2
Hartington Rd B2
Haverton Hill Rd A1
Hey Wood St B1
Highfield Rd C3
Hillstreet Centre B2
Holwick Rd B1
Hutton Rd C3
Ironmasters Way B1
Lambton Rd C3
Lancaster Rd C2
Lansdowne Rd C3
Latham Rd C2
Law Courts B2/B3
Lees Rd B2
Leeway B3
Library B2/C2
Linthorpe Cemetery C1
Linthorpe Rd B2
Lloyd St B2
Longford St C2
Longlands Rd C3
Lower East St A3
Lower Lake C3
Macmillan Acad C1
Maldon Rd C1
Manor St B2
Marsh St B2
Marton Rd B3
Middlesbrough By-Pass B2/C1
Middlesbrough Coll B3
Middlesbrough Dock B3
Middlesbrough Leisure Park B3
Middlesbrough Station B2
Middletown Park C2
MIMA B3
Mulgrave Rd C2
Newport Bridge B1
Newport Bridge Approach Rd B1
Newport Rd B2
North Ormesby Rd B3
North Rd B2
Northern Rd C1
Outram St B2
Oxford Rd C2
Park La C2
Park Rd North C2
Park Rd South C2
Park Vale Rd C3
Parliament Rd B1
Police Station A2
Port Clarence Rd A3
Portman St B2
Post Office B3/C1/C2
Princes Rd B2
Python A2
Riverside Park Rd A1
Riverside Stadium (Middlesbrough FC) B3
Rockliffe Rd C2
Romaldkirk Rd B1
Roman Rd C2
Roseberry Rd C3
St Barnabas' Rd C2
St Paul's Rd B2
Saltwells Rd B3
Scott's Rd A3
Seaton Carew Rd A3
Shepherdson Way B3
Shopmobility B2
Snowdon Rd A2
South West Ironmasters Park B1
Southfield Rd B2
Southwell Rd C2
Springfield Rd C1
Startforth Rd A2
Stockton Rd C1
Stockton St A2
Superstore B2
Surrey St C2
Sycamore Rd C2
Tax Offices B3
Tees Viaduct C1
Teessaurus Park A2
Teesside Tertiary College C3
Temenos B3
Thornfield Rd C1
Town Hall B2
Transporter Bridge (Toll) A3
Union St B2
Univ of Teesside B2
Upper Lake C2
Valley Rd C3
Ventnor Rd C2
Victoria Rd B2
Vulcan St A2
Warwick St C2
Wellesley Rd B3
West La C1
West Lane Hosp C1
Westminster Rd C2
Wilson St B2
Windward Way B3
Woodlands Rd B2
York Rd C3

Milton Keynes 191

Abbey Way A1
Arbrook Ave B1
Armourer Dr A3
Arncliffe Dr A1
Avebury C2
Avebury Blvd C2
Bankfield B3
Bayard Ave A2
Belvedere A2
Bishopstone A1
Blundells Rd A1
Boundary, The C3
Boycott Ave C2
Bradwell Common Boulevard B1
Bradwell Rd C1
Bramble Ave A2
Brearley Ave C2
Breckland A1
Brill Place B1
Burnham Dr B1
Campbell Park B3
Cantle Ave A3
Central Retail Park C1
Century Ave C2
Chaffron Way C3
Childs Way C1
Christ the Cornerstone B2
Cineworld B2
Civic Offices B2
Cleavers Ave B2
Colesbourne Dr A3
Conniburrow Blvd B2
Currier Dr A2
Dansteed Way A2/A3/B1
Deltic Ave B1
Downs Barn A2
Downs Barn Blvd A3
Eaglestone C3
Eelbrook Ave B1
Elder Gate B1
Evans Gate C2
Fairford Cres A3
Falcon Ave B3
Fennel Dr A2
Fishermead Blvd C3
Food Centre B3
Fulwoods Dr C3
Glazier Dr A2
Glovers La A1
Grafton Gate C1
Grafton St A1/C2
Gurnards Ave B3
Harrier Dr C3
The Hub Leisure Quarter B2/C2
Ibstone Ave B1
intu Milton Keynes B2
Langcliffe Dr A1
Leisure Centre C3
Leisure Plaza C1
Leys Rd C1
Library B2
Linceslade Grove C1
Linford Wood A2
Magistrates Court B2
Marlborough Gate B3
Marlborough St A2/B3
Mercers Dr A1
Midsummer C2
Midsummer Blvd B2
Milton Keynes Central C1
Milton Keynes Hospital (A&E) C3
Monks Way A1
Mullen Ave A3
Mullion Place C3
Neath Hill A3
North Elder C1
North Grafton B1
North Overgate A3
North Row B2
North Saxon B2
North Secklow B2
North Skeldon A3
North Witan B1
Oakley Gdns A3
Odeon B2
Oldbrook Blvd C2
Open-Air Theatre B3
Overgate A3
Overstreet A3
Patriot Dr B1
Pencarrow Place B3
Penryn Ave B3
Perran Ave C3
Pitcher La C1
Place Retail Pk, The C1
Police Station B2
Portway B2
Post Office A2/B2/B3
Precedent Dr B1
Quinton Dr B1
Ramsons Ave B2
Retail Park C2
Rockingham Dr A2
Rooksley B1
Saxon Gate B2
Saxon St A1/C3
Secklow Gate B2
Shackleton Place C2
Shopmobility B2
Silbury Blvd B2
Skeldon A3
South Enmore B3
South Grafton C2
South Row C2
South Saxon C2
South Secklow B3
South Witan C2
Springfield B3
Stainton Dr A1/B1
Stanton Wood A1
Stantonbury A1
Stantonbury Leisure Centre A1
Strudwick Dr C2
Sunrise Parkway A2
Superstore C1/C2
Theatre & Art Gallery B3
theCentre:mk B2
Tolcarne Ave C3
Towan Ave C3
Trueman Place C2
Vauxhall A1
Winterhill Retail Park C2
Witan Gate B2
Xscape B3

Newcastle upon Tyne 191

Albert St B3
Argyle St B3
Back New Bridge St B3
BALTIC Centre for Contemporary Art C3
Barker St A3
Barrack Rd B1
Bath La B1
Bessie Surtees House C2
Bigg Market C2
Biscuit Factory B3
Black Gate C2
Blackett St B2
Blandford Sq C1
Boating Lake A1
Boyd St B3
Brandling Park A2
Bus Station B2
Buxton St B3
Byron St A3
Camden St B2
Castle Keep C2
Central C1
Central Library B2
Central Motorway B2
Chester St A3
Cineworld B1
City Hall B2
City Rd B3/C3
City Walls C1
Civic Centre A2
Claremont Rd A1
Clarence St B3
Clarence Walk B3
Clayton St C1/B1
Clayton St West C1
Close, The C2
Coach Station C1
College St B2
Collingwood St C2
Copland Terr B3
Coppice Way B3
Corporation St B1
Courts C3
Crawhall Rd B3
Dean St C2
Dental Hospital A1
Dinsdale Place A3
Dinsdale Rd A3
Discovery C1
Doncaster Rd A3
Durant Rd B2
Eldon Sq B1
Ellison Place B2
Eskdale Terr A2
Eslington Terr A1
Exhibition Park A1
Falconar St B3
Fenkle St C1
Forth Banks C1
Forth St C1
Gallowgate B1
Gate, The B1
Gateshead Millennium Bridge C3
Gateshead Quays C3
Gibson St B3
Goldspink La A3
Grainger Market B2
Grainger St B2
Grantham Rd A3
Granville Rd A3
Great North Children's Hospital A1
Great North Mus:Hancock A2
Grey St B2
Groat Market C2
Guildhall C2
Hancock St A2
Hanover St C2
Hatton Gallery A1
Hawks Rd C3
Haymarket B2
Heber St B1
Helmsley Rd A3
High Bridge B2
High Level Bridge C2
Hillgate C3
Howard St B3
Hutton Terr A3
intu Eldon Square Shopping Centre B2
Jesmond A2
Jesmond Rd A2/A3
John Dobson St B2
Jubilee Rd B3
Kelvin Grove A3
Kensington Terr A2
Laing Gallery B2
Lambton Rd A2
Leazes Cres B1
Leazes La B1
Leazes Park B1
Leazes Park Rd B1
Leazes Terr B1
Library A2
Life Science Ctr C1
Live C2
Low Friar St C1
Manor Chare C2
Manors C2
Manors Station B2
Market St B2
Melbourne St B2
Mill Rd C3
Monument B2
Monument Mall Shopping Centre B2
Morpeth St A2
Mosley St C2
Napier St A3
New Bridge St West B2/B3
Newcastle Central Station C1
Newcastle Univ A1
Newgate St B1
Newington Rd A3
Northern Design Ctr C3
Northern Stage Theatre A2
Northumberland Rd B2
Northumberland St B2
Northumbria Univ A2
Northwest Radial Rd A1
O2 Academy C1
Oakwellgate C3
Open Univ C3
Orchard St C2
Osborne Rd A2
Osborne Terr A3
Pandon C3
Pandon Bank B3
Park Terr A1
Percy St B1
Pilgrim St B2
Pipewellgate C2
Pitt St B1
Plummer Tower A2
Police Station C1
Portland Rd A3/B3
Portland Terr A3
Post Office B1/B2
Pottery La C1
Prudhoe Place B1
Prudhoe St B1
Quayside C2
Queen Elizabeth II Bridge C2
Queen Victoria Rd A1
Richardson Rd A1
Ridley Place B2
Rock Terr B3
Rosedale Terr A3
Royal Victoria Infirmary A1
Sage Gateshead C3
St Andrew's St B1
St James B1
St James' Blvd C1
St James' Park (Newcastle Utd FC) B1
St Mary's Heritage Centre C3
St Mary's (RC) C1
St Mary's Place B2
St Nicholas C2
St Nicholas St C2
St Thomas' St B1
Sandyford Rd A2/A3
Shield St B3
Shieldfield B3
Shopmobility B1
Side, The C2
Simpson Terr B3
South Shore Rd C3
South St C1
Starbeck Ave A3
Stepney Rd B3
Stoddart St B3
Stowell St B1
Strawberry Place B1
Swing Bridge C2
Temple St C1
Terrace Place B1
Theatre Royal B2
Times Sq C1
Tower St B3
Trinity House C2
Tyne Bridge C2
Tyne Bridges C2
Tyne Theatre & Opera House C1
Tyneside B2
Victoria Square A2
Warwick St A3
Waterloo St C1
Wellington St B1
Westgate Rd C1/C2
Windsor Terr A2
Worswick St B2
Wretham Place B3

Newport
Casnewydd 191

Albert Terr B1
Allt-yr-Yn Ave A1
Alma St C2
Ambulance Station C3
Bailey St B2
Barrack Hill A2
Bath St A3
Bedford Rd B3
Belle Vue La C1
Belle Vue Park C1
Bishop St A3
Blewitt St B1
Bolt Close C3
Bolt St C3
Bond St A2
Bosworth Dr A1
Bridge St B1
Bristol St A3
Bryngwyn Rd B1
Brynhyfryd Ave C1
Brynhyfryd Rd C1
Bus Station B2
Caerau Cres C1
Caerau Rd B1
Caerleon Rd A3
Capel Cres C2
Cardiff Rd C2
Caroline St B3
Castle (Remains) A2
Cedar Rd B3
Charles St B2
Charlotte Dr C2
Chepstow Rd A3
Church Rd A3
Cineworld B2
Civic Centre B1
Clarence Place A2
Clifton Place B1
Clifton Rd C1
Clyffard Cres B1
Clytha Park Rd B1
Clytha Sq C2
Coldra Rd C1
Collier St A3
Colne St B3
Comfrey Close A1
Commercial Rd C3
Commercial St B2
Corelli St A3
Corn St B2
Corporation Rd B3
Coulson Close C2
County Court A2
Courts A1
Courts B1
Crawford St A3
Cyril St B3
Dean St A3
Devon Place B1
Dewsland Park Rd C2
Dolman B2
Dolphin St C3
East Dock Rd C3
East St B1
East Usk Rd A3
Ebbw Vale Wharf B3
Emlyn St B2
Enterprise Way C3
Eton Rd B3
Evans St A2
Factory Rd A2
Fields Rd B1
Francis Dr C2
Frederick St C3
Friars Rd C1
Friars Walk B2
Gaer La C1
George St C3
George St Bridge C3
Godfrey Rd B1
Gold Tops B1
Gore St A3
Gorsedd Circle C1
Grafton Rd A3
Graham St B1
Granville St C3
Harlequin Dr A1
Harrow Rd B3
Herbert Rd A3
Herbert Walk C2
Hereford St A3
High St B2
Hill St B2
Hoskins St A2
Information Ctr B2
Ivor St B2
Jones St B1
Junction Rd A3
Keynshaw Ave C2
King St C2
Kingsway B2
Kingsway Centre B2
Ledbury Dr A2
Library A3
Library, Museum & Art Gallery B2
Liverpool Wharf B3
Llanthewy Rd B1
Llanvair Rd A3
Locke St A2
Lower Dock St C3
Lucas St A2
Manchester St A3
Market B2
Marlborough Rd B3
Mellon St C3
Mill St A2
Morgan St A3
Mountjoy Rd C2
Newport Bridge A2
Newport Ctr B2
Newport RFC B3
Newport Station B2
North St B2
Oakfield Rd B1
Park Sq C2
Police Sta A3/C2
Post Office B2/C3
Power St A1
Prince St A3
Pugsley St A2
Queen St C2
Queen's Close A1
Queen's Hill A1
Queen's Hill Cres A1
Queensway B2
Railway St B2
Riverfront Theatre & Arts Centre, The B2
Riverside A3
Rodney Rd B2
Royal Gwent (A&E) C2
Rudry St A3
Rugby Rd B3
Ruperra La C3
Ruperra St C3
St Edmund St B1
St Mark's Cres A1
St Mary St B1
St Vincent Rd A3
St Woolos C2
St Woolos General (no A&E) C1
St Woolos Rd B1
School La B2
Serpentine Rd B1
Shaftesbury Park A2
Sheaf La A3
Skinner St B2
Sorrel Dr A1
South Market St C3
Spencer Rd B1
Stow Hill B2/C1/C2
Stow Park Ave C1
Stow Park Dr C1
TA Centre A1
Talbot St B2
Tennis Club A1
Tregare St A3
Trostrey St A3
Tunnel Terr B1
Turner St A3
Univ of Wales Newport City Campus B3
Upper Dock St B2
Usk St A3
Usk Way B3/C3
Victoria Cres B1
War Memorial A3
Waterloo Rd C1
West St B1
Wharves B2
Wheeler St A2
Whitby Place A3
Windsor Terr B1
York Place C1

Newquay 192

Agar Rd B2
Alma Place B1
Ambulance Station B2
Anthony Rd C1
Atlantic Hotel A1
Bank St B1
Barrowfields A3
Bay View Terr B2
Beach Rd B1
Beachfield Ave B1
Beacon Rd A1
Belmont Place A1
Berry Rd B2
Blue Reef Aquarium B1
Boating Lake C2
Bus Station B1
Chapel Hill B1
Chester Rd A3
Cheviot Rd C1/C2
Chichester Cres C2
Chynance Dr C1
Chyverton Close C1
Cliff Rd B2
Coach Park B2
Colvreath Rd A3
Cornwall College Newquay B3
Council Offices B1
Crantock St B1
Crescent, The B1
Criggar Rocks A3
Dale Close C3
Dale Rd C3
Dane Rd A1
East St B2
Edgcumbe Ave B3
Edgcumbe Gdns B3
Eliot Gdns B3
Elm Close C3
Ennor's Rd B1
Fernhill Rd B1
Fire Station B1
Fore St B1
Gannel Rd C2
Golf Driving Range B3
Gover La B1
Great Western Beach A2
Grosvenor Ave B2
Harbour A1
Hawkins Rd C2
Headleigh Rd B2
Hilgrove Rd A3/B3
Holywell Rd B3
Hope Terr B1
Huer's Hut, The A1
Information Ctr B1
Island Cres B2
Jubilee St B1
Kew Close C3
Killacourt Cove A2
King Edward Cres A1
Lanhenvor Ave B2
Library B1
Lifeboat Station A1
Lighthouse B1
Linden Ave C2
Listry Rd C2
Lusty Glaze Beach A3
Lusty Glaze Rd A3
Manor Rd B1
Marcus Hill B2
Mayfield Rd B2
Meadowside C3
Mellanvrane La C2
Michell Ave B2
Miniature Golf Course C3
Miniature Railway B3
Mount Wise B1
Mowhay Close C3
Narrowcliff A3
Newquay B2
Newquay Hosp B2
Newquay Town Football Ground B1
Newquay Zoo B3
North Pier A1
North Quay Hill A1
Oakleigh Terr B2
Pargolla Rd B2

Pendragon Cres . . . C3
Pengannel Close . . C1
Penina Ave C3
Pirate's Quest 🏰 . . B1
Police Station & Courts B2
Post Office . . . B1/B2
Quarry Park Rd . . . B3
Rawley La C2
Reeds Way A3
Robartes Rd A2
St Anne's Rd A3
St Aubyn Cres B3
St George's Rd . . . B1
St John's Rd B1
St Mary's Rd B1
St Michael's Rd . . . B1
St Michael's Rd . . . B1
StThomas' Rd B2
Seymour Ave B2
South Pier A1
South Quay Hill. . . A1
Superstore A1
Sweet Briar Cres . . C3
Sydney Rd. A1
Tolcarne Beach . . . A2
Tolcarne Point . . . A2
Tolcarne Rd A2
Tor Rd A2
Towan Beach A1
Towan Blystra Rd . . B3
Tower Rd A1
Trebarwith Cres . . . B2
Tredour Rd C2
Treforda Rd C3
Tregoss Rd B2
Tregunnel Hill . . B1/C1
Tregunnel Saltings. . C1
Trelawney Rd B2
Treloggan La C2
Treloggan Rd C3
Trembath Cres C1
Trenance Ave B2
Trenance Gardens . B2
Trenance La C2
Trenance Leisure Pk B2
Trenance Rd B2
Trenarth Rd B2
Treninnick Hill . . . C3
Tretherras Rd B3
Tretheway Way . . . C1
Trevemper Rd C3
Ulalia Rd B2
Vivian Close B3
Waterworld B3
Whitegate Rd B3
Wych Hazel Way . . . C1

Northampton 192
78 Derngate 🏛 . . . B3
Abington Sq B3
Abington St. B3
Alcombe St A3
All Saints' ⛪ B2
Ambush St B1
Angel St B2
Army Reserve Ctr . . A3
Arundel St. A2
Ash St A2
Auctioneers Way . . C2
Bailiff St B3
Barrack Rd A2
BBOB Rugby FC . . . A1
Beaconsfield Terr . . A1
Becket's Park C3
Bedford Rd B3
Billing Rd B3
Brecon St A1
Brewery B2
Bridge St. C2
Broad St B2
Burns St B3
Bus Station B2
Campbell St B2
Castle (Site of) . . . B2
Castle St B2
Cattle Market Rd . . C2
Central Museum & Art Gallery 🏛 . . . B2
Charles St A3
Cheyne Walk. C3
Church La A2
Clare St A3
Cloutsham St A3
College St A3
Colwyn Rd. A3
Cotton End C2
Countess Rd A1
County Hall A3
Court. A3
Craven St A3
Crown & County Courts B3
Denmark Rd B3
Derngate 🏛 B3
Doddridge Church B2
Drapery,The B2
Duke St. A3
Dunster St. A3
Earl St A3
Euston Rd C2
Fire Station B1
Foot Meadow A2
Gladstone Rd A1
Gold St B2
Grafton St A2
Gray St A3
Green St B1
Greenwood Rd B1
Greyfriars B2
Grosvenor Centre. . B2
Grove Rd A3
Guildhall 🏛 B2
Hampton St A2
Harding Terr A2
Hazelwood Rd B2
Herbert St B2
Hester St A3
Holy Sepulchre ⛪ . B2
Hood St A3
Horse Market B2
Hunter St A3
Information Ctr 🛈 . . B1
Kettering Rd A3
Kingswell St B2
Lady's La B2
Leicester St A2
Leslie Rd A1
Library B3
Lorne Rd A2
Lorry Park B1
Louise Rd A2
Lower Harding St . . A2
Lower Hester St . . . A2
Lower Mounts B3
Lower Priory St . . . A2
Main Rd. C1
Marefair B2
Market Sq B2
Marlboro Rd A1
Marriott St A2
Millers Meadow . . . A1
Military Rd A3
Mounts Baths Leisure Centre . . . A3
NeneValley Retail Park C1
New South Bridge Rd C2
Northampton General Hospital (A&E) 🏥 . . B3
Northampton Marina C3
Northampton Sta ⟐ B1
Northcote St A2
Nunn Mills Rd. . . . C3
OldTowcester Rd . . C2
Overstone Rd A3
Pembroke Rd A1
Penn Court A3
Police Station 🏛 . . B1
Post Office ⊠ . . A1/B3
Quorn Way A2
Ransome Rd C3
Regent Sq A2
Ridings,The B2
Robert St. A2
Royal & Derngate Theatres 🎭 B3
St Andrew's Rd . . . B1
St Andrew's St A2
St Edmund's Rd . . . B3
St George's St. . . . B3
St Giles ⛪ B3
St Giles St B3
St Giles'Terr B3
St James Park Rd . . B1
St James Rd B1
St James Retail Pk . C1
St James' Mill Rd . . C1
St James' Mill Rd East C1
St Leonard's Rd . . . C2
St Mary's St B2
St Michael's Rd . . . A3
St Peter's Way Shopping Precinct . B2
St Peter's Way B2
Salisbury St A2
Scarletwell St. . . . B2
Semilong Rd. A2
Sheep St B2
Sol Central (Leisure Centre) . . B2
Somerset St A3
South Bridge C2
Southfield Ave C3
Spencer Bridge Rd. . A1
Spencer Rd A2
Spring Gdns A3
Spring La A2
Superstore C2
Swan St A1
Tintern Ave A1
Towcester Rd C2
Univ of Northampton (Waterside Campus) C3
Upper Bath St B2
Upper Mounts A2
Victoria Park A1
Victoria Promenade . B2
Victoria Rd B3
Victoria St. A2
Wellingborough Rd . B3
West Bridge C2
York Rd B3

Norwich 192
Albion Way C3
All Saints Green . . . C2
Anchor St A3
Anglia Sq A2
Argyle St C3
Arts Centre 🏛 B1
Ashby St C2
Assembly House 🏛 . B1
Bank Plain B2
Barker St A1
Barn Rd B1
Barrack St A3
Ber St C2
Bethel St B1
Bishop Bridge B3
Bishopbridge Rd . . A3
Bishopgate B3
Blackfriars St B2
Botolph St. A2
Bracondale C3
Brazen Gate C2
Bridewell Mus 🏛 . . B2
Brunswick Rd C1
Bull Close Rd B2
Bus Station C2
Calvert St A2
Cannell Green A3
Carrow Rd C3
Castle & Mus 🏛 . . . B2
Castle Mall B2
Castle Meadow . . . B2
Cathedral ✝ B2
Cathedral (RC) ✝ . . B1
Cath Retail Park . . . A1
Cattlemarket St . . . B2
Chantry Rd C1
Chapel Loke C2
Chapelfield East . . . C1
Chapelfield Gdns . . C1
Chapelfield North . . B1
Chapelfield Rd C1
Cinema City 🎬 B2
City Hall ⟐ B1
City Rd C2
City Wall C1/C3
Close,The B2/B3
Colegate A2
Coslany St B1
Cow Hill. B1
CowTower A3
Cowgate A2
Crown & Magistrates' Courts A2
Dragon Hall Heritage Centre 🏛 C3
Duke St B1
Edward St A2
Elm Hill B2
Erpingham Gate ✦ . B2
Fishergate A2
Forum,The B1
Foundry Bridge . . . B3
Fye Bridge A2
Garden St C2
Gas Hill B3
Gentlemans Walk. . B2
Grapes Hill B1
Great Hospital Halls,The A3
Grove Ave C1
Grove Rd C1
Guildhall ✦ B1
Gurney Rd. A3
Hall Rd C2
Heathgate. A3
Heigham St A1
Hollywood 🎬 A2
Horn's La C2
Hungate Medieval Art ✦ B2
Information 🛈 B2
intu Chapelfield . . . B1
Ipswich Rd C1
ITV Anglia B3
James Stuart Gdns . B3
King St B2
King St C3
Koblenz Ave C3
Leisure Centre A1
Library B1
London St B2
Lower Clarence Rd . B3
Maddermarket 🎭 . . B1
Magdalen St A2
Mariners La C2
Market B2
Market Ave B2
Mountergate B2
Mousehold St A3
Newmarket Rd C1
Norfolk St C1
Norwich City FC . . . C3
Norwich Gallery 🏛 . B2
Norwich School ✦ . B2
Norwich Station ⟐ . B3
Oak St A1
Odeon 🎬 C3
Palace St A2
Pitt St A2
Playhouse 🎭 A2
Police Station B1
Post Office ⊠ . . . A2/B2/B3/C1
Pottergate B1
Prince of Wales Rd. . B2
Princes St B2
Pull's Ferry ✦ B3
Puppet Theatre 🎭 . . A2
Queen St. B2
Queens Rd C2
Recorder Rd B3
Riverside Entertainment Ctr . C3
Riverside Leisure Centre C3
Riverside Rd B3
Riverside Retail Pk. . C3
Rosary Rd B3
Rose La B2
Rouen Rd C2
St Andrews St B2
St Augustines St . . A1
St Benedicts St . . . B1
St Crispins Road . . A1
St Ethelbert's Gate ✦ B2
St Faiths La B2
St Georges St B1
St Giles St B1
St James Close . . . A2
St Julians C2
St Leonards St B3
St Martin's La A1
St Peter Mancroft ⛪ B2
St Peters St B1
St Stephens Rd . . . C1
St Stephens St C1
Shopmobility C1
Silver Rd A3
Silver St A2
Southwell Rd C2
St. Andrew's & Blackfriars' Hall ✦ . B2
Strangers' Hall 🏛 . . B1
Superstore C2
Surrey St C2
Sussex St A2
Theatre Royal 🎭 . . . B1
Theatre St B1
Thorn La C2
Thorpe Rd B3
Tombland B2
Union St C1
Vauxhall St B1
Victoria St C1
Vue 🎬 B2
Walpole St B1
Waterfront,The . . . C2
Wensum St A2
Wessex St C1
Westwick St B1
Wherry Rd C3
Whitefriars A2
Willow La B1

Nottingham 192
Abbotsford Dr. . . . A3
Addison St A1
Albert Hall ✦ B1
Alfred St Central . . A3
Alfreton Rd A1
All Saints St A1
Annesley Grove . . . A1
Arboretum ✤ A1
Arboretum St A1
Arthur St A1
ArtsTheatre 🎭 B3
Ashforth St A2
Balmoral Rd A1
Barker Gate B3
Bath St B3
BBC Nottingham . . C2
Beacon Hill Rise . . B3
Belgrave Rooms . . . B1
Bellar Gate B3
Belward St B3
Brewhouse Yard 🏛 . C2
Broad Marsh Bus Station. C2
Broad St B3
Brook St B3
Burns St A1
Burton St B2
Bus Station C3
Canal St C2
Carlton St B3
Carrington St C2
Castle 🏛 C2
Castle Boulevard . . C1
Castle Gate C2
Castle Meadow Rd . C1
Castle Meadow Retail Park C1
Castle Rd. C2
Castle Wharf. C2
Cavendish Rd East . C1
Cemetery A1/B1
Chaucer St B2
Cheapside B2
Church Rd A3
City Link C3
City of Caves ✦ . . . C2
Clarendon St B2
Cliff Rd C2
Clumber Rd East. . . C1
Clumber St B2
College St B1
Collin St C2
Contemporary 🏛 . . C3
Conway Close A2
Cornerhouse, The 🎬 B2
Council House 🏛 . . B2
Cranbrook St B3
Cranmer St A2
Cromwell St B1
Curzon St B3
Derby Rd B1
Dryden St A2
Exchange Ctr,The . . B2
Fishpond Dr C1
Fletcher Gate B3
Forest Rd East A1
Forest Rd West . . . A1
Friar La C2
Gedling Grove A1
Gedling St B3
George St B3
Gill St A2
Glasshouse St B2
Goldsmith St B2
Goose Gate. B3
Great Freeman St . . A2
Guildhall B2
Hamilton Dr C1
Hampden St A1
Heathcote St B3
High Pavement . . . C3
High School ✦ A1
HM Revenue & Customs B2
Holles Cres C1
Hope Dr. C1
Hungerhill Rd A3
Huntingdon Dr . . . C1
Huntingdon St A2
Information Ctr 🛈 . . B2
Instow Rise A3
International Community Ctr . . . A2
intu Broadmarsh . . C2
intu Victoria Centre . B2
Kent St B3
King St B2
Lace Market 🏛 . . . B3
Lace Mkt Theatre 🎭 C3
Lamartine St B3
Lenton Rd C1
Lewis Close A3
Lincoln St B2
London Rd C3
Long Row B2
Low Pavement . . . C2
Lower Parliament St B3
Magistrates'Court. . C2
Maid Marian Way . . B2
Mansfield Rd . . A2/B2
Middle Hill C2
Milton St B2
Mount St B2
National Ice Centre & Motorpoint Arena . C3
National Justice Museum 🏛 C3
Newcastle Dr B1
Newstead Grove . . . A1
North Sherwood St . A2
Nottingham Arena . C3
Nottingham Cathedral ✝ B1
Nottingham Coll. . . C2
Nottingham Trent University . . . A2/B2
Old Mkt Square ⟐ . B2
Oliver St A1
Park Dr C1
Park Row B1
ParkTerr C1
ParkValley C1
Peas Hill Rd A3
Peel St A1
Pelham St B3
Peveril Dr C1
Plantagenet St A3
Playhouse Theatre 🎭 B1
Plumptre St C3
Police Sta ⟐ . . . B1/B2
Poplar St C3
Portland Rd B1
Post Office ⊠ A2
Queen's Rd C3
Raleigh St A1
Regent St B1
Rick St B3
Robin Hood St B3
Robin Hood Statue ✦ C2
Ropewalk,The B1
Royal Centre ⟐ . . . B2
Royal Children Inn 🏛 C1
Royal Concert Hall . B2
St Ann's Hill Rd . . . A2
St Ann's Way A3
St Ann's Well Rd . . . A3
St James' St B2
St Mark's St A3
St Mary's Rest Gdn . B3
St Mary's Gate C3
St Nicholas ⛪ C2
St Peter's ⛪ B2
St Peter's Gate B2
Salutation Inn 🏛 . . C2
Shakespeare St . . . B2
Shelton St A2
Shopmobility B2
South Parade B2
South Rd C1
South Sherwood St . B2
Station Street ⟐ . . C3
Stoney St B3
Talbot St B1
Tattershall Dr C1
Tennis Dr C1
Tennyson St A1
Theatre Royal 🎭 . . B2
Trent St C2
Trent University ⟐ . B2
Union Rd A3
Upper Parliament St B2
Victoria Leisure Ctr . B3
Victoria Park B3
Victoria St B2
Walter St. A1
Warser Gate B3
Watkin St A2
Waverley St A1
Wheeler Gate B2
Wilford Rd C2
Wilford St C2
Wollaton St B1
Woodborough Rd. . A2
Woolpack La B3
Ye OldTrip to Jerusalem ✦ C2
York St A2

Oxford 193
Adelaide St A1
Albert St A1
All Souls (Coll) B2
Ashmolean Mus 🏛 . B1
Balliol (Coll) A2
Banbury Rd A1
Bate Collection of Musical Instruments 🏛 C2
Beaumont St B1
Becket St. B1
Blackhall Rd A2
Blue Boar St B2
Bodleian Library 🏛 . B2
Botanic Garden ✤ . . B3
Brasenose (Coll) . . . B2
Brewer St C2
Broad St B2
Burton-Taylor Theatre 🎭 B2
Bus Station B1
Canal St A1
Cardigan St A1
Carfax Tower ✦ . . . B2
Castle 🏛 B1
Castle St B2
Catte St B2
Cemetery C1
Christ Church (Coll) B2
Christ Church Cathedral ✝ C2
Christ Church Meadow C2
City of Oxford Coll . C1
Clarendon Centre . . B2
Cornmarket St B2
Corpus Christi (Coll) B2
County Hall B1
Covered Market . . . B2
Cowley Place C3
Cranham St A1
Cranham Terr A1
Cricket Ground . . . C1
Crown & County Courts B1
Deer Park B3
Exeter (Coll) B2
Fire Sta B1
Folly Bridge C2
George St B1
Great Clarendon St . A1
Harris Manchester (Coll) B2
Hart St A1
Hertford (Coll) B2
High St B3
Hollybush Row . . . B1
Holywell St B2
Hythe Bridge St . . . B1
Ice Rink B1
Information Ctr 🛈 . . B2
Jericho St A1
Jesus (Coll) B2
Jowett Walk B3
Juxon St A1
Keble (Coll) A2
Keble Rd A2
Library B2
Linacre (Coll) A3
Lincoln (Coll) B2
Little Clarendon St . A1
Longwall St. B3
Magdalen (Coll) . . . B3
Magdalen Bridge . . B3
Magdalen St B2
Magistrate's Court. . C2
Manor Rd B3
Mansfield (Coll) . . . A2
Mansfield Rd A2
Market B2
Marlborough Rd . . . C2
Martyrs' Meml ✦ . . B2
Merton (Coll) B2
Merton Field C2
Merton St B2
Museum of Modern Art 🏛 . . . B2
Mus of Oxford 🏛 . . B2
Museum Rd A2
New College (Coll) . B2
New Inn Hall St . . . B2
New Rd B1
NewTheatre 🎭 . . . B2
Norfolk St C1
Nuffield (Coll) B1
Observatory A1
Observatory St . . . A1
Odeon 🎬 B1/B2
Old Fire Station 🎭 . B1
Old Greyfriars St . . C2
Oriel (Coll) B2
Oxford Castle & Prison 🏛 B1
Oxford Station ⟐ . . B1
Oxford University Research Centres 🏛 A1
Oxpens Rd C1
Paradise Sq C1
Paradise St B1
Park End St B1
Parks Rd A2/B2
Pembroke (Coll) . . . B2
Phoenix 🎬 A1
Picture Gallery 🏛 . . C2
Plantation Rd A1
Playhouse 🎭 B2
Police Station 🏛 . . B1
Post Office ⊠ . . A1/B2
Pusey St A1
Queen's (Coll) B2
Radcliffe Camera 🏛 B2
Rewley Rd B1
Richmond Rd A1
Rose La B3
Ruskin (Coll) A1
Said Bsns School . . A1
St Aldates C2
St Anne's (Coll) . . . A1
St Antony's (Coll) . . A1
St Bernard's Rd . . . A1
St Cross Building . . A2
St Cross Rd A2
St Edmund Hall (Coll) B3
St Giles St A2
St Hilda's (Coll) . . . C3
St John St B2
St John's (Coll) . . . A2
St Mary the Virgin ⛪ B2
St Michael at the Northgate ⛪ . . . B2
St Peter's (Coll) . . . B1
StThomas St B1
Science Area A2
Science Museum 🏛 . B2
Sheldonian Theatre 🏛 B2
Somerville (Coll) . . A1
South Parks Rd . . . A2
Speedwell St C2
Sports Ground C1
Thames St C1
Town Hall B2
Trinity (Coll) B2
Turl St B2
Univ Coll (Coll) . . . B2
Univ Natural History Museum & Pitt Rivers Museum 🏛 A2
University Parks. . . A2
Wadham (Coll) . . . B2
Walton Cres A1
Walton St A1
Western Rd C2
Westgate C2
Woodstock Rd A1
Worcester (Coll) . . . B1

Perth 193
AK Bell Library . . . B2
Abbot Cres C1
Abbot St C1
AlbanyTerr A1
Albert Monument . A2
Alexandra St B2
Atholl St A2
Balhousie Ave. . . . A2
Balhousie Castle & Black Watch Museum 🏛 A2
Balhousie St A2
Ballantine Place. . . B1
Barossa Place A2
Barossa St A2
Barrack St B2
Bell's Sports Ctr . . A2
Bellwood C3
Blair St B1
Burn Park C1
Bus Station B2
Caledonian Rd . . . B1
Canal Cres B2
Canal St. B2
Cavendish Ave . . . C1
Charles St B2
Charlotte Place . . . A2
Charlotte St A2
Church St A1
City Hall B2
Club House C1
Clyde Place. C3
Coach Park C2
Commercial St . . . A2
Concert Hall ✦ . . . B3
Council Chambers . B2
County Place B1
Court. B2
Craigie Place C2
Crieff Rd A1
Croft Park C2
Cross St. B2
Darnhall Cres C1
Darnhall Dr C1
Dewars Centre . . . B1
Dundee Rd B3
Dunkeld Rd A1
Earl's Dykes B1
Edinburgh Rd C3
Elibank St C1
Fair Maid's Ho ✦ . . A3
Fergusson 🏛 B2
Feus Rd A1
Fire Station B1
Foundary La C1
Friar St C1
George St B3
Glamis Place C1
Glasgow Rd B1
Glenearn Rd C2
Glover St B1/C1
Golf Course A3
Gowrie St A3
Gray St A3
Graybank Rd C1
Hay St A2
High St B2/B3
Inchaffray St A1
Ind/Retail Park . . . B1
Information Ctr 🛈 . . B2
Isla Rd A3
James St B2
Keir St B1
King Edward St . . . B2
King James VI Golf Course C3
King St C2
Kings Place. C2
Kinnoull Causeway . B1
Kinnoull St B2
Knowlea Place C1
KnowleaTerr C1
Ladeside Bsns Ctr . B1
Leisure Pool A2
Leonard St B1
Lickley St B2
Lochie Brae A3
Long Causeway . . . A1
Low St A2
Main St A2
Marshall Place . . . C2
Melville St B2
Mill St B2
Milne St. B2
Murray Cres B3
Murray St B2
Needless Rd C1
North Inch A3
North Methven St . C2
Park Place C1
Perth ⟐ B2
Perth Bridge. A2
Perth Business Pk . B1
Perth Museum & Art Gallery 🏛 . . . B3
Perth Station ⟐ . . . B1
Pickletullum Rd . . C1
Pitheavlis Cres . . . C1
Playhouse 🎬 B2
Police Station A2
Pomarium St B1
Post Office ⊠ . . B2/C2
Princes St B3
Priory Place C2
Queen St. C1
Queen's Bridge . . . B3
Riggs Rd C1
Rose Terr A2
St Catherine's Rd A1/A2
St Catherine's Retail Park B1
St John St B2
St John's ⛪ B2
St John's Kirk 🏛 . . B2
St Leonards Bridge . C2
St Ninians Cath ✝ . A1
Scott Monument . . C2
Scott St B2
Sheriff Court B2
Shore Rd C3
Skate Park A2
South Inch C2
South Inch Bsns Ctr C2
South Inch Park . . C2
South InchView . . . C2
South Methven St . B2
South St B2
South William St . . B2
Stables,The A1
Stanners,The A3
Stormont St A2
Strathmore St A3
Stuart Ave C1
Superstore . . . B1/B2
Tay St. B3
Union La B2
Victoria St B2
Watergate. B3
Wellshill Cemetery . A1
West Bridge St . . . A3
West Mill St B2
Whitefriars Cres. . . A1
Whitefriars St A1
Wilson St C1
Windsor Terr C1
Woodside Cres . . . A1
York Place B2
Young St C1

Peterborough 193
Athletics Arena . . . A3
Bishop's Palace 🏛 . B2
Bishop's Rd. . . . B2/B3
Boongate A3
Bourges Boulevard . A1
Bourges Retail Park B1/B2
Bridge House (Council Offices) . . B2
Bridge St. B2
Bright St A1
Broadway A2
Broadway 🎭 B2
Brook St A2
Burghley Rd A2
Bus Station B2
Cavendish St A3
Charles St A2
Church St B2
Church Walk B2
Cobden Ave C1
Cobden St C1
Cowgate B2
Craig St A2
Crawthorne Rd . . . A2
Cromwell Rd A1
Dickens St A2
Eastfield Rd A3
Eastgate B2
East Station Road. . C2
Fire Station A2
Fletton Ave C2
Frank Perkins Parkway C3
Geneva St A2
George St C1
Gladstone St A1
Glebe Rd C2
Gloucester Rd C2
Granby St B3
Grove St C1
Guildhall 🏛 B2
Gwydir St A1
Hadrians Ct C3
Hawksbill Way . . . C1
Henry St A1
Hereward Cross (shopping) B2
Hoe Approach B3
Hoe Rd B3
Hoe,The B3
Hoegate St B3
Houndiscombe Rd . A2
Information Ctr 🛈 . . C3
Information Ctr 🛈 . . B2
James St A2
Kensington Rd . . . A3
King St B2
Lincoln Rd. A1
London Rd C1
Long Causeway . . . B2
Lower Bridge St . . C2
Magistrates Court . B2
Manor House St . . A1
Mayor's Walk A1
Midland Rd B1
Monument St A2
Morris St A2
Mus & Art Gallery 🏛 B2
NeneValley Railway ⟐ C1
New Rd A2
New Rd A2
Northminster A2
Old Customs Ho ⟐ . C2
Oundle Rd C1
Padholme Rd A3
Palmerston Rd . . . C1
Park Rd A2
Passport Office . . . C2
Peterborough Cathedral ✝ B2
Peterborough NeneValley B2
Peterborough Station ⟐ B1
Police Station 🏛 . . B2
Post Office ⊠ . . A3/B2
Priestgate B2
Queen's Walk C2
Queensgate Centre . B2
Railworld Wildlife Haven 🏛 C1
Regional Fitness & Swimming Centre . B3
River La B1
Rivergate Shopping Centre . . B2
Riverside Mead . . . C3
Russell St A1
St John's St B2
St John's ⛪ B2
St Marks St A2
St Peter's Rd. B2
Saxon Rd. A1
Spital Bridge A1
Stagshaw Dr. C3
Star Rd A3
Superstore B1
Thorpe Lea Rd . . . B1
Thorpe Rd. B1
Thorpe's Lea Rd . . B1
Tower St A2
Town Hall B2
Viersen Platz B2
Vineyard Rd B3
Wake Rd C3
Wellington St A3
Wentworth St B2
Westgate A2
Weston Homes Stadium (Peterborough United FC)The . . . C2
Whalley St. A3
Wharf Rd. C1
Whitsed St A3
YMCA A3

Plymouth 193
Alma Rd A1
Anstis St A1
Armada Shopping Centre A2
Armada St A3
Armada Way B2
Arts Centre B2
Athenaeum 🏛 B2
Athenaeum St. . . . C2
Barbican C3
Baring St A3
Bath St C1
Beaumont Park . . . B3
Beaumont Rd B3
Black Friars Gin Distillery ✦ . . C3
Box,The 🏛 A2
Breton Side. B3
Coach Sta B1
Castle St C3
Chapel La B2
Church St A1
Cinnamon La B1
Citadel Rd C2
Citadel Rd East . . . C2
Civic Centre ✦ . . . B2
Cliff Rd C1
Clifton Place A3
Cobourg St A2
College of Art A2
Cornwall St B2
Crescent,The B1
Dale Rd A2
Deptford Place . . . A3
Derry Ave A2
Derry's Cross ⟐ . . B2
Drake Circus A2
Drake Circus Shopping Centre . B2
Drake Statue ✦ . . . B2
Eastlake St B2
Ebrington St B3
Elizabethan Ho 🏛 . C3
Elliot St C2
Endsleigh Place . . . A2
Exeter St B3
Fire Station B3
Fish Quay C3
Gibbons St A3
Glen Park Ave A2
Grand Parade C2
Great Western Rd . . C1
Greenbank Rd . . . A3
GreenbankTerr . . . A3
Guildhall B2
Hampton St B3
Harwell St B1
Hill Park Cres A3
Hoe Approach C2
Hoe Rd C1
Hoe,The C2
Hoegate St C3
Market Ave B1
Martin St B1
Mayflower St B2
Mayflower Stone & Steps ✦ C3
Mayflower 🏛 C3
Merchant's Rd . . . B2
Millbay Rd C1
National Marine Aquarium C3
Neswick St B1
New George St . . . B2
New St B2
North Cross ⟐ . . . B2
North Hill B1
North Quay B1
North Rd East A1
North Rd West . . . A1
Notte St B2
Octagon,The ⟐ . . . A1
Octagon St A1
Pennycomequick . . A1
Pier St C2
Plymouth Naval Memorial ✦ C1
Plymouth Pavilions . B1
Plymouth Sta ⟐ . . A2
Police Station A1
Post Office ⊠ . . B2/C1,C3
Princess St B2
Promenade,The . . . C2
Prysten House 🏛 . . B3
Queen Anne's Battery Watersports C3
Radford Rd C1
Regent St B3
Rope Walk C3
Royal Citadel 🏛 . . C3
Royal Pde B2
RoyalTheatre 🎭 . . B2
Russell Place A1
St Andrew's ⛪ . . . B3
St Andrew's Cross ⟐ B2
St Andrew's St . . . B2
St Lawrence Rd . . . A2
Saltash Rd A1
Shopmobility B2
Smeaton's Tower ✦ C2
Southern Terr A3
Southside St C3
Stuart Rd A1
Sutherland Rd A3
Sydney St A1
Teats Hill Rd C3
Tothill Ave A3
Union St B1
Univ of Plymouth . . A2
Vauxhall St B2/3
Victoria Park A2
WalkerTerr C2
West Hoe Rd C1
Western Approach . B1
Whittington St . . . A1
Wyndham St A1

Poole 194
Ambulance Station . A3
Baiater Gdns C3
Baiter Park C3
Ballard Close B3
Ballard Rd C2
Bay Hog La B1
BMIThe Harbour Hospital A3
Bridge Approach . . C1
Bus Station B2
Castle St B2
Catalina Dr C3
Chapel La B2
Church St B2
Colborne Close . . . B3
Dear Hay La B2
Denmark La A3
Denmark Rd A3
Dolphin Ctr B2
East St B2
Elizabeth Rd A3
Emerson Rd B2
Ferry Rd C1
FerryTerminal C1
Fire Station A2
Freightliner Terminal A1
Furnell Rd A3
Garland Rd A3
Green Rd B2
Heckford La A3
Heckford Rd A3
High St B2
High St North B2
Hill St B2
Holes Bay Rd A1
Hospital (A&E) 🏥 . . A3
Information Ctr 🛈 . . B2
Kingland Rd B3
Kingston Rd A3
Labrador Dr C3
Lagland St B2
Lander Close B3
Lighthouse, Poole Ctr for the Arts ✦ . B2
Longfleet Rd A3
Maple Rd A3
Market Close B2
Market St B2
Mount Pleasant Rd . B3
New Harbour Rd . . C1
New Harbour Rd South C1
New Harbour Rd West C1
New Orchard B2
New Quay Rd C1
New St B2
Newfoundland Dr . . B1
Old Lifeboat 🏛 . . . C1
Old Orchard B2
Parish Rd A3
Park Lake Rd B3
Parkstone Rd A3
Perry Gdns C2
Pitwines Close . . . B3
Police Station ⟐ . . . A3
Poole Station ⟐ . . . A2
Poole Central Liby . B2
Poole Lifting Bridge . C1
Poole Park C3
Poole Museum 🏛 . . C1
Post Office ⊠ B2
Quay,The C1
RNLI College B1
St John's Rd A3
St Margaret's Rd . . A3
St Mary's Maternity Unit . . A3
St Mary's Rd A3
Seldown Bridge . . . B3
Seldown La B3
Seldown Rd B3
Serpentine Rd C2
Scaplen's Court 🏛 . C1
Shaftesbury Rd . . . A2
Skinner St B2
Slipway B1
Stanley Rd B2
Sterte Ave A1
Sterte Ave West . . . A1
Sterte Close A1
Sterte Esplanade . . C1
Sterte Rd A2
Strand St C1
Superstore B3
Swimming Pool . . . B3
Taverner Close . . . C3
Thames St C1
Towngate Bridge . . B2
Twin Sails Bridge . . B1
Vallis Close C3
Waldren Close . . . B3
West Quay B1
West Quay Rd B1
West St B1
WestView Rd B1
Whatleigh Close . . B2
Wimborne Rd A3

Portsmouth 194
Action Stations ✦ . B1
Admiralty Rd A1
Alfred Rd A2
Anglesea Rd B2
Arundel St. B2
Aspex 🏛 C1
Bishop St C1
Broad St C1
Buckingham Ho ✦ . C1
Burnaby Rd B2
Bus Station C1
Camber Dock C1
Cambridge Rd B2
Car Ferry to Isle of Wight B1
Cascades Shopping Centre A3
Castle Rd B3
Civic Offices B3
Clarence Pier C2
College St B1
Commercial Rd . . . B3
Cottage Grove B3
Cross St C1
Cumberland St . . . A2
Duisbury Way C2
Durham St A3
East St C1
Edinburgh Rd B2
Elm Grove C3
Emirates Spinnaker Tower ✦ B1
Governor's Grn. . . . C1
Great Southsea St . C3
Green Rd B2
Greetham St B2
Grosvenor St B2
Groundlings 🎭 . . . A2
Guildhall B2
Guildhall Walk . . . B1
Gunwharf Quays Designer Outlet . . B1
Gunwharf Rd B1
Hambrook St C2
Hampshire Terr . . . B2
Hanover St A2
Hard,The A1
High St C1
HM Naval Base . . . A1
HMS Nelson (Royal Naval Barracks) . . A1
HMS Monitor M.33 ⚓ A1
HMSVictory ⚓ . . . A1
HMS Warrior ⚓ . . . A1
Hovercraft Terminal C2
Hyde Park Rd C2
Information Ctr 🛈 . . A1/B3
Isambard Brunel Rd . B2
Isle of Wight Car Ferry Terminal . . . C1
Kent Rd C3
Kent St B3
King St B3
King's Rd B3
King'sTerr B3
Lake Rd A3
Law Courts B2
Library B2
Long Curtain Rd . . C2
Marina A1
Market Way A2
Marmion Rd C3
Mary Rose 🏛 A1
Middle St B3
Millennium Promenade Walk B1/C1
Museum Rd B2
National Museum of the Royal Navy 🏛 . C2
Naval Rec Gd C2
Nightingale Rd . . . C3
Norfolk St B3
North St A2
Osborne Rd C3
Paradise St A3
Park Rd B2
Passenger Catamaran to Isle of Wight . . B1
Passenger Ferry to Gosport B1
Pelham Rd B3
Pembroke Gdns . . C2
Pier Rd C2
Point Battery C1
Police Station A3
Portsmouth & Southsea Sta A3
Portsmouth Harbour Station A1
Portsmouth Historic Dockyard A1
Portsmouth Museum & Art Gallery B2

Post Office A1/A3/B3
Queen St A1
Queen's Cres C3
Ravelin Park B2
Register Office B2
Round Tower C1
Royal Garrison Church C1
St Edward's Rd C3
St George's Rd B2
St George's Sq B1
St George's Way B2
St James's Rd B3
St James's St A2
St John's Cathedral (RC) A3
St Thomas's Cath C1
St Thomas's St B2
Shopmobility A3/B1
Somers Rd B3
Southsea Common C2
Southsea Terr C2
Square Tower C1
Station St A3
Town Fortifications C1
Unicorn Rd A2
United Services Recreation Ground B2
University of Portsmouth A2/B2
University of Portsmouth B3
Upper Arundel St A3
Victoria Ave C2
Victoria Park A2
Victory Gate A1
Vue B1
Warblington St B1
Western Pde C2
White Hart Rd C1
Winston Churchill Ave B3

Preston 194

Adelphi St A2
Anchor Ct B3
Aqueduct St A1
Ardee Rd C1
Arthur St B2
Ashton St A1
Avenham La B3
Avenham Park C3
Avenham Rd B3
Avenham St B3
Bairstow St B3
Balderstone Rd C1
Beamont Dr A1
Beech St South C2
Bird St C1
Bow La B2
Brieryfield Rd A1
Broadgate C1
Brook St A2
Bus Station A3
Butler St B2
Cannon St B3
Carlton St A1
Chaddock St B3
Channel Way B1
Chapel St B3
Christ Church St B2
Christian Rd B2
Cold Bath St A2
Coleman Ct C1
Connaught Rd C2
Corporation St A2/B2
County Hall B2
Cricket Ground C2
Croft St A1
Cross St B3
Crown Court A3
Crown St A3
East Cliff C3
East Cliff Rd B3
Edward St A2
Elizabeth St A3
Euston St B1
Fishergate B2/B3
Fishergate Hill B2
Fishergate Shopping Centre B2
Fitzroy St B1
Fleetwood St A1
Friargate A3
Fylde Rd A1/A2
Gerrard St B2
Glover's Ct B3
Good St B2
Grafton St B2
Great George St A3
Great Shaw St A3
Greenbank St A2
Guild Way B1
Guild Hall & Charter B3
Guildhall St B3
Harrington St A2
Harris Museum B3
Hartington Rd B1
Hasset Close C2
Heatley St B2
Hind St C2
Information Ctr B3
Kilruddery Rd C1
Lancashire Archives B2
Lancaster Rd A3/B3
Latham St B3
Lauderdale St C2
Lawson St A3
Leighton St A2
Leyland Rd C1
Library A1
Library B3
Liverpool Rd C1
Lodge St B2
Lune St B3
Magistrate's Court A3
Main Sprit West B3
Maresfield Rd C1
Market St West A3
Marsh La B1/B2
Maudland Bank A2
Maudland Rd A2
Meadow Ct C2
Meath Rd C1
Miller Arcade B3
Miller Park C3
Moor La A3
Mount St B3
North Rd A3
North St A3
Northcote Rd B1
Old Milestones B1
Old Tram Rd C3
Pedder St A1/A2
Peel St A2
Penwortham Bridge C2
Penwortham New Bridge C1
Pitt St B2
Playhouse A3
Police Station A3
Portway B1
Post Office B3
Preston Station B2
Retail Park B2
Ribble Bank St B2
Ribble Viaduct C2
Ribblesdale Place B3
Ringway B3
River Parade C1
Riverside C2
St George's Shopping Centre B3
St Georges B3
St John's Minster B3
St Johns Shopping Centre A3
St Mark's Rd A1
St Walburges A1
Salisbury Rd B1
Sessions House B3
Snow Hill A3
South End C2
South Meadow La C2
Spa Rd B1
Sports Ground C2
Strand Rd B1
Syke St B3
Talbot Rd B1
Taylor St C1
Tithebarn St A3
Town Hall B3
Tulketh Brow A1
University of Central Lancashire A2
Valley Rd C1
Victoria St A2
Walker St A3
Walton's Parade B2
Warwick St A3
Wellfield Business Park A1
Wellfield Rd A1
Wellington St A1
West Cliff C2
West Strand A1
Winckley Rd C1
Winckley Square B3
Wolseley Rd C2

Reading 194

Abbey Ruins B2
Abbey Sq B2
Abbey St B2
Abbot's Walk B2
Acacia Rd C2
Addington Rd C3
Addison Rd A1
Allcroft Rd C3
Alpine St C2
Baker St B1
Berkeley Ave C1
Bridge St B1
Brigham Rd A1
Broad St B1
Broad Street Mall B1
Carey St B1
Castle Hill C1
Castle St B1
Causeway, The A3
Caversham Rd A1
Christchurch Meadows A2
Civic Offices B1
Coley Hill C1
Coley Place C1
Craven Rd C3
Crown St C2
De Montfort Rd A1
Denmark Rd C3
Duke St B2
East St B2
Edgehill St C2
Eldon Rd B3
Eldon Terr B3
Elgar Rd C1
Erleigh Rd C3
Field Rd C1
Fire Station A1
Fobney St B1
Forbury Gdns B1
Forbury Rd B2
Forbury Retail Park B2
Francis St C1
Friar St B1
Garrard St B1
Gas Works Rd B3
George St A2
Great Knollys St B1
Greyfriars B1
Grove, The B2
Gun St B1
Henry St C1
Hexagon Theatre, The B1
Hill's Meadow A2
Howard St B1
Inner Distribution Rd B1
Katesgrove La C1
Kenavon Dr B2
Kendrick Rd C2
King's Meadow Recreation Gd A2
King's Rd B2
Library B2
London Rd C3
London St B2
Lynmouth Rd A1
Magistrate's Court B1
Market Place B2
Mill La B2
Mill Rd A2
Minster St B1
Morgan Rd C3
Mount Pleasant C2
Museum of English Rural Life (MERL) C3
Napier Rd A2
Newark St C2
Newport Rd A1
Oracle Shopping Centre, The B1
Orts Rd B3
Oxford Road B1
Pell St C1
Post Office B1
Queen Victoria St B1
Queen's Rd A2
Queen's Rd B2
Randolph Rd A1
Reading Bridge A2
Reading College B3
Reading Station A1
Redlands Rd C3
Riverside Mus B3
Rose Kiln La C1
Royal Berkshire Medical Mus C3
Royal Berks Hospital (A&E) C3
St Giles C2
St Laurence B2
St Mary's B1
St Mary's Butts B1
St Saviour's Rd C1
Send Rd A3
Sherman Rd C2
Sidmouth St B2
Silver St C2
South St B2
South St Arts Ctr B2
Southampton St C2
Station Rd B1
Superstore A3
Swansea Rd A1
Thames Lido A2
Tudor Road A1
Univ of Reading C3
Valpy St B2
Vastern Rd A1
Vue B2
Waldeck St C2
Watlington St B3
West St B1
Whitby Dr C3
Wolseley St C1
York Rd A1
Zinzan St B1

St Andrews 195

Abbey St B2
Abbey Walk B3
Abbotsford Cres A1
Albany Pk C3
Allan Robertson Dr C2
Ambulance Station C1
Anstruther Rd C3
Argyle St B1
Auld Burn Rd B2
Bassaguard Ind Est B1
Bell St B2
Blackfriars Chapel (Ruins) B2
Boase Ave B2
Braid Cres C3
Brewster Place C3
Bridge St B1
British Golf Mus A1
Broomfaulds Ave C1
Bruce Embankment A1
Bruce St C2
Bus Station A1
Byre Theatre B2
Canongate C1
Cathedral and Priory (Ruins) B3
Cemetery B3
Chamberlain St C1
Church St B2
Churchill Cres C2
City Rd A1
Claybraes C1
Cockshaugh Public Park B1
Cosmos Com Ctr B3
Council Office A2
Crawford Gdns C1
Doubledykes Rd B1
Drumcarrow Rd C1
East Sands B3
East Scores A3
Fire Station C1
Forrest St C1
Fraser Ave C1
Freddie Tait St C2
Gateway Centre A1
Glebe Rd B2
Golf Place A1
Grange Rd C3
Greenside Place B2
Greyfriars Gdns A2
Hamilton Ave C2
Hepburn Gdns B1
Holy Trinity B2
Horseleys Park C1
Information Ctr B2
Irvine Cres C3
James Robb Ave C1
James St B1
John Knox Rd C1
Kennedy Gdns B1
Kilrymont Close C3
Kilrymont Place C3
Kilrymont Rd C3
Kinburn Park B1
Kinkell Terr C3
Kinnesburn Rd B2
Ladebraes Walk B2
Lady Buchan's Cave A3
Lamberton Place C1
Lamond Dr C2
Langlands Rd B2
Largo Rd C1
Learmonth Place C1
Library B2
Links Clubhouse A1
Links, The A1
Livingstone Cres B2
Long Rocks A2
Madras College B2
Market St A2
Martyr's Monument A1
Murray Pk A2
Murray Place A2
Museum of the University of St Andrews (MUSA) A2
Nelson St B2
New Course, The A1
New Picture Ho A2
North Castle St A3
North St A2
Old Course, The A1
Old Station Rd A1
Pends, The B3
Pilmour Links A1
Pipeland Rd B2/C2
Police Sta A2/C1
Post Office B2
Preservation Trust B2
Priestden Park C3
Priestden Place C3
Priestden Rd C3
Queen's Gdns B2
Queen's Terr B2
Roundhill Rd C2
Royal & Ancient Golf Club A1
St Andrews B1
St Andrews Aquarium A2
St Andrews Botanic Garden B1
St Andrews Castle (Ruins) & Visitor Centre A2
St Leonard's Sch B3
St Mary St B3
St Mary's College B2
St Nicholas St C3
St Rules Tower B3
St Salvator's Coll A2
Sandyhill Cres C2
Sandyhill Rd C2
Scooniehill Rd C2
Scores, The A2
Shields Ave C3
Shoolbraids C2
Shore, The B3
Sloan St B1
South St B2
Spottiswoode Gdns C1
Station Rd A1
Swilcen Bridge A1
Tom Morris Dr C2
Tom Stewart La C1
Town Hall B2
Union St A2
Univ Chapel A2
University Library A2
Univ of St Andrews A1
Viaduct Walk B1
War Memorial A3
Wardlaw Gdns B1
Warrack St C3
Watson Ave B2
West Port B2
West Sands A1
Westview B2
Windmill Rd A1
Winram Place C1
Wishart Gdns C2
Woodburn Pk B3
Woodburn Place B3
Woodburn Terr B3
Younger Hall A2

Salisbury 195

Albany Rd A2
Arts Centre A3
Ashley Rd A1
Avon Approach A2
Ayleswade Rd C2
Bedwin St A2
Belle Vue A2
Bishops Walk B2
Blue Boar Row B2
Bourne Ave A3
Bourne Hill A3
Britford La C2
Broad Walk C2
Brown St B2
Castle St A2
Catherine St B2
Chapter House B2
Church House B2
Churchfields Rd B1
Churchill Gdns C3
Churchill Way East B3
Churchill Way North A3
Churchill Way South C2
Churchill Way West A1
City Hall B2
Close Wall B2
Coldharbour La A1
College St A3
Council and Registry Offices A3
Court A1
Crane Bridge Rd B2
Crane St B2
Cricket Ground C1
Culver St South B3
De Vaux Place C2
Devizes Rd A1
Dews Rd B1
Elm Grove B3
Elm Grove Rd A3
Endless St A2
Estcourt Rd A3
Exeter St C2
Fairview Rd A3
Fire Station A1
Fisherton St A1
Folkestone Rd C1
Fowlers Hill B3
Fowlers Rd B3
Friary La B2
Friary, The B3
Gas La A1
Gigant St B3
Greencroft B3
Greencroft St A3
Guildhall B2
Hall of John Halle B2
Hamilton Rd A2
Harnham Mill B1
Harnham Rd C1/C2
High St B2
House of John A'Port B2
Information Ctr B2
Kelsey Rd A3
King's Rd A3
Laverstock Rd B3
Library B2
London Rd A3
Lower St C1
Maltings, The B2
Manor Rd A3
Marsh La A1
Medieval Hall B2
Milford Hill B3
Milford St B3
Mill Rd B1
Mill Stream App A2
Mompesson House B2
New Bridge Rd C2
New Canal B2
New Harnham Rd C2
New St B2
North Canonry B2
North Gate B2
North Walk B2
Old Blandford Rd C1
Old Deanery B2
Old George Hall B2
Park St A3
Parsonage Green C1
Playhouse Theatre A2
Police Station A3
Post Office A2/B2
Poultry Cross B2
Queen Elizabeth Gdns B1
Queen's Rd A3
Rampart Rd B3
Rifles, The B2
St Ann St B2
St Ann's Gate B2
St Marks Rd A3
St Martins B3
St Paul's A1
St Paul's Rd A1
St Thomas B2
Salisbury Cathedral B2
Salisbury Cathedral School (Bishop's Palace) C2
Salisbury Museum, The B2
Salisbury Sta A1
Salt La A3
Saxon Rd C1
Scots La A2
Shady Bower B3
Shopmobility B2
South Canonry C2
South Gate C2
Southampton Rd B2
Spire View A1
Sports Ground C3
Tollgate Rd B3
Town Path B1
Wain-a-Long Rd A3
Wessex Rd A3
West Walk C2
Wilton Rd A1
Wiltshire College B3
Winchester St B3
Windsor Rd A1
Wyndham Rd A2
YHA B3
York Rd A1

Scarborough 195

Aberdeen Walk B2
Albert Rd A2
Albion Rd C2
Auborough St B2
Balmoral Ctr B2
Belle Vue St C1
Belmont Rd C2
Blenheim Terrace A2
Brunswick Shopping Centre B2
Castle Dykes B3
Castle Hill A3
Castle Rd B2
Castle Walls A3
Castlegate B3
Cemetery C1
Central Tramway B2
Coach Park B1
Columbus Ravine A1
Court B1
Crescent, The C2
Cricket Ground A1
Cross St B2
Crown Terr C2
Dean Rd B1
Devonshire Dr A1
East Harbour B3
East Pier B3
Eastborough B2
Elmville Ave B1
Esplanade C2
Falconers Rd B2
Falsgrave Rd C1
Fire Station B2
Foreshore Rd B2
Friargate B2
Gladstone Rd B1
Gladstone St B1
Hollywood Plaza A1
Holms, The A3
Hoxton Rd B1
King St B2
Library B2
Lifeboat Station B3
Londesborough Rd C1
Longwestgate B3
Marine Dr A3
Luna Park B3
Miniature Railway A1
Nelson St B1
Newborough B2
Nicolas St B2
North Marine Rd A1
North St B2
Northway B1
Old Harbour B3
Olympia Leisure B2
Peasholm Park A1
Peasholm Rd A1
Police Station B1
Post Office B2
Princess St B3
Prospect Rd B1
Queen St B2
Queen's Parade A2
Queen's Tower (Remains) A3
Ramshill Rd C2
Roman Signal Sta A3
Roscoe St C1
Rotunda Mus C2
Royal Albert Dr A2
Royal Albert Park A2
St Martin-on-the-Hill C2
St Martin's Ave C2
St Mary's B3
St Thomas St B2
Sandside B3
Scarborough Art Gallery C2
Scarborough Bowls Centre A1
Scarborough Castle A3
Shopmobility C2
Somerset Terr C2
South Cliff Lift C2
Spa Theatre, The C2
Spa, The C2
Stephen Joseph Theatre C1
Tennyson Ave B1
Tollergate B2
Town Hall B2
Trafalgar Rd B1
Trafalgar Square A1
Trafalgar St West B1
Valley Bridge Par C2
Valley Rd C1
Vernon Rd C2
Victoria Park Mount A1
Victoria Rd B1
West Pier B3
Westborough C1
Westover Rd C1
Westwood C1
Woodall Ave A1
YMCA Theatre B2
York Place B2
Yorkshire Coast College (Westwood Campus) C1

Sheffield 196

Addy Dr A2
Addy St A2
Adelphi St A3
Albert Terrace Rd A3
Albion St A2
Aldred Rd A1
Allen St A4
Alma St A4
Angel St B5
Arundel Gate B5
Arundel St C4
Ashberry Rd A2
Ashdell Rd C1
Ashgate Rd C1
Athletics Centre B2
Attercliffe Rd A6
Bailey St B4
Ball St A4
Balm Green B4
Bank St B4
Barber Rd A2
Bard St B5
Barker's Pool B4
Bates St A1
Beech Hill Rd C1
Beet St B3
Bellefield St A3
Bernard Rd A6
Bernard St B6
Birkendale A2
Birkendale Rd A2
Birkendale View A1
Bishop St C4
Blackwell Place B6
Blake St A2
Blonk St A5
Bolsover St B2
Botanical Gdns C1
Bower Rd A1
Bradley St A1
Bramall La C4
Bramwell St A3
Bridge St A4/A5
Brighton Terrace Rd A1
Broad La B3
Broad St B6
Brocco St A3
Brook Hill B3
Broomfield Rd C1
Broomgrove Rd C2
Broomhall Place C3
Broomhall Rd C2
Broomhall St C3
Broomspring La C2
Brown St C5
Brunswick St B3
Burgess St B4
Burlington St A2
Burns Rd A2
Cadman St A6
Cambridge St B4
Campo La B4
Carver St B4
Castle Square B5
Castlegate A5
Cathedral B4
Cathedral (RC) B4
Cavendish St B3
Charles St C4
Charter Row C4
Children's Hosp B2
Church St B4
City Hall B4
City Hall B4
City Rd C6
Claremont Cres B2
Claremont Place B2
Clarke St C3
Clarkegrove Rd C2
Clarkehouse Rd C1
Clarkson St B2
Cobden View Rd A1
Collegiate Cres C2
Commercial St B5
Commonside A1
Conduit Rd B1
Cornish St A3
Corporation St A4
Cricket Inn Rd B6
Cromwell St A1
Crookes Rd B1
Crookes Valley Park B2
Crookes Valley Rd B2
Crookesmoor Rd A2
Crown Court A4
Crucible Theatre B5
Cutlers' Hall B4
Cutlers Gate A6
Daniel Hill A2
Dental Hospital B2
Derek Dooley Way A5
Devonshire Green B3
Devonshire St B3
Division St B4
Dorset St C2
Dover St A3
Duchess Rd C5
Duke St B5
Duncombe St A1
Durham Rd B2
Earl St C4
Earl Way C4
Ecclesall Rd C3
Edward St B3
Effingham Rd A6
Effingham St A6
Egerton St C3
Eldon St B3
Elmore Rd B1
Exchange St B5
Eyre St C4
Fargate B4
Farm Rd C5
Fawcett St A3
Filey St B3
Fir St A1
Fire Station C4
Fitzalan Square/Ponds Forge B5
Fitzwater Rd C6
Fitzwilliam Gate C4
Fitzwilliam St B3
Flat St B5
Foley St A6
Foundry Climbing Centre A4
Fulton Rd A1
Furnace Hill A4
Furnival Rd A5
Furnival Sq C4
Furnival St C4
Garden St B3
Gell St B3
Gibraltar St A4
Glebe Rd B1
Glencoe Rd C6
Glossop Rd B2/B3/C1
Gloucester St C2
Government Offices C4
Granville Rd C6
Granville Rd / The Sheffield Coll C5
Graves Gallery B5
Green La A4
Hadfield St A1
Hanover St C3
Hanover Way C3
Harcourt Rd B1
Harmer La B5
Havelock St C2
Hawley St B4
Haymarket B5
Headford St C3
Heavygate Rd A1
Henry St A3
High St B4
Hodgson St C3
Holberry Gdns C2
Hollis Croft B4
Holly St B4
Hounsfield Rd B3
Howard Rd A1
Hoyle St A3
Hyde Park A6
Infirmary Rd A3
Infirmary Rd A3
Jericho St A3
Johnson St A5
Kelham Island Industrial Mus A4
Lawson Rd C1
Leadmill Rd C5
Leadmill St C5
Leadmill, The C5
Leamington St A1
Leavygreave Rd B3
Lee Croft B4
Leopold St B4
Leveson St A6
Library A2/B5/C1
Light, The C4
Lyceum Theatre B5
Malinda St A3
Maltravers St A5
Manor Oaks Rd B6
Mappin St B3
Marlborough Rd B1
Mary St C4
Matilda St C4
Matlock Rd A1
Meadow St A3
Melbourn Rd A1
Melbourne Ave C1
Millennium Galleries B5
Milton St C3
Mitchell St B3
Mona Ave A1
Mona Rd A1
Montgomery Terrace Rd A3
Montgomery Theatre B4
Monument Grounds C6
Moor Oaks Rd B1
Moor, The C4
Moor Market C4
Moore St C3
Mowbray St A4
Mushroom La B2
National Emergency Service A4
National Videogame Museum B5
Netherthorpe Rd B3
Netherthorpe Rd B3
Newbould La C1
Nile St C1
Norfolk Park Rd C6
Norfolk Rd C6
Norfolk St B4
North Church St B4
Northfield Rd A1
Northumberland Rd B1
Nursery St A5
O2 Academy B5
Oakholme Rd C1
Octagon B2
Odeon B5
Old St B6
Orchard Square Shopping Centre B4
Oxford St A2
Paradise St B4
Park La C2
Park Sq B5
Parker's Rd B1
Pearson Building (Univ) C2
Penistone Rd A3
Pinstone St B4
Pitt St B3
Police Station B5
Pond Hill B5
Pond St B5
Ponds Forge International Sports Centre B5
Pondorosa, The A2
Portobello St B3
Post Office A2/B3/B5/C1/C3/C4/C6
Powell St A2
Queen St B4
Queen's Rd C5
Ramsey Rd B1
Red Hill B3
Redcar Rd B1
Regent St B3
Rockingham St B4
Roebuck Rd A2
Royal Hallamshire Hospital C2
Russell St A4
Rutland Park C1
St George's Close B3
St Mary's Gate C3
St Mary's Rd C4/C5
St Philip's Rd A3
Savile St A5
School Rd B1
Scotland St A4
Severn Rd B1
Shalesmoor A4
Shalesmoor A3
Sheaf St B5
Sheffield Cath B4
Sheffield Hallam University B5
Sheffield Ice Sports Ctr – Skate Central C5
Sheffield Institute of Arts B5
Sheffield Interchange B5
Sheffield Parkway A6
Sheffield Station C5
Sheffield Station/Sheffield Hallam University B5
Sheffield University B2
Shepherd St A3
Shipton St A2
Shopmobility B3
Shoreham St C4
Showroom C5
Shrewsbury Rd C5
Sidney St C4
Site Gallery C5
Slinn St A1
Smithfield A4
Snig Hill A5
Snow La A4
Solly St B3
South La C4
South Street Park B5
Southbourne Rd C1
Spital Hill A5
Spital St A5
Spring Hill B1
Spring Hill Rd B1
Springvale Rd A1
Stafford Rd C6
Stafford St B6
Suffolk Rd C5
Summer St B2
Sunny Bank C3
Superstore A3/C3
Surrey St B4
Sussex St A6
Sutton St B3
Sydney Rd A2
Sylvester St C4
Talbot St B5
Taptonville Rd B1
Tenter St B4
Town Hall B4
Townend St A1
Townhead St B4
Trafalgar St B4
Tree Root Walk B2
Trinity St A4
Trippet La B4
Turner Museum of Glass B3
Union St B4
University Drama Studio B2
Univ of Sheffield B3
Upper Allen St A3
Upper Hanover St B3
Upperthorpe Rd A2/A3
Verdon St A5
Victoria Rd C2
Victoria St B3
Waingate B5
Watery St A3
Watson Rd C1
Wellesley Rd B2
Wellington St C3
West Bar A4
West Bar Green A4
West One Plaza B3
West St B3
West St B3
Westbourne Rd C1
Western Bank B2
Western Rd A1
Weston Park B2
Weston Park Hospital B2
Weston Park Mus B2
Weston St B2
Wharncliffe Rd C3
Whitham Rd B1
Wicker A5
Wilkinson St B2
William St C3
Winter Garden B4
Winter St B2
York St B4
Yorkshire Artspace C5
Young St C4

Shrewsbury 195

Abbey Foregate B3
Abbey Gardens B2
Abbey Lawn Business Park B3
Abbots House B2
Albert St A2
Alma St B1
Ashley St A3
Ashton Rd C1
Avondale Dr A3
Bage Way C3
Barker St B1
Beacall's La A2
Beeches La C2
Beehive La C1
Belle Vue Gdns C2
Belle Vue Rd C2
Belmont Bank C1
Berwick Ave A1
Berwick Rd A1
Betton St C2
Bishop St B3
Bradford St B3
Bridge St B1
Burton St A3
Bus Station B2
Butcher Row B2
Butler Rd C1
Bynner St C2
Canon St B3
Canonbury C1
Castle Business Park, The A2
Castle Foregate A2
Castle Gates B2
Castle Walk B3
Castle St B2
Cathedral (RC) C1
Chester St A2
Cineworld C3
Claremont Bank B1
Claremont Hill B1
Cleveland St B3
Coleham Head B2
Coleham Pumping Station C2
College Hill B1
Corporation La A1
Coton Cres A1
Coton Hill A2
Coton Mount A1
Crescent La C1
Crewe St A2
Cross Hill B1
Dana, The B2
Darwin Centre B2
Dingle, The B1
Dogpole B2
English Bridge B2
Fish St B2
Frankwell B1
Gateway Ctr, The A2
Gravel Hill La A1
Greenhous West Mid Showground A1
Greyfriars Rd C2
Hampton Rd A3
Haycock Way C3
High St B1
Hills La B1
Holywell St B3
Hunter St A1
Information Ctr B1
Ireland's Mansion & Bear Steps B1
John St A3
Kennedy Rd C1
King St B3
Kingsland Bridge C1
Kingsland Bridge (toll) C1
Kingsland Rd C1
Library B2
Lime St C2
Longden Coleham C2
Longden Rd C1
Longner St B1
Luciefelde Rd C1
Mardol B1
Marine Terr C2
Market B1
Monkmoor Rd B3
Moreton Cres C2
Mount St A1
New Park Close A3
New Park Rd A2
New Park St A3
North St A2
Oakley St C1
Old Coleham C2
Old Market Hall B1
Old Potts Way C3
Parade Shopping Centre, The B2
Police Station B1
Post Office B1/B2/B3
Pride Hill B1
Pride Hill Centre B1
Priory Rd B1
Pritchard Way C3
Queen St A2
Queensway Swimming & Fitness Centre, The B1
Raby Cres C2
Rad Brook C1
Rea Brook C3
Rea Brook Valley Country Park & Local Nature Reserve C3
Riverside B1
Roundhill La A1
St Alkmund's B2
St Chad's B1
St Chad's Terr B1
St John's Hill B1
St Julians Friars C2
St Mary's B2
St Mary's St B2
Salters La C2
Scott St C3
Severn Theatre B1
Severn Bank A3
Severn St A2
Shrewsbury B2
Shrewsbury Abbey B3
Shrewsbury High School C1
Shrewsbury Mus & Art Gallery B1
Shrewsbury Prison Tours B2
Shrewsbury School C1
Shropshire Regimental Museum B2
Shropshire Wildlife Trust B3
Smithfield Rd B1
South Hermitage C1
Square, The B1
Superstore C3
Swan Hill B1
Sydney Ave A3
Tankerville St B3
Tilbrook Dr A3
Town Walls C1
Trinity St C2
Underdale Rd B3
University Centre Shrewsbury (Guildhall) B1
Victoria Ave B1
Victoria Quay B1
Victoria St B2
Welsh Bridge B1
Whitehall St B3
Wood St A2
Wyle Cop B2

Southampton 196

Above Bar St A2
Albert Rd North B3
Albert Rd South C3
Andersons Rd B3
Argyle Rd A2
Arundel Tower B1
Bargate, The B2
BBC South A1
Bedford Place A1
Belvidere Rd A3
Bernard St C2
Blechynden Terr A1
Brinton's Rd A2
Britannia Rd A3
Briton St C2
Brunswick Place A2
Bugle St C1
Canute Rd C3
Castle Way C2
Catchcold Tower B1
Central Bridge C3
Central Rd C2
Channel Way C3
Chapel Rd B3
City Art Gallery A1
City College B3
City Cruise Terminal C1
Civic Centre A1
Civic Centre Rd A1
Coach Station B1
Commercial Rd A1
Cumberland Place A1
Cunard Rd C2
Derby Rd A3
Devonshire Rd A1
Dock Gate 4 C2
Dock Gate 8 B1
East Park (Andrew's Park) A2
East Park Terr A2
East St B2
Endle St B3
European Way C2
Fire Station A2
Floating Bridge Rd C3
God's House Tower C2
Golden Grove A3
Graham Rd A2
Guildhall A1
Hanover Bldgs B2
Harbour Lights C3
Harbour Pde B1
Hartington Rd A3
Havelock Rd A1
Henstead Rd A1
Herbert Walker Ave B1
High St B2
Hoglands Park B2
Holy Rood (Rems), Merchant Navy Memorial B2
Houndwell Park B2
Houndwell Place B2
Hythe Ferry C2
Isle of Wight Ferry Terminal C1
James St B3
Kingsway A2
Leisure World B1
Library A1
Lime St B2
London Rd A2
Marine Pde B3
Marlands Shopping Centre, The A1
Marsh La B2
Mayflower Memorial C1
Mayflower Park C1
Mayflower Theatre, The A1
Medieval Merchant's House C1
Melbourne St B3
Morris Rd A1
National Oceanography Centre C3
Neptune Way C3
New Rd A2
Nichols Rd A3
North Front A2
Northam Rd A3
Ocean Dock C2
Ocean Village Marina C3
Ocean Way C3
Odeon B1
Ogle Rd B1
Old Northam Rd A2
Orchard La B2
Oxford Ave A2
Oxford St C2
Palmerston Park A2
Palmerston Rd A2
Parsonage Rd A3
Peel St A3
Platform Rd C2
Polygon, The A1
Portland Terr B1
Post Office B2
Pound Tree Rd B2
Quays Swimming & Diving Complex, The B1
Queen's Park C2
Queen's Peace Fountain A2
Queen's Terr C2
Queensway B2
Radcliffe Rd A3
Rochester St A3
Royal Pier C1
Royal South Hants Hospital A2
St Andrew's Rd A2
St Mary's B3
St Mary St A2
St Mary's Leisure Centre A2
St Mary's Place B2
St Mary's Rd A2
St Mary's Stadium (Southampton FC) A3
St Michael's C1
Sea City Mus A1
Showcase Cinema de Lux B1
Solent Sky C3
South Front B2
Southampton Central Station A1
Southampton Solent University A2

Terminus Terr C2
Threefield La B2
Titanic Engineers' Memorial ✦ A2
Town Quay C1
Town Walls B2
Tudor House C1
Vincent's Walk B2
Westgate Hall C1
West Marlands Rd A1
West Park A1
West Park Rd A1
West Quay Rd B1
West Quay Retail Park B1
Western Esplanade B1
Westquay Shopping Centre B1
Westquay South B1
White Star Way C2
Winton St A2

Southend-on-Sea 197

Adventure Island ✦ C3
Albany Ave A1
Albert Rd C3
Alexandra Rd C2
Alexandra St C2
Alexandra Yacht Club ✦ C2
Ashburnham Rd B2
Ave Rd B1
Avenue Terr B1
Balmoral Rd B1
Baltic Ave B3
Baxter Ave A2/B2
Beecroft Art Gallery B2
Bircham Rd A2
Boscombe Rd B3
Boston Ave A1/B2
Bournemouth Park Rd A3
Browning Ave A3
Bus Station C3
Byron Ave A3
Cambridge Rd C1/C2
Canewdon Rd B1
Carnarvon Rd A2
Central Ave A3
Central Museum B2
Chelmsford Ave A1
Chichester Rd B2
Church Rd C3
Civic Centre A2
Clarence Rd C2
Clarence St C2
Cliff Ave B1
Cliffs Pavilion C1
Clifftown Parade C2
Clifftown Rd C2
Colchester Rd A1
Coleman St B3
College Way B2
County Court B3
Cromer Rd B3
Crowborough Rd A2
Dryden Ave A3
East St A2
Elmer App B2
Elmer Ave B2
Forum, The B2
Gainsborough Dr A1
Gayton Rd A2
Glenhurst Rd A2
Gordon Place B2
Gordon Rd B2
Grainger Rd A2
Greyhound Way A3
Grove, The A3
Guildford Rd B3
Hamlet Ct Rd B1
Hamlet Rd C1
Harcourt Ave A1
Hartington Rd C3
Hastings Rd B3
Herbert Grove C3
Heygate Ave C3
High St B2/C2
Information Ctr C3
Kenway A2
Kilworth Ave B3
Lancaster Gdns B3
London Rd B1
Lucy Rd C3
MacDonald Ave A1
Magistrates' Court A2
Maldon Rd A2
Marine Ave C1
Marine Parade C3
Marine Rd C1
Milton Rd B1
Milton St B2
Napier Ave B2
North Ave A3
North Rd A1/B1
Odeon B2
Osborne Rd B1
Park Cres B1
Park Rd B1
Park St B1
Park Terr B1
Pier Hill C3
Pleasant Rd C3
Police Station A2
Post Office B2/B3
Princes St B2
Queens Rd B2
Queensway B2/B3/C3
Radio Essex C2
Rayleigh Ave A1
Redstock Rd A2
Rochford Ave A1
Royal Mews C2
Royal Terr C2
Royals Shopping Centre, The C3
Ruskin Ave A3
St Ann's Rd B3
St Helen's Rd B1
St John's Rd B1
St Leonard's Rd C3
St Lukes Rd A3
St Vincent's Rd C1
Salisbury Ave A1/B1
Scratton Rd C2
Shakespeare Dr A1
Shopmobility B2
Short St A2
South Ave A3
Southchurch Rd B3
Southend Central ≥ B2
Southend Pier Railway C3
Southend United FC A1
Southend Victoria ≥ B2
Stanfield Rd A2
Stanley Rd C3
Sutton Rd A3/B3
Swanage Rd B3
Sweyne Ave A1
Sycamore Grove A3
Tennyson Ave A3
Tickfield Ave A2
Tudor Rd A1
Tunbridge Rd A2
Tylers Ave B3
Tyrrel Dr B3
Univ of Essex B2/C2
Vale Ave A2
Victoria Ave A2
Victoria Shopping Centre, The B2
Warrior Sq B3
Wesley Rd C3
West Rd A1
West St A1
Westcliff Ave C1
Westcliff Parade C1
Western Esplanade C1
Weston Rd C2
Whitegate Rd B3
Wilson Rd C1
Wimborne Rd B3
York Rd C3

Stirling 197

Abbey Rd A3
Abbotsford Place A3
Abercromby Place C1
Albert Halls B1
Albert Place B1
Alexandra Place A3
Allan Park C2
Ambulance Station A2
AMF Ten Pin Bowling ✦ B2
Argyll Ave A3
Argyll's Lodging ✦ B1
Back O' Hill Ind Est A1
Back O' Hill Rd A1
Baker St B2
Ballengeich Pass A1
Balmoral Place B1
Barn Rd B1
Barnton St B2
Bastion, The ✦ C2
Bow St B1
Bruce St A2
Burghmuir Retail Park C2
Burghmuir Rd A2/B2/C2
Bus Station B2
Cambuskenneth Bridge A3
Castle Ct B1
Causewayhead Rd A2
Cemetery A1
Changing Room, The B1
Church of the Holy Rude B1
Clarendon Place C1
Club House B1
Colquhoun St C3
Corn Exchange B2
Council Offices C2
Court B2
Cowane Ctr A2
Cowane St A2
Cowane's Hosp B1
Crofthead Rd A1
Dean Cres A3
Douglas St A2
Drip Rd A1
Drummond La C1
Drummond Place C1
Drummond Place La C1
Dumbarton Rd C2
Eastern Access Rd B2
Edward Ave A3
Edward Rd A2
Forrest Rd A2
Fort A1
Forth Cres B2
Forth St A2
Gladstone Place C1
Glebe Ave C1
Glebe Cres C1
Golf Course C1
Goosecroft Rd B2
Gowanhill A1
Greenwood Ave B1
Harvey Wynd A1
Information Ctr B1
Irvine Place B2
James St A2
John St B1
Kerse Rd C3
King's Knot ✦ B1
King's Park C1
King's Park Rd C1
Laurencecroft Rd A2
Leisure Pool B2
Library B2
Linden Ave C2
Lovers Wk A2
Lower Back Walk B1
Lower Bridge St A2
Lower Castlehill A1
Mar Place B1
Meadow Place A3
Meadowforth Rd C3
Middlemuir Rd C3
Millar Place A3
Morris Terr B2
Mote Hill A1
Murray Place B2
Nelson Place C2
Old Town Cemetery B1
Old Town Jail ✦ B1
Park Terr C1
Phoenix Ind Est C3
Players Rd C3
Port St C2
Post Office B2
Princes St B2
Queen St B2
Queen's Rd B1
Queenshaugh Dr A3
Ramsay Place A2
Riverside Dr A3
Ronald Place A1
Rosebery Place A2
Royal Gardens B1
Royal Gardens B1
St Mary's Wynd B1
St Ninian's Rd C2
Scott St A2
Seaforth Place B2
Shore Rd B2
Smith Art Gallery & Museum B1
Snowdon Place C1
Snowdon Place La C1
Spittal St B2
Springkerse Ind Est C3
Springkerse Rd C3
Stirling Arcade B2
Stirling Business Centre C2
Stirling Castle A1
Stirling County Rugby Football Club A3
Stirling Enterprise Park B3
Stirling Old Bridge A2
Stirling Station ≥ B2
Superstore A1/A2
Sutherland Ave A3
TA Centre C3
Tannery La A2
Thistle Ind Est C3
Thistles Shopping Centre, The B2
Tolbooth ✦ B1
Town Wall B1
Union St A2
Upper Back Walk B1
Upper Bridge St A1
Upper Castlehill B1
Upper Craigs C2
Victoria Place C1
Victoria Rd B1
Victoria Sq B1/C1
Vue B2
Wallace St A2
Waverley Cres A3
Wellgreen Rd C2
Windsor Place C1
YHA B1

Stoke-on-Trent (Hanley) 196

Acton St A3
Albion St B2
Argyle St C1
Ashbourne Grove A2
Avoca St A3
Baskerville Rd B3
Bedford Rd C1
Bedford St C1
Bethesda St B2
Bexley St A2
Birches Head Rd A3
Botteslow St C3
Boundary St A2
Broad St C2
Broom St A3
Bryan St A2
Bucknall New Rd B3
Bucknall Old Rd B3
Bus Station C3
Cannon St C2
Castlefield St C1
Cavendish St B1
Central Forest Park A2
Century Retail Park B1
Charles St B3
Cheapside B2
Chell St A3
Cinema A2
Clarke St C1
Cleveland Rd C2
Clifford St C3
Clough St B2
Clough St East B2
Clyde St C1
College Rd C2
Cooper St C2
Corbridge Rd A1
Cutts St C2
Davis St C1
Denbigh St A1
Derby St C3
Dilke St A3
Dudson Ctr, The A2
Dundas St A3
Dundee Rd C1
Dyke St B3
Eastwood Rd C3
Eaton St A3
Etruria Park B1
Etruria Rd B1
Etruria Vale Rd C1
Festing St A3
Festival Heights Retail Park A1
Festival Retail Park A1
Fire Station C2
Foundry St B2
Franklyn St C3
Garnet St B1
Garth St B3
George St A3
Gilman St B3
Glass St B3
Goodson St B3
Greyhound Way A1
Grove Place C1
Hampton St C3
Hanley Park C2
Hanley Park C2
Harding Rd C2
Hassall St B3
Havelock Place C1
Hazlehurst St C3
Hinde St C2
Hope St B2
Houghton St C2
Hulton St A3
Information Ctr B2
intu Potteries Shopping Centre B2
Jasper St C2
Jervis St A3
John Bright St A3
John St B2
Keelings Rd A3
Kimberley Rd C1
Ladysmith Rd C1
Lawrence St C2
Leek Rd C3
Library C2
Lichfield St C3
Linfield Rd B3
Loftus St A2
Lower Bedford St C1
Lower Bryan St A2
Lower Mayer St A3
Lowther St A1
Magistrates Court C2
Malham St A2
Marsh St B2
Matlock St C3
Mayer St A3
Milton St C1
Mitchell Arts Ctr B2
Moston St A3
Mount Pleasant C1
Mulgrave St A1
Mynors St B3
Nelson Place B3
New Century St B1
Octagon Retail Park B1
Ogden Rd C3
Old Hall St B3
Old Town Rd A3
Pall Mall B2
Palmerston St C3
Park and Ride C2
Parkway, The C2
Pavilion Dr A1
Pelham St C3
Percy St B2
Piccadilly B2
Picton St B3
Plough St A3
Police Station C2
Portland St A1
Post Office A3/B2
Potteries Museum & Art Gallery B2
Potteries Way B1
Powell St A1
Pretoria Rd C1
Quadrant Rd B2
Ranelagh St C2
Raymond St C2
Rectory Rd C1
Regent Rd C2
Regent Theatre B2
Richmond Terr C2
Ridgehouse Dr A1
Robson St C2
St Ann St B3
St Luke St B3
Sampson St B2
Shaw St A1
Sheaf St C2
Shearer St C1
Shelton New Rd C1
Shirley Rd C2
Slippery La B2
Snow Hill C2
Spur St C3
Stafford St B2
Stubbs La C3
Sun St C1
Supermarket A1/B2
Superstore B2
Talbot St C3
Town Hall B2
Town Rd A3
Trinity St B2
Union St A2
Upper Hillchurch St A3
Upper Huntbach St B3
Victoria Hall B3
Warner St C2
Warwick St C1
Waterloo Rd A1
Waterloo St B3
Well St B3
Wellesley St C2
Wellington Rd B3
Wellington St B3
Whitehaven Dr A2
Whitmore St C1
Windermere St A1
Woodall St A1
Yates St C2
York St A2

Stratford-upon-Avon 197

Albany Rd B1
Alcester Rd B1
Ambulance Station B1
Arden St B1
Avenue Farm A1
Ave Farm Ind Est A1
Avenue Rd A1
Baker Ave A1
Bandstand C3
Benson Rd A3
Birmingham Rd A2
Boat Club B3
Borden Place C1
Bridge St B2
Bridgetown Rd C3
Bridgeway B3
Broad St C2
Broad Walk C2
Brookvale Rd C1
Brunel Way B1
Bull St C2
Butterfly Farm ✦ C3
Cemetery C1
Chapel La B2
Cherry Orchard C1
Chestnut Walk B2
Children's Playground C3
Church St C2
Civic Hall B2
Clarence Rd B1
Clopton Bridge ✦ B3
Clopton Rd A2
College B1
College La C2
College St C2
Com Sports Centre B1
Council Offices (District) B2
Courtyard, The C2
Cox's Yard ✦ B3
Cricket Ground C3
Ely Gdns B2
Ely St B2
Evesham Rd C1
Fire Station B1
Foot Ferry C3
Fordham Ave A2
Garrick Way C1
Gower Memorial ✦ B3
Great William St B2
Greenhill St B2
Greenway, The C2
Grove Rd B2
Guild St B2
Guildhall & School B2
Hall's Croft C2
Harvard House B2
Henley St B2
Hertford Rd C1
High St B2
Holton St C2
Holy Trinity C2
Information Ctr B3
Jolyffe Park Rd A2
Kipling Rd C3
Library B2
Lodge Rd B1
Maidenhead Rd A2
Mansell St B2
Masons Court B2
Masons Rd A1
Maybird Shopping Park A2
Maybrook Retail Park A2
Maybrook Rd A1
Mayfield Ave A2
Meer St B2
Mill La C2
Moat House Hotel B3
Narrow La C2
Nash's House & New Place B2
New St C2
Old Town C2
Orchard Way C1
Other Place, The C2
Paddock La C1
Park Rd A1
Payton St B2
Percy St A2
Police Station B2
Post Office B2
Recreation Ground C2
Regal Road A2
Rother St B2
Rowley Cres A3
Royal Shakespeare Theatre B3
Ryland St C2
Saffron Meadow C2
St Andrew's Cres B1
St Gregory's A3
St Gregory's Rd A3
St Mary's Rd A2
Sanctus Dr C2
Sanctus St C1
Sandfield Rd C2
Scholars La B2
Seven Meadows Rd C2
Shakespeare Inst C2
Shakespeare St B2
Shakespeare's Birthplace ✦ B2
Sheep St B2
Shelley Rd C3
Shipston Rd C3
Shottery Rd C1
Slingates Rd A2
Southern La C2
Station Rd B1
Stratford Healthcare B2
Stratford Hosp B2
Stratford Leisure Centre B3
Stratford Sports Club B1
Stratford-upon-Avon Station ≥ B1
Swan Theatre B3
Swan's Nest La B3
Talbot Rd A2
Tiddington Rd B3
Timothy's Bridge Industrial Estate A1
Timothy's Bridge Rd A1
Town Hall & Council Offices B2
Town Sq B2
Trinity Close C2
Tyler St B2
War Memorial Gdns B3
Warwick Rd B3
Waterside B3
Welcombe Rd A3
West St C2
Western Rd A2
Wharf Rd A2
Willows North, The B1
Willows, The B1
Wood St B2

Sunderland 197

Albion Place C2
Alliance Place B1
Argyle St C2
Ashwood St C1
Athenaeum St B2
Azalea Terr C2
Beach St A1
Bedford St B2
Beechwood Terr C1
Belvedere Rd C2
Blandford St B2
Borough Rd B3
Bridge Cres B2
Bridge St B2
Bridges, The B2
Brooke St A2
Brougham St B2
Burdon Rd C2
Burn Park C1
Burn Park Rd C1
Burn Park Technology Park C1
Carol St B1
Charles St A3
Chester Rd C1
Chester Terr B1
Church St A3
Civic Centre C2
Cork St B3
Coronation St B3
Cowan Terr C2
Dame Dorothy St A2
Deptford Rd B1
Deptford Terr A1
Derby St C2
Derwent St C2
Dock St A3
Dundas St A2
Durham Rd C1
Easington St A2
Egerton St C3
Empire B3
Empire Theatre B2
Farringdon Row B1
Fawcett St B2
Fire Station B1
Fox St C1
Foyle St B3
Frederick St B3
Hanover Place A1
Havelock Terr C1
Hay St A2
Headworth Square B3
Hendon Rd B3
High St East B3
High St West B2/B3
Holmeside B2
Hylton Rd B1
Information Ctr B2
John St B3
Kier Hardie Way A2
Lambton St B3
Laura St C3
Lawrence St B3
Library & Arts Ctr B3
Lily St B1
Lime St B1
Livingstone Rd B2
Low Row B2
Magistrates' Court B2
Matamba Terr B1
Millburn St B1
Millennium Way A2
Minster B2
Monkwearmouth Sta Museum A2
Mowbray Park C3
Mowbray Rd C3
Murton St C3
National Glass Centre ✦ A3
New Durham Rd C1
Newcastle Rd A2
Nile St B3
Norfolk St B3
North Bridge St A2
Northern Gallery for Contemporary Art (NGCA) B3
Otto Terr C1
Park La C2
Park Lane B2
Park Rd C2
Paul's Rd B3
Peel St C3
Point, The ✦ B2
Police Station B2
Priestly Cres A1
Queen St B2
Railway Row B1
Retail Park B1
Richmond St A2
Roker Ave A2
Royalty Theatre C1
Royalty, The C1
Ryhope Rd C2
St Mary's Way B2
St Michael's Way B2
St Peter's A3
St Peter's A2
St Peter's Way A3
St Vincent St C3
Salem Rd C3
Salem St C3
Salisbury St C3
Sans St B3
Shopmobility B2
Silkworth Row B1
Southwick Rd A2
Stadium of Light (Sunderland AFC) A2
Stadium Way A2
Stobart St A2
Stockton Rd C2
Suffolk St C3
Sunderland B2
Sunderland Aquatic Centre A2
Sunderland College C2
Sunderland Museum B3
Sunderland St B3
Sunderland Sta ≥ B2
Tatham St C3
Tavistock Place B3
Thelma St C1
Thomas St North A2
Thornholme Rd C1
Toward Rd C3
Transport Interchange C2
Trimdon St Way B1
Tunstall Rd C2
University C1
University Library C1
Univ of Sunderland (City Campus) B1
Univ of Sunderland (St Peter's Campus) A3
University of Sunderland (Sir Tom Cowie Campus) A3
Vaux Brewery Way A2
Villiers St B3
Villiers St South B3
Vine Place C2
Violet St B1
Walton La B3
Waterworks Rd B1
Wearmouth Bridge B2
West Sunniside B3
West Wear St B3
Westbourne Rd B1
Western Hill C1
Wharncliffe B1
Whickham St A3
White House Rd C3
Wilson St North A2
Winter Gdns C3
Wreath Quay A1

Swansea Abertawe 198

Adelaide St C3
Albert Row C3
Alexandra Rd B3
Argyle St C1
Baptist Well Place A2
Beach St C1
Belle Vue Way B3
Berw Rd A1
Berwick Terr A2
Bond St C1
Brangwyn Concert Hall C1
Bridge St A3
Brooklands Terr B1
Brunswick St C1
Bryn-Syfi Terr A2
Bryn-y-Mor Rd C1
Bullins La B1
Burrows Rd C1
Bus Station C2
Bus/Rail link A3
Cadfan Rd A1
Cadrawd Rd A1
Caer St B3
Carig Cres A1
Carlton Terr B2
Carmarthen Rd A3
Castle Square B3
Castle St B3
Catherine St C1
Cinema C3
Civic Ctr & Library C2
Clarence St C2
Colbourne Terr A2
Constitution Hill B1
Court B3
Creidiol Rd A2
Cromwell St B2
Crown Courts C1
Duke St B1
Dunvant Place C2
Dyfatty Park A3
Dyfatty St A3
Dyfed Ave A1
Dylan Thomas Centre ✦ B3
Dylan Thomas Theatre C3
Eaton Cres C1
Eigen Cres A1
Elfed Rd A1
Emlyn Rd A1
Evans Terr A3
Fairfield Terr B1
Ffynone Dr B1
Ffynone Rd B1
Fire Station B3
Firm St A2
Fleet St C1
Francis St C1
Fullers Row B2
George St B2
Glamorgan St C2
Glynn Vivian Art Gallery B3
Gower Coll Swansea C1
Graig Terr A3
Grand Theatre C2
Granogwen Rd A2
Guildhall C1
Guildhall Rd South C1
Gwent Rd A1
Gwynedd Ave A1
Hafod St A3
Hanover St B1
Harcourt St B2
Harries St A2
Heathfield B2
Henrietta St B2
Hewson St B2
High St A3/B3
High View A2
Hill St A2
Historic Ships Berth C3
HM Prison C2
Information Ctr C2
Islwyn Rd A1
King Edward's Rd C1
Kingsway, The B2
LC, The C3
Long Ridge A2
Madoc St C2
Mansel St B2
Maritime Quarter C3
Market B3
Mayhill Gdns B1
Mayhill Rd A1
Milton Terr A2
Mission Gallery C3
Montpelier Terr B1
Morfa Rd A3
Mount Pleasant B2
National Waterfront Museum C3
New Cut Rd A3
New St A3
Nicander Parade A2
Nicander Place A2
Nicholl St B2
Norfolk St B2
North Hill Rd A2
Northampton La B2
Observatory ✦ C3
Orchard St B3
Oxford St B2
Oystermouth Rd C1
Page St B2
Pant-y-Celyn Rd B1
Parc Tawe North B3
Parc Tawe Shopping & Leisure Centre B3
Patti Pavilion C1
Paxton St C2
Pen-y-Graig Rd A1
Penmaen Terr B1
Phillips Pde C1
Picton Terr B2
Plantasia B3
Plantasia B3
Police Station B2
Post Office A1/A2/C1/C2
Powys Ave A1
Primrose St B2
Princess Way B3
Promenade B2
Pryder Gdns A1
Quadrant Shopping Centre C2
Quay Park B3
Rhianfa La B1
Rhondda St B2
Richardson St C2
Rodney St C1
Rose Hill B1
Rosehill Terr B1
Russell St B1
St Helen's Ave C1
St Helen's Cres C1
St Helen's Rd C1
St James Gdns B1
St James's Cres B1
St Mary's B3
Sea View Terr A3
Singleton St C2
South Dock C3
Stanley Place B2
Strand B3
Swansea Castle B3
Swansea Metropolitan University B2
Swansea Mus C3
Swansea Station ≥ A3
Taliesyn Rd B1
Tan y Marian Rd A1
Tegid Rd A2
Teilo Cres A1
Tenpin Bowling ✦ B3
Terrace Rd B1/B2
Tontine St A3
Townhill Rd A1
Tramshed, The C3
Trawler Rd C3
Union St B2
Upper Strand A3
Vernon St A3
Victoria Quay C3
Victoria Rd B3
Vincent St C1
Walter Rd B1
Watkin St A2
Waun-Wen Rd A2
Wellington St C2
Westbury St C1
Western St C1
Westway C2
William St C2
Wind St B3
Woodlands Terr B1
YMCA B2
York St C3

Swindon 198

Albert St C3
Albion St C1
Alfred St A2
Alvescot Rd C3
Art Gallery & Museum C3
Ashford Rd C1
Aylesbury St A2
Bath Rd C2
Bathampton St B1
Bathurst Rd B3
Beatrice St A2
Beckhampton St B3
Bowood Rd C1
Bristol St B1
Broad St A3
Brunel Shopping Centre, The B2
Brunel Statue B2
Brunswick St C2
Bus Station B2
Cambria Bridge Rd B1
Cambria Place B1
Canal Walk B2
Carr St B1
Cemetery C1/C3
Chandler Close C3
Chapel C1
Chester St B1
Christ Church C3
Church Place B1
Cirencester Way A3
Clarence St B2
Clifton St C1
Cockleberry A2
Colbourne A3
Colbourne St A3
College St B2
Commercial Rd B2
Corporation St A2
Council Offices B3
County Cricket Gd A3
County Rd A3
Courts B2
Cricklade Street C3
Crombey St B1/C2
Cross St C2
Curtis St B1
Deacon St C1
Designer Outlet (Great Western) B1
Dixon St C2
Dover St C2
Dowling St C2
Drove Rd C3
Dryden St C1
Durham St C3
East St B1
Eastcott Hill C2
Eastcott Rd C2
Edgeware Rd B2
Edmund St C2
Elmina Rd A3
Emlyn Square B1
English Heritage National Monuments Record Centre B1
Euclid St B3
Exeter St B1
Fairview C1
Faringdon Rd B1
Farnsby St B1
Fire Station C3
Fleet St B2
Fleming Way B2/B3
Florence St A2
Gladstone St A3
Gooch St A2
Graham St A3
Great Western Way A1/A2
Groundwell Rd B3
Hawksworth Way A1
Haydon St A2
Henry St B2
Hillside Ave C1
Holbrook Way B2
Hunt St C3
Hydro B1
Hythe Rd C2
Information Ctr B2
Joseph St C1
Kent Rd C2
King William St C2
Kingshill Rd C1
Lansdown Rd C2
Lawn, The C3
Leicester St B3
Library B2
Lincoln St B3
Little London C3
London St B1
Magic A3
Maidstone Rd C2
Manchester Rd A3
Maxwell St B1
Milford St B2
Milton Rd B1
Morse St C2
Newcastle St B3
Newcombe Drive A1
Hawsworth Ind Est A1
Newhall St C2
North St C2
North Star A1
North Star Ave A1
Northampton St B3
Nurseries, The C1
Oasis Leisure Ctr A1
Ocotal Way A3
Okus Rd C1
Old Town C3
Oxford St B1
Parade, The B2
Park Lane B1
Park Lane B1
Park, The B1
Pembroke St C2
Plymouth St B3
Polaris Way A2
Police Station B2
Ponting St A2
Post Office B1/B2/C3
Poulton St A3
Princes St B2
Prospect Hill C2
Prospect Place C2
Queen St B2
Queen's Park C3
Radnor St C1
Read St C1
Reading St B1
Regent Circus C2
Regent St B2
Retail Park A2/A3/B3
Rosebery St A3
St Mark's B1
Salisbury St A3
Savernake St C2
Science & Technology Facilities Council HQ A2
Shelley St C1
Sheppard St B1
Shopmobility B2
South St C2
Southampton St B3
Spring Gardens B3
Stafford Street C2
Stanier St C2
Station Road A2
STEAM GWR B1
Swindon College A2
Swindon Rd C2
Swindon Station ≥ A2
Swindon Town Football Club A3
TA Centre B1
Tennyson St B1
Theobald St B1
Town Hall B2
Transfer Bridges A3
Union St C2
Upham Rd C3
Victoria Rd C3
Walcot Rd B3
War Memorial ✦ B2
Wells St B3
Western St C2
Westmorland Rd B3
Whalebridge B2
Whitehead St C1
Whitehouse Rd A2
William St C1
Wood St C3
Wyvern Theatre & Arts Centre B2
York Rd B3

Taunton 198

Addison Grove A1
Albemarle Rd A1
Alfred St B3
Alma St C2
Avenue, The A1
Bath Place C1
Belvedere Rd A1
Billet St B2
Billetfield C2
Birch Grove A1
Brewhouse Theatre B2
Bridge St B1
Bridgwater & Taunton Canal A2
Broadlands Rd C1
Burton Place C1
Bus Station B1
Canal Rd A2
Cann St C1
Canon St B2
Castle St B1
Cheddon Rd A2
Chip Lane A1
Clarence St B1
Cleveland St B1
Clifton Terr A2
Coleridge Cres C3
Compass Hill C1
Compton Close A2
Corporation St B1
Council Offices A1
County Walk Shopping Centre C2
Courtyard B2
Cranmer Rd B2
Crescent, The C1
Critchard Way B3
Cyril St A1
Deller's Wharf B1
Duke St B2
East Reach B3
East St B3
Eastbourne Rd B2
Eastleigh Rd C3
Eaton Cres A2
Elm Grove A1
Elms Close A1
Fons George C1
Fore St B2
Fowler St A1
French Weir Recreation Gd B1
Geoffrey Farrant Walk A2
Gray's Almshouses B2
Grays Rd B3
Greenway Ave A1
Guildford Place C1
Hammet St B2
Haydon Rd B3
Heavitree Way A2
Herbert St A1
High St C2
Holway Ave C3
Hugo St B3
Huish's Almshouses B2
Hurdle Way C2
Information Ctr C2
Jubilee St A1
King's College C3
Kings Close C3
Laburnum St B2
Lambrook Rd B3
Lansdowne Rd A3
Leslie Ave A1
Leycroft Rd B3
Library C2
Linden Grove A1
Magdalene St B2
Magistrates Court B1
Malvern Terr A2
Market House B2
Mary St C2
Middle St B2
Mitre Court B3
Mount Nebo C1
Mount St C2
Mount, The C2
Mountway C2
Museum of Somerset B1
North St B2
Northfield Ave B1
Northfield Rd B1
Northleigh Rd C3
Obridge Allotments A3
Obridge Lane A3
Obridge Rd A3
Obridge Viaduct A3
Orch Shopping Ctr C2
Osborne Way C1
Park St C1
Paul St C2
Plais St A2
Playing Field C3
Police Station A1
Portland St B1
Post Office B1/B2
Priorswood Ind Est A3
Priorswood Rd A2
Priory Ave B2
Priory Bridge Rd B2
Priory Fields Retail Park A3
Priory Park A2
Priory Way A3
Queen St B3
Railway St A1
Records Office A2
Recreation Grd A1
Riverside Place B2
St Augustine St B2
St George's C2
St Georges Sq C2
St James B2
St James St B2
St John's C1
St John's Rd B1
St Josephs Field C2
St Mary Magdalene's B2
Samuels Ct A1
Shire Hall & Law Courts C1
Somerset County Cricket Ground B2
Somerset County Hall C1
Somerset Cricket B2
South Rd C3
South St C3
Staplegrove Rd B1
Station Approach A2
Station Rd A1
Stephen St B2
Stephen Way B2
Superstore C2
Swimming Pool A1
Tancred St B2
Tangier Way B1
Tauntfield Close C3
Taunton Castle B1
Taunton Dean Cricket Club C2
Taunton Station ≥ A2
Thomas St A1
Toneway A3
Tower St C1
Trenchard Way A1
Trevor Smith Place C3
Trinity Business Centre C3
Trinity Rd C3
Trinity St B3
Trull Rd C1
Tudor House B2
Upper High St C1
Venture Way A3
Victoria Gate B3
Victoria Park B3
Victoria St B3
Viney St B3
Vivary Pk Golf Club C2
Vivary Rd C1
War Memorial ✦ C1
Wellesley St A2
Wheatley Cres A3
Whitehall A1
Wilfred Rd B3
William St A1
Wilton Church C1
Wilton Close C1
Wilton Grove C1
Wilton St C1
Winchester St B2
Winters Field B2
Wood St B1
Yarde Place B1

Telford 198

Alma Ave C1
Amphitheatre C2
Bowling Alley B2
Brandsfarm Way C3
Brunel Rd B1
Bus Station B2
Buxton Rd C1
Central Park A2
Chelsea Gardens B2
Coach Central B2
Coachwell Close B1
Colliers Way A1
Courts B2
Dale Acre Way B3
Darliston C3
Deepdale B3
Deercote B2
Dinthill C3
Doddington C3
Dodmoor Grange C3
Downemead B3
Duffryn B3
Dunsheath B3
Euston Way A3
Eyton Mound C1
Eyton Rd C1
Forgegate A2

Grange Central B2
Hall Park Way B1
Hinkshay Rd C2
Hollinsworth Rd A2
Holyhead Rd A3
Housing Trust A1
Ice Rink B2
Information Ctr B2
Ironmasters Way A2
Job Centre B1
Land Registry B1
Lawn Central B2
Lawnswood C1
Library B2
Malinsgate B1
Matlock Ave C1
Moor Rd C1
Mount Rd C1
Odeon B2
Park Lane A1
Police Station B1
Post Office A2/B2/C1
Priorslee Ave A3
Queen Elizabeth Ave C3
Queen Elizabeth Way B1
Queensway A2/B3
QEII Arena C2
Rampart Way A2
Randlay Ave C3
Randlay Wood C3
Rhodes Ave C1
Royal Way B1
St Leonards Rd B1
St Quentin Gate B2
Shifnal Rd A3
Silkin Way C2
Sixth Ave A1
Southwater Leisure Complex B2
Southwater Way B1
Spout Lane C1
Spout Mound B1
Spout Way C1
Stafford Court B3
Stafford Park B3
Stirchley Ave C3
Stone Row C1
Superstore B1
Telford Bridge Retail Park A1
Telford Central Station A3
Telford Centre, The B2
Telford Forge Shopping Park A1
Telford Hornets RFC C2
Telford Int Ctr C2
Telford Way A3
Third Ave A2
Town Park C2
Town Park Visitor Centre B2
Wellswood Ave A2
West Centre Way B1
Withywood Drive C1
Wonderland C2
Woodhouse Central B2
Yates Way A1

Torquay 199

Abbey Rd B2
Alexandra Rd A2
Alpine Rd B3
AMF Bowling C3
Ash Hill Rd A2
Babbacombe Rd B3
Bampfylde Rd B1
Barton Rd A1
Beacon Quay C2
Belgrave Rd A1/B1
Belmont Rd A3
Berea Rd A3
Braddons Hill Rd East B3
Brewery Park A3
Bronshill Rd A2
Carlton Rd A3
Castle Circus A2
Castle Rd A2
Cavern Rd A3
Central B2
Chatsworth Rd A2
Chestnut Ave B1
Church St A1
Coach Station A1
Corbyn Head C1
Croft Hill B1
Croft Rd B1
East St A1
Egerton Rd A3
Ellacombe Church Rd A3
Ellacombe Rd A2
Falkland Rd B1
Fleet St B2
Fleet Walk Shopping Centre B2
Grafton Rd B3
Grange Rd A3
Haldon Pier C2
Hatfield Rd A2
Highbury Rd A2
Higher Warberry Rd A3
Hillesdon Rd B3
Hoxton Rd A3
Hunsdon Rd B3
Information Ctr B2
Inner Harbour C3
Kenwyn Rd A3
King's Drive, The B1
Laburnum St A1
Law Courts A2
Library A2
Lime Ave B1
Living Coasts C3
Lower Warberry Rd B3
Lucius St B1
Lymington Rd A1
Magdalene Rd A1
Marina C2
Market Forum, The B2
Market St B2
Meadfoot Lane C3
Meadfoot Rd C3
Melville St B2
Middle Warberry Rd B3
Mill Lane A1
Montpellier Rd B3
Morgan Ave A1
Museum Rd B3
Newton Rd A1
Oakhill Rd A1
Outer Harbour C2
Parkhill Rd C3
Pimlico B2
Police Station A1
Post Office A1/B2
Prince of Wales Steps C3
Princes Rd A3
Princes Rd East A3
Princes Rd West A3
Princess Gdns C2
Princess Pier C2
Princess Theatre C2
Rathmore Rd B1
Recreation Grd B1
Riviera Int Ctr B1
Rock End Ave C3
Rock Rd B2
Rock Walk B2
Rosehill Rd A3
South West Coast Path C3
St Efride's Rd A1
St John's B3
St Luke's Rd B2
St Luke's Rd North B2
St Luke's Rd South B2
St Marychurch Rd A2
Scarborough Rd B1
Shedden Hill B2
South Pier C2
South St A1
Spanish Barn B1
Stitchill Rd B3
Strand B3
Sutherland Rd B3
Teignmouth Rd A1
Temperance St B2
Terrace, The B3
Thurlow Rd A1
Tor Bay B1
Tor Church Rd A1
Tor Hill Rd A1
Torbay Rd B2
Torquay Mus B3
Torquay Station C1
Torquay Tennis Club B1
Torre Abbey B1
Torre Abbey Meadows B1
Torre Abbey Sands B1
Torwood Gardens B3
Torwood St C3
Town Hall A2
Union Square Shopping Centre A2
Union St A1
Upton Hill A2
Upton Park A1
Upton Rd A1
Vanehill Rd C3
Vansittart Rd A1
Vaughan Parade C2
Victoria Parade C3
Victoria Rd A2
Warberry Rd West B2
Warren Rd B2
Windsor Rd A2/A3
Woodville Rd A3

Truro 199

Adelaide Ter B1
Agar Rd B3
Arch Hill C2
Arundell Place C2
Avenue, The A3
Avondale Rd B1
Back Quay B3
Barrack La C3
Barton Meadow A1
Benson Rd A2
Bishops Close A2
Bosvean Gdns B1
Bosvigo Gardens B1
Bosvigo La A1
Bosvigo Rd B2
Broad St A3
Burley Close C3
Bus Station B3
Calenick St B2
Campfield Hill B3
Carclew St B3
Carew Rd A2
Carey Park B2
Carlyon Rd A2
Carvoza Rd A3
Castle St B2
Cathedral View A2
Chainwalk Dr A2
Chapel Hill B1
Charles St B2
City Hall B3
City Rd B2
Coinage Hall B3
Comprigney Hill A1
Coosebean La A1
Copes Gdns A2
County Hall B1
Courtney Rd A2
Crescent Rd B1
Crescent Rise B1
Crescent, The B1
Daniell Court C2
Daniell Rd C2
Daniell St C2
Daubuz Close A2
Daubuz Moors Nature Reserve A3
Dobbs La B1
Edward St B2
Eliot Rd A2
Elm Court A3
Enys Close A1
Enys Rd A1
Fairmantle St B3
Falmouth Rd C2
Ferris Town B2
Fire Station B1
Frances St B2
George St B2
Green Close C2
Green La C1
Grenville Rd A2
Hall for Cornwall B3
Hendra Rd A2
Hendra Vean A1
High Cross B3
Higher Newham La C3
Higher Trehaverne A2
Hillcrest Ave B1
Hospital B2
Hunkin Close A2
Hurland Rd C3
Infirmary Hill B2
James Place B3
Kenwyn Church Rd A1
Kenwyn Hill A1
Kenwyn Rd A2
Kenwyn St B2
Kerris Gdns A1
King St B3
Leats, The B2
Lemon Quay B3
Lemon St Gallery B3
Library B1/B3
Malpas Rd B3
Magistrates Court A3
Market B3
Merrifield Close B1
Mitchell Hill A3
Moresk Close A3
Moresk Rd A3
Morlaix Ave C3
Nancemere Rd A3
Newham Business Park C3
Newham Ind Est C3
Newham Rd C3
Northfield Dr C3
Oak Way A3
Pal's Terr A3
Park View C2
Pendarves Rd A2
Plaza Cinema B3
Police Sta A2/B3
Post Office B3
Prince's St B3
Pydar St B2
Quay St B3
Redannick Cres C2
Redannick La B2
Richard Lander Monument C2
Richmond Hill B1
River St B2
Rosedale Rd A2
Royal Cornwall Museum B2
St Aubyn Rd C3
St Clement St B3
St George's Rd A1
School La C2
Spires, The A2
Station Rd B1
Stokes Rd A2
Strangways Terr C3
Tabernacle St B3
Trehaverne La A2
Tremayne Rd A2
Treseder's Gdns A3
Treworder Rd B1
Treyew Rd B1
Truro Cathedral B3
Truro Harbour Office B3
Truro Station B3
Union St B3
Upper School La C2
Victoria Gdns B2
Waterfall Gdns B2

Winchester 199

Andover Rd A2
Andover Road Retail Park A2
Archery La C2
Arthur Rd A2
Bar End Rd C3
Beaufort Rd C2
Beggar's La B3
Bereweeke Ave A1
Bereweeke Rd A1
Boscobel Rd A2
Brassey Rd A2
Broadway B3
Brooks Shopping Centre, The B3
Bus Station B3
Butter Cross B2
Canon St C2
Castle Wall C2/C3
Cathedral C2
Cheriton Rd A1
Chesil St C3
Chesil Theatre C3
Christchurch Rd C1
City Mill B3
City Museum B2
City Rd B2
Clifton Rd B1
Clifton Terr B2
Close Wall C2/C3
Coach Park A2
Colebrook St C3
College St C2
College Walk C3
Compton Rd C2
Council Offices C3
County Council Offices B2
Cranworth Rd A2
Cromwell Rd C1
Culver Rd C2
Discovery Centre B2
Domum Rd C3
Durngate Place B3
Eastgate St B3
East Hill C3
Edgar Rd C2
Egbert Rd A2
Elm Rd B1
Everyman B2
Fairfield Rd A1
Fire Station B3
Fordington Ave B1
Fordington Rd A1
Friarsgate B3
Gordon Rd B3
Great Hall & Round Table, The B2
Greenhill Rd B1
Guildhall B3
Hatherley Rd A1
High St B2
Hillier Way A3
HM Prison B1
Hyde Abbey (Remains) A2
Hyde Abbey Rd B2
Hyde Close A2
Hyde St A2
Information Ctr B3
Jane Austen's House C2
Jewry St B2
King Alfred Place A2
Kingsgate Arch C2
Kingsgate Park C2
Kingsgate Rd C2
Kingsgate St C2
Lankhills Rd A2
Law Courts B2
Library B2
Lower Brook St B3
Magdalen Hill B3
Market La B2
Mews La B1
Middle Brook St B3
Middle Rd B1
Military Museums B2
Milland Rd C3
Milverton Rd B1
Monks Rd A3
North Hill Close A2
North Walls B2
North Walls Recreation Gnd A3
Nuns Rd A3
Oram's Arbour B1
Owens Rd A2
Parchment St B2
Park & Ride C3
Park Ave B3
Playing Field A1
Police HQ B1
Portal Rd C3
Post Office B2/C1
Ranelagh Rd C1
Regimental Museum B2
River Park Leisure Ctr B3
Romans' Rd C2
Romsey Rd B1
Royal Hampshire County Hospital (A&E) B1
St Cross Rd C2
St George's St B2
St Giles Hill C3
St James Villas C2
St James' La B1
St James' Terr B1
St John's B3
St John's St B3
St Michael's Rd C2
St Paul's Hill B1
St Peter St B2
St Swithun St C2
St Thomas St C2
Saxon Rd A2
School of Art B3
Sleepers Hill Rd C1
Southgate St B2
Sparkford Rd C1
Square, The B2
Staple Gdns B2
Station Rd B2
Step Terr B1
Stockbridge Rd A1
Stuart Cres C1
Sussex St B2
Swan Lane B2
Tanner St B3
Theatre Royal B2
Tower St B2
Union St B3
University of Southampton (Winchester School of Art) B3
University of Winchester (King Alfred Campus) C1
Upper Brook St B2
Wales St B3
Water Lane B3
Weirs, The C3
West End Terr B1
Western Rd B1
Westgate B2
Wharf Hill C3
Winchester Sta A2
Winnall Moors Wildlife Reserve A3
Wolvesey Castle C3
Worthy Lane A2
Worthy Rd A2

Windsor 199

Adelaide Sq C3
Albany Rd C2
Albert St B1
Alexandra Gdns B2
Alexandra Rd C2
Alma Rd B2
Arthur Rd B2
Bachelors Acre B3
Barry Ave B2
Beaumont Rd C2
Bexley St B1
Boat House B2
Brocas St B2
Brocas, The A2
Brook St C3
Bulkeley Ave C1
Castle Hill B3
Charles St B2
Claremont Rd C2
Clarence Cres B2
Clarence Rd B1
Clewer Court Rd B1
Coach Park B2
College Cres C1
Cricket Ground C3
Dagmar Rd C2
Datchet Rd B3
Devereux Rd C2
Dorset Rd C2
Duke St B1
Elm Rd C1
Eton College A3
Eton College Natural History Mus A2
Eton Ct A2
Eton Sq A2
Eton Wick Rd A2
Farm Yard B3
Fire Station C2
Frances Rd C2
Frogmore Dr B3
Gloucester Place C3
Goslar Way C1
Goswell Hill B2
Goswell Rd B2
Green La C1
Grove Rd C2
Guildhall B3
Helena Rd C2
Helston La B1
High St A2/B3
Holy Trinity C2
Home Park, The A3/C3
Household Cavalry C2
Imperial Rd C1
Information Ctr B2
Keats La A2
King Edward VII Ave A3
King Edward VII Hospital C2
King George V Memorial B3
King Stable St A2
King's Rd C3
Library A2/B2
Long Walk, The C3
Maidenhead Rd B1
Meadow La A2
Municipal Offices C3
Nell Gwynne's House B3
Osborne Rd C2
Oxford Rd B1
Park St B3
Peascod St B2
Police Station C2
Post Office A2/C1
Princess Margaret Hosp (private) C2
Old Court Art Space, The C2
Queen Elizabeth Bridge A1
Queen Victoria's Walk B3
Queen's Rd C2
River St B2
Romney Island A3
Romney Lock A3
Romney Lock Rd A3
Russell St C2
St George's Chapel B3
St John's B3
St John's Chapel A2
St Leonards Rd C2
St Mark's Rd C2
Sheet St C3
Shopmobility B2
South Meadow A2
South Meadow La A2
Springfield Rd C1
Stovell Rd B1
Sunbury Rd A3
Tangier La A2
Temple Rd C2
Thames St B3
Theatre Royal B3
Trinity Place C2
Vansittart Rd B1/C1
Victoria Barracks C2
Victoria St C2
Westmead C1
White Lilies Island A1
William St B2
Windsor & Eton Central B2
Windsor & Eton Riverside A3
Windsor Bridge B3
Windsor Castle B3
Windsor Leisure Ctr B1
Windsor Relief Rd A1
Windsor Royal Station Shopping Centre B2
Windsor Yards B2
York Ave C1
York Rd C1

Wolverhampton 200

Albion St B3
Arena B2
Art Gallery B2
Ashland St C1
Austin St A1
Badger Dr A3
Bailey St B3
Bath Ave B1
Bath Rd B1
Bell St C2
Berry St B3
Bilston Rd C3
Bilston St C3
Birmingham Canal A3
Bone Mill La A2
Brewery Rd B1
Bright St A1
Burton Cres B3
Bus Station B3
Cambridge St A3
Camp St B2
Cannock Rd A3
Castle St C2
Chapel Ash C1
Cherry St C1
Chester St A1
Church La C2
Church St C2
Civic Centre B2
Civic Hall B2
Clarence Rd B2
Cleveland St C2
Clifton St C1
Coach Station B2
Compton Rd B1
Corn Hill B3
Coven St A3
Craddock St A1
Cross St North A2
Crown & County Courts C3
Crown St A2
Culwell St B3
Dale St C1
Darlington St C1
Devon Rd A1
Drummond St B2
Dudley Rd C2
Dudley St B2
Duke St C3
Dunkley St B1
Dunstall Ave A2
Dunstall Hill A2
Dunstall Rd A1/A2
Evans St A1
Fawdry St A1
Field St B3
Fire Station C1
Fiveways A2
Fowler Playing Fields A3
Fox's La A2
Francis St A2
Fryer St B3
Gloucester St A1
Gordon St C3
Graiseley St C1
Grand B3
Grand Station B3
Granville St C3
Great Brickkiln St C1
Great Hampton St A1
Great Western St A2
Grimstone St B3
Harrow St A1
Hilton St A3
Hive Liby The B2
Horseley Fields C3
Humber Rd C1
Information Ctr B2
Jack Hayward Way A2
Jameson St A1
Jenner St C3
Kennedy Rd B3
Kimberley St C1
King St B2
Laburnum St C1
Lansdowne Rd B1
Leicester St A1
Lever St C3
Library C3
Lichfield St B2
Light House B3
Little's La B3
Lock St B3
Lord St C1
Lowe St A1
Maltings, The B2
Mander Centre C2
Mander St C1
Market C2
Market St B2
Maxwell Rd C3
Merridale St C1
Middlecross C3
Molineux St B2
Mostyn St A1
Newhampton Arts Centre B1
New Hampton Rd East A1
Nine Elms La A3
North Rd A2
Oaks Cres C1
Oxley St A2
Paget St A1
Park Ave B1
Park Road East A1
Park Road West B1
Paul St C2
Pelham St C1
Penn Rd C2
Piper's Row B3
Piper's Row C3
Pitt St C2
Police Station C3
Pool St C2
Poole St A3
Post Office A1/B2/B2/C2/C3
Powlett St C3
Queen St B2
Raby St C3
Railway Dr B3
Red Hill St A2
Red Lion St B2
Retreat St C1
Ring Rd B2
Royal, The C3
Rugby St A1
Russell St C1
St Andrew's B1
St David's B3
St George's C3
St George's Parade C2
St James St C3
St John's C2
St John's C2
St John's Retail Pk C2
St John's Square C2
St Mark's C1
St Marks Rd C1
St Marks St C1
St Patrick's B2
St Peter's B2
St Peter's B2
Salisbury St C1
Salop St C2
School St C2
Sherwood St A2
Smestow St A3
Snow Hill C2
Springfield Rd A3
Stafford St A2/B2
Staveley Rd A1
Steelhouse La C3
Stephenson St C1
Stewart St C2
Sun St B3
Tempest St C2
Temple St C2
Tettenhall Rd B1
Thomas St C2
Thornley St B2
Tower St C2
University B2
Upper Zoar St C1
Vicarage Rd C3
Victoria St C2
Walpole St A1
Walsall St C3
Ward St C3
Warwick St C3
Water St A3
Waterloo Rd B2
Wednesfield Rd B3
West Park (not A&E) B1
West Park Swimming Pool B1
Wharf St C3
Whitmore Hill B2
Wolverhampton B3
Wolverhampton B3
Wolverhampton St George's C3
Wolverhampton Wanderers Football Gnd (Molineux) B2
Worcester St C2
Wulfrun Centre C2
Yarwell Close A3
York St C3
Zoar St C1

Worcester 200

Albany Terr A1
Angel Place B2
Angel St B2
Ashcroft Rd A2
Athelstan Rd C3
Avenue, The C1
Back Lane North A1
Back Lane South A1
Barbourne Rd A2
Bath Rd C2
Battenhall Rd C3
Bridge St B2
Britannia Sq A1
Broad St B2
Bromwich La C1
Bromwich Rd C1
Bromyard Rd C1
Bus Station B2
Butts, The B2
Carden St B3
Castle St A2
Cathedral C2
Cathedral Plaza B2
Charles St B3
Chequers La B1
Chestnut St A2
Chestnut Walk A2
Citizens' Advice Bureau B2
City Walls Rd B2
Cole Hill C3
College St C2
Commandery, The C3
Cripplegate Park B1
Croft Rd B1
Cromwell St B3
Cross, The B2
Crowngate Ctr B2
Deansway B2
Diglis Pde C2
Diglis Rd C2
Edgar Tower C2
Farrier St A2
Foregate St B2
Fort Royal Hill C3
Fort Royal Park C3
Foundry St B3
Friar St C2
George St B3
Grand Stand Rd B1
Greenhill C3
Greyfriars B2
Guildhall B2
Henwick Rd B1
High St B2
Hill St B3
Hive, The B2
Huntingdon Hall B2
Hylton Rd B1
Information Ctr B2
King Charles Place Shopping Centre C1
King's School C2
King's School Playing Field C2
Kleve Walk C2
Lansdowne Cres A3
Lansdowne Rd A3
Lansdowne Walk A3
Laslett St A3
Little Chestnut St A2
Little London A2
London Rd C3
Lowell St A3
Lowesmoor B2
Lowesmoor Terrace A3
Lowesmoor Wharf A3
Magistrates Court A2
Midland Rd B3
Mill St C2
Moors Severn Terrace, The A1
Museum & Art Gallery A2
Museum of Royal Worcester C2
New Rd C1
New St B2
Northfield St A2
Odeon B2
Old Palace The C2
Padmore St B3
Park St C3
Pheasant St B3
Pitchcroft Racecourse A1
Police Station A2
Portland St C2
Post Office B2
Quay St B2
Queen St B2
Rainbow Hill A3
Recreation Ground A2
Reindeer Court B2
Rogers Hill A3
Sabrina Terr A1
St Dunstan's Cres C3
St John's C1
St Martin's Gate B3
St Martin's Quarter B3
St Oswald's Rd A2
St Paul's St B3
St Swithin's Church B2
St Wulstans Cres C3
Sansome Walk A2
Severn St C2
Shambles, The B2
Shaw St B2
Shire Hall Crown Court A2
Shrub Hill Rd B3
Shrub Hill Retail Pk B3
Slingpool Walk C1
South Parade B2
Southfield St A2
Sports Centre A3
Stanley Rd B3
Swan, The A1
Swimming Pool A2
Tallow Hill B3
Tennis Walk A2
Tolladine Rd B3
Tudor House B2
Tybridge St B1
Tything, The A2
Univ of Worcester B2
Vincent Rd B3
Vue C2
Washington St A3
Woolhope Rd C3
Worcester Bridge B2
Worcester County Cricket Club C1
Worcester Foregate Street B2
Worcester Shrub Hill B3
Worcester Royal Grammar School A2
Wylds La C3

Wrexham Wrecsam 200

Abbot St B2
Acton Rd A3
Albert St C3
Alexandra Rd C1
Aran Rd A3
Barnfield C3
Bath Rd C2
Beeches, The A3
Beechley Rd C3
Belgrave Rd C2
Belle Vue Park C2
Belle Vue Rd C2
Belvedere Dr A1
Bennion's Rd C3
Berse Rd A1
Bersham Rd C1
Birch St C3
Bodhyfryd B3
Border Retail Park B3
Bradley Rd C2
Bright St B1
Bron-y-Nant B1
Brook St C2
Bryn-y-Cabanau Rd C3
Bury St C3
Bus Station B2
Butchers Market B3
Caia Rd C3
Cambrian Ind Est C3
Caxton Place B2
Cemetery C1
Centenary Rd C1
Central Retail Park B2
Chapel St C2
Charles St B3
Chester Rd A3
Chester St B3
Cilcen Grove A3
Citizens Advice Bureau B2
Cobden Rd B1
Council Offices B3
County C2
Crescent Rd B3
Crispin La A2
Croesnewyth Rd B1
Cross St A2
Cunliffe St A2
Derby Rd C3
Dolydd Rd B1
Duke St B2
Eagles Meadow C3
Earle St C2
East Ave A2
Edward St C2
Egerton St B2
Empress Rd C1
Erddig Rd C2
Fairy Rd C2
Fire Station B2
Foster Rd A3
Foxwood Dr C1
Garden Rd A2
General Market B3
Gerald St B2
Gibson St C1
Glyndwr University Plas Coch Campus A1
Greenbank St C3
Greenfield A2
Grosvenor Rd B2
Grove Park B3
Grove Park Rd B3
Grove Rd A3
Guildhall B2
Haig Rd C3
Hampden Rd C2
Hazel Grove A3
Henblas St B3
High St B3
Hightown Rd C3
Hill St B2
Holt Rd B3
Holt St B3
Hope St B2
Huntroyde Ave C3
Information Ctr B3
Island Green Shopping Centre B2
Jobcentre Plus B2
Jubilee Rd B2
King St B2
Kingsmills Rd C3
Lambpit St B3
Law Courts B3
Lawson Close A3
Lawson Rd A3
Lea Rd C2
Library & Arts Ctr B2
Lilac Way B1
Llys David Lord B1
Lorne St A2
Maesgwyn Rd B1
Maesydre Rd A3
Manley Rd B3
Market St B3
Mawddy Ave A2
Mayville Ave A2
Meml Gallery B2
Memorial Hall B3
Mold Rd A1
Mount St C3
Neville Cres A3
New Rd A2
North Wales Regional Tennis Centre A1
Oak Dr A3
Odeon C3
Park Ave A3
Park St A2
Peel St C1
Pen y Bryn C2
Pentre Felin C2
Penymaes Ave A3
Peoples Market B3
Percy St C2
Plas Coch Rd A1
Plas Coch Retail Pk A1
Police Station B3
Poplar Rd C2
Post Office A2/B3/C3
Powell Rd B3
Poyser St C2
Price's La A2
Primose Way B1
Princess St C1
Queen St B3
Queens Sq B2
Regent St B2
Rhosddu Rd A2/B2
Rhosnesni La A3
Rivulet Rd C3
Ruabon Rd C2
Ruthin Rd C1/C2
St Giles C3
St Giles Way C3
St James Ct A2
St Mary's B2
Salisbury Rd C3
Salop Rd C3
Sontley Rd C2
Spring Rd A2
Stanley St C3
Stansty Rd A2
Station Approach B2
Studio B2
Superstore B3/C1
Talbot Rd C2
Techniquest Glyndwr A2
Town Hill C2
Trevor St C2
Trinity St B2
Tuttle St C3
Vale Park A1
Vernon St B2
Vicarage Hill B2
Victoria Rd C2
Walnut St A2
War Memorial B3
Waterworld Leisure Centre B3
Watery Rd B1/B2
Wellington Rd C2
Westminster Dr A3
William Aston Hall A1
Windsor Rd A1
Wrecsam
Wrexham AFC A1
Wrexham Central B2
Wrexham General B2
Wrexham Maelor Hospital (A&E) B1
Wrexham Technology Park B1
Wynn Ave C2
Yale College B3
Yale Grove A3
Yorke St C3

York 200

Aldwark B2
Barbican Rd C3
Bar Convent Living Heritage Centre C1
Barley Hall B2
Bishopgate St C2
Bishopshill Senior C2
Bishopthorpe Rd C2
Blossom St C1
Bootham A1
Bootham Cres A1
Bootham Terr A1
Bridge St B2
Brook St A2
Brownlow St A2
Burton Stone La A1
Castle Museum C2
Castlegate B2
Cemetery Rd C3
Cherry St C2
City Screen B2
City Wall A2/B1/C3
Clarence St A2
Clementhorpe C2
Clifford St B2
Clifford's Tower B2
Clifton A1
Coach park A2
Coney St B2
Coppergate Ctr B2
Cromwell Rd C2
Crown Court C2
Davygate B2
Deanery Gdns A2
DIG B2
Dodsworth Ave A3
Eboracum Way A3
Ebor Industrial Est B3
Eldon St A2
Everyman C1
Fairfax House B2
Fire Station C3
Fishergate C3
Foss Islands Rd B3
Foss Islands Retail Park B3
Fossbank A3
Garden St A2
George St C3
Gillygate A2
Goodramgate B2
Grand Opera House B2
Grosvenor Terr A1
Guildhall B2
Hallfield Rd A3
Heslington Rd C3
Heworth Green A3
Holy Trinity B2
Hope St C3
Huntington Rd A3
Information Ctr B2
James St B3
Jorvik Viking Ctr B2
Kent St C3
Lawrence St C3
Layerthorpe A3
Leeman Rd B1
Lendal B2
Lendal Bridge B1
Library A2/B1
Longfield Terr A1
Lord Mayor's Walk A2
Lowther St A2
Mansion House B2
Margaret St C3
Marygate A1
Melbourne St C3
Merchant Adventurers' Hall B2
Merchant Taylors' Hall B2
Micklegate B1
Micklegate Bar C1
Monkgate A2
Moss St C1
Museum Gdns B1
Museum St B1
National Railway Museum B1
Navigation Rd B3
Newton Terr C2
North Pde A1
North St B2
Nunnery La C1
Nunthorpe Rd C1
Ouse Bridge B2
Paragon St C3
Park Grove A3
Park St C1
Parliament St B2
Peasholme Green B3
Penley's Grove St A2
Piccadilly B2
Police Station B2
Post Office B1/B2/C3
Priory St B1
Queen Anne's Rd A1
Regimental Mus B2
Richard III Experience at Monk Bar A2
Roman Bath B2
Rowntree Park C2
St Andrewgate B2
St Benedict Rd C1
St John St A2
St Olave's Rd A1
St Peter's Grove A1
St Saviourgate B2
Scarcroft Hill C1
Scarcroft Rd C1
Shambles, The B2
Shopmobility B2
Skeldergate C2
Skeldergate Bridge C2
Station Rd B1
Stonebow, The B2
Stonegate B2
Superstore A3
Sycamore Terrace A1
Terry Ave C2
Theatre Royal B2
Thorpe St C1
Toft Green B1
Tower St C2
Townend St A2
Treasurer's House A2
Trinity La B1
Undercroft Museum A2
Union Terrace A2
Victor St C2
Vine St C2
Walmgate B3
War Memorial B1
Wellington St C3
York Art Gallery A1
York Barbican C3
York Brewery B1
York Dungeon, The B2
York Minster A2
York St John University A2
York Station B1

Abbreviations used in the index

Aberdeen	Aberdeen City
Aberds	Aberdeenshire
Ald	Alderney
Anglesey	Isle of Anglesey
Angus	Angus
Argyll	Argyll and Bute
Bath	Bath and North East Somerset
BCP	Bournemouth, Christchurch and Poole
Bedford	Bedford
Blackburn	Blackburn with Darwen
Blackpool	Blackpool
Bl Gwent	Blaenau Gwent
Borders	Scottish Borders
Brack	Bracknell
Bridgend	Bridgend
Brighton	City of Brighton and Hove
Bristol	City and County of Bristol
Bucks	Buckinghamshire
Caerph	Caerphilly
Cambs	Cambridgeshire
Cardiff	Cardiff
Carms	Carmarthenshire
C Beds	Central Bedfordshire
Ceredig	Ceredigion
Ches E	Cheshire East
Ches W	Cheshire West and Chester
Clack	Clackmannanshire
Conwy	Conwy
Corn	Cornwall
Cumb	Cumbria
Darl	Darlington
Denb	Denbighshire
Derby	City of Derby
Derbys	Derbyshire
Devon	Devon
Dorset	Dorset
Dumfries	Dumfries and Galloway
Dundee	Dundee City
Durham	Durham
E Ayrs	East Ayrshire
Edin	City of Edinburgh
E Dunb	East Dunbartonshire
E Loth	East Lothian
E Renf	East Renfrewshire
Essex	Essex
E Sus	East Sussex
E Yorks	East Riding of Yorkshire
Falk	Falkirk
Fife	Fife
Flint	Flintshire
Glasgow	City of Glasgow
Glos	Gloucestershire
Gtr Man	Greater Manchester
Guern	Guernsey
Gwyn	Gwynedd
Halton	Halton
Hants	Hampshire
Hereford	Herefordshire
Herts	Hertfordshire
Highld	Highland
Hrtlpl	Hartlepool
Hull	Hull
Invclyd	Inverclyde
IoM	Isle of Man
IoW	Isle of Wight
Jersey	Jersey
Kent	Kent
Lancs	Lancashire
Leicester	City of Leicester
Leics	Leicestershire
Lincs	Lincolnshire
London	Greater London
Luton	Luton
Mbro	Middlesbrough
Medway	Medway
Mers	Merseyside
Midloth	Midlothian
M Keynes	Milton Keynes
Mon	Monmouthshire
Moray	Moray
M Tydf	Merthyr Tydfil
N Ayrs	North Ayrshire
Neath	Neath Port Talbot
NE Lincs	North East Lincolnshire
Newport	City and County of Newport
N Lanark	North Lanarkshire
N Lincs	North Lincolnshire
N Nhants	North Northamptonshire
Norf	Norfolk
Northumb	Northumberland
Nottingham	City of Nottingham
Notts	Nottinghamshire
N Som	North Somerset
N Yorks	North Yorkshire
Orkney	Orkney
Oxon	Oxfordshire
Pboro	Peterborough
Pembs	Pembrokeshire
Perth	Perth and Kinross
Plym	Plymouth
Powys	Powys
Ptsmth	Portsmouth
Reading	Reading
Redcar	Redcar and Cleveland
Renfs	Renfrewshire
Rhondda	Rhondda Cynon Taff
Rutland	Rutland
S Ayrs	South Ayrshire
Scilly	Scilly
S Glos	South Gloucestershire
Shetland	Shetland
Shrops	Shropshire
S Lanark	South Lanarkshire
Slough	Slough
Som	Somerset
Soton	Southampton
Southend	Southend-on-Sea
Staffs	Staffordshire
Stirling	Stirling
Stockton	Stockton-on-Tees
Stoke	Stoke-on-Trent
Suff	Suffolk
Sur	Surrey
Swansea	Swansea
Swindon	Swindon
S Yorks	South Yorkshire
T&W	Tyne and Wear
Telford	Telford and Wrekin
Thurrock	Thurrock
Torbay	Torbay
Torf	Torfaen
V Glam	The Vale of Glamorgan
Warks	Warwickshire
Warr	Warrington
W Berks	West Berkshire
W Dunb	West Dunbartonshire
Wilts	Wiltshire
Windsor	Windsor and Maidenhead
W Isles	Western Isles
W Loth	West Lothian
W Mid	West Midlands
W Nhants	West Northamptonshire
Wokingham	Wokingham
Worcs	Worcestershire
Wrex	Wrexham
W Sus	West Sussex
W Yorks	West Yorkshire
York	City of York

How to use the index

Example

Trudoxhill Som **24** E2

- grid square
- page number
- county or unitary authority

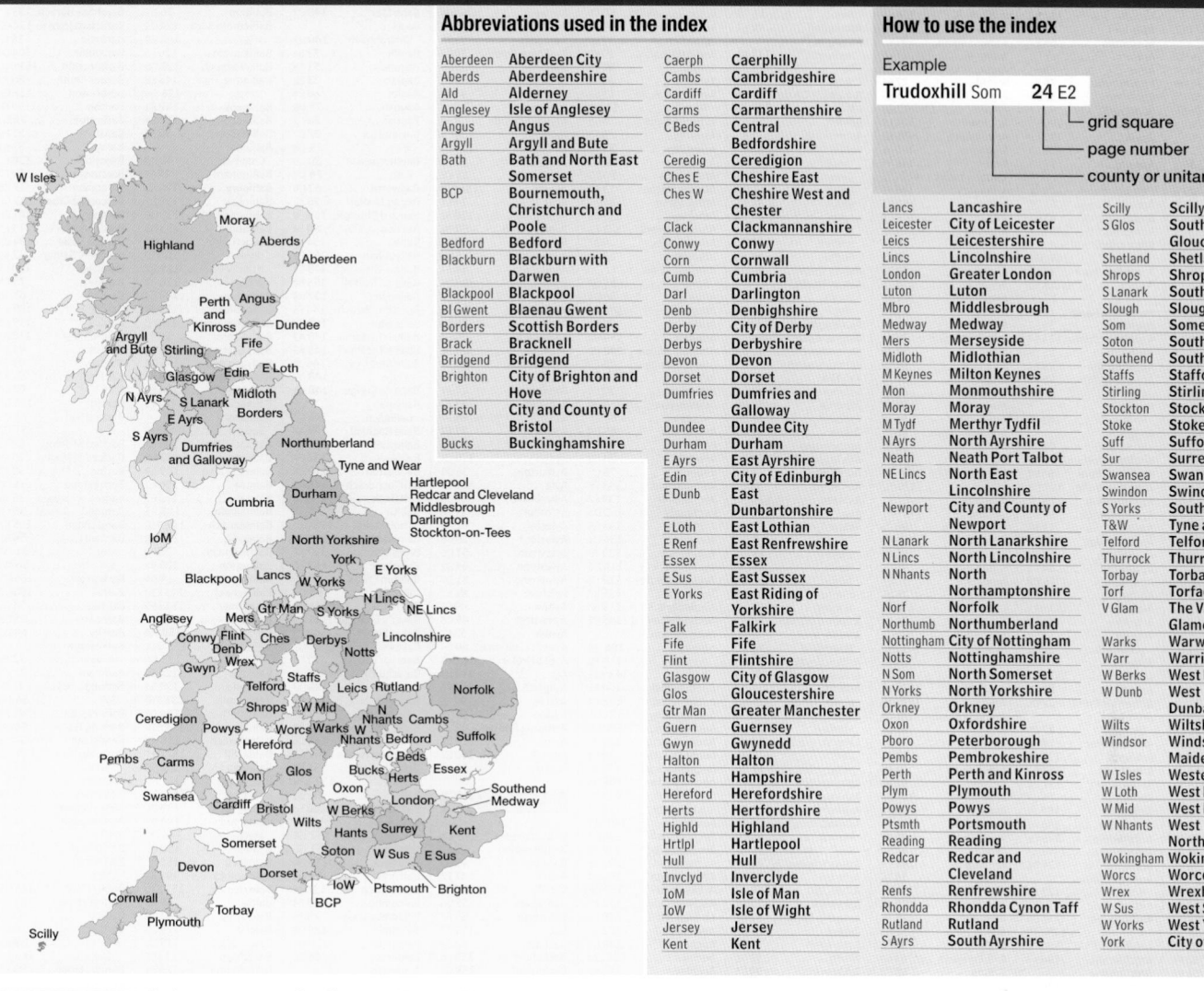

A

Abbas Combe 12 B5
Abberley 50 C2
Abberton Essex 43 C6
Worcs 50 D4
Abberwick 117 C7
Abbess Roding 42 C1
Abbey 11 C6
Abbey-cwm-hir . . . 48 B2
Abbeydale 88 F4
Abbey Dore 49 F5
Abbey Field 43 B5
Abbey Hulton 75 E6
Abbey St Bathans 122 C3
Abbeystead 93 D5
Abbey Town 107 D8
Abbey Village 86 B4
Abbey Wood 29 B5
Abbots Bickington . . 9 C5
Abbots Bromley . . . 62 B4
Abbotsbury 12 F3
Abbotsham 9 B6
Abbotskerswell 7 C6
Abbots Langley 40 D3
Abbots Leigh 23 B7
Abbotsley 54 D3
Abbots Morton 50 D5
Abbots Ripton 54 B3
Abbots Salford 51 D5
Abbotswood 14 B4
Abbotts Ann 25 E8
Abcott 49 B5
Abdon 61 F5
Aber 46 E3
Aberaeron 46 C3
Aberaman 34 D4
Aberangell 58 C5
Aber-Arad 46 F2
Aberarder 137 F7
Aberarder House . 138 B2
Aberarder Lodge . 137 F8
Aberargie 128 C3
Aberarth 46 C3
Aberavon 33 E8
Aber-banc 46 E2
Aberbeeg 35 D6
Abercanaid 34 D4
Abercarn 35 E6
Abercastle 44 B3
Abercegir 58 D5
Aberchirder 152 C6
Aber Cowarch 59 C5
Abercraf 34 C2
Abercrombie 129 D7
Abercych 45 E4
Abercynafon 34 C4
Abercynon 34 E4
Aberdalgie 128 B2
Aberdâr = Aberdare 34 D3
Aberdare = Aberdâr 34 D3
Aberdaron 70 E2
Aberdaugleddau = Milford Haven . . . 44 E4
Aberdeen 141 D8
Aberdesach 82 F4
Aberdour 128 F3
Aberdovey 58 E3
Aberdulais 34 D1
Aberedw 48 E2
Abereiddy 44 B2
Abererch 70 D4
Aberfan 34 D4
Aberfeldy 133 E5
Aberffraw 82 E3
Aberffrwd 47 B5
Aberford 95 F7
Aberfoyle 126 D4
Abergavenny = Y Fenni 35 C6
Abergele 72 B3
Aber-Giâr 46 E4
Abergorlech 46 F4
Abergwaun = Fishguard 44 B4
Abergwesyn 47 D7
Abergwili 33 B5
Abergwynant 58 C3
Aber-gwynfi 34 E2
Abergwyngregyn . . 83 D6
Abergynolwyn 58 D3
Aber-Hirnant 72 F3
Aberhonddu = Brecon 34 B4
Aberhosan 58 E5
Aberkenfig 34 F2
Aberlady 129 F6
Aberlemno 135 D5
Aberllefenni 58 D4
Abermagwr 47 B5
Abermaw = Barmouth 58 C3
Abermeurig 46 D4
Abermule 59 E8
Abernaint 59 B8
Abernant 32 B4
Aber-nant 34 D4
Abernethy 128 C3
Abernyte 134 F2
Aberpennar = Mountain Ash . . . 34 E4
Aberporth 45 D4
Aber-Rhiwlech 59 B6
Abersoch 70 E4
Abersychan 35 D6
Abertawe = Swansea 33 E7
Aberteifi = Cardigan 45 E3
Aberthin 22 B2
Abertillery = Abertyleri 35 D6
Abertridwr Caerph . . 35 F5
Powys 59 C7
Abertyleri = Abertillery 35 D6
Abertysswg 35 D5
Aberuthven 127 C8
Aber-Village 35 B5
Aberyscir 34 B3
Aberystwyth 58 F2
Abhainn Suidhe . . 154 G5
Abingdon-on-Thames 38 E4
Abinger Common . 28 E2
Abinger Hammer . . 27 E8
Abington 114 B2
Abington Pigotts . . 54 E4
Ab Kettleby 64 B4
Ab Lench 50 D5
Ablington Glos 37 D8
Wilts 25 E6
Abney 75 B8
Aboyne 140 E4
Abram 86 D4
Abriachan 151 H8
Abridge 41 E7
Abronhill 119 B7
Abson 24 B2
Abthorpe 52 E4
Abune-the-Hill . . 159 F3
Aby 79 B7
Acaster Malbis 95 E8
Acaster Selby 95 E8
Accrington 87 B5
Acha 146 F4
Achabraid 145 E7
Achachork 149 D9
Achafolla 124 D3
Achagary 157 D10
Achahoish 144 F6
Achalader 133 E8
Achallader 131 E7
Acha Mor 155 E8
Achanalt 150 E5
Achanamara 144 E6
Achandunie 151 D9
Ach'an Todhair . . . 130 B4
Achany 157 J8
Achaphubuil 130 B4
Acharacle 147 E9
Acharn Highld 147 F10
Perth 132 E4
Acharole 158 E4
Achath 141 C6
Achavanich 158 F3
Achavraat 151 G12
Achddu 33 D5
Achduart 156 J3
Achentoul 157 F11
Achfary 156 F5
Achgarve 155 H13
Achiemore Highld . 156 C6
Highld 157 D11
A'Chill 148 H7
Achiltibuie 156 J3
Achina 157 C10
Achinduich 157 J8
Achinduin 124 B4
Achingills 158 D3
Achintee Highld . . . 131 B5
Highld 150 G2
Achintraid 149 E13
Achlean 138 E4
Achleck 146 G7
Achluachrach 137 F5
Achlyness 156 D5
Achmelvich 156 G3
Achmore Highld . . 149 E13
Stirling 132 F2
Achnaba Argyll 124 B5
Argyll 145 E8
Achnabat 151 H8
Achnacarnin 156 F3
Achnacarry 136 F4
Achnacloich Argyll 125 B5
Highld 149 H10
Achnaconeran . . . 137 C7
Achnacraig 146 G7
Achnacroish 130 E2
Achnadrish 146 F7
Achnafalnich 125 C8
Achnagarron 151 E9
Achnaha 146 E7
Achnahanat 151 B8
Achnahannet 139 B5
Achnairn 157 H8
Achnaluachrach . . 157 J9
Achnasaul 136 F4
Achnasheen 150 F4
Achosnich 146 E7
Achranich 147 G10
Achreamie 157 C13
Achriabhach 131 C5
Achriesgill 156 D5
Achrimsdale 157 J12
Achtoty 157 C9
Achurch 65 F7
Achuvoldrach 157 D8
Achvaich 151 B10
Achvarasdal 157 C12
Ackergill 158 E5
Acklam Mbro 102 C2
N Yorks 96 C3
Ackleton 61 E7
Acklington 117 D8
Ackton 88 B5
Ackworth Moor Top 88 C5
Acle 69 C7
Acock's Green 62 F5
Acol 31 C7
Acomb Northumb . . 110 C2
York 95 D8
Aconbury 49 F7
Acre 87 B5
Acrefair 73 E6
Acre Street 15 E8
Acton Ches E 74 D3
Dorset 13 G7
London 41 F5
Shrops 60 F3
Suff 56 E2
Wrex 73 D7
Acton Beauchamp . 49 D8
Acton Bridge 74 B2
Acton Burnell 60 D5
Acton Green 49 D8
Acton Pigott 60 D5
Acton Round 61 E6
Acton Scott 60 F4
Acton Trussell 62 C3
Acton Turville 37 F5
Adbaston 61 B7
Adber 12 B3
Adderley 74 E3
Adderstone 123 F7
Addiewell 120 C2
Addingham 94 E3
Addington Bucks . . . 39 B7
Kent 29 D7
London 28 C4
Addinston 121 D8
Addiscombe 28 C4
Addlestone 27 C8
Addlethorpe 79 C8
Adel 95 F5
Adeney 61 C7
Adfa 59 D7
Adforton 49 B6
Adisham 31 D6
Adlestrop 38 B2
Adlingfleet 90 B2
Adlington 86 C4
Admaston Staffs . . . 62 B4
Telford 61 C6
Admington 51 E7
Adstock 52 F5
Adstone 52 D3
Adversane 16 B4
Advie 152 E1
Adwalton 88 B3
Adwell 39 E6
Adwick le Street . . . 89 D6
Adwick upon Dearne 89 D5
Adziel 153 C9
Ae Village 114 F2
Affleck 141 B7
Affpuddle 13 E6
Affric Lodge 136 B4
Afon-wen 72 B5
Afton 14 F4
Agglethorpe 101 F5
Agneash 84 D4
Aigburth 85 F4
Aiginis 155 D9
Aike 97 E6
Aikerness 159 C5
Aikers 159 J5
Aiketgate 108 E4
Aikton 108 D2
Ailey 48 E5
Ailstone 51 D7
Ailsworth 65 E8
Ainderby Quernhow 102 F1
Ainderby Steeple . 101 E8
Aingers Green 43 B7
Ainsdale 85 C4
Ainsdale-on-Sea . . 85 C4
Ainstable 108 E5
Ainsworth 87 C5
Ainthorpe 103 D5
Aintree 85 E4
Aird Argyll 124 E3
Dumfries 104 C4
Highld 149 A12
W Isles 155 D10
Aird a Mhachair . . 148 D2
Aird a' Mhulaidh . . 154 F6
Aird Asaig 154 G6
Aird Dhail 155 A9
Airdens 151 B9
Aird Mhidhinis . . . 148 H2
Aird Mhighe
W Isles 154 H6
W Isles 154 J5
Aird Mhor 148 H2
Aird of Sleat 149 H10
Airdrie 119 C7
Aird Thunga 155 D9
Airdtorrisdale 157 C9
Aird Uig 154 D5
Airidh a Bhruaich . 154 F7
Airieland 106 D4
Airmyn 89 B8
Airntully 133 F7
Airor 149 H12
Airth 127 F7
Airton 94 D2
Airyhassen 105 E7
Aisby Lincs 78 F3
Lincs 90 E2
Aisgernis 148 F2
Aiskew 101 F7
Aislaby N Yorks 103 D6
N Yorks 103 F5
Stockton 102 C2
Aisthorpe 78 A2
Aith Orkney 159 G3
Shetland 160 D8
Shetland 160 H5
Aithsetter 160 K6
Aitkenhead 112 D3
Aitnoch 151 H12
Akeld 117 B5
Akeley 52 F5
Akenham 56 E5
Albaston 6 B2
Alberbury 60 C3
Albourne 17 C6
Albrighton Shrops . . 60 C4
Shrops 62 D2
Alburgh 69 F5
Albury Herts 41 B7
Sur 27 E8
Albury End 41 B7
Alby Hill 81 D7
Alcaig 151 F8
Alcaston 60 F4
Alcester 51 D5
Alciston 18 E2
Alcombe Som 21 E8
Wilts 24 C3
Alconbury 54 B2
Alconbury Weald
Cambs 54 B3
Alconbury Weston . 54 B2
Aldbar Castle 135 D5
Aldborough Norf . . . 81 D7
N Yorks 95 C7
Aldbourne 25 B7
Aldbrough 97 F8
Aldbrough St John 101 C7
Aldbury 40 C2
Aldcliffe 92 C4
Aldclune 133 C6
Aldeburgh 57 D8
Aldeby 69 E7
Aldenham 40 E4
Alderbury 14 B2
Aldercar 76 E4
Alderford 68 C4
Alderholt 14 C2
Alderley 36 E4
Alderley Edge 74 B5
Aldermaston 26 C3
Aldermaston Wharf 26 C4
Alderminster 51 E7
Alder's End 49 E8
Aldersey Green 73 D8
Aldershot 27 D6
Alderton Glos 50 F5
Shrops 60 B4
Suff 57 E7
Wilts 37 F5
W Nhants 52 E5
Alderwasley 76 D3
Aldfield 95 C5
Aldford 73 D8
Aldham Essex 43 B5
Suff 56 E4
Aldie 151 C10
Aldingbourne 16 D3
Aldingham 92 B2
Aldington Kent 19 B7
Worcs 51 E5
Aldington Frith 19 B7
Aldochlay 126 E2
Aldreth 54 B5
Aldridge 62 D4
Aldringham 57 C8
Aldsworth 38 C1
Aldunie 140 B2
Aldwark Derbys 76 D2
N Yorks 95 C7
Aldwick 16 E3
Aldwincle 65 F7
Aldworth 26 B3
Alexandria 118 B3
Alfardisworthy 8 C4
Alfington 11 E6
Alfold 27 F8
Alfold Bars 27 F8
Alfold Crossways . . 27 F8
Alford Aberds 140 C4
Lincs 79 B7
Som 23 F8
Alfreton 76 D4
Alfrick 50 D2
Alfrick Pound 50 D2
Alfriston 18 E2
Algaltraig 145 F9
Algarkirk 79 F5
Alhampton 23 F8
Aline Lodge 154 F6
Alisary 147 D10
Alkborough 90 B2
Alkerton 51 E8
Alkham 31 E6
Alkington 74 F2
Alkmonton 75 F8
Alladale Lodge . . . 150 C7
Allaleigh 7 D6
Allanaquoich 139 E7
Allangrange Mains 151 F9
Allanton Borders . . 122 D4
N Lanark 119 D8
Allathasdal 148 H1
All Cannings 25 C5
Allendale Town . . . 109 D8
Allenheads 109 E8
Allensford 110 D3
Allens Green 41 C7
Allensmore 49 F6
Allenton 76 F3
Aller 12 B2
Allerby 107 F7
Allerford 21 E8
Allerston 103 F6
Allerthorpe 96 E3
Allerton Mers 86 F2
W Yorks 94 F4
Allerton Bywater . . 88 B5
Allerton Mauleverer 95 D7
Allesley 63 F7
Allestree 76 F3
Allet 3 B6
Allexton 64 D5
Allgreave 75 C6
Allhallows 30 B2
Allhallows-on-Sea 30 B2
Alligin Shuas 149 C13
Allimore Green 62 C2
Allington Lincs 77 E8

Allington *continued*
Wilts 25 C5
Wilts 25 F7
Allithwaite 92 B3
Alloa 127 E7
Allonby 107 E7
Alloway 112 C3
All Saints South Elmham . . . 69 F6
All Stretton 60 E4
Allt 33 D6
Alltchaorunn 131 D5
Alltforgan 59 B6
Alltmawr 48 E2
Alltnacaillich 156 E7
Allt na h-Airbhe . . 150 B4
Allt-nan-sùgh . . . 136 B2
Alltsigh 137 C7
Alltwalis 46 F3
Alltwen 33 D8
Alltyblaca 46 E4
Allwood Green 56 B4
Almeley 48 D5
Almer 13 E7
Almholme 89 D6
Almington 74 F4
Alminstone Cross . . . 8 B5
Almondbank 128 B2
Almondbury 88 C2
Almondsbury 36 F3
Alne 95 C7
Alness 151 E9
Alnham 117 C5
Alnmouth 117 C8
Alnwick 117 C7
Alperton 40 F4
Alphamstone 56 F2
Alpheton 56 D2
Alphington 10 E4
Alport 76 C2
Alpraham 74 D2
Alresford 43 B6
Alrewas 63 C5
Alsager 74 D4
Alsagers Bank 74 E5
Alsop en le Dale . . . 75 D8
Alston Cumb 109 E7
Devon 11 D8
Alstone 50 F4
Alstonefield 75 D8
Alswear 10 B2
Altandhu 156 H2
Altanduin 157 G11
Altarnun 8 F4
Altass 156 J7
Alterwall 158 D4
Altham 93 F7
Althorne 43 E5
Althorpe 90 D2
Alticry 105 D6

Altnabreac Station 157 E13
Altnacealgach Hotel 156 H5
Altnacraig 124 C4
Altnafeadh 131 D6
Altnaharra 157 F8
Altofts 88 B4
Alton Derbys 76 C3
Hants 26 F5
Staffs 75 E7
Alton Pancras 12 D5
Alton Priors 25 C6
Altrincham 87 F5
Altrua 136 F5
Altskeith 126 D3
Altyre House 151 F13
Alva 127 E7
Alvanley 73 B8
Alvaston 76 F3
Alvechurch 50 B5
Alvecote 63 D6
Alvediston 13 B7
Alveley 61 F7
Alverdiscott 9 B7
Alverstoke 15 E7
Alverstone 15 F6
Alverton 77 E7
Alves 152 B1
Alvescot 38 D2
Alveston S Glos 36 F3
Warks 51 D7
Alvie 138 D4
Alvingham 91 E7
Alvington 36 D3
Alwalton 65 E8
Alweston 12 C4
Alwinton 116 D5
Alwoodley 95 E5
Alyth 134 E2
Amatnatua 150 B7
Am Baile 148 G2
Ambergate 76 D3
Amber Hill 78 E5
Amberley Glos 37 D5
W Sus 16 C4
Amble 117 D8
Amblecote 62 F2
Ambler Thorn 87 B8
Ambleside 99 D5
Ambleston 44 C5
Ambrosden 39 C6
Am Buth 124 C4
Amcotts 90 C2
Amersham 40 E2
Amesbury 25 E6
Amington 63 D6
Amisfield 114 F2
Amlwch 82 B4
Amlwch Port 82 B4
Ammanford =Rhydaman 33 C7
Amod 143 E8
Amotherby 96 B3
Ampfield 14 B5
Ampleforth 95 B8
Ampney Crucis 37 D7
Ampney St Mary 37 D7
Ampney St Peter 37 D7
Amport 25 E7
Ampthill 53 F8
Ampton 56 B2
Amroth 32 D2
Amulree 133 F5
Anagach 139 B6
Anaheilt 130 C2
Anancaun 150 E3
An Caol 149 C11
Ancaster 78 E2
Anchor 59 F8
Anchorsholme 92 E3
An Cnoc 155 D9
Ancroft 123 E5
Ancrum 116 B2
Anderby 79 B8
Anderson 13 E6
Anderton 74 B3
Andover 25 E8
Andover Down 25 E8
Andoversford 37 C7
Andreas 84 C4
Anfield 85 E4
Angersleigh 11 C6
Angle 44 E3
An Gleann Ur 155 D9
Angmering 16 D4
Angram N Yorks 95 E8
N Yorks 100 E3
Anie 126 C4
Ankerville 151 D11
Anlaby 90 B4
Anmer 80 E3
Annan 107 C8
Annat Argyll 125 C6
Highld 149 C13
Anna Valley 25 E8
Annbank 112 B4
Annesley 76 D5
Annesley Woodhouse 76 D4
Annfield Plain 110 D4
Annifirth 160 J3
Annitsford 111 B5
Annscroft 60 D4
Ansdell 85 B4
Ansford 23 F8
Ansley 63 E6
Anslow 63 B6
Anslow Gate 63 B5
Anstey Herts 54 F5
Leics 64 D2
Anstruther Easter 129 D7
Anstruther Wester 129 D7
Ansty Hants 26 E5
Warks 63 F7
Wilts 13 B7
W Sus 17 B6
Anthill Common 15 C7
Anthorn 107 D8
Antingham 81 D8
An t-Ob =Leverburgh 154 J5
Anton's Gowt 79 E5
Antonshill 127 F7
Antony 5 D8
Anwick 78 D4
Anwoth 106 D2
Aoradh 142 B3
Apes Hall 67 E5
Apethorpe 65 E7
Apeton 62 C2
Apley 78 B4
Apperknowle 76 B3
Apperley 37 B5
Apperley Bridge 94 F4
Appersett 100 E3
Appin 130 E3
Appin House 130 E3
Appleby 90 C3
Appleby-in-Westmorland 100 B1
Appleby Magna 63 D7
Appleby Parva 63 D7
Applecross 149 D12
Applecross House 149 D12
Appledore Devon 11 C5
Devon 20 F3
Kent 19 C6
Appledore Heath 19 B6
Appleford 39 E5
Applegarthtown 114 F4
Appleshaw 25 E8
Applethwaite 98 B4
Appleton Halton 86 F3
Oxon 38 D4
Appleton-le-Moors 103 F5
Appleton-le-Street 96 B3
Appleton Roebuck 95 E8
Appleton Thorn 86 F4
Appleton Wiske 102 D1
Appletreehall 115 C8
Appletreewick 94 C3
Appley 11 B5
Appley Bridge 86 D3
Apse Heath 15 F6
Apsley End 54 F2
Apuldram 16 D2
Aquhythie 141 C6
Arabella 151 D11
Arbeadie 141 E5
Arberth =Narberth 32 C2
Arbirlot 135 E6
Arboll 151 C11
Arborfield 27 C5
Arborfield Cross 27 C5
Arborfield Garrison 27 C5
Arbourthorne 88 F4
Arbroath 135 E6
Arbuthnott 135 B7
Archiestown 152 D2
Arclid 74 C4
Ardachu 157 J9
Ardalanish 146 K6
Ardanaiseig 125 C6
Ardaneaskan 149 E13
Ardanstur 124 D4
Ardargie House Hotel 128 C2
Ardarroch 149 E13
Ardbeg Argyll 142 D5
Argyll 145 E10
Ardcharnich 150 C4
Ardchiavaig 146 K6
Ardchullarie More 126 C4
Ardchyle 126 B4
Ard-dhubh 149 D12
Arddleen 60 C2
Ardechvie 136 E4
Ardeley 41 B6
Ardelve 149 F13
Arden 126 F2
Ardens Grafton 51 D6
Ardentinny 145 E10
Ardentraive 145 F9
Ardeonaig 132 F3
Ardersier 151 F10
Ardessie 150 C3
Ardfern 124 E4
Ardgartan 125 E8
Ardgay 151 B8
Ardgour 130 C4
Ardheslaig 149 C12
Ardiecow 152 B5
Ardindrean 150 C4
Ardingly 17 B7
Ardington 38 F4
Ardlair 140 B4
Ardlamont House 145 G8
Ardleigh 43 B6
Ardler 134 E2
Ardley 39 B5
Ardlui 126 C2
Ardlussa 144 E5
Ardmair 150 B4
Ardmay 125 E8
Ardminish 143 D7
Ardmolich 147 D10
Ardmore Argyll 124 C3
Highld 151 C10
Highld 156 D5
Ardnacross 147 G8
Ardnadam 145 F10
Ardnagrask 151 G8
Ardnarff 149 E13
Ardnastang 130 C2
Ardnave 142 A3
Ardno 125 E7
Ardo 153 E8
Ardoch 133 F7
Ardochy House 136 D5
Ardo House 141 B8
Ardoyne 141 B5
Ardpatrick 144 G6
Ardpatrick House 144 H6
Ardpeaton 145 E11
Ardrishaig 145 E7
Ardross Fife 129 D7
Highld 151 D9
Ardrossan 118 E2
Ardross Castle 151 D9
Ardshealach 147 E9
Ardsley 88 D4
Ardslignish 147 E8
Ardtalla 142 C5
Ardtalnaig 132 F4
Ardtoe 147 D9
Ardtrostan 127 B5
Arduaine 124 D3
Ardullie 151 E8
Ardvasar 149 H11
Ardvorlich 126 B5
Ardwell 104 E5
Ardwell Mains 104 E5
Ardwick 87 E6
Areley Kings 50 B3
Arford 27 F6
Argoed Caerph 35 E5
Powys 47 C8
Arichamish 124 E5
Arichastlich 125 B8
Aridhglas 146 J6
Arileod 146 F4
Arinacrinachd 149 C12
Arinagour 146 F5
Arion 159 G3
Arisaig 147 C9
Ariundle 130 C2
Arkendale 95 C6
Arkesden 55 F5
Arkholme 93 B5
Arkleton 115 E6
Arkle Town 101 D5
Arkley 41 E5
Arksey 89 D6
Arkwright Town 76 B4
Arle 37 B6
Arlecdon 98 C2
Arlesey 54 F2
Arleston 61 C6
Arley 86 F4
Arlingham 36 C4
Arlington Devon 20 E5
E Sus 18 E2
Glos 37 D8
Armadale Highld 157 C10
W Loth 120 C2
Armadale Castle 149 H11
Armathwaite 108 E5
Arminghall 69 D5
Armitage 62 C4
Armley 95 F5
Armscote 51 E7
Armthorpe 89 D7
Arnabost 146 F5
Arncliffe 94 B2
Arncroach 129 D7
Arne 13 F7
Arnesby 64 E3
Arngask 128 C3
Arnisdale 149 G13
Arnish 149 D10
Arniston Engine 121 C6
Arnol 155 C8
Arnold E Yorks 97 E7
Notts 77 E5
Arnprior 126 E5
Arnside 92 B4
Aros Mains 147 G8
Arowry 73 F8
Arpafeelie 151 F9
Arrad Foot 99 F5
Arram 97 E6
Arrathorne 101 E7
Arreton 15 F6
Arrington 54 D4
Arrivain 125 B8
Arrochar 125 E8
Arrow 51 D5
Arthington 95 E5
Arthingworth 64 F4
Arthog 58 C3
Arthrath 153 E9
Arthurstone 134 E2
Artrochie 153 E10
Arundel 16 D4
Aryhoulan 130 C4
Asby 98 B2
Ascog 145 G10
Ascot 27 C7
Ascott 51 F8
Ascott-under-Wychwood 38 C3
Asenby 95 B6
Asfordby 64 C4
Asfordby Hill 64 C4
Asgarby Lincs 78 E4
Lincs 79 C6
Ash Kent 29 C6
Kent 31 D6
Som 12 B2
Sur 27 D6
Ashampstead 26 B3
Ashbocking 57 D5
Ashbourne 75 E8
Ashbrittle 11 B5
Ash Bullayne 10 D2
Ashburton 7 C5
Ashbury Devon 9 E7
Oxon 38 F2
Ashby 90 D3
Ashby by Partney 79 C7
Ashby cum Fenby 91 D6
Ashby de la Launde 78 D3
Ashby-de-la-Zouch 63 C7
Ashby Folville 64 C4
Ashby Magna 64 E2
Ashby Parva 64 F2
Ashby Puerorum 79 B6
Ashby St Ledgers 52 C3
Ashby St Mary 69 D6
Ashchurch 50 F4
Ashcombe 7 B7
Ashcott 23 F6
Ashdon 55 E6
Ashe 26 E3
Asheldham 43 D5
Ashen 55 E8
Ashendon 39 C7
Ashfield Carms 33 B7
Stirling 127 D6
Suff 57 C6
Ashfield Green 57 B6
Ashfold Crossways 17 B6
Ashford Devon 20 F4
Hants 14 C2
Kent 30 E4
Sur 27 B8
Ashford Bowdler 49 B7
Ashford Carbonell 49 B7
Ashford Hill 26 C3
Ashford in the Water 75 C8
Ashgill 119 E7
Ash Green 63 F7
Ashill Devon 11 C5
Norf 67 D8
Som 11 C8
Ashingdon 42 E4
Ashington Northumb 117 F8
Som 12 B3
W Sus 16 C5
Ashintully Castle 133 C8
Ashkirk 115 B7
Ashlett 15 D5
Ashleworth 37 B5
Ashley Cambs 55 C7
Ches E 87 F5
Devon 9 C8
Dorset 14 D2
Glos 37 E6
Hants 14 E3
Hants 25 F8
N Nhants 64 E4
Staffs 74 F4
Ashley Green 40 D2
Ashley Heath Dorset 14 D2
Staffs 74 F4
Ash Magna 74 F2
Ashmanhaugh 69 B6
Ashmansworth 26 D2
Ashmansworthy 8 C5
Ash Mill 10 B2
Ashmore 13 C7
Ashorne 51 D8
Ashover 76 C3
Ashow 51 B8
Ashprington 7 D6
Ash Priors 11 B6
Ashreigney 9 C8
Ash Street 56 E4
Ashtead 28 D2
Ash Thomas 10 C5
Ashton Ches W 74 C2
Corn 2 D5
Hants 15 C6
Hereford 49 C7
Invclyd 118 B2
N Nhants 65 F7
W Nhants 53 E5
Ashton Common 24 D3
Ashton-in-Makerfield 86 E3
Ashton Keynes 37 E7
Ashton under Hill 50 F4
Ashton-under-Lyne 87 E7
Ashton upon Mersey 87 E5
Ashurst Hants 14 C4
Kent 18 B2
W Sus 17 C5
Ashurstwood 28 F5
Ash Vale 27 D6
Ashwater 9 E5
Ashwell Herts 54 F3
Rutland 65 C5
Som 11 C8
Ashwellthorpe 68 E4
Ashwick 23 E8
Ashwicken 67 C7
Ashybank 115 C8
Askam in Furness 92 B2
Askern 89 C6
Askerswell 12 E3
Askett 39 D8
Askham Cumb 99 B7
Notts 77 B7
Askham Bryan 95 E8
Askham Richard 95 E8
Asknish 145 D8
Askrigg 100 E4
Askwith 94 E4
Aslackby 78 F3
Aslacton 68 E4
Aslockton 77 F7
Asloun 140 C4
Aspatria 107 E8
Aspenden 41 B6
Asperton 79 F5
Aspley Guise 53 F7
Aspley Heath 53 F7
Aspull 86 D4
Asselby 89 B8
Asserby 79 B7
Assington 56 F3
Assynt House 151 E8
Astbury 74 C5
Astcote 52 D4
Asterley 60 D3
Asterton 60 E3
Asthall 38 C2
Asthall Leigh 38 C3
Astley Shrops 60 C5
Warks 63 F7
Worcs 50 C2
Astley Abbotts 61 E7
Astley Bridge 86 C5
Astley Cross 50 C3
Astley Green 86 E5
Aston Ches E 74 E3
Ches W 74 B2
Derbys 88 F2
Hereford 49 B6
Herts 41 B5
Oxon 38 D3
Shrops 60 B5
Staffs 74 E4
S Yorks 89 F5
Telford 61 D6
W Mid 62 F4
Wokingham 39 F7
Aston Abbotts 39 B8
Aston Botterell 61 F6
Aston-by-Stone 75 F6
Aston Cantlow 51 D6
Aston Clinton 40 C1
Aston Crews 36 B3
Aston Cross 50 F4
Aston End 41 B5
Aston Eyre 61 E6
Aston Fields 50 C4
Aston Flamville 63 E8
Aston Ingham 36 B3
Aston juxta Mondrum 74 D3
Aston le Walls 52 D2
Aston Magna 51 F6
Aston Munslow 60 F5
Aston on Clun 60 F3
Aston-on-Trent 63 B8
Aston Rogers 60 D3
Aston Rowant 39 E7
Aston Sandford 39 D7
Aston Somerville 50 F5
Aston Subedge 51 E6
Aston Tirrold 39 F5
Aston Upthorpe 39 F5
Astrop 52 F3
Astwick 54 F3
Astwood M Keynes 53 E7
Worcs 50 D3
Astwood Bank 50 C5
Aswarby 78 F3
Aswardby 79 B6
Atcham 60 D5
Atch Lench 50 D5
Athelhampton 13 E5
Athelington 57 B6
Athelney 11 B8
Athelstaneford 121 B8
Atherington 9 B7
Atherstone 63 E7
Atherstone on Stour 51 D7
Atherton 86 D4
Atley Hill 101 D7
Atlow 76 E2
Attadale 150 H2
Attadale House 150 H2
Attenborough 76 F5
Atterby 90 E3
Attercliffe 88 F4
Attleborough Norf 68 E3
Warks 63 E7
Attlebridge 68 C4
Atwick 97 D7
Atworth 24 C3
Aubourn 78 C2
Auchagallon 143 E9
Auchallater 139 F7
Aucharnie 153 D6
Auchattie 141 E5
Auchavan 134 C1
Auchbreck 139 B8
Auchenback 118 D5
Auchenbainzie 113 E8
Auchenblae 135 B7
Auchenbrack 113 E7
Auchenbreck 145 E9
Auchencairn Dumfries 106 D4
Dumfries 114 F2
N Ayrs 143 F11
Auchencrosh 104 B5
Auchencrow 122 C4
Auchendinny 121 C5
Auchengray 120 D2
Auchenhalrig 152 B3
Auchenheath 119 E8
Auchenlochan 145 F8
Auchenmalg 105 D6
Auchensoul 112 E2
Auchentiber 118 E3
Auchertyre 149 F13
Auchgourish 138 C5
Auchincarroch 126 F3
Auchindrain 125 E6
Auchindrean 150 C4
Auchininna 153 D6
Auchinleck 113 B5
Auchinloch 119 B6
Auchinroath 152 C2
Auchintoul 140 C4
Auchiries 153 E10
Auchlee 141 E7
Auchleven 140 B5
Auchlochan 119 F8
Auchlossan 140 D4
Auchlunies 141 E7
Auchlyne 126 B4
Auchmacoy 153 E9
Auchmair 140 B2
Auchmantle 105 C5
Auchmillan 112 B5
Auchmithie 135 E6
Auchmuirbridge 128 D4
Auchmull 135 B5
Auchnacree 134 C4
Auchnagallin 151 H13
Auchnagatt 153 D9
Auchnaha 145 E8
Auchnashelloch 127 C6
Aucholzie 140 E2
Auchrannie 134 D2
Auchroisk 139 B6
Auchronie 140 F3
Auchterarder 127 C8
Auchteraw 137 D6
Auchterderran 128 E4
Auchterhouse 134 F3
Auchtermuchty 128 C4
Auchterneed 150 F7
Auchtertool 128 E4
Auchtertyre 152 C1
Auchtubh 126 B4
Auckengill 158 D5
Auckley 89 D7
Audenshaw 87 E7
Audlem 74 E3
Audley 74 D4
Audley End 56 F2
Auds 153 B6
Aughton E Yorks 96 F3
Lancs 85 D4
Lancs 93 C5
S Yorks 89 F5
Wilts 25 D7
Aughton Park 86 D2
Auldearn 151 F12
Aulden 49 D6
Auldgirth 114 F2
Auldhame 129 F7
Auldhouse 119 D6
Ault a'chruinn 136 B2
Aultanrynie 156 F6
Aultbea 155 J13
Aultdearg 150 E5
Aultgrishan 155 J12
Aultguish Inn 150 D6
Aultibea 157 G13
Aultiphurst 157 C11
Aultmore 152 C4
Aultnagoire 137 B8
Aultnamain Inn 151 C9
Aultnaslat 136 D4
Aulton 140 B5
Aundorach 139 C5
Aunsby 78 F3
Auquhorthies 141 B7
Aust 36 F2
Austendike 66 B2
Austerfield 89 E7
Austrey 63 D6
Austwick 93 C7
Authorpe 91 F8
Authorpe Row 79 B8
Avebury 25 C6
Aveley 42 F1
Avening 37 E5
Averham 77 D7
Aveton Gifford 6 E4
Avielochan 138 C5
Aviemore 138 C4
Avington Hants 26 F3
W Berks 25 C8
Avoch 151 F10
Avon 14 E2
Avonbridge 120 B2
Avon Dassett 52 E2
Avonmouth 23 B7
Avonwick 6 D5
Awbridge 14 B4
Awhirk 104 D4
Awkley 36 F2
Awliscombe 11 D6
Awre 36 D4
Awsworth 76 E4
Axbridge 23 D6
Axford Hants 26 E4
Wilts 25 B7
Axminster 11 E7
Axmouth 11 E7
Axton 85 F2
Aycliff 31 E7
Aycliffe 101 B7
Aydon 110 C3
Aylburton 36 D3
Ayle 109 E7
Aylesbeare 10 E5
Aylesbury 39 C8
Aylesby 91 D6
Aylesford 29 D8
Aylesham 31 D6
Aylestone 64 D2
Aylmerton 81 D7
Aylsham 81 E7
Aylton 49 F8
Aymestrey 49 C6
Aynho 52 F3
Ayot St Lawrence 40 C4
Ayot St Peter 41 C5
Ayr 112 B3
Aysgarth 101 F5
Ayside 99 F5
Ayston 65 D5
Aythorpe Roding 42 C1
Ayton 122 C5
Aywick 160 E7
Azerley 95 B5

B

Babbacombe 7 C7
Babbinswood 73 F7
Babcary 12 B3
Babel 47 F7
Babell 73 B5
Babraham 55 D6
Babworth 89 F7
Bac 155 C9
Bachau 82 C4
Backaland 159 E6
Backaskaill 159 C5
Backbarrow 99 F5
Backe 32 C3
Backfolds 153 C10
Backford 73 B8
Backford Cross 73 B7
Backhill Aberds 153 E7
Aberds 153 E10
Backhill of Clackriach 153 D9
Backhill of Fortree 153 D9
Backhill of Trustach 140 E5
Backies 157 J11
Backlass 158 E4
Back of Keppoch 147 C9
Back Rogerton 113 B5
Backwell 23 C6
Backworth 111 B6
Bacon End 42 C2
Baconsthorpe 81 D7
Bacton Hereford 49 F5
Norf 81 D9
Suff 56 C4
Bacton Green 56 C4
Bacup 87 B6
Badachro 149 A12
Badanloch Lodge 157 F10
Badavanich 150 F4
Badbury 38 F1
Badby 52 D3
Badcall 156 D5
Badcaul 150 B3
Baddeley Green 75 D6
Baddesley Clinton 51 B7
Baddesley Ensor 63 E6
Baddidarach 156 G3
Baddoch 139 F7
Baddock 151 F10
Badenscoth 153 E7
Badenyon 140 C2
Badger 61 E7
Badger's Mount 29 C5
Badgeworth 37 C6
Badgworth 23 D5
Badicaul 149 F12
Badingham 57 C7
Badlesmere 30 D4
Badlipster 158 F4
Badluarach 150 B2
Badminton 37 F5
Badnaban 156 G3
Badninish 151 B10
Badrallach 150 B3
Badsey 51 E5
Badshot Lea 27 E6
Badsworth 89 C5
Badwell Ash 56 C3
Bae Colwyn =Colwyn Bay 83 D8
Bagby 102 F2
Bag Enderby 79 B6
Bagendon 37 D7
Bagh a Chaisteil =Castlebay 148 J1
Baghasdal 148 G2
Bagh Mor 148 C3
Bagh Shiarabhagh 148 H2
Baghillt 73 B6
Baginton 51 B8
Baglan 33 E8
Bagley 60 B4
Bagnall 75 D6
Bagnor 26 C2
Bagshot Sur 27 C7
Wilts 25 C8
Bagthorpe Norf 80 D3
Notts 76 D4
Bagworth 63 D8
Bagwy Llydiart 35 B8
Bail Àrd Bhuirgh 155 B9
Baildon 94 F4
Baile 154 J4
Baile Ailein 155 E7
Baile a Mhanaich 148 C2
Baile an Truiseil 155 B8
Bailebeag 137 C8
Baile Boidheach 144 F6
Baile Glas 148 C3
Baile Mhartainn 148 A2
Baile Mhic Phail 148 A3
Baile Mor Argyll 146 J5
W Isles 148 B2
Baile na Creige 148 H1
Baile nan Cailleach 148 C2
Baile Raghaill 148 A2
Baileyhead 108 B5
Bailiesward 152 E4
Baillieston 119 C6
Bail'lochdrach 148 C3
Bail Uachdraich 148 B3
Bail'Ur Tholastaidh 155 C10
Bainbridge 100 E4
Bainsford 127 F7
Bainshole 152 E6
Bainton E Yorks 97 D5
Pboro 65 D7
Bairnkine 116 C2
Baker's End 41 C6
Baker Street 42 F2
Bakewell 76 C2
Bala =Y Bala 72 F3
Balachuirn 149 D10
Balavil 138 D3
Balbeg Highld 137 B7
Highld 150 H7
Balbeggie 128 B3
Balbithan 141 C6
Balbithan House 141 C7
Balblair Highld 151 B8
Highld 151 E10
Balby 89 D6
Balchladich 156 F3
Balchraggan Highld 151 G8
Highld 151 H8
Balchrick 156 D4
Balchrystie 129 D6
Balcladaich 137 B5
Balcombe 28 F4
Balcombe Lane 28 F4
Balcomie 129 C8
Balcurvie 128 D5
Baldersby 95 B6
Baldersby St James 95 B6
Balderstone 93 F6
Balderton Ches W 73 C7
Notts 77 D8
Baldhu 3 B6
Baldinnie 129 C6
Baldock 54 F3
Baldovie 134 F4
Baldrine 84 D4
Baldslow 18 D4
Baldwin 84 D3
Baldwinholme 108 D3
Baldwin's Gate 74 E4
Bale 81 D6
Balearn 153 C10
Balemartine 146 G2
Balephuil 146 G2
Balerno 120 C4
Balevullin 146 G2
Balfield 135 C5
Balfour 159 G5
Balfron 126 F4
Balfron Station 126 F4
Balgaveny 153 D6
Balgavies 135 D5
Balgonar 128 E2
Balgove 153 E8
Balgowan 138 E2
Balgown 149 B8
Balgrochan 119 B6
Balgy 149 C13
Balhaldie 127 D7
Balhalgardy 141 B6
Balham 28 B3
Balhary 134 E2
Baliasta 160 C8
Baligill 157 C11
Balintore Angus 134 D2
Highld 151 D11
Balintraid 151 D10
Balk 102 F2
Balkeerie 134 E3
Balkemback 134 F3
Balkholme 89 B8
Balkissock 104 A5
Ball 60 B3
Ballabeg 84 E2
Ballacannel 84 D4
Ballachulish 130 D4
Ballajora 84 C4
Ballaleigh 84 D3
Ballamodha 84 E2
Ballantrae 104 A4
Ballaquine 84 D4
Ballards Gore 43 E5
Ballasalla IoM 84 C3
IoM 84 E2
Ballater 140 E2
Ballaugh 84 C3
Ballaveare 84 E3
Ballcorach 139 B7
Ballechin 133 D6
Balleigh 151 C10
Ballencrieff 121 B7
Ballentoul 133 C5
Ball Haye Green 75 D6
Ball Hill 26 C2
Ballidon 76 D2
Balliemore Argyll 124 C4
Argyll 145 E9
Ballikinrain 126 F4
Ballimeanoch 125 D6
Ballimore Argyll 145 E8
Stirling 126 C4
Ballinaby 142 B3
Ballindean 128 B4
Ballingdon 56 E2
Ballinger Common 40 D2
Ballingham 49 F7
Ballingry 128 E3
Ballinlick 133 E6
Ballinluig 133 D6
Ballintuim 133 D8
Balloch Angus 134 D3
Highld 151 G10
N Lanark 119 B7
W Dunb 126 F2
Ballochan 140 E4
Ballochford 152 E3
Ballochmorrie 112 F2
Balls Cross 16 B3
Balls Green 43 B6
Ballygowan 146 G7
Ballygrant 142 B4
Ballyhaugh 146 F4
Balmacara 149 F13
Balmacara Square 149 F13
Balmaclellan 106 B3
Balmacneil 133 D6
Balmacqueen 149 A9
Balmae 106 E3
Balmaha 126 E3
Balmalcolm 128 D5
Balmeanach 149 D10
Balmedie 141 C8
Balmer Heath 73 F8
Balmerino 129 B5
Balmerlawn 14 D4
Balmichael 143 E10
Balmirmer 135 F5
Balmore Highld 149 D7
Highld 150 H6
Highld 151 G11
Perth 133 D6
Balmule 128 F4
Balmullo 129 B6
Balmungie 151 F10
Balnaboth 134 C3
Balnabruaich 151 E10
Balnabruich 158 H3
Balnacoil 157 H11
Balnacra 150 G2
Balnafoich 151 H9
Balnagall 151 C11
Balnaguard 133 D6
Balnahard Argyll 144 D3
Argyll 146 H7
Balnain 150 H7
Balnakeil 156 C6
Balnaknock 149 B9
Balnapaling 151 E10
Balne 89 C6
Balochroy 143 C8
Balone 129 C6
Balornock 119 C6
Balquharn 133 F7
Balquhidder 126 B4
Balsall 51 B7
Balsall Common 51 B7
Balsall Heath 62 F4
Balscott 51 E8
Balsham 55 D6
Baltasound 160 C8
Balterley 74 D4
Baltersan 105 C8
Balthangie 153 C8
Baltonsborough 23 F7
Balvaird 151 F8
Balvicar 124 D3
Balvraid Highld 149 G13
Highld 151 H11
Bamber Bridge 86 B3
Bambers Green 42 B1
Bamburgh 123 F7
Bamff 134 D2
Bamford Derbys 88 F3
Gtr Man 87 C6
Bampton Cumb 99 C7
Devon 10 B4
Oxon 38 D3
Bampton Grange 99 C7
Banavie 131 B5
Banbury 52 E2
Bancffosfelen 33 C5
Banchory 141 E5
Banchory-Devenick 141 D8
Bancycapel 33 C5
Bancyfelin 32 C4
Bancyffordd 46 F3
Bandirran 134 F2
Banff 153 B6
Bangor 83 D5
Bangor-is-y-coed =Bangor-on-Dee 73 E7
Bangor-on-Dee =Bangor-is-y-coed 73 E7
Banham 68 F3
Bank 14 D3
Bankend 107 C7
Bankfoot 133 F7
Bankglen 113 C6
Bankhead Aberdeen 141 C7
Aberds 141 D5
Bank Newton 94 D2
Banknock 119 B7
Banks Cumb 109 C5
Lancs 85 B4
Bankshill 114 F4
Bank Street 49 C8
Banningham 81 E8
Banniskirk House 158 E3
Bannister Green 42 B2
Bannockburn 127 E7
Banstead 28 D3
Bantham 6 E4
Banton 119 B7
Banwell 23 D5
Banyard's Green 57 B6
Bapchild 30 C3
Barabhas 155 C8
Barabhas Iarach 155 C8
Barabhas Uarach 155 B8
Barachandroman 124 C2
Barassie 118 F3
Baravullin 124 E4
Barbaraville 151 D10
Barber Booth 88 F2
Barbieston 112 C4
Barbon 99 F8
Barbridge 74 D3
Barbrook 21 E6
Barby 52 B3
Barcaldine 130 E3
Barcheston 51 F7
Barcombe 17 C8
Barcombe Cross 17 C8
Barden 101 E6
Bardennoch 113 E5
Barden Scale 94 D3
Bardfield Saling 42 B2
Bardister 160 F5
Bardney 78 C4
Bardon 63 C8
Bardon Mill 109 C7
Bardowie 119 B5
Bardrainney 118 B3
Bardsea 92 B3
Bardsey 95 E6
Bardwell 56 B3
Bare 92 C4
Barfad 145 G7
Barford Norf 68 D4
Warks 51 C7
Barford St John 52 F2
Barford St Martin 25 F5
Barford St Michael 52 F2
Barfrestone 31 D6
Bargod =Bargoed 35 E5
Bargoed =Bargod 35 E5
Bargrennan 105 B7
Barham Cambs 54 B2
Kent 31 D6
Suff 56 D5
Barharrow 106 D3
Barhill 106 C5
Bar Hill 54 C4
Barholm 65 C7
Barkby 64 D3
Barkestone-le-Vale 77 F7
Barkham 27 C5
Barking London 41 F7
Suff 56 D4
Barkingside 41 F7
Barking Tye 56 D4
Barkisland 87 C8
Barkston Lincs 78 E2
N Yorks 95 F7
Barkway 54 F4
Barlaston 75 F5
Barlavington 16 C3
Barlborough 76 B4
Barlby 96 F2
Barlestone 63 D8
Barley Herts 54 F4
Lancs 93 E8
Barley Mow 111 D5
Barleythorpe 64 D5
Barling 43 F5
Barlow Derbys 76 B3
N Yorks 89 B7
T&W 110 C4
Barmby Moor 96 E3
Barmby on the Marsh 89 B7
Barmer 80 D4
Barmoor Castle 123 F5
Barmoor Lane End 123 F6
Barmouth =Abermaw 58 C3
Barmpton 101 C8
Barmston 97 D7
Barnack 65 D7
Barnacle 63 F7
Barnard Castle 101 C5
Barnard Gate 38 C4
Barnardiston 55 E8
Barnbarroch 106 D5
Barnburgh 89 D5
Barnby 69 F7
Barnby Dun 89 D7
Barnby in the Willows 77 D8
Barnby Moor 89 F7
Barnes Street 29 E7
Barnet 41 E5
Barnetby le Wold 90 D4
Barney 81 D5
Barnham Suff 56 B2
W Sus 16 D3
Barnham Broom 68 D3
Barnhead 135 D6
Barnhill Ches W 73 D8
Dundee 134 F4
Moray 152 C1
Barnhills 104 B3
Barningham Durham 101 C5
Suff 56 B3
Barnoldby le Beck 91 D6
Barnoldswick 93 E8
Barns Green 16 B5
Barnsley Glos 37 D7
S Yorks 88 D4
Barnstaple 20 F4
Barnston Essex 42 C2
Mers 85 F3
Barnstone 77 F7
Barnt Green 50 B5
Barnton Ches W 74 B3
Edin 120 B4
Barnwell All Saints 65 F7
Barnwell St Andrew 65 F7
Barnwood 37 C5
Barochreal 124 C4
Barons Cross 49 D6
Barr 112 E2
Barra Castle 141 B6
Barrachan 105 E7
Barrack 153 D8
Barraglom 154 D6
Barrahormid 144 E6
Barran 124 C4
Barrapol 146 G2
Barras Aberds 141 F7

Barras *continued*
Cumb 100 C3
Barrasford 110 B2
Barravullin 124 E4
Barregarrow 84 D3
Barrhead 118 D4
Barrhill 112 F2
Barrington Cambs 54 E4
Som 11 C8
Barripper 2 C5
Barrmill 118 D3
Barrock 158 C4
Barrock House 158 D4
Barrow Lancs 93 F7
Rutland 65 C5
Suff 55 C8
Barroway Drove 67 D5
Barrowburn 116 C4
Barrowby 77 F8
Barrowcliff 103 F8
Barrowden 65 D6
Barrowford 93 F8
Barrow Green 30 C3
Barrow Gurney 23 C7
Barrow Haven 90 B4
Barrow-in-Furness 92 C2
Barrow Island 92 C1
Barrow Nook 86 D2
Barrows Green
Ches E 74 D3
Cumb 99 F7
Barrow's Green 86 F3
Barrow Street 24 F3
Barrow upon Humber 90 B4
Barrow upon Soar 64 C2
Barrow upon Trent 63 B7
Barry 135 F5
Barry = *Y Barri* 22 C3
Barry Island 22 C3
Barsby 64 C3
Barsham 69 F6
Barston 51 B7
Bartestree 49 E7
Barthol Chapel 153 E8
Barthomley 74 D4
Bartley 14 C4
Bartley Green 62 F4
Bartlow 55 E6
Barton Cambs 54 D5
Ches W 73 D8
Glos 37 B8
Lancs 85 D4
Lancs 92 F5
N Yorks 101 D7
Oxon 39 D5
Torbay 7 C7
Warks 51 D6
Barton Bendish 67 D7
Barton Hartshorn 52 F4
Barton in Fabis 76 F5
Barton in the Beans 63 D7
Barton-le-Clay 53 F8
Barton-le-Street 96 B3
Barton-le-Willows 96 C3
Barton Mills 55 B8
Barton on Sea 14 E3
Barton on the Heath 51 F7
Barton St David 23 F7
Barton Seagrave 53 B6
Barton Stacey 26 E2
Barton Turf 69 B6
Barton-under-Needwood 63 C5
Barton-upon-Humber 90 B4
Barton Waterside 90 B4
Barugh 88 D4
Barway 55 B6
Barwell 63 E8
Barwick Herts 41 C6
Som 12 C3
Barwick in Elmet 95 F6
Baschurch 60 B4
Bascote 52 C2
Basford Green 75 D6
Bashall Eaves 93 E6
Bashley 14 E3
Basildon 42 F3
Basingstoke 26 D4
Baslow 76 B2
Bason Bridge 22 E5
Bassaleg 35 F6
Bassenthwaite 108 F2
Bassett 14 C5
Bassingbourn 54 E4
Bassingfield 77 F6
Bassingham 78 C2
Bassingthorpe 65 B6
Basta 160 D7
Baston 65 C8
Bastwick 69 C7
Baswick Steer 97 E6
Batchworth Heath 40 E3
Batcombe Dorset 12 D4
Som 23 F8
Bate Heath 74 B3
Batford 40 C4
Bath 24 C2
Bathampton 24 C2
Bathealton 11 B5
Batheaston 24 C2
Bathford 24 C2
Bathgate 120 C2
Bathley 77 D7
Bathpool Corn 5 B7
Som 11 B7
Bathville 120 C2
Batley 88 B3
Batsford 51 F6
Battersby 102 D3
Battersea 28 B3
Battisborough Cross 6 E3
Battisford 56 D4
Battisford Tye 56 D4
Battle E Sus 18 D4
Powys 48 F2
Battledown 37 B6
Battlefield 60 C5
Battlesbridge 42 E3
Battlesden 40 B2
Battlesea Green 57 B6
Battleton 10 B4
Battram 63 D8
Battramsley 14 E4
Baughton 50 E3
Baughurst 26 D3
Baulking 38 E3
Baumber 78 B5
Baunton 37 D7
Baverstock 24 F5
Bawburgh 68 D4
Bawdeswell 81 E6
Bawdrip 22 F5
Bawdsey 57 E7
Bawtry 89 E7
Baxenden 87 B5
Baxterley 63 E6
Baybridge 15 B6
Baycliff 92 B2
Baydon 25 B7
Bayford Herts 41 D6
Som 12 B5
Bayles 109 E7
Baylham 56 D5
Baynard's Green 39 B5
Bayston Hill 60 D4
Baythorn End 55 E8
Bayton 49 B8
Beach 130 D1
Beachampton 53 F5
Beachamwell 67 D7
Beachans 151 G13
Beacharr 143 D7
Beachborough 19 B8
Beachley 36 E2
Beacon 11 D6
Beacon End 43 B5
Beacon Hill 27 F6
Beacon's Bottom 39 E7
Beaconsfield 40 F2
Beacrabhaic 154 H6
Beadlam 102 F4
Beadlow 54 F2
Beadnell 117 B8
Beaford 9 C7
Beal Northumb 123 E6
N Yorks 89 B6
Beamhurst 75 F7
Beaminster 12 D2
Beamish 110 D5
Beamsley 94 D3
Bean 29 B6
Beanacre 24 C4
Beanley 117 C6
Beaquoy 159 F4
Bear Cross 13 E8
Beardwood 86 B4
Beare Green 28 E2
Bearley 51 C6
Bearnus 146 G6
Bearpark 110 E5
Bearsbridge 109 D7
Bearsden 118 B5
Bearsted 29 D8
Bearstone 74 F4
Bearwood BCP 13 E8
Hereford 49 D5
W Mid 62 F4
Beattock 114 D3
Beauchamp Roding 42 C1
Beauchief 88 F4
Beaufort 35 C5
Beaufort Castle 151 G8
Beaulieu 14 D4
Beauly 151 G8
Beaumaris 83 D6
Beaumont Cumb 108 D3
Essex 43 B7
Beaumont Hill 101 C7
Beausale 51 B7
Beauworth 15 B6
Beaworthy 9 E6
Beazley End 42 B3
Bebington 85 F4
Bebside 117 F8
Beccles 69 E7
Becconsall 86 B2
Beckbury 61 D7
Beckenham 28 C4
Beckermet 98 D2
Beckfoot Cumb 98 D3
Cumb 107 E7
Beck Foot 99 E8
Beckford 50 F4
Beckhampton 25 C5
Beck Hole 103 D6
Beckingham Lincs 77 D8
Notts 89 F8
Beckington 24 D3
Beckley E Sus 19 C5
Hants 14 E3
Oxon 39 C5
Beck Row 55 B7
Beck Side 98 F4
Beckton 41 F7
Beckwithshaw 95 D5
Becontree 41 F7
Bedale 101 F7
Bedburn 110 F4
Bedchester 13 C6
Beddau 34 F4
Beddgelert 71 C6
Beddingham 17 D8
Beddington 28 C4
Bedfield 57 C6
Bedford 53 D8
Bedham 16 B4
Bedhampton 15 D8
Bedingfield 57 C5
Bedlam 95 C5
Bedlington 117 F8
Bedlington Station 117 F8
Bedlinog 34 D4
Bedminster 23 B7
Bedmond 40 D3
Bednall 62 C3
Bedrule 116 C2
Bedstone 49 B5
Bedwas 35 F5
Bedworth 63 F7
Bedworth Heath 63 F7
Bed-y-coedwr 71 E8
Beeby 64 D3
Beech Hants 26 F4
Staffs 75 F5
Beech Hill Gtr Man 86 D3
W Berks 26 C4
Beechingstoke 25 D5
Beedon 26 B2
Beeford 97 D7
Beeley 76 C2
Beelsby 91 D6
Beenham 26 C3
Beeny 8 E3
Beer 11 F7
Beercrocombe 11 B8
Beer Hackett 12 C3
Beesands 7 E6
Beesby 91 F8
Beeson 7 E6
Beeston C Beds 54 E2
Ches W 74 D2
Norf 68 C2
Notts 76 F5
W Yorks 95 F5
Beeston Regis 81 C7
Beeswing 107 C5
Beetham 92 B4
Beetley 68 C2
Begbroke 38 C4
Begelly 32 D2
Beggar's Bush 48 C4
Beguildy 48 B3
Beighton Norf 69 D6
S Yorks 88 F5
Beighton Hill 76 D2
Beith 118 D3
Bekesbourne 31 D5
Belaugh 69 C5
Belbroughton 50 B4
Belchamp Otten 56 E2
Belchamp St Paul 55 E8
Belchamp Walter 56 E2
Belchford 79 B5
Belford 123 F7
Belhaven 122 B2
Belhelvie 141 C8
Belhinnie 140 B3
Bellabeg 140 C2
Bellamore 112 F2
Bellanoch 144 D6
Bellaty 134 D2
Bell Bar 41 D5
Bell Busk 94 D2
Belleau 79 B7
Bellehiglash 152 E1
Bell End 50 B4
Bellerby 101 E6
Bellever 6 B4
Belliehill 135 C5
Bellingdon 40 D2
Bellingham 116 F4
Belloch 143 E7
Bellochantuy 143 E7
Bell o'th'Hill 74 E2
Bellsbank 112 D4
Bellshill N Lanark 119 C7
Northumb 123 F7
Bellspool 120 F4
Bellsquarry 120 C3
Bells Yew Green 18 B3
Belmaduthy 151 F9
Belmesthorpe 65 C7
Belmont Blackburn 86 C4
London 28 C3
S Ayrs 112 B3
Shetland 160 C7
Belnacraig 140 C2
Belowda 4 C4
Belper 76 E3
Belper Lane End 76 E3
Belsay 110 B4
Belses 115 B8
Belsford 7 D5
Belstead 56 E5
Belston 112 B3
Belstone 9 E8
Belthorn 86 B5
Beltinge 31 C5
Beltoft 90 D2
Belton Leics 63 B8
Lincs 78 F2
N Lincs 89 D8
Norf 69 D7
Belton in Rutland 64 D5
Beltring 29 E7
Belts of Collonach 141 E5
Belvedere 29 B5
Belvoir 77 F8
Bembridge 15 F7
Bemersyde 121 F8
Bemerton 25 F6
Bempton 97 B7
Benacre 69 F8
Ben Alder Lodge 132 B2
Ben Armine Lodge 157 H10
Benbuie 113 E7
Ben Casgro 155 E9
Benderloch 124 B5
Bendronaig Lodge 150 H3
Benenden 18 B5
Benfield 105 C7
Bengate 69 B6
Bengeworth 50 E5
Benhall Green 57 C7
Benhall Street 57 C7
Benholm 135 C8
Beningbrough 95 D8
Benington Herts 41 B5
Lincs 79 E6
Benllech 82 C5
Benmore Argyll 145 E10
Stirling 126 B3
Benmore Lodge 156 H6
Bennacott 8 E4
Bennan 143 F10
Benniworth 91 F6
Benover 29 E8
Bensham 110 C5
Benslie 118 E3
Benson 39 E6
Bent 135 B6
Bent Gate 87 B5
Benthall Northumb 117 B8
Shrops 61 D6
Bentham 37 C6
Benthoul 141 D7
Bentlawnt 60 D3
Bentley E Yorks 97 F6
Hants 27 E5
Suff 56 F5
S Yorks 89 D6
Warks 63 E6
Worcs 50 C4
Bentley Heath 51 B6
Benton 21 F5
Bentpath 115 E6
Bents 120 C2
Bentworth 26 E4
Benvie 134 F3
Benwick 66 E3
Beoley 51 C5
Beoraidbeg 147 B9
Bepton 16 C2
Berden 41 B7
Bere Alston 6 C2
Bere Ferrers 6 C2
Berepper 3 D5
Bere Regis 13 E6
Bergh Apton 69 D6
Berinsfield 39 E5
Berkeley 36 E3
Berkhamsted 40 D2
Berkley 24 E3
Berkswell 51 B7
Bermondsey 28 B4
Bernera 149 F13
Bernice 145 D10
Bernisdale 149 C9
Berrick Salome 39 E6
Berriedale 158 H3
Berrier 99 B5
Berriew 59 D8
Berrington Northumb 123 E6
Shrops 60 D5
Berrow 22 D5
Berrow Green 50 D2
Berry Down Cross 20 E4
Berryfield 39 C7
Berry Hill Glos 36 C2
Pembs 45 E2
Berryhillock 152 B5
Berrynarbor 20 E4
Berry Pomeroy 7 C6
Bersham 73 E7
Berstane 159 G5
Berwick 18 E2
Berwick Bassett 25 B5
Berwick Hill 110 B4
Berwick St James 25 F5
Berwick St John 13 B7
Berwick St Leonard 24 F4
Berwick-upon-Tweed 123 D5
Bescar 85 C4
Besford 50 E4
Bessacarr 89 D7
Bessels Leigh 38 D4
Bessingby 97 C7
Bessingham 81 D7
Bestbeech Hill 18 B3
Besthorpe Norf 68 E3
Notts 77 C8
Bestwood 77 E5
Bestwood Village 77 E5
Beswick 97 E6
Betchworth 28 E3
Bethania Ceredig 46 C4
Gwyn 71 C8
Gwyn 83 F6
Bethel Anglesey 82 D3
Gwyn 72 F3
Gwyn 82 E5
Bethersden 30 E3
Bethesda Gwyn 83 E6
Pembs 32 C1
Bethlehem 33 B7
Bethnal Green 41 F6
Betley 74 E4
Betsham 29 B7
Betteshanger 31 D7
Bettiscombe 11 E8
Bettisfield 73 F8
Betton Shrops 60 D3
Shrops 74 F3
Bettws Bridgend 34 F3
Mon 35 C6
Newport 35 E6
Bettws Cedewain 59 E8
Bettws Gwerfil Goch 72 E4
Bettws Ifan 46 E2
Bettws Newydd 35 D7
Bettws-y-crwyn 60 F2
Bettyhill 157 C10
Betws 33 C7
Betws Bledrws 46 D4
Betws-Garmon 82 F5
Betws-y-Coed 83 F7
Betws-yn-Rhos 72 B3
Beulah Ceredig 45 E4
Powys 47 D8
Bevendean 17 D7
Bevercotes 77 B6
Beverley 97 F6
Beverston 37 E5
Bevington 36 E3
Bewaldeth 108 F2
Bewcastle 109 B5
Bewdley 50 B2
Bewerley 94 C4
Bewholme 97 D7
Bexhill 18 E4
Bexley 29 B5
Bexleyheath 29 B5
Bexwell 67 D6
Beyton 56 C3
Bhaltos 154 D5
Bhatarsaigh 148 J1
Bibury 37 D8
Bicester 39 B5
Bickenhall 11 C7
Bickenhill 63 F5
Bicker 78 F5
Bickershaw 86 D4
Bickerstaffe 86 D2
Bickerton Ches E 74 D2
N Yorks 95 D7
Bickington Devon 7 B5
Devon 20 F4
Bickleigh Devon 6 C3
Devon 10 D4
Bickleton 20 F4
Bickley 28 C5
Bickley Moss 74 E2
Bicknacre 42 D3
Bicknoller 22 F3
Bicknor 30 D2
Bickton 14 C2
Bicton Shrops 60 C4
Shrops 60 F2
Bidborough 29 E6
Biddenden 19 B5
Biddenham 53 E8
Biddestone 24 B3
Biddisham 23 D5
Biddlesden 52 E4
Biddlestone 117 D5
Biddulph 75 D5
Biddulph Moor 75 D6
Bideford 9 B6
Bidford-on-Avon 51 D6
Bidston 85 E3
Bielby 96 E3
Bieldside 141 D7
Bierley IoW 15 G6
W Yorks 94 F4
Bierton 39 C8
Bigbury 6 E4
Bigbury on Sea 6 E4
Bigby 90 D4
Biggar Cumb 92 C1
S Lanark 120 F3
Biggin Derbys 75 D8
Derbys 76 E2
N Yorks 95 F8
Biggings 160 G3
Biggin Hill 28 D5
Biggleswade 54 E2
Bighouse 157 C11
Bighton 26 F4
Bignor 16 C3
Big Sand 149 A12
Bigton 160 L5
Bilberry 4 C5
Bilborough 76 E5
Bilbrook 22 E2
Bilbrough 95 E8
Bilbster 158 E4
Bildershaw 101 B7
Bildeston 56 E3
Billericay 42 E2
Billesdon 64 D4
Billesley 51 D6
Billingborough 78 F4
Billinge 86 D3
Billingford 81 E6
Billingham 102 B2
Billinghay 78 D4
Billingley 88 D5
Billingshurst 16 B4
Billingsley 61 F7
Billington C Beds 40 B2
Lancs 93 F7
Billockby 69 C7
Billy Row 110 F4
Bilsborrow 92 F5
Bilsby 79 B7
Bilsham 16 D3
Bilsington 19 B7
Bilson Green 36 C3
Bilsthorpe 77 C6
Bilsthorpe Moor 77 D6
Bilston Midloth 121 C5
W Mid 62 E3
Bilstone 63 D7
Bilting 30 E4
Bilton E Yorks 97 F7
Northumb 117 C8
Warks 52 B2
Bilton in Ainsty 95 E7
Bimbister 159 G4
Binbrook 91 E6
Binchester Blocks 110 F5
Bincombe 12 F4
Bindal 151 C12
Binegar 23 E8
Binfield 27 B6
Binfield Heath 26 B5
Bingfield 110 B2
Bingham 77 F7
Bingley 94 F4
Bings Heath 60 C5
Binham 81 D5
Binley Hants 26 D2
W Mid 51 B8
Binley Woods 51 B8
Binniehill 119 B8
Binsoe 94 B5
Binstead 15 E6
Binsted 27 E5
Binton 51 D6
Bintree 81 E6
Binweston 60 D3
Birch Essex 43 C5
Gtr Man 87 D6
Bircham Newton 80 D3
Bircham Tofts 80 D3
Birchanger 41 B8
Birchencliffe 88 C2
Bircher 49 C6
Birch Green 43 C5
Birchgrove Cardiff 22 B3
Swansea 33 E8
Birch Heath 74 C2
Birch Hill 74 B2
Birchington 31 C6
Birchmoor 63 D6
Birchover 76 C2
Birch Vale 87 F8
Birchwood Lincs 78 C2
Warr 86 E4
Bircotes 89 E7
Birdbrook 55 E8
Birdforth 95 B7
Birdham 16 E2
Birdholme 76 C3
Birdingbury 52 C2
Birdlip 37 C6
Birdsall 96 C4
Birds Edge 88 D3
Birdsgreen 61 F7
Birdsmoor Gate 11 D8
Birdston 119 B6
Birdwell 88 D4
Birdwood 36 C4
Birgham 122 F3
Birkby 101 D8
Birkdale 85 C4
Birkenhead 85 F4
Birkenhills 153 D7
Birkenshaw N Lanark 119 C6
W Yorks 88 B3
Birkhall 140 E2
Birkhill Angus 134 F3
Borders 114 C5
Birkholme 65 B6
Birkin 89 B6
Birley 49 D6
Birling Kent 29 C7
Northumb 117 D8
Birling Gap 18 F2
Birlingham 50 E4
Birmingham 62 F4
Birnam 133 E7
Birse 140 E4
Birsemore 140 E4
Birstall Leics 64 D2
W Yorks 88 B3
Birstwith 94 D5
Birthorpe 78 F4
Birtley Hereford 49 C5
Northumb 109 B8
T&W 111 D5
Birts Street 50 F2
Bisbrooke 65 E5
Biscathorpe 91 F6
Biscot 40 B3
Bisham 39 F8
Bishampton 50 D4
Bish Mill 10 B2
Bishop Auckland 101 B7
Bishopbridge 90 E4
Bishopbriggs 119 C6
Bishop Burton 97 F5
Bishop Middleham 111 F6
Bishopmill 152 B2
Bishop Monkton 95 C6
Bishop Norton 90 E3
Bishopsbourne 31 D5
Bishops Cannings 24 C5
Bishop's Castle 60 F3
Bishop's Caundle 12 C4
Bishop's Cleeve 37 B6
Bishops Frome 49 E8
Bishop's Green 42 C2
Bishop's Hull 11 B7
Bishop's Itchington 51 D8
Bishops Lydeard 11 B6
Bishops Nympton 10 B2
Bishop's Offley 61 B7
Bishop's Stortford 41 B7
Bishop's Sutton 26 F4
Bishop's Tachbrook 51 C8
Bishops Tawton 20 F4
Bishopsteignton 7 B7
Bishopstoke 15 C5
Bishopston 33 F6
Bishopstone Bucks 39 C8
E Sus 17 D8
Hereford 49 E6
Swindon 38 F2
Wilts 13 B8
Bishopstrow 24 E3
Bishop Sutton 23 D7
Bishop's Waltham 15 C6
Bishopswood 11 C7
Bishop's Wood 62 D2
Bishopsworth 23 C7
Bishop Thornton 95 C5
Bishopthorpe 95 E8
Bishopton Darl 102 B1
Dumfries 105 E8
N Yorks 95 B6
Renfs 118 B4
Warks 51 D6
Bishop Wilton 96 D3
Bishton 35 F7
Bisley Glos 37 D6
Sur 27 D7
Bispham 92 E3
Bispham Green 86 C2
Bissoe 3 B6
Bisterne Close 14 D3
Bitchfield 65 B6
Bittadon 20 E4
Bittaford 6 D4
Bittering 68 C2
Bitterley 49 B7
Bitterne 15 C5
Bitteswell 64 F2
Bitton 23 C8
Bix 39 F7
Bixter 160 H5
Blaby 64 E2
Blackacre 114 E3
Blackadder West 122 D4
Blackawton 7 D6
Blackborough 11 D5
Blackborough End 67 C6
Black Bourton 38 D2
Blackboys 18 C2
Blackbrook Derbys 76 E3
Mers 86 E3
Staffs 74 F4
Blackburn Aberds 141 C7
Aberds 152 E5
Blackburn 86 B4
W Loth 120 C2
Black Callerton 110 C4
Black Clauchrie 112 F2
Black Corries Lodge 131 D6
Blackcraig 113 F7
Black Crofts 124 B5
Blackden Heath 74 B4
Blackdog 141 C8
Black Dog 10 D3
Blackfell 111 D5
Blackfield 14 D5
Blackford Cumb 108 C3
Perth 127 D7
Som 12 B4
Som 23 E6
Blackfordby 63 C7
Blackgang 15 G5
Blackhall Colliery 111 F7
Blackhall Mill 110 D4
Blackhall Rocks 111 F7
Blackham 29 F5
Blackhaugh 121 F7
Blackheath Essex 43 B6
Suff 57 B8
Sur 27 E8
W Mid 62 F3
Black Heddon 110 B3
Blackhill Aberds 153 C10
Aberds 153 D10
Highld 149 C8
Blackhills Highld 151 F12
Moray 152 C2
Blackhorse 23 B8
Blackland 24 C5
Black Lane 87 D5
Blacklaw 153 C6
Blackley 87 D6
Blacklunans 134 C1
Black Marsh 60 E3
Blackmill 34 F3
Blackmoor 27 F5
Blackmoor Gate 21 E5
Blackmore 42 D2
Blackmore End
Essex 55 F8
Herts 40 C4
Black Mount 131 E6
Blackness 120 B3
Blacknest 27 E5
Black Notley 42 B3
Blacko 93 E8
Black Pill 33 E7
Blackpool Blackpool 92 F3
Devon 7 E6
Pembs 32 C1
Blackpool Gate 108 B5
Blackridge 119 C8
Blackrock Argyll 142 B4
Mon 35 C6
Blackrod 86 C4
Blackshaw 107 C7
Blackshaw Head 87 B7
Blacksmith's Green 56 C5
Blackstone 17 C6
Black Tar 44 E4
Blackthorn 39 C6
Blackthorpe 56 C3
Blacktoft 90 B2
Blacktop 141 D7
Black Torrington 9 D6
Blacktown 35 F6
Blackwall Tunnel 41 F6
Blackwater Corn 3 B6
Hants 27 D6
IoW 15 F6
Blackwaterfoot 143 F9
Blackwell Darl 101 C7
Derbys 75 B8
Derbys 76 D4
Warks 51 E7
Worcs 50 B4
W Sus 28 F4
Blackwood 119 E7
Blackwood
= *Coed Duon* 35 E5
Blackwood Hill 75 D6
Blacon 73 C7
Bladnoch 105 D8
Bladon 38 C4
Blaenannerch 45 E4
Blaenau Ffestiniog 71 C8
Blaenavon 35 D6
Blaencelyn 46 D2
Blaendyryn 47 F8
Blaenffos 45 F3
Blaengarw 34 E3
Blaengwrach 34 D2
Blaen-gwynfi 34 E2
Blaenpennal 46 C5
Blaenplwyf 46 B4
Blaenporth 45 E4
Blaenrhondda 34 D3
Blaen-waun 32 B3
Blaen-y-coed 32 B4
Blaenycwm 47 B7
Blaen-y-Cwm Denb 72 F4
Gwyn 71 E8
Powys 59 B7
Blagdon N Som 23 D7
Torbay 7 C6
Blagdon Hill 11 C7
Blagill 109 E7
Blaguegate 86 D2
Blaich 130 B4
Blain 147 E9
Blaina 35 D6
Blair Atholl 133 C5
Blairbeg 143 E11
Blairdaff 141 C5
Blair Drummond 127 E6
Blairglas 126 F2
Blairgowrie 134 E1
Blairhall 128 F2
Blairingone 127 E8
Blairland 118 E3
Blairlogie 127 E7
Blairlomond 125 F7
Blairmore 145 E10
Blairnamarrow 139 C8
Blairquhosh 126 F4
Blair's Ferry 145 G8
Blairskaith 119 B5
Blaisdon 36 C4
Blakebrook 50 B3
Blakedown 50 B3
Blakelaw 122 F3
Blakeley 62 E2
Blakeley Lane 75 E6
Blakemere 49 E5
Blakeney Glos 36 D3
Norf 81 C6
Blakenhall Ches E 74 E4
W Mid 62 E3
Blakeshall 62 F2
Blakesley 52 D4
Blanchland 110 D2
Blandford Forum 13 D6
Blandford St Mary 13 D6
Bland Hill 94 D5
Blanefield 119 B5
Blankney 78 C3
Blantyre 119 D6
Blar a'Chaorainn 131 C5
Blaran 124 D4
Blarghour 125 D5
Blarmachfoldach 130 C4
Blarnalearoch 150 B4
Blashford 14 D2
Blaston 64 E5
Blatherwycke 65 E6
Blawith 98 F4
Blaxhall 57 D7
Blaxton 89 D7
Blaydon 110 C4
Bleadney 23 E6
Bleadon 22 D5
Bleak Hey Nook 87 D8
Blean 30 C5
Bleasby Lincs 90 F5
Notts 77 E7
Bleasdale 93 E5
Bleatarn 100 C2
Blebocraigs 129 C6
Bleddfa 48 C4
Bledington 38 B2
Bledlow 39 D7
Bledlow Ridge 39 E7
Blegbie 121 C7
Blencarn 109 F6
Blencogo 107 E8
Blendworth 15 C8
Blenheim Park 80 D4
Blennerhasset 107 E8
Blervie Castle 151 F13
Bletchingdon 39 C5
Bletchingley 28 D4
Bletchley M Keynes 53 F6
Shrops 74 F3
Bletherston 32 B1
Bletsoe 53 D8
Blewbury 39 F5
Blickling 81 E7
Blidworth 77 D5
Blindburn 116 C4
Blindcrake 107 F8
Blindley Heath 28 E4
Blisland 5 B6
Blissford 14 C2
Bliss Gate 50 B2
Blisworth 52 D5
Blithbury 62 B4
Blitterlees 107 D8
Blockley 51 F6
Blofield 69 D6
Blofield Heath 69 C6
Blo' Norton 56 B4
Bloomfield 115 B8
Blore 75 E8
Blount's Green 75 F7
Blowick 85 C4
Bloxham 52 F2
Bloxholm 78 D3
Bloxwich 62 D3
Bloxworth 13 E6
Blubberhouses 94 D4
Blue Anchor Som 22 E2
Swansea 33 E6
Blue Row 43 C6
Blundeston 69 E8
Blunham 54 D2
Blunsdon St Andrew 37 F8
Bluntington 50 B3
Bluntisham 54 B4
Blunts 5 C8
Blyborough 90 E3
Blyford 57 B8
Blymhill 62 C2
Blyth Northumb 117 F9
Notts 89 F7
Blyth Bridge 120 E4
Blythburgh 57 B8
Blythe 121 E8
Blythe Bridge 75 E6
Blyton 90 E2
Boarhills 129 C7
Boarhunt 15 D7
Boarshead 18 B2
Boars Head 86 D3
Boars Hill 38 D4
Boarstall 39 C6
Boasley Cross 9 E6
Boath 151 D8
Boat of Garten 138 C5
Bobbing 30 C2
Bobbington 62 E2
Bobbingworth 41 D8
Bocaddon 5 D6
Bochastle 126 D5
Bocking 42 B3
Bocking Churchstreet 42 B3
Boddam Aberds 153 D11
Shetland 160 M5
Boddington 37 B5
Bodedern 82 C3
Bodelwyddan 72 B4
Bodenham
Hereford 49 D7
Wilts 14 B2
Bodenham Moor 49 D7
Bodermid 70 E2
Bodewryd 82 B3
Bodfari 72 B4
Bodffordd 82 D4
Bodham 81 C7
Bodiam 18 C4
Bodicote 52 F2
Bodieve 4 B4
Bodinnick 5 D6
Bodle Street Green 18 D3
Bodmin 5 C5
Bodney 67 E8
Bodorgan 82 E3
Bodsham 30 E5
Boduan 70 D4
Bodymoor Heath 63 E5
Bogallan 151 F9
Bogbrae 153 E10
Bogend Borders 122 E3
S Ayrs 118 F3
Boghall 120 C2
Boghead 119 E7
Bogmoor 152 B3
Bogniebrae 152 D5
Bognor Regis 16 E3
Bograxie 141 C6
Bogside 119 D8
Bogton 153 C6
Bogue 113 F6
Bohenie 137 F5
Bohortha 3 C7
Bohuntine 137 F5
Boirseam 154 J5
Bojewyan 2 C2
Bolam Durham 101 B6
Northumb 117 F6
Bolberry 6 F4
Bold Heath 86 F3
Boldon 111 C6
Boldon Colliery 111 C6
Boldre 14 E4
Boldron 101 C5
Bole 89 F8
Bolehill 76 D2
Boleside 121 F7
Bolham 10 C4
Bolham Water 11 C6
Bolingey 4 D2
Bollington 75 B6
Bollington Cross 75 B6
Bolney 17 B6
Bolnhurst 53 D8
Bolshan 135 D6
Bolsover 76 B4
Bolsterstone 88 E3
Bolstone 49 F7
Boltby 102 F2
Bolter End 39 E7
Bolton Cumb 99 B8
E Loth 121 B8
E Yorks 96 D3
Gtr Man 86 D5
Northumb 117 C7
Bolton Abbey 94 D3
Bolton Bridge 94 D3
Bolton-by-Bowland 93 E7
Boltonfellend 108 C4
Boltongate 108 E2
Bolton-le-Sands 92 C4
Bolton Low Houses 108 E2
Bolton-on-Swale 101 E7
Bolton Percy 95 E8
Bolton Town End 92 C4
Bolton upon Dearne 89 D5
Bolventor 5 B6
Bomere Heath 60 C4
Bonar Bridge 151 B9
Bonawe 125 B6
Bonby 90 C4
Boncath 45 F4
Bonchester Bridge 115 C8
Bonchurch 15 G6
Bondleigh 9 D8
Bonehill Devon 6 B5
Staffs 63 D5
Bo'ness 127 F8
Bonhill 118 B3
Boningale 62 D2
Bonjedward 116 B2
Bonkle 119 D8
Bonnavoulin 147 F8
Bonnington Edin 120 C4
Kent 19 B7
Bonnybank 129 D5
Bonnybridge 127 F7
Bonnykelly 153 C8
Bonnyrigg and Lasswade 121 C6
Bonnyton Aberds 153 E6
Angus 134 F3
Angus 135 D6
Bonsall 76 D2
Bonskeid House 133 C5
Bont 35 C7
Bontddu 58 C3
Bont-Dolgadfan 59 D5
Bont-goch 58 F3
Bonthorpe 79 B7
Bontnewydd
Ceredig 46 C5
Gwyn 82 F4
Bont-newydd 72 B4
Bont Newydd Gwyn 71 C8
Gwyn 71 E8
Bontuchel 72 D4
Bonvilston 22 B2
Bon-y-maen 33 E7
Booker 39 E8
Boon 121 E8
Boosbeck 102 C4
Boot 98 D3
Booth 87 B8
Boothby Graffoe 78 D2
Boothby Pagnell 78 F2
Boothen 75 E5
Boothferry 89 B8
Boothville 53 C5
Booth Wood 87 C8
Bootle Cumb 98 F3
Mers 85 E4
Booton 81 E7
Boot Street 57 E6
Boquhan 126 F4
Boraston 49 B8
Borden Kent 30 C2
W Sus 16 B2
Bordley 94 C2
Bordon 27 F6
Bordon Camp 27 F5
Boreham Essex 42 D3
Wilts 24 E3
Boreham Street 18 D3
Borehamwood 40 E4
Boreland Dumfries 114 E4
Stirling 132 F2
Borgh W Isles 148 H1
W Isles 154 J4
Borghastan 154 C7
Borgie 157 D9
Borgue Dumfries 106 E3
Highld 158 H3
Borley 56 E2
Bornais 148 F2
Bornesketaig 149 A8
Borness 106 E3
Boroughbridge 95 C6
Borough Green 29 D7
Borras Head 73 D7
Borreraig 148 C6
Borrobol Lodge 157 G11
Borrowash 76 F4
Borrowby 102 F2
Borrowdale 98 C4
Borrowfield 141 E7
Borth 58 E3
Borthwickbrae 115 C7
Borthwickshiels 115 C7
Borth-y-Gest 71 D6
Borve 149 D9
Borve Lodge 154 H5
Borwick 92 B5
Bosavern 2 C2
Bosbury 49 E8
Boscastle 8 E3
Boscombe BCP 14 E2
Wilts 25 F7
Boscoppa 4 D5
Bosham 16 D2
Bosherston 44 F4
Boskenna 2 D3
Bosley 75 C6
Bossall 96 C3
Bossiney 8 F2
Bossingham 31 E5
Bossington 21 E7
Bostock Green 74 C3

Boston 79 E6
Boston Long Hedges 79 E6
Boston Spa 95 E7
Boston West 79 E5
Boswinger 3 B8
Botallack 2 C2
Botany Bay 41 E5
Botcherby 108 D4
Botcheston 63 D8
Botesdale 56 B4
Bothal 117 F8
Bothamsall 77 B6
Bothel 107 F8
Bothenhampton 12 E2
Bothwell 119 D7
Botley Bucks 40 D2
Hants 15 C6
Oxon 38 D4
Botolph Claydon 39 B7
Botolphs 17 D5
Bottacks 150 E7
Bottesford Leics 77 F8
N Lincs 90 D2
Bottisham 55 C6
Bottlesford 25 D6
Bottom Boat 88 B4
Bottomcraig 129 B5
Bottom House 75 D7
Bottom of Hutton 86 B2
Bottom o'th'Moor 86 C4
Botusfleming 6 C2
Botwnnog 70 D3
Bough Beech 29 E5
Boughrood 48 F3
Boughspring 36 E2
Boughton Norf 67 D6
Notts 77 C6
W Nhants 53 C5
Boughton Aluph 30 E4
Boughton Lees 30 E4
Boughton Malherbe 30 E2
Boughton Monchelsea 29 D8
Boughton Street 30 D4
Boulby 103 C5
Boulden 60 F5
Boulmer 117 C8
Boulston 44 D4
Boultenstone 140 C3
Boultham 78 C2
Bourn 54 D4
Bourne 65 B7
Bourne End Bucks 40 F1
C Beds 53 E7
Herts 40 D3
Bournemouth 13 E8
Bournes Green Glos 37 D6
Southend 43 F5
Bournheath 50 B4
Bournmoor 111 D6
Bournville 62 F4
Bourton Dorset 24 F2
N Som 23 C5
Oxon 38 F2
Shrops 61 E5
Bourton on Dunsmore 52 B2
Bourton on the Hill 51 F6
Bourton-on-the-Water 38 B1
Bousd 146 E5
Boustead Hill 108 D2
Bouth 99 F5
Bouthwaite 94 B4
Boveney 27 B7
Boverton 21 C8
Bovey Tracey 7 B6
Bovingdon 40 D3
Bovingdon Green Bucks 39 F8
Herts 40 D3
Bovinger 41 D8
Bovington Camp 13 F6
Bow Borders 121 E7
Devon 10 D2
Orkney 159 J4
Bowbank 100 B4
Bow Brickhill 53 F7
Bowburn 111 F6
Bowcombe 15 F5
Bowd 11 E6
Bowden Borders 121 F8
Devon 7 E6
Bowden Hill 24 C4
Bowderdale 100 D1
Bowdon 87 F5
Bower 116 F3
Bowerchalke 13 B8
Bowerhill 24 C4
Bower Hinton 12 C2
Bowermadden 158 D4
Bowers Gifford 42 F3
Bowershall 128 E2
Bowertower 158 D4
Bowes 100 C4
Bowgreave 92 E4
Bowgreen 87 F5
Bowhill 115 B7
Bowhouse 107 C7
Bowland Bridge 99 F6
Bowley 49 D7
Bowlhead Green 27 F7
Bowling W Dunb 118 B4
W Yorks 94 F4
Bowling Bank 73 E7
Bowling Green 50 D3
Bowmanstead 99 E5
Bowmore 142 C4
Bowness-on-Solway 108 C2
Bowness-on-Windermere 99 E6
Bow of Fife 128 C5
Bowsden 123 E5
Bowside Lodge 157 C11
Bowston 99 E6
Bow Street 58 F3
Bowthorpe 68 D4
Box Glos 37 D5
Wilts 24 C3
Boxbush 36 C4
Box End 53 E8
Boxford Suff 56 E3
W Berks 26 B2
Boxgrove 16 D3
Boxley 29 D8
Boxmoor 40 D3
Boxted Essex 56 F4
Suff 56 D2
Boxted Cross 56 F4
Boxted Heath 56 F4
Boxworth 54 C4
Boxworth End 54 C4
Boyden Gate 31 C6
Boylestone 75 F8
Boyndie 153 B6
Boynton 97 C7
Boysack 135 E6
Boyton Corn 8 E5
Suff 57 E7
Wilts 24 F4
Boyton Cross 42 D2
Boyton End 55 E8
Bozeat 53 D7
Braaid 84 E3
Braal Castle 158 D3
Brabling Green 57 C6
Brabourne 30 E4
Brabourne Lees 30 E4
Brabster 158 D5
Bracadale 149 E8
Bracara 147 B10
Braceborough 65 C7
Bracebridge 78 C2
Bracebridge Heath 78 C2
Bracebridge Low Fields 78 C2
Braceby 78 F3
Bracewell 93 E8
Brackenfield 76 D3
Brackenthwaite Cumb 108 E2
N Yorks 95 D5
Bracklesham 16 E2
Brackletter 136 F4
Brackley Argyll 143 D8
W Nhants 52 F3
Brackloch 156 G4
Bracknell 27 C6
Braco 127 D7
Bracobrae 152 C5
Bracon Ash 68 E4
Bracorina 147 B10
Bradbourne 76 D2
Bradbury 101 B8
Bradda 84 F1
Bradden 52 E4
Braddock 5 C6
Bradeley 75 D5
Bradenham Bucks 39 E8
Norf 68 D2
Bradenstoke 24 B5
Bradfield Essex 56 F5
Norf 81 D8
W Berks 26 B4
Bradfield Combust 56 D2
Bradfield Green 74 D3
Bradfield Heath 43 B7
Bradfield St Clare 56 D3
Bradfield St George 56 C3
Bradford Corn 5 B6
Derbys 76 C2
Devon 9 D6
Northumb 123 F7
W Yorks 94 F4
Bradford Abbas 12 C3
Bradford Leigh 24 C3
Bradford-on-Avon 24 C3
Bradford-on-Tone 11 B6
Bradford Peverell 12 E4
Brading 15 F7
Bradley Derbys 76 E2
Hants 26 E4
NE Lincs 91 D6
Staffs 62 C2
W Mid 62 E3
W Yorks 88 B2
Bradley Green 50 C4
Bradley in the Moors 75 E7
Bradley Stoke 36 F3
Bradlow 50 F2
Bradmore Notts 77 F5
W Mid 62 E2
Bradninch 10 D5
Bradnop 75 D7
Bradpole 12 E2
Bradshaw Gtr Man 86 C5
W Yorks 87 C8
Bradstone 9 F5
Bradwall Green 74 C4
Bradway 88 F4
Bradwell Derbys 88 F2
Essex 42 B4
M Keynes 53 F6
Norf 69 D8
Staffs 74 E5
Bradwell Grove 38 D2
Bradwell on Sea 43 D6
Bradwell Waterside 43 D5
Bradworthy 8 C5
Bradworthy Cross 8 C5
Brae Dumfries 107 B5
Highld 155 J13
Highld 156 J7
Shetland 160 G5
Braeantra 151 D8
Braedownie 134 B2
Braefield 150 H7
Braegrum 128 B2
Braehead Dumfries 105 D8
Orkney 159 D5
Orkney 159 H6
S Lanark 119 F8
S Lanark 120 D2
Braehead of Lunan 135 D6
Braehoulland 160 F4
Braehungie 158 G3
Braelangwell Lodge 151 B8
Braemar 139 E7
Braemore Highld 150 D4
Highld 158 G2
Brae of Achnahaird 156 H3
Brae Roy Lodge 137 E6
Braeside 118 B2
Braes of Enzie 152 C3
Braeswick 159 E7
Braewick 160 H5
Brafferton Darl 101 B7
N Yorks 95 B7
Brafield-on-the-Green 53 D6
Bragar 155 C7
Bragbury End 41 B5
Bragleenmore 124 C5
Braichmelyn 83 E6
Braid 120 C5
Braides 92 D4
Braidley 101 F5
Braidwood 119 E8
Braigo 142 B3
Brailsford 76 E2
Brainshaugh 117 D8
Braintree 42 B3
Braiseworth 56 B5
Braishfield 14 B4
Braithwaite Cumb 98 B4
S Yorks 89 C7
W Yorks 94 E3
Braithwell 89 E6
Bramber 17 C5
Bramcote Notts 76 F5
Warks 63 F8
Bramdean 15 B7
Bramerton 69 D5
Bramfield Herts 41 C5
Suff 57 B7
Bramford 56 E5
Bramhall 87 F6
Bramham 95 E7
Bramhope 95 E5
Bramley Hants 26 D4
Sur 27 E8
S Yorks 89 E5
W Yorks 94 F5
Bramling 31 D6
Brampford Speke 10 E4
Brampton Cambs 54 B3
Cumb 100 B1
Cumb 108 C5
Derbys 76 B3
Hereford 49 F6
Lincs 77 B8
Norf 81 E8
Suff 69 F7
S Yorks 88 D5
Brampton Abbotts 36 B3
Brampton Ash 64 F4
Brampton Bryan 49 B5
Brampton en le Morthen 89 F5
Bramshall 75 F7
Bramshaw 14 C3
Bramshill 26 C5
Bramshott 27 F6
Branault 147 E8
Brancaster 80 C3
Brancaster Staithe 80 C3
Brancepeth 110 F5
Branch End 110 C3
Branchill 151 F13
Branderburgh 152 A2
Brandesburton 97 E7
Brandeston 57 C6
Brand Green 36 B4
Brandhill 49 B6
Brandis Corner 9 D6
Brandiston 81 E7
Brandon Durham 110 F5
Lincs 78 E2
Northumb 117 C6
Suff 67 F7
Warks 52 B2
Brandon Bank 67 F6
Brandon Creek 67 E6
Brandon Parva 68 D3
Brandsby 95 B8
Brandy Wharf 90 E4
Brane 2 D3
Bran End 42 B2
Branksome 13 E8
Branksome Park 13 E8
Bransby 77 B8
Branscombe 11 F6
Bransford 50 D2
Bransgore 14 E2
Branshill 127 E7
Bransholme 97 F7
Branson's Cross 51 B5
Branston Leics 64 B5
Lincs 78 C3
Staffs 63 B6
Branston Booths 78 C3
Branstone 15 F6
Bransty 98 C1
Brant Broughton 78 D2
Brantham 56 F5
Branthwaite Cumb 98 B2
Cumb 108 F2
Brantingham 90 B3
Branton Northumb 117 C6
S Yorks 89 D7
Branxholme 115 C7
Branxholm Park 115 C7
Branxton 122 F4
Brassey Green 74 C2
Brassington 76 D2
Brasted 29 D5
Brasted Chart 29 D5
Brathens 141 E5
Bratoft 79 C7
Brattleby 90 F3
Bratton Telford 61 C6
Wilts 24 D4
Bratton Clovelly 9 E6
Bratton Fleming 20 F5
Bratton Seymour 12 B4
Braughing 41 B6
Braunston 52 C3
Braunstone Town 64 D2
Braunston-in-Rutland 64 D5
Braunton 20 F3
Brawby 96 B3
Brawl 157 C11
Brawlbin 158 E2
Bray 27 B7
Braybrooke 64 F4
Braye Ald 16
Brayford 21 F5
Bray Shop 5 B8
Braystones 98 D2
Braythorn 94 E5
Brayton 95 F9
Bray Wick 27 B6
Brazacott 8 E4
Breach 30 C2
Breachacha Castle 146 F4
Breachwood Green 40 B4
Breacleit 154 D6
Breaden Heath 73 F8
Breadsall 76 F3
Breadstone 36 D4
Breage 2 D5
Breakachy 150 G7
Bream 36 D3
Breamore 14 C2
Brean 22 D4
Breanais 154 E4
Brearton 95 C6
Breascleit 154 D7
Breaston 76 F4
Brechfa 46 F4
Brechin 135 C5
Breckan 159 H3
Breck of Cruan 159 G4
Breckrey 149 B10
Brecon = Aberhonddu 34 B4
Bredbury 87 E7
Brede 18 D5
Bredenbury 49 D8
Bredfield 57 D6
Bredgar 30 C2
Bredhurst 29 C8
Bredicot 50 D4
Bredon 50 F4
Bredon's Norton 50 F4
Bredwardine 48 E5
Breedon on the Hill 63 B8
Breibhig W Isles 148 J1
W Isles 155 D9
Breich 120 C2
Breightmet 86 D5
Breighton 96 F3
Breinton 49 F6
Breinton Common 49 E6
Breiwick 160 J6
Bremhill 24 B4
Bremirehoull 160 L6
Brenchley 29 E7
Brendon 21 E6
Brenkley 110 B5
Brent Eleigh 56 E3
Brentford 28 B2
Brentingby 64 C4
Brent Knoll 22 D5
Brent Pelham 54 F5
Brentwood 42 E1
Brenzett 19 C7
Brereton 62 C4
Brereton Green 74 C4
Brereton Heath 74 C5
Bressingham 68 F3
Bretby 63 B6
Bretford 52 B2
Bretforton 51 E5
Bretherdale Head 99 D7
Bretherton 86 B2
Brettabister 160 H6
Brettenham Norf 68 F2
Suff 56 D3
Bretton Derbys 76 B2
Flint 73 C7
Brewer Street 28 D4
Brewlands Bridge 134 C1
Brewood 62 D2
Briach 151 F13
Briants Puddle 13 E6
Brick End 42 B1
Brickendon 41 D6
Bricket Wood 40 D4
Bricklehampton 50 E4
Bride 84 B4
Bridekirk 107 F8
Bridell 45 E3
Bridestowe 9 F7
Brideswell 152 E5
Bridford 10 F3
Bridfordmills 10 F3
Bridge 31 D5
Bridge End 78 F4
Bridgefoot Angus 134 F3
Cumb 98 B2
Bridge Green 55 F5
Bridgehampton 12 B3
Bridge Hewick 95 B6
Bridgehill 110 D3
Bridgemary 15 D6
Bridgemont 87 F8
Bridgend Aberds 140 C4
Aberds 152 E5
Angus 135 C5
Argyll 142 B4
Argyll 143 E8
Argyll 145 D7
Cumb 99 C5
Fife 129 C5
Moray 152 E3
N Lanark 119 B6
Pembs 45 E3
W Loth 120 B3
Bridgend = Pen-y-Bont Ar Ogwr 21 B8
Bridgend of Lintrathen 134 D2
Bridge of Alford 140 C4
Bridge of Allan 127 E6
Bridge of Avon 152 E1
Bridge of Awe 125 C6
Bridge of Balgie 132 E2
Bridge of Cally 133 D8
Bridge of Canny 141 E5
Bridge of Craigisla 134 D2
Bridge of Dee 106 D4
Bridge of Don 141 C8
Bridge of Dun 135 D6
Bridge of Dye 141 F5
Bridge of Earn 128 C3
Bridge of Ericht 132 D2
Bridge of Feugh 141 E6
Bridge of Forss 157 C13
Bridge of Gairn 140 E2
Bridge of Gaur 132 D2
Bridge of Muchalls 141 E7
Bridge of Oich 137 D6
Bridge of Orchy 125 B8
Bridge of Waith 159 G3
Bridge of Walls 160 H4
Bridge of Weir 118 C3
Bridgerule 8 D4
Bridges 60 E3
Bridge Sollers 49 E6
Bridge Street 56 E2
Bridgeton 119 C6
Bridgetown Corn 8 F5
Som 21 F8
Bridge Trafford 73 B8
Bridge Yate 23 B8
Bridgham 68 F2
Bridgnorth 61 E7
Bridgtown 62 D3
Bridgwater 22 F5
Bridlington 97 C7
Bridport 12 E2
Bridstow 36 B2
Brierfield 93 F8
Brierley Glos 36 C3
Hereford 49 D6
S Yorks 88 C5
Brierley Hill 62 F3
Briery Hill 35 D5
Brigg 90 D4
Briggswath 103 D6
Brigham Cumb 107 F7
E Yorks 97 D6
Brighouse 88 B2
Brighstone 14 F5
Brightgate 76 D2
Brighthampton 38 D3
Brightling 18 C3
Brightlingsea 43 C6
Brighton Brighton 17 D7
Corn 4 D4
Brighton Hill 26 E4
Brightons 120 B2
Brightwalton 26 B2
Brightwell 57 E6
Brightwell Baldwin 39 E6
Brightwell cum Sotwell 39 E5
Brignall 101 C5
Brig o'Turk 126 D4
Brigsley 91 D6
Brigsteer 99 F6
Brigstock 65 F6
Brill 39 C6
Brilley 48 E4
Brimaston 44 C4
Brimfield 49 C7
Brimington 76 B4
Brimley 7 B5
Brimpsfield 37 C6
Brimpton 26 C3
Brims 159 K3
Brimscombe 37 D5
Brimstage 85 F4
Brinacory 147 B10
Brind 96 F3
Brindister Shetland 160 H4
Shetland 160 K6
Brindle 86 B4
Brindley Ford 75 D5
Brineton 62 C2
Bringhurst 64 E5
Brington 53 B8
Brinian 159 F5
Briningham 81 D6
Brinkhill 79 B6
Brinkley 55 D7
Brinklow 52 B2
Brinkworth 37 F7
Brinmore 138 B2
Brinscall 86 B4
Brinsea 23 C6
Brinsley 76 E4
Brinsop 49 E6
Brinsworth 88 F5
Brinton 81 D6
Brisco 108 D4
Brisley 81 E5
Brislington 23 B8
Bristol 23 B7
Briston 81 D6
Britannia 87 B6
Britford 14 B2
Brithdir 58 C4
British Legion Village 29 D8
Briton Ferry 33 E8
Britwell Salome 39 E6
Brixham 7 D7
Brixton Devon 6 D3
London 28 B4
Brixton Deverill 24 F3
Brixworth 52 B5
Brize Norton 38 D3
Broad Blunsdon 38 E1
Broadbottom 87 E7
Broadbridge 16 D2
Broadbridge Heath 28 F2
Broad Campden 51 F6
Broad Chalke 13 B8
Broadclyst 10 E4
Broadfield Gtr Man 87 C6
Lancs 86 B3
Pembs 32 D2
W Sus 28 F3
Broadford 149 F11
Broadford Bridge 16 B4
Broad Green C Beds 53 E7
Essex 42 B4
Worcs 50 D2
Broadhaugh 115 D7
Broadhaven 158 E5
Broad Haven 44 D3
Broadheath 87 F5
Broad Heath 49 C8
Broadhembury 11 D6
Broadhempston 7 C6
Broad Hill 55 B6
Broad Hinton 25 B6
Broadholme Derbys 76 E3
Lincs 77 B8
Broadland Row 18 D5
Broadlay 32 D4
Broad Laying 26 C2
Broadley Lancs 87 C6
Moray 152 B3
Broadley Common 41 D7
Broad Marston 51 E6
Broadmayne 12 F5
Broadmeadows 121 F7
Broadmere 26 E4
Broadmoor 32 D1
Broadoak 31 C5
Broad Oak Carms 33 B6
Cumb 98 E3
Dorset 12 E2
Dorset 13 C5
E Sus 18 C3
E Sus 18 D5
Hereford 36 B1
Mers 86 E3
Broadrashes 152 C4
Broadsea 153 B9
Broadstairs 31 C7
Broadstone BCP 13 E8
Shrops 60 F5
Broad Street 30 D2
Broad Street Green 42 D4
Broad Town 25 B5
Broadtown Lane 25 B5
Broadwas 50 D2
Broadwater Herts 41 B5
W Sus 17 D5
Broadway Carms 32 D3
Pembs 44 D3
Som 11 C8
Suff 57 B7
Worcs 51 F5
Broadwell Glos 36 C2
Glos 38 B2
Oxon 38 D2
Warks 52 C2
Broadwell House 110 D2
Broadwey 12 F4
Broadwindsor 12 D2
Broadwood Kelly 9 D8
Broadwoodwidger 9 F6
Brobury 48 E5
Brochel 149 D10
Brochloch 113 E5
Brochroy 125 B6
Brockamin 50 D2
Brockbridge 15 C7
Brockdam 117 B7
Brockdish 57 B6
Brockenhurst 14 D4
Brocketsbrae 119 F8
Brockford Street 56 C5
Brockhall 52 C4
Brockham 28 E2
Brockhampton Glos 37 B7
Hereford 49 F7
Brockholes 88 C2
Brockhurst Derbys 76 C3
Hants 15 D7
Brocklebank 108 E3
Brocklesby 90 C5
Brockley 23 C6
Brockley Green 56 D2
Brockleymoor 108 F4
Brockton Shrops 60 D3
Shrops 60 F3
Shrops 61 D7
Shrops 61 E5
Telford 61 C7
Brockweir 36 D2
Brockwood 15 B7
Brockworth 37 C5
Brocton 62 C3
Brodick 143 E11
Brodsworth 89 D6
Brogaig 149 B9
Brogborough 53 F7
Brokenborough 37 F6
Broken Cross Ches E 75 B5
Ches W 74 B3
Bromborough 85 F4
Brome 56 B5
Brome Street 57 B5
Bromeswell 57 D7
Bromfield Cumb 107 E8
Shrops 49 B6
Bromham Bedford 53 D8
Wilts 24 C4
Bromley London 28 C5
W Mid 62 F3
Bromley Common 28 C5
Bromley Green 19 B6
Brompton Medway 29 C8
N Yorks 102 E1
N Yorks 103 F7
Brompton-on-Swale 101 E7
Brompton Ralph 22 F2
Brompton Regis 21 F8
Bromsash 36 B3
Bromsberrow Heath 50 F2
Bromsgrove 50 B4
Bromyard 49 D8
Bromyard Downs 49 D8
Bronaber 71 D8
Brongest 46 E2
Bronington 73 F8
Bronllys 48 F3
Bronnant 46 C5
Bronwydd Arms 33 B5
Bronydd 48 E4
Bronygarth 73 F6
Brook Carms 32 D3
Hants 14 B4
Hants 14 C3
IoW 14 F4
Kent 30 E4
Sur 27 E8
Sur 27 F7
Brooke Norf 69 E5
Rutland 64 D5
Brookenby 91 E6
Brookend 36 E2
Brook End 53 C8
Brookfield 118 C4
Brook Hill 14 C3
Brookhouse 92 C5
Brookhouse Green 74 C5
Brookland 19 C6
Brooklands Dumfries 106 B5
Gtr Man 87 E5
Shrops 74 E2
Brookmans Park 41 D5
Brooks 59 E8
Brooks Green 16 B5
Brook Street Kent 19 B6
Kent 29 E6
W Sus 17 B7
Brookthorpe 37 C5
Brookville 67 E7
Brookwood 27 D7
Broom C Beds 54 E2
S Yorks 88 E5
Warks 51 D5
Worcs 50 B4
Broome Norf 69 E6
Shrops 60 F4
Broomedge 86 F5
Broome Park 117 C7
Broomer's Corner 16 B5
Broomfield Aberds 153 E9
Essex 42 C3
Kent 30 D2
Kent 31 C5
Som 22 F4
Broomfleet 90 B2
Broom Green 81 E5
Broomhall Ches E 74 E3
Windsor 27 C7
Broomhaugh 110 C3
Broomhill Norf 67 D6
Northumb 117 D8
S Yorks 88 D5
Broom Hill 13 D8
Broomholm 81 D9
Broomley 110 C3
Broompark 110 E5
Broom's Green 50 F2
Broomy Lodge 14 C3
Brora 157 J12
Broseley 61 D6
Brotherhouse Bar 66 C2
Brotherstone 122 F2
Brothertoft 79 E5
Brotherton 89 B5
Brotton 102 C4
Broubster 157 C13
Brough Cumb 100 C2
Derbys 88 F2
E Yorks 90 B3
Highld 158 C4
Notts 77 D8
Orkney 159 G4
Shetland 160 F6
Shetland 160 F7
Shetland 160 G7
Shetland 160 H6
Shetland 160 J7
Broughall 74 E2
Brough Lodge 160 D7
Brough Sowerby 100 C2
Broughton Borders 120 F4
Cambs 54 B3
Flint 73 C7
Hants 25 F8
Lancs 92 F5
M Keynes 53 E6
N Lincs 90 D3
N Nhants 53 B6
N Yorks 94 D2
N Yorks 96 B3
Orkney 159 D5
Oxon 52 F2
V Glam 21 B8
Broughton Astley 64 E2
Broughton Beck 98 F4
Broughton Common 24 C3
Broughton Gifford 24 C3
Broughton Hackett 50 D4
Broughton in Furness 98 F4
Broughton Mills 98 E4
Broughton Moor 107 F7
Broughton Park 87 D6
Broughton Poggs 38 D2
Broughtown 159 D7
Broughty Ferry 134 F4
Browhouses 108 C2
Browland 160 H4
Brown Candover 26 F3
Brown Edge Lancs 85 C4
Staffs 75 D6
Brown Heath 73 C8
Brownhill Aberds 153 D6
Aberds 153 D8
Blackburn 93 F6
Shrops 60 B4
Brownhills Fife 129 C7
W Mid 62 D4
Brownlow 74 C5
Brownlow Heath 74 C5
Brownmuir 135 B7
Brown's End 50 F2
Brownshill 37 D5
Brownston 6 D4
Brownyside 117 B7
Broxa 103 E7
Broxbourne 41 D6
Broxburn E Loth 122 B2
W Loth 120 B3
Broxholme 78 B2
Broxted 42 B1
Broxton 73 D8
Broxwood 49 D5
Broyle Side 17 C8
Brù 155 C8
Bruairnis 148 H2
Bruan 158 G5
Bruar Lodge 133 B5
Brucehill 118 B3
Bruera 73 C8
Bruern Abbey 38 B2
Bruichladdich 142 B3
Bruisyard 57 C7
Brumby 90 D2
Brund 75 C8
Brundall 69 D6
Brundish 57 C6
Brundish Street 57 B6
Brunery 147 D10
Brunshaw 93 F8
Brunswick Village 110 B5
Bruntcliffe 88 B3
Bruntingthorpe 64 E3
Brunton Fife 128 B5
Northumb 117 B8
Wilts 25 D7
Brushford Devon 9 D8
Som 10 B4
Bruton 23 F8
Bryanston 13 D6
Brydekirk 107 B8
Bryher 2 E3
Brymbo 73 D6
Brympton 12 C3
Bryn Carms 33 D6
Gtr Man 86 D3
Neath 34 E2
Shrops 60 F2
Brynamman 33 C8
Brynberian 45 F3
Brynbryddan 34 E1
Brynbuga = Usk 35 D7
Bryncae 34 F3
Bryncethin 34 F3
Bryncir 71 C5
Bryn-coch 33 E8
Bryncroes 70 D3
Bryncrug 58 D3
Bryn Du 82 D3
Bryneglwys 72 E5
Brynford 73 B5
Bryn Gates 86 D3
Bryn-glas 83 E8
Bryn Golau 34 F3
Bryngwran 82 D3
Bryngwyn Ceredig 45 E4
Mon 35 D7
Powys 48 E3
Brynhenllan 45 F2
Brynhoffnant 46 D2
Brynithel 35 D6
Bryn-Iwan 46 F2
Brynmawr 35 C5
Bryn-mawr 70 D3
Brynmenyn 34 F3
Brynmill 33 E7
Brynna 34 F3
Bryn-nantllech 72 C3
Bryn-penarth 59 D8
Brynrefail Anglesey 82 C4
Gwyn 83 E5
Bryn Rhyd-yr-Arian 72 C3
Brynsadler 34 F4
Bryn Saith Marchog 72 D4
Brynsiencyn 82 E4
Bryn Sion 59 C5
Brynteg Anglesey 82 C4
Ceredig 46 E3
Bryn-y-gwenin 35 C7
Bryn-y-maen 83 D8
Bryn-yr-eryr 70 C4
Buaile nam Bodach 148 H2
Bualintur 149 F9
Buarthmeini 72 F2
Bubbenhall 51 B8
Bubwith 96 F3
Buccleuch 115 C6
Buchanhaven 153 D11
Buchanty 127 B8
Buchlyvie 126 E4
Buckabank 108 E3
Buckden Cambs 54 C2
N Yorks 94 B2
Buckenham 69 D6
Buckerell 11 D6
Buckfast 6 C5
Buckfastleigh 6 C5
Buckhaven 129 E5
Buckholm 121 F7
Buckholt 36 C2
Buckhorn Weston 13 B5
Buckhurst Hill 41 E7
Buckie 152 B4
Buckies 158 D3
Buckingham 52 F4
Buckland Bucks 40 C1
Devon 6 E4
Glos 51 F5
Hants 14 E4
Herts 54 F4
Kent 31 E7
Oxon 38 E3
Sur 28 D3
Buckland Brewer 9 B6
Buckland Common 40 D2
Buckland Dinham 24 D2
Buckland Filleigh 9 D6
Buckland in the Moor 6 B5
Buckland Monachorum 6 C2
Buckland Newton 12 D4
Buckland St Mary 11 C7
Bucklebury 26 B3
Bucklegate 79 F6
Bucklerheads 134 F4
Bucklers Hard 14 E5
Bucklesham 57 E6
Buckley = Bwcle 73 C6
Bucklow Hill 86 F5
Buckminster 65 B5
Bucknall Lincs 78 C4
Stoke 75 E6
Bucknell Oxon 39 B5
Shrops 49 B5
Buckpool 152 B4
Bucksburn 141 D7
Buck's Cross 8 B5
Bucks Green 27 F8
Buckshaw Village 86 B3
Bucks Horn Oak 27 E6
Buckskin 26 D4
Buck's Mills 9 B5
Buckton E Yorks 97 B7
Hereford 49 B5
Northumb 123 F6
Buckworth 54 B2
Budbrooke 51 C7
Budby 77 C6
Budd's Titson 8 D4
Bude 8 D4
Budlake 10 E4
Budle 123 F7
Budleigh Salterton 11 F5
Budock Water 3 C6
Buerton 74 E3
Buffler's Holt 52 F4
Bugbrooke 52 D4
Buglawton 75 C5
Bugle 4 D5
Bugley 24 E3
Bugthorpe 96 D3
Buildwas 61 D6
Builth Road 48 D2
Builth Wells = Llanfair-ym-Muallt 48 D2
Buirgh 154 H5
Bulby 65 B7
Bulcote 77 E6
Buldoo 157 C12
Bulford 25 E6
Bulford Camp 25 E6
Bulkeley 74 D2
Bulkington Warks 63 F7
Wilts 24 D4
Bulkworthy 9 C5
Bullamoor 102 E1
Bullbridge 76 D3
Bullbrook 27 C6
Bulley 36 C4
Bullgill 107 F7
Bull Hill 14 E4
Bullington Hants 26 E2
Lincs 78 B3
Bull's Green 41 C5
Bullwood 145 F10
Bulmer Essex 56 E2
N Yorks 96 C2
Bulmer Tye 56 F2
Bulphan 42 F2
Bulverhythe 18 E4
Bulwark 153 D9
Bulwell 76 E5
Bulwick 65 E6
Bumble's Green 41 D7
Bun Abhainn Eadarra 154 G6
Bunacaimb 147 C9
Bun a'Mhuillin 148 G2
Bunarkaig 136 F4
Bunbury 74 D2
Bunbury Heath 74 D2
Bunchrew 151 G9
Bundalloch 149 F13
Buness 160 C8
Bunessan 146 J6
Bungay 69 F6
Bunkers Hill 38 C4
Bunker's Hill Lincs 78 B2
Lincs 79 D5
Bunloit 137 B8
Bun Loyne 136 D5
Bunnahabhain 142 A5
Bunny 64 B2
Buntait 150 H6
Buntingford 41 B6
Bunwell 68 E4
Burbage Derbys 75 B7
Leics 63 E8
Wilts 25 C7
Burchett's Green 39 F8
Burcombe 25 F5
Burcot 39 E5
Burcott 40 B1
Burdon 111 D6
Bures 56 F3
Bures Green 56 F3
Burford Ches E 74 D3
Oxon 38 C2
Shrops 49 C7
Burg 146 G6
Burgar 159 F4
Burgate Hants 14 C2
Suff 56 B4
Burgess Hill 17 C7
Burgh 57 D6
Burgh by Sands 108 D3
Burgh Castle 69 D7
Burghclere 26 C2
Burghead 151 E14
Burghfield 26 C4
Burghfield Common 26 C4
Burghfield Hill 26 C4
Burgh Heath 28 D3
Burghill 49 E6
Burgh le Marsh 79 C8
Burgh Muir 141 B6
Burgh next Aylsham 81 E8
Burgh on Bain 91 F6
Burgh St Margaret 69 C7
Burgh St Peter 69 E7
Burghwallis 89 C6
Burham 29 C8
Buriton 15 B8
Burland 74 D3
Burlawn 4 B4
Burleigh 27 C6
Burlescombe 11 C5
Burleston 13 E5
Burley Hants 14 D3
Rutland 65 C5
W Yorks 95 F5
Burleydam 74 E3
Burley Gate 49 E7
Burley in Wharfedale 94 E4
Burley Lodge 14 D3
Burley Street 14 D3
Burlingjobb 48 D4
Burlow 18 D2
Burlton 60 B4
Burmarsh 19 B7
Burmington 51 F7
Burn 89 B6
Burnaston 76 F2
Burnbank 119 D7
Burnby 96 E4
Burncross 88 E4
Burneside 99 E7
Burness 159 D7
Burneston 101 F8
Burnett 23 C8
Burnfoot Borders 115 C7
Borders 115 C8
E Ayrs 112 D4
Perth 127 D8
Burnham Bucks 40 F2
N Lincs 90 C4
Burnham Deepdale 80 C4
Burnham Green 41 C5
Burnham Market 80 C4
Burnham Norton 80 C4
Burnham-on-Crouch 43 E5
Burnham-on-Sea 22 E5
Burnham Overy Staithe 80 C4
Burnham Overy Town 80 C4
Burnham Thorpe 80 C4
Burnhead Dumfries 113 E8
S Ayrs 112 D2

Burnhervie 141 C6
Burnhill Green 61 D7
Burnhope 110 E4
Burnhouse 118 D3
Burniston 103 E8
Burnlee 88 D2
Burnley 93 F8
Burnley Lane 93 F8
Burnmouth 123 C5
Burn of Cambus 127 D6
Burnopfield 110 D4
Burnsall 94 C3
Burnside Angus 135 D5
E Ayrs 113 C5
Fife 128 D3
Shetland 160 F4
S Lanark 119 C6
W Loth 120 B3
Burnside of Duntrune 134 F4
Burnswark 107 B8
Burntcommon 27 D8
Burnt Heath 76 B2
Burnthouse 3 C6
Burnt Houses 101 B6
Burntisland 128 F4
Burnton 112 D4
Burntwood 62 D4
Burnt Yates 95 C5
Burnwynd 120 C4
Burpham Sur 27 D8
W Sus 16 D4
Burradon
Northumb 117 D5
T&W 111 B5
Burrafirth 160 B8
Burraland Shetland 160 F5
Shetland 160 J4
Burras 3 C5
Burravoe Shetland 160 F7
Shetland 160 G5
Burray Village 159 J5
Burrells 100 C1
Burrelton 134 F2
Burridge Devon 20 F4
Hants 15 C6
Burrill 101 F7
Burringham 90 D2
Burrington Devon 9 C8
Hereford 49 B6
N Som 23 D6
Burrough Green 55 D7
Burrough on the Hill 64 C4
Burrow-bridge 11 B8
Burrowhill 27 C7
Burry 33 E5
Burry Green 33 E5
Burry Port =Porth Tywyn 33 D5
Burscough 86 C2
Burscough Bridge 86 C2
Bursea 96 F4
Burshill 97 E6
Bursledon 15 D5
Burslem 75 E5
Burstall 56 E4
Burstock 12 D2
Burston Norf 68 F4
Staffs 75 F6
Burstow 28 E4
Burstwick 91 B6
Burtersett 100 F3
Burtle 23 E5
Burton BCP 14 E2
Ches W 73 B7
Ches W 74 C2
Lincs 78 B2
Northumb 123 F7
Pembs 44 E4
Som 22 E3
Wilts 24 B3
Burton Agnes 97 C7
Burton Bradstock 12 F2
Burton Dassett 51 D8
Burton Fleming 97 B6
Burton Green
W Mid 51 B7
Wrex 73 D7
Burton Hastings 63 E8
Burton-in-Kendal 92 B5
Burton in Lonsdale 93 B6
Burton Joyce 77 E6
Burton Latimer 53 B7
Burton Lazars 64 C4
Burton-le-Coggles 65 B6
Burton Leonard 95 C6
Burton on the Wolds 64 B2
Burton Overy 64 E3
Burton Pedwardine 78 E4
Burton Pidsea 97 F8
Burton Salmon 89 B5
Burton Stather 90 C2
Burton upon Stather 90 C2
Burton upon Trent 63 B6
Burtonwood 86 E3
Burwardsley 74 D2
Burwarton 61 F6
Burwash 18 C3
Burwash Common 18 C3
Burwash Weald 18 C3
Burwell Cambs 55 C6
Lincs 79 B6
Burwen 82 B4
Burwick 159 K5
Bury Cambs 66 F2
Gtr Man 87 C6
Som 10 B4
W Sus 16 C4
Bury Green 41 B7
Bury St Edmunds 56 C2
Burythorpe 96 C3
Busby 119 D5
Buscot 38 E2
Bush Bank 49 D6
Bushbury 62 D3
Bushby 64 D3
Bush Crathie 139 E8
Bushey 40 E4
Bushey Heath 40 E4
Bush Green 68 F5
Bushley 50 F3
Bushton 25 B5
Buslingthorpe 90 F4
Busta 160 G5
Butcher's Cross 18 C2
Butcombe 23 C7
Butetown 22 B3
Butleigh 23 F7
Butleigh Wootton 23 F7
Butler's Cross 39 D8
Butler's End 63 F6
Butlers Marston 51 E8
Butley 57 D7
Butley High Corner 57 E7
Butterburn 109 B6
Buttercrambe 96 D3
Butterknowle 101 B6
Butterleigh 10 D4
Buttermere Cumb 98 C3
Wilts 25 C8
Buttershaw 88 B2
Butterstone 133 E7
Butterton 75 D7
Butterwick
Durham 102 B1
Lincs 79 E6
N Yorks 96 B3
N Yorks 97 B5
Butt Green 74 D3
Buttington 60 D2
Buttonoak 50 B2
Buttsash 14 D5
Butt's Green 14 B4
Buxhall 56 D4
Buxhall Fen Street 56 D4
Buxley 122 D4
Buxted 17 B8
Buxton Derbys 75 B7
Norf 81 E8
Buxworth 87 F8
Bwcle =Buckley 73 C6
Bwlch 35 B5
Bwlchgwyn 73 D6
Bwlch-Llan 46 D4
Bwlchnewydd 32 B4
Bwlchtocyn 70 E4
Bwlch-y-cibau 59 C8
Bwlchyddar 59 B8
Bwlch-y-fadfa 46 E3
Bwlch-y-ffridd 59 E7
Bwlchygroes 45 F4
Bwlch-y-sarnau 48 B2
Byermoor 110 D4
Byers Green 110 F5
Byfield 52 D3
Byfleet 27 C8
Byford 49 E5
Bygrave 54 F3
Byker 111 C5
Bylchau 72 C3
Byley 74 C4
Bynea 33 E6
Byrness 116 D3
Bythorn 53 B8
Byton 49 C5
Byworth 16 B3

C

Cabharstadh 155 E8
Cablea 133 F6
Cabourne 90 D5
Cabrach Argyll 144 G3
Moray 140 B2
Cabrich 151 G8
Cabus 92 E4
Cackle Street 17 B8
Cadbury 10 D4
Cadbury Barton 9 C8
Cadder 119 B6
Caddington 40 C3
Caddonfoot 121 F7
Cadeby Leics 63 D8
S Yorks 89 D6
Cadeleigh 10 D4
Cade Street 18 C3
Cadgwith 3 E6
Cadham 128 D4
Cadishead 86 E5
Cadle 33 E7
Cadley Lancs 92 F5
Wilts 25 C7
Wilts 25 D7
Cadmore End 39 E7
Cadnam 14 C3
Cadney 90 D4
Cadole 73 C6
Cadoxton 22 C3
Cadoxton-Juxta-Neath 34 E1
Cadshaw 86 C5
Cadzow 119 D7
Caeathro 82 E4
Caehopkin 34 C2
Caenby 90 F4
Caenby Corner 90 F3
Caerau Bridgend 34 E2
Cardiff 22 B3
Caér-bryn 33 C6
Caerdeon 58 C3
Caerdydd =Cardiff 22 B3
Caerfarchell 44 C2
Caerffili =Caerphilly 35 F5
Caerfyrddin =Carmarthen 33 B5
Caergeiliog 82 D3
Caergwrle 73 D7
Caergybi =Holyhead 82 C2
Caerleon =Caerllion 35 E7
Caer Llan 36 D1
Caerllion =Caerleon 35 E7
Caernarfon 82 E4
Caerphilly =Caerffili 35 F5
Caersws 59 E7
Caerwedros 46 D2
Caerwent 36 E1
Caerwych 71 D7
Caerwys 72 B5
Caethle 58 E3
Caim 83 C6
Caio 47 F5
Cairinis 148 B3
Cairisiadar 154 D5
Cairminis 154 J5
Cairnbaan 145 D7
Cairnbanno House 153 D8
Cairnborrow 152 D4
Cairnbrogie 141 B7
Cairnbulg Castle 153 B10
Cairncross Angus 134 B4
Borders 122 C4
Cairndow 125 D7
Cairness 153 B10
Cairneyhill 128 F2
Cairnfield House 152 B4
Cairngaan 104 F5
Cairngarroch 104 E4
Cairnhill 153 E6
Cairnie Aberds 141 D7
Aberds 152 D4
Cairnorrie 153 D8
Cairnpark 141 C7
Cairnryan 104 C4
Cairnton 159 H4
Caister-on-Sea 69 C8
Caistor 90 D5
Caistor St Edmund 68 D5
Caistron 117 D5
Caitha Bowland 121 E7
Calais Street 56 F3
Calanais 154 D7
Calbost 155 F9
Calbourne 14 F5
Calceby 79 B6
Calcot Row 26 B4
Calcott 31 C5
Caldback 160 C8
Caldbeck 108 F3
Caldbergh 101 F5
Caldecote Cambs 54 D4
Cambs 65 F8
Herts 54 F3
W Nhants 52 D4
Caldecott N Nhants 53 C7
Oxon 38 E4
Rutland 65 E5
Calderbank 119 C7
Calder Bridge 98 D2
Calderbrook 87 C7
Caldercruix 119 C8
Calder Hall 98 D2
Calder Mains 158 E2
Caldermill 119 E6
Calder Vale 92 E5
Calderwood 119 D6
Caldhame 134 E4
Caldicot 36 F1
Caldwell Derbys 63 C6
N Yorks 101 C6
Caldy 85 F3
Caledrhydiau 46 D3
Calfsound 159 E6
Calgary 146 F6
Califer 151 F13
California Falk 120 B2
Norf 69 C8
Calke 63 B7
Callakille 149 C11
Callaly 117 D6
Callander 126 D5
Callaughton 61 E6
Callestick 4 D2
Calligarry 149 H11
Callington 5 C8
Callow 49 F6
Callow End 50 E3
Callow Hill Wilts 37 F7
Worcs 50 B2
Callows Grave 49 C7
Calmore 14 C4
Calmsden 37 D7
Calne 24 B5
Calow 76 B4
Calshot 15 D5
Calstock 6 C2
Calstone Wellington 24 C5
Calthorpe 81 D7
Calthwaite 108 E4
Calton N Yorks 94 D2
Staffs 75 D8
Calveley 74 D2
Calver 76 B2
Calverhall 74 F3
Calver Hill 49 E5
Calverleigh 10 C4
Calverley 94 F5
Calvert 39 B6
Calverton M Keynes 53 F5
Notts 77 E6
Calvine 133 C5
Calvo 107 D8
Cam 36 E4
Camas-luinie 136 B2
Camasnacroise 130 D2
Camastianavaig 149 E10
Camasunary 149 G10
Camault Muir 151 G8
Camb 160 D7
Camber 19 D6
Camberley 27 C6
Camberwell 28 B4
Camblesforth 89 B7
Cambo 117 F6
Cambois 117 F9
Camborne 3 B5
Cambourne 54 D4
Cambridge Cambs 55 D5
Glos 36 D4
Cambridge Town 43 F5
Cambus 127 E7
Cambusavie Farm 151 B10
Cambusbarron 127 E6
Cambuskenneth 127 E7
Cambuslang 119 C6
Cambusmore Lodge 151 B10
Camden 41 F5
Camelford 8 F3
Camelsdale 27 F6
Camerory 151 H13
Camer's Green 50 F2
Camerton Bath 23 D8
Cumb 107 F7
E Yorks 91 B6
Camghouran 132 D2
Cammachmore 141 E8
Cammeringham 90 F3
Camore 151 B10
Campbeltown 143 F8
Camperdown 111 B5
Camp Hill 63 E7
Campmuir 134 F2
Campsall 89 C6
Campsey Ash 57 D7
Campton 54 F2
Camptown 116 C2
Camrose 44 C4
Camserney 133 E5
Camster 158 F4
Camuschoirk 130 C1
Camuscross 149 G11
Camusnagaul Highld 130 B4
Highld 150 C3
Camusrory 147 B11
Camusteel 149 D12
Camusterrach 149 D12
Camusvrachan 132 E3
Canada 14 C3
Canadia 18 D4
Canal Side 89 C7
Candacraig House 140 C2
Candlesby 79 C7
Candy Mill 120 E3
Cane End 26 B4
Canewdon 42 E4
Canford Bottom 13 D8
Canford Cliffs 13 F8
Canford Magna 13 E8
Canham's Green 56 C4
Canholes 75 B7
Canisbay 158 C5
Cann 13 B6
Cannard's Grave 23 E8
Cann Common 13 B6
Cannich 150 H6
Cannington 22 F4
Cannock 62 D3
Cannock Wood 62 C4
Canonbie 108 B3
Canon Bridge 49 E6
Canon Frome 49 E8
Canon Pyon 49 E6
Canons Ashby 52 D3
Canonstown 2 C4
Canterbury 30 D5
Cantley Norf 69 D6
S Yorks 89 D7
Cantlop 60 D5
Canton 22 B3
Cantraybruich 151 G10
Cantraydoune 151 G10
Cantraywood 151 G10
Cantsfield 93 B6
Canvey Island 42 F3
Canwick 78 C2
Canworthy Water 8 E4
Caol 131 B5
Caolas 146 G3
Caolas Scalpaigh 154 H7
Caolas Stocinis 154 H6
Caol Ila 142 A5
Capel 28 E2
Capel Bangor 58 F3
Capel Betws Lleucu 46 D5
Capel Carmel 70 E2
Capel Coch 82 C4
Capel Curig 83 F7
Capel Cynon 46 E2
Capel Dewi Carms 33 B5
Ceredig 46 E3
Ceredig 58 F3
Capel Garmon 83 F8
Capel-gwyn 82 D3
Capel Gwyn 33 B5
Capel Gwynfe 33 B8
Capel Hendre 33 C6
Capel Hermon 71 E8
Capel Isaac 33 B6
Capel Iwan 45 F4
Capel le Ferne 31 F6
Capel Llanilltern 34 F4
Capel Mawr 82 D4
Capel St Andrew 57 E7
Capel St Mary 56 F4
Capel Seion 46 B5
Capel Tygwydd 45 E4
Capel Uchaf 70 C5
Capelulo 83 D7
Capel-y-graig 82 E5
Capenhurst 73 B7
Capernwray 92 B5
Capheaton 117 F6
Cappercleuch 115 B5
Capplegill 114 D4
Capton 7 D6
Caputh 133 F7
Carbis Bay 2 C4
Carbost Highld 149 D9
Highld 149 E8
Carbrook 88 F4
Carbrooke 68 D2
Carburton 77 B6
Carcant 121 D6
Carcary 135 D6
Carclaze 4 D5
Car Colston 77 E7
Carcroft 89 C6
Cardenden 128 E4
Cardeston 60 C3
Cardiff =Caerdydd 22 B3
Cardigan =Aberteifi 45 E3
Cardington Bedford 53 E8
Shrops 60 E5
Cardinham 5 C6
Cardonald 118 C5
Cardow 152 D1
Cardrona 121 F6
Cardross 118 B3
Cardurnock 107 D8
Careby 65 C7
Careston Castle 135 D5
Carew 32 D1
Carew Cheriton 32 D1
Carew Newton 32 D1
Carey 49 F7
Carfrae 121 C8
Cargenbridge 107 B6
Cargill 134 F1
Cargo 108 D3
Cargreen 6 C2
Carham 122 F4
Carhampton 22 E2
Carharrack 3 B6
Carie Perth 132 D3
Perth 132 F3
Carines 4 D2
Carisbrooke 15 F5
Cark 92 B3
Carlabhagh 154 C7
Carland Cross 4 D3
Carlby 65 C7
Carlecotes 88 D2
Carlesmoor 94 B4
Carleton Cumb 99 B7
Cumb 108 D4
Lancs 92 F3
N Yorks 94 E2
Carleton Forehoe 68 D3
Carleton Rode 68 E4
Carlingcott 23 D8
Carlin How 103 C5
Carlisle 108 D4
Carlops 120 D4
Carlton Bedford 53 D7
Cambs 55 D7
Leics 63 D7
Notts 77 E6
N Yorks 89 B7
N Yorks 101 C6
N Yorks 101 F5
N Yorks 102 F4
Stockton 102 B1
Suff 57 C7
S Yorks 88 C4
W Yorks 88 B4
Carlton Colville 69 F8
Carlton Curlieu 64 E3
Carlton Husthwaite 95 B7
Carlton in Cleveland 102 D3
Carlton in Lindrick 89 F6
Carlton le Moorland 78 D2
Carlton Miniott 102 F1
Carlton on Trent 77 C7
Carlton Scroop 78 E2
Carluke 119 D8
Carmarthen =Caerfyrddin 33 B5
Carmel Anglesey 82 C3
Carms 33 C6
Flint 73 B5
Guern 16
Gwyn 82 F4
Carmont 141 F7
Carmunnock 119 D6
Carmyle 119 C6
Carmyllie 135 E5
Carnaby 97 C7
Carnach Highld 136 B3
Highld 150 B3
W Isles 154 H7
Carnachy 157 D10
Càrnais 154 D5
Carnbee 129 D7
Carnbo 128 D2
Carnbrea 3 B5
Carnduff 119 E6
Carnduncan 142 B3
Carne 3 C8
Carnforth 92 B4
Carn-gorm 136 B2
Carnhedryn 44 C3
Carnhell Green 2 C5
Carnkie Corn 3 C5
Corn 3 C6
Carno 59 E6
Carnoch Highld 150 F5
Highld 150 H6
Carnock 128 F2
Carnon Downs 3 B6
Carnousie 153 C6
Carnoustie 135 F5
Carnwath 120 E2
Carnyorth 2 C2
Carperby 101 F5
Carpley Green 100 F4
Carr 89 E6
Carradale 143 E9
Carragraich 154 H6
Carrbridge 138 B5
Carrefour Selous Jersey 17
Carreglefn 82 C3
Carreg-wen 45 E4
Carr Hill 111 C5
Carrick Argyll 145 E8
Fife 129 B6
Carrick Castle 145 D10
Carrick House 159 E6
Carriden 128 F2
Carrington Gtr Man 86 E5
Lincs 79 D6
Midloth 121 C6
Carrog Conwy 71 C8
Denb 72 E5
Carron Falk 127 F7
Moray 152 D2
Carronbridge 113 E8
Carron Bridge 127 F6
Carronshore 127 F7
Carrshield 109 E8
Carrutherstown 107 B8
Carrville 111 E6
Carsaig Argyll 144 E6
Argyll 147 J8
Carscreugh 105 D6
Carsegowan 105 D8
Carse Gray 134 D4
Carse House 144 G6
Carseriggan 105 C7
Carsethorn 107 D6
Carshalton 28 C3
Carsington 76 D2
Carskiey 143 H7
Carsluith 105 D8
Carsphairn 113 E5
Carstairs 120 E2
Carstairs Junction 120 E2
Carswell Marsh 38 E3
Carter's Clay 14 B4
Carterton 38 D2
Carterway Heads 110 D3
Carthew 4 D5
Carthorpe 101 F8
Cartington 117 D6
Cartland 119 E8
Cartmel 92 B3
Cartmel Fell 99 F6
Carway 33 D5
Cary Fitzpaine 12 B3
Cascob 48 C4
Cas-gwent =Chepstow 36 E2
Cashlie 132 E1
Cashmoor 13 C7
Casnewydd =Newport 35 F7
Cassey Compton 37 C7
Cassington 38 C4
Cassop 111 F6
Castell 72 C5
Castellau 34 F4
Castell-Howell 46 E3
Castell-Nedd =Neath 33 E8
Castell Newydd Emlyn =Newcastle Emlyn 46 E2
Castell-y-bwch 35 E6
Casterton 93 B6
Castle Acre 67 C8
Castle Ashby 53 D6
Castlebay =Bagh a Chaisteil 148 J1
Castle Bolton 101 E5
Castle Bromwich 62 F5
Castle Bytham 65 C6
Castlebythe 32 B1
Castle Caereinion 59 D8
Castle Camps 55 E7
Castle Carrock 108 D5
Castlecary 119 B7
Castle Cary 23 F8
Castle Combe 24 B3
Castlecraig 151 E11
Castle Donington 63 B8
Castle Douglas 106 C4
Castle Eaton 37 E8
Castle Eden 111 F7
Castlefairn 113 F7
Castle Forbes 140 C5
Castleford 88 B5
Castle Frome 49 E8
Castle Green 27 C7
Castle Gresley 63 C6
Castle Heaton 122 E5
Castle Hedingham 55 F8
Castlehill Borders 120 F5
Highld 158 D3
W Dunb 118 B3
Castle Hill 29 E7
Castle Huntly 128 B5
Castle Kennedy 104 D5
Castlemaddy 113 F5
Castlemartin 44 F4
Castlemilk Dumfries 107 B8
Glasgow 119 D6
Castlemorris 44 B4
Castlemorton 50 F2
Castle O'er 115 E5
Castle Pulverbatch 60 D4
Castle Rising 67 B6
Castleside 110 E3
Castle Stuart 151 G10
Castlethorpe 53 E6
Castleton Angus 134 E3
Argyll 145 E7
Derbys 88 F2
Gtr Man 87 C6
Newport 35 F6
N Yorks 102 D4
Castletown Ches W 73 D8
Highld 151 G10
Highld 158 D3
IoM 84 F2
T&W 111 D6
Castleweary 115 D7
Castley 95 E5
Caston 68 E2
Castor 65 E8
Catacol 143 D10
Catbrain 36 F2
Catbrook 36 D2
Catchall 2 D3
Catchems Corner 51 B7
Catchgate 110 D4
Catcleugh 116 D3
Catcliffe 88 F5
Catcott 23 F5
Caterham 28 D4
Catfield 69 B6
Catfirth 160 H6
Catford 28 B4
Catforth 92 F4
Cathays 22 B3
Cathcart 119 C5
Cathedine 35 B5
Catherington 15 C7
Catherton 49 B8
Catlodge 138 E2
Catlowdy 108 B4
Catmore 38 F4
Caton 92 C5
Caton Green 92 C5
Catrine 113 B5
Cat's Ash 35 E7
Catsfield 18 D4
Catshill 50 B4
Cattal 95 D7
Cattawade 56 F5
Catterall 92 E4
Catterick 101 E7
Catterick Bridge 101 E7
Catterick Garrison 101 E6
Catterlen 108 F4
Catterline 135 B8
Catterton 95 E8
Catthorpe 52 B3
Cattistock 12 E3
Catton Northumb 109 D8
N Yorks 95 B6
Catwick 97 E7
Catworth 53 B8
Caudlesprings 68 D2
Caulcott 39 B5
Cauldcots 135 E6
Cauldhame 126 E5
Cauldmill 115 C8
Cauldon 75 E7
Caulkerbush 107 D6
Caulside 115 F7
Caunsall 62 F2
Caunton 77 D7
Causewayend 120 F3
Causeway End 105 C8
Causeway Foot 94 F3
Causewayhead Cumb 107 D8
Stirling 127 E6
Causeyend 141 C8
Causey Park Bridge 117 E7
Cautley 100 E1
Cavendish 56 E2
Cavendish Bridge 63 B8
Cavenham 55 C8
Caversfield 39 B5
Caversham 26 B5
Caverswall 75 E6
Cavil 96 F3
Cawdor 151 F11
Cawkwell 79 B5
Cawood 95 F8
Cawsand 6 D2
Cawston 81 E7
Cawthorne 88 D3
Cawthorpe 65 B7
Cawton 96 B2
Caxton 54 D4
Caynham 49 B7
Caythorpe Lincs 78 E2
Notts 77 E6
Cayton 103 F8
Ceann a Bhaigh 148 B2
Ceannacroc Lodge 136 C5
Ceann a Deas Loch Baghasdail 148 G2
Ceann Shiphoirt 155 F7
Ceann Tarabhaigh 154 F7
Cearsiadair 155 E8
Cefn Berain 72 C3
Cefn-brith 72 D3
Cefn Canol 73 F6
Cefn-coch 83 E8
Cefn Coch 59 B8
Cefn-coed-y-cymmer 34 D4
Cefn Cribbwr 34 F2
Cefn Cross 34 F2
Cefn-ddwysarn 72 F3
Cefn Einion 60 F2
Cefneithin 33 C6
Cefn-gorwydd 47 E8
Cefn-mawr 73 E6
Cefn-y-bedd 73 D7
Cefn-y-pant 32 B2
Cei-bach 46 D3
Ceinewydd =New Quay 46 D2
Ceint 82 D4
Cellan 46 E5
Cellarhead 75 E6
Cemaes 82 B3
Cemmaes 58 D5
Cemmaes Road 58 D5
Cenarth 45 E4
Cenin 71 C5
Central 118 B2
Ceos 155 E8
Ceres 129 C6
Cerne Abbas 12 D4
Cerney Wick 37 E7
Cerrigceinwen 82 D4
Cerrigydrudion 72 E3
Cessford 116 B3
Ceunant 82 E5
Chaceley 50 F3
Chacewater 3 B6
Chackmore 52 F4
Chacombe 52 E2
Chadderton 87 D7
Chadderton Fold 87 D6
Chaddesden 76 F3
Chaddesley Corbett 50 B3
Chaddleworth 26 B2
Chadlington 38 B3
Chadshunt 51 D8
Chad Valley 62 F4
Chadwell 64 B4
Chadwell St Mary 29 B7
Chadwick End 51 B7
Chadwick Green 86 E3
Chaffcombe 11 C8
Chagford 10 F2
Chailey 17 C7
Chainbridge 66 D4
Chain Bridge 79 E6
Chainhurst 29 E8
Chalbury 13 D8
Chalbury Common 13 D8
Chaldon 28 D4
Chaldon Herring 13 F5
Chale 15 G5
Chale Green 15 G5
Chalfont Common 40 E3
Chalfont St Giles 40 E2
Chalfont St Peter 40 E3
Chalford 37 D5
Chalgrove 39 E6
Chalk 29 B7
Challacombe 21 E5
Challoch 105 C7
Challock 30 D4
Chalton C Beds 40 B3
Hants 15 C8
Chalvington 18 E2
Chancery 46 B4
Chandler's Ford 14 B5
Channel Tunnel 19 B8
Channerwick 160 L6
Chantry Som 24 E2
Suff 56 E5
Chapel 128 E4
Chapel Allerton Som 23 D6
W Yorks 95 F6
Chapel Amble 4 B4
Chapel Brampton 52 C5
Chapel Chorlton 74 F5
Chapel End 63 E7
Chapel-en-le-Frith 87 F8
Chapelgate 66 B4
Chapel Green Warks 52 C2
Warks 63 F6
Chapel Haddlesey 89 B6
Chapelhall 119 C7
Chapel Head 66 F3
Chapelhill Dumfries 114 E3
Highld 151 D11
N Ayrs 118 E2
Perth 128 B4
Perth 133 F7
Chapel Hill Aberds 153 E10
Lincs 78 D5
Mon 36 E2
N Yorks 95 E6
Chapelknowe 108 B3
Chapel Lawn 48 B5
Chapel-le-Dale 93 B7
Chapel Milton 87 F8
Chapel of Garioch 141 B6
Chapel Row 26 C3
Chapel St Leonards 79 B8
Chapel Stile 99 D5
Chapelton Angus 135 E6
Devon 9 B7
Highld 138 C5
S Lanark 119 E6
Chapeltown Blackburn 86 C5
Moray 139 B8
S Yorks 88 E4
Chapmanslade 24 E3
Chapmans Well 9 E5
Chapmore End 41 C6
Chappel 42 B4
Chard 11 D8
Chardstock 11 D8
Charfield 36 E4
Charford 50 C4
Charing 30 E3
Charing Cross 14 C2
Charing Heath 30 E3
Charingworth 51 F7
Charlbury 38 C3
Charlcombe 24 C2
Charlecote 51 D7
Charles 21 F5
Charlesfield 107 C8
Charleston Angus 134 E3
Renfs 118 C4
Charlestown Aberdeen 141 D8
Corn 4 D5
Derbys 87 E8
Dorset 12 G4
Fife 128 F2
Gtr Man 87 D6
Highld 149 A13
Highld 151 G9
W Yorks 87 B7
Charlestown of Aberlour 152 D2
Charles Tye 56 D4
Charlesworth 87 E8
Charleton 7 E5
Charlton Hants 25 E8
Herts 40 B4
London 28 B5
Northumb 116 F4
Som 23 D8
Telford 61 C5
Wilts 13 B7
Wilts 25 D6
Wilts 37 F6
W Nhants 52 F3
Worcs 50 E5
W Sus 16 C2
Charlton Abbots 37 B7
Charlton Adam 12 B3
Charlton-All-Saints 14 B2
Charlton Down 12 E4
Charlton Horethorne 12 B4
Charlton Kings 37 B6
Charlton Mackerell 12 B3
Charlton Marshall 13 D6
Charlton Musgrove 12 B5
Charlton on Otmoor 39 C5
Charltons 102 C4
Charlwood 28 E3
Charlynch 22 F4
Charminster 12 E4
Charmouth 11 E8
Charndon 39 B6
Charney Bassett 38 E3
Charnock Richard 86 C3
Charsfield 57 D6
Chart Corner 29 D8
Charter Alley 26 D3
Charterhouse 23 D6
Charterville Allotments 38 C3
Chartham 30 D5
Chartham Hatch 30 D5
Chartridge 40 D2
Chart Sutton 30 E2
Charvil 27 B5
Charwelton 52 D3
Chasetown 62 D4
Chastleton 38 B2
Chasty 8 D5
Chatburn 93 E7
Chatcull 74 F4
Chatham 29 C8
Chathill 117 B7
Chattenden 29 B8
Chatteris 66 F3
Chattisham 56 E4
Chatto 116 C3
Chatton 117 B6
Chawleigh 10 C2
Chawley 38 D4
Chawston 54 D2
Chawton 26 F5
Cheadle Gtr Man 87 F6
Staffs 75 E7
Cheadle Heath 87 F6
Cheadle Hulme 87 F6
Cheam 28 C3
Cheapside 27 D8
Chearsley 39 C7
Chebsey 62 B2
Checkendon 39 F6
Checkley Ches E 74 E4
Hereford 49 F7
Staffs 75 F7
Chedburgh 55 D8
Cheddar 23 D6
Cheddington 40 C2
Cheddleton 75 D6
Cheddon Fitzpaine 11 B7
Chedglow 37 E6
Chedgrave 69 E6
Chedington 12 D2
Chediston 57 B7
Chedworth 37 C7
Chedzoy 22 F5
Cheeklaw 122 D3
Cheeseman's Green 19 B7
Cheglinch 20 E4
Cheldon 10 C2
Chelford 74 B5
Chellaston 76 F3
Chell Heath 75 D5
Chellington 53 D7
Chelmarsh 61 F7
Chelmer Village 42 D3
Chelmondiston 57 F6
Chelmorton 75 C8
Chelmsford 42 D3
Chelsea 28 B3
Chelsfield 29 C5
Chelsworth 56 E3
Cheltenham 37 B6
Chelveston 53 C7
Chelvey 23 C6
Chelwood 23 C8
Chelwood Common 17 B8
Chelwood Gate 17 B8
Chelworth 37 E6
Chelworth Green 37 E7
Chemistry 74 E2
Chenies 40 E3
Cheny Longville 60 F4
Chepstow =Cas-gwent 36 E2
Chequerfield 89 B5
Cherhill 24 B5
Cherington Glos 37 E6
Warks 51 F7
Cheriton Devon 21 E6
Hants 15 B6
Kent 19 B8
Swansea 33 E5
Cheriton Bishop 10 E2
Cheriton Fitzpaine 10 D3
Cheriton or Stackpole Elidor 44 F4
Cherrington 61 B6
Cherrybank 128 B3
Cherry Burton 97 E5
Cherry Hinton 55 D5
Cherry Orchard 50 D3
Cherry Willingham 78 B3
Chertsey 27 C8
Cheselbourne 13 E5
Chesham 40 D2
Chesham Bois 40 E2
Cheshunt 41 D6
Cheslyn Hay 62 D3
Chessington 28 C2
Chester 73 C8
Chesterblade 23 E8
Chesterfield 76 B3
Chester-le-Street 111 D5
Chester Moor 111 E5
Chesters Borders 116 B2
Borders 116 C2
Chesterton Cambs 55 C5
Cambs 65 E8
Glos 37 D7
Oxon 39 B5
Shrops 61 E7
Staffs 74 E5
Warks 51 D8
Chesterwood 109 C8
Chestfield 30 C5
Cheston 6 D4
Cheswardine 61 B7
Cheswick 123 E6
Chetnole 12 D4
Chettiscombe 10 C4
Chettisham 66 F5
Chettle 13 C7
Chetton 61 E6
Chetwode 39 B6
Chetwynd Aston 61 C7
Cheveley 55 C7
Chevening 29 D5
Chevington 55 D8
Chevithorne 10 C4
Chew Magna 23 C7
Chew Stoke 23 C7
Chewton Keynsham 23 C8
Chewton Mendip 23 D7
Chicheley 53 E7
Chichester 16 D2
Chickerell 12 F4
Chicklade 24 F4
Chicksgrove 24 F4
Chidden 15 C7
Chiddingfold 27 F7
Chiddingly 18 D2
Chiddingstone 29 E5
Chiddingstone Causeway 29 E6
Chiddingstone Hoath 29 E5
Chideock 12 E2
Chidham 15 D8
Chidswell 88 B3
Chieveley 26 B2
Chignall St James 42 D2
Chignall Smealy 42 C2
Chigwell 41 E7
Chigwell Row 41 E7
Chilbolton 25 F8
Chilcomb 15 B6
Chilcombe 12 E3
Chilcompton 23 D8
Chilcote 63 C6
Childer Thornton 73 B7
Child Okeford 13 C6
Childrey 38 F3
Child's Ercall 61 B6
Childswickham 51 F5
Childwall 86 F2
Childwick Green 40 C4
Chilfrome 12 E3
Chilgrove 16 C2
Chilham 30 D4
Chilhampton 25 F5
Chilla 9 D6
Chillaton 9 F6
Chillenden 31 D6

Chillerton 15 F5
Chillesford 57 D7
Chillingham 117 B6
Chillington Devon 7 E5
Som 11 C8
Chilmark 24 F4
Chilson 38 C3
Chilsworthy Corn 6 B2
Devon 8 D5
Chilthorne Domer 12 C3
Chiltington 17 C7
Chilton Bucks 39 C6
Durham 101 B7
Oxon 38 F4
Chilton Cantelo 12 B3
Chilton Foliat 25 B8
Chilton Lane 111 F6
Chilton Polden 23 F5
Chilton Street 55 E8
Chilton Trinity 22 F4
Chilvers Coton 63 E7
Chilwell 76 F5
Chilworth Hants 14 C5
Sur 27 E8
Chimney 38 D3
Chineham 26 D4
Chingford 41 E6
Chinley 87 F8
Chinley Head 87 F8
Chinnor 39 D7
Chipnall 74 F4
Chippenhall Green 57 B6
Chippenham Cambs 55 C7
Wilts 24 B4
Chipperfield 40 D3
Chipping Herts 54 F4
Lancs 93 E6
Chipping Campden 51 F6
Chipping Hill 42 C4
Chipping Norton 38 B3
Chipping Ongar 42 D1
Chipping Sodbury 36 F4
Chipping Warden 52 E2
Chipstable 10 B5
Chipstead Kent 29 D5
Sur 28 D3
Chirbury 60 E2
Chirk = Y Waun 73 F6
Chirk Bank 73 F6
Chirmorrie 105 B6
Chirnside 122 D4
Chirnsidebridge 122 D4
Chirton 25 D5
Chisbury 25 C7
Chiselborough 12 C2
Chiseldon 25 B6
Chiserley 87 B8
Chislehampton 39 E5
Chislehurst 28 B5
Chislet 31 C6
Chiswell Green 40 D4
Chiswick 28 B3
Chiswick End 54 E4
Chisworth 87 E7
Chithurst 16 B2
Chittering 55 B5
Chitterne 24 E4
Chittlehamholt 9 B8
Chittlehampton 9 B8
Chittoe 24 C4
Chivenor 20 F4
Chobham 27 C7
Choicelee 122 D3
Cholderton 25 E7
Cholesbury 40 D2
Chollerford 110 B2
Chollerton 110 B2
Cholmondeston 74 C3
Cholsey 39 F5
Cholstrey 49 D6
Chop Gate 102 E3
Choppington 117 F8
Chopwell 110 D4
Chorley Ches E 74 D2
Lancs 86 C3
Shrops 61 F6
Staffs 62 C4
Chorleywood 40 E3
Chorlton cum Hardy 87 E6
Chorlton Lane 73 E8
Choulton 60 F3
Chowdene 111 D5
Chowley 73 D8
Chrishall 54 F5
Christchurch BCP 14 E2
Cambs 66 E4
Glos 36 C2
Newport 35 F7
Christian Malford 24 B4
Christleton 73 C8
Christmas Common 39 E7
Christon 23 D5
Christon Bank 117 B8
Christow 10 F3
Chryston 119 B6
Chudleigh 7 B6
Chudleigh Knighton 7 B6
Chulmleigh 9 C8
Chunal 87 E8
Church 86 B5
Churcham 36 C4
Church Aston 61 C7
Churchbank 48 B4
Church Brampton 52 C5
Churchbridge 62 D3
Church Broughton 76 F2
Church Crookham 27 D6
Churchdown 37 C5
Church Eaton 62 C2
Churchend Essex 42 B2
Essex 43 E6
S Glos 36 E4
Church End Cambs 66 D3
Cambs 66 F2
C Beds 40 B2
C Beds 53 F7
C Beds 54 F2
Essex 42 B3
Essex 55 E6
E Yorks 97 D6
Hants 26 D4
Lincs 78 F5
Warks 63 E6
Warks 63 E6
Church End continued
Wilts 24 B5
Church Enstone 38 B3
Church Fenton 95 F8
Churchfield 62 E4
Churchgate Street 41 C7
Church Green
Devon 11 E6
Norf 68 E3
Church Gresley 63 C6
Church Hanborough 38 C4
Church Hill 74 C3
Church Houses 102 E4
Churchill Devon 11 D8
Devon 20 E4
N Som 23 D6
Oxon 38 B2
Worcs 50 B3
Worcs 50 D4
Churchinford 11 C7
Church Knowle 13 F7
Church Laneham 77 B8
Church Langton 64 E4
Church Lawford 52 B2
Church Lawton 74 D5
Church Leigh 75 F7
Church Lench 50 D5
Church Mayfield 75 E8
Church Minshull 74 C3
Church Norton 16 E2
Churchover 64 F2
Church Preen 60 E5
Church Pulverbatch 60 D4
Churchstanton 11 C6
Church Stoke 60 E2
Churchstow 6 E5
Church Stowe 52 D4
Church Street 29 B8
Church Stretton 60 E4
Churchtown Derbys 76 C2
IoM 84 C4
Lancs 92 E4
Mers 85 C4
Church Town
N Lincs 89 D8
Sur 28 D4
Church Village 34 F4
Church Warsop 77 C5
Churnsike Lodge 109 B6
Churston Ferrers 7 D7
Churt 27 F6
Churton 73 D8
Churwell 88 B3
Chute Standen 25 D8
Chwilog 70 D5
Chyandour 2 C3
Cilan Uchaf 70 E3
Cilcain 73 C5
Cilcennin 46 C4
Cilfor 71 D7
Cilfrew 34 D1
Cilfynydd 34 E4
Cilgerran 45 E3
Cilgwyn Carms 33 B8
Gwyn 82 F4
Pembs 45 F2
Ciliau Aeron 46 D3
Cill Donnain 148 F2
Cille Bhrighde 148 G2
Cille Pheadair 148 G2
Cilmery 48 D2
Cilsan 33 B6
Ciltalgarth 72 E2
Cilwendeg 45 F4
Cilybebyll 33 D8
Cilycwm 47 F6
Cimla 34 E1
Cinderford 36 C3
Cippyn 45 E3
Circebost 154 D6
Cirencester 37 D7
Ciribhig 154 C6
City London 41 F6
Powys 60 F2
City Dulas 82 C4
Clachaig 145 E10
Clachan Argyll 124 D3
Argyll 125 D7
Argyll 130 E2
Argyll 144 H6
Highld 149 E10
W Isles 148 D2
Clachaneasy 105 B7
Clachanmore 104 E4
Clachan na Luib 148 B3
Clachan of Campsie 119 B6
Clachan of Glendaruel 145 E8
Clachan-Seil 124 D3
Clachan Strachur 125 E6
Clachbreck 144 F6
Clachnabrain 134 C3
Clachtoll 156 G3
Clackmannan 127 E8
Clacton-on-Sea 43 C7
Cladach Chireboist 148 B2
Claddach-knockline 148 B2
Cladich 125 C6
Claggan Highld 131 B5
Highld 147 G9
Claigan 148 C7
Claines 50 D3
Clandown 23 D8
Clanfield Hants 15 C7
Oxon 38 D2
Clanville 25 E8
Claonaig 145 H7
Claonel 157 J8
Clapgate Dorset 13 D8
Herts 41 B7
Clapham Bedford 53 D8
London 28 B3
N Yorks 93 C7
W Sus 16 D4
Clap Hill 19 B7
Clappers 122 D5
Clappersgate 99 D5
Clapton 12 D2
Clapton-in-Gordano 23 B6
Clapton-on-the-Hill 38 C1
Clapworthy 9 B8
Clarach 58 F3
Clara Vale 110 C4
Clarbeston 32 B1
Clarbeston Road 32 B1
Clarborough 89 F8
Clardon 158 D3
Clare 55 E8
Clarebrand 106 C4
Clarencefield 107 C7
Clarilaw 115 C8
Clark's Green 28 F2
Clarkston 119 D5
Clashandorran 151 G8
Clashcoig 151 B9
Clashindarroch 152 E4
Clashmore
Highld 151 C10
Highld 156 F3
Clashnessie 156 F3
Clashnoir 139 B8
Clate 160 G7
Clathy 127 C8
Clatt 140 B4
Clatter 59 E6
Clatterford 15 F5
Clatterin Bridge 135 B6
Clatworthy 22 F2
Claughton Lancs 92 E5
Lancs 93 C5
Mers 85 F4
Claverdon 51 C6
Claverham 23 C6
Clavering 55 F5
Claverley 61 E7
Claverton 24 C2
Clawdd-newydd 72 D4
Clawthorpe 92 B5
Clawton 9 E5
Claxby Lincs 79 B7
Lincs 90 E5
Claxton Norf 69 D6
N Yorks 96 C2
Claybokie 139 E6
Claybrooke Magna 63 F8
Claybrooke Parva 63 F8
Clay Common 69 F7
Clay Coton 52 B3
Clay Cross 76 C3
Claydon Oxon 52 D2
Suff 56 D5
Claygate Dumfries 108 B3
Kent 29 E8
Sur 28 C2
Claygate Cross 29 D7
Clayhanger Devon 10 B5
W Mid 62 D4
Clayhidon 11 C6
Clayhill E Sus 18 C5
Hants 14 D4
Clay Hill 26 B3
Clay Lake 66 B2
Clayock 158 E3
Claypole 77 E8
Clayton Staffs 75 E5
S Yorks 89 D5
W Sus 17 C6
W Yorks 94 F4
Clayton Green 86 B3
Clayton-le-Moors 93 F7
Clayton-le-Woods 86 B3
Clayton West 88 C3
Clayworth 89 F8
Cleadale 146 C7
Cleadon 111 C6
Clearbrook 6 C3
Clearwell 36 D2
Cleasby 101 C7
Cleat 159 K5
Cleatlam 101 C6
Cleator 98 C2
Cleator Moor 98 C2
Clebrig 157 F8
Cleckheaton 88 B2
Cleedownton 61 F5
Cleehill 49 B7
Clee St Margaret 61 F5
Cleethorpes 91 D7
Cleeton St Mary 49 B8
Cleeve 23 C6
Cleeve Hill 37 B6
Cleeve Prior 51 E5
Clegyrnant 59 D6
Clehonger 49 F6
Cleish 128 E2
Cleland 119 D8
Clench Common 25 C6
Clenchwarton 67 B5
Clent 50 B4
Cleobury Mortimer 49 B8
Cleobury North 61 F6
Cleongart 143 E7
Clephanton 151 F11
Clerklands 115 B8
Clestrain 159 H4
Cleuch Head 115 C8
Cleughbrae 107 B7
Clevancy 25 B5
Clevedon 23 B6
Cleveley 38 B3
Cleveleys 92 E3
Cleverton 37 F6
Clevis 21 B7
Clewer 23 D6
Cley next the Sea 81 C6
Cliaid 148 H1
Cliasmol 154 G5
Cliburn 99 B7
Click Mill 159 F4
Cliddesden 26 E4
Cliffburn 135 E6
Cliffe Medway 29 B8
N Yorks 96 F2
Cliff End 19 D5
Cliffe Woods 29 B8
Clifford Hereford 48 E4
W Yorks 95 E7
Clifford Chambers 51 D6
Clifford's Mesne 36 B4
Cliffsend 31 C7
Clifton Bristol 23 B7
C Beds 54 F2
Cumb 99 B7
Derbys 75 E8
Lancs 92 F4
Northumb 117 F8
Nottingham 77 F5
N Yorks 94 E4
Oxon 52 F2
Stirling 131 F7
Clifton continued
S Yorks 89 E6
Worcs 50 E3
York 95 D8
Clifton Campville 63 C6
Cliftoncote 116 B4
Clifton Green 87 D5
Clifton Hampden 39 E5
Clifton Reynes 53 D7
Clifton upon Dunsmore 52 B3
Clifton upon Teme 50 C2
Cliftonville 31 B7
Climaen gwyn 33 D8
Climping 16 D4
Climpy 120 D2
Clink 24 E2
Clint 95 D5
Clint Green 68 C3
Clintmains 122 F2
Cliobh 154 D5
Clippesby 69 C7
Clipsham 65 C6
Clipston 64 F4
Clipstone 77 C5
Clitheroe 93 E7
Cliuthar 154 H6
Clive 60 B5
Clivocast 160 C8
Clixby 90 D5
Clocaenog 72 D4
Clochan 152 B4
Clock Face 86 E3
Clockmill 122 D3
Cloddiau 60 D2
Clodock 35 B7
Clola 153 D10
Clophill 53 F8
Clopton N Nhants 65 F7
Suff 57 D6
Clopton Corner 57 D6
Clopton Green 55 D8
Closeburn 113 E8
Close Clark 84 E2
Closworth 12 C3
Clothall 54 F3
Clotton 74 C2
Clough Foot 87 B7
Cloughton 103 E8
Cloughton Newlands 103 E8
Clousta 160 H5
Clouston 159 G3
Clova Aberds 140 B3
Angus 134 B3
Clovelly 8 B5
Clove Lodge 100 C4
Clovenfords 121 F7
Clovenstone 141 C6
Clovullin 130 C4
Clow Bridge 87 B6
Clowne 76 B4
Clows Top 50 B2
Cloy 73 E7
Cluanie Inn 136 C3
Cluanie Lodge 136 C3
Clun 60 F3
Clunbury 60 F3
Clunderwen 32 C2
Clune 138 B3
Clunes 136 F5
Clungunford 49 B5
Clunie Aberds 153 C6
Perth 133 E8
Clunton 60 F3
Cluny 128 E4
Cluny Castle 138 E2
Clutton Bath 23 D8
Ches W 73 D8
Clwt-grugoer 72 C3
Clwt-y-bont 83 E5
Clydach Mon 35 C6
Swansea 33 D7
Clydach Vale 34 E3
Clydebank 118 B4
Clydey 45 F4
Clyffe Pypard 25 B5
Clynder 145 E11
Clyne 34 D2
Clynelish 157 J11
Clynnog-fawr 82 F4
Clyro 48 E4
Clyst Honiton 10 E4
Clyst Hydon 10 D5
Clyst St George 10 F4
Clyst St Lawrence 10 D5
Clyst St Mary 10 E4
Cnoc Amhlaigh 155 D10
Cnwch-coch 47 B5
Coachford 152 D4
Coad's Green 5 B7
Coal Aston 76 B3
Coalbrookdale 61 D6
Coalbrookvale 35 D5
Coalburn 119 F8
Coalburns 110 C4
Coalcleugh 109 E8
Coaley 36 D4
Coalhall 112 C4
Coalhill 42 E3
Coalpit Heath 36 F3
Coalport 61 D6
Coalsnaughton 127 E8
Coaltown of Balgonie 128 E4
Coaltown of Wemyss 128 E5
Coalville 63 C8
Coalway 36 C2
Coat 12 B2
Coatbridge 119 C7
Coatdyke 119 C7
Coate Swindon 38 F1
Wilts 24 C5
Coates Cambs 66 E3
Glos 37 D6
Lancs 93 E8
Notts 90 F2
W Sus 16 C3
Coatham 102 B3
Coatham Mundeville 101 B7
Coatsgate 114 D3
Cobbaton 9 B8
Cobbler's Green 69 E5
Coberley 37 C6
Cobham Kent 29 C7
Sur 28 C2
Cobholm Island 69 D8
Cobleland 126 E4
Cobnash 49 C6
Coburty 153 B9
Cockayne 102 E4
Cockayne Hatley 54 E3
Cock Bank 73 E7
Cock Bridge 139 D8
Cockburnspath 122 B3
Cock Clarks 42 D4
Cockenzie and Port Seton 121 B7
Cockerham 92 D4
Cockermouth 107 F8
Cockernhoe Green 40 B4
Cockfield Durham 101 B6
Suff 56 D3
Cockfosters 41 E5
Cocking 16 C2
Cockington 7 C6
Cocklake 23 E6
Cockley Beck 98 D4
Cockley Cley 67 D7
Cockshutt 60 B4
Cockthorpe 81 C5
Cockwood 10 F4
Cockyard 49 F6
Codda 5 B6
Coddenham 56 D5
Coddington
Ches W 73 D8
Hereford 50 E2
Notts 77 D8
Codford St Mary 24 F4
Codford St Peter 24 F4
Codicote 41 C5
Codmore Hill 16 B4
Codnor 76 E4
Codrington 24 B2
Codsall 62 D2
Codsall Wood 62 D2
Coed Duon = Blackwood 35 E5
Coedely 34 F4
Coedkernew 35 F6
Coed Mawr 83 D5
Coed Morgan 35 C7
Coedpoeth 73 D6
Coed-Talon 73 D6
Coedway 60 C3
Coed-y-bryn 46 E2
Coed-y-paen 35 E7
Coed-yr-ynys 35 B5
Coed Ystumgwern 71 E6
Coelbren 34 C2
Coffinswell 7 C6
Cofton Hackett 50 B5
Cogan 22 B3
Cogenhoe 53 C6
Cogges 38 D3
Coggeshall 42 B4
Coggeshall Hamlet 42 B4
Coggins Mill 18 C2
Coignafearn Lodge 138 C2
Coig Peighinnean 155 A10
Coig Peighinnean Bhuirgh 155 B9
Coilacriech 140 E2
Coilantogle 126 D4
Coilleag 148 G2
Coillore 149 E8
Coity 34 F3
Col 155 C9
Colaboll 157 H8
Colan 4 C3
Colaton Raleigh 11 F5
Colbost 148 D7
Colburn 101 E6
Colby Cumb 100 B1
IoM 84 E2
Norf 81 D8
Colchester 43 B6
Colcot 22 C3
Cold Ash 26 C3
Cold Ashby 52 B4
Cold Ashton 24 B2
Cold Aston 37 C8
Coldbackie 157 D9
Coldbeck 100 D2
Coldblow 29 B6
Cold Blow 32 C2
Cold Brayfield 53 D7
Coldean 17 D7
Coldeast 7 B6
Colden 87 B7
Colden Common 15 B5
Coldfair Green 57 C8
Coldham 66 D4
Cold Hanworth 90 F4
Coldharbour Glos 36 D2
Kent 29 D6
Sur 28 E2
Cold Harbour 78 F2
Cold Hatton 61 B6
Cold Hesledon 111 E7
Cold Higham 52 D4
Coldingham 122 C5
Cold Kirby 102 F3
Cold Newton 64 D4
Cold Northcott 8 F4
Cold Norton 42 D4
Cold Overton 64 C5
Coldrain 128 D2
Coldred 31 E6
Coldridge 9 D8
Coldstream Angus 134 F3
Borders 122 F4
Coldwaltham 16 C4
Coldwells 153 D11
Coldwells Croft 140 B4
Coldyeld 60 E3
Cole 23 F8
Colebatch 60 F3
Colebrook 10 D5
Colebrooke 10 E2
Coleby Lincs 78 C2
N Lincs 90 C2
Coleford Devon 10 D2
Glos 36 C2
Som 23 E8
Cole Green 41 C5
Cole Henley 26 D2
Colehill 13 D8
Coleman's Hatch 29 F5
Colemere 73 F8
Colemore 26 F5
Coleorton 63 C8
Colerne 24 B3
Colesbourne 37 C6
Colesden 54 D2
Coles Green 56 E4
Cole's Green 57 C6
Coleshill Bucks 40 E2
Oxon 38 E2
Warks 63 F6
Colestocks 11 D5
Colgate 28 F3
Colgrain 126 F2
Colinsburgh 129 D6
Colinton 120 C5
Colintraive 145 F9
Colkirk 80 E5
Collace 134 F2
Collafirth 160 G6
Collaton St Mary 7 D6
College Milton 119 D6
Collessie 128 C4
Collier Row 41 E8
Collier's End 41 B6
Collier's Green 18 B4
Collier Street 29 E8
Colliery Row 111 E6
Collieston 141 B9
Collin 107 B7
Collingbourne Ducis 25 D7
Collingbourne Kingston 25 D7
Collingham Notts 77 C8
W Yorks 95 E6
Collington 49 C8
Collingtree 53 D5
Collins Green 86 E3
Colliston 135 E6
Collycroft 63 F7
Collynie 153 E8
Collyweston 65 D6
Colmonell 104 A5
Colmworth 54 D2
Colnabaichin 139 D8
Colnbrook 27 B8
Colne Cambs 54 B4
Lancs 93 E8
Colne Edge 93 E8
Colne Engaine 56 F2
Colney 68 D4
Colney Heath 41 D5
Colney Street 40 D4
Coln Rogers 37 D7
Coln St Aldwyn's 37 D8
Coln St Dennis 37 C7
Colpy 153 E6
Colquhar 121 E6
Colsterdale 101 F6
Colsterworth 65 B6
Colston Bassett 77 F6
Coltfield 151 E14
Colthouse 99 E5
Coltishall 69 C5
Coltness 119 D8
Colton Cumb 99 F5
Norf 68 D4
N Yorks 95 E8
Staffs 62 B4
W Yorks 95 F6
Col Uarach 155 D9
Colva 48 D4
Colvend 107 D5
Colvister 160 D7
Colwall Green 50 E2
Colwall Stone 50 E2
Colwell 110 B2
Colwich 62 B4
Colwick 77 E6
Colwinston 21 B8
Colworth 16 D3
Colwyn Bay = Bae Colwyn 83 D8
Colyford 11 E7
Colyton 11 E7
Combe Hereford 48 C5
Oxon 38 C4
W Berks 25 C8
Combe Common 27 F7
Combe Down 24 C2
Combe Florey 22 F3
Combe Hay 24 D2
Combeinteignhead 7 B7
Combe Martin 20 E4
Combe Moor 49 C5
Combe Raleigh 11 D6
Comberbach 74 B3
Comberton Cambs 54 D4
Hereford 49 C6
Combe St Nicholas 11 C8
Combpyne 11 E7
Combridge 75 F7
Combrook 51 D8
Combs Derbys 75 B7
Suff 56 D4
Combs Ford 56 D4
Combwich 22 E4
Comers 141 D5
Comins Coch 58 F3
Commercial End 55 C6
Commins Capel Betws 46 D5
Commins Coch 58 D5
Commondale 102 C4
Common Edge 92 F3
Commonmoor 5 C7
Commonside 74 B2
Common Side 76 B3
Compstall 87 E7
Compton Devon 7 C6
Hants 15 B5
Sur 27 E6
Sur 27 E7
W Berks 26 B3
Wilts 25 D6
W Sus 15 C8
Compton Abbas 13 C6
Compton Abdale 37 C7
Compton Bassett 24 B5
Compton Beauchamp 38 F2
Compton Bishop 23 D5
Compton Chamberlayne 13 B8
Compton Dando 23 C8
Compton Dundon 23 F6
Compton Martin 23 D7
Compton Pauncefoot 12 B4
Compton Valence 12 E3
Comrie Fife 128 F2
Comrie continued
Perth 127 B6
Conaglen House 130 C4
Conchra 145 E9
Concraigie 133 E8
Conder Green 92 D4
Conderton 50 F4
Condicote 38 B1
Condorrat 119 B7
Condover 60 D4
Coneyhurst 16 B5
Coneysthorpe 96 B3
Coneythorpe 95 D6
Coney Weston 56 B3
Conford 27 F6
Congash 139 B6
Congdon's Shop 5 B7
Congerstone 63 D7
Congham 80 E3
Congleton 75 C5
Congl-y-wal 71 C8
Congresbury 23 C6
Congreve 62 C3
Conicavel 151 F12
Coningsby 78 D5
Conington Cambs 54 C4
Cambs 65 F8
Conisbrough 89 E6
Conisby 142 B3
Conisholme 91 E8
Coniston Cumb 99 E5
E Yorks 97 F7
Coniston Cold 94 D2
Conistone 94 C2
Connah's Quay 73 C6
Connel 124 B5
Connel Park 113 C6
Connor Downs 2 C4
Conon Bridge 151 F8
Conon House 151 F8
Cononley 94 E2
Conordan 149 E10
Consall 75 E6
Consett 110 D4
Constable Burton 101 E6
Constantine 3 D6
Constantine Bay 4 B3
Contin 150 F7
Contlaw 141 D7
Conwy 83 D7
Conyer 30 C3
Conyers Green 56 C2
Cooden 18 E4
Cooil 84 E3
Cookbury 9 D6
Cookham 40 F1
Cookham Dean 40 F1
Cookham Rise 40 F1
Cookhill 51 D5
Cookley Suff 57 B7
Worcs 62 F2
Cookley Green 39 E6
Cookney 141 E7
Cookridge 95 E5
Cooksbridge 17 C8
Cooksmill Green 42 D2
Coolham 16 B5
Cooling 29 B8
Coombe Corn 4 D4
Corn 8 C4
Hants 15 B7
Wilts 25 D6
Coombe Bissett 14 B2
Coombe Hill 37 B5
Coombe Keynes 13 F6
Coombes 17 D5
Coopersale Common 41 D7
Cootham 16 C4
Copdock 56 E5
Copford Green 43 B5
Copgrove 95 C6
Copister 160 F6
Cople 54 E2
Copley 101 B5
Coplow Dale 75 B8
Copmanthorpe 95 E8
Coppathorne 8 D4
Coppenhall 62 C3
Coppenhall Moss 74 D4
Copperhouse 2 C4
Coppingford 65 F8
Copplestone 10 D2
Coppull 86 C3
Coppull Moor 86 C3
Copsale 17 B5
Copster Green 93 F6
Copston Magna 63 F8
Copt Heath 51 B6
Copt Hewick 95 B6
Copthorne Shrops 60 C4
Sur 28 F4
Copt Oak 63 C8
Copy's Green 80 D5
Copythorne 14 C4
Corbets Tey 42 F1
Corbridge 110 C2
Corby 65 F5
Corby Glen 65 B6
Cordon 143 E11
Coreley 49 B8
Cores End 40 F2
Corfe 11 C7
Corfe Castle 13 F7
Corfe Mullen 13 E7
Corfton 60 F4
Corgarff 139 D8
Corhampton 15 B7
Corlae 113 E6
Corley 63 F7
Corley Ash 63 F6
Corley Moor 63 F6
Cornaa 84 D4
Cornabus 142 D4
Cornel 83 E7
Corner Row 92 F4
Corney 98 E3
Cornforth 111 F6
Cornhill 152 C5
Cornhill-on-Tweed 122 F4
Cornholme 87 B7
Cornish Hall End 55 F7
Cornquoy 159 J6
Cornsay 110 E4
Cornsay Colliery 110 E4
Corntown Highld 151 F8
V Glam 21 B8
Cornwell 38 B2
Cornwood 6 D4
Cornworthy 7 D6
Corpach 130 B4
Corpusty 81 D7
Corran Highld 130 C4
Highld 149 H13
Corranbuie 145 G7
Corrany 84 D4
Corrie 143 D11
Corrie Common 114 F5
Corriecravie 143 F10
Corriemoillie 150 E6
Corriemulzie Lodge 150 B6
Corrievarkie Lodge 132 B2
Corrievorrie 138 B3
Corrimony 150 H6
Corringham Lincs 90 E2
Thurrock 42 F3
Corris 58 D4
Corris Uchaf 58 D4
Corrour Shooting Lodge 131 C8
Corrow 125 E7
Corry 149 F11
Corrykinloch 156 G6
Corrymuckloch 133 F5
Corrynachenchy 147 G9
Corry of Ardnagrask 151 G8
Corsback 158 C4
Corscombe 12 D3
Corse Aberds 152 D6
Glos 36 B4
Corse Lawn 50 F3
Corse of Kinnoir 152 D5
Corsewall 104 C4
Corsham 24 B3
Corsindae 141 D5
Corsley 24 E3
Corsley Heath 24 E3
Corsock 106 B4
Corston Bath 23 C8
Wilts 37 F6
Corstorphine 120 B4
Cors-y-Gedol 71 E6
Cortachy 134 D3
Corton Suff 69 E8
Wilts 24 E4
Corton Denham 12 B4
Coruanan Lodge 130 C4
Corunna 148 B3
Corwen 72 E4
Coryton Devon 9 F6
Thurrock 42 F3
Cosby 64 E2
Coseley 62 E3
Cosgrove 53 E5
Cosham 15 D7
Cosheston 32 D1
Cossall 76 E4
Cossington Leics 64 C3
Som 23 E5
Costa 159 F4
Costessey 68 C4
Costock 64 B2
Coston 64 B5
Cote 38 D3
Cotebrook 74 C2
Cotehill 108 D4
Cotes Cumb 99 F6
Leics 64 B2
Staffs 74 F5
Cotesbach 64 F2
Cotgrave 77 F6
Cothall 141 C7
Cotham 77 E7
Cothelstone 22 F3
Cotherstone 101 C5
Cothill 38 E4
Cotleigh 11 D7
Cotmanhay 76 E4
Cotmaton 11 F6
Coton Cambs 54 D5
Staffs 62 B2
Staffs 75 F6
W Nhants 52 B4
Coton Clanford 62 B2
Coton Hill Shrops 60 C4
Staffs 75 F6
Coton in the Elms 63 C6
Cott 7 C5
Cottam E Yorks 97 C5
Lancs 92 F5
Notts 77 B8
Cottartown 151 H13
Cottenham 54 C5
Cotterdale 100 E3
Cottered 41 B6
Cotteridge 50 B5
Cotterstock 65 E7
Cottesbrooke 52 B5
Cottesmore 65 C6
Cotteylands 10 C4
Cottingham
E Yorks 97 F6
N Nhants 64 E5
Cottingley 94 F4
Cottisford 52 F3
Cotton Staffs 75 E7
Suff 56 C4
Cotton End 53 E8
Cottown Aberds 140 B4
Aberds 141 C6
Aberds 153 D8
Cotwalton 75 F6
Couch's Mill 5 D6
Coughton Hereford 36 B2
Warks 51 C5
Coulaghailtro 144 G6
Coulags 150 G2
Coulby Newham 102 C3
Coulderton 98 D1
Coulin 150 F3
Coull Aberds 140 D4
Argyll 142 B3
Coulport 145 E11
Coulsdon 28 D3
Coulston 24 D4
Coulter 120 F3
Coulton 96 B2
Cound 61 D5
Coundon Durham 101 B7
W Mid 63 F7
Coundon Grange 101 B7
Countersett 100 F4
Countess 25 E6
Countess Wear 10 F4
Countesthorpe 64 E2
Countisbury 21 E6
County Oak 28 F3
Coupar Angus 134 E2
Coup Green 86 B3
Coupland 122 F5
Cour 143 D9
Courance 114 E3
Court-at-Street 19 B7
Courteenhall 53 D5
Court Henry 33 B6
Courtsend 43 E6
Courtway 22 F4
Cousland 121 C6
Cousley Wood 18 B3
Cove Argyll 145 E11
Borders 122 B3
Devon 10 C4
Hants 27 D6
Highld 155 H13
Cove Bay 141 D8
Cove Bottom 57 B8
Covehithe 69 F8
Coven 62 D3
Coveney 66 F4
Covenham St Bartholomew 91 E7
Covenham St Mary 91 E7
Coventry 51 B8
Coverack 3 E6
Coverham 101 F6
Covesea 152 A1
Covington Cambs 53 B8
S Lanark 120 F2
Cowan Bridge 93 B6
Cow Ark 93 E6
Cowbeech 18 D3
Cowbit 66 C2
Cowbridge Lincs 79 E6
Som 21 E8
Cowbridge = Y Bont-Faen 21 B8
Cowdale 75 B7
Cowden 29 E5
Cowdenbeath 128 E3
Cowdenburn 120 D5
Cowers Lane 76 E3
Cowes 15 E5
Cowesby 102 F2
Cowfold 17 B6
Cowgill 100 F2
Cowie Aberds 141 F7
Stirling 127 F7
Cowley Devon 10 E4
Glos 37 C6
London 40 F3
Oxon 39 D5
Cowleymoor 10 C4
Cowling Lancs 86 C3
N Yorks 94 E2
N Yorks 101 F7
Cowlinge 55 D8
Cowpe 87 B6
Cowpen 117 F8
Cowpen Bewley 102 B2
Cowplain 15 C7
Cowshill 109 E8
Cowslip Green 23 C6
Cowstrandburn 128 E2
Cowthorpe 95 D7
Coxbank 74 E3
Coxbench 76 E3
Cox Common 69 F6
Coxford Norf 80 E4
Soton 14 C4
Cox Green 27 B6
Coxheath 29 D8
Coxhill 31 E6
Coxhoe 111 F6
Coxley 23 E7
Cox Moor 76 D5
Coxwold 95 B8
Coychurch 21 B8
Coylton 112 B4
Coylumbridge 138 C5
Coynach 140 D3
Coynachie 152 E4
Coytrahen 34 F2
Crabadon 7 D5
Crabbs Cross 50 C5
Crabtree 17 B6
Crackenthorpe 100 B1
Crackington Haven 8 E3
Crackley 51 B7
Crackleybank 61 C7
Crackpot 100 E4
Cracoe 94 C2
Craddock 11 C5
Cradhlastadh 154 D5
Cradley 50 E2
Cradley Heath 62 F3
Crafthole 5 D8
Craggan 139 B6
Craggie Highld 151 H10
Highld 157 H11
Cragg Vale 87 B8
Craghead 110 D5
Crai 34 B2
Craibstone 152 C4
Craichie 135 E5
Craig Dumfries 106 B3
Dumfries 106 C3
Highld 150 G3
Craiganor Lodge 132 D3
Craig Castle 140 B3
Craig-cefn-parc 33 D7
Craigdam 153 E8
Craigdarroch
Dumfries 113 E7
Highld 150 F7
Craigdhu 150 G7
Craigearn 141 C6
Craigellachie 152 D2
Craigencross 104 C4
Craigend Perth 128 B3
Stirling 127 F6
Craigendive 145 E9
Craigendoran 126 F2
Craigends 118 C4
Craigens Argyll 142 B3
E Ayrs 113 C5
Craighat 126 F3
Craighead 129 D8
Craighlaw Mains 105 C7
Craighouse 144 G4
Craigie Aberds 141 C8
Dundee 134 F4
Perth 128 B3
Perth 133 E8

Craigie *continued*
S Ayrs 118 F4
Craigiefield 159 G5
Craigielaw 121 B7
Craiglockhart 120 B5
Craigmalloch 112 E4
Craigmaud 153 C8
Craigmillar 121 B5
Craigmore 145 G10
Craignant 73 F6
Craigneuk
N Lanark 119 C7
N Lanark 119 D7
Craignure 124 B3
Craigo 135 C6
Craigow 128 D2
Craig Penllyn 21 B8
Craigrothie 129 C5
Craigroy 151 F14
Craigruie 126 B3
Craigston Castle 153 C7
Craigton Aberdeen 141 D7
Angus 134 D3
Angus 135 F5
Highld 151 B9
Craigtown 157 D11
Craig-y-don 83 C7
Craig-y-nos 34 C2
Craik 115 D6
Crail 129 D8
Crailing 116 B2
Crailinghall 116 B2
Craiselound 89 E8
Crakehill 95 B7
Crakemarsh 75 F7
Crambe 96 C3
Cramlington 111 B5
Cramond 120 B4
Cramond Bridge 120 B4
Cranage 74 C4
Cranberry 74 F5
Cranborne 13 C8
Cranbourne 27 B7
Cranbrook Devon 10 E5
Kent 18 B4
Cranbrook Common 18 B4
Crane Moor 88 D4
Crane's Corner 68 C2
Cranfield 53 E7
Cranford 28 B2
Cranford St Andrew 53 B7
Cranford St John 53 B7
Cranham Glos 37 C5
London 42 F1
Crank 86 E3
Crank Wood 86 D4
Cranleigh 27 F8
Cranley 57 B5
Cranmer Green 56 B4
Cranmore 14 F4
Cranna 153 C6
Crannich 147 G8
Crannoch 152 C4
Cranoe 64 E4
Cransford 57 C7
Cranshaws 122 C2
Cranstal 84 B4
Crantock 4 C2
Cranwell 78 E3
Cranwich 67 E7
Cranworth 68 D2
Craobh Haven 124 E3
Crapstone 6 C3
Crarae 125 F5
Crask Inn 157 G8
Craskins 140 D4
Crask of Aigas 150 G7
Craster 117 C8
Craswall 48 F4
Cratfield 57 B7
Crathes 141 E6
Crathie Aberds 139 E8
Highld 137 E8
Crathorne 102 D2
Craven Arms 60 F4
Crawcrook 110 C4
Crawford Lancs 86 D2
S Lanark 114 B2
Crawfordjohn 113 B8
Crawick 113 C7
Crawley Hants 26 F2
Oxon 38 C3
W Sus 28 F3
Crawley Down 28 F4
Crawleyside 110 E2
Crawshawbooth 87 B6
Crawton 135 B8
Cray N Yorks 94 B2
Perth 133 C8
Crayford 29 B6
Crayke 95 B8
Crays Hill 42 E3
Cray's Pond 39 F6
Creacombe 10 C3
Creagan 130 E3
Creag Ghoraidh 148 D2
Creaguaineach Lodge 131 C7
Creaksea 43 E5
Creaton 52 B5
Creca 108 B2
Credenhill 49 E6
Crediton 10 D3
Creebridge 105 C8
Creech Heathfield 11 B7
Creech St Michael 11 B7
Creed 3 B8
Creekmouth 41 F7
Creeting Bottoms 56 D5
Creeting St Mary 56 D4
Creeton 65 B7
Creetown 105 D8
Creggans 125 E6
Cregneash 84 F1
Creg-ny-Baa 84 D3
Cregrina 48 D3
Creich 128 B5
Creigiau 34 F4
Cremyll 6 D2
Creslow 39 B8
Cressage 61 D5
Cressbrook 75 B8
Cresselly 32 D1
Cressing 42 B3
Cresswell Northumb 117 E8
Staffs 75 F6
Cresswell Quay 32 D1
Creswell 76 B5
Cretingham 57 C6
Cretshengan 144 G6
Crewe Ches E 74 D4
Ches W 73 D8
Crewgreen 60 C3
Crewkerne 12 D2
Crianlarich 126 B2
Cribyn 46 D4
Criccieth 71 D5
Crich 76 D3
Crichie 153 D9
Crichton 121 C6
Crick Mon 36 E1
W Nhants 52 B3
Crickadarn 48 E2
Cricket Malherbie 11 C8
Cricket St Thomas 11 D8
Crickheath 60 B2
Crickhowell 35 C6
Cricklade 37 E8
Cricklewood 41 F5
Cridling Stubbs 89 B6
Crieff 127 B7
Criggion 60 C2
Crigglestone 88 C4
Crimond 153 C10
Crimonmogate 153 C10
Crimplesham 67 D6
Crinan 144 D6
Cringleford 68 D4
Cringles 94 E3
Crinow 32 C2
Cripplesease 2 C4
Cripplestyle 13 C8
Cripp's Corner 18 C4
Croasdale 98 C2
Crockenhill 29 C6
Crockernwell 10 E2
Crockerton 24 E3
Crocketford or Ninemile Bar 106 B5
Crockey Hill 96 E2
Crockham Hill 28 D5
Crockleford Heath 43 B6
Crockness 159 J4
Crock Street 11 C8
Croeserw 34 E2
Croes-goch 44 B3
Croes-lan 46 E2
Croesor 71 C7
Croesyceiliog Carms 33 C5
Torf 35 E7
Croes-y-mwyalch 35 E7
Croesywaun 82 F5
Croft Leics 64 E2
Lincs 79 C8
Pembs 45 E3
Warr 86 E4
Croftamie 126 F3
Croftmalloch 120 C2
Crofton Wilts 25 C7
W Yorks 88 C4
Croft-on-Tees 101 D7
Crofts of Benachielt 158 G3
Crofts of Haddo 153 E8
Crofts of Inverthernie 153 D7
Crofts of Meikle Ardo 153 D8
Crofty 33 E6
Croggan 124 C3
Croglin 109 E5
Croich 150 B7
Crois Dughaill 148 F2
Cromarty 151 E10
Cromblet 153 E7
Cromdale 139 B6
Cromer Herts 41 B5
Norf 81 C8
Cromford 76 D2
Cromhall 36 E3
Cromhall Common 36 F3
Cromor 155 E9
Cromra 137 E8
Cromwell 77 C7
Cronberry 113 B6
Crondall 27 E5
Cronk-y-Voddy 84 D3
Cronton 86 F2
Crook Cumb 99 E6
Durham 110 F4
Crookedholm 118 F4
Crookes 88 F4
Crookham Northumb 122 F5
W Berks 26 C3
Crookham Village 27 D5
Crookhaugh 114 B4
Crookhouse 116 B3
Crooklands 99 F7
Crook of Devon 128 D2
Cropredy 52 E2
Cropston 64 C2
Cropthorne 50 E4
Cropton 103 F5
Cropwell Bishop 77 F6
Cropwell Butler 77 F6
Cros 155 A10
Crosbost 155 E8
Crosby Cumb 107 F7
IoM 84 E3
N Lincs 90 C2
Crosby Garrett 100 D2
Crosby Ravensworth 99 C8
Crosby Villa 107 F7
Croscombe 23 E7
Cross 23 D6
Crossaig 143 C9
Crossal 149 E9
Crossapol 146 G2
Cross Ash 35 C8
Cross-at-Hand 29 E8
Crossburn 119 B8
Crossbush 16 D4
Crosscanonby 107 F7
Crossdale Street 81 D8
Crossens 85 C4
Crossflatts 94 E4
Crossford Fife 128 F2
S Lanark 119 E8
Crossgate 66 B2
Crossgatehall 121 C6
Crossgates Fife 128 F3
Powys 48 C2
Crossgill 93 C5
Cross Green Devon 9 F5
Suff 56 D2
Suff 56 D3
Warks 51 D8
Cross-hands 32 B2
Cross Hands Carms 33 C6
Pembs 32 C1
Crosshill E Ayrs 112 B4
Fife 128 E3
S Ayrs 112 D3
Cross Hill 76 E4
Crosshouse 118 F3
Cross Houses 60 D5
Crossings 108 B5
Cross in Hand E Sus 18 C2
Leics 64 F2
Cross Inn Ceredig 46 C4
Ceredig 46 D2
Rhondda 34 F4
Crosskeys 35 E6
Cross Keys 29 D6
Crosskirk 157 B13
Cross Lane Head 61 E7
Crosslanes 60 C3
Cross Lanes Corn 3 D5
N Yorks 95 C8
Wrex 73 E7
Crossle 118 C4
Crosslee 115 C6
Crossmichael 106 C4
Crossmoor 92 F4
Cross Oak 35 B5
Cross of Jackston 153 E7
Cross o'th'hands 76 E2
Crossroads Aberds 141 E6
E Ayrs 118 F4
Cross Street 57 B5
Crossway Hereford 49 F8
Mon 35 C8
Powys 48 D2
Crossway Green 50 C3
Crossways 13 F5
Crosswell 45 F3
Crosswood 47 B5
Crosthwaite 99 E6
Croston 86 C2
Crostwick 69 C5
Crostwight 69 B6
Crothair 154 D6
Crouch 29 D7
Croucheston 13 B8
Crouch Hill 12 C5
Crouch House Green 28 E5
Croughton 52 F3
Crovie 153 B8
Crowan 2 C5
Crowborough 18 B2
Crowcombe 22 F3
Crowdecote 75 C8
Crowden 87 E8
Crow Edge 88 D2
Crowell 39 E7
Crowfield Suff 56 D5
W Nhants 52 E4
Crow Hill 36 B3
Crowhurst E Sus 18 D4
Sur 28 E4
Crowhurst Lane End 28 E4
Crowland 66 C2
Crowlas 2 C4
Crowle N Lincs 89 C8
Worcs 50 D4
Crowmarsh Gifford 39 F6
Crown Corner 57 B6
Crownhill 6 D2
Crownland 56 C4
Crownthorpe 68 D3
Crowntown 2 C5
Crows-an-wra 2 D2
Crowshill 68 D2
Crowsnest 60 D3
Crowthorne 27 C6
Crowton 74 B2
Croxall 63 C5
Croxby 91 E5
Croxdale 111 F5
Croxden 75 F7
Croxley Green 40 E3
Croxton Cambs 54 C3
N Lincs 90 C4
Norf 67 F8
Staffs 74 F4
Croxtonbank 74 F4
Croxton Kerrial 64 B5
Croy Highld 151 G10
N Lanark 119 B7
Croyde 20 F3
Croydon Cambs 54 E4
London 28 C4
Crubenmore Lodge 138 E2
Cruckmeole 60 D4
Cruckton 60 C4
Cruden Bay 153 E10
Crudgington 61 C6
Crudwell 37 E6
Crug 48 B3
Crugmeer 4 B4
Crugybar 47 F5
Crulabhig 154 D6
Crumlin = *Crymlyn* 35 E6
Crumpsall 87 D6
Crundale Kent 30 E4
Pembs 44 D4
Cruwys Morchard 10 C3
Crux Easton 26 D2
Crwbin 33 C5
Crya 159 H4
Cryers Hill 40 E1
Crymlyn 83 D6
Crymlyn = *Crumlin* 35 E6
Crymych 45 F3
Crynant 34 D1
Crynfryn 46 C4
Cuaig 149 C12
Cuan 124 D3
Cubbington 51 C8
Cubeck 100 F4
Cubert 4 D2
Cubley 88 D3
Cubley Common 75 F8
Cublington Bucks 39 B8
Hereford 49 F6
Cuckfield 17 B7
Cucklington 13 B5
Cuckney 77 B5
Cuckoo Hill 89 E8
Cuddesdon 39 D6
Cuddington Bucks 39 C7
Ches W 74 B3
Cuddington Heath 73 E8
Cuddy Hill 92 F4
Cudham 28 D5
Cudliptown 6 B3
Cudworth Som 11 C8
S Yorks 88 D4
Cuffley 41 D6
Cuiashader 155 B10
Cuidhir 148 H1
Cuidhtinis 154 J5
Culbo 151 E9
Culbokie 151 F9
Culburnie 150 G7
Culcabock 151 G9
Culcairn 151 E9
Culcharry 151 F11
Culcheth 86 E4
Culdrain 152 E5
Culduie 149 D12
Culford 56 B2
Culgaith 99 B8
Culham 39 E5
Culkein 156 F3
Culkein Drumbeg 156 F4
Culkerton 37 E6
Cullachie 139 B5
Cullen 152 B5
Cullercoats 111 B6
Cullicudden 151 E9
Cullingworth 94 F3
Cullipool 124 D3
Cullivoe 160 C7
Culloch 127 C6
Culloden 151 G10
Cullompton 10 D5
Culmaily 151 B11
Culmazie 105 D7
Culmington 60 F4
Culmstock 11 C6
Culnacraig 156 J3
Culnaknock 149 B10
Culpho 57 E6
Culrain 151 B8
Culross 127 F8
Culroy 112 C3
Culsh Aberds 140 E2
Aberds 153 D8
Culshabbin 105 D7
Culswick 160 J4
Cultercullen 141 B8
Cults Aberdeen 141 D7
Aberds 152 E5
Dumfries 105 E8
Culverstone Green 29 C7
Culverthorpe 78 E3
Culworth 52 E3
Culzie Lodge 151 D8
Cumbernauld 119 B7
Cumbernauld Village 119 B7
Cumberworth 79 B8
Cuminestown 153 C8
Cumlewick 160 L6
Cummersdale 108 D3
Cummertrees 107 C8
Cummingston 152 B1
Cumnock 113 B5
Cumnor 38 D4
Cumrew 108 D5
Cumwhinton 108 D4
Cumwhitton 108 D5
Cundall 95 B7
Cunninghamhead 118 E3
Cunnister 160 D7
Cupar 129 C5
Cupar Muir 129 C5
Cupernham 14 B4
Curbar 76 B2
Curbridge Hants 15 C6
Oxon 38 D3
Curdridge 15 C6
Curdworth 63 E5
Curland 11 C7
Curlew Green 57 C7
Currarie 112 E1
Curridge 26 B2
Currie 120 C4
Curry Mallet 11 B8
Curry Rivel 11 B8
Curtisden Green 29 E8
Curtisknowle 6 D5
Cury 3 D5
Cushnie 153 B7
Cushuish 22 F3
Cusop 48 E4
Cutcloy 105 F8
Cutcombe 21 F8
Cutgate 87 C6
Cutiau 58 C3
Cutlers Green 55 F6
Cutnall Green 50 C3
Cutsdean 51 F5
Cutthorpe 76 B3
Cutts 160 K6
Cuxham 39 E6
Cuxton 29 C8
Cuxwold 91 D5
Cwm Bl Gwent 35 D5
Denb 72 B4
Swansea 33 E7
Cwmafan 34 E1
Cwmaman 34 E4
Cwmann 46 E4
Cwmavon 35 D6
Cwmbach Carms 32 B3
Carms 33 D5
Powys 48 D2
Powys 48 F3
Cwmbâch 34 D4
Cwmbelan 59 F6
Cwmbran = *Cwmbrân* 35 E6
Cwmbrân = *Cwmbran* 35 E6
Cwmbrwyno 58 F4
Cwm-byr 46 F5
Cwmcarn 35 E6
Cwmcarvan 36 D1
Cwm-Cewydd 59 C5
Cwm-cou 45 E4
Cwmcych 45 F4
Cwmdare 34 D3
Cwmderwen 59 D6
Cwmdu Carms 46 F5
Powys 35 B5
Swansea 33 E7
Cwmduad 46 F2
Cwm-Dulais 33 D7
Cwmdwr 47 F6
Cwmfelin Bridgend 34 F2
M Tydf 34 D4
Cwmfelin Boeth 32 C2
Cwm-felin-fach 35 E5
Cwmfelin Mynach 32 B3
Cwmffrwd 33 C5
Cwm Ffrwd-oer 35 D6
Cwmgiedd 34 C1
Cwmgors 33 C8
Cwmgwili 33 C6
Cwmgwrach 34 D2
Cwm-hesgen 71 E8
Cwmhiraeth 46 F2
Cwm-hwnt 34 D3
Cwmifor 33 B7
Cwm Irfon 47 E7
Cwmisfael 33 C5
Cwm-Llinau 58 D5
Cwmllynfell 33 C8
Cwm-mawr 33 C6
Cwmorgan 45 F4
Cwm-parc 34 E3
Cwmpengraig 46 F2
Cwm Penmachno 71 C8
Cwmrhos 35 B5
Cwmsychpant 46 E3
Cwmtillery 35 D6
Cwm-twrch Isaf 34 C1
Cwm-twrch Uchaf 34 C1
Cwmwysg 34 B2
Cwm-y-glo Carms 33 C6
Gwyn 82 E5
Cwmyoy 35 B6
Cwmystwyth 47 B6
Cwrt 58 D3
Cwrt-newydd 46 E3
Cwrt-y-cadno 47 E5
Cwrt-y-gollen 35 C6
Cydweli = *Kidwelly* 33 D5
Cyffordd Llandudno = *Llandudno Junction* 83 D7
Cyffylliog 72 D4
Cyfronydd 59 D8
Cymer 34 E2
Cyncoed 35 F5
Cynghordy 47 E7
Cynheidre 33 D5
Cynwyd 72 E4
Cynwyl Elfed 32 B4
Cywarch 59 C5

D

Dacre Cumb 99 B6
N Yorks 94 C4
Dacre Banks 94 C4
Daddry Shield 109 F8
Dadford 52 F4
Dadlington 63 E8
Dafarn Faig 71 C5
Dafen 33 D6
Daffy Green 68 D2
Dagenham 41 F7
Daglingworth 37 D6
Dagnall 40 C2
Dail Beag 154 C7
Dail bho Dheas 155 A9
Dail bho Thuath 155 A9
Daill 142 B4
Dailly 112 D2
Dail Mor 154 C7
Dairsie or Osnaburgh 129 C6
Daisy Hill 86 D4
Dalabrog 148 F2
Dalavich 125 D5
Dalbeattie 106 C5
Dalblair 113 C6
Dalbog 135 B5
Dalbury 76 F2
Dalby IoM 84 E2
N Yorks 96 B2
Dalchalloch 132 C4
Dalchalm 157 J12
Dalchenna 125 E6
Dalchirach 152 E1
Dalchork 157 H8
Dalchreichart 137 C5
Dalchruin 127 C6
Dalderby 78 C5
Dale 44 E3
Dale Abbey 76 F4
Dale Head 99 C6
Dalelia 147 E10
Dale of Walls 160 H3
Daless 151 H11
Dalfaber 138 C5
Dalgarven 118 E2
Dalgety Bay 128 F3
Dalginross 127 B6
Dalguise 133 E6
Dalhalvaig 157 D11
Dalham 55 C8
Dalinlongart 145 E10
Dalkeith 121 C6
Dallam 86 E3
Dallas 151 F14
Dalleagles 113 C5
Dallinghoo 57 D6
Dallington E Sus 18 D3
W Nhants 52 C5
Dallow 94 B4
Dalmadilly 141 C6
Dalmally 125 C7
Dalmarnock 119 C6
Dalmary 126 E4
Dalmellington 112 D4
Dalmeny 120 B4
Dalmigavie 138 C3
Dalmigavie Lodge 138 B3
Dalmore 151 E9
Dalmuir 118 B4
Dalnabreck 147 E9
Dalnacardoch Lodge 132 B4
Dalnacroich 150 F6
Dalnaglar Castle 133 C8
Dalnahaitnach 138 B4
Dalnaspidal Lodge 132 B3
Dalnavaid 133 C7
Dalnavie 151 D9
Dalnawillan Lodge 157 E13
Dalness 131 D5
Dalnessie 157 H9
Dalqueich 128 D2
Dalreavoch 157 J10
Dalry 118 E2
Dalrymple 112 C3
Dalserf 119 D8
Dalston 108 D3
Dalswinton 114 F2
Dalton Dumfries 107 B8
Lancs 86 D2
Northumb 110 B4
Northumb 110 D2
N Yorks 95 B7
N Yorks 101 D6
S Yorks 89 E5
Dalton-in-Furness 92 B2
Dalton-le-Dale 111 E7
Dalton-on-Tees 101 D7
Dalton Piercy 111 F7
Dalveich 126 B5
Dalvina Lodge 157 E9
Dalwhinnie 138 F2
Dalwood 11 D7
Dalwyne 112 E3
Damerham 14 C2
Damgate 69 D7
Dam Green 68 F3
Damnaglaur 104 F5
Damside 120 E4
Dam Side 92 E4
Danbury 42 D3
Danby 103 D5
Danby Wiske 101 E8
Dandaleith 152 D2
Danderhall 121 C6
Danebridge 75 C6
Dane End 41 B6
Danehill 17 B8
Danemoor Green 68 D3
Danesford 61 E7
Daneshill 26 D4
Dangerous Corner 86 C3
Danskine 121 C8
Darcy Lever 86 D5
Darenth 29 B6
Daresbury 86 F3
Darfield 88 D5
Darfoulds 77 B5
Dargate 30 C4
Dargavel Renfs 118 B3
Darite 5 C7
Darlaston 62 E3
Darley 94 D5
Darley Bridge 76 C2
Darley Head 94 D4
Darlingscott 51 E7
Darlington 101 C7
Darliston 74 F2
Darlton 77 B7
Darnall 88 F4
Darnick 121 F8
Darowen 58 D5
Darra 153 D7
Darracott 20 F3
Darras Hall 110 B4
Darrington 89 B5
Darsham 57 C8
Dartford 29 B6
Dartford Crossing 29 B6
Dartington 7 C5
Dartmeet 6 B4
Dartmouth 7 D6
Darton 88 D4
Darvel 119 F5
Darwell Hole 18 D3
Darwen 86 B4
Datchet 27 B7
Datchworth 41 C5
Datchworth Green 41 C5
Daubhill 86 D5
Daugh of Kinermony 152 D2
Dauntsey 37 F6
Dava 151 H13
Davenham 74 B3
Davenport Green 74 B5
Daventry 52 C3
Davidson's Mains 120 B5
Davidstow 8 F3
David's Well 48 B2
Davington 115 D5
Daviot Aberds 141 B6
Highld 151 H10
Davoch of Grange 152 C4
Davyhulme 87 E5
Dawley 61 D6
Dawlish 7 B7
Dawlish Warren 7 B7
Dawn 83 D8
Daws Heath 42 F4
Daw's House Corn 8 F5
Dawsmere 79 F7
Dayhills 75 F6
Daylesford 38 B2
Ddôl-Cownwy 59 C7
Ddrydwy 82 D3
Deadwater 116 E2
Deaf Hill 111 F6
Deal 31 D7
Deal Hall 43 E6
Dean Cumb 98 B2
Devon 6 C5
Devon 20 E4
Dorset 13 C7
Hants 15 C6
Som 23 E8
Deanburnhaugh 115 C6
Deane Gtr Man 86 D4
Hants 26 D3
Deanich Lodge 150 C6
Deanland 13 C7
Dean Prior 6 C5
Dean Row 87 F6
Deans 120 C3
Deanscales 98 B2
Deanshanger 53 F5
Deanston 127 D6
Dearham 107 F7
Debach 57 D6
Debden Essex 41 E7
Essex 55 F6
Debden Cross 55 F6
Debenham 57 C5
Dechmont 120 B3
Deddington 52 F2
Dedham 56 F4
Dedham Heath 56 F4
Deebank 141 E5
Deene 65 E6
Deenethorpe 65 E6
Deepcar 88 E3
Deepcut 27 D7
Deepdale 100 F2
Deeping Gate 65 D8
Deeping St James 65 D8
Deeping St Nicholas 66 C2
Deerhill 152 C4
Deerhurst 37 B5
Deerness 159 H6
Defford 50 E4
Defynnog 34 B3
Deganwy 83 D7
Deighton N Yorks 102 D1
W Yorks 88 C2
York 96 E2
Deiniolen 83 E5
Delabole 8 F2
Delamere 74 C2
Delfrigs 141 B8
Delliefure 151 H13
Dell Lodge 139 C6
Delnabo 139 C7
Delnadamph 139 D8
Delph 87 D7
Delves 110 E4
Delvine 133 E8
Dembleby 78 F3
Denaby Main 89 E5
Denbigh = *Dinbych* 72 C4
Denbury 7 C6
Denby 76 E3
Denby Dale 88 D3
Denchworth 38 E3
Dendron 92 B2
Denel End 53 F8
Denend 152 E6
Denford 53 B7
Dengie 43 D5
Denham Bucks 40 F3
Suff 55 C8
Suff 57 B5
Denham Street 57 B5
Denhead Aberds 153 C9
Fife 129 C6
Denhead of Arbilot 135 E5
Denhead of Gray 134 F3
Denholm 115 C8
Denholme 94 F3
Denholme Clough 94 F3
Denio 70 D4
Denmead 15 C7
Denmore 141 C8
Denmoss 153 D6
Dennington 57 C6
Denny 127 F7
Dennyloanhead 127 F7
Denny Lodge 14 D4
Denshaw 87 C7
Denside 141 E7
Densole 31 E6
Denston 55 D8
Denstone 75 E8
Dent 100 F2
Denton Cambs 65 F8
Darl 101 C7
E Sus 17 D8
Gtr Man 87 E7
Kent 31 E6
Lincs 77 F8
Norf 69 F5
N Yorks 94 E4
Oxon 39 D5
W Nhants 53 D6
Denton's Green 86 E2
Denver 67 D6
Denwick 117 C8
Deopham 68 D3
Deopham Green 68 E3
Depden 55 D8
Depden Green 55 D8
Deptford London 28 B4
Wilts 24 F5
Derby 76 F3
Derbyhaven 84 F2
Dereham 68 C2
Deri 35 D5
Derril 8 D5
Derringstone 31 E6
Derrington 62 B2
Derriton 8 D5
Derryguaig 146 H7
Derry Hill 24 B4
Derrythorpe 90 D2
Dersingham 80 D2
Dervaig 146 F7
Derwen 72 D4
Derwenlas 58 E4
Desborough 64 F5
Desford 63 D8
Detchant 123 F6
Detling 29 D8
Deuddwr 60 C2
Devauden 36 E1
Devil's Bridge 47 B6
Devizes 24 C5
Devol 118 B3
Devonport 6 D2
Devonside 127 E8
Devoran 3 C6
Dewar 121 E6
Dewlish 13 E5
Dewsbury 88 B3
Dewsbury Moor 88 B3
Dewshall Court 49 F6
Dhoon 84 D4
Dhoor 84 C4
Dhowin 84 B4
Dial Post 17 C5
Dibden 14 D5
Dibden Purlieu 14 D5
Dickleburgh 68 F4
Didbrook 51 F5
Didcot 39 F5
Diddington 54 C2
Diddlebury 60 F5
Didley 49 F6
Didling 16 C2
Didmarton 37 F5
Didsbury 87 E6
Didworthy 6 C4
Digby 78 D3
Digg 149 B9
Diggle 87 D8
Digmoor 86 D2
Digswell Park 41 C5
Dihewyd 46 D3
Dilham 69 B6
Dilhorne 75 E6
Dillarburn 119 E8
Dillington 54 C2
Dilston 110 C2
Dilton Marsh 24 E3
Dilwyn 49 D6
Dinas Carms 45 F4
Gwyn 70 D3
Dinas Cross 45 F2
Dinas Dinlle 82 F4
Dinas-Mawddwy 59 C5
Dinas Powys 22 B3
Dinbych = *Denbigh* 72 C4
Dinbych-y-Pysgod = *Tenby* 32 D2
Dinder 23 E7
Dinedor 49 F7
Dingestow 36 C1
Dingle 85 F4
Dingleden 18 B5
Dingley 64 F4
Dingwall 151 F8
Dinlabyre 115 E8
Dinmael 72 E4
Dinnet 140 E3
Dinnington Som 12 C2
S Yorks 89 F6
T&W 110 B5
Dinorwic 83 E5
Dinton Bucks 39 C7
Wilts 24 F5
Dinwoodie Mains 114 E4
Dinworthy 8 C5
Dippen 143 F11
Dippenhall 27 E6
Dipple Moray 152 C3
S Ayrs 112 D2
Diptford 6 D5
Dipton 110 D4
Dirdhu 139 B6
Dirleton 129 F7
Dirt Pot 109 E8
Discoed 48 C4
Diseworth 63 B8
Dishes 159 F7
Dishforth 95 B6
Disley 87 F7
Diss 56 B5
Disserth 48 D2
Distington 98 B2
Ditchampton 25 F5
Ditcheat 23 F8
Ditchingham 69 E6
Ditchling 17 C7
Ditherington 60 C5
Dittisham 7 D6
Ditton Halton 86 F2
Kent 29 D8
Ditton Green 55 D7
Ditton Priors 61 F6
Divach 137 B7
Divlyn 47 F6
Dixton Glos 50 F4
Mon 36 C2
Dobcross 87 D7
Dobwalls 5 C7
Doccombe 10 F2
Dochfour House 151 H9
Dochgarroch 151 G9
Docking 80 D3
Docklow 49 D7
Dockray 99 B5
Dockroyd 94 F3
Doc Penfro = *Pembroke Dock* 44 E4
Dodburn 115 D7
Doddinghurst 42 E1
Doddington Cambs 66 E3
Kent 30 D3
Lincs 78 B2
Northumb 123 F5
Shrops 49 B8
Doddiscombsleigh 10 F3
Dodford W Nhants 52 C4
Worcs 50 B4
Dodington 24 A2
Dodleston 73 C7
Dods Leigh 75 F7
Dodworth 88 D4
Doe Green 86 F3
Doe Lea 76 C4
Dogdyke 78 D5
Dogmersfield 27 D5
Dogridge 37 F7
Dogsthorpe 65 D8
Dog Village 10 E4
Dolanog 59 C7
Dolau Powys 48 C3
Rhondda 34 F3
Dolbenmaen 71 C6
Dolfach 59 D6
Dolfor 59 F8
Dol-fôr 58 D5
Dolgarrog 83 E7
Dolgellau 58 C4
Dolgran 46 F3
Dolhendre 72 F2
Doll 157 J11
Dollar 127 E8
Dolley Green 48 C4
Dollwen 58 F3
Dolphin 73 B5
Dolphinholme 92 D5
Dolphinton 120 E4
Dolton 9 C7
Dolwen Conwy 83 D8
Powys 59 D6
Dolwyd 83 D8
Dolwyddelan 83 F7
Dôl-y-Bont 58 F3
Dol-y-cannau 48 E4
Dolyhir 48 D4
Doncaster 89 D6
Dones Green 74 B3
Donhead St Andrew 13 B7
Donhead St Mary 13 B7
Donibristle 128 F3
Donington 78 F5
Donington on Bain 91 F6
Donington South Ing 78 F5
Donisthorpe 63 C7
Donkey Town 27 C7
Donnington Glos 38 B1
Hereford 50 F2
Shrops 61 D5
Telford 61 C7
W Berks 26 C2
W Sus 16 D2
Donnington Wood 61 C7
Donyatt 11 C8
Doonfoot 112 C3
Dorback Lodge 139 C6
Dorchester Dorset 12 E4
Oxon 39 E5
Dordon 63 D6
Dore 88 F4
Dores 151 H8
Dorking 28 E2
Dormansland 28 E5
Dormanstown 102 B3
Dormington 49 E7
Dormston 50 D4
Dornal 105 B6
Dorney 27 B7
Dornie 149 F13
Dornoch 151 C10
Dornock 108 C2
Dorrery 158 E2
Dorridge 51 B6
Dorrington Lincs 78 D3
Shrops 60 D4
Dorsington 51 E6
Dorstone 48 E5
Dorton 39 C6
Dorusduain 136 B2
Dosthill 63 E6
Dottery 12 E2
Doublebois 5 C6
Dougarie 143 E9
Doughton 37 E5
Douglas IoM 84 E3
S Lanark 119 F8
Douglas & Angus 134 F4
Douglastown 134 E4
Douglas Water 119 F8
Douglas West 119 F8
Doulting 23 E8
Dounby 159 F3
Doune Highld 156 J7
Stirling 127 D6
Doune Park 153 B7
Douneside 140 D3
Dounie 151 B8
Dounreay 157 C12
Dousland 6 C3
Dovaston 60 B3
Dove Holes 75 B7
Dovenby 107 F7
Dover 31 E7
Dovercourt 57 F6
Doverdale 50 C3
Doveridge 75 F8
Doversgreen 28 E3
Dowally 133 E7
Dowbridge 92 F4
Dowdeswell 37 C6
Dowlais 34 D4
Dowland 9 C7
Dowlish Wake 11 C8
Down Ampney 37 E8
Downcraig Ferry 145 H10
Downderry 5 D8
Downe 28 C5
Downend IoW 15 F6
S Glos 23 B8
W Berks 26 B2
Downfield 134 F3
Downgate 5 B8
Downham Essex 42 E3
Lancs 93 E7
Northumb 122 F4
Downham Market 67 D6
Down Hatherley 37 B5
Downhead 23 E8
Downhill Perth 133 F7
T&W 111 D6
Downholland Cross 85 D4
Downholme 101 E6
Downies 141 E8
Downley 39 E8
Down St Mary 10 D2
Downside Som 23 E8
Sur 28 D2
Down Thomas 6 D3
Downton Hants 14 E3
Wilts 14 B2
Downton on the Rock 49 B6
Dowsby 65 B8
Dowsdale 66 C2
Dowthwaitehead 99 B5
Doxey 62 B3
Doxford 117 B7
Doxford Park 111 D6
Doynton 24 B2
Draffan 119 E7
Dragonby 90 C3
Drakeland Corner 6 D3
Drakemyre 118 D2
Drake's Broughton 50 E4
Drakes Cross 51 B5
Drakewalls 6 B2
Draughton N Yorks 94 D3
W Nhants 53 B5
Drax 89 B7
Draycote 52 B2
Draycott Derbys 76 F4
Glos 51 F6
Som 23 D6
Draycott in the Clay 63 B5
Draycott in the Moors 75 E6
Drayford 10 C2
Drayton Leics 64 E5
Lincs 78 F5

Drayton *continued*
Norf 68 C4
Oxon 38 E4
Oxon 52 E2
Ptsmth 15 D7
Som 12 B2
Worcs 50 B4
Drayton Bassett 63 D5
Drayton Beauchamp 40 C2
Drayton Parslow 39 B8
Drayton St Leonard 39 E5
Drebley 94 D3
Dreemskerry 84 C4
Dreenhill 44 D4
Drefach Carms 33 C6
Carms 46 F2
Dre-fach Carms 33 C7
Ceredig 46 E4
Drefelin 46 F2
Dreghorn 118 F3
Drellingore 31 E6
Drem 121 B8
Dresden 75 E6
Dreumasdal 148 E2
Drewsteignton 10 E2
Driby 79 B6
Driffield EYorks 97 D6
Glos 37 E7
Drigg 98 E2
Drighlington 88 B3
Drimnin 147 F8
Drimpton 12 D2
Drimsynie 125 E7
Drinisiadar 154 H6
Drinkstone 56 C3
Drinkstone Green 56 C3
Drishaig 125 D7
Drissaig 124 D5
Drochil 120 E4
Drointon 62 B4
Droitwich Spa 50 C3
Droman 156 D4
Dron 128 C3
Dronfield 76 B3
Dronfield Woodhouse 76 B3
Drongan 112 C4
Dronley 134 F3
Droxford 15 C7
Droylsden 87 E7
Druid 72 E4
Druidston 44 D3
Druimarbin 130 B4
Druimavuic 130 E4
Druimdrishaig 144 F6
Druimindarroch 147 C9
Druimyeon More 143 C7
Drum Argyll 145 F8
Perth 128 D2
Drumbeg 156 F4
Drumblade 152 D5
Drumblair 153 D6
Drumbuie
Dumfries 113 F5
Highld 149 E12
Drumburgh 108 D2
Drumburn 107 C6
Drumchapel 118 B5
Drumchardine 151 G8
Drumchork 155 J13
Drumclog 119 F6
Drumderfit 151 F9
Drumeldrie 129 D6
Drumelzier 120 F4
Drumfearn 149 G11
Drumgask 138 E2
Drumgley 134 D4
Drumguish 138 E3
Drumin 152 E1
Drumlasie 140 D5
Drumlemble 143 G7
Drumligair 141 C8
Drumlithie 141 F6
Drummoddie 105 E7
Drummond 151 E9
Drummore 104 F5
Drummuir 152 D3
Drummuir Castle 152 D3
Drumnadrochit 137 B8
Drumnagorrach 152 C5
Drumoak 141 E6
Drumpark 107 A5
Drumphail 105 C6
Drumrash 106 B3
Drumrunie 156 J4
Drums 141 B8
Drumsallie 130 B3
Drumstinchall 107 D5
Drumsturdy 134 F4
Drumtochty Castle 135 B6
Drumtroddan 105 E7
Drumuie 149 D9
Drumuillie 138 B5
Drumvaich 127 D5
Drumwhindle 153 E9
Drunkendub 135 E6
Drury 73 C6
Drury Square 68 C2
Drybeck 100 C1
Drybridge Moray 152 B4
N Ayrs 118 F3
Drybrook 36 C3
Dryburgh 121 F8
Dry Doddington 77 E8
Dry Drayton 54 C4
Dryhope 115 B5
Drylaw 120 B5
Drym 2 C5
Drymen 126 F3
Drymuir 153 D9
Drynoch 149 E9
Dryslwyn 33 B6
Dryton 61 D5
Dubford 153 B8
Dubton 135 D5
Duchally 156 H6
Duchlage 126 F2
Duck Corner 57 E7
Duckington 73 D8
Ducklington 38 D3
Duckmanton 76 B4
Duck's Cross 54 D2
Duddenhoe End 55 F5
Duddingston 121 B5
Duddington 65 D6
Duddleswell 17 B8
Duddo 122 E5
Duddon 74 C2
Duddon Bridge 98 F4
Dudleston 73 F7
Dudleston Heath 73 F7
Dudley T&W 111 B5
W Mid 62 E3
Dudley Port 62 E3
Duffield 76 E3
Duffryn Neath 34 E2
Newport 35 F6
Dufftown 152 E3
Duffus 152 B1
Dufton 100 B1
Duggleby 96 C4
Duirinish 149 E12
Duisdalemore 149 G12
Duisky 130 B4
Dukestown 35 C5
Dukinfield 87 E7
Dulas 82 C4
Dulcote 23 E7
Dulford 11 D5
Dull 133 E5
Dullatur 119 B7
Dullingham 55 D7
Dulnain Bridge 139 B5
Duloe Bedford 54 C2
Corn 5 D7
Dulsie 151 G12
Dulverton 10 B4
Dulwich 28 B4
Dumbarton 118 B3
Dumbleton 50 F5
Dumcrieff 114 D4
Dumfries 107 B6
Dumgoyne 126 F4
Dummer 26 E3
Dumpford 16 B2
Dumpton 31 C7
Dun 135 D6
Dunain House 151 G9
Dunalastair 132 D4
Dunan 149 F10
Dunans 145 D9
Dunball 22 E5
Dunbar 122 B2
Dunbeath 158 H3
Dunbeg 124 B4
Dunblane 127 D6
Dunbog 128 C4
Duncanston 151 F8
Duncanstone 140 B4
Dun Charlabhaigh 154 C6
Dunchurch 52 B2
Duncote 52 D4
Duncow 114 F2
Duncraggan 126 D4
Duncrievie 128 D3
Duncton 16 C3
Dundas House 159 K5
Dundee 134 F4
Dundeugh 113 F5
Dundon 23 F6
Dundonald 118 F3
Dundonnell 150 C3
Dundonnell Hotel 150 C3
Dundonnell House 150 C4
Dundraw 108 E2
Dundreggan 137 C6
Dundreggan Lodge 137 C6
Dundrennan 106 E4
Dundry 23 C7
Dunecht 141 D6
Dunfermline 128 F2
Dunfield 37 E8
Dunford Bridge 88 D2
Dungworth 88 F3
Dunham 77 B8
Dunham-on-the-Hill 73 B8
Dunhampton 50 C3
Dunham Town 86 F5
Dunholme 78 B3
Dunino 129 C7
Dunipace 127 F7
Dunira 127 B6
Dunkeld 133 E7
Dunkerton 24 D2
Dunkeswell 11 D6
Dunkeswick 95 E6
Dunkirk Kent 30 D4
Norf 81 E8
Dunk's Green 29 D7
Dunlappie 135 C5
Dunley Hants 26 D2
Worcs 50 C2
Dunlichity Lodge 151 H9
Dunlop 118 E4
Dunmaglass Lodge 137 B8
Dunmore Argyll 144 G6
Falk 127 F7
Dunnet 158 C4
Dunnichen 135 E5
Dunninald 135 D7
Dunning 128 C2
Dunnington
EYorks 97 D7
Warks 51 D5
York 96 D2
Dunnockshaw 87 B6
Dunollie 124 B4
Dunoon 145 F10
Dunragit 105 D5
Dunrostan 144 E6
Duns 122 D3
Dunsby 65 B8
Dunscore 113 F8
Dunscroft 89 D7
Dunsdale 102 C4
Dunsden Green 26 B5
Dunsfold 27 F8
Dunsford 10 F3
Dunshalt 128 C4
Dunshillock 153 D9
Dunskey House 104 D4
Dunsley 103 C6
Dunsmore 40 D1
Dunsop Bridge 93 D6
Dunstable 40 B3
Dunstall 63 B5
Dunstall Common 50 E3
Dunstall Green 55 C8
Dunstan 117 C8
Dunstan Steads 117 B8
Dunster 21 E8
Duns Tew 38 B4
Dunston Lincs 78 C3
Norf 68 D5
Staffs 62 C3
T&W 110 C5
Dunsville 89 D7
Dunswell 97 F6
Dunsyre 120 E3
Dunterton 5 B8
Duntisbourne Abbots 37 D6
Duntisbourne Leer 37 D6
Duntisbourne Rouse 37 D6
Duntish 12 D4
Duntocher 118 B4
Dunton Bucks 39 B8
C Beds 54 E3
Norf 80 D4
Dunton Bassett 64 E2
Dunton Green 29 D6
Dunton Wayletts 42 E2
Duntulm 149 A9
Dunure 112 C2
Dunvant 33 E6
Dunvegan 148 D7
Dunwich 57 B8
Dunwood 75 D6
Dupplin Castle 128 C2
Durdar 108 D4
Durgates 18 B3
Durham 111 E5
Durisdeer 113 D8
Durisdeermill 113 D8
Durkar 88 C4
Durleigh 22 F4
Durley Hants 15 C6
Wilts 25 C7
Durnamuck 150 B3
Durness 156 C7
Durno 141 B6
Duror 130 D3
Durran Argyll 125 E5
Highld 158 D3
Durrington Wilts 25 E6
W Sus 16 D5
Dursley 36 E4
Durston 11 B7
Durweston 13 D6
Dury 160 G6
Duston 52 C5
Duthil 138 B5
Dutlas 48 B4
Duton Hill 42 B2
Dutson 8 F5
Dutton 74 B2
Duxford Cambs 55 E5
Oxon 38 E3
Dwygyfylchi 83 D7
Dwyran 82 E4
Dyce 141 C7
Dye House 110 D2
Dyffryn Bridgend 34 E2
Carms 32 B4
Pembs 44 B4
Dyffryn Ardudwy 71 E6
Dyffryn Castell 58 F4
Dyffryn Ceidrych 33 B8
Dyffryn Cellwen 34 D2
Dyke Lincs 65 B8
Moray 151 F12
Dykehead Angus 134 C3
N Lanark 119 D8
Stirling 126 E4
Dykelands 135 C7
Dykends 134 D2
Dykeside 153 D7
Dykesmains 118 E2
Dylife 59 E5
Dymchurch 19 C7
Dymock 50 F2
Dyrham 24 B2
Dysart 128 E5
Dyserth 72 B4

E

Eadar Dha Fhadhail 154 D5
Eagland Hill 92 E4
Eagle 77 C8
Eagle Barnsdale 77 C8
Eagle Moor 77 C8
Eaglescliffe 102 C2
Eaglesfield Cumb 98 B2
Dumfries 108 B2
Eaglesham 119 D5
Eaglethorpe 65 E7
Eairy 84 E2
Eakley Lanes 53 D6
Eakring 77 C6
Ealand 89 C8
Ealing 40 F4
Eals 109 D6
Eamont Bridge 99 B7
Earby 94 E2
Earcroft 86 B4
Eardington 61 E7
Eardisland 49 D6
Eardisley 48 E5
Eardiston Shrops 60 B3
Worcs 49 C8
Earith 54 B4
Earle 117 B5
Earley 27 B5
Earlham 68 D5
Earlish 149 B8
Earls Barton 53 C6
Earls Colne 42 B4
Earl's Croome 50 E3
Earlsdon 51 B8
Earlsferry 129 E6
Earlsfield 78 F2
Earlsford 153 E8
Earl's Green 56 C4
Earlsheaton 88 B3
Earl Shilton 63 E8
Earlsmill 151 F12
Earl Soham 57 C6
Earl Sterndale 75 C7
Earlston Borders 121 F8
E Ayrs 118 F4
Earl Stonham 56 D5
Earlswood Mon 36 E1
Earlswood *continued*
Sur 28 E3
Warks 51 B6
Earnley 16 E2
Earsairidh 148 J2
Earsdon 111 B6
Earsham 69 F6
Earswick 96 D2
Eartham 16 D3
Easby N Yorks 101 D6
N Yorks 102 D3
Easdale 124 D3
Easebourne 16 B2
Easenhall 52 B2
Eashing 27 E7
Easington Bucks 39 C6
Durham 111 E7
E Yorks 91 C7
Northumb 123 F7
Oxon 39 E6
Oxon 52 F2
Redcar 103 C5
Easington Colliery 111 E7
Easington Lane 111 E6
Easingwold 95 C8
Easole Street 31 D6
Eassie 134 E3
East Aberthaw 22 C2
East Adderbury 52 F2
East Allington 7 E5
East Anstey 10 B3
East Appleton 101 E7
East Ardsley 88 B4
East Ashling 16 D2
East Auchronie 141 D7
East Ayton 103 F7
East Bank 35 D6
East Barkwith 91 F5
East Barming 29 D8
East Barnby 103 C6
East Barnet 41 E5
East Barns 122 B3
East Barsham 80 D5
East Beckham 81 D7
East Bedfont 27 B8
East Bergholt 56 F4
East Bilney 68 C2
East Blatchington 17 D8
East Boldre 14 D4
Eastbourne 18 F3
East Brent 22 D5
Eastbridge 57 C8
East Bridgford 77 E6
East Buckland 21 F5
East Budleigh 11 F5
Eastburn 94 E3
East Burrafirth 160 H5
East Burton 13 F6
Eastbury London 40 E3
W Berks 25 B8
East Butsfield 110 E4
East Butterwick 90 D2
Eastby 94 D3
East Cairnbeg 135 B7
East Calder 120 C3
East Carleton 68 D4
East Carlton
N Nhants 64 F5
W Yorks 94 E5
East Chaldon 13 F5
East Challow 38 F3
East Chiltington 17 C7
East Chinnock 12 C2
East Chisenbury 25 D6
Eastchurch 30 B3
East Clandon 27 D8
East Claydon 39 B7
East Clyne 157 J12
East Coker 12 C3
Eastcombe 37 D5
East Combe 22 F3
East Common 96 F2
East Compton 23 E8
Eastcote London 40 F4
W Mid 51 B6
W Nhants 52 D4
Eastcott Corn 8 C4
Wilts 24 D5
East Cottingwith 96 E3
Eastcourt Wilts 25 C7
Wilts 37 E6
East Cowes 15 E6
East Cowick 89 B7
East Cowton 101 D8
East Cramlington 111 B5
East Cranmore 23 E8
East Creech 13 F7
East Croachy 138 B2
East Croftmore 139 C5
East Curthwaite 108 E3
East Dean E Sus 18 F2
Hants 14 B3
W Sus 16 C3
East Down 20 E5
East Drayton 77 B7
East Ella 90 B4
East End Dorset 13 E7
E Yorks 91 B6
Hants 14 E4
Hants 15 B7
Hants 26 C2
Herts 41 B7
Kent 18 B5
N Som 23 B6
Oxon 38 C3
Easter Ardross 151 D9
Easter Balmoral 139 E8
Easter Boleskine 137 B8
Easter Compton 36 F2
Easter Cringate 127 F6
Easter Davoch 140 D3
Easter Earshaig 114 D3
Easter Fearn 151 C9
Easter Galcantray 151 G11
Eastergate 16 D3
Easterhouse 119 C6
Easter Howgate 120 C5
Easter Howlaws 122 E3
Easter Kinkell 151 F8
Easter Lednathie 134 C3
Easter Milton 151 F12
Easter Moniack 151 G8
Eastern Green 63 F6
Easter Ord 141 D7
Easter Quarff 160 K6
Easter Rhynd 128 C3
Easter Row 127 E6
Easter Silverford 153 B7
Easter Skeld 160 J5
Easterton 24 D5
Eastertown 22 D5
Eastertown of Auchleuchries 153 E10
Easter Whyntie 152 B6
East Farleigh 29 D8
East Farndon 64 F4
East Ferry 90 E2
Eastfield N Lanark 119 C8
N Yorks 103 F8
Eastfield Hall 117 D8
East Fortune 121 B8
East Garston 25 B8
Eastgate Durham 110 F2
Norf 81 E7
East Ginge 38 F4
East Goscote 64 C3
East Grafton 25 C7
East Grimstead 14 B3
East Grinstead 28 F4
East Guldeford 19 C6
East Haddon 52 C4
East Hagbourne 39 F5
East Halton 90 C5
Eastham 85 F4
East Ham 41 F7
Eastham Ferry 85 F4
Easthampstead 27 C6
East Hanney 38 E4
East Hanningfield 42 D3
East Hardwick 89 C5
East Harling 68 F2
East Harlsey 102 E2
East Harnham 14 B2
East Harptree 23 D7
East Hartford 111 B5
East Harting 15 C8
East Hatley 54 D3
East Hauxwell 101 E6
East Haven 135 F5
Eastheath 27 C6
East Heckington 78 E4
East Hedleyhope 110 E4
East Hendred 38 F4
East Herrington 111 D6
East Heslerton 96 B5
East Hoathly 18 D2
Easthope 61 E5
Easthorpe Essex 43 B5
Leics 77 F8
Notts 77 D7
East Horrington 23 E7
East Horsley 27 D8
East Horton 123 F6
Easthouses 121 C6
East Huntspill 22 E5
East Hyde 40 C4
East Ilkerton 21 E6
East Ilsley 38 F4
Eastington Devon 10 D2
Glos 36 D4
Glos 37 C8
East Keal 79 C6
East Kennett 25 C6
East Keswick 95 E6
East Kilbride 119 D6
East Kirkby 79 C6
East Knapton 96 B4
East Knighton 13 F6
East Knoyle 24 F3
East Kyloe 123 F6
East Lambrook 12 C2
East Lamington 151 D10
East Langdon 31 E7
East Langton 64 E4
East Langwell 157 J10
East Lavant 16 D2
East Lavington 16 C3
East Layton 101 D6
Eastleach Martin 38 D2
Eastleach Turville 38 D1
East Leake 64 B2
East Learmouth 122 F4
Eastleigh Devon 9 B6
Hants 14 C5
East Leigh 9 D8
East Lexham 67 C8
East Lilburn 117 B6
Eastling 30 D3
East Linton 121 B8
East Liss 15 B8
East Looe 5 D7
East Lound 89 E8
East Lulworth 13 F6
East Lutton 96 C5
East Lydford 23 F7
East Mains 141 E5
East Malling 29 D8
East March 134 F4
East Marden 16 C2
East Markham 77 B7
East Marton 94 D2
East Meon 15 B7
East Mere 10 C4
East Mersea 43 C6
East Mey 158 C5
East Molesey 28 C2
Eastmoor Derbys 76 B3
Norf 67 D7
East Morden 13 E7
East Morton 94 E3
East Ness 96 B2
East Newton 97 F8
Eastney 15 E7
Eastnor 50 F2
East Norton 64 D4
East Nynehead 11 B6
East Oakley 26 D3
Eastoft 90 C2
East Ogwell 7 B6
Eastoke 15 E8
Easton Cambs 54 B2
Cumb 108 B4
Cumb 108 D2
Devon 10 F2
Dorset 12 G4
Hants 26 F3
Lincs 65 B6
Norf 68 C4
Som 23 E7
Suff 57 D6
Wilts 24 B3
Easton Grey 37 F5
Easton-in-Gordano 23 B7
Easton Maudit 53 D6
Easton on the Hill 65 D7
Easton Royal 25 C7
East Orchard 13 C6
East Ord 123 D5
East Panson 9 E5
Eastpark 107 C7
East Peckham 29 E7
East Pennard 23 F7
East Perry 54 C2
East Portlemouth 6 F5
East Prawle 7 F5
East Preston 16 D4
East Putford 9 C5
East Quantoxhead 22 E3
East Rainton 111 E6
East Ravendale 91 E6
East Raynham 80 E4
Eastrea 66 E2
East Rhidorroch Lodge 150 B5
Eastriggs 108 C2
East Rigton 95 E6
Eastrington 89 B8
East Rounton 102 D2
East Row 103 C6
East Rudham 80 E4
East Runton 81 C7
East Ruston 69 B6
Eastry 31 D7
East Saltoun 121 C7
East Sleekburn 117 F8
East Somerton 69 C7
East Stockwith 89 E8
East Stoke Dorset 13 F6
Notts 77 E7
East Stour 13 B6
East Stourmouth 31 C6
East Stowford 9 B8
East Stratton 26 F3
East Studdal 31 E7
East Suisnish 149 E10
East Taphouse 5 C6
East-the-Water 9 B6
East Thirston 117 E7
East Tilbury 29 B7
East Tisted 26 F5
East Torrington 90 F5
East Tuddenham 68 C3
East Tytherley 14 B3
East Tytherton 24 B4
East Village 10 D3
Eastville Bristol 23 B8
Lincs 79 D7
East Wall 60 E5
East Walton 67 C7
Eastwell 64 B4
East Wellow 14 B4
East Wemyss 128 E5
East Whitburn 120 C2
Eastwick Herts 41 C7
Shetland 160 F5
East Williamston 32 D1
East Winch 67 C6
East Winterslow 25 F7
East Wittering 15 E8
East Witton 101 F6
Eastwood Notts 76 E4
Southend 42 F4
W Yorks 87 B7
East Woodburn 116 F5
East Woodhay 26 C2
East Worldham 26 F5
East Worlington 10 C2
East Worthing 17 D5
Eathorpe 51 C8
Eaton Ches E 75 C5
Ches W 74 C2
Leics 64 B4
Norf 68 D5
Notts 77 B7
Oxon 38 D4
Shrops 60 F3
Shrops 60 F5
Eaton Bishop 49 F6
Eaton Bray 40 B2
Eaton Constantine 61 D5
Eaton Green 40 B2
Eaton Hastings 38 E2
Eaton on Tern 61 B6
Eaton Socon 54 D2
Eavestone 94 C5
Ebberston 103 F6
Ebbesbourne Wake 13 B7
Ebbw Vale = *Glyn Ebwy* 35 D5
Ebchester 110 D4
Ebford 10 F4
Ebley 37 D5
Ebnal 73 E8
Ebrington 51 E6
Ecchinswell 26 D2
Ecclaw 122 C3
Ecclefechan 107 B8
Eccles Borders 122 E3
Gtr Man 87 E5
Kent 29 C8
Ecclesall 88 F4
Ecclesfield 88 E4
Ecclesgreig 135 C7
Eccleshall 62 B2
Eccleshill 94 F4
Ecclesmachan 120 B3
Eccles on Sea 69 B7
Eccles Road 68 E3
Eccleston Ches W 73 C8
Lancs 86 C3
Mers 86 E2
Eccleston Park 86 E2
Eccup 95 E5
Echt 141 D6
Eckford 116 B3
Eckington Derbys 76 B4
Worcs 50 E4
Ecton 53 C6
Edale 88 F2
Edburton 17 C6
Edderside 107 E7
Edderton 151 C10
Eddistone 8 B4
Eddleston 120 E5
Edenbridge 28 E5
Edenfield 87 C5
Edenhall 109 F5
Edenham 65 B7
Eden Park 28 C4
Edensor 76 C2
Edentaggart 126 E2
Edenthorpe 89 D7
Edentown 108 D3
Ederline 124 E4
Edern 70 D3
Edgarley 23 F7
Edgbaston 62 F4
Edgcott Bucks 39 B6
Som 21 F7
Edge 60 D3
Edgebolton 61 B5
Edge End 36 C2
Edgefield 81 D6
Edgefield Street 81 D6
Edge Green 73 D8
Edge Hill 85 F4
Edgeside 87 B6
Edgeworth 37 D6
Edgmond 61 C7
Edgmond Marsh 61 B7
Edgton 60 F3
Edgware 40 E4
Edgworth 86 C5
Edinample 126 B4
Edinbane 149 C8
Edinburgh 121 B5
Edingale 63 C6
Edingight House 152 C5
Edingley 77 D6
Edingthorpe 69 A6
Edingthorpe Green 69 A6
Edington Som 23 F5
Wilts 24 D4
Edintore 152 D4
Edithmead 22 E5
Edith Weston 65 D6
Edlesborough 40 C2
Edlingham 117 D7
Edlington 78 B5
Edmondsham 13 C8
Edmondsley 110 E5
Edmondthorpe 65 C5
Edmonstone 159 F6
Edmonton 41 E6
Edmundbyers 110 D3
Ednam 122 F3
Ednaston 76 E2
Edradynate 133 D5
Edrom 122 D4
Edstaston 74 F2
Edstone 51 C6
Edvin Loach 49 D8
Edwalton 77 F5
Edwardstone 56 E3
Edwinsford 46 F5
Edwinstowe 77 C6
Edworth 54 E3
Edwyn Ralph 49 D8
Edzell 135 C5
E Eachwick 110 B4
Efail Isaf 34 F4
Efailnewydd 70 D4
Efailwen 32 B2
Efenechtyd 72 D5
Effingham 28 D2
Effirth 160 H5
Efford 10 D3
Egdon 50 D4
Egerton Gtr Man 86 C5
Kent 30 E3
Egerton Forstal 30 E2
Eggborough 89 B6
Eggbuckland 6 D3
Eggington 40 B2
Egginton 63 B6
Egglescliffe 102 C2
Eggleston 100 B4
Egham 27 B8
Egleton 65 D5
Eglingham 117 C7
Egloshayle 4 B5
Egloskerry 8 F4
Eglwysbach 83 D8
Eglwys-Brewis 22 C2
Eglwys Cross 73 E8
Eglwys Fach 58 E3
Eglwyswen 45 F3
Eglwyswrw 45 F3
Egmanton 77 C7
Egremont Cumb 98 C2
Mers 85 E4
Egton 103 D6
Egton Bridge 103 D6
Eight Ash Green 43 B5
Eignaig 130 E1
Eil 138 C4
Eilanreach 149 G13
Eileanach Lodge 151 E8
Eilean Darach 150 C4
Einacleite 154 E6
Eisgean 155 F8
Eisingrug 71 D7
Elan Village 47 C8
Elberton 36 F3
Elburton 6 D3
Elcho 128 B3
Elcombe 37 F8
Eldernell 66 E3
Eldersfield 50 F3
Eldersli 118 C4
Eldon 101 B7
Eldrick 112 F2
Eldroth 93 C7
Eldwick 94 E4
Elfhowe 99 E6
Elford Northumb 123 F7
Staffs 63 C5
Elgin 152 B2
Elgol 149 G10
Elham 31 E5
Elie 129 D6
Elim 82 C3
Eling 14 C4
Elishader 149 B10
Elishaw 116 E4
Elkesley 77 B6
Elkstone 37 C6
Ellan 138 B4
Elland 88 B2
Ellary 144 F6
Ellastone 75 E8
Ellemford 122 C3
Ellenbrook 84 E3
Ellenhall 62 B2
Ellen's Green 27 F8
Ellerbeck 102 E2
Ellerburn 103 F6
Ellerby 103 C5
Ellerdine Heath 61 B6
Ellerhayes 10 D4
Elleric 130 E4
Ellerker 90 B3
Ellerton E Yorks 96 F3
Shrops 61 B7
Ellesborough 39 D8
Ellesmere 73 F8
Ellesmere Port 73 B8
Ellingham Norf 69 E6
Northumb 117 B7
Ellingstring 101 F6
Ellington Cambs 54 B2
Northumb 117 E8
Elliot 135 F6
Ellisfield 26 E4
Ellistown 63 C8
Ellon 153 E9
Ellonby 108 F4
Ellough 69 F7
Elloughton 90 B3
Ellwood 36 D2
Elm 66 D4
Elmbridge 50 C4
Elmdon Essex 55 F5
W Mid 63 F5
Elmdon Heath 63 F5
Elmers End 28 C4
Elmesthorpe 63 E8
Elmfield 15 E7
Elm Hill 13 B6
Elmhurst 62 C5
Elmley Castle 50 E4
Elmley Lovett 50 C3
Elmore 36 C4
Elmore Back 36 C4
Elm Park 41 F8
Elmscott 8 B4
Elmsett 56 E4
Elmstead Market 43 B6
Elmsted 30 E5
Elmstone 31 C6
Elmstone Hardwicke 37 B6
Elmswell E Yorks 97 D5
Suff 56 C3
Elmton 76 B5
Elphin 156 H5
Elphinstone 121 B6
Elrick 141 D7
Elrig 105 E7
Elsdon 117 E5
Elsecar 88 E4
Elsenham 41 B8
Elsfield 39 C5
Elsham 90 C4
Elsing 68 C3
Elslack 94 E2
Elson 73 F7
Elsrickle 120 E3
Elstead 27 E7
Elsted 16 C2
Elsthorpe 65 B7
Elstob 101 B8
Elston Notts 77 E7
Wilts 25 E5
Elstone 9 C8
Elstow 53 E8
Elstree 40 E4
Elstronwick 97 F8
Elswick 92 F4
Elsworth 54 C4
Elterwater 99 D5
Eltham 28 B5
Eltisley 54 D3
Elton Cambs 65 E7
Ches W 73 B8
Derbys 76 C2
Glos 36 C4
Hereford 49 B6
Notts 77 F7
Stockton 102 C2
Elton Green 73 B8
Elvanfoot 114 C2
Elvaston 76 F4
Elveden 56 B2
Elvingston 121 B7
Elvington Kent 31 D6
York 96 E2
Elwick Hrtlpl 111 F7
Northumb 123 F7
Elworth 74 C4
Elworthy 22 F2
Ely Cambs 66 F5
Cardiff 22 B3
Emberton 53 E6
Embleton Cumb 107 F8
Northumb 117 B8
Embo 151 B11
Emborough 23 D8
Embo Street 151 B11
Embsay 94 D3
Emersons Green 23 B8
Emery Down 14 D3
Emley 88 C3
Emmbrook 27 C5
Emmer Green 26 B5
Emmington 39 D7
Emneth 66 D4
Emneth Hungate 66 D5
Empingham 65 D6
Empshott 27 F5
Emstrey 60 C5
Emsworth 15 D8
Enborne 26 C2
Enchmarsh 60 E5
Enderby 64 E2
Endmoor 99 F7
Endon 75 D6
Endon Bank 75 D6
Enfield 41 E6
Enfield Wash 41 E6
Enford 25 D6
Engamoor 160 H4
Engine Common 36 F3
Englefield 26 B4
Englefield Green 27 B7
Englesea-brook 74 D4
English Bicknor 36 C2
Englishcombe 24 C2
English Frankton 60 B4
Enham Alamein 25 E8
Enmore 22 F4
Ennerdale Bridge 98 C2
Enoch 113 D8
Enochdhu 133 C7
Ensay 146 G6
Ensbury 13 E8
Ensdon 60 C4
Ensis 9 B7
Enstone 38 B3
Enterkinfoot 113 D8
Enterpen 102 D2
Enville 62 F2
Eolaigearraidh 148 H2
Eorabus 146 J6
Eòropaidh 155 A10
Epperstone 77 E6
Epping 41 D7
Epping Green
Essex 41 D7
Herts 41 D5
Epping Upland 41 D7
Eppleby 101 C6
Eppleworth 97 F6
Epsom 28 C3
Epwell 51 E8
Epworth 89 D8
Epworth Turbary 89 D8
Erbistock 73 E7
Erbusaig 149 F12
Erchless Castle 150 G7
Erdington 62 E5
Eredine 125 E5
Eriboll 156 D7
Ericstane 114 C3
Eridge Green 18 B2
Erines 145 F7
Eriswell 55 B8
Erith 29 B6
Erlestoke 24 D4
Ermine 78 B2
Ermington 6 D4
Erpingham 81 D7
Errogie 137 B8
Errol 128 B4
Erskin 118 B4
Erskine Bridg 118 B4
Ervie 104 C4
Erwarton 57 F6
Erwood 48 E2
Eryholme 101 D8
Eryrys 73 D6
Escomb 101 B6
Escrick 96 E2
Esgairdawe 46 E5
Esgairgeiliog 58 D4
Esh 110 E4
Esher 28 C2
Esholt 94 E4
Eshott 117 E8
Eshton 94 D2
Esh Winning 110 E4
Eskadale 150 H7
Eskbank 121 C6
Eskdale Green 98 D3
Eskdalemuir 115 E5
Eske 97 E6
Eskham 91 E7
Esk Valley 103 D6
Esprick 92 F4
Essendine 65 C7
Essendon 41 D5
Essich 151 H9
Essington 62 D3
Esslemont 141 B8
Eston 102 C3
Eswick 160 H6
Etal 122 F5
Etchilhampton 24 C5
Etchingham 18 C4
Etchinghill Kent 19 B8
Staffs 62 C4
Ethie Castle 135 E6
Ethie Mains 135 E6
Etling Green 68 C3
Eton 27 B7
Eton Wick 27 B7
Etteridge 138 E2
Ettersgill 100 B3
Ettingshall 62 E3
Ettington 51 E7
Etton E Yorks 97 E5
Pboro 65 D8
Ettrick 115 C5
Ettrickbridge 115 B6
Ettrickhill 115 C5
Etwall 76 F2
Euston 56 B2
Euximoor Drove 66 E4
Euxton 86 C3
Evanstown 34 F3
Evanton 151 E9
Evedon 78 E3
Evelix 151 B10
Evenjobb 48 C4
Evenley 52 F3
Evenlode 38 B2
Evenwood 101 B6
Evenwood Gate 101 B6
Everbay 159 F7
Evercreech 23 F8
Everdon 52 D3
Everingham 96 E4
Everleigh 25 D7
Everley 103 F7
Eversholt 53 F7
Evershot 12 D3
Eversley 27 C5
Eversley Cross 27 C5
Everthorpe 96 F5
Everton C Beds 54 D3
Hants 14 E3
Mers 85 E4
Notts 89 E7
Evertown 108 B3
Evesbatch 49 E8
Evesham 50 E5
Evington 64 D3
Ewden Village 88 E3
Ewell 28 C3
Ewell Minnis 31 E6
Ewelme 39 E6
Ewen 37 E7
Ewenny 21 B8
Ewerby 78 E4
Ewerby Thorpe 78 E4
Ewes 115 E6
Ewesley 117 E6
Ewhurst 27 E8
Ewhurst Green
E Sus 18 C4
Sur 27 F8
Ewloe 73 C7
Ewloe Green 73 C6
Ewood 86 B4
Eworthy 9 E6
Ewshot 27 E6
Ewyas Harold 35 B7
Exbourne 9 D8
Exbury 14 E5

Exebridge . . . 10 B4
Exelby . . . 101 F7
Exeter . . . 10 E4
Exford . . . 21 F7
Exhall . . . 51 D6
Exley Head . . . 94 F3
Exminster . . . 10 F4
Exmouth . . . 10 F5
Exnaboe . . . 160 M5
Exning . . . 55 C7
Exton Devon . . . 10 F4
Hants . . . 15 B7
Rutland . . . 65 C6
Som . . . 21 F8
Exwick . . . 10 E4
Eyam . . . 76 B2
Eydon . . . 52 D3
Eye Hereford . . . 49 C6
Pboro . . . 66 D2
Suff . . . 56 B5
Eye Green . . . 66 D2
Eyemouth . . . 122 C5
Eyeworth . . . 54 E3
Eyhorne Street . . . 30 D2
Eyke . . . 57 D7
Eynesbury . . . 54 D2
Eynort . . . 149 F8
Eynsford . . . 29 C6
Eynsham . . . 38 D4
Eype . . . 12 E2
Eyre Highld . . . 149 C9
Highld . . . 149 E10
Eythorne . . . 31 E6
Eyton Hereford . . . 49 C6
Shrops . . . 60 F3
Wrex . . . 73 E7
Eyton upon the Weald Moors . . . 61 C6

F

Faceby . . . 102 D2
Facit . . . 87 C6
Faddiley . . . 74 D2
Fadmoor . . . 102 F4
Faerdre . . . 33 D7
Failand . . . 23 B7
Failford . . . 112 B4
Failsworth . . . 87 D6
Fain . . . 150 D4
Fairbourne . . . 58 C3
Fairburn . . . 89 B5
Fairfield Derbys . . . 75 B7
Stockton . . . 102 C2
Worcs . . . 50 B4
Worcs . . . 50 E5
Fairford . . . 38 D1
Fair Green . . . 67 C6
Fairhaven . . . 85 B4
Fair Hill . . . 108 F5
Fairlie . . . 118 D2
Fairlight . . . 19 D5
Fairlight Cove . . . 19 D5
Fairmile . . . 11 E5
Fairmilehead . . . 120 C5
Fairoak . . . 74 F4
Fair Oak . . . 15 C5
Fair Oak Green . . . 26 C4
Fairseat . . . 29 C7
Fairstead Essex . . . 42 C3
Norf . . . 67 C6
Fairwarp . . . 17 B8
Fairy Cottage . . . 84 D4
Fairy Cross . . . 9 B6
Fakenham . . . 80 E5
Fakenham Magna . . . 56 B3
Fala . . . 121 C7
Fala Dam . . . 121 C7
Falahill . . . 121 D6
Falcon . . . 49 F8
Faldingworth . . . 90 F4
Falfield . . . 36 E3
Falkenham . . . 57 F6
Falkirk . . . 119 B8
Falkland . . . 128 D4
Falla . . . 116 C3
Fallgate . . . 76 C3
Fallin . . . 127 E7
Fallowfield . . . 87 E6
Fallsidehill . . . 122 E2
Falmer . . . 17 D7
Falmouth . . . 3 C7
Falsgrave . . . 103 F8
Falstone . . . 116 F3
Fanagmore . . . 156 E4
Fangdale Beck . . . 102 E3
Fangfoss . . . 96 D3
Fankerton . . . 127 F6
Fanmore . . . 146 G7
Fannich Lodge . . . 150 E5
Fans . . . 122 E2
Far Bank . . . 89 C7
Far Bletchley . . . 53 F6
Farcet . . . 66 E2
Far Cotton . . . 52 D5
Farden . . . 49 B7
Fareham . . . 15 D6
Farewell . . . 62 C4
Far Forest . . . 50 B2
Farforth . . . 79 B6
Faringdon . . . 38 E2
Farington . . . 86 B3
Farlam . . . 109 D5
Farlary . . . 157 J10
Far Laund . . . 76 E3
Farleigh N Som . . . 23 C6
Sur . . . 28 C4
Farleigh Hungerford . . . 24 D3
Farleigh Wallop . . . 26 E4
Farlesthorpe . . . 79 B7
Farleton Cumb . . . 99 F7
Lancs . . . 93 C5
Farley Shrops . . . 60 D3
Staffs . . . 75 E7
Wilts . . . 14 B3
Farley Green . . . 27 E8
Farley Hill Luton . . . 40 B3
Wokingham . . . 26 C5
Farleys End . . . 36 C4
Farlington . . . 96 C2
Farlow . . . 61 F6
Farmborough . . . 23 C8
Farmcote Glos . . . 37 B7
Shrops . . . 61 E7
Farmington . . . 37 C8
Farmoor . . . 38 D4
Farmtown . . . 152 C5
Farnborough Hants . . . 27 D6
London . . . 28 C5
Warks . . . 52 E2
W Berks . . . 38 F4
Farnborough Green . . . 27 D6
Farncombe . . . 27 E7
Farndish . . . 53 C7
Farndon Ches W . . . 73 D8
Notts . . . 77 D7
Farnell . . . 135 D6
Farnham Dorset . . . 13 C7
Essex . . . 41 B7
N Yorks . . . 95 C6
Suff . . . 57 C7
Sur . . . 27 E6
Farnham Common . . . 40 F2
Farnham Green . . . 41 B7
Farnham Royal . . . 40 F2
Farnhill . . . 94 E3
Farningham . . . 29 C6
Farnley N Yorks . . . 94 E5
W Yorks . . . 95 F5
Farnley Tyas . . . 88 C2
Farnsfield . . . 77 D6
Farnworth Gtr Man . . . 86 D5
Halton . . . 86 F3
Farr Highld . . . 138 D4
Highld . . . 151 H9
Highld . . . 157 C10
Farr House . . . 151 H9
Farringdon . . . 10 E5
Farrington Gurney . . . 23 D8
Far Sawrey . . . 99 E5
Farsley . . . 94 F5
Farthinghoe . . . 52 F3
Farthingloe . . . 31 E6
Farthingstone . . . 52 D4
Fartown . . . 88 C2
Farway . . . 11 E6
Fasag . . . 149 C13
Fascadale . . . 147 D8
Faslane Port . . . 145 E11
Fasnacloich . . . 130 E4
Fasnakyle Ho . . . 137 B6
Fassfern . . . 130 B4
Fatfield . . . 111 D6
Fattahead . . . 153 C6
Faugh . . . 108 D5
Fauldhouse . . . 120 C2
Faulkbourne . . . 42 C3
Faulkland . . . 24 D2
Fauls . . . 74 F2
Faversham . . . 30 C4
Favillar . . . 152 E2
Fawdington . . . 95 B7
Fawfieldhead . . . 75 C7
Fawkham Green . . . 29 C6
Fawler . . . 38 C3
Fawley Bucks . . . 39 F7
Hants . . . 15 D5
W Berks . . . 38 F3
Fawley Chapel . . . 36 B2
Faxfleet . . . 90 B2
Faygate . . . 28 F3
Fazakerley . . . 85 E4
Fazeley . . . 63 D6
Fearby . . . 101 F6
Fearn . . . 151 D11
Fearnan . . . 132 E4
Fearnbeg . . . 149 C12
Fearnhead . . . 86 E4
Fearn Lodge . . . 151 C9
Fearnmore . . . 149 B12
Fearn Station . . . 151 D11
Featherstone Staffs . . . 62 D3
W Yorks . . . 88 B5
Featherwood . . . 116 D4
Feckenham . . . 50 C5
Feering . . . 42 B4
Feetham . . . 100 E4
Feizor . . . 93 C7
Felbridge . . . 28 F4
Felbrigg . . . 81 D8
Felcourt . . . 28 E4
Felden . . . 40 D3
Felin-Crai . . . 34 B2
Felindre Carms . . . 33 B6
Carms . . . 33 B8
Carms . . . 46 F2
Carms . . . 47 F5
Ceredig . . . 46 D4
Powys . . . 59 F8
Swansea . . . 33 D7
Felindre Farchog . . . 45 F3
Felinfach Ceredig . . . 46 D4
Powys . . . 48 F2
Felinfoel . . . 33 D6
Felingwmisaf . . . 33 B6
Felingwmuchaf . . . 33 B6
Felinwynt . . . 45 D4
Felixkirk . . . 102 F2
Felixstowe . . . 57 F6
Felixstowe Ferry . . . 57 F7
Felkington . . . 122 E5
Felkirk . . . 88 C4
Felling . . . 111 C5
Fell Side . . . 108 F3
Felmersham . . . 53 D7
Felmingham . . . 81 E8
Felpham . . . 16 E3
Felsham . . . 56 D3
Felsted . . . 42 B2
Feltham . . . 28 B2
Felthorpe . . . 68 C4
Felton Hereford . . . 49 E7
Northumb . . . 117 D7
N Som . . . 23 C7
Felton Butler . . . 60 C3
Feltwell . . . 67 E7
Fenay Bridge . . . 88 C2
Fence . . . 93 F8
Fence Houses . . . 111 D6
Fen Ditton . . . 55 C5
Fen Drayton . . . 54 C4
Fen End . . . 51 B7
Fengate Norf . . . 81 E7
Pboro . . . 66 E2
Fenham . . . 123 E6
Fenhouses . . . 79 E5
Feniscliffe . . . 86 B4
Feniscowles . . . 86 B4
Feniton . . . 11 E6
Fenlake . . . 53 E8
Fenny Bentley . . . 75 D8
Fenny Bridges . . . 11 E6
Fenny Compton . . . 52 D2
Fenny Drayton . . . 63 E7
Fenny Stratford . . . 53 F6
Fenrother . . . 117 E7
Fen Side . . . 79 D6
Fenstanton . . . 54 C4
Fenton Cambs . . . 54 B4
Lincs . . . 77 B8
Lincs . . . 77 D8
Stoke . . . 75 E5
Fenton Barns . . . 129 F7
Fenton Town . . . 123 F5
Fenwick E Ayrs . . . 118 E4
Northumb . . . 110 B3
Northumb . . . 123 E6
S Yorks . . . 89 C6
Feochaig . . . 143 G8
Feock . . . 3 C7
Feolin Ferry . . . 144 G3
Ferindonald . . . 149 H11
Feriniquarrie . . . 148 C6
Ferlochan . . . 130 E3
Fern . . . 134 C4
Ferndale . . . 34 E4
Ferndown . . . 13 D8
Ferness . . . 151 G12
Ferney Green . . . 99 E6
Fernham . . . 38 E2
Fernhill Heath . . . 50 D3
Fernhurst . . . 16 B2
Fernie . . . 128 C5
Ferniegair . . . 119 D7
Fernilea . . . 149 E8
Fernilee . . . 75 B7
Ferrensby . . . 95 C6
Ferring . . . 16 D4
Ferrybridge . . . 89 B5
Ferryden . . . 135 D7
Ferryhill Aberdeen . . . 141 D8
Durham . . . 111 F5
Ferry Hill . . . 66 F3
Ferryhill Station . . . 111 F6
Ferry Point . . . 151 C10
Ferryside . . . 32 C4
Fersfield . . . 68 F3
Fersit . . . 131 B7
Ferwig . . . 45 E3
Feshiebridge . . . 138 D4
Fetcham . . . 28 D2
Fetterangus . . . 153 C9
Fettercairn . . . 135 B6
Fettes . . . 151 F8
Fewcott . . . 39 B5
Fewston . . . 94 D4
F Faccombe . . . 25 D8
Ffairfach . . . 33 B7
Ffair-Rhos . . . 47 C6
Ffaldybrenin . . . 46 E5
Ffarmers . . . 47 E5
Ffawyddog . . . 35 C6
Fforest . . . 33 D6
Fforest-fâch . . . 33 E7
Ffostrasol . . . 46 E2
Ffos-y-ffi . . . 46 C3
Ffridd-Uchaf . . . 83 F5
Ffrith . . . 73 D6
Ffrwd . . . 82 F4
Ffynnon ddrain . . . 33 B5
Ffynnongroyw . . . 85 F2
Ffynnon-oer . . . 46 D4
Fidden . . . 146 J6
Fiddes . . . 141 F7
Fiddington Glos . . . 50 F4
Som . . . 22 E4
Fiddleford . . . 13 C6
Fiddlers Hamlet . . . 41 D7
Field . . . 75 F7
Field Broughton . . . 99 F5
Field Dalling . . . 81 D6
Field Head . . . 63 D8
Fifehead Magdalen . . . 13 B5
Fifehead Neville . . . 13 C5
Fifield Oxon . . . 38 C2
Wilts . . . 25 D6
Windsor . . . 27 B7
Fifield Bavant . . . 13 B8
Figheldean . . . 25 E6
Filands . . . 37 F6
Filby . . . 69 C7
Filey . . . 97 A7
Filgrave . . . 53 E6
Filkins . . . 38 D2
Filleigh Devon . . . 9 B8
Devon . . . 10 C2
Fillingham . . . 90 F3
Fillongley . . . 63 F6
Filton . . . 23 B8
Fimber . . . 96 C4
Finavon . . . 134 D4
Finchairn . . . 124 E5
Fincham . . . 67 D6
Finchampstead . . . 27 C5
Finchdean . . . 15 C8
Finchingfield . . . 55 F7
Finchley . . . 41 E5
Findern . . . 76 F3
Findhorn . . . 151 E13
Findhorn Bridge . . . 138 B4
Findochty . . . 152 B4
Findo Gask . . . 128 B2
Findon Aberds . . . 141 E8
W Sus . . . 16 D5
Findon Mains . . . 151 E9
Findrack House . . . 140 D5
Finedon . . . 53 B7
Fingal Street . . . 57 C6
Fingask . . . 141 B6
Fingerpost . . . 50 B2
Fingest . . . 39 E7
Finghall . . . 101 F6
Fingland Cumb . . . 108 D2
Dumfries . . . 113 C7
Finglesham . . . 31 D7
Fingringhoe . . . 43 B6
Finlarig . . . 132 F2
Finmere . . . 52 F4
Finnart . . . 132 D2
Finningham . . . 56 C4
Finningley . . . 89 E7
Finnygaud . . . 152 C5
Finsbury . . . 41 F6
Finstall . . . 50 C4
Finsthwaite . . . 99 F5
Finstock . . . 38 C3
Finstown . . . 159 G4
Fintry Aberds . . . 153 C7
Dundee . . . 134 F4
Stirling . . . 126 F5
Finzean . . . 140 E5
Fionnphort . . . 146 J6
Fionnsbhagh . . . 154 J5
Firbeck . . . 89 F6
Firby N Yorks . . . 96 C3
N Yorks . . . 101 F7
Firgrove . . . 87 C7
Firsby . . . 79 C7
Firsdown . . . 25 F7
First Coast . . . 150 B2
Fir Tree . . . 110 F4
Fishbourne IoW . . . 15 E6
W Sus . . . 16 D2
Fishburn . . . 111 F6
Fishcross . . . 127 E7
Fisherford . . . 153 E6
Fisher Place . . . 99 C5
Fisher's Pond . . . 15 B5
Fisherstreet . . . 27 F7
Fisherton Highld . . . 151 F10
S Ayrs . . . 112 C2
Fishguard = Abergwaun . . . 44 B4
Fishlake . . . 89 C7
Fishleigh Barton . . . 9 B7
Fishponds . . . 23 B8
Fishpool . . . 36 B3
Fishtoft . . . 79 E6
Fishtoft Drove . . . 79 E6
Fishtown of Usan . . . 135 D7
Fishwick . . . 122 D5
Fiskavaig . . . 149 E8
Fiskerton Lincs . . . 78 B3
Notts . . . 77 D7
Fitling . . . 97 F8
Fittleton . . . 25 E6
Fittleworth . . . 16 C4
Fitton End . . . 66 C4
Fitz . . . 60 C4
Fitzhead . . . 11 B6
Fitzwilliam . . . 88 C5
Fiunary . . . 147 G9
Five Acres . . . 36 C2
Five Ashes . . . 18 C2
Fivecrosses . . . 74 B2
Fivehead . . . 11 B8
Five Oak Green . . . 29 E7
Five Oaks Jersey . . . 17
W Sus . . . 16 B4
Five Roads . . . 33 D5
Flack's Green . . . 42 C3
Flackwell Heath . . . 40 F1
Fladbury . . . 50 E4
Fladdabister . . . 160 K6
Flagg . . . 75 C8
Flamborough . . . 97 B8
Flamstead . . . 40 C3
Flamstead End . . . 41 D6
Flansham . . . 16 D3
Flanshaw . . . 88 B4
Flasby . . . 94 D2
Flash . . . 75 C7
Flashader . . . 149 C8
Flask Inn . . . 103 D7
Flaunden . . . 40 D3
Flawborough . . . 77 E7
Flawith . . . 95 C7
Flax Bourton . . . 23 C7
Flaxby . . . 95 D6
Flaxholme . . . 76 E3
Flaxley . . . 36 C3
Flaxpool . . . 22 F3
Flaxton . . . 96 C2
Fleckney . . . 64 E3
Flecknoe . . . 52 C3
Fledborough . . . 77 B8
Fleet Hants . . . 15 D8
Hants . . . 27 D6
Lincs . . . 66 B3
Fleetham . . . 117 B7
Fleet Hargate . . . 66 B3
Fleetlands . . . 15 D6
Fleetville . . . 40 D4
Fleetwood . . . 92 E3
Flemingston . . . 22 B2
Flemington . . . 119 D6
Flempton . . . 56 C2
Fleoideabhagh . . . 154 J5
Fletchertown . . . 108 E2
Fletching . . . 17 B8
Flexbury . . . 8 D4
Flexford . . . 27 E7
Flimby . . . 107 F7
Flimwell . . . 18 B4
Flint = Y Fflint . . . 73 B6
Flintham . . . 77 E7
Flint Mountain . . . 73 B6
Flinton . . . 97 F8
Flintsham . . . 48 D5
Flitcham . . . 80 E3
Flitton . . . 53 F8
Flitwick . . . 53 F8
Flixborough . . . 90 C2
Flixborough Stather . . . 90 C2
Flixton Gtr Man . . . 86 E5
N Yorks . . . 97 B6
Suff . . . 69 F6
Flockton . . . 88 C3
Flodaigh . . . 148 C3
Flodden . . . 122 F5
Flodigarry . . . 149 A9
Flood's Ferry . . . 66 E3
Flookburgh . . . 92 B3
Florden . . . 68 E4
Flore . . . 52 C4
Flotterton . . . 117 D5
Flowton . . . 56 E4
Flush House . . . 88 D2
Flushing Aberds . . . 153 D10
Corn . . . 3 C7
Flyford Flavell . . . 50 D4
Foals Green . . . 57 B6
Fobbing . . . 42 F3
Fochabers . . . 152 C3
Fochriw . . . 35 D5
Fockerby . . . 90 C2
Fodderletter . . . 139 B7
Fodderty . . . 151 F8
Foel . . . 59 C6
Foel-gastell . . . 33 C6
Foffarty . . . 134 E4
Foggathorpe . . . 96 F3
Fogo . . . 122 E3
Fogorig . . . 122 E3
Foindle . . . 156 E4
Folda . . . 134 C1
Fole . . . 75 F7
Foleshill . . . 63 F7
Folke . . . 12 C4
Folkestone . . . 31 F6
Folkingham . . . 78 F3
Folkington . . . 18 E2
Folksworth . . . 65 F8
Folkton . . . 97 B6
Folla Rule . . . 153 E7
Follifoot . . . 95 D6
Folly Gate . . . 9 E7
Fonthill Bishop . . . 24 F4
Fonthill Gifford . . . 24 F4
Fontmell Magna . . . 13 C6
Fontwell . . . 16 D3
Foolow . . . 75 B8
Foots Cray . . . 29 B5
Forbestown . . . 140 C2
Force Mills . . . 99 E5
Forcett . . . 101 C6
Ford Argyll . . . 124 E4
Bucks . . . 39 D7
Devon . . . 9 B6
Glos . . . 37 B7
Northumb . . . 122 F5
Shrops . . . 60 C4
Staffs . . . 75 D7
Wilts . . . 24 B3
W Sus . . . 16 D3
Fordcombe . . . 29 E6
Fordell . . . 128 F3
Forden . . . 60 D2
Ford End . . . 42 C2
Forder Green . . . 7 C5
Fordham Cambs . . . 55 B7
Essex . . . 43 B5
Norf . . . 67 E6
Fordhouses . . . 62 D3
Fordingbridge . . . 14 C2
Fordon . . . 97 B6
Fordoun . . . 135 B7
Ford's Green . . . 56 C4
Fordstreet . . . 43 B5
Ford Street . . . 11 C6
Fordwells . . . 38 C3
Fordwich . . . 31 D5
Fordyce . . . 152 B5
Forebridge . . . 62 B3
Forest . . . 109 F8
Forest Becks . . . 93 D7
Forestburn Gate . . . 117 E6
Foresterseat . . . 152 C1
Forest Gate . . . 41 F7
Forest Green . . . 28 E2
Forest Hall . . . 99 D7
Forest Head . . . 109 D5
Forest Hill . . . 39 D5
Forest Lane Head . . . 95 D6
Forest Lodge Argyll . . . 131 E6
Highld . . . 139 C6
Perth . . . 133 B6
Forest Mill . . . 127 E8
Forest Row . . . 28 F5
Forestside . . . 15 C8
Forest Town . . . 77 C5
Forfar . . . 134 D4
Forgandenny . . . 128 C2
Forge . . . 58 E4
Forge Side . . . 35 D6
Forgewood . . . 119 D7
Forgie . . . 152 C3
Forglen House . . . 153 C6
Formby . . . 85 D4
Forncett End . . . 68 E4
Forncett St Mary . . . 68 E4
Forncett St Peter . . . 68 E4
Forneth . . . 133 E7
Fornham All Saints . . . 56 C2
Fornham St Martin . . . 56 C2
Forres . . . 151 F13
Forrestfield . . . 119 C8
Forrest Lodge . . . 113 F5
Forsbrook . . . 75 E6
Forse . . . 158 G4
Forse House . . . 158 G4
Forsinain . . . 157 E12
Forsinard . . . 157 E11
Forsinard Station . . . 157 E11
Forston . . . 12 E4
Fort Augustus . . . 137 D6
Forteviot . . . 128 C2
Fort George Guern . . . 16
Highld . . . 151 F10
Forth . . . 120 D2
Forthampton . . . 50 F3
Forth Road Bridge . . . 120 B4
Fortingall . . . 132 E4
Forton Hants . . . 26 E2
Lancs . . . 92 D4
Shrops . . . 60 C4
Som . . . 11 D8
Staffs . . . 61 B7
Forton Heath . . . 60 C4
Fortrie . . . 153 D6
Fortrose . . . 151 F10
Fortuneswell . . . 12 G4
Fort William . . . 131 B5
Forty Green . . . 40 E2
Forty Hill . . . 41 E6
Forward Green . . . 56 D4
Fosbury . . . 25 D8
Fosdyke . . . 79 F6
Foss . . . 132 D4
Foss Cross . . . 37 D7
Fossebridge . . . 37 C7
Fosterhouses . . . 89 C7
Foster Street . . . 41 D7
Foston Derbys . . . 75 F8
Lincs . . . 77 E8
N Yorks . . . 96 C2
Foston on the Wolds . . . 97 D7
Fotherby . . . 91 E7
Fotheringhay . . . 65 E7
Foubister . . . 159 H6
Foulby . . . 88 C4
Foulden Borders . . . 122 D5
Norf . . . 67 E7
Foulis Castle . . . 151 E8
Foul Mile . . . 18 D3
Foulridge . . . 93 E8
Foulsham . . . 81 E6
Fountainhall . . . 121 E7
Four Ashes Staffs . . . 62 F2
Suff . . . 56 B4
Four Crosses Powys . . . 59 D7
Powys . . . 60 C2
Wrex . . . 73 D6
Four Elms . . . 29 E5
Four Forks . . . 22 F4
Four Gotes . . . 66 C4
Fourlane Ends . . . 76 D3
Four Lane Ends . . . 74 C2
Four Lanes . . . 3 C5
Fourlanes End . . . 74 D5
Four Marks . . . 26 F4
Four Mile Bridge . . . 82 D2
Four Oaks E Sus . . . 19 C5
W Mid . . . 62 E5
W Mid . . . 63 F6
Fourpenny . . . 151 B11
Four Roads Carms . . . 33 D5
IoM . . . 84 F2
Fourstones . . . 109 C8
Four Throws . . . 18 C4
Fovant . . . 13 B8
Foveran . . . 141 B8
Fowey . . . 5 D6
Fowley Common . . . 86 E4
Fowlis . . . 134 F3
Fowlis Wester . . . 127 B8
Fowlmere . . . 54 E5
Fownhope . . . 49 F7
Foxbar . . . 118 C4
Foxcombe Hill . . . 38 D4
Fox Corner . . . 27 D7
Foxdale . . . 84 E2
Foxearth . . . 56 E2
Foxfield . . . 98 F4
Foxham . . . 24 B4
Foxhole Corn . . . 4 D4
Swansea . . . 33 E7
Foxholes . . . 97 B6
Foxhunt Green . . . 18 D2
Fox Lane . . . 27 D6
Foxley Norf . . . 81 E6
Wilts . . . 37 F5
Fox Street . . . 43 B6
Foxt . . . 75 E7
Foxton Cambs . . . 54 E5
Durham . . . 102 B1
Leics . . . 64 E4
Foxup . . . 93 B8
Foxwist Green . . . 74 C3
Foxwood . . . 49 B8
Foy . . . 36 B2
Foyers . . . 137 B7
Fraddam . . . 2 C4
Fraddon . . . 4 D4
Fradley . . . 63 C5
Fradswell . . . 75 F6
Fraisthorpe . . . 97 C7
Framfield . . . 17 B8
Framingham Earl . . . 69 D5
Framingham Pigot . . . 69 D5
Framlingham . . . 57 C6
Frampton Dorset . . . 12 E4
Lincs . . . 79 F6
Frampton Cotterell . . . 36 F3
Frampton Mansell . . . 37 D6
Frampton on Severn . . . 36 D4
Frampton West End . . . 79 E5
Framsden . . . 57 D5
Framwellgate Moor . . . 111 E5
Franche . . . 50 B3
Frankby . . . 85 F3
Frankley . . . 62 F3
Frank's Bridge . . . 48 D3
Frankton . . . 52 B2
Frant . . . 18 B2
Fraserburgh . . . 153 B9
Frating Green . . . 43 B6
Fratton . . . 15 E7
Freathy . . . 5 D8
Freckenham . . . 55 B7
Freckleton . . . 86 B2
Freeby . . . 64 B5
Freehay . . . 75 E7
Freeland . . . 38 C4
Freester . . . 160 H6
Freethorpe . . . 69 D7
Freiston . . . 79 E6
Fremington Devon . . . 20 F4
N Yorks . . . 101 E5
Frenchay . . . 23 B8
Frenchbeer . . . 9 F8
Frenich . . . 126 D3
Frensham . . . 27 E6
Fresgoe . . . 157 C12
Freshfield . . . 85 D3
Freshford . . . 24 C2
Freshwater . . . 14 F4
Freshwater Bay . . . 14 F4
Freshwater East . . . 32 E1
Fressingfield . . . 57 B6
Freston . . . 57 F5
Freswick . . . 158 D5
Fretherne . . . 36 D4
Frettenham . . . 68 C5
Freuchie . . . 128 D4
Freuchies . . . 134 C2
Freystrop . . . 44 D4
Friar's Gate . . . 29 F5
Friarton . . . 128 B3
Friday Bridge . . . 66 D4
Friday Street . . . 18 E3
Fridaythorpe . . . 96 D4
Friern Barnet . . . 41 E5
Friesland . . . 146 F4
Friesthorpe . . . 90 F4
Frieston . . . 78 E2
Frieth . . . 39 E7
Frilford . . . 38 E4
Frilsham . . . 26 B3
Frimley . . . 27 D6
Frimley Green . . . 27 D6
Frindsbury . . . 29 B8
Fring . . . 80 D3
Fringford . . . 39 B6
Frinsted . . . 30 D2
Frinton-on-Sea . . . 43 B8
Friockheim . . . 135 E5
Friog . . . 58 C3
Frisby on the Wreake . . . 64 C3
Friskney . . . 79 D7
Friskney Eaudike . . . 79 D7
Friskney Tofts . . . 79 D7
Friston E Sus . . . 18 F2
Suff . . . 57 C8
Fritchley . . . 76 D3
Fritham . . . 14 C3
Frith Bank . . . 79 E6
Frith Common . . . 49 C8
Frithelstock . . . 9 C6
Frithelstock Stone . . . 9 C6
Frithville . . . 79 D6
Frittenden . . . 30 E2
Frittiscombe . . . 7 E6
Fritton Norf . . . 68 E5
Norf . . . 69 D7
Fritwell . . . 39 B5
Frizinghall . . . 94 F4
Frizington . . . 98 C2
Frocester . . . 36 D4
Frodesley . . . 60 D5
Frodingham . . . 90 C2
Frodsham . . . 74 B2
Frogden . . . 116 B3
Froggatt . . . 76 B2
Froghall . . . 75 E7
Frogmore Devon . . . 7 E5
Hants . . . 27 D6
Frognall . . . 65 C8
Frogshail . . . 81 D8
Frolesworth . . . 64 E2
Frome . . . 24 E2
Frome St Quintin . . . 12 D3
Fromes Hill . . . 49 E8
Fron Denb . . . 72 C4
Gwyn . . . 70 D4
Gwyn . . . 82 F5
Powys . . . 48 C2
Powys . . . 59 E8
Powys . . . 60 D2
Froncysyllte . . . 73 E6
Frongoch . . . 72 F3
Frostenden . . . 69 F7
Frosterley . . . 110 F3
Frotoft . . . 159 F5
Froxfield . . . 25 C7
Froxfield Green . . . 15 B8
Froyle . . . 27 E5
Fryerning . . . 42 D2
Fryton . . . 96 B2
Fulbeck . . . 78 D2
Fulbourn . . . 55 D6
Fulbrook . . . 38 C2
Fulford Som . . . 11 B7
Staffs . . . 75 F6
York . . . 96 E2
Fulham . . . 28 B3
Fulking . . . 17 C6
Fullarton Glasgow . . . 119 C6
N Ayrs . . . 118 F3
Fuller's Moor . . . 73 D8
Fuller Street . . . 42 C3
Fullerton . . . 25 F8
Fulletby . . . 79 B5
Full Sutton . . . 96 D3
Fullwood . . . 118 D4
Fulmer . . . 40 F2
Fulmodestone . . . 81 D5
Fulnetby . . . 78 B3
Fulstow . . . 91 E7
Fulwell . . . 111 D6
Fulwood Lancs . . . 92 F5
S Yorks . . . 88 F4
Fundenhall . . . 68 E4
Fundenhall Street . . . 68 E4
Funtington . . . 15 D8
Funtley . . . 15 D6
Funtullich . . . 127 B6
Funzie . . . 160 D8
Furley . . . 11 D7
Furnace Argyll . . . 125 E6
Carms . . . 33 D6
Furnace End . . . 63 E6
Furneaux Pelham . . . 41 B7
Furness Vale . . . 87 F8
Furze Platt . . . 21 E6
Furze Platt . . . 40 F1
Fyfett . . . 11 C7
Fyfield Essex . . . 42 D1
Glos . . . 38 D2
Hants . . . 25 E7
Oxon . . . 38 E4
Wilts . . . 25 C6
Fylingthorpe . . . 103 D7
Fyvie . . . 153 E7

G

Gabhsann bho Dheas . . . 155 B9
Gabhsann bho Thuath . . . 155 B9
Gablon . . . 151 B10
Gabroc Hill . . . 118 D4
Gaddesby . . . 64 C3
Gadebridge . . . 40 D3
Gaer . . . 35 B5
Gaerllwyd . . . 35 E8
Gaerwen . . . 82 D4
Gagingwell . . . 38 B4
Gaick Lodge . . . 138 F3
Gailey . . . 62 C3
Gainford . . . 101 C6
Gainsborough Lincs . . . 90 E2
Suff . . . 57 E5
Gainsford End . . . 55 F8
Gairloch . . . 149 A13
Gairlochy . . . 136 F4
Gairney Bank . . . 128 E3
Gairnshiel Lodge . . . 139 D8
Gaisgill . . . 99 D8
Gaitsgill . . . 108 E3
Galashiels . . . 121 F7
Galgate . . . 92 D4
Galhampton . . . 12 B4
Gallaberry . . . 114 F2
Gallachoille . . . 144 E6
Gallanach Argyll . . . 124 C4
Argyll . . . 146 E5
Gallantry Bank . . . 74 D2
Gallatown . . . 128 E4
Galley Common . . . 63 E7
Galleyend . . . 42 D3
Galley Hill . . . 54 C4
Galleywood . . . 42 D3
Gallin . . . 132 E2
Gallowfauld . . . 134 E4
Gallows Green . . . 75 E7
Galltair . . . 149 F13
Galmisdale . . . 146 C7
Galmpton Devon . . . 6 E4
Torbay . . . 7 D6
Galphay . . . 95 B5
Galston . . . 118 F5
Galtrigill . . . 148 C6
Gamblesby . . . 109 E6
Gamesley . . . 87 E8
Gamlingay . . . 54 D3
Gammersgill . . . 101 F5
Gamston . . . 77 B7
Ganarew . . . 36 C2
Ganavan . . . 124 B4
Gang . . . 5 C8
Ganllwyd . . . 71 E8
Gannochy Angus . . . 135 B5
Perth . . . 128 B3
Gansclet . . . 158 F5
Ganstead . . . 97 F7
Ganthorpe . . . 96 B2
Ganton . . . 97 B5
Garbat . . . 150 E7
Garbhallt . . . 125 F6
Garboldisham . . . 68 F3
Garden City . . . 73 C7
Gardenstown . . . 153 B7
Garden Village Wrex . . . 73 D7
W Yorks . . . 95 F7
Garderhouse . . . 160 J5
Gardham . . . 97 E5
Gardin . . . 160 G6
Gare Hill . . . 24 E2
Garelochhead . . . 145 D11
Garford . . . 38 E4
Garforth . . . 95 F7
Gargrave . . . 94 D2
Gargunnock . . . 127 E6
Garlic Street . . . 68 F5
Garlieston . . . 105 E8
Garlinge Green . . . 30 D5
Garlogie . . . 141 D6
Garmond . . . 153 C8
Garmony . . . 147 G9
Garmouth . . . 152 B3
Garnant . . . 33 C7
Garndiffaith . . . 35 D6
Garndolbenmaen . . . 71 C5
Garnedd . . . 83 F7
Garnett Bridge . . . 99 E7
Garnfadryn . . . 70 D3
Garnkirk . . . 119 C6
Garnlydan . . . 35 C5
Garnswllt . . . 33 D7
Garn-yr-erw . . . 35 C6
Garrabost . . . 155 D10
Garraron . . . 124 E4
Garras . . . 3 D6
Garreg . . . 71 C7
Garrick . . . 127 C7
Garrigill . . . 109 E7
Garriston . . . 101 E6
Garroch . . . 113 F5
Garrogie Lodge . . . 137 C8
Garros . . . 149 B9
Garrow . . . 133 E5
Garryhorn . . . 113 E5
Garsdale . . . 100 F2
Garsdale Head . . . 100 E2
Garsdon . . . 37 F6
Garshall Green . . . 75 F6
Garsington . . . 39 D5
Garstang . . . 92 E4
Garston . . . 86 F2
Garswood . . . 86 E3
Gartcosh . . . 119 C6
Garth Bridgend . . . 34 E2
Gwyn . . . 83 D5
Powys . . . 47 E8
Shetland . . . 160 H4
Wrex . . . 73 E6
Garthamlock . . . 119 C6
Garthbrengy . . . 48 F2
Garthdee . . . 141 D8
Garthieli . . . 46 D4
Garthmyl . . . 59 E8
Garthorpe Leics . . . 64 B5
N Lincs . . . 90 C2
Garth Row . . . 99 E7
Gartly . . . 152 E5
Gartmore . . . 126 E4
Gartnagrenach . . . 144 H6
Gartness N Lanark . . . 119 C7
Stirling . . . 126 F4
Gartocharn . . . 126 F3
Garton . . . 97 F8
Garton-on-the-Wolds . . . 97 D5
Gartsherrie . . . 119 C7
Gartymore . . . 157 H13
Garvald . . . 121 B8
Garvamore . . . 137 E8
Garvard . . . 144 D2
Garvault Hotel . . . 157 F10
Garve . . . 150 E6
Garvestone . . . 68 D3
Garvock Aberds . . . 135 B7
Invclyd . . . 118 B2
Garway . . . 36 B1
Garway Hill . . . 35 B8
Gaskan . . . 130 B1
Gastard . . . 24 C3
Gasthorpe . . . 68 F2
Gatcombe . . . 15 F5
Gateacre . . . 86 F2
Gatebeck . . . 99 F7
Gate Burton . . . 90 F2
Gateford . . . 89 F6
Gateforth . . . 89 B6
Gatehead . . . 118 F3
Gate Helmsley . . . 96 D2
Gatehouse . . . 116 F3
Gatehouse of Fleet . . . 106 D3
Gatelawbridge . . . 114 E2
Gateley . . . 81 E5
Gatenby . . . 101 F8
Gateshead . . . 111 C5
Gatesheath . . . 73 C8
Gateside Aberds . . . 140 C5
Angus . . . 134 E4
E Renf . . . 118 D4
Fife . . . 128 D3
N Ayrs . . . 118 D3
Gathurst . . . 86 D3
Gatley . . . 87 F6
Gattonside . . . 121 F8
Gatwick Airport . . . 28 E3
Gaufron . . . 47 C8
Gaulby . . . 64 D3
Gauldry . . . 129 B5
Gaunt's Common . . . 13 D8
Gautby . . . 78 B4
Gavinton . . . 122 D3
Gawber . . . 88 D4
Gawcott . . . 52 F4
Gawsworth . . . 75 C5
Gawthorpe . . . 88 B3
Gawthrop . . . 100 F1
Gawthwaite . . . 98 F4
Gaydon . . . 51 D8
Gayfield . . . 159 C5
Gayhurst . . . 53 E6
Gayle . . . 100 F3
Gayles . . . 101 D6
Gay Street . . . 16 B4
Gayton Mers . . . 85 F3
Norf . . . 67 C7
Staffs . . . 62 B3
W Nhants . . . 52 D5
Gayton le Marsh . . . 91 F8
Gayton le Wold . . . 91 F6
Gayton Thorpe . . . 67 C7
Gaywood . . . 67 B6
Gazeley . . . 55 C8
Geanies House . . . 151 D11
Gearraidh Bhailteas . . . 148 F2
Gearraidh Bhaird . . . 155 E8
Gearraidh na h-Aibhne . . . 154 D7
Gearraidh na Monadh . . . 148 G2
Geary . . . 148 B7
Geddes House . . . 151 F11
Gedding . . . 56 D3
Geddington . . . 65 F5
Gedintailor . . . 149 E10
Gedling . . . 77 E6
Gedney . . . 66 B4
Gedney Broadgate . . . 66 B4
Gedney Drove End . . . 66 B4
Gedney Dyke . . . 66 B4
Gedney Hill . . . 66 C3
Gee Cross . . . 87 E7
Geilston . . . 118 B3
Geirinis . . . 148 D2
Geise . . . 158 D3
Geisiadar . . . 154 D6
Geldeston . . . 69 E6
Gell . . . 83 E8
Gelli Pembs . . . 32 C1
Rhondda . . . 34 E3
Gellideg . . . 34 D4
Gellifor . . . 72 C5
Gelligaer . . . 35 E5
Gellilydan . . . 71 D7
Gellinudd . . . 33 D8
Gellyburn . . . 133 F7
Gellywen . . . 32 B3
Gelston Dumfries . . . 106 D4
Lincs . . . 78 E2
Gembling . . . 97 D7
Gentleshaw . . . 62 C4
Geocrab . . . 154 H6
George Green . . . 40 F3
Georgefield . . . 115 E5
Georgeham . . . 20 F3
George Nympton . . . 10 B2
Georgetown . . . 35 D5
Gerlan . . . 83 E6
Germansweek . . . 9 E6
Germoe . . . 2 D4
Gerrans . . . 3 C7
Gerrards Cross . . . 40 F3
Gestingthorpe . . . 56 F2
Geuffordd . . . 60 C2
Gibbet Hill . . . 64 F2
Gibbshill . . . 106 B4
Gib Hill . . . 74 B3
Gidea Park . . . 41 F8
Gidleigh . . . 9 F8
Giffnock . . . 119 D5
Gifford . . . 121 C8
Giffordland . . . 118 E2
Giffordtown . . . 128 C4
Giggleswick . . . 93 C8
Gilberdyke . . . 90 B2
Gilchriston . . . 121 C7
Gilcrux . . . 107 F8
Gildersome . . . 88 B3
Gildingwells . . . 89 F6
Gileston . . . 22 C2
Gilfach . . . 35 E5
Gilfach Goch . . . 34 F3
Gilfachrheda . . . 46 D3
Gillamoor . . . 102 F4
Gillar's Green . . . 86 E2
Gillen . . . 148 C7
Gilling East . . . 96 B2
Gillingham Dorset . . . 13 B6
Medway . . . 29 C8
Norf . . . 69 E7
Gilling West . . . 101 D6
Gillock . . . 158 E4
Gillow Heath . . . 75 D5
Gills . . . 158 C5
Gill's Green . . . 18 B4
Gilmanscleuch . . . 115 B6
Gilmerton Edin . . . 121 C5
Perth . . . 127 B7
Gilmonby . . . 100 C4
Gilmorton . . . 64 F2
Gilmourton . . . 119 E6
Gilsland . . . 109 C6
Gilsland Spa . . . 109 C6
Gilston Borders . . . 121 D7
Herts . . . 41 C7
Gilwern . . . 35 C6
Gimingham . . . 81 D8
Giosla . . . 154 E6
Gipping . . . 56 C4
Gipsey Bridge . . . 79 E5
Girdle Toll . . . 118 E3
Girlsta . . . 160 H6
Girsby . . . 102 D1
Girtford . . . 54 D2
Girthon . . . 106 D3
Girton Cambs . . . 54 C5
Notts . . . 77 C8
Girvan . . . 112 E1
Gisburn . . . 93 E8
Gisleham . . . 69 F8
Gislingham . . . 56 B4
Gissing . . . 68 F4
Gittisham . . . 11 E6
Gladestry . . . 48 D4
Gladsmuir . . . 121 B7
Glais . . . 33 D8
Glaisdale . . . 103 D5
Glame . . . 149 D10
Glamis . . . 134 E3

Glan Adda . . . 83 D5
Glanaman . . . 33 C7
Glan Conwy Conwy . 83 D8
Conwy . . . 83 F8
Glandford . . . 81 C6
Glan-Duar . . . 46 E4
Glandwr . . . 32 B2
Glan-Dwyfach . . . 71 C5
Glandy Cross . . . 32 B2
Glandyfi . . . 58 E3
Glan Gors . . . 82 D4
Glangrwyney . . . 35 C6
Glanmule . . . 59 E8
Glanrafon . . . 58 F3
Glanrhyd Gwyn . . . 70 D3
Pembs . . . 45 E3
Glan-rhyd . . . 82 F4
Glanton . . . 117 C6
Glanton Pike . . . 117 C6
Glan-traeth . . . 82 D2
Glanvilles
Wootton . . . 12 D4
Glan-y-don . . . 73 B5
Glan-y-nant . . . 59 F6
Glan-yr-afon
Anglesey . . . 83 C6
Gwyn . . . 72 E3
Gwyn . . . 72 E4
Glan-y-wern . . . 71 D7
Glapthorn . . . 65 E7
Glapwell . . . 76 C4
Glas-allt Shiel . . . 139 F8
Glasbury . . . 48 F3
Glaschoil . . . 151 H13
Glascoed Denb . . . 72 B3
Mon . . . 35 D7
Powys . . . 59 C8
Glascorrie . . . 140 E2
Glascote . . . 63 D6
Glascwm . . . 48 D3
Glasdrum . . . 130 E4
Glasfryn . . . 72 D3
Glasgow . . . 119 C5
Glashvin . . . 149 B9
Glasinfryn . . . 83 E5
Glasnacardoch . . . 147 B9
Glasnakille . . . 149 G10
Glasphein . . . 148 D6
Glaspwll . . . 58 E4
Glassburn . . . 150 H6
Glasserton . . . 105 F8
Glassford . . . 119 E7
Glasshouse Hill . . . 36 B4
Glasshouses . . . 94 C4
Glasslie . . . 128 D4
Glasson Cumb . . . 108 C2
Lancs . . . 92 D4
Glassonby . . . 109 F5
Glasterlaw . . . 135 D5
Glaston . . . 65 D5
Glastonbury . . . 23 F7
Glatton . . . 65 F8
Glazebrook . . . 86 E4
Glazebury . . . 86 E4
Glazeley . . . 61 F7
Gleadless . . . 88 F4
Gleadsmoss . . . 74 C5
Gleann
Tholàstaidh . . . 155 C10
Gleaston . . . 92 B2
Gleiniant . . . 59 E6
Glemsford . . . 56 E2
Glen Dumfries . . . 106 B5
Dumfries . . . 106 D2
Glenamachrie . . . 124 C5
Glen Auldyn . . . 84 C4
Glenbarr . . . 143 E7
Glenbeg Highld . . . 139 B6
Highld . . . 147 E8
Glen Bernisdale . . 149 D9
Glenbervie . . . 141 F6
Glenboig . . . 119 C7
Glenborrodale . . . 147 E9
Glenbranter . . . 125 F7
Glenbreck . . . 114 B3
Glenbrein Lodge . 137 C7
Glenbrittle House 149 F9
Glenbuchat
Lodge . . . 140 C2
Glenbuck . . . 113 B7
Glenburn . . . 118 C4
Glencalvie Lodge . 150 C7
Glencanisp
Lodge . . . 156 G4
Glencaple . . . 107 C6
Glencarron
Lodge . . . 150 F3
Glencarse . . . 128 B3
Glencassley
Castle . . . 156 J7
Glenceitlein . . . 131 E5
Glencoe . . . 130 D4
Glencraig . . . 128 E3
Glencripesdale . . . 147 F9
Glencrosh . . . 113 F7
Glendavan House 140 D3
Glendevon . . . 127 D8
Glendoebeg . . . 137 D7
Glendoe Lodge . . . 137 D7
Glendoick . . . 128 B4
Glendoll Lodge . . . 134 B2
Glendoune . . . 112 E1
Glenduckie . . . 128 C4
Glendye Lodge . . . 140 F5
Gleneagles Hotel . 127 C8
Gleneagles
House . . . 127 D8
Glenegedale . . . 142 C4
Glenelg . . . 149 G13
Glenernie . . . 151 G13
Glenfarg . . . 128 C3
Glenfarquhar
Lodge . . . 141 F6
Glenferness
House . . . 151 G12
Glenfeshie Lodge 138 E4
Glenfield . . . 64 D2
Glenfinnan . . . 147 C11
Glenfoot . . . 128 C3
Glenfyne Lodge . . 125 D8
Glengap . . . 106 D3
Glengarnock . . . 118 D3
Glengorm Castle . 146 F7
Glengrasco . . . 149 D9
Glenhead Farm . . 134 C2
Glen Ho . . . 121 F5
Glenhoul . . . 113 F6
Glenhurich . . . 130 C2
Glenkerry . . . 115 C5
Glenkiln . . . 106 B5
Glenkindie . . . 140 C3
Glenlatterach . . . 152 C1
Glenlee . . . 113 F6
Glenlichorn . . . 127 C6
Glenlivet . . . 139 B7
Glenlochsie . . . 133 B7
Glenloig . . . 143 E10
Glenluce . . . 105 D6
Glenmallan . . . 125 F8
Glenmarksie . . . 150 F6
Glenmassan . . . 145 E10
Glenmavis . . . 119 C7
Glenmaye . . . 84 E2
Glenmidge . . . 113 F8
Glen Mona . . . 84 D4
Glenmore Argyll . . 124 D4
Highld . . . 149 D9
Glenmore Lodge . 139 D5
Glenmoy . . . 134 C4
Glen Nevis House . 131 B5
Glenogil . . . 134 C4
Glen Parva . . . 64 E2
Glenprosen
Lodge . . . 134 C2
Glenprosen
Village . . . 134 C3
Glenquiech . . . 134 C4
Glenreasdell
Mains . . . 145 H7
Glenree . . . 143 F10
Glenridding . . . 99 C5
Glenrossal . . . 156 J7
Glenrothes . . . 128 D4
Glensanda . . . 130 E2
Glensaugh . . . 135 B6
Glenshero Lodge . 137 E8
Glen Sluain . . . 125 F6
Glenstockadale . . 104 C4
Glenstriven . . . 145 F9
Glentaggart . . . 113 B8
Glen Tanar
House . . . 140 E3
Glentham . . . 90 E4
Glentirranmuir . . . 127 E5
Glenton . . . 140 B5
Glentress . . . 121 F5
Glentromie
Lodge . . . 138 E3
Glen Trool Lodge . 112 F4
Glentrool Village . 105 B7
Glentruan . . . 84 B4
Glentruim House . 138 E2
Glentworth . . . 90 F3
Glenuig . . . 147 D9
Glenurquhart . . . 151 E10
Glen Village . . . 119 B8
Glen Vine . . . 84 E3
Glespin . . . 113 B8
Gletness . . . 160 H6
Glewstone . . . 36 B2
Glinton . . . 65 D8
Glooston . . . 64 E4
Glororum . . . 123 F7
Glossop . . . 87 E8
Gloster Hill . . . 117 D8
Gloucester . . . 37 C5
Gloup . . . 160 C7
Glusburn . . . 94 E3
Glutt Lodge . . . 157 F12
Glutton Bridge . . . 75 C7
Glympton . . . 38 B4
Glynarthen . . . 46 E2
Glynbrochan . . . 59 F6
Glyn-Ceiriog . . . 73 F6
Glyncoch . . . 34 E4
Glyncorrwg . . . 34 E2
Glyn-cywarch . . . 71 D7
Glynde . . . 17 D8
Glyndebourne . . . 17 C8
Glyndyfrdwy . . . 72 E5
Glyn Ebwy
= Ebbw Vale . . . 35 D5
Glynedd
= Glynneath . . . 34 D2
Glyn-neath
= Glynedd . . . 34 D2
Glynogwr . . . 34 F3
Glyntaff . . . 34 F4
Glyntawe . . . 34 C2
Gnosall . . . 62 B2
Gnosall Heath . . . 62 B2
Goadby . . . 64 E4
Goadby Marwood . 64 B4
Goatacre . . . 24 B5
Goathill . . . 12 C4
Goathland . . . 103 D6
Goathurst . . . 22 F4
Goat Lees . . . 30 E4
Gobernuisgach
Lodge . . . 156 E7
Gobhaig . . . 154 G5
Gobowen . . . 73 F7
Godalming . . . 27 E7
Godley . . . 87 E7
Godmanchester . . . 54 B3
Godmanstone . . . 12 E4
Godmersham . . . 30 D4
Godney . . . 23 E6
Godolphin Cross . . . 2 C5
Godre'r-graig . . . 34 D1
Godshill Hants . . . 14 C2
IoW . . . 15 F6
Godstone . . . 28 D4
Godwinscroft . . . 14 E2
Goetre . . . 35 D7
Goferydd . . . 82 C2
Goff's Oak . . . 41 D6
Gogar . . . 120 B4
Goginan . . . 58 F3
Golan . . . 71 C6
Golant . . . 5 D6
Golberdon . . . 5 B8
Golborne . . . 86 E4
Golcar . . . 88 C2
Goldcliff . . . 35 F7
Golden Cross . . . 18 D2
Golden Green . . . 29 E7
Golden Grove . . . 33 C6
Goldenhill . . . 75 D5
Golden Hill . . . 14 E3
Golden Pot . . . 26 E5
Golden Valley . . . 37 B6
Golders Green . . . 41 F5
Goldhanger . . . 43 D5
Gold Hill . . . 66 E5
Golding . . . 60 D5
Goldington . . . 53 D8
Goldsborough
N Yorks . . . 95 D6
N Yorks . . . 103 C6
Goldsithney . . . 2 C4
Goldsworthy . . . 9 B5
Goldthorpe . . . 89 D5
Gollanfield . . . 151 F11
Golspie . . . 157 J11
Golval . . . 157 C11
Gomeldon . . . 25 F6
Gomersal . . . 88 B3
Gomshall . . . 27 E8
Gonalston . . . 77 E6
Gonfirth . . . 160 G5
Good Easter . . . 42 C2
Gooderstone . . . 67 D7
Goodleigh . . . 20 F5
Goodmanham . . . 96 E4
Goodnestone Kent . 30 C4
Kent . . . 31 D6
Goodrich . . . 36 C2
Goodrington . . . 7 D6
Goodshaw . . . 87 B6
Goodwick = Wdig . . 44 B4
Goodworth
Clatford . . . 25 E8
Goole . . . 89 B8
Goonbell . . . 3 B6
Goonhavern . . . 4 D2
Goose Eye . . . 94 E3
Goose Green
Gtr Man . . . 86 D3
Norf . . . 68 F4
W Sus . . . 16 C5
Gooseham . . . 8 C4
Goosey . . . 38 E3
Goosnargh . . . 93 F5
Goostrey . . . 74 B4
Gorcott Hill . . . 51 C5
Gord . . . 160 L6
Gordon . . . 122 E2
Gordonbush . . . 157 J11
Gordonsburgh . . . 152 B4
Gordonstoun . . . 152 B1
Gordonstown
Aberds . . . 152 C5
Aberds . . . 153 E7
Gore . . . 31 D7
Gorebridge . . . 121 C6
Gore Cross . . . 24 D5
Gorefield . . . 66 C4
Gore Pit . . . 42 C4
Gorey Jersey . . . 17
Gorgie . . . 120 B5
Goring . . . 39 F6
Goring-by-Sea . . . 16 D5
Goring Heath . . . 26 B4
Gorleston-on-Sea 69 D8
Gornalwood . . . 62 E3
Gorrachie . . . 153 C7
Gorran Churchtown . 3 B8
Gorran Haven . . . 3 B9
Gorrenberry . . . 115 E7
Gors . . . 46 B5
Gorsedd . . . 73 B5
Gorse Hill . . . 38 F1
Gorseinon . . . 33 E6
Gorseness . . . 159 G5
Gorsgoch . . . 46 D3
Gorslas . . . 33 C6
Gorsley . . . 36 B3
Gorstan . . . 150 E6
Gorstanvorran . . . 130 B2
Gorsteyhill . . . 74 D4
Gorsty Hill . . . 62 B5
Gortantaoid . . . 142 A4
Gorton . . . 87 E6
Gosbeck . . . 57 D5
Gosberton . . . 78 F5
Gosberton Clough . 65 B8
Gosfield . . . 42 B3
Gosford . . . 49 C7
Gosforth Cumb . . . 98 D2
T&W . . . 110 C5
Gosmore . . . 40 B4
Gosport . . . 15 E7
Gossabrough . . . 160 E7
Gossington . . . 36 D4
Goswick . . . 123 E6
Gotham . . . 76 F5
Gotherington . . . 37 B6
Gott . . . 160 J6
Goudhurst . . . 18 B4
Goulceby . . . 79 B5
Gourdas . . . 153 D7
Gourdon . . . 135 B8
Gourock . . . 118 B2
Govan . . . 119 C5
Govanhill . . . 119 C5
Goveton . . . 7 E5
Govilon . . . 35 C6
Gowanhill . . . 153 B10
Gowdall . . . 89 B7
Gowerton . . . 33 E6
Gowkhall . . . 128 F2
Gowthorpe . . . 96 D3
Goxhill E Yorks . . . 97 E7
N Lincs . . . 90 B5
Goxhill Haven . . . 90 B5
Goytre . . . 34 F1
Grabhair . . . 155 F8
Graby . . . 65 B7
Grade . . . 3 E6
Graffham . . . 16 C3
Grafham Cambs . . . 54 C2
Sur . . . 27 E8
Grafton Hereford . . . 49 F6
N Yorks . . . 95 C7
Oxon . . . 38 D2
Shrops . . . 60 C4
Worcs . . . 49 C7
Grafton Flyford . . . 50 D4
Grafton Regis . . . 53 E5
Grafton
Underwood . . . 65 F6
Grafty Green . . . 30 E2
Graianrhyd . . . 73 D6
Graig Conwy . . . 83 D8
Denb . . . 72 B4
Graig-fechan . . . 72 D5
Grain . . . 30 B2
Grainsby . . . 91 E6
Grainthorpe . . . 91 E7
Grampound . . . 3 B8
Grampound Road . . 4 D4
Gramsdal . . . 148 C3
Granborough . . . 39 B7
Granby . . . 77 F7
Grandborough . . . 52 C2
Grandtully . . . 133 D6
Grange Cumb . . . 98 C4
E Ayrs . . . 118 F4
Medway . . . 29 C8
Mers . . . 85 F3
Perth . . . 128 B4
Grange
Crossroads . . . 152 C4
Grange Hall . . . 151 E13
Grange Hill . . . 41 E7
Grangemill . . . 76 D2
Grange Moor . . . 88 C3
Grangemouth . . . 127 F8
Grange of
Lindores . . . 128 C4
Grange-
over-Sands . . . 92 B4
Grangepans . . . 128 F2
Grangetown Cardiff 22 B3
Redcar . . . 102 B3
Grange Villa . . . 110 D5
Granish . . . 138 C5
Gransmoor . . . 97 D7
Granston . . . 44 B3
Grantchester . . . 54 D5
Grantham . . . 78 F2
Grantley . . . 94 C5
Grantlodge . . . 141 C6
Granton Dumfries . . 114 D3
Edin . . . 120 B5
Grantown-
on-Spey . . . 139 B6
Grantshouse . . . 122 C4
Grappenhall . . . 86 F4
Grasby . . . 90 D4
Grasmere . . . 99 D5
Grasscroft . . . 87 D7
Grassendale . . . 85 F4
Grassholme . . . 100 B4
Grassington . . . 94 C3
Grassmoor . . . 76 C4
Grassthorpe . . . 77 C7
Grateley . . . 25 E7
Gratwich . . . 75 F7
Graveley Cambs . . . 54 C3
Herts . . . 41 B5
Gravelly Hill . . . 62 E5
Gravels . . . 60 D3
Graven . . . 160 F6
Graveney . . . 30 C4
Gravesend Herts . . . 41 B7
Kent . . . 29 B7
Grayingham . . . 90 E3
Grayrigg . . . 99 E7
Grays . . . 29 B7
Grayshott . . . 27 F6
Grayswood . . . 27 F7
Graythorp . . . 102 B3
Grazeley . . . 26 C4
Greasbrough . . . 88 E5
Greasby . . . 85 F3
Great Abington . . . 55 E6
Great Addington . . . 53 B7
Great Alne . . . 51 D6
Great Altcar . . . 85 D4
Great Amwell . . . 41 C6
Great Asby . . . 100 C1
Great Ashfield . . . 56 C3
Great Ayton . . . 102 C3
Great Baddow . . . 42 D3
Great Bardfield . . . 55 F7
Great Barford . . . 54 D2
Great Barr . . . 62 E4
Great Barrington . . 38 C2
Great Barrow . . . 73 C8
Great Barton . . . 56 C2
Great Barugh . . . 96 B3
Great Bavington . . 117 F5
Great Bealings . . . 57 E6
Great Bedwyn . . . 25 C7
Great Bentley . . . 43 B7
Great Billing . . . 53 C6
Great Bircham . . . 80 D3
Great Blakenham . . 56 D5
Great Blencow . . . 108 F4
Great Bolas . . . 61 B6
Great Bookham . . . 28 D2
Great Bourton . . . 52 E2
Great Bowden . . . 64 F4
Great Bradley . . . 55 D7
Great Braxted . . . 42 C4
Great Bricett . . . 56 D4
Great Brickhill . . . 53 F7
Great Bridge . . . 62 E3
Great Bridgeford . . 62 B2
Great Brington . . . 52 C4
Great Bromley . . . 43 B6
Great Broughton
Cumb . . . 107 F7
N Yorks . . . 102 D3
Great Budworth . . . 74 B3
Great Burdon . . . 101 C8
Great Burgh . . . 28 D3
Great Burstead . . . 42 E2
Great Busby . . . 102 D3
Great Canfield . . . 42 C1
Great Carlton . . . 91 F8
Great Casterton . . . 65 D7
Great Chart . . . 30 E3
Great Chatwell . . . 61 C7
Great Chesterford . 55 E6
Great Cheverell . . . 24 D4
Great Chishill . . . 54 F5
Great Clacton . . . 43 C7
Great Cliff . . . 88 C4
Great Clifton . . . 98 B2
Great Coates . . . 91 D6
Great Comberton . . 50 E4
Great Corby . . . 108 D4
Great Cornard . . . 56 E2
Great Cowden . . . 97 E8
Great Coxwell . . . 38 E2
Great Crakehall . . . 101 E7
Great Cransley . . . 53 B6
Great
Cressingham . . . 67 D8
Great Crosby . . . 85 E4
Great Cubley . . . 75 F8
Great Dalby . . . 64 C4
Great Denham . . . 53 E8
Great Doddington . 53 C6
Great Dunham . . . 67 C8
Great Dunmow . . . 42 B2
Great Durnford . . . 25 F6
Great Easton Essex . 42 B2
Leics . . . 64 E5
Great Eccleston . . . 92 E4
Great Edstone . . . 103 F5
Great Ellingham . . . 68 E3
Great Elm . . . 24 E2
Greater Doward . . . 36 C2
Great Eversden . . . 54 D4
Great Fencote . . . 101 E7
Great Finborough . 56 D4
Greatford . . . 65 C7
Great Fransham . . . 67 C8
Great Gaddesden . . 40 C3
Greatgate . . . 75 E7
Great Gidding . . . 65 F8
Great Givendale . . . 96 D4
Great Glemham . . . 57 C7
Great Glen . . . 64 E3
Great Gonerby . . . 77 F8
Great Gransden . . . 54 D3
Great Green Norf . . . 69 F5
Suff . . . 56 D3
Great Habton . . . 96 B3
Great Hale . . . 78 E4
Great Hallingbury . 41 C8
Greatham Hants . . . 27 F5
Hrtlpl . . . 102 B2
W Sus . . . 16 C4
Great Hampden . . . 39 D8
Great Harrowden . . 53 B6
Great Harwood . . . 93 F7
Great Haseley . . . 39 D6
Great Hatfield . . . 97 E7
Great Haywood . . . 62 B4
Great Heath . . . 63 F7
Great Heck . . . 89 B6
Great Henny . . . 56 F2
Great Hinton . . . 24 D4
Great Hockham . . . 68 E2
Great Holland . . . 43 C8
Great Horkesley . . . 56 F3
Great Hormead . . . 41 B6
Great Horton . . . 94 F4
Great Horwood . . . 53 F5
Great Houghton
S Yorks . . . 88 D5
W Nhants . . . 53 D5
Great Hucklow . . . 75 B8
Great Kelk . . . 97 D7
Great Kimble . . . 39 D8
Great Kingshill . . . 40 E1
Great Langton . . . 101 E7
Great Leighs . . . 42 C3
Great Lever . . . 86 D5
Great Limber . . . 90 D5
Great Linford . . . 53 E6
Great Livermere . . . 56 B2
Great Longstone . . 76 B2
Great Lumley . . . 111 E5
Great Lyth . . . 60 D4
Great Malvern . . . 50 E2
Great Maplestead . 56 F2
Great Marton . . . 92 F3
Great Massingham 80 E3
Great Melton . . . 68 D4
Great Milton . . . 39 D6
Great Missenden . . 40 D1
Great Mitton . . . 93 F7
Great Mongeham . . 31 D7
Great Moulton . . . 68 E4
Great Munden . . . 41 B6
Great Musgrave . . 100 C2
Great Ness . . . 60 C3
Great Notley . . . 42 B3
Great Oakley Essex . 43 B7
N Nhants . . . 65 F5
Great Offley . . . 40 B4
Great Ormside . . . 100 C2
Great Orton . . . 108 D3
Great Ouseburn . . . 95 C7
Great Oxendon . . . 64 F4
Great Oxney
Green . . . 42 D2
Great Palgrave . . . 67 C8
Great Parndon . . . 41 D7
Great Paxton . . . 54 C3
Great Plumpton . . . 92 F3
Great Plumstead . . 69 C6
Great Ponton . . . 78 F2
Great Preston . . . 88 B5
Great Raveley . . . 66 F2
Great Rissington . . 38 C1
Great Rollright . . . 51 F8
Great Ryburgh . . . 81 E5
Great Ryle . . . 117 C6
Great Ryton . . . 60 D4
Great Saling . . . 42 B3
Great Salkeld . . . 109 F5
Great Sampford . . . 55 F7
Great Sankey . . . 86 F3
Great Saxham . . . 55 C8
Great Shefford . . . 25 B8
Great Shelford . . . 55 D5
Great Smeaton . . . 101 D8
Great Snoring . . . 80 D5
Great Somerford . . 37 F6
Great Stainton . . . 101 B8
Great Stambridge . 42 E4
Great Staughton . . 54 C2
Great Steeping . . . 79 C7
Great Stonar . . . 31 D7
Greatstone on Sea . 19 C7
Great Strickland . . . 99 B7
Great Stukeley . . . 54 B3
Great Sturton . . . 78 B5
Great Sutton
Ches W . . . 73 B7
Shrops . . . 60 F5
Great Swinburne . 110 B2
Great Tew . . . 38 B3
Great Tey . . . 42 B4
Great Thurkleby . . . 95 B7
Great Thurlow . . . 55 D7
Great Torrington . . . 9 C6
Great Tosson . . . 117 D6
Great Totham
Essex . . . 42 C4
Essex . . . 42 C4
Great Tows . . . 91 E6
Great Urswick . . . 92 B2
Great Wakering . . . 43 F5
Great Waldingfield 56 E3
Great Walsingham . 80 D5
Great Waltham . . . 42 C2
Great Warley . . . 42 E1
Great Washbourne 50 F4
Great Weldon . . . 65 F6
Great Welnetham . 56 D2
Great Wenham . . . 56 F4
Great
Whittington . . . 110 B3
Great Wigborough 43 C5
Great Wilbraham . . 55 D6
Great Wishford . . . 25 F5
Great Witcombe . . 37 C6
Great Witley . . . 50 C2
Great Wolford . . . 51 F7
Greatworth . . . 52 E3
Great Wratting . . . 55 E7
Great Wymondley . 41 B5
Great Wyrley . . . 62 D3
Great Wytheford . . 61 C5
Great Yarmouth . . . 69 D8
Great Yeldham . . . 55 F8
Greave . . . 87 B6
Greeba . . . 84 D3
Green . . . 72 C4
Greenbank . . . 160 C7
Greenburn . . . 120 C2
Greendikes . . . 117 B6
Green End . . . 54 D2
Greenfield C Beds . . 53 F8
Flint . . . 73 B5
Gtr Man . . . 87 D7
Highld . . . 136 D5
Oxon . . . 39 E7
Greenford . . . 40 F4
Greengairs . . . 119 B7
Greenham . . . 26 C2
Green Hammerton 95 D7
Greenhaugh . . . 116 F3
Greenhead . . . 109 C6
Greenhill Falk . . . 119 B8
Kent . . . 31 C5
Leics . . . 63 C8
London . . . 40 F4
Greenhills . . . 118 D3
Greenhithe . . . 29 B6
Greenholm . . . 118 F5
Greenholme . . . 99 D7
Greenhouse . . . 115 B8
Greenhow Hill . . . 94 C4
Greenigoe . . . 159 H5
Greenland . . . 158 D4
Greenlands . . . 39 F7
Green Lane . . . 59 E8
Greenlaw Aberds . . 153 C6
Borders . . . 122 E3
Greenlea . . . 107 B7
Greenloaning . . . 127 D7
Greenmount . . . 87 C5
Greenmow . . . 160 L6
Greenock . . . 118 B2
Greenock West . . . 118 B2
Greenodd . . . 99 F5
Green Ore . . . 23 D7
Greenrow . . . 107 D8
Green St Green . . . 29 C5
Greenside . . . 110 C4
Greensidehill . . . 117 C5
Greens Norton . . . 52 E4
Greenstead Green . 42 B4
Greensted . . . 41 D8
Green Street . . . 40 E4
Greenwich . . . 28 B4
Greet . . . 50 F5
Greete . . . 49 B7
Greetham Lincs . . . 79 B6
Rutland . . . 65 C6
Greetland . . . 87 B8
Gregg Hall . . . 99 E6
Gregson Lane . . . 86 B3
Greinetobht . . . 148 A3
Greinton . . . 23 F6
Gremista . . . 160 J6
Grenaby . . . 84 E2
Grendon N Nhants . . 53 C6
Warks . . . 63 D6
Grendon Common . 63 E6
Grendon Green . . . 49 D7
Grendon
Underwood . . . 39 B6
Grenofen . . . 6 B2
Grenoside . . . 88 E4
Greosabhagh . . . 154 H6
Gresford . . . 73 D7
Gresham . . . 81 D7
Greshornish . . . 149 C8
Gressenhall . . . 68 C2
Gressingham . . . 93 C5
Gresty Green . . . 74 D4
Greta Bridge . . . 101 C5
Gretna . . . 108 C3
Gretna Green . . . 108 C3
Gretton Glos . . . 50 F5
N Nhants . . . 65 E5
Shrops . . . 60 E5
Grewelthorpe . . . 94 B5
Greygarth . . . 94 B4
Grey Green . . . 89 D8
Greynor . . . 33 D6
Greysouthen . . . 98 B2
Greystoke . . . 108 F4
Greystone Angus . . 135 E5
Dumfries . . . 107 B6
Greywell . . . 26 D5
Griais . . . 155 C9
Grianan . . . 155 D9
Gribthorpe . . . 96 F3
Gridley Corner . . . 9 E5
Griff . . . 63 F7
Griffithstown . . . 35 E6
Grimbister . . . 159 G4
Grimblethorpe . . . 91 F6
Grimeford Village . 86 C4
Grimethorpe . . . 88 D5
Griminis . . . 148 C2
Grimister . . . 160 D6
Grimley . . . 50 C3
Grimness . . . 159 J5
Grimoldby . . . 91 F7
Grimpo . . . 60 B3
Grimsargh . . . 93 F5
Grimsbury . . . 52 E2
Grimsby . . . 91 C6
Grimscote . . . 52 D4
Grimscott . . . 8 D4
Grimsthorpe . . . 65 B7
Grimston E Yorks . . . 97 F8
Leics . . . 64 B3
Norf . . . 80 E3
York . . . 96 D2
Grimstone . . . 12 E4
Grinacombe Moor . . 9 E6
Grindale . . . 97 B7
Grindigar . . . 159 H6
Grindiscol . . . 160 K6
Grindle . . . 61 D7
Grindleford . . . 76 B2
Grindleton . . . 93 E7
Grindley . . . 62 B4
Grindley Brook . . . 74 E2
Grindlow . . . 75 B8
Grindon Northumb . 122 E5
Staffs . . . 75 D7
Grindonmoor Gate 75 D7
Gringley on the
Hill . . . 89 E8
Grinsdale . . . 108 D3
Grinshill . . . 60 B5
Grinton . . . 101 E5
Griomsidar . . . 155 E8
Grishipoll . . . 146 F4
Grisling Common . . 17 B8
Gristhorpe . . . 103 F8
Griston . . . 68 E2
Gritley . . . 159 H6
Grittenham . . . 37 F7
Grittleton . . . 37 F5
Grizebeck . . . 98 F4
Grizedale . . . 99 E5
Grobister . . . 159 F7
Groby . . . 64 D2
Groes Conwy . . . 72 C4
Neath . . . 34 F1
Groes-faen . . . 34 F4
Groesffordd Marli . 72 B4
Groeslon Gwyn . . . 82 E5
Gwyn . . . 82 F4
Groes-lwyd . . . 60 C2
Grogport . . . 143 D9
Gromford . . . 57 D7
Gronant . . . 72 A4
Groombridge . . . 18 B2
Grosmont Mon . . . 35 B8
N Yorks . . . 103 D6
Groton . . . 56 E3
Grougfoot . . . 120 B3
Grouville Jersey . . . 17
Grove Dorset . . . 12 G5
Kent . . . 31 C6
Notts . . . 77 B7
Oxon . . . 38 E4
Grove Park . . . 28 B5
Grovesend . . . 33 D6
Grove Vale . . . 62 E4
Grudie . . . 150 E6
Gruids . . . 157 J8
Gruinard House . . 150 B2
Grula . . . 149 F8
Gruline . . . 147 G8
Grunasound . . . 160 K5
Grundisburgh . . . 57 D6
Grunsagill . . . 93 D7
Gruting . . . 160 J4
Grutness . . . 160 N6
Gualachulain . . . 131 E5
Gualin House . . . 156 D6
Guardbridge . . . 129 C6
Guarlford . . . 50 E3
Guay . . . 133 E7
Guestling Green . . . 19 D5
Guestling Thorn . . . 18 D5
Guestwick . . . 81 E6
Guestwick Green . . 81 E6
Guide . . . 86 B5
Guide Post . . . 117 F8
Guilden Morden . . . 54 E3
Guilden Sutton . . . 73 C8
Guildford . . . 27 E7
Guildtown . . . 133 F8
Guilsborough . . . 52 B4
Guilsfield . . . 60 C2
Guilton . . . 31 D6
Guineaford . . . 20 F4
Guisborough . . . 102 C4
Guiseley . . . 94 E4
Guist . . . 81 E5
Guith . . . 159 E6
Guiting Power . . . 37 B7
Gulberwick . . . 160 K6
Gullane . . . 129 F6
Gulval . . . 2 C3
Gulworthy . . . 6 B2
Gumfreston . . . 32 D2
Gumley . . . 64 E3
Gummow's Shop . . . 4 D3
Gunby E Yorks . . . 96 F3
Lincs . . . 65 B6
Gundleton . . . 26 F4
Gun Hill . . . 18 D2
Gunn . . . 20 F5
Gunnerside . . . 100 E4
Gunnerton . . . 110 B2
Gunness . . . 90 C2
Gunnislake . . . 6 B2
Gunnista . . . 160 J7
Gunthorpe Norf . . . 81 D6
Notts . . . 77 E6
Pboro . . . 65 D8
Gunville . . . 15 F5
Gunwalloe . . . 3 D5
Gurnard . . . 15 E5
Gurnett . . . 75 B6
Gurney Slade . . . 23 E8
Gurnos . . . 34 D1
Gussage All Saints . 13 C8
Gussage
St Michael . . . 13 C7
Guston . . . 31 E7
Gutcher . . . 160 D7
Guthrie . . . 135 D5
Guyhirn . . . 66 D3
Guyhirn Gull . . . 66 D3
Guy's Head . . . 66 B4
Guy's Marsh . . . 13 B6
Guyzance . . . 117 D8
Gwaenysgor . . . 72 A4
Gwalchmai . . . 82 D3
Gwaun-Cae-
Gurwen . . . 33 C8
Gwaun-Leision . . . 33 C8
Gwbert . . . 45 E3
Gweek . . . 3 D6
Gwehelog . . . 35 D7
Gwenddwr . . . 48 E2
Gwennap . . . 3 C6
Gwenter . . . 3 E6
Gwernaffield . . . 73 C6
Gwernesney . . . 35 D8
Gwernogle . . . 46 F4
Gwernymynydd . . . 73 C6
Gwersyllt . . . 73 D7
Gwespyr . . . 85 F2
Gwithian . . . 2 B4
Gwredog . . . 82 C4
Gwyddelwern . . . 72 E4
Gwyddgrug . . . 46 F3
Gwydyr Uchaf . . . 83 E7
Gwynfryn . . . 73 D6
Gwystre . . . 48 C2
Gwytherin . . . 83 E8
Gyfelia . . . 73 E7
Gyffi . . . 83 D7
Gyre . . . 159 H4
Gyrn-goch . . . 70 C5

H

Habberley . . . 60 D3
Habergham . . . 93 F8
Habrough . . . 90 C5
Haceby . . . 78 F3
Hacheston . . . 57 D7
Hackbridge . . . 28 C3
Hackenthorpe . . . 88 F5
Hackford . . . 68 D3
Hackforth . . . 101 E7
Hackland . . . 159 F4
Hackleton . . . 53 D6
Hackness N Yorks . . 103 E7
Orkney . . . 159 J4
Hackney . . . 41 F6
Hackthorn . . . 90 F3
Hackthorpe . . . 99 B7
Haconby . . . 65 B8
Hacton . . . 41 F8
Hadden . . . 122 F3
Haddenham Bucks . 39 D7
Cambs . . . 55 B5
Haddington
E Loth . . . 121 B8
Lincs . . . 78 C2
Haddiscoe . . . 69 E7
Haddon Cambs . . . 65 E8
Ches E . . . 75 C6
Hade Edge . . . 88 D2
Hademore . . . 63 D5
Hadfield . . . 87 E8
Hadham Cross . . . 41 C7
Hadham Ford . . . 41 B7
Hadleigh Essex . . . 42 F4
Suff . . . 56 E4
Hadley . . . 61 C6
Hadley End . . . 62 B5
Hadlow . . . 29 E7
Hadlow Down . . . 18 C2
Hadnall . . . 60 C5
Hadstock . . . 55 E6
Hady . . . 76 B3
Hadzor . . . 50 C4
Haffenden Quarter 30 E2
Hafod-Dinbych . . . 83 F8
Hafod-Iom . . . 83 D8
Haggate . . . 93 F8
Haggbeck . . . 108 B4
Haggerston . . . 123 E6
Haggrister . . . 160 F5
Hagley Hereford . . . 49 E7
Worcs . . . 62 F3
Hagworthingham . 79 C6
Haigh Gtr Man . . . 86 D4
S Yorks . . . 88 C3
Haigh Moor . . . 88 B3
Haighton Green . . . 93 F5
Haile . . . 98 D2
Hailes . . . 50 F5
Hailey Herts . . . 41 C6
Oxon . . . 38 C3
Hailsham . . . 18 E2
Hail Weston . . . 54 C2
Haimer . . . 158 D3
Hainault . . . 41 E7
Hainford . . . 68 C5
Hainton . . . 91 F5
Hairmyres . . . 119 D6
Haisthorpe . . . 97 C7
Hakin . . . 44 E3
Halam . . . 77 D6
Halbeath . . . 128 F3
Halberton . . . 10 C5
Halcro . . . 158 D4
Hale Gtr Man . . . 87 F5
Halton . . . 86 F2
Hants . . . 14 C2
Hale Bank . . . 86 F2
Halebarns . . . 87 F5
Hales Norf . . . 69 E6
Staffs . . . 74 F4
Halesfield . . . 61 D7
Halesgate . . . 66 B3
Halesowen . . . 62 F3
Hales Place . . . 30 D5
Hale Street . . . 29 E7
Halesworth . . . 57 B7
Halewood . . . 86 F2
Halford Shrops . . . 60 F4
Warks . . . 51 E7
Halfpenny Furze . . 32 C3
Halfpenny Green . . 62 E2
Halfway Carms . . . 46 F5
Carms . . . 47 F7
W Berks . . . 26 C2
Halfway Bridge . . . 16 B3
Halfway House . . . 60 C3
Halfway Houses . . . 30 B3
Halifax . . . 87 B8
Halket . . . 118 D4
Halkirk . . . 158 E3
Halkyn . . . 73 B6
Halland . . . 18 D2
Hallaton . . . 64 E4
Hallatrow . . . 23 D8
Hallbankgate . . . 109 D5
Hall Dunnerdale . . . 98 E4
Hallen . . . 36 F2
Hall Green W Mid . . . 62 F5
W Yorks . . . 88 C4
Hall Grove . . . 41 C5
Halliburton . . . 122 E2
Hallin . . . 148 C7
Halling . . . 29 C8
Hallington Lincs . . . 91 F7
Northumb . . . 110 B2
Halliwell . . . 86 C5
Hall of
Tankerness . . . 159 H6
Hall of the Forest . . 60 F2
Halloughton . . . 77 D6
Hallow . . . 50 D3
Hallrule . . . 115 C8
Halls . . . 122 B2
Hallsands . . . 7 F6
Hall's Green . . . 41 B5
Hallthwaites . . . 98 F3
Hallworthy . . . 8 F3
Hallyburton
House . . . 134 F2
Hallyne . . . 120 E4
Halmer End . . . 74 E4
Halmore . . . 36 D3
Halmyre Mains . . . 120 E4
Halnaker . . . 16 D3
Halsall . . . 85 C4
Halse Som . . . 11 B6
W Nhants . . . 52 E3
Halsetown . . . 2 C4
Halsham . . . 91 B6
Halsinger . . . 20 F4
Halstead Essex . . . 56 F2
Kent . . . 29 C5
Leics . . . 64 D4
Halstock . . . 12 D3
Haltham . . . 78 C5
Haltoft End . . . 79 E6
Halton Bucks . . . 40 C1
Halton . . . 86 F3
Lancs . . . 92 C5
Northumb . . . 110 C2
Wrex . . . 73 F7
W Yorks . . . 95 F6
Halton East . . . 94 D3
Halton Gill . . . 93 B8
Halton Holegate . . 79 C7
Halton Lea Gate . . 109 D6
Halton West . . . 93 D8
Haltwhistle . . . 109 C7
Halvergate . . . 69 D7
Halwell . . . 7 D5
Halwill . . . 9 E6
Halwill Junction . . . 9 D6
Ham Devon . . . 11 D7
Glos . . . 36 E3
Highld . . . 158 C4
Kent . . . 31 D7
London . . . 28 B2
Shetland . . . 160 K1
Wilts . . . 25 C8
Hambleden . . . 39 F7
Hambledon Hants . . 15 C7
Sur . . . 27 F7
Hamble-le-Rice . . . 15 D5
Hambleton Lancs . . . 92 E3
N Yorks . . . 95 F8
Hambridge . . . 11 B8
Hambrook S Glos . . . 23 B8
W Sus . . . 15 D8
Ham Common . . . 13 B6
Hameringham . . . 79 C6
Hamerton . . . 54 B2
Hametoun . . . 160 K1
Ham Green
Hereford . . . 50 E2
Kent . . . 19 C5
Kent . . . 30 C2
N Som . . . 23 B7
Worcs . . . 50 C5
Hamilton . . . 119 D7
Hammer . . . 27 F6
Hammerpot . . . 16 D4
Hammersmith . . . 28 B3
Hammerwich . . . 62 D4
Hammerwood . . . 28 F5
Hammond Street . . 41 D6
Hammoon . . . 13 C6
Hamnavoe
Shetland . . . 160 E4
Shetland . . . 160 E6
Shetland . . . 160 F6
Shetland . . . 160 K5
Hampden Park . . . 18 E3
Hamperden End . . . 55 F6
Hampnett . . . 37 C7
Hampole . . . 89 C6
Hampreston . . . 13 E8
Hampstead . . . 41 F5
Hampstead
Norreys . . . 26 B3
Hampsthwaite . . . 95 D5
Hampton Pboro . . . 65 E8
London . . . 28 C2
Shrops . . . 61 F7
Worcs . . . 50 E5
Hampton Bishop . . 49 F7
Hampton Heath . . . 73 E8
Hampton in Arden . 63 F6
Hampton Loade . . . 61 F7
Hampton Lovett . . . 50 C3
Hampton Lucy . . . 51 D7
Hampton on the
Hill . . . 51 C7
Hampton Poyle . . . 39 C5
Hamrow . . . 80 E5
Hamsey . . . 17 C8
Hamsey Green . . . 28 D4
Hamstall Ridware . 62 C5
Hamstead IoW . . . 14 E5
W Mid . . . 62 E4
Hamstead
Marshall . . . 26 C2
Hamsterley
Durham . . . 110 D4
Durham . . . 110 F4
Hamstreet . . . 19 B7
Ham Street . . . 23 F7
Hamworthy . . . 13 E7
Hanbury Staffs . . . 63 B5
Worcs . . . 50 C4
Hanbury Woodend 63 B5
Hanby . . . 78 F3
Hanchurch . . . 74 E5
Handbridge . . . 73 C8
Handcross . . . 17 B6
Handforth . . . 87 F6
Handley . . . 73 D8
Handsacre . . . 62 C4
Handsworth
S Yorks . . . 88 F5
W Mid . . . 62 E4
Handy Cross . . . 9 B6
Hanford . . . 75 E5
Hanging Langford . 24 F5
Hangleton . . . 16 D4
Hanham . . . 23 B8
Hankelow . . . 74 E3
Hankerton . . . 37 E6
Hankham . . . 18 E3
Hanley . . . 75 E5
Hanley Castle . . . 50 E3
Hanley Child . . . 49 C8
Hanley Swan . . . 50 E3
Hanley William . . . 49 C8
Hanlith . . . 94 C2
Hanmer . . . 73 F8
Hannah . . . 79 B8
Hannington Hants . . 26 D3
Swindon . . . 38 E1

Hannington *continued*
W Nhants 53 B6
Hannington Wick 38 E1
Hansel Village 118 F3
Hanslope 53 E6
Hanthorpe 65 B7
Hanwell London 40 F4
Oxon 52 E2
Hanwood 60 D4
Hanworth London 28 B2
Norf 81 D7
Happendon 119 F8
Happisburgh 69 A6
Happisburgh Common 69 B6
Hapsford 73 B8
Hapton Lancs 93 F7
Norf 68 E4
Harberton 7 D5
Harbertonford 7 D5
Harbledown 30 D5
Harborne 62 F4
Harborough Magna 52 B2
Harbottle 117 D5
Harbury 51 D8
Harby Leics 77 F7
Notts 77 B8
Harcombe 11 E6
Harden W Mid 62 D4
W Yorks 94 F3
Hardenhuish 24 B4
Hardgate 141 D6
Hardham 16 C4
Hardingham 68 D3
Hardingstone 53 D5
Hardington 24 D2
Hardington Mandeville 12 C3
Hardington Marsh 12 D3
Hardley 14 D5
Hardley Street 69 D6
Hardmead 53 E7
Hardrow 100 E3
Hardstoft 76 C4
Hardway Hants 15 D7
Som 24 F2
Hardwick Bucks 39 C8
Cambs 54 D4
N Nhants 53 C6
Norf 67 C6
Norf 68 F5
Notts 77 B6
Oxon 38 D3
Oxon 39 B5
W Mid 62 E4
Hardwicke Glos 36 C4
Glos 37 B6
Hereford 48 E4
Hardy's Green 43 B5
Hareby 79 C6
Hareden 93 D6
Harefield 40 E3
Hare Green 43 B6
Hare Hatch 27 B6
Harehills 95 F6
Harehope 117 B6
Hareseugh 109 E6
Harescombe 37 C5
Haresfield 37 C5
Hareshaw 119 C8
Hareshaw Head 116 F4
Hare Street 41 B6
Harewood 95 E6
Harewood End 36 B2
Harford Carms 46 E5
Devon 6 D4
Hargate 68 E4
Hargatewall 75 B8
Hargrave Ches W 73 C8
N Nhants 53 B8
Suff 55 D8
Harker 108 C3
Harkland 160 E6
Harkstead 57 F5
Harlaston 63 C6
Harlaw House 141 B6
Harlaxton 77 F8
Harlech 71 D6
Harlequin 77 F6
Harlescott 60 C5
Harlesden 41 F5
Harleston Devon 7 E5
Norf 68 F5
Suff 56 D4
Harlestone 52 C5
Harle Syke 93 F8
Harley Shrops 61 D5
S Yorks 88 E4
Harleyholm 120 F2
Harlington C Beds 53 F8
London 27 B8
S Yorks 89 D5
Harlosh 149 D7
Harlow 41 C7
Harlow Hill Northumb 110 C3
N Yorks 95 D5
Harlthorpe 96 F3
Harlton 54 D4
Harman's Cross 13 F7
Harmby 101 F6
Harmer Green 41 C5
Harmer Hill 60 B4
Harmondsworth 27 B8
Harmston 78 C2
Harnham 110 B3
Harnhill 37 D7
Harold Hill 41 E8
Haroldston West 44 D3
Haroldswick 160 B8
Harold Wood 41 E8
Harome 102 F4
Harpenden 40 C4
Harpford 11 E5
Harpham 97 C6
Harpley Norf 80 E3
Worcs 49 C8
Harpole 52 C4
Harpsdale 158 E3
Harpsden 39 F7
Harpswell 90 F3
Harpurhey 87 D6
Harpur Hill 75 B7
Harraby 108 D4
Harrapool 149 F11
Harrier 160 J1
Harrietfield 127 B8
Harrietsham 30 D2
Harrington Cumb 98 B1
Lincs 79 B6
N Nhants 64 F4
Harringworth 65 E6
Harris 146 B6
Harrogate 95 D6
Harrold 53 D7
Harrow 40 F4
Harrowbarrow 5 C8
Harrowden 53 E8
Harrowgate Hill 101 C7
Harrow on the Hill 40 F4
Harrow Street 56 F3
Harrow Weald 40 E4
Harston Cambs 54 D5
Leics 77 F8
Harswell 96 E4
Hart 111 F7
Hartburn Northumb 117 F6
Stockton 102 C2
Hart Common 86 D4
Hartest 56 D2
Hartfield 29 F5
Hartford Cambs 54 B3
Ches W 74 B3
Hartfordbridge 27 D5
Hartford End 42 C2
Hartforth 101 D6
Harthill Ches W 74 D2
N Lanark 120 C2
S Yorks 89 F5
Hart Hill 40 B4
Hartington 75 C8
Hartland 8 B4
Hartlebury 50 B3
Hartlepool 111 F8
Hartley Cumb 100 D2
Kent 18 B4
Kent 29 C7
Northumb 111 B6
Hartley Westpall 26 D4
Hartley Wintney 27 D5
Hartlip 30 C2
Hartoft End 103 E5
Harton N Yorks 96 C3
Shrops 60 F4
T&W 111 C6
Hartpury 36 B4
Hartshead 88 B2
Hartshill 63 E7
Hartshorne 63 B7
Hartsop 99 C6
Hart Station 111 F7
Hartwell 53 D5
Hartwood 119 D8
Harvieston 126 F4
Harvington 51 E5
Harvington Cross 51 E5
Harwell 38 F4
Harwich 57 F6
Harwood Durham 109 F8
Gtr Man 86 C5
Harwood Dale 103 E7
Harworth 89 E7
Hasbury 62 F3
Hascombe 27 E7
Haselbech 52 B5
Haselbury Plucknett 12 C2
Haseley 51 C7
Haselor 51 D6
Hasfield 37 B5
Hasguard 44 E3
Haskayne 85 D4
Hasketon 57 D6
Hasland 76 C3
Haslemere 27 F7
Haslingden 87 B5
Haslingfield 54 D5
Haslington 74 D4
Hassall 74 D4
Hassall Green 74 D4
Hassell Street 30 E4
Hassendean 115 B8
Hassingham 69 D6
Hassocks 17 C6
Hassop 76 B2
Hastigrow 158 D4
Hastingleigh 30 E4
Hastings 18 E5
Hastingwood 41 D7
Hastoe 40 D2
Haswell 111 E6
Haswell Plough 111 E6
Hatch C Beds 54 E2
Hants 26 D4
Wilts 13 B7
Hatch Beauchamp 11 B8
Hatch End 40 E4
Hatchet Gate 14 D4
Hatch Green 11 C8
Hatching Green 40 C4
Hatchmere 74 B2
Hatcliffe 91 D6
Hatfield Hereford 49 D7
Herts 41 D5
S Yorks 89 D7
Worcs 50 D3
Hatfield Broad Oak 41 C8
Hatfield Garden Village 41 D5
Hatfield Heath 41 C8
Hatfield Hyde 41 C5
Hatfield Peverel 42 C3
Hatfield Woodhouse 89 D7
Hatford 38 E3
Hatherden 25 D8
Hatherleigh 9 D7
Hathern 63 B8
Hatherop 38 D1
Hathersage 88 F3
Hathershaw 87 D7
Hatherton Ches E 74 E3
Staffs 62 C3
Hatley St George 54 D3
Hatt 5 C8
Hattingley 26 F4
Hatton Aberds 153 E10
Derbys 63 B6
Lincs 78 B4
Shrops 60 E4
Warks 51 C7
Warr 86 F3
Hatton Castle 153 D7
Hattoncrook 141 B7
Hatton Heath 73 C8
Hatton of Fintray 141 C7
Haugh E Ayrs 112 B4
Gtr Man 87 C7
Lincs 79 B7
Haugham 91 F7
Haugh Head 117 B6
Haughley 56 C4
Haughley Green 56 C4
Haugh of Glass 152 E4
Haugh of Urr 106 C5
Haughs of Clinterty 141 C7
Haughton Notts 77 B6
Shrops 60 B3
Shrops 61 C5
Shrops 61 D7
Shrops 61 E6
Staffs 62 B2
Haughton Castle 110 B2
Haughton Green 87 E7
Haughton Moss 74 D2
Haultwick 41 B6
Haunn Argyll 146 G6
W Isles 148 G2
Haunton 63 C6
Hauxley 117 D8
Hauxton 54 D5
Havant 15 D8
Haven 49 D6
Haven Bank 78 D5
Haven Side 91 B5
Havenstreet 15 E6
Havercroft 88 C4
Haverfordwest = *Hwlffordd* 44 D4
Haverhill 55 E7
Haverigg 92 B1
Havering-atte-Bower 41 E8
Haveringland 81 E7
Haversham 53 E6
Haverthwaite 99 F5
Haverton Hill 102 B2
Hawarden = *Penarlâg* 73 C7
Hawcoat 92 B2
Hawen 46 E2
Hawes 100 F3
Hawes' Green 68 E5
Hawes Side 92 F3
Hawford 50 C3
Hawick 115 C8
Hawkchurch 11 D8
Hawkedon 55 D8
Hawkenbury Kent 18 B2
Kent 30 E2
Hawkeridge 24 D3
Hawkerland 11 F5
Hawkesbury S Glos 36 F4
Warks 63 F7
Hawkesbury Upton 36 F4
Hawkes End 63 F7
Hawk Green 87 F7
Hawkhill 117 C8
Hawkhurst 18 B4
Hawkinge 31 F6
Hawkley 15 B8
Hawkridge 21 F7
Hawkshead 99 E5
Hawkshead Hill 99 E5
Hawksland 119 F8
Hawkswick 94 B2
Hawksworth Notts 77 E7
W Yorks 94 E4
W Yorks 95 F5
Hawkwell 42 E4
Hawley Hants 27 D6
Kent 29 B6
Hawling 37 B7
Hawnby 102 F3
Haworth 94 F3
Hawstead 56 D2
Hawthorn Durham 111 E7
Rhondda 35 F5
Wilts 24 C3
Hawthorn Hill Brack 27 B6
Lincs 78 D5
Hawthorpe 65 B7
Hawton 77 D7
Haxby 96 D2
Haxey 89 D8
Haydock 86 E3
Haydon 12 C4
Haydon Bridge 109 C8
Haydon Wick 37 F8
Haye 5 C8
Hayes London 28 C5
London 40 F4
Hayfield Derbys 87 F8
Fife 128 E4
Hay Green 66 C5
Hayhill 112 C4
Hayhillock 135 E5
Hayle 2 C4
Haynes 53 E8
Haynes Church End 53 E8
Hay-on-Wye = *Y Gelli Gandryll* 48 E4
Hayscastle 44 C3
Hayscastle Cross 44 C4
Hayshead 135 E6
Hay Street 41 B6
Hayton Aberdeen 141 D8
Cumb 107 E8
Cumb 108 D5
E Yorks 96 E4
Notts 89 F8
Hayton's Bent 60 F5
Haytor Vale 7 B5
Haywards Heath 17 B7
Haywood 89 C6
Haywood Oaks 77 D6
Hazelbank 119 E8
Hazelbury Bryan 12 D5
Hazeley 26 D5
Hazel Grove 87 F7
Hazelhurst 87 D7
Hazelslade 62 C4
Hazel Street 18 B3
Hazelton 37 C7
Hazelton Walls 128 B5
Hazelwood 76 E3
Hazlemere 40 E1
Hazlerigg 110 B5
Hazlewood 94 D3
Hazon 117 D7
Heacham 80 D2
Headbourne Worthy 26 F2
Headbrook 48 D5
Headcorn 30 E2
Headingley 95 F5
Headington 39 D5
Headlam 101 C6
Headless Cross 50 C5
Headley Hants 26 C3
Hants 27 F6
Sur 28 D3
Head of Muir 127 F7
Headon 77 B7
Heads 119 E7
Heads Nook 108 D4
Heage 76 D3
Healaugh N Yorks 95 E7
N Yorks 101 E5
Heald Green 87 F6
Heale Devon 20 E5
Som 23 E8
Healey Gtr Man 87 C6
Northumb 110 D3
N Yorks 101 F6
Healing 91 C6
Heamoor 2 C3
Heanish 146 G3
Heanor 76 E4
Heanton Punchardon 20 F4
Heapham 90 F2
Hearthstane 114 B4
Heasley Mill 21 F6
Heast 149 G11
Heath Cardiff 22 B3
Derbys 76 C4
Heath and Reach 40 B2
Heathcote 75 C8
Heath End Hants 26 C3
Sur 27 E6
Warks 51 C7
Heather 63 C7
Heatherfield 149 D9
Heathfield Devon 7 B6
E Sus 18 C2
Som 11 B6
Heathhall 107 B6
Heath Hayes 62 C4
Heath Hill 61 C7
Heath House 23 E6
Heathrow Airport 27 B8
Heathstock 11 D7
Heathton 62 E2
Heath Town 62 E3
Heatley 86 F5
Heaton Lancs 92 C4
Staffs 75 C6
T&W 111 C5
W Yorks 94 F4
Heaton Moor 87 E6
Heaverham 29 D6
Heaviley 87 F7
Heavitree 10 E4
Hebburn 111 C6
Hebden 94 C3
Hebden Bridge 87 B7
Hebron Anglesey 82 C4
Carms 32 B2
Northumb 117 F7
Heck 114 F3
Heckfield 26 C5
Heckfield Green 57 B5
Heckfordbridge 43 B5
Heckington 78 E4
Heckmondwike 88 B3
Heddington 24 C4
Heddle 159 G4
Heddon-on-the-Wall 110 C4
Hedenham 69 E6
Hedge End 15 C5
Hedgerley 40 F2
Hedging 11 B8
Hedley on the Hill 110 D3
Hednesford 62 C4
Hedon 91 B5
Hedsor 40 F2
Hedworth 111 C6
Hegdon Hill 49 D7
Heggerscales 100 C3
Heglibister 160 H5
Heighington Darl 101 B7
Lincs 78 C3
Heights of Brae 151 E8
Heights of Kinlochewe 150 E3
Heilam 156 C7
Heiton 122 F3
Hele Devon 10 D4
Devon 20 E4
Helensburgh 145 E11
Helford 3 D6
Helford Passage 3 D6
Helhoughton 80 E4
Helions Bumpstead 55 E7
Hellaby 89 E6
Helland 5 B5
Hellesdon 68 C5
Hellidon 52 D3
Hellifield 93 D8
Hellingly 18 D2
Hellington 69 D6
Hellister 160 J5
Helm 117 E7
Helmdon 52 E3
Helmingham 57 D5
Helmington Row 110 F4
Helmsdale 157 H13
Helmshore 87 B5
Helmsley 102 F4
Helperby 95 C7
Helperthorpe 97 B5
Helpringham 78 E4
Helpston 65 D8
Helsby 73 B8
Helsey 79 B8
Helston 3 D5
Helstone 8 F2
Helton 99 B7
Helwith Bridge 93 C8
Hemblington 69 C6
Hemel Hempstead 40 D3
Hemingbrough 96 F2
Hemingby 78 B5
Hemingford Abbots 54 B3
Hemingford Grey 54 B3
Hemingstone 57 D5
Hemington Leics 63 B8
N Nhants 65 F7
Som 24 D2
Hemley 57 E6
Hemlington 102 C3
Hemp Green 57 C7
Hempholme 97 D6
Hempnall 68 E5
Hempnall Green 68 E5
Hempriggs House 158 F5
Hempstead Essex 55 F7
Medway 29 C8
Norf 69 B7
Norf 81 D7
Hempsted 37 C5
Hempton Norf 80 E5
Oxon 52 F2
Hemsby 69 C7
Hemswell 90 E3
Hemswell Cliff 90 F3
Hemsworth 88 C5
Hemyock 11 C6
Henbury Bristol 23 B7
Ches E 75 B5
Hendon London 41 F5
T&W 111 D7
Hendre 73 C5
Hendre-ddu 83 E8
Hendreforgan 34 F3
Hendy 33 D6
Heneglwys 82 D4
Hen-feddau fawr 45 F4
Henfield 17 C6
Henford 9 E5
Henghurst 19 B6
Hengoed Caerph 35 E5
Powys 48 D4
Shrops 73 F6
Hengrave 56 C2
Henham 41 B8
Heniarth 59 D8
Henlade 11 B7
Henley Shrops 49 B7
Som 23 F6
Suff 57 D5
W Sus 16 B2
Henley-in-Arden 51 C6
Henley-on-Thames 39 F7
Henley's Down 18 D4
Henllan Ceredig 46 E2
Denb 72 C4
Henllan Amgoed 32 B2
Henllys 35 E6
Henlow 54 F2
Hennock 10 F3
Henny Street 56 F2
Henryd 83 D7
Henry's Moat 32 B1
Hensall 89 B6
Henshaw 109 C7
Hensingham 98 C1
Henstead 69 F7
Henstridge 12 C5
Henstridge Ash 12 B5
Henstridge Marsh 12 B5
Henton Oxon 39 D7
Som 23 E6
Henwood 5 B7
Heogan 160 J6
Heol-las 33 E7
Heol Senni 34 B3
Heol-y-Cyw 34 F3
Hepburn 117 B6
Hepple 117 D5
Hepscott 117 F8
Heptonstall 87 B7
Hepworth Suff 56 B3
W Yorks 88 D2
Herbrandston 44 E3
Hereford 49 E7
Heriot 121 D6
Hermiston 120 B4
Hermitage Borders 115 E8
Dorset 12 D4
W Berks 26 B3
W Sus 15 D8
Hermon Anglesey 82 E3
Carms 33 B7
Carms 46 F2
Pembs 45 F4
Herne 31 C5
Herne Bay 31 C5
Herner 9 B7
Hernhill 30 C4
Herodsfoot 5 C7
Herongate 42 E2
Heronsford 104 A5
Herriard 26 E4
Herringfleet 69 E7
Herringswell 55 B8
Hersden 31 C6
Hersham Corn 8 D4
Sur 28 C2
Herstmonceux 18 D3
Herston 159 J5
Hertford 41 C6
Hertford Heath 41 C6
Hertingfordbury 41 C6
Hesketh Bank 86 B2
Hesketh Lane 93 E6
Hesket Newmarket 108 F3
Heskin Green 86 C3
Hesleden 111 F7
Hesleyside 116 F4
Heslington 96 D2
Hessay 95 D8
Hessenford 5 D8
Hessett 56 C3
Hessle 90 B4
Hest Bank 92 C4
Heston 28 B2
Hestwall 159 G3
Heswall 85 F3
Hethe 39 B5
Hethersett 68 D4
Hethersgill 108 C4
Hethpool 116 B4
Hett 111 F5
Hetton 94 D2
Hetton-le-Hole 111 E6
Hetton Steads 123 F6
Heugh 110 B3
Heugh-head 140 C2
Heveningham 57 B7
Hever 29 E5
Heversham 99 F6
Hevingham 81 E7
Hewas Water 3 B8
Hewelsfield 36 D2
Hewish N Som 23 C6
Som 12 D2
Heworth 96 D2
Hexham 110 C2
Hextable 29 B6
Hexton 54 F2
Hexworthy 6 B4
Hey 93 E8
Heybridge Essex 42 D4
Essex 42 E2
Heybridge Basin 42 D4
Heybrook Bay 6 E3
Heydon Cambs 54 E5
Norf 81 E7
Heydour 78 F3
Heyford Park Oxon 39 B5
Heylipol 146 G2
Heylor 160 E4
Heysham 92 C4
Heyshott 16 C2
Heyside 87 D7
Heytesbury 24 E4
Heythrop 38 B3
Heywood Gtr Man 87 C6
Wilts 24 D3
Hibaldstow 90 D3
Hickleton 89 D5
Hickling Norf 69 B7
Notts 64 B3
Hickling Green 69 B7
Hickling Heath 69 B7
Hickstead 17 B6
Hidcote Boyce 51 E6
High Ackworth 88 C5
Higham Derbys 76 D3
Kent 29 B8
Lancs 93 F8
Suff 55 C8
Suff 56 F4
Higham Dykes 110 B4
Higham Ferrers 53 C7
Higham Gobion 54 F2
Higham on the Hill 63 E7
Highampton 9 D6
Higham Wood 29 E6
High Angerton 117 F6
High Bankhill 109 E5
High Barnes 111 D6
High Beach 41 E7
High Bentham 93 C6
High Bickington 9 B8
High Birkwith 93 B7
High Blantyre 119 D6
High Bonnybridge 119 B8
High Bradfield 88 E3
High Bray 21 F5
Highbridge Highld 136 F4
Som 22 E5
Highbrook 28 F4
High Brooms 29 E6
High Bullen 9 B7
Highburton 88 C2
Highbury 23 E8
High Buston 117 D8
High Callerton 110 B4
High Catton 96 D3
Highclere 26 C2
Highcliffe 14 E3
High Cogges 38 D3
High Coniscliffe 101 C7
High Cross Hants 15 B8
Herts 41 C6
High Easter 42 C2
High Eggborough 89 B6
High Ellington 101 F6
Higher Ansty 13 D5
Higher Ashton 10 F3
Higher Ballam 92 F3
Higher Bartle 92 F5
Higher Boscaswell 2 C2
Higher Burwardsley 74 D2
High Ercall 61 C5
Higher Clovelly 8 B5
Higher End 86 D3
Higher Kinnerton 73 C7
Higher Penwortham 86 B3
Higher Town 2 E4
Higher Walreddon 6 B2
Higher Walton Lancs 86 B3
Warr 86 F3
Higher Wheelton 86 B4
Higher Whitley 86 F4
Higher Wincham 74 B3
Higher Wych 73 E8
High Etherley 101 B6
Highfield E Yorks 96 F3
Gtr Man 86 D5
N Ayrs 118 D3
Oxon 39 B5
S Yorks 88 F4
T&W 110 D4
Highfields Cambs 54 D4
Northumb 123 D5
High Garrett 42 B3
Highgate 41 F5
High Grange 110 F4
High Green Norf 68 D4
S Yorks 88 E4
Worcs 50 E3
High Halden 19 B5
High Halstow 29 B8
High Ham 23 F6
High Harrington 98 B2
High Hatton 61 B6
High Hawsker 103 D7
High Hesket 108 E4
High Hesleden 111 F7
High Hoyland 88 C3
High Hunsley 97 F5
High Hurstwood 17 B8
High Hutton 96 C3
High Ireby 108 F2
High Kelling 81 C7
High Kilburn 95 B8
High Lands 101 B6
Highlane Ches E 75 C5
Derbys 88 F5
High Lane Gtr Man 87 F7
Worcs 49 C8
High Laver 41 D8
Highlaws 107 E8
Highleadon 36 B4
High Legh 86 F5
Highleigh 16 E2
High Leven 102 C2
Highley 61 F7
High Littleton 23 D8
High Lorton 98 B3
High Marishes 96 B4
High Marnham 77 B8
High Melton 89 D6
High Mickley 110 C3
High Mindork 105 D7
Highmoor Cross 39 F7
Highmoor Hill 36 F1
Highnam 36 C4
Highnam Green 36 B4
High Newton 99 F6
High Newton-by-the-Sea 117 B8
High Nibthwaite 98 F4
High Offley 61 B7
High Ongar 42 D1
High Onn 62 C2
High Roding 42 C2
High Row 108 F3
High Salvington 16 D5
High Sellafield 98 D2
High Shaw 100 E3
High Spen 110 D4
Highsted 30 C3
High Stoop 110 E4
High Street Corn 4 D4
Kent 18 B4
Suff 56 E2
Suff 57 B8
Suff 57 D8
Highstreet Green 55 F8
High Street Green 56 D4
Hightae 107 B7
High Throston 111 F7
Hightown Ches E 75 C5
Mers 85 D4
Hightown Green 56 D3
High Toynton 79 C5
High Trewhitt 117 D6
High Valleyfield 128 F2
Highway 24 B5
Highweek 7 B6
High Westwood 110 D4
Highworth 38 E2
High Wray 99 E5
High Wych 41 C7
High Wycombe 40 E1
Hilborough 67 D8
Hilcote 76 D4
Hilcott 25 D6
Hildenborough 29 E6
Hilden Park 29 E6
Hildersham 55 E6
Hilderstone 75 F6
Hilderthorpe 97 C7
Hilfield 12 D4
Hilgay 67 E6
Hill Pembs 32 D2
S Glos 36 E3
W Mid 62 E5
Hillam 89 B6
Hillbeck 100 C2
Hillborough 31 C6
Hillbrae Aberds 141 B6
Aberds 152 D6
Hill Brow 15 B8
Hillbutts 13 D7
Hillclifflane 76 E2
Hillcommon 11 B6
Hill Dale 86 C2
Hill Dyke 79 E6
Hillend 128 F3
Hill End Durham 110 F3
Fife 128 E2
N Yorks 94 D3
Hillerton 10 E2
Hillesden 39 B6
Hillesley 36 F4
Hillfarrance 11 B6
Hillhead Aberds 152 E5
Devon 7 D7
S Ayrs 112 C4
Hill Head Hants 15 D6
Northumb 110 C2
Hillhead of Auchentumb 153 C9
Hillhead of Cocklaw 153 D10
Hillhouse 121 D8
Hilliclay 158 D3
Hillingdon 40 F3
Hillington Glasgow 118 C5
Norf 80 E3
Hillmorton 52 B3
Hill Mountain 44 E4
Hillockhead Aberds 140 C3
Aberds 140 D2
Hill of Beath 128 E3
Hill of Fearn 151 D11
Hill of Mountblairy 153 C6
Hill Ridware 62 C4
Hillside Aberds 141 E8
Angus 135 C7
Mers 85 C4
Orkney 159 J5
Shetland 160 G6
Hillswick 160 F4
Hill Top Durham 100 B4
Hants 14 D5
W Mid 62 E3
W Yorks 88 C4
Hill View 13 E7
Hillway 15 F7
Hillwell 160 M5
Hilmarton 24 B5
Hilperton 24 D3
Hilsea 15 D7
Hilston 97 F8
Hilton Aberds 153 E9
Cambs 54 C3
Cumb 100 B2
Derbys 76 F2
Dorset 13 D5
Durham 101 B6
Highld 151 C10
Shrops 61 E7
Stockton 102 C2
Hilton of Cadboll 151 D11
Himbleton 50 D4
Himley 62 E2
Hincaster 99 F7
Hinckley 63 E8
Hinderclay 56 B4
Hinderton 73 B7
Hinderwell 103 C5
Hindford 73 F7
Hindhead 27 F6
Hindley 86 D4
Hindley Green 86 D4
Hindlip 50 D3
Hindolveston 81 E6
Hindon 24 F4
Hindringham 81 D5
Hingham 68 D3
Hinstock 61 B6
Hintlesham 56 E4
Hinton Hants 14 E3
Hereford 48 F5
S Glos 24 B2
Shrops 60 D4
W Nhants 52 D3
Hinton Ampner 15 B6
Hinton Blewett 23 D7
Hinton Charterhouse 24 D2
Hinton-in-the-Hedges 52 F3
Hinton Martell 13 D8
Hinton on the Green 50 E5
Hinton Parva 38 F2
Hinton St George 12 C2
Hinton St Mary 13 C5
Hinton Waldrist 38 E3
Hints Shrops 49 B8
Staffs 63 D5
Hinwick 53 C7
Hinxhill 30 E4
Hinxton 55 E5
Hinxworth 54 E3
Hipperholme 88 B2
Hipswell 101 E6
Hirael 83 D5
Hiraeth 32 B2
Hirn 141 D6
Hirnant 59 B7
Hirst N Lanark 119 C8
Northumb 117 F8
Hirst Courtney 89 B7
Hirwaen 72 C5
Hirwaun 34 D3
Hiscott 9 B7
Histon 54 C5
Hitcham 56 D3
Hitchin 40 B4
Hither Green 28 B4
Hittisleigh 10 E2
Hive 96 F4
Hixon 62 B4
Hoaden 31 D6
Hoaldalbert 35 B7
Hoar Cross 62 B5
Hoarwithy 36 B2
Hoath 31 C6
Hobarris 48 B5
Hobbister 159 H4
Hobkirk 115 C8
Hobson 110 D4
Hoby 64 C3
Hockering 68 C3
Hockerton 77 D7
Hockley 42 E4
Hockley Heath 51 B6
Hockliffe 40 B2
Hockwold cum Wilton 67 F7
Hockworthy 10 C5
Hoddesdon 41 D6
Hoddlesden 86 B5
Hoddomcross 107 B8
Hoddom Mains 107 B8
Hodgeston 32 E1
Hodley 59 E8
Hodnet 61 B6
Hodthorpe 76 B5
Hoe Hants 15 C6
Norf 68 C2
Hoe Gate 15 C7
Hoff 100 C1
Hoggard's Green 56 D2
Hoggeston 39 B8
Hogha Gearraidh 148 A2
Hoghton 86 B4
Hognaston 76 D2
Hog Patch 27 E6
Hogsthorpe 79 B8
Holbeach 66 B3
Holbeach Bank 66 B3
Holbeach Clough 66 B3
Holbeach Drove 66 C3
Holbeach Hurn 66 B3
Holbeach St Johns 66 C3
Holbeach St Marks 79 F6
Holbeach St Matthew 79 F7
Holbeck Notts 76 B5
W Yorks 95 F5
Holbeck Woodhouse 76 B5
Holberrow Green 50 D5
Holbeton 6 D4
Holborn 41 F6
Holbrook Derbys 76 E3
Suff 57 F5
S Yorks 88 F5
Holburn 123 F6
Holbury 14 D5
Holcombe Devon 7 B7
Som 23 E8
Holcombe Rogus 11 C5
Holcot 53 C5
Holden 93 E7
Holdenby 52 C4
Holdenhurst 14 E2
Holdgate 61 F5
Holdingham 78 E3
Holditch 11 D8
Holefield 122 F4
Holehouses 74 B4
Hole-in-the-Wall 36 B3
Holemoor 9 D6
Holestane 113 E8
Holford 22 E3
Holgate 95 D8
Holker 92 B3
Holkham 80 C4
Hollacombe 9 D5
Holland Orkney 159 C5
Holland *continued*
Orkney 159 F7
Holland Fen 78 E5
Holland-on-Sea 43 C8
Hollandstoun 159 C8
Hollee 108 C2
Hollesley 57 E7
Hollicombe 7 C6
Hollingbourne 30 D2
Hollington Derbys 76 F2
E Sus 18 D4
Staffs 75 F7
Hollington Grove 76 F2
Hollingworth 87 E8
Hollins 87 D6
Hollinsclough 75 C7
Hollins Green 86 E4
Hollins Lane 92 D4
Hollinwood Gtr Man 87 D7
Shrops 74 F2
Hollocombe 9 C8
Holloway 76 D3
Hollowell 52 B4
Hollow Meadows 88 F3
Hollybush Caerph 35 D5
E Ayrs 112 C3
Worcs 50 F2
Holly End 66 D4
Holly Green 50 E3
Hollym 91 B7
Hollywood 51 B5
Holmbridge 88 D2
Holmbury St Mary 28 E2
Holmbush 4 D5
Holmcroft 62 B3
Holme Cambs 65 F8
Cumb 92 B5
Notts 77 D8
N Yorks 102 F1
W Yorks 88 D2
Holme Chapel 87 B6
Holme Green 95 E8
Holme Hale 67 D8
Holme Lacy 49 F7
Holme Marsh 48 D5
Holme next the Sea 80 C3
Holme-on-Spalding-Moor 96 F4
Holme on the Wolds 97 E5
Holme Pierrepont 77 F6
Holmer 49 E7
Holmer Green 40 E2
Holme St Cuthbert 107 E8
Holmes Chapel 74 C4
Holmesfield 76 B3
Holmeswood 86 C2
Holmewood 76 C4
Holme Wood 94 F4
Holmfirth 88 D2
Holmhead Dumfries 113 F7
E Ayrs 113 B5
Holmisdale 148 D6
Holmpton 91 B7
Holmrook 98 E2
Holmsgarth 160 J6
Holmwrangle 108 E5
Holne 6 C5
Holnest 12 D4
Holsworthy 8 D5
Holsworthy Beacon 9 D5
Holt Dorset 13 D8
Norf 81 D6
Wilts 24 C3
Worcs 50 C3
Wrex 73 D8
Holtby 96 D2
Holt End Hants 26 F4
Worcs 51 C5
Holt Fleet 50 C3
Holt Heath 50 C3
Holton Oxon 39 D6
Som 12 B4
Suff 57 B7
Holton cum Beckering 90 F5
Holton Heath 13 E7
Holton le Clay 91 D6
Holton le Moor 90 E4
Holton St Mary 56 F4
Holt Park 95 E5
Holwell Dorset 12 C5
Herts 54 F2
Leics 64 B4
Oxon 38 D2
Holwick 100 B4
Holworth 13 F5
Holybourne 26 E5
Holy Cross 50 B4
Holyhead = *Caergybi* 82 C2
Holy Island 123 E7
Holymoorside 76 C3
Holyport 27 B6
Holystone 117 D5
Holytown 119 C7
Holywell Cambs 54 B4
Corn 4 D2
Dorset 12 D3
E Sus 18 F2
Northumb 111 B6
Holywell = *Treffynnon* 73 B5
Holywell Green 87 C8
Holywell Lake 11 B6
Holywell Row 55 B8
Holywood 114 F2
Homer 61 D6
Homersfield 69 F5
Hom Green 36 B2
Homington 14 B2
Honeyborough 44 E4
Honeybourne 51 E6
Honeychurch 9 D8
Honey Hill 30 C5
Honey Street 25 C6
Honey Tye 56 F3
Honiley 51 B7
Honing 69 B6
Honingham 68 C4
Honington Lincs 78 E2
Suff 56 B3

Honington continued
Warks 51 E7
Honiton 11 D6
Honley 88 C2
Hood Green 88 D4
Hooe E Sus 18 E3
Plym 6 D3
Hooe Common 18 D3
Hoo Green 86 F5
Hook E Yorks 89 B8
Hants 26 D5
London 28 C2
Pembs 44 D4
Wilts 37 F7
Hooke 12 E3
Hookgate 74 F4
Hook Green Kent 18 B3
Kent 29 C7
Hook Norton 51 F8
Hookway 10 E3
Hookwood 28 E3
Hoole 73 C8
Hooley 28 D3
Hoop 36 D2
Hoo St Werburgh 29 B8
Hooton 73 B7
Hooton Levitt 89 E6
Hooton Pagnell 89 D5
Hooton Roberts 89 E5
Hope Derbys 88 F2
Devon 6 F4
Highld 156 B7
Powys 60 D2
Shrops 60 D3
Staffs 75 D8
Hope = Yr Hôb 73 D7
Hope Bagot 49 B7
Hope Bowdler 60 E4
Hope End Green 42 B1
Hope Green 87 F7
Hopeman 152 B1
Hope Mansell 36 C3
Hopesay 60 F3
Hope's Green 42 F3
Hope under Dinmore 49 D7
Hopley's Green 48 D5
Hopperton 95 D7
Hop Pole 65 C8
Hopstone 61 E7
Hopton Shrops 60 B3
Shrops 61 B5
Staffs 62 B3
Suff 56 B3
Hopton Cangeford 60 F5
Hopton Castle 49 B5
Hoptonheath 49 B5
Hopton on Sea 69 D8
Hopton Wafers 49 B8
Hopwas 63 D5
Hopwood Gtr Man 87 D6
Worcs 50 B5
Horam 18 D2
Horbling 78 F4
Horbury 88 C3
Horcott 38 D1
Horden 111 E7
Horderley 60 F4
Hordle 14 E3
Hordley 73 F7
Horeb Carms 33 B6
Carms 33 D5
Ceredig 46 E2
Horfield 23 B8
Horham 57 B6
Horkesley Heath 43 B5
Horkstow 90 C3
Horley Oxon 52 E2
Sur 28 E3
Hornblotton Green 23 F7
Hornby Lancs 93 C5
N Yorks 101 E7
N Yorks 102 D1
Horncastle 79 C5
Hornchurch 41 F8
Horncliffe 122 E5
Horndean Borders 122 E4
Hants 15 C8
Horndon 6 B3
Horndon on the Hill 42 F2
Horne 28 E4
Horniehaugh 134 C4
Horning 69 C6
Horninghold 64 E5
Horninglow 63 B6
Horningsea 55 C5
Horningsham 24 E3
Horningtoft 80 E5
Hornsby 108 D5
Horns Corner 18 C4
Horns Cross Devon 9 B5
E Sus 18 C5
Hornsea 97 E8
Hornsea Bridge 97 E8
Hornsey 41 F6
Hornton 51 E8
Horrabridge 6 C3
Horringer 56 C2
Horringford 15 F6
Horsebridge Devon 6 B2
Hants 25 F8
Horse Bridge 75 D6
Horsebrook 62 C2
Horsehay 61 D6
Horseheath 55 E7
Horsehouse 101 F5
Horsell 27 D7
Horseman's Green 73 E8
Horseway 66 F4
Horsey 69 B7
Horsford 68 C4
Horsforth 94 F5
Horsham Worcs 50 D2
W Sus 28 F2
Horsham St Faith 68 C5
Horsington Lincs 78 C4
Som 12 B5
Horsley Derbys 76 E3
Glos 37 E5
Northumb 110 C3
Northumb 116 E4
Horsley Cross 43 B7
Horsleycross Street 43 B7
Horsleyhill 115 C8
Horsleyhope 110 E3
Horsley Woodhouse 76 E3
Horsmonden 29 E7
Horspath 39 D5
Horstead 69 C5
Horsted Keynes 17 B7
Horton Bucks 40 C2
Dorset 13 D8
Lancs 93 D8
S Glos 36 F4
Shrops 60 B4
Som 11 C8
Staffs 75 D6
Swansea 33 F5
Wilts 25 C5
Windsor 27 B8
W Nhants 53 D6
Horton-cum-Studley 39 C5
Horton Green 73 E8
Horton Heath 15 C5
Horton in Ribblesdale 93 B8
Horton Kirby 29 C6
Hortonlane 60 C4
Horwich 86 C4
Horwich End 87 F8
Horwood 9 B7
Hose 64 B4
Hoselaw 122 F4
Hoses 98 E4
Hosh 127 B7
Hosta 148 A2
Hoswick 160 L6
Hotham 96 F4
Hothfield 30 E3
Hoton 64 B2
Houbie 160 D8
Houdston 112 E1
Hough Ches E 74 D4
Ches E 75 B5
Hougham 77 E8
Hough Green 86 F2
Hough-on-the-Hill 78 E2
Houghton Cambs 54 B3
Cumb 108 D4
Hants 25 F8
Pembs 44 E4
W Sus 16 C4
Houghton Conquest 53 E8
Houghton Green E Sus 19 C6
Warr 86 E4
Houghton-le-Side 101 B7
Houghton-le-Spring 111 E6
Houghton on the Hill 64 D3
Houghton Regis 40 B3
Houghton St Giles 80 D5
Houlland Shetland 160 F7
Shetland 160 H5
Houlsyke 103 D5
Houlton Warks 52 B3
Hound 15 D5
Hound Green 26 D5
Houndslow 122 E2
Houndwood 122 C4
Hounslow 28 B2
Hounslow Green 42 C2
Housay 160 F8
House of Daviot 151 G10
House of Glenmuick 140 E2
Housetter 160 E5
Houss 160 K5
Houston 118 C4
Houstry 158 G3
Houton 159 H4
Hove 17 D6
Hoveringham 77 E6
Hoveton 69 C6
Hovingham 96 B2
How 108 D5
Howbrook 88 E4
How Caple 49 F8
Howden Borders 116 B2
E Yorks 89 B8
Howden-le-Wear 110 F4
Howe Highld 158 D5
Norf 69 D5
N Yorks 101 F8
Howe Bridge 86 D4
Howe Green 42 D3
Howell 78 E4
How End 53 E8
Howe of Teuchar 153 D7
Howe Street Essex 42 C2
Essex 55 F7
Howey 48 D2
Howgate 120 D5
How Green 29 E5
Howick 117 C8
Howle Durham 101 B5
Telford 61 B6
Howlett End 55 F6
Howley 11 D7
Hownam 116 C3
Hownam Mains 116 B3
Howpasley 115 D6
Howsham N Lincs 90 D4
N Yorks 96 C3
Howslack 114 D3
Howtel 122 F4
Howton 35 B8
Howtown 99 C6
Howwood 118 C3
Hoxne 57 B5
Hoy 159 H3
Hoylake 85 F3
Hoyland 88 D4
Hoylandswaine 88 D3
Hubberholme 94 B2
Hubbert's Bridge 79 E5
Huby N Yorks 95 C8
N Yorks 95 E5
Hucclecote 37 C5
Hucking 30 D2
Hucknall 76 E5
Huddersfield 88 C2
Huddington 50 D4
Hudswell 101 D6
Huggate 96 D4
Hugglescote 63 C8
Hughenden Valley 40 E1
Hughley 61 E5
Hugh Town 2 E4
Huish Devon 9 C7
Wilts 25 C6
Huish Champflower 11 B5
Huish Episcopi 12 B2
Huisinis 154 F4
Hulcott 40 C1
Hulland 76 E2
Hulland Ward 76 E2
Hullavington 37 F5
Hullbridge 42 E4
Hulme 87 E6
Hulme End 75 D8
Hulme Walfield 74 C5
Hulverstone 14 F4
Hulver Street 69 F7
Humber 49 D7
Humber Bridge 90 B4
Humberston 91 D7
Humbie 121 C7
Humbleton E Yorks 97 F8
Northumb 117 B5
Humby 78 F3
Hume 122 E3
Humshaugh 110 B2
Huna 158 C5
Huncoat 93 F7
Huncote 64 E2
Hundalee 116 C2
Hunderthwaite 100 B4
Hundleby 79 C6
Hundle Houses 79 D5
Hundleton 44 E4
Hundon 55 E8
Hundred Acres 15 C6
Hundred End 86 B2
Hundred House 48 D3
Hungarton 64 D3
Hungerford Hants 14 C2
W Berks 25 C8
Hungerford Newtown 25 B8
Hungerton 65 B5
Hungladder 149 A8
Hunmanby 97 B6
Hunmanby Moor 97 B7
Hunningham 51 C8
Hunny Hill 15 F5
Hunsdon 41 C7
Hunsingore 95 D7
Hunslet 95 F6
Hunsonby 109 F5
Hunspow 158 C4
Hunstanton 80 C2
Hunstanworth 110 E2
Hunsterson 74 E3
Hunston Suff 56 C3
W Sus 16 D2
Hunstrete 23 C8
Hunt End 50 C5
Hunter's Quay 145 F10
Hunthill Lodge 134 B4
Huntingdon 54 B3
Huntingfield 57 B7
Huntingford 24 F3
Huntington E Loth 121 B7
Hereford 48 D4
Staffs 62 C3
York 96 D2
Huntingtower 128 B2
Huntley 36 C4
Huntly 152 E5
Huntlywood 122 E2
Hunton Kent 29 E8
N Yorks 101 E6
Hunt's Corner 68 F3
Hunt's Cross 86 F2
Huntsham 10 B5
Huntspill 22 E5
Huntworth 22 F5
Hunwick 110 F4
Hunworth 81 D6
Hurdsfield 75 B6
Hurley Warks 63 E6
Windsor 39 F8
Hurlford 118 F4
Hurliness 159 K3
Hurn 14 E2
Hurn's End 79 E7
Hursley 14 B5
Hurst N Yorks 101 D5
Som 12 C2
Wokingham 27 B5
Hurstbourne Priors 26 E2
Hurstbourne Tarrant 25 D8
Hurst Green E Sus 18 C4
Lancs 93 F6
Hurstpierpoint 17 C6
Hurst Wickham 17 C6
Hurstwood 93 F8
Hurtmore 27 E7
Hurworth Place 101 D7
Hury 100 C4
Husabost 148 C7
Husbands Bosworth 64 F3
Husborne Crawley 53 F7
Husthwaite 95 B8
Hutchwns 21 B7
Huthwaite 76 D4
Huttoft 79 B8
Hutton Borders 122 D5
Cumb 99 B6
Essex 42 E2
E Yorks 97 D6
Lancs 86 B2
N Som 22 D5
Hutton Buscel 103 F7
Hutton Conyers 95 B6
Hutton Cranswick 97 D6
Hutton End 108 F4
Hutton Gate 102 C3
Hutton Henry 111 F7
Hutton-le-Hole 103 E5
Hutton Magna 101 C6
Hutton Roof Cumb 93 B5
Cumb 108 F3
Hutton Rudby 102 D2
Hutton Sessay 95 B7
Hutton Village 102 C3
Hutton Wandesley 95 D8
Huxley 74 C2
Huxter Shetland 160 G7
Shetland 160 H5
Huxton 122 C4
Huyton 86 E2
Hwlffordd = Haverfordwest 44 D4
Hycemoor 98 F2
Hyde Glos 37 D5
Gtr Man 87 E7
Hants 14 C2
Hyde Heath 40 D2
Hyde Park 89 D6
Hydestile 27 E7
Hylton Castle 111 D6
Hyndford Bridge 120 E2
Hynish 146 H2
Hyssington 60 E3
Hythe Hants 14 D5
Kent 19 B8
Hythe End 27 B8
Hythie 153 C10

I

Ibberton 13 D5
Ible 76 D2
Ibsley 14 D2
Ibstock 63 C8
Ibstone 39 E7
Ibthorpe 25 D8
Ibworth 26 D3
Ichrachan 125 B6
Ickburgh 67 E8
Ickenham 40 F3
Ickford 39 D6
Ickham 31 D6
Ickleford 54 F2
Icklesham 19 D5
Ickleton 55 E5
Icklingham 55 B8
Ickwell Green 54 E2
Icomb 38 B2
Idbury 38 C2
Iddesleigh 9 D7
Ide 10 E3
Ideford 7 B6
Ide Hill 29 D5
Iden 19 C6
Iden Green Kent 18 B4
Kent 18 B5
Idle 94 F4
Idlicote 51 E7
Idmiston 25 F6
Idole 33 C5
Idridgehay 76 E2
Idrigill 149 B8
Idstone 38 F2
Idvies 135 E5
Iffley 39 D5
Ifield 28 F3
Ifold 27 F8
Iford 17 D8
Ifton Heath 73 F7
Ightfield 74 F2
Ightham 29 D6
Iken 57 D8
Ilam 75 D8
Ilchester 12 B3
Ilderton 117 B6
Ilford 41 F7
Ilfracombe 20 E4
Ilkeston 76 E4
Ilketshall St Andrew 69 F6
Ilketshall St Lawrence 69 F6
Ilketshall St Margaret 69 F6
Ilkley 94 E4
Illey 62 F3
Illingworth 87 B8
Illogan 3 B5
Illston on the Hill 64 E4
Ilmer 39 D7
Ilmington 51 E7
Ilminster 11 C8
Ilsington 7 B5
Ilston 33 E6
Ilton N Yorks 94 B4
Som 11 C8
Imachar 143 D9
Imeraval 142 D4
Immingham 91 C5
Impington 54 C5
Ince 73 B8
Ince Blundell 85 D4
Ince in Makerfield 86 D3
Inchbare 135 C6
Inchberry 152 C3
Inchbraoch 135 D7
Incheril 150 E3
Inchgrundle 134 B4
Inchina 150 B2
Inchinnan 118 C4
Inchkinloch 157 E8
Inchlaggan 136 D4
Inchlumpie 151 D8
Inchmore 150 G6
Inchnacardoch Hotel 137 C6
Inchnadamph 156 G5
Inch of Arnhall 135 B6
Inchree 130 C4
Inchture 128 B4
Inchyra 128 B3
Indian Queens 4 D4
Inerval 142 D4
Ingatestone 42 E2
Ingbirchworth 88 D3
Ingestre 62 B3
Ingham Lincs 90 F3
Norf 69 B6
Suff 56 B2
Ingham Corner 69 B6
Ingleborough 66 C4
Ingleby Derbys 63 B7
Lincs 77 B8
Ingleby Arncliffe 102 D2
Ingleby Barwick 102 C2
Ingleby Greenhow 102 D3
Inglemire 97 F6
Inglesbatch 24 C2
Inglesham 38 E2
Ingleton Durham 101 B6
N Yorks 93 B6
Inglewhite 92 E5
Ingliston 120 B4
Ingoe 110 B3
Ingol 92 F5
Ingoldisthorpe 80 D2
Ingoldmells 79 C8
Ingoldsby 78 F3
Ingon 51 D7
Ingram 117 C6
Ingrow 94 F3
Ings 99 E6
Ingst 36 F2
Ingworth 81 E7
Inham's End 66 E2
Inkberrow 50 D5
Inkpen 25 C8
Inkstack 158 C4
Inn 99 D6
Innellan 145 F10
Innerleithen 121 F6
Innerleven 129 D5
Innermessan 104 C4
Innerwick E Loth 122 B3
Perth 132 E2
Innis Chonain 125 C7
Insch 140 B5
Insh 138 D4
Inshore 156 C6
Inskip 92 F4
Instoneville 89 C6
Instow 20 F3
Intake 89 D6
Inver Aberds 139 E8
Highld 151 C11
Perth 133 E7
Inverailort 147 C10
Inveraldie 134 F4
Inveralligin 149 C13
Inverallochy 153 B10
Inveran 151 B8
Inveraray 125 E6
Inverarish 149 E10
Inverarity 134 E4
Inverarnan 126 C2
Inverasdale 155 J13
Inverbeg 126 E2
Inverbervie 135 B8
Inverboyndie 153 B6
Inverbroom 150 C4
Invercassley 156 J7
Invercauld House 139 E7
Inverchaolain 145 F9
Invercharnan 131 E5
Inverchoran 150 F5
Invercreran 130 E4
Inverdruie 138 C5
Inverebrie 153 E9
Invereck 145 E10
Inverernan House 140 C2
Invereshie House 138 D4
Inveresk 121 B6
Inverey 139 F6
Inverfarigaig 137 B8
Invergarry 137 D6
Invergelder 139 E8
Invergeldie 127 B6
Invergordon 151 E10
Invergowrie 134 F3
Inverguseran 149 H12
Inverhadden 132 D3
Inverharroch 152 E3
Inverherive 126 B2
Inverie 147 B10
Inverinan 125 D5
Inverinate 136 B2
Inverkeilor 135 E6
Inverkeithing 128 F3
Inverkeithny 153 D6
Inverkip 118 B2
Inverkirkaig 156 H3
Inverlael 150 C4
Inverlochlarig 126 C3
Inverlochy Argyll 125 C7
Highld 131 B5
Inverlussa 144 E5
Inver Mallie 136 F4
Invermark Lodge 140 F3
Invermoidart 147 D9
Invermoriston 137 C7
Invernaver 157 C10
Inverneill 145 E7
Inverness 151 G9
Invernettie 153 D11
Invernoaden 125 F7
Inveroran Hotel 131 E6
Inverpolly Lodge 156 H3
Inverquharity 134 D4
Inverquhomery 153 D10
Inverroy 137 F5
Inversanda 130 D3
Invershiel 136 C2
Invershin 151 B8
Inversnaid Hotel 126 D2
Inverugie 153 D11
Inveruglas 126 D2
Inveruglass 138 D4
Inverurie 141 B6
Invervar 132 E3
Inverythan 153 D7
Inwardleigh 9 E7
Inworth 42 C4
Iochdar 148 D2
Iping 16 B2
Ipplepen 7 C6
Ipsden 39 F6
Ipsley 51 C5
Ipstones 75 D7
Ipswich 57 E5
Irby 85 F3
Irby in the Marsh 79 C7
Irby upon Humber 91 D5
Irchester 53 C7
Ireby Cumb 108 F2
Lancs 93 B6
Ireland Orkney 159 H4
Shetland 160 L5
Ireland's Cross 74 E4
Ireleth 92 B2
Ireshopeburn 109 F8
Irlam 86 E5
Irnham 65 B7
Iron Acton 36 F3
Ironbridge 61 D6
Iron Cross 51 D5
Irongray 107 B6
Ironmacannie 106 B3
Ironside 153 C8
Ironville 76 D4
Irstead 69 B6
Irthington 108 C4
Irthlingborough 53 B7
Irton 103 F8
Irvine 118 F3
Isauld 157 C12
Isbister Orkney 159 F3
Orkney 159 G4
Shetland 160 D5
Shetland 160 G7
Isfield 17 C8
Isham 53 B6
Isle Abbotts 11 B8
Isle Brewers 11 B8
Isleham 55 B7
Isle of Whithorn 105 F8
Isleornsay 149 G12
Islesburgh 160 G5
Islesteps 107 B6
Isleworth 28 B2
Isley Walton 63 B8
Islibhig 154 E4
Islington 41 F6
Islip N Nhants 53 B7
Oxon 39 C5
Istead Rise 29 C7
Isycoed 73 D8
Itchen 14 C5
Itchen Abbas 26 F3
Itchen Stoke 26 F3
Itchingfield 16 B5
Itchington 36 F3
Itteringham 81 D7
Itton 9 E8
Itton Common 36 E1
Ivegill 108 E4
Iver 40 F3
Iver Heath 40 F3
Iveston 110 D4
Ivinghoe 40 C2
Ivinghoe Aston 40 C2
Ivington 49 D6
Ivington Green 49 D6
Ivybridge 6 D4
Ivy Chimneys 41 D7
Ivychurch 19 C7
Ivy Cross 13 B6
Ivy Hatch 29 D6
Iwade 30 C3
Iwerne Courtney or Shroton 13 C6
Iwerne Minster 13 C6
Ixworth 56 B3
Ixworth Thorpe 56 B3

J

Jack Hill 94 D5
Jack in the Green 10 E5
Jacksdale 76 D4
Jackstown 153 E7
Jacobstow 8 E3
Jacobstowe 9 D7
Jameston 32 E1
Jamestown Dumfries 115 E6
Highld 150 F7
W Dunb 126 F2
Jarrow 111 C6
Jarvis Brook 18 C2
Jasper's Green 42 B3
Java 124 B3
Jawcraig 119 B8
Jaywick 43 C7
Jealott's Hill 27 B6
Jedburgh 116 B2
Jeffreyston 32 D1
Jellyhill 119 B6
Jemimaville 151 E10
Jersey Farm 40 D4
Jesmond 111 C5
Jevington 18 E2
Jockey End 40 C3
Johnby 108 F4
John o'Groats 158 C5
John's Cross 18 C4
Johnshaven 135 C7
Johnston E Renfs 118 C4
Pembs 44 D4
Johnstonebridge 114 E3
Johnstown Carms 33 C5
Wrex 73 E7
Joppa Edin 121 B6
S Ayrs 112 C4
Jordans 40 E2
Jordanthorpe 88 F4
Jump 88 D4
Jumpers Green 14 E2
Juniper Green 120 C4
Jurby East 84 C3
Jurby West 84 C3

K

Kaber 100 C2
Kaimend 120 E2
Kaimes 121 C5
Kalemouth 116 B3
Kames Argyll 124 D4
Argyll 145 F8
E Ayrs 113 B6
Kea 3 B7
Keadby 90 C2
Keal Cotes 79 C6
Kearsley 87 D5
Kearstwick 99 F8
Kearton 100 E4
Kearvaig 156 B5
Keasden 93 C7
Keckwick 86 F3
Keddington 91 F7
Kedington 55 E8
Kedleston 76 E3
Keelby 91 C5
Keele 74 E5
Keeley Green 53 E8
Keeston 44 D4
Keevil 24 D4
Kegworth 63 B8
Kehelland 2 B5
Keig 140 C5
Keighley 94 E3
Keil 130 D3
Keilarsbrae 127 E7
Keilhill 153 C7
Keillmore 144 E5
Keillor 134 E2
Keillour 127 B8
Keills 142 B5
Keils 144 G4
Keinton Mandeville 23 F7
Keir Mill 113 E8
Keisby 65 B7
Keiss 158 D5
Keith 152 C4
Keith Inch 153 D11
Keithock 135 C6
Kelbrook 94 E2
Kelby 78 E3
Keld Cumb 99 C7
N Yorks 100 D3
Keldholme 103 F5
Kelfield N Lincs 90 D2
N Yorks 95 F8
Kelham 77 D7
Kellan 147 G8
Kellas Angus 134 F4
Moray 152 C1
Kellaton 7 F6
Kelleth 100 D1
Kelleythorpe 97 D5
Kelling 81 C6
Kellingley 89 B6
Kellington 89 B6
Kelloe 111 F6
Kelloholm 113 C7
Kelly 9 F5
Kelly Bray 5 B8
Kelmarsh 52 B5
Kelmscot 38 E2
Kelsale 57 C7
Kelsall 74 C2
Kelsall Hill 74 C2
Kelshall 54 F4
Kelsick 107 D8
Kelso 122 F3
Kelstedge 76 C3
Kelstern 91 E6
Kelston 24 C2
Keltneyburn 132 E4
Kelton 107 B6
Kelty 128 E3
Kelvedon 42 C4
Kelvedon Hatch 42 E1
Kelvin 119 D6
Kelvinside 119 C5
Kelynack 2 C2
Kemback 129 C6
Kemberton 61 D7
Kemble 37 E6
Kemerton 50 F4
Kemeys Commander 35 D7
Kemnay 141 C6
Kempley 36 B3
Kempsey 50 E3
Kempsford 38 E1
Kemps Green 51 B6
Kempshott 26 D4
Kempston 53 E8
Kempston Hardwick 53 E8
Kempton 60 F3
Kemp Town 17 D7
Kemsing 29 D6
Kemsley 30 C3
Kenardington 19 B6
Kenchester 49 E6
Kencot 38 D2
Kendal 99 E7
Kendoon 113 F6
Kendray 88 D4
Kenfig 34 F2
Kenfig Hill 34 F2
Kenilworth 51 B7
Kenknock 132 F1
Kenley London 28 D4
Shrops 61 D5
Kenmore Highld 149 C12
Perth 132 E4
Kenn Devon 10 F4
N Som 23 C6
Kennacley 154 H6
Kennacraig 145 G7
Kennerleigh 10 D3
Kennet 127 E8
Kennethmont 140 B4
Kennett 55 C7
Kennford 10 F4
Kenninghall 68 F3
Kenninghall Heath 68 F3
Kennington Kent 30 E4
Oxon 39 D5
Kennoway 129 D5
Kenny Hill 55 B7
Kennythorpe 96 C3
Kenovay 146 G2
Kensaleyre 149 C9
Kensington 28 B3
Kensworth 40 C3
Kensworth Common 40 C3
Kentallen 130 D4
Kentchurch 35 B8
Kentford 55 C8
Kentisbeare 11 D5
Kentisbury 20 E5
Kentisbury Ford 20 E5
Kentmere 99 D6
Kenton Devon 10 F4
Suff 57 C5
T&W 110 C5
Kenton Bankfoot 110 C5
Kentra 147 E9
Kents Bank 92 B3
Kent's Green 36 B4
Kent's Oak 14 B4
Kent Street E Sus 18 D4
Kent 29 D7
W Sus 17 B6
Kenwick 73 F8
Kenwyn 3 B7
Keoldale 156 C6
Keppanach 130 C4
Keppoch 136 B2
Keprigan 143 G7
Kepwick 102 E2
Kerchesters 122 F3
Keresley 63 F7
Kernborough 7 E5
Kerne Bridge 36 C2
Kerris 2 D3
Kerry 59 F8
Kerrycroy 145 G10
Kerrysdale 149 A13
Kerry's Gate 49 F5
Kersall 77 C7
Kersey 56 E4
Kershopefoot 115 F7
Kersoe 50 F4
Kerswell 11 D5
Kerswell Green 50 E3
Kesgrave 57 E6
Kessingland 69 F8
Kessingland Beach 69 F8
Kessington 119 B5
Kestle 3 B8
Kestle Mill 4 D3
Keston 28 C5
Keswick Cumb 98 B4
Norf 68 D5
Norf 81 D9
Ketley 61 C6
Ketley Bank 61 C6
Ketsby 79 B6
Kettering 53 B6
Ketteringham 68 D4
Kettins 134 F2
Kettlebaston 56 D3
Kettlebridge 128 D5
Kettleburgh 57 C6
Kettlehill 128 D5
Kettleholm 107 B8
Kettleness 103 C6
Kettleshume 75 B6
Kettlesing Bottom 94 D5
Kettlesing Head 94 D5
Kettlestone 81 D5
Kettlethorpe 77 B8
Kettletoft 159 E7
Kettlewell 94 B2
Ketton 65 D6
Kew 28 B2
Kew Bridge 28 B2
Kewstoke 22 C5
Kexbrough 88 D4
Kexby Lincs 90 F2
York 96 D3
Key Green 75 C5
Keyham 64 D3
Keyhaven 14 E4
Keyingham 91 B6
Keymer 17 C7
Keynsham 23 C8
Keysoe 53 C8
Keysoe Row 53 C8
Keyston 53 B8
Keyworth 77 F6
Kibblesworth 110 D5
Kibworth Beauchamp 64 E3
Kibworth Harcourt 64 E3
Kidbrooke 28 B5
Kiddemore Green 62 D2
Kidderminster 50 B3
Kiddington 38 B4
Kidlington 38 C4
Kidmore End 26 B4
Kidsgrove 74 D5
Kidstones 100 F4
Kidwelly = Cydweli 33 D5
Kiel Crofts 124 B5
Kielder 116 E2
Kierfiold Ho 159 G3
Kilbagie 127 F8
Kilbarchan 118 C4
Kilbeg 149 H11
Kilberry 144 G6
Kilbirnie 118 D3
Kilbride Argyll 124 C4
Argyll 124 C5
Highld 149 F10
Kilburn Angus 134 C3
Derbys 76 E3
London 41 F5
N Yorks 95 B8
Kilby 64 E3
Kilchamaig 145 G7
Kilchattan 144 D2
Kilchattan Bay 145 H10
Kilchenzie 143 F7
Kilcheran 124 B4
Kilchiaran 142 B3
Kilchoan Argyll 124 D3
Highld 146 E7
Kilchoman 142 B3
Kilchrenan 125 C6
Kilconquhar 129 D6
Kilcot 36 B3
Kilcoy 151 F8
Kilcreggan 145 E11
Kildale 102 D4
Kildalloig 143 G8
Kildary 151 D10
Kildermorie Lodge 151 D8
Kildonan 143 F11
Kildonan Lodge 157 G12
Kildonnan 146 C7
Kildrummy 140 C3
Kildwick 94 E3
Kilfinan 145 F8
Kilfinnan 137 E5
Kilgetty 32 D2
Kilgwrrwg Common 36 E1
Kilham E Yorks 97 C6
Northumb 122 F4
Kilkenneth 146 G2
Kilkerran 143 G8
Kilkhampton 9 E6
Killamarsh 89 F5
Killay 33 E7
Killbeg 147 G9
Killean 143 D7
Killearn 126 F4
Killen 151 F9
Killerby 101 C6
Killichonan 132 D2
Killiechonate 136 F5
Killiechronan 147 G8
Killiecrankie 133 C6
Killiemor 146 H7
Killiemore House 146 J7
Killilan 150 H2
Killimster 158 E5
Killin 132 F2
Killinallan 142 A4
Killinghall 95 D5
Killington 99 F8
Killingworth 111 B5
Killin Lodge 137 D8
Killmahumaig 144 D6
Killochyett 121 E7
Killocraw 143 E7
Killundine 147 G8
Kilmacolm 118 C3
Kilmaha 124 E5
Kilmahog 126 D5
Kilmalieu 130 D2
Kilmaluag 149 A9
Kilmany 129 B5
Kilmarie 149 G10
Kilmarnock 118 F4
Kilmaron Castle 129 C5
Kilmartin 124 F4
Kilmaurs 118 E4
Kilmelford 124 D4
Kilmeny 142 B4
Kilmersdon 23 D8
Kilmeston 15 B6
Kilmichael 143 F7
Kilmichael Glassary 145 D7
Kilmichael of Inverlussa 144 E6
Kilmington Devon 11 E7
Wilts 24 F2
Kilmonivaig 136 F4
Kilmorack 150 G7
Kilmore Argyll 124 C4
Highld 149 H11
Kilmory Argyll 144 F6
Highld 147 D8
Highld 149 H8
N Ayrs 143 F10
Kilmuir Highld 148 D7
Highld 149 A8
Highld 151 D10
Highld 151 G9
Kilmun Argyll 124 D5
Argyll 145 E10
Kilncadzow 119 E8
Kilndown 18 B4
Kilnhurst 89 E5
Kilninian 146 G6
Kilninver 124 C4
Kiln Pit Hill 110 D3
Kilnsea 91 C8
Kilnsey 94 C2
Kilnwick 97 E5
Kilnwick Percy 96 D4
Kiloran 144 D2
Kilpatrick 143 F10
Kilpeck 49 F6
Kilphedir 157 H12
Kilpin 89 B8
Kilpin Pike 89 B8
Kilrenny 129 D7
Kilsby 52 B3
Kilspindie 128 B4
Kilsyth 119 B7
Kiltarlity 151 G8
Kilton Notts 77 B5
Som 22 E3
Kilton Thorpe 102 C4
Kilvaxter 149 B8
Kilve 22 E3
Kilvington 77 E7
Kilwinning 118 E3
Kimberley Norf 68 D3
Notts 76 E5
Kimberworth 88 E5
Kimblesworth 111 E5
Kimble Wick 39 D8
Kimbolton Cambs 53 C8
Hereford 49 C7
Kimcote 64 F2
Kimmeridge 13 G7
Kimmerston 123 F5
Kimpton Hants 25 E7
Herts 40 C4
Kinbrace 157 F11
Kinbuck 127 D6
Kincaple 129 C6
Kincardine Fife 127 F8
Highld 151 C9
Kincardine Bridge 127 F8
Kincardine O'Neil 140 E4
Kinclaven 134 F1
Kincorth 141 D8
Kincorth House 151 E13
Kincraig 138 D4
Kincraigie 133 E6
Kindallachan 133 E6
Kineton Glos 37 B7
Warks 51 D8
Kinfauns 128 B3
Kingairloch 130 D2
Kingarth 145 H9
Kingcoed 35 D8
King Edward 153 C7
Kingerby 90 E4
Kingham 38 B2
Kingholm Quay 107 B6
Kinghorn 128 F4
Kingie 136 D4
Kinglassie 128 E4
Kingoodie 128 B5
King's Acre 49 E6
Kingsand 6 D2
Kingsbarns 129 C7
Kingsbridge Devon 6 E5
Som 21 F8
King's Bromley 62 C5
Kingsburgh 149 C8
Kingsbury London 41 F5
Warks 63 E6
Kingsbury Episcopi 12 B2
King's Caple 36 B2
Kingsclere 26 D3
King's Cliffe 65 E7
Kingscote 37 E5
Kingscott 9 C7
King's Coughton 51 D5
Kingscross 143 F11
Kingsdon 12 B3
Kingsdown 31 E7
Kingseat 128 E3
Kingsey 39 D7
Kingsfold 28 F2
Kingsford E Ayrs 118 E4
Worcs 62 F2
Kingsforth 90 C4
Kingsgate 31 B7
Kingsheanton 20 F4
King's Heath 62 F4
Kings Hedges 55 C5
King's Hill 29 D7
Kingshouse Hotel 131 D6
Kingside Hill 107 D8
Kingskerswell 7 C6
Kingskettle 128 D5
Kingsland Anglesey 82 C2

Kingsland *continued*
Hereford 49 C6
Kings Langley 40 D3
Kingsley Ches W 74 B2
Hants 27 F5
Staffs 75 E7
Kingsley Green 27 F6
Kingsley Holt 75 E7
Kingsley Park 53 C5
King's Lynn 67 B6
King's Meaburn 99 B8
King's Mills 73 E7
Kingsmuir Angus 134 E4
Fife 129 D7
Kings Muir 121 F5
King's Newnham 52 B2
King's Newton 63 B7
Kingsnorth 19 B7
King's Norton Leics 64 D3
W Mid 51 B5
King's Nympton 9 C8
King's Pyon 49 D6
King's Ripton 54 B3
King's Somborne 25 F8
King's Stag 12 C5
King's Stanley 37 D5
King's Sutton 52 F2
Kingstanding 62 E4
Kingsteignton 7 B6
King Sterndale 75 B7
King's Thorn 49 F7
Kingsthorpe 53 C5
Kingston Cambs 54 D4
Devon 6 E4
Dorset 13 D5
Dorset 13 G7
E Loth 129 F7
Hants 14 D2
IoW 15 F5
Kent 31 D5
Moray 152 B3
Kingston Bagpuize 38 E4
Kingston Blount 39 E7
Kingston by Sea 17 D6
Kingston Deverill 24 F3
Kingstone Hereford 49 F6
Som 11 C8
Staffs 62 B4
Kingston Gorse 16 D4
Kingston Lisle 38 F3
Kingston
Maurward 12 E5
Kingston near
Lewes 17 D7
Kingston on Soar 64 B2
Kingston Russell 12 E3
Kingston St Mary 11 B7
Kingston Seymour 23 C6
Kingston upon
Hull 90 B4
Kingston upon
Thames 28 C2
Kingston Vale 28 B3
Kingstown 108 D3
King's Walden 40 B4
Kingswear 7 D6
Kingswells 141 D7
Kingswinford 62 F2
Kingswood Bucks 39 C6
Glos 36 E4
Hereford 48 D4
Kent 30 D2
Powys 60 D2
S Glos 23 B8
Sur 28 D3
Warks 51 B6
Kings Worthy 26 F2
Kingthorpe 78 B4
Kington Hereford 48 D4
Worcs 50 D4
Kington Langley 24 B4
Kington Magna 13 B5
Kington
St Michael 24 B4
Kingussie 138 D3
Kingweston 23 F7
Kininvie House 152 D3
Kinkell Bridge 127 C8
Kinknockie 153 D10
Kinlet 61 F7
Kinloch Fife 128 C4
Highld 146 B6
Highld 149 G11
Highld 156 F6
Perth 133 E8
Perth 134 E2
Kinlochan 130 C2
Kinlochard 126 D3
Kinlochbeoraid 147 C11
Kinlochbervie 156 D5
Kinlocheil 130 B3
Kinlochewe 150 E3
Kinloch Hourn 136 D2
Kinloch Laggan 137 F8
Kinlochleven 131 C5
Kinloch Lodge 157 D8
Kinlochmoidart 147 D10
Kinlochmorar 147 B11
Kinlochmore 131 C5
Kinloch Rannoch 132 D3
Kinlochspelve 124 C2
Kinloid 147 C9
Kinloss 151 E13
Kinmel Bay 72 A3
Kinmuck 141 C7
Kinmundy 141 C7
Kinnadie 153 D9
Kinnaird 128 B4
Kinnaird Castle 135 D6
Kinneff 135 B8
Kinnelhead 114 D3
Kinnell 135 D6
Kinnerley 60 B3
Kinnersley Hereford 48 E5
Worcs 50 E3
Kinnerton 48 C4
Kinnesswood 128 D3
Kinninvie 101 B5
Kinnordy 134 D3
Kinoulton 77 F6
Kinross 128 D3
Kinrossie 134 F1
Kinsbourne Green 40 C4
Kinsey Heath 74 E3
Kinsham Hereford 49 C5
Worcs 50 F4
Kinsley 88 C5
Kinson 13 E8
Kintbury 25 C8
Kintessack 151 E12
Kintillo 128 C3
Kintocher 140 D4
Kinton Hereford 49 B6
Shrops 60 C3
Kintore 141 C6
Kintour 142 C5
Kintra Argyll 142 D4
Argyll 146 J6
Kintraw 124 E4
Kinuachdrachd 124 F3
Kinveachy 138 C5
Kinver 62 F2
Kippax 95 F7
Kippen 127 E5
Kippford or
Scaur 106 D5
Kirbister Orkney 159 F7
Orkney 159 H4
Kirbuster 159 F3
Kirby Bedon 69 D5
Kirby Bellars 64 C4
Kirby Cane 69 E6
Kirby Cross 43 B8
Kirby Grindalythe 96 C5
Kirby Hill N Yorks 95 C6
N Yorks 101 D6
Kirby Knowle 102 F2
Kirby-le-Soken 43 B8
Kirby Misperton 96 B3
Kirby Muxloe 64 D2
Kirby Row 69 E6
Kirby Sigston 102 E2
Kirby Underdale 96 D4
Kirby Wiske 102 F1
Kirdford 16 B4
Kirk 158 E4
Kirkabister 160 K6
Kirkandrews 106 E3
Kirkandrews upon
Eden 108 D3
Kirkbampton 108 D3
Kirkbean 107 D6
Kirk Bramwith 89 C7
Kirkbride 108 D2
Kirkbuddo 135 E5
Kirkburn Borders 121 F5
E Yorks 97 D5
Kirkburton 88 C2
Kirkby Lincs 90 E4
Mers 86 E2
N Yorks 102 D3
Kirkby Fleetham 101 E7
Kirkby Green 78 D3
Kirkby-in-Ashfield 76 D5
Kirkby-in-Furness 98 F4
Kirkby la Thorpe 78 E3
Kirkby Lonsdale 93 B6
Kirkby Malham 93 C8
Kirkby Mallory 63 D8
Kirkby Malzeard 94 B5
Kirkby Mills 103 F5
Kirkbymoorside 102 F4
Kirkby on Bain 78 C5
Kirkby Overflow 95 E6
Kirkby Stephen 100 D2
Kirkby Thore 99 B8
Kirkby Underwood 65 B7
Kirkby Wharfe 95 E8
Kirkcaldy 128 E4
Kirkcambeck 108 C5
Kirkcarswell 106 E4
Kirkcolm 104 C4
Kirkconnel 113 C7
Kirkconnell 107 C6
Kirkcowan 105 C7
Kirkcudbright 106 D3
Kirkdale 85 E4
Kirk Deighton 95 D6
Kirk Ella 90 B4
Kirkfieldbank 119 E8
Kirkgunzeon 107 C5
Kirk Hallam 76 E4
Kirkham Lancs 92 F4
N Yorks 96 C3
Kirkhamgate 88 B3
Kirk Hammerton 95 D7
Kirkharle 117 F6
Kirkheaton
Northumb 110 B3
W Yorks 88 C2
Kirkhill Angus 135 C6
Highld 151 G8
Midloth 120 C5
Moray 152 E2
Kirkhope 115 B6
Kirkhouse 121 F6
Kirkiboll 157 D8
Kirkibost 149 G10
Kirkinch 134 E3
Kirkinner 105 D8
Kirkintilloch 119 B6
Kirk Ireton 76 D2
Kirkland Cumb 98 C2
Cumb 109 F6
Dumfries 113 C7
Dumfries 113 E8
Kirk Langley 76 F2
Kirkleatham 102 B3
Kirklevington 102 D2
Kirkley 69 E8
Kirklington Notts 77 D6
N Yorks 101 F8
Kirklinton 108 C4
Kirkliston 120 B4
Kirkmaiden 104 F5
Kirk Merrington 111 F5
Kirkmichael Perth 133 D7
S Ayrs 112 D3
Kirk Michael 84 C3
Kirkmuirhill 119 E7
Kirknewton
Northumb 122 F5
W Loth 120 C4
Kirkney 152 E5
Kirk of Shotts 119 C8
Kirkoswald Cumb 109 E5
S Ayrs 112 D2
Kirkpatrick
Durham 106 B4
Kirkpatrick-
Fleming 108 B2
Kirk Sandall 89 D7
Kirksanton 98 F3
Kirk Smeaton 89 C6
Kirkstall 95 F5
Kirkstead 78 C4
Kirkstile 152 E5
Kirkstyle 158 C5
Kirkton Aberds 140 B5
Aberds 153 D6
Angus 134 E4
Angus 134 F4
Borders 115 C8
Dumfries 114 F2
Fife 129 B5
Highld 149 F13
Highld 150 G2
Highld 151 B10
Highld 151 F10
Perth 127 C8
S Lanark 114 B2
Stirling 126 D4
Kirktonhill 121 D7
Kirkton Manor 120 F5
Kirkton of Airlie 134 D3
Kirkton of
Auchterhouse 134 F3
Kirkton of
Auchterless 153 D7
Kirkton of
Barevan 151 G11
Kirkton of
Bourtie 141 B7
Kirkton of
Collace 134 F1
Kirkton of Craig 135 D7
Kirkton of
Culsalmond 153 E6
Kirkton of Durris 141 E6
Kirkton of
Glenbuchat 140 C2
Kirkton of
Glenisla 134 C2
Kirkton of
Kingoldrum 134 D3
Kirkton of Largo 129 D6
Kirkton of
Lethendy 133 E8
Kirkton of Logie
Buchan 141 B8
Kirkton of
Maryculter 141 E7
Kirkton of
Menmuir 135 C5
Kirkton of
Monikie 135 F5
Kirkton of Oyne 141 B5
Kirkton of Rayne 153 F6
Kirkton of Skene 141 D7
Kirkton of Tough 140 C5
Kirktown 153 C10
Kirktown of
Alvah 153 B6
Kirktown of
Deskford 152 B5
Kirktown of
Fetteresso 141 F7
Kirktown of
Mortlach 152 E3
Kirktown of
Slains 141 B9
Kirkurd 120 E4
Kirkwall 159 G5
Kirkwhelpington 117 F5
Kirk Yetholm 116 B4
Kirmington 90 C5
Kirmond le Mire 91 E5
Kirn 145 F10
Kirriemuir 134 D3
Kirstead Green 69 E5
Kirtlebridge 108 B2
Kirtleton 115 F5
Kirtling 55 D7
Kirtling Green 55 D7
Kirtlington 38 C4
Kirtomy 157 C10
Kirton Lincs 79 F6
Notts 77 C6
Suff 57 F6
Kirton End 79 E5
Kirton Holme 79 E5
Kirton in Lindsey 90 E3
Kislingbury 52 D4
Kites Hardwick 52 C2
Kittisford 11 B5
Kittle 33 F6
Kitt's Green 63 F5
Kitt's Moss 87 F6
Kittybrewster 141 D8
Kitwood 26 F4
Kivernoll 49 F6
Kiveton Park 89 F5
Knaith 90 F2
Knaith Park 90 F2
Knap Corner 13 B6
Knaphill 27 D7
Knapp Perth 134 F2
Som 11 B8
Knapthorpe 77 D7
Knapton Norf 81 D9
York 95 D8
Knapton Green 49 D6
Knapwell 54 C4
Knaresborough 95 D6
Knarsdale 109 D6
Knauchland 152 C5
Knaven 153 D8
Knayton 102 F2
Knebworth 41 B5
Knedlington 89 B8
Kneesall 77 C7
Kneesworth 54 E4
Kneeton 77 E7
Knelston 33 F5
Knenhall 75 F6
Knettishall 68 F2
Knightacott 21 F5
Knightcote 51 D8
Knightley Dale 62 B2
Knighton Devon 6 E3
Leicester 64 D2
Staffs 61 B7
Staffs 74 E4
Knighton
= *Tref-y-Clawdd* 48 B4
Knightswood 118 C5
Knightwick 50 D2
Knill 48 C4
Knipton 77 F8
Knitsley 110 E4
Kniveton 76 D2
Knock Argyll 147 H8
Cumb 100 B1
Moray 152 C5
Knockally 158 H3
Knockan 156 H5
Knockandhu 139 B8
Knockando 152 D1
Knockando
House 152 D2
Knockbain 151 F9
Knockbreck 148 B7
Knockbrex 106 E2
Knockdee 158 D3
Knockdolian 104 A5
Knockenkelly 143 F11
Knockentiber 118 F3
Knockespock
House 140 B4
Knockfarrel 151 F8
Knockglass 104 D4
Knockholt 29 D5
Knockholt Pound 29 D5
Knockie Lodge 137 C7
Knockin 60 B3
Knockinlaw 118 F4
Knocklearn 106 B4
Knocknaha 143 G7
Knocknain 104 C3
Knockrome 144 F4
Knocksharry 84 D2
Knodishall 57 C8
Knolls Green 74 B5
Knolton 73 F7
Knolton Bryn 73 F7
Knook 24 E4
Knossington 64 D5
Knott End-on-Sea 92 E3
Knotting 53 C8
Knotting Green 53 C8
Knottingley 89 B6
Knotts Cumb 99 B6
Lancs 93 D7
Knotty Ash 86 E2
Knotty Green 40 E2
Knowbury 49 B7
Knowe 105 B7
Knowehead 113 E6
Knowesgate 117 F5
Knowes of Elrick 152 C6
Knoweton 119 D7
Knowhead 153 C9
Knowle Bristol 23 B8
Devon 10 D2
Devon 11 F5
Devon 20 F3
Shrops 49 B7
W Mid 51 B6
Knowle Green 93 F6
Knowle Park 94 E3
Knowl Hill 27 B6
Knowlton Dorset 13 C8
Kent 31 D6
Knowsley 86 E2
Knowstone 10 B3
Knox Bridge 29 E8
Knucklas 48 B4
Knuston 53 C7
Knutsford 74 B4
Knutton 74 E5
Knypersley 75 D5
Kuggar 3 E6
Kyleakin 149 F12
Kyle of Lochalsh 149 F12
Kylerhea 149 F12
Kylesknoydart 147 B11
Kylesku 156 F5
Kylesmorar 147 B11
Kylestrome 156 F5
Kyllachy House 138 B3
Kynaston 60 B3
Kynnersley 61 C6
Kyre Magna 49 C8

L

Labost 155 C7
Lacasaidh 155 E8
Lacasdal 155 D9
Laceby 91 D6
Lacey Green 39 E8
Lach Dennis 74 B4
Lackford 55 B8
Lacock 24 C4
Ladbroke 52 D2
Laddingford 29 E7
Lade Bank 79 D6
Ladock 4 D3
Lady 159 D7
Ladybank 128 C5
Ladykirk 122 E4
Ladysford 153 B9
La Fontenelle Guern 16
Laga 147 E9
Lagalochan 124 D4
Lagavulin 142 D5
Lagg Argyll 144 F4
N Ayrs 143 F10
Laggan Argyll 142 C3
Highld 137 E5
Highld 138 E2
Highld 147 D10
S Ayrs 112 F2
Lagganulva 146 G7
Laide 155 H13
Laigh Fenwick 118 E4
Laigh Glengall 112 C3
Laighmuir 118 E4
Laindon 42 F2
Lair 150 G3
Lairg 157 J8
Lairg Lodge 157 J8
Lairgmore 151 H8
Lairg Muir 157 J8
Laisterdyke 94 F4
Laithes 108 F4
Lake IoW 15 F6
Wilts 25 F6
Lakenham 68 D5
Lakenheath 67 F7
Lakesend 66 E5
Lakeside 99 F5
Laleham 27 C8
Laleston 21 B7
Lamarsh 56 F2
Lamas 81 E8
Lambden 122 E3
Lamberhurst 18 B3
Lamberhurst
Quarter 18 B3
Lamberton 123 D5
Lambeth 28 B4
Lambhill 119 C5
Lambley Northumb 109 D6
Notts 77 E6
Lamborough Hill 38 D4
Lambourn 25 B8
Lambourne End 41 E7
Lambs Green 28 F3
Lambston 44 D4
Lambton 111 D5
Lamerton 6 B2
Lamesley 111 D5
Laminess 159 E7
Lamington
Highld 151 D10
S Lanark 120 F2
Lamlash 143 E11
Lamloch 112 E5
Lamonby 108 F4
Lamorna 2 D3
Lamorran 3 B7
Lampardbrook 57 C6
Lampeter = *Llanbedr
Pont Steffan* 46 E4
Lampeter Velfrey 32 C2
Lamphey 32 D1
Lamplugh 98 B2
Lamport 53 B5
Lamyatt 23 F8
Lana 8 E5
Lanark 119 E8
Lancaster 92 C4
Lanchester 110 E4
Lancing 17 D5
Landbeach 55 C5
Landcross 9 B6
Landerberry 141 D6
Landford 14 C3
Landford Manor 14 B3
Landimore 33 E5
Landkey 20 F4
Landore 33 E7
Landrake 5 C8
Landscove 7 C5
Landshipping 32 C1
Landshipping
Quay 32 C1
Landulph 6 C2
Landwade 55 C7
Lane 4 C3
Laneast 8 F4
Lane End Bucks 39 E8
Cumb 98 E3
Dorset 13 E6
Hants 15 B6
IoW 15 F7
Lancs 93 E8
Lane Ends Lancs 93 D7
Lancs 93 F7
N Yorks 94 E2
Laneham 77 B8
Lanehead Durham 109 E8
Northumb 116 F3
Lane Head Derbys 75 B8
Durham 101 C6
Gtr Man 86 E4
W Yorks 88 D2
Lanercost 109 C5
Laneshaw Bridge 94 E2
Lane Side 87 B5
Lanfach 35 E6
Langar 77 F7
Langbank 118 B3
Langbar 94 D3
Langburnshiels 115 D8
Langcliffe 93 C8
Langdale 157 E9
Langdale End 103 E7
Langdon 8 F5
Langdon Beck 109 F8
Langdon Hills 42 F2
Langdyke 128 D5
Langenhoe 43 C6
Langford C Beds 54 E2
Devon 10 D5
Essex 42 D4
Notts 77 D8
Oxon 38 D2
Langford Budville 11 B6
Langham Essex 56 F4
Norf 81 C6
Rutland 64 C5
Suff 56 C3
Langhaugh 120 F5
Langho 93 F7
Langholm 115 F6
Langleeford 117 B5
Langley Ches E 75 B6
Hants 14 D5
Herts 41 B5
Kent 30 D2
Northumb 109 C8
Slough 27 B8
Warks 51 C6
W Sus 16 B2
Langley Burrell 24 B4
Langley Common 76 F2
Langley Heath 30 D2
Langley Lower
Green 54 F5
Langley Marsh 11 B5
Langley Park 110 E5
Langley Street 69 D6
Langley Upper
Green 54 F5
Langney 18 E3
Langold 89 F6
Langore 8 F5
Langport 12 B2
Langrick 79 E5
Langridge 24 C2
Langridge Ford 9 B7
Langrigg 107 E8
Langrish 15 B8
Langsett 88 D3
Langshaw 121 F8
Langside 127 C6
Langskaill 159 D5
Langstone Hants 15 D8
Newport 35 E7
Langthorne 101 E7
Langthorpe 95 C6
Langthwaite 101 D5
Langtoft E Yorks 97 C6
Lincs 65 C8
Langton Durham 101 C6
Lincs 78 C5
Lincs 79 B6
N Yorks 96 C3
Langton by
Wragby 78 B4
Langton Green
Kent 18 B2
Langton Green
continued
Suff 56 B5
Langton Herring 12 F4
Langton
Matravers 13 G8
Langtree 9 C6
Langwathby 109 F5
Langwell House 158 H3
Langwell Lodge 156 J4
Langwith 76 C5
Langwith Junction 76 C5
Langworth 78 B3
Lanivet 4 C5
Lanlivery 5 D5
Lanner 3 C6
Lanreath 5 D6
Lansallos 5 D6
Lansdown 37 B6
Lanteglos Highway 5 D6
Lanton Borders 116 B2
Northumb 122 F5
Lapford 10 D2
Laphroaig 142 D4
La Planque Guern 16
Lapley 62 C2
Lapworth 51 B6
Larachbeg 147 G9
Larbert 127 F7
Larden Green 74 D2
Largie 152 E6
Largiemore 145 E8
Largoward 129 D6
Largs 118 D2
Largybeg 143 F11
Largymore 143 F11
Larkfield 118 B2
Larkhall 119 D7
Larkhill 25 E6
Larling 68 F2
Larriston 115 E8
Lartington 101 C5
Lary 140 D2
Lasham 26 E4
Lashenden 30 E2
Lassington 36 B4
Lassodie 128 E3
Lastingham 103 E5
Latcham 23 E6
Latchford Herts 41 B6
Warr 86 F4
Latchingdon 42 D4
Latchley 6 B2
Lately Common 86 E4
Lathbury 53 E6
Latheron 158 G3
Latheronwheel 158 G3
Latheronwheel
House 158 G3
Lathones 129 D6
Latimer 40 E3
Latteridge 36 F3
Lattiford 12 B4
Latton 37 E7
Latton Bush 41 D7
Lauchintilly 141 C6
Lauder 121 E8
Laugharne 32 C4
Laughterton 77 B8
Laughton E Sus 18 D2
Leics 64 F3
Lincs 78 F3
Lincs 90 E2
Laughton Common 89 F6
Laughton en le
Morthen 89 F6
Launcells 8 D4
Launceston 8 F5
Launton 39 B6
Laurencekirk 135 B7
Laurieston
Dumfries 106 C3
Falk 120 B2
Lavendon 53 D7
Lavenham 56 E3
Laverhay 114 E4
Laversdale 108 C4
Laverstock 25 F6
Laverstoke 26 E2
Laverton Glos 51 F5
N Yorks 94 B5
Som 24 D2
Lavister 73 D7
Law 119 D8
Lawers Perth 127 B6
Perth 132 F3
Lawford 56 F4
Lawhitton 9 F5
Lawkland 93 C7
Lawley 61 D6
Lawnhead 62 B2
Lawrenny 32 D1
Lawshall 56 D2
Lawton 49 D6
Laxey 84 D4
Laxfield 57 B6
Laxfirth Shetland 160 H6
Shetland 160 J6
Laxford Bridge 156 E5
Laxo 160 G6
Laxobigging 160 F6
Laxton E Yorks 89 B8
N Nhants 65 E6
Notts 77 C7
Laycock 94 E3
Layer Breton 43 C5
Layer de la Haye 43 C5
Layer Marney 43 C5
Layham 56 E4
Laylands Green 25 C8
Laytham 96 F3
Layton 92 F3
Lazenby 102 B3
Lazonby 108 F5
Lea Derbys 76 D3
Hereford 36 B3
Lincs 90 F2
Shrops 60 D4
Shrops 60 F3
Wilts 37 F6
Leabrooks 76 D4
Leac a Li 154 H6
Leachkin 151 G9
Leadburn 120 D5
Leadenham 78 D2
Leaden Roding 42 C1
Leadgate Cumb 109 E7
Durham 110 D4
T&W 110 D4
Leadhills 113 C8
Leafield 38 C3
Leagrave 40 B3
Leake 102 E2
Leake
Commonside 79 D6
Lealholm 103 D5
Lealt Argyll 144 D5
Highld 149 B10
Lea Marston 63 E6
Leamington
Hastings 52 C2
Leamonsley 62 D5
Leamside 111 E6
Leanaig 151 F8
Leargybreck 144 F4
Leasgill 99 F6
Leasingham 78 E3
Leasingthorne 101 B7
Leasowe 85 E3
Leatherhead 28 D2
Leatherhead
Common 28 D2
Leathley 94 E5
Leaton 60 C4
Lea Town 92 F4
Leaveland 30 D4
Leavening 96 C3
Leaves Green 28 C5
Leazes 110 D4
Lebberston 103 F8
Lechlade-on-
Thames 38 E2
Leck 93 B6
Leckford 25 F8
Leckfurin 157 D10
Leckgruinart 142 B3
Leckhampstead
Bucks 52 F5
W Berks 26 B2
Leckhampstead
Thicket 26 B2
Leckhampton 37 C6
Leckie 150 E3
Leckmelm 150 B4
Leckwith 22 B3
Leconfield 97 E6
Ledaig 124 B5
Ledburn 40 B2
Ledbury 50 F2
Ledcharrie 126 B4
Ledgemoor 49 D6
Ledicot 49 C6
Ledmore 156 H5
Lednagullin 157 C10
Ledsham Ches W 73 B7
W Yorks 89 B5
Ledston 88 B5
Ledston Luck 95 F7
Ledwell 38 B4
Lee Argyll 146 J7
Devon 20 E3
Hants 14 C4
Lancs 93 D5
Shrops 73 F8
Leeans 160 J5
Leebotten 160 L6
Leebotwood 60 E4
Lee Brockhurst 60 B5
Leece 92 C2
Leechpool 44 D4
Lee Clump 40 D2
Leeds Kent 30 D2
W Yorks 95 F5
Leedstown 2 C5
Leek 75 D6
Leekbrook 75 D6
Leek Wootton 51 C7
Lee Mill 6 D4
Leeming 101 F7
Leeming Bar 101 E7
Lee Moor 6 C3
Lee-on-the-
Solent 15 D6
Lees Derbys 76 F2
Gtr Man 87 D7
W Yorks 94 F3
Leeswood 73 C6
Legbourne 91 F7
Legerwood 121 E8
Legsby 90 F5
Leicester 64 D2
Leicester Forest
East 64 D2
Leigh Dorset 12 D4
Glos 37 B5
Gtr Man 86 D4
Kent 29 E6
Shrops 60 D3
Sur 28 E3
Wilts 37 E7
Worcs 50 D2
Leigh Beck 42 F4
Leigh Common 12 B5
Leigh Delamere 24 B3
Leigh Green 19 B6
Leigh on Sea 42 F4
Leigh Park 15 D8
Leigh Sinton 50 D2
Leighswood 62 D4
Leighterton 37 E5
Leighton N Yorks 94 B4
Powys 60 D2
Shrops 61 D6
Som 24 E2
Leighton
Bromswold 54 B2
Leighton Buzzard 40 B2
Leigh upon
Mendip 23 E8
Leigh Woods 23 B7
Leinthall Earls 49 C6
Leinthall Starkes 49 C6
Leintwardine 49 B6
Leire 64 E2
Leirinmore 156 C7
Leiston 57 C8
Leitfie 134 E2
Leith 121 B5
Leitholm 122 E3
Lelant 2 C4
Lelley 97 F8
Lem Hill 50 B2
Lemmington Hall 117 C7
Lempitlaw 122 F3
Lenchwick 50 E5
Lendalfoot 112 F1
Lendrick Lodge 126 D4
Lenham 30 D2
Lenham Heath 30 E3
Lennel 122 E4
Lennoxtown 119 B6
Lenton Lincs 78 F3
Nottingham 77 F5
Lentran 151 G8
Lenwade 68 C3
Leny House 126 D5
Lenzie 119 B6
Leoch 134 F3
Leochel-Cushnie 140 C4
Leominster 49 D6
Leonard Stanley 37 D5
Leorin 142 D4
Lepe 15 E5
Lephin 148 D6
Lephinchapel 145 D8
Lephinmore 145 D8
Le Planel Guern 16
Leppington 96 C3
Lepton 88 C3
Lerryn 5 D6
Lerwick 160 J6
Lesbury 117 C8
Le Skerne
Haughton 101 C8
Leslie Aberds 140 B4
Fife 128 D4
Lesmahagow 119 F8
Lesnewth 8 E3
Lessendrum 152 D5
Lessingham 69 B6
Lessonhall 108 D2
Leswalt 104 C4
Letchmore Heath 40 E4
Letchworth Garden
City 54 F3
Letcombe Bassett 38 F3
Letcombe Regis 38 F3
Letham Angus 135 E5
Falk 127 F7
Fife 128 C5
Perth 128 B2
Letham Grange 135 E6
Lethenty 153 D8
Letheringham 57 D6
Letheringsett 81 D6
Lettaford 10 F2
Lettan 159 D8
Letterewe 150 D2
Letterfearn 149 F13
Letterfinlay 137 E5
Lettermorar 147 C10
Lettermore 146 G7
Letters 150 C4
Letterston 44 C4
Lettoch Highld 139 C6
Highld 151 H13
Letton Hereford 48 E5
Hereford 49 B5
Letton Green 68 D2
Letty Green 41 C5
Letwell 89 F6
Leuchars 129 B6
Leuchars House 152 B2
Leumrabhagh 155 F8
Levan 118 B2
Levaneap 160 G6
Levedale 62 C2
Leven E Yorks 97 E7
Fife 129 D5
Levencorroch 143 F11
Levens 99 F6
Levens Green 41 B6
Levenshulme 87 E6
Levenwick 160 L6
Leverburgh
= *An t-Ob* 154 J5
Leverington 66 C4
Leverton 79 E7
Leverton Highgate 79 E7
Leverton
Lucasgate 79 E7
Leverton Outgate 79 E7
Le Villocq Guern 16
Levington 57 F6
Levisham 103 E6
Levishie 137 C7
Lew 38 D3
Lewannick 8 F4
Lewdown 9 F6
Lewes 17 C8
Leweston 44 C4
Lewisham 28 B4
Lewiston 137 B8
Lewistown 34 F3
Lewknor 39 E7
Leworthy Devon 8 D5
Devon 21 F5
Lewtrenchard 9 F6
Lexden 43 B5
Ley Aberds 140 C4
Corn 5 C6
Leybourne 29 D7
Leyburn 101 E6
Leyfields 63 D6
Leyhill 40 D2
Leyland 86 B3
Leylodge 141 C6
Leymoor 88 C2
Leys Aberds 153 C10
Perth 134 F2
Leys Castle 151 G9
Leysdown-on-Sea 30 B4
Leysmill 135 E6
Leys of Cossans 134 E3
Leysters Pole 49 C7
Leyton 41 F6
Leytonstone 41 F6
Lezant 5 B8
Leziate 67 C6
Lhanbryde 152 B2
Liatrie 150 H5
Libanus 34 B3
Libberton 120 E2
Liberton 121 C5
Liceasto 154 H6
Lichfield 62 D5
Lickey 50 B4
Lickey End 50 B4
Lickfold 16 B3
Liddel 159 K5
Liddesdale 130 D1
Liddington 38 F2
Lidgate 55 D8
Lidget 89 D7
Lidget Green 94 F4
Lidgett 77 C6
Lidlington 53 F7
Lidstone 38 B3
Lieurary 158 D2
Liff 134 F3
Lifton 9 F5
Liftondown 9 F5
Lighthorne 51 D8
Lightwater 27 C7
Lightwood 75 E6
Lightwood Green
Ches E 74 E3
Wrex 73 E7
Lilbourne 52 B3
Lilburn Tower 117 B6
Lilleshall 61 C7
Lilley Herts 40 B4
W Berks 26 B2
Lilliesleaf 115 B8
Lillingstone
Dayrell 52 F5
Lillingstone Lovell 52 E5
Lillington Dorset 12 C4
Warks 51 C8
Lilliput 13 E8
Lilstock 22 E3
Lilyhurst 61 C7
Limbury 40 B3
Limebrook 49 C5
Limefield 87 C6
Limekilnburn 119 D7
Limekilns 128 F2
Limerigg 119 B8
Limerstone 14 F5
Limington 12 B3
Limpenhoe 69 D6
Limpley Stoke 24 C2
Limpsfield 28 D5
Limpsfield Chart 28 D5
Linby 76 D5
Linchmere 27 F6
Lincluden 107 B6
Lincoln 78 B2
Lincomb 50 C3
Lincombe 6 D5
Lindale 99 F6
Lindal in Furness 92 B2
Lindean 121 F7
Lindfield 17 B7
Lindford 27 F6
Lindifferon 128 C5
Lindley 88 C2
Lindley Green 94 E5
Lindores 128 C4
Lindridge 49 C8
Lindsell 42 B2
Lindsey 56 E3
Linford Hants 14 D2
Thurrock 29 B7
Lingague 84 E2
Lingards Wood 87 C8
Lingbob 94 F3
Lingdale 102 C4
Lingen 49 C5
Lingfield 28 E4
Lingreabhagh 154 J5
Lingwood 69 D6
Linicro 149 B8
Linkenholt 25 D8
Linkhill 18 C5
Linkinhorne 5 B8
Linklater 159 K5
Linksness 159 H3
Linktown 128 E4
Linley 60 E3
Linley Green 49 D8
Linlithgow 120 B3
Linlithgow
Bridge 120 B2
Linshiels 116 D4
Linsiadar 154 D7
Linsidemore 151 B8
Linslade 40 B2
Linstead Parva 57 B7
Linstock 108 D4
Linthwaite 88 C2
Lintlaw 122 D4
Lintmill 152 B5
Linton Borders 116 B3
Cambs 55 E6
Derbys 63 C6
Hereford 36 B3
Kent 29 E8
Northumb 117 E8
N Yorks 94 C2
W Yorks 95 E6
Linton-on-Ouse 95 C7
Linwood Hants 14 D2
Lincs 90 F5
Renfs 118 C4
Lionacleit 148 D2
Lional 155 A10
Liphook 27 F6
Liscard 85 E4
Liscombe 21 F7
Liskeard 5 C7
L'Islet Guern 16
Liss 15 B8
Lissett 97 D7
Liss Forest 15 B8
Lissington 90 F5
Lisvane 35 F5
Liswerry 35 F7
Litcham 67 C8
Litchborough 52 D4
Litchfield 26 D2
Litherland 85 E4
Litlington Cambs 54 E4
E Sus 18 E2
Little Abington 55 E6
Little Addington 53 B7
Little Alne 51 C6
Little Altcar 85 D4
Little Asby 100 D1
Little Assynt 156 G4
Little Aston 62 D4
Little Atherfield 15 F5
Little Ayre 159 J4
Little-ayre 160 G5
Little Ayton 102 C3
Little Baddow 42 D3
Little Badminton 37 F5
Little Ballinluig 133 D6
Little Bampton 108 D2
Little Bardfield 55 F7
Little Barford 54 D2
Little Barningham 81 D7
Little Barrington 38 C2

Little Barrow 73 B8
Little Barugh 96 B3
Little Bavington 110 B2
Little Bealings 57 E6
Littlebeck 103 D6
Little Bedwyn 25 C7
Little Bentley 43 B7
Little Berkhamsted 41 D5
Little Billing 53 C6
Little Birch 49 F7
Little Blakenham 56 E5
Little Blencow 108 F4
Little Bollington 86 F5
Little Bookham 28 D2
Littleborough
Gtr Man 87 C7
Notts 90 F2
Littlebourne 31 D6
Little Bowden 64 F4
Little Bradley 55 D7
Little Brampton 60 F3
Little Brechin 135 C5
Littlebredy 12 F3
Little Brickhill 53 F7
Little Brington 52 C4
Little Bromley 43 B6
Little Broughton 107 F7
Little Budworth 74 C2
Little Burstead 42 E2
Littlebury 55 F6
Littlebury Green 55 F5
Little Bytham 65 C7
Little Carlton Lincs 91 F7
Notts 77 D7
Little Casterton 65 D7
Little Cawthorpe 91 F7
Little Chalfont 40 E2
Little Chart 30 E3
Little Chesterford 55 E6
Little Cheverell 24 D4
Little Chishill 54 F5
Little Clacton 43 C7
Little Clifton 98 B2
Little Colp 153 D7
Little Comberton 50 E4
Little Common 18 E4
Little Compton 51 F7
Little Cornard 56 F2
Little Cowarne 49 D8
Little Coxwell 38 E2
Little Crakehall 101 E7
Little Cressingham 67 D8
Little Crosby 85 D4
Little Dalby 64 C4
Little Dawley 61 D6
Littledean 36 C3
Little Dens 153 D10
Little Dewchurch 49 F7
Little Downham 66 F5
Little Driffield 97 D6
Little Dunham 67 C8
Little Dunkeld 133 E7
Little Dunmow 42 B2
Little Easton 42 B2
Little Eaton 76 E3
Little Eccleston 92 E4
Little Ellingham 68 E3
Little End 41 D8
Little Eversden 54 D4
Little Faringdon 38 D2
Little Fencote 101 E7
Little Fenton 95 F8
Littleferry 151 B11
Little Finborough 56 D4
Little Fransham 68 C2
Little Gaddesden 40 C2
Little Gidding 65 F8
Little Glemham 57 D7
Little Glenshee 133 F6
Little Gransden 54 D3
Little Green 24 E2
Little Grimsby 91 E7
Little Gruinard 150 C2
Little Habton 96 B3
Little Hadham 41 B7
Little Hale 78 E4
Little Hallingbury 41 C7
Littleham Devon 9 B6
Devon 10 F5
Little Hampden 40 D1
Littlehampton 16 D4
Little Harrowden 53 B6
Little Haseley 39 D6
Little Hatfield 97 E7
Little Hautbois 81 E8
Little Haven 44 D3
Little Hay 62 D5
Little Hayfield 87 F8
Little Haywood 62 B4
Little Heath 63 F7
Littlehempston 7 C6
Little Hereford 49 C7
Little Horkesley 56 F3
Little Horsted 17 C8
Little Horton 94 F4
Little Horwood 53 F5
Littlehoughton 117 C8
Little Houghton
S Yorks 88 D5
W Nhants 53 D6
Little Hucklow 75 B8
Little Hulton 86 D5
Little Humber 91 B5
Little Hungerford 26 B3
Little Irchester 53 C7
Little Kimble 39 D8
Little Kineton 51 D8
Little Kingshill 40 E1
Little Langdale 99 D5
Little Langford 25 F5
Little Laver 41 D8
Little Leigh 74 B3
Little Leighs 42 C3
Little Lever 87 D5
Little London Bucks 39 C6
E Sus 18 D2
Hants 25 E8
Hants 26 D4
Lincs 66 B2
Lincs 66 B4
Norf 81 E7
Powys 59 F7
Little Longstone 75 B8
Little Lynturk 140 C4
Little Malvern 50 E2
Little Maplestead 56 F2
Little Marcle 49 F8
Little Marlow 40 F1
Little Marsden 93 F8
Little Massingham 80 E3
Little Melton 68 D4
Littlemill Aberds 140 E2
E Ayrs 112 C4
Highld 151 F12
Northumb 117 C8
Little Mill 35 D7
Little Milton 39 D6
Little Missenden 40 E2
Littlemoor 12 F4
Littlemore 39 D5
Little Musgrave 100 C2
Little Ness 60 C4
Little Neston 73 B6
Little Newcastle 44 C4
Little Newsham 101 C6
Little Oakley Essex 43 B8
N Nhants 65 F5
Little Orton 108 D3
Little Ouseburn 95 C7
Littleover 76 F3
Little Paxton 54 C2
Little Petherick 4 B4
Little Pitlurg 152 D4
Little Plumpton 92 F3
Little Plumstead 69 C6
Little Ponton 78 F2
Littleport 67 F5
Little Raveley 54 B3
Little Reedness 90 B2
Little Ribston 95 D6
Little Rissington 38 C1
Little Ryburgh 81 E5
Little Ryle 117 C6
Little Salkeld 109 F5
Little Sampford 55 F7
Little Sandhurst 27 C6
Little Saxham 55 C8
Little Scatwell 150 F6
Little Sessay 95 B7
Little Shelford 54 D5
Little Singleton 92 F3
Little Skillymarno 153 C9
Little Smeaton 89 C6
Little Snoring 81 D5
Little Sodbury 36 F4
Little Somborne 25 F8
Little Somerford 37 F6
Little Stainforth 93 C8
Little Stainton 101 B8
Little Stanney 73 B8
Little Staughton 54 C2
Little Steeping 79 C7
Little Stoke 75 F6
Littlestone on Sea 19 C7
Little Stonham 56 C5
Little Stretton Leics 64 D3
Shrops 60 E4
Little Strickland 99 C7
Little Stukeley 54 B3
Little Sutton 73 B7
Little Tew 38 B3
Little Thetford 55 B6
Little Thirkleby 95 B7
Littlethorpe Leics 64 E2
N Yorks 95 C6
Little Thurlow 55 D7
Little Thurrock 29 B7
Littleton Ches W 73 C8
Hants 26 F2
Perth 134 F2
Som 23 F6
Sur 27 C8
Sur 27 E7
Littleton Drew 37 F5
Littleton-on-Severn 36 F2
Littleton Pannell 24 D5
Little Torboll 151 B10
Little Torrington 9 C6
Little Totham 42 C4
Little Toux 152 C5
Littletown 111 E6
Little Town Cumb 98 C4
Lancs 93 F6
Little Urswick 92 B2
Little Wakering 43 F5
Little Walden 55 E6
Little Waldingfield 56 E3
Little Walsingham 80 D5
Little Waltham 42 C3
Little Warley 42 E2
Little Weighton 97 F5
Little Weldon 65 F6
Little Welnetham 56 C2
Little Wenlock 61 D6
Little Whittingham Green 57 B6
Littlewick Green 27 B6
Little Wilbraham 55 D6
Little Wishford 25 F5
Little Witley 50 C2
Little Wittenham 39 E5
Little Wolford 51 F7
Littleworth Bedford 53 E8
Glos 37 D5
Oxon 38 E3
Staffs 62 C4
Worcs 50 D3
Little Wratting 55 E7
Little Wymington 53 C7
Little Wymondley 41 B5
Little Wyrley 62 D4
Little Yeldham 55 F8
Litton Derbys 75 B8
N Yorks 94 B2
Som 23 D7
Litton Cheney 12 E3
Liurbost 155 E8
Liverpool 85 E4
Liverpool Airport 86 F2
Liversedge 88 B3
Liverton Devon 7 B6
Redcar 103 C5
Livingston 120 C3
Livingston Village 120 C3
Lixwm 73 B5
Lizard 3 E6
Llaingoch 82 C2
Llaithddu 59 F7
Llan 59 D5
Llanaber 58 C3
Llanaelhaearn 70 C4
Llanafan 47 B5
Llanafan-fawr 47 D8
Llanallgo 82 C4
Llanandras = Presteigne 48 C5
Llanarmon 70 D5
Llanarmon Dyffryn Ceiriog 73 F5
Llanarmon-yn-Ial 73 D5
Llanarth Ceredig 46 D3
Mon 35 C7
Llanarthne 33 B6
Llanasa 85 F2
Llanbabo 82 C3
Llanbadarn Fawr 58 F3
Llanbadarn Fynydd 48 B3
Llanbadarn-y-Garreg 48 E3
Llanbadoc 35 E7
Llanbadrig 82 B3
Llanbeder 35 E7
Llanbedr Gwyn 71 E6
Powys 35 B6
Powys 48 E3
Llanbedr-Dyffryn-Clwyd 72 D5
Llanbedrgoch 82 C5
Llanbedrog 70 D4
Llanbedr Pont Steffan = Lampeter 46 E4
Llanbedr-y-cennin 83 E7
Llanberis 83 E5
Llanbethêry 22 C2
Llanbister 48 B3
Llanblethian 21 B8
Llanboidy 32 B3
Llanbradach 35 E5
Llanbrynmair 59 D5
Llancarfan 22 B2
Llancayo 35 D7
Llancloudy 36 B1
Llancynfelyn 58 E3
Llandaff 22 B3
Llandanwg 71 E6
Llandarcy 33 E8
Llandawke 32 C3
Llanddaniel Fab 82 D4
Llanddarog 33 C6
Llanddeiniol 46 B4
Llanddeiniolen 82 E5
Llandderfel 72 F3
Llanddeusant Anglesey 82 C3
Carms 34 B1
Llanddew 48 F2
Llanddewi 33 F5
Llanddewi-Brefi 47 D5
Llanddewi'r Cwm 48 E2
Llanddewi Rhydderch 35 C7
Llanddewi Velfrey 32 C2
Llanddoged 83 E8
Llanddona 83 D5
Llanddowror 32 C3
Llanddulas 72 B3
Llanddwywe 71 E6
Llanddyfynan 82 D5
Llandefaelog Fach 48 F2
Llandefaelog-tre'rgraig 35 B5
Llandefalle 48 F3
Llandegai 83 D5
Llandegfan 83 D5
Llandegla 73 D5
Llandegley 48 C3
Llandegveth 35 E7
Llandegwning 70 D3
Llandeilo 33 B7
Llandeilo Graban 48 E2
Llandeilo'r Fan 47 F7
Llandeloy 44 C3
Llandenny 35 D8
Llandevenny 35 F8
Llandewednock 3 E6
Llandewi Ystradenny 48 C3
Llandinabo 36 B2
Llandinam 59 F7
Llandissilio 32 B2
Llandogo 36 D2
Llandough V Glam 21 B8
V Glam 22 B3
Llandovery = Llanymddyfri 47 F6
Llandow 21 B8
Llandre Carms 47 E5
Ceredig 58 F3
Llandrillo 72 F4
Llandrillo-yn-Rhos 83 C8
Llandrindod = Llandrindod Wells 48 C2
Llandrindod Wells = Llandrindod 48 C2
Llandrinio 60 C2
Llandudno 83 C7
Llandudno Junction = Cyffordd Llandudno 83 D7
Llandwrog 82 F4
Llandybie 33 C7
Llandyfaelog 33 C5
Llandyfan 33 C7
Llandyfriog 46 E2
Llandyfrydog 82 C4
Llandygwydd 45 E4
Llandynan 73 E5
Llandyrnog 72 C5
Llandysilio 60 C2
Llandyssil 59 E8
Llandysul 46 E3
Llanedeyrn 35 F6
Llanedi 33 D6
Llaneglwys 48 F2
Llanegryn 58 D2
Llanegwad 33 B6
Llaneilian 82 B4
Llanelian-yn-Rhos 83 D8
Llanelidan 72 D5
Llanelieu 48 F3
Llanellen 35 C7
Llanelli 33 E6
Llanelltyd 58 C4
Llanelly 35 C6
Llanelly Hill 35 C6
Llanelwedd 48 D2
Llanelwy = St Asaph 72 B4
Llanenddwyn 71 E6
Llanengan 70 E3
Llanerchymedd 82 C4
Llanerfyl 59 D7
Llanfachraeth 82 C3
Llanfachreth 71 E8
Llanfaelog 82 D3
Llanfaelrhys 70 E3
Llanfaenor 35 C8
Llanfaes Anglesey 83 D6
Powys 34 B4
Llanfaethlu 82 C3
Llanfaglan 82 E4
Llanfair 71 E6
Llanfair-ar-y-bryn 47 F7
Llanfair Caereinion 59 D8
Llanfair Clydogau 46 D5
Llanfair-Dyffryn-Clwyd 72 D5
Llanfairfechan 83 D6
Llanfair Kilgheddin 35 D7
Llanfair-Nant-Gwyn 45 F3
Llanfairpwllgwyngyll 82 D5
Llanfair Talhaiarn 72 B3
Llanfair Waterdine 48 B4
Llanfair-ym-Muallt = Builth Wells 48 D2
Llanfairyneubwll 82 D3
Llanfairynghornwy 82 B3
Llanfallteg 32 C2
Llanfaredd 48 D2
Llanfarian 46 B4
Llanfechain 59 B8
Llanfechan 47 D8
Llanfechell 82 B3
Llanfendigaid 58 D2
Llanferres 73 C5
Llan Ffestiniog 71 C8
Llanfflewyn 82 C3
Llanfihangel-ararth 46 F3
Llanfihangel-Crucorney 35 B7
Llanfihangel Glyn Myfyr 72 E3
Llanfihangel Nant Bran 47 F8
Llanfihangel-nant-Melan 48 D3
Llanfihangel Rhydithon 48 C3
Llanfihangel Rogiet 35 F8
Llanfihangel Tal-y-llyn 35 B5
Llanfihangel-uwch-Gwili 33 B5
Llanfihangel-y-Creuddyn 47 B5
Llanfihangel-yn-Ngwynfa 59 C7
Llanfihangel yn Nhowyn 82 D3
Llanfihangel-ypennant Gwyn 58 D3
Gwyn 71 C6
Llanfihangel-ytraethau 71 D6
Llanfilo 48 F3
Llanfoist 35 C6
Llanfor 72 F3
Llanfrechfa 35 E7
Llanfrothen 71 C7
Llanfrynach 34 B4
Llanfwrog Anglesey 82 C3
Denb 72 D5
Llanfyllin 59 C8
Llanfynydd Carms 33 B6
Flint 73 D6
Llanfyrnach 45 F4
Llangadfan 59 C7
Llangadog 33 B8
Llangadwaladr Anglesey 82 E3
Powys 73 F5
Llangaffo 82 E4
Llangain 32 C4
Llangammarch Wells 47 E8
Llangan 21 B8
Llangarron 36 B2
Llangasty Talyllyn 35 B5
Llangathen 33 B6
Llangattock 35 C6
Llangattock Lingoed 35 B7
Llangattock nigh Usk 35 D7
Llangattock-Vibon-Avel 36 C1
Llangedwyn 59 B8
Llangefni 82 D4
Llangeinor 34 F3
Llangeitho 46 D5
Llangeler 46 F2
Llangelynin 58 D2
Llangendeirne 33 C5
Llangennech 33 D6
Llangennith 33 E5
Llangenny 35 C6
Llangernyw 83 E8
Llangian 70 E3
Llanglydwen 32 B2
Llangoed 83 D6
Llangoedmor 45 E3
Llangollen 73 E6
Llangolman 32 B2
Llangors 35 B5
Llangovan 36 D1
Llangower 72 F3
Llangrannog 46 D2
Llangristiolus 82 D4
Llangrove 36 C2
Llangua 35 B7
Llangunllo 48 B4
Llangunnor 33 C5
Llangurig 47 B8
Llangwm Conwy 72 E3
Mon 35 D8
Pembs 44 E4
Llangwnnadl 70 D3
Llangwyfan 72 C5
Llangwyfan-isaf 82 E3
Llangwyllog 82 D4
Llangwyryfon 46 B4
Llangybi Ceredig 46 D5
Gwyn 70 C5
Mon 35 E7
Llangyfelach 33 E7
Llangynhafal 72 C5
Llangynidr 35 C5
Llangynin 32 C3
Llangynog Carms 32 C4
Powys 59 B7
Llangynwyd 34 F2
Llanhamlach 34 B4
Llanharan 34 F4
Llanharry 34 F4
Llanhennock 35 E7
Llanhiledd = Llanhilleth 35 D6
Llanhilleth = Llanhiledd 35 D6
Llanidloes 59 F6
Llaniestyn 70 D3
Llanifyny 59 F5
Llanigon 48 F4
Llanilar 46 B5
Llanilid 34 F3
Llanilltud Fawr = Llantwit Major 21 C8
Llanishen Cardiff 35 F5
Mon 36 D1
Llanllawddog 33 B5
Llanllechid 83 E6
Llanllowell 35 E7
Llanllugan 59 D7
Llanllwch 32 C4
Llanllwchaiarn 59 E8
Llanllwni 46 F3
Llanllyfni 82 F4
Llanmadoc 33 E5
Llanmaes 21 C8
Llanmartin 35 F7
Llanmihangel 21 B8
Llanmorlais 33 E6
Llannefydd 72 B3
Llannon 33 D6
Llannor 70 D4
Llanon 46 C4
Llanover 35 D7
Llanpumsaint 33 B5
Llanreithan 44 C3
Llanrhaeadr 72 C4
Llanrhaeadr-ym-Mochnant 59 B8
Llanrhian 44 B3
Llanrhidian 33 E5
Llanrhos 83 C7
Llanrhyddlad 82 C3
Llanrhystud 46 C4
Llanrosser 48 F4
Llanrothal 36 C1
Llanrug 82 E5
Llanrumney 35 F6
Llanrwst 83 E8
Llansadurnen 32 C3
Llansadwrn Anglesey 83 D5
Carms 47 F5
Llansaint 32 D4
Llansamlet 33 E7
Llansanffraid-ym-Mechain 60 B2
Llansannan 72 C3
Llansannor 21 B8
Llansantffraed Ceredig 46 C4
Powys 35 B5
Llansantffraed Cwmdeuddwr 47 C8
Llansantffraed-in-Elvel 48 D2
Llansawel 46 F5
Llansilin 60 B2
Llansoy 35 D8
Llanspyddid 34 B4
Llanstadwell 44 E4
Llansteffan 32 C4
Llanstephan 48 E3
Llantarnam 35 E7
Llanteg 32 C2
Llanthony 35 B6
Llantilio Crossenny 35 C7
Llantilio Pertholey 35 C7
Llantood 45 E3
Llantrisant Anglesey 82 C3
Mon 35 E7
Rhondda 34 F4
Llantrithyd 22 B2
Llantwit Fardre 34 F4
Llantwit Major = Llanilltud Fawr 21 C8
Llanuwchllyn 72 F2
Llanvaches 35 E8
Llanvair Discoed 35 E8
Llanvapley 35 C7
Llanvetherine 35 C7
Llanveynoe 48 F5
Llanvihangel Gobion 35 D7
Llanvihangel-Ystern-Llewern 35 C8
Llanwarne 36 B2
Llanwddyn 59 C7
Llanwenog 46 E3
Llanwern 35 F7
Llanwinio 32 B3
Llanwnda Gwyn 82 F4
Pembs 44 B4
Llanwnnen 46 E4
Llanwnog 59 E7
Llanwrda 47 F6
Llanwrin 58 D4
Llanwrthwl 47 C8
Llanwrtud = Llanwrtyd Wells 47 E7
Llanwrtyd 47 E7
Llanwrtyd Wells = Llanwrtud 47 E7
Llanwyddelan 59 D7
Llanyblodwel 60 B2
Llanybri 32 C4
Llanybydder 46 E4
Llanycefn 32 B1
Llanychaer 44 B4
Llanycil 72 F3
Llanycrwys 46 E5
Llanymawddwy 59 C6
Llanymddyfri = Llandovery 47 F6
Llanymynech 60 B2
Llanynghenedl 82 C3
Llanynys 72 C5
Llan-y-pwll 73 D7
Llanyre 48 C2
Llanystumdwy 71 D5
Llanywern 35 B5
Llawhaden 32 C1
Llawnt 73 F6
Llawr Dref 70 E3
Llawryglyn 59 E6
Llay 73 D7
Llechcynfarwy 82 C3
Llecheiddior 71 C5
Llechfaen 34 B4
Llechryd Caerph 35 D5
Ceredig 45 E4
Llechrydau 73 F6
Lledrod 46 B5
Llenmerewig 59 E8
Llethrid 33 E6
Llidiad Nenog 46 F4
Llidiardau 72 F2
Llidiart-y-parc 72 E5
Llithfaen 70 C4
Llong 73 C6
Llowes 48 E3
Llundain-fach 46 D4
Llwydcoed 34 D3
Llwyn 60 F2
Llwyncelyn 46 D3
Llwyndafydd 46 D2
Llwynderw 60 D2
Llwyn-du 35 C6
Llwyndyrys 70 C4
Llwyngwril 58 D2
Llwyn-hendy 33 E6
Llwynmawr 73 F6
Llwyn-têg 33 D6
Llwyn-y-brain 32 C2
Llwyn-y-groes 46 D4
Llwynypia 34 E3
Llynclys 60 B2
Llynfaes 82 D4
Llysfaen 83 D8
Llyswen 48 F3
Llysworney 21 B8
Llys-y-frân 32 B1
Llywel 47 F7
Loan 120 B2
Loanend 122 D5
Loanhead 121 C5
Loans 118 F3
Loans of Tullich 151 D11
Lobb 20 F3
Loch a Charnain 148 D3
Loch a' Ghainmhich 155 E7
Lochailort 147 C10
Lochaline 147 G9
Lochanhully 138 B5
Lochans 104 D4
Locharbriggs 114 F2
Lochassynt Lodge 156 G4
Lochavich House 124 D5
Lochawe 125 C7
Loch Baghasdail = Lochboisdale 148 G2
Lochboisdale = Loch Baghasdail 148 G2
Lochbuie 124 C2
Lochcarron 149 E13
Loch Choire Lodge 157 F9
Lochdhu 157 E13
Lochdochart House 126 B3
Lochdon 124 B3
Lochdrum 150 D5
Lochead 144 F6
Lochearnhead 126 B4
Lochee 134 F3
Lochend Highld 151 H8
Highld 158 D4
Locherben 114 E2
Loch Euphoirt 148 B3
Lochfoot 107 B5
Lochgair 145 D8
Lochgarthside 137 C8
Lochgelly 128 E3
Lochgilphead 145 E7
Lochgoilhead 125 E8
Loch Head 105 E7
Lochhill 152 B2
Lochindorb Lodge 151 H12
Lochinver 156 G3
Lochlane 127 B7
Loch Loyal Lodge 157 E9
Lochluichart 150 E6
Lochmaben 114 F3
Lochmaddy = Loch nam Madadh 148 B4
Lochmore Cottage 158 F2
Lochmore Lodge 156 F5
Loch nam Madadh = Lochmaddy 148 B4
Lochore 128 E3
Lochportain 148 A4
Lochranza 143 C10
Lochs Crofts 152 B3
Loch Sgioport 148 E3
Lochside Aberds 135 C7
Highld 151 F11
Highld 156 D7
Highld 157 F11
Lochslin 151 C11
Lochstack Lodge 156 E5
Lochton 141 E6
Lochty Angus 135 C5
Fife 129 D7
Perth 128 B2
Lochuisge 130 D1
Lochurr 113 F7
Lochwinnoch 118 D3
Lochwood 114 E3
Lochyside 131 B5
Lockengate 4 C5
Lockerbie 114 F4
Lockeridge 25 C6
Lockerley 14 B3
Locking 23 D5
Lockinge 38 F4
Lockington E Yorks 97 E5
Leics 63 B8
Lockleywood 61 B6
Locks Heath 15 D6
Lockton 103 E6
Lockwood 88 C2
Loddington Leics 64 D4
N Nhants 53 B6
Loddiswell 6 E5
Loddon 69 E6
Lode 55 C6
Loders 12 E2
Lodsworth 16 B3
Lofthouse N Yorks 94 B4
W Yorks 88 B4
Loftus 103 C5
Logan 113 B5
Loganlea 120 C2
Logan Mains 104 E4
Loggerheads 74 F4
Logie Angus 135 C6
Fife 129 B6
Moray 151 F13
Logiealmond Lodge 133 F6
Logie Coldstone 140 D3
Logie Hill 151 D10
Logie Newton 153 E6
Logie Pert 135 C6
Logierait 133 D6
Login 32 B2
Lolworth 54 C4
Lonbain 149 C11
Londesborough 96 E4
London Colney 40 D4
Londonderry 101 F8
Londonthorpe 78 F2
Londubh 155 J13
Lonemore 151 C10
Long Ashton 23 B7
Longbar 118 D3
Long Bennington 77 E8
Longbenton 111 C5
Longborough 38 B1
Long Bredy 12 E3
Longbridge Warks 51 C7
W Mid 50 B5
Longbridge Deverill 24 E3
Long Buckby 52 C4
Longburton 12 C4
Long Clawson 64 B4
Longcliffe 76 D2
Long Common 15 C6
Long Compton Staffs 62 B2
Warks 51 F7
Longcot 38 E2
Long Crendon 39 D6
Long Crichel 13 C7
Longcroft 119 B7
Longden 60 D4
Long Ditton 28 C2
Longdon Staffs 62 C4
Worcs 50 F3
Longdon Green 62 C4
Longdon on Tern 61 C6
Longdown 10 E3
Longdowns 3 C6
Long Drax 89 B7
Long Duckmanton 76 B4
Long Eaton 76 F4
Longfield Kent 29 C7
Shetland 160 M5
Longford Derbys 76 F2
Glos 37 B5
London 27 B8
Shrops 74 F3
Telford 61 C7
W Mid 63 F7
Longfordlane 76 F2
Longforgan 128 B5
Longformacus 122 D2
Longframlington 117 D7
Long Green 50 F3
Longham Dorset 13 E8
Norf 68 C2
Long Hanborough 38 C4
Longhaven 153 E11
Longhill 153 C9
Longhirst 117 F8
Longhope Glos 36 C3
Orkney 159 J4
Longhorsley 117 E7
Longhoughton 117 C8
Long Itchington 52 C2
Longlane Derbys 76 F2
W Berks 26 B2
Long Lawford 52 B2
Longlevens 37 B5
Longley 88 D2
Longley Green 50 D2
Long Load 12 B2
Longmanhill 153 B7
Long Marston Herts 40 C1
N Yorks 95 D8
Warks 51 E6
Long Marton 100 B1
Long Melford 56 E2
Longmoor Camp 27 F5
Longmorn 152 C2
Long Newnton 37 E6
Longnewton Borders 115 B8
Stockton 102 C1
Long Newton 121 C8
Longney 36 C4
Longniddry 121 B7
Longnor Shrops 60 D4
Staffs 75 C7
Longparish 26 E2
Longport 75 E5
Long Preston 93 D8
Longridge Lancs 93 F6
Staffs 62 C3
W Loth 120 C2
Longriggend 119 B8
Long Riston 97 E7
Longrock 2 C4
Longsdon 75 D6
Longshaw 86 D3
Longside 153 D10
Long Sight 87 D7
Longstanton 54 C4
Longstock 25 F8
Longstone 32 D2
Longstowe 54 D4
Long Stratton 68 E4
Long Street 53 E5
Long Sutton Hants 26 E5
Lincs 66 B4
Som 12 B2
Longthorpe 65 E8
Long Thurlow 56 C4
Longthwaite 99 B6
Longton Lancs 86 B2
Stoke 75 E6
Longtown Cumb 108 C3
Hereford 35 B7
Longview 86 E2
Longville in the Dale 60 E5
Long Whatton 63 B8
Longwick 39 D7
Long Wittenham 39 E5
Longwitton 117 F6
Longwood 61 D6
Longworth 38 E3
Longyester 121 C8
Lonmay 153 C10
Lonmore 148 D7
Looe 5 D7
Loose 29 D8
Loosley Row 39 D8
Lopcombe Corner 25 F7
Lopen 12 C2
Loppington 60 B4
Lopwell 6 C2
Lorbottle 117 D6
Lorbottle Hall 117 D6
Lornty 134 E1
Loscoe 76 E4
Losgaintir 154 H5
Lossiemouth 152 A2
Lossit 142 C2
Lostford 74 F3
Lostock Gralam 74 B3
Lostock Green 74 B3
Lostock Hall 86 B3
Lostock Junction 86 D4
Lostwithiel 5 D6
Loth 159 E7
Lothbeg 157 H12
Lothersdale 94 E2
Lothmore 157 H12
Loudwater 40 E2
Loughborough 64 C2
Loughor 33 E6
Loughton Essex 41 E7
M Keynes 53 F6
Shrops 61 F6
Lound Lincs 65 C7
Notts 89 F7
Suff 69 E8
Lount 63 C7
Louth 91 F7
Love Clough 87 B6
Lovedean 15 C7
Lover 14 B3
Loversall 89 E6
Loves Green 42 D2
Lovesome Hill 102 E1
Loveston 32 D1
Lovington 23 F7
Low Ackworth 89 C5
Low Barlings 78 B3
Low Bentham 93 C6
Low Bradfield 88 E3
Low Bradley 94 E3
Low Braithwaite 108 E4
Lowbridge House 99 D7
Low Brunton 110 B2
Low Burnham 89 D8
Low Burton 101 F7
Low Buston 117 D8
Lowca 98 B1
Low Catton 96 D3
Low Clanyard 104 F5
Low Coniscliffe 101 C7
Low Crosby 108 D4
Low Dalby 103 F6
Lowdham 77 E6
Low Dinsdale 101 C8
Lowe 74 F2
Lowe Hill 75 D6
Low Ellington 101 F7
Lower Aisholt 22 F4
Lower Arncott 39 C6
Lower Ashton 10 F3
Lower Assendon 39 F7
Lower Badcall 156 E4
Lower Bartle 92 F4
Lower Basildon 26 B4
Lower Beeding 17 B6
Lower Benefield 65 F6
Lower Boddington 52 D2
Lower Brailes 51 F8
Lower Breakish 149 F11
Lower Broadheath 50 D3
Lower Bullingham 49 F7
Lower Cam 36 D4
Lower Chapel 48 F2
Lower Chute 25 D8
Lower Cragabus 142 D4
Lower Crossings 87 F8
Lower Cumberworth 88 D3
Lower Darwen 86 B4
Lower Dean 53 C8
Lower Diabaig 149 B12
Lower Dicker 18 D2
Lower Dinchope 60 F4
Lower Down 60 F3
Lower Drift 2 D3
Lower Dunsforth 95 C7
Lower Egleton 49 E8
Lower Elkstone 75 D7
Lower End 40 B2
Lower Everleigh 25 D6
Lower Farringdon 26 F5
Lower Foxdale 84 E2
Lower Frankton 73 F7
Lower Froyle 27 E5
Lower Gledfield 151 B8
Lower Green 81 D5
Lower Hacheston 57 D7
Lower Halistra 148 C7
Lower Halstow 30 C2
Lower Hardres 31 D5
Lower Hawthwaite 98 F4
Lower Heath 75 C5
Lower Hempriggs 151 E14
Lower Hergest 48 D4
Lower Heyford 38 B4
Lower Higham 29 B8
Lower Holbrook 57 F5
Lower Hordley 60 B3
Lower Horsebridge 18 D2
Lower Killeyan 142 D3
Lower Kingswood 28 D3
Lower Kinnerton 73 C7
Lower Langford 23 C6
Lower Largo 129 D6
Lower Leigh 75 F7
Lower Lemington 51 F7
Lower Lenie 137 B8
Lower Lydbrook 36 C2
Lower Lye 49 C6
Lower Machen 35 F6
Lower Maes-coed 48 F5
Lower Mayland 43 D5
Lower Midway 63 B7
Lower Milovaig 148 C6
Lower Moor 50 E4
Lower Nazeing 41 D6
Lower Netchwood 61 E6
Lower Ollach 149 E10
Lower Penarth 22 B3
Lower Penn 62 E2
Lower Pennington 14 E4
Lower Peover 74 B4
Lower Pexhill 75 B5
Lower Place 87 C7
Lower Quinton 51 E6
Lower Rochford 49 C8
Lower Seagry 37 F6
Lower Shelton 53 E7
Lower Shiplake 27 B5
Lower Shuckburgh 52 C2
Lower Slaughter 38 B1
Lower Stanton St Quintin 37 F6
Lower Stoke 30 B2
Lower Stondon 54 F2
Lower Stow Bedon 68 E2
Lower Street Norf 69 C6
Norf 81 D8
Lower Strensham 50 E4
Lower Stretton 86 F4
Lower Sundon 40 B3
Lower Swanwick 15 D5
Lower Swell 38 B1
Lower Tean 75 F7
Lower Thurlton 69 E7
Lower Tote 149 B10
Lower Town 44 B4
Lower Tysoe 51 E8
Lower Upham 15 C6
Lower Vexford 22 F3
Lower Weare 23 D6
Lower Welson 48 D4
Lower Whitley 74 B3
Lower Wield 26 E4
Lower Winchendon 39 C7
Lower Withington 74 C5
Lower Woodend 39 F8
Lower Woodford 25 F6
Lower Wyche 50 E2
Lowesby 64 D4
Lowestoft 69 E8
Loweswater 98 B3
Low Etherley 101 B6
Low Fell 111 D5
Lowford 15 C5
Low Fulney 66 B2
Low Garth 103 D5
Low Gate 110 C2
Lowgill Cumb 99 E8
Lancs 93 C6
Low Grantley 94 B5
Low Habberley 50 B3
Low Ham 12 B2
Low Hesket 108 E4
Low Hesleyhurst 117 E6
Low Hutton 96 C3
Lowick N Nhants 65 F6
Northumb 123 F6
Lowick Bridge 98 F4
Lowick Green 98 F4
Low Laithe 94 C4
Lowlands 35 E6
Low Leighton 87 F8
Low Lorton 98 B3
Low Marishes 96 B4
Low Marnham 77 C8
Low Mill 102 E4
Low Moor Lancs 93 E7
W Yorks 88 B2
Lowmoor Row 99 B8
Low Moorsley 111 E6
Low Newton 99 F6
Low Newton-by-the-Sea 117 B8
Lownie Moor 134 E4
Low Row Cumb 108 F3
Cumb 109 C5
N Yorks 100 E4
Low Salchrie 104 C4
Low Smerby 143 F8
Lowsonford 51 C6
Lowther 99 B7
Lowthorpe 97 C6
Lowton 86 E4
Lowton Common 86 E4
Low Torry 128 F2
Low Worsall 102 D1
Low Wray 99 D5
Loxbeare 10 C4
Loxhill 27 F8
Loxhore 20 F5
Loxley 51 D7
Loxton 23 D5
Loxwood 27 F8
Lubcroy 156 J6
Lubenham 64 F4
Luccombe 21 E8
Luccombe Village 15 G6
Lucker 123 F7
Luckett 5 B8
Luckington 37 F5
Lucklawhill 129 B6
Luckwell Bridge 21 F8
Lucton 49 C6
Ludag 148 G2
Ludborough 91 E6
Ludchurch 32 C2
Luddenden 87 B8
Luddenden Foot 87 B8
Luddesdown 29 C7
Luddington N Lincs 90 C2
Warks 51 D6
Luddington in the Brook 65 F8
Lude House 133 C5
Ludford Lincs 91 F6
Shrops 49 B7
Ludgershall Bucks 39 C6

Ludgershall *continued*
Wilts 25 D7
Ludgvan 2 C4
Ludham 69 C6
Ludlow 49 B7
Ludwell 13 B7
Ludworth 111 E6
Luffincott 8 E5
Lugar 113 B5
Luggate Burn 122 B2
Lugg Green 49 C6
Luggiebank 119 B7
Lugton 118 D4
Lugwardine 49 E7
Luib 149 F10
Lulham 49 E6
Lullenden 28 E5
Lullington Derbys 63 C6
Som 24 D2
Lulsgate Bottom 23 C7
Lulsley 50 D2
Lumb 87 B8
Lumby 95 F7
Lumloch 119 C6
Lumphanan 140 D4
Lumphinnans 128 E3
Lumsdaine 122 C4
Lumsden 140 B3
Lunan 135 D6
Lunanhead 134 D4
Luncarty 128 B2
Lund E Yorks 97 E5
N Yorks 96 F2
Shetland 160 C7
Lunderton 153 D11
Lundie Angus 134 F2
Highld 136 C4
Lundin Links 129 D6
Lunga 124 E3
Lunna 160 G6
Lunning 160 G7
Lunnon 33 F6
Lunsford's Cross 18 D4
Lunt 85 D4
Luntley 49 D5
Luppitt 11 D6
Lupset 88 C4
Lupton 99 F7
Lurgashall 16 B3
Lusby 79 C6
Luson 6 E4
Luss 126 E2
Lussagiven 144 E5
Lusta 149 C7
Lustleigh 10 F2
Luston 49 C6
Luthermuir 135 C6
Luthrie 128 C5
Luton Devon 7 B7
Luton 40 B3
Medway 29 C8
Lutterworth 64 F2
Lutton Devon 6 D3
Lincs 66 B4
N Nhants 65 F8
Lutworthy 10 C2
Luxborough 21 F8
Luxulyan 5 D5
Lybster 158 G4
Lydbury North 60 F3
Lydcott 21 F5
Lydd 19 C7
Lydden 31 E6
Lyddington 65 E5
Lydd on Sea 19 C7
Lydeard
St Lawrence 22 F3
Lyde Green 26 D5
Lydford 9 F7
Lydford-on-Fosse 23 F7
Lydgate 87 B7
Lydham 60 E3
Lydiard Green 37 F7
Lydiard Millicent 37 F7
Lydiate 85 D4
Lydlinch 12 C5
Lydney 36 D3
Lydstep 32 E1
Lye 62 F3
Lye Green Bucks 40 D2
E Sus 18 B2
Lyford 38 E3
Lymbridge Green 30 E5
Lyme Regis 11 E8
Lyminge 31 E5
Lymington 14 E4
Lyminster 16 D4
Lymm 86 F4
Lymore 14 E3
Lympne 19 B8
Lympsham 22 D5
Lympstone 10 F4
Lynchat 138 D3
Lyndale House 149 C8
Lyndhurst 14 D4
Lyndon 65 D6
Lyne 27 C8
Lyneal 73 F8
Lyne Down 49 F8
Lyneham Oxon 38 B2
Wilts 24 B5
Lynemore 139 B6
Lynemouth 117 E8
Lyne of
Gorthleck 137 B8
Lyne of Skene 141 C6
Lyness 159 J4
Lyng Norf 68 C3
Som 11 B8
Lynmouth 21 E6
Lynsted 30 C3
Lynton 21 E6
Lyon's Gate 12 D4
Lyonshall 48 D5
Lytchett Matravers 13 E7
Lytchett Minster 13 E7
Lyth 158 D4
Lytham 85 B4
Lytham St Anne's 85 B4
Lythe 103 C6
Lythes 159 K5

M

Mabe Burnthouse 3 C6
Mabie 107 B6
Mablethorpe 91 F9
Macclesfield 75 B6
Macclesfield
Forest 75 B6
Macduff 153 B7
Mace Green 56 E5
Macharioch 143 H8
Machen 35 F6
Machrihanish 143 F7
Machynlleth 58 D4
Machynys 33 E6
Mackerel's
Common 16 B4
Mackworth 76 F3
Macmerry 121 B7
Madderty 127 B8
Maddiston 120 B2
Madehurst 16 C3
Madeley Staffs 74 E4
Telford 61 D6
Madeley Heath 74 E4
Madeley Park 74 E4
Madingley 54 C4
Madley 49 F6
Madresfield 50 E3
Madron 2 C3
Maenaddwyn 82 C4
Maenclochog 32 B1
Maendy 22 B2
Maentwrog 71 C7
Maen-y-groes 46 D2
Maer 74 F4
Maerdy Conwy 72 E4
Rhondda 34 E3
Maesbrook 60 B2
Maesbury 60 B3
Maesbury Marsh 60 B3
Maesgwyn-Isaf 59 C8
Maesgwynne 32 B3
Maeshafn 73 C6
Maesllyn 46 E2
Maesmynis 48 E2
Maesteg 34 E2
Maestir 46 E4
Maes-Treylow 48 C4
Maesybont 33 C6
Maesycrugiau 46 E3
Maesy cwmmer 35 E5
Maesymeillion 46 E3
Magdalen Laver 41 D8
Maggieknockater 152 D3
Magham Down 18 D3
Maghull 85 D4
Magor 35 F8
Magpie Green 56 B4
Maiden Bradley 24 F3
Maidencombe 7 C7
Maidenhall 57 E5
Maidenhead 40 F1
Maiden Law 110 E4
Maiden Newton 12 E3
Maidens 112 D2
Maidensgrave 57 E6
Maiden's Green 27 B6
Maidenwell Corn 5 B6
Lincs 79 B6
Maiden Wells 44 F4
Maidford 52 D4
Maids Moreton 52 F5
Maidstone 29 D8
Maidwell 52 B5
Mail 160 L6
Main 59 C8
Maindee 35 F7
Mainsforth 111 F6
Mains of Airies 104 C3
Mains of
Allardice 135 B8
Mains of
Annochie 153 D9
Mains of Ardestie 135 F5
Mains of Balhall 135 C5
Mains of
Ballindarg 134 D4
Mains of
Balnakettle 135 B6
Mains of Birness 153 E9
Mains of Burgie 151 F13
Mains of Clunas 151 G11
Mains of Crichie 153 D9
Mains of Dalvey 151 H14
Mains of
Dellavaird 141 F6
Mains of Drum 141 E7
Mains of
Edingight 152 C5
Mains of
Fedderate 153 D8
Mains of Inkhorn 153 E9
Mains of Mayen 152 D5
Mains of
Melgund 135 D5
Mains of
Thornton 135 B6
Mains of Watten 158 E4
Mainsriddle 107 D6
Mainstone 60 F2
Maisemore 37 B5
Malacleit 148 A2
Malborough 6 F5
Malcoff 87 F8
Maldon 42 D4
Malham 94 C2
Maligar 149 B9
Mallaig 147 B9
Malleny Mills 120 C4
Malling 126 D4
Malltraeth 82 E4
Mallwyd 59 C5
Malmesbury 37 F6
Malmsmead 21 E6
Malpas Ches W 73 E8
Corn 3 B7
Newport 35 E7
Malswick 36 B4
Maltby Stockton 102 C2
S Yorks 89 E6
Maltby le Marsh 91 F8
Malting Green 43 B5
Maltman's Hill 30 E3
Malton 96 B3
Malvern Link 50 E2
Malvern Wells 50 E2
Mamble 49 B8
Manaccan 3 D6
Manafon 59 D8
Manais 154 J6
Manar House 141 B6
Manaton 10 F2
Manby 91 F7
Mancetter 63 E7
Manchester 87 E6
Manchester
Airport 87 F6
Mancot 73 C7
Mandally 137 D5
Manea 66 F4
Manfield 101 C7
Mangaster 160 F5
Mangotsfield 23 B8
Mangurstadh 154 D5
Mankinholes 87 B7
Manley 74 B2
Manmoel 35 D5
Mannal 146 G2
Mannerston 120 B3
Manningford
Bohune 25 D6
Manningford
Bruce 25 D6
Manningham 94 F4
Mannings Heath 17 B6
Mannington 13 D8
Manningtree 56 F4
Mannofield 141 D8
Manor 41 F7
Manorbier 32 E1
Manordeilo 33 B7
Manor Estate 88 F4
Manorhill 122 F2
Manorowen 44 B4
Manselfield 33 F6
Mansel Lacy 49 E6
Mansell Gamage 49 E5
Mansergh 99 F8
Mansfield E Ayrs 113 C6
Notts 76 C5
Mansfield
Woodhouse 76 C5
Mansriggs 98 F4
Manston Dorset 13 C6
Kent 31 C7
W Yorks 95 F6
Manswood 13 D7
Manthorpe Lincs 65 C7
Lincs 78 F2
Manton N Lincs 90 D3
Notts 77 B5
Rutland 65 D5
Wilts 25 C6
Manuden 41 B7
Maperton 12 B4
Maplebeck 77 C7
Maple Cross 40 E3
Mapledurham 26 B4
Mapledurwell 26 D4
Maplehurst 17 B5
Maplescombe 29 C6
Mapleton 75 E8
Mapperley 76 E4
Mapperley Park 77 E5
Mapperton 12 E3
Mappleborough
Green 51 C5
Mappleton 97 E8
Mappowder 12 D5
Maraig 154 G6
Marazanvose 4 D3
Marazion 2 C4
Marbhig 155 F9
Marbury 74 E2
March Cambs 66 E4
S Lanark 114 C2
Marcham 38 E4
Marchamley 61 B5
Marchington 75 F8
Marchington
Woodlands 62 B5
Marchroes 70 E4
Marchwiel 73 E7
Marchwood 14 C4
Marcross 21 C8
Marden Hereford 49 E7
Kent 29 E8
T&W 111 B6
Wilts 25 D5
Marden Beech 29 E8
Marden Thorn 29 E8
Mardy 35 C7
Marefield 64 D4
Mareham le Fen 79 C5
Mareham on
the Hill 79 C5
Marehay 76 E3
Marehill 16 C4
Maresfield 17 B8
Marfleet 90 B5
Marford 73 D7
Margam 34 F1
Margaret Marsh 13 C6
Margaret Roding 42 C1
Margaretting 42 D2
Margate 31 B7
Margnaheglish 143 E11
Margrove Park 102 C4
Marham 67 C7
Marhamchurch 8 D4
Marholm 65 D8
Mariandyrys 83 C6
Marianglas 82 C5
Mariansleigh 10 B2
Marionburgh 141 D6
Marishader 149 B9
Marjoriebanks 114 F3
Mark Dumfries 104 D5
S Ayrs 104 B4
Som 23 E5
Markbeech 29 E5
Markby 79 B7
Mark Causeway 23 E5
Mark Cross E Sus 17 C8
E Sus 18 B2
Market Bosworth 63 D8
Market Deeping 65 D8
Market Drayton 74 F3
Market
Harborough 64 F4
Markethill 134 F2
Market Lavington 24 D5
Market Overton 65 C5
Market Rasen 90 F5
Market Stainton 78 B5
Market Warsop 77 C5
Market Weighton 96 E4
Market Weston 56 B3
Markfield 63 C8
Markham 35 D5
Markham Moor 77 B7
Markinch 128 D4
Markington 95 C5
Marksbury 23 C8
Marks Tey 43 B5
Markyate 40 C3
Marland 87 C6
Marlborough 25 C6
Marlbrook Hereford 49 D7
Worcs 50 B4
Marlcliff 51 D5
Marldon 7 C6
Marlesford 57 D7
Marley Green 74 E2
Marley Hill 110 D5
Marley Mount 14 E3
Marlingford 68 D4
Mar Lodge 139 E6
Marloes 44 E2
Marlow Bucks 39 F8
Hereford 49 B6
Marlow Bottom 40 F1
Marlpit Hill 28 E5
Marlpool 76 E4
Marnhull 13 C5
Marnoch 152 C5
Marnock 119 C7
Marple 87 F7
Marple Bridge 87 F7
Marr 89 D6
Marrel 157 H13
Marrick 101 E5
Marrister 160 G7
Marros 32 D3
Marsden T&W 111 C6
W Yorks 87 C8
Marsett 100 F4
Marsh Devon 11 C7
W Yorks 94 F3
Marshall's Heath 40 C4
Marshalsea 11 D8
Marshalswick 40 D4
Marsham 81 E7
Marshaw 93 D5
Marsh Baldon 39 E5
Marshborough 31 D7
Marshbrook 60 F4
Marshchapel 91 E7
Marshfield Newport 35 F6
S Glos 24 B2
Marshgate 8 E3
Marsh Gibbon 39 B6
Marsh Green Devon 10 E5
Kent 28 E5
Staffs 75 D5
Marshland
St James 66 D5
Marsh Lane 76 B4
Marshside 85 C4
Marsh Street 21 E8
Marshwood 11 E8
Marske 101 D6
Marske-by-
the-Sea 102 B4
Marston Ches W 74 B3
Hereford 49 D5
Lincs 77 E8
Oxon 39 D5
Staffs 62 B3
Staffs 62 C2
Warks 63 E6
Wilts 24 D4
Marston Doles 52 D2
Marston Green 63 F5
Marston Magna 12 B3
Marston Meysey 37 E8
Marston
Montgomery 75 F8
Marston
Moretaine 53 E7
Marston on Dove 63 B6
Marston
St Lawrence 52 E3
Marston Stannett 49 D7
Marston Trussell 64 F3
Marstow 36 C2
Marsworth 40 C2
Marten 25 D7
Marthall 74 B5
Martham 69 C7
Martin Hants 13 C8
Kent 31 E7
Lincs 78 C5
Lincs 78 D4
Martin Dales 78 C4
Martin Drove End 13 B8
Martinhoe 21 E5
Martinhoe Cross 21 E5
Martin
Hussingtree 50 C3
Martin Mill 31 E7
Martinscroft 86 F4
Martinstown 12 F4
Martlesham 57 E6
Martlesham Heath 57 E6
Martletwy 32 C1
Martley 50 D2
Martock 12 C2
Marton Ches E 75 C5
E Yorks 97 F7
Lincs 90 F2
Mbro 102 C3
N Yorks 95 C7
N Yorks 103 F5
Shrops 60 B4
Shrops 60 D2
Warks 52 C2
Marton-le-Moor 95 B6
Martyr's Green 27 D8
Martyr Worthy 26 F3
Marwick 159 F3
Marwood 20 F4
Marybank 150 F7
Maryburgh 151 F8
Maryhill 119 C5
Marykirk 135 C6
Marylebone 86 D3
Marypark 152 E1
Maryport Cumb 107 F7
Dumfries 104 F5
Mary Tavy 6 B3
Maryton 135 D6
Marywell Aberds 140 E4
Aberds 141 E8
Angus 135 E6
Masham 101 F7
Mashbury 42 C2
Masongill 93 B6
Masonhill 112 B3
Mastin Moor 76 B4
Mastrick 141 D7
Matching 41 C8
Matching Green 41 C8
Matching Tye 41 C8
Matfen 110 B3
Matfield 29 E7
Mathern 36 E2
Mathon 50 E2
Mathry 44 B3
Matlaske 81 D7
Matlock 76 C2
Matlock Bath 76 D2
Matson 37 C5
Matterdale End 99 B5
Mattersey 89 F7
Mattersey Thorpe 89 F7
Mattingley 26 D5
Mattishall 68 C3
Mattishall Burgh 68 C3
Mauchline 112 B4
Maud 153 D9
Maugersbury 38 B2
Maughold 84 C4
Mauld 150 H7
Maulden 53 F8
Maulds Meaburn 99 C8
Maunby 102 F1
Maund Bryan 49 D7
Maundown 11 B5
Mautby 69 C7
Mavis Enderby 79 C6
Mawbray 107 E7
Mawdesley 86 C2
Mawdlam 34 F2
Mawgan 3 D6
Maw Green 74 D4
Mawla 3 B6
Mawnan 3 D6
Mawnan Smith 3 D6
Mawsley 53 B6
Maxey 65 D8
Maxstoke 63 F6
Maxton Borders 122 F2
Kent 31 E7
Maxwellheugh 122 F3
Maxwelltown 107 B6
Maxworthy 8 E4
Mayals 33 E7
May Bank 75 E5
Maybole 112 D3
Mayfield E Sus 18 C2
Midloth 121 C6
Staffs 75 E8
W Loth 120 C2
Mayford 27 D7
Mayland 43 D5
Maynard's Green 18 D2
Maypole Mon 36 C1
Scilly 2 E4
Maypole Green
Essex 43 B5
Norf 69 E7
Suff 57 C6
Maywick 160 L5
Meadle 39 D8
Meadowtown 60 D3
Meaford 75 F5
Mealabost 155 D9
Mealabost
Bhuirgh 155 B9
Meal Bank 99 E7
Mealsgate 108 E2
Meanwood 95 F5
Mearbeck 93 C8
Meare 23 E6
Meare Green 11 B8
Mears Ashby 53 C6
Measham 63 C7
Meath Green 28 E3
Meathop 99 F6
Meaux 97 F6
Meavy 6 C3
Medbourne 64 E4
Medburn 110 B4
Meddon 8 C4
Meden Vale 77 C5
Medlam 79 D6
Medmenham 39 F8
Medomsley 110 D4
Medstead 26 F4
Meerbrook 75 C6
Meer End 51 B7
Meers Bridge 91 F8
Meesden 54 F5
Meeth 9 D7
Meggethead 114 B4
Meidrim 32 B3
Meifod Denb 72 D4
Powys 59 C8
Meigle N Ayrs 118 C1
Perth 134 E2
Meikle Earnock 119 D7
Meikle Ferry 151 C10
Meikle Forter 134 C1
Meikle Gluich 151 C9
Meikleour 134 F1
Meikle Pinkerton 122 B3
Meikle Strath 135 B6
Meikle Tarty 141 B8
Meikle Wartle 153 E7
Meinciau 33 C5
Meir 75 E6
Meir Heath 75 E6
Melbourn 54 E4
Melbourne Derbys 63 B7
E Yorks 96 E3
S Lanark 120 E3
Melbury Abbas 13 B6
Melbury Bubb 12 D3
Melbury Osmond 12 D3
Melbury Sampford 12 D3
Melby 160 H3
Melchbourne 53 C8
Melcombe
Bingham 13 D5
Melcombe Regis 12 F4
Meldon Devon 9 E7
Northumb 117 F7
Meldreth 54 E4
Meldrum House 141 B7
Melfort 124 D4
Melgarve 137 E7
Meliden 72 A4
Melinbyrhedyn 58 E5
Melincourt 34 D2
Melin-y-coed 83 E8
Melin-y-ddôl 59 D7
Melin-y-grug 59 D7
Melin-y-Wig 72 E4
Melkinthorpe 99 B7
Melkridge 109 C7
Melksham 24 C4
Melldalloch 145 F8
Melling Lancs 93 B5
Mers 85 D4
Melling Mount 86 D2
Mellis 56 B5
Mellon Charles 155 H13
Mellon Udrigle 155 H13
Mellor Gtr Man 87 F7
Lancs 93 F6
Mellor Brook 93 F6
Mells 24 E2
Melmerby Cumb 109 F6
N Yorks 95 B6
N Yorks 101 F5
Melplash 12 E2
Melrose 121 F8
Melsetter 159 K3
Melsonby 101 D6
Meltham 88 C2
Melton 57 D6
Meltonby 96 D3
Melton Constable 81 D6
Melton Mowbray 64 C4
Melton Ross 90 C4
Melvaig 155 J12
Melverley 60 C3
Melverley Green 60 C3
Melvich 157 C11
Membury 11 D7
Memsie 153 B9
Memus 134 D4
Menabilly 5 D5
Menai Bridge
= *Porthaethwy* 83 D5
Mendham 69 F5
Mendlesham 56 C5
Mendlesham
Green 56 C4
Menheniot 5 C7
Mennock 113 D8
Menston 94 E4
Menstrie 127 E7
Menthorpe 96 F2
Mentmore 40 C2
Meoble 147 C10
Meole Brace 60 C4
Meols 85 E3
Meonstoke 15 C7
Meopham 29 C7
Meopham Station 29 C7
Mepal 66 F4
Meppershall 54 F2
Merbach 48 E5
Mere Ches E 86 F5
Wilts 24 F3
Mere Brow 86 C2
Mereclough 93 F8
Mere Green 62 E5
Mereside 92 F3
Mereworth 29 D7
Mergie 141 F6
Meriden 63 F6
Merkadale 149 E8
Merkland
Dumfries 106 B4
S Ayrs 112 E2
Merkland Lodge 156 G7
Merley 13 E8
Merlin's Bridge 44 D4
Merrington 60 B4
Merrion 44 F4
Merriott 12 C2
Merrivale 6 B3
Merrow 27 D8
Merrymeet 5 C7
Mersham 19 B7
Merstham 28 D3
Merston 16 D2
Merstone 15 F6
Merther 3 B7
Merthyr 32 B4
Merthyr Cynog 47 F8
Merthyr-Dyfan 22 C3
Merthyr Mawr 21 B7
Merthyr Tudful
= *Merthyr Tydfil* 34 D4
Merthyr Tydfil
= *Merthyr Tudful* 34 D4
Merthyr Vale 34 E4
Merton Devon 9 C7
London 28 B3
Norf 68 E2
Oxon 39 C5
Mervinslaw 116 C2
Meshaw 10 C2
Messing 42 C4
Messingham 90 D2
Metfield 69 F5
Metheringham 78 C3
Methil 129 E5
Methlem 70 D2
Methley 88 B4
Methlick 153 E8
Methven 128 B2
Methwold 67 E7
Methwold Hythe 67 E7
Mettingham 69 F6
Mevagissey 3 B9
Mewith Head 93 C7
Mexborough 89 D5
Mey 158 C4
Meysey Hampton 37 E8
Miabhag W Isles 154 G5
W Isles 154 H6
Miabhig 154 D5
Michaelchurch 36 B2
Michaelchurch
Escley 48 F5
Michaelchurch
on Arrow 48 D4
Michaelston-
le-Pit 22 B3
Michaelston-
y-Fedw 35 F6
Michaelstow 5 B5
Michealston-
super-Ely 22 B3
Micheldever 26 F3
Michelmersh 14 B4
Mickfield 56 C5
Micklebring 89 E6
Mickleby 103 C6
Mickleham 28 D2
Mickleover 76 F3
Micklethwaite 94 E4
Mickleton Durham 100 B4
Glos 51 E6
Mickletown 88 B4
Mickle Trafford 73 C8
Mickley 95 B5
Mickley Square 110 C3
Mid Ardlaw 153 B9
Mid Auchinlech 118 B3
Midbea 159 D5
Mid Beltie 140 D5
Mid Calder 120 C3
Mid Cloch Forbie 153 C7
Mid Clyth 158 G4
Middle Assendon 39 F7
Middle Aston 38 B4
Middle Barton 38 B4
Middlebie 108 B2
Middle
Cairncake 153 D8
Middle Claydon 39 B7
Middle Drums 135 D5
Middleforth Green 86 B3
Middleham 101 F6
Middle Handley 76 B4
Middlehope 60 F4
Middle Littleton 51 E5
Middle Maes-coed 48 F5
Middlemarsh 12 D4
Middle Mill 44 C3
Middlemuir 141 B8
Middle Rasen 90 F4
Middle Rigg 128 D2
Middlesbrough 102 B2
Middleshaw Cumb 99 F7
Dumfries 107 B8
Middlesmoor 94 B3
Middlestone 111 F5
Middlestone
Moor 110 F5
Middlestown 88 C3
Middlethird 122 E2
Middleton Aberds 141 C7
Argyll 146 G2
Cumb 99 F8
Derbys 75 C8
Derbys 76 D2
Essex 56 F2
Gtr Man 87 D6
Hants 26 E2
Hereford 49 C7
Lancs 92 D4
Midloth 121 D6
N Nhants 64 F5
Norf 67 C6
Northumb 117 F6
Northumb 123 F7
N Yorks 94 E4
N Yorks 103 F5
Perth 128 D3
Perth 133 E8
Shrops 49 B7
Shrops 60 B3
Shrops 60 E2
Suff 57 C8
Swansea 33 F5
Warks 63 E5
W Yorks 88 B3
Middleton Cheney 52 E2
Middleton Green 75 F6
Middleton Hall 117 B5
Middleton-in-
Teesdale 100 B4
Middleton Moor 57 C8
Middleton
One Row 102 C1
Middleton-
on-Leven 102 D2
Middleton-on-Sea 16 D3
Middleton on the
Hill 49 C7
Middleton-on-
the-Wolds 96 E5
Middleton Priors 61 E6
Middleton
Quernham 95 B6
Middleton
St George 101 C8
Middleton Scriven 61 F6
Middleton Stoney 39 B5
Middleton Tyas 101 D7
Middletown Cumb 98 D1
Powys 60 C3
Middle Tysoe 51 E8
Middle Wallop 25 F7
Middlewich 74 C3
Middle Winterslow 25 F7
Middle Woodford 25 F6
Middlewood
Green 56 C4
Middlezoy 23 F5
Middridge 101 B7
Midfield 157 C8
Midge Hall 86 B3
Midgeholme 109 D6
Midgham 26 C3
Midgley W Yorks 87 B8
W Yorks 88 C3
Midhopestones 88 E3
Midhurst 16 B2
Mid Lavant 16 D2
Midlem 115 B8
Mid Main 150 H7
Midmar 141 D5
Midsomer Norton 23 D8
Midton 118 B2
Midtown Highld 155 J13
Highld 157 C8
Midtown of
Buchromb 152 D3
Mid Urchany 151 G11
Midville 79 D6
Mid Walls 160 H4
Midway 87 F7
Mid Yell 160 D7
Migdale 151 B9
Migvie 140 D3
Milarrochy 126 E3
Milborne Port 12 C4
Milborne
St Andrew 13 E6
Milborne Wick 12 B4
Milbourne 110 B4
Milburn 100 B1
Milbury Heath 36 E3
Milcombe 52 F2
Milden 56 E3
Mildenhall Suff 55 B8
Wilts 25 C7
Milebrook 48 B5
Milebush 29 E8
Mile Cross 68 C5
Mile Elm 24 C4
Mile End Essex 43 B5
Glos 36 C2
Mileham 68 C2
Mile Oak 17 D6
Milesmark 128 F2
Milfield 122 F5
Milford Derbys 76 E3
Devon 8 B4
Powys 59 E7
Staffs 62 B3
Sur 27 E7
Wilts 14 B2
Milford Haven =
Aberdaugleddau 44 E4
Milford on Sea 14 E3
Milkwall 36 D2
Milkwell 13 B7
Milland 16 B2
Millarston 118 C4
Millbank Aberds 153 D11
Highld 158 D3
Mill Bank 87 B8
Millbeck 98 B4
Millbounds 159 E6
Millbreck 153 D10
Millbridge 27 E6
Millbrook C Beds 53 F8
Corn 6 D2
Soton 14 C4
Millburn 112 B4
Millcombe 7 E6
Mill Common 69 F7
Millcorner 18 C5
Milldale 75 D8
Millden Lodge 135 B5
Milldens 135 D5
Mill End Bucks 39 F7
Herts 54 F4
Millerhill 121 C6
Miller's Dale 75 B8
Miller's Green 76 D2
Millgreen 61 B6
Mill Green Essex 42 D2
Norf 68 F4
Suff 56 E3
Millhalf 48 E4
Millhayes 11 D7
Millhead 92 B4
Millheugh 119 D7
Mill Hill 41 E5
Millholme 99 E7
Millhouse Argyll 145 F8
Cumb 108 F3
Millhousebridge 114 F4
Millhouse Green 88 D3
Millhouses 88 F4
Millikenpark 118 C4
Millin Cross 44 D4
Millington 96 D4
Mill Lane 27 D5
Millmeece 74 F5
Mill of
Kingoodie 141 B7
Mill of Muiresk 153 D6
Mill of Sterin 140 E2
Mill of Uras 141 F7
Millom 98 F3
Millook 8 E3
Mill Place 90 D3
Millpool 5 B6
Millport 145 H10
Millquarter 113 F6
Mill Side 99 F6
Mill Street 68 C3
Millthorpe 78 F4
Millthrop 100 E1
Milltimber 141 D7
Milltown Corn 5 D6
Derbys 76 C3
Devon 20 F4
Dumfries 108 B3
Milltown of
Aberdalgie 128 B2
Milltown of
Auchindoun 152 D3
Milltown of
Craigston 153 C7
Milltown of
Edinvillie 152 D2
Milltown of
Kildrummy 140 C3
Milltown of
Rothiemay 152 D5
Milltown of
Towie 140 C3
Milnathort 128 D3
Milner's Heath 73 C8
Milngavie 119 B5
Milnrow 87 C7
Milnshaw 87 B5
Milnthorpe 99 F6
Milo 33 C6
Milson 49 B8
Milstead 30 D3
Milston 25 E6
Milton Angus 134 E3
Cambs 55 C5
Cumb 109 C5
Derbys 63 B7
Dumfries 105 D6
Dumfries 106 B5
Dumfries 113 F8
Highld 150 F6
Highld 150 H7
Highld 151 D10
Highld 151 G8
Highld 158 E5
Moray 152 B5
Notts 77 B7
N Som 22 C5
Oxon 38 E4
Oxon 52 F2
Pembs 32 D1
Perth 127 C8
Ptsmth 15 E7
Stirling 126 D4
Stoke 75 D6
W Dunb 118 B4
Milton Abbas 13 D6
Milton Abbot 6 B2
Milton Bridge 120 C5
Milton Bryan 53 F7
Milton Clevedon 23 F8
Milton Coldwells 153 E9
Milton Combe 6 C2
Milton Damerel 9 C5
Miltonduff 152 B1
Milton End 37 D8
Milton Ernest 53 D8
Milton Green 73 D8
Miltonhill 151 E13
Milton Hill 38 E4
Miltonise 105 B5
Milton Keynes 53 F6
Milton Keynes
Village 53 F6
Milton Lilbourne 25 C6
Milton Malsor 52 D5
Milton Morenish 132 F3
Milton of
Auchinhove 140 D4
Milton of
Balgonie 128 D5
Milton of
Buchanan 126 E3
Milton of
Campfield 140 D5
Milton of
Campsie 119 B6
Milton of
Corsindae 141 D5
Milton of
Cushnie 140 C4
Milton of
Dalcapon 133 D6
Milton of
Edradour 133 D6
Milton of
Gollanfield 151 F10
Milton of
Lesmore 140 B3
Milton of Logie 140 D3
Milton of Murtle 141 D7
Milton of Noth 140 B4
Milton of Tullich 140 E2
Milton on Stour 13 B5
Milton Regis 30 C3
Milton under
Wychwood 38 C2
Milverton Som 11 B6
Warks 51 C8
Milwich 75 F6
Minard 125 F5
Minchinhampton 37 D5
Mindrum 122 F4
Minehead 21 E8
Minera 73 D6
Minety 37 E7
Minffordd Gwyn 58 C4
Gwyn 71 D6
Gwyn 83 D5
Miningsby 79 C6
Minions 5 B7
Minishant 112 C3
Minllyn 59 C5
Minnes 141 B8
Minngearraidh 148 F2
Minnigaff 105 C8
Minnonie 153 B7
Minskip 95 C6
Minstead 14 C3
Minsted 16 B2
Minster Kent 30 B3
Kent 31 C7
Minsterley 60 D3
Minster Lovell 38 C3
Minsterworth 36 C4
Minterne Magna 12 D4
Minting 78 B4
Mintlaw 153 D9
Minto 115 B8
Minton 60 E4
Minwear 32 C1
Minworth 63 E5
Mirbister 159 F4
Mirehouse 98 C1
Mireland 158 D5
Mirfield 88 C3
Miserden 37 D6
Miskin 34 F4
Misson 89 E7
Misterton Leics 64 F2
Notts 89 E8
Som 12 D2
Mistley 56 F5
Mitcham 28 C3
Mitcheldean 36 C3
Mitchell 4 D3
Mitchel Troy 36 C1
Mitcheltroy
Common 36 D1
Mitford 117 F7
Mithian 4 D2
Mitton 62 C2
Mixbury 52 F4
Moat 108 B4
Moats Tye 56 D4
Mobberley Ches E 74 B4
Staffs 75 E7
Moccas 49 E5
Mochdre Conwy 83 D8
Powys 59 F7
Mochrum 105 E7
Mockbeggar 14 D2
Mockerkin 98 B2
Modbury 6 D4
Moddershall 75 F6
Moelfre Anglesey 82 C5
Powys 59 B8
Moffat 114 D3
Moggerhanger 54 E2
Moira 63 C7
Molash 30 D4
Mol-chlach 149 G9
Mold =
Yr Wyddgrug 73 C6
Moldgreen 88 C2
Molehill Green 42 B1
Molescroft 97 E6
Molesden 117 F7
Molesworth 53 B8
Moll 149 E10
Molland 10 B3
Mollington Ches W 73 B7
Oxon 52 E2
Mollinsburn 119 B7
Monachty 46 C4
Monachylemore 126 C3
Monar Lodge 150 G5
Monaughty 48 C4
Monboddo House 135 B7
Mondynes 135 B7
Monewechadan 125 E7
Monewden 57 D6
Moneydie 128 B2

Moniaive 113 E7
Monifieth 134 F4
Monikie 135 F4
Monimail 128 C4
Monington 45 E3
Monk Bretton 88 D4
Monken Hadley 41 E5
Monk Fryston 89 B6
Monkhopton 61 E6
Monkland 49 D6
Monkleigh 9 B6
Monknash 21 B8
Monkokehampton 9 D7
Monkseaton 111 B6
Monks Eleigh 56 E3
Monk's Gate 17 B6
Monks Heath 74 B5
Monk Sherborne 26 D4
Monkshill 153 D7
Monksilver 22 F2
Monks Kirby 63 F8
Monk Soham 57 C6
Monkspath 51 B6
Monks Risborough 39 D8
Monk Street 42 B2
Monkswood 35 D7
Monkton Devon 11 D6
Kent 31 C6
Pembs 44 E4
S Ayrs 112 B3
Monkton Combe 24 C2
Monkton Deverill 24 F3
Monkton Farleigh 24 C3
Monkton Heathfield 11 B7
Monkton Up Wimborne 13 C8
Monkwearmouth 111 D6
Monkwood 26 F4
Monmouth = *Trefynwy* 36 C2
Monmouth Cap 35 B7
Monnington on Wye 49 E5
Monreith 105 E7
Monreith Mains 105 E7
Montacute 12 C2
Montcoffer House 153 B6
Montford Argyll 145 G10
Shrops 60 C4
Montford Bridge 60 C4
Montgarrie 140 C4
Montgomery = *Trefaldwyn* 60 E2
Montrave 129 D5
Montrose 135 D7
Mont Saint Guern 16
Montsale 43 E6
Monxton 25 E8
Monyash 75 C8
Monymusk 141 C5
Monzie 127 B7
Monzie Castle 127 B7
Moodiesburn 119 B6
Moonzie 128 C5
Moor Allerton 95 F5
Moorby 79 C5
Moor Crichel 13 D7
Moordown 13 E8
Moore 86 F3
Moorend 36 D4
Moor End E Yorks 96 F4
York 96 D2
Moorends 89 C7
Moorgate 88 E5
Moorgreen 76 E4
Moorhall 76 B3
Moorhampton 49 E5
Moorhead 94 F4
Moorhouse Cumb 108 D3
Notts 77 C7
Moorlinch 23 F5
Moor Monkton 95 D8
Moor of Granary 151 F13
Moor of Ravenstone 105 E7
Moor Row 98 C2
Moorsholm 102 C4
Moorside 87 D7
Moor Street 30 C2
Moorthorpe 89 C5
Moortown Hants 14 D2
IoW 14 F5
Lincs 90 E4
Morangie 151 C10
Morar 147 B9
Morborne 65 E8
Morchard Bishop 10 D2
Morcombelake 12 E2
Morcott 65 D6
Morda 60 B2
Morden Dorset 13 E7
London 28 C3
Mordiford 49 F7
Mordon 101 B8
More 60 E3
Morebath 10 B4
Morebattle 116 B3
Morecambe 92 C4
Morefield 150 B4
Moreleigh 7 D5
Morenish 132 F2
Moresby 98 B1
Moresby Parks 98 C1
Morestead 15 B6
Moreton Dorset 13 F6
Essex 41 D8
Mers 85 E3
Oxon 39 D6
Staffs 61 C7
Moreton Corbet 61 B5
Moretonhampstead 10 F2
Moreton-in-Marsh 51 F7
Moreton Jeffries 49 E8
Moreton Morrell 51 D8
Moreton on Lugg 49 E7
Moreton Pinkney 52 E3
Moreton Say 74 F3
Moreton Valence 36 D4
Morfa Carms 33 C6
Carms 33 E6
Morfa Bach 32 C4
Morfa Bychan 71 D6
Morfa Dinlle 82 F4
Morfa Glas 34 D2
Morfa Nefyn 70 C3
Morfydd 72 E5
Morgan's Vale 14 B2
Moriah 46 B5
Morland 99 B7
Morley Derbys 76 E3
Durham 101 B6
W Yorks 88 B3
Morley Green 87 F6
Morley St Botolph 68 E3
Morningside Edin 120 B5
N Lanark 119 D8
Morningthorpe 68 E5
Morpeth 117 F8
Morphie 135 C7
Morrey 62 C5
Morris Green 55 F8
Morriston 33 E7
Morston 81 C6
Mortehoe 20 E3
Mortimer 26 C4
Mortimer's Cross 49 C6
Mortimer West End 26 C4
Mortlake 28 B3
Morton Cumb 108 D3
Derbys 76 C4
Lincs 65 B7
Lincs 77 C8
Lincs 90 E2
Norf 68 C4
Notts 77 D7
S Glos 36 E3
Shrops 60 B2
Morton Bagot 51 C6
Morton-on-Swale 101 E8
Morvah 2 C3
Morval 5 D7
Morvich Highld 136 B2
Highld 157 J10
Morville 61 E6
Morville Heath 61 E6
Morwenstow 8 C4
Mosborough 88 F5
Moscow 118 E4
Mosedale 108 F3
Moseley W Mid 62 E3
W Mid 62 F4
Worcs 50 D3
Moss Argyll 146 G2
Highld 147 E9
S Yorks 89 C6
Wrex 73 D7
Mossat 140 C3
Mossbank 160 F6
Moss Bank 86 E3
Mossbay 98 B1
Mossblown 112 B4
Mossbrow 86 F5
Mossburnford 116 C2
Mossdale 106 B3
Moss Edge 92 E4
Mossend 119 C7
Moss End 27 B6
Mosser 98 B3
Mossfield 151 D9
Mossgiel 112 B4
Mosside 134 D4
Mossley Ches E 75 C5
Gtr Man 87 D7
Mossley Hill 85 F4
Moss of Barmuckity 152 B2
Moss Pit 62 B3
Moss-side 151 F11
Moss Side 92 F3
Mosstodloch 152 B3
Mosston 135 E5
Mossy Lea 86 C3
Mosterton 12 D2
Moston Gtr Man 87 D6
Shrops 61 B5
Moston Green 74 C4
Mostyn 85 F2
Mostyn Quay 85 F2
Motcombe 13 B6
Mothecombe 6 E4
Motherby 99 B6
Motherwell 119 D7
Mottingham 28 B5
Mottisfont 14 B4
Mottistone 14 F5
Mottram in Longdendale 87 E7
Mottram St Andrew 75 B5
Mouilpied Guern 16
Mouldsworth 74 B2
Moulin 133 D6
Moulsecoomb 17 D7
Moulsford 39 F5
Moulsoe 53 E7
Moulton Ches W 74 C3
Lincs 66 B3
N Yorks 101 D7
Suff 55 C7
V Glam 22 B2
W Nhants 53 C5
Moulton Chapel 66 C2
Moulton Eaugate 66 C3
Moulton St Mary 69 D6
Moulton Seas End 66 B3
Mounie Castle 141 B6
Mount Corn 4 D2
Corn 5 C6
Highld 151 G12
Mountain 94 F3
Mountain Ash = *Aberpennar* 34 E4
Mountain Cross 120 E4
Mountain Water 44 C4
Mountbenger 115 B6
Mount Bures 56 F3
Mount Canisp 151 D10
Mountfield 18 C4
Mountgerald 151 E8
Mount Hawke 3 B6
Mountjoy 4 C3
Mountnessing 42 E2
Mounton 36 E2
Mount Pleasant Ches E 74 D5
Derbys 63 C6
Derbys 76 E3
Flint 73 B6
Hants 14 E3
W Yorks 88 B3
Mountsorrel 64 C2
Mount Sorrel 13 B8
Mount Tabor 87 B8
Mousehole 2 D3
Mousen 123 F7
Mouswald 107 B7
Mow Cop 75 D5
Mowhaugh 116 B4
Mowsley 64 F3
Moxley 62 E3
Moy Highld 137 F7
Highld 151 H10
Moy Hall 151 H10
Moy House 151 E13
Moyles Court 14 D2
Moylgrove 45 E3
Moy Lodge 137 F7
Muasdale 143 D7
Muchalls 141 E8
Much Birch 49 F7
Much Cowarne 49 E8
Much Dewchurch 49 F6
Muchelney 12 B2
Much Hadham 41 C7
Much Hoole 86 B2
Muchlarnick 5 D7
Much Marcle 49 F8
Muchrachd 150 H5
Much Wenlock 61 D6
Muckernich 151 F8
Mucking 42 F2
Muckleford 12 E4
Mucklestone 74 F4
Muckleton 61 B5
Muckletown 140 B4
Muckley Corner 62 D4
Muckton 91 F7
Mudale 157 F8
Muddiford 20 F4
Mudeford 14 E2
Mudford 12 C3
Mudgley 23 E6
Mugdock 119 B5
Mugeary 149 E9
Mugginton 76 E2
Muggleswick 110 E3
Muie 157 J9
Muir 139 F6
Muirden 153 C7
Muirdrum 135 F5
Muirhead Angus 134 F3
Fife 128 D4
N Lanark 119 C6
S Ayrs 118 F3
Muirhouselaw 116 B2
Muirhouses 128 F2
Muirkirk 113 B6
Muirmill 127 F6
Muir of Fairburn 150 F7
Muir of Fowlis 140 C4
Muir of Ord 151 F8
Muir of Pert 134 F4
Muirshearlich 136 F4
Muirskie 141 E7
Muirtack 153 E9
Muirton Highld 151 E10
Perth 127 C8
Perth 128 B3
Muirton Mains 150 F7
Muirton of Ardblair 134 E1
Muirton of Ballochy 135 C6
Muiryfold 153 C7
Muker 100 E4
Mulbarton 68 D4
Mulben 152 C3
Mulindry 142 C4
Mullardoch House 150 H5
Mullion 3 E5
Mullion Cove 3 E5
Mumby 79 B8
Munderfield Row 49 D8
Munderfield Stocks 49 D8
Mundesley 81 D9
Mundford 67 E8
Mundham 69 E6
Mundon 42 D4
Mundurno 141 C8
Munerigie 137 D5
Muness 160 C8
Mungasdale 150 B2
Mungrisdale 108 F3
Munlochy 151 F9
Munsley 49 E8
Munslow 60 F5
Murchington 9 F8
Murcott 39 C5
Murkle 158 D3
Murlaggan Highld 136 E3
Highld 137 F6
Murra 159 H3
Murrayfield 120 B5
Murrow 66 D3
Mursley 39 B8
Murthill 134 D4
Murthly 133 F7
Murton Cumb 100 B2
Durham 111 E6
Northumb 123 E5
York 96 D2
Musbury 11 E7
Muscoates 102 F4
Musdale 124 C5
Musselburgh 121 B6
Muston Leics 77 F8
N Yorks 97 B6
Mustow Green 50 B3
Mutehill 106 E3
Mutford 69 F7
Muthill 127 C7
Mutterton 10 D5
Muxton 61 C7
Mybster 158 E3
Myddfai 34 B1
Myddle 60 B4
Mydroilyn 46 D3
Myerscough 92 F4
Mylor Bridge 3 C7
Mynachlog-ddu 45 F3
Myndtown 60 F3
Mynydd Bach 47 B6
Mynydd-bach 36 E1
Mynydd Bodafon 82 C4
Mynydd Isa 73 C6
Mynyddygarreg 33 D5
Mynytho 70 D4
Myrebird 141 E6
Myrelandhorn 158 E4
Myreside 128 B4
Myrtle Hill 47 F6
Mytchett 27 D6
Mytholm 87 B7
Mytholmroyd 87 B8
Myton-on-Swale 95 C7
Mytton 60 C4

N

Naast 155 J13
Naburn 95 E8
Nackington 31 D5
Nacton 57 E6
Nafferton 97 D6
Na Gearrannan 154 C6
Nailbridge 36 C3
Nailsbourne 11 B7
Nailsea 23 B6
Nailstone 63 D8
Nailsworth 37 E5
Nairn 151 F11
Nalderswood 28 E3
Nancegollan 2 C5
Nancledra 2 C3
Nanhoron 70 D3
Nannau 71 E8
Nannerch 73 C5
Nanpantan 64 C2
Nanpean 4 D4
Nanstallon 4 C5
Nant-ddu 34 C4
Nanternis 46 D2
Nantgaredig 33 B5
Nantgarw 35 F5
Nant-glas 47 C8
Nantglyn 72 C4
Nantgwyn 47 B8
Nantlle 82 F5
Nantmawr 60 B2
Nantmel 48 C2
Nantmor 71 C7
Nant Peris 83 F6
Nant Uchaf 72 D4
Nantwich 74 D3
Nant-y-Bai 47 E6
Nant-y-cafn 34 D2
Nantycaws 33 C5
Nant-y-derry 35 D7
Nant-y-ffi 46 F4
Nantyffyllon 34 E2
Nantyglo 35 C5
Nant-y-moel 34 E3
Nant-y-pandy 83 D6
Naphill 39 E8
Nappa 93 D8
Napton on the Hill 52 C2
Narberth = *Arberth* 32 C2
Narborough Leics 64 E2
Norf 67 C7
Nasareth 82 F4
Naseby 52 B4
Nash Bucks 53 F5
Hereford 48 C5
Newport 35 F7
Shrops 49 B8
Nash Lee 39 D8
Nassington 65 E7
Nasty 41 B6
Nateby Cumb 100 D2
Lancs 92 E4
Natland 99 F7
Naughton 56 E4
Naunton Glos 37 B8
Worcs 50 F3
Naunton Beauchamp 50 D4
Navenby 78 D2
Navestock Heath 41 E8
Navestock Side 42 E1
Navidale 157 H13
Nawton 102 F4
Nayland 56 F3
Nazeing 41 D7
Neacroft 14 E2
Neal's Green 63 F7
Neap 160 H7
Near Sawrey 99 E5
Neasham 101 C8
Neath = *Castell-Nedd* 33 E8
Neath Abbey 33 E8
Neatishead 69 B6
Nebo Anglesey 82 B4
Ceredig 46 C4
Conwy 83 F8
Gwyn 82 F4
Necton 67 D8
Nedd 156 F4
Nedderton 117 F8
Nedging Tye 56 E4
Needham 68 F5
Needham Market 56 D4
Needingworth 54 B4
Needwood 63 B5
Neen Savage 49 B8
Neen Sollars 49 B8
Neenton 61 F6
Nefyn 70 C4
Neilston 118 D4
Neinthirion 59 D6
Neithrop 52 E2
Nelly Andrews Green 60 D2
Nelson Caerph 35 E5
Lancs 93 F8
Nelson Village 111 B5
Nemphlar 119 E8
Nempnett Thrubwell 23 C7
Nene Terrace 66 D2
Nenthall 109 E7
Nenthead 109 E7
Nenthorn 122 F2
Nerabus 142 C3
Nercwys 73 C6
Nerston 119 D6
Nesbit 123 F5
Ness 73 B7
Nesscliffe 60 C3
Neston Ches W 73 B6
Wilts 24 C3
Nether Alderley 74 B5
Netheravon 25 E6
Nether Blainslie 121 E8
Nether Booth 88 F2
Netherbrae 153 C7
Netherbrough 159 G4
Nether Broughton 64 B3
Netherburn 119 E8
Nether Burrow 93 B6
Netherbury 12 E2
Netherby Cumb 108 B3
N Yorks 95 E6
Nether Cerne 12 E4
Nether Compton 12 C3
Nethercote 52 C3
Nethercott 20 F3
Nether Crimond 141 B7
Nether Dalgliesh 115 D5
Nether Dallachy 152 B3
Netherend 36 D2
Nether Exe 10 D4
Netherfield 18 D4
Nether Glasslaw 153 C8
Netherhampton 14 B2
Nether Handwick 134 E3
Nether Haugh 88 E5
Nether Heage 76 D3
Nether Heyford 52 D4
Nether Hindhope 116 C3
Nether Howecleuch 114 C3
Nether Kellet 92 C5
Nether Kinmundy 153 D10
Nether Langwith 76 B5
Netherlaw 106 E4
Nether Leask 153 E10
Nether Lenshie 153 D6
Netherley Aberds 141 E7
Mers 86 F2
Nethermill 114 F3
Nether Monynut 122 C3
Nethermuir 153 D9
Nether Padley 76 B2
Nether Park 153 C10
Netherplace 118 D5
Nether Poppleton 95 D8
Netherseal 63 C6
Nether Silton 102 E2
Nether Stowey 22 F3
Netherthird 113 C5
Netherthong 88 D2
Netherthorpe 89 F6
Netherton Angus 135 D5
Devon 7 B6
Hants 25 D8
Mers 85 D4
Northumb 117 D5
Oxon 38 E4
Perth 133 D8
Stirling 119 B5
W Mid 62 F3
Worcs 50 E4
W Yorks 88 C2
W Yorks 88 C3
Nethertown Cumb 98 D1
Highld 158 C5
Nether Urquhart 128 D3
Nether Wallop 25 F8
Nether Wasdale 98 D3
Nether Whitacre 63 E6
Netherwitton 117 E7
Netherwood 113 B6
Nether Worton 52 F2
Nethy Bridge 139 B6
Netley 15 D5
Netley Marsh 14 C4
Netteswell 41 C7
Nettlebed 39 F7
Nettlebridge 23 E8
Nettlecombe 12 E3
Nettleden 40 C3
Nettleham 78 B3
Nettlestead 29 D7
Nettlestead Green 29 D7
Nettlestone 15 E7
Nettlesworth 111 E5
Nettleton Lincs 90 D5
Wilts 24 B3
Neuadd 33 B7
Nevendon 42 E3
Nevern 45 E2
New Abbey 107 C6
New Aberdour 153 B8
New Addington 28 C4
Newall 94 E4
New Alresford 26 F3
New Alyth 134 E2
Newark Orkney 159 D8
Pboro 66 D2
Newark-on-Trent 77 D7
New Arley 63 F6
Newarthill 119 D7
New Ash Green 29 C7
New Barn 29 C7
New Barnetby 90 C4
Newbarns 92 B2
New Barton 53 C6
Newbattle 121 C6
New Bewick 117 B6
Newbiggin Cumb 92 C2
Cumb 98 E2
Cumb 99 B6
Cumb 99 B8
Cumb 109 E5
Durham 100 B4
N Yorks 100 E4
N Yorks 100 F4
Newbiggin-by-the-Sea 117 F9
Newbigging Angus 134 E2
Angus 134 F4
Angus 134 F4
S Lanark 120 E3
Newbiggin-on-Lune 100 D2
New Bilton 52 B2
Newbold Derbys 76 B3
Leics 63 C8
Newbold on Avon 52 B2
Newbold on Stour 51 E7
Newbold Pacey 51 D7
Newbold Verdon 63 D8
New Bolingbroke 79 D6
Newborough Anglesey 82 E4
Pboro 66 D2
Staffs 62 B5
Newbottle T&W 111 D6
W Nhants 52 F3
New Boultham 78 B2
Newbourne 57 E6
New Bradwell 53 E6
New Brancepeth 110 E5
Newbridge Caerph 35 E6
Ceredig 46 D4
Corn 2 C3
Corn 5 C8
Dumfries 107 B6
Edin 120 B4
Hants 14 C3
IoW 14 F5
Pembs 44 B4
New Bridge 73 E6
Newbridge Green 50 F3
Newbridge-on-Usk 35 E7
Newbridge on Wye 48 D2
New Brighton Flint 73 C6
Mers 85 E4
New Brinsley 76 D4
Newbrough 109 C8
New Broughton 73 D7
New Buckenham 68 E3
Newbuildings 10 D2
Newburgh Aberds 141 B8
Aberds 153 C9
Borders 115 C6
Fife 128 C4
Lancs 86 C2
Newburn 110 C4
Newbury 26 C2
Newbury Park 41 F7
Newby Cumb 99 B7
Lancs 93 E8
N Yorks 93 B7
N Yorks 102 C3
N Yorks 103 E8
Newby Bridge 99 F5
Newby East 108 D4
New Byth 153 C8
Newby West 108 D3
Newby Wiske 102 F1
Newcastle Mon 35 C8
Shrops 60 F2
Newcastle Emlyn = *Castell Newydd Emlyn* 46 E2
Newcastleton or Copshaw Holm 115 F7
Newcastle-under-Lyme 74 E5
Newcastle upon Tyne 110 C5
New Catton 68 C5
Newchapel Pembs 45 F4
Powys 59 F6
Staffs 75 D5
Sur 28 E4
New Cheriton 15 B6
Newchurch Carms 32 B4
IoW 15 F6
Kent 19 B7
Lancs 93 F8
Mon 36 E1
Powys 48 D4
Staffs 62 B5
New Costessey 68 C4
Newcott 11 D7
New Cowper 107 E8
Newcraighall 121 B6
New Cross Ceredig 46 B5
London 28 B4
New Cumnock 113 C6
New Deer 153 D8
New Delaval 111 B5
Newdigate 28 E2
New Duston 52 C5
New Earswick 96 D2
New Edlington 89 E6
New Elgin 152 B2
New Ellerby 97 F7
Newell Green 27 B6
New Eltham 28 B5
New End 51 D5
Newenden 18 C5
Newent 36 B4
Newerne 36 D3
New Farnley 94 F5
New Ferry 85 F4
Newfield Durham 110 F5
Highld 151 D10
Newford 2 E4
Newfound 26 D3
New Fryston 89 B5
Newgale 44 C3
New Galloway 106 B3
Newgate 81 C6
Newgate Street 41 D6
New Gilston 129 D6
New Grimsby 2 E3
New Hainford 68 C5
Newhall Ches E 74 E3
Derbys 63 B6
Newhall House 151 E9
Newhall Point 151 E10
Newham 117 B7
Newham Hall 117 B7
New Hartley 111 B6
Newhaven Derbys 75 D8
Edin 121 B5
E Sus 17 D8
New Haw 27 C8
New Hedges 32 D2
New Herrington 111 D6
Newhey 87 C7
New Hinksey 39 D5
New Holkham 80 D4
New Holland 90 B4
Newholm 103 C6
New Houghton Derbys 76 C4
Norf 80 E3
Newhouse 119 C7
New Houses 93 B8
New Humberstone 64 D3
New Hutton 99 E7
New Hythe 29 D8
Newick 17 B8
Newingreen 19 B8
Newington Kent 19 B8
Kent 30 C2
Kent 31 C7
Notts 89 E7
Oxon 39 E6
Shrops 60 F4
New Inn Carms 46 F3
Mon 36 D1
Pembs 45 F2
Torf 35 E7
New Invention Shrops 48 B4
W Mid 62 D3
New Kelso 150 G2
New Kingston 64 B2
New Lanark 119 E8
Newland Glos 36 D2
Hull 97 F6
N Yorks 89 B7
Worcs 50 E2
Newlandrig 121 C6
Newlands Borders 115 E8
Highld 151 G10
Moray 152 C3
Northumb 110 D3
Newland's Corner 27 E8
Newlandsmuir 119 D6
Newlands of Geise 158 D2
Newlands of Tynet 152 B3
Newlands Park 82 C2
New Lane 86 C2
New Lane End 86 E4
New Leake 79 D7
New Leeds 153 C9
New Longton 86 B3
Newlot 159 G6
New Luce 105 C5
Newlyn 2 D3
Newmachar 141 C7
Newmains 119 D8
New Malden 28 C3
Newmarket Suff 55 C7
W Isles 155 D9
New Marske 102 B4
New Marton 73 F7
New Micklefield 95 F7
Newmill Borders 115 C7
Corn 2 C3
Moray 152 C4
New Mill Aberds 141 F6
Herts 40 C2
Wilts 25 C6
W Yorks 88 D2
Newmill of Inshewan 134 C4
New Mills Ches E 87 F5
Corn 4 D3
Derbys 87 F7
Powys 59 D7
Newmills of Boyne 152 C5
Newmiln 133 F8
Newmilns 118 F5
New Milton 14 E3
New Moat 32 B1
Newnham Cambs 54 D5
Glos 36 C3
Hants 26 D5
Herts 54 F3
Kent 30 D3
W Nhants 52 D3
Newnham Bridge 49 C8
New Ollerton 77 C6
New Oscott 62 E4
Newpark 129 C6
New Park 95 D5
New Pitsligo 153 C8
New Polzeath 4 B4
Newport Devon 20 F4
Essex 55 F6
E Yorks 96 F4
Highld 158 H3
IoW 15 F6
Norf 69 C8
Telford 61 C7
Newport = *Casnewydd* 35 F7
Newport = *Trefdraeth* 45 F2
Newport-on-Tay 129 B6
Newport Pagnell 53 E6
Newpound Common 16 B4
Newquay 4 C3
New Quay = *Ceinewydd* 46 D2
New Rackheath 69 C5
New Radnor 48 C4
New Rent 108 F4
New Ridley 110 D3
New Road Side 94 E2
New Romney 19 C7
New Rossington 89 E7
New Row Ceredig 47 B6
Lancs 93 F6
N Yorks 102 C4
New Sarum 25 F6
Newsbank 74 C5
Newseat Aberds 153 D10
Aberds 153 E7
Newsham Northumb 111 B6
N Yorks 101 C6
N Yorks 102 F1
Newsholme E Yorks 89 B8
Lancs 93 D8
New Silksworth 111 D6
Newsome 88 C2
Newstead Borders 121 F8
Northumb 117 B7
Notts 76 D5
New Stevenston 119 D7
New Street 75 D7
New Street Lane 74 F3
New Swanage 13 F8
Newthorpe 95 F7
Newton Argyll 125 F6
Borders 116 B2
Bridgend 21 B7
Cambs 54 E5
Cambs 66 C4
Cardiff 22 B4
Ches W 73 C8
Ches W 74 B2
Ches W 74 D2
Cumb 92 B2
Derbys 76 D4
Dorset 13 C5
Dumfries 108 B2
Dumfries 114 E4
Gtr Man 87 E7
Hereford 48 F5
Hereford 49 D7
Highld 151 E10
Highld 151 G10
Highld 156 F5
Newton *continued*
Highld 158 F5
Lancs 92 F4
Lancs 93 B5
Lancs 93 D6
Lincs 78 F3
Moray 152 B1
N Nhants 65 F5
Norf 67 C8
Northumb 110 C3
Notts 77 E6
Perth 133 F5
S Lanark 119 C6
S Lanark 120 F2
Staffs 62 B4
Suff 56 E3
Swansea 33 F7
S Yorks 89 D6
Warks 52 B3
Wilts 14 B3
W Loth 120 B3
Newton Abbot 7 B6
Newtonairds 113 F8
Newton Arlosh 107 D8
Newton Aycliffe 101 B7
Newton Bewley 102 B2
Newton Blossomville 53 D7
Newton Bromswold 53 C7
Newton Burgoland 63 D7
Newton by Toft 90 F4
Newton Ferrers 6 E3
Newton Flotman 68 E5
Newtongrange 121 C6
Newton Hall 110 C3
Newton Harcourt 64 E3
Newton Heath 87 D6
Newtonhill Aberds 141 E8
Highld 151 G8
Newton House 141 B5
Newton Kyme 95 E7
Newton-le-Willows Mers 86 E3
N Yorks 101 F7
Newton Longville 53 F6
Newton Mearns 118 D5
Newtonmill 135 C6
Newtonmore 138 E3
Newton Morrell 101 D7
Newton Mulgrave 103 C5
Newton of Ardtoe 147 D9
Newton of Balcanquhal 128 C3
Newton of Falkland 128 D4
Newton on Ayr 112 B3
Newton on Ouse 95 D8
Newton-on-Rawcliffe 103 E6
Newton-on-the-Moor 117 D7
Newton on Trent 77 B8
Newton Park 145 G10
Newton Poppleford 11 F5
Newton Purcell 52 F4
Newton Regis 63 D6
Newton Reigny 108 F4
Newton St Cyres 10 E3
Newton St Faith 68 C5
Newton St Loe 24 C2
Newton St Petrock 9 C6
Newton Solney 63 B6
Newton Stacey 26 E2
Newton Stewart 105 C8
Newton Tony 25 E7
Newton Tracey 9 B7
Newton under Roseberry 102 C3
Newton upon Derwent 96 E3
Newton Valence 26 F5
New Totley 76 B3
Newtown Argyll 125 E6
BCP 13 E8
Ches W 74 B2
Corn 3 D6
Cumb 107 E7
Cumb 108 C5
Derbys 87 F7
Devon 10 B2
Glos 36 D3
Glos 50 F4
Hants 14 B4
Hants 14 C3
Hants 15 C6
Hants 15 C7
Hants 15 D5
Hants 26 C2
Hereford 49 E8
Highld 137 D6
IoM 84 E3
IoW 14 E5
Northumb 117 B6
Northumb 117 D6
Northumb 123 F5
Shrops 73 F8
Staffs 75 C6
Staffs 75 C7
Wilts 13 B7
New Town 121 B7
Newtown = *Y Drenewydd* 59 E8
Newtown Linford 64 D2
Newtown St Boswells 121 F8
Newtown Unthank 63 D8
New Tredegar = *Tredegar Newydd* 35 D5
New Trows 119 F8
Newtyle 134 E2
New Ulva 144 E6
New Walsoken 66 D4
New Waltham 91 D6
New Whittington 76 B3
New Wimpole 54 E4
New Winton 121 B7
New Yatt 38 C3
New York Lincs 78 D5
N Yorks 94 C4
Neyland 44 E4
Niarbyl 84 E2
Nibley 36 F3
Nibley Green 36 E4
Nibon 160 F5
Nicholashayne 11 C6
Nicholaston 33 F6
Nidd 95 C6
Nigg Aberdeen 141 D8
Highld 151 D11
Nigg Ferry 151 E10
Nightcott 10 B3
Nilig 72 D4
Nine Ashes 42 D1
Ninebanks 109 D7
Nine Mile Burn 120 D4
Nine Wells 44 C2
Ninfield 18 D4
Ningwood 14 F4
Nisbet 116 B2
Nisthouse Orkney 159 G4
Shetland 160 G7
Niton 15 G6
Nitshill 118 C5
Noak Hill 41 E8
Noblethorpe 88 D3
Nobottle 52 C4
Nocton 78 C3
Noke 39 C5
Nolton 44 D3
Nolton Haven 44 D3
No Man's Heath Ches W 74 E2
Warks 63 D6
Nomansland Devon 10 C3
Wilts 14 C3
Noneley 60 B4
Nonikiln 151 D9
Nonington 31 D6
Noonsbrough 160 H4
Norbreck 92 E3
Norbridge 50 E2
Norbury Ches E 74 E2
Derbys 75 E8
Shrops 60 E3
Staffs 61 B7
Nordelph 67 D5
Norden 87 C6
Norden Heath 13 F7
Nordley 61 E6
Norham 122 E5
Norley 74 B2
Norleywood 14 E4
Normanby N Lincs 90 C2
N Yorks 103 F5
Redcar 102 C3
Normanby-by-Spital 90 F4
Normanby by Stow 90 F2
Normanby le Wold 90 E5
Norman Cross 65 E8
Normandy 27 D7
Norman's Bay 18 E3
Norman's Green 11 D5
Normanstone 69 E8
Normanton Derby 76 F3
Leics 77 E8
Lincs 78 E2
Notts 77 D7
Rutland 65 D6
W Yorks 88 B4
Normanton le Heath 63 C7
Normanton on Soar 64 B2
Normanton-on-the-Wolds 77 F6
Normanton on Trent 77 C7
Normoss 92 F3
Norney 27 E7
Norrington Common 24 C3
Norris Green 85 E4
Norris Hill 63 C7
Northacre 68 E2
Northallerton 102 E1
Northam Devon 9 B6
Soton 14 C5
Northampton 53 C5
North Anston 89 F6
North Aston 38 B4
Northaw 41 D5
North Baddesley 14 C4
North Ballachulish 130 C4
North Barrow 12 B4
North Barsham 80 D5
Northbeck 78 E3
North Benfleet 42 F3
North Bersted 16 D3
North Berwick 129 F7
North Boarhunt 15 C7
Northborough 65 D8
Northbourne 31 D7
North Bovey 10 F2
North Bradley 24 D3
North Brentor 9 F6
North Brewham 24 F2
Northbridge Street 18 C4
North Buckland 20 E3
North Burlingham 69 C6
North Cadbury 12 B4
North Cairn 104 B3
North Carlton 78 B2
North Carrine 143 H7
North Cave 96 F4
North Cerney 37 D7
Northchapel 16 B3
North Charford 14 C2
North Charlton 117 B7
North Cheriton 12 B4
Northchurch 40 D2
North Cliff 97 E8
North Cliffe 96 F4
North Clifton 77 B8
North Cockerington 91 E7
North Coker 12 C3
North Collafirth 160 E5
North Common 17 B7
North Connel 124 B5
North Cornelly 34 F2
North Cotes 91 D7
Northcott 8 E5
North Cove 69 F7
North Cowton 101 D7
North Crawley 53 E7
North Cray 29 B5
North Creake 80 D4
North Curry 11 B8
North Dalton 96 D5
North Dawn 159 H5

North Deighton 95 D6
Northdown 31 B7
North Duffield 96 F2
Northdyke 159 F3
North Elkington 91 E6
North Elmham 81 E5
North Elmshall 89 C5
Northend Bath 24 C2
Bucks 39 E7
Warks 51 D8
North End Bucks 39 B8
Essex 42 C2
E Yorks 97 F8
Hants 26 C2
Lincs 78 E5
N Som 23 C6
Ptsmth 15 D7
Som 11 B7
W Sus 16 D5
Northenden 87 E6
North Erradale 155 J12
North Fambridge 42 E4
North Fearns 149 E10
North Featherstone 88 B5
North Ferriby 90 B3
Northfield Aberdeen 141 D8
Borders 122 C5
E Yorks 90 B4
W Mid 50 B5
Northfields 65 D7
Northfleet 29 B7
North Frodingham 97 D7
Northgate 65 B8
North Gluss 160 F5
North Gorley 14 C2
North Green Norf 68 F5
Suff 57 C7
North Greetwell 78 B3
North Grimston 96 C4
North Halley 159 H6
North Halling 29 C8
North Hayling 15 D8
North Hazelrigg 123 F6
North Heasley 21 F6
North Heath 16 B4
North Hill Cambs 55 B5
Corn 5 B7
North Hinksey 38 D4
North Holmwood 28 E2
Northhouse 115 D7
North Howden 96 F3
North Huish 6 D5
North Hykeham 78 C2
Northiam 18 C5
Northill 54 E2
Northington 26 F3
North Johnston 44 D4
North Kelsey 90 D4
North Kelsey Moor 90 D4
North Kessock 151 G9
North Killingholme 90 C5
North Kilvington 102 F2
North Kilworth 64 F3
North Kirkton 153 C11
North Kiscadale 143 F11
North Kyme 78 D4
North Lancing 17 D5
Northlands 79 D6
Northlea 111 D7
Northleach 37 C8
North Lee 39 D8
Northleigh 11 E6
North Leigh 38 C3
North Leverton with Habblesthorpe 89 F8
Northlew 9 E7
North Littleton 51 E5
North Lopham 68 F3
North Luffenham 65 D6
North Marden 16 C2
North Marston 39 B7
North Middleton Midloth 121 D6
Northumb 117 B6
North Molton 10 B2
Northmoor 38 D4
Northmoor Green or Moorland 22 F5
North Moreton 39 F5
Northmuir 134 D3
North Mundham 16 D2
North Muskham 77 D7
North Newbald 96 F5
North Newington 52 F2
North Newnton 25 D6
North Newton 22 F4
Northney 15 D8
North Nibley 36 E4
North Oakley 26 D3
North Ockendon 42 F1
Northolt 40 F4
Northop 73 C6
Northop Hall 73 C6
North Ormesby 102 B3
North Ormsby 91 E6
Northorpe Lincs 65 C7
Lincs 78 F5
Lincs 90 E2
North Otterington 102 F1
Northover Som 12 B3
Som 23 F6
North Owersby 90 E4
Northowram 88 B2
North Perrott 12 D2
North Petherton 22 F4
North Petherwin 8 F4
North Pickenham 67 D8
North Piddle 50 D4
North Poorton 12 E3
Northport 13 F7
North Port 125 C6
Northpunds 160 L6
North Queensferry 128 F3
North Radworthy 21 F6
North Rauceby 78 E3
Northrepps 81 D8
North Reston 91 F7
North Rigton 95 E5
North Rode 75 C5
North Roe 160 E5
North Runcton 67 C6
North Sandwick 160 D7
North Scale 92 C1
North Scarle 77 C8
North Seaton 117 F8
North Shian 130 E3
North Shields 111 C6
North Shoebury 43 F5
North Shore 92 F3
North Side Cumb 98 B2
Pboro 66 E2
North Skelton 102 C4
North Somercotes 91 E8
North Stainley 95 B5
North Stainmore 100 C3
North Stifford 42 F2
North Stoke Bath 24 C2
Oxon 39 F6
W Sus 16 C4
Northstowe 54 C5
North Street Hants 26 F4
Kent 30 D4
Medway 30 B2
W Berks 26 B4
North Sunderland 123 F8
North Tamerton 8 E5
North Tawton 9 D8
North Thoresby 91 E6
North Tidworth 25 E7
North Togston 117 D8
Northtown 159 J5
North Tuddenham 68 C3
North Walbottle 110 C4
North Walsham 81 D8
North Waltham 26 E3
North Warnborough 26 D5
North Water Bridge 135 C6
North Watten 158 E4
Northway 50 F4
North Weald Bassett 41 D7
North Wheatley 89 F8
North Whilborough 7 C6
Northwich 74 B3
Northwick 36 F2
North Wick 23 C7
North Willingham 91 F5
North Wingfield 76 C4
North Witham 65 B6
Northwold 67 E7
Northwood Derbys 76 C2
IoW 15 E5
Kent 31 C7
London 40 E3
Shrops 73 F8
Northwood Green 36 C4
North Woolwich 28 B5
North Wootton Dorset 12 C4
Norf 67 B6
Som 23 E7
North Wraxall 24 B3
North Wroughton 38 F1
Norton E Sus 17 D8
Glos 37 B5
Halton 86 F3
Herts 54 F3
IoW 14 F4
Mon 35 C8
Notts 77 B5
Powys 48 C5
Shrops 60 F4
Shrops 61 D5
Shrops 61 D7
Stockton 102 B2
Suff 56 C3
S Yorks 89 C6
Wilts 37 F5
W Nhants 52 C4
Worcs 50 D3
Worcs 50 E5
W Sus 16 D3
W Sus 16 E2
Norton Bavant 24 E4
Norton Bridge 75 F5
Norton Canes 62 D4
Norton Canon 49 E5
Norton Corner 81 E6
Norton Disney 77 D8
Norton East 62 D4
Norton Ferris 24 F2
Norton Fitzwarren 11 B6
Norton Green 14 F4
Norton Hawkfield 23 C7
Norton Heath 42 D2
Norton in Hales 74 F4
Norton-in-the-Moors 75 D5
Norton-Juxta-Twycross 63 D7
Norton-le-Clay 95 B7
Norton Lindsey 51 C7
Norton Malreward 23 C8
Norton Mandeville 42 D1
Norton-on-Derwent 96 B3
Norton St Philip 24 D2
Norton sub Hamdon 12 C2
Norton Woodseats 88 F4
Norwell 77 C7
Norwell Woodhouse 77 C7
Norwich 68 D5
Norwick 160 B8
Norwood 89 F5
Norwood Hill 28 E3
Norwoodside 66 E4
Noseley 64 E4
Noss 160 M5
Noss Mayo 6 E3
Nosterfield 101 F7
Nostie 149 F13
Notgrove 37 B8
Nottage 21 B7
Nottingham 77 F5
Nottington 12 F4
Notton Wilts 24 C4
W Yorks 88 C4
Nounsley 42 C3
Noutard's Green 50 C2
Novar House 151 E9
Nox 60 C4
Nuffield 39 F6
Nunburnholme 96 E4
Nuncargate 76 D5
Nuneaton 63 E7
Nuneham Courtenay 39 E5
Nun Hills 87 B6
Nun Monkton 95 D8
Nunney 24 E2
Nunnington 96 B2
Nunnykirk 117 E6
Nunsthorpe 91 D6
Nunthorpe Mbro 102 C3
York 96 D2
Nunton 14 B2
Nunwick 95 B6
Nupend 36 D4
Nursling 14 C4
Nursted 15 B8
Nutbourne W Sus 15 D8
W Sus 16 C4
Nutfield 28 D4
Nuthall 76 E5
Nuthampstead 54 F5
Nuthurst 17 B5
Nutley E Sus 17 B8
Hants 26 E4
Nutwell 89 D7
Nybster 158 D5
Nyetimber 16 E2
Nyewood 16 B2
Nymet Rowland 10 D2
Nymet Tracey 10 D2
Nympsfield 37 D5
Nynehead 11 B6
Nyton 16 D3

O

Oadby 64 D3
Oad Street 30 C2
Oakamoor 75 E7
Oakbank 120 C3
Oak Cross 9 E7
Oakdale 35 E5
Oake 11 B6
Oaken 62 D2
Oakenclough 92 E5
Oakengates 61 C7
Oakenholt 73 B6
Oakenshaw Durham 110 F5
W Yorks 88 B2
Oakerthorpe 76 D3
Oakes 88 C2
Oakfield 35 E7
Oakford Ceredig 46 D3
Devon 10 B4
Oakfordbridge 10 B4
Oakgrove 75 C6
Oakham 65 D5
Oakhanger 27 F5
Oakhill 23 E8
Oakhurst 29 D6
Oakington 54 C5
Oaklands Herts 41 C5
Powys 48 D2
Oakle Street 36 C4
Oakley BCP 13 E8
Bedford 53 D8
Bucks 39 C6
Fife 128 F2
Hants 26 D3
Oxon 39 D7
Suff 57 B5
Oakley Green 27 B7
Oakley Park 59 F6
Oakmere 74 C2
Oakridge Glos 37 D6
Hants 26 D4
Oaks 60 D4
Oaksey 37 E6
Oaks Green 75 F8
Oakthorpe 63 C7
Oakwoodhill 28 F2
Oakworth 94 F3
Oape 156 J7
Oare Kent 30 C4
Som 21 E7
W Berks 26 B3
Wilts 25 C6
Oasby 78 F3
Oathlaw 134 D4
Oatlands 95 D6
Oban Argyll 124 C4
Highld 147 C11
Oborne 12 C4
Obthorpe 65 C7
Occlestone Green 74 C3
Occold 57 B5
Ochiltree 112 B5
Ochtermuthill 127 C7
Ochtertyre 127 B7
Ockbrook 76 F4
Ockham 27 D8
Ockle 147 D8
Ockley 28 F2
Ocle Pychard 49 E7
Octon 97 C6
Octon Cross Roads 97 C6
Odcombe 12 C3
Odd Down 24 C2
Oddendale 99 C7
Odder 78 B2
Oddingley 50 D4
Oddington Glos 38 B2
Oxon 39 C5
Odell 53 D7
Odie 159 F7
Odiham 26 D5
Odstock 14 B2
Odstone 63 D7
Offchurch 51 C8
Offenham 51 E5
Offham E Sus 17 C7
Kent 29 D7
W Sus 16 D4
Offord Cluny 54 C3
Offord Darcy 54 C3
Offton 56 E4
Offwell 11 E6
Ogbourne Maizey 25 B6
Ogbourne St Andrew 25 B6
Ogbourne St George 25 B7
Ogil 134 C4
Ogle 110 B4
Ogmore 21 B7
Ogmore-by-Sea 21 B7
Ogmore Vale 34 E3
Okeford Fitzpaine 13 C6
Okehampton 9 E7
Okehampton Camp 9 E7
Okraquoy 160 K6
Old 53 B5
Old Aberdeen 141 D8
Old Alresford 26 F3
Oldany 156 F4
Old Arley 63 E6
Old Basford 76 E5
Old Basing 26 D4
Oldberrow 51 C6
Old Bewick 117 B6
Old Bolingbroke 79 C6
Oldborough 10 D2
Old Bramhope 94 E5
Old Brampton 76 B3
Old Bridge of Tilt 133 C5
Old Bridge of Urr 106 C4
Old Buckenham 68 E3
Old Burghclere 26 D2
Oldbury Shrops 61 E7
Warks 63 E7
W Mid 62 F3
Oldbury-on-Severn 36 E3
Oldbury on the Hill 37 F5
Old Byland 102 F3
Old Cassop 111 F6
Oldcastle Bridgend 21 B8
Mon 35 B7
Old Castleton 115 E8
Old Catton 68 C5
Old Clee 91 D6
Old Cleeve 22 E2
Old Clipstone 77 C6
Old Colwyn 83 D8
Oldcotes 89 F6
Old Coulsdon 28 D4
Old Crombie 152 C5
Old Dailly 112 E2
Old Dalby 64 B3
Old Deer 153 D9
Old Denaby 89 E5
Old Edlington 89 E6
Old Eldon 101 B7
Old Ellerby 97 F7
Oldfallow 62 C3
Old Felixstowe 57 F7
Oldfield 50 C3
Old Fletton 65 E8
Oldford 24 D2
Old Glossop 87 E8
Old Goole 89 B8
Old Hall 59 F6
Oldham 87 D7
Oldhamstocks 122 B3
Old Heath 43 B6
Old Heathfield 18 C2
Old Hill 62 F3
Old Hunstanton 80 C2
Old Hurst 54 B3
Old Hutton 99 F7
Old Kea 3 B7
Old Kilpatrick 118 B4
Old Kinnernie 141 D6
Old Knebworth 41 B5
Oldland 23 B8
Old Langho 93 F7
Old Laxey 84 D4
Old Leake 79 D7
Old Malton 96 B3
Oldmeldrum 141 B7
Old Micklefield 95 F7
Old Milton 14 E3
Old Milverton 51 C7
Old Monkland 119 C7
Old Netley 15 D5
Old Philpstoun 120 B3
Old Quarrington 111 F6
Old Radnor 48 D4
Old Rattray 153 C10
Old Rayne 141 B5
Old Romney 19 C7
Oldshore Beg 156 D4
Oldshoremore 156 D5
Old Sodbury 36 F4
Old Somerby 78 F2
Oldstead 102 F3
Old Stratford 53 E5
Old Thirsk 102 F2
Oldtown 140 B4
Old Town Cumb 99 F7
Cumb 108 E4
Northumb 116 E4
Scilly 2 E4
Oldtown of Ord 152 C6
Old Trafford 87 E6
Old Tupton 76 C3
Old Warden 54 E2
Oldway 33 F6
Oldways End 10 B3
Old Weston 53 B8
Oldwhat 153 C8
Old Whittington 76 B3
Old Wick 158 E5
Old Windsor 27 B7
Old Wives Lees 30 D4
Old Woking 27 D8
Old Woodhall 78 C5
Olgrinmore 158 E2
Oliver's Battery 15 B5
Ollaberry 160 E5
Ollerton Ches E 74 B4
Notts 77 C6
Shrops 61 B6
Olmarch 46 D5
Olney 53 D6
Olrig House 158 D3
Olton 62 F5
Olveston 36 F3
Olwen 46 E4
Ombersley 50 C3
Ompton 77 C6
Onchan 84 E3
Onecote 75 D7
Onen 35 C8
Ongar Hill 67 B5
Ongar Street 49 C5
Onibury 49 B6
Onich 130 C4
Onllwyn 34 C2
Onneley 74 E4
Onslow Village 27 E7
Onthank 118 E4
Openwoodgate 76 E3
Opinan Highld 149 A12
Highld 155 H13
Orange Lane 122 E3
Orange Row 66 B5
Orasaigh 155 F8
Orbliston 152 C3
Orbost 148 D7
Orby 79 C7
Orchard Hill 9 B6
Orchard Portman 11 B7
Orcheston 25 E5
Orcop 36 B1
Orcop Hill 36 B1
Ord 149 G11
Ordhead 141 C5
Ordie 140 D3
Ordiequish 152 C3
Ordsall 89 F7
Ore 18 D5
Oreton 61 F6
Orford Suff 57 E8
Warr 86 E4
Orgreave 63 C5
Orlestone 19 B6
Orleton Hereford 49 C6
Worcs 49 C8
Orlingbury 53 B6
Ormesby 102 C3
Ormesby St Margaret 69 C7
Ormesby St Michael 69 C7
Ormiclate Castle 148 E2
Ormiscaig 155 H13
Ormiston 121 C7
Ormsaigbeg 146 E7
Ormsaigmore 146 E7
Ormsary 144 F6
Ormsgill 92 B1
Ormskirk 86 D2
Orpington 29 C5
Orrell Gtr Man 86 D3
Mers 85 E4
Orrisdale 84 C3
Orroland 106 E4
Orsett 42 F2
Orslow 62 C2
Orston 77 E7
Orthwaite 108 F2
Ortner 92 D5
Orton Cumb 99 D8
N Nhants 53 B6
Orton Longueville 65 E8
Orton-on-the-Hill 63 D7
Orton Waterville 65 E8
Orwell 54 D4
Osbaldeston 93 F6
Osbaldwick 96 D2
Osbaston 60 B3
Osbournby 78 F3
Oscroft 74 C2
Ose 149 D8
Osgathorpe 63 C8
Osgodby Lincs 90 E4
N Yorks 96 F2
N Yorks 103 F8
Oskaig 149 E10
Oskamull 146 G7
Osmaston Derby 76 F3
Derbys 76 E2
Osmington 12 F5
Osmington Mills 12 F5
Osmotherley 102 E2
Ospisdale 151 C10
Ospringe 30 C4
Ossett 88 B3
Ossington 77 C7
Ostend 43 E5
Oswaldkirk 96 B2
Oswaldtwistle 86 B5
Oswestry 60 B2
Otford 29 D6
Otham 29 D8
Othery 23 F5
Otley Suff 57 D6
W Yorks 94 E5
Otterbourne 15 B5
Otterburn Northumb 116 E4
N Yorks 93 D8
Otterburn Camp 116 E4
Otter Ferry 145 E8
Otterham 8 E3
Otterhampton 22 E4
Ottershaw 27 C8
Otterswick 160 E7
Otterton 11 F5
Ottery St Mary 11 E6
Ottinge 31 E5
Ottringham 91 B6
Oughterby 108 D2
Oughtershaw 100 F3
Oughterside 107 E8
Oughtibridge 88 E4
Oughtrington 86 F4
Oulston 95 B8
Oulton Cumb 108 D2
Norf 81 E7
Staffs 75 F6
Suff 69 E8
W Yorks 88 B4
Oulton Broad 69 E8
Oulton Street 81 E7
Oundle 65 F7
Ousby 109 F6
Ousdale 158 H2
Ousden 55 D8
Ousefleet 90 B2
Ouston Durham 111 D5
Northumb 110 B3
Outertown 159 G3
Outgate 99 E5
Outhgill 100 D2
Outlane 87 C8
Out Newton 91 B7
Out Rawcliffe 92 E4
Outwell 66 D5
Outwick 14 C2
Outwood Sur 28 E4
W Yorks 88 B4
Outwoods 61 C7
Ovenden 87 B8
Ovenscloss 121 F7
Over Cambs 54 B4
Ches W 74 C3
S Glos 36 F2
Overbister 159 D7
Overbury 50 F4
Overcombe 12 F4
Over Compton 12 C3
Overgreen 76 B3
Over Green 63 E5
Over Haddon 76 C2
Over Hulton 86 D4
Over Kellet 92 B5
Over Kiddington 38 B4
Over Knutsford 74 B4
Overleigh 23 F6
Overley Green 51 D5
Over Monnow 36 C2
Over Norton 38 B3
Over Peover 74 B4
Overpool 73 B7
Overscaig Hotel 156 G7
Overseal 63 C6
Over Silton 102 E2
Oversland 30 D4
Overstone 53 C6
Over Stowey 22 F3
Overstrand 81 C8
Over Stratton 12 C2
Over Tabley 86 F5
Overthorpe 52 E2
Overton Aberdeen 141 C7
Ches W 74 B2
Dumfries 107 C6
Hants 26 E3
Lancs 92 D4
N Yorks 95 D8
Shrops 49 B7
Swansea 33 F5
W Yorks 88 C3
Overton = Owrtyn 73 E7
Overton Bridge 73 E7
Overtown 119 D8
Over Wallop 25 F7
Over Whitacre 63 E6
Over Worton 38 B4
Oving Bucks 39 B7
W Sus 16 D3
Ovingdean 17 D7
Ovingham 110 C3
Ovington Durham 101 C6
Essex 55 E8
Hants 26 F3
Norf 68 D2
Northumb 110 C3
Ower 14 C4
Owermoigne 13 F5
Owlbury 60 E3
Owler Bar 76 B2
Owlerton 88 F4
Owl's Green 57 C6
Owlswick 39 D7
Owmby 90 D4
Owmby-by-Spital 90 F4
Owrtyn = Overton 73 E7
Owslebury 15 B6
Owston Leics 64 D4
S Yorks 89 C6
Owston Ferry 90 D2
Owstwick 97 F8
Owthorne 91 B7
Owthorpe 77 F6
Oxborough 67 D7
Oxcombe 79 B6
Oxenholme 99 F7
Oxenhope 94 F3
Oxen Park 99 F5
Oxenton 50 F4
Oxenwood 25 D8
Oxford 39 D5
Oxhey 40 E4
Oxhill 51 E8
Oxley 62 D3
Oxley Green 43 C5
Oxley's Green 18 C3
Oxnam 116 C2
Oxshott 28 C2
Oxspring 88 D3
Oxted 28 D4
Oxton Borders 121 D7
Notts 77 D6
Oxwich 33 F5
Oxwick 80 E5
Oykel Bridge 156 J6
Oyne 141 B5

P

Pabail Iarach 155 D10
Pabail Uarach 155 D10
Pace Gate 94 D4
Packington 63 C7
Padanaram 134 D4
Padbury 52 F5
Paddington 41 F5
Paddlesworth 19 B8
Paddockhaugh 152 C2
Paddockhole 115 F5
Paddock Wood 29 E7
Padfield 87 E8
Padiham 93 F7
Padog 83 F8
Padside 94 D4
Padstow 4 B4
Padworth 26 C4
Page Bank 110 F5
Pagelsham Eastend 43 E5
Pagham 16 E2
Paglesham Churchend 43 E5
Paibeil 148 B2
Paible 154 H5
Paignton 7 C6
Pailton 63 F8
Painscastle 48 E3
Painshawfield 110 C3
Painsthorpe 96 D4
Painswick 37 D5
Pairc Shiaboist 154 C7
Paisley 118 C4
Pakefield 69 E8
Pakenham 56 C3
Pale 72 F3
Palestine 25 E7
Paley Street 27 B6
Palfrey 62 E4
Palgowan 112 F3
Palgrave 56 B5
Pallion 111 D6
Palmarsh 19 B8
Palnackie 106 D5
Palnure 105 C8
Palterton 76 C4
Pamber End 26 D4
Pamber Green 26 D4
Pamber Heath 26 C4
Pamphill 13 D7
Pampisford 55 E5
Pan 159 J4
Panbride 135 F5
Pancrasweek 8 D4
Pandy Gwyn 58 D3
Mon 35 B7
Powys 59 D6
Wrex 73 F5
Pandy Tudur 83 E8
Panfield 42 B3
Pangbourne 26 B4
Pannal 95 D6
Panshanger 41 C5
Pant 60 B2
Pant-glas Carms 33 B6
Gwyn 71 C5
Pant-glâs 58 E4
Pant-glas 73 F6
Pantgwyn Carms 33 B6
Ceredig 45 E4
Pant-lasau 33 E7
Pant Mawr 59 F5
Panton 78 B4
Pantperthog 58 D4
Pant-teg 33 B5
Pant-y-Caws 32 B2
Pant-y-dwr 47 B8
Pant-y-ffridd 59 D8
Pantyffynnon 33 C7
Pantymwyn 73 C5
Pant-yr-awel 34 F3
Pant-y-Wacco 72 B5
Panxworth 69 C6
Papcastle 107 F8
Papigoe 158 E5
Papil 160 K5
Papley 159 J5
Papple 121 B8
Papplewick 76 D5
Papworth Everard 54 C3
Papworth St Agnes 54 C3
Par 5 D5
Parbold 86 C2
Parbrook Som 23 F7
W Sus 16 B4
Parc 72 F2
Parcllyn 45 D4
Parc-Seymour 35 E8
Parc-y-rhôs 46 E4
Pardshaw 98 B2
Parham 57 C7
Park 114 E2
Park Corner Oxon 39 F6
Windsor 40 F1
Parkend 36 D3
Park End Mbro 102 C3
Northumb 109 B8
Parkeston 57 F6
Parkgate Ches W 73 B6
Dumfries 114 F3
Kent 19 B5
Sur 28 E3
Park Gate 15 D6
Parkham 9 B5
Parkham Ash 9 B5
Park Hill Notts 77 D6
N Yorks 95 C6
Parkhill House 141 C7
Parkhouse 36 D1
Parkhouse Green 76 C4
Parkhurst 15 E5
Parkmill 33 F6
Parkneuk 135 B7
Parkstone 13 E8
Park Street 28 F2
Parley Cross 13 E8
Parracombe 21 E5
Parrog 45 F2
Parsley Hay 75 C8
Parsonage Green 42 D3
Parsonby 107 F8
Parson Cross 88 E4
Parson Drove 66 D3
Parson's Heath 43 B6
Partick 119 C5
Partington 86 E5
Partney 79 C7
Parton Cumb 98 B1
Dumfries 106 B3
Glos 37 B5
Partridge Green 17 C5
Parwich 75 D8
Passenham 53 F5
Paston 81 D9
Patchacott 9 E6
Patcham 17 D7
Patching 16 D4
Patchole 20 E5
Pateley Bridge 94 C4
Paternoster Heath 43 C5
Pathe 23 F5
Pathhead Aberds 135 C7
E Ayrs 113 C6
Fife 128 E4
Midloth 121 C6
Path of Condie 128 C2
Pathstruie 128 C2
Patna 112 C4
Patney 25 D5
Patrick 84 D2
Patrick Brompton 101 E7
Patrington 91 B7
Patrixbourne 31 D5
Patterdale 99 C5
Pattingham 62 E2
Pattishall 52 D4
Pattiswick Green 42 B4
Patton Bridge 99 E7
Paul 2 D3
Paulerspury 52 E5
Paull 91 B5
Paulton 23 D8
Pavenham 53 D7
Pawlett 22 E5
Pawston 122 F4
Paxford 51 F6
Paxton 122 D5
Payhembury 11 D5
Paythorne 93 D8
Peacehaven 17 D8
Peak Dale 75 B7
Peak Forest 75 B8
Peakirk 65 D8
Pearsie 134 D3
Peasedown St John 24 D2
Peasemore 26 B2
Peasenhall 57 C7
Pease Pottage 28 F3
Peaslake 27 E8
Peasley Cross 86 E3
Peasmarsh 19 C5
Peaston 121 C7
Peastonbank 121 C7
Peathill 153 B9
Peat Inn 129 D6
Peatling Magna 64 E2
Peatling Parva 64 F2
Peaton 60 F5
Peats Corner 57 C5
Pebmarsh 56 F2
Pebworth 51 E6
Pecket Well 87 B7
Peckforton 74 D2
Peckham 28 B4
Peckleton 63 D8
Pedlinge 19 B8
Pedmore 62 F3
Pedwell 23 F6
Peebles 121 E5
Peel 84 D2
Peel Common 15 D6
Peel Park 119 D6
Peening Quarter 19 C5
Pegsdon 54 F2
Pegswood 117 F8
Pegwell 31 C7
Peinchorran 149 E10
Peinlich 149 C9
Pelaw 111 C5
Pelcomb Bridge 44 D4
Pelcomb Cross 44 D4
Peldon 43 C5
Pellon 87 B8
Pelsall 62 D4
Pelton 111 D5
Pelutho 107 E8
Pelynt 5 D7
Pemberton 86 D3
Pembrey 33 D5
Pembridge 49 D5
Pembroke = Penfro 44 E4
Pembroke Dock = Doc Penfro 44 E4
Pembury 29 E7
Penallt 36 C2
Penally 32 E2
Penalt 36 B2
Penare 3 B8
Penarlâg = Hawarden 73 C7
Penarth 22 B3
Pen-bont Rhydybeddau 58 F3
Penbryn 45 D4
Pencader 46 F3
Pencaenewydd 70 C5
Pencaitland 121 C7
Pencarnisiog 82 D3
Pencarreg 46 E4
Pencelli 34 B4
Pen-clawdd 33 E6
Pencoed 34 F3
Pencombe 49 D7
Pencoyd 36 B2
Pencraig Hereford 36 B2
Powys 59 B7
Pendeen 2 C2
Penderyn 34 D3
Pendine 32 D3
Pendlebury 87 D5
Pendleton 93 F7
Pendock 50 F2
Pendoggett 4 B5
Pendomer 12 C3
Pendoylan 22 B2
Pendre 34 F3
Penegoes 58 D4
Pen-ffordd 32 B1
Penfro = Pembroke 44 E4
Pengam 35 E5
Penge 28 B4
Pengenffordd 48 F3
Pengorffwysfa 82 B4
Pengover Green 5 C7
Pen-groes-oped 35 D7
Penhale Corn 3 E5
Corn 4 D4
Penhalvaen 3 C6
Penhill 38 F1
Penhow 35 E8
Penhurst 18 D3
Peniarth 58 D3
Penicuik 120 C5
Peniel Carms 33 B5
Denb 72 C4
Penifiler 149 D9
Peninver 143 F8
Penisarwaun 83 E5
Penistone 88 D3
Penjerrick 3 C6
Penketh 86 F3
Penkill 112 E2
Penkridge 62 C3
Penley 73 F8
Penllergaer 33 E7
Penllyn 21 B8
Pen-llyn 82 C3
Pen-lon 82 E4
Penmachno 83 F7
Penmaen 33 F6
Penmaenan 83 D7
Penmaenmawr 83 D7
Penmaenpool 58 C3
Penmark 22 C2
Penmarth 3 C6
Penmon 83 C6
Penmore Mill 146 F7
Penmorfa Ceredig 46 D2
Gwyn 71 C6
Penmynydd 82 D5
Penn Bucks 40 E2
W Mid 62 E2
Pennal 58 D4
Pennan 153 B8
Pennant Ceredig 46 C4
Denb 72 D4
Denb 72 F4
Powys 59 E5
Pennant Melangell 59 B7
Pennar 44 E4
Pennard 33 F6
Pennerley 60 E3
Pennington Cumb 92 B2
Gtr Man 86 E4
Hants 14 E4
Penn Street 40 E2
Penny Bridge 99 F5
Pennycross 147 J8
Pennygate 69 B6
Pennygown 147 G8
Pennymoor 10 C3
Pennywell 111 D6
Penparc Ceredig 45 E4
Pembs 44 B3
Penparcau 58 F2
Penperlleni 35 D7
Penpillick 5 D5
Penpol 3 C7
Penpoll 5 D6
Penpont Dumfries 113 E8
Powys 34 B3
Penrherber 45 F4
Penrhiwceiber 34 E4
Penrhiw goch 33 C6
Penrhiw-llan 46 E2
Penrhiw-pâl 46 E2
Penrhos 70 D4
Penrhôs 35 C8
Penrhos 34 C1
Penrhosfeilw 82 C2
Penrhyn Bay 83 C8
Penrhyn-coch 58 F3
Penrhyndeudraeth 71 D7
Penrhynside 83 C8
Penrice 33 F5
Penrith 108 F5
Penrose 4 B3
Penruddock 99 B6
Penryn 3 C6
Pensarn Carms 33 C5
Conwy 72 B3
Pen-sarn Gwyn 70 C5
Gwyn 71 E6
Pensax 50 C2
Pensby 85 F3
Penselwood 24 F2
Pensford 23 C8
Penshaw 111 D6
Penshurst 29 E6
Pensilva 5 C7
Penston 121 B7
Pentewan 3 B9
Pentir 83 E5
Pentire 4 C2
Pentlow 56 E2
Pentney 67 C7
Penton Mewsey 25 E8
Pentraeth 82 D5
Pentre Carms 33 C6
Powys 59 F7
Powys 60 E2
Rhondda 34 E3
Shrops 60 C3
Wrex 72 F5
Wrex 73 E6
Pentrebach M Tydf 34 D4
Swansea 33 D7
Pentre-bâch 46 E4
Pentre-bach 47 F8
Pentrebeirdd 59 C8
Pentre Berw 82 D4
Pentre-bont 83 F7
Pentrecagal 46 E2
Pentre-celyn Denb 72 D5
Powys 59 D5
Pentre-chwyth 33 E7
Pentre-cwrt 46 F2
Pentre Dolau-Honddu 47 E8
Pentredwr 73 E5
Pentre-dwr 33 E7
Pentrefelin Carms 33 B6
Ceredig 46 E5
Conwy 83 D8
Gwyn 71 D6
Pentrefoelas 83 F8
Pentre-galar 45 F3
Pentregat 46 D2
Pentre-Gwenlais 33 C7
Pentre Gwynfryn 71 E6
Pentre Halkyn 73 B6
Pentreheyling 60 E2
Pentre-Isaf 83 E8
Pentre Llanrhaeadr 72 C4
Pentre-llwyn-llŵyd 47 D8
Pentre-llyn 46 B5
Pentre-llyn cymmer 72 D3
Pentre Meyrick 21 B8
Pentre-poeth 35 F6
Pentre'r Felin 83 E8
Pentre'r-felin 47 F8
Pentre-rhew 47 D5
Pentre-tafarn-y-fedw 83 E8
Pentre-ty-gwyn 47 F7
Pentrich 76 D3
Pentridge 13 C8
Pen-twyn 36 D2
Pentyrch 35 F5
Penuchadre 21 B7
Penuwch 46 C4
Penwithick 4 D5
Penwyllt 34 C2
Penybanc 33 C7
Pen-y-banc 33 B7
Penybont 48 C3
Pen-y-bont Carms 32 B4
Gwyn 58 D4
Gwyn 71 E7
Powys 60 B2
Pen-y-Bont Ar Ogwr = Bridgend 21 B8
Penybontfawr 59 B7
Pen-y-bryn Gwyn 58 C3
Pembs 45 E3
Penycae 73 E6
Pen-y-cae 34 C2
Pen-y-cae-mawr 35 E8
Pen-y-cefn 72 B5
Pen-y-clawdd 36 D1
Pen-y-coedcae 34 F4
Penycwm 44 C3
Pen-y-fai 34 F2
Penyffordd 73 C7
Penyffridd 82 F5
Pen-y-garn Carms 46 F4
Ceredig 58 F3
Penygarnedd 59 B8
Pen-y-garnedd 82 D5

Pen-y-gop 72 E3
Penygraig 34 E3
Pen-y-graig 70 D2
Penygroes Gwyn 82 F4
Pembs 45 F3
Pen-y-groes 33 C6
Pen-y-groeslon 70 D3
Pen-y-Gwryd Hotel 83 F6
Penyrheol 35 F5
Pen-yr-heol 35 C8
Pen-yr-Heolgerrig 34 D4
Penysarn 82 B4
Pen-y-stryt 73 D5
Penywaun 34 D3
Penzance 2 C3
Peopleton 50 D4
Peover Heath 74 B4
Peper Harow 27 E7
Perceton 118 E3
Percie 140 E4
Percyhorner 153 B9
Periton 21 E8
Perivale 40 F4
Perkinsville 111 D5
Perlethorpe 77 B6
Perranarworthal 3 C6
Perranporth 4 D2
Perranuthnoe 2 D4
Perranzabuloe 4 D2
Perry Barr 62 E4
Perryfoot 88 F2
Perry Green Herts 41 C7
Wilts 37 F6
Perry Street 29 B7
Pershall 74 F5
Pershore 50 E4
Pert 135 C6
Pertenhall 53 C8
Perth 128 B3
Perthy 73 F7
Perton 62 E2
Pertwood 24 F3
Peterborough 65 E8
Peterburn 155 J12
Peterchurch 48 F5
Peterculter 141 D7
Peterhead 153 D11
Peterlee 111 E7
Petersfield 15 B8
Peter's Green 40 C4
Peters Marland 9 C6
Peterstone Wentlooge 35 F6
Peterston-super-Ely 22 B2
Peterstow 36 B2
Peter Tavy 6 B3
Petertown 159 H4
Petham 30 D5
Petrockstow 9 D7
Pett 19 D5
Pettaugh 57 D5
Petteridge 29 E7
Pettinain 120 E2
Pettistree 57 D6
Petton Devon 10 B5
Shrops 60 B4
Petts Wood 28 C5
Petty 153 E7
Pettycur 128 F4
Pettymuick 141 B8
Petworth 16 B3
Pevensey 18 E3
Pevensey Bay 18 E3
Pewsey 25 C6
Philham 8 B4
Philiphaugh 115 B7
Phillack 2 C4
Philleigh 3 C7
Philpstoun 120 B3
Phocle Green 36 B3
Phoenix Green 27 D5
Pica 98 B2
Piccotts End 40 D3
Pickering 103 F5
Picket Piece 25 E8
Picket Post 14 D2
Pickhill 101 F8
Picklescott 60 E4
Pickletillem 129 B6
Pickmere 74 B3
Pickney 11 B6
Pickstock 61 B7
Pickwell Devon 20 E3
Leics 64 C4
Pickworth Lincs 78 F3
Rutland 65 C6
Picton Ches W 73 B8
Flint 85 F2
N Yorks 102 D2
Piddinghoe 17 D8
Piddington Oxon 39 C6
W Nhants 53 D6
Piddlehinton 12 E5
Piddletrenthide 12 E5
Pidley 54 B4
Piercebridge 101 C7
Pierowall 159 D5
Pigdon 117 F7
Pikehall 75 D8
Pilgrims Hatch 42 E1
Pilham 90 E2
Pill 23 B7
Pillaton 5 C8
Pillerton Hersey 51 E8
Pillerton Priors 51 E7
Pilleth 48 C4
Pilley Hants 14 E4
S Yorks 88 D4
Pilling 92 E4
Pilling Lane 92 E3
Pillowell 36 D3
Pillwell 13 C5
Pilning 36 F2
Pilsbury 75 C8
Pilsdon 12 E2
Pilsgate 65 D7
Pilsley Derbys 76 B2
Derbys 76 C4
Pilton Devon 20 F4
N Nhants 65 F7
Rutland 65 D6
Som 23 E7
Pilton Green 33 F5
Pimperne 13 D7
Pinchbeck 66 B2
Pinchbeck Bars 65 B8
Pinchbeck West 66 B2
Pincheon Green 89 C7
Pinehurst 38 F1
Pinfold 85 C4
Pinged 33 D5
Pinhoe 10 E4
Pinkneys Green 40 F1
Pinley 51 B8
Pin Mill 57 F6
Pinminnoch 112 E1
Pinmore 112 E2
Pinmore Mains 112 E2
Pinner 40 F4
Pinvin 50 E4
Pinwherry 112 F1
Pinxton 76 D4
Pipe and Lyde 49 E7
Pipe Gate 74 E4
Piperhill 151 F11
Piper's Pool 8 F4
Pipewell 64 F5
Pippacott 20 F4
Pipton 48 F3
Pirbright 27 D7
Pirnmill 143 D9
Pirton Herts 54 F2
Worcs 50 E3
Pisgah Ceredig 47 B5
Stirling 127 D6
Pishill 39 F7
Pistyll 70 C4
Pitagowan 133 C5
Pitblae 153 B9
Pitcairngreen 128 B2
Pitcalnie 151 D11
Pitcaple 141 B6
Pitchcombe 37 D5
Pitchcott 39 B7
Pitchford 60 D5
Pitch Green 39 D7
Pitch Place 27 D7
Pitcombe 23 F8
Pitcorthie 129 D7
Pitcox 122 B2
Pitcur 134 F2
Pitfichie 141 C5
Pitforthie 135 B8
Pitgrudy 151 B10
Pitkennedy 135 D5
Pitkevy 128 D4
Pitkierie 129 D7
Pitlessie 128 D5
Pitlochry 133 D6
Pitmachie 141 B5
Pitmain 138 D3
Pitmedden 141 B7
Pitminster 11 C7
Pitmuies 135 E5
Pitmunie 141 C5
Pitney 12 B2
Pitscottie 129 C6
Pitsea 42 F3
Pitsford 53 C5
Pitsmoor 88 F4
Pitstone 40 C2
Pitstone Green 40 C2
Pittendreich 152 B1
Pittentrail 157 J10
Pittenweem 129 D7
Pittington 111 E6
Pittodrie 141 B5
Pitton 25 F7
Pittswood 29 E7
Pittulie 153 B9
Pityme 4 B4
Pity Me 111 E5
Pityoulish 138 C5
Pixey Green 57 B6
Pixham 28 D2
Pixley 49 F8
Place Newton 96 B4
Plaidy 153 C7
Plains 119 C7
Plaish 60 E5
Plaistow 27 F8
Plaitford 14 C3
Plank Lane 86 E4
Plas-canol 58 C2
Plas Gogerddan 58 F3
Plas Llwyngwern 58 D4
Plas Nantyr 73 F5
Plastow Green 26 C3
Plas-yn-Cefn 72 B4
Platt 29 D7
Platt Bridge 86 D4
Platts Common 88 D4
Plawsworth 111 E5
Plaxtol 29 D7
Playden 19 C6
Playford 57 E6
Play Hatch 26 B5
Playing Place 3 B7
Playley Green 50 F2
Plealey 60 D4
Plean 127 F7
Pleasington 86 B4
Pleasley 76 C5
Pleckgate 93 F6
Plenmeller 109 C7
Pleshey 42 C2
Plockton 149 E13
Plocrapol 154 H6
Ploughfield 49 E5
Plowden 60 F3
Ploxgreen 60 D3
Pluckley 30 E3
Pluckley Thorne 30 E3
Plumbland 107 F8
Plumley 74 B4
Plumpton Cumb 108 F4
E Sus 17 C7
Plumpton Green 17 C7
Plumpton Head 108 F5
Plumstead London 29 B5
Norf 81 D7
Plumtree 77 F6
Plungar 77 F7
Plush 12 D5
Plwmp 46 D2
Plymouth 6 D2
Plympton 6 D3
Plymstock 6 D3
Plymtree 11 D5
Pockley 102 F4
Pocklington 96 E4
Pode Hole 66 B2
Podimore 12 B3
Podington 53 C7
Podmore 74 F4
Point Clear 43 C6
Pointon 78 F4
Pokesdown 14 E2
Pol a Charra 148 G2
Polbae 105 B6
Polbain 156 H2
Polbathic 5 D8
Polbeth 120 C3
Polchar 138 D4
Polebrook 65 F7
Pole Elm 50 E3
Polegate 18 E2
Poles 151 B10
Polesworth 63 D6
Polgigga 2 D2
Polglass 156 J3
Polgooth 4 D4
Poling 16 D4
Polkerris 5 D5
Polla 156 D6
Pollington 89 C7
Polloch 130 C1
Pollok 118 C5
Pollokshields 119 C5
Polmassick 3 B8
Polmont 120 B2
Polnessan 112 C4
Polnish 147 C10
Polperro 5 D7
Polruan 5 D6
Polsham 23 E7
Polstead 56 F3
Poltalloch 124 F4
Poltimore 10 E4
Polton 121 C5
Polwarth 122 D3
Polyphant 8 F4
Polzeath 4 B4
Pondersbridge 66 E2
Ponders End 41 E6
Pondtail 27 D6
Ponsanooth 3 C6
Ponsworthy 6 B5
Pont Aber 33 B8
Pont Aber-Geirw 71 E8
Pontamman 33 C7
Pontantwn 33 C5
Pontardawe 33 D8
Pontarddulais 33 D6
Pont-ar-gothi 33 B6
Pont ar Hydfer 34 B2
Pont-ar-llechau 33 B8
Pontarsais 33 B5
Pontblyddyn 73 C6
Pontbren Araeth 33 B7
Pontbren Llwyd 34 D3
Pont Cwm Pydew 72 F4
Pont Cyfyng 83 F7
Pont Cysyllte 73 E6
Pont Dolydd Prysor 71 D8
Pontefract 89 B5
Ponteland 110 B4
Ponterwyd 58 F4
Pontesbury 60 D3
Pontfadog 73 F6
Pontfaen 45 F2
Pont-faen 47 F8
Pont Fronwydd 58 B5
Pont-gareg 45 E3
Pontgarreg 46 D2
Pont-Henri 33 D5
Ponthir 35 E7
Ponthirwaun 45 E4
Pontllanfraith 35 E5
Pontlliw 33 D7
Pont-Llogel 59 C7
Pontllyfni 82 F4
Pontlottyn 35 D5
Pontneddfechan 34 D3
Pontnewydd 35 E6
Pont Pen-y-benglog 83 E6
Pontrhydfendigaid 47 C6
Pont Rhyd-goch 83 E6
Pont-Rhyd-sarn 59 B5
Pont Rhyd-y-cyff 34 F2
Pontrhydyfen 34 E1
Pont-rhyd-y-groes 47 B6
Pontrilas 35 B7
Pontrobert 59 C8
Pont-rug 82 E5
Pont Senni = Sennybridge 34 B3
Ponts Green 18 D3
Pontshill 36 B3
Pont-siân 46 E3
Pontsticill 34 C4
Pontwgan 83 D7
Pontyates 33 D5
Pontyberem 33 C6
Pontyclun 34 F4
Pontycymer 34 E3
Pontyglasier 45 F3
Pont-y-gwaith 34 E4
Pont-y-pant 83 F7
Pont y Pennant 59 B6
Pontypool = Pont-y-pŵl 35 D6
Pontypridd 34 F4
Pont-y-pŵl = Pontypool 35 D6
Pont yr Afon-Gam 71 C8
Pont-yr-hafod 44 C4
Pontywaun 35 E6
Pooksgreen 14 C4
Pool Corn 3 B5
W Yorks 94 E5
Poole 13 E8
Poole Keynes 37 E6
Poolend 75 D6
Poolewe 155 J13
Pooley Bridge 99 B6
Poolfold 75 D5
Poolhill 36 B4
Pool o'Muckhart 128 D2
Pool Quay 60 C2
Poolsbrook 76 B4
Pootings 29 E5
Pope Hill 44 D4
Popeswood 27 C6
Popham 26 E3
Poplar 41 F6
Popley 26 D4
Porchester 77 E5
Porchfield 14 E5
Porin 150 F6
Poringland 69 D5
Porkellis 3 C5
Porlock 21 E7
Porlock Weir 21 E7
Portachoillan 144 H6
Port Ann 145 E8
Port Appin 130 E3
Port Arthur 160 K5
Port Askaig 142 B5
Portavadie 145 G8
Port Bannatyne 145 G9
Portbury 23 B7
Port Carlisle 108 C2
Port Charlotte 142 C3
Portchester 15 D7
Portclair 137 C7
Port Clarence 102 B2
Port Driseach 145 F8
Port Ellen 142 D4
Port Elphinstone 141 C6
Portencalzie 104 B4
Portencross 118 E1
Port Erin 84 F1
Port Erroll 153 E10
Portesham 12 F4
Portessie 152 B4
Port e Vullen 84 C4
Port-Eynon 33 F5
Portfield Gate 44 D4
Portgate 9 F6
Port Gaverne 8 F2
Port Glasgow 118 B3
Portgordon 152 B3
Portgower 157 H13
Porth Corn 4 C3
Rhondda 34 E4
Porthaethwy = Menai Bridge 83 D5
Porthallow Corn 3 D6
Corn 5 D7
Porthcawl 21 B7
Porthcothan 4 B3
Porthcurno 2 D2
Port Henderson 149 A12
Porthgain 44 B3
Porthill 60 C4
Porthkerry 22 C2
Porthleven 2 D5
Porthllechog 82 B4
Porthmadog 71 D6
Porthmeor 2 C3
Porth Navas 3 D6
Portholland 3 B8
Porthoustock 3 D7
Porthpean 4 D5
Porthtowan 3 B5
Porth Tywyn = Burry Port 33 D5
Porthyrhyd Carms 33 C6
Carms 47 F6
Porth-y-waen 60 B2
Portincaple 145 D11
Portington 96 F3
Portinnisherrich 125 D5
Portinscale 98 B4
Port Isaac 4 A4
Portishead 23 B6
Portkil 145 E11
Portknockie 152 B4
Port Lamont 145 F9
Portlethen 141 E8
Portling 107 D5
Port Lion 44 E4
Portloe 3 C8
Port Logan 104 E4
Portmahomack 151 C12
Portmeirion 71 D6
Portmellon 3 B9
Port Mholair 155 D10
Port Mor 146 D7
Portmore 14 E4
Port Mulgrave 103 C5
Portnacroish 130 E3
Portnahaven 142 C2
Portnalong 149 E8
Portnaluchaig 147 C9
Portnancon 156 C7
Port Nan Giùran 155 D10
Port nan Long 148 A3
Portnellan 126 B3
Port Nis 155 A10
Portobello 121 B6
Port of Menteith 126 D4
Porton 25 F6
Portpatrick 104 D4
Port Quin 4 A4
Port Ramsay 130 E2
Portreath 3 B5
Portree 149 D9
Port St Mary 84 F2
Portscatho 3 C7
Portsea 15 D7
Portskerra 157 C11
Portskewett 36 F2
Portslade 17 D6
Portslade-by-Sea 17 D6
Portsmouth Ptsmth 15 D7
W Yorks 87 B7
Portsonachan 125 C6
Portsoy 152 B5
Port Sunlight 85 F4
Portswood 14 C5
Port Talbot 34 E1
Porttanachy 152 B3
Port Tennant 33 E7
Portuairk 146 E7
Portway Hereford 49 F6
Worcs 51 B5
Port Wemyss 142 C2
Port William 105 E7
Portwrinkle 5 D8
Poslingford 55 E8
Postbridge 6 B4
Postcombe 39 E7
Postling 19 B8
Postwick 69 D5
Potholm 115 F6
Potsgrove 40 B2
Potten End 40 D3
Potter Brompton 97 B5
Potterhanworth 78 C3
Potterhanworth Booths 78 C3
Potter Heigham 69 C7
Potterne 24 D4
Potterne Wick 24 D5
Potternewton 95 F6
Potters Bar 41 D5
Potter's Cross 62 F2
Potterspury 53 E5
Potter Street 41 D7
Potterton Aberds 141 C8
W Yorks 95 F7
Potto 102 D2
Potton 54 E3
Pott Row 80 E3
Pott Shrigley 75 B6
Poughill Corn 8 D4
Devon 10 D3
Poulshot 24 D4
Poulton Glos 37 D8
Mers 85 E4
Poulton-le-Fylde 92 F3
Pound Bank 50 B2
Poundbury 12 E4
Poundfield 18 B2
Pound Green E Sus 18 C2
IoW 14 F4
Worcs 50 B2
Pound Hill 28 F3
Poundland 112 F1
Poundon 39 B6
Poundsgate 6 B5
Poundstock 8 E4
Powburn 117 C6
Powderham 10 F4
Powerstock 12 E3
Powfoot 107 C8
Powick 50 D3
Powmill 128 E2
Poxwell 12 F5
Poyle 27 B8
Poynings 17 C6
Poyntington 12 C4
Poynton 87 F7
Poynton Green 61 C5
Poystreet Green 56 D3
Praa Sands 2 D4
Pratt's Bottom 29 C5
Praze 2 C4
Praze-an-Beeble 2 C5
Predannack Wollas 3 E5
Prees 74 F2
Preesall 92 E3
Prees Green 74 F2
Preesgweene 73 F6
Prees Heath 74 F2
Prees Higher Heath 74 F2
Prees Lower Heath 74 F2
Prenderguest 122 D5
Prendwick 117 C6
Prengwyn 46 E3
Prenteg 71 C6
Prenton 85 F4
Prescot 86 E2
Prescott 60 B4
Pressen 122 F4
Prestatyn 72 A4
Prestbury Ches E 75 B6
Glos 37 B6
Presteigne = Llanandras 48 C5
Presthope 61 E5
Prestleigh 23 E8
Preston Borders 122 D3
Brighton 17 D7
Devon 7 B6
Dorset 12 F5
E Loth 121 B8
E Yorks 97 F7
Glos 37 D7
Glos 49 F8
Herts 40 B4
Kent 30 C4
Kent 31 C6
Lancs 86 B3
Northumb 117 B7
Rutland 65 D5
Shrops 60 C5
Wilts 24 B5
Wilts 25 B7
Preston Bagot 51 C6
Preston Bissett 39 B6
Preston Bowyer 11 B6
Preston Brockhurst 60 B5
Preston Brook 86 F3
Preston Candover 26 E4
Preston Capes 52 D3
Preston Crowmarsh 39 E6
Preston Gubbals 60 C4
Prestonmill 107 D6
Preston on Stour 51 E7
Preston on the Hill 86 F3
Preston on Wye 49 E5
Prestonpans 121 B6
Preston Plucknett 12 C3
Preston St Mary 56 D3
Preston-under-Scar 101 E5
Preston upon the Weald Moors 61 C6
Preston Wynne 49 E7
Prestwich 87 D6
Prestwick Northumb 110 B4
S Ayrs 112 B3
Prestwood 40 D1
Price Town 34 E3
Prickwillow 67 F5
Priddy 23 D7
Priesthaugh 115 D7
Priest Hutton 92 B5
Priest Weston 60 E2
Primethorpe 64 E2
Primrose Green 68 C3
Primrosehill 40 D3
Primrose Valley 97 B7
Princes Gate 32 C2
Princes Risborough 39 D8
Princethorpe 52 B2
Princetown Caerph 35 C5
Devon 6 B3
Prion 72 C4
Prior Muir 129 C7
Prior Park 123 D5
Priors Frome 49 F7
Priors Hardwick 52 D2
Priorslee 61 C7
Priors Marston 52 D2
Priory Wood 48 E4
Priston 23 C8
Pristow Green 68 F4
Prittlewell 42 F4
Privett 15 B7
Prixford 20 F4
Probus 3 B7
Proncy 151 B10
Prospect 107 E8
Prudhoe 110 C3
Ptarmigan Lodge 126 D2
Pubil 132 E1
Puckeridge 41 B6
Puckington 11 C8
Pucklechurch 23 B8
Pucknall 14 B4
Puckrup 50 F3
Puddinglake 74 C4
Puddington Ches W 73 B7
Devon 10 C3
Puddledock 68 E3
Puddletown 13 E5
Pudleston 49 D7
Pudsey 94 F5
Pulborough 16 C4
Puleston 61 B7
Pulford 73 D7
Pulham 12 D5
Pulham Market 68 F4
Pulham St Mary 68 F5
Pulloxhill 53 F8
Pumpherston 120 C3
Pumsaint 47 E5
Puncheston 32 B1
Puncknowle 12 F3
Punnett's Town 18 C3
Purbrook 15 D7
Purewell 14 E2
Purfleet 29 B6
Puriton 22 E5
Purleigh 42 D4
Purley London 28 C4
W Berks 26 B4
Purlogue 48 B4
Purls Bridge 66 F4
Purse Caundle 12 C4
Purslow 60 F3
Purston Jaglin 88 C5
Purton Glos 36 D3
Glos 36 D3
Wilts 37 F7
Purton Stoke 37 E7
Pury End 52 E5
Pusey 38 E3
Putley 49 F8
Putney 28 B3
Putsborough 20 E3
Puttenham Herts 40 C1
Sur 27 E7
Puxton 23 C6
Pwll 33 D5
Pwllcrochan 44 E4
Pwll-glas 72 D5
Pwllgloyw 48 F2
Pwllheli 70 D4
Pwllmeyric 36 E2
Pwll-trap 32 C3
Pwll-y-glaw 34 E1
Pyecombe 17 C6
Pye Corner 35 F7
Pye Green 62 C3
Pyewipe 91 C6
Pyle 15 G5
Pyle = Y Pîl 34 F2
Pylle 23 F8
Pymoor 66 F4
Pyrford 27 D8
Pyrton 39 E6
Pytchley 53 B6
Pyworthy 8 D5

Q

Quabbs 60 F2
Quadring 78 F5
Quainton 39 C7
Quarley 25 E7
Quarndon 76 E3
Quarrier's Homes 118 C3
Quarrington 78 E3
Quarrington Hill 111 F6
Quarry Bank 62 F3
Quarryford 121 C8
Quarryhill 151 C10
Quarrywood 152 B1
Quarter 119 D7
Quatford 61 E7
Quatt 61 F7
Quebec 110 E4
Quedgeley 37 C5
Queen Adelaide 67 F5
Queenborough 30 B3
Queen Camel 12 B3
Queen Charlton 23 C8
Queen Dart 10 C3
Queenhill 50 F3
Queen Oak 24 F2
Queensbury 94 F4
Queensferry Edin 120 B4
Flint 73 C7
Queensferry Crossing 120 B4
Queen's Head 60 B3
Queen's Park Bedford 53 E8
W Nhants 53 C5
Queenstown 92 F3
Queen Street Kent 29 E7
Wilts 37 F7
Queenzieburn 119 B6
Quemerford 24 C5
Quendale 160 M5
Quendon 55 F6
Queniborough 64 C3
Quenington 37 D8
Quernmore 92 D5
Quethiock 5 C8
Quholm 159 G3
Quicks Green 26 B3
Quidenham 68 F3
Quidhampton Hants 26 D3
Wilts 25 F6
Quilquox 153 E9
Quina Brook 74 F2
Quindry 159 J5
Quinton W Mid 62 F3
Quinton *continued*
W Nhants 53 D5
Quintrell Downs 4 C3
Quixhill 75 E8
Quoditch 9 E6
Quoig 127 B7
Quorndon 64 C2
Quothquan 120 F2
Quoyloo 159 F3
Quoyness 159 H3
Quoys Shetland 160 B8
Shetland 160 G6

R

Raasay House 149 E10
Rabbit's Cross 29 E8
Raby 73 B7
Rachan Mill 120 F4
Rachub 83 E6
Rackenford 10 C3
Rackham 16 C4
Rackheath 69 C5
Racks 107 B7
Rackwick Orkney 159 D5
Orkney 159 J3
Radbourne 76 F2
Radcliffe Gtr Man 87 D5
Northumb 117 D8
Radcliffe on Trent 77 F6
Radclive 52 F4
Radcot 38 E2
Raddery 151 F10
Radernie 129 D6
Radford Semele 51 C8
Radipole 12 F4
Radlett 40 E4
Radley 39 E5
Radmanthwaite 76 C5
Radmoor 61 B6
Radmore Green 74 D2
Radnage 39 E7
Radstock 23 D8
Radstone 52 E3
Radway 51 E8
Radway Green 74 D4
Radwell Bedford 53 D8
Herts 54 F3
Radwinter 55 F7
Radyr 35 F5
Rafford 151 F13
Ragdale 64 C3
Raglan 35 D8
Ragnall 77 B8
Rahane 145 E11
Rainford 86 D2
Rainford Junction 86 D2
Rainham London 41 F8
Medway 30 C2
Rainhill 86 E2
Rainhill Stoops 86 E3
Rainow 75 B6
Rainton 95 B6
Rainworth 77 D5
Raisbeck 99 D8
Raise 109 E7
Rait 128 B4
Raithby Lincs 79 C6
Lincs 91 F7
Rake 16 B2
Rakewood 87 C7
Ram 46 E4
Ramasaig 148 D6
Rame Corn 3 C6
Corn 6 E2
Rameldry Mill Bank 128 D5
Ram Lane 30 E3
Ramnageo 160 C8
Rampisham 12 D3
Rampside 92 C2
Rampton Cambs 54 C5
Notts 77 B7
Ramsbottom 87 C5
Ramsbury 25 B7
Ramscraigs 158 H3
Ramsdean 15 B8
Ramsdell 26 D3
Ramsden 38 C3
Ramsden Bellhouse 42 E3
Ramsden Heath 42 E3
Ramsey Cambs 66 F2
Essex 57 F6
IoM 84 C4
Ramseycleuch 115 C5
Ramsey Forty Foot 66 F3
Ramsey Heights 66 F2
Ramsey Island 43 D5
Ramsey Mereside 66 F2
Ramsey St Mary's 66 F2
Ramsgate 31 C7
Ramsgill 94 B4
Ramshorn 75 E7
Ramsnest Common 27 F7
Ranais 155 E9
Ranby Lincs 78 B5
Notts 89 F7
Rand 78 B4
Randwick 37 D5
Ranfurly 118 C3
Rangag 158 F3
Rangemore 63 B5
Rangeworthy 36 F3
Rankinston 112 C4
Ranmoor 88 F4
Ranmore Common 28 D2
Rannerdale 98 C3
Rannoch Station 131 D8
Ranochan 147 C11
Ranskill 89 F7
Ranton 62 B2
Ranworth 69 C6
Raploch 127 E6
Rapness 159 D6
Rascal Moor 96 F4
Rascarrel 106 E4
Rashiereive 141 B8
Raskelf 95 B7
Rassau 35 C5
Rastrick 88 B2
Ratagan 136 C2
Ratby 64 D2
Ratcliffe Culey 63 E7
Ratcliffe on Soar 63 B8
Ratcliffe on the Wreake 64 C3
Rathen 153 B10
Rathillet 129 B5
Rathmell 93 D8
Ratho 120 B4
Ratho Station 120 B4
Rathven 152 B4
Ratley 51 E8
Ratlinghope 60 E4
Rattar 158 C4
Ratten Row 92 E4
Rattery 6 C5
Rattlesden 56 D3
Rattray 134 E1
Raughton Head 108 E3
Raunds 53 B7
Ravenfield 89 E5
Ravenglass 98 E2
Raveningham 69 E6
Ravenscar 103 D7
Ravenscraig 118 B2
Ravensdale 84 C3
Ravensden 53 D8
Ravenseat 100 D3
Ravenshead 77 D5
Ravensmoor 74 D3
Ravensthorpe W Nhants 52 B4
W Yorks 88 B3
Ravenstone Leics 63 C8
M Keynes 53 D6
Ravenstonedale 100 D2
Ravenstown 92 B3
Ravenstruther 120 E2
Ravensworth 101 D6
Raw 103 D7
Rawcliffe E Yorks 89 B7
York 95 D8
Rawcliffe Bridge 89 B7
Rawdon 94 F5
Rawmarsh 88 E5
Rawreth 42 E3
Rawridge 11 D7
Rawtenstall 87 B6
Raxton 153 E8
Raydon 56 F4
Raylees 117 E5
Rayleigh 42 E4
Rayne 42 B3
Rayners Lane 40 F4
Raynes Park 28 C3
Reach 55 C6
Read 93 F7
Reading 26 B5
Reading Street 19 B6
Reagill 99 C8
Rearquhar 151 B10
Rearsby 64 C3
Reaster 158 D4
Reawick 160 J5
Reay 157 C12
Rechullin 149 C13
Reculver 31 C6
Redberth 32 D1
Redbourn 40 C4
Redbourne 90 E3
Redbrook Mon 36 C2
Wrex 74 E2
Redburn Highld 151 E8
Highld 151 G12
Northumb 109 C7
Redcar 102 B4
Redcastle Angus 135 D6
Highld 151 G8
Redcliff Bay 23 B6
Red Dial 108 E2
Redding 120 B2
Reddingmuirhead 120 B2
Reddish 87 E6
Redditch 50 C5
Rede 56 D2
Redenhall 69 F5
Redesdale Camp 116 E4
Redesmouth 116 F4
Redford Aberds 135 B7
Angus 135 E5
Durham 110 F3
Redfordgreen 115 C6
Redgorton 128 B2
Redgrave 56 B4
Redhill Aberds 141 D6
Aberds 153 E6
N Som 23 C7
Sur 28 D3
Red Hill 50 D3
Redhouse 145 G7
Redhouses 142 B4
Red Houses Jersey 17
Redisham 69 F7
Redland Bristol 23 B7
Orkney 159 F4
Redlingfield 57 B5
Red Lodge 55 B7
Redlynch Som 23 F9
Wilts 14 B3
Redmarley D'Abitot 50 F2
Redmarshall 102 B1
Redmile 77 F7
Redmire 101 E5
Redmoor 5 C5
Rednal 60 B3
Redpath 121 F8
Redpoint 149 B12
Red Rail 36 B2
Red Rock 86 D3
Red Roses 32 C3
Red Row 117 E8
Redruth 3 B5
Red Street 74 D5
Redvales 87 D6
Red Wharf Bay 82 C5
Redwick Newport 35 F8
S Glos 36 F2
Redworth 101 B7
Reed 54 F4
Reedham 69 D7
Reedness 89 B8
Reeds Beck 78 C5
Reepham Lincs 78 B3
Norf 81 E6
Reeth 101 E5
Regaby 84 C4
Regoul 151 F11
Reiff 156 H2
Reigate 28 D3
Reighton 97 B7
Reighton Gap 97 B7
Reinigeadal 154 G7
Reiss 158 E5
Rejerrah 4 D2
Releath 3 C5
Relubbus 2 C4
Relugas 151 G12
Remenham 39 F7
Remenham Hill 39 F7
Remony 132 E4
Rempstone 64 B2
Rendcomb 37 D7
Rendham 57 C7
Rendlesham 57 D7
Renfrew 118 C5
Renhold 53 D8
Renishaw 76 B4
Rennington 117 C8
Renton 118 B3
Renwick 109 E5
Repps 69 C7
Repton 63 B7
Reraig 149 F13
Rescobie 135 D5
Resipole 147 E10
Resolis 151 E9
Resolven 34 D2
Reston 122 C4
Reswallie 135 D5
Retew 4 D4
Retford 89 F8
Rettendon 42 E3
Rettendon Place 42 E3
Revesby 79 C5
Revesby Bridge 79 C6
Rewe 10 E4
Rew Street 15 E5
Reydon 57 B8
Reydon Smear 57 B8
Reymerston 68 D3
Reynalton 32 D1
Reynoldston 33 E5
Rezare 5 B8
Rhaeadr Gwy = Rhayader 47 C8
Rhandirmwyn 47 E6
Rhayader = Rhaeadr Gwy 47 C8
Rhedyn 70 D3
Rhemore 147 F8
Rhencullen 84 C3
Rhes-y-cae 73 B5
Rhewl Denb 72 C5
Denb 73 E5
Rhian 157 H8
Rhicarn 156 G3
Rhiconich 156 D5
Rhicullen 151 D9
Rhidorroch House 150 B4
Rhifail 157 E10
Rhigos 34 D3
Rhilochan 157 J10
Rhiroy 150 C4
Rhisga = Risca 35 E6
Rhiw 70 E3
Rhiwabon = Ruabon 73 E7
Rhiwbina 35 F5
Rhiwbryfdir 71 C7
Rhiwderin 35 F6
Rhiwlas Gwyn 72 F3
Gwyn 83 E5
Powys 73 F5
Rhodes 87 D6
Rhodesia 77 B5
Rhodes Minnis 31 E5
Rhodiad 44 C2
Rhondda 34 E3
Rhonehouse or Kelton Hill 106 D4
Rhoose = Y Rhws 22 C2
Rhôs Carms 46 F2
Neath 33 D8
Rhosaman 33 C8
Rhosbeirio 82 B3
Rhoscefnhir 82 D5
Rhoscolyn 82 D2
Rhoscrowther 44 E4
Rhosesmor 73 C6
Rhos-fawr 70 D4
Rhosgadfan 82 F5
Rhosgoch 82 C4
Rhos-goch 48 E3
Rhos-hill 45 E3
Rhoshirwaun 70 E2
Rhoslan 71 C5
Rhoslefain 58 D2
Rhosllanerchrugog 73 E6
Rhosmaen 33 B7
Rhosmeirch 82 D4
Rhosneigr 82 D3
Rhosnesni 73 D7
Rhos-on-Sea 83 C8
Rhosrobin 73 D7
Rhossili 33 F5
Rhosson 44 C2
Rhostryfan 82 F4
Rhostyllen 73 E7
Rhosybol 82 C4
Rhos-y-brithdir 59 B8
Rhos-y-garth 46 B5
Rhos-y-gwaliau 72 F3
Rhos-y-llan 70 D3
Rhos-y-Madoc 73 E7
Rhos-y-meirch 48 C4
Rhu Argyll 145 E11
Argyll 145 G7
Rhualt 72 B4
Rhuddall Heath 74 C2
Rhuddlan Ceredig 46 E3
Denb 72 B4
Rhue 150 B3
Rhulen 48 E3
Rhunahaorine 143 D8
Rhuthun = Ruthin 72 D5
Rhyd Gwyn 71 C7
Powys 59 D6
Rhydaman = Ammanford 33 C7
Rhydargaeau 33 B5
Rhydcymerau 46 F4
Rhydd 50 E3
Rhyd-Ddu 83 F5
Rhydding 33 E8
Rhydfudr 46 C4
Rhydlewis 46 E2
Rhydlios 70 D2
Rhydlydan 83 F8
Rhyd-moel-ddu 48 B2

Rhydness 48 E3
Rhydowen 46 E3
Rhyd-Rosser 46 C4
Rhydspence 48 E4
Rhydtalog 73 D6
Rhyd-uchaf 72 F3
Rhyd-wen 58 C4
Rhydwyn 82 C3
Rhyd-y-clafdy 70 D4
Rhydycroesau 73 F6
Rhydyfelin Ceredig 46 B4
Rhondda 34 F4
Rhyd-y-foel 72 B3
Rhyd-y-fro 33 D8
Rhyd-y-gwin 33 D7
Rhydymain 58 B5
Rhyd-y-meirch 35 D7
Rhyd-y-meudwy 72 D5
Rhydymwyn 73 C6
Rhyd-y-pandy 33 D7
Rhyd-yr-onen 58 D3
Rhyd-y-sarn 71 C7
Rhyl = Y Rhyl 72 A4
Rhymney
= Rhymni 35 D5
Rhymni
= Rhymney 35 D5
Rhynd Fife 129 B6
Perth 128 B3
Rhynie Aberds 140 B3
Highld 151 D11
Ribbesford 50 B2
Ribblehead 93 B7
Ribbleton 93 F5
Ribchester 93 F6
Ribigill 157 D8
Riby 91 D5
Riby Cross Roads 91 D5
Riccall 96 F2
Riccarton 118 F4
Richards Castle 49 C6
Richings Park 27 B8
Richmond London 28 B2
N Yorks 101 D6
Rickarton 141 F7
Rickinghall 56 B4
Rickleton 111 D5
Rickling 55 F5
Rickmansworth 40 E3
Riddings Cumb 108 B4
Derbys 76 D4
Riddlecombe 9 C8
Riddlesden 94 E3
Riddrie 119 C6
Ridge Dorset 13 F7
Hants 14 C4
Wilts 24 F4
Ridgebourne 48 C2
Ridge Green 28 E4
Ridgehill 23 C7
Ridge Lane 63 E6
Ridgeway Cross 50 E2
Ridgewell 55 E8
Ridgewood 17 C8
Ridgmont 53 F7
Riding Mill 110 C3
Ridleywood 73 D8
Ridlington Norf 69 A6
Rutland 64 D5
Ridsdale 116 F5
Riechip 133 E7
Riemore 133 E7
Rienachait 156 F3
Rievaulx 102 F3
Rift House 111 F7
Rigg 108 C2
Riggend 119 B7
Rigsby 79 B7
Rigside 119 F8
Riley Green 86 B4
Rileyhill 62 C5
Rilla Mill 5 B7
Rillington 96 B4
Rimington 93 E8
Rimpton 12 B4
Rimswell 91 B7
Rinaston 44 C4
Ringasta 160 M5
Ringford 106 D3
Ringinglow 88 F3
Ringland 68 C4
Ringles Cross 17 B8
Ringmer 17 C8
Ringmore 6 E4
Ringorm 152 D2
Ring's End 66 D3
Ringsfield 69 F7
Ringsfield Corner 69 F7
Ringshall Herts 40 C2
Suff 56 D4
Ringshall Stocks 56 D4
Ringstead N Nhants 53 B7
Norf 80 C3
Ringwood 14 D2
Ringwould 31 E7
Rinmore 140 C3
Rinnigill 159 J4
Rinsey 2 D4
Riof 154 D6
Ripe 18 D2
Ripley Derbys 76 D3
Hants 14 E2
N Yorks 95 C5
Sur 27 D8
Riplingham 97 F5
Ripon 95 B6
Rippingale 65 B7
Ripple Kent 31 E7
Worcs 50 F3
Ripponden 87 C8
Rireavach 150 B3
Risabus 142 D4
Risbury 49 D7
Risby 55 C8
Risca = Rhisga 35 E6
Rise 97 E7
Riseden 18 B3
Risegate 66 B2
Riseholme 78 B2
Riseley Bedford 53 C8
Wokingham 26 C5
Rishangles 57 C5
Rishton 93 F7
Rishworth 87 C8
Rising Bridge 87 B5
Risley Derbys 76 F4
Warr 86 E4
Risplith 94 C5
Rispond 156 C7
Rivar 25 C8
Rivenhall End 42 C4
River Bank 55 C6
Riverhead 29 D6
Rivington 86 C4
Roachill 10 B3
Roade 53 D5
Road Green 69 E5
Roadhead 108 B5
Roadmeetings 119 E8
Roadside 158 D3
Roadside of
Catterline 135 B8
Roadside of
Kinneff 135 B8
Roadwater 22 F2
Roag 149 D7
Roa Island 92 C2
Roath 22 B3
Roberton Borders 115 C7
S Lanark 114 B2
Robertsbridge 18 C4
Roberttown 88 B2
Robeston Cross 44 E3
Robeston Wathen 32 C1
Robin Hood 88 B4
Robin Hood's
Bay 103 D7
Roborough Devon 6 C3
Devon 9 C7
Roby 86 E2
Roby Mill 86 D3
Rocester 75 F8
Roch 44 C3
Rochdale 87 C6
Roche 4 C4
Rochester Medway 29 C8
Northumb 116 E4
Rochford 42 E4
Roch Gate 44 C3
Rock Corn 4 B4
Northumb 117 B8
Worcs 50 B2
W Sus 16 C5
Rockbeare 10 E5
Rockbourne 14 C2
Rockcliffe Cumb 108 C3
Dumfries 107 D5
Rock Ferry 85 F4
Rockfield Highld 151 C12
Mon 36 C1
Rockford 14 D2
Rockhampton 36 E3
Rockingham 65 E5
Rockland All
Saints 68 E2
Rockland St Mary 69 D6
Rockland St Peter 68 E2
Rockley 25 B6
Rockwell End 39 F7
Rockwell Green 11 B6
Rodborough 37 D5
Rodbourne Swindon 37 F8
Wilts 37 F6
Rodbourne Cheney 37 F8
Rodd 48 C5
Roddam 117 B6
Rodden 12 F4
Rode 24 D3
Rodeheath 75 C5
Rode Heath 74 D5
Roden 61 C5
Rodhuish 22 F2
Rodington 61 C5
Rodley Glos 36 C4
W Yorks 94 F5
Rodmarton 37 E6
Rodmell 17 D8
Rodmersham 30 C3
Rodney Stoke 23 D6
Rodsley 76 E2
Rodway 22 F4
Rodwell 12 G4
Roecliffe 95 C6
Roe Green 54 F4
Roehampton 28 B3
Roesound 160 G5
Roffey 28 F2
Rogart 157 J10
Rogart Station 157 J10
Rogate 16 B2
Rogerstone 35 F6
Roghadal 154 J5
Rogiet 36 F1
Rogue's Alley 66 D3
Roke 39 E6
Roker 111 D7
Rollesby 69 C7
Rolleston Leics 64 D4
Notts 77 D7
Rolleston-
on-Dove 63 B6
Rolston 97 E8
Rolvenden 18 B5
Rolvenden Layne 19 B5
Romaldkirk 100 B4
Romanby 102 E1
Romannobridge 120 E4
Romansleigh 10 B2
Romford 41 F8
Romiley 87 E7
Romsey 14 B4
Romsey Town 55 D5
Romsley Shrops 61 F7
Worcs 50 B4
Ronague 84 E2
Rookhope 110 E2
Rookley 15 F6
Rooks Bridge 23 D5
Roos 97 F8
Roosebeck 92 C2
Rootham's Green 54 D2
Rootpark 120 D2
Ropley 26 F4
Ropley Dean 26 F4
Ropsley 78 F2
Rora 153 C10
Rorandle 141 C5
Rorrington 60 D3
Roscroggan 3 B5
Rose 4 D2
Roseacre Kent 29 D8
Lancs 92 F4
Rose Ash 10 B2
Rosebank 119 E8
Rosebrough 117 B7
Rosebush 32 B1
Rosecare 8 E3
Rosedale Abbey 103 E5
Roseden 117 B6
Rosefield 151 F1
Rose Green 16 E3
Rose Grove 93 F8
Rosehall 156 J7
Rosehaugh
Mains 151 F9
Rosehearty 153 B9
Rosehill 74 F3
Rose Hill E Sus 17 C8
Lancs 93 F8
Suff 57 E5
Roseisle 152 B1
Roselands 18 E3
Rosemarket 44 E4
Rosemarkie 151 F10
Rosemary Lane 11 C6
Rosemount 134 E1
Rosenannon 4 C4
Rosewell 121 C5
Roseworth 102 B2
Roseworthy 2 C5
Rosgill 99 C7
Roshven 147 D10
Roskhill 149 D7
Roskill House 151 F9
Rosley 108 E3
Roslin 121 C5
Rosliston 63 C6
Rosneath 145 E11
Ross Dumfries 106 E3
Northumb 123 F7
Perth 127 B6
Rossett 73 D7
Rossett Green 95 D6
Rossie Ochill 128 C2
Rossie Priory 134 F2
Rossington 89 E7
Rosskeen 151 E9
Rossland 118 B4
Ross-on-Wye 36 B3
Roster 158 G4
Rostherne 86 F5
Rosthwaite 98 C4
Roston 75 E8
Rosyth 128 F3
Rothbury 117 D6
Rotherby 64 C3
Rotherfield 18 C2
Rotherfield Greys 39 F7
Rotherfield
Peppard 39 F7
Rotherham 88 E5
Rothersthorpe 52 D5
Rotherwick 26 D5
Rothes 152 D2
Rothesay 145 G9
Rothiebrisbane 153 E7
Rothienorman 153 E7
Rothiesholm 159 F7
Rothley Leics 64 C2
Northumb 117 F6
Rothley Shield
East 117 E6
Rothmaise 153 E6
Rothwell Lincs 91 E5
N Nhants 64 F5
W Yorks 88 B4
Rothwell Haigh 88 B4
Rotsea 97 D6
Rottal 134 C3
Rotten End 57 C7
Rottingdean 17 D7
Rottington 98 C1
Roud 15 F6
Rougham Norf 80 E4
Suff 56 C3
Rougham Green 56 C3
Roughburn 137 F6
Rough Close 75 F6
Rough Common 30 D5
Roughlee 93 E8
Roughley 62 E5
Roughsike 108 B5
Roughton Lincs 78 C5
Norf 81 D8
Shrops 61 E7
Roughton Moor 78 C5
Roundhay 95 F6
Roundstonefoot 114 D4
Roundstreet
Common 16 B4
Roundway 24 C5
Rous Lench 50 D5
Rousdon 11 E7
Routenburn 118 C1
Routh 97 E6
Row Corn 5 B5
Cumb 99 F6
Rowanburn 108 B4
Rowardennan 126 E2
Rowde 24 C4
Rowen 83 D7
Rowfoot 109 C6
Row Heath 43 C7
Rowhedge 43 B6
Rowhook 28 F2
Rowington 51 C7
Rowland 76 B2
Rowlands Castle 15 C8
Rowlands Gill 110 D4
Rowledge 27 E6
Rowlestone 35 B7
Rowley E Yorks 97 F5
Shrops 60 D3
Rowley Hill 88 C2
Rowley Regis 62 F3
Rowly 27 E8
Rowney Green 50 B5
Rownhams 14 C4
Rowrah 98 C2
Rowsham 39 C8
Rowsley 76 C2
Rowstock 38 F4
Rowston 78 D3
Rowton Ches W 73 C8
Shrops 60 C3
Telford 61 C6
Roxburgh 122 F3
Roxby N Lincs 90 C3
N Yorks 103 C5
Roxton 54 D2
Roxwell 42 D2
Royal Leamington
Spa 51 C8
Royal Oak Darl 101 B7
Lancs 86 D2
Royal Tunbridge
Wells 18 B2
Royal Wootton
Bassett 37 F7
Roybridge 137 F5
Roydhouse 88 C3
Roydon Essex 41 D7
Norf 68 F3
Norf 80 E3
Roydon Hamlet 41 D7
Royston Herts 54 E4
S Yorks 88 C4
Royton 87 D7
Rozel Jersey 17
Ruabon
= Rhiwabon 73 E7
Ruaig 146 G3
Ruan Lanihorne 3 B7
Ruan Minor 3 E6
Ruarach 136 B2
Ruardean 36 C3
Ruardean
Woodside 36 C3
Rubery 50 B4
Ruckcroft 108 E5
Ruckhall 49 F6
Ruckinge 19 B7
Ruckland 79 B6
Ruckley 60 D5
Rudbaxton 44 C4
Rudby 102 D2
Ruddington 77 F5
Rudford 36 B4
Rudge Shrops 62 E2
Som 24 D3
Rudgeway 36 F3
Rudgwick 27 F8
Rudhall 36 B3
Rudheath 74 B3
Rudley Green 42 D4
Rudry 35 F5
Rudston 97 C6
Rudyard 75 D6
Rufford 86 C2
Rufforth 95 D8
Rugby 52 B3
Rugeley 62 C4
Ruglen 112 D2
Ruilick 151 G8
Ruishton 11 B7
Ruisigearraidh 154 J4
Ruislip 40 F3
Ruislip Common 40 F3
Rumbling Bridge 128 E2
Rumburgh 69 F6
Rumford 4 B3
Rumney 22 B4
Runcorn 86 F3
Runcton 16 D2
Runcton Holme 67 D6
Rundlestone 6 B3
Runfold 27 E6
Runhall 68 D3
Runham Norf 69 C7
Norf 69 D8
Runnington 11 B6
Runsell Green 42 D3
Runswick Bay 103 C6
Runwell 42 E3
Ruscombe 27 B5
Rushall Hereford 49 F8
Norf 68 F4
Wilts 25 D6
W Mid 62 D4
Rushbrooke 56 C2
Rushbury 60 E5
Rushden Herts 54 F4
N Nhants 53 C7
Rushenden 30 B3
Rushford 68 F2
Rush Green 41 F8
Rush-head 153 D8
Rushlake Green 18 D3
Rushmere 69 F7
Rushmere
St Andrew 57 E6
Rushmoor 27 E6
Rushock 50 B3
Rusholme 87 E6
Rushton Ches W 74 C2
N Nhants 64 F5
Shrops 61 D6
Rushton Spencer 75 C6
Rushwick 50 D3
Rushyford 101 B7
Ruskie 126 D5
Ruskington 78 D3
Rusland 99 F5
Rusper 28 F3
Ruspidge 36 C3
Russell's Water 39 F7
Russel's Green 57 B6
Rusthall 18 B2
Rustington 16 D4
Ruston 103 F7
Ruston Parva 97 C6
Ruswarp 103 D6
Rutherford 122 F2
Rutherglen 119 C6
Ruthernbridge 4 C5
Ruthin = Rhuthun 72 D5
Ruthrieston 141 D8
Ruthven Aberds 152 D5
Angus 134 E2
Highld 138 E3
Highld 151 H11
Ruthven House 134 E3
Ruthvoes 4 C4
Ruthwell 107 C7
Ruyton-XI-Towns 60 B3
Ryal 110 B3
Ryal Fold 86 B4
Ryall 12 E2
Ryarsh 29 D7
Rydal 99 D5
Ryde 15 E6
Rye 19 C6
Ryecroft Gate 75 C6
Rye Foreign 19 C5
Rye Harbour 19 D6
Ryehill 91 B6
Rye Park 41 C6
Rye Street 50 F2
Ryhall 65 C7
Ryhill 88 C4
Ryhope 111 D7
Rylstone 94 D2
Ryme Intrinseca 12 C3
Ryther 95 F8
Ryton Glos 50 F2
N Yorks 96 B3
Ryton *continued*
Shrops 61 D7
T&W 110 C4
Ryton-on-
Dunsmore 51 B8

S

Sabden 93 F7
Sacombe 41 C6
Sacriston 110 E5
Sadberge 101 C8
Saddell 143 E8
Saddington 64 E3
Saddle Bow 67 C6
Saddlescombe 17 C6
Sadgill 99 D6
Saffron Walden 55 F6
Sageston 32 D1
Saham Hills 68 D2
Saham Toney 68 D2
Saighdinis 148 B3
Saighton 73 C8
St Abbs 122 C5
St Abb's Haven 122 C5
St Agnes Corn 4 D2
Scilly 2 F3
St Albans 40 D4
St Allen 4 D3
St Andrews 129 C7
St Andrew's
Major 22 B3
St Anne Ald 16
St Annes 85 B4
St Ann's 114 E3
St Ann's Chapel
Corn 6 B2
Devon 6 E4
St Anthony-in-
Meneage 3 D6
St Anthony's Hill 18 E3
St Arvans 36 E2
St Asaph
= Llanelwy 72 B4
St Athan 22 C2
St Aubin Jersey 17
St Austell 4 D5
St Bees 98 C1
St Blazey 5 D5
St Boswells 121 F8
St Brelade Jersey 17
St Breock 4 B4
St Breward 5 B5
St Briavels 36 D2
St Bride's 44 D3
St Brides Major 21 B7
St Bride's
Netherwent 35 F8
St Brides-
super-Ely 22 B2
St Brides
Wentlooge 35 F6
St Budeaux 6 D2
Saintbury 51 F6
St Buryan 2 D3
St Catherine 24 B2
St Catherine's 125 E7
St Clears = Sanclêr 32 C3
St Cleer 5 C7
St Clement 3 B7
St Clements Jersey 17
St Clether 8 F4
St Colmac 145 G9
St Columb Major 4 C4
St Columb Minor 4 C3
St Columb Road 4 D4
St Combs 153 B10
St Cross South
Elmham 69 F5
St Cyrus 135 C7
St David's 127 B8
St David's
= Tyddewi 44 C2
St Day 3 B6
St Dennis 4 D4
St Devereux 49 F6
St Dogmaels 45 E3
St Dogwells 44 C4
St Dominick 6 C2
St Donat's 21 C8
St Edith's 24 C4
St Endellion 4 B4
St Enoder 4 D3
St Erme 4 D3
St Erney 5 D8
St Erth 2 C4
St Ervan 4 B3
St Eval 4 C3
St Ewe 3 B8
St Fagans 22 B3
St Fergus 153 C10
St Fillans 127 B5
St Florence 32 D1
St Genny's 8 E3
St George 72 B3
St George's 22 B2
St Germans 5 D8
St Giles 78 B2
St Giles in
the Wood 9 C7
St Giles on
the Heath 9 E5
St Harmon 47 B8
St Helena 63 D6
St Helen
Auckland 101 B6
St Helens IoW 15 F7
Mers 86 E3
St Helen's 18 D5
St Helier Jersey 17
London 28 C3
St Hilary Corn 2 C4
V Glam 22 B2
Saint Hill 28 F4
St Illtyd 35 D6
St Ippollytts 40 B4
St Ishmael's 44 E3
St Issey 4 B4
St Ive 5 C8
St Ives Cambs 54 B4
Corn 2 B4
Dorset 14 D2
St James South
Elmham 69 F6
St Jidgey 4 C4
St John 6 D2
St John's IoM 84 D2
Jersey 17
St John's *continued*
Sur 27 D7
Worcs 50 D3
St John's Chapel 109 F8
St John's Fen End 66 C5
St John's Highway 66 C5
St John's Town of
Dalry 113 F6
St Judes 84 C3
St Just 2 C2
St Just in Roseland 3 C7
St Katherine's 153 E7
St Keverne 3 D6
St Kew 4 B5
St Kew Highway 4 B5
St Keyne 5 C7
St Lawrence Corn 4 C5
Essex 43 D5
IoW 15 G6
St Leonards Dorset 14 D2
E Sus 18 E4
S Lanark 119 D6
St Leonard's 40 D2
St Levan 2 D2
St Lythans 22 B3
St Mabyn 4 B5
St Madoes 128 B3
St Margarets 41 C6
St Margaret's 49 F5
St Margaret's at
Cliffe 31 E7
St Margaret's
Hope 159 J5
St Margaret South
Elmham 69 F6
St Mark's 84 E2
St Martin 5 D7
St Martins Corn 3 D6
Perth 134 F1
St Martin's Jersey 17
Shrops 73 F7
St Mary Bourne 26 D2
St Mary Church 22 B2
St Mary Cray 29 C5
St Mary Hill 21 B8
St Mary Hoo 30 B2
St Mary in the
Marsh 19 C7
St Mary's Jersey 17
Orkney 159 H5
St Mary's Bay 19 C7
St Maughans 36 C1
St Mawes 3 C7
St Mawgan 4 C3
St Mellion 5 C8
St Mellons 35 F6
St Merryn 4 B3
St Mewan 4 D4
St Michael
Caerhays 3 B8
St Michael Penkevil 3 B7
St Michaels 49 C7
St Michael's 19 B5
St Michael's on
Wyre 92 E4
St Michael South
Elmham 69 F6
St Minver 4 B4
St Monans 129 D7
St Neot 5 C6
St Neots 54 C2
St Newlyn East 4 D3
St Nicholas Pembs 44 B3
V Glam 22 B2
St Nicholas at
Wade 31 C6
St Ninians 127 E6
St Osyth 43 C7
St Osyth Heath 43 C7
St Ouens Jersey 17
St Owens Cross 36 B2
St Paul's Cray 29 C5
St Paul's Walden 40 B4
St Peter Port Guern 16
St Peter's Jersey 17
Kent 31 C7
St Petrox 44 F4
St Pinnock 5 C7
St Quivox 112 B3
St Ruan 3 E6
St Sampson Guern 16
St Stephen 4 D4
St Stephens Corn 6 D2
Herts 40 D4
St Stephen's 8 F5
St Teath 8 F2
St Thomas 10 E4
St Tudy 5 B5
St Twynnells 44 F4
St Veep 5 D6
St Vigeans 135 E6
St Wenn 4 C4
St Weonards 36 B1
Salcombe 6 F5
Salcombe Regis 11 F6
Salcott 43 C5
Sale 87 E5
Saleby 79 B7
Sale Green 50 D4
Salehurst 18 C4
Salem Carms 33 B7
Ceredig 58 F3
Salen Argyll 147 G8
Highld 147 E9
Salesbury 93 F6
Salford C Beds 53 F7
Gtr Man 87 E6
Oxon 38 B2
Salford Priors 51 D5
Salfords 28 E3
Salhouse 69 C6
Saline 128 E2
Salisbury 14 B2
Sallachan 130 C3
Sallachy Highld 150 H2
Highld 157 J8
Salle 81 E7
Salmonby 79 B6
Salmond's Muir 135 F5
Salperton 37 B7
Salph End 53 D8
Salsburgh 119 C8
Salt 62 B3
Saltaire 94 F4
Saltash 6 D2
Saltburn 151 E10
Saltburn-by-
the-Sea 102 B4
Saltby 65 B5
Saltcoats Cumb 98 E2
N Ayrs 118 E2
Saltdean 17 D7
Salt End 91 B5
Salter 93 C6
Salterforth 93 E8
Salterswall 74 C3
Saltfleet 91 E8
Saltfleetby All
Saints 91 E8
Saltfleetby
St Clements 91 E8
Saltfleetby
St Peter 91 F8
Saltford 23 C8
Salthouse 81 C6
Saltmarshe 89 B8
Saltney 73 C7
Salton 96 B3
Saltwick 110 B4
Saltwood 19 B8
Salum 146 G3
Salvington 16 D5
Salwarpe 50 C3
Salwayash 12 E2
Sambourne 51 C5
Sambrook 61 B7
Samhla 148 B2
Samlesbury 93 F5
Samlesbury
Bottoms 86 B4
Sampford Arundel 11 C6
Sampford Brett 22 E2
Sampford
Courtenay 9 D8
Sampford Peverell 10 C5
Sampford Spiney 6 B3
Sampool Bridge 99 F6
Samuelston 121 B7
Sanachan 149 D13
Sanaigmore 142 A3
Sanclêr = St Clears 32 C3
Sancreed 2 D3
Sancton 96 F5
Sand Highld 150 B2
Shetland 160 J5
Sandaig 149 H12
Sandale 108 E2
Sandal Magna 88 C4
Sandbach 74 C4
Sandbank 145 E10
Sandbanks 13 F8
Sandend 152 B5
Sanderstead 28 C4
Sandfields 37 B6
Sandford Cumb 100 C2
Devon 10 D3
Dorset 13 F7
IoW 15 F6
N Som 23 D6
Shrops 74 F2
S Lanark 119 E7
Sandfordhill 153 D11
Sandford on
Thames 39 D5
Sandford Orcas 12 B4
Sandford
St Martin 38 B4
Sandgate 19 B8
Sandgreen 106 D2
Sandhaven 153 B9
Sandhead 104 E4
Sandhills 27 F7
Sandhoe 110 C2
Sand Hole 96 F4
Sandholme E Yorks 96 F4
Lincs 79 F6
Sandhurst Brack 27 C6
Glos 37 B5
Kent 18 C4
Sandhurst Cross 18 C4
Sandhutton 102 F1
Sand Hutton 96 D2
Sandiacre 76 F4
Sandilands Lincs 91 F9
S Lanark 119 F8
Sandiway 74 B3
Sandleheath 14 C2
Sandling 29 D8
Sandlow Green 74 C4
Sandness 160 H3
Sandon Essex 42 D3
Herts 54 F4
Staffs 75 F6
Sandown 15 F6
Sandplace 5 D7
Sandridge Herts 40 C4
Wilts 24 C4
Sandringham 67 B6
Sandsend 103 C6
Sandside
House 157 C12
Sandsound 160 J5
Sandtoft 89 D8
Sandway 30 D2
Sandwell 62 F4
Sandwich 31 D7
Sandwick Cumb 99 C6
Orkney 159 K5
Shetland 160 L6
Sandwith 98 C1
Sandy Carms 33 D5
C Beds 54 E2
Sandy Bank 79 D5
Sandycroft 73 C7
Sandyford
Dumfries 114 E5
Stoke 75 D5
Sandygate 84 C3
Sandy Haven 44 E3
Sandyhills 107 D5
Sandylands 92 C4
Sandy Lane Wilts 24 C4
Wrex 73 E7
Sandypark 10 F2
Sandysike 108 C3
Sangobeg 156 C7
Sangomore 156 C7
Sanna 146 E7
Sanndabhaig
W Isles 148 D3
W Isles 155 D9
Sannox 143 D11
Sanquhar 113 D7
Santon 90 C3
Santon Bridge 98 D3
Santon Downham 67 F8
Sapcote 63 E8
Sapey Common 50 C2
Sapiston 56 B3
Sapley 54 B3
Sapperton Glos 37 D6
Lincs 78 F3
Saracen's Head 66 B3
Sarclet 158 F5
Sardis 33 D6
Sarn Bridgend 34 F3
Powys 60 E2
Sarnau Carms 32 C4
Ceredig 46 D2
Gwyn 72 F3
Powys 48 F2
Powys 60 C2
Sarn Bach 70 E4
Sarnesfield 49 D5
Sarn Meyllteyrn 70 D3
Saron Carms 33 C7
Carms 46 F2
Denb 72 C4
Gwyn 82 E5
Gwyn 82 F4
Sarratt 40 E3
Sarre 31 C6
Sarsden 38 B2
Sarsgrum 156 C6
Satley 110 E4
Satron 100 E4
Satterleigh 9 B8
Satterthwaite 99 E5
Satwell 39 F7
Sauchen 141 C5
Saucher 134 F1
Sauchie 127 E7
Sauchieburn 135 C6
Saughall 73 B7
Saughtree 115 E8
Saul 36 D4
Saundby 89 F8
Saundersfoot 32 D2
Saunderton 39 D7
Saunton 20 F3
Sausthorpe 79 C6
Saval 157 J8
Savary 147 G9
Savile Park 87 B8
Sawbridge 52 C3
Sawbridgeworth 41 C7
Sawdon 103 F7
Sawley Derbys 76 F4
Lancs 93 E7
N Yorks 94 C5
Sawston 55 E5
Sawtry 65 F8
Saxby Leics 64 C5
Lincs 90 F4
Saxby All Saints 90 C3
Saxelbye 64 B4
Saxham Street 56 C4
Saxilby 77 B8
Saxlingham 81 D6
Saxlingham Green 68 E5
Saxlingham
Nethergate 68 E5
Saxlingham
Thorpe 68 E5
Saxmundham 57 C7
Saxondale 77 F6
Saxon Street 55 D7
Saxtead 57 C6
Saxtead Green 57 C6
Saxthorpe 81 D7
Saxton 95 F7
Sayers Common 17 C6
Scackleton 96 B2
Scadabhagh 154 H6
Scaftworth 89 E7
Scagglethorpe 96 B4
Scaitcliffe 87 B5
Scalasaig 144 D2
Scalby E Yorks 90 B2
N Yorks 103 E8
Scaldwell 53 B5
Scaleby 108 C4
Scaleby Hill 108 C4
Scale Houses 109 E5
Scales Cumb 92 B2
Cumb 99 B5
Lancs 92 F4
Scalford 64 B4
Scaling 103 C5
Scallastle 124 B2
Scalloway 160 K6
Scalpay 154 H7
Scalpay House 149 F11
Scalpsie 145 H9
Scamadale 147 B10
Scamblesby 79 B5
Scamodale 130 B2
Scampston 96 B4
Scampton 78 B2
Scapa 159 H5
Scapegoat Hill 87 C8
Scar 159 D7
Scarborough 103 F8
Scarcliffe 76 C4
Scarcroft 95 E6
Scarcroft Hill 95 E6
Scardroy 150 F5
Scarff 160 E4
Scarfskerry 158 C4
Scargill 101 C5
Scarinish 146 G3
Scarisbrick 85 C4
Scarning 68 C2
Scarrington 77 E7
Scartho 91 D6
Scarwell 159 F3
Scatness 160 M5
Scatraig 151 H10
Scawby 90 D3
Scawsby 89 D6
Scawton 102 F3
Scayne's Hill 17 B7
Scethrog 35 B5
Scholar Green 74 D5
Scholes W Yorks 88 B2
W Yorks 88 D2
W Yorks 95 F6
School Green 74 C3
Scleddau 44 B4
Scofton 89 F7
Scole 56 B5
Scolpaig 148 A2
Scone 128 B3
Sconser 149 E10
Scoonie 129 D5
Scoor 146 K7
Scopwick 78 D3
Scoraig 150 B3
Scorborough 97 E6
Scorrier 3 B6
Scorton Lancs 92 E5
N Yorks 101 D7
Sco Ruston 81 E8
Scotbheinn 148 C3
Scotby 108 D4
Scotch Corner 101 D7
Scotforth 92 D4
Scothern 78 B3
Scotland Gate 117 F8
Scotlandwell 128 D3
Scotsburn 151 D10
Scotscalder
Station 158 E2
Scotscraig 129 B6
Scots' Gap 117 F6
Scotston Aberds 135 B7
Perth 133 E6
Scotstoun 118 C5
Scotstown 130 C2
Scotswood 110 C4
Scottas 149 H12
Scotter 90 D2
Scotterthorpe 90 D2
Scottlethorpe 65 B7
Scotton Lincs 90 E2
N Yorks 95 D6
N Yorks 101 E6
Scottow 81 E8
Scoughall 129 F8
Scoulag 145 H10
Scoulton 68 D2
Scourie 156 E4
Scourie More 156 E4
Scousburgh 160 M5
Scrabster 158 C2
Scrafield 79 C6
Scrainwood 117 D5
Scrane End 79 E6
Scraptoft 64 D3
Scratby 69 C8
Scrayingham 96 C3
Scredington 78 E3
Scremby 79 C7
Scremerston 123 E6
Screveton 77 E7
Scrivelsby 79 C5
Scriven 95 D6
Scrooby 89 E7
Scropton 75 F8
Scrub Hill 78 D5
Scruton 101 E7
Sculcoates 97 F6
Sculthorpe 80 D4
Scunthorpe 90 C2
Scurlage 33 F5
Seaborough 12 D2
Seacombe 85 E4
Seacroft Lincs 79 C8
W Yorks 95 F6
Seadyke 79 F6
Seafield S Ayrs 112 B3
W Loth 120 C3
Seaford 17 E8
Seaforth 85 E4
Seagrave 64 C3
Seaham 111 E7
Seahouses 123 F8
Seal 29 D6
Sealand 73 C7
Seale 27 E6
Seamer N Yorks 102 C2
N Yorks 103 F8
Seamill 118 E2
Sea Palling 69 B7
Searby 90 D4
Seasalter 30 C4
Seascale 98 D2
Seathorne 79 C8
Seathwaite Cumb 98 C4
Cumb 98 E4
Seatoller 98 C4
Seaton Corn 5 D8
Cumb 107 F7
Devon 11 F7
Durham 111 D6
E Yorks 97 E7
Northumb 111 B6
Rutland 65 E6
Seaton Burn 110 B5
Seaton Carew 102 B3
Seaton Delaval 111 B6
Seaton Ross 96 E3
Seaton Sluice 111 B6
Seatown Aberds 152 B5
Dorset 12 E2
Seave Green 102 D3
Seaview 15 E7
Seaville 107 D8
Seavington
St Mary 12 C2
Seavington
St Michael 12 C2
Sebergham 108 E3
Seckington 63 D6
Second Coast 150 B2
Sedbergh 100 E1
Sedbury 36 E2
Sedbusk 100 E3
Sedgeberrow 50 F5
Sedgebrook 77 F8
Sedgefield 102 B1
Sedgeford 80 D3
Sedgehill 13 B6
Sedgley 62 E3
Sedgwick 99 F7
Sedlescombe 18 D4
Sedlescombe
Street 18 D4
Seend 24 C4
Seend Cleeve 24 C4
Seer Green 40 E2
Seething 69 E6
Sefton 85 D4
Seghill 111 B5
Seifton 60 F4
Seighford 62 B2
Seilebost 154 H5
Seion 82 E5
Seisdon 62 E2
Seisiadar 155 D10
Selattyn 73 F6
Selborne 26 F5
Selby 96 F2

Selham 16 B3
Selhurst 28 C4
Selkirk 115 B7
Sellack 36 B2
Sellafirth 160 D7
Sellibister 159 D8
Sellindge 19 B7
Sellindge Lees 19 B8
Selling 30 D4
Sells Green 24 C4
Selly Oak 62 F4
Selmeston 18 E2
Selsdon 28 C4
Selsey 16 E2
Selsfield Common 28 F4
Selsted 31 E6
Selston 76 D4
Selworthy 21 E8
Semblister 160 H5
Semer 56 E3
Semington 24 C3
Semley 13 B6
Send 27 D8
Send Marsh 27 D8
Senghenydd 35 E5
Sennen 2 D2
Sennen Cove 2 D2
Sennybridge =Pont Senni 34 B3
Serlby 89 F7
Sessay 95 B7
Setchey 67 C6
Setley 14 D4
Setter Shetland 160 E6
Shetland 160 H5
Shetland 160 J7
Settiscarth 159 G4
Settle 93 C8
Settrington 96 B4
Sevenhampton 37 B7
Seven Kings 41 F7
Sevenoaks 29 D6
Sevenoaks Weald 29 D6
Seven Sisters 34 D2
Severn Beach 36 F2
Severnhampton 38 E2
Severn Stoke 50 E3
Sevington 30 E4
Sewards End 55 F6
Sewardstone 41 E6
Sewardstonebury 41 E6
Sewerby 97 C7
Seworgan 3 C6
Sewstern 65 B5
Sezincote 51 F6
Sgarasta Mhor 154 H5
Sgiogarstaigh 155 A10
Shabbington 39 D6
Shackerstone 63 D7
Shackleford 27 E7
Shade 87 B7
Shadforth 111 E6
Shadingfield 69 F7
Shadoxhurst 19 B6
Shadsworth 86 B5
Shadwell Norf 68 F2
W Yorks 95 F6
Shaftesbury 13 B6
Shafton 88 C4
Shalbourne 25 C8
Shalcombe 14 F4
Shalden 26 E4
Shaldon 7 B7
Shalfleet 14 F5
Shalford Essex 42 B3
Sur 27 E8
Shalford Green 42 B3
Shallowford 21 E6
Shalmsford Street 30 D4
Shalstone 52 F4
Shamley Green 27 E8
Shandon 145 E11
Shandwick 151 D11
Shangton 64 E4
Shankhouse 111 B5
Shanklin 15 F6
Shanquhar 152 E5
Shanzie 134 D2
Shap 99 C7
Shapwick Dorset 13 D7
Som 23 F6
Shardlow 76 F4
Shareshill 62 D3
Sharlston 88 C4
Sharlston Common 88 C4
Sharnbrook 53 D7
Sharnford 63 E8
Sharoe Green 92 F5
Sharow 95 B6
Sharpenhoe 53 F8
Sharperton 117 D5
Sharpness 36 D3
Sharp Street 69 B6
Sharpthorne 28 F4
Sharrington 81 D6
Shatterford 61 F7
Shaugh Prior 6 C3
Shavington 74 D4
Shaw Gtr Man 87 D7
W Berks 26 C2
Wilts 24 C3
Shawbury 61 B5
Shawdon Hall 117 C6
Shawell 64 F2
Shawford 15 B5
Shawforth 87 B6
Shaw Green 86 C3
Shawhead 107 B5
Shawhill 108 C2
Shaw Mills 95 C5
Shawton 119 E6
Shawtonhill 119 E6
Shear Cross 24 E3
Shearington 107 C7
Shearsby 64 E3
Shebbear 9 D6
Shebdon 61 B7
Shebster 157 C13
Sheddens 119 D5
Shedfield 15 C6
Sheen 75 C8
Sheepscar 95 F6
Sheepscombe 37 C5
Sheepstor 6 C3
Sheepwash 9 D6
Sheepway 23 B6
Sheepy Magna 63 D7
Sheepy Parva 63 D7
Sheering 41 C8
Sheerness 30 B3
Sheet 15 B8
Sheffield 88 F4
Sheffield Bottom 26 C4
Sheffield Green 17 B8
Shefford 54 F2
Shefford Woodlands 25 B8
Sheigra 156 C4
Sheinton 61 D6
Shelderton 49 B6
Sheldon Derbys 75 C8
Devon 11 D6
W Mid 63 F5
Sheldwich 30 D4
Shelf 88 B2
Shelfanger 68 F4
Shelfield Warks 51 C6
W Mid 62 D4
Shelford 77 E6
Shellacres 122 E4
Shelley Essex 42 D1
Suff 56 F4
W Yorks 88 C3
Shellingford 38 E3
Shellow Bowells 42 D2
Shelsley Beauchamp 50 C2
Shelsley Walsh 50 C2
Shelthorpe 64 C2
Shelton Bedford 53 C8
Norf 68 E5
Notts 77 E7
Shrops 60 C4
Shelton Green 68 E5
Shelve 60 E3
Shelwick 49 E7
Shenfield 42 E2
Shenington 51 E8
Shenley 40 D4
Shenley Brook End 53 F6
Shenleybury 40 D4
Shenley Church End 53 F6
Shenmore 49 F5
Shennanton 105 C7
Shenstone Staffs 62 D5
Worcs 50 B3
Shenton 63 D7
Shenval Highld 137 B7
Moray 139 B8
Shepeau Stow 66 C3
Shephall 41 B5
Shepherd's Green 39 F7
Shepherd's Port 80 D2
Shepherdswell 31 E6
Shepley 88 D2
Shepperdine 36 E3
Shepperton 27 C8
Shepreth 54 E4
Shepshed 63 C8
Shepton Beauchamp 12 C2
Shepton Mallet 23 E8
Shepton Montague 23 F8
Shepway 29 D8
Sheraton 111 F7
Sherborne Dorset 12 C4
Glos 38 C1
Sherborne St John 26 D4
Sherbourne 51 C7
Sherburn Durham 111 E6
N Yorks 97 B5
Sherburn Hill 111 E6
Sherburn in Elmet 95 F7
Shere 27 E8
Shereford 80 E4
Sherfield English 14 B3
Sherfield on Loddon 26 D4
Sherford 7 E5
Sheriffhales 61 C7
Sheriff Hutton 96 C2
Sheringham 81 C7
Sherington 53 E6
Shernal Green 50 C4
Shernborne 80 D3
Sherrington 24 F4
Sherston 37 F5
Sherwood Green 9 B7
Shettleston 119 C6
Shevington 86 D3
Shevington Moor 86 C3
Shevington Vale 86 D3
Sheviock 5 D8
Shide 15 F5
Shiel Bridge 136 C2
Shieldaig Highld 149 A13
Highld 149 C13
Shieldhill Dumfries 114 F3
Falk 119 B8
S Lanark 120 E3
Shielfoot 147 E9
Shielhill Angus 134 D4
Invclyd 118 B2
Shifford 38 D3
Shifnal 61 D7
Shilbottle 117 D7
Shildon 101 B7
Shillingford Devon 10 B4
Oxon 39 E5
Shillingford St George 10 F4
Shillingstone 13 C6
Shillington 54 F2
Shillmoor 116 D4
Shilton Oxon 38 D2
Warks 63 F8
Shilvington 117 F7
Shimpling Norf 68 F4
Suff 56 D2
Shimpling Street 56 D2
Shincliffe 111 E5
Shiney Row 111 D6
Shinfield 26 C5
Shingham 67 D7
Shingle Street 57 E7
Shinner's Bridge 7 C5
Shinness 157 H8
Shipbourne 29 D6
Shipdham 68 D2
Shipham 23 D6
Shiphay 7 C6
Shiplake 27 B5
Shipley Derbys 76 E4
Northumb 117 C7
Shrops 62 E2
W Sus 16 B5
W Yorks 94 F4
Shipley Shiels 116 E3
Shipmeadow 69 F6
Shippea Hill Station 67 F6
Shippon 38 E4
Shipston-on-Stour 51 E7
Shipton Glos 37 C7
N Yorks 95 D8
Shrops 61 E5
Shipton Bellinger 25 E7
Shipton Gorge 12 E2
Shipton Green 16 D2
Shipton Moyne 37 F5
Shipton on Cherwell 38 C4
Shipton Solers 37 C7
Shiptonthorpe 96 E4
Shipton-under-Wychwood 38 C2
Shirburn 39 E6
Shirdley Hill 85 C4
Shirebrook 76 C5
Shiregreen 88 E4
Shirehampton 23 B7
Shiremoor 111 B6
Shirenewton 36 E1
Shireoaks 89 F6
Shirkoak 19 B6
Shirland 76 D3
Shirley Derbys 76 E2
London 28 C4
Soton 14 C5
W Mid 51 B6
Shirl Heath 49 D6
Shirrell Heath 15 C6
Shirwell 20 F4
Shirwell Cross 20 F4
Shiskine 143 F10
Shobdon 49 C6
Shobnall 63 B6
Shobrooke 10 D3
Shoby 64 C3
Shocklach 73 E8
Shoeburyness 43 F5
Sholden 31 D7
Sholing 14 C5
Shoot Hill 60 C4
Shop Corn 4 B3
Corn 8 C4
Shop Corner 57 F6
Shoreditch 41 F6
Shoreham 29 C6
Shoreham-by-Sea 17 D6
Shore Mill 151 E10
Shoresdean 123 E5
Shoreswood 122 E5
Shoreton 151 E9
Shorncote 37 E7
Shorne 29 B7
Shortacombe 9 F7
Shortgate 17 C8
Short Heath 62 D3
Shortlanesend 3 B7
Shortlees 118 F4
Shortstown 53 E8
Shorwell 15 F5
Shoscombe 24 D2
Shotatton 60 B3
Shotesham 69 E5
Shotgate 42 E3
Shotley 57 F6
Shotley Bridge 110 D3
Shotleyfield 110 D3
Shotley Gate 57 F6
Shottenden 30 D4
Shottermill 27 F6
Shottery 51 D6
Shotteswell 52 E2
Shottisham 57 E7
Shottle 76 E3
Shottlegate 76 E3
Shotton Durham 111 F7
Flint 73 C7
Northumb 122 F4
Shotton Colliery 111 E6
Shotts 119 C8
Shotwick 73 B7
Shouldham 67 D6
Shouldham Thorpe 67 D6
Shoulton 50 D3
Shover's Green 18 B3
Shrawardine 60 C4
Shrawley 50 C3
Shrewley Common 51 C7
Shrewsbury 60 C4
Shrewton 25 E5
Shripney 16 D3
Shrivenham 38 F2
Shropham 68 E2
Shrub End 43 B5
Shucknall 49 E7
Shudy Camps 55 E7
Shulishadermor 149 D9
Shurdington 37 C6
Shurlock Row 27 B6
Shurrery 157 D13
Shurrery Lodge 157 D13
Shurton 22 E4
Shustoke 63 E6
Shute Devon 10 D3
Devon 11 E7
Shutford 51 E8
Shuthonger 50 F3
Shutlanger 52 D5
Shuttington 63 D6
Shuttlewood 76 B4
Siabost bho Dheas 154 C7
Siabost bho Thuath 154 C7
Siadar 155 B8
Siadar Iarach 155 B8
Siadar Uarach 155 B8
Sibbaldbie 114 F4
Sibbertoft 64 F3
Sibdon Carwood 60 F4
Sibford Ferris 51 F8
Sibford Gower 51 F8
Sible Hedingham 55 F8
Sibsey 79 D6
Sibson Cambs 65 E7
Leics 63 D7
Sibthorpe 77 E7
Sibton 57 C7
Sibton Green 57 B7
Sicklesmere 56 C2
Sicklinghall 95 E6
Sid 11 F6
Sidbury Devon 11 E6
Shrops 61 F6
Sidcot 23 D6
Sidcup 29 B5
Siddick 107 F7
Siddington Ches E 74 B5
Glos 37 E7
Sidemoor 50 B4
Sidestrand 81 D8
Sidford 11 E6
Sidlesham 16 E2
Sidley 18 E4
Sidlow 28 E3
Sidmouth 11 F6
Sigford 7 B5
Sigglesthorne 97 E7
Sighthill 120 B4
Sigingstone 21 B8
Signet 38 C2
Silchester 26 C4
Sildinis 155 F7
Sileby 64 C2
Silecroft 98 F3
Silfield 68 E4
Silian 46 D4
Silkstone 88 D3
Silkstone Common 88 D3
Silk Willoughby 78 E3
Silloth 107 D8
Sills 116 D4
Sillyearn 152 C5
Siloh 47 F6
Silpho 103 E7
Silsden 94 E3
Silsoe 53 F8
Silverburn 120 C5
Silverdale Lancs 92 B4
Staffs 74 E5
Silver End 42 C4
Silvergate 81 E7
Silverhill 18 D4
Silverley's Green 57 B6
Silverstone 52 E4
Silverton 10 D4
Silvington 49 B8
Silwick 160 J4
Simmondley 87 E8
Simonburn 109 B8
Simonsbath 21 F6
Simonstone 93 F7
Simprim 122 E4
Simpson 53 F6
Simpson Cross 44 D3
Sinclair's Hill 122 D4
Sinclairston 112 C4
Sinderby 101 F8
Sinderhope 109 D8
Sindlesham 27 C5
Singdean 115 D8
Singleborough 53 F5
Singleton Lancs 92 F3
W Sus 16 C2
Singlewell 29 B7
Sinkhurst Green 30 E2
Sinnahard 140 C3
Sinnington 103 F5
Sinton Green 50 C3
Sipson 27 B8
Sirhowy 35 C5
Sisland 69 E6
Sissinghurst 18 B4
Sisterpath 122 E3
Siston 23 B8
Sithney 2 D5
Sittingbourne 30 C2
Six Ashes 61 F7
Sixhills 91 F5
Six Hills 64 B3
Six Mile Bottom 55 D6
Sixpenny Handley 13 C7
Sizewell 57 C8
Skail 157 E10
Skaill Orkney 159 E5
Orkney 159 G3
Orkney 159 H6
Skares 113 C5
Skateraw 122 B3
Skaw 160 G7
Skeabost 149 D9
Skeabrae 159 F3
Skeeby 101 D7
Skeffington 64 D4
Skeffling 91 C7
Skegby 76 C4
Skegness 79 C8
Skelberry 160 M5
Skelbo 151 B10
Skelbrooke 89 C6
Skeldyke 79 F6
Skellingthorpe 78 B2
Skellister 160 H6
Skellow 89 C6
Skelmanthorpe 88 C3
Skelmersdale 86 D2
Skelmonae 153 E8
Skelmorlie 118 C1
Skelmuir 153 D9
Skelpick 157 D10
Skelton Cumb 108 F4
E Yorks 89 B8
N Yorks 101 D5
Redcar 102 C4
York 95 D8
Skelton-on-Ure 95 C6
Skelwick 159 D5
Skelwith Bridge 99 D5
Skendleby 79 C7
Skene House 141 D6
Skenfrith 36 B1
Skerne 97 D6
Skeroblingarry 143 F8
Skerray 157 C9
Skerton 92 C4
Sketchley 63 E8
Sketty 33 E7
Skewen 33 E8
Skewsby 96 B2
Skeyton 81 E8
Skiag Bridge 156 G5
Skibo Castle 151 C10
Skidbrooke 91 E8
Skidbrooke North End 91 E8
Skidby 97 F6
Skilgate 10 B4
Skillington 65 B5
Skinburness 107 D8
Skinflats 127 F8
Skinidin 148 D7
Skinnet 157 C8
Skinningrove 103 B5
Skipness 145 H7
Skippool 92 E3
Skipsea 97 D7
Skipsea Brough 97 D7
Skipton 94 D2
Skipton-on-Swale 95 B6
Skipwith 96 F2
Skirbeck 79 E6
Skirbeck Quarter 79 E6
Skirlaugh 97 F7
Skirling 120 F3
Skirmett 39 F7
Skirpenbeck 96 D3
Skirwith 109 F6
Skirza 158 D5
Skulamus 149 F11
Skullomie 157 C9
Skyborry Green 48 B4
Skye of Curr 139 B5
Skyreholme 94 C3
Slackhall 87 F8
Slackhead 152 B4
Slad 37 D5
Slade Devon 20 E4
Pembs 44 D4
Slade Green 29 B6
Slaggyford 109 D6
Slaidburn 93 D7
Slaithwaite 87 C8
Slaley 110 D2
Slamannan 119 B8
Slapton Bucks 40 B2
Devon 7 E6
W Nhants 52 E4
Slatepit Dale 76 C3
Slattocks 87 D6
Slaugham 17 B6
Slaughterford 24 B3
Slawston 64 E4
Sleaford Hants 27 F6
Lincs 78 E3
Sleagill 99 C7
Sleapford 61 C6
Sledge Green 50 F3
Sledmere 96 C5
Sleightholme 100 C4
Sleights 103 D6
Slepe 13 E7
Slickly 158 D4
Sliddery 143 F10
Sligachan Hotel 149 F9
Slimbridge 36 D4
Slindon Staffs 74 F5
W Sus 16 D3
Slinfold 28 F2
Sling 83 E6
Slingsby 96 B2
Slioch 152 E5
Slip End C Beds 40 C3
Herts 54 F3
Slipton 53 B7
Slitting Mill 62 C4
Slochd 138 B4
Slockavullin 124 F4
Sloley 81 E8
Sloothby 79 B7
Slough 27 B7
Slough Green 17 B6
Sluggan 138 B4
Slumbay 149 E13
Slyfield 27 D7
Slyne 92 C4
Smailholm 122 F2
Smallbridge 87 C7
Smallburgh 69 B6
Smallburn Aberds 153 D10
E Ayrs 113 B6
Small Dole 17 C6
Smalley 76 E4
Smallfield 28 E4
Small Hythe 19 B5
Smallridge 11 D8
Smannell 25 E8
Smardale 100 D2
Smarden 30 E2
Smarden Bell 30 E2
Smeatharpe 11 C6
Smeeth 19 B7
Smeeton Westerby 64 E3
Smercleit 148 G2
Smerral 158 G3
Smethwick 62 F4
Smirisary 147 D9
Smisby 63 C7
Smithfield 108 C4
Smith Green 92 D4
Smithincott 11 C5
Smith's Green 42 B1
Smithstown 149 A12
Smithton 151 G10
Smithy Green 74 B4
Smockington 63 F8
Smoogro 159 H4
Smythe's Green 43 C5
Snaigow House 133 E7
Snailbeach 60 D3
Snailwell 55 C7
Snainton 103 F7
Snaith 89 B7
Snape N Yorks 101 F7
Suff 57 D7
Snape Green 85 C4
Snarestone 63 D7
Snarford 90 F4
Snargate 19 C6
Snave 19 C7
Snead 60 E3
Sneath Common 68 F4
Sneaton 103 D6
Sneatonthorpe 103 D7
Snelland 90 F4
Snelston 75 E8
Snettisham 80 D2
Sniseabhal 148 E2
Snitter 117 D6
Snitterby 90 E3
Snitterfield 51 D7
Snitton 49 B7
Snodhill 48 E5
Snodland 29 C7
Snowden Hill 88 D3
Snowdown 31 D6
Snowshill 51 F5
Snydale 88 C5
Soar Anglesey 82 D3
Carms 33 B7
Devon 6 F5
Soar-y-Mynydd 47 D6
Soberton 15 C7
Soberton Heath 15 C7
Sockbridge 99 B7
Sockburn 101 D8
Soham 55 B6
Soham Cotes 55 B6
Solas 148 A3
Soldon Cross 8 C5
Soldridge 26 F4
Sole Street Kent 29 C7
Kent 30 E4
Solihull 51 B6
Sollers Dilwyn 49 D6
Sollers Hope 49 F8
Sollom 86 C2
Solva 44 C2
Somerby Leics 64 C4
Lincs 90 D4
Somercotes 76 D4
Somerford 14 E2
Somerford Keynes 37 E7
Somerley 16 E2
Somerleyton 69 E7
Somersal Herbert 75 F8
Somersby 79 B6
Somersham Cambs 54 B4
Suff 56 E4
Somerton Oxon 38 B4
Som 12 B2
Sompting 17 D5
Sonning 27 B5
Sonning Common 39 F7
Sonning Eye 27 B5
Sontley 73 E7
Sopley 14 E2
Sopwell 40 D4
Sopworth 37 F5
Sorbie 105 E8
Sordale 158 D3
Sorisdale 146 E5
Sorn 113 B5
Sornhill 118 F5
Sortat 158 D4
Sotby 78 B5
Sots Hole 78 C4
Sotterley 69 F7
Soudley 61 B7
Soughton 73 C6
Soulbury 40 B1
Soulby 100 C2
Souldern 52 F3
Souldrop 53 C7
Sound Ches E 74 E3
Shetland 160 H5
Shetland 160 J6
Sound Heath 74 E3
Soundwell 23 B8
Sourhope 116 B4
Sourin 159 E5
Sourton 9 E7
Soutergate 98 F4
South Acre 67 C8
Southall 40 F4
South Allington 7 F5
South Alloa 127 E7
Southam Glos 37 B6
Warks 52 C2
South Ambersham 16 B3
Southampton 14 C5
South Anston 89 F6
South Ascot 27 C7
South Ballachulish 130 D4
South Balloch 112 E3
South Bank 102 B3
South Barrow 12 B4
South Beach 70 D4
South Benfleet 42 F3
South Bersted 16 D3
Southborough 29 E6
Southbourne BCP 14 E2
W Sus 15 D8
South Brent 6 C4
South Brewham 24 F2
South Broomhill 117 E8
Southburgh 68 D2
South Burlingham 69 D6
Southburn 97 D5
South Cadbury 12 B4
South Cairn 104 C3
South Carlton 78 B2
South Cave 96 F5
South Cerney 37 E7
South Chard 11 D8
South Charlton 117 B7
South Cheriton 12 B4
Southchurch 43 F5
South Cliffe 96 F4
South Clifton 77 B8
South Cockerington 91 F7
South Cornelly 34 F2
Southcott 25 D6
Southcourt 39 C8
South Cove 69 F7
South Creagan 130 E3
South Creake 80 D4
South Croxton 64 C3
South Croydon 28 C4
South Dalton 97 E5
South Darenth 29 C6
Southdean 116 D2
Southdene 86 E2
South Duffield 96 F2
Southease 17 D8
South Elkington 91 F6
South Elmsall 89 C5
Southend Argyll 143 H7
W Berks 26 B3
Wilts 25 B6
South End Bucks 40 B1
Cumb 92 C2
N Lincs 90 B5
Southend-on-Sea 42 F4
Southernden 30 E2
Southerndown 21 B7
Southerness 107 D6
South Erradale 149 A12
Southery 67 E6
South Fambridge 42 E4
South Fawley 38 F3
South Ferriby 90 B3
Southfield 111 B5
Southfleet 29 B7
South Garth 160 D7
South Garvan 130 B3
Southgate Ceredig 46 B4
London 41 E5
Norf 81 E7
Swansea 33 F6
South Glendale 148 G2
South Godstone 28 E4
South Gorley 14 C2
South Green Essex 42 E2
Kent 30 C2
South-haa 160 E5
South Ham 26 D4
South Hanningfield 42 E3
South Harting 15 C8
South Hatfield 41 D5
South Hayling 15 E8
South Hazelrigg 123 F6
South Heath 40 D2
South Heighton 17 D8
South Hetton 111 E6
South Hiendley 88 C4
South Hill 5 B8
South Hinksey 39 D5
South Hole 8 B4
South Holme 96 B2
South Holmwood 28 E2
South Hornchurch 41 F8
South Hykeham 78 C2
South Hylton 111 D6
Southill 54 E2
South Kelsey 90 E4
South Kessock 151 G9
South Killingholme 91 C5
South Kilvington 102 F2
South Kilworth 64 F3
South Kirkby 88 C5
South Kirkton 141 D6
South Kiscadale 143 F11
South Kyme 78 E4
South Lancing 17 D5
Southleigh 11 E7
South Leigh 38 D3
South Leverton 89 F8
South Littleton 51 E5
South Lopham 68 F3
South Luffenham 65 D6
South Malling 17 C8
South Marston 38 F1
South Middleton 117 B5
South Milford 95 F7
South Millbrex 153 D8
South Milton 6 E5
South Mimms 41 D5
Southminster 43 E5
South Molton 10 B2
Southmoor 38 E3
South Moreton 39 F5
South Mundham 16 D2
South Muskham 77 D7
South Newbald 96 F5
South Newington 52 F2
South Newton 25 F5
South Normanton 76 D4
South Norwood 28 C4
South Nutfield 28 E4
South Ockendon 42 F1
Southoe 54 C2
Southolt 57 C5
South Ormsby 79 B6
Southorpe 65 D7
South Otterington 102 F1
South Owersby 90 E4
Southowram 88 B2
South Oxhey 40 E4
South Perrott 12 D2
South Petherton 12 C2
South Petherwin 8 F5
South Pickenham 67 D8
South Pool 7 E5
Southport 85 C4
South Port 125 C6
Southpunds 160 L6
South Radworthy 21 F6
South Rauceby 78 E3
South Raynham 80 E4
Southrepps 81 D8
South Reston 91 F8
Southrey 78 C4
Southrop 38 D1
Southrope 26 E4
South Runcton 67 D6
South Scarle 77 C8
Southsea 15 E7
South Shian 130 E3
South Shields 111 C6
South Shore 92 F3
South Somercotes 91 E8
South Stainley 95 C6
South Stainmore 100 C3
South Stifford 29 B7
Southstoke 24 C2
South Stoke Oxon 39 F5
W Sus 16 D4
South Street E Sus 17 C7
Kent 30 C5
Kent 30 D4
London 28 D5
South Tawton 9 E8
South Thoresby 79 B7
South Tidworth 25 E7
Southtown Norf 69 D8
Orkney 159 J5
South Town 26 F4
South View 26 D4
Southwaite 108 E4
South Walsham 69 C6
Southwark 28 B4
South Warnborough 26 E5
Southwater 17 B5
Southwater Street 17 B5
Southway 23 E7
South Weald 42 E1
Southwell Dorset 12 G4
Notts 77 D6
South Weston 39 E7
South Wheatley Corn 8 E4
Notts 89 F8
South Whiteness 160 J5
Southwick Hants 15 D7
N Nhants 65 E7
T&W 111 D6
Wilts 24 D3
W Sus 17 D6
South Widcombe 23 D7
South Wigston 64 E2
South Willingham 91 F5
South Wingfield 76 D3
South Witham 65 C6
Southwold 57 B9
South Wonston 26 F2
Southwood Norf 69 D6
Som 23 F7
South Woodham Ferrers 42 E4
South Wootton 67 B6
South Wraxall 24 C3
South Zeal 9 E8
Soval Lodge 155 E8
Sowber Gate 102 F1
Sowerby N Yorks 102 F2
W Yorks 87 B8
Sowerby Bridge 87 B8
Sowerby Row 108 F3
Sowood 87 C8
Sowton 10 E4
Soyal 151 B8
Spacey Houses 95 D6
Spa Common 81 D8
Spadeadam Farm 109 B5
Spalding 66 B2
Spaldington 96 F3
Spaldwick 54 B2
Spalford 77 C8
Spanby 78 F3
Sparham 68 C3
Spark Bridge 99 F5
Sparkford 12 B4
Sparkhill 62 F4
Sparkwell 6 D3
Sparrow Green 68 C2
Sparrowpit 87 F8
Sparsholt Hants 26 F2
Oxon 38 F3
Spartylea 109 E8
Spaunton 103 F5
Spaxton 22 F4
Spean Bridge 136 F5
Spear Hill 16 C5
Speen Bucks 39 E8
W Berks 26 C2
Speeton 97 B7
Speke 86 F2
Speldhurst 29 E6
Spellbrook 41 C7
Spelsbury 38 B3
Spelter 34 E2
Spencers Wood 26 C5
Spennithorne 101 F6
Spennymoor 111 F5
Spetchley 50 D3
Spetisbury 13 D7
Spexhall 69 F6
Spey Bay 152 B3
Speybridge 139 B6
Speyview 152 D2
Spilsby 79 C7
Spindlestone 123 F7
Spinkhill 76 B4
Spinningdale 151 C9
Spirthill 24 B4
Spital Hill 89 E7
Spital in the Street 90 F3
Spithurst 17 C8
Spittal Dumfries 105 D7
E Loth 121 B7
Highld 158 E3
Northumb 123 D6
Pembs 44 C4
Stirling 126 F4
Spittalfield 133 E8
Spittal of Glenmuick 140 F2
Spittal of Glenshee 133 B8
Spixworth 68 C5
Splayne's Green 17 B8
Spofforth 95 D6
Spondon 76 F4
Spon End 51 B8
Spon Green 73 C6
Spooner Row 68 E3
Sporle 67 C8
Spott 122 B2
Spratton 52 B5
Spreakley 27 E6
Spreyton 9 E8
Spridlington 90 F4
Springburn 119 C6
Springfield Dumfries 108 C3
Essex 42 D3
Fife 128 C5
Moray 151 F13
W Mid 62 F4
Springhill 62 D3
Springholm 106 C5
Springkell 108 B2
Springside 118 F3
Springthorpe 90 F2
Spring Vale 88 D3
Spring Valley 84 E3
Springwell 111 D5
Sproatley 97 F7
Sproston Green 74 C4
Sprotbrough 89 D6
Sproughton 56 E5
Sprouston 122 F3
Sprowston 68 C5
Sproxton Leics 65 B5
N Yorks 102 F4
Spurstow 74 D2
Spynie 152 B2
Squires Gate 92 F3
Srannda 154 J5
Sronphadruig Lodge 132 B4
Stableford Shrops 61 E7
Staffs 74 F5
Stacey Bank 88 E3
Stackhouse 93 C8
Stackpole 44 F4
Staddiscombe 6 D3
Staddlethorpe 90 B2
Stadhampton 39 E6
Stadhlaigearraidh 148 E2
Staffi 149 B9
Staffield 108 E5
Stafford 62 B3
Stagsden 53 E7
Stainburn Cumb 98 B2
N Yorks 94 E5
Stainby 65 B6
Staincross 88 C4
Staindrop 101 B6
Staines-upon-Thames 27 B8
Stainfield Lincs 65 B7
Lincs 78 B4
Stainforth N Yorks 93 C8
S Yorks 89 C7
Staining 92 F3
Stainland 87 C8
Stainsacre 103 D7
Stainsby 76 C4
Stainton Cumb 99 B6
Cumb 99 F7
Durham 101 C5
Mbro 102 C2
N Yorks 101 E6
S Yorks 89 E6
Stainton by Langworth 78 B3
Staintondale 103 E7
Stainton le Vale 91 E5
Stainton with Adgarley 92 B2
Stair Cumb 98 B4
E Ayrs 112 B4
Stairhaven 105 D6
Staithes 103 C5
Stakeford 117 F8
Stake Pool 92 E4
Stalbridge 12 C5
Stalbridge Weston 12 C5
Stalham 69 B6
Stalham Green 69 B6
Stalisfield Green 30 D3
Stallingborough 91 C5
Stalling Busk 100 F4
Stalmine 92 E3
Stalybridge 87 E7
Stambourne 55 F8
Stambourne Green 55 F8
Stamford 65 D7
Stamford Bridge Ches W 73 C8
E Yorks 96 D3
Stamfordham 110 B3
Stanah 99 C5
Stanborough 41 C5
Stanbridge C Beds 40 B2
Dorset 13 D8
Stanbrook 50 E3
Stanbury 94 F3
Stand Gtr Man 87 D5
N Lanark 119 C7
Standburn 120 B2
Standeford 62 D3
Standen 30 E2
Standford 27 F6
Standingstone 107 F7
Standish 86 C3
Standlake 38 D3
Standon Hants 14 B5
Herts 41 B6
Staffs 74 F5
Stane 119 D8
Stanfield 80 E5
Stanford C Beds 54 E2
Kent 19 B8
Stanford Bishop 49 D8
Stanford Bridge 50 C2
Stanford Dingley 26 B3
Stanford in the Vale 38 E3
Stanford-le-Hope 42 F2
Stanford on Avon 52 B3
Stanford on Soar 64 B2
Stanford on Teme 50 C2
Stanford Rivers 41 D8
Stanfree 76 B4
Stanghow 102 C4
Stanground 66 E2
Stanhoe 80 D4
Stanhope Borders 114 B4
Durham 110 F2
Stanion 65 F6
Stanley Derbys 76 E4
Durham 110 D4
Lancs 86 D2
Perth 133 F8
Staffs 75 D6
W Yorks 88 B4
Stanley Common 76 E4
Stanley Gate 86 D2
Stanley Hill 49 E8
Stanlow 73 B8
Stanmer 17 D7
Stanmore Hants 15 B5
London 40 E4
W Berks 26 B2
Stannergate 134 F4
Stanningley 94 F5
Stannington Northumb 110 B5
S Yorks 88 F4
Stansbatch 48 C5
Stansfield 55 D8
Stanstead 56 E2
Stanstead Abbotts 41 C6
Stansted 29 C7
Stansted Airport 42 B1
Stansted Mountfitchet 41 B8
Stanton Glos 51 F5
Mon 35 B7
Northumb 117 F7
Staffs 75 E8
Suff 56 B3
Stanton by Bridge 63 B7
Stanton-by-Dale 76 F4
Stanton Drew 23 C7
Stanton Fitzwarren 38 E1
Stanton Harcourt 38 D4
Stanton Hill 76 C4
Stanton in Peak 76 C2
Stanton Lacy 49 B6
Stanton Long 61 E5
Stanton-on-the-Wolds 77 F6
Stanton Prior 23 C8
Stanton St Bernard 25 C5
Stanton St John 39 D5

Stanton St Quintin 24 B4
Stanton Street 56 C3
Stanton under Bardon 63 C8
Stanton upon Hine Heath 61 B5
Stanton Wick 23 C8
Stanwardine in the Fields 60 B4
Stanwardine in the Wood 60 B4
Stanway Essex 43 B5
Glos 51 F5
Stanway Green 57 B6
Stanwell 27 B8
Stanwell Moor 27 B8
Stanwick 53 B7
Stanwick-St-John 101 C6
Stanwix 108 D4
Stanydale 160 H4
Staoinebrig 148 E2
Stape 103 E5
Stapehill 13 D8
Stapeley 74 E3
Stapenhill 63 B6
Staple Kent 31 D6
Som 22 E3
Staple Cross 18 C4
Staplefield 17 B6
Staple Fitzpaine 11 C7
Stapleford Cambs 55 D5
Herts 41 C6
Leics 64 C5
Lincs 77 D8
Notts 76 F4
Wilts 25 F5
Stapleford Abbotts 41 E8
Stapleford Tawney 41 E8
Staplegrove 11 B7
Staplehay 11 B7
Staplehurst 29 E8
Staplers 15 F6
Stapleton Bristol 23 B8
Cumb 108 B5
Hereford 48 C5
Leics 63 E8
N Yorks 101 C7
Shrops 60 D4
Som 12 B2
Stapley 11 C6
Staploe 54 C2
Staplow 49 E8
Star Fife 128 D5
Pembs 45 F4
Som 23 D6
Stara 159 F3
Starbeck 95 D6
Starbotton 94 B2
Starcross 10 F4
Stareton 51 B8
Starkholmes 76 D3
Starlings Green 55 F5
Starston 68 F5
Startforth 101 C5
Startley 37 F6
Stathe 11 B8
Stathern 77 F7
Station Town 111 F7
Staughton Green 54 C2
Staughton Highway 54 C2
Staunton Glos 36 B4
Glos 36 C2
Staunton in the Vale 77 E8
Staunton on Arrow 49 C5
Staunton on Wye 49 E5
Staveley Cumb 99 E6
Cumb 99 F5
Derbys 76 B4
N Yorks 95 C6
Staverton Devon 7 C5
Glos 37 B5
Wilts 24 C3
W Nhants 52 C3
Staverton Bridge 37 B5
Stawell 23 F5
Staxigoe 158 E5
Staxton 97 B6
Staylittle 59 E5
Staynall 92 E3
Staythorpe 77 D7
Stean 94 B3
Stearsby 96 B2
Steart 22 E4
Stebbing 42 B2
Stebbing Green 42 B2
Stedham 16 B2
Steele Road 115 E8
Steen's Bridge 49 D7
Steep 15 B8
Steeple Dorset 13 F7
Essex 43 D5
Steeple Ashton 24 D4
Steeple Aston 38 B4
Steeple Barton 38 B4
Steeple Bumpstead 55 E7
Steeple Claydon 39 B6
Steeple Gidding 65 F8
Steeple Langford 24 F5
Steeple Morden 54 E3
Steep Marsh 15 B8
Steeton 94 E3
Stein 148 C7
Steinmanhill 153 D7
Stelling Minnis 30 E5
Stemster 158 D3
Stemster House 158 D3
Stenalees 4 D5
Stenhousemuir 127 F7
Stenigot 91 F6
Stenness 160 F4
Stenscholl 149 B9
Stenso 159 F4
Stenson 63 B7
Stenton E Loth 122 B2
Fife 128 E4
Stenwith 77 F8
Stepaside 32 D2
Stepping Hill 87 F7
Steppingley 53 F8
Stepps 119 C6
Sterndale Moor 75 C8
Sternfield 57 C7
Sterridge 20 E4
Stert 24 D5
Stetchworth 55 D7
Stevenage 41 B5
Stevenston 118 E2
Steventon Hants 26 E3
Oxon 38 E4
Stevington 53 D7
Stewartby 53 E8
Stewarton Argyll 143 G7
E Ayrs 118 E4
Stewkley 40 B1
Stewton 91 F7
Steyne Cross 15 F7
Steyning 17 C5
Steynton 44 E4
Stibb 8 C4
Stibbard 81 E5
Stibb Cross 9 C6
Stibb Green 25 C7
Stibbington 65 E7
Stichill 122 F3
Sticker 4 D4
Stickford 79 D6
Sticklepath 9 E8
Stickney 79 D6
Stiffkey 81 C5
Stifford's Bridge 50 E2
Stillingfleet 95 E8
Stillington N Yorks 95 C8
Stockton 102 B1
Stilton 65 F8
Stinchcombe 36 E4
Stinsford 12 E5
Stirchley 61 D7
Stirkoke House 158 E5
Stirling Aberds 153 D11
Stirling 127 E6
Stisted 42 B3
Stithians 3 C6
Stittenham 151 D9
Stivichall 51 B8
Stixwould 78 C4
Stoak 73 B8
Stobieside 119 F6
Stobo 120 F4
Stoborough 13 F7
Stoborough Green 13 F7
Stobshiel 121 C7
Stobswood 117 E8
Stock 42 E2
Stockbridge 25 F8
Stockbury 30 C2
Stockcross 26 C2
Stockdalewath 108 E3
Stockerston 64 E5
Stock Green 50 D4
Stockheath 15 D8
Stockiemuir 126 F4
Stockingford 63 E7
Stocking Pelham 41 B7
Stockland 11 D7
Stockland Bristol 22 E4
Stockleigh English 10 D3
Stockleigh Pomeroy 10 D3
Stockley 24 C5
Stocklinch 11 C8
Stockport 87 E6
Stocksbridge 88 E3
Stocksfield 110 C3
Stockton Hereford 49 C7
Norf 69 E6
Shrops 60 D2
Shrops 61 E7
Warks 52 C2
Wilts 24 F4
Stockton Heath 86 F4
Stockton-on-Tees 102 C2
Stockton on Teme 50 C2
Stockton on the Forest 96 D2
Stock Wood 50 D5
Stodmarsh 31 C6
Stody 81 D6
Stoer 156 G3
Stoford Som 12 C3
Wilts 25 F5
Stogumber 22 F2
Stogursey 22 E4
Stoke Devon 8 B4
Hants 15 D8
Hants 26 D2
Medway 30 B2
Suff 57 E5
Stoke Abbott 12 D2
Stoke Albany 64 F5
Stoke Ash 56 B5
Stoke Bardolph 77 E6
Stoke Bliss 49 C8
Stoke Bruerne 52 E5
Stoke by Clare 55 E8
Stoke-by-Nayland 56 F3
Stoke Canon 10 E4
Stoke Charity 26 F2
Stoke Climsland 5 B8
Stoke D'Abernon 28 D2
Stoke Doyle 65 F7
Stoke Dry 65 E5
Stoke Farthing 13 B8
Stoke Ferry 67 E7
Stoke Fleming 7 E6
Stokeford 13 F6
Stoke Gabriel 7 D6
Stoke Gifford 23 B8
Stoke Golding 63 E7
Stoke Goldington 53 E6
Stoke Green 40 F2
Stokeham 77 B7
Stoke Hammond 40 B1
Stoke Heath 61 B6
Stoke Holy Cross 68 D5
Stokeinteignhead 7 B7
Stoke Lacy 49 E8
Stoke Lyne 39 B5
Stoke Mandeville 39 C8
Stokenchurch 39 E7
Stoke Newington 41 F6
Stokenham 7 E6
Stoke on Tern 61 B6
Stoke-on-Trent 75 E5
Stoke Orchard 37 B6
Stoke Poges 40 F2
Stoke Prior Hereford 49 D7
Worcs 50 C4
Stoke Rivers 20 F5
Stoke Rochford 65 B6
Stoke Row 39 F6
Stoke St Gregory 11 B8
Stoke St Mary 11 B7
Stoke St Michael 23 E8
Stoke St Milborough 61 F5
Stokesay 60 F4
Stokesby 69 C7
Stokesley 102 D3
Stoke sub Hamdon 12 C2
Stoke Talmage 39 E6
Stoke Trister 12 B5
Stoke Wake 13 D5
Stolford 22 E4
Stondon Massey 42 D1
Stone Bucks 39 C7
Glos 36 E3
Kent 19 C6
Kent 29 B6
Staffs 75 F6
S Yorks 89 F6
Worcs 50 B3
Stone Allerton 23 D6
Ston Easton 23 D8
Stone Bridge Corner 66 D2
Stonebroom 76 D4
Stone Chair 88 B2
Stone Cross E Sus 18 E3
Kent 31 D7
Stone-edge Batch 23 B6
Stoneferry 97 F7
Stonefield 119 D6
Stonegate E Sus 18 C3
N Yorks 103 D5
Stonegrave 96 B2
Stonehaugh 109 B7
Stonehaven 141 F7
Stonehouse Glos 37 D5
Northumb 109 D6
S Lanark 119 E7
Stone House 100 F2
Stoneleigh 51 B8
Stonely 54 C2
Stoner Hill 15 B8
Stonesby 64 B5
Stonesfield 38 C3
Stone's Green 43 B7
Stone Street Kent 29 D6
Suff 56 F3
Suff 69 F6
Stonethwaite 98 C4
Stoneybreck 160 N8
Stoneyburn 120 C2
Stoney Cross 14 C3
Stoneygate Aberds 153 E10
Leicester 64 D3
Stoneyhills 43 E5
Stoneykirk 104 D4
Stoney Middleton 76 B2
Stoney Stanton 63 E8
Stoney Stoke 24 F2
Stoney Stratton 23 F8
Stoney Stretton 60 D3
Stoneywood Aberdeen 141 C7
Falk 127 F6
Stonganess 160 C7
Stonham Aspal 56 D5
Stonnall 62 D4
Stonor 39 F7
Stonton Wyville 64 E4
Stony Cross 50 E2
Stonyfield 151 D9
Stony Stratford 53 E5
Stoodleigh 10 C4
Stopes 88 F3
Stopham 16 C4
Stopsley 40 B4
Stores Corner 57 E7
Storeton 85 F4
Stornoway 155 D9
Storridge 50 E2
Storrington 16 C4
Storrs 99 E5
Storth 99 F6
Storwood 96 E3
Stotfield 152 A2
Stotfold 54 F3
Stottesdon 61 F6
Stoughton Leics 64 D3
Sur 27 D7
W Sus 16 C2
Stoul 147 B10
Stoulton 50 E4
Stourbridge 62 F3
Stourpaine 13 D6
Stourport on Severn 50 B3
Stour Provost 13 B5
Stour Row 13 B6
Stourton Staffs 62 F2
Warks 51 F7
Wilts 24 F2
Stourton Caundle 12 C5
Stove Orkney 159 E7
Shetland 160 L6
Stoven 69 F7
Stow Borders 121 E7
Lincs 78 F3
Lincs 90 F2
Stow Bardolph 67 D6
Stow Bedon 68 E2
Stowbridge 67 D6
Stow cum Quy 55 C6
Stowe 48 B5
Stowe-by-Chartley 62 B4
Stowe Green 36 D2
Stowell 12 B4
Stowford 9 F6
Stowlangtoft 56 C3
Stow Longa 54 B2
Stow Maries 42 E4
Stowmarket 56 D4
Stow-on-the-Wold 38 B1
Stowting 30 E5
Stowupland 56 D4
Straad 145 G9
Strachan 141 E5
Stradbroke 57 B6
Stradishall 55 D8
Stradsett 67 D6
Stragglethorpe 78 D2
Straid 112 E1
Straith 113 F8
Straiton Edin 121 C5
S Ayrs 112 D3
Straloch Aberds 141 B7
Perth 133 C7
Stramshall 75 F7
Strang 84 E3
Stranraer 104 C4
Stratfield Mortimer 26 C4
Stratfield Saye 26 C4
Stratfield Turgis 26 D4
Stratford 41 F6
Stratford St Andrew 57 C7
Stratford St Mary 56 F4
Stratford Sub Castle 25 F6
Stratford Tony 13 B8
Stratford-upon-Avon 51 D6
Strath Highld 149 A12
Highld 158 E4
Strathan Highld 136 E2
Highld 156 G3
Highld 157 C8
Strathaven 119 E7
Strathblane 119 B5
Strathcanaird 156 J4
Strathcarron 150 G2
Strathcoil 124 B2
Strathdon 140 C2
Strathellie 153 B10
Strathkinness 129 C6
Strathmashie House 137 E8
Strathmiglo 128 C4
Strathmore Lodge 158 F3
Strathpeffer 150 F7
Strathrannoch 150 D6
Strathtay 133 D6
Strathvaich Lodge 150 D6
Strathwhillan 143 E11
Strathy 157 C11
Strathyre 126 C4
Stratton Corn 8 D4
Dorset 12 E4
Glos 37 D7
Stratton Audley 39 B6
Stratton on the Fosse 23 D8
Stratton St Margaret 38 F1
Stratton St Michael 68 E5
Stratton Strawless 81 E8
Stravithie 129 C7
Streat 17 C7
Streatham 28 B4
Streatley C Beds 40 B3
W Berks 39 F5
Street Lancs 92 D5
N Yorks 103 D5
Som 23 F6
Street Dinas 73 F7
Street End Kent 30 D5
W Sus 16 E2
Street Gate 110 D5
Streethay 62 C5
Streetlam 101 E8
Streetly 62 E4
Street Lydan 73 F8
Streetly End 55 E7
Strefford 60 F4
Strelley 76 E5
Strensall 96 C2
Stretcholt 22 E4
Strete 7 E6
Stretford 87 E6
Strethall 55 F5
Stretham 55 B6
Strettington 16 D2
Stretton Ches W 73 D8
Derbys 76 C3
Rutland 65 C6
Staffs 62 C2
Staffs 63 B6
Warr 86 F4
Stretton Grandison 49 E8
Stretton-on-Dunsmore 52 B2
Stretton-on-Fosse 51 F7
Stretton Sugwas 49 E6
Stretton under Fosse 63 F8
Stretton Westwood 61 E5
Strichen 153 C9
Strines 87 F7
Stringston 22 E3
Strixton 53 C7
Stroat 36 E2
Stromeferry 149 E13
Stromemore 149 E13
Stromness 159 H3
Stronaba 136 F5
Stronachlachar 126 C3
Stronchreggan 130 B4
Stronchrubie 156 H5
Strone Argyll 145 E10
Highld 136 F4
Highld 137 B8
Invclyd 118 B2
Stronmilchan 125 C7
Strontian 130 C2
Strood 29 C8
Strood Green Sur 28 E3
W Sus 16 B4
W Sus 28 F2
Stroud Glos 37 D5
Hants 15 B8
Stroud Green 42 E4
Stroxton 78 F2
Struan Highld 149 E8
Perth 133 C5
Strubby 91 F8
Strumpshaw 69 D6
Strutherhill 119 E7
Struy 150 H6
Stryt-issa 73 E6
Stuartfield 153 D9
Stubbington 15 D6
Stubbins 87 C5
Stubbs Cross 19 B6
Stubbs Green 69 E6
Stubb's Green 69 E5
Stubhampton 13 C7
Stub Place 98 E2
Stubton 77 E8
Stuckgowan 126 D2
Stuckton 14 C2
Stud Green 27 B6
Studham 40 C3
Studland 13 F8
Studley Warks 51 C5
Wilts 24 B4
Studley Roger 95 B5
Stump Cross 55 E6
Stuntney 55 B6
Sturbridge 74 F5
Sturmer 55 E7
Sturminster Marshall 13 D7
Sturminster Newton 13 C5
Sturry 31 C5
Sturton 90 D3
Sturton by Stow 90 F2
Sturton le Steeple 89 F8
Stuston 56 B5
Stutton N Yorks 95 E7
Suff 57 F5
Styal 87 F6
Styrrup 89 E7
Suainebost 155 A10
Suardail 155 D9
Succoth Aberds 152 E4
Argyll 125 E8
Suckley 50 D2
Suckquoy 159 K5
Sudborough 65 F6
Sudbourne 57 D8
Sudbrook Lincs 78 E2
Mon 36 F2
Sudbrooke 78 B3
Sudbury Derbys 75 F8
London 40 F4
Suff 56 E2
Suddie 151 F9
Sudgrove 37 D6
Suffield Norf 81 D8
N Yorks 103 E7
Sugnall 74 F4
Suladale 149 C8
Sulaisiadar 155 D10
Sulby 84 C3
Sulgrave 52 E3
Sulham 26 B4
Sulhamstead 26 C4
Sulland 159 D6
Sullington 16 C4
Sullom 160 F5
Sullom Voe Oil Terminal 160 F5
Sully 22 C3
Sumburgh 160 N6
Summer Bridge 94 C5
Summercourt 4 D3
Summerfield 80 D3
Summergangs 97 F7
Summer-house 101 C7
Summerleaze 35 F8
Summersdale 16 D2
Summerseat 87 C5
Summertown 39 D5
Summit 87 D7
Sunbury-on-Thames 28 C2
Sundaywell 113 F8
Sunderland Argyll 142 B3
Cumb 107 F8
T&W 111 D6
Sunderland Bridge 111 F5
Sundhope 115 B6
Sundon Park 40 B3
Sundridge 29 D5
Sunipol 146 F6
Sunk Island 91 C6
Sunningdale 27 C7
Sunninghill 27 C7
Sunningwell 38 D4
Sunniside Durham 110 F4
T&W 110 D5
Sunnyhurst 86 B4
Sunnylaw 127 E6
Sunnyside 28 F4
Sunton 25 D7
Surbiton 28 C2
Surby 84 E2
Surfleet 66 B2
Surfleet Seas End 66 B2
Surlingham 69 D6
Sustead 81 D7
Susworth 90 D2
Sutcombe 8 C5
Suton 68 E3
Sutors of Cromarty 151 E11
Sutterby 79 B6
Sutterton 79 F5
Sutton Cambs 54 B5
C Beds 54 E3
Kent 31 E7
London 28 C3
Mers 86 E3
Norf 69 B6
Notts 77 F7
Notts 89 F7
N Yorks 89 B5
Oxon 38 D4
Pboro 65 E7
Shrops 61 F7
Shrops 74 F3
Som 23 F8
Staffs 61 B7
Suff 57 E7
Sur 27 E8
S Yorks 89 C6
W Sus 16 C3
Sutton at Hone 29 B6
Sutton Bassett 64 E4
Sutton Benger 24 B4
Sutton Bonington 64 B2
Sutton Bridge 66 B4
Sutton Cheney 63 D8
Sutton Coldfield 62 E5
Sutton Courtenay 39 E5
Sutton Crosses 66 B4
Sutton Grange 95 B5
Sutton Green 27 D8
Sutton Howgrave 95 B6
Sutton in Ashfield 76 D4
Sutton-in-Craven 94 E3
Sutton Ings 97 F7
Sutton in the Elms 64 E2
Sutton Lane Ends 75 B6
Sutton Leach 86 E3
Sutton Maddock 61 D7
Sutton Mallet 23 F5
Sutton Mandeville 13 B7
Sutton Manor 86 E3
Sutton Montis 12 B4
Sutton on Hull 97 F7
Sutton on Sea 91 F9
Sutton-on-the-Forest 95 C8
Sutton on the Hill 76 F2
Sutton on Trent 77 C7
Sutton St Edmund 66 C3
Sutton St James 66 C3
Sutton St Nicholas 49 E7
Sutton Scarsdale 76 C4
Sutton Scotney 26 F2
Sutton under Brailes 51 F8
Sutton-under-Whitestonecliffe 102 F2
Sutton upon Derwent 96 E3
Sutton Valence 30 E2
Sutton Veny 24 E3
Sutton Waldron 13 C6
Sutton Weaver 74 B2
Sutton Wick 23 D7
Swaby 79 B6
Swadlincote 63 C7
Swaffham 67 D8
Swaffham Bulbeck 55 C6
Swaffham Prior 55 C6
Swafield 81 D8
Swainby 102 D2
Swainshill 49 E6
Swainsthorpe 68 D5
Swainswick 24 C2
Swalcliffe 51 F8
Swalecliffe 30 C5
Swallow 91 D5
Swallowcliffe 13 B7
Swallowfield 26 C5
Swallownest 89 F5
Swallows Cross 42 E2
Swanage 13 G8
Swanbister 159 H4
Swanbourne 39 B8
Swan Green Ches W 74 B4
Suff 57 B6
Swanland 90 B3
Swanley 29 C6
Swanley Village 29 C6
Swanmore 15 C6
Swannington Leics 63 C8
Norf 68 C4
Swanscombe 29 B7
Swansea = Abertawe 33 E7
Swanton Abbott 81 E8
Swanton Morley 68 C3
Swanton Novers 81 D6
Swanton Street 30 D2
Swanwick Derbys 76 D4
Hants 15 D6
Swarby 78 E3
Swardeston 68 D5
Swarister 160 E7
Swarkestone 63 B7
Swarland 117 D7
Swarland Estate 117 D7
Swarthmoor 92 B2
Swathwick 76 C3
Swaton 78 F4
Swavesey 54 C4
Sway 14 E3
Swayfield 65 B6
Swaythling 14 C5
Sweet Green 49 C8
Sweetham 10 E3
Sweethouse 5 C5
Sweffling 57 C7
Swepstone 63 C7
Swerford 51 F8
Swettenham 74 C5
Swetton 94 B4
Swffryd 35 E6
Swiftsden 18 C4
Swilland 57 D5
Swillington 95 F6
Swimbridge 9 B8
Swimbridge Newland 20 F5
Swinbrook 38 C2
Swinderby 77 C8
Swindon Glos 37 B6
Staffs 62 E2
Swindon 38 F1
Swine 97 F7
Swinefleet 89 B8
Swineshead Bedford 53 C8
Lincs 78 E5
Swineshead Bridge 78 E5
Swiney 158 G4
Swinford Leics 52 B3
Oxon 38 D4
Swingate 76 E5
Swingfield Minnis 31 E6
Swingfield Street 31 E6
Swinhoe 117 B8
Swinhope 91 E6
Swining 160 G6
Swinithwaite 101 F5
Swinnow Moor 94 F5
Swinscoe 75 E8
Swinside Hall 116 C3
Swinstead 65 B7
Swinton Borders 122 E4
Gtr Man 87 D5
N Yorks 94 B5
N Yorks 96 B3
S Yorks 88 E5
Swintonmill 122 E4
Swithland 64 C2
Swordale 151 E8
Swordland 147 B10
Swordly 157 C10
Sworton Heath 86 F4
Swyddffynnon 47 C5
Swynnerton 75 F5
Swyre 12 F3
Sychtyn 59 D6
Syde 37 C6
Sydenham London 28 B4
Oxon 39 D7
Sydenham Damerel 6 B2
Syderstone 80 D4
Sydling St Nicholas 12 E4
Sydmonton 26 D2
Syerston 77 E7
Syke 87 C6
Sykehouse 89 C7
Sykes 93 D6
Syleham 57 B6
Sylen 33 D6
Symbister 160 G7
Symington S Ayrs 118 F3
S Lanark 120 F2
Symondsbury 12 E2
Symonds Yat 36 C2
Synod Inn 46 D3
Syre 157 E9
Syreford 37 B7
Syresham 52 E4
Syston Leics 64 C3
Lincs 78 E2
Sytchampton 50 C3
Sywell 53 C6

T

Taagan 150 E3
Tàbost 155 A10
Tabost 155 F8
Tackley 38 B4
Tacleit 154 D6
Tacolneston 68 E4
Tadcaster 95 E7
Taddington 75 B8
Taddiport 9 C6
Tadley 26 C4
Tadlow 54 E3
Tadmarton 51 F8
Tadworth 28 D3
Tafarnau-bach 35 C5
Tafarn-y-gelyn 73 C5
Taff's Well 35 F5
Tafolwern 59 D5
Tai 83 E7
Taibach 34 F1
Tai-bach 59 B8
Taigh a Ghearraidh 148 A2
Tai-mawr 72 E3
Tain Highld 151 C10
Highld 158 D4
Tainant 73 E6
Tainlon 82 F4
Tairbeart = Tarbert 154 G6
Tai'r-Bull 34 B3
Tairgwaith 33 C8
Tai-Ucha 72 D4
Takeley 42 B1
Takeley Street 41 B8
Talachddu 48 F2
Talacre 85 F2
Talardd 59 B5
Talaton 11 E5
Talbenny 44 D3
Talbot Green 34 F4
Talbot Village 13 E8
Tale 11 D5
Talerddig 59 D6
Talgarreg 46 D3
Talgarth 48 F3
Talisker 149 E8
Talke 74 D5
Talkin 109 D5
Talladale 150 D2
Talla Linnfoots 114 B4
Tallarn Green 73 E8
Tallentire 107 F8
Talley 46 F5
Tallington 65 D7
Talmine 157 C8
Talog 32 B4
Talsarn 34 B1
Tal-sarn 46 D4
Talsarnau 71 D7
Talskiddy 4 C4
Talwrn Anglesey 82 D4
Wrex 73 E6
Tal-y-bont Ceredig 58 F3
Conwy 83 E7
Gwyn 71 E6
Gwyn 83 D6
Talybont-on-Usk 35 B5
Tal-y-cafn 83 D7
Talygarn 34 F4
Talyllyn 35 B5
Tal-y-llyn 58 D4
Talysarn 82 F4
Talywain 35 D6
Tal-y-wern 58 D5
Tame Bridge 102 D3
Tamerton Foliot 6 C2
Tamworth 63 D6
Tandem 88 C2
Tanden 19 B6
Tandridge 28 D4
Tanerdy 33 B5
Tanfield 110 D4
Tanfield Lea 110 D4
Tangasdal 148 J1
Tangiers 44 D4
Tangley 25 D8
Tanglwst 46 F2
Tangmere 16 D3
Tangwick 160 F4
Tan Hinon 59 F5
Tankersley 88 D4
Tankerton 30 C5
Tan-lan Conwy 83 E7
Gwyn 71 C7
Tannach 158 F5
Tannachie 141 F6
Tannadice 134 D4
Tannington 57 C6
Tansley 76 D3
Tansley Knoll 76 C3
Tansor 65 E7
Tantobie 110 D4
Tanton 102 C3
Tanworth-in-Arden 51 B6
Tan-y-bwlch 71 C7
Tan-y-fron 72 C3
Tan-y-graig Anglesey 82 D5
Gwyn 70 D4
Tanygrisiau 71 C7
Tan-y-groes 45 E4
Tan-y-pistyll 59 B7
Tan-yr-allt 82 F4
Tanyrhydiau 47 C6
Taobh a Chaolais 148 G2
Taobh a'Ghlinne 155 F8
Taobh a Thuath Loch Aineort 148 F2
Taobh a Tuath Loch Baghasdail 148 F2
Taobh Tuath 154 J4
Taplow 40 F2
Tapton 76 B3
Tarbat House 151 D10
Tarbert Argyll 143 C7
Argyll 144 E5
Argyll 145 G7
Tarbert = Tairbeart 154 G6
Tarbet Argyll 126 D2
Highld 147 B10
Highld 156 E4
Tarbock Green 86 F2
Tarbolton 112 B4
Tarbrax 120 D3
Tardebigge 50 C5
Tarfside 134 B4
Tarland 140 D3
Tarleton 86 B2
Tarlogie 151 C10
Tarlscough 86 C2
Tarlton 37 E6
Tarnbrook 93 D5
Tarporley 74 C2
Tarr 22 F3
Tarrant Crawford 13 D7
Tarrant Gunville 13 C7
Tarrant Hinton 13 C7
Tarrant Keyneston 13 D7
Tarrant Launceston 13 D7
Tarrant Monkton 13 D7
Tarrant Rawston 13 D7
Tarrant Rushton 13 D7
Tarrel 151 C11
Tarring Neville 17 D8
Tarrington 49 E8
Tarsappie 128 B3
Tarskavaig 149 H10
Tarves 153 E8
Tarvie Highld 150 F7
Perth 133 C7
Tarvin 73 C8
Tasburgh 68 E5
Tasley 61 E6
Taston 38 B3
Tatenhill 63 B6
Tathall End 53 E6
Tatham 93 C6
Tathwell 91 F7
Tatling End 40 F3
Tatsfield 28 D5
Tattenhall 73 D8
Tattenhoe 53 F6
Tatterford 80 E4
Tattersett 80 D4
Tattershall 78 D5
Tattershall Bridge 78 D4
Tattershall Thorpe 78 D5
Tattingstone 56 F5
Tatworth 11 D8
Taunton 11 B7
Taverham 68 C4
Tavernspite 32 C2
Tavistock 6 B2
Taw Green 9 E8
Tawstock 9 B7
Taxal 75 B7
Tay Bridge 129 B6
Tayinloan 143 D7
Taymouth Castle 132 E4
Taynish 144 E6
Taynton Glos 36 B4
Oxon 38 C2
Taynuilt 125 B6
Tayport 129 B6
Tayvallich 144 E6
Tealby 91 E5
Tealing 134 F4
Teangue 149 H11
Teanna Mhachair 148 B2
Tebay 99 D8
Tebworth 40 B2
Tedburn St Mary 10 E3
Teddington Glos 50 F4
London 28 B2
Tedstone Delamere 49 D8
Tedstone Wafre 49 D8
Teeton 52 B4
Teffont Evias 24 F4
Teffont Magna 24 F4
Tegryn 45 F4
Teigh 65 C5
Teigncombe 9 F8
Teigngrace 7 B6
Teignmouth 7 B7
Telford 61 D6
Telham 18 D4
Tellisford 24 D3
Telscombe 17 D8
Telscombe Cliffs 17 D7
Templand 114 F3
Temple Corn 5 B6
Glasgow 118 C5
Midloth 121 D6
Temple Balsall 51 B7
Temple Bar Carms 33 C6
Ceredig 46 D4
Temple Cloud 23 D8
Temple Combe 12 B5
Temple Ewell 31 E6
Temple Grafton 51 D6
Temple Guiting 37 B7
Templehall 128 E4
Temple Herdewyke 51 D8
Temple Hirst 89 B7
Temple Normanton 76 C4
Temple Sowerby 99 B8
Templeton Devon 10 C3
Pembs 32 C2
Templeton Bridge 10 C3
Templetown 110 D4
Tempsford 54 D2
Tenbury Wells 49 C7
Tenby = Dinbych-y-Pysgod 32 D2
Tendring 43 B7
Tendring Green 43 B7
Ten Mile Bank 67 E6
Tenston 159 G3
Tenterden 19 B5
Terling 42 C3
Ternhill 74 F3
Terregles Banks 107 B6
Terrick 39 D8
Terrington 96 B2
Terrington St Clement 66 C5
Terrington St John 66 C5
Teston 29 D8
Testwood 14 C4
Tetbury 37 E5
Tetbury Upton 37 E5
Tetchill 73 F7
Tetcott 8 E5
Tetford 79 B6
Tetney 91 D7
Tetney Lock 91 D7
Tetsworth 39 D6
Tettenhall 62 E2
Teuchan 153 E10
Teversal 76 C4
Teversham 55 D5
Teviothead 115 D7
Tewel 141 F7
Tewin 41 C5
Tewkesbury 50 F3
Teynham 30 C3
Thackthwaite 98 B3
Thainston 135 B6
Thakeham 16 C5
Thame 39 D7
Thames Ditton 28 C2
Thames Haven 42 F3
Thamesmead 41 F7
Thanington 30 D5
Thankerton 120 F2
Tharston 68 E4
Thatcham 26 C3
Thatto Heath 86 E3
Thaxted 55 F7
The Aird 149 C9
Theakston 101 F8
Thealby 90 C2
Theale Som 23 E6
W Berks 26 B4
The Arms 67 E8
Thearne 97 F6
The Bage 48 E4
The Balloch 127 C7
The Barony 159 F3
Theberton 57 C8
The Bog 60 E3
The Bourne 27 E6
The Braes 149 E10
The Broad 49 C6
The Butts 24 E2
The Camp Glos 37 D6
Herts 40 D4
The Chequer 73 E8
The City 39 E7
The Common 25 F7
The Craigs 150 B7
The Cronk 84 C3
Theddingworth 64 F3
Theddlethorpe All Saints 91 F8
Theddlethorpe St Helen 91 F8
The Dell 69 E7
The Den 118 D3
The Eals 116 F3
The Eaves 36 D3
The Flatt 109 B5
The Four Alls 74 F3
The Garths 160 B8
The Green Cumb 98 F3
Wilts 24 F3
The Grove 107 B6
The Hall 160 D8
The Haven 27 F8
The Heath Norf 81 E7
Suff 56 F5
The Hill 98 F3
The Howe Cumb 99 F6
IoM 84 F1
The Hundred 49 C7
Thelbridge Barton 10 C2
The Lee 40 D2
The Lhen 84 B3
Thelnetham 56 B4
Thelveton 68 F4
Thelwall 86 F4
The Marsh Powys 60 E3
Wilts 37 F7
Themelthorpe 81 E6
The Middles 110 D5
The Moor 18 C4
The Mumbles = Y Mwmbwls 33 F7
The Murray 119 D6
The Neuk 141 E6
Thenford 52 E3
The Oval 24 C2
The Pole of Itlaw 153 C6
The Quarry 36 E4
Therfield 54 F4
The Rhos 32 C1
The Rock 61 D6
The Ryde 41 D5
The Sands 27 E6
The Stocks 19 C6
Thetford Lincs 65 C8
Norf 67 F8
The Throat 27 C6
The Vauld 49 E7
The Wyke 61 D7
Theydon Bois 41 E7
Thickwood 24 B3
Thimbleby Lincs 78 C5
N Yorks 102 E2
Thingwall 85 F3
Thirdpart 118 E1
Thirlby 102 F2
Thirlestane 121 E8
Thirn 101 F7
Thirsk 102 F2
Thirtleby 97 F7
Thistleton Lancs 92 F4
Rutland 65 C6
Thistley Green 55 B7
Thixendale 96 C4

Thockrington 110 B2
Tholomas Drove 66 D3
Tholthorpe 95 C7
Thomas Chapel 32 D2
Thomas Close 108 E4
Thomastown 152 E5
Thompson 68 E2
Thomshill 152 C2
Thong 29 B7
Thongsbridge 88 D2
Thoralby 101 F5
Thoresway 91 E5
Thorganby Lincs 91 E6
N Yorks 96 E2
Thorgill 103 E5
Thorington 57 B8
Thorington Street 56 F4
Thorlby 94 D2
Thorley 41 C7
Thorley Street
Herts 41 C7
IoW 14 F4
Thormanby 95 B7
Thornaby-on-Tees 102 C2
Thornage 81 D6
Thornborough
Bucks 52 F5
N Yorks 95 B5
Thornbury Devon 9 D6
Hereford 49 D8
S Glos 36 E3
W Yorks 94 F4
Thornby 52 B4
Thorncliffe 75 D7
Thorncombe
Dorset 11 D8
Dorset 13 D6
Thorncombe Street 27 E8
Thorncote Green 54 E2
Thorncross 14 F5
Thorndon 56 C5
Thorndon Cross 9 E7
Thorne 89 C7
Thorner 95 E6
Thorne St Margaret 11 B5
Thorney Notts 77 B8
Pboro 66 D2
Thorney Crofts 91 B6
Thorney Green 56 C4
Thorney Hill 14 E2
Thorney Toll 66 D3
Thornfalcon 11 B7
Thornford 12 C4
Thorngumbald 91 B6
Thornham 80 C3
Thornham Magna 56 B5
Thornham Parva 56 B5
Thornhaugh 65 D7
Thornhill Cardiff 35 F5
Cumb 98 D2
Derbys 88 F2
Dumfries 113 E8
Soton 15 C5
Stirling 127 E5
W Yorks 88 C3
Thornhill Edge 88 C3
Thornhill Lees 88 C3
Thornholme 97 C7
Thornley Durham 110 F4
Durham 111 F6
Thornliebank 118 D5
Thorns 55 D8
Thornsett 87 F8
Thorns Green 87 F5
Thornthwaite
Cumb 98 B4
N Yorks 94 D4
Thornton Angus 134 E3
Bucks 53 F5
E Yorks 96 E3
Fife 128 E4
Lancs 92 E3
Leics 63 D8
Lincs 78 C5
Mbro 102 C2
Mers 85 D4
Northumb 123 E5
Pembs 44 E4
W Yorks 94 F4
Thornton Curtis 90 C4
Thorntonhall 119 D5
Thornton Heath 28 C4
Thornton Hough 85 F4
Thornton in Craven 94 E2
Thornton-le-Beans 102 E1
Thornton-le-Clay 96 C2
Thornton-le-Dale 103 F6
Thornton le Moor 90 E4
Thornton-le-Moor 102 F1
Thornton-le-Moors 73 B8
Thornton-le-Street 102 F2
Thorntonloch 122 B3
Thorntonpark 122 E5
Thornton Rust 100 F4
Thornton Steward 101 F6
Thornton Watlass 101 F7
Thornwood Common 41 D7
Thornydykes 122 E2
Thoroton 77 E7
Thorp Arch 95 E7
Thorpe Derbys 75 D8
E Yorks 97 E5
Lincs 91 F8
Norf 69 E7
Notts 77 E7
N Yorks 94 C3
Sur 27 C8
Thorpe Abbotts 57 B5
Thorpe Acre 64 B2
Thorpe Arnold 64 B4
Thorpe Audlin 89 C5
Thorpe Bassett 96 B4
Thorpe Bay 43 F5
Thorpe by Water 65 E5
Thorpe Common 57 F6
Thorpe Constantine 63 D6
Thorpe Culvert 79 C7
Thorpe End 69 C5
Thorpe Fendykes 79 C7
Thorpe Green
Essex 43 B7
Suff 56 D3
Thorpe Hesley 88 E4
Thorpe in Balne 89 C6
Thorpe in the Fallows 90 F3
Thorpe Langton 64 E4
Thorpe Larches 102 B1
Thorpe-le-Soken 43 B7
Thorpe le Street 96 E4
Thorpe Malsor 53 B6
Thorpe Mandeville 52 E3
Thorpe Market 81 D8
Thorpe Marriot 68 C4
Thorpe Morieux 56 D3
Thorpeness 57 D8
Thorpe on the Hill 78 C2
Thorpe St Andrew 69 D5
Thorpe St Peter 79 C7
Thorpe Salvin 89 F6
Thorpe Satchville 64 C4
Thorpe Thewles 102 B2
Thorpe Tilney 78 D4
Thorpe Underwood 95 D7
Thorpe Waterville 65 F7
Thorpe Willoughby 95 F8
Thorrington 43 C6
Thorverton 10 D4
Thrandeston 56 B5
Thrapston 53 B7
Thrashbush 119 C7
Threapland Cumb 107 F8
N Yorks 94 C2
Threapwood
Ches W 73 E8
Staffs 75 E7
Three Ashes 36 B2
Three Bridges 28 F3
Three Burrows 3 B6
Three Chimneys 18 B5
Three Cocks 48 F3
Three Crosses 33 E6
Three Cups Corner 18 C3
Threehammer Common 69 C6
Three Holes 66 D5
Threekingham 78 F3
Three Leg Cross 18 B3
Three Legged Cross 13 D8
Threemile Cross 26 C5
Threemilestone 3 B6
Threemiletown 120 B3
Three Oaks 18 D5
Threlkeld 99 B5
Threshfield 94 C2
Thrigby 69 C7
Thringarth 100 B4
Thringstone 63 C8
Thrintoft 101 E8
Thriplow 54 E5
Throckenholt 66 D3
Throcking 54 F4
Throckley 110 C4
Throckmorton 50 E4
Throphill 117 F7
Thropton 117 D6
Throsk 127 E7
Throwleigh 9 E8
Throwley 30 D3
Thrumpton 76 F5
Thrumster 158 F5
Thrunton 117 C6
Thrupp Glos 37 D5
Oxon 38 C4
Thrushelton 9 F6
Thrussington 64 C3
Thruxton Hants 25 E7
Hereford 49 F6
Thrybergh 89 E5
Thulston 76 F4
Thundergay 143 D9
Thundersley 42 F3
Thundridge 41 C6
Thurcaston 64 C2
Thurcroft 89 F5
Thurgarton Norf 81 D7
Notts 77 E6
Thurgoland 88 D3
Thurlaston Leics 64 E2
Warks 52 B2
Thurlbear 11 B7
Thurlby Lincs 65 C8
Lincs 78 C2
Thurleigh 53 D8
Thurlestone 6 E4
Thurloxton 22 F4
Thurlstone 88 D3
Thurlton 69 E7
Thurlwood 74 D5
Thurmaston 64 D3
Thurnby 64 D3
Thurne 69 C7
Thurnham Kent 30 D2
Lancs 92 D4
Thurning N Nhants 65 F7
Norf 81 E6
Thurnscoe 89 D5
Thurnscoe East 89 D5
Thursby 108 D3
Thursford 81 D5
Thursley 27 F7
Thurso 158 D3
Thurso East 158 D3
Thurstaston 85 F3
Thurston 56 C3
Thurstonfield 108 D3
Thurstonland 88 C2
Thurton 69 D6
Thurvaston 76 F2
Thuxton 68 D3
Thwaite N Yorks 100 E3
Suff 56 C5
Thwaites 94 E3
Thwaite St Mary 69 E6
Thwaites Brow 94 E3
Thwing 97 B6
Tibbermore 128 B2
Tibberton Glos 36 B4
Telford 61 B6
Worcs 50 D4
Tibenham 68 F4
Tibshelf 76 C4
Tibthorpe 97 D5
Ticehurst 18 B3
Tichborne 26 F3
Tickencote 65 D6
Tickenham 23 B6
Tickhill 89 E6
Ticklerton 60 E4
Ticknall 63 B7
Tickton 97 E6
Tidcombe 25 D7
Tiddington Oxon 39 D6
Warks 51 D7
Tidebrook 18 C3
Tideford 5 D8
Tideford Cross 5 C8
Tidenham 36 E2
Tideswell 75 B8
Tidmarsh 26 B4
Tidmington 51 F7
Tidpit 13 C8
Tidworth 25 E7
Tiers Cross 44 D4
Tiffield 52 D4
Tifty 153 D7
Tigerton 135 C5
Tigh-na-Blair 127 C6
Tighnabruaich 145 F8
Tighnafiline 155 J13
Tigley 7 C5
Tilbrook 53 C8
Tilbury 29 B7
Tilbury Juxta Clare 55 E8
Tile Cross 63 F5
Tile Hill 51 B7
Tilehurst 26 B4
Tilford 27 E6
Tilgate 28 F3
Tilgate Forest Row 28 F3
Tillathrowie 152 E4
Tilley 60 B5
Tillicoultry 127 E8
Tillingham 43 D5
Tillington Hereford 49 E6
W Sus 16 B3
Tillington Common 49 E6
Tillyarblet 135 C5
Tillybirloch 141 D5
Tillycorthie 141 B8
Tillydrine 140 E5
Tillyfour 140 C4
Tillyfourie 140 C5
Tillygarmond 140 E5
Tillygreig 141 B7
Tillykerrie 141 B7
Tilmanstone 31 D7
Tilney All Saints 67 C5
Tilney High End 67 C5
Tilney St Lawrence 66 C5
Tilshead 24 E5
Tilstock 74 F2
Tilston 73 D8
Tilstone Fearnall 74 C2
Tilsworth 40 B2
Tilton on the Hill 64 D4
Timberland 78 D4
Timbersbrook 75 C5
Timberscombe 21 E8
Timble 94 D4
Timperley 87 F5
Timsbury Bath 23 D8
Hants 14 B4
Timsgearraidh 154 D5
Timworth Green 56 C2
Tincleton 13 E5
Tindale 109 D6
Tingewick 52 F4
Tingley 88 B3
Tingrith 53 F8
Tingwall 159 F4
Tinhay 9 F5
Tinshill 95 F5
Tinsley 88 E5
Tintagel 8 F2
Tintern Parva 36 D2
Tintinhull 12 C3
Tintwistle 87 E8
Tinwald 114 F3
Tinwell 65 D7
Tipperty 141 B8
Tipsend 66 E5
Tipton 62 E3
Tipton St John 11 E5
Tiptree 42 C4
Tirabad 47 E7
Tiraghoil 146 J6
Tirley 37 B5
Tirphil 35 D5
Tirril 99 B7
Tir-y-dail 33 C7
Tisbury 13 B7
Tisman's Common 27 F8
Tissington 75 D8
Titchberry 8 B4
Titchfield 15 D6
Titchmarsh 53 B8
Titchwell 80 C3
Tithby 77 F6
Titley 48 C5
Titlington 117 C7
Titsey 28 D5
Tittensor 75 F5
Tittleshall 80 E4
Tiverton Ches W 74 C2
Devon 10 C4
Tivetshall St Margaret 68 F4
Tivetshall St Mary 68 F4
Tividale 62 E3
Tivy Dale 88 D3
Tixall 62 B3
Tixover 65 D6
Toab Orkney 159 H6
Shetland 160 M5
Toadmoor 76 D3
Tobermory 147 F8
Toberonochy 124 E3
Tobha Mor 148 E2
Tobhtarol 154 D6
Tobson 154 D6
Tocher 153 E6
Tockenham 24 B5
Tockenham Wick 37 F7
Tockholes 86 B4
Tockington 36 F3
Tockwith 95 D7
Todber 13 B6
Todding 49 B6
Toddington C Beds 40 B3
Glos 50 F5
Todenham 51 F7
Todhills 108 C3
Todlachie 141 C5
Todmorden 87 B7
Todrig 115 C7
Todwick 89 F5
Toft Cambs 54 D4
Lincs 65 C7
Toft Hill Durham 101 B6
Lincs 78 C5
Toft Monks 69 E7
Toft next Newton 90 F4
Toftrees 80 E4
Tofts 158 D5
Toftwood 68 C2
Togston 117 D8
Tokavaig 149 G11
Tokers Green 26 B5
Tolastadh a Chaolais 154 D6
Tolastadh bho Thuath 155 C10
Tolland 22 F3
Tollard Royal 13 C7
Toll Bar 89 D6
Tollbar End 51 B8
Toll End 62 E3
Toller Fratrum 12 E3
Toller Porcorum 12 E3
Tollerton Notts 77 F6
N Yorks 95 C8
Tollesbury 43 C5
Tolleshunt D'Arcy 43 C5
Tolleshunt Major 43 C5
Toll of Birness 153 E10
Tolm 155 D9
Tolpuddle 13 E5
Tolvah 138 E4
Tolworth 28 C2
Tomatin 138 B4
Tombreck 151 H9
Tomchrasky 137 C5
Tomdoun 136 D4
Tomich Highld 137 B6
Highld 151 D9
Tomich House 151 G8
Tomintoul Aberds 139 E7
Moray 139 C7
Tomnaven 152 E4
Tomnavoulin 139 B8
Tonbridge 29 E6
Tondu 34 F2
Tonfanau 58 D2
Tong Shrops 61 D7
W Yorks 94 F5
Tonge 63 B8
Tongham 27 E6
Tongland 106 D3
Tong Norton 61 D7
Tongue 157 D8
Tongue End 65 C8
Tongwynlais 35 F5
Tonna 34 E1
Ton-Pentre 34 E3
Tonwell 41 C6
Tonypandy 34 E3
Tonyrefail 34 F4
Toot Baldon 39 D5
Toot Hill 41 D8
Toothill 14 C4
Topcliffe 95 B7
Topcroft 69 E5
Topcroft Street 69 E5
Top of Hebers 87 D6
Toppesfield 55 F8
Toppings 86 C5
Topsham 10 F4
Torbay 7 D7
Torbeg 143 F10
Torboll Farm 151 B10
Torbrex 127 E6
Torbryan 7 C6
Torcross 7 E6
Tore 151 F9
Torinturk 145 G7
Torksey 77 B8
Torlum 148 C2
Torlundy 131 B5
Tormarton 24 B2
Tormisdale 142 C2
Tormitchell 112 E2
Tormore 143 E9
Tornagrain 151 G10
Tornahaish 139 D8
Tornaveen 140 D5
Torness 137 B8
Toronto 110 F4
Torpenhow 108 F2
Torphichen 120 B2
Torphins 140 D5
Torpoint 6 D2
Torquay 7 C7
Torquhan 121 E7
Torran Argyll 124 E4
Highld 149 D10
Highld 151 D10
Torrance 119 B6
Torrans 146 J7
Torranyard 118 E3
Torre 7 C7
Torridon 150 F2
Torridon House 149 C13
Torrin 149 F10
Torrisdale 157 C9
Torrisdale-Square 143 E8
Torrish 157 H12
Torrisholme 92 C4
Torroble 157 J8
Torry Aberdeen 141 D8
Aberds 152 E4
Torryburn 128 F2
Torterston 153 D10
Torthorwald 107 B7
Tortington 16 D4
Tortworth 36 E4
Torvaig 149 D9
Torver 98 E4
Torwood 127 F7
Torworth 89 F7
Tosberry 8 B4
Toscaig 149 E12
Toseland 54 C3
Tosside 93 D7
Tostock 56 C3
Totaig Highld 148 C7
Highld 149 F13
Tote 149 D9
Totegan 157 C11
Tothill 91 F8
Totland 14 F4
Totnes 7 C6
Toton 76 F5
Totronald 146 F4
Totscore 149 B8
Tottenham 41 E6
Tottenhill 67 C6
Tottenhill Row 67 C6
Totteridge 41 E5
Totternhoe 40 B2
Tottington 87 C5
Totton 14 C4
Touchen End 27 B6
Tournaig 155 J13
Toux 153 C9
Tovil 29 D8
Toward 145 G10
Towcester 52 E4
Towednack 2 C3
Tower End 67 C6
Towersey 39 D7
Towie Aberds 140 C3
Aberds 153 B8
Towiemore 152 D3
Tow Law 110 F4
Townend 118 B4
Town End Cambs 66 E4
Cumb 99 F6
Towngate 65 C8
Townhead Cumb 108 F5
Dumfries 106 E3
S Ayrs 112 D2
S Yorks 88 D2
Townhead of Greenlaw 106 C4
Townhill 128 F3
Town Row 18 B2
Townsend Bucks 39 D7
Herts 40 D4
Townshend 2 C4
Town Yetholm 116 B4
Towthorpe 96 D2
Towton 95 F7
Towyn 72 B3
Toxteth 85 F4
Toynton All Saints 79 C6
Toynton Fen Side 79 C6
Toynton St Peter 79 C7
Toy's Hill 29 D5
Trabboch 112 B4
Traboe 3 D6
Tradespark
Highld 151 F11
Orkney 159 H5
Trafford Park 87 E5
Trallong 34 B3
Tranent 121 B7
Tranmere 85 F4
Trantlebeg 157 D11
Trantlemore 157 D11
Tranwell 117 F7
Trapp 33 C7
Traprain 121 B8
Traquair 121 F6
Trawden 94 F2
Trawsfynydd 71 D8
Trealaw 34 E4
Treales 92 F4
Trearddur 82 D2
Treaslane 149 C8
Trebanog 34 E4
Trebanos 33 D8
Trebartha 5 B7
Trebarwith 8 F2
Trebetherick 4 B4
Treborough 22 F2
Trebudannon 4 C3
Trebullett 5 B8
Treburley 5 B8
Trebyan 5 C5
Trecastle 34 B2
Trecenydd 35 F5
Trecwn 44 B4
Trecynon 34 D3
Tredavoe 2 D3
Treddiog 44 C3
Tredegar 35 D5
Tredegar = Newydd
New Tredegar 35 D5
Tredington Glos 37 B6
Warks 51 E7
Tredinnick 4 B4
Tredomen 48 F3
Tredunnock 35 E7
Tredustan 48 F3
Treen 2 D2
Treeton 88 F5
Trefaldwyn = Montgomery 60 E2
Trefasser 44 B3
Trefdraeth 82 D4
Trefdraeth = Newport 45 F2
Trefecca 48 F3
Trefechan 58 F2
Trefeglwys 59 E6
Trefenter 46 C5
Treffgarne 44 C4
Treffynnon 44 C3
Treffynnon = Holywell 73 B5
Trefgarn Owen 44 C3
Trefi 44 B3
Trefil 35 C5
Trefilan 46 D4
Trefin 44 B3
Treflach 60 B2
Trefnanney 60 C2
Trefnant 72 B4
Trefonen 60 B2
Trefor Anglesey 82 C3
Gwyn 70 C4
Treforest 34 F4
Trefriw 83 E7
Tref-y-Clawdd = Knighton 48 B4
Trefynwy = Monmouth 36 C2
Tregadillett 8 F4
Tregaian 82 D4
Tregare 35 C8
Tregaron 47 D5
Tregarth 83 E6
Tregeare 8 F4
Tregeiriog 73 F5
Tregele 82 B3
Tre-Gibbon 34 D3
Tregidden 3 D6
Treglemais 44 C3
Tregole 8 E3
Tregonetha 4 C4
Tregony 3 B8
Tregoss 4 C4
Tregoyd 48 F4
Tregroes 46 E3
Tregurrian 4 C3
Tregynon 59 E7
Trehafod 34 E4
Treharris 34 E4
Treherbert 34 E3
Trekenner 5 B8
Treknow 8 F2
Trelan 3 E6
Trelash 8 E3
Trelassick 4 D3
Trelawnyd 72 B4
Trelech 45 F4
Treleddyd-fawr 44 C2
Trelewis 35 E5
Treligga 8 F2
Trelights 4 B4
Trelill 4 B5
Trelissick 3 C7
Trellech 36 D2
Trelleck Grange 36 D1
Trelogan 85 F2
Trelystan 60 D2
Tremadog 71 C6
Tremail 8 F3
Tremain 45 E4
Tremaine 8 F4
Tremar 5 C7
Trematon 5 D8
Tremeirchion 72 B4
Trenance 4 C3
Trenarren 3 B9
Trench 61 C6
Treneglos 8 F4
Trenewan 5 D6
Trent 12 C3
Trentham 75 E5
Trentishoe 20 E5
Trent Vale 75 E5
Treoes 21 B8
Treorchy = Treorci 34 E3
Treorci = Treorchy 34 E3
Tre'r-ddôl 58 E3
Trerulefoot 5 D8
Tresaith 45 D4
Tresawle 3 B7
Trescott 62 E2
Trescowe 2 C4
Tresham 36 E4
Tresillian 3 B7
Tresinwen 44 A4
Treskinnick Cross 8 E4
Tresmeer 8 F4
Tresparrett 8 E3
Tresparrett Posts 8 E3
Tressait 133 C5
Tresta Shetland 160 D8
Shetland 160 H5
Treswell 77 B7
Tre-Taliesin 58 E3
Trethosa 4 D4
Trethurgy 4 D5
Tretio 44 C2
Tretire 36 B2
Tretower 35 B5
Treuddyn 73 D6
Trevalga 8 F2
Trevalyn 73 D7
Trevanson 4 B4
Trevarren 4 C4
Trevarrian 4 C3
Trevarrick 3 B8
Trevaughan 32 C2
Tre-vaughan 32 B4
Treveighan 5 B5
Trevellas 4 D2
Treverva 3 C6
Trevethin 35 D6
Trevigro 5 C8
Treviscoe 4 D4
Trevone 4 B3
Trewarmett 8 F2
Trewassa 8 F3
Trewellard 2 C2
Trewen 8 F4
Trewennack 3 D5
Trewern 60 C2
Trewethern 4 B5
Trewidland 5 D7
Trewint Corn 8 E3
Corn 8 F4
Trewithian 3 C7
Trewoofe 2 D3
Trewoon 4 D4
Treworga 3 B7
Treworlas 3 C7
Tre-wyn 35 B7
Treyarnon 4 B3
Treyford 16 C2
Trezaise 4 D4
Triangle 87 B8
Trickett's Cross 13 D8
Triffleton 44 C4
Trimdon 111 F6
Trimdon Colliery 111 F6
Trimdon Grange 111 F6
Trimingham 81 D8
Trimley Lower Street 57 F6
Trimley St Martin 57 F6
Trimley St Mary 57 F6
Trimpley 50 B2
Trimsaran 33 D5
Trimstone 20 E3
Trinafour 132 C4
Trinant 35 D6
Tring 40 C2
Tring Wharf 40 C2
Trinity Angus 135 C6
Jersey 17
Trisant 47 B6
Trislaig 130 B4
Trispen 4 D3
Tritlington 117 E8
Trochry 133 E6
Trodigal 143 F7
Troed-rhiwdalar 47 D8
Troedyraur 46 E2
Troedyrhiw 34 D4
Tromode 84 E3
Trondavoe 160 F5
Troon Corn 3 C5
S Ayrs 118 F3
Trosaraidh 148 G2
Trossachs Hotel 126 D4
Troston 56 B2
Trottiscliffe 29 C7
Trotton 16 B2
Troutbeck Cumb 99 B5
Cumb 99 D6
Troutbeck Bridge 99 D6
Trowbridge 24 D3
Trowell 76 F4
Trow Green 36 D2
Trowle Common 24 D3
Trowley Bottom 40 C3
Trows 122 F2
Trowse Newton 68 D5
Trudoxhill 24 E2
Trull 11 B7
Trumaisgearraidh 148 A3
Trumpan 148 B7
Trumpet 49 F8
Trumpington 54 D5
Trunch 81 D8
Trunnah 92 E3
Truro 3 B7
Trusham 10 F3
Trusley 76 F2
Trusthorpe 91 F9
Trysull 62 E2
Tubney 38 E4
Tuckenhay 7 D6
Tuckhill 61 F7
Tuckingmill 3 B5
Tuddenham 55 B8
Tuddenham St Martin 57 E5
Tudeley 29 E7
Tudhoe 111 F5
Tudorville 36 B2
Tudweiliog 70 D3
Tuesley 27 E7
Tuffley 37 C5
Tufton Hants 26 E2
Pembs 32 B1
Tugby 64 D4
Tugford 61 F5
Tullibardine 127 C8
Tullibody 127 E7
Tullich Argyll 125 D6
Highld 138 B2
Tullich Muir 151 D10
Tulliemet 133 D6
Tulloch Aberds 135 B7
Aberds 153 E8
Perth 128 B2
Tulloch Castle 151 E8
Tullochgorm 125 F5
Tulloes 135 E5
Tullybannocher 127 B6
Tullybelton 133 F7
Tullyfergus 134 E2
Tullymurdoch 134 D1
Tullynessle 140 C4
Tumble 33 C6
Tumby Woodside 79 D5
Tummel Bridge 132 D4
Tunga 155 D9
Tunstall E Yorks 97 F9
Kent 30 C2
Lancs 93 B6
Norf 69 D7
N Yorks 101 E7
Stoke 75 D5
Suff 57 D7
T&W 111 D6
Tunstead Derbys 75 B8
Gtr Man 87 D8
Norf 81 E8
Tunworth 26 E4
Tupsley 49 E7
Tupton 76 C3
Turgis Green 26 D4
Turin 135 D5
Turkdean 37 C8
Tur Langton 64 E4
Turleigh 24 C3
Turn 87 C6
Turnastone 49 F5
Turnberry 112 D2
Turnditch 76 E2
Turners Hill 28 F4
Turners Puddle 13 E6
Turnford 41 D6
Turnhouse 120 B4
Turnworth 13 D6
Turriff 153 C7
Turton Bottoms 86 C5
Turves 66 E3
Turvey 53 D7
Turville 39 E7
Turville Heath 39 E7
Turweston 52 F4
Tushielaw 115 C6
Tutbury 63 B6
Tutnall 50 B4
Tutshill 36 E2
Tuttington 81 E8
Tutts Clump 26 B3
Tuxford 77 B7
Twatt Orkney 159 F3
Shetland 160 H5
Twechar 119 B7
Tweedmouth 123 D5
Tweedsmuir 114 B3
Twelve Heads 3 B6
Twemlow Green 74 C4
Twenty 65 B8
Twerton 24 C2
Twickenham 28 B2
Twigworth 37 B5
Twineham 17 C6
Twinhoe 24 D2
Twinstead 56 F2
Twinstead Green 56 F2
Twiss Green 86 E4
Twiston 93 E8
Twitchen Devon 21 F6
Shrops 49 B5
Two Bridges 6 B4
Two Dales 76 C2
Two Mills 73 B7
Twycross 63 D7
Twyford Bucks 39 B6
Derbys 63 B7
Hants 15 B5
Leics 64 C4
Twyford *continued*
Lincs 65 B6
Norf 81 E6
Wokingham 27 B5
Twyford Common 49 F7
Twynholm 106 D3
Twyning 50 F3
Twyning Green 50 F4
Twynllanan 34 B1
Twynmynydd 33 C7
Twyn-y-Sheriff 35 D8
Twywell 53 B7
Tyberton 49 F5
Tyburn 62 E5
Tycroes 33 C7
Tycrwyn 59 C8
Tyddewi = St David's 44 C2
Tydd Gote 66 C4
Tydd St Giles 66 C4
Tydd St Mary 66 C4
Tyddyn-mawr 71 C6
Ty-draw 83 F8
Tye Green Essex 41 D7
Essex 42 B3
Essex 55 F6
Ty-hen Carms 32 B4
Gwyn 70 D2
Tyldesley 86 D4
Tyler Hill 30 C5
Tylers Green 40 E2
Tylorstown 34 E4
Tylwch 59 F6
Ty-mawr 82 C4
Ty Mawr 46 E4
Ty Mawr Cwm 72 E3
Ty-nant Conwy 72 E3
Gwyn 59 B6
Tyncelyn 46 C5
Tyndrum 131 F7
Tyneham 13 F6
Tynehead 121 D6
Tynemouth 111 C6
Tyne Tunnel 111 C6
Tynewydd 34 E3
Tyninghame 122 B2
Tynron 113 E8
Tyn-y-celyn 73 F5
Tyn-y-coed 60 B2
Tyn-y-fedwen 72 F5
Tyn-y-ffridd 72 F5
Tynygongl 82 C5
Tynygraig 47 C5
Tyn-y-graig 48 D2
Ty'n-y-groes 83 D7
Ty'n-y-maes 83 E6
Tyn-y-pwll 82 C4
Ty'n-yr-eithin 47 C5
Ty'r-felin-isaf 83 E8
Tyrie 153 B9
Tyringham 53 E6
Tythecott 9 C6
Tythegston 21 B7
Tytherington
Ches E 75 B6
S Glos 36 F3
Som 24 E2
Wilts 24 E4
Tytherleigh 11 D8
Ty-uchaf 59 B7
Tywardreath 5 D5
Tywyn Conwy 83 D7
Gwyn 58 D2

U

Uachdar 148 C2
Uags 149 E12
Ubbeston Green 57 B7
Ubley 23 D7
Uckerby 101 D7
Uckfield 17 B8
Uckington 37 B6
Uddingston 119 C6
Uddington 119 F8
Udimore 19 D5
Udny Green 141 B7
Udny Station 141 B8
Udston 119 D6
Udstonhead 119 E7
Uffcott 25 B6
Uffculme 11 C5
Uffington Lincs 65 D7
Oxon 38 F3
Shrops 60 C5
Ufford Pboro 65 D7
Suff 57 D6
Ufton 51 C8
Ufton Nervet 26 C4
Ugadale 143 F8
Ugborough 6 D4
Uggeshall 69 F7
Ugglebarnby 103 D6
Ughill 88 E3
Ugley 41 B8
Ugley Green 41 B8
Ugthorpe 103 C5
Uidh 148 J1
Uig Argyll 145 E10
Highld 148 C6
Highld 149 B8
Uigen 154 D5
Uigshader 149 D9
Uisken 146 K6
Ulbster 158 F5
Ulceby Lincs 79 B7
N Lincs 90 C5
Ulceby Skitter 90 C5
Ulcombe 30 E2
Uldale 108 F2
Uley 36 E4
Ulgham 117 E8
Ullapool 150 B4
Ullenhall 51 C6
Ullenwood 37 C6
Ulleskelf 95 E8
Ullesthorpe 64 F2
Ulley 89 F5
Ullingswick 49 E7
Ullinish 149 E8
Ullock 98 B2
Ulnes Walton 86 C3
Ulpha 98 E3
Ulrome 97 D7
Ulsta 160 E6
Ulva House 146 H7
Ulverston 92 B2
Ulwell 13 F8
Umberleigh 9 B8
Unapool 156 F5
Unasary 148 F2
Underbarrow 99 E6
Undercliffe 94 F4
Underhoull 160 C7
Underriver 29 D6
Underwood 76 D4
Undy 35 F8
Unifirth 160 H4
Union Cottage 141 E7
Union Mills 84 E3
Union Street 18 B4
Unstone 76 B3
Unstone Green 76 B3
Unthank Cumb 108 F4
Cumb 109 E6
Unthank End 108 F4
Upavon 25 D6
Up Cerne 12 D4
Upchurch 30 C2
Upcott 48 D5
Upend 55 D7
Up Exe 10 D4
Upgate 68 C4
Uphall 120 B3
Uphall Station 120 B3
Upham Devon 10 D3
Hants 15 B6
Uphampton 50 C3
Up Hatherley 37 B6
Uphill 22 D5
Up Holland 86 D3
Uplawmoor 118 D4
Upleadon 36 B4
Upleatham 102 C4
Uplees 30 C3
Uploders 12 E3
Uplowman 10 C5
Uplyme 11 E8
Up Marden 15 C8
Upminster 42 F1
Up Nately 26 D4
Upnor 29 B8
Upottery 11 D7
Upper Affcot 60 F4
Upper Ardchronie 151 C9
Upper Arley 61 F7
Upper Arncott 39 C6
Upper Astrop 52 F3
Upper Badcall 156 E4
Upper Basildon 26 B3
Upper Beeding 17 C5
Upper Benefield 65 F6
Upper Bighouse 157 D11
Upper Boddington 52 D2
Upper Borth 58 F3
Upper Boyndlie 153 B9
Upper Brailes 51 F8
Upper Breakish 149 F11
Upper Breinton 49 E6
Upper Broadheath 50 D3
Upper Broughton 64 B3
Upper Bucklebury 26 C3
Upper Burnhaugh 141 E7
Upperby 108 D4
Upper Caldecote 54 E2
Upper Catesby 52 D3
Upper Chapel 48 E2
Upper Church Village 34 F4
Upper Chute 25 D7
Upper Clatford 25 E8
Upper Clynnog 71 C5
Upper Cumberworth 88 D3
Upper Cwmbran 35 E6
Upper Dallachy 152 B3
Upper Dean 53 C8
Upper Denby 88 D3
Upper Denton 109 C6
Upper Derraid 151 H13
Upper Dicker 18 E2
Upper Dovercourt 57 F6
Upper Druimfi 147 F8
Upper Dunsforth 95 C7
Upper Eathie 151 E10
Upper Elkstone 75 D7
Upper End 75 B7
Upper Farringdon 26 F5
Upper Framilode 36 C4
Upper Glenfintaig 137 F5
Upper Gornal 62 E3
Upper Gravenhurst 54 F2
Upper Green Mon 35 C7
W Berks 25 C8
Upper Grove Common 36 B2
Upper Hackney 76 C2
Upper Hale 27 E6
Upper Halistra 148 C7
Upper Halling 29 C7
Upper Hambleton 65 D6
Upper Hardres Court 31 D5
Upper Hartfield 29 F5
Upper Haugh 88 E5
Upper Heath 61 F5
Upper Hellesdon 68 C5
Upper Helmsley 96 D2
Upper Hergest 48 D4
Upper Heyford
Oxon 38 B4
W Nhants 52 D4
Upper Hill 49 D6
Upper Hopton 88 C2
Upper Horsebridge 18 D2
Upper Hulme 75 C7
Upper Inglesham 38 E2
Upper Inverbrough 151 H11
Upper Killay 33 E6
Upper Knockando 152 D1
Upper Lambourn 38 F3
Upper Leigh 75 F7
Upper Lenie 137 B8
Upper Lochton 141 E5
Upper Longdon 62 C4
Upper Lybster 158 G4
Upper Lydbrook 36 C3
Upper Maes-coed 48 F5
Upper Midway 63 B6

Uppermill 87 D7
Upper Milovaig 148 D6
Upper Minety 37 E7
Upper Mitton 50 B3
Upper North Dean 39 E8
Upper Obney 133 F7
Upper Ollach 149 E10
Upper Padley 76 B2
Upper Pollicott 39 C7
Upper Poppleton 95 D8
Upper Quinton 51 E6
Upper Ratley 14 B4
Upper Rissington 38 C2
Upper Rochford 49 C8
Upper Sandaig 149 G12
Upper Sanday 159 H6
Upper Sapey 49 C8
Upper Saxondale 77 F6
Upper Seagry 37 F6
Upper Shelton 53 E7
Upper Sheringham 81 C7
Upper Skelmorlie 118 C2
Upper Slaughter 38 B1
Upper Soudley 36 C3
Uppersound 160 J6
Upper Stondon 54 F2
Upper Stowe 52 D4
Upper Stratton 38 F1
Upper Street Hants 14 C2
Norf 69 C6
Norf 69 C6
Suff 56 F5
Upper Strensham 50 F4
Upper Sundon 40 B3
Upper Swell 38 B1
Upper Tean 75 F7
Upperthong 88 D2
Upperthorpe 89 D8
Upper Tillyrie 128 D3
Upperton 16 B3
Upper Tooting 28 B3
Upper Tote 149 C10
Uppertown Derbys 76 C3
Highld 158 C5
Orkney 159 J5
Upper Town 23 C7
Upper Treverward 48 B4
Upper Tysoe 51 E8
Upper Upham 25 B7
Upper Wardington 52 E2
Upper Weald 53 F5
Upper Weedon 52 D4
Upper Wield 26 F4
Upper Winchendon 39 C7
Upper Witton 62 E4
Upper Woodend 141 C5
Upper Woodford 25 F6
Upper Wootton 26 D3
Upper Wyche 50 E2
Uppingham 65 E5
Uppington 61 D6
Upsall 102 F2
Upshire 41 D7
Up Somborne 25 F8
Upstreet 31 C6
Up Sydling 12 D4
Upthorpe 56 B3
Upton Cambs 54 B2
Ches W 73 C8
Corn 8 D4
Dorset 12 F5
Dorset 13 E7
Hants 14 C4
Hants 25 D8
Leics 63 E7
Lincs 90 F2
Mers 85 F3
Norf 69 C6
Notts 77 B7
Notts 77 D7
Oxon 39 F5
Pboro 65 D8
Slough 27 B7
Som 10 B4
W Nhants 52 C5
W Yorks 89 C5
Upton Bishop 36 B3
Upton Cheyney 23 C8
Upton Cressett 61 E6
Upton Cross 5 B7
Upton Grey 26 E4
Upton Hellions 10 D3
Upton Lovell 24 E4
Upton Magna 61 C5
Upton Noble 24 F2
Upton Pyne 10 E4
Upton St Leonard's 37 C5
Upton Scudamore 24 E3
Upton Snodsbury 50 D4
Upton upon Severn 50 E3
Upton Warren 50 C4
Upwaltham 16 C3
Upware 55 B6
Upwell 66 D4
Upwey 12 F4
Upwood 66 F2
Uradale 160 K6
Urafirth 160 F5
Urchfont 24 D5
Urdimarsh 49 E7
Ure 160 F4
Ure Bank 95 B6
Urgha 154 H6
Urishay Common 48 F5
Urlay Nook 102 C1
Urmston 87 E5
Urpeth 110 D5
Urquhart Highld 151 F8
Moray 152 B2
Urra 102 D3
Urray 151 F8
Ushaw Moor 110 E5
Usk = *Brynbuga* 35 D7
Usselby 90 E4
Usworth 111 D6
Utkinton 74 C2
Utley 94 E3
Uton 10 E3
Utterby 91 E7
Uttoxeter 75 F7
Uwchmynydd 70 E2
Uxbridge 40 F3
Uyeasound 160 C7
Uzmaston 44 D4

V

Valley 82 D2
Valleyfield 106 D3
Valley Truckle 8 F2
Valsgarth 160 B8
Valtos 149 B10
Van 59 F6
Vange 42 F3
Varteg 35 D6
Vatten 149 D7
Vaul 146 G3
Vaynor 34 C4
Veensgarth 160 J6
Velindre 48 F3
Vellow 22 F2
Veness 159 F6
Venn Green 9 C5
Vennington 60 D3
Venn Ottery 11 E5
Venny Tedburn 10 E3
Ventnor 15 G6
Vernham Dean 25 D8
Vernham Street 25 D8
Vernolds Common 60 F4
Verwood 13 D8
Veryan 3 C8
Vicarage 11 F7
Vickerstown 92 C1
Victoria Corn 4 C4
S Yorks 88 D2
Vidlin 160 G6
Viewpark 119 C7
Vigo Village 29 C7
Vinehall Street 18 C4
Vine's Cross 18 D2
Viney Hill 36 D3
Virginia Water 27 C8
Virginstow 9 E5
Vobster 24 E2
Voe Shetland 160 E5
Shetland 160 G6
Vowchurch 49 F5
Voxter 160 F5
Voy 159 G3

W

Wackerfield 101 B6
Wacton 68 E4
Wadbister 160 J6
Wadborough 50 E4
Waddesdon 39 C7
Waddingham 90 E3
Waddington Lancs 93 E7
Lincs 78 C2
Wadebridge 4 B4
Wadeford 11 C8
Wadenhoe 65 F7
Wadesmill 41 C6
Wadhurst 18 B3
Wadshelf 76 B3
Wadsley 88 E4
Wadsley Bridge 88 E4
Wadworth 89 E6
Waen Denb 72 C3
Denb 72 C5
Waen Fach 60 C2
Waen Goleugoed 72 B4
Wag 157 G13
Wainfleet All Saints 79 D7
Wainfleet Bank 79 D7
Wainfleet St Mary 79 D8
Wainfleet Tofts 79 D7
Wainhouse Corner 8 E3
Wainscott 29 B8
Wainstalls 87 B8
Waitby 100 D2
Waithe 91 D6
Wakefield 88 B4
Wake Lady Green 102 E4
Wakerley 65 E6
Wakes Colne 42 B4
Walberswick 57 B8
Walberton 16 D3
Walbottle 110 C4
Walcot Lincs 78 F3
N Lincs 90 B2
Shrops 60 F3
Swindon 38 F1
Telford 61 C5
Walcote Leics 64 F2
Warks 51 D6
Walcot Green 68 F4
Walcott Lincs 78 D4
Norf 69 A6
Walden 101 F5
Walden Head 100 F4
Walden Stubbs 89 C6
Waldersey 66 D4
Walderslade 29 C8
Walderton 15 C8
Walditch 12 E2
Waldley 75 F8
Waldridge 111 D5
Waldringfield 57 E6
Waldringfield Heath 57 E6
Waldron 18 D2
Wales 89 F5
Walesby Lincs 90 E5
Notts 77 B6
Walford Hereford 36 B2
Hereford 49 B5
Shrops 60 B4
Walford Heath 60 C4
Walgherton 74 E3
Walgrave 53 B6
Walhampton 14 E4
Walkden 86 D5
Walker 111 C5
Walker Barn 75 B6
Walkerburn 121 F6
Walker Fold 93 E6
Walkeringham 89 E8
Walkerith 89 E8
Walkern 41 B5
Walker's Green 49 E7
Walkerville 101 E7
Walkford 14 E3
Walkhampton 6 C3
Walkington 97 F5
Walkley 88 F4
Walk Mill 93 F8
Wall Northumb 110 C2
Staffs 62 D5
Wallaceton 113 F8
Wallacetown
S Ayrs 112 B3
S Ayrs 112 D2
Wallands Park 17 C8
Wallasey 85 E4
Wall Bank 60 E5
Wallcrouch 18 B3
Wall Heath 62 F2
Wallingford 39 F6
Wallington Hants 15 D6
Herts 54 F3
London 28 C3
Wallis 32 B1
Walliswood 28 F2
Walls 160 J4
Wallsend 111 C5
Wallston 22 B3
Wall under Heywood 60 E5
Wallyford 121 B6
Walmer 31 D7
Walmer Bridge 86 B2
Walmersley 87 C6
Walmley 62 E5
Walpole 57 B7
Walpole Cross Keys 66 C5
Walpole Highway 66 C5
Walpole Marsh 66 C4
Walpole St Andrew 66 C5
Walpole St Peter 66 C5
Walsall 62 E4
Walsall Wood 62 D4
Walsden 87 B7
Walsgrave on Sowe 63 F7
Walsham le Willows 56 B3
Walshaw 87 C5
Walshford 95 D7
Walsoken 66 C4
Walston 120 E3
Walsworth 54 F3
Walters Ash 39 E8
Walterston 22 B2
Walterstone 35 B7
Waltham Kent 30 E5
NE Lincs 91 D6
Waltham Abbey 41 D6
Waltham Chase 15 C6
Waltham Cross 41 D6
Waltham on the Wolds 64 B5
Waltham St Lawrence 27 B6
Walthamstow 41 F6
Walton Cumb 108 C5
Derbys 76 C3
Leics 64 F2
Mers 85 E4
M Keynes 53 F6
Pboro 65 D8
Powys 48 D4
Som 23 F6
Staffs 75 F5
Suff 57 F6
Telford 61 C5
Warks 51 D7
W Yorks 88 C4
W Yorks 95 E7
Walton Cardiff 50 F4
Walton East 32 B1
Walton-in-Gordano 23 B6
Walton-le-Dale 86 B3
Walton-on-Thames 28 C2
Walton on the Hill
Staffs 62 B3
Sur 28 D3
Walton-on-the-Naze 43 B8
Walton on the Wolds 64 C2
Walton-on-Trent 63 C6
Walton West 44 D3
Walwen 73 B6
Walwick 110 B2
Walworth 101 C7
Walworth Gate 101 B7
Walwyn's Castle 44 D3
Wambrook 11 D7
Wanborough Sur 27 E7
Swindon 38 F2
Wandsworth 28 B3
Wangford 57 B8
Wanlockhead 113 C8
Wansford E Yorks 97 D6
Pboro 65 E7
Wanstead 41 F7
Wanstrow 24 E2
Wanswell 36 D3
Wantage 38 F3
Wapley 24 B2
Wappenbury 51 C8
Wappenham 52 E4
Warbleton 18 D3
Warblington 15 D8
Warborough 39 E5
Warboys 66 F3
Warbreck 92 F3
Warbstow 8 E4
Warburton 86 F5
Warcop 100 C2
Warden Kent 30 B4
Northumb 110 C2
Ward End 62 F5
Ward Green 56 C4
Wardhill 159 F7
Wardington 52 E2
Wardlaw 115 C5
Wardle Ches E 74 D3
Gtr Man 87 C7
Wardley 64 D5
Wardlow 75 B8
Wardy Hill 66 F4
Ware Herts 41 C6
Kent 31 C6
Wareham 13 F7
Warehorne 19 B6
Warenford 117 B7
Waren Mill 123 F7
Warenton 123 F7
Wareside 41 C6
Waresley Cambs 54 D3
Worcs 50 B3
Warfield 27 B6
Warfleet 7 D6
Wargrave 27 B5
Warham 80 C5
Warhill 87 E7
Wark Northumb 109 B8
Northumb 122 F4
Warkleigh 9 B8
Warkton 53 B6
Warkworth
Northumb 117 D8
W Nhants 52 E2
Warlaby 101 E8
Warland 87 B7
Warleggan 5 C6
Warlingham 28 D4
Warmfield 88 B4
Warmingham 74 C4
Warmington
N Nhants 65 E7
Warks 52 E2
Warminster 24 E3
Warmlake 30 D2
Warmley 23 B8
Warmley Tower 23 B8
Warmonds Hill 53 C7
Warmsworth 89 D6
Warmwell 13 F5
Warndon 50 D3
Warnford 15 B7
Warnham 28 F2
Warninglid 17 B6
Warren Ches E 75 B5
Pembs 44 F4
Warren Heath 57 E6
Warren Row 39 F8
Warren Street 30 D3
Warrington
M Keynes 53 D6
Warr 86 F4
Warsash 15 D5
Warslow 75 D7
Warter 96 D4
Warthermarske 94 B5
Warthill 96 D2
Wartling 18 E3
Wartnaby 64 B4
Warton Lancs 86 B2
Lancs 92 B4
Northumb 117 D6
Warks 63 D6
Warwick 51 C7
Warwick Bridge 108 D4
Warwick on Eden 108 D4
Wasbister 159 E4
Wasdale Head 98 D3
Washaway 4 C5
Washbourne 7 D5
Wash Common 26 C2
Washfield 10 C4
Washfold 101 D5
Washford 22 E2
Washford Pyne 10 C3
Washingborough 78 B3
Washington T&W 111 D6
W Sus 16 C5
Wasing 26 C3
Waskerley 110 E3
Wasperton 51 D7
Wasps Nest 78 C3
Wass 95 B8
Watchet 22 E2
Watchfield Oxon 38 E2
Som 22 E5
Watchgate 99 E7
Watchhill 107 E8
Watcombe 7 C7
Watendlath 98 C4
Water Devon 10 F2
Lancs 87 B6
Waterbeach 55 C5
Waterbeck 108 B2
Waterden 80 D4
Water End E Yorks 96 F3
Herts 40 C3
Herts 41 D5
Waterfall 75 D7
Waterfoot E Renf 119 D5
Lancs 87 B6
Waterford Hants 14 E4
Herts 41 C6
Waterhead Cumb 99 D5
Dumfries 114 E4
Waterheads 120 D5
Waterhouses
Durham 110 E4
Staffs 75 D7
Wateringbury 29 D7
Waterloo BCP 13 E8
Gtr Man 87 D7
Highld 149 F11
Mers 85 E4
N Lanark 119 D8
Norf 68 C5
Perth 133 F7
Shrops 74 F2
Waterloo Port 82 E4
Waterlooville 15 D7
Watermeetings 114 C2
Watermillock 99 B6
Water Newton 65 E8
Water Orton 63 E5
Waterperry 39 D6
Waterrow 11 B5
Watersfield 16 C4
Waterside Aberds 141 B9
Blackburn 86 B5
Cumb 108 E2
E Ayrs 112 D4
E Ayrs 118 E4
E Dunb 119 B6
E Renf 118 D5
Water's Nook 86 D4
Waterstock 39 D6
Waterston 44 E4
Water Stratford 52 F4
Waters Upton 61 C6
Water Yeat 98 F4
Watford Herts 40 E4
W Nhants 52 C4
Watford Gap 62 D5
Wath N Yorks 94 C4
N Yorks 95 B6
N Yorks 96 B2
Wath Brow 98 C2
Wath upon Dearne 88 D5
Watlington Norf 67 C6
Oxon 39 E6
Watnall 76 E5
Watten 158 E4
Wattisfield 56 B4
Wattisham 56 D4
Wattlesborough Heath 60 C3
Watton E Yorks 97 D6
Norf 68 D2
Watton at Stone 41 C6
Wattston 119 B7
Wattstown 34 E4
Wauchan 136 F2
Waulkmill Lodge 159 H4
Waun 59 D5
Waunarlwydd 33 E7
Waunclunda 47 F5
Waunfawr 82 F5
Waungron 33 D6
Waunlwyd 35 D5
Waun-y-clyn 33 D5
Wavendon 53 F7
Waverbridge 108 E2
Waverley S Yorks 88 F5
Waverton Ches W 73 C8
Cumb 108 E2
Wavertree 85 F4
Wawne 97 F6
Waxham 69 B7
Waxholme 91 B7
Way 31 C7
Wayfield 29 C8
Wayford 12 D2
Waymills 74 E2
Wayne Green 35 C8
Way Village 10 C3
Wdig = *Goodwick* 44 B4
Weachyburn 153 C6
Weald 38 D3
Wealdstone 40 F4
Weardley 95 E5
Weare 23 D6
Weare Giffard 9 B6
Wearhead 109 F8
Weasdale 100 D1
Weasenham All Saints 80 E4
Weasenham St Peter 80 E4
Weatherhill 28 E4
Weaverham 74 B3
Weaverthorpe 97 B5
Webheath 50 C5
Wedderlairs 153 E8
Wedderlie 122 D2
Weddington 63 E7
Wedhampton 25 D5
Wedmore 23 E6
Wednesbury 62 E3
Wednesfield 62 D3
Weedon 39 C8
Weedon Bec 52 D4
Weedon Lois 52 E4
Weeford 62 D5
Week 10 C2
Weeke 26 F2
Weekley 65 F5
Week St Mary 8 E4
Weel 97 F6
Weeley 43 B7
Weeley Heath 43 B7
Weem 133 E5
Weeping Cross 62 B3
Weethley Gate 51 D5
Weeting 67 F7
Weeton E Yorks 91 B7
Lancs 92 F3
N Yorks 95 E5
Weetwood Hall 117 B6
Weir 87 B6
Weir Quay 6 C2
Welborne 68 D3
Welbourn 78 D2
Welburn N Yorks 96 C3
N Yorks 102 F4
Welbury 102 D1
Welby 78 F2
Welches Dam 66 F4
Welcombe 8 C4
Weld Bank 86 C3
Weldon 117 E7
Welford W Berks 26 B2
W Nhants 64 F3
Welford-on-Avon 51 D6
Welham Leics 64 E4
Notts 89 F8
Welham Green 41 D5
Well Hants 27 E5
Lincs 79 B7
N Yorks 101 F7
Welland 50 E2
Wellbank 134 F4
Welldale 107 C8
Well End 40 F1
Wellesbourne 51 D7
Well Heads 94 F3
Well Hill 29 C5
Welling 29 B5
Wellingborough 53 C6
Wellingham 80 E4
Wellingore 78 D2
Wellington Cumb 98 D2
Hereford 49 E6
Som 11 B6
Telford 61 C6
Wellington Heath 50 E2
Wellington Hill 95 F6
Wellow Bath 24 D2
IoW 14 F4
Notts 77 C6
Wellpond Green 41 B7
Wells 23 E7
Wellsborough 63 D7
Wells Green 74 D3
Wells-next-the-Sea 80 C5
Wellswood 7 C7
Well Town 10 D4
Wellwood 128 F2
Welney 66 E5
Welshampton 73 F8
Welsh Bicknor 36 C2
Welsh End 74 F2
Welsh Frankton 73 F7
Welsh Hook 44 C4
Welsh Newton 36 C1
Welshpool = *Y Trallwng* 60 D2
Welsh St Donats 22 B2
Welton Cumb 108 E3
E Yorks 90 B3
Welton *continued*
Lincs 78 B3
W Nhants 52 C3
Welton Hill 90 F4
Welton le Marsh 79 C7
Welton le Wold 91 F6
Welwick 91 B7
Welwyn 41 C5
Welwyn Garden City 41 C5
Wem 60 B5
Wembdon 22 F4
Wembley 40 F4
Wembury 6 E3
Wembworthy 9 D8
Wemyss Bay 118 C1
Wenallt Ceredig 47 B5
Gwyn 72 E3
Wendens Ambo 55 F6
Wendlebury 39 C5
Wendling 68 C2
Wendover 40 D1
Wendron 3 C5
Wendy 54 E4
Wenfordbridge 5 B5
Wenhaston 57 B8
Wennington Cambs 54 B3
Lancs 93 B6
London 41 F8
Wensley Derbys 76 C2
N Yorks 101 F5
Wentbridge 89 C5
Wentnor 60 E3
Wentworth Cambs 55 B5
S Yorks 88 E4
Wenvoe 22 B3
Weobley 49 D6
Weobley Marsh 49 D6
Wereham 67 D6
Wergs 62 D2
Wern Powys 59 C6
Powys 60 C2
Wernffrwd 33 E6
Wernyrheolydd 35 C7
Werrington Corn 8 F5
Pboro 65 D8
Staffs 75 E6
Wervin 73 B8
Wesham 92 F4
Wessington 76 D3
Westacott 20 F4
West Acre 67 C7
West Adderbury 52 F2
West Allerdean 123 E5
West Alvington 6 E5
West Amesbury 25 E6
West Anstey 10 B3
West Ashby 79 B5
West Ashling 16 D2
West Ashton 24 D3
West Auckland 101 B6
West Ayton 103 F7
West Bagborough 22 F3
West Barkwith 91 F5
West Barnby 103 C6
West Barns 122 B2
West Barsham 80 D5
West Bay 12 E2
West Beckham 81 D7
West Bedfont 27 B8
West Benhar 119 C8
Westbere 31 C5
West Bergholt 43 B5
West Bexington 12 F3
West Bilney 67 C7
West Blatchington 17 D6
Westborough 77 E8
Westbourne BCP 13 E8
Suff 56 E5
W Sus 15 D8
West Bowling 94 F4
West Bradford 93 E7
West Bradley 23 F7
West Bretton 88 C3
West Bridgford 77 F5
West Bromwich 62 E4
Westbrook 26 B2
West Buckland
Devon 21 F5
Som 11 B6
West Burrafirth 160 H4
West Burton
N Yorks 101 F5
W Sus 16 C3
Westbury Bucks 52 F4
Shrops 60 D3
Wilts 24 D3
Westbury Leigh 24 D3
Westbury-on-Severn 36 C4
Westbury on Trym 23 B7
Westbury-sub-Mendip 23 E7
West Butterwick 90 D2
Westby 92 F3
West Byfleet 27 C8
West Caister 69 C8
West Calder 120 C3
West Camel 12 B3
West Challow 38 F3
West Chelborough 12 D3
West Chevington 117 E8
West Chiltington 16 C4
West Chiltington Common 16 C4
West Chinnock 12 C2
West Chisenbury 25 D6
West Clandon 27 D8
West Cliffe 31 E7
Westcliff-on-Sea 42 F4
West Clyne 157 J11
West Clyth 158 G4
West Coker 12 C3
Westcombe 23 F8
West Compton
Dorset 12 E3
Som 23 E7
Westcote 38 B2
Westcott Bucks 39 C7
Devon 10 D5
Sur 28 E2
Westcott Barton 38 B4
West Cowick 89 B7
West Cranmore 23 E8
West Cross 33 F7
West Cullery 141 D6
West Curry 8 E4
West Curthwaite 108 E3
West Darlochan 143 F7
Westdean 18 F2
West Dean Wilts 14 B3
W Sus 16 C2
West Deeping 65 D8
Westdene 17 D6
West Derby 85 E4
West Dereham 67 D6
West Didsbury 87 E6
West Ditchburn 117 B7
West Down 20 E4
West Drayton
London 27 B8
Notts 77 B7
West Ella 90 B4
West End Bedford 53 D7
E Yorks 96 F5
E Yorks 97 F7
Hants 15 C5
Lancs 86 B5
Norf 68 D2
Norf 69 C8
N Som 23 C6
N Yorks 94 D4
Oxon 38 D4
S Lanark 120 E2
Suff 69 F7
Sur 27 C7
S Yorks 89 D7
Wilts 13 B7
Wilts 24 B4
W Sus 17 C6
West End Green 26 C4
Wester Aberchalder 137 B8
Wester Balgedie 128 D3
Wester Culbeuchly 153 B6
Westerdale Highld 158 E3
N Yorks 102 D4
Wester Dechmont 120 C3
Wester Denoon 134 E3
Westerfield
Shetland 160 H5
Suff 57 E5
Wester Fintray 141 C7
Westergate 16 D3
Wester Gruinards 151 B8
Westerham 28 D5
Westerhope 110 C4
Wester Lealty 151 D9
Westerleigh 23 B9
Wester Milton 151 F12
Wester Newburn 129 D6
Wester Quarff 160 K6
Wester Skeld 160 J4
Westerton Angus 135 D6
Durham 110 F5
W Sus 16 D2
Westerwick 160 J4
West Farleigh 29 D8
West Felton 60 B3
West Fenton 129 F6
West Ferry 134 F4
Westfield Cumb 98 B1
E Sus 18 D5
Hereford 50 E2
Highld 158 D2
N Lanark 119 B7
Norf 68 D2
W Loth 120 B2
Westfields 12 D5
Westfields of Rattray 134 E1
West Firle 17 D8
Westgate Durham 110 F2
N Lincs 89 D8
Norf 80 C4
Norf 81 C5
Westgate on Sea 31 B7
West Ginge 38 F4
West Grafton 25 C7
West Green 26 D5
West Greenskares 153 B7
West Grimstead 14 B3
West Grinstead 17 B5
West Haddlesey 89 B6
West Haddon 52 B4
West Hagbourne 39 F5
West Hagley 62 F3
Westhall Aberds 141 B5
Suff 69 F7
West Hall 109 C5
West Hallam 76 E4
West Halton 90 B3
Westham Dorset 12 G4
E Sus 18 E3
Som 23 E6
West Ham 41 F7
Westhampnett 16 D2
West Handley 76 B3
West Hanney 38 E4
West Hanningfield 42 E3
West Hardwick 88 C5
West Harnham 14 B2
West Harptree 23 D7
West Hatch 11 B7
Westhay 23 E6
Westhead 86 D2
West Head 67 D5
West Heath Ches E 74 C5
Hants 26 D3
Hants 27 D6
West Helmsdale 157 H13
West Hendred 38 F4
West Heslerton 96 B5
Westhide 49 E7
Westhill Aberds 141 D7
Highld 151 G10
West Hill Devon 11 E5
E Yorks 97 C7
N Som 23 B6
West Hoathly 28 F4
West Holme 13 F6
Westhope Hereford 49 D6
Shrops 60 F4
West Horndon 42 F2
Westhorpe Lincs 78 F5
Suff 56 C4
West Horrington 23 E7
West Horsley 27 D8
West Horton 123 F6
West Hougham 31 E6
Westhoughton 86 D4
West Houlland 160 H4
Westhouse 93 B6
Westhouses 76 D4
Westhumble 28 D2
West Huntington 96 D2
West Hythe 19 B8
West Ilsley 38 F4
Westing 160 C7
West Itchenor 15 D8
West Keal 79 C6
West Kennett 25 C6
West Kilbride 118 E2
West Kingsdown 29 C6
West Kington 24 B3
West Kinharrachie 153 E9
West Kirby 85 F3
West Knapton 96 B4
West Knighton 12 F5
West Knoyle 24 F3
West Kyloe 123 E6
Westlake 6 D4
West Lambrook 12 C2
West Langdon 31 E7
West Langwell 157 J9
West Lavington
Wilts 24 D5
W Sus 16 B2
West Layton 101 D6
West Lea 111 E7
West Leake 64 B2
West Learmouth 122 F4
Westleigh Devon 9 B6
Devon 11 C5
Gtr Man 86 D4
West Leigh 9 D8
Westleton 57 C8
West Lexham 67 C8
Westley Shrops 60 D3
Suff 56 C2
Westley Waterless 55 D7
West Lilling 96 C2
Westlington 39 C7
Westlinton 108 C3
West Linton 120 D4
West Liss 15 B8
West Littleton 24 B2
West Looe 5 D7
West Luccombe 21 E7
West Lulworth 13 F6
West Lutton 96 C5
West Lydford 23 F7
West Lyng 11 B8
West Lynn 67 B6
West Malling 29 D7
West Malvern 50 E2
West Marden 15 C8
West Marina 18 E4
West Markham 77 B7
Westmarsh 31 C6
West Marsh 91 C6
West Marton 93 D8
West Meon 15 B7
West Mersea 43 C6
Westmeston 17 C7
Westmill 41 B6
West Milton 12 E3
Westminster 28 B4
West Minster 30 B3
West Molesey 28 C2
West Monkton 11 B7
West Moors 13 D8
West Morriston 122 E2
Westmuir 134 D3
West Muir 135 C5
Westness 159 F4
West Ness 96 B2
West Newham 110 B3
Westnewton Cumb 107 E8
Northumb 122 F5
West Newton
E Yorks 97 F7
Norf 67 B6
West Norwood 28 B4
Westoe 111 C6
West Ogwell 7 B6
Weston Bath 24 C2
Ches E 74 D4
Devon 11 F6
Dorset 12 G4
Halton 86 F3
Hants 15 B8
Herts 54 F3
Lincs 66 B2
Notts 77 C7
N Yorks 94 E4
Shrops 61 B5
Shrops 61 E5
Staffs 62 B3
W Berks 25 B8
W Nhants 52 E3
Weston Beggard 49 E7
Westonbirt 37 F5
Weston by Welland 64 E4
Weston Colville 55 D7
Westoncommon 60 B4
Weston Coyney 75 E6
Weston Favell 53 C5
Weston Green
Cambs 55 D7
Norf 68 C4
Weston Heath 61 C7
Weston Hills 66 B2
Westoning 53 F8
Weston-in-Gordano 23 B6
Weston Jones 61 B7
Weston Longville 68 C4
Weston Lullingfields 60 B4
Weston-on-the-Green 39 C5
Weston-on-Trent 63 B8
Weston Patrick 26 E4
Weston Rhyn 73 F6
Weston-sub-Edge 51 E6
Weston-super-Mare 22 C5
Weston Turville 40 C1
Weston under Lizard 62 C2
Weston under Penyard 36 B3
Weston under Wetherley 51 C8
Weston Underwood
Derbys 76 E2
M Keynes 53 D6
Westonzoyland 23 F5
West Orchard 13 C6
West Overton 25 C6
Westow 96 C3
West Park 111 F7
West Parley 13 E8
West Peckham 29 D7
West Pelton 110 D5
West Pennard 23 F7
West Pentire 4 C2
West Perry 54 C2
Westport Argyll 143 F7
Som 11 C8
West Putford 9 C5
West Quantoxhead 22 E3
West Rainton 111 E6
West Rasen 90 F4
West Raynham 80 E4
West Retford 89 F7
Westrigg 120 C2
West Rounton 102 D2
West Row 55 B7
West Rudham 80 E4
West Runton 81 C7
Westruther 122 E2
Westry 66 E3
West Saltoun 121 C7
West Sandwick 160 E6
West Scrafton 101 F5
West Sleekburn 117 F8
West Somerton 69 C7
West Stafford 12 F5
West Stockwith 89 E8
West Stoke 16 D2
West Stonesdale 100 D3
West Stoughton 23 E6
West Stour 13 B5
West Stourmouth 31 C6
West Stow 56 B2
West Stowell 25 C6
West Strathan 157 C8
West Stratton 26 E3
West Street 30 D3
West Tanfield 95 B5
West Taphouse 5 C6
West Tarbert 145 G7
West Thirston 117 E7
West Thorney 15 D8
West Thurrock 29 B6
West Tilbury 29 B7
West Tisted 15 B7
West Tofts Norf 67 E8
Perth 133 F8
West Torrington 90 F5
West Town Hants 15 E8
N Som 23 C6
West Tytherley 14 B3
West Tytherton 24 B4
Westville 76 E5
West Walton 66 C4
West Walton Highway 66 C4
Westward 108 E2
Westward Ho! 9 B6
Westwell Kent 30 E3
Oxon 38 D2
Westwell Leacon 30 E3
West Wellow 14 C3
West Wemyss 128 E5
Westwick Cambs 54 C5
Durham 101 C5
Norf 81 E8
West Wick 23 C5
West Wickham
Cambs 55 E7
London 28 C4
West Williamston 32 D1
West Willoughby 78 E2
West Winch 67 C6
West Winterslow 25 F7
West Wittering 15 E8
West Witton 101 F5
Westwood Devon 10 E5
Wilts 24 D3
West Woodburn 116 F4
West Woodhay 25 C8
West Woodlands 24 E2
Westwoodside 89 E8
West Worldham 26 F5
West Worlington 10 C2
West Worthing 16 D5
West Wratting 55 D7
West Wycombe 39 E8
West Wylam 110 C4
West Yell 160 E6
Wetheral 108 D4
Wetherby 95 E7
Wetherden 56 C4
Wetheringsett 56 C5
Wethersfield 55 F8
Wethersta 160 G5
Wetherup Street 56 C5
Wetley Rocks 75 E6
Wettenhall 74 C3
Wetton 75 D8
Wetwang 96 D5
Wetwood 74 F4
Wexcombe 25 D7
Wexham Street 40 F2
Weybourne 81 C7
Weybread 68 F5
Weybridge 27 C8
Weycroft 11 E8
Weydale 158 D3
Weyhill 25 E8
Weymouth 12 G4
Whaddon Bucks 53 F6
Cambs 54 E4
Glos 37 C5
Wilts 14 B2
Whale 99 B7
Whaley 76 B5
Whaley Bridge 87 F8
Whaley Thorns 76 B5
Whaligoe 158 F5
Whalley 93 F7
Whalton 117 F7
Wham 93 C7
Whaplode 66 B3
Whaplode Drove 66 C3
Whaplode St Catherine 66 B3
Wharfe 93 C7
Wharles 92 F4
Wharncliffe Side 88 E3
Wharram le Street 96 C4
Wharton 74 C3
Wharton Green 74 C3
Whashton 101 D6
Whatcombe 13 D6

Whatcote ... 51 E8
Whatfield ... 56 E4
Whatley Som. ... 11 D8
Som ... 24 E2
Whatlington ... 18 D4
Whatstandwell ... 76 D3
Whatton ... 77 F7
Whauphill ... 105 E8
Whaw ... 100 D4
Wheatacre ... 69 E7
Wheatcroft ... 76 D3
Wheathampstead ... 40 C4
Wheathill ... 61 F6
Wheatley Devon ... 10 E4
Hants ... 27 E5
Oxon ... 39 D5
S Yorks ... 89 D6
W Yorks ... 87 B8
Wheatley Hill ... 111 F6
Wheaton Aston ... 62 C2
Wheddon Cross ... 21 F8
Wheedlemont ... 140 B3
Wheelerstreet ... 27 E7
Wheelock ... 74 D4
Wheelock Heath ... 74 D4
Wheelton ... 86 B4
Wheen ... 134 B3
Wheldrake ... 96 E2
Whelford ... 38 E1
Whelpley Hill ... 40 D2
Whempstead ... 41 B6
Whenby ... 96 C2
Whepstead ... 56 D2
Wherstead ... 57 E5
Wherwell ... 25 E8
Wheston ... 75 B8
Whetsted ... 29 E7
Whetstone ... 64 E2
Whicham ... 98 F3
Whichford ... 51 F8
Whickham ... 110 C5
Whiddon Down ... 9 E8
Whigstreet ... 134 E4
Whilton ... 52 C4
Whimble ... 9 D5
Whim Farm ... 120 D5
Whimple ... 10 E5
Whimpwell Green ... 69 B6
Whinburgh ... 68 D3
Whinnieliggate ... 106 D4
Whinnyfold ... 153 E10
Whippingham ... 15 E6
Whipsnade ... 40 C3
Whipton ... 10 E4
Whirlow ... 88 F4
Whisby ... 78 C2
Whissendine ... 64 C5
Whissonsett ... 80 E5
Whistlefield
Argyll ... 145 D10
Argyll ... 145 E11
Whistley Green ... 27 B5
Whiston Mers ... 86 E2
Staffs ... 62 C2
Staffs ... 75 E7
S Yorks ... 88 F5
W Nhants ... 53 C6
Whitbeck ... 98 F3
Whitbourne ... 50 D2
Whitburn T&W ... 111 C7
W Loth ... 120 C2
Whitburn
Colliery ... 111 C7
Whitby Ches W ... 73 B7
N Yorks ... 103 C6
Whitbyheath ... 73 B7
Whitchurch Bath ... 23 C8
Bucks ... 39 B7
Cardiff ... 35 F5
Devon ... 6 B2
Hants ... 26 E2
Hereford ... 36 C2
Oxon ... 26 B4
Pembs ... 44 C2
Shrops ... 74 E2
Whitchurch
Canonicorum ... 11 E8
Whitchurch Hill ... 26 B4
Whitcombe ... 12 F5
Whitcott Keysett ... 60 F2
Whiteacen ... 152 D2
Whiteacre Heath ... 63 E6
Whitebridge ... 137 C7
Whitebrook ... 36 D2
Whiteburn ... 121 E8
Whitecairn ... 105 E6
Whitecairns ... 141 C8
Whitecastle ... 120 E3
Whitechapel ... 93 E5
Whitecleat ... 159 H6
White Coppice ... 86 C4
Whitecraig ... 121 B6
Whitecroft ... 36 D3
Whitecross Corn ... 4 B4
Falk ... 120 B2
Staffs ... 62 B2
Whiteface ... 151 C10
Whitefarland ... 143 D9
Whitefaulds ... 112 D2
Whitefield Gtr Man ... 87 D6
Perth ... 134 F1
Whiteford ... 141 B6
Whitegate ... 74 C3
Whitehall Blackburn ... 86 B4
W Sus ... 16 B5
Whitehall Village ... 159 F7
Whitehaven ... 98 C1
Whitehill ... 27 F5
Whitehills Aberds ... 153 B6
S Lanark ... 119 D6
Whitehough ... 87 F8
Whitehouse
Aberds ... 140 C5
Argyll ... 145 G7
Whiteinch ... 118 C5
Whitekirk ... 129 F7
White Lackington ... 12 E5
White Ladies
Aston ... 50 D4
Whitelaw ... 119 E6
Whiteleas ... 111 C6
Whiteley Bank ... 15 F6
Whiteley Green ... 75 B6
Whiteley Village ... 27 C8
White Lund ... 92 C4
Whitemans Green ... 17 B7

White Mill ... 33 B5
Whitemire ... 151 F12
Whitemoor ... 4 D4
Whitemore ... 75 C5
Whitenap ... 14 B4
White Ness ... 160 J5
White Notley ... 42 C3
Whiteoak Green ... 38 C3
Whiteparish ... 14 B3
White Pit ... 79 B6
White Post ... 77 D6
Whiterashes ... 141 B7
White Rocks ... 35 B8
White Roding ... 42 C1
Whiterow ... 158 F5
Whiteshill ... 37 D5
Whiteside
Northumb ... 109 C7
W Loth ... 120 C2
Whitesmith ... 18 D2
Whitestaunton ... 11 C7
Whitestone Devon ... 10 E3
Devon ... 20 E3
Warks ... 63 F7
Whitestones ... 153 C8
Whitestreet Green ... 56 F3
Whitewall Corner ... 96 B3
Whiteway Glos ... 37 C6
Glos ... 37 E5
Whitewell Aberds ... 153 B9
Lancs ... 93 E6
Whitewell Bottom ... 87 B6
Whiteworks ... 6 B4
Whitfield Kent ... 31 E7
Northumb ... 109 D7
S Glos ... 36 E3
W Nhants ... 52 F4
Whitford Devon ... 11 E7
Flint ... 72 B5
Whitgift ... 90 B2
Whitgreave ... 62 B2
Whithorn ... 105 E8
Whiting Bay ... 143 F11
Whitkirk ... 95 F6
Whitland ... 32 C2
Whitletts ... 112 B3
Whitley N Yorks ... 89 B6
Reading ... 26 B5
Wilts ... 24 C3
Whitley Bay ... 111 B6
Whitley Chapel ... 110 D2
Whitley Lower ... 88 C3
Whitley Row ... 29 D5
Whitlock's End ... 51 B6
Whitminster ... 36 D4
Whitmore ... 74 E5
Whitnage ... 10 C5
Whitnash ... 51 C8
Whitney-on-Wye ... 48 E4
Whitrigg Cumb ... 108 D2
Cumb ... 108 F2
Whitsbury ... 14 C2
Whitsome ... 122 D4
Whitson ... 35 F7
Whitstable ... 30 C5
Whitstone ... 8 E4
Whittingham ... 117 C6
Whittingslow ... 60 F4
Whittington Glos ... 37 B7
Lancs ... 93 B6
Norf ... 67 E7
Shrops ... 73 F7
Staffs ... 62 F2
Staffs ... 63 D5
Worcs ... 50 D3
Whittlebury ... 52 E4
Whittle-le-Woods ... 86 B3
Whittlesey ... 66 E2
Whittlesford ... 55 E5
Whittlestone Head ... 86 C5
Whitton Borders ... 116 B3
N Lincs ... 90 B3
Northumb ... 117 D6
Powys ... 48 C4
Shrops ... 49 B7
Stockton ... 102 B1
Suff ... 56 E5
Whittonditch ... 25 B7
Whittonstall ... 110 D3
Whitway ... 26 D2
Whitwell Derbys ... 76 B5
Herts ... 40 B4
IoW ... 15 G6
N Yorks ... 101 E7
Rutland ... 65 D6
Whitwell-on-the-
Hill ... 96 C3
Whitwell Street ... 81 E7
Whitwick ... 63 C8
Whitwood ... 88 B5
Whitworth ... 87 C6
Whixall ... 74 F2
Whixley ... 95 D7
Whoberley ... 51 B8
Whorlton Durham ... 101 C6
N Yorks ... 102 D2
Whygate ... 109 B7
Whyle ... 49 C7
Whyteleafe ... 28 D4
Wibdon ... 36 E2
Wibsey ... 88 A2
Wibtoft ... 63 F8
Wichenford ... 50 C2
Wichling ... 30 D3
Wick BCP ... 14 E2
Devon ... 11 C6
Highld ... 158 E5
S Glos ... 24 B2
Shetland ... 160 K6
V Glam ... 21 B8
Wilts ... 14 B2
W Sus ... 16 D4
Wick Hill ... 27 C5
Wicken Bonhunt ... 55 F5
Wickenby ... 90 F4
Wicken Green
Village ... 80 D4
Wickersley ... 89 E5
Wickford ... 42 E3
Wickham Hants ... 15 C6
W Berks ... 25 B8
Wickham Bishops ... 42 C4
Wickhambreaux ... 31 D6
Wickhambrook ... 55 D8
Wickhamford ... 51 E5
Wickham Market ... 57 D7

Wickhampton ... 69 D7
Wickham St Paul ... 56 F2
Wickham Skeith ... 56 C4
Wickham Street
Suff ... 55 D8
Suff ... 56 C4
Wick Hill ... 27 C5
Wicklewood ... 68 D3
Wickmere ... 81 D7
Wick St Lawrence ... 23 C5
Wickwar ... 36 F4
Widdington ... 55 F6
Widdrington ... 117 E8
Widdrington
Station ... 117 E8
Widecombe in the
Moor ... 6 B5
Widegates ... 5 D7
Widemouth Bay ... 8 D4
Wide Open ... 110 B5
Widewall ... 159 J5
Widford Essex ... 42 D2
Herts ... 41 C7
Widham ... 37 F7
Widmer End ... 40 E1
Widmerpool ... 64 B3
Widnes ... 86 F3
Wigan ... 86 D3
Wiggaton ... 11 E6
Wiggenhall
St Germans ... 67 C5
Wiggenhall St Mary
Magdalen ... 67 C5
Wiggenhall St Mary
the Virgin ... 67 C5
Wigginton Herts ... 40 C2
Oxon ... 51 F8
Staffs ... 63 D6
York ... 95 D8
Wigglesworth ... 93 D8
Wiggonby ... 108 D2
Wiggonholt ... 16 C4
Wighill ... 95 E7
Wighton ... 80 D5
Wigley ... 14 C4
Wigmore Hereford ... 49 C6
Medway ... 30 C2
Wigsley ... 77 B8
Wigsthorpe ... 65 F7
Wigston ... 64 E3
Wigthorpe ... 89 F6
Wigtoft ... 79 F5
Wigton ... 108 E2
Wigtown ... 105 D8
Wigtwizzle ... 88 E3
Wike ... 95 E6
Wike Well End ... 89 C7
Wilbarston ... 64 F5
Wilberfoss ... 96 D3
Wilberlee ... 87 C8
Wilburton ... 55 B5
Wilby N Nhants ... 53 C6
Norf ... 68 F3
Suff ... 57 B6
Wilcot ... 25 C6
Wilcott ... 60 C3
Wilcrick ... 35 F8
Wilday Green ... 76 B3
Wildboarclough ... 75 C6
Wilden Bedford ... 53 D8
Worcs ... 50 B3
Wildhern ... 25 D8
Wildhill ... 41 D5
Wildmoor ... 50 B4
Wildsworth ... 90 E2
Wilford ... 77 F5
Wilkesley ... 74 E3
Wilkhaven ... 151 C12
Wilkieston ... 120 C4
Willand ... 10 C5
Willaston Ches E ... 74 D3
Ches W ... 73 B7
Willen ... 53 E6
Willenhall W Mid ... 51 B8
W Mid ... 62 E3
Willerby E Yorks ... 97 F6
N Yorks ... 97 B6
Willersey ... 51 F6
Willersley ... 48 E5
Willesborough ... 30 E4
Willesborough
Lees ... 30 E4
Willesden ... 41 F5
Willett ... 22 F3
Willey Shrops ... 61 E6
Warks ... 63 F8
Willey Green ... 27 D7
Williamscott ... 52 E2
Willian ... 54 F3
Willingale ... 42 D1
Willingdon ... 18 E2
Willingham ... 54 B4
Willingham by
Stow ... 90 F2
Willington Bedford ... 54 E2
Derbys ... 63 B6
Durham ... 110 F4
T&W ... 111 C6
Warks ... 51 F7
Willington Corner ... 74 C2
Willisham Tye ... 56 D4
Willitoft ... 96 F3
Williton ... 22 E2
Willoughbridge ... 74 E4
Willoughby Lincs ... 79 B7
Warks ... 52 C3
Willoughby-on-
the-Wolds ... 64 B3
Willoughby
Waterleys ... 64 E2
Willoughton ... 90 E3
Willows Green ... 42 C3
Willsbridge ... 23 B8
Willsworthy ... 9 F7
Wilmcote ... 51 D6
Wilmington Devon ... 11 E7
E Sus ... 18 E2
Kent ... 29 B6
Wilminstone ... 6 B2
Wilmslow ... 87 F6
Wilnecote ... 63 D6
Wilpshire ... 93 F6
Wilsden ... 94 F3
Wilsford Lincs ... 78 E3
Wilts ... 25 D6
Wilts ... 25 F6
Wilsill ... 94 C4
Wilsley Pound ... 18 B4
Wilsom ... 26 F5

Wilson ... 63 B8
Wilsontown ... 120 D2
Wilstead ... 53 E8
Wilsthorpe ... 65 C7
Wilstone ... 40 C2
Wilton Borders ... 115 C7
Cumb ... 98 C2
N Yorks ... 103 F6
Redcar ... 102 C3
Wilts ... 25 C7
Wilts ... 25 F5
Wimbish ... 55 F6
Wimbish Green ... 55 F7
Wimblebury ... 62 C4
Wimbledon ... 28 B3
Wimblington ... 66 E4
Wimborne Minster ... 13 E8
Wimborne
St Giles ... 13 C8
Wimbotsham ... 67 D6
Wimpson ... 14 C4
Wimpstone ... 51 E7
Wincanton ... 12 B5
Wincham ... 74 B3
Winchburgh ... 120 B3
Winchcombe ... 37 B7
Winchelsea ... 19 D6
Winchelsea Beach ... 19 D6
Winchester ... 15 B5
Winchet Hill ... 29 E8
Winchfield ... 27 D5
Winchmore Hill
Bucks ... 40 E2
London ... 41 E6
Wincle ... 75 C6
Wincobank ... 88 E4
Windermere ... 99 E6
Winderton ... 51 E8
Windhill ... 151 G8
Windhouse ... 160 D6
Windlehurst ... 87 F7
Windlesham ... 27 C7
Windley ... 76 E3
Windmill Hill
E Sus ... 18 D3
Som ... 11 C8
Windrush ... 38 C1
Windsor N Lincs ... 89 C8
Windsor ... 27 B7
Windsoredge ... 37 D5
Windygates ... 128 D5
Windyknowe ... 120 C2
Windywalls ... 122 F3
Wineham ... 17 B6
Winestead ... 91 B6
Winewall ... 94 E2
Winfarthing ... 68 F4
Winford IoW ... 15 F6
N Som ... 23 C7
Winforton ... 48 E4
Winfrith
Newburgh ... 13 F6
Wing Bucks ... 40 B1
Rutland ... 65 D5
Wingate ... 111 F7
Wingates Gtr Man ... 86 D4
Northumb ... 117 E7
Wingerworth ... 76 C3
Wingfield C Beds ... 40 B2
Suff ... 57 B6
Wilts ... 24 D3
Wingham ... 31 D6
Wingmore ... 31 E5
Wingrave ... 40 C1
Winkburn ... 77 D7
Winkfield ... 27 B7
Winkfield Row ... 27 B6
Winkhill ... 75 D7
Winklebury ... 26 D4
Winkleigh ... 9 D8
Winksley ... 95 B5
Winkton ... 14 E2
Winlaton ... 110 C4
Winless ... 158 E5
Winmarleigh ... 92 E4
Winnal ... 49 F6
Winnall ... 15 B5
Winnersh ... 27 B5
Winscales ... 98 B2
Winscombe ... 23 D6
Winsford Ches W ... 74 C3
Som ... 21 F8
Winsham ... 11 D8
Winshill ... 63 B6
Winskill ... 109 F5
Winslade ... 26 E4
Winsley ... 24 C3
Winslow ... 39 B7
Winson ... 37 D7
Winson Green ... 62 F4
Winsor ... 14 C4
Winster Cumb ... 99 E6
Derbys ... 76 C2
Winston Durham ... 101 C6
Suff ... 57 C5
Winstone ... 37 D6
Winston Green ... 57 C5
Winswell ... 9 C6
Winterborne
Clenston ... 13 D6
Winterborne
Herringston ... 12 F4
Winterborne
Houghton ... 13 D6
Winterborne
Kingston ... 13 E6
Winterborne
Monkton ... 12 F4
Winterborne
Stickland ... 13 D6
Winterborne
Whitechurch ... 13 D6
Winterborne
Zelston ... 13 E6
Winterbourne
S Glos ... 36 F3
W Berks ... 26 B2
Winterbourne
Abbas ... 12 E4
Winterbourne
Bassett ... 25 B6
Winterbourne
Dauntsey ... 25 F6
Winterbourne
Down ... 23 B8
Winterbourne
Earls ... 25 F6
Winterbourne
Gunner ... 25 F6

Winterbourne
Monkton ... 25 B6
Winterbourne
Steepleton ... 12 F4
Winterbourne
Stoke ... 25 E5
Winter Gardens ... 42 F3
Winteringham ... 90 B3
Winterley ... 74 D4
Wintersett ... 88 C4
Wintershill ... 15 C6
Winterton ... 90 C3
Winterton-on-Sea ... 69 C7
Winthorpe Lincs ... 79 C8
Notts ... 77 D8
Winton BCP ... 13 E8
Cumb ... 100 C2
N Yorks ... 102 E2
Wintringham ... 96 B4
Winwick Cambs ... 65 F8
Warr ... 86 E4
W Nhants ... 52 B4
Wirksworth ... 76 D2
Wirksworth Moor ... 76 D3
Wirswall ... 74 E2
Wisbech ... 66 D4
Wisbech St Mary ... 66 D4
Wisborough Green ... 16 B4
Wiseton ... 89 F8
Wishaw N Lanark ... 119 D7
Warks ... 63 E5
Wisley ... 27 D8
Wispington ... 78 B5
Wissenden ... 30 E3
Wissett ... 57 B7
Wistanstow ... 60 F4
Wistanswick ... 61 B6
Wistaston ... 74 D3
Wistaston Green ... 74 D3
Wiston Pembs ... 32 C1
S Lanark ... 120 F2
W Sus ... 16 C5
Wistow Cambs ... 66 F2
N Yorks ... 95 F8
Wiswell ... 93 F7
Witcham ... 66 F4
Witchampton ... 13 D7
Witchford ... 55 B6
Witham ... 42 C4
Witham Friary ... 24 E2
Witham on the Hill ... 65 C7
Withcall ... 91 F6
Withdean ... 17 D7
Witherenden Hill ... 18 C3
Witheridge ... 10 C3
Witherley ... 63 E7
Withern ... 91 F8
Withernsea ... 91 B7
Withernwick ... 97 E7
Withersdale Street ... 69 F5
Withersfield ... 55 E7
Witherslack ... 99 F6
Withiel ... 4 C4
Withiel Florey ... 21 F8
Withington Glos ... 37 C7
Hereford ... 49 E7
Gtr Man ... 87 E6
Shrops ... 61 C5
Staffs ... 75 F7
Withington Green ... 74 B5
Withleigh ... 10 C4
Withnell ... 86 B4
Withybrook ... 63 F8
Withycombe ... 22 E2
Withycombe
Raleigh ... 10 F5
Witham ... 31 B6
Withypool ... 21 F7
Witley ... 27 F7
Witnesham ... 57 D5
Witney ... 38 C3
Wittering ... 65 D7
Witton Angus ... 135 B5
Witton Worcs ... 50 C3
Witton Bridge ... 69 A6
Witton Gilbert ... 110 E5
Witton-le-Wear ... 110 F4
Witton Park ... 110 F4
Wiveliscombe ... 11 B5
Wivelrod ... 26 F4
Wivelsfield ... 17 B7
Wivelsfield Green ... 17 B7
Wivenhoe ... 43 B6
Wivenhoe Cross ... 43 B6
Wiveton ... 81 C6
Wix ... 43 B7
Wixford ... 51 D5
Wixhill ... 61 B5
Wixoe ... 55 E8
Woburn ... 53 F7
Woburn Sands ... 53 F7
Wokefield Park ... 26 C4
Woking ... 27 D8
Wokingham ... 27 C6
Wolborough ... 7 B6
Woldingham ... 28 D4
Wold Newton
E Yorks ... 97 B6
NE Lincs ... 91 E6
Wolfclyde ... 120 F3
Wolferton ... 67 B6
Wolfhill ... 134 F1
Wolf's Castle ... 44 C4
Wolfsdale ... 44 C4
Woll ... 115 B7
Wollaston
N Nhants ... 53 C7
Shrops ... 60 C3
Wollaton ... 76 F5
Wollerton ... 74 F3
Wollescote ... 62 F3
Wolsingham ... 110 F3
Wolstanton ... 75 E5
Wolston ... 52 B2
Wolvercote ... 38 D4
Wolverhampton ... 62 E3
Wolverley Shrops ... 73 F8
Worcs ... 50 B3
Wolverton Hants ... 26 D3
M Keynes ... 53 E6
Warks ... 51 C7
Wolverton
Common ... 26 D3
Wolvesnewton ... 36 E1
Wolvey ... 63 F8
Wolviston ... 102 B2
Wombleton ... 102 F4
Wombourne ... 62 E2

Wombwell ... 88 D4
Womenswold ... 31 D6
Womersley ... 89 C6
Wonastow ... 36 C1
Wonersh ... 27 E8
Wonson ... 9 F8
Wooburn ... 40 F2
Wooburn Green ... 40 F2
Woodacott ... 9 D5
Woodale ... 94 B3
Woodbank ... 143 G7
Woodbastwick ... 69 C6
Woodbeck ... 77 B7
Woodborough
Notts ... 77 E6
Wilts ... 25 D6
Woodbridge Dorset ... 12 C5
Suff ... 57 E6
Woodbury ... 10 F5
Woodbury
Salterton ... 10 F5
Woodchester ... 37 D5
Woodchurch Kent ... 19 B6
Mers ... 85 F3
Woodcombe ... 21 E8
Woodcote ... 39 F6
Woodcott ... 26 D2
Woodcroft ... 36 E2
Woodcutts ... 13 C7
Wood Dalling ... 81 E6
Woodditton ... 55 D7
Woodeaton ... 39 C5
Woodend Cumb ... 98 E3
W Nhants ... 52 E4
W Sus ... 16 D2
Wood End Herts ... 41 B6
Warks ... 51 B6
Warks ... 63 E6
Wood Enderby ... 79 C5
Woodend Green ... 52 E4
Woodfalls ... 14 B2
Woodfield Oxon ... 39 B5
S Ayrs ... 112 B3
Wood Field ... 28 D2
Woodford Corn. ... 8 C4
Devon ... 7 D5
Glos ... 36 E3
Gtr Man ... 87 F6
London ... 41 E7
N Nhants ... 53 B7
Woodford Bridge ... 41 E7
Woodford Halse ... 52 D3
Woodgate Norf ... 68 C3
W Mid ... 62 F3
Worcs ... 50 C4
W Sus ... 16 D3
Woodgreen ... 14 C2
Wood Green ... 41 E6
Woodhall Herts ... 41 C5
Involyd ... 118 B3
N Yorks ... 100 E4
Woodhall Spa ... 78 C4
Woodham ... 27 D8
Woodham Ferrers ... 42 E3
Woodham
Mortimer ... 42 D4
Woodham Walter ... 42 D4
Woodhaven ... 129 B6
Wood Hayes ... 62 D3
Woodhead ... 153 E7
Woodhey ... 87 C5
Woodhill ... 61 F7
Woodhorn ... 117 F8
Woodhouse Leics ... 64 C2
N Lincs ... 89 D8
S Yorks ... 88 F5
W Yorks ... 88 B4
W Yorks ... 95 F5
Woodhouse Eaves ... 64 C2
Woodhouselee ... 120 C5
Woodhouselees ... 108 B3
Woodhouse Park ... 87 F6
Woodhouses ... 63 C5
Woodhurst ... 54 B4
Woodingdean ... 17 D7
Woodkirk ... 88 B3
Woodland Devon ... 7 C5
Durham ... 101 B5
Woodlands Aberds ... 141 E6
Dorset ... 13 D8
Hants ... 14 C4
Highld ... 151 E8
N Yorks ... 95 D6
S Yorks ... 89 D6
Woodlands Park ... 27 B6
Woodlands
St Mary ... 25 B8
Woodlane ... 62 B5
Wood Lanes ... 87 F7
Woodleigh ... 6 E5
Woodlesford ... 88 B4
Woodley Gtr Man ... 87 E7
Wokingham ... 27 B5
Woodmancote Glos ... 36 E4
Glos ... 37 B6
Glos ... 37 D7
W Sus ... 15 D8
W Sus ... 17 C6
Woodmancott ... 26 E3
Woodmansey ... 97 F6
Woodmansterne ... 28 D3
Woodminton ... 13 B8
Woodnesborough ... 31 D7
Woodnewton ... 65 E7
Wood Norton ... 81 E6
Woodplumpton ... 92 F5
Woodrising ... 68 D2
Woodseaves Shrops ... 74 F3
Staffs ... 61 B7
Woodsend ... 25 B7
Woodsetts ... 89 F6
Woodsford ... 13 E5
Wood's Green ... 18 B3
Woodside
Aberdeen ... 141 D8
Aberds ... 153 D10
Brack. ... 27 B7
Fife ... 129 D6
Hants ... 14 E4
Herts ... 41 D5
Perth ... 134 F2
Woodside of
Arbeadie ... 141 E6
Woodstock Oxon ... 38 C4
Pembs ... 32 B1
Wood Street Norf ... 69 B6
Sur. ... 27 D7
Woodthorpe Derbys ... 76 B4

Woodthorpe continued
Leics ... 64 C2
Lincs ... 91 F8
York ... 95 D8
Woodton ... 69 E5
Woodtown ... 9 B6
Woodvale ... 85 C4
Woodville ... 63 C7
Wood Walton ... 66 F2
Woodyates ... 13 C8
Woofferton ... 49 C7
Wookey ... 23 E7
Wookey Hole ... 23 E7
Wool ... 13 F6
Woolacombe ... 20 E3
Woolage Green ... 31 E6
Woolaston ... 36 E2
Woolavington ... 22 E5
Woolbeding ... 16 B2
Wooldale ... 88 D2
Wooler ... 117 B5
Woolfardisworthy
Devon ... 8 B5
Devon ... 10 D3
Woolfords
Cottages ... 120 D3
Woolhampton ... 26 C3
Woolhope ... 49 F8
Woolhope
Cockshoot ... 49 F8
Woolland ... 13 D5
Woollaton ... 9 C6
Woolley Bath. ... 24 C2
Cambs ... 54 B2
Corn. ... 8 C4
Derbys ... 76 C3
W Yorks ... 88 C4
Woolmer Green ... 41 C5
Woolmere Green ... 50 C4
Woolpit ... 56 C3
Woolscott ... 52 C2
Woolsington ... 110 C4
Woolstanwood ... 74 D3
Woolstaston ... 60 E4
Woolsthorpe Lincs ... 65 B6
Lincs ... 77 F8
Woolston Devon ... 6 E5
Shrops ... 60 B3
Shrops ... 60 F4
Soton ... 14 C5
Warr ... 86 F4
Woolstone M Keynes ... 53 F6
Oxon ... 38 F2
Woolton ... 86 F2
Woolton Hill ... 26 C2
Woolverstone ... 57 F5
Woolverton ... 24 D2
Woolwich ... 28 B5
Woolwich Ferry ... 28 B5
Woonton ... 49 D5
Wooperton ... 117 B6
Woore ... 74 E4
Wootten Green ... 57 B6
Wootton Bedford ... 53 E8
Hants ... 14 E3
Hereford ... 48 D5
Kent ... 31 E6
N Lincs ... 90 C4
Oxon ... 38 C4
Oxon ... 38 D4
Shrops ... 49 B6
Shrops ... 60 B3
Staffs ... 62 B2
Staffs ... 75 E8
Wootton Bridge ... 15 E6
Wootton Common ... 15 E6
Wootton
Courtenay ... 21 E8
Wootton Fitzpaine ... 11 E8
Wootton Rivers ... 25 C6
Wootton
St Lawrence ... 26 D3
Wootton Wawen ... 51 C6
Worcester ... 50 D3
Worcester Park ... 28 C3
Wordsley ... 62 F2
Worfield ... 61 E7
Work ... 159 G5
Workington ... 98 B1
Worksop ... 77 B5
Worlaby ... 90 C4
World's End ... 26 B2
Worle ... 23 C5
Worleston ... 74 D3
Worlingham ... 69 F7
Worlington ... 55 B7
Worlingworth ... 57 C6
Wormald Green ... 95 C6
Wormbridge ... 49 F6
Wormegay ... 67 C6
Wormelow Tump ... 49 F6
Wormhill ... 75 B8
Wormingford ... 56 F3
Worminghall ... 39 D6
Wormington ... 50 F5
Worminster ... 23 E7
Wormit ... 129 B5
Wormleighton ... 52 D2
Wormley Herts ... 41 D6
Sur. ... 27 F7
Wormley West
End ... 41 D6
Wormshill ... 30 D2
Wormsley ... 49 E6
Worplesdon ... 27 D7
Worrall ... 88 E4
Worsbrough ... 88 D4
Worsbrough
Common ... 88 D4
Worsley ... 86 D5
Worstead ... 69 B6
Worsthorne ... 93 F8
Worston ... 93 E7
Worswell ... 6 E3
Wortham ... 56 B4
Worthen ... 60 D3
Worthenbury ... 73 E8
Worthing Norf ... 68 C2
W Sus ... 16 D5
Worthington ... 63 B8
Worth Matravers ... 13 G7
Worting ... 26 D4
Wortley S Yorks ... 88 E4
W Yorks ... 95 F5

Worton N Yorks ... 100 E4
Wilts ... 24 D4
Wortwell ... 69 F5
Wotherton ... 60 D2
Wotter ... 6 C3
Wotton ... 28 E2
Wotton-
under-Edge ... 36 E4
Wotton
Underwood ... 39 C6
Woughton on
the Green ... 53 F6
Wouldham ... 29 C8
Wrabness ... 57 F5
Wrafton ... 20 F3
Wragby Lincs ... 78 B4
W Yorks ... 88 C5
Wragholme ... 91 E7
Wramplingham ... 68 D4
Wrangbrook ... 89 C5
Wrangham ... 153 E6
Wrangle ... 79 D7
Wrangle Bank ... 79 D7
Wrangle Lowgate ... 79 D7
Wrangway ... 11 C6
Wrantage ... 11 B8
Wrawby ... 90 D4
Wraxall Dorset ... 12 D3
N Som ... 23 B6
Som ... 23 E8
Wray ... 93 C6
Wraysbury ... 27 B8
Wrayton ... 93 B6
Wrea Green ... 92 F3
Wreay Cumb ... 99 B6
Cumb ... 108 E4
Wrecclesham ... 27 E6
Wrecsam
= Wrexham ... 73 D7
Wrekenton ... 111 D5
Wrelton ... 103 F5
Wrenbury ... 74 E2
Wrench Green ... 103 F7
Wreningham ... 68 E4
Wrentham ... 69 F7
Wrenthorpe ... 88 B4
Wrentnall ... 60 D4
Wressle E Yorks ... 96 F3
N Lincs ... 90 D3
Wrestlingworth ... 54 E3
Wretham ... 68 F2
Wretton ... 67 E6
Wrexham
Industrial Estate. ... 73 E7
= Wrecsam ... 73 D7
Wribbenhall ... 50 B2
Wrightington Bar. ... 86 C3
Wrinehill ... 74 E4
Wrington ... 23 C6
Writhlington ... 24 D2
Writtle ... 42 D2
Wrockwardine ... 61 C6
Wroot ... 89 D8
Wrotham ... 29 D7
Wrotham Heath ... 29 D7
Wroughton ... 37 F8
Wroxall IoW ... 15 G6
Warks ... 51 B7
Wroxeter ... 61 D5
Wroxham ... 69 C6
Wroxton ... 52 E2
Wyaston ... 75 E8
Wyberton ... 79 E6
Wyboston ... 54 D2
Wybunbury ... 74 E4
Wychbold ... 50 C4
Wych Cross ... 28 F5
Wyck ... 27 F5
Wyck Rissington ... 38 B1
Wycoller ... 94 F2
Wycomb ... 64 B4
Wycombe Marsh ... 40 E1
Wyddial ... 54 F4
Wye ... 30 E4
Wyesham ... 36 C2
Wyfordby ... 64 C4
Wyke Dorset ... 13 B5
Shrops ... 61 D6
Sur. ... 27 D7
W Yorks ... 88 B2
Wykeham N Yorks ... 96 B4
N Yorks ... 103 F7
Wyken ... 63 F7
Wyke Regis ... 12 G4
Wykey ... 60 B3
Wylam ... 110 C4
Wylde Green ... 62 E5
Wyllie ... 35 E5
Wylye ... 24 F5
Wymering ... 15 D7
Wymeswold ... 64 B3
Wymington ... 53 C7
Wymondham Leics ... 65 C5
Norf ... 68 D4
Wyndham ... 34 E3
Wynford Eagle ... 12 E3
Wyng ... 159 J4
Wynyard Village ... 102 B2
Wyre Piddle ... 50 E4
Wysall ... 64 B3
Wyson ... 49 C7
Wythall ... 51 B5
Wytham ... 38 D4
Wythburn ... 99 C5
Wythenshawe ... 87 F6
Wythop Mill ... 98 B3
Wyton ... 54 B3
Wyverstone ... 56 C4
Wyverstone Street. ... 56 C4
Wyville ... 65 B5
Wyvis Lodge ... 150 D7

Yarkhill ... 49 E8
Yarlet ... 62 B3
Yarlington ... 12 B4
Yarlside ... 92 C2
Yarm ... 102 C2
Yarnbrook ... 24 D3
Yarmouth ... 14 F4
Yarnacombe ... 9 B7
Yarnfield ... 75 F5
Yarnscombe ... 9 B7
Yarnton ... 38 C4
Yarpole ... 49 C6
Yarrow ... 115 B6
Yarrow Feus ... 115 B6
Yarsop ... 49 E6
Yarwell ... 65 E7
Yate ... 36 F4
Yateley ... 27 C6
Yatesbury ... 25 B5
Yattendon ... 26 B3
Yatton Hereford ... 49 C6
N Som ... 23 C6
Yatton Keynell ... 24 B3
Yaverland ... 15 F7
Yaxham ... 68 C3
Yaxley Cambs. ... 65 E8
Suff ... 56 B5
Yazor ... 49 E6

Y

Y Bala = Bala ... 72 F3
Y Barri = Barry ... 22 C3
Y Bont-Faen
= Cowbridge. ... 21 B8
Y Drenewydd
= Newtown ... 59 E8
Yeading ... 40 F4
Yeadon ... 94 E5
Yealand Conyers ... 92 B5
Yealand
Redmayne ... 92 B5
Yealmpton ... 6 D3
Yearby ... 102 B4
Yearsley ... 95 B8
Yeaton ... 60 C4
Yeaveley ... 75 E8
Yedingham ... 96 B4
Yeldon ... 53 C8
Yelford ... 38 D3
Yelland ... 20 F3
Yelling ... 54 C3
Yelvertoft ... 52 B3
Yelverton Devon ... 6 C3
Norf. ... 69 D5
Yenston ... 12 B5
Yeoford ... 10 E2
Yeolmbridge ... 8 F5
Yeo Mill ... 10 B3
Yeovil ... 12 C3
Yeovil Marsh ... 12 C3
Yeovilton ... 12 B3
Yerbeston ... 32 D1
Yesnaby ... 159 G3
Yetlington ... 117 D6
Yetminster ... 12 C3
Yettington ... 11 F5
Yetts o'Muckhart. ... 128 D2
Y Felinheli ... 82 E5
Y Fenni
= Abergavenny... ... 35 C6
Y Fflint = Flint ... 73 B6
Y Ffôr ... 70 D4
Y-Ffrith ... 72 A4
Y Gelli Gandryll
= Hay-on-Wye ... 48 E4
Yieldshields ... 119 D8
Yiewsley ... 40 F3
Y Mwmbwls
= The Mumbles ... 33 F7
Ynysboeth ... 34 E4
Ynysddu ... 35 E5
Ynysgyfflog ... 58 C3
Ynyshir ... 34 E4
Ynyslas ... 58 E3
Ynys-meudwy ... 33 D8
Ynystawe ... 33 D7
Ynysybwl ... 34 E4
Yockenthwaite ... 94 B2
Yockleton ... 60 C3
Yokefleet ... 90 B2
Yoker ... 118 C5
Yonder Bognie ... 152 D5
York ... 95 D8
Yorkletts ... 30 C4
Yorkley ... 36 D3
York Town ... 27 C6
Yorton ... 60 B5
Youlgreave ... 76 C2
Youlstone ... 8 C4
Youlthorpe ... 96 D3
Youlton ... 95 C7
Young's End ... 42 C3
Young Wood ... 78 B4
Yoxall ... 62 C5
Yoxford ... 57 C7
Y Pîl = Pyle ... 34 F2
Yr Hôb = Hope... ... 73 D7
Y Rhws = Rhoose. ... 22 C2
Y Rhyl = Rhyl ... 72 A4
Yr Wyddgrug
= Mold... ... 73 C6
Ysbyty-Cynfyn ... 47 B6
Ysbyty Ifan ... 72 E2
Ysbyty Ystwyth ... 47 B6
Ysceifiog ... 73 B5
Yspitty ... 33 E6
Ystalyfera ... 34 D1
Ystrad ... 34 E3
Ystrad Aeron ... 46 D4
Ystradfellte ... 34 C3
Ystradffin ... 47 E6
Ystradgynlais ... 34 C1
Ystradmeurig ... 47 C6
Ystrad-mynach. ... 35 E5
Ystradowen Carms ... 33 C8
V Glam. ... 22 B2
Ystumtuen ... 47 B6
Ythanbank ... 153 E9
Ythanwells ... 153 E6
Ythsie ... 153 E8
Y Trallwng
= Welshpool ... 60 D2
Y Waun = Chirk ... 73 F6

Z

Zeal Monachorum. ... 10 D2
Zeals ... 24 F2
Zelah ... 4 D3
Zennor ... 2 C3